Handbook of Antitrust Economics

Handbook of Antitrust Economics

edited by Paolo Buccirossi

The MIT Press
Cambridge, Massachusetts
London, England

This book was set in Times New Roman and Syntax on 3B2 by Asco Typesetters, Hong Kong.

Library of Congress Cataloging-in-Publication Data

Handbook of antitrust economics / edited by Paolo Buccirossi.
    p.   cm.
Includes bibliographical references and index.
ISBN 978-0-262-02627-7 (hardcover : alk. paper)—ISBN 978-0-262-52477-3 (pbk. : alk. paper) 1. Consolidation and merger of corporations. 2. Industrial organization (Economic theory) 3. Antitrust law—Economic aspects. I. Buccirossi, Paolo.
HD2746.5.H3584   2007
338.8—dc22   2007002665

The MIT Press is pleased to keep this title available in print by manufacturing single copies, on demand, via digital printing technology.

Contents

Contributors

Mark Armstrong, University College London

Jonathan B. Baker, American University

Timothy F. Bresnahan, Stanford University

Paolo Buccirossi, Lear (Laboratorio di economia, antitrust, regolamentazione)

Nicholas Economides, New York University

Hans W. Friederiszick, European School of Management and Technology, Berlin

Luke M. Froeb, Vanderbilt University

Richard J. Gilbert, University of California at Berkeley

Joseph E. Harrington Jr., Johns Hopkins University

Paul Klemperer, Oxford University and UK Competition Commission

Kai-Uwe Kühn, University of Michigan

Francine Lafontaine, University of Michigan

Damien J. Neven, Graduate Institute of International Studies, Geneva, and DG Competition of the European Commision

Patrick Rey, Toulouse University (IDEI-GREMAQ)

Michael H. Riordan, Columbia University

Jean-Charles Rochet, Toulouse University (IDEI-GREMAQ)

Lars-Hendrik Röller, European School of Management and Technology, Berlin and Humboldt University

Margaret Slade, University of Warwick

Giancarlo Spagnolo, University of Rome at Tor Vergata and Stockholm School of Economics

Jean Tirole, Toulouse University (IDEI-GREMAQ) and MIT

Thibaud Vergé, CREST-LEI

Vincent Verouden, Chief Economist Team of the European Commission, Directorate-General for Competition

John Vickers, Oxford University

Gregory J. Werden, US Department of Justice

Introduction

Paolo Buccirossi

Economics lies at the heart of competition, or antitrust, law. While in the early days the application of antitrust rules was almost entirely left to the wit of people with only a legal background, it is now widely accepted that the proper interpretation of these rules requires an understanding of how markets work and of how firms can alter their efficient functioning. This knowledge is the realm of economic science. As the awareness of the central role of economics in antitrust has progressed, so has the research. An industrial economist would probably say that the growth in the demand for economic knowledge coming from administrative bodies, courts, companies, and lawyers (in short, the antitrust community) has led to a reorganization of the industry, with a sharp increase in the supply of new theoretical models and more reliable empirical methods. This reorganization has taken place mostly over the last twenty years or so, and has significantly changed the landscape. Now seems the appropriate time to provide the antitrust community, which recognizes the economist as one of its members, with an updated map of the territory. This *Handbook* serves this purpose.

Different Jurisdictions, Same Economics: Aims and Scope of the *Handbook*

Not all jurisdictions have experienced an increase in the use of economics with the same intensity, rapidity, and scope, and some may still lag behind. The essays contained in this *Handbook* relate the economic theory to the application of competition, or antitrust, law mostly in two jurisdictions: the United States and the European Union. Between these two jurisdictions, there are nevertheless important differences in the way competition, or antitrust, rules are interpreted and applied. Even the name that identifies the relevant legislation differs: in the United States it is generally referred to as "antitrust law," whereas in the European Union it is normally referred to as "competition law." In this *Handbook* both terms are used interchangeably, and the choice of the title does not express a bias in favor of the United States.[1] It rather advocates the opinion that for the subject matter of this volume the many and notable differences between these two jurisdictions (and between them and all those that are not cited) are not pertinent. This idea needs to be explained.

The differences between the United States and the European Union, and more generally between jurisdictions, arise from three sources. The first is the institutional setting, which includes the nature of the public bodies empowered to apply these rules, their role in the process, the procedural rules and the sanction policy. The second is the political background and refers to the goals that are pursued by those that are in the position to shape the content of the legislation or to influence its application. The third is the language of the statutes and their interpretation.

At the institutional level, the US and the EU systems differ considerably.[2] First and foremost, the US system is a judiciary enforcement law system whereby the public agencies, the Antitrust Division of the Department of Justice and the Federal Trade Commission, have only the power to litigate a case before a court.[3] On the contrary in the European Union, at the community level and in many member states, competition laws are enforced through an administrative system in which the relevant competition authority has the power to make decisions that immediately produce effects on the parties. Therefore the European Commission, and many national competition authorities, act in the double role of "prosecutor" and "adjudicator." It is true that these administrative decisions are subject to a judicial review, so the last word rests in the hands of a court. However, the role of the courts, given their ex post intervention and the very episodic new gathering of evidence, is necessarily limited and, in the case of mergers, is de facto ineffective against negative decisions.[4]

The second important institutional difference concerns the nature and the severity of the sanctions that can be imposed in the two jurisdictions. In the United States, violations of Sections 1 and 2 of the Sherman Act are punishable with criminal fines for both companies and individuals and with imprisonment for individuals. In the European Union, violations of Articles 81 and 82 of the EC Treaty are not of a criminal law nature. Hence the Commission can only levy fines on undertakings, though this is not true for all member states.[5]

A third striking difference between the two jurisdictions regards the role private enforcement plays in fostering the effectiveness of competition law. A recent study commissioned by the European Commission, describes the state of damage actions for breaches of competition law in the enlarged EU as one of "total underdevelopment."[6] On the contrary, in the United States the actions brought by private plaintiffs, where the claimants can recover treble damages, represent the principal way in which the antitrust law is enforced.[7]

The differences stemming from the political background are also significant but less pronounced. At the heart of a different treatment of some business practices there may be the political objective of the creation of a EU-wide common market, a role that antitrust law in the United States did not need to play for obvious historical reasons. This peculiar political goal has lead to the development of a per se rule that bans as anticompetitive any attempt undertaken by private companies to partition the market along national boundaries. This rule may have little to do with any serious competitive concern.

Apart from this different development and to the extent that politics reflect some deeper cultural characteristics, the juxtaposition of the United States to the European Union is likely to be inappropriate. The Sherman Act has its roots in the English common law, which prohibits monopolies and other "combinations in restraint of trade" and the same may be true for other jurisdictions with the same historical and cultural roots. In continental Europe, competition law was primarily advocated by the German ordo-liberal school, which considered it as a means to curb the power of private companies (and its connection with public powers) and to prevent risks to the development of a stable democracy.[8] The fruits of these early seeds may still grow in some corner of the field and explain different attitudes toward the proper application of competition law.

The third source, the language of the statutes and their interpretation, is the cause of differences that are mostly superficial. By digging a little beneath the surface, one finds that the scope of the legal norms, even if drafted with different words, is now very similar and is becoming increasingly so. This similarity is due to the widespread use of the economic reasoning to distinguish lawful from unlawful conduct. Therefore it also explains why the content of this *Handbook* is applicable in both US and EU jurisdictions and in many others. Indeed, if by antitrust, or competition, law we intend a set of rules that aims at protecting competition as a means to achieve some well-defined economic goal, then these rules should prohibit those conducts that run against the goal and permit those that do not. The identification of these "anticompetitive" conducts, whatever is the language used to prohibit them, must hinge on some theoretical models that are able to predict the consequences of each conduct that may be scrutinized. Moreover the theory has to indicate what is the evidence that allows to choose the appropriate model and what facts are relevant to decide any specific case. This *Handbook* has been written under the assumption that what makes a conduct competitive, or anticompetitive, does not depend on how the legislator phrased the prohibitions and with the conviction that the economic science is the only body of knowledge that provides the rational foundation for the proper interpretation of any substantive antitrust rule. Since this point of view tends to be shared by both US and EU antitrust practitioners, and the validity of the economic science is not confined to one particular jurisdiction, the interpretation of the substantive provisions moves along a convergent path.[9] Hence this *Handbook*'s primary objective is to provide a comprehensive account of the economic models and of the economic evidence that allow one to determine whether a conduct is anticompetitive in any jurisdiction where an antitrust law exists.

Notwithstanding this convergence, the antitrust treatment of some practices is still different in the two jurisdictions, and in some cases the same facts have led to conflicting findings.[10] The explanation may be found in any of the three sources discussed above. The different conclusions reached by the competition authorities in the United States and in the European Union may be due to institutional or political differences, or to the different reliance placed on economic theory and economic evidence, or to the reference to different economic models or evidence to predict the likely consequences of a business practice or a merger.[11] I believe that the first two causes explain most of the divergent outcomes. However, there are cases where the institutional setting and the political background do not provide an exhaustive explanation. When the different decisions are due to the economic basis on which the relevant prohibition is interpreted, we must distinguish between the lack of appropriate economic reasoning behind a finding of illegality and the use of alternative economic models and evidence. While the former represents a curse, the latter may even be a blessing as it poses questions that spur the advancement of economics. Some contrasts are the genuine consequence of unsettled theoretical and empirical questions. This provides another motivation for this *Handbook*, that is, to highlight those issues that are not yet fully understood or settled and that should be on the research agenda of industrial and competition economists.

This *Handbook* covers the contribution of "industrial organization" researches to the identification of anticompetitive conducts and the enforcement of competition law. Industrial organization models aim at explaining the functioning of markets. These models are not inherently normative, as their intended aim is to understand the relationship between firms' conducts and the market outcome and to identify the market and institutional characteristics that influence them. However, these models provide the foundations for a normative theory, once a clear objective is defined. Before discussing this preliminary issue, I want to clarify what topics this *Handbook* does not cover and explain why.

As I have argued before, the actual day-to-day enforcement of antitrust law depends on the institutional setting and on the political or cultural background in which individuals and institutions act. One can refer to the analysis of these aspects of the application of the substantive antitrust norms as the analysis of the antitrust *policy*. Economics can contribute and has contributed to our understanding of the functioning of this larger and more complex system. And it can and has done so with both positive and normative theories. To clarify, some questions that may benefit from an economic analysis are: What motives explain the decisions of antitrust authorities and courts? How private and public interests shape the conduct of competition authorities or other agents involved in the application of antitrust rules? What standard of proof should be required in antitrust cases? Why in some jurisdictions the private enforcement of antitrust law is more frequent than in other jurisdictions? Which of the two types of enforcement is more effective in deterring anticompetitive conducts? Who should be qualified to present economic evidence in a trial? What is the best way to compute antitrust damages? This list could go on for many pages. Economics alone may prove insufficient to answer them all, but provides a unified and consistent framework to deal with them.

These questions are clearly different from the questions addressed in this *Handbook*: What conducts should be deemed anticompetitive? In what circumstances? and How can we identify them? These are the central questions of competition law. The reason why this *Handbook* is confined to these central questions (with one notable exception) is that the other questions mentioned above are much more general and not relevant to antitrust alone. For instance, the analysis of the motives behind the behavior of competition authorities and courts has been investigated in the "public choice" literature.[12] However, much of this literature is not about competition policy, and some important theoretical and empirical results stem from the analysis of other public policies. Therefore, had these issues been included in the project of the book, one would have had to choose whether to limit the exposition to the researches that had explicitly investigated the antitrust policy, running the risk of missing some fundamental results, or extend the coverage of the book to other areas. The second choice, while attractive in principle, would have made the entire project unmanageable. This explains the scope of the *Handbook* and its omissions. The only exception is the essay of Spagnolo that is about the application of whistleblower and leniency programs in antitrust. The reason for this exception will be given in the roadmap of the book.

The Economic Goals of Antitrust

In order to build a coherent interpretation of antitrust law, based on economics, we need to define its breadth and its objective. Antitrust is generally viewed as a public policy aimed at a fostering a public good: that is, competition. This explains why in almost all jurisdictions one or more public bodies have the task of overseeing the functioning of markets and the power to act against any violations of the antitrust laws. In the United States the Supreme Court has awarded the antitrust statutes near-constitutional status, while in the European Union the Court of Justice has affirmed the supremacy of the articles of the EC Treaty that contain the substantive antitrust prohibitions over national legislations. Yet competition is a fuzzy concept and some naïve or narrow notions of competition may induce interventions that are against the ultimate intended goal of the law or impede interventions that would be beneficial. For instance, if one believes that the essence of competition lies in the parties' freedom of contract, long-term relationships that hamper the future contractual freedom of one of the two parties can be considered anticompetitive regardless of their efficiency properties and justifications; if competition is seen as a process of discovery or a selection mechanism that is altered whenever the government interferes with it, then any antitrust intervention contrasts with its intended aim of protecting competition.

This problem can be overcome by recognizing that the chain that links means and objectives is longer. A first additional ring is added to the chain once we recognize that competition should not be intended as a goal in itself, but rather as a means to achieve some other goal that is in the interest of the public. If antitrust laws protect competition as a means to foster a different pubic goal, the interpretation of these laws must be based on a two-pronged criterion: one prong requires to establish whether a conduct hinders competition; the other prong requires to ascertain whether as a consequence of the impaired competition the other goal is not reached. Both prongs need to be qualified. Most of the current debate focuses on the second prong as if this alone would suffice to guide the interpretation of antitrust norms. This debate sees two positions confronting each other: one argues that antitrust law's final aim should be to maximize total welfare (which includes consumers' and firms surpluses with equal weight) or, equivalently, that its goal is allocative efficiency; the other argues that the goal of antitrust is to defend consumers so that consumer welfare represents the proper objective function. It is apparent that neither position suffices to decide whether a conduct violates antitrust law. Two examples make this clear. Suppose that a firm markets a product that is unsafe, and that it turns out that consumers are worse off because their health is exposed to some risk and that, in the end, also the firm is worse off as it must compensate the victims for the damage incurred. It is apparent that this conduct is against the welfare objective of competition law (whatever it is), but this does not make the firm liable under antitrust law. Many mergers fail to produce the synergies they promise and may even disrupt the efficient functioning of previously separated organizations so that eventually they create a less efficient firm. Nonetheless, I would be very surprised if an antitrust authority challenged a merger only on the grounds that it is likely to raise the cost of production of the merging firms, even though the merger is against some well-defined economic goal. In both examples the adverse effects on welfare do not stem from a reduction of competition, and therefore competition law should not be concerned. They clarify that before establishing what welfare notion is more apt to guide the interpretation of antitrust norms, we must restrict the set of conducts that may fall under the scrutiny of antitrust law, namely clarify the first prong.

While competition is a fuzzy concept, economists have found a clever way to say what a perfectly competitive market is. Perfect competition occurs when the market clears at a price equal to the marginal cost of production. When this does not happen, firms are said to possess market power. Market power, however, is not an absolute concept. It may exist to different degrees depending on the extent to which prices are above costs and on the time period during which a firm is able to maintain such level of price. The notion of market power defines the first prong. Competition law applies to those conducts that are aimed at creating, increasing, defending, or exploiting a significant market power.[13] Not all conducts that have these effects constitute an antitrust infringement, as many of these conducts are likely to foster both efficiency and consumer welfare. For instance, R&D investments, advertising and product differentiation, and other similar strategies are means used by firms to gain the ability to raise prices above costs, or in our terminology to obtain some market power. However, they are also likely to improve the welfare of consumers and of the overall society. As a consequence antitrust authorities rarely, if ever, challenge them.

Having clarified the first prong, I can turn to the total welfare versus consumer welfare debate. Although I do not have any reliable statistics,[14] my educated guess is that among economists the opinion that the ultimate goal of antitrust law should be to promote total welfare (allocative efficiency) prevails.[15] However, there are noteworthy exceptions.[16] The controversy boils down to the question of whether distributive issues should matter for the application of competition law. As pointed out by Martin (2006), this is a genuine policy question that cannot and should not be solved by economists. Economists can, however, try to identify the costs and benefits of using antitrust also as a distributive tool. On the costs side, I would list: the loss in the efficient allocation of resources caused by the prohibition of efficient conducts;[17] the risk of redistributing income from (relatively) poor firms' stakeholders to (relatively) rich consumers; and in the intermediate market, the unwarranted transfer of wealth from the seller's stakeholders to the buyers' one, where both sellers and buyers are firms. On the benefits side I can find only one convincing argument: if we believe that any transfer of wealth due to an anticompetitive conduct is unjust (independent of the other sources of wealth of the subjects involved in the transfer), its neutralization would be extremely difficult, if not impossible, through other public policies. I believe that the costs outweigh the benefits, and I enroll myself in the category of those that favor total welfare.

A different attitude may arise if we add an additional ring to the chain of means and goals. According to some recent contributions, which focus on mergers, even if total welfare is the ultimate goal of antitrust law, in some cases this goal is better pursued by endowing competition authorities with the objective of maximizing consumer welfare. Putting it differently, there may be a difference between the economic goal aimed at by antitrust law and the welfare *standard* that competition authorities have to adopt to interpret and enforce the law. This position rests on two different arguments. The first argument posits a strategic interaction between a competition authority and firms. The former announces its enforcement strategy, that is, the welfare standard on which it will assess a merger. The latter decides what merger to propose from a set of alternative mergers. Fridolfsson (2001) and Lyons (2002) show that there may be instances of this strategic interaction in which the adoption of a consumer welfare standard induces firms to select a merger with a higher total surplus than the merger they would have proposed had the competition authority adopted the other available standard. Suppose, indeed, that firms can choose between two profitable mergers, A and B. Merger A increases profits more than merger B. Consumers would be harmed if merger A takes place while they would benefit from the other merger. Finally, suppose that merger B is more efficient, in the sense that it leads to a higher level total welfare but that both mergers improve total welfare with respect to the case in which no merger at all takes place. If the competition authority adopts the total welfare standard, firms know that both mergers would be approved. Therefore they choose the merger with the highest increase in profits, that is, merger A. If the competition authority adopts the consumer welfare standard, firms know that merger A would be blocked and merger B would be allowed. Since from their point of view merger B is better than no merger, they would go for it. In this case the consumer welfare standard induces the firms to select the merger that yields the highest total welfare.

The second argument supporting a consumer standard, even in the absence of distributive ends, rests on political economy considerations. Neven and Röller (2005) argue that the parties to a merger can influence the outcome of the review through lobbying. In their model, consumers who are uninformed and dispersed do not "bid" to obtain their preferred outcome, while the merging firms and their rivals do and they are willing to devote resources to this activity up to the gain they would get from the merger. The competition authority is influenced by the lobbying activity to a degree that depends on the level of accountability of the authority and of the transparency in the procedure. If there is no perfect transparency, and the competition authority adopts a total welfare standard, the welfare of the merging firms and their rivals is counted more than once: it enters in the total welfare calculation, and (though only to some degree) in the bids of the parties. In this case there might exist inefficient mergers, in which the sum of the (positive) effect on firms' profits and the (negative) effect on consumers is negative, that are allowed by the competition authority because the first positive effect is given a greater weight than the second negative effect. If the competition authority adopts a consumer welfare standard, this double counting does not occur and such inefficient mergers would be blocked. From this short and simplified description of this model, it is apparent that in some circumstances the first best is achieved only with a standard defined by the weighted sum of the two components of the total welfare, profits, and consumer surplus, where the weights are set so as to balance the extent to which firms profits are overevaluated by the competition authority because of the lack of transparency.

A similar conclusion is reached by Baker (2005), who describes competition policy as a political bargain emerging from the interaction between two diffuse interest groups: producers and consumers. Through this bargain the two groups share the efficiency gains that competition policy brings about in such a way that neither group can perform better by reneging on the bargain. As a consequence competition authorities should enforce competition laws with the view to maximize aggregate welfare, subject to the constraint that the equilibrium attained in the bargaining process is not disrupted. This requires to provide both producers and consumers with a level of surplus that is above the level they would obtain in the absence of a competition regime. Since, after the change in the courts' attitude provoked by the Chicago School, the prevalent antitrust doctrine has removed the risk that antitrust rules are exploited by consumers, the protection of consumers' interest identifies the most important constraint. Hence the welfare standard to be adopted has to contain a qualified emphasis on the welfare of consumers.

To sum up, these recent researches show that in some circumstances competition law performs better if consumer surplus is given a higher weight than produces surplus because of (1) the strategic interaction between firms and competition authorities, (2) the need to balance the firms' ability to influence the activity of the enforcement agencies, and (3) the necessity of guaranteeing political support for competition policy from the constituency that is more likely to withdraw it. These considerations are important but not conclusive.

Indeed they only prove that in some cases, a standard that is more consumer-orientated is preferable even where only efficiency matters. They trigger new questions and indicate new research themes. A first question is empirical: How frequent are the cases where the consumer welfare standard yields more efficient decisions? If they are exceptional, we should avoid creating a potentially risky and confusing misalignment between the ultimate goal of competition law and the standard adopted to interpret its prohibitions. Even if we find that these cases are a rule more than an exception, we may want to know if we can keep a more consistent mind-set by changing other features of competition policy. For instance, if a consumer welfare standard is justified by the existence of a potential bias in favor of firms in the decision-making process of competition authorities, can we cure this bias instead of abandoning a total welfare standard? Which of the two options is more efficient?

These questions do not have an answer yet. The reader may be led to think that the attempt to base the application of competition law on a solid economic theory is doomed to fail. Indeed a critic may say: if the definition of a clear economic goal is a prerequisite to a rational effect-based interpretation of the norms, the unsettled state of the economic debate on this point renders unstable the foundations of the entire edifice. This criticism is unwarranted. First, the choice of the economic goal of antitrust law, and of its guiding welfare standard, is a policy decision. Once this has been made, economists can keep quarreling about it but cannot change it. And when we have clearly defined goals and standards, the economic theory has to be applied to discern those conducts that are against them from those that are not. Second, whatever is the adopted standard, industrial organization models try to predict the consequences of given conducts on the market equilibrium and therefore on each component of the social welfare. The same models can and should be applied whatever is the welfare standard. Having reassured the reader on the usefulness of this *Handbook*, I can now describe its content.

Roadmap of the *Handbook*

There are three ways in which the public good that antitrust aims to protect may be jeopardized by firms' behavior. The first is the sheer creation and exploitation of market power by individual firms, the second is the joint exploitation of market power by a group of firms, and the third is the partial or total exclusion of competitors from the market aimed at creating or protecting the market power of a dominant firm. Usually antitrust issues are treated within a different framework that follows the typical formal structure of competition law, which contains norms dealing with mergers, agreements (either horizontal or vertical), and unilateral conducts. For instance, in the European Union, mergers are subject to an ex ante control regime that is set in the EC Regulation No 139/2004 (replacing the initial EC Regulation 4064/1989). Article 81 of the EC Treaty prohibits agreements that have as their object or effect a restriction of competition. This prohibition covers cartels, other horizontal agreements, and vertical agreements. Article 82 prohibits abuses of dominant position both in the form of "exploitative" abuses and in the form of "exclusionary" abuses. In the United States, the main antitrust prohibition are set in Sections 1 and 2 of the Sherman Act (1890). Section 1 prohibits "every contract, combination..., or conspiracy, in restraint of trade...." This provision applies to a wide range of agreements both horizontal and vertical. Section 2 prohibits monopolization or an attempt to monopolize. It applies to unilateral actions undertaken by firms with a dominant position. Mergers, although they may be also covered by Section 1, have been more specifically disciplined by the Clayton Act, passed in 1914, and then by the Hart-Scott-Rodino Act passed in 1976.

For the sake of simplicity, this book follows these formal structure even if it is recognized that the same conduct (including mergers) can give rise to different competitive concerns and that the same competitive concern may be at the heart of the antitrust discipline of different conducts.

Chapter 1 sets the scene, because whatever is the conduct to be investigated, the central empirical question is how we can identify the existence of market power. A seemingly different question that emerges in almost all antitrust cases is how can we correctly draw the product and geographic boundaries of a market, namely how to delineate the antitrust relevant market. Jonathan Baker and Timothy Bresnahan discuss these two topics in the broader context of the use of empirical methods in antitrust cases.

The first part of the book is formed by three groups of chapters that deals with mergers (chapters 2–5), agreements (chapters 6–10), and abuses of dominance or unilateral conducts (chapters 11–13).

In chapter 2, Gregory Werden and Luke Froeb review the theory underlying the unilateral competitive effects of mergers and two classes of empirical methods used to make quantitative predictions about these effects: merger simulations and reduced-form empirical models. Chapter 3, by Kai-Uwe Kühn, deals with the economic theory of the coordinated effects of mergers. He surveys the relevant empirical work on this topic and evaluates the policy rules developed in the United States and in the European Union to assess the risk of the pro-collusive effects of mergers. Chapter 4, by Michael Riordan, takes up the analysis of the competitive effects of vertical mergers, surveying the economic theory on the risk of foreclosure and tacit collusion and relating these theories to some actual cases. This first group of chapters is closed by the analysis of the competitive effects of conglomerate mergers made by Damien Neven (chapter 5). Neven's contribution focuses mostly on the treatment of conglomerate mergers in the European Union, but his review of the literature covers issues that are relevant in all jurisdictions.

The first theme addressed in the second group of chapters is cartels. Hard-core cartels in the form of price-fixing or market-sharing agreements constitute one the most pernicious forms of anticompetitive behavior and are generally prohibited per se. Therefore the main question for the application of antitrust law is not whether they are anticompetitive, but how to detect and how to deter them. Joe Harrington, in chapter 6, addresses the first issue. His contribution is devoted to the quest for empirical methods that may provide circumstantial evidence of a cartelized market. This evidence would direct the (scarce) resources of the competition authorities toward those industries in which explicit collusion is more likely, to filter allegations and pursue only those that are more likely to be correct, or finally to corroborate other forms of evidence in the legal process.

The best antitrust policy, however, is not that which is able to detect all cartels but that in which no cartels are detected because none is ever formed. Chapter 7, by Giancarlo Spagnolo, describes how well-designed leniency and whistleblower programs can be exploited to increase the deterrence properties of an antitrust law and the related sanction policy. This chapter is the only one in which the main focus is on some institutional features of antitrust policy. However, the issue is of such importance for the antitrust treatment of cartels that its omission would have been unforgivable. Chapter 8, which I have written, deals with facilitating practices, namely business conducts that favor the emergence of an anticompetitive equilibrium, such as pre-play communications, information sharing, partial ownership arrangements, and best-price policies. Chapter 9, by Patrick Rey and Thibaud Vergé, surveys the economic theory of vertical restraints. These are contractual arrangements among firms operating at different levels in the production process that may be aimed at restricting the set of strategies the parties can undertake. Rey and Vergé explore the pro- and anticompetitive motives that might explain the adoption of such contractual restrictions and derive their implications for the application of competition rules. The same issue is investigated from a different angle by Francine Lafontaine and Margaret Slade in chapter 10. They discuss the empirical methods that can be used to assess the competitive consequences of vertical restraints and survey the findings of empirical studies that have addressed the effect of restraints in the context of exclusive retail relationships.

Chapters 9 and 10 form a bridge from the second to the third group of chapters, because, as Rey and Vergé point out, vertical restraints are scrutinized both under the norms that prohibit anticompetitive agreements and under the abuse of dominance prohibitions. Chapters 11 and 12 focus more specifically on business practices that may constitute a violation of these prohibition. In chapter 11 John Vickers discusses the advantages and disadvantages of three criteria that can be used to separate competitive unilateral conducts from anticompetitive ones: the sacrifice test, the as efficient competitor test, and the consumer harm test. In chapter 12 Mark Armstrong examines the welfare consequences of conducts that allow firms to price-discriminate, including bundling.

The last part of the *Handbook* is devoted to the analysis of some market features that have a great impact on the way firms compete and may influence the proper application of antitrust rules. Nicholas Economides (chapter 13) discusses how antitrust law and regulatory rules should be applied to industries characterized by the presence of network effects. Richard Gilbert (chapter 14) examines the intricate, and sometime conflicting, relationship between competition law and the defense of intellectual property. Jean-Charles

Rochet and Jean Tirole (chapter 15) present an overview of the recent literature on two-sided markets and derive its implications for competition policy. Paul Klemperer (chapter 16) takes up the analysis of markets organized through auctions and bidding processes and consider if, and to what extent, the application of competition law should differ in these markets. Finally, since competition can be hurt not only from the conducts of firms but also from inappropriate state interferences, and in the European Union state aid control is considered an integral part of its competition law and policy, chapter 17, by Hans Friederiszick, Lars-Hendrik Röller, and Vincent Verouden, is devoted to this issue and discusses the contribution of economic theory that could enhance the effectiveness of this policy.

I believe that researchers and practitioners will find this *Handbook* useful for their work. Especially the latter are likely to find in the chapters of this handbook many instances and examples of which they have had some significant experience they can share with or question the authors about. I invite them to write me at paolo.buccirossi@learlab.it to provide comments and suggestions.

Acknowledgments

My primary debt is to the authors of the chapters in the *Handbook*. Some of them provided valuable suggestions at a very early stage of the project and I am indebted to them for their encouragement. They are Joe Harrington, Patrick Rey, and especially Giancarlo Spagnolo. I would like to thank also those who contributed to this book at different stages in various, but all important ways. In no significant order, they are Dana Andrus, John Covell, Carlo Cambini, Michele Grillo, Yan Ho, Pierluigi Sabbatini, and Simona Ventullo. Finally, I thank all the participants to the 2005 Lear Conference on the Economics of Competition Law where many of the chapters of this *Handbook* were initially presented and discussed.

Notes

1. The use of "antitrust" in the title of this volume reflects a personal bias. In Italy the administrative body that is in charge of the application of competition law, where I worked as an economist and was initially exposed to this fascinating field, is generally referred to as the Autorità Antitrust.

2. The following discussion is necessarily cursory. The interested reader can consult the encyclopedic Areeda and Hovenkamp (2000–2006), Holmes (2006), or Sullivan and Grimes (2006), among others, for a detailed description of the US antitrust law system, and Jones and Sufrin (2001) or Whish (2003), among others, for the EU system.

3. There are, however, important differences between the DOJ and the FTC: only the DOJ can file criminal cases. FTC actions are initially adjudicated by an Administrative Law Judge, whose decisions can be either approved or disapproved by the Commission itself. Only the subsequent FTC decision can be appealed before a federal court. Further it has to be noted that not all cases are actually litigated. In civil cases the public agencies and the defendants, in order to avoid litigation, can enter a consent decree that is a binding out-of-court settlement approved by the court.

4. Although recently the Court of First Instance has annulled several Commission's mergers prohibitions (i.e., *Airtours/First Choice*; *Tetra Laval/Sidel*; *Schneider/Legrand*, and to some extent *Ge/Hobeywell*), none of these mergers were consummated as the annulment decision intervened at a time that could not allow a firm to resurrect

a deal blocked by the Commission. For a critical view of the limited role of the EU judiciary review system in the merger regulation, see Patterson and Shapiro (2003).

5. Criminal sanctions have been recently introduced in some EU member states (e.g., the United Kingdom and Ireland) leading to what has been referred to as the "criminalization of EU competition law." For a detailed analysis of this tendency and a discussion of its pros and cons, see the contributions in Cseres et al. (2006), Buccirossi and Spagnolo (2007), and references therein.

6. Waelbroeck, Slater, and Even-Shoshan (2004).

7. According to Hovenkamp (1994, p. 542), in the US "roughly 90% of antitrust cases are brought by private plaintiffs."

8. See Amato (1997) for an interesting account of these origins of competition law in Europe.

9. A further signal of this convergent trend is the activity of the International Competition Network (ICN), an informal forum that gathers national and multinational competition authorities from over 80 jurisdictions. The main scope of the ICN is to create cooperation among enforcement agencies and to develop best practices in order to foster a coherent application of competition law (see ⟨www.internationalcompetitionnetwork.org⟩).

10. Much of the most recent debate over the differences between US and EU competition law took place in the aftermath of the *GE/Honeywell* merger that lead to opposite decisions in the two jurisdictions. In the United States the merger was not challenged in court, whereas the European Commission blocked it. The spring–summer 2004 issue of the *Antitrust Bulletin* is entirely devoted to this theme and reports other noteworthy divergent decisions.

11. Of course there might be a strong relationship among these factors as the accurate use of economic reasoning is influenced by the institutional characteristics of the antitrust system. Neven (2006) provides a through analysis of how some institutional features of the EU prosecutorial system of antitrust enforcement have negatively affected the application of rigorous economic analysis in the enforcement of EU competition law.

12. See Tollison (1985) for an early analysis and the works in McChesney and Shugart II (1994) for more recent contributions.

13. Driving a car is a risky activity. However, the law does not prohibit this activity but only restricts it to reduce the degree of risk. This choice is justified because the expected benefits of a strict prohibition would be smaller relative to the costs it would impose on society. Similarly antitrust law is not concerned with any instance of market power because such a wide scope would entail costs that are lager than the expected benefits. This explains why antitrust law only deals with those cases in which the degree of market power is substantial.

14. Any attempt to assess the weight of the two groups is complicated by a confusion provoked by the influential work of Bork (1978). In his book he argues that efficiency (total welfare) is the only legitimate end of antitrust but then qualifies this objective function as the maximization of consumer welfare. Since the publication of Bork's book many commentators have taken a stance in favor of the total welfare standard and have dubbed it as the maximization of consumer welfare.

15. Whinston (2006, pp. 6–7) writes: "To an economist the thought of designing antitrust policy to maximize aggregate surplus comes naturally and, indeed, much of the economics literature implicitly has taken this to be the appropriate objective for antitrust policy". This position has been taken explicitly by Motta (2004), and by Farrell and Katz (2006).

16. Among them, Lande (1989) and Salop (2005). Their position is mainly based on a positive analysis of the original motives behind the antitrust statutes in the United States.

17. This represents an obvious cost and is at the core of the debate. It is therefore surprising to find statements that affirm that the objective of competition law is to maximize consumer welfare *and* guarantee the optimal allocation of resources. These statements are not infrequent in soft law or policy documents issued by the enforcement agencies. For instance: "The objective of Article 81 is to protect competition on the market as a means of enhancing consumer welfare and of ensuring an efficient allocation of resources" (EC Guidelines on Article 81.3). "The modern consensus is that the objective of antitrust policy is to maximize consumer welfare and promote economic efficiency through the optimal allocation of resources in a competitive market context" (US "Objectives of U.S. Antitrust Law," in OECD 2003). These statements define two objectives of antitrust law. If these two objectives were never in conflict, the entire debate over the welfare standard would be pointless. Arguing that they are rarely in conflict does not solve the problem either, because the only reason for the debate is to find the proper solution when this conflict arises.

References

Amato, G. 1997. *Antitrust and the Bounds of Power: The Dilemma of Liberal Democracy in the History Market.* Portland, OR: Hart Publishing.

Areeda, P., and H. Hovenkamp. 2000–2006. *Antitrust Law: An Analysis of Antitrust Principles and Their Application.* Boston: Little, Brown, 1978–1999; 2nd ed., New York: Aspen Law and Business, 2000–2006.

Baker, J. B. 2005. Competition Policy as a Political Bargain. Mimeo. Available at SSRN ⟨http://ssrn.com/abstract=649442⟩.

Bork, R. H. 1978. *The Antitrust Paradox.* New York: Basic Books.

Buccirossi, P., and G. Spagnolo. 2007. Optimal fines in the era of whistleblowers. Should Price fixers still go to prison? In V. Ghosal and J. Stennek, eds., *The Political Economy of Antitrust.* Amsterdam: Elsevier.

Cseres, K. J., Schinkel, M. P., and Vogelaar, F. O. W., eds. 2006. *Criminalization of Competition Law Enforcement—Economic and Legal Implications for the EU Member States.* London: Edwar Elgar.

Farrell, J., and M. L. Katz. 2006. The economics of welfare standards in antitrust. CPC Paper 06-061. University of California, Berkley.

Fridolfsson, S. O. 2001. A consumer surplus defense in merger control. In Essays on Endogenous Market Theory, Ph.D. dissertation. Stockholm University.

Holmes, W. C. 2006. *Antitrust Law Handbook: 2006 Edition.* Antitrust Law Library. St. Paul, MN: West Publishing.

Hovenkamp, H. 1994. *Federal Antitrust Policy: The Law of Competition and its Practice.* St. Paul, MN: West Publishing.

Jones, A., and B. Sufrin. 2001. *EC Competition Law: Text, Cases, and Materials.* Oxford: Oxford University Press.

Lande, R. H. 1989. Chicago's false foundation: Wealth transfers (not just efficiency) should guide antitrust. *Antitrust Law Journal* 58: 631–44.

Lyons, B. R. 2002. Could politicians be more right than economists? A theory of merger standards. Working Paper CCR 02-1. University of East Anglia.

Martin, S. 2006. The goals of antitrust policy. In W. D. Collins, ed., *ABA Competition Law and Policy*, ABA, forthcoming.

McChesney, F. S., and W. F. Shughart II, eds. 1994. *The Causes and Consequences of Antitrust: The Public-Choice Perspective.* Chicago: University of Chicago Press.

Motta, M. 2004. *Competition Policy: Theory and Practice.* Cambridge: Cambridge University Press.

Neven, D. 2006. Competition economics and antitrust in Europe. *Economic Policy* (October): 741–91.

Neven, D., and L.-H. Röller. 2005. Consumer surplus vs. welfare standard in a political economy model of merger control. *International Journal of Industrial Organization* 23 (9–10): 665–68.

OECD. 2003. The objectives of competition law and policy and optimal design of a competition agency. *Global Forum on Competition.* Paris: OECD.

Patterson, D. E., and C. Shapiro. 2003. Transatlantic divergence in *GE/Honeywell*: Causes and lessons. *Antitrust* (Fall): 18–26.

Salop, S. C. 2005. Question: What is the real and proper antitrust welfare standard? Answer: The *true* consumer welfare standard. Statement before the Antitrust Modernization Commission, November 2, 2005, available at ⟨www.amc.gov/public_strudies_fr28902/exclus_conduct_pdf/051104_Salop_Mergers.pdf⟩.

Sullivan, L. A., and W. S. Grimes. 2006. *The Law of Antitrust. An Integrated Handbook.* St. Paul, MN: West Publishing.

Tollison, R. D. 1985. Public choice and antitrust. *Cato Journal* 3 (4): 905–16.

Waelbroeck, D., D. Slater, and G. Even-Shoshan. 2004. *Study on the Conditions of Claims for Damages in Case of Infringement of EC Competition Rules*, DG Comp, European Commission, Brussels. Available at ⟨http://ec.europa.eu/comm/competition/antitrust/others/actions_for_damages/study.html⟩.

Whinston, M. D. 2006. *Lectures on Antitrust Economics.* Cambridge: MIT Press.

Whish, R. 2003. *Competition Law.* London: Butterworths.

1 Economic Evidence in Antitrust: Defining Markets and Measuring Market Power

Jonathan B. Baker and Timothy F. Bresnahan

Antitrust law, policy, and practice are the product of a long and fruitful interdisciplinary collaboration between law and economics. Our chapter addresses an important aspect of that collaboration: the use courts can and should make of two bodies of knowledge in empirical industrial organization economics, as that academic discipline has evolved over the last few decades. Our examples focus on the US experience, which we know best. But we are confident that the broad considerations we discuss apply to any competition policy regime.

The first body of economic knowledge we discuss involves methods of distinguishing among alternative explanations for market outcomes or firm conduct. This is termed the problem of "identification" in empirical economics. We show how courts can apply what economists have learned about identification to the problems of defining markets and determining whether market power has been exercised. We show that the same analytic issues arise regardless of whether the evidence on these concepts is quantitative or qualitative.

The second relevant body of economic knowledge derives from the empirical economics research literature, taken as a whole. That literature demonstrates that differences among industries are important, making the industry the appropriate unit of analysis for addressing economic issues related to competition policy. A similar conclusion was reached long ago in antitrust law, when market definition became central to reasonableness analysis. But, as we explain, the research literature goes further in a way that has not yet been fully appreciated in antitrust: it suggests generalizations across closely related industries that can be exploited to help evaluate evidence and resolve cases.

We conclude by considering ways of increasing the institutional capacity of the judicial system to make use of these two bodies of economic learning. These include a possible limited role for neutral economic experts in litigation, and a role for the antitrust enforcement agencies in identifying and codifying relevant generalizations about industries from the empirical economic literature to make that learning available to courts.

1.1 Antitrust as an Interdisciplinary Collaboration

Antitrust law, more than most legal fields, looks like an outpost of economics. Competition policy decision-makers today rely extensively on economic concepts, reasoning, and evidence. Economic terms like elasticity of demand, marginal cost, and oligopoly behavior have become part of the language of antitrust.

The importance of economics is most evident when antitrust cases are resolved in litigation. In deciding individual cases, courts routinely undertake a detailed economic inquiry into the nature of competition and the effect of challenged practices on that competition. This is most evident in merger analysis, where modern examples are numerous.[1] Economic concepts, reasoning, and evidence are central to modern antitrust analysis outside the merger context as well.[2] In enforcement agency investigations as well as antitrust litigation, the development and interpretation of evidence about industry market power and conditions of entry, and about the likely effects of a merger or business practice, are importantly exercises in applied economics.

Economic reasoning also plays an important role in framing legal rules. Perhaps the most notable example occurred in 1977 when the Supreme Court overruled the per se prohibition against nonprice vertical restraints, causing such practices to be evaluated under the rule of reason.[3] The Court emphasized that a blanket prohibition was inappropriate given that manufacturers can use such contractual restrictions to promote competition by inducing retailers to provide point-of-sale services like promotion and after-sale service, through preventing dealer free-riding.

When industrial organization economists create new tools and methodological approaches, the antitrust field pays attention. For example, as new empirical methods of detecting and measuring market power have been developed, and as advances in computerization have facilitated the collection and manipulation of data, empirical economic tools have increasingly been applied to measure market power in antitrust enforcement and litigation. Since our own experience using empirical methods in antitrust began during the mid-1980s,[4] and since we last surveyed the topic in 1992,[5] the use of such methods has grown rapidly. It is no longer a surprise to see empirical analyses presented to the antitrust enforcement agencies by outside parties during the course of an investigation, developed by enforcers to analyze a matter, or presented as part of expert economic testimony in litigation.

Just as antitrust has become infused with economics, industrial organization economics—the economics field most closely related to antitrust—has turned its attention to the legal system. Over the past few decades many of the issues and problems addressed in the research literature on industrial organization economists have been suggested or framed by antitrust cases. In one widely used undergraduate industrial organization text, for example, the index listing legal cases most involving antitrust goes on for three pages.[6] Moreover many academic economists in the industrial organization field undertake litigation-related consulting projects involving antitrust issues.

Rather than viewing antitrust law as another victory for economic imperialism, or industrial organization economics as captured by the concerns of well-heeled corporate clients with antitrust problems, we understand these developments as the natural result of a long and successful interdisciplinary collaboration between law and economics. That deep engagement was probably inevitable. Most modern competition law regimes have economic goals, such as promoting economic efficiency or consumer welfare, in whole or substantial part.[7]

An emphasis on economic goals inevitably brings economics to bear, leading courts to frame antitrust issues in terms of economic concepts such as market power, competitive effects, entry, and efficiencies, and to interpret the detailed facts involving a particular industry and specific challenged practices through application of the logical framework supplied by economics.[8] Courts have become analytically rigorous about the effects of the challenged conduct on competition: identifying the market or markets in which competition has or will likely be harmed and the mechanism by which the challenged conduct does so. In US antitrust law the use of an economic framework was abetted by the development of the "antitrust injury" doctrine, which requires plaintiffs in many cases to explain how their injury flows from the antitrust violation they have alleged.[9] This doctrine implements the key analytical distinction from economics between protecting competition and merely protecting competitors, as it ensures that plaintiffs may not recover damages merely because they have been harmed.

Antitrust analysis also reflects the concerns of the legal system, leading judges at times to approach issues in ways that differ from how we economists might act on our own. Courts may, for example, undertake the step of defining markets even in settings where the competitive effects of business conduct can be measured directly, settings where economists might find market definition unnecessary. Economists often prefer to bring all the available information to bear, whereas courts at times adopt truncated analyses that exclude certain relevant inquiries in order to reduce the costs of administering the legal system and to specify clear and simple rules that give more guidance to courts and firms. The legal system will not fine-tune particular industries to achieve specific economic goals through regulatory determinations, as some economists have suggested. Antitrust policy properly rejects frequent suggestions that courts or regulators attempt to determine that a particular price be achieved, that a particular entrant come in, or that a particular industry structure is efficient. Rather, to the extent possible, the legal system trusts the competitive mechanism to achieve economic goals. For example, merger law does not seek to identify and create the most efficient industry structure; it merely attempts to determine whether a particular merger in an industry would harm competition.

1.2 The Empirical Problem of Identification

1.2.1 Empirical Economic Methods in Antitrust

Economic methods are valuable to antitrust because they encourage precise measurement and analysis of key economic relationships and effects.[10] In antitrust enforcement and litigation the use of economic methods helps focus the attention of decision-makers and litigants on the connection between the economic theory of the case and the evidence. Economic methods help clarify what hypotheses are in dispute and what evidence can help test them. Economic methods also encourage analytical rigor.[11] Careful articulation of the theory can clarify thinking by laying bare key assumptions and reasoning steps, and by structuring the collection of evidence.

Our chapter addresses two facets of empirical economic methods of testing theories with evidence that have particular relevance for antitrust analysis: decision-making when information is "local" and identification. First, economic methods bring to the surface the background assumptions that underlie any particular articulation of the link between economic evidence and the theory of the case. Antitrust policy-making, whether conducted by enforcers or courts, invariably takes place under conditions of uncertainty using what we term "local" information. Information is local for the obvious reason that the record in any investigation or case is necessarily limited in scope. Litigants have neither infinite time nor infinite resources to gather information. Information is also local for a more subtle reason: inferences about economic concepts like market power or efficiencies, whether quantitative or qualitative, are never made in a vacuum. Rather, these inferences are necessarily predicated on assumptions that permit estimation of the magnitude of the effects.

Economic reasoning connecting theory and evidence lays bare those assumptions, allowing them to be recognized. This in turn facilitates evaluation of the plausibility of such assumptions and the extent to which conclusions depend on them. Accordingly, empirical economists routinely test the robustness of their conclusions to alternative assumptions, and identify the key assumptions underlying their analysis. This reasoning process has obvious application to the evaluation of economic evidence in the courtroom, and much of what goes on in the back and forth over empirical work between expert economists can also be understood this way.

The need to make decisions when information is local has another implication for investigations and litigation: it heightens the importance of using all available evidence, whether quantitative or qualitative, in antitrust decision-making. For this reason we give qualitative and quantitative evidence equal attention below when we discuss identification with respect to the market definition and market power inquiries. Moreover the need to make decisions when information is local heightens the value of relying on generalizations based on studies of related industries when reaching conclusions about industry performance and firm conduct, as we will also discuss further below.

In the remainder of this section we address a second important facet of empirical economic methods with particular relevance when evidence is analyzed in nonexperimental contexts such as antitrust: identification. We begin with a perspective on quantitative data analysis, but the conclusions we reach also apply to the analysis of qualitative evidence. Antitrust analysis, like most work in empirical social science, is best viewed generally as making inferences from evidence without the benefit of performing experiments like those that are routine in high school chemistry.

When data are analyzed in both experimental and nonexperimental contexts, the analysis must address a number of difficulties, including specification (what are the range of sensible general forms for the relationship under evaluation, including the relevant variables, the way they could interact, and the nature of errors or uncertainty?),[12] observation (how well do the measures approximate the variables they are intended to represent?), and estimation (what do the data in the sample suggest as to the range of plausible relationships among variables?). But inference in the social sciences, including economics, must also confront a distinctive problem, difficulties in identification, which are largely not issues in the experimental context of the physical sciences.[13] The identification problem arises because empirical economists can rarely perform experiments on economic actors; they must instead look carefully for settings in which nature has created an experiment for them. In planning an empirical test, economists must therefore explain why it is reasonable to interpret the data as having been created by an implicit experiment, and describe the nature of that experiment. This explanation—identification—is an important part of empirical economic analysis.

More generally, identification can be understood as clarifying the basis on which one theory can be preferred to another in nonexperimental evidence. This problem in data analysis has obvious relevance for antitrust analysis, when a court must select between alternative interpretations of industry behavior. All antitrust cases that go to trial involve a contest between at least two distinct theories explaining firm conduct, one in which the challenged behavior lessens competition and one in which it is efficient. The economic principle of identification focuses attention on the correspondence between the evidence and the competing economic theories, and thus on whether the evidence can be used to distinguish between competing theories of the case.

We illustrate these points through a close analysis of identification strategies in two areas of antitrust practice: defining markets and measuring market power. The first area focuses on identifying demand-side attributes of the industry at issue; the second on identifying supply-side attributes. Our chapter does not address the measurement of damages, the problem of inferring agreement from circumstantial evidence or the many other areas of antitrust practice where economic evidence is routinely employed.

1.2.2 Identifying Buyer Substitution in Market Definition

The empirical problem of identifying the extent of buyer substitution is ubiquitous in antitrust analysis. It is central not only to market definition, our primary example in this section, but also to the identification of unilateral effects of merger among sellers of differentiated products, an issue to which we will also refer. In both settings a key empirical question is whether demand grows less elastic when price increases are coordinated across a more extensive scope of products or locations. This is the question that determines whether the products and locations constitution an antitrust market or whether a merger would create unilateral effects by lessening localized competition.

Notwithstanding the close similarity of the economic questions addressed in these two inquiries, the types of evidence commonly relied upon to answer differ substantially. In practice, the unilateral effects inquiry gravitates toward quantitative evidence,[14] while the market definition inquiry commonly looks first and often exclusively to qualitative evidence. This difference—on its surface something of a paradox—may have a number of explanations. First, market definition may tend toward qualitative evidence because it was recognized as a central question in antitrust litigation long before quantitative evidence became important, while the unilateral effects theory became persuasive only with the development of empirical tools that allowed precise measurement of the extent of localized competition and with the widespread availability of point-of-sale scanner data for retail products (which are commonly differentiated, often by brand name).[15] Second, unilateral effects analysis may gravitate toward quantitative evidence because it can be difficult to delineate market boundaries convincingly in industries characterized by extensive product differentiation. With market shares difficult to determine (and not necessarily meaningful in any event),[16] quantitative methods generally provide more convincing evidence of competitive problems than do market shares.[17] Third, market definition may tend toward qualitative evidence because it is frequently (though improperly) assessed in a vacuum, unmoored from the theory of harm to competition. By contrast, the assessment of unilateral effects involves the direct evaluation of a competitive effects theory, and this connection is readily made evident when quantitative evidence is analyzed. In principle, there is no good reason for ignoring quantitative evidence in market definition or ignoring qualitative evidence in evaluating unilateral effects; depending on industry circumstances and the nature of the available information, either type of evidence could be the most compelling in any particular case. Accordingly our discussion will focus on the empirical economic issues at stake in identifying a market, without regard to whether the evidence is qualitative or quantitative. But we will often employ quantitative examples to illustrate methodological points, when that is how the issues can be made most clear. Our discussion of market definition is limited to settings in which the alleged harm to competition is prospective, and to those in which the theory of why competition is harmed involves cooperative rather than exclusionary conduct. Accordingly we do not consider, among other things, the *Cellophane* fallacy.

It is obvious to economists that there is an implicit economic argument underlying market definition, and that this argument is closely related to the economic and legal theory of a particular case. In a horizontal effects merger case, for example, the relevant question is whether competitive incentives of the merging firms will change following their transaction. If there is a great deal of competition for the merging firms' products from other firms, competitive incentives will change little. Market definition offers one way to get at this question, albeit an imperfect or incomplete one.[18] By contrast, courts do not always see the market definition exercise as related to the economic theory of harm. Instead, they may think of market definition largely in a legally analytical way, as one of the things that must be proved for the reasonableness analysis in an antitrust case.

Regardless of how market definition is understood, it is often a useful component of the way antitrust doctrine is implemented in court. It requires the plaintiff in the antitrust suit to state, with reasonable specificity, what competition might be harmed by the challenged practices—by a merger, by allegedly exclusionary acts and practices, by an agreement on practices said to facilitate coordination, and so forth. Indeed market definition can be useful in this procedural sense even when market shares are not strongly probative of the magnitude of likely competitive harm. The market definition requirement also permits the defendant to rebut the idea that competition is fragile enough to be harmed, by attempting to establish a wider market.

The US merger guidelines adopt a conceptual approach to market definition that emphasizes an analysis of buyer substitution.[19] This approach is generally but not invariably followed by US courts.[20] By this methodology a candidate market does not qualify as a relevant antitrust market unless the firms participating would find it profitable to raise price for some or all of their products, at some or all of their locations, after accounting for the likely buyer response to a higher price. This analysis turns on the elasticity of candidate market demand. In particular, to first order, it would be profitable for the firms participating in the candidate market to raise price if and only if the inverse elasticity of the residual demand facing the firms[21] exceeds their Lerner index of price–cost margin $(1/ > L)$.[22] In the event this condition is not met, because candidate market demand is too elastic, the candidate market is expanded to include demand substitutes (additional products or additional locations). The candidate market expansion continues until demand grows sufficiently less elastic as to satisfy the condition for a price increase to be profitable.

The economic problem in evaluating unilateral competitive effects of mergers among sellers of differentiated products is similar to that of market definition. In differentiated products industries, competition may be localized: buyers may view some products as closer substitutes to each other, and individual sellers may, in consequence, compete more directly with those rivals selling the closest demand substitutes. A merger of firms selling two products in localized competition may lead to higher prices for each product, since the merged firm can now recoup some of the profit it would previously have lost as a result of buyer substitution were it to raise price. Before the merger (assume here single-product firms) each firms sets price such that the inverse elasticity of its residual demand function equals its Lerner index of price–cost margin. If the two products are in localized competition, the residual demand for one or both grows less elastic, giving the merged firm the incentive to raise one or both prices.

As should be evident, in order to define markets or assess unilateral effects, it is essential to determine the extent of buyer substitution caused by a price increase. A complete quantitative assessment would also require information about the price–cost margin.[23] But the central economic issue at stake in market definition or unilateral competitive effects is the likely magnitude of demand substitution.

In the remainder of this section we examine strategies for identifying the magnitude of buyer substitution in the event of a price increase. We look first at how demand substitution is identified, and separated from other causes of price increases, when two common quantitative approaches are employed: estimation of demand elasticities and inference about buyer substitution from the way prices vary as firm conduct or market structure changes. We then show how the same and other approaches to identification apply when evidence as to demand substitution is qualitative.

Identification When Evidence Is Quantitative

Estimating Demand Elasticities   To focus our discussion of how buyer substitution is identified, we first sketch a hypothetical study seeking to provide evidence as to whether the retail sale of beer in Chicago constitutes an antitrust market by identifying the elasticity of beer demand in that city. The proposed study is purposely oversimplified relative to how one might be set up in practice.

The study employs monthly data on total retail revenues and total retail quantities of beer in the Chicago metropolitan area over a five-year period. Average revenue is computed from these data. Data on the average prices for soft drinks are also collected, along with data on the average unemployment rate in the region. All variables are transformed into their logarithms, and the following equation is estimated:

$$\ln(\text{quantity beer}) = \alpha + \beta \ln(\text{price beer}) + \gamma \ln(\text{price soft drinks})$$
$$+ \delta \ln(\text{unemployment rate}) + u.$$

The equation is estimated using two-stage least squares, with a time series on the logged average revenue from the retail sale of beer in Cleveland as an instrument for the price of beer in Chicago. The resulting estimate of β is interpreted as the elasticity of demand for beer in Chicago.

A number of important issues related to the probative value of evidence aside from identification are embedded even in this simple, straightforward econometric approach to developing evidence on the magnitude of buyer substitution. We will note a few, but our list is not exhaustive. Some involve observation. Beers are differentiated products, sold in a range of unit prices. In consequence, variation in average revenue, the proxy for price, could reflect variation in the market share of various brands even if no prices change. Assuming the resulting measurement error is not correlated with the other independent variables in the equation, it can be expected to lead to a downward bias in the estimate of β, toward finding little buyer substitution.[24] Also the regional unemployment rate might not be the best measure of the way changing local economic conditions affect beer demand. For example, if beer consumption is concentrated within particular demographic groups, the aggregate unemployment rate might not reflect the financial situation of those buyers most interested in the product.

Other possible problems with this approach to learning about buyer substitution involve specification. The estimated equation does not account for advertising, by brewers or the producers of soft drinks, yet advertising may well affect demand. Nor does it allow for substitution to other beverages such as wine. Possible seasonal variation in the demand for beer is unaccounted for.[25] And the double-log specification, while convenient for interpreting coefficients (as elasticities), builds in an arbitrary assumption about the curvature of demand and the form of the error term (multiplicative not additive) that could be incorrect. These problems could lead to biased estimates of the key parameter, the coefficient β. A more subtle specification problem involves the monthly sample. A one-month reduction in the average price of beer—for example, if multiple producers place beer on sale at the same time—might lead to a different quantity response from a more permanent price reduction. If a brief price cut would expand purchases temporarily, as buyers stock up their refrigerators and pantries, the monthly demand elasticity might overstate the intermediate or long-term buyer response that might be more relevant to questions that arise in antitrust decision-making.[26]

Estimation problems could also be important. In a monthly sample, unobservable demand shocks might be serially correlated, making estimates of β appear more precise than the data actually allow. Or the prices of beer and soft drinks could be correlated, making it difficult to disentangle the demand parameter associated with either price individually.

In addition this method of assessing the magnitude of likely buyer substitution raises the distinctive social science difficulty of identification, our primary focus in this chapter. The instrumental variable technique used to identify demand in the hypothetical example operates in effect by removing variation in price where price changes are unlikely to reflect buyer substitution (removing variation unlikely to cause movements along a demand curve). In particular, the experiment created by the instrument used in the hypothetical example presumes that when beer prices in Chicago move in the same way as price changes in Cleveland, the price changes result from common production or distribution cost variation (which induce movements along a demand curve) and not from shifts in demand. If that assumption is correct, the output response to these price changes will reveal the magnitude of buyer substitution. Unfortunately, this is a suspect assumption in an advertising-intensive industry like brewing.[27] If it is incorrect, demand can appear to be more responsive to price (more elastic) than it is in fact.

This type of study of buyer substitution patterns is not exclusively employed in market definition. Demand elasticities can also be estimated in order to make inferences about the scope of localized competition and the potential for adverse unilateral effects of mergers. Defendants may argue, for example, that unilateral effects are unlikely because the cross-elasticity of demand between the products of the merger partners is low.[28] More sophisticated approaches along similar lines estimate the parameters of demand systems involving a large set of products, and simulate the effects of merger after incorporating information (or assumptions) about marginal cost and the nature of oligopoly conduct.[29]

Relating Price to Market Structure   The likely magnitude of demand substitution in the event of a price rise is sometimes assessed quantitatively using a different type of identifying experiment, involving changes in conduct or market structure. One example of such an experiment arises if there is a cartel that was in effect for only a given time period or only in particular places. A related identifying experiment can be used if market structure differs across otherwise similar locations, or changes over time. If prices increase when the number of firms selling the products in a candidate market (or at the locations in a candidate market, or in the times or locations of the cartel) decline, then it may be reasonable to infer that a hypothetical monopolist of those products would find it profitable to raise price at locations where the number of firms has not decreased.

This approach was employed in the *Staples* litigation to analyze market definition and the likelihood of unilateral competitive effects of merger.[30] The market definition question in that case was whether consumable office supplies sold through office superstores should be deemed a market, or whether to expand that candidate market to include other distribution channels such as discount mass merchandisers and warehouse club stores. Analysis of the data by the FTC's econometric witness showed that prices were higher in locations and at times with only one superstore chain present than in locations and at times with multiple superstore chains present. If so, a hypothetical monopolist of consumable office supplies sold through office superstores in locations and at times with multiple superstore chains present could profitably raise price, allowing the inference of a market limited to the superstore distribution channel.[31]

Success for this research strategy depends on finding the same product or products being sold, either in multiple locations or over time, and also on finding variation in market structure, either across markets or over time, that change competition in an observable way. Identification then results from the assumption, which must be defended, that variation in market structure—particularly the decisions by office superstore chains on where to locate—does not reflect variation in the marginal costs of doing business in those locations (beyond factors that can be accounted for in the statistical analysis). That is, in order to identify the influence of demand on prices, the appropriate econometric practice is to use only those observable movements in market structure that correspond to exogenous supply side changes, in this case, changes in competitive incentives. In the analysis undertaken by the government in *Staples*, identification in comparisons of same-city prices over time was based on the assumption that any unobservable factors affecting cost likely changed little from quarter to quarter over a few years. This assumption was plausible on the facts of the case and was shared by both parties to the litigation. Identification in comparisons across cities was based on the measurement of all significant cost variables mentioned in merging firm documents as the basis for pricing and location decisions. Moreover the estimates of price changes based on cross-city comparisons and same-city comparisons over time were similar, corroborating each other's identification strategy.

Other Quantitative Approaches   These two quantitative measures of buyer responses to changes in relative prices—estimation of demand elasticities and the comparison of prices across markets thought to be similar except for differences in market structure—do not exhaust the possible methodological approaches. Other quantitative possibilities suggested in the economics literature are potentially available for antitrust analysis. For example, beginning with the influential work of Berry, Levinsohn, and Pakes, a number of articles model the structure of product differentiation to attempt to measure long-run substitution behavior by buyers.[32] Other studies use information about price dispersion to study price discrimination.[33] Perhaps the largest literature concerns the strategic determination of prices in auctions.[34]

Identification When Evidence Is Qualitative   Market definition is more often conducted without these types of systematic empirical analyses than with them.[35] This should be no surprise: good data are not always available, key parameters in the estimation can be difficult to pin down (accompanied by large standard errors), and some tribunals are less comfortable than others with the problem of sorting out conflicting econometric testimony. Moreover qualitative evidence can be compelling, at times more probative than quantitative evidence. But when qualitative evidence is employed, the underlying economic logic of the identification strategy is often analogous to an approach to identification taken in the empirical economics literature with respect to quantitative evidence.

Demand Response to Price   A qualitative analogue to the estimation of demand elasticities may come from anecdotal evidence involving buyer responses. A firm's marketing executives may be able to report on the results of an experiment with a price increase,[36] or that their price increased following what they perceived as firm-specific increase in marginal cost. The executives may have an understanding of whether they lost share following a price increase, and if so, which rivals benefited the most from buyer substitution. To identify these responses as providing information about buyer substitution, there must be good reason to believe that the price or cost changes were exogenous.

Relating Price to Market Structure   A comparison of prices across markets thought to be similar except for differences in market structure similarly does not invariably require sophisticated data analysis. The court opinion in *Staples*, for example, evaluates this evidence based solely on party pricing documents, without reference to the econometric evidence in the record analyzing pricing systematically. The court found, based on the documentary evidence, that office superstore prices were higher when fewer superstore chains were competing. This conclusion was based both on comparisons across markets that varied in the number of competing superstore chains at a given time and on comparisons within markets in which the number of superstore varied over time. The latter price comparisons, made based on the anecdotes and raw data presented in the documentary evidence, identified the influence of demand on prices (or, in this case, the lack of influence of demand on prices) under the same assumption adopted in the econometric work that any unobservable factors affecting cost likely changed little over the time period studied.

Structure of Product Differentiation   Market definition might also be based on qualitative information about the distribution of product characteristics and seller locations, and information on how much more buyers value products that are exactly what the buyer wants relative to products that are not quite what buyers are looking for. This approach would be analogous to econometric methods of inferring the distribution of the valuations buyers place on unobservable product characteristics from market shares and buyer characteristics.[37] This methodology requires that buyers differ from each other in their valuations of product characteristics, and that those differences or the basis for them be observable.

Under some circumstances this kind of analysis can be conducted without sophisticated modeling. For example, seller marketing documents may describe the geographic location of seller plants, the geographic distribution of buyers, and shipping costs. That information could be used to identify those buyers that view any pair of firms as their first and second choices, and to assess the likely profitability of a unilateral increase in price at either location following their merger. The econometric literature emphasizes the inferential problems arising from the presence of characteristics known to buyer and seller but unobservable to the analyst, as those characteristics are likely correlated with price. Accordingly, to identify the results of this kind of qualitative calculation as depicting buyer substitution patterns, it is important to have confidence that the most important product and buyer characteristics—locations in the example above—are observable.

Buyer Surveys and Bidding Records   Another method of assessing the likely response of buyers to price changes, buyer surveys, has both quantitative and qualitative analogues. One quantitative possibility might involve sampling of retail customers at shopping malls using a carefully constructed survey instrument, for example.[38] But surveys can also be informal, based on customer interviews. The latter approach was adopted by the Irish Competition Authority as the basis for market definition and unilateral effects analysis in a recent decision preventing IBM from acquiring another firm in the business recovery hotsite industry.[39] If there is some basis for concluding that the customer views are informed, representative, and account for a reasonable fraction of the relevant business, even an informal survey may provide a reliable guide to likely buyer substitution patterns. The identification problem in these survey contexts, whether the evidence is quantitative or qualitative, would be addressed with an argument as to why the reported buyer responses are reliable guides to future buyer conduct under the conditions likely then to prevail in the marketplace.

A different approach to a buyer survey of demand, of particular applicability to the analysis of unilateral competitive effects of merger, involves the examination of bidding records to identify buyer preferences and substitution possibilities. If many buyers routinely solicited bids from the same two sellers in the past, that evidence may identify localized competition between the two today, at least if product characteristics and relative prices among all sellers (including those two firms) have not changed (the identification assumption). That a particular buyer who bought from firm A in the past included firm B in a final round of bidding indicates that firm B may be its second choice—more reliably, in some circumstances, than if the buyer were simply to opine about its second choice. As with other methods of assessing buyer substitution, the identification issue is similar regardless of whether the evidence is quantitative, derived from a systematic analysis of buyer bidding records (or by comparing the records of the sellers), or qualitative, developed from an informal survey of an informed and representative group of customers.

Business Executive Views and Identification   Even when the evidence is primarily quantitative, the argument for identification may turn on qualitative evidence, particularly the views of business executives.[40] Experienced marketing executives may be able to explain which price changes likely result primarily from shifts in supply, whether all the significant cost-shift variables are observable, whether buyer valuations of product characteristics are observable and unchanging, and the like. For example, while we were working for one of the parties in a merger investigation over two decades ago, we sought econometrically to estimate the degree to which the potential exercise of market power for products of the parties had been disciplined by substitution to third-party products. We used a product-specific price and quantity data set. But we also asked managers to explain the changes in prices in the data set. We sought to use only the exogenous changes in prices that managers chose to implement for supply-side reasons, excluding their reactions to shifting demand conditions and to the exogenous movements of other firms.[41]

As a general rule, it is sensible to suppose that business executives have a reasonable basis for their opinions. But in principle, the reliability of those views could be tested and buttressed by asking the same kind of questions that would naturally arise were such conclusions reached by an expert economist based on an empirical study. Suppose, for example, that likely buyer substitution in the event of a price rise—a key issue in market definition and the evaluation of the unilateral effects of merger among sellers of differentiated products—is assessed not through a quantitative study of demand but through the testimony of an industry marketing executive. Like the econometrician thinking about market definition, the marketing executive concerned with pricing needs to how customers would react to a price change undertaken by the company in an effort to increase profit margins. Would customers substitute away, and if so, to which competitors' products? Would that substitution be much lessened if a particular competitor were (coincidentally or through conscious parallelism or otherwise) to raise prices at the same time? Marketing executives very frequently think about the first two questions, perhaps less frequently about the third, and draw on a wide variety of different sources of knowledge. In assessing the marketing executive's testimony and documents, the key questions of identification turn on the executive's familiarity with this and related markets, the depth of investigation undertaken by the executive, the plausibility of the background assumptions the executive relies upon, and the clarity with which evidence was linked to the business purpose of assessing a pricing decision.

If an executive were testifying about the output effects of past increases in price, one important question would be whether his or her views are based on observations as to past supply-side shocks.[42] If past price changes were instead largely the result of shifts in demand, one might question whether the executive would have much basis for developing an informed opinion as to buyer substitution from observing buyer responses to price fluctuations.[43] Ultimately the linkage of the analysis of buyer responses to price changes that come from the supply side—cost or strategy changes at the firm or at its competitors— determines its suitability for the pricing business purpose and its suitability as evidence in an antitrust enquiry.

To see how such a conversation about identification might play out in practice with evidence in a merger case where unilateral effects are alleged, suppose that the government or other plaintiff can show that a number of customers report that products of merging firms are their first and second choices, the two firms' products have common characteristics valued by customers that distinguish them from the products of most rivals, and the two firms monitor and respond to each other's business decisions more closely than they respond to the decisions of other rivals. This qualitative and anecdotal evidence should be sufficient to draw an inference that the demand curve for one or both products will grow less elastic with merger, creating a unilateral incentive to raise price.

The merging firms could respond by undermining the probative value of the government's evidence, showing that the government's evidence misleads, by raising the same kind of problems that might undermine identification were the government's evidence quantitative. The merging firms might show, for example, that the customers are not informed and representative and that unobservable product characteristics are also important in determining buyer substitution patterns in the industry.[44] In this hypothetical litigation context, either side might supplement its position with quantitative evidence, for example, as to the magnitude of the demand cross-elasticities between the two products. But identification is no more and no less important when the evidence is anecdotal and qualitative as when the evidence is systematic and statistical.

The procedural context of antitrust lawsuits typically does not permit the multiyear data-building process sometimes needed for cutting edge academic industry studies; it must deal with the available information. Nor does it permit the scholarly tactic of selecting for study industries where data are available or where a particularly attractive identification strategy presents itself. An antitrust investigation or lawsuit is about a particular industry, all evidentiary inferences are made conditional on background assumptions (knowledge is local), and even if the appropriate statistical technique from the academic literature is clear, the data may not be available to employ that technique within the time and resource constraints of litigation. In short, courts must decide antitrust cases reasonably expeditiously, for good public policy reasons, which sometimes constrains the amount of information and especially data available for analysis. This makes the use of multiple sources of evidence particularly valuable.

1.2.3   Identifying and Measuring Market Power

Market power—the ability of firms to raise price above the competitive level for a sustained period—is a part of the legal framework in multiple antitrust contexts. Monopoly power is an element of the monopolization offense under Sherman Act, Section 2.[45] In addition market power is often frequently assessed under Sherman Act, Section 1 to determine whether conduct undertaken pursuant to an agreement was reasonable. The market power inquiry may apply to a firm individually or to a number of firms as a group. Historically, in the antitrust world, market power has most commonly been identified through inference from a high market share. But direct evidence has increasingly become important as an alternative, in part because academic economists have developed a number of econometric approaches for measuring market power.[46]

It is worth emphasizing that the ultimate economic question in antitrust litigation is almost never whether a firm or set of firms have market power. The case almost invariably concerns an economic objection to the challenged conduct—an agreement among rivals, a merger, exclusionary tactics, and the like—that turns on whether the conduct has increased (in a retrospective case) or is likely to increase (in a prospective case) market power. Accordingly the economic question is not the level of market power but the change. Antitrust law at times relies upon presumptions that if the level of market power is high, various types of conduct will increase it, and if the level of market power is low, they will not. That is, in legal terms, anticompetitive effect is at times inferred from proof of market power.[47] Whether or not such inferences are justified empirically, they shift attention from the ultimate economic question of whether market power has increased. Our discussion of identification when measuring market power also focuses on levels for expositional clarity. Nonetheless, it is important not to lose sight of the ultimate question. Accordingly, when it is possible, economic methods should be used to assess changes in market power, examining a historical counterfactual without the challenged practices in a retrospective case or providing an analysis of the change in incentives in a prospective one.

As with identifying buyer substitution, quantitative methods of measuring market power through direct evidence have parallels involving the use of qualitative evidence. In this section we discuss a number of approaches to identifying market and highlight characteristic econometric issues that arise with each approach, regardless of whether the available evidence is quantitative or qualitative. We emphasize the method of identification.

A Formal Framework for Market Power Measurement   Many methods of measuring market power can be understood as growing out of a two-equation model with an industry demand function and industry quasi-supply function:

$$P = f(Q, Y, u), \tag{1.1}$$

$$P = C(Q, W, v) + h(f(\cdot), C(\cdot), Z). \tag{1.2}$$

Equation (1.1) is an inverse demand function, relating industry price P to industry output Q, a vector of observable demand-shift variables Y, and stochastic error u. In a homogeneous product industry, both P and Q are scalars. If the industry is differentiated, they have as many elements as there are products in the industry.[48]

Equation (1.2) is a quasi-supply function. It describes price as equal to industry marginal cost C, which is viewed as a function of a vector of cost-shift variables W and a stochastic error v, plus a markup, the function $h(\cdot)$. The markup function in equation (1.2) depends on marginal cost, demand, and exogenous variables Z. The models adopted in the literature typically allow perfect competition (price-taking) as a special case, by permitting the markup function to equal zero. If the markup is positive, price exceeds the competitive level. In both equations (1.1) and (1.2) we have suppressed the unknown parameters that will be estimated.

Both equations in this two equation system can provide information relevant to making inferences about market power. Incentives for exercising market power are related to the slope or elasticity of the demand function, equation (1.1). The extent to which a firm or firms have taken advantage of those incentives is related to the markup function in equation (1.2). The nature of the oligopoly interaction (e.g., static Bertrand or Cournot, or some form of coordination) is also related to the markup function, and also bears on the extent to which firms have exercised market power.

We have previously discussed issues involving the identification of demand, in connection with market definition, though will return to them briefly in this section. We will also discuss strategies for identifying parameters related to market power in equation (1.2). Before doing so, we will describe some general strategies for inferring market power related to this two-equation setup.

Estimating Quasi-Supply   The empirical economic literature employs several approaches to estimating the quasi-supply function, equation (1.2).[49] Some studies specify (1.2) as derived from a particular game-theoretic model of market power. For example, when the investigation involves unilateral market power, Bertrand (price-setting) competition is the most common assumption. The Bertrand assumption leads to prices in excess of marginal cost only if products are differentiated or if firms have increasing marginal cost functions.[50] The antitrust purpose of estimating (1.2) is to discriminate between higher costs and a higher markup as the source of higher prices.

The markup function $h(\cdot)$ can take a variety of forms, depending on various aspects of industry structure and the range of plausible ways in which firms might interact. The simplest models are competition ($h(\cdot) = 0$) and monopoly ($P - h(\cdot) = MR$). For some game-theoretic models the markup function depends only on demand and cost elasticities. Other theories are more complex, potentially leading $h(\cdot)$ to depend on complex unobservables such as firms' information. A number of theories suggest that firm conduct will vary with market conditions. Accordingly some approaches allow the markup to vary with observables (variables in the vector Z), which might include, for example, measures of market concentration (like the Herfindahl-Hirschman index) or negative demand shocks (negative realizations of u), as suggested by various theories of oligopoly. But when quasi-supply during any particular time period arises as the single-period realization of a repeated game, the markup function may depend in a complex way on time preferences, information, and other variables; under such circumstances researchers tend to approximate that dependence in a simple way.

One useful generalization has structured much of the empirical literature on estimating quasi-supply: game-theoretic models of supply commonly indicate that there is more market power with less elastic industry demand. This generalization leads many empirical economists to include the term $-Qf'(\cdot)$ in the markup function, to capture the pricing incentive that lies in the difference between price and marginal revenue (MR).[51]

Estimating Demand   Variation in the slope of the demand curve, equation (1.1), and the resulting incentive for market power, can be assessed at the individual firm level as well as at the market level. The distinction is particularly important in product differentiated industries. One approach is to estimate a multiple-price, multiple-quantity version of equation (1.1). This approach is well suited for data-rich environments in which the identification problem at issue in measuring buyer substitution can readily be solved.

Another approach is to estimate the slope of the residual demand curve facing a particular firm or a small number of firms.[52] A residual demand function can be defined for a firm or a candidate market. It is derived from the structural demand function by substituting best response functions for the output of rivals, thus projecting rival output on demand and cost-shift variables. Its elasticity reflects the response of a firm to cost variation after accounting for two economic forces: buyer substitution (the parameters of demand) and rival reactions (incorporated through the determinants of rival best responses). If a firm's (or group of firms) residual demand function is perfectly elastic, it does not exercise market power. It cannot raise price on its own, and the combination of buyer substitution and output expansion of rivals would make any such effort ineffective. But a downward-sloping residual demand function indicates that the firm (or group) has the ability to raise price by reducing output, and thus can exercise market power.

In econometric terms, the elasticity of a firm's residual demand is identified by a movement in an exogenous variable affecting the supply of that firm and no other. The intuition is that a higher marginal cost for the firm of interest (and that firm alone) gives the firm an incentive to raise price, but price will not rise in fact unless the firm also has the ability to increase price after accounting for the expected response of buyers and all rivals (none of which experienced a similar cost increase, so none of which have an incentive to raise price on their own).

The empirical literature has made progress in two very different areas in estimating residual demand functions. One is in product differentiated industries. Here the largest advantage of the residual demand curve approach is that it economizes on identifying variation. The source of single-firm market power is differentiation. In other words, there is little distinction between what is learned about market power from estimating the residual demand curve and what is learned from estimating structural demand curves.

The empirical literature has also made progress where a single firm's residual demand curve is sloped because the supply curves of other firms rise steeply. This approach has been deployed in studies of wholesale electricity markets, for example. In those markets observable measures of the height and slope of other firms' supply curve are available. For example, the capacity of other firms' plants, the capacity of their most efficient plants, and so on, are in some data sets. A firm competing against only capacity-constrained rivals will face the industry demand elasticity and thus generally have more market power than a firm whose competitors might expand if price were to rise. The literature has taken advantage of that feature in estimating residual demand curves. Empirical economists have also estimated residual demand curves in the intermediate case of a firm facing only competitors whose more efficient plants are at capacity.[53]

Direct Measurement of Accounting Margins   Another approach to measuring market power is an alternative to statistical estimation: to attempt to measure directly the departure of price from an accounting estimate of marginal cost. The common measure is the Lerner Index, defined as $L = (P - C)/P$. L is related to the markup function $h(\cdot)$ discussed above. In the special case of perfect competition, both $h(\cdot)$ and L are zero. Let the elasticity of industry demand be denoted ε in absolute value. In homogeneous good industries, the magnitude of market power is often taken to equal the product $L\varepsilon$. This expression calibrates the Lerner Index by recognizing that a high value for L is unlikely if industry demand is relatively elastic, and that a low value of L does not reflect much success in raising price toward the monopoly level if industry demand is relatively inelastic.

Cost-based measures of market power such as the Lerner index will be more meaningful when market power arises mainly from product differentiation (in which case the nature of oligopoly conduct is relatively unimportant in explaining markup), from static noncooperative behavior (e.g., Cournot quantity-setting behavior) when the demand function is steep, or when the industry is behaving close to perfect competition or monopoly. They will be least meaningful when conduct is coordinated in ways that lead markups to vary over time (unless changes in $L\varepsilon$ can be correlated with the economic determinants of successful coordination).[54]

Inference about Oligopoly Conduct   With an estimate of both L and ε, it may be possible to make inferences about the nature of firm behavior of relevance to antitrust analysis. For example, it may be possible to test the hypothesis that firm supply is close to the monopoly level, close to perfect competition, close to Bertrand supply, and so on.[55] For this purpose the estimate of the Lerner index can either come from cost data or, more typically in the literature, can come from an estimate of firms' supply behavior. For an industry that might be collusive, the literature has tested the hypothesis that behavior is closer to the monopoly level in some time periods but not in others (Bresnahan 1987; Porter 1983) because that is the implication of oligopoly supergame theory.

This method of inference depends on a wide range of assumptions. First, it incorporates an estimate of the demand elasticity, and thus depends in part on the probative value of the evidence as to buyer substitution from which that elasticity estimate derives. Second, any implementation must address a number of practical problems.[56] Third, the Lerner Index can be difficult to measure because of well-known problems in the measurement of marginal cost. These include conceptual difficulties in relating accounting measures to economic concepts. For example, accountants define cost categories for audit purposes that do not necessarily track economist's concepts, that present difficulties in the accounting treatment of depreciation, that may not capture opportunity costs in accounting data, and that show average variable costs not equal to marginal cost where the marginal cost curve is not horizontal.[57] Indeed the academic literature in empirical industrial organization economics commonly treats the level of marginal cost as unobservable even when some of its determinants, like input prices and scale, can be observed.[58]

1.2.4 Identification Issues

We focus our discussion of identification of market power on the problem of determining the nature of firm conduct when marginal cost is not observable. This is the problem of identifying the markup function in equation (1.2). We emphasize the possibility that marginal cost is not observable because that is the dominant perspective in the empirical economics literature. As with our discussion of identifying the magnitude of buyer substitution, we treat quantitative and qualitative evidence analogously.

Rotations in Demand   To identify firm conduct in equation (1.2) when marginal cost is unobservable, empirical economists often identify oligopoly conduct from the response of price to rotations in demand (or changes in demand elasticity produced by that rotation).[59] If price rises as demand grows less elastic, industry conduct is not competitive. Less elastic demand creates room for firms to exercise market power, if they possess it.

This insight is perhaps most familiar as a method of inferring market power from anecdotal evidence, when price discrimination (as defined by economists) is viewed as evidence of market power.[60] Qualitative information could also be used to make this inference: if firm marketing executives routinely refer to value-of-service pricing rather than cost-based or competitor-based pricing, they may well be taking advantage of less elastic buyer demand to raise price.

The econometric literature on implementing this approach to measuring market power emphasizes the importance of distinguishing price increases arising when firms take advantage of less elastic demand—which reflect market power—from price increases that result from increases in cost.[61] This identification problem also arises when the evidence is qualitative. Price increases for certain customers, at certain times, or in certain markets could come about because firms hit capacity constraints or input costs are high, even if higher costs happen to be correlated with less elastic demand. This possibility must be accounted for in order to infer market power from price increases in markets in which demand grows less elastic.

Variation in Observable Cost Components   Even when firm or industry marginal cost is difficult to observe, some of its major determinants, such as key input prices, may be observable. Under such circumstances movements in price that remain after accounting for variation in factors likely affecting cost may be used to make inferences about market power. This approach identifies market power from observing price rises not likely explained by cost increases.

This type of reasoning has been adopted in antitrust cases, using anecdotal evidence. One example comes from *American Tobacco*,[62] a midtwentieth century case in which the Supreme Court upheld a jury finding that the leading tobacco firms had conspired to monopolize by fixing cigarette prices and excluded competition. The conclusion relied in part on evidence that cigarette prices rose during the Great Depression, a time when the costs of tobacco leaf were unusually low and manufacturing costs were declining. Tobacco leaf and cigarette manufacturing costs were implicitly treated as observable factors affecting cigarette costs but not affecting the costs of producing demand substitutes.

The early antitrust decision in *Addyston Pipe*[63] illustrates the inference of market power through a similar comparison made across markets rather than over time. The six defendants in the case manufactured cast iron pipe, which they sold to local gas and water utilities in procurement auctions. The firms divided markets: they agreed on which firm would enter the lowest bid in procurements in certain "reserved" cities. But cities more than 500 miles from the firms' foundries ("free" cities) were not allocated to any individual seller. Prices were higher in the reserved cities than the free cities, even though costs were lower in the reserved cities, allowing the inference that the firms had exercised market power. The econometric evidence presented by the FTC in *Staples*, discussed above, provides an example of how systematic empirical evidence can be used to make a similar comparison.

In the kind of comparisons undertaken in *American Tobacco* or *Addyston*, whether with anecdotal evidence as in those cases or through a systematic empirical study as in *Staples*, the identification problem is ruling out cost increases as the explanation for price increases, so it is sometimes framed as an omitted variable issue or a measurement error problem. In *Addyston*, for example, what if certain important costs were greater in the reserved cities but not observed by the court? This possibility is not entirely far-fetched. According to the court, defendants claimed that prices in at least one reserved city were higher because specifications were detailed and precise, requiring custom production rather than use of stock on hand. Hence it is possible that custom production was on average more likely to be required in reserved than free cities. Or suppose that reserved cities tended to have a different geology than free cities, requiring pipe manufacturers to employ more costly manufacturing techniques. This could also mean that input costs were greater in reserved cities for a reason not observed by the court. In the tobacco example, the cost of a key input was declining, and manufacturing costs were falling, but what if distribution costs were instead increasing? Not surprisingly, measurement error and omitted variable issues like these were central to the econometric argument between the parties in *Staples*.[64]

Comparison with the Conduct of Competitive Firms   Another way to interpret the methods of identifying market power employed in *American Tobacco* and *Addyston Pipe* is to view what the courts did as comparing the way firms behaved with the way competitive firms would likely behave. If there is a difference, the firms likely exercised market power. The essence of the identification problem does not change with this change in perspective, as a perfectly competitive industry would raise price only if marginal costs increased.

This alternative interpretation is worth highlighting because it has been employed in the empirical economic literature. For example, a similar approach has long been a staple of cartel detection using qualitative methods. According to one story, the infamous electrical equipment cartel involving General Electric and Westinghouse, uncovered around 1960, was discovered by a journalist who noticed that the unsuccessful bidders in one procurement had submitted bids that were identical to the last digit.[65] This pricing pattern was consistent with a bid-rigging scheme—the firms had presumably chosen their bids to avoid undercutting the colluding firm that had been selected to win that particular procurement—and hard to rationalize with competition.

A comparable strategy for identifying market power has been adopted in the empirical economics literature to detect price-fixing in auction markets. Those studies look at the way firms form bids in markets or at times thought to be competitive—at the factors that affect bidding strategies—and compare the results with the way bids are formed in markets where market power might be exercised.[66] The competitive benchmark might be identified empirically, through analysis of the bidding strategies actually adopted by firms thought to behave in a competitive manner. Firms that respond to factors like variation in costs or the determinants of buyer willingness to pay differently in the test markets than in the control markets would be identified as likely exercising market power. For example, Porter and Zona (1999) used this method to identify a partial bid-rigging conspiracy among sellers of school milk in Ohio. They found that members of the bid-rigging cartel behaved differently, along several dimensions of behavior, when the nearest competitors to any particular school district were other members of the cartel than when there was a nearby nonparticipant. Alternatively, the competitive benchmark might be identified based on a theoretical model of how competitive firms would act. For example, firms that do not raise their bids when their costs go up, or firms that systematically raise their bids when a rival lowers its bid, might be thought not to be acting the way a competitor would. Either way, this strategy for identifying market power requires a great deal of confidence in the competitive benchmark, and confidence that cost differences across bidders (that might affect how aggressively they would bid) are accounted for.

Another antitrust application of the idea that price formation inconsistent with competition can be used to identify market power comes in the analysis of the coordinated effects of merger. In a market in which coordination is imperfect and incomplete—as coordinated oligopoly conduct would be expected to be, given difficulties firms subject to the antitrust laws have in communicating and making side payments—one firm, termed the maverick, may constrain the effectiveness of coordinated pricing when its rivals would be willing to coordinate more completely (as by raising the industry price closer to the monopoly level). Coordinated effects analysis is often concerned with identifying the maverick and analyzing the effects of the merger on its incentives to prevent more effective coordination.[67] To infer a maverick's identity from its marketplace behavior, that behavior must be compared with a competitive benchmark, much as is done in the auction literature on identifying bid-rigging. For example, if industry prices change in response to pricing decisions by one firm but not those of its rivals (or to the determinants of such decisions, such as firm-specific costs facing one firm but not those of its rivals), the firm that appears to be constraining industry pricing is a likely maverick.[68]

Unusual Movements in Price   Another way to identify market power when cost is unobservable to isolate changes in price that cannot be explained by observable factors influencing cost and demand, and that are so large or unusual in their distribution as to have no plausible interpretation other than variation in quasi-supply (equation 1.2) resulting from changes in conduct. Again, identification of market power in essence turns on ruling out alternative, cost-based explanations for the price changes.

This strategy was adopted by Porter (1983) to identify coordinated conduct among nineteenth-century railroads. Porter found occasional short-term declines in price that could not be explained as the result of declines in demand in a competitive market, and could not be explained by reductions in the observable determinants of cost. Rather, he concluded, they were consistent with a model in which firms occasionally engage in price wars, set off by unexpected declines in market demand, in order to deter cheating that would undermine cooperative pricing during other periods. He identified these periods econometrically by showing that multiple pricing regimes (one during high price periods and one during price wars) fit the unexplained variation in price (the error) better than did a single price regime.[69] Any single large price decline could reflect random chance, but multiple declines otherwise unexplained could reasonably be attributed to shifts in seller conduct.[70]

One could imagine exploiting the same ideas about the properties of unexplained price changes to identify market power in a industry experiencing occasional price wars, with qualitative instead of quantitative evidence. If industry participants routinely respond to low prices not by pointing to lower costs but instead by complaining about pricing break-downs and calling for improved pricing discipline, and if such comments in the trade press are commonly followed by increasing prices shortly thereafter, that evidence could suggest that the participants see themselves as engaged in coordinated pricing punctuated by occasional price wars.

1.3 The Nature and Significance of Industry Differences

A large empirical literature in industrial organization economics has systematically studied market power, entry barriers, collusion, and other topics relevant to antitrust. In the previous section we reviewed a number of the methodologies empirical economists have employed for studying buyer substitution and market power. Most of this work does not have antitrust policy formation as its primary goal.[71] Almost all of this work studies a single industry or a group of closely related industries, such as inherently local businesses observed in a number of different cities or counties. This literature offers a great deal of support to the basic antitrust paradigm of applying a general economic framework to analyze a particular industry in which harm to competition is alleged. The empirical economic literature itself uses the same paradigm by employing different subsets of the same broad, general body of economic and econometric tools to analyze particular industries. In this section we review what has been learned about the nature and significance of industry differences. We describe the failure of the research effort to identify broad empirical generalizations across all industries. We also describe the successful and ongoing (if less well known in antitrust circles) effort to identify generalizations across closely related industries that can be exploited in antitrust to help evaluate evidence and resolve cases.

One important finding of the economics literature is of substantial variation across industries in features most relevant to antitrust. Studies of market power find more of it in some industries than others, and some studies find more market power for some products in the same product differentiated markets than for others.[72] Studies of entry similarly find that the conditions of entry vary across industries.[73] At the broadest level the empirical economic literature therefore demonstrates that there are important industry differences in the economic concepts that matter most to antitrust analysis. This confirms the importance of an industry-specific fact-based antitrust enquiry into such matters as market definition, market power, and entry barriers.

1.3.1 Unsuccessful Efforts to Generalize Broadly across Industries

From both an academic and a policy perspective, an obvious question arises. Can econo-mists reach a more detailed and specific answer than "it varies across industries?" Could economists, instead, systematically predict which industries are more likely to depart from competition? From an academic perspective, this would involve learning the underlying causes of why certain industries have more market power (higher entry barriers, etc.) than others. From an antitrust policy perspective, this would support the more rapid identifica-tion of industries in which a detailed enquiry was likely to find market power (entry bar-riers, etc.) It could also lead to the development of useful policy rules of thumb, "safe harbors," presumptions, and other abbreviated enquiries.

In industrial organization economics there flourished until the early 1970s a large-scale, sustained effort that attempted to provide a detailed and specific set of answers to these important questions. That effort was called the structure-conduct performance (SCP) approach. It sought to establish a set of presumptions to identify which markets have market power and entry barriers by looking for simple, easily observed indicia. One exten-sively explored hypothesis was that capital-intensive, R&D intensive, or advertising-intensive industries might be those with high entry barriers. That hypothesis was never convincingly demonstrated, however, in large part because it looked only to information about firms' costs, oblivious to what we now know: that entry barriers have roots in stra-tegic interaction as well as in costs.[74] Another SCP hypothesis, explored with equal fervor, attempted to connect firm or industry market power reliably with market concentration. That hypothesis too was not convincingly demonstrated. Here a large part of the SCP approach's difficulties derived from the use of accounting profit as the indicator of poor industry performance resulting from the exercise of market power.

The SCP methods ultimately failed because the empirical methods used to establish both hypotheses were subject to fatal identification critiques from Chicago school economists, a school of industrial organization economics that flourished until the mid-1970s. These economists explained that instead of measuring only market power and barriers to entry, structure-conduct performance methods also left open the possibility of another interpreta-tion. Under that alternative view all industries have free entry and perform competitively, but there is a wide range in the productive efficiency of firms within capital-intensive, advertising-intensive, and R&D-intensive industries.[75] Firms could have large market shares and be profitable because they had achieved low costs or other efficiencies rather than because they exploited market power. The Chicago identification argument has carried the day, and empirical structure-conduct performance methods have largely been discarded in economics. In consequence modern studies relating price to market concentra-tion, perhaps the only area in which descendants of empirical structure-conduct perfor-mance methods are pursued today, are generally limited to the examination of related industries, rather than seeking broad generalizations across the economy.[76]

The structure-conduct performance project in industrial organization economics proceeded in parallel with a related legal project. The legal project, characteristic of antitrust's post–World War II structural era, sought to develop broad legal rules to be applied to all industries, framed around measures of market concentration.[77] The legal project was unsuccessful for two reasons. First, it eventually became clear that the rules that were adopted served to deter much efficient, pro-competitive conduct. Second, reliance only on structural measures to detect market power also became clearly problematic. The Chicago school of antitrust analysis, an intellectual movement that has dominated the antitrust field in the United States since the mid- to late 1970s and confusingly shares a name and some participants with the earlier Chicago school of industrial organization economics, played a major role in raising discomfort with structural era legal rules. These antitrust commentators created a number of case studies of leading antitrust decisions that showed how the challenged conduct could alternatively be interpreted as efficient and pro-competitive.[78]

The doctrines of antitrust's structural era came under pressure from both this legal critique and from the economic critique of the parallel structure-conduct performance project in empirical industrial organization economics. In consequence, after the mid-1970s, many if not most antitrust rules were modified, and some were overruled. Antitrust doctrine generally moved away from bright line rules and toward open-ended reasonableness standards. For example, per se rules against vertical nonprice restraints and maximum resale price maintenance have been overruled, the per se prohibition against horizontal price-fixing has been narrowed, and the structural presumption in merger analysis, once a near–per se prohibition against all but the smallest horizontal mergers, has eroded.

Some Chicago school antitrust commentators have sought to replace the discarded structural era bright line rules with new ones, reflecting a new set of broad, economywide presumptions in favor of interpreting most conduct as reflecting efficiencies achieved in competitive markets.[79] While these efforts have achieved some success,[80] on the whole, antitrust law examines much more firm conduct under a reasonableness standard today than was true a generation ago.[81] We suspect that most economists think that this leads to better antitrust policy formation (at least if the higher costs of running the legal system to decide cases under reasonableness standards are ignored).

Leading developments in the post-Chicago evolution of antitrust generally continue to push doctrine away from bright line rules and toward an economic-based reasonableness analysis. These include use of the "raising rivals' costs" framework for evaluating exclusionary conduct,[82] recognition of the possibility of unilateral competitive effects of mergers among sellers of differentiated products,[83] establishment of the possibility that predatory pricing could be a rational strategy,[84] attention to understanding how a merger affects the incentives of the "maverick" seller when evaluating coordinated competitive effects,[85] the use of direct evidence of market power to trump evidence of low market shares in exclusion cases,[86] and the evaluation of the potential loss of research and development competition in innovation markets.[87] The main post-Chicago development going the other way, toward bright line rules, is the application of truncated or structured legal rules to condemn the conduct of a monopolist who excludes a rival without an adequate business justification, without need for direct proof of harm to competition.[88]

In the adversarial context of competition policy implementation, the choice between bright line rules and unstructured standards presents a decision-theoretic trade-off.[89] Bright line rules, including antitrust's per se rules, promise to lower transactions costs. They give guidance to firms seeking to comply with the law and to generalist judges seeking to apply it. They do so by limiting what must be shown to prove or disprove an offense—for example, by excluding certain arguments that a litigant might wish to proffer and in consequence excluding evidence related to those arguments—thereby also promising to reduce the transactions costs of litigation. But these advantages come at the price of greater errors in classifying firm conduct, either false convictions (finding violations when the conduct was pro-competitive) or false acquittals (failing to find a violation when the conduct harmed competition). By contrast, unstructured standards, including reasonableness tests, promise to make fewer errors by allowing courts to review all relevant evidence and arguments. But they may achieve this benefit at the price of reducing guidance to courts and firms, and raising transactions costs of litigation.

The advantages of reasonableness analysis were particularly apparent in the wake of economic criticisms of the bright line doctrinal rules that were characteristic of antitrust's structural era. The effort by some Chicago school antitrust commentators to convince courts instead to codify bright line doctrinal rules based on a new set of broad presumptions, more accepting of a wide range of firm conduct, may have been stalled by the inability of Chicago school economists to convince the economics profession that new presumptions had deep empirical economic support. Chicago school antitrust scholars listened to Chicago school economists explain that "structure-conduct performance methods cannot show market power," but formulated policy recommendations as though the lesson had been the overstatement "there is little or no market power in the economy."

1.3.2 Limited Generalizations across Related Industries
Since the late 1970s mainstream industrial organization economics have adopted the industry case study methodology previously employed fruitfully by Chicago school economists in the preceding era, but now with improved empirical methods. The "new empirical industrial organization" emphasized the creation of empirical tools that could be adapted to analyze individual industries, for purposes that included the identification and measurement of market power.[90] The large and varied literature that resulted has identified market power in many industries, thereby undermining the possibility of an empirical basis for broad bright line antitrust rules raising high bars to antitrust challenges across the board.[91] At the same time, theoretical industrial organization economists, deploying the game-

theoretic tools through which microeconomics has been reconstructed since the 1970s, have shown that a wide range of business conduct that Chicago school economists view as consistent with the competitive model could be understood as competitive under some conditions but as reflecting the exercise or creation of market power under others. This theoretical development has also militated against the project undertaken by Chicago school antitrust commentators of identifying broad presumptions that could be codified in antitrust rules.

The application of reasonableness standards in antitrust decision-making and the modern empirical literature in industrial organization economics have an important commonality: both treat the industry as the appropriate unit of observation. Both fields recognize that a one-size-fits-all approach to analyzing business conduct won't do, since so much variation in outcomes arises from factors specific to each individual industry. Empirical investigation of game-theoretic models of competition in a variety of industries shows that some of these factors are strategic. The most plausible competitive or efficiency theory of any particular industry's structure and business practices is as likely to be idiosyncratic to that industry as the most plausible strategic theory with market power. In addition the probative value of various types of evidence as to market power, entry, efficiencies, and the like, including the relative availability and usefulness of qualitative and quantitative evidence, often differs from one industry to the next.

This perspective does not mean that each industry must be analyzed afresh, without reference to what is known about other industries. Both antitrust law and industrial organization economics have come to recognize that related industries often are sufficiently similar to provide useful guidance. Many of the same legal and economic questions arise, for example, in understanding firm behavior in markets in which products are sold at retail, in markets for basic metals with cyclical demand, in markets for high-tech products sold in aftermarkets, and in any number of similar categories. One key challenge for both antitrust analysis and empirical industrial organization economics going forward is to exploit similarities among related industries. Focused inquiry involving the industry besides the firms under study is not recognized in antitrust to the extent it is understood in economics.

For instance, it is widely recognized that product-differentiated industries as a class present certain common behaviors and analytical problems, but few economists would argue that any particular product-differentiated industry could be analyzed for market power, competitive effects, or demand substitution without industry-specific analysis. What the research literature has done is identify a set of industries in which broadly the same tool kit can be used to examine market power. Within this set of industries, an enquiry that looks only at demand substitution to address market definition and identify market power, ignoring supply-side factors like costs and strategic conduct, is in general likely to be largely right.[92]

Another example of the value of information about related industries comes from the large literature on pharmaceutical markets studying the entry of generic drugs in competition with previously patent-protected brand-name drugs.[93] This literature establishes a presumption about the relevant product market in a merger, such as between the brand-name producer and the first generic entrant. In particular, if that merger occurs around the time that a drug goes off patent, the relevant product market for the merger analysis is likely to be exactly this drug, not including other drugs in the same therapeutic category, making the transaction a merger to monopoly. Similarly the literature establishes a presumption that the likely competitive effects of such a merger are to prevent price declines in the form of cheaper generics. These presumptions could be overcome in the detailed review of facts surrounding a particular merger, of course. However, the generalizations from an academic literature that has looked at differences in market outcomes in many pharmaceutical markets when drugs go off patent should be treated as a legitimate and potentially persuasive basis for reaching conclusions in any particular investigation.

Another example, taken from the *Microsoft* litigation, illustrates how a presumption, reasonably derived from a generalization across related industries, can be rebutted. In his testimony for Microsoft, Richard Schmalensee relied upon generalizations from the software industry as a whole to inform his views about market power and entry in operating systems, the particular software category that Microsoft was accused of monopolizing. Schmalensee testified that "[c]ompetition in the software industry is based on sequential races for the leadership of categories such as word processing, spreadsheets, personal financial software, games, operating systems and utilities." Although there may be some switching costs, "the history and reality of the microcomputer industry" show that superior alternatives, for which consumers are willing to abandon their investment in the products of the category leader, "come often." Indeed "[h]istory has shown that when faced with a superior alternative, software users switch and do so in droves." Accordingly, Schmalensee concluded, Microsoft's success and high share in the operating-system category does not mean it has monopoly power. "Rather, like other firms in this industry, it is in a constant struggle for competitive survival," including its struggle "to maintain its leadership in operating systems."[94]

As these excerpts suggest, Schmalensee recognized, correctly, that many software markets can be characterized by leapfrog competition, in which the winner obtains a high share for a time, only to be supplanted when a superior product comes along. He applied this generalization about software markets to the particular software category, operating systems, that was the subject of the monopolization litigation. In short, Schmalensee did what we suggest: he used what he learned about related industries to focus the inquiry about operating systems software. Based on how competition often works in software markets generally, it was reasonable to approach this case initially as Schmalensee did, by adopting a presumption that competition works similarly in operating systems software. The government actually adopted a version of the same presumption in its theory of competitive harm, which posited the possibility of leapfrog competition in the operating system market if new Internet technologies, such as Netscape's browser or Sun's Java, were to come into widespread use.

But along with the court, we think the presumption as used by Schmalensee was rebutted by the evidence presented by the Justice Department and state plaintiffs demonstrating that operating systems in the period at issue were a monopoly. Microsoft's leading position in operating systems was buttressed by the so-called applications barrier to entry that gives consumers reason to prefer the dominant operating system, Microsoft's Windows, even if they would prefer another operating system if all or most applications programs available for Windows were rewritten for that operating system. When Microsoft took steps to impede the success of a new technology (Netscape's Internet browser combined with Sun's Java programming langauge) that had the potential for reducing the applications barrier to entry, those acts allowed Microsoft to maintain its operating systems monopoly.

Our point here is not to reargue the *Microsoft* case. It is to show how a generalization taken from the experiences of related industries can create a presumption about how competition works in the industry under study—and to show that the presumption can be rebutted with industry-specific evidence to explain why it does not apply in the specific case under review.

1.4   Design of Institutions for Antitrust Decision-Making

Antitrust decision-making relies centrally upon economic reasoning and upon economic evidence. Economic reasoning in antitrust decision-making puts a premium on ensuring that decision-makers are capable of that task.

The institutional structure of the US courts and antitrust enforcement agencies presents a mixed picture of the sophistication of economic thinking. The enforcement agencies have a well-developed institutional capacity to obtain economic input from a professional staff of PhD economists, and antitrust lawyers in leadership roles often have developed a substantial facility with economic reasoning from their long engagement with the antitrust field.[95] Indeed many attorneys in the antitrust bar show considerable economic sophistication. But the courts do not have these advantages. Judges are generalists. Most lack experience with antitrust or economics and do not generally have the same training as professional economists.[96] Unlike agency officials, judges do not have much access to economic support. Accordingly, there is a serious discrepancy between tasks judges are called upon to do in antitrust cases—evaluating or even undertaking economic reasoning—and the capabilities of many judges to perform that task.

Moreover the litigation context in which much antitrust analysis occurs can direct the attention of a court away from the most important issues in evaluating economic evidence. The litigation setting encourages precision in the details, more so than the academic setting, where a small computational mistake, for example, would be unlikely to raise a question about the credibility of the researcher. The litigation context can undervalue the importance of the big picture—of linking the economic evidence with a theory of the case, or measuring key economic relationships and effects using sensible methods. These problems, which could be of great significance in the academic setting, may be dismissed as merely another disagreement among experts.

Recognition of the difficulties courts face in evaluating economic evidence in antitrust cases is not new. Frank Easterbrook (1984) has termed the difficulties of making correct judgments under a reasonableness standard in any individual case the "limits of antitrust." Easterbrook's solution was to recommend that courts adopt simple and general bright line doctrinal rules in the antitrust field, rather than endorsing a wide-ranging reasonableness analysis in individual cases. We do not object, in principle, to bright line rules based on convincing economic generalizations from a substantial program of careful empirical research. But absent progress in developing such rules, we propose two other approaches to this problem that do not avoid the detailed analysis of industry evidence.

Our first proposal is that empirical economists—both academics and economists at the antitrust enforcement agencies—work to unify the tool kit used in academic work and in antitrust work and begin to create a catalog of generalizations about various industry structures—a set of stylized facts and (rebuttable) presumptions about groups of related industries. We have already provided two examples of the kind of generalizations and presumptions we have in mind. One is a presumption about the likely loss of competition from a merger involving the producer of a brand-name drug producer and the first generic entrant, which could be expressed in the form of a narrow product market. Another is the generalization that shifts in retail prices in differentiated consumer products industries resulting from horizontal merger will generally reflect the effect of the merger on the pricing constraint imposed by demand substitution, not supply-side changes in cost or the oligopoly solution concept. These kinds of generalizations would be used to structure the analysis in individual antitrust cases and suggest the kind of evidence that would be most appropriate. The antitrust agencies could assume the job of organizing conferences of empirical economists to identify the consensus view of the economics profession, and write reports to codify the resulting generalizations and presumptions, and making them available to help judges and litigants.[97]

Our second proposal involves helping judges interpret economic evidence and assess its probative value.[98] Various methods of doing so have been tried, including the use of court-appointed economic experts,[99] the use of judicial law clerks with economic expertise,[100] and direct questioning of one economic expert by another. The legal debate over options for giving courts greater access to economic expertise has mainly addressed the pros and cons of court-appointed experts. The commentary highlights the importance of finding an independent expert acceptable to the parties (particularly in fields where basic principles are in dispute), making any independent expert's views transparent to the litigants and giving the parties an opportunity to comment on those views. One concern is that otherwise, a district court judge, having selected an independent expert, may in practice give that expert's views too much deference. Another is the difficulty finding a neutral independent expert, free from conflicts and strong ideological presumptions, who could be available at the court's convenience. Many of the best potential experts—well versed in aspects of economics most relevant to antitrust and sufficiently experienced with antitrust litigation to understand how to assist a court—have a high opportunity cost of taking on new projects and may not find it attractive to work for the court, perhaps excluding high-profile cases, unless they are able to limit the time they must commit. A third concern is that utilization of a court-appointed independent expert may add to the length and cost of litigation.

We suspect that the most pressing need for improvement in the design of institutions for antitrust decision-making is to find a way to clarify for generalist judges the nature of the dispute between economic experts for opposing parties. This observation suggests that a court-appointed economic expert would confer substantial value by undertaking a limited task: reviewing the reports of opposing experts, and writing his or her own report for the court that supplements the work of party experts by explaining where those experts disagree and why (without necessarily taking a view of his or her own on the resolution of key disputes). Party experts could be allowed to comment on the independent expert's report, but oral testimony and cross-examination of the independent expert would not be necessary.

This proposal for what might be termed a "clarifying expert" would have a number of advantages. It would give the judge help in understanding the economic arguments in the case. The limited scope for the court-appointed expert would encourage the judge to view the expert as providing help, rather than as an authority to be deferred to.[101] The limited assignment would also encourage a strong and deep pool of potential independent experts to make themselves available for consideration for the clarifying expert role. If the clarifying expert's report is made public (presumably after redacting confidential business information), that would encourage high-quality analysis by the clarifying expert, by allowing for peer review of his or her output, and encourage high-quality analysis by the party experts, by creating a public record of an independent view of their economic work.[102]

A number of important details would still have to be worked out to implement this suggestion—such as how the independent clarifying expert is selected (must the parties agree? can they wield a veto?), what materials the expert may review (just the expert reports?), how much direction the court will provide (perhaps by indicating where the judge would most benefit from clarification), and at what stage in the proceeding should a clarifying expert be involved.[103] We have sketched our proposal to encourage further deliberation about the way institutional design affects the ability of judges to undertake sound economic reasoning in antitrust litigation.[104]

Attention to the capacity of courts to apply economic reasoning is important because of the central role that judges play in shaping and implementing US antitrust policy. The success of the antitrust enforcement agencies owes much to the way decision-makers in those institutions are able to interact with economists.[105] Courts have done so too, but only indirectly, through what judges learn from the experts in their courtroom, economic articles cited by the litigants, and the economic reasoning embedded in the doctrinal rules that they employ. Our proposals seek to bring judges even closer to how economists think and what economists know.

Notes

1. For example, *Hospital Corp. v. Federal Trade Commission*, 807 F.2d 1381 (7th Cir. 1986) (Posner, J.) (upholding FTC determination that a hospital merger would likely harm competition by facilitating coordination was upheld based on a detailed review of postmerger market structure, integrating a wide range of factors beyond market concentration); *Federal Trade Commission v. Staples, Inc.*, 970 F. Supp. 1066 (DDC 1997) (enjoining a merger between office superstore chains based on evidence that head-to-head competition between the merging firms led to lower prices, regardless of the presence of warehouse club stores, mass merchandisers, or independent retail office supply stores in the area); *United States v. Waste Management, Inc.*, 743 F.2d 976 (2d Cir. 1984) (overturning lower court injunction barring a merger between two Dallas-area waste disposal firms that would result in high market concentration, since easy entry into the market made the exercise of market power unlikely).

2. For example, *United States v. Microsoft Corp.*, 253 F.3d 34 (DC Cir. 2001) (upholding lower court finding of liability against Microsoft based on detailed economic analysis of the way the exclusion of Microsoft's browser rival from access to the most important channels of distribution protected Microsoft's operating system monopoly from a significant long-term competitive threat, thus allowing it to maintain its market power); *Blomkest Fertilizer, Inc. v. Potash Corp.*, 203 F.2d 1028 (8th Cir. 2000) (relying on economic analysis of factors including market structure affecting the ability of firms to coordinate successfully to uphold award of summary judgment to defendants in a horizontal price-fixing case); *National Collegiate Athletic Association v. Board of Regents*, 468 US 85 (1984) (concluding that the association regulating college sports had effectively created a cartel by selling television rights for all college football games, and preventing schools or conferences from contracting with television networks on their own).

3. *Continental Television, Inc. v. GTE Sylvania, Inc.*, 433 US 36 (1977), overruling *United States v. Arnold, Schwinn & Co.*, 388 US 365 (1967).

4. The empirical revolution in antitrust analysis was arguably ushered in by our development of empirical methods of estimating residual demand elasticities during the mid-1980s. Baker and Bresnahan (1985, 1988).

5. Baker and Bresnahan (1992). For a more recent survey, see Baker and Rubinfeld (1999).

6. Carlton and Perloff (2005).

7. Noneconomic goals played a greater role in the United States prior to the late 1970s than they do today, but even then economic goals were important.

8. See generally, Lopatka and Page (2005).

9. The antitrust injury requirement was introduced in *Brunswick Corp. v. Pueblo Bowl-O-Mat, Inc.*, 429 US 477 (1977) in a setting where a rival sought damages from a merger alleged to harm competition by facilitating horizontal coordination. Later decisions have extended the requirement substantially. Gavil, Kovacic, and Baker (2002, pp. 777–88). For example, in *Microsoft*, the appeals court interpreted *Brunswick* as requiring proof that the monopolist's conduct harmed competition not just competitors. *United States v. Microsoft Corp.*, 243 F.3d 34, 589–59 (DC Cir. 2001). In that case, the antitrust injury requirement was applied to an allegation of exclusionary (not collusive) conduct challenged under the Sherman Act (not the Clayton Act) by a government plaintiff (not a private plaintiff) seeking injunctive relief (not damages)—a setting far indeed from that of *Brunswick*.

10. Here we view economic methods broadly, as going beyond theoretical modeling and econometric data analysis to include experimental and simulation methods.

11. Rigorous analysis is important regardless of whether the economic theory of the case is presented informally or through a formal model. In some sense a model is always lurking in the background when an economist, attorney or judge interprets evidence. (We use the term "model" broadly to include all abstract frameworks. In appropriate circumstances a table or a verbal articulation of an economic story would both count as models.)

12. Specification includes a full description of the economic model and an account of the nature of stochastic components (errors). See Reiss and Wolak (2005, secs. 4.1, 4.2).

13. Manski (1995) defines "identification" as the range of conclusions that could be drawn if one could use the sampling process to obtain an unlimited number of observations (as distinct from the additional "statistical" problems in making inferences arising from the fact that samples are finite). His definition includes the use we make of the term identification, namely whether a model that distinguishes between policy-relevant conclusions and alternative explanations of the same phenomena can be estimated.

14. The Merger Guidelines suggest an algorithm for inferring unilateral effects from market shares, but this algorithm is rarely if ever employed, as it depends on the generally unrealistic assumption that each product's market share reflects not only its relative appeal as a first choice to buyers but also its relative appeal as a second choice, and hence as a competitive constraint.

15. Baker (2003a) explores why the antitrust enforcement agencies adopted unilateral effects theories in merger analysis.

16. On the limited probative value of market shares in assessing likely unilateral effects, see Baker (1997b).

17. However, some remain skeptical of the possibility of unilateral effects when market shares are low. *United States v. Oracle Corp.*, 331 F. Supp. 1098 (ND Cal. 2004).

18. In a monopolization case the inquiry would be different, typically asking whether there is market power in the industry already that might be sustained by an anticompetitive act or practice. Market definition offers an imperfect way to get at this question too. For a discussion of market definition in cases in which the alleged harm is retrospective and the alleged anticompetitive conduct is exclusionary, see Baker (2007).

19. US Department of Justice and Federal Trade Commission Horizontal Merger Guidelines (1992, revised 1997), available at ⟨http://www.ftc.gov/bc/doc/horizmer.htm⟩.

20. Market definition is exclusively concerned with the economic force of demand substitution under the methodology of the merger guidelines. In nonmerger contexts, some US courts also incorporate considerations of supply substitution in the market definition step, rather than later in antitrust analysis. The use of supply substitution to define markets is criticized in Baker (2007).

21. The firm's residual demand function is the demand curve that results after accounting for the best response of nonmerging rivals.

22. This condition follows from the first order condition for profit maximization, assuming differences in price and price–cost margin among sellers within the group can be ignored. For a general discussion of related issues, see Werden (1998).

23. As will be discussed, calculations of the Lerner index must deal with a range of issues including aggregation problems (as arise from heterogeneity in prices and costs among the market participants) and the difficulties associated with inferring a sensible economic measure of marginal cost from accounting data.

24. If the errors are correlated with other independent variables, the bias could go in either direction.

25. Empirical studies of retailer behavior find that products generally decline in price during predictable periods of peak demand (such as seasons for some products or certain holidays for others). See Hosken and Reiffen (2004a,b), Chevalier, Kashyap, and Rossi (2003), MacDonald (2000), Warner and Barsky (1995). The literature interprets this observation as typically resulting from a reduction in the retailer's per-customer distribution costs (which decline as the density of customers grows). (Alternative explanations—that demand tends to grow more elastic at predictable peaks, or that manufacturers choose to compete more aggressively—appear inconsistent with evidence that promotion levels typically surge and manufacturer margins generally do not decline.) In consequence the model may need to account for the possibility that marginal cost as well as demand varies seasonally or that both marginal cost and demand could be related to the level of promotional activity. Alternatively, a model in which interactions between buyers and sellers are explicitly dynamic (i.e., one in which price is not determined in the one period run) might be employed.

26. Hendel and Nevo (2002).

27. For detailed discussions of the identification issues, see Reiss and Wolak (2005, sec. 7.1) and Bresnahan (1998).

28. This type of argument was successful in *New York v. Kraft General Foods, Inc.*, 926 F. Supp. 321 (SD NY 1995). A similar argument was advanced by defendants in responding to the FTC's challenge to the merger of two baby food producers, Beech-Nut and Heinz. See Baker (2004).

29. For surveys, see Werden and Froeb (2005) and Epstein and Rubinfeld (2004). The quantitative analysis underlying a merger simulation is closely related to the quantitative analysis underlying a market definition or market power assessment. In the merger setting, key inputs include estimates of the substitution possibilities between the products of the merging firms and among the products of the merging firms and other sellers and estimates of the competitive response to a merger by other firms. The simulation methodology takes those inputs and puts them in a helpful and policy-relevant form, facilitating interpretation and the evaluation of the practical economic significance of alternative assumptions, but it cannot substitute for weaknesses in the estimates. In the market definition setting, a simple simulation methodology called "critical loss analysis," based on estimate of the magnitude of demand substitution, is sometimes employed. In practice, however, the approach commonly embodies a number of simplifying assumptions that do not invariably hold, and can in consequence lead to misleading results. For a discussion, see Baker (2007).

30. See, generally, Ashenfelter et al. (2006) and Baker (1999).

31. The empirical study of natural experiments involving changes in market structure can also provide an indication of the likely price effects from the loss of localized competition, by facilitating a comparison between prices with and without the presence of that localized competition. This is an alternative interpretation of the econometric study relied upon by the FTC in *Staples*. A similar study was introduced by defendants in the baby food merger case. Baker (2004).

32. For example, Bresnahan (1987), Berry, Levinsohn, and Pakes (1995), Goldberg (1995), Nevo (2000), Petrin (2002), and Trajtenberg (1990).

33. For example, Borenstein and Rose (1994), Leslie (2004), and Shephard (1991).

34. For example, Athey and Levin (2001), Bajari and Hortacsu (2003), Guerre, Perrigne, and Vuong (2000), and Hedricks and Porter (1988). Identification for auction models is discussed in Athey and Haile (2001).

35. The types of evidence available for assessing demand substitution in market definition are surveyed in Baker (2007).

36. We describe an anecdote of this sort taken from our consulting experience in Baker and Bresnahan (1992, p. 6).

37. Berry and Pakes (1993), Berry, Levinsohn, and Pakes (1995), Bresnahan, Stern, and Trajtenberg (1997), and Nevo (2000, 2001).

38. See the discussion of conjoint survey methods in Baker and Rubinfeld (1999).

39. Notification M/04/032, Proposed Acquisition of IBM Ireland Limited Of Schlumberger Business Continuity Services (Ireland) Limited, Irish Competition Authority (October 28, 2004), available at ⟨http://www.tca.ie/⟩.

40. Whether the most convincing evidence about economic concepts, like market power or efficiencies, is systematic empirical evidence derived from econometric analysis or more qualitative, as with much evidence derived from documents and testimony, such evidence is necessarily predicated on a set of assumptions that permit inference. As we noted previously when describing information as local, empirical analysis cannot be conducted in a vacuum. Even when systematic empirical methods are employed, documents and testimony invariably and appropriately play a role in specifying a model and interpreting its results.

41. Another example of such a data set, from outside the litigation context, comes from Bresnahan and Ramey (1994), who use information on managers' reported motives for temporary automobile plant closings and shift changes in the automobile industry. The economic literature on the study of sales and on couponing (e.g., Nevo and Wolfram 2002) has made progress on understanding these phenomena without managerial information.

42. If the views of industry experts (e.g., including the views of sellers of complementary products) are used to judge the likely buyer substitution responses to prices, their reliability as evidence would be assessed similarly to what is inferred from seller conduct: based on whether the experts are in a position to gather direct information about buyers, and on whether they base costly business decisions on that information.

43. Of course, the absence of supply shifters would equally prevent identification of the demand elasticity using quantitative methods.

44. The defense might also raise problems with the government's inference other than identification. For example, a defense showing that the firms monitor other rivals nearly as much as they monitor each other can be thought of as a qualitative analogue to problems with estimation in data analysis.

45. Some commentators view monopoly power as another term for market power; others view it as market power of more than some threshold magnitude. Either way, proof of monopoly power requires proof of market power.

46. Many of these methodologies are surveyed in Reiss and Wolak (2005), Porter (2005), Bresnahan (1989), and, less technically, in Baker and Bresnahan (1992).

47. If a firm (or group of firms) with market power (collectively) excludes a rival with no legitimate (procompetitive) justification, antitrust law will not require proof that price has increased. The best economic interpretation comes from a decision-theoretic framework: false acquittals are unlikely (since the firms involved could exercise or be exercising market power) and false convictions are unlikely (since there is no procompetitive reason for the conduct).

48. Thus, with n products, equation (1.1) is from R^n to R^n.

49. In many studies of product differentiated industries, however, equation (1.2) is not estimated. Alternative methods that might be employed in studying such industries are discussed below under the headings "estimating demand" and "direct measurement."

50. Much of the literature focuses on differentiated products, but a substantial new literature looks at the implications for market power of increasing firm marginal costs. The electricity industry has proven fertile ground for such studies, because good observable indicators of cost-related variables like (the other) firms' capacity and variety in the efficiency of plants are often available. See, for example, Borenstein, Bushnell, and Wolak (2002), Borenstein and Bushnell (1999), and Wolfram (1999).

51. In the context of a homogeneous goods industry, this is the slope of the industry demand curve times industry quantity. In a product-differentiated industry, it depends on the slopes of individual products and on which products are provided by a particular firm. See Bresnahan (1982) for details.

52. Baker and Bresnahan (1985, 1988).

53. See, for example, Wolfram's (1999) study of duopoly pricing in electricity. Wolfram's careful analysis shows that marginal costs are rising at the firm level because plants vary in efficiency, leading to strategic pricing. See also Wolak (2003) for discussion of the California energy crisis emphasizing unilateral market power that arose because of capacity constraints. As weather shocks constrained the capacity of hydroelectric producers, fossil-fuel producers faced less elastic residual demand curves.

54. Coordinating firms that find it difficult to reach consensus and deter deviation may, moreover, adopt inflexible pricing rules. Then simple methods of inferring L based on observing price responses to changes in the elasticity of demand or observable components of cost (discussed below) may not be able to distinguish coordination from competition.

55. For example, a test for monopoly could be based on the prediction that a monopolist that sells a single product and does not discriminate in price would set its price such that $L = 1/\varepsilon$ or, equivalently, such that $L\varepsilon = 1$. See Genesove and Mullin (1999) for an implementation of this test.

56. The Lerner index estimate is presumably derived as an average of the price–cost margins in a number of transactions, over which price and cost vary because of shifts in the exogenous variables Y, W, and Z and the stochastic terms u and v. In general, the precision of the inference about firm conduct will depend on the variation in L from transaction to transaction, and on whether this variation can be linked empirically to variation in the important determinants of firm conduct across those transactions. Moreover the Lerner index for an industry is not well defined unless price plays an allocative role in transactions, so this method of inference is difficult to employ in the presence of certain forms of price discrimination such as volume discounts and loyalty discounts across multiple products sold by a single firm.

57. Special problems in relating a measure of the Lerner index to market power arise in industries with high fixed costs and low (and nonincreasing) marginal costs. These might include computer software, airline transportation, or some entertainment industries, for example. In such industries, some or all buyers will likely be charged a price in excess of marginal cost, even when there is free entry, if the fixed costs are so high that an increase in competition would lead a new entrant to be unprofitable. One problem that arises under such circumstances is that it is theoretically possible that the threat of entry constrains existing firms. More precisely, the average prices of incumbent firms might be constrained not to exceed entrant average cost. In that case the competitive price would need to be defined relative to the incremental cost associated with an entrant, a variant of marginal cost. This problem is unlikely to be important in practice, however, as the presence of such a powerful constraint by potential entrants has not been identified in any market studied in the empirical economics literature and appears to call for extreme assumptions theoretically.

Another problem that arises under such circumstances is that the exercise of market power can theoretically be efficient. If the fixed costs of entry are large relative to the size of the market, adding competitors may reduce welfare, even though price is above marginal cost. This result suggests a possible efficiency justification for an acquisition in an industry with high fixed and low marginal costs. Such a justification should be considered only with great caution, for demonstrating empirically that a less competitive market structure is more efficient is very difficult. Such a justification should almost never be considered in technologically progressive industries. This is because the efficiency conclusion can only follow if there were no benefits of innovation rivalry among active firms.

58. These difficulties with measuring the appropriate economic concept of marginal cost also arise when accounting information on marginal cost is used as an input into the simulation of price increases. This may occur in antitrust litigation, in the analysis of competitive effects of firm conduct, or in market definition, where "critical loss" simulations are sometimes employed.

59. Bresnahan (1982) and Lau (1982). For example, Reiss and Wolak (2005) show that if equation (1.1) is specified as $P = \alpha_0 + \alpha_1 Y + \beta Q^{1/\gamma} + u$, and marginal cost is specified as $C = c_0 + c_1 W + v$, a function that does not depend on output, then the quasi-supply function (1.2) simplifies to the reduced form $P = [1/(\gamma + \theta)][(\alpha_0 \theta + \gamma c_0) + \alpha_1 \theta Y + \gamma c_1 W + (\theta u + \gamma v)]$. If the demand curve parameters α_1 and γ have been estimated, then θ, an estimator of $L\varepsilon$, can be inferred from the coefficient on Y in this equation, so θ is identified. The key to econometric identification of θ in this example is the presence of a variable Y, which allows the demand function to rotate in observable ways.

60. Economists recognize that price discrimination can occur in markets where entry competes the long-run profit rate to zero for marginal entrants. Restaurants in a large city, which often discount entrees for "early bird" customers, might present an example. (In this case we assume that such discounts are greater than might be explained by any reduction in marginal cost, as might reflect the lower probability of reaching a capacity constraint during off-peak periods.) Baker (2003b) describes this limiting case as an example of the exercise of market power without the possibility of anticompetitive effect. (Product differentiation could similarly compete profits to zero, as in the model of monopolistic competition, but it more commonly allows firms to create niches for their products that rivals could not profitably enter, allowing the firm to earn economic profits. The limiting case of monopolistic competition again represents the exercise of market power without anticompetitive effect.)

61. This is evident from the example in note 59. Without the presence of a variable Y that rotates demand, it would be impossible to infer θ, the estimator of $L\varepsilon$. The parameter cannot be backed out of the intercept term $[1/(\gamma + \theta)][(\alpha_0 \theta + \gamma c_0)]$ because that term depends both on θ and on c_0, the average level of marginal cost.

62. *American Tobacco Co. v. United States*, 328 US 781 (1946).

63. *United States v. Addyston Pipe & Steel Co.*, 85 F. 271 (6th Cir. 1898) (Taft, J.).

64. See Baker (1999).

65. Carlton and Perloff (2005, pp. 128–30).

66. Bajari and Summers (2002), Porter and Zona (1993), and Porter and Zona (1999).

67. Baker (2002b). When coordinated effects of merger are alleged, it is important to understand more than merely whether the industry structure is conducive to coordination—whether firms can plausibly reach consensus as to the terms of coordination, deter deviation (cheating) on those terms, and prevent new competition (entry)—but also to understand the mechanism by which coordinated competitive effects of mergers might arise. The latter question may be addressed by identifying a maverick firm that constrains coordination from becoming more effective, and evaluating how the merger affect the pricing incentives of that firm.

68. Baker (2002b) terms this the revealed preference strategy (when based on prices) or the natural experiment strategy (when based on costs) for identifying a maverick. An example in which the revealed preference strategy was applied based on qualitative evidence appears in Bresnahan (2002). Another approach, termed by Baker the a priori factors strategy, identifies a maverick firm from structural characteristics tending to suggest that it has more incentive than its rivals to keep coordination from becoming fully effective or complete. For example, if excess capacity creates price pressure in the view of industry participants, a merger of firms intending to reduce capacity could be understood as a transaction likely to alter the incentives facing firms likely to spoil attempts at more effective coordination. See *FTC v. Cardinal Health, Inc.*, 12 F. Supp. 2d 34, 63–64 (DDC 1998).

69. Similarly, using data from the steel industry during the Great Depression, Baker (1989) shows that unexpected declines in demand (inferred from an estimated demand function) reduced price more than would be explained merely by the effects of a demand decline on price, holding conduct constant, and concludes that the negative demand shocks led firms to act more competitively for a time. The firms switched from a high-price to a low-price regime, at the same time as unexpected negative demand shocks, suggesting a causal connection.

70. See Porter (2005) for a more nuanced and complete discussion of this topic. This methodology could alternatively be thought of as a way of comparing observed conduct with that of competitive firms, which would not be expected to experience occasional large reductions in price unrelated to shifts in cost or demand.

71. See Bresnahan (1989) and Reiss and Wolak (2005) for reviews of some of this literature.

72. See, for example, Bresnahan (1987) and Berry, Levinsohn, and Pakes (1995) on variation in market power within the US automobile industry.

73. See Bresnahan and Reiss (1987) or Sutton (1991).

74. The strategic approach to understanding entry conditions transcended an older debate between pioneering industrial organization economists Joe S. Bain and George Stigler. Bain emphasized the role of structural factors in creating entry barriers, including absolute cost advantages of incumbents, product differentiation and economies of scale. Stigler's definition of entry barriers was limited to costs that must be borne by an entrant though not an incumbent. Stigler also questioned whether high capital requirements could prevent entry given the wide range of financing opportunities from well-funded participants in financial and credit markets. Modern industrial organization economists see Stigler's framework as including disadvantages to entrants that arise from the strategic forces determining industry structure. Many of these entry barriers are closely linked to costs, as strategic entry problems can arise particularly when the fixed costs of entry are sunk and can be exacerbated by information asymmetries in financial and credit markets. For example, Sutton (1991) shows that the presence of sunk costs, including irreversible expenditures on research and development, capital and advertising, is a precondition for one form of strategic entry barriers.

75. Accordingly, this effort could be thought of as more than a critique of the structure-conduct performance approach. It could be viewed instead as a second effort to establish a broad presumption, this time that few industries exercise market power and possess entry barriers.

76. See, for example, the chapters in Weiss (1989).

77. For a brief survey of the three major eras in US antitrust enforcement, classical, structural, and Chicago school, see Baker (2002a).

78. As a strategy for learning about antitrust enforcement generally, this approach has significant limitations. The primary benefits of enforcement may come from deterring anticompetitive conduct among nondefendants rather than from identifying and remedying specific problems in the markets in which enforcement occurred, and in which the benefits of enforcement (or lack thereof) might be observed. Also we should expect antitrust enforcers to be selective if markets vary. Deterrence and selection make identification difficult. Suppose, for example, we were to find that past mergers had no effect on competition. That could either mean that competition policy authorities are doing a good job screening out anticompetitive mergers, or that their policies are far too stringent in some dimension. To resolve the question, we would like to know what would happen if a different set of mergers had been permitted. but cannot perform that experiment. In Baker (2003a) this identification problem is addressed using qualitative evidence on the behavior of US firms during four periods or situations without effective antitrust enforcement, and by examining the behavior of firms across national antitrust regimes with different degrees of effectiveness.

79. Easterbrook (1984) and Posner (1981).

80. For example, the legal rules concerning predatory pricing have been modified over the past few decades to create nearly insurmountable hurdles for plaintiffs. New procedural rules involving antitrust injury have combined with rules involving summary judgment standards in conspiracy cases to make it difficult for a dealer to challenge its termination by a manufacturer as resulting from a vertical agreement between the manufacturer and rival dealers as to price. Also the legal rules concerning vertical nonprice agreements, which formally require a reasonableness analysis, have been applied in practice to make successful challenges extremely rare.

81. On the other hand, the recent development of structured inquiries like quick look rules for Sherman Act analysis can be understood as moving some antitrust doctrine in the direction of bright line rules. The current dispute as to whether "profit sacrifice" is a good guide to monopolization can also be understood as an effort by the federal enforcement agencies to encourage adoption of a bright line rule. For criticism, see Gavil (2005) and Salop (2005).

82. Krattenmaker and Salop (1986).

83. For example, Baker and Bresnahan (1985).

84. Brodley, Bolton, and Riordan (2000).

85. Baker (2002b).

86. For example, *Toys 'R' Us v. FTC*, 221 F.3d 928 (7th Cir. 2000).

87. Gilbert and Sunshine (1995).

88. For example, United States v. Microsoft Corp., 253 F.3d 34 (DC Cir. 2001). In this case the government alleged that a number of Microsoft's actions maintained high entry barriers into its operating system monopoly. The court's standard was truncated in the sense that it did not require the government to show that lower entry barriers would necessarily have led to entry and new competition, instead requiring only a showing that the challenged conduct was exclusionary. (Of course, this standard permits a defense based on a procompetitive justification of the challenged practices.)

89. On the decision-theoretic framework for developing antitrust rules, see, for example, Beckner and Salop (1999).

90. See Bresnahan (1989) and Reiss and Wolak (2005) for literature reviews.

91. In consequence the only principled argument against antitrust enforcement generally is the contested claim, made by some antitrust opponents, that government actions seeking to remedy anticompetitive acts almost invariably leave the economy worse off than the anticompetitive conduct itself, even after accounting for additional harm that would arise from removing the deterrent effect of antitrust enforcement in industries where no violation was found to remedy. For an analysis of the benefits and costs of antitrust that reaches the opposite conclusion, see Baker (2003c).

92. See the discussion in Bresnahan (1989). The subsequent literature on product-differentiated consumer products industries has, with a few exceptions, assumed Bertrand competition. Peters (2003) and Nevo (2004) compare the predicted price change under Bertrand competition to the actual price change ex post mergers in the Airline and RTE cereals industries.

Careful attention to the supply side along with demand becomes important only when the question shifts from whether the firm or firms exercise market power—the issue in market definition or unilateral effects of merger among sellers of differentiated products—to whether changes in supply, as from the efficiencies that may result from firm conduct or the increased competition that could result from proposed remedies, would counteract the exercise of market power in such markets.

93. For example, Scott-Morton (1997, 1999, 2000).

94. Schmalensee (1999, at paras. 33, 34, 37, 59, 135).

95. In this connection we applaud the recent decision of the European Union's antitrust authority to deepen its economics capability and to appoint a chief competition economist.

96. There are occasional exceptions, for there are a number of very economically oriented attorneys and judges who are not PhD economists.

97. The Federal Trade Commission frequently hosts workshops and conferences on antitrust topics, often inviting participation from academic economists.

98. The value of improving the economic expertise available to judges deciding antitrust cases is heightened by the recent increase in challenges to admissibility of expert economic testimony in the wake of *Daubert v. Merrell Dow Pharmaceuticals*, 509 US 579 (1993), where the Supreme Court encouraged such challenges as a means of weeding out complaints based on "junk science." Issues related to Daubert challenges are surveyed in Gavil (2000).

99. This approach has been encouraged by both Justice Breyer, *General Electric Co. v. Joiner*, 522 US 136, 149–50 (1997) (Breyer, J., concurring) and Judge Posner (1999), two economically sophisticated antitrust experts. For an antitrust example, see *New York v. Kraft General Foods, Inc.*, 926 F. Supp. 321, 351–52 (SDNY 1995) (testimony of court-appointed expert economist, Dr. Alfred Kahn, relied upon in evaluating merger challenge). The *CASE* (Court Appointed Scientific Experts) program of the American Association for the Advancement of Science, while primarily focused on health and physical sciences, has facilitated the connection of court-appointed economists in legal proceedings. Through this program, economist Frank Wolak was selected to serve as a court-appointed expert in the *High Fructose Corn Syrup* antitrust litigation. Wolak provided highly helpful assistance to the district court judge during the pretrial litigation that preceded a settlement.

100. Economist Carl Kaysen assisted the district court judge who decided *United States v. United Shoe Machinery Corp.*, 110 F. Supp. 295 (D. Mass. 1953), *aff'd per curium*, 347 US 521 (1954), a major monopolization case. Kaysen (1987).

101. The court might also request the clarifying expert to address specific questions of concern to the judge.

102. Party experts would also be encouraged to explain the bases of their opinions more fully, for fear of having omissions exposed in the clarifying expert's report (as well as exposed during cross-examination, as occurs today).

103. If the clarifying expert's report were filed before Daubert challenges to the admissibility of expert testimony were resolved, it could aid the court in that task, for example.

104. A possible alternative for achieving this end would be to require the opposing experts to negotiate and file with the court a pre-trial statement clarifying where they agree and where they disagree. It may be difficult to negotiate such a statement in an adversarial context, however, unless it is written vaguely, reducing its usefulness.

105. Baker (1997a) argues that the deep engagement of economists in agency decision-making confers the benefits of applying cost–benefit analysis even absent a formal requirement to do so.

References

Ashenfelter, O., D. Ashmore, J. B. Baker, S. Gleason, and D. S. Hosken. 2006. Empirical methods in merger analysis: Econometric analysis of pricing in *FTC v. Staples. International Journal of the Economics of Business* 13: 265–79.

Athey, S., and P. A. Haile. 2002. Identification of standard auction models. *Econometrica* 70: 2107–40.

Athey, S., and J. Levin. 2001. Information and competition in U.S. Forest Service Timber auctions. *Journal of Political Economy* 109: 375–417.

Bajari, P., and A. Hortacsu. 2003. The winner's curse, reserve prices and endogenous entry: Empirical insights from eBay auctions. *RAND Journal of Economics* 3(2): 329–55.

Bajari, P. L., and G. Summers. 2002. Detecting collusion in procurement auctions. *Antitrust Law Journal* 70: 143–70.

Baker, J. B. 2007. Market definition. *Antitrust Law Journal* 74: 129–73.

Baker, J. B. 2004. Efficiencies and high concentration: Heinz proposes to acquire Beech-Nut (2001). In J. E. Kwoka Jr. and L. J. White, eds., *The Antitrust Revolution*, 4th ed. New York: Oxford University Press, pp. 150–69.

Baker, J. B. 2003a. Why did the antitrust agencies embrace unilateral effects? *George Mason University Law Review* 12: 31–38.

Baker, J. B. 2003b. Competitive price discrimination: The exercise of market power without anticompetitive effects (comment on Klein and Wiley). *Antitrust Law Journal* 70: 643–54.

Baker, J. B. 2003c. The case for antitrust enforcement. *Journal of Economic Perspectives* 17: 27–50.

Baker, J. B. 2002a. A preface to post-Chicago antitrust. In R. van den Bergh, R. Pardolesi, and A. Cucinotta, eds., *Post Chicago Developments in Antitrust Analysis*. London: Edward Elgar, pp. 60–75.

Baker, J. B. 2002b. Mavericks, mergers, and exclusion: Proving coordinated competitive effects under the antitrust laws. *New York University Law Review* 77: 135–203.

Baker, J. B. 1999. Econometric analysis in *FTC v. Staples. Journal of Public Policy and Marketing* 18: 11–21.

Baker, J. B. 1997a. "Continuous" regulatory reform at the Federal Trade Commission. *Administrative Law Review* 49: 859–74.

Baker, J. B. 1997b. Product differentiation through space and time: Some antitrust policy issues. *Antitrust Bulletin* 42: 177–96.

Baker, J. B. 1989. Identifying cartel policing under uncertainty: The U.S. steel industry 1933–1939. *Journal of Law and Economics* 32(2, pt. 2): S47–76.

Baker, J. B., and T. F. Bresnahan. 1985. The gains from merger or collusion in product differentiated industries. *Journal of Industrial Economics* 33: 427–44.

Baker, J. B., and T. F. Bresnahan. 1988. Estimating the residual demand curve facing a single firm. *International Journal of Industrial Organization* 6: 283–300.

Baker, J. B., and T. F. Bresnahan. 1992. Empirical methods of identifying and measuring market power. *Antitrust Law Journal* 61: 3–16.

Baker, J. B., and D. L. Rubinfeld. 1999. Empirical methods in antitrust litigation: Review and critique. *American Law and Economics Review* 1: 386–435.

Beckner III, C. F., and S. C. Salop. 1999. Decision theory and antitrust rules. *Antitrust Law Journal* 67: 41–76.

Berry, S., and A. Pakes. 1993. Automobile prices in market equilibrium. *Econometrica* 63: 841–90.

Berry, S. T., J. Levinsohn, and A. Pakes. 1995. Automobile prices in market equilibrium. *Econometrica* 63: 841–90.

Borenstein, S., J. B. Bushnell, and F. A. Wolak. 2002. Measuring market inefficiencies in California's restructured wholesale electricity market. *American Economic Review* 92: 1376–1405.

Borenstein, S., and J. B. Bushnell. 1999. An empirical analysis of market power in a deregulated California electricity market. *Journal of Industrial Economics* 47: 285–323.

Borenstein, S., and N. E. Rose. 1994. Competition and price dispersion in the U.S. airline industry. *Journal of Political Economy* 102: 653–83.

Bresnahan, T. F. 2002. Comments on "Reforming European merger review: Targeting problem areas in policy outcomes" by Kai-Uwe Kühn. Working manuscript. Available at ⟨http://www.stanford.edu/~tbres/research.htm⟩.

Bresnahan, T. F. 1998. The apple-cinnamon Cheerios war: Valuing new goods, identifying market power, and economic measurement. Working manuscript. Available at ⟨http://www.stanford.edu/~tbres/research.htm⟩.

Bresnahan, T. F. 1989. Empirical studies of industries with market power. In R. Schmalensee and R. D. Willig, eds., *Handbook of Industrial Organization*, vol. 2. Amsterdam: North-Holland, pp. 1011–57.

Bresnahan, T. F. 1987. Competition and collusion in the American automobile market: The 1955 price war. *Journal of Industrial Economics* 35: 457–82.

Bresnahan, T. F. 1982. The oligopoly solution concept is identified. *Economics Letters* 10: 87–92.

Bresnahan, T. F., and V. Ramey. 1994. Output fluctuations at the plant level. *Quarterly Journal of Economics* 109: 593–624.

Bresnahan, T. F., and P. C. Reiss. 1987. Do entry conditions vary across markets? *Brookings Papers on Economic Activity: Special Issue on Microeconomics*, pp. 833–71.

Bresnahan, T. F., S. Stern, and M. Trajtenberg. 1997. Market segmentation and the sources of rents from innovation: Personal computers in the late 1980s. *RAND Journal of Economics* 28: S17–44.

Brodley, J. F., P. Bolton, and M. H. Riordan. 2000. Predatory pricing: Strategic theory and legal policy. *Georgetown Law Journal* 88: 2239–2330.

Carlton, D. W., and J. M. Perloff. 2005. *Modern Industrial Organization*, 4th ed. Boston: Pearson/Addison Wesley.

Chevalier, J. A., A. K. Kashyap, and P. E. Rossi. 2003. Why don't prices rise during periods of peak demand? Evidence from scanner data. *American Economic Review* 93: 15–37.

Easterbrook, F. H. 1984. The limits of antitrust. *Texas Law Review* 63: 1–40.

Epstein, R. J., and D. L. Rubinfeld. 2004. Technical report: Effects of mergers involving differentiated products. European Commission, DG Competition, COMP/B1/2003/07, October 7, 2004. Available at ⟨http://europa.eu.int/comm/competition/mergers/others/effects_mergers_involving_differentiated_products.pdf⟩.

Gavil, A. I. 2005. Exclusionary distribution strategies by dominant firms: Striking a better balance. *Antitrust Law Journal* 72: 3–81.

Gavil, A. I., W. E. Kovacic, and J. B. Baker. 2002. Antitrust law in perspective: Cases, concepts and problems in competition policy. Thomson West.

Gavil, A. I. 2000. Defining reliable forensic economics in the post Daubert-Kumho Tire era case studies from antitrust. *Washington and Lee Law Review* 57: 831–78.

Genesove, D., and W. P. Mullin. 1998. Testing static oligopoly models: Conduct and cost in the sugar industry, 1890–1914. *RAND Journal of Economics* 29(2): 355–77.

Gilbert, R. J., and S. Sunshine. 1995. Incorporating dynamic efficiency concerns in merger analysis: The use of innovation markets. *Antitrust Law Journal* 63: 569–601.

Goldberg, P. K. 1995. Product differentiation and oligopoly in international markets: The case of the U.S. automobile industry. *Econometrica* 63: 891–951.

Guerre, E., I. Perrigne, and Q. Vuong. 2000. Optimal nonparametric estimation of first-price auctions. *Econometrica* 68: 525–74.

Hendel, I. and A. Nevo. 2002. Sales and consumer inventory. Working Paper 9048. NBER Working Paper Series.

Hendricks, K., and R. H. Porter. 1988. An empirical study of an auction with asymmetric information. *American Economic Review* 78: 865–83.

Hosken, D., and D. Reiffen. 2004a. Patterns of retail price variation. *RAND Journal of Economics* 35: 128–46.

Hosken, D., and D. Reiffen. 2004b. How retailers determine which products should go on sale: Evidence from store-level data. *Journal of Consumer Policy* 27: 141–77.

Kaysen, C. 1987. In memorium: Charles E. Wyzanski Jr. *Harvard Law Review* 100: 713–16.

Krattenmaker, T., and S. Salop. 1986. Anticompetitive exclusion: Raising rivals' costs to achieve power over price. *Yale Law Journal* 96: 209–93.

Lau, L. J. 1982. On identifying the degree of industry competitiveness from industry price and output data. *Economics Letters* 10: 93–99.

Leslie, P. 2004. Price discrimination in Broadway theatre. *RAND Journal of Economics* 35: 520–41.

Lopatka, J. E., and W. H. Page. 2005. Economic authority and the limits of expertise in antitrust cases. *Cornell Law Review* 90: 617–703.

MacDonald, J. M. 2000. Demand, information, and competition: Why do food prices fall at seasonal demand peaks? *Journal of Industrial Economics* 48: 27–45.

Manski, C. F. 1995. *Identification Problems in the Social Sciences*. Cambridge: Harvard University Press.

Scott-Morton, F. 2000. Barriers to entry, brand advertising, and generic entry in the U.S. pharmaceutical industry. *International Journal of Industrial Organization* 18: 1085–1104.

Scott-Morton, F. 1999. Entry decisions in the generic drug industry. *RAND Journal of Economics* 30: 421–40.

Scott-Morton, F. 1997. The strategic response by pharmaceutical firms to the medicaid most-favored-customer rules. *RAND Journal of Economics* 28: 269–90.

Nevo, A. 2001. Measuring market power in the ready-to-eat cereal industry. *Econometrica* 69: 307–42.

Nevo, A. 2000. Mergers with differentiated products: The case of the ready-to-eat cereal industry. *RAND Journal of Economics* 31: 395–421.

Nevo, A., and C. Wolfram. 2002. Why do manufacturers issue coupons? An empirical analysis of breakfast cereals. *RAND Journal of Economics* 33: 319–39.

Peters, C. T. 2003. Evaluating the performance of merger simulation: Evidence from the U.S. airline industry. DOJ Antitrust Division Economic Analysis Group Discussion Paper 03-1.

Petrin, A. 2002. Quantifying the benefits of new products: The case of the minivan. *Journal of Political Economy* 110: 705–29.

Porter, R. H. 2005. Detecting collusion. *Review of Industrial Organization* 26: 147–67.

Porter, R., and D. Zona. 1999. Ohio school milk markets: An analysis of bidding. *RAND Journal of Economics* 30: 263–88.

Porter, R., and D. Zona. 1993. Detection of bid rigging in procurement auctions. *Journal of Political Economy* 101: 518–38.

Porter, R. 1983. A study of cartel stability: The Joint Executive Committee 1880–1886. *Bell Journal of Economics* 14: 301–14.

Posner, R. A. 1999. An economic approach to the law of evidence. *Stanford Law Review* 51: 1477–1546.

Posner, R. A. 1981. The next step in antitrust treatment of restricted distribution: Per se legality. *University of Chicago Law Review* 48: 6–26.

Reiss, P. C., and F. A. Wolak. 2006. Structural econometric modeling: Rationales and examples from industrial organization. *Handbook of Econometrics*, vol. 6, forthcoming.

Salop, S. C. 2006. Exclusionary conduct, effect on consumers, and the flawed profit-sacrifice standard. *Antitrust Law Journal* 73: 311–74.

Schmalensee, R. L. 1999. Direct testimony. *United States v. Microsoft* (DDC 2000).

Shepard, A. 1991. Price discrimination and retail configuration. *Journal of Political Economy* 99: 30–53.

Sutton, J. 1991. *Sunk Costs and Market Structure: Price Competition, Advertising, and the Evolution of Concentration*. Cambridge: MIT Press.

Trajtenberg, M. 1990. *Economic Analysis of Product Innovation: The Case of CT Scanners*. Cambridge: Harvard University Press.

Warner, E. J., and R. B. Barsky. 1995. The timing and magnitude of retail store markdowns: Evidence from weekends and holidays. *Quarterly Journal of Economics* 110: 321–52.

Weiss, L. W. ed. 1989. *Concentration and Price*. Cambridge: MIT Press.

Werden, G. J. 1998. Demand elasticities in antitrust analysis. *Antitrust Law Journal* 66: 363.

Wolak, F. A. 2003. Measuring unilateral market power in wholesale electricity markets: The California market 1998 to 2000. *American Economic Review* 93: 425–30.

Wolfram, C. 1999. Measuring duopoly power in the British electricity spot market. *American Economic Review* 89: 805–26.

2 Unilateral Competitive Effects of Horizontal Mergers

Gregory J. Werden and Luke M. Froeb

Horizontal mergers—those of direct competitors—give rise to unilateral anticompetitive effects if they cause the merged firm to charge a higher price, produce a lower output, or otherwise act less intensely competitive than the merging firms, while nonmerging rivals do not alter their strategies. Unilateral effects contrast with coordinated effects arising if a merger induces rivals to alter their strategies, resulting in some form of coordination or reinforcement of ongoing coordination. The term "unilateral" is used because the merged firm and its rivals both pursue their unilateral self-interests.

Unilateral merger effects flow from internalization of the competition between the merging firms. The simplest case is the merger of duopolists when the pre-merger oligopoly game yields a unique equilibrium more competitive in some sense than the monopoly equilibrium. Through the merged firm's pursuit of self-interest, the merger causes a shift from the duopoly equilibrium to the less competitive monopoly equilibrium. Although merger to monopoly is the simplest example of unilateral effects, it may be the least common and least interesting, so the remainder of this chapter considers mergers not resulting in monopoly.

Unilateral effects of mergers arise in one-shot oligopoly games with Nash noncooperative equilibria, including the classic models of Cournot (1838), Bertrand (1888), and Forchheimer (1908, dominant firm). In Bertrand oligopoly, for example, a merger combining two competing brands of a differentiated consumer product, and not reducing costs, necessarily leads to unilateral price increases, even if only very small price increases. The merged firm accounts for the increase in sales of either of the two brands resulting from an increase in the price of the other, and therefore finds it in its unilateral self-interest to raise the prices of both. Pursuing the unchanging strategies optimal in the Bertrand model, firms selling competing brands respond by raising their prices. The postmerger equilibrium reflects the merged firm's response to the responses of nonmerging competitors, the nonmerging competitors' responses to those responses, and so forth.

Although unilateral effects theories are based on ideas that are quite old as economic theory goes, explicit application of these ideas to merger policy was limited prior to the release of the Horizontal Merger Guidelines (1992). One reason unilateral effects theories did not become prominent until recently is that most economists paid little attention to the Cournot and Bertrand models during the formative era for merger enforcement policy in the United States—from the late 1940s through the late 1960s. Only coordinated effects were predicted by the then-prevailing view of oligopoly theory (Chamberlin 1929; 1933, ch. 3; Fellner 1949), which held that cooperation would tend to emerge spontaneously when the number of competitors was sufficiently small. The Cournot model was dismissed almost from the start as positing irrational behavior (see Fisher 1898, pp. 126–27). It was (mis)understood to assume that competitors myopically treated rival's outputs as fixed, when in fact each competitor's output depended—even in the model—on the outputs of the others. Although Nash noncooperative equilibrium was well known by game theorists in the 1950s and 1960s, industrial organization economists did not understand and embrace it until later, and only then did they appreciate the wisdom of the Cournot and Bertrand models (see Leonard 1994; Meyerson 1999).

As detailed by Werden (1997, 2005), merger policy developed without any clear foundation in economic theory, but rather with a general abhorrence of industrial concentration. *Columbia Steel* (1948) introduced the term "relevant market" and was the first horizontal merger case to focus on market shares. *Brown Shoe* (1962, p. 335) held that "the proper definition of the market is a 'necessary predicate' to an examination of the competition that may be affected by the horizontal aspects of the merger." And *Philadelphia National Bank* (1963, p. 363) established a presumption of illegality for a merger that "produces a firm controlling an undue percentage share of the relevant market, and results in a significant increase in the concentration of firms in the market." These decisions remain significant, particularly because the US Supreme Court has not had the occasion to address merger policy for three decades.

This chapter first reviews the economic theory underlying the unilateral competitive effects of mergers, focusing on the Cournot model, commonly applied to homogeneous products; the Bertrand model, commonly applied to differentiated consumer products; and models of auctions and bargaining, commonly applied when a bidding process or negotiation is used to set prices. This chapter then reviews two classes of empirical methods used to make quantitative predictions of the unilateral effects of proposed mergers.

Merger simulation calibrates a model of a one-shot noncooperative oligopoly game to match critical features of the industry, such as prices and outputs. The calibrated model is then used to compute the postmerger equilibrium that internalizes competition between the merging firms. With differentiated consumer products, to which merger simulation principally has been applied, calibration involves selecting values for the own- and cross-price elasticities of demand for relevant products. Typically used for this purpose are econometric estimates derived from high-frequency consumer purchase data. Over the past decade, merger simulation and econometric estimation of demand elasticities both have become common in the analysis of differentiated products mergers, and as Robert Willig (Merger Enforcement Workshop, February 19, p. 124) declared, "the biggest change in the analytic framework used for merger enforcement has been the advent of simulation analysis."

Another class of methods for predicting unilateral merger effects is reduced-form empirical modeling, which predicts unilateral merger effects without reliance on any particular model of competitor interaction. Inferences, instead, are drawn from experiments performed by nature. Such experiments can consist of any significant variation in market structure across markets or over time. The most prominent example of this approach is the FTC's prediction of the likely price effects in the *Staples* (1997) case. The FTC based its prediction on the relationship between particular stores' prices and the number and identity of their competitors. Although reduced-form modeling can be useful, significant conceptual issues must be confronted if the experiments performed by nature are not mergers. It is likely to be far from straightforward to extrapolate from the observed relationship between price and structure across markets, or even over time, to the likely price effects of a merger.

2.1 Theoretical Analysis of Unilateral Effects

2.1.1 A Formal Definition of Unilateral Effects

Consider a simultaneous-move oligopoly game, in which n competing firms choose "actions" represented by real numbers. Firm i's action is a_i, and $\boldsymbol{a}_{-i}$ is the $(n-1)$-tuple of actions taken by the other firms. The profits of firm i are denoted $\Pi^i(a_i, \boldsymbol{a}_{-i})$ to indicate their dependence on not just firm i's own action but also on the actions of its rivals. To ensure the existence and uniqueness of equilibrium, $\Pi^i(a_i, \boldsymbol{a}_{-i})$ is assumed to be twice continuously differentiable and strictly concave.

The necessary and sufficient conditions for Nash equilibrium are that for all i,

$$\frac{\partial \Pi^i(a_i, \boldsymbol{a}_{-i})}{\partial a_i} \equiv \Pi_i^i(a_i, \boldsymbol{a}_{-i}) = 0.$$

Each of these partial derivatives is taken with rivals' actions being held constant, but this does not mean that firms actually treat rivals' actions as fixed. For any actions by its rivals, firm i's optimal action is given by its reaction function, or best-response function, which solves $\Pi_i^i(a_i, \boldsymbol{a}_{-i}) = 0$ for a_i as a function of $\boldsymbol{a}_{-i}$. Best-response functions may be implicit, although some profit functions permit an explicit solution

$$a_i = R_i(\boldsymbol{a}_{-i}).$$

The Nash noncooperative equilibrium is the n-tuple of actions, such that each firm operates on its best-response function.

The merger of firms i and j produces a new firm choosing a_i and a_j to maximize $\Pi^i + \Pi^j$. For the merged firm, the necessary and sufficient conditions for Nash equilibrium are

$$\frac{\partial \Pi^i(a_i, \boldsymbol{a}_{-i})}{\partial a_i} + \frac{\partial \Pi^j(a_j, \boldsymbol{a}_{-j})}{\partial a_i} = 0,$$

$$\frac{\partial \Pi^i(a_i, \boldsymbol{a}_{-i})}{\partial a_j} + \frac{\partial \Pi^j(a_j, \boldsymbol{a}_{-j})}{\partial a_j} = 0.$$

The merger alters the optimal choice of a_i and a_j because the merged firm accounts for the effect of a_i on Π^j and the effect of a_j on Π^i. Unless both effects are negligible, the merger affects the choice of both a_i and a_j. Consequently it affects the actions of nonmerging competitors as well, to the extent that the first derivatives of their profit functions are affected by changes in a_i or a_j. The postmerger equilibrium fully reflects all competitors' responses to others' responses, and so forth.

What makes the merger anticompetitive is that it internalizes the rivalry between the merging firms and thereby causes them to alter their actions. What makes the anticompetitive effect "unilateral" is that the actions of nonmerging competitors are determined by the same, Nash equilibrium, best-response functions before and after the merger. The effects are unilateral even though nonmerging competitors do not take the same actions after the merger that they took before it, and even if the changes in their actions increase the merged firm's profit. Merger effects also would be unilateral even if the merged firm played an oligopoly game different than that the merging firms had played (e.g., see Daughety 1990; Levin 1990).

2.1.2 Mergers in Cournot Industries

Mergers in the Basic Cournot Model   In 1838 Antoine Augustin Cournot published the first systematic analysis of oligopoly, positing that the actions of competitors are their outputs. Cournot considered an industry with a homogeneous product, and it is to such an industry that the model generally is applied. In what follows, a "Cournot industry" is one in which competing producers of a homogeneous product simultaneously chose outputs in a one-shot game. Shapiro (1989, pp. 333–39) and Vives (1999, ch. 4) usefully analyze competition in a Cournot industry, and Szidarovszky and Yakowitz (1982) offer a technical treatment of the subject.

Firm i in a Cournot industry has output x_i and is completely characterized by its cost function $C_i(x_i)$. The industry has aggregate output X and is characterized the set of incumbent firms and the inverse demand $p = D(X)$. The profits of firm i are

$$\Pi^i(x_i, X) = x_i D(X) - C_i(x_i).$$

Denoting the first derivatives of the demand and cost functions with primes, the necessary conditions for the Nash noncooperative equilibrium are that for all i,

$$\frac{\partial \Pi^i(x_i, X)}{\partial x_i} = p + x_i D'(X) - C_i'(x_i) = 0.$$

If ϵ is the industry's elasticity of demand, $m_i \equiv [p - C_i'(x_i)]/p$ is firm i's price–cost margin, and $s_i \equiv x_i/X$ is firm i's output share, these equilibrium conditions can be written

$$m_i = \frac{-s_i}{\epsilon}.$$

In equilibrium therefore the larger a firm's output share, the larger is its margin and the lower its marginal cost.

If m is the share-weighted industry average margin, and $H \equiv \sum s_i^2$ is the Herfindahl-Hirschman index of output concentration, multiplying both sides of each firm's equilibrium condition by its output share, and summing over all firms in the industry, yields

$$m = \frac{-H}{\epsilon}.$$

If the pre- and postmerger demand elasticities are the same, and the merger does not affect the industry average marginal cost, it follows that

$$\frac{\Delta p}{p} = \frac{-(H_{post} - H_{pre})}{\epsilon + H_{post}}.$$

This result, however, is not useful for predicting the price effects of *proposed* mergers. If a merger is significantly anticompetitive, the unobservable, postmerger output shares that go into H_{post} are different than the observable, pre-merger output shares. Moreover the assumption that industry average marginal cost is constant cannot be maintained unless all firms in the industry have the same, constant marginal cost.

If the merged firm's output is x_m, and its marginal cost is $C_m'(\cdot)$, its equilibrium condition is

$$p + x_m D'(X) - C_m'(x_m) = 0,$$

and the sum of the pre-merger equilibrium conditions for firms i and j is

$$2p + (x_i + x_j)D'(X) - C_i'(x_i) - C_j'(x_j) = 0.$$

Assuming that the merger of those two firms induces neither the entry of a new competitor nor investments affecting the marginal costs of nonmerging incumbents, the effect of the merger on price can be gleaned by subtracting the former condition from the latter. If x_i and x_j are the pre-merger outputs of the merging firms, the output of the merged firm is less than $x_i + x_j$ and the merger increases price unless

$$C_m'(x_i + x_j) < C_i'(x_i) + C_j'(x_j) - p.$$

Substituting the conditions for pre-merger equilibrium margins into this inequality yields the conclusion that the merger increases price unless

$$C'_m(x_i + x_j) < p\left(1 - \frac{s_i + s_j}{\epsilon}\right),$$

with the right-hand side evaluated at the pre-merger equilibrium. Farrell and Shapiro (1990a) derive this result and also demonstrate, as a general matter, that mergers in Cournot industries cause prices to rise unless they generate sufficient offsetting synergies, in the sense that the merged firm can produce a given level of output at a lower total cost than the two separate merging firms can when optimally rationalizing production between them. Absent synergies, the merged firm chooses an output less than the sum of the outputs of the merging firms; nonmerging competitors increase their output, but the net effect is a lower aggregate output and hence a higher price.

For a Cournot industry Froeb and Werden (1998) show that

$$\frac{-2s_i s_j}{\epsilon(s_i + s_j) + (s_i^2 + s_j^2)}$$

is the amount of the reduction in marginal cost, as a proportion of the share-weighted average of the merging firms' marginal costs, required to prevent a merger from increasing price. As a proportion of the pre-merger price, the required reduction in marginal cost is

$$\frac{-2s_i s_j}{\epsilon(s_i + s_j)}.$$

In the symmetric case, $s_i = s_j = s$, so the former expression simplifies to $-s/(\epsilon + s)$ and the latter to $-s/\epsilon$, which equals the pre-merger margin of both merging firms. This final result provides a handy rule-of-thumb: To prevent a price increase following a merger in a Cournot industry, merger synergies must reduce the merged firm's marginal cost, in absolute terms, by at least as much as the pre-merger price exceeds the merging firms' marginal costs.

Significance of Cost Functions   Just as firms in the Cournot model are characterized by their cost functions, the impact of a merger in the model is reflected in the difference between the cost function of the merged firm and those of the merging firms. If the merging firms have constant marginal cost and no capacity constraints, the merged firm is endowed with the lower of the two marginal costs. The effect of the merger is simply to destroy the higher cost merging firm, and nothing of value is acquired when the lower cost firm purchases the stock or assets of the higher cost firm. While real-world corporate acquisitions on rare occasions may be designed to accomplish no more than destroying assets, that is certainly not the usual case. Hence the Cournot model is apt to be of interest to merger policy only if marginal costs are increasing in the relevant range of output, or if there are significant capacity constraints. As a description of real-world industries the latter circumstance is apt to be more realistic than the former.

An interesting special case, analyzed by Werden (1991) and McAfee and Williams (1992), combines linear demand with quadratic costs of the form $x_i^2/2k_i$, where k_i is a constant proportional to the capital stock or capacity of firm i. The marginal cost of firm i is x_i/k_i, and the merger of firms i and j combines their capital stock, yielding a marginal cost of $x_m/(k_i + k_j)$. Defining $\kappa_i = k_i/(1 + k_i)$, $\kappa_m = (k_i + k_j)/(1 + k_i + k_j)$, $\kappa = \sum \kappa_i$, and $\Delta\kappa = \kappa_m - \kappa_i - \kappa_j < 0$, it is easy to show that the proportionate effect of the merger on the equilibrium price, $\Delta p/p$, is given by $-\Delta\kappa/(1 + \kappa_{pre} + \Delta\kappa)$. Thus the larger $\Delta\kappa$ in absolute value, the greater the effect of the merger on price. From this, Werden (1991) demonstrates that $\Delta p/p$ is increased by (1) replacing either merging firm with a nonmerging competitor with a larger share of industry capital stock, (2) increasing the equality of the merging firms' shares of industry capital, while holding their total capital constant, or (3) transferring capital between two nonmerging competitors in a manner that increases the inequality of their capital holdings.

Profitability, Partial Acquisitions, and Entry   The academic literature on mergers in Cournot industries has concentrated on their profitability. Salant, Switzer, and Reynolds (1983) show that in a symmetric Cournot industry, with linear demand, constant marginal costs, and no capacity constraints, mergers are unprofitable for the merging firms unless they involve at least 80 percent of the industry. But, as Perry and Porter (1985) note, those assumptions produce an unrealistic notion of a merger. Perry and Porter consider instead a model in which a firm's marginal cost is increasing with a slope inversely proportional to a its capital stock, and they find greater scope for profitable mergers. In addition Fauli-Oller (1997) and Hennessy (2000) show there is greater scope for profitable mergers in Cournot industries when demand is convex. Furthermore the profitability of a real-world merger may derive from sources assumed away in these models, including cost reductions or other synergy gains in businesses of the merging firms other than those producing the anticompetitive effects.

Partial equity interests and joint ventures in Cournot industries are analyzed by Bresnahan and Salop (1986), Farrell and Shapiro (1990b), Flath (1992), Nye (1992), O'Brien and Salop (2000), and Reynolds and Snapp (1986). One insight of this literature is that a purely financial interest in a competitor causes a firm to restrict its own output without directly affecting the behavior of the competitor in which the interest is held.

There also have been attempts to address the generally unrealistic assumption that competitors' only actions are their outputs. Models have been analyzed in which competitors first make investment decisions determining their capacities, and then choose prices. The equilibrium in such models depends on which consumers pay what price, when different firms charge different prices and the low-price firm cannot satisfy total market demand. Kreps and Scheinkman (1983) and Osborne and Pitchik (1986) show that the equilibrium is the same as that in the Cournot model if the available low-price units of output are used to satisfy the demand of consumers willing to pay the most. Davidson and Deneckere (1986), however, show that first-come–first-served rationing produces an equilibrium more intensely competitive than the Cournot model.

Even if this last class of models yields the same equilibrium as the Cournot model, it does not follow that it makes the same predictions for the effects of mergers. If the pre-merger capacities are the Cournot outputs, it follows that nonmerging competitors are capacity constrained immediately following a merger. Considerable time may be required to adjust capacities to postmerger equilibrium levels, and until they adjust, the merged firm may find that a substantial price increase maximizes short-run profits.

The literature has begun to explore the incentive for, and effects of, entry following merger in a Cournot industry. Werden and Froeb (1998) analyze a model in which entry necessarily results in a net price reduction, and in that model, a merger producing significant price increases is unlikely to induce entry. They also argue that the merging firms account for the effect of their merger on prospects for entry, so the decision to merge implies either the expectation of substantial cost reductions or the belief that significant entry would be unprofitable. Spector (2003) posits a model in which entry could leave the post-merger, postentry price above the pre-merger level and shows that a merger is profitable, and thus occurs, only if any entry leaves price at a higher level. Gowrisankaran (1999) analyzes the very long-run outcome of a Cournot game with endogenous investment, entry, exit, and mergers. His numerical analysis suggests that mergers are likely to occur in Cournot industries (unless prevented by the legal system) and their price increasing effects are unlikely to be reversed by investment or entry.

2.1.3 Mergers in Bertrand Industries

Mergers in the Basic Bertrand Model   In an 1883 review of Cournot's book, Joseph Louis François Bertrand argued that it was more natural for competitors' actions to be their prices. Although Bertrand presumed a homogeneous product, the model that bears his name is considered most relevant with differentiated products, and in what follows, a "Bertrand industry" is one in which competitors in a one-shot game simultaneously chose prices for competing brands of a differentiated product. Vives (1999, ch. 6) usefully analyzes competition in a Bertrand industry. As Edgeworth (1925, pp. 116–21) pointed out, price competition need not produce an equilibrium in pure strategies, and conditions necessary to ensure existence of equilibrium are assumed below.

Deneckere and Davidson (1985) provide a reasonably general proof that mergers of substitutes in Bertrand industries raise prices and are profitable for the merging firms, although the mergers are even more profitable for nonmerging competitors. The basic intuition for the price-raising effect of mergers can be gleaned from consideration of a Bertrand industry with single-brand firms. Suppose that brand i's price is p_i, the vector of prices for its competing brands is $\boldsymbol{p}_{-i}$, the demand for brand i is $D_i(p_i, \boldsymbol{p}_{-i})$, and the cost of producing brand i is $C_i(D_i(p_i, \boldsymbol{p}_{-i}))$. Consequently the profits for brand i are

$$\Pi^i(p_i, \boldsymbol{p}_{-i}) = p_i D_i(p_i, \boldsymbol{p}_{-i}) - C_i(D_i(p_i, \boldsymbol{p}_{-i})).$$

The necessary conditions for the Nash noncooperative equilibrium are that for all i,

$$\frac{\partial \Pi^i(p_i, \boldsymbol{p}_{-i})}{\partial p_i} = D_i(p_i, \boldsymbol{p}_{-i}) + [p_i - C_i'(D_i(p_i, \boldsymbol{p}_{-i}))] \left[\frac{\partial D_i(p_i, \boldsymbol{p}_{-i})}{\partial p_i} \right] = 0.$$

If ϵ_{ji} is the elasticity of the demand for brand j with respect to the price of brand i, and $m_i \equiv [p_i - C_i'(\cdot)]/p_i$ is brand i's price–cost margin, the necessary conditions can be written

$$m_i = \frac{-1}{\epsilon_{ii}},$$

which is the familiar inverse-elasticity rule or Lerner (1934) condition for equilibrium in monopoly.

If brands i and j are merged together, the postmerger necessary conditions for equilibrium are

$$m_i = \frac{-1}{\epsilon_{ii}} + \frac{m_j d_{ij} p_i}{p_j},$$

$$m_j = \frac{-1}{\epsilon_{jj}} + \frac{m_i d_{ji} p_j}{p_i},$$

in which d_{ij} is the diversion ratio from brand i to brand j, that is, the ratio of the increase in quantity of brand j sold to the decrease in the quantity of brand i sold, when the price of brand i is increased slightly, or more formally,

$$d_{ij} = \frac{-\epsilon_{ji} D_j}{\epsilon_{ii} D_i}.$$

The last term in the equilibrium conditions is positive if brands i and j are substitutes. It follows that the merger raises the prices of both products unless it also reduces marginal costs or induces the entry of a new brand or investments that alter consumer perceptions about incumbent brands (termed "repositioning"). The postmerger equilibrium conditions for single-brand firms provide useful intuition about what determines the magnitudes of the price increases. Larger price increases result from larger diversion ratios and larger pre-merger margins for the merging brands (implying less elastic pre-merger demands). Shapiro (1996), who introduced the concept of the "diversion ratio," usefully outlines the foregoing.

Significance of Demand Curvature   In the symmetric case of $m_i = m_j = m$ and $d_{ji} = d_{ij} = d$, simple expressions give the price effects of mergers of single-brand firms when the mergers neither affect costs nor induce entry or repositioning. Shapiro (1996) shows that with iso-elastic demand,

$$\frac{\Delta p}{p} = \frac{md}{1 - m - d},$$

and with linear demand,

$$\frac{\Delta p}{p} = \frac{md}{2(1 - d)}.$$

For all positive values for m and d, isoelastic demand results in price increases more than twice those with linear demand. These expressions thus illustrate the importance of the higher order or "curvature" properties of demand in determining the effects of differenti-ated products mergers.

Froeb, Tschantz, and Werden (2005) systematically examine the impact of demand cur-vature on the price effects of mergers in Bertrand industries and on the extent to which marginal-cost reductions are passed through to consumers in the form of lower prices. The analysis is much like that for the monopoly case, which has the same inverse-elasticity equilibrium condition as a Bertrand industry with single-product firms. The only difference between the two cases is that in a Bertrand industry, a reduction in the marginal cost of producing either of the merged firm's brands affects the postmerger equilibrium prices of all competing brands, and these cross-price effects depend on idiosyncratic proper-ties of the functional form of demand.

Letting $\epsilon(p)$ be the elasticity of demand, the monopoly equilibrium condition can be written

$$-\epsilon(p) = \frac{p}{p - c} \equiv \frac{1}{m}.$$

If $\eta(p) \equiv \epsilon'(p)p/\epsilon(p)$ is the elasticity of the elasticity of demand, total differentiation of the equilibrium condition reveals that the derivative of the equilibrium price with respect to a constant marginal cost is

$$\frac{1}{1 + (\eta(p) - 1)m} = \frac{\epsilon(p)}{1 + \epsilon(p) - \eta(p)} \equiv \gamma.$$

This result is derived by Werden, Froeb, and Tschantz (2005), and Bulow and Pfleiderer (1983) present the result with plus sign where the minus sign should be. It follows that

$\gamma < 1$ if $\eta(p) > 1$, as with linear demand, for which $\gamma = \frac{1}{2}$;
$\gamma = 1$ if $\eta(p) = 1$, as with $D(p) = a \exp(-bp)$ and $a, b > 0$;
$\gamma > 1$ if $\eta(p) < 1$, as with isoelastic demand.

Among demand curves yielding the same competitive equilibrium and same value of $\epsilon(c)$, it is also the case that the monopoly-equilibrium margin is higher, the lower is the elasticity of the elasticity of demand.

While both the price and pass-through effects of mergers in Bertrand industries depend on the curvature of demand, that is not true of the magnitude of marginal-cost reductions that exactly restore pre-merger prices, provided that the merger induces neither the entry of a new brand nor repositioning of existing brands. Because all prices remain the same, so too do all demand elasticities, which makes these compensating marginal cost reductions (CMCRs) robust to the form of demand. Werden (1998) derives a general expression for the CMCRs. Defining m and d as before, the CMCRs for both merging brands in the symmetric case are

$$\frac{md}{(1-m)(1-d)},$$

when expressed as a proportion of pre-merger marginal cost. Expressed instead as a proportion of pre-merger price, the CMCRs are

$$\frac{md}{1-d}.$$

If $d = \frac{1}{2}$, making the merging brands exceptionally close substitutes, this implies the same rule-of-thumb as in a Cournot industry: To prevent postmerger price increases, the marginal costs of both the merging brands must fall in absolute terms by at least as much as the pre-merger prices exceed the pre-merger marginal costs. Merging brands typically are far less close substitutes, so much smaller cost reductions prevent price increases.

Bertrand Mergers with Logit Demand   Werden and Froeb (1994) analyze mergers among single-brand competitors in the context of logit demand, which generally is motivated by a random utility model of consumer choice. As formalized by Manski (1977), each consumer in this class of models makes a single choice from an exhaustive set of alternatives A, consisting of some particular alternatives plus "none of the above." In this formulation every alternative in A is necessarily a substitute for all the others. Consumers maximize utility, and the utility associated with each alternative is the sum of a "systematic" or "representative" component V_i common to all consumers, and a component specific to the individual consumer, which is treated as random to the outside observer. If and only if the random component of utility has the Gumbel (extreme value) distribution, McFadden (1974, pp. 111–12) and Anderson, de Palma, and Thisse (1992, pp. 39–40) have shown that result is the logit model, in which case, the probability of choosing brand i, over the entire population of consumers, is

$$\pi_i = \frac{\exp(V_i)}{\sum_{k \in A} \exp(V_k)}.$$

The simplest logit model specifies the systematic component of utility as

$$V_i = \alpha_i - \beta p_i,$$

in which α_i is a constant that indicates, roughly, brand i's average preference and β is a constant that determines the degree of substitutability among alternatives. The own-price elasticity of demand for brand i is

$$-\beta p_i (1 - \pi_i),$$

and the cross-price elasticity of the demand for brand i with respect to the price of brand j is

$$\beta p_j \pi_j.$$

With a very large β, competing brands are nearly perfect substitutes, so competition from nonmerging brands prevents a merger from increasing prices. And with a very small β, there is essentially no competition to lose from merging two brands.

With single-brand firms, logit demand, and constant marginal costs c_i, Werden and Froeb (1994) show that necessary conditions for Bertrand-Nash equilibrium are

$$p_i - c_i = \frac{1}{\beta(1 - \pi_i)}.$$

Before the merger, the markup for brand i, $p_i - c_i$, is higher the larger is its choice probability. The necessary conditions for equilibrium for the firm formed by merging brands i and j are

$$p_i - c_i = p_j - c_j = \frac{1}{\beta(1 - \pi_i - \pi_j)}.$$

Because both of the merged firm's brands have the same markup, it follows that the merger causes a larger increase (in absolute terms) in the price of the merging brand with the smaller pre-merger choice probability. The primary reason for this relates to pattern of switching between the two brands in response to a price increase: for any given loss in sales from a price increase for the merging brands, a larger portion is recaptured by the brand with the larger choice probability. A second reason is that the brand with the larger choice probability has the larger markup in the pre-merger equilibrium, making any given sales recapture more profitable. The same factors apply in general, although without logit demand, they may not be controlling.

Werden and Froeb (1994) also show that the slope of the best-response function for non-merging brand k, to an increase in price of merging brand i, is given by

$$\frac{\pi_i \pi_k}{1 - \pi_k}.$$

This expression is positive and increasing in both choice probabilities. Consequently the prices of nonmerging brands increase in response to increases in the prices of merging brands, with greater increases for brands with larger pre-merger choice probabilities. For nonmerging brands with choice probabilities less than those of both merging brands, the slope of the best-response function is less than one-sixth, so the prices of nonmerging brands are apt to increase much less than those of the merging brands, and that typically is the case with other demand assumptions.

Independence of Irrelevant Alternatives and Closeness of Substitutes   The logit model exhibits independence of irrelevant alternatives (IIA), meaning that for any alternatives i and j and any subset S of the choice set A,

$$\frac{\text{Prob}(i|S)}{\text{Prob}(j|S)} = \frac{\text{Prob}(i|A)}{\text{Prob}(j|A)}.$$

The IIA property was introduced by Luce (1959, pp. 5–6, 12–15), who termed it the "choice axiom" and found it consistent with some experimental evidence. Debreu (1960) immediately noted that the IIA property cannot hold in some choice problems, and much economic literature has considered the IIA property unreasonably restrictive.

The IIA property, however, can be made far less restrictive by formulating the choice problem so that there is only a limited range of choices over which the IIA property is assumed to apply. One way to do this is to model the choice problem hierarchically, as in the nested version of the logit model. The IIA property then is assumed to apply at each stage of the choice problem. A very simple way to limit the range of choices over which the IIA property is assumed to apply is to model only a portion of the choice problem. For example, rather than modeling choice among all automobiles, it may suffice to model choice among just economy cars.

In practical terms, the IIA property implies substitution proportionate to relative choice probabilities: if alternatives i and j have choice probabilities 0.3 and 0.1, the IIA property implies that an increase in the price of any other alternative in the choice set necessarily induces three times as much substitution to i as to j. Because an increase in the price of one alternative induces equiproportionate increases in the consumption of all other alternatives in the choice set, there are equal cross-price elasticities of demand for every alternative in the choice set with respect to the price of a given alternative.

The IIA property provides the most useful definition of what it means for all alternatives to be equally close substitutes for each other. There are, however, other possible definitions. For example, one might say all alternatives are equally close substitutes if an increase in the price of one induces equal absolute increases in the consumption (or the value of the consumption) of all other alternatives in the choice set.

A common misconception reflected by the court's analysis in *Oracle* (2004, pp. 1117, 1166–68, 1172–73) is that mergers have significant unilateral anticompetitive effects in

Bertrand industries only when competition is highly localized as in a spatial model, the merger involves adjacent brands, and the merging brands are widely separated from non-merging brands. Analysis of the logit model, with its IIA property, explodes this notion.

Consider a symmetric, six-brand industry in which marginal costs are constant, all brands are priced at $1, the demand elasticity at the industry level is 0.5, and the logit β is 2.9. These assumptions produce plausible pre-merger price–cost margins of 0.4. Each brand has five equally close substitutes, but the merger of any two brands causes their prices to increase by 5.7 percent. All brands are not equally close substitutes in the mind of an individual consumer, and a significant number of consumers find any two brands to be their first and second choices.

Entry, Repositioning, and Other Dimensions of Competition Werden and Froeb (1998) explore the possibility of entry following merger in randomly generated Bertrand industries with logit demand. Their results suggest that mergers are unlikely to induce entry unless entry was nearly profitable pre-merger. Cabral (2003) considers the possibility of entry following mergers in a spatially differentiated Bertrand industry, and finds that merger to monopoly is reasonably likely to induce entry, leading to lower prices than before the merger.

Thus far it has been assumed that price is the only dimension of competition, but price is only one of several dimensions of competition in consumer goods industries—a fact stressed in the field of marketing. Little work has been done on the effects of mergers among competitors that choose both price and another strategic variable, such as product positioning or the level of promotion. Analyzing a merger solely in terms of price competition seems to be a reasonable simplification in many cases, but little theoretical or empirical analysis currently supports that view.

Gandhi et al. (forthcoming) analyze mergers between firms competing by simultaneously choosing price and location, which is modeled using the Hotelling (1929) line. Consumer choice in their model is determined by distance and a random factor capturing idiosyncratic tastes. They find that products combined by a merger are repositioned away from each other to reduce cannibalization, and nonmerging substitutes are, in response, repositioned between the merged products. This repositioning greatly reduces the merged firm's incentive to raise prices and thus substantially mitigates the anticompetitive effects of the merger. The repositioning also reduces the merger's benefit to nonmerging competitors and may make them worse off.

Gandhi et al. assume that changing location is costless, which is highly unrealistic in many industries. Altering product characteristics can be both expensive and risky, and it can take sufficiently long that ignoring that possibility altogether yields a good prediction of a merger's short-term effects. However, Berry and Waldfogel (2001) find that mergers among radio stations resulted in increased format variety within a short period of time. The increase in variety likely benefited listeners, but it could have harmed advertisers by making radio stations more distant substitutes and thereby leading to an increase in advertising rates.

2.1.4   Mergers in Auction Models
The Cournot and Bertrand models characterize equilibrium outcomes of a competitive process without detailing the process itself, while auction models specify in detail how bidders interact under rules dictated by the auctioneer. William Vickery (1961, 1962) initially formalized the analysis of competition in a bidding setting, with significant elaboration provided, in particular, by Milgrom and Weber (1982). The vast auction literature is usefully summarized by Klemperer (2004).

Different auction rules yield different models. In the model principally considered here, the auctioneer sells an item through ascending oral bidding. As illustrated below, essentially nothing changes if the auctioneer procures an item from the bidders rather than sells an item to them. Switching to sealed bidding introduces significant computational complexity with asymmetric bidders but might not have much impact on the effects of mergers.

In the model principally considered here, bidders have "private values" for the item auctioned, meaning that the value a particular bidder places on the item does not depend on how much rival bidders value the item. The literature on auctions with "common values," which do depend on rival bidders' values, remains largely undeveloped in the critical case of asymmetric bidders.

Mergers in Ascending Oral Auctions   When the auctioneer sells an item to bidders with private values, each bidder is modeled as drawing its value for the item from a specified joint distribution. A bidder's optimal strategy in an ascending oral auction is to bid until the level of the bidding reaches the value the bidder places on the item, or until all other bidders have dropped out. For example, suppose four bidders value an item at 1, 2, 3, and 4. The first bidder drops out as the bidding reaches 1, the second as it reaches 2, and the third as it reaches 3. When the third bidder drops out, the auction is over, and the remaining active bidder wins the auction at a bid of 3. The winner of an ascending oral auction is the bidder who places the highest value on the item, and the winning bid is the maximum of the values placed on the item by the losing bidders. Adding or subtracting a bidder need not affect the outcome of the auction; bidders who value the item at less than 3 affect neither who wins the auction nor the winning bid.

A merger in an auction context generally is modeled as the formation of a coalition of bidders, each of which continues to take a separate draw from the joint value distribution. The coalition, however, makes only a single bid. A merger modeled in this manner affects the winning bid if, and only if, the merged bidders draw both the highest and second-highest values. In the simple numerical example, merging the bidders with the values of 3 and 4 reduces the winning bid to 2 while all other mergers have no effect. The reduction in the winning bid is a profit increase to the merged firm, and Mailith and Zemsky (1991) show that a bidding coalition in an ascending oral auction cannot be unprofitable.

If bidders compete in many separate auctions, the average effect of a merger is the frequency with which the merging bidders draw the two highest values multiplied by the difference between the second- and third-highest values when they do. Both quantities depend on the joint value distribution, which plays much the same role as the demand function in the differentiated products Bertrand model. While the closeness of merging products in the latter model is determined by cross-price elasticities of demand, closeness of bidders in an auction model is determined by the frequency with which one draws the second-highest value when the other draws the highest value.

Mergers with Power-Related Distributions   A useful simplification models bidder asymmetries as if bidders differ in the number of draws they take from a common distribution, with the maximum of a bidder's draws being the value that bidder places on an item. This results in "power-related" value distributions. Cumulative value distribution functions $F_1(v)$ and $F_2(v)$ are power related if $F_1(v) = [F_2(v)]^r \equiv F_2^r(v)$, for all v, and $r > 0$. Froeb and Tschantz (2002) and Waehrer and Perry (2003) make use of the convenient properties of power-related distributions to analyze the effects of mergers in auctions.

The private value of bidder i, v_i, can be modeled as having the distribution $F(v)$ raised to the power t_i. Since t_i is a parameter reflecting bidder i's strength, and not literally the number of draws bidder i takes, it can be any positive real number. If bidders' values are mutually independent, the distribution of the maximum values across all bidders is $F^t(v) \equiv F_{max}(v_{max})$, $t \equiv \sum t_i$. Waehrer and Perry (2003) show that the probability that bidder i draws the maximum value, and wins the auction, is $\pi_i = t_i/t$. It follows immediately that the IIA property holds: π_i/π_j does not depend on the presence or absence of other bidders.

For purpose of merger simulation, a convenient normalization sets $t = 1$ so that $t_i = \pi_i$. Equivalently, $F_{max}(v_{max})$ can be used as the base distribution in place of $F(v)$ so that $F_i(v_i)$ equals $F_{max}(v_{max})$ raised to the power π_i. A family of power-related distributions consists of the set of all distributions, $F_i(v)$, such that $F_i(v) = F^r(v)$, when r is a positive real number; any of the $F_i(v)$ in a family can deemed the base distribution, $F(v)$, for the family.

Letting $v_{-i} = \max(v_1, \ldots, v_{i-1}, v_{i+1}, \ldots, v_n)$ be the maximum value among the losing bidders when bidder i's wins, Froeb, Tschantz, and Crooke (2001) show that the distribution of B_i, the winning bid when bidder i wins, is

$$F(B_i) = F(v_{-i} \mid v_i > v_{-i}) = F_{max}(v_{max}) - \frac{F_{max}(v_{max}) - F_{-i}(v_{-i})}{\pi_i}.$$

Define $\mu(r)$ as the expectation of the maximum from the distribution $F^r(v)$ and $t_{-i} = t - t_i$. It follows that

$$\mathbf{E}[B_i] = \mathbf{E}[v_{-i} \mid v_i > v_{-i}] = \mu(t) - \frac{\mu(t) - \mu(t_{-i})}{\pi_i}.$$

Bidder i's expected profit is its winning probability times the expectation of the difference between its value and its winning bid:

$$\pi_i \mathbf{E}[v_{max} - B_i] = \mu(t) - \mu(t_{-i}) = \mu(t) - \mu(t(1 - \pi_i)) \equiv h(\pi_i).$$

Thus more successful bidders earn higher expected profits, much as equilibrium margins in Cournot and Bertrand models tend to be greater for firms with larger shares.

The foregoing results yield closed-form expressions for the effects of a merger. The winning probability of the firm formed by merging bidders i and j is simply $\pi_i + \pi_j$, so the merged firm's expected winning bid and its expected profit can be computed directly from these equations. The total expected profits of all bidders is the sum of the $h(\pi_i)$, which the merger increases by

$$h(\pi_i + \pi_j) - h(\pi_i) - h(\pi_j),$$

and all of this increase accrues to the merged firm. Oral auctions are efficient in that the bidder drawing the highest value always wins the auction, so the bidders' gain from the merger precisely equals the auctioneer's loss. As Froeb and Tschantz (2002) show, the magnitudes of the price and profit effects are determined by the curvature of the $h(\cdot)$ function, which in turn is determined by the properties of the underlying distribution $F(v)$.

The foregoing analysis presumes that there is no reserve price. Waehrer and Perry (2003) show that the use of an optimal reserve price can cause the expected winning bid to increase following a merger in a private values oral auction. In that event the merger is unprofitable for the merging firms, but it nevertheless makes the auctioneer worse off because it increases the probability that no sale is made.

Two Useful Families of Power-Related Distributions   For some particular families of value distributions, it is possible to solve explicitly for the corresponding $h(\cdot)$ function. Froeb, Tschantz, and Crooke (2001) assume a family of Gumbel (extreme value) distributions and construct a logit auction model by combining $F(v) = \exp[-\exp(-\lambda v)]$ with $t_i = \exp(\lambda \zeta_i)$, so that

$$F_i(v_i) = \exp[-\exp(-\lambda(v - \zeta_i))].$$

The winning probabilities take the familiar logit form:

$$\pi_i = \frac{\exp(\lambda \zeta_i)}{\sum \exp(\lambda \zeta_j)}.$$

The maximum of independent draws from the Gumbel distribution also has a Gumbel distribution, and it has the same variance as distribution from which the draws are taken, although this is not true for any other power-related distributions. Defining $\sigma^2 \equiv 6\,\mathrm{Var}(v)/\pi^2$, Froeb, Tschantz, and Crooke (2001) show that

$$h(\pi_i) \equiv -\sigma \log(1 - \pi_i).$$

This function is increasing in the standard deviation of the underlying value distribution because a higher variance causes a greater expected spread between the two highest private values. The effect of a merger of bidders i and j on expected profits is

$$-\sigma[\log(1 - \pi_i - \pi_j) - \log(1 - \pi_i) - \log(1 - \pi_j)].$$

A higher standard deviation for the value distribution causes a greater effect from the merger because it causes a greater expected spread between the second- and third-highest private values.

A uniform family of power-related distributions also yields a simple solution. With base distribution

$$F(v) = \frac{v - a}{b - a}, \qquad a \le v \le b,$$

Froeb, Tschantz, and Crooke (2001) show that the value distribution for a bidder taking t_i draws has mean $(a + bt_i)/(t_i + 1)$, and variance $(b - a)^2 t_i/(t_i + 1)^2(t_i + 2)$, and for that bidder,

$$h(\pi_i) \equiv \frac{\pi_i(b - a)t}{(t + 1)(t(1 - \pi_i) + 1)}.$$

It is simple to use this function to calculate the effect of a merger. That effect depends on the variance of the value distribution, as is seen in the term $(b - a)$, which is the range of the support for v.

Mergers in Procurement and Sealed-Bid Auctions The foregoing analysis changes little when adapted to procurement auctions, in which bidders typically are modeled as drawing the cost of serving a particular customer from a specified joint cost distribution. The results of the two previous sections with power-related distributions are easily adapted, and Waehrer and Perry (2003) analyze the effects of mergers with power-related cost distributions. Cumulative cost distribution functions $F_1(c)$ and $F_2(c)$ are power related if there exists a positive r such that $F_1(c) = 1 - [1 - F_2(c)]^r$ for all c. $F(B_i)$ and $\mathbf{E}[B_i]$ are exactly the same as before, except that the value distributions are replaced by cost distributions and the maximum value is replaced by the minimum cost. Bidder i's expected profit is

$$\pi_i \mathbf{E}[B_i - c_{min}] = \mu(t_{-i}) - \mu(t) = \mu(t(1 - \pi_i)) - \mu(t) \equiv h(\pi_i).$$

The $h(\cdot)$ functions with extreme value and uniform distributions are as before, although other things change when the minimum of multiple draws, rather than the maximum, is relevant. For example, if $F(c)$ is uniform, the cost distribution for a bidder taking t_i draws has the mean $(at_i + b)/(t_i + 1)$.

Alternatively, bidders in a procurement auction could compete to supply an auctioneer who draws from a joint distribution of the differing values placed on each bidder's product. If bidders can observe the values drawn (even if with error), the resulting model differs significantly from the Bertrand model applied to differentiated consumer products, since there is a separate competition to supply each customer/auctioneer.

A first-price, sealed-bid, procurement auction requires a different bidding strategy than an oral auction. The winner pays the amount actually bid. In order for the expected payoff from participating in the auction to be positive, bids must be less than, rather than equal to, the values drawn. Although bidders find it optimal to bid differently in oral versus sealed-bid auctions, the revenue equivalence theorem, originally proved by Vickery (1961) and later generalized by Riley and Samuelson (1981), states that the expected winning bid is the same for the two types of auctions. Proofs of the theorem, however, assume symmetric bidders, and Maskin and Riley (2000) show that the theorem does not hold with asymmetric bidders. Rather, either type of auction may result in the higher expected winning bid, depending on how bidders' value distributions relate to each other.

Because bidding functions depend on the specific value distributions assumed, there are few general results for asymmetric sealed-bid auctions. Marshall et al. (1994) and Dalkir, Logan, and Masson (2000) compute sealed-bid equilibria using power-related uniform distributions. Tschantz, Crooke, and Froeb (2000) do so for the logit auction model. Conditioning on the merging firms' pre-merger shares, they find that the price effects of mergers in a sealed-bid auction are almost perfectly predicted by taking 85 percent of the price effect predicted using the corresponding oral auction model.

Mergers in Auctions versus Mergers in Bertrand Industries   There is much in common between the effects of mergers in Bertrand industries and the effects of mergers in auctions, but there are differences. All customers face the same prices in Bertrand industries, while each faces its own set of prices in an oral auction. The contrast between the effects of mergers in Bertrand industries and their effects in auctions is greater the more bidders know about customer-specific competitive conditions, and that contrast may be nil for sealed-bid auctions.

The unilateral exercise of market power following a merger in an industry using oral auctions does not affect the identity of the winner bidder in any auction. In contrast, some customers switch their purchases in response to higher prices following a merger in a Bertrand industry. Consequently a merger in a Bertrand industry reduces total surplus, but at least in the short-run, that is not true in an industry employing oral auctions.

The effect of synergies also differs. In a Bertrand industry, reductions in marginal costs for the merging brands are passed through to some extent in the form of lower prices on all sales of those brands. In procurement auctions, reductions in marginal costs similarly cause the merged firm to lower its bids, but when the merged firm wins the auction, the winning bid is the cost of the second-lowest bidder, not the merged firm's cost. Merger synergies affect the winning bid if the synergies cause the merged firm to be the low-cost supplier when it otherwise would not have been. Merger synergies also affect the winning bid if the merged firm has the second-lowest cost and therefore sets the winning bid in the auction, which is lower because the merged firm's bid is lower.

In some auction models (e.g., Brannman and Froeb 2000) substantial price effects from mergers leaving at least two bidders require an implausibly high variance in the underlying value or cost distribution. But this does not suggest that auctions are inherently more competitive than Bertrand industries. Rather, the substantial degree of differentiation in many industries to which the Bertrand model is applied simply is not matched in many of the industries to which auction models are applied.

2.1.5 Mergers in Bargaining Models

John F. Nash Jr. (1950, 1953) developed the theory of bargaining, and Osborne and Rubinstein (1990) usefully present Nash's contributions and subsequent developments. From first principles, Nash's axiomatic bargaining theory identifies a reasonable solution to a bargaining game. In sharp contrast to auction models, this solution abstracts from the process of bargaining completely. Strategic bargaining theory, however, resembles auction theory in its attention to detail about how the game is played.

A simple strategic bargaining game involves splitting a pie. Suppose that players 1 and 2 make alternating offers, with player 1 going first. The game ends either when an offer is accepted, and the game ends if three offers are rejected, in which case neither player gets any pie. The equilibrium is identified by backward induction. In the third round, player 1 optimally offers player 2 nothing, which is all player 2 can get by rejecting the offer. In the second round, player 1 optimally rejects player 2's offer if it is for less than the whole pie, since player 1 can get the whole pie by waiting until the third round. In the first round, player 1 offers player 2 nothing, knowing that offer would be accepted in the last round, and player 2 accepts, knowing that nothing can be gained by prolonging the game.

The equilibrium to this strategic bargaining game is drastically different if the order of play or number of rounds is changed, yet the real world normally has no fixed number of rounds nor a designated first-mover. This contrasts with an auction in which the auctioneer dictates the rules and commits to deal only under those rules. Nash (1953) posited axioms for reasonable solutions to the bargaining game, which eliminate sensitivity to arbitrary conditions. Defining z as the outcome of the bargaining game, $V_i(z)$ as the value player i places on outcome z, and d_i as player i's "disagreement value" or payoff if no bargain is reached, Nash showed that any solution satisfying these axioms maximizes the value of

$$[V_1(z) - d_1][V_2(z) - d_2],$$

which is the product of the incremental surpluses the players derive from reaching a bargain. In the example of splitting a pie, the disagreement values are zero, and the problem is to maximize $z(1 - z)$. The solution therefore is that each player gets half.

Nash hypothesized that his axiomatic solution was also the equilibrium of some larger strategic game, and Rubinstein (1982) took a major step toward confirming Nash's hypothesis by identifying the subgame-perfect equilibrium in the infinite-round, alternating-offer game to split a pie. The value of the pie is assumed at the end of each period to be $\delta < 1$ times its value at the beginning, and Rubinstein proved that equilibrium fraction of the pie going to player making the first offer is

$$\frac{1 - \delta}{1 - \delta^2}.$$

For discount factors close to 1, this is close to Nash's axiomatic solution of $\frac{1}{2}$. The player making the first offer can bargain for slightly more than half of the pie because its value declines slightly between that first offer and any counter by other player. Binmore, Rubinstein, and Wolinsky (1986) show that the unique subgame-perfect equilibrium of the alternating-offer game converges to Nash's axiomatic solution as the time period between offers, and hence the decline in the pie's value, approaches zero.

Nash's axiomatic solution provides intuition as to how a merger can affect the outcome of bargaining, and one possibility is no effect at all. Suppose that players $A_1, \ldots, A_n$ bargain with their counterparts $B_1, \ldots, B_n$ over the splitting of n pies, and assume that two or more of the A players form a coalition. This coalition does not affect the outcomes of any of the bargaining games because it has no effect on the incremental surplus to either the A players or the B players from striking a bargain. Some mergers, however, do affect the incremental surplus of one of the parties.

Vistnes (2000) explains that the merger of two hospitals could allow them to achieve a better bargain if they serve as substitutes in the networks of managed care plans. The merger increases the plans' incremental surplus from striking a bargain because it means that neither merging hospital will be in the network if no bargain is struck. Raskovich (2003) shows that roughly the reverse also can occur if merging firms bargain with a supplier with substantial fixed, but not yet sunk, costs. He posits that the merged firm becomes "pivotal" to the supplier, in the sense that the supplier can cover its fixed costs only by striking a bargain with the merged firm. Ironically the merger allows the supplier to achieve a better bargain. The merged firm covers all of the supplier's fixed costs, since they otherwise would not be incurred and the merged firm would lose all surplus from making a bargain.

A merger that reduces the marginal cost of supplying a customer increases the incremental surplus to the merged firm from striking a bargain with that customer, causing marginal-cost reductions to be partially passed through. The rate of pass-through in Nash's axiomatic solution is determined by the curvature of value functions. In a constant-sum game, such as splitting a pie, Nash's axiomatic bargaining solution yields a pass-through rate of 50 percent, just as in a Bertrand industry with linear demand. Moreover savings of fixed, but not sunk, costs may be passed through in Nash's solution, although not in a Bertrand or Cournot industry. If a customer is large enough that there is a recurring fixed cost associated with its particular account, merger-related reductions in that fixed cost are shared with the customer. Reductions in account-specific fixed costs are passed through because the entire account is the relevant margin for decision-making purposes.

2.2 Merger Simulation

2.2.1 The Rationale for, and Mechanics of, Merger Simulation

The Rationale of Merger Simulation   Merger simulation has been used primarily with differentiated consumer products, and the rationale for its use in that context is illustrated by the *Kraft* (1995) case, in which the court rejected a challenge to Kraft's consummated acquisition of Nabisco. To assess the unilateral effects of the combination of Post Grape-Nuts, owned by Kraft, with Nabisco Shredded Wheat, the economic expert testifying for the merging firms estimated the relevant elasticities of demand. He opined that the cross-price elasticities of demand between the two brands were too low to produce significant anticompetitive effects (see Rubinfeld 2000), and the court agreed.

A subsequent analysis by Nevo (2000b), based on his own elasticity estimates, predicted price increases of 3.1 percent and 1.5 percent for Shredded Wheat and Grape-Nuts, absent any marginal-cost reductions. It is unclear how these predictions compare to what either the expert or the court gleaned from the raw cross-price elasticity estimates; both may well have believed that much smaller price increases were implied. The key point, however, is that the court did not have the benefit of any systematic analysis of the implications of the elasticity estimates. Although it may have been correct, the court's decision was uninformed. Merger simulation could have usefully substituted objective and verifiable calculation for subjective and unverifiable intuition.

Merger simulation is particularly useful with differentiated consumer products because that is the context in which the focus on market shares and concentration is most problematic in the traditional legal analysis of mergers. The competitive effect of merging two differentiated product depends largely on the cross-price elasticities of demand between those products, which are only very roughly suggested by market shares. Werden and Froeb (1996) illustrate the point by simulating mergers in randomly generated industries with logit demand. Logit demand makes shares the best predictors they can be, since it causes substitution away from any brand to be distributed among competing brands in proportion to their relative shares. Nevertheless, Werden and Froeb find a huge variance in the price effects of differentiated products mergers for a given set of market shares, depending on the values of the parameters of the logit demand function.

Werden and Rozanski (1994) explain why market delineation is likely to obscure more than illuminate when highly differentiated consumer products are involved. Consumers typically have differing and complex preferences, and available alternatives appear over a broad and fairly continuous range of prices and attributes. Under these conditions the merging firms often argue that no meaningful boundaries can be drawn within a price and quality continuum, as the court found to be the case in *Brown Shoe* (1963, p. 326). Yet shares of a very broadly delineated market can mask an intense competitive interaction between the merging brands. And if the merging brands are particularly close substitutes, the plaintiff generally argues for a very narrow market. Yet shares in such a market ignore the potentially significant competitive impact of brands outside the delineated market.

A major advantage of merger simulation with differentiated consumer products is that it eliminates the need for market delineation. It is necessary to designate which brands are included in a merger simulation, but the competitive significance of a brand is accounted for, even if it is excluded. In the context of merger simulation, the word "shares" refers to included-brand shares. Relative shares matter, but they are invariant to which brands are included.

Only included brands interact strategically, so only their prices can change as a result of the merger. The prices of excluded brands are held constant, and competition from them is incorporated through the own-price elasticities of demand of the included brands. As indicated by Werden and Froeb (1994), the predicted effects of mergers generally are insensitive to which nonmerging brands are included. The reason is that the prices of nonmerging brands generally change far less, often an order of magnitude less, than those of the merging brands.

Merger simulation also permits an explicit trade-off between the anticompetitive effects of internalizing competition between the merging products and the pro-competitive effects of cost reductions resulting from the merger. In a traditional analysis focusing on market shares, there is no explicit way to trade-off cost reductions, no matter what sort of tradeoff is deemed appropriate. With merger simulation, it is simple to predict the price effects of a merger after accounting for any marginal-cost reductions, and under certain demand assumptions, it is easy to compute the net effect of a merger on standard measures of economic welfare. Similarly it is straightforward to predict the net effect of both a merger and a curative divestiture, as done by Jayaratne and Shapiro (2000).

Like any formal modeling, merger simulation forces assumptions to be made explicit. That, in turn, adds focus to the analysis by identifying what really matters, why it matters, and how much it matters. Performing simulation helps guide a merger investigation by indicating both the kinds of evidence usefully gathered and how to interpret what has been gathered. At the same time the evidence gathered indicates what modeling assumptions are appropriate. While merger simulation applies abstract theoretical models, its proper use ensures that the specific facts of each case play a central role in merger analysis. Merger simulation clarifies the implications of established facts for the likely unilateral effects of proposed mergers by combining those facts with reasonable assumptions about what is not known and evaluating their significance in a precise, objective manner.

Notwithstanding all of the foregoing advantages of merger simulation, there are serious limitations. The predictions of merger simulation are *at best* reasonable, but rough, estimates of the likely effects of mergers. Price-increase predictions always are subject to modeling error, stemming from assumptions that are never exactly right and can be terribly wrong, as well as from sampling error in the statistical estimation of model parameters. These two sources of error imply, for example, that price increase predictions close to zero cannot be meaningfully distinguished from zero.

At the current state of the art, merger simulation also predicts only the immediate price and output effects of mergers. Issues relating to the longer-term evolution of the industry, such as entry, product repositioning, and other changes in marketing strategy are assumed away in merger simulation and hence must be separately considered. The limitations of merger simulation must be assessed within the factual context of any particular case.

Mechanics of Cournot Merger Simulation The Cournot model is rarely used to simulate mergers, but its simplicity makes it useful for introducing the basic ideas, mechanics, and capabilities of merger simulation. Assuming that a proposed merger occurs in Cournot industry, simulating its effects proceeds in three steps: (1) specification of functional forms for demand and cost, (2) calibration of the parameters of these functions to make them fit the pre-merger equilibrium, and (3) computation of the postmerger equilibrium.

Because a Cournot industry is characterized by the demand for the industry and the cost functions of the firms, the first step in simulating a Cournot merger is specifying functional forms for both. With today's desktop computing power, computation places no constraints on functional form, but calibration may. The less there is about demand and cost that can be observed or inferred, the greater is the amount of structure that must be imposed through the assumption of simple functional forms. One of the virtues of merger simulation is that strong assumptions permit calibration from information likely to be amassed in the typical merger investigation. One of the main limitations of merger simulation is that its predictions can be highly sensitive to these assumptions.

A merger investigation can be expected to yield basic descriptive information about an industry, including an average price, an aggregate annual output, and the output shares of the firms in the industry. These quantities may vary significantly over time, yet it is necessary to characterize the pre-merger equilibrium with a single price, aggregate output, and set of shares. That is typically done by averaging historical data over a period such as the most recent twelve months for which the data are available. Averaging over a longer time period may be best if shares are volatile, and averaging over a shorter time period may be best if the data exhibit trends or structural shifts causing the near future to be unlikely to resemble the past of just a year ago. In exceptional cases, there may be sufficient grounds for adjusting historical data to reflect anticipated near-term changes in price or shares but for the merger. For example, one incumbent may be about to bring new capacity on line, or a new firm may be about to enter.

Unlike the situation with differentiated consumer products, merger simulation in a Cournot industry requires the specification of industry boundaries. Traditional merger analysis supplies them through the delineation of a relevant market, and as explained by Werden (1998, pp. 384–98), that requires either estimating or intuiting the elasticity of demand for any candidate market: to declare that any group of products in any area constitutes a relevant market is to declare that demand for the products in that area is no more elastic than some critical value (which depends on the functional form of the demand curve). With the rough estimate of the industry's elasticity of demand supplied by market delineation, along with a but-for equilibrium, it is straightforward to calibrate a Cournot model, provided that simple functional forms for demand and cost are assumed. The demand elasticity and shares are critical to the simulation, but important predictions, including the percentage change in price and output caused by the merger, are independent of the but-for price and aggregate output.

For example, inverse demand may be of the form $p = a - bX$, where p and X are the industry price and quantity, and the parameters a and b are positive. Values for these parameters are implied by the but-for industry price (p_0), aggregate output (X_0), and elasticity of demand (ϵ_0): $a = p_0(\epsilon_0 + 1)/\epsilon_0$, $b = -p_0/\epsilon_0 X_0$. An isoelastic demand function can be calibrated similarly. Of course, either the demand elasticity or b itself can be estimated with suitable data, and if b were estimated, the calibration would use the point estimate of b. If the sample means of the data used to estimate b are used for p_0 and X_0, the calibration uses the standard point estimate of a, but p_0 and X_0 typically are not the sample means.

The marginal-cost functions are calibrated using the Cournot equilibrium conditions, which can be written $c_{i0} = p_0(\epsilon_0 + s_{i0})/\epsilon_0$, with c_{i0} denoting firm i's marginal cost in the but-for equilibrium, and s_{i0} its output share. If marginal costs are assumed to be invariant to output, this expression gives the marginal costs directly. If instead the marginal cost of firm i is assumed to take the form x_i/k_i, it is straightforward to calculate the k_i's from the equilibrium conditions.

As an illustration of Cournot merger simulation, suppose that the two largest firms propose to merge in an industry with output shares of 0.4, 0.3, 0.2, and 0.1, and a demand elasticity of -1.5. The predicted effect of the merger is the difference between the computed postmerger equilibrium and the but-for equilibrium used to calibrate the model. Assuming linear demand, no merger synergies, and marginal costs proportionate to capital stock, it is simple to calculate that the merger would cause industry price to increase by 5.5 percent.

Simulating the merger facilitates the examination of sensitivity to the elasticity of demand. If the demand elasticity is −3 and everything else is the same, the predicted price increase is just 1.8 percent. Simulating the merger also facilitates the examination of sensitivity to the functional form of demand. With isoelastic demand and a pre-merger elasticity of −1.5, the predicted price increase is 8.3 percent. Simulation also makes it fairly simple to compute the effects of the merger on consumer and total surplus.

As noted above, the most realistic marginal-cost assumption can be constant marginal cost up to a capacity constraint. Adding capacity constraints to the simulation could lead to much larger price-increase predictions because nonmerging competitors could be unable to expand output significantly following a merger. The analysis by the US Department of Justice in the *Georgia-Pacific* (2001) case was heavily influenced by tight constraints on the ability of the nonmerging competitors to expand output. Suppose in the foregoing hypothetical that each firm has constant marginal cost up to a capacity constraint at 110 percent of its but-for output. With a demand elasticity of −1.5, the merger causes price to rise 9.0 percent with linear demand and 18.7 percent with isoelastic demand. In contrast, without the capacity constraints, the merger causes price to increase by 5.0 percent with linear demand and 8.5 percent with isoelastic demand. While capacity constraints can add critical realism to a merger simulation, they require more complex calculations to compute the postmerger equilibrium.

Mechanics of Bertrand Merger Simulation   Merger simulation in a Bertrand industry proceeds in the same three steps as merger simulation in a Cournot industry, but the first two steps raise quite different issues. Because the unilateral effects of a merger in a Bertrand industry arise from the internalization of competition among the brands combined by the merger, the focus in a Bertrand merger simulation is almost entirely on the demand side of the industry. Modeling and estimating demand, or otherwise calibrating it, raise important, and often difficult, issues in a Bertrand industry that simply do not arise in a Cournot industry. The demand side in a Cournot industry is relatively simple, with only a single demand elasticity, while the demand side with differentiated products can be quite complex.

Furthermore the simplest cost assumption—constant marginal costs with no capacity constraints—generally is not problematic in a Bertrand industry, whereas it is in a Cournot industry. With differentiated consumer products, marginal costs typically are essentially constant throughout the relevant range of output. And while nonmerging competitors may have capacity constraints, they are unlikely to bind because the outputs of nonmerging competitors are unlikely to change much following a merger.

After the functional forms of the demand and cost functions are specified, their parameters are calibrated to make them fit the industry under review. The selection of a set of prices and shares to reflect the equilibrium but for the merger is done much as it is in a Cournot simulation, except that the particular demand model chosen may dictate a particular basis for assigning shares in a Bertrand industry. With a choice model, such as logit, shares are assigned on the basis of a physical unit that serves as a common denominator for alternatives in the choice set, for example, pounds of bread. Other demand models require that shares be assigned on the basis of expenditures. Unit and revenues shares commonly differ substantially for differentiated consumer products, so attention must be paid to the basis for their assignment.

Another issue in the calibration of a Bertrand simulation is deciding which brands to include. As noted above, the prices of excluded brands are held constant. Since the prices of all substitutes for the merging brands increase following a merger in a Bertrand industry, any exclusion of substitutes biases downward the price-increasing effects of the merger. But, since the prices of most nonmerging brands change little, their exclusion generally imparts only a slight bias. Excluding minor brands and brands thought to be more distant substitutes for the merging brands is a useful way to simplify the calibration of a Bertrand simulation.

Bertrand merger simulations typically are calibrated by estimating the parameters of an assumed demand specification. The point estimates of the relevant slope parameters (e.g., the elasticities within an isoelastic demand system) are used in the simulation. The estimated intercept, or shift, parameters are replaced by values calculated from the prices, shares, and elasticities used as the but-for equilibrium. Once the demand side of the model is calibrated, no additional information on the cost side is required, since marginal costs are assumed to be constant. The pre-merger equilibrium conditions are solved for the marginal costs, and the pre-merger marginal costs are assumed to be those in the postmerger equilibrium as well, apart from any cost reductions the merger produces.

Calibration of a Bertrand simulation does not require estimation. Accounting data on the variable costs associated with the production of branded consumer products commonly provide reasonable estimates of the relevant short-run marginal costs. In some cases, however, significant conceptual issues can make it difficult to estimate marginal costs, such as when there are significant opportunity costs because scarce factors of production have profitable alternative uses. Once the cost side of a Bertrand simulation is calibrated, the equilibrium conditions can be solved for the implied demand parameters, provided that suitable restrictions are placed on demand. Without restrictions, the n equilibrium conditions cannot be solved for n^2 demand elasticities. As discussed below, placing restrictions on demand is often desirable even when estimation is used to calibrate the model.

In a calibrated simulation model it is a simple matter to incorporate the impact of a merger on the equilibrium conditions and compute the postmerger equilibrium. The merger adds terms to the equilibrium conditions for merging brands relating to the cross-price elasticities of demand between pairs of products that are combined by the merger.

The predicted price effects of the merger are the differences between the prices in the simulated postmerger equilibrium, and those in the but-for equilibrium. If a merger is likely to produce marginal-cost reductions, it is simple to account for them.

Mechanics of Simulation in the Auction Model Merger simulation with an auction model is like that in a Cournot or Bertrand industry, but value or cost distributions for competing bidders are specified instead of functional forms for demand and cost. Athey and Haile (2002) develop techniques for nonparametric estimation of auction models from bid data. However, calibration with minimal data is also possible with certain families of power-related distributions. For those families the parameters of all the relevant distributions can be recovered from just the variance of a single value or cost distribution in the family. That variance can be inferred from data on a single bidder's profits (e.g., its cost minus its winning bid), or estimated from bid data. The only other data required for calibration are the winning bid probabilities of the merging firms. The probabilities used to calibrate the model are those expected to prevail without the merger, and they are based on historical data, just as in other merger simulations.

Consider a procurement auction in which bidders draw costs from a power-related family with base distribution $F(c)$. Because the distributions are power related, it suffices to calibrate any one of them. It is convenient to focus on the distribution of the minimum cost, $F_{min}(c_{min})$, which is $1 - [1 - F(c)]^t$. Merging bidder i's cost distribution is $1 - [1 - F_{min}(c_{min})]^r$ with $r = \pi_i = t_i/t$. Using the $h(\cdot)$ function corresponding to the specified $F(c)$, one can compute the variance from the winning probability and average profit of either merging bidder. If $F_{min}(c_{min})$ is uniform on the interval $[a, b]$, the relevant $h(\cdot)$ function is that given above with $t = 1$, specifically $\pi_i(b - a)/2(2 - \pi_i)$, which is easily solved for $b - a$, and the variance is $(b - a)^2/12$. The logit model is even simpler, since the variance itself appears in the relevant $h(\cdot)$ function. If a firm with a winning probability of 0.5 has an average profit of 5 over all auctions, the implied standard deviation of the underlying value distribution is easily calculated to be 9.25.

The *Oracle* case (2004, pp. 1169–70) is the only US merger case in which a merger simulation was introduced at trial. The government's economic expert, R. Preston McAfee, modeled competition among vendors of highly complex business software as an oral procurement auction. The court rejected the predictions of his simulation on the sole ground that basic inputs into it—the winning bid shares—were "unreliable."

2.2.2   The "Fit" between the Oligopoly Model and the Industry

General "Fit" Considerations As argued by Werden, Froeb, and Scheffman (2004), a merger simulation should not be given significant weight by an enforcement agency or court unless the oligopoly model at the heart of the simulation fits the industry. Among other things, this means that the model must reflect critical features of the competitive landscape, such as whether the product is homogeneous or highly differentiated. But it does not mean that the model must capture every institutional detail of an industry.

Models are useful analytical tools because they abstract from the minutiae of real-world complexity. Elaborate attempts to incorporate industry details cause models to lose their value in merger analysis; calibration likely becomes infeasible with available information, and there may no longer be any clear predictions. Fine details of competitor behavior also are unlikely to affect the big picture of how the proposed merger affects competition. Finally, competitor behavior (especially in fine detail) tends to be observed with error by an enforcement agency or a court, so allowance must be made for the possibility of facts that do not fit because they are not true.

The most important test for whether a model fits an industry is whether it explains the past well enough to provide useful predictions of the future. When a merger simulation is used to predict changes in the prices of merging brands, the underlying oligopoly model must explain reasonably well the average level of prices for these brands over a substantial period of time before the merger. However, it is wholly unnecessary for the model to explain week-to-week price movements or special promotions.

In general, the proponent of a merger simulation should be prepared to justify each modeling choice on some basis. For most choices, the justification should relate to the factual setting of the industry. For some, ample justification can come from an axiom of economics, for example, that firms maximize profits. For any remaining choices, some sort of sensitivity analysis should be conducted to indicate whether and how the particular choice matters. Evaluating justifications for modeling choices requires an appreciation of the artistic nature of economic modeling. Different observers of an industry might reasonably perceive the competitive process differently, and different modelers might reasonably come to different conclusions about how best to capture that process.

Fit of Cournot, Auction, and Bargaining Models   Although oligopolists probably never literally set outputs, the Cournot model can be a reasonably good predictor of the effects of mergers in some industries. A useful test is how well it explains the intensity of competition as reflected in industry margins. The Cournot model predicts that the price–cost margin of each competitor equals its output share divided by the absolute value of the elasticity of demand. It should not be difficult to determine whether the average level of margins in an industry is roughly as predicted by the Cournot model and whether larger firms have larger margins, also as predicted. Of course, high margins can be observed for a limited time if demand temporarily presses against industry capacity. Therefore strong support for the Cournot model requires that margins be roughly as predicted by the model for a substantial time. Another useful indication of the utility of the Cournot model may be how well it predicts reactions to entry and exit.

The Cournot model, apparently, has not been used in any court for the purpose of simulating a merger, but in nonmerger antitrust cases two courts have evaluated the fit of

Cournot models employed in analogous tasks. The leading example is *Concord Boat* (2000, pp. 1056–57), in which the court held that a symmetric Cournot model was "not grounded in the economic reality" of an industry in which competitors were highly asymmetric. And in *Heary Bros.* (2003, pp. 1066–68), the court held that a "Cournot model does not 'fit' the economic reality" of an industry in which highly asymmetric shares were not associated with significant differences in margins.

An auction or bargaining model may fit an industry better than the Cournot model if an intermediate good is traded through bidding or negotiations. This is especially true if the good is customized to a significant extent, or otherwise not subject to arbitrage, so that prices vary significantly across different transactions. An auction or bargaining model can accurately reflect observed price dispersion in an industry, whereas the Cournot model cannot. Just as the Cournot model can fit an industry reasonably well even if competitors' actions are not literally their quantities, an auction model can fit an industry reasonably well even if competitors' actions are not limited to the submission of bids. An auction model can fit better than a bargaining model, even if negotiations follow the submission of bids, when the winner is determined by the bidding process alone or the party accepting the bids dictates the rules of the game.

An examination of the relationship between winning bids and bidders' costs or private values is useful in assessing the fit of an auction or bargaining model, much as an examination of margins is useful with a Cournot model. It should be possible to determine whether bidders' profits are related to their winning probabilities in the manner predicted by the model. For certain families of power-related distributions, one test involves computing the implied variance separately from data on both merging bidders. If data on costs or values are available, it is also useful to estimate the variance of the cost or value distribution and to compare that to the variance inferred from margins. If such data are not available, one can still ask whether the implied variance makes sense. If bidders in a procurement setting appear to have very similar costs in different procurements, an auction model may not be able to explain high observed profits.

An issue in evaluating the fit of an auction model relates to the manner in which the merger itself is modeled. The theoretical discussion above modeled a merger as a coalition submitting a single bid after taking the same draws from the cost or value distribution that the merging firms would have taken. In some industries this is an entirely sensible way to model a merger, for example, because the cost of supplying a customer depends on the location from which it is supplied, and the merged firm has all of the merging firms' locations. In other industries, this can prove to be highly unrealistic. In that event it may be possible to model mergers differently than has been done in the literature, for example, as the destruction of one of the merging firms. But just as in a Cournot industry, that is not normally how a merger really works.

There is limited experience in modeling mergers with bargaining models, and less can be said about when a bargaining model, in general, and any specific bargaining model in particular, is appropriate. Even if a merger clearly alters bargaining power, an analysis predicated on Nash's axiomatic bargaining solution is not necessarily appropriate, since it might not reflect the specific strategic bargaining game being played in the industry.

Fit of the Bertrand Model   In evaluating the Bertrand model's fit, an examination of price–cost margins can be very useful. Bertrand merger simulations generally infer, rather than measure or estimate, brand-level marginal costs. When that is done, a test for the fit of the model is how well the inferred marginal costs match the available evidence on actual marginal costs. If the two match reasonably well, the Bertrand model, as calibrated, can be said to reflect the observed intensity of competition.

It is important that the model satisfactorily explain the pricing of the merging firm's brands. If it does not, the reason may be that one or more of the merging brands is not being priced pre-merger as the Bertrand model predicts. In this case the model cannot be relied upon to predict postmerger prices. Two other explanations that should be considered are that the functional form of demand has been seriously misspecified, and that demand has been poorly calibrated.

None of the many known problems with using accounting data to measure economic costs is necessarily significant in measuring short-run marginal costs for differentiated consumer products. Thus data that the merging firms can readily supply typically provide a reasonable indication of the marginal costs for their brands.

Cost data from nonmerging competitors is less likely to be available, but it may be apparent without any cost data that the inferred marginal costs for one or more nonmerging brands are implausible. Although negative marginal cost is wildly improbable, negative marginal costs sometimes are implied by the Bertrand equilibrium conditions combined with estimated demand elasticities. The inference of a negative marginal cost, despite a plausible value for a brand's own-price elasticity of demand, indicates that the brand is priced far more aggressively than the Bertrand model predicts. A comparison of the inferred marginal costs across brands can reveal implausibly large inter-brand differences. When the Bertrand model fails to explain only the pricing of relatively minor nonmerging brands, a simple and satisfactory solution is to drop those brands out of the simulation. When the prices of such brands cannot be satisfactorily modeled, they can be held constant.

Several published merger simulations have tested the fit of the Bertrand model in essentially the foregoing manner. Pinske and Slade (2004) conducted a formal statistical test on the average margin, based on detailed price and cost data, and found that the hypothesis of Bertrand competition could not be rejected. The Bertrand assumption made by Nevo (2000b) was supported by a similar test, albeit with comparatively poor cost data, performed by Nevo (2001).

Other aspects of the fit of the Bertrand model also should be considered. The Bertrand model can be used to predict responses to new product introductions and other such shocks. If there are such events in the available data, it is straightforward to examine the accuracy the model's predictions. In addition it is important to consider whether non-price competition is so important that the predictions of the Bertrand model are likely to be seriously misleading. Finally, in the vast majority of cases in which merging manufacturers of differentiated consumer products do not sell directly to consumers, it is essential to investigate the relationship between the merging manufacturers and retailers.

Published merger simulations, such as Nevo (2000b) and Saha and Simon (2000), typically have modeled consumer products industries as if the manufacturers sell directly to consumers. This is a harmless simplification if retailers apply a constant percentage markup to the prices paid to manufacturers, as Werden (2000) found was their practice in the *Interstate Bakeries* (1995) case. Froeb, Tschantz, and Werden (2007) and O'Brien and Shaffer (2005) analyze other scenarios, but only involving a monopoly retailer supplied by competing manufacturers. In these models the effect of a manufacturer merger depends on the contracting arrangements between the manufacturers and the retailer, and on the retailer's freedom to decide which brands to carry.

If nonlinear contracts are used, with marginal prices and fixed fees, the merger of the manufacturers might have no effect on retail prices, or it might have the same effect as if the manufacturers sold directly to consumers. Retail prices can be unaffected by the merger if the retailer is entirely free to choose which brands to carry and therefore can credibly threaten to deal exclusively with one manufacturer. The analysis in that case is essentially that of O'Brien and Shaffer (1997) and Bernheim and Winston (1998). If the retailer carries both merging brands in the pre-merger equilibrium, the merger increases the merging manufacturers' share of total profits but has no effect on marginal wholesale prices or retail prices, since the same retail prices maximize total profits before and after the merger. Things are different with restrictions on the retailer's freedom to refuse to carry particular brands, since such restrictions shift the bargaining power to the manufacturers. Then, the pre-merger equilibrium is such that marginal wholesale prices induce the retail prices that the manufacturers would set if they sold directly to consumers, and fixed fees transfer all profits to the manufacturers. The merger has the same effects on retail prices as if the manufacturers sold directly to consumers.

If only linear contracts can be used, a double-marginalization problem arises. Competition among manufacturers determines the degree to which they raise prices above their marginal costs, and the retailer acts as a monopolist facing the wholesale prices as its brand-specific marginal costs. The effect of a manufacturer merger is to raise the retailer's marginal costs, and the effect on retail prices is determined by the curvature properties of retail demand, just as the pass-through of marginal-cost reductions. Besanko, Dubé, and Gupta (2005) find average pass-through rates of about 60 percent, and some rates over 100 percent are found by Stenneck and Verboven (2006, p. 289). Besanko, Dubé, and Gupta also find wide variation in cross-brand pass through rates, which is not surprising in light of their sensitivity to the idiosyncratic properties of particular functional forms.

The various retailer-manufacturer scenarios imply different retail margins. So one or more of these scenarios might be rejected empirically. Sudhir (2001) and Villas-Boas (2007) perform empirical analyses along these lines.

2.2.3 Merger Simulation with Differentiated Consumer Products

Illustrative Merger Simulations An extensive literature makes quantitative predictions of the unilateral competitive effects of mergers using real-world data. Some of the mergers analyzed are actual proposed mergers, and others are hypothetical mergers used to illustrate the methodology. Some analyses only approximate the postmerger equilibrium and therefore are technically not merger simulations, as that termed is defined here. Nearly all the literature considers differentiated consumer products, and much of it focuses primarily on demand estimation of a variety of models. An exception is the analysis of Brannman and Froeb (2000), which uses an auction model to simulate hypothetical mergers of spatially differentiated competitors.

The simplest and least data-intensive demand model is logit. For purposes of merger simulation, Werden and Froeb (1994, 2002) introduced the ALM (antitrust logit model), a convenient reparameterization of the conventional logit model. The version of the logit model we presented above has the "none of the above" alternative in the choice set, making the choice probabilities unconditional. The ALM replaces the unconditional choice probabilities with choice probabilities conditioned on one of the inside goods being chosen, that is, with inside-good "shares." Shares are convenient to use, whereas the probability of choosing "none of the above" is not otherwise considered in merger analysis and poses conceptual difficulties. The ALM treats that choice probability as a scaling factor determined by the aggregate elasticity of demand for the inside goods, ϵ. If s_i is the share of good i and p is the average price of all inside goods, the own-price elasticity of demand for brand i in the ALM is

$$\frac{[\beta p(1 - s_i) + \epsilon s_i] p_i}{p},$$

and the cross-price elasticity of the demand for brand i with respect to the price of brand j is

$$\frac{s_j(\beta p - \epsilon) p_j}{p}.$$

Werden (2000) provides a shortened version of his analysis for the US Department of Justice as an expert in the *Interstate Bakeries* (1995) case. In the first application of merger simulation by an enforcement agency to an actual proposed merger, he prepared to testify against the merger partly on the basis of simulations using the ALM. The merging firms were leading US bakers of premium brands of white pan bread, which competed with

Table 2.1
Predicted average wholesale price increases for white pan bread in the Chicago and Los Angeles areas

Brand group	Chicago	Los Angeles
Continental's premium white pan breads	10.3%	10.0%
Interstate's premium white pan breads	5.5%	8.3%
All premium brands of white pan bread	6.5%	8.3%
All brands of white pan bread	3.1%	5.9%

other premium brands as well as with lower priced private labels (store brands). In the Los Angeles area, the merging firms were the only significant sellers of premium brands, each accounting for about a third of pounds sold, with private labels accounting for almost all the rest. In the Chicago area, private labels accounted for almost exactly the same share total pounds sold, but the merging firms faced more competition from other premium brands.

Separately for the Los Angeles and Chicago areas, retail scanner data were used to estimate the aggregate elasticity of demand for premium white pan bread and the logit β. Since the data reflected retail prices, but the merging firms sold at wholesale, the calibrated prices were the average retail prices minus the 28 percent margin generally taken by retailers. Table 2.1 presents the wholesale price increases predicted by the simulation, using the point estimates for the two demand parameters. The first two rows give the average price increases for the premium brands of the merging firms (Continental Baking Co. and Interstate Bakeries Corp.), and the last two rows give average price increases for broader aggregates. The last row includes private label bread, for which prices were held constant in the simulation.

Had the case gone to trial, the merging firms undoubtedly would have argued that competition from private label white breads and competition from breads other than white pan bread would have prevented the merged firm from raising prices. Both contentions are addressed by merger simulation in a manner likely to be far more reliable than the sorts of impressionistic evidence a court otherwise would have relied upon.

Less restrictive demand models often are preferred to the ALM when abundant data are available, along with abundant time for analyzing it. However, at the outset of a merger investigation, when little is known about patterns of substitution and no data have been analyzed, the IIA property is the natural assumption. Using the ALM, which is based on the IIA property, a merger can be quickly and cheaply simulated for a wide range of values for the two demand parameters. Such simulations indicate what must be true for the merger to produce significant price increases if the Bertrand model applies, for example, whether the merging brands must be especially close substitutes. Werden and Froeb (2002, pp. 74–77) present such simulations for the proposed merger of two brewers in Sweden, and Werden, Froeb, and Scheffman (2004) present such simulations for the *World-Com* (2000) case.

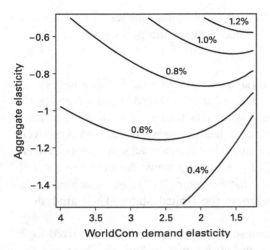

Figure 2.1
Industry average price increases predicted from the WorldCom-Sprint merger

The latter merger would have combined the second- and third-largest residential long-distance telecommunication carriers in the United States and was abandoned after a challenge by the US Department of Justice. In the course of the investigation various approaches to merger simulation, some based on demand estimation, were taken by proponents, opponents, and government agencies, and some are discussed by the ABA (2005, pp. 373–96) and Pelcovits (2004). Abstracting from many issues actually confronted in the case, it is interesting to consider the sort of analysis that could have been done during the first week of the investigation using publically available data. Academic estimates indicate that demand for residential long-distance service is slightly inelastic, so the interval $[-1.5, -0.5]$ should contain every plausible value for this aggregate elasticity. The logit β can be calibrated from any brand-level demand elasticity, and WorldCom's own-price elasticity of demand is used. In keeping with the range of estimates frequently found in empirical studies, values between -4 and -1.25 are considered. For these two elasticity ranges, figure 2.1 provides a contour plot of predicted price increases, averaged over the entire industry. The predicted price increases for the merging brands, of course, are substantially greater that the industry average, and the likely price increases for those brands could have been much greater if consumers perceived them as especially close substitutes, contrary to the IIA assumption.

Quantitative analyses of proposed mergers involving differentiated consumer products are commonly performed under the assumption of Bertrand competition, using a choice model related to the ALM. Froeb, Tardiff, and Werden (1996) simulate hypothetical mergers of Japanese long-distance carriers using a logit model that incorporates brand characteristics. Froeb, Tschantz, and Crooke (2003) simulate the merger of parking lots using a logit model that incorporates travel distance between the parking lots and consumers' final destinations. Their simulation also accounts for the effects of capacity constraints on optimal prices.

Several published merger simulations use a version of the logit model with a nest structure that allows some products to be especially close substitutes. Werden and Froeb (1994) simulate hypothetical mergers of US long-distance carriers with such a model. Feldman (1994) simulates the merger of two managed care health plans. Ivaldi and Verboven (2005) simulate the *Volvo/Scania* (2000) merger involving heavy trucks in Europe. Hausman (2005) critiques their analysis. On behalf of the merging firms, Andrew Joskow and Robert Willig simulated the merger challenged in the *Echostar* (2002) case, which involved the only two direct satellite television broadcasters in the United States. Their analysis is outlined by the ABA (2005, pp. 152–60).

Nevo (2000b) uses the model of Berry, Levinsohn, and Pakes (1995), a mixed-logit model incorporating both brand characteristics and an interaction between them and the random component of utility. He analyzes actual and hypothetical mergers of ready-to-eat cereal producers in the United States, including the merger challenged in the *Kraft* (1995) case. Gaynor and Vogt (2003) take a similar approach in simulating an actual hospital merger, as does Dubé (2005) who exploits household level data in simulating actual and hypothetical mergers in the carbonated soft drink industry. Similar in spirit is the model of Pinkse and Slade (2004), which constrains the relevant demand elasticities to be functions of a closeness metric defined on brand characteristics. They use their model to simulate mergers of brewers in the United Kingdom.

Many quantitative analyses of proposed mergers in Bertrand industries use flexible functions forms, especially the AIDS (almost ideal demand system) model developed by Deaton and Muellbauer (1980). Hausman, Leonard, and Zona (1994) pioneered the modeling of differentiated consumer products using AIDS for the bottom level of a multi-stage budgeting system, as suggested by Gorman (1995). Hausman, Leonard, and Zona analyze hypothetical mergers of brewers in North America. Hausman and Leonard (1997a) use the AIDS model to simulate the merger of US producers of bathroom tissue in the *Kimberly-Clark* (1995) case. Abere et al. (2002) use both AIDS and another flexible functional form to analyze the Canadian effects of the merger of leading producers of carbonated beverages. Capps et al. (2003) use the same demand systems to analyze hypothetical mergers of US spaghetti sauce producers.

Merger simulation is also done using the PCAIDS (proportionately calibrated AIDS) model, which assumes AIDS demand but calibrates the pre-merger demand elasticities using the IIA property (making the pre-merger demand elasticities the same as those in the ALM). Epstein and Rubinfeld (2002) propose this model and use it to simulate the mergers in the *Kimberly-Clark* (1995) and *Heinz* (2001) cases. The latter merger involved the second- and third-largest producers of baby food in the United States. It was challenged by the Federal Trade Commission and enjoined on the basis of its likely coordinated effects. Epstein and Rubinfeld (2004) use a version of the PCAIDS model with nests to simulate the hypothetical beer mergers considered by Hausman, Leonard, and Zona (1994).

Baker and Bresnahan (1985) also predict the price effects of hypothetical beer mergers. Although their analysis is akin to merger simulation, it differs in critical ways. Most important is that they do not base their prediction on a one-shot oligopoly model with a Nash noncooperative equilibrium. Indeed the main point of their approach is to estimate best-response functions differing from those derived from the assumption of Nash equilibrium.

Higher Order Properties of Demand Specifications   In simulating a merger involving differentiated consumer products, the focus generally is the specification and calibration of demand. Academic work has strongly favored the demand forms best fitting the data and best explaining the observed equilibrium. While those are important considerations, more important in merger simulation are the various idiosyncratic properties of any demand form that is used to model consumer demand. The magnitudes of the price changes from a merger are determined not by just the own- and cross-price elasticities of demand at the pre-merger equilibrium but also by how those elasticities change as prices change, and the higher order, "curvature" properties of demand are preordained by all conventional functional-form assumptions.

The impact of functional-form assumptions is easily seen with single-product demand. Figure 2.2, taken from Crooke et al. (1999), shows segments of four demand curves that have been calibrated to have a common competitive equilibrium. These demand curves share the same price, quantity, and elasticity of demand (−2) at the right endpoints of the plotted segments, and at that common point, the demand curves intersect an arbitrary

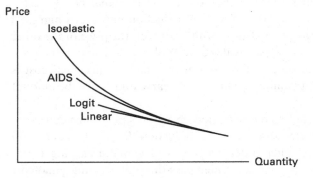

Figure 2.2
Four demand curves plotted between the competitive and monopoly prices

Table 2.2
Average price increase for the merged firm and pass-through rates for the WorldCom-Sprint merger

Demand form	Price increase	Pass-through rate from Sprint cost to		
		Sprint	WorldCom	AT&T
Linear	2.3%	0.502	0.001	0.007
AIDS	13.8%	1.807	0.032	0.046
Isoelastic	16.4%	3.838	−0.343	0

constant marginal cost curve. Given this marginal cost, the monopoly prices with each of the four demand curves are the left endpoints of the plotted segments. Functional form for demand may appear more important in figure 2.2 than it really is, because the axes have been translated to enlarge the relevant range of demand. The lowest monopoly price, the price with linear demand, is 25 percent greater than the competitive price, while the highest monopoly price, that with isoelastic demand, is twice the competitive price. The implication of the foregoing for merger simulation is immediate: merger simulations predict relatively low price increases with linear and logit demand functions, in which the own-price elasticities increase relatively rapidly as prices increases. And merger simulations predict relatively high price increases with AIDS and isoelastic demand functions, in which the own-price elasticities increase relatively slowly, or not at all, as prices increases. Crooke et al. (1999) illustrate this by simulating mergers in randomly generated industries, and that exercise demonstrates roughly what figure 2.2 suggests.

Also interesting is an illustration based on the *WorldCom* (2000) case. Froeb, Tschantz, and Werden (2005) simulated the merger under three different demand assumptions, using elasticity estimates supplied by Jerry Hausman in a submission opposing the merger before the Federal Communications Commission. The second column in table 2.2 indicates the huge differences in predicted increases, absent any marginal-cost reductions, with the three demand functions. The third through fifth columns indicate the marginal effect, at the postmerger equilibrium without cost reductions, of a small reduction in Sprint's marginal cost. The table displays the effect on the price of the Sprint brand, on the price of the other merging brand, and on the price of the principal rival brand. With linear demand, the price of the Sprint brand would be reduced by half the amount by which its marginal cost is reduced, and with isoelastic demand, it would be reduced by nearly four times the amount of the marginal-cost reduction.

It is not coincidental that the impact of a cost reduction on Sprint's price is roughly proportional to amount of the price increases absent the cost reduction. Froeb, Tschantz, and Werden (2005) demonstrate that the higher order properties of demand causing larger price increase absent a cost reduction also cause greater pass-through of a marginal-cost reduction. With isoelastic demand, Sprint's marginal-cost reduction notably causes an *in-*

crease in the price of its merger partner. The same result is observed with logit demand and is simply an idiosyncratic property of the two demand forms.

While isoelastic demand appears never to have been explicitly assumed in any published merger simulation, it is reasonably common to approximate the postmerger equilibrium in a manner that effectively assumes both isoelastic demand and that shares are unaffected by the merger. Hausman and Leonard (1997a) argue that such an approximation is quite close to the exactly computed postmerger equilibrium. But they assume that the true demand is AIDS, which yields predictions reasonably close to those with isoelastic demand, and they consider a merger with small predicted price effects, which minimizes the error of approximation.

Parameter Parsimony in Demand Specifications   The number of own- and cross-price elasticities in a differentiated products merger simulation is the square of the number of products, and even a fairly narrow product category may have hundreds of products at the level of UPCs (universal product codes). The number of elasticities can exceed the number of observations. Even if there are several times as many observations as elasticities, imposing structure on demand may be desirable to reduce the variances of the elasticity estimators. The art of demand estimation is achieving necessary and desirable parameter parsimony without sacrificing critical flexibility.

At one extreme in the balance between flexibility and parameter parsimony is the use of a flexible functional form such as an AIDS model (see Pollak and Wales 1992, pp. 60–67), which, in theory, does not constrain the elasticities. Of course, flexible functional forms are flexible only to the second-order, meaning they locally approximate arbitrary functions at a single point. Their flexibility does not extend to the higher order properties critical in determining the price effects from a merger. Moreover White (1980) has shown that the particular flexible form assumed affects the elasticity estimates obtained.

In practice, the use of flexible functional forms also requires imposing considerable structure on the data. Many separate UPCs are aggregated up to the brand level, by which it is essentially assumed all the aggregated products have the same elasticities. Multi-stage budgeting is assumed in order to further limit the number of brands at the bottom level, although that imposes potentially unrealistic substitution patterns on pairs of brands not together at the bottom level. This imposition of structure on the data, however, still is not sufficient to preclude point estimates inconsistent with strong prior beliefs. Brand-level demands may be estimated to be inelastic, and pairs of obviously substitute brands may be estimated to be complements. For example, the estimates of Abere et al. (2002) indicate a complementary relationship between Coca-Cola's brands of carbonated beverages and those of Cadbury Schweppes. A finding of that sort should give one pause.

At the other extreme in the balance between flexibility and parameter parsimony is the use of the ALM, in which two parameters determine all of the own-price and cross-price elasticities of demand for the included brands. The imposition of the IIA property is only natural in the absence of data, but when data, time, and resources allow the closeness of the merging brands to be investigated empirically, it is certainly desirable do so. Imposing the IIA property assumes away both the possibility that the merging brands are especially close substitutes and the possibility that they are especially distant substitutes.

Several less restrictive alternatives to the ALM incorporate brand characteristics in potentially useful ways. In the nested logit model, developed by McFadden (1977) and discussed by Anderson, de Palma, and Thisse (1992, pp. 46–48), brands can be placed together in a nest based on shared attributes, and whether these brands are especially close substitutes can be determined empirically. Similarly Bresnahan, Stern, and Trajtenberg (1997) specify "principles of differentiation" that distinguish brands, for example, on the basis of whether they have strong customer recognition, and they estimate the importance of these dimensions of differentiation. Their approach is somewhat more flexible than the nested logit model, but both rely on a priori segmentation of an industry. Such a priori segmentation is not employed by the most popular approach in the academic literature, which is to generalize random utility models by treating the coefficients of the indirect utility function as random variables. This results in a mixed-logit model, with the random component of utility reflecting brand characteristics observable to the consumer but not the econometrician and assumed to be distributed just as in the logit model.

The best known mixed-logit model, that of Berry, Levinsohn, and Pakes (1995), assumes that consumers differ in the weights they place on individual brand characteristics. The coefficients on characteristics are assumed to be normally distributed over the population of consumers, and a brand's aggregate demand is obtained by integrating over the population distribution. The estimates of the means and variances of the coefficient distributions are those best fitting the moments of the data. Although the implications of the normality assumption for merger simulations do not appear to have been investigated, Nevo (2001) replaces that assumption with the assumption that those distributions are determined by the distributions of relevant consumer demographics. He exploits cross-sectional demographic variation in census data to estimate those distributions. Like Berry, Levinsohn, and Pakes, Nevo assumes that the distributions of individual random coefficients are independent.

While the foregoing analysis is based on aggregated data, McFadden and Train (1999) and Berry, Levinsohn, and Pakes (2004) estimate mixed-logit models with individual data. This allows demographic characteristics at the level of individual consumers to explain their choices. With aggregate data, demand can be estimated on the basis of intertemporal movements in prices, which can result from various exogenous factors, including changes in the distribution of consumer characteristics. While Berry, Levinsohn, and Pakes (1995) exploit changes in the choice set over time to estimate the means of the random coefficients on brand characteristics, data on the characteristics and choices of individual consumers allows demand to be estimated from a single cross section. Berry, Levinsohn, and Pakes (2004) use survey data on second choices.

Mixed-logit models have potentially significant advantages over the ALM. Because of the more flexible way they model consumer heterogeneity, mixed-logit models permit merging products to be particularly close or distant substitutes, as indicated by the data. They also make it possible to have niche products with high prices despite low shares. Moreover, as Petrin (2002) illustrates, mixed-logit models may provide more reasonable estimates of the consumer welfare effects of adding or subtracting brands. The logit model assumes that a major component of utility is a random variable with a Gumbel (extreme value) distribution. One implication is that *some* consumers derive significant additional utility from switching to a new product that differs little from many preexisting products. If brand characteristics explain choices well, this occurs far less often in a mixed-logit model than in a logit model.

The distributional assumption for unobserved brand characteristics shared by logit and mixed-logit models may be a source of difficulty. Making many of the assumptions employed to estimate a mixed-logit model from aggregate data, Bajari and Benkard (2005) develop a two-step estimator for a hedonic model without an error term capturing unobserved product characteristics. The first step estimates the hedonic price equation, and the second backs out the parameters of the indirect utility function from the derivatives of the hedonic price equation and the conditions for utility maximization.

Empirical research in industrial organization has tended to employ complex demand forms. The mathematical properties that assure existence, uniqueness, and simple computation of equilibrium in the ALM may be lost when complex models are used. It is notable that Nevo (2000b), for example, does not actually compute postmerger equilibria in his analysis of ready-to-eat cereal mergers. Berry (1994) showed that equilibrium conditions can be used to identify a demand model without computing the equilibrium, but computing the equilibrium is central to merger simulation.

Estimation Issues with Scanner Data   The data most often used in merger cases to estimate consumer demand is generated by Information Resources, Inc. and ACNielsen through checkout scanners at the point of sale, primarily in grocery retailers. As detailed by Baron and Lock (1995) and Bucklin and Gupta (1999), the marketing departments of major corporations, which are the main customers for the data, rely heavily on such data, as do marketing researchers. Although some less aggregated data have been provided to researchers, a merger investigation typically has several years of weekly data on the number of units sold and average revenue aggregated over all sampled stores in a metropolitan area. These data typically are aggregated to the level of "products," which include many individual UPCs, and they do not reflect price reductions from the use of coupons. IRI and Nielsen also provide data on special promotions for products, such as the proportion of stores using in-store displays and whether local newspapers had free-standing inserts, although that information may not be employed in the estimation.

As documented by Hosken and Reiffen (2004), grocery prices in the United States vary over time largely due to temporary price reductions (TPRs). In nonpublic data used to compile the consumer price index, they find that prices within twenty categories of products are at their annual modal value about 60 percent of the time and at least 10 percent below their modal value about 15 percent of the time. They also find that for the vast majority of categories, 20 to 50 percent of the intertemporal variation in prices results from TPRs. Pesendorfer (2002) finds a similar pattern in daily scanner data for a single product category—ketchup. He argues, similarly to Sobel (1984), that the observed timing and duration of TPRs is explained by a model in which retailers price discriminate among consumers who sort themselves on the basis of their willingness to postpone purchasing until a TPR.

Because so much of the price variation in scanner data arises from TPRs, questions arise about whether these data are suitable for estimating the demand elasticities are relevant to competitors' postmerger decisions on permanent price changes. If TPRs work as intended, the quantity response should be greater than the quantity response to a permanent price change. This is true whether TPRs are used to price discriminate or to induce consumers to try new things in the hope that some will continue to purchase without the TPRs. Nevo and Wolfram (2002) find that coupons have the latter effect.

Even if TPRs are random events associated with mixed-strategy equilibria, as suggested by Varian (1980), they pose a challenge in estimation because they allow thrifty consumers to stockpile storable products during TPRs and draw down inventories during periods of regular prices. Indeed Van Heerde et al. (2004) estimate that about a third of the quantity increases from TPRs stem from the time shifting of purchases by consumers. As Hendel and Nevo (2006a) demonstrate, failing to account for consumer inventory behavior can lead to large errors in estimating the relevant demand elasticities.

An ad hoc solution is to aggregate the weekly data up four-week periods, but this entirely eliminates the problem only in the extraordinary case of consumer inventories varying over precisely the same four-week cycle. Even in that extraordinary case, aggregating to four-week periods can eliminate most of the price and quantity variation in the data and greatly increase the standard errors of the estimated coefficients. Erdem, Imai, and Keane (2003), Hendel and Nevo (2006b), Sun, Neslin, and Srinivasan (2003), and Romeo and Sullivan (2004) all make efforts to incorporate inventories into econometric models of consumer demand. Clearly, that is unnecessary for products likely to have minimal inventorying, particularly highly perishable food items.

As generally provided by IRI and Nielsen, scanner data are aggregated over products, stores, and time. As noted by Hosken et al. (2002) and ABA (2005, pp. 434–44), all three types of aggregation potentially create estimation problems because the prices series aggregated are far from perfectly correlated. Although TPRs are commonly sponsored by the manufacturers, Chevalier, Kashyap, and Rossi (2003) find that retailer margins decreased along with retail prices. Different retailers may take manufacturer-sponsored TPRs to different degrees, at different times, and accompany them with different sorts of in-store and advertising promotions. Pesendorfer (2002) finds a correlation of prices for Heinz ketchup across stores within a chain of only about 0.5 and a correlation across chains near zero. Consequently average revenue for a given product in a given week may reflect purchases made by different consumers facing significantly different relative prices.

For the foregoing reasons scanner data inherently present aggregation issues (see generally Stoker 1993). The fundamental problem is that scanner data employ a particular price index, average revenue, that is unlikely to be the correct price index. Consider, for example, the case of n identical stores indexed by i, each charging a single price p_i. If the stores have identical demands of the form $x_i = a - bp_i$, aggregate demand per store is $a - b \sum p_i / n$. The price index provided by the scanner data is $\sum p_i x_i / \sum x_i$, which does not equal $\sum p_i / n$ if the stores charge different prices. Regressing quantity on the scanner data price index therefore yields a biased estimate of b. The actual aggregation problem is obviously far more complex than this, and it not so clear what the impact aggregation really is.

That scanner data reflect retail prices, while mergers generally involve manufacturers selling at wholesale prices, presents the serious challenges discussed above concerning the impact of different contractual relationships. But if such challenges, and the problems presented by demand estimation, can be overcome, observing retail rather than wholesale prices is more of a blessing than a curse. The demand of final consumers is fundamentally what drives wholesale pricing, and retail data may be a far richer source of information. Wholesale price data for competing manufacturers can have so little independent variation that they are unhelpful in estimating demand. As noted above, manufacturers rely on retail data to inform pricing and other marketing decisions. Merger investigations should be able to rely on the same data for similar purposes.

2.3 Reduced-Form Estimation

2.3.1 Rationale of Reduced-Form Estimation
Merger simulation is an application of deductive reasoning. Based on axioms about competitor behavior, assumptions about functional forms, and data reflecting key parameters, merger simulation logically deduces what the effect of a merger must be. Alhough useful, merger simulation, like any economic modeling, has inherent limitations. Competing models may offer differing predictions, and tractable models may be so simplified that they cannot usefully predict real-world events.

The alternative to deductive reasoning is inductive reasoning, which generalizes from specific events. Rather than predict the effect of proposed mergers on the basis of axioms and assumptions, one could forecast those effects on the basis of historical evidence. In principle, a quantitative prediction of the likely effects of a proposed merger can be derived inductively, by carefully measuring the effects of prior mergers, but two factors greatly limit the practical value of that approach.

First, prior mergers are unlikely to be similar to those for which a challenge is seriously contemplated. Active antitrust enforcement causes the most anticompetitive mergers never to be proposed and prevents the consummation of the vast majority of mergers to which enforcement agencies object. Second, it is difficult for a variety of reasons to generate reliable estimates of the price and output effects from many prior mergers. One important reason is that suitable data are not publically available in most industries.

Published studies directly measuring the competitive effects of prior mergers in the United States have focused on the data-rich airline, banking, and hospital industries. Studies of airline mergers include those of Borenstein (1990), Kim and Singal (1993), and Werden, Joskow, and Johnson (1991). Prager and Hannan (1998) study bank mergers, and Vita and Sacher (2001) study a hospital merger. One of the few published studies of a US merger in any other industry is that of Barton and Sherman (1984). These studies find that mergers had anticompetitive effects, but there are far too few such studies to provide a solid foundation for predicting the effects of specific future mergers even in just the airline, banking, and hospital industries.

Because of the difficulty of performing controlled experiments, economics has long relied on what Haavelmo (1944, p. 14) called "the stream of experiments that Nature is steadily turning out from her own enormous laboratory, and which we merely watch as passive observers." For empirical evidence on the likely effects of mergers, one could consider a broad class of "natural experiments," and exploit any significant variation in market structure either over time or among markets. Data generated by all sorts of natural experiments can be analyzed through what is often termed "reduced-form estimation," in which prices, or possibly price–cost margins, are regressed on explanatory variables, including market concentration.

Structural variation across markets is observed in many industries with multiple regional or local markets. The FTC exploited such variation to produce a quantitative estimate of the likely unilateral price effects of the *Staples* (1997) merger. Structural variation across markets is also observed when auctions are used in procurement, and the European Commission exploited such variation in the *GE/Instrumentarium* (2003) case. Structural variation over time is less commonly observed, but may be exploited when there has been entry or exit. Jerry Hausman exploited such variation in his analysis (discussed in the next section) on behalf of the merging firms in the *Staples* case.

Econometrics like that in *Staples* and *GE/Instrumentarium* can play a useful role in the analysis of the unilateral effects of mergers, but when the experiments performed by nature are not mergers, careful attention must be paid to sources of variation in price and market structure and to the implications of the estimated relationship for the effects of proposed mergers. The remainder of this section illustrates many reasons why the effects of mergers can be very different from any prediction that could be derived from reduced-form estimation.

Reduced-form estimation can be contrasted with what Goldberger (1972, p. 979) termed "structural estimation" in which "each equation represents a causal link, rather than a mere empirical association." Reiss and Wolak (forthcoming) outline the extensive literature on structural econometric modeling in industrial organization. They also argue that to qualify as a "reduced form," a regression specification must be reduced from a fully specified structural model, which is not characteristic of the regressions discussed here or those employed in much of the industrial organization literature.

2.3.2 Exploiting Variation across Local Markets

Inter-industry studies relating a measure of industry or firm profitability to concentration were a mainstay of empirical industrial organization for decades, and Schmalensee (1989), Scherer and Ross (1990, ch. 11), and Weiss (1974) review this huge literature. But measurement problems and conceptual difficulties eventually led economists to turn their attention elsewhere. One alternative has been *intra*-industry studies, which avoid many of the measurement problems and conceptual difficulties of inter-industry studies by examining a single industry and using price, rather than profitability, as the dependent variable. Weiss (1989) provides several such studies and reviews prior literature.

Intra-industry concentration-price studies sometime are performed in the course of a merger investigation. The goals of such studies can be quite modest. For example, a study aimed essentially at market delineation would estimate the impact of other products on the prices of the merging firms' products. Alternatively, the goal of such estimation can be to generate a quantitative prediction of the price effect of a proposed merger. Intra-industry studies often utilize panel data, which may permit the exploitation of both cross-sectional and time-series variations in price and market structure, but intra-industry studies, like inter-industry studies, mainly have been cross-sectional studies.

The *Staples* (1997) Case   In 1996 the two largest US chains of "office supply superstores" (OSSs)—Staples and Office Depot—announced their intention to merge. The FTC sought a preliminary injunction against the merger, which was granted by the district court. The basic facts and analysis of the case are presented by Dalkir and Warren-Boulton (2004). As the FTC argued, the court found that the merger would have substantially lessened competition in the sale of consumable office supplies (e.g., pens and paper) by OSSs in forty-two metropolitan areas. In some areas the merger would have reduced the number of OSSs to one, and in others the merger would have reduced that number to two.

Because OSSs accounted for less than 6 percent of total sales of consumable office supplies in the United States, the court's (*Staples* 1997, p. 1075) "initial gut reaction" was that competition from other retailers would prevent any price increases following the merger. But the evidence at trial persuaded the court that its gut reaction was wrong. The evidence cited by the court (*Staples* 1997, pp. 1075–78) indicated that prices were substantially higher in areas with a single OSS than in areas with two or three. Although substantial econometric evidence was introduced on this point, the court cited only less systematic evidence.

The *Staples* case was the first in which regressions of price on market structure variables were introduced at trial (although other sorts of econometric evidence had been introduced in prior merger cases). ABA Section of Antitrust Law (2005, pp. 351–72), Ashenfelter et al. (2006), Baker (1999), and Hausman and Leonard (1997b) detail the analyses of the opposing parties. The FTC's analysis was conducted by its staff economists and by Orley Ashenfelter, who testified on the analysis. The analysis for the merging firms was conducted by Jerry Hausman, who testified on their behalf, and by his associates. Both teams worked with weekly price indexes for over four hundred Staples stores, in over forty metropolitan areas, spanning roughly eighteen months.

The FTC's team initially regressed the log of the price index on market structure variables, with fixed time effects. The defendants' team ran a similar regression with fixed store effects instead of fixed time effects. The former approach essentially sought to exploit the cross-sectional variation in the data, observing the relationship between price and different arrays of competitors. The latter approach, which both sides took at trial, essentially sought to exploit the time-series variation in the data, observing the effect on price of opening or closing stores.

Both teams included variables reflecting the presence or absence of OSS competitors, as well as non-OSS competitors such as WalMart. A major reason for including the latter variables was to test whether those competitors affected the OSSs' prices. There were, however, significant differences in the two teams' market structure variables. Based on evidence that the OSSs set prices at the level of metropolitan areas, the FTC's market structure variables reflected that level and consisted of dummy variables for the presence of particular competitors as well as variables based on the number of each competitor's stores in the area. Because different individual OSS locations faced different arrays of competitors, the defendants' measures of market structure were dummy variables for the presence of particular competitors within various radii around each Staples store.

A consequence of this difference in approach is that the two teams identified different lists of Staples stores that faced competition from an Office Depot store. This appears to have been partly responsible for fact that the two approaches yielded significantly different predicted price effects for the merger. A second reason for their different predictions was that the FTC calculated an average effect over all time periods in the data, while Hausman calculated an effect only as of the last sampled time period. Hausman's approach appears preferable because the FTC's calculation gives weight to competitive conditions no longer existing at the time of the merger. Finally, the predictions differed substantially depending on whether the Staples stores in California were included in the same regression as the rest of the country. Why that was so, remains unclear.

Conceptual Issues with Variation across Local Markets Nature does not perform the experiment of varying the size distribution of competitors across otherwise identical local markets. As indicated by Schmalensee (1989, p. 953), the usual motivation for cross-sectional studies is that markets are observed in long-run equilibrium, with the number of competitors having been determined by exogenous market characteristics. For example, local markets exogenously vary in size (e.g., in population), and Bresnahan and Reiss (1988, 1991) empirically demonstrate that larger markets allow greater numbers of competitors to cover both the sunk costs of entry and the recurring fixed costs of remaining active. The determinants of equilibrium structure in real-world markets likely include other market characteristics as well as the interaction of market characteristics with firm characteristics (see Berry 1992).

A simple illustration is provided by Sutton's (1991, pp. 29–32) analysis of a symmetric Cournot model. Using the notation above, let inverse demand be $p = a/X$, and assume that competitors have constant marginal costs c. In equilibrium with n competitors,

$$p = \frac{nc}{n-1}.$$

If H is the Herfindahl-Hirschman index of output concentration, this condition can be rewritten

$$\frac{p-c}{p} = \frac{1}{n} = H.$$

With isoelastic demand, as in this model from Sutton, the size of the market does not directly affect the equilibrium price, and equilibrium price–cost margins are determined entirely by concentration. If a firm incurs a fixed cost of F to produce a positive output, its profits are

$$\frac{a}{n^2} - F,$$

so the number of active firms in long-run equilibrium is the integer part of $\sqrt{a/F}$.

If local markets differ only with respect to the size parameter a, the long-run equilibrium price is a decreasing step function of market size. Because a merger in this model merely destroys an incumbent firm, the effect of a merger can be predicted directly from the observed relationship across markets between prices or margins and concentration. Of course, only the short-run effect of a merger can be predicted this way. The same number of firms can be supported by any given market size after a merger as before it, so a firm merged out of existence is replaced and pre-merger prices restored.

The foregoing model minimizes the conceptual difficulties of interpreting the observed relationship between price and concentration. Sutton uses this model as a point of departure for his (Sutton 1991, ch. 3) analysis of endogenous sunk costs, illustrated by adding advertising to the simple Cournot model. The optimal advertising outlay becomes a sunk cost that depends on the number of incumbent competitors. This considerably complicates the relationship between market size and the long-run equilibrium number of competitors, which need not be monotonic. But it is not necessary to add complications like endogenous sunk costs to demonstrate serious difficulties in interpreting the observed price-concentration relationship.

Consider an n-firm Cournot industry with inverse demand $p = a - X$, and let firm i have output x_i and marginal cost x_i/k_i. If all firms have $k_i = 1$, it is easy to show that in equilibrium,

$$p = \frac{2a}{n+2}.$$

With linear demand, both the equilibrium price and the elasticity of demand depend on the size of the market. If a firm incurs a cost of F to produce a positive output, its profits are

$$\frac{3a^2}{2(n+2)^2} - F,$$

and the long-run equilibrium number of active firms is the integer part of $a\sqrt{3/2F} - 2$. This result differs critically from that with the prior model. Setting $F = 3/2$ for illustrative purposes, there is a range of demand levels,

$$n + 2 \leq a < n + 3,$$

supporting n competitors. If $a = n + 2$, demand is just great enough to allow n firms to break even, and the long-run equilibrium price is 2 for any n. Within the range of demand levels supporting a given number of competitors, equilibrium price is increasing in a, and the range of possible prices shrinks as a and n increase. With $n = 1$, $2 \leq p < 2.67$, and with $n = 3$, $2 \leq p < 2.4$.

If the foregoing is the true model, the observed relationship between prices or margins and concentration cannot provide a useful predictor of the effect of a particular merger. A positive correlation between p and H may be observed, but that is only because technology is lumpy (see Newmark 2004; Lamson 1987). The observed relationship tells us nothing about the price effects of a merger. In a local market with three competitors, the merger of any two causes the price to rise over 15 percent in the short run. Although the size of the market is sufficient to support three firms with $k_i = 1$, it may not be able to support both the merged firm with $k_i = 2$ and two rivals with $k_i = 1$. Thus the long-run effect of the merger may be the same as the short-run effect. If the size of the market is sufficient to support three firms after the merger, the long-run effect of the merger is to reduce price by over 6 percent. The observed relationship between p and H provides no basis for predicting the 15 percent price increase without entry, the 6 percent price decrease with entry, or the likelihood of entry.

The experiments performed by nature may be much more complex than the foregoing models, and one important complication may be economies of scale. Economies of scale arise if firms can lower their marginal costs by investing in greater capacity, or if firms can acquire larger blocks of capacity at lower costs per unit. In either case the long-run equilibrium is more complex because larger markets are populated by larger competitors with lower costs. Across local markets the price may be observed to fall rapidly as the number of competitors increases, but much of that effect is accounted for by lower costs rather than greater competition. This possibility is mentioned by Bresnahan (1989, pp. 1045–46) and is closely related to the critique of inter-industry profit-concentration studies made by Demsetz (1973).

Even if economies of scale are not important, nature is likely to vary not just the number of competitors across local markets but also the market shares for any given number of competitors. In fact H can be decomposed into $1/n$ plus the variance of market shares in the data, and much of the observed variation in measured concentration across local markets may not stem from variation in the number of competitors. Consider a two-firm Cournot model with inverse demand $p = a - X$. (Isoelastic demand produces the same sort of results.) Assume that competitors have constant marginal costs c_1 and c_2 with $c_1 < c_2$. It is easy to see that the equilibrium price is $(a + c_1 + c_2)/3$, which is increasing in a, and the equilibrium output shares are

$$s_1 = \frac{a - 2c_1 + c_2}{2a - c_1 - c_2},$$

$$s_2 = \frac{a + c_1 - 2c_2}{2a - c_1 - c_2}.$$

Since $c_1 < c_2$ implies $s_1 > s_2$, it is not difficult to verify that increasing a leads to a *decrease* in s_1 and an *increase* in s_2, which reduces H. Thus across local markets differing only in the value of a, one can observe a *negative* correlation between p and H, but a merger does not lower price. Absent entry, the merger of the only two competitors in any of the local markets causes a substantial price increase. If local markets instead differ only with respect to c_1, much the same can be said. Equilibrium price is increasing in c_1, and it is not difficult to see that increasing c_1 causes H to fall in equilibrium.

The use of reduced-form estimation could be motivated by the belief that models like the foregoing are highly unrealistic or by the belief that static oligopoly theory is utterly useless. But even if the real world is nothing like these models, the basic insights from these models are important. For many reasons the observed relationship between price and concentration across local markets may not provide a straightforward and reliable predictor of the likely price effect of a merger within a given local market.

Econometric Issues with Variation across Local Markets   The foregoing is not framed in econometric terms because conceptual issues in exploiting variation across local markets can arise without errors in any of the underlying relationships. Nevertheless, regression models generally are assumed to have error terms, and econometric issues arise when the measure of concentration in a regression is correlated with the error term. In regressions exploiting variation across local markets, such a correlation may result from intertemporal feedback effects between price and concentration or from contemporaneous co-determination of price and concentration. As discussed by Schmalensee (1989, pp. 954–56), the co-determination of profits and concentration was identified as a significant issue in earlier inter-industry studies. In contrast to the reduced-form approach discussed here, some of those studies estimated systems of simultaneous equations (see Martin 2002, pp. 173–77).

As explained by Froeb and Werden (1991), the number of competitors and their cost functions are elements of market structure, but outcomes of the competitive process, such as the outputs of individual competitors, are not. Commonly used measures of concentration are functions of competitors' outputs, and therefore are endogenous. Outputs and prices are co-determined by demand curves and equilibrium conditions. Consequently stochastic factors, such as the random error in the industry demand curve, affect both price and commonly used measures of concentration. This in turn induces a correlation between measured concentration and the error term in a price-concentration regression equation. Evans, Froeb, and Werden (1983) note this problem and illustrate its impact on the price-concentration relationship in the airline industry. The problem, however, can be avoided by using measures of concentration based entirely on elements of market structure, such as the number of competitors and their capacities.

Feedback between price and concentration is a more vexing problem, especially if local markets are observed in states of partial adjustment to shocks of various sorts rather than in long-run equilibrium. Competitors come and go as markets expand and contract, as technology changes, and as new ideas succeed and fail, with prevailing levels of prices and profits serving as critical factors in entry and exit decisions. The survey by Siegfried and Evans (1994, pp. 124–29) finds substantial empirical evidence indicating that both market growth and high profits are associated with relatively high rates of entry. Thus the principal targets for entry may be rapidly growing markets in which prices are high because capacity has not kept up with demand. Prices may fall as entry occurs, although the bulk of the price decrease may be due to additions to capacity by incumbents, rather than the entry of new competitors.

Even if local markets are observed in long-run equilibrium, concentration measures still may be correlated with the error term of the regression equation because a host of unobserved cost and demand determinants effectively go into the error term. Through a variety of direct and indirect causal mechanisms, these cost and demand determinants also affect market structure. For example, small towns may be expensive to serve in a retailing industry because of significant economies of density in supplying stores. Small towns also can be expected to have few competitors, so the unobserved cost factors can be highly correlated with market structure. The inclusion of cost- and demand-shift variables, such as population, mitigates such problems, and the inclusion of fixed market effects solves them entirely if the omitted cost and demand determinants are invariant over time.

Concentration-price regressions are also apt to suffer from errors-in-variables. A common source of error is observing price and market structure over arbitrary geographic areas. Antitrust law may overemphasize market delineation, but variation across local markets can inform merger policy only if observations of prices and market structure are made within geographic areas that constitute relevant markets. Academic studies often have paid insufficient attention to market definition. Considerable attention was paid to market definition in the *Staples* case, but neither of the approaches taken was entirely satisfactory. Newmark (2001, 2004) argues that there may be significant, unobserved differences in product quality across markets that account for price differences.

Despite these issues, exploiting variation across local markets in panel data can offer advantages over exploiting time-series variation. If, as is common, market structure varies significantly across local markets but not over time, little can be gleaned from the time-series variation. In addition, much of the intertemporal variation in price may be due to unobserved or poorly measured cost and demand shocks, which likely are correlated with measured concentration. Hence bias from correlation between measures of market structure and the error term can be even greater when time-series variation is exploited than when variation across local markets is exploited.

2.3.3 Exploiting Variation within Markets over Time

Conceptual Issues with Variation over Time   Exploiting variation within markets over time also raises significant conceptual issues when that variation does not stem from mergers. Entry and exit are likely to have effects quite different from those of mergers for the simple reason that the two truly are different things. In the *Staples* case it is unlikely that Staples would have closed all the Office Depot stores after the merger, and the FTC's analysis assumed that none of them would close. The merger would not have been the mirror image of Office Depot's entry, so the price effect of Office Depot's entry estimated by the defendants was not a reliable predictor of the price effect of the merger.

In a homogeneous product industry, the critical insight is that entry normally entails the addition of physical capacity, which itself has an effect on prices. Consider again the Cournot model with inverse demand $p = a - X$, and again, let firm i have marginal cost x_i/k_i. If there are initially two competitors, each with $k_i = 1$, and an identical third competitor enters, equilibrium price falls 20 percent. This price decrease is partly due to the increase in the intensity of competition, and it is partly due to the decrease in the industry's marginal cost at any given level of output. If the entrant's capacity is acquired by an incumbent, equilibrium price increases 15.4 percent. This increase is entirely due to a reduction in the intensity of competition, since the merged firm cannot produce any given level of output at a lower marginal cost than the two merging firms could. After both the entry and the merger, price is 7.7 percent below its original level because the entrant's capacity remains in the market and keeps industry marginal cost below its pre-merger level.

In a differentiated consumer products industry, the critical insight is that the factors that determine the price effects of a new brand's entry differ from those that determine the price effects of incumbent brands' merger. A merger internalizes the competition between the merging brands, and large cross-price elasticities of demand between merging brands lead to significant price increases. The entry of a new brand does not have a mirror image effect, and large cross elasticities with an entering brand do not necessarily imply significant price changes in response to entry (although they would have such an implication with logit demand).

The optimal price responses by incumbent brands to entry are determined by the effect of the entry on their own-price elasticities of demand. Entry of a major new brand may not cause significant price decreases for incumbent brands because it may have little effect on the incumbent brands' own-price elasticities. Entry of a new brand can even lead to price increases for an incumbent brand if the entrant attracts away its marginal customers while leaving the most loyal customers. Frank and Salkever (1997) find this patten occurring with the entry of generic pharmaceuticals.

Econometric Issues with Variation over Time   Exploiting variation within markets over time raises several econometric issues. One is that the price-concentration relationship may not be stable; for example, there may be drift in the elasticity of industry demand as markets expand or contract. A more significant issue is that cost shocks and demand shifts cause many industries to experience substantial intertemporal variation in prices. Cost shocks and demand shifts create noise that masks the impact of changes in market structure, and far more important, cost shocks and demand shifts can be confounding events. Significant changes in market structure are apt to be infrequent and to occur at about the same time as cost shocks or demand shifts. This can make it impossible to identify the separate effects of changes in market structure and changes cost or demand.

One way of separating these effects is a "differences-in-differences" estimator such as that used by Bamberger, Carlton, and Neumann (2004). The idea is to filter out the effects of cost shocks and demand shifts by using a control group of markets. In one set of markets, prices before a change in market structure are compared to prices after the change. For a second set of markets without the changes in market structure but with the same cost shocks and demand shifts as the first set of markets, prices are compared for the same two time periods. The estimated effect of the change in market structure is then the difference between the two differences.

The GAO's (2004, app. IV) study of the price-concentration relationship for gasoline wholesaling in the US takes a different approach. Observing market structure only annually and having several missing observations, the GAO estimates the price-concentration relationship using weekly data. The GAO study has the major advantage of observing variation in market structure primarily from mergers, and the major disadvantage of having to cope with substantial price variation from huge swings in crude oil prices and from seasonal and other shifts in demand. The GAO study also is handicapped by serious errors in variables. The market structure data used by the GAO reflect only competition among refineries within broad regions, with no accounting for interregional shipments of gasoline. Moreover price is observed for numerous local areas instead of a few broad regions. The geographic scope of either the local areas or the broad regions can correspond reasonably well with the scope of the relevant markets, whereas certainly both cannot.

2.3.4   Exploiting Variation across Auctions

GE/Instrumentarium **(2003)**   In the recent GE/Instrumentarium merger decision, the European Commission found the proposed merger would have a significant anticompetitive effect in peri-operative patient monitors (PPMs) used to monitor the vital signs of patients receiving anesthesia. Competing PPMs differ in technical and design characteristics over which customers have preferences. Customers purchase PPMs through an auction-like process in which tenders are made in response to customers' technical specifications. Both the Commission and outside consultants performed econometric analyses on data collected by the PPM suppliers competing in that process.

The data identified individual competitors as participating or not participating (although perhaps neither consistently nor entirely reliably), apparently based on whether they submitted a tender. Reasoning that a competitor participates only when its product matches up well with a customer's preferences, the Commission evaluated the closeness of the merging firms' products by examining frequencies (in various data sets) with which (1) both merging firms participated, (2) they were the only participants, and (3) either merging firm was identified as the second choice when the other was the first choice (*GE/ Instrumentarium* 2003, para. 131–47, 212–17). To quantify the price effect of the merger, the Commission econometrically examined the relationship between prices (in the form of discounts off of list price) and competitors' participation (para. 166–86, 216). The Commission's decision, however, does not state what merger-effects predictor the Commission derived from the observed relationship.

Conceptual Issues with Variation across Auctions   The Commission described the tender process as an "auction" (*GE/Instrumentarium* 2003, para. 132, 179), and at least for purposes of discussion, it is useful to view it as an auction. As the Commission noted, which competitors find it in their interests to participate in a particular auction, or which are invited to participate, depends on the particular circumstances of each auction. For this reason great care must be taken in the analysis of bidding data. Such data can be highly informative, for example, by indicating the frequency with which either merging firm's bid is second-best when the other merging firm wins the auction, but reduced-form estimation with bidding data provides no useful predictor of a merger's likely price effects.

The most critical insight is that the winning bid is determined not by the number of active participants in an auction but rather by the number of draws figuratively taken from the relevant value or cost distribution. Consider the case of a procurement auction in which it is costless for a potential bidder to take a draw (i.e., it is easy to know the costs of serving every particular customer) but it is costly to submit a bid. Under these circumstances every potential bidder takes a draw. However, some do not submit bids because their cost draws are so high that they know they cannot win by submitting a profitable bid. The winning bid is determined by all of the cost draws taken, no matter whether two or twenty bids actually are submitted.

A more likely scenario may be that potential bidders learn the distribution from which they would draw their costs through an examination of the bid solicitation, and they actually take their cost draws through costly bid preparation. Under such circumstances the correlation between winning bids and the number of active bidders can be even more misleading. Suppose in such an industry that auctions differ only with respect to the variance of the cost distribution from which bidders draw. The higher the variance associated with an auction, the greater is the expected gross profit from winning, so the greater is the number of bidders that elect to incur the cost of participating in the auction. Bidding data can therefore be expected to exhibit a positive correlation between profits and the number of bidders, although that in no way implies that mergers are likely to cause profits to fall.

There is also no direct way to generate a meaningful prediction of the likely effect of a merger from the coefficients on bidder presence in regressions like those in the *GE/Instrumentarium* (2003) case. Consider a world in which there are two types of customers differing with respect to their preferences for the products of potential bidders. With H customers, bidders draw from a value distribution with a high variance, and with L customers, the distribution has a low variance. Bidders drawing low private values either are not invited to participate in the auction or elect not to do so. Over many auctions each bidder actively bids against each other bidder more frequently with L customers than with H customers. A regression such as that used in *GE/Instrumentarium* might find what the Commission found, but there would be no direct implication for the likely price effect of the merger. Nevertheless, the observation that GE bid, for example, 10 percent less when Instrumentarium also bid, could have significant implications for the underlying value distributions.

Note

The views expressed herein are not purported to reflect those of the US Department of Justice.

References

Abere, A., O. Capps Jr., J. Church, and H. A. Love. 2002. Mergers and market power: Estimating the effect on market power of the proposed acquisition of the Coca-Cola Company of Cadbury Schwepps' carbonated soft drinks in Canada. In D. Slottje, ed., *Measuring Market Power.* Amsterdam: Elsevier.

ABA Section of Antitrust Law. 2005. *Econometrics.* Chicago: American Bar Association.

Anderson, S. P., A. de Palma, and J.-F. Thisse. 1992. *Discrete Choice Theory of Product Differentiation.* Cambridge: MIT Press.

Ashenfelter, O., D. Ashmore, J. B. Baker, S. Gleason, and D. S. Hosken. 2006. Empirical methods in merger analysis: Econometric analysis of pricing in *FTC v. Staples. International Journal of the Economics of Business* 13: 265–79.

Athey, S., and P. A. Haile. 2002. Identification of standard auction models. *Econometrica* 70: 2107–40.

Bajari, P., and C. L. Benkard. 2005. Demand estimation with heterogeneous consumers and unobserved product characteristics: A hedonic approach. *Journal of Political Economy* 113: 1239–76.

Baker, J. B. 1997. Contemporary empirical merger analysis. *George Mason Law Review* 5: 347–61.

Baker, J. B. 1997. Unilateral competitive effects theories in merger analysis. *Antitrust* 11(2): 21–26.

Baker, J. B. 1999. Econometric analysis in *FTC v. Staples. Journal of Public Policy and Marketing* 18: 11–21.

Baker, J. B., and T. F. Bresnahan. 1985. The gains from merger or collusion in product-differentiated industries. *Journal of Industrial Economics* 33: 427–300.

Baron, S., and A. Lock. 1995. The challenges of scanner data. *Journal of the Operations Research Society* 46: 50–61.

Bernheim, B. D., and M. D. Whinston. 1998. Exclusive dealing. *Journal of Political Economy* 106: 64–103.

Bamberger, G. E., D. W. Carlton, and L. R. Neumann. 2004. An empirical investigation of the competitive effects of domestic airline alliances. *Journal of Law and Economics* 47: 195–222.

Barton, D. M., and R. Sherman. 1984. The price and profit effects of a horizontal merger: A case study. *Journal of Industrial Economics* 23: 165–77.

Berry, S. T. 1992. Estimating of a model of entry in the airline industry. *Econometrica* 60: 889–917.

Berry, S. T. 1993. Some application and limitation of recent advances of empirical industrial organization: Merger analysis. *American Economic Review, Papers and Proceedings* 83: 247–52.

Berry, S. T. 1994. Estimating discrete choice models of product differentiation. *RAND Journal of Economics* 25: 242–62.

Berry, S. T., J. Levinsohn, and A. Pakes. 1995. Automobile prices in market equilibrium. *Econometrica* 63: 841–90.

Berry, S. T., J. Levinsohn, and A. Pakes. 2004. Differentiated products demand systems from a combination of micro and macro data: The new car market. *Journal of Political Economy* 112: 68–105.

Berry, S. T., and J. Waldfogel. 2001. Do mergers increase product variety? Evidence from radio broadcasting. *Quarterly Journal of Economics* 116: 1009–25.

Bertrand, J. L. F. 1883. Review of "Théorie mathématique de la richesse sociale" and "Recherches sur les principes mathématiques de la théorie des richesses." *Journal des Savants* 67: 499–508. Trans. by J. Friedman, in A. Daughety, ed., *Cournot Oligopoly,* Cambridge: Cambridge University Press, 1988.

Besanko, D., J.-P. Dubé, and S. Gupta. 2005. Own-brand and cross-brand retail pass-through. *Marketing Science* 24: 123–37.

Binmore, K., A. Rubinstein, and A. Wolinsky. 1986. The Nash bargaining solution in economic modelling. *RAND Journal of Economics* 17: 176–88.

Borenstein, S. 1990. Airline mergers, airport dominance, and market power. *American Economics Review, Papers and Proceedings* 80: 400–404.

Brannman, L., and L. M. Froeb. 2000. Mergers, cartels, set-asides, and bidding preferences in asymmetric oral auctions. *Review of Economics and Statistics* 82: 283–90.

Bresnahan, T. F. 1989. Empirical studies of industries with market power. In R. Schmalensee and R. Willig, eds., *Handbook of Industrial Organization*, vol. 2. Amsterdam: North-Holland.

Bresnahan, T. F., and P. C. Reiss. 1988. Do entry conditions vary across markets? *Brookings Papers on Economic Activity, Microeconomics* 833–71.

Bresnahan, T. F., and P. C. Reiss. 1991. Entry and competition in concentrated markets. *Journal of Political Economy* 99: 977–1009.

Bresnahan, T. F., and S. C. Salop. 1986. Quantifying the competitive effects of production joint ventures. *International Journal of Industrial Organization* 4: 155–75.

Bresnahan, T. F., S. Stern, and M. Trajtenberg. 1997. Market segmentation and the sources of rents from innovation: Personal computers in the late 1980s. *RAND Journal of Economics* 28: S17–44.

Bucklin, R. E., and S. Gupta. 1999. Commercial use of UPC scanner data: Industry and academic perspectives. *Marketing Science* 18: 247–73.

Bulow, J. I., and P. Pfleiderer. 1983. A note on the effect of cost changes on prices. *Journal of Political Economy* 91: 182–85.

Cabral, L. M. B. 2003. Horizontal mergers with free-entry: Why cost efficiencies may be a weak defense and asset sales a poor remedy. *International Journal of Industrial Organization* 21: 607–23.

Capps, O. Jr., J. Church, and H. A. Love. 2003. Specification issues and confidence intervals in unilateral price effects analysis. *Journal of Econometrics* 113: 3–31.

Chamberlin, E. H. 1933. *The Theory of Monopolistic Competition*. Cambridge: Harvard University Press.

Chamberlin, E. H. 1929. Duopoly: Value where sellers are few. *Quarterly Journal of Economics* 44: 63–100.

Chevalier, J. A., A. K. Kashyap, and P. E. Rossi. 2003. Why don't prices rise during periods of peak demand? Evidence from scanner data. *American Economic Review* 93: 15–37.

Cournot, A. A. 1838. *Researches into the Mathematical Principles of the Theory of Wealth* (trans. N. T. Bacon, New York: Augustus M. Kelley, 1971).

Crooke, P., L. Froeb, S. Tschantz, and G. J. Werden. 1999. The effects of assumed demand form on simulated post-merger equilibria. *Review of Industrial Organization* 15: 205–17.

Dalkir, S., and F. R. Warren-Boulton. 2004. Prices, market definition, and the effects of merger: Staples–Office Depot. In J. Kwoka Jr. and L. White, eds., *The Antitrust Revolution*, 4th ed. New York: Oxford University Press.

Dalkir, S., J. Logan, and R. T. Masson. 2000. Mergers in symmetric and asymmetric noncooperative auction markets: The effects on prices and efficiency. *International Journal of Industrial Organization* 18: 383–413.

Daughety, A. F. 1985. Reconsidering Cournot: The Cournot equilibrium is consistent. *RAND Journal of Economics* 16: 368–79.

Daughety, A. F. 1990. Beneficial concentration. *American Economic Review* 80: 1231–37.

Davidson, C., and R. Deneckere. 1986. Long-run competition in capacity, short-run competition in price, and the Cournot model. *RAND Journal of Economics* 17: 404–15.

Deaton, A., and J. Muellbauer. 1980. An almost ideal demand system. *American Economic Review* 70: 312–26.

Debreu, G. 1960. Review of *Individual Choice Behavior: A Theoretical Analysis* by R. Duncan Luce. *American Economic Review* 50: 186–88.

Demsetz, H. 1973. Industry structure, market rivalry, and public policy. *Journal of Law and Economics* 16: 1–9.

Deneckere, R., and C. Davidson. 1985. Incentives to form coalitions with Bertrand competition. *RAND Journal of Economics* 16: 473–86.

Dubé, J.-P. 2005. Product differentiation and mergers in the carbonated soft drink industry. *Journal of Economics and Management Strategy* 14: 879–904.

Edgeworth, F. Y. 1925. *Papers Relating to Political Economy*, vol. 1. London: Macmillan.

Epstein, R. J., and D. L. Rubinfeld. 2002. Merger simulation: A simplified approach with new applications. *Antitrust Law Journal* 69: 833–919.

Epstein, R. J., and D. L. Rubinfeld. 2004. Merger simulation with brand-level margin data: Extending PCAIDS with nests. *Advances in Economic Analysis and Policy* 4. Available at ⟨http://www.bepress.com/bejeap/advances/vol4/iss1/art2⟩.

Erdem, T., S. Imai, and M. Keane. 2003. A model of consumer brand and quantity choice dynamics under price uncertainty. *Quantitative Marketing and Economics* 1: 5–64.

Evans, W. N., L. M. Froeb, and G. J. Werden. 1983. Endogeneity in the concentration-price relationship: Causes and cures. *Journal of Industrial Economics* 61: 431–38.

European Commission. 2004. Guidelines on the assessment of horizontal mergers under the Council regulation on the control of concentrations between undertakings. *Official Journal* C 31/03.

Farrell, J., and C. Shapiro. 1990a. Horizontal mergers: An equilibrium analysis. *American Economic Review* 80: 107–26.

Farrell, J., and C. Shapiro. 1990b. Asset ownership and market structure in oligopoly. *RAND Journal of Economics* 21: 275–92.

Fauli-Oller, R. 1997. On merger profitability in a Cournot setting. *Economics Letters* 54: 75–79.

Feldman, R. 1994. The welfare economics of a health plan merger. *Journal of Regulatory Economics* 6: 67–86.

Fellner, W. J. 1949. *Competition among the Few.* New York: Knopf.

Fisher, I. 1898. Cournot and mathematical economics. *Quarterly Journal of Economics* 12: 119–38.

Flath, D. 1992. Horizontal shareholding interlocks. *Managerial and Decision Economics* 13: 75–77.

Forchheimer, K. 1908. Theoretishes zum unvollständigen Monopole. *Jahrbuch für Gesetzgebung, Verwaltung und Volkswirtschaft* 32: 1–12.

Frank, R. G., and D. S. Salkever. 1997. Generic entry and the pricing of pharmaceuticals. *Journal of Economics and Management Strategy* 6: 75–90.

Froeb, L. M., T. J. Tardiff, and G. J. Werden. 1996. The Demsetz postulate and the welfare effects of mergers in differentiated products. In F. S. McChesney, ed., *Economic Inputs, Legal Outputs: The Role of Economists in Modern Antitrust.* New York: Wiley.

Froeb, L., and S. Tschantz. 2002. Mergers among bidders with correlated values. In D. Slottje, ed., *Measuring Market Power.* Amsterdam: Elsevier.

Froeb, L., S. Tschantz, and P. Crooke. 2001. Second-price auctions with mixtures of power-related distributions. Unpublished paper. Available at ⟨http://www2.owen.vanderbilt.edu/lukefroeb/papers/prdist.pdf⟩.

Froeb, L., S. Tschantz, and P. Crooke. 2003. Bertrand competition with capacity constraints: Mergers among parking lots. *Journal of Econometrics* 113: 49–67.

Froeb, L. M., S. Tschantz, and G. J. Werden. 2005. Pass through rates and the price effects of mergers. *International Journal of Industrial Organization* 23: 703–15.

Froeb, L., S. Tschantz, and G. J. Werden. 2007. Vertical restraints and the effects of upstream horizontal mergers. In V. Ghosal and J. Stennek, eds., *The Political Economy of Antitrust.* Amsterdam: Elsevier.

Froeb, L. M., and G. J. Werden. 1991. Endogeneity in the concentration-price relationship: Causes and consequences. Economic Analysis Group discussion paper EAG 91-7. US Department of Justice, Antitrust Division.

Froeb, L. M., and G. J. Werden. 1998. A robust test for consumer welfare enhancing mergers among sellers of a homogeneous product. *Economics Letters* 58: 367–69.

Gandhi, A., L. M. Froeb, S. Tschantz, and G. J. Werden. Forthcoming. Post-merger product repositioning. *Journal of Industrial Economics.*

Gaynor, M., and W. B. Vogt. 2003. Competition among hospitals. *RAND Journal of Economics* 34: 764–85.

Goldberger, A. S. 1972. Structural equations methods in the social sciences. *Econometrica* 40: 979–1001.

Gorman, W. M. 1995. Two-stage budgeting. In C. Blackorby and A. F. Shorrocks, eds., *Separability and Aggregation: 1 Collected Works of W. M. Gorman.* Oxford: Clarendon Press.

Gowrisankaran, G. 1999. A dynamic model of endogenous horizontal mergers. *RAND Journal of Economics* 30: 56–83.

Haavelmo, T. 1944. The probability approach in econometrics. *Econometrica* 12 (supp.): iii–115.

Hausman, J. A. 2005. Using merger simulation models: Testing the underlying assumptions. *International Journal of Industrial Organization* 23: 693–98.

Hausman, J. A., and G. K. Leonard. 1997a. Economic analysis of differentiated products mergers using real world data. *George Mason Law Review* 5: 321–46.

Hausman, J. A., and G. K. Leonard. 1997b. Documents versus econometrics in *Staples*. Unpublished paper. Available at ⟨htttp://www.nera.com/Publication.asp?p_ID=2744⟩.

Hausman, J., G. Leonard, and J. D. Zona. 1994. Competitive analysis with differentiated products. *Annales d'Economie et Statistique* 34: 159–80.

Hendel, I., and A. Nevo. 2006a. Sales and consumer inventory. *RAND Journal of Econonics* 37: 543–61.

Hendel, I., and A. Nevo. 2006b. Measuring the implications of sales and consumer inventory behavior. *Econometrica* 74: 1637–73.

Hendel, I., and A. Nevo. 2004. Inter-temporal substitution and storable products. *Journal of the European Economic Association* 2: 536–47.

Hennessy, D. A. 2000. Cournot oligopoly conditions under which any horizontal merger is profitable. *Review of Industrial Organization* 17: 277–84.

Hosken, D., and D. Reiffen. 2004. Patterns of retail price variation. *RAND Journal of Economics* 35: 128–46.

Hosken, D., D. O'Brien, D. Scheffman, and M. Vita. 2002. Demand system estimation and its application to horizontal merger analysis. Working paper 246, Federal Trade Commission, Bureau of Economics. Available at ⟨http://www.ftc.gov/be/workpapers/wp246.pdf⟩.

Hotelling, H. 1929. Stability and competition. *Economic Journal* 39: 41–57.

Ivaldi, M., and F. Verboven. 2005. Quantifying the effects from horizontal mergers in European competition policy. *International Journal of Industrial Organization* 23: 669–91.

Ivaldi, M., B. Jullien, P. Rey, P. Seabright, and J. Tirole. 2003. The economics of unilateral effects. Unpublished paper. Available at ⟨http://europa.eu.int/comm/competition/mergers/review/the_economics_of_unilateral_effects _en.pdf⟩.

Jayaratne, J., and C. Shapiro. 2000. Simulating partial asset divestitures to "fix" mergers. *International Journal of the Economics of Business* 7: 179–200.

Kim, E. H., and V. Singal. 1993. Mergers and market power: Evidence from the airline industry. *American Economic Review* 83: 549–69.

Kimmel, S. 1992. Effects of cost changes on oligopolists' profits. *Journal of Industrial Economics* 40: 441–49.

Klemperer, P. 2004. *Auctions: Theory and Practice*. Princeton: Princeton University Press.

Kreps, D. M., and J. Scheinkman. 1983. Quantity precommitment and Bertrand competition yield Cournot outcomes. *Bell Journal of Economics* 14: 326–37.

Lambson, V. E. 1987. Is the concentration-profit correlation partly an artifact of lumpy technology? *American Economic Review* 77: 731–33.

Leonard, R. J. 1994. Reading Cournot, reading Nash: The creation and stabilization of the Nash equilibrium. *Economic Journal* 104: 492–511.

Lerner, A. P. 1934. The concept and measurement of monopoly power. *Review of Economic Studies* 1: 157–75.

Levin, D. 1990. Horizontal mergers: The 50-percent benchmark. *American Economic Review* 80: 1238–45.

Luce, R. D. 1959. *Individual Choice Behavior: Theoretical Analysis*. New York: Wiley.

Mailath, G. J., and P. Zemsky. 1991. Collusion in second price auctions with heterogeneous bidders. *Games and Economic Behavior* 3: 467–86.

Manski, C. F. 1977. The structure of random utility models. *Theory and Decision* 8: 229–54.

Marshall, R. C., M. J. Meurer, J.-F. Richard, and W. Stromquist. 1994. Numerical analysis of asymmetric first price auctions. *Games and Economic Behavior* 7: 193–220.

Martin, S. 2002. *Advanced Industrial Economics*, 2nd ed. Oxford: Blackwell.

Maskin, E. S., and J. C. Riley. 2000. Asymmetric auctions. *Review of Economic Studies* 67: 413–38.

McAfee, R. P., and M. A. Williams. 1992. Horizontal mergers and antitrust policy. *Journal of Industrial Economics* 40: 181–87.

McFadden, D. 1974. Conditional logit analysis of qualitative choice behavior. In P. Zarembka, ed., *Frontiers in Econometrics*. New York: Academic Press.

McFadden, D. 1978. Modelling the choice of residential location. In A. Karquist, L. Lundqvist, F. Snickars, and J. W. Weibull, eds. *Spatial Interaction Theory and Planning Models*. Amsterdam: North-Holland.

McFadden, D., and K. Train. 1999. Mixed MNL models for discrete response. *Journal of Applied Econometrics* 89: 109–29.

Merger Enforcement Workshop. 2004. Available at ⟨http://www.ftc.gov/bc/mergerenforce/index.html⟩.

Milgrom, P. R., and R. J. Weber. 1982. A theory of auctions and competitive bidding. *Econometrica* 50: 1089–122.

Myerson, R. B. 1999. Nash equilibrium and the history of economic theory. *Journal of Economic Literature* 37: 1067–82.

Nash, J. 1950. The bargaining problem. *Econometrica* 18: 155–62.

Nash, J. 1951. Non-cooperative games. *Annals of Mathematics* 54: 286–95. Reprinted in A. Daughety, ed., *Cournot Oligopoly*. Cambridge: Cambridge University Press, 1988.

Nash, J. 1953. Two-person cooperative games. *Econometrica* 21: 128–40.

Nevo, A. 2000a. A practitioner's guide to estimation of random-coefficients logit models of demand. *Journal of Economics and Management Strategy* 9: 513–48.

Nevo, A. 2000b. Mergers with differentiated products: The case of the ready-to-eat cereal industry. *RAND Journal of Economics* 31: 395–421.

Nevo, A. 2001. Measuring market power in the ready-to-eat cereal industry. *Econometrica* 69: 307–42.

Nevo, A., and C. Wolfram. 2002. Why do manufacturers issue coupons? An empirical analysis of breakfast cereals. *RAND Journal of Economics* 33: 319–39.

Newmark, C. M. 2001. The positive correlation of price and concentration in Staples: Market power or indivisibility?" Unpublished paper. Available at ⟨http://www.independent.org/tii/WorkingPapers/Newmark.pdf⟩.

Newmark, C. M. 2004. Price-concentration studies: There you go again. Unpublished paper. Available at ⟨http://papers.ssrn.com/sol3/papers.cfm?abstract_id=503522⟩.

Nye, W. 1992. Can a joint venture lessen competition more than a merger? *Economics Letters* 40: 487–89.

O'Brien, D. P., and S. C. Salop. 2000. Competitive effects of partial ownership: Financial and corporate control. *Antitrust Law Journal* 67: 559–614.

O'Brien, D. P., and G. Shaffer. 1997. Nonlinear supply contracts, exclusive dealing, and equilibrium market foreclosure. *Journal of Economics and Management Strategy* 6: 755–85.

O'Brien, D. P., and G. Shaffer. 2005. Bargaining, bundling, and clout: The portfolio effects of horizontal mergers. *RAND Journal of Economics* 36: 573–95.

Osborne, M. J., and C. Pitchik. 1986. Price competition in a capacity-constrained duopoly. *Journal of Economic Theory* 38: 238–60.

Osborne, M. J., and A. Rubinstein. 1990. *Bargaining and Markets*. San Diego: Academic Press.

Pelcovits, M. D. 2004. The long-distance industry: One merger too many? MCI WorldCom and Sprint. In J. Kwoka Jr. and L. White, eds., *The Antitrust Revolution*, 4th ed. New York: Oxford University Press.

Perry, M. K., and R. H. Porter. 1985. Oligopoly and the incentive for horizontal merger. *American Economic Review* 75: 219–27.

Pesendorfer, M. 2002. Retail sales: A study of pricing behavior in supermarkets. *Journal of Business* 75: 33–66.

Petrin, A. 2002. Quantifying the benefits of new products: The case of the minivan. *Journal of Political Economy* 110: 705–29.

Pinkse, J., and M. E. Slade. 2004. Mergers, brand competition, and the price of a pint. *European Economic Review* 48: 617–43.

Pollak, R. A., and T. J. Wales. 1992. *Demand System Specification and Estimation*. Oxford: Oxford University Press.

Prager, R. A., and T. H. Hannan. 1998. Do substantial horizontal mergers generate significant price effects? Evidence from the banking industry. *Journal of Industrial Economics* 46: 433–52.

Raskovich, A. 2003. Pivotal buyers and bargaining position. *Journal of Industrial Economics* 51: 405–26.

Reiss, P. C., and F. A. Wolak. Forthcoming. Structural econometric modeling: Rationales and examples from industrial organization. In J. Heckman and E. Leamer, eds., *Handbook of Econometrics*, vol. 6. Amsterdam: North-Holland.

Reynolds, R. J., and B. R. Snapp. 1986. The competitive effects of partial equity interests and joint ventures. *International Journal of Industrial Organization* 4: 141–53.

Riley, J. G., and W. F. Samuelson. 1981. Optimal auctions. *American Economic Review* 71: 381–92.

Romeo, C. J., and M. W. Sullivan. 2004. Controlling for temporary promotions in a differentiated products model of consumer demand. Economic Analysis Group discussion paper EAG 04-10, US Department of Justice, Antitrust Division.

Rubinfeld, D. L. 2000. Market definition with differentiated products: The Post/Nabisco cereal merger. *Antitrust Law Journal* 50: 163–85.

Rubinstein, A. 1982. Perfect equilibrium in a bargaining model. *Econometrica* 50: 97–109.

Saha, A., and P. Simon. 2000. Predicting the price effects of mergers with polynomial logit demand. *International Journal of the Economics of Business* 7: 149–57.

Salant, S. W., S. Switzer, and R. J. Reynolds. 1983. Losses from horizontal merger: The effects of an exogenous change in industry structure on Cournot-Nash equilibrium. *Quarterly Journal of Economics* 98: 185–99.

Scherer, F. M., D. Ross. 1990. *Industrial Market Structure and Economic Performance*. Boston: Houghton Mifflin.

Schmalensee, R. 1989. Inter-industry studies of structure and performance. In R. Schmalensee and R. Willig, eds., *Handbook of Industrial Organization*, vol. 2. Amsterdam: North-Holland.

Shapiro, C. 1989. Theories of oligopoly behavior. In R. Schmalensee and R. Willig, eds., *Handbook of Industrial Organization*, vol. 1. Amsterdam: North-Holland.

Shapiro, C. 1996. Mergers with differentiated products. *Antitrust* 10(2): 23–30.

Siegfried, J. J., and L. B. Evans. 1994. Empirical studies of entry and exit: A survey of the evidence. *Review of Industrial Organization* 9: 121–55.

Sobel, J. 1984. The timing of sales. *Review of Economic Studies* 51: 353–68.

Spector, D. 2003. Horizontal mergers, entry, and efficiency defenses. *International Journal of Industrial Organization* 21: 1591–1600.

Stenneck, J., and F. Verboven. 2006. Merger control and enterprise competitiveness: Empirical analysis and policy recommendations. In F. Ilzkovitz and R. Meikeljohn, eds., *European Merger Control*. Cheltenham, UK: Edward Elgar.

Stoker, T. M. 1993. Empirical approaches to the problem of aggregation over individuals. *Journal of Economic Literature* 31: 1827–74.

Sudhir, K. 2001. Structural analysis of manufacturer pricing in the presence of a strategic retailer. *Marketing Science* 20: 244–64.

Sun, B., S. A. Neslin, and K. Srinivasan. 2003. Measuring the impact of promotions on brand switching when consumers are forward-looking. *Journal of Marketing Research* 40: 389–405.

Sutton, John. 1991. *Sunk Costs and Market Structure*. Cambridge, Mass.: MIT Press.

Szidarovszky, T., and S. Yakowitz. 1982. Contributions to Cournot oligopoly. *Journal of Economic Theory* 28: 51–70.

Thomas, C. J. 2004. The competitive effects of mergers between asymmetric firms. *International Journal of Industrial Organization* 22: 679–92.

Tschantz, S., P. Crooke, and L. Froeb. 2000. Mergers in sealed versus oral auctions. *International Journal of the Economics of Business* 7: 201–12.

US Department of Justice and Federal Trade Commission. 1992. *Horizontal Merger Guidelines*.

US General Accounting Office. 2004. *Energy Markets: Effects of Mergers and Market Concentration in the U.S. Petroleum Industry*. Available at ⟨http://www.gao.gov/new.items/d0496.pdf⟩.

Van Heerde, H. J., P. S. H. Leeflang, and D. R. Wittink. 2004. Decomposing the sales promotion bump with store data. *Marketing Science* 23: 317–34.

Varian, H. R. 1980. A model of sales. *American Economic Review* 70: 651–59.

Vickrey, W. 1961. Counterspeculation, auctions, and competitive sealed tenders. *Journal of Finance* 16: 8–37.

Vickery, W. 1962. Auctions and bidding games. In O. Morgenstern and A. Tucker, eds., *Recent Advances in Game Theory*. Princeton: Princeton University Press.

Villas-Boas, S. B. 2007. Vertical relationships between manufacturers and retailers: Inference with limited data. *Review of Economic Studies* 74: 625–52.

Vistnes, G. 2000. Hospitals, mergers, and two-stage competition. *Antitrust Law Journal* 67: 671–92.

Vita, M. G., and S. Sacher. 2001. The competitive effects of not-for-profit hospital mergers: A case study. *Journal of Industrial Economics* 49: 63–84.

Vives, X. 1999. *Oligopoly Pricing: Old Ideas and New Tools*. Cambridge: MIT Press.

Weiss, L. W. 1989. *Concentration and Price*. Cambridge: MIT Press.

Weiss, L. W. 1974. The concentration-profits relationship and antitrust. In H. Goldschmid, H. M. Mann, and J. F. Weston, eds., *Industrial Concentration: The New Learning*. Boston: Little, Brown.

Waehrer, K., and M. K. Perry. 2003. The effects of mergers in open-auction markets. *RAND Journal of Economics* 38: 287–304.

Weiskopf, D. A. 2003. Merger simulation. *Antitrust* 17(2): 57–60.

Werden, G. J. 1991. Horizontal mergers: Comment. *American Economic Review* 81: 1002–06.

Werden, G. J. 1996. A robust test for consumer welfare enhancing mergers among sellers of differentiated products. *Journal of Industrial Economics* 44: 409–13.

Werden, G. J. 1997. Simulating the effects of differentiated products mergers: A practical alternative to structural merger policy. *George Mason Law Review* 5: 363–86.

Werden, G. J. 1998. Demand elasticities in antitrust analysis. *Antitrust Law Journal* 66: 363–96.

Werden, G. J. 2000. Expert report in *United States v. Interstate Bakeries Corp. and Continental Baking Co. International Journal of the Economics of Business* 7: 139–48.

Werden, G. J. 2005. Merger simulation: Potentials and pitfalls. In P. van Bergeijk and E. Kloosterhuis, eds., *Modelling European Mergers: Theory: Competition Policy and Cases*. Cheltenham, UK: Edward Elgar.

Werden, G. J., and L. M. Froeb. 1994. The effects of mergers in differentiated products industries: Logit demand and merger policy. *Journal of Law, Economics, and Organization* 10: 407–26.

Werden, G. J., and L. M. Froeb. 1996. Simulation as an alternative to structural merger policy in differentiated products industries. In M. Coate and A. Kleit, eds., *The Economics of the Antitrust Process*. Boston: Kluwer Academic.

Werden, G. J., and L. M. Froeb. 1998. The entry-inducing effects of horizontal mergers. *Journal of Industrial Economics* 46: 525–43.

Werden, G. J., and L. M. Froeb. 2002. Calibrated economic models add focus, accuracy, and persuasiveness to merger analysis. In *The Pros and Cons of Merger Control*. Stockholm: Swedish Competition Authority.

Werden, G. J., L. M. Froeb, and D. T. Scheffman. 2004. A *Daubert* discipline for merger simulation. *Antitrust* 18(3): 89–95.

Werden, G. J., L. M. Froeb, and S. Tschantz. 2005. The effects of merger efficiencies on consumers of differentiated products. *European Competition Journal* 1: 245–64.

Werden, G. J., L. M. Froeb, and T. J. Tardiff. 1996. The use of the logit model in applied industrial organization. *International Journal of the Economics of Business* 3: 83–105.

Werden, G. J., A. S. Joskow, and R. L. Johnson. 1991. The effects of mergers on price and output: Two case studies from the airline industry. *Managerial and Decision Economics* 12: 341–52.

Werden, G. J., and G. Rozanski. 1994. The application of Section 7 to differentiated products industries: The market delineation dilemma. *Antitrust* 8(3): 40–43.

White, H. 1980. Using least squares to approximate unknown regression functions. *International Economic Review* 21: 149–70.

Willig, R. D. 1991. Merger analysis, industrial organization theory, and merger guidelines. *Brookings Papers on Economic Activity, Microeconomics* 281–332.

Cases

Brown Shoe Co. v. United States (1962). 370 US 294.

Concord Boat v. Brunswick Corp. (2000). 207 F.3d 1039 (8th Cir.).

FTC v. H.J. Heinz Co. (2001). 246 F.3d 708 (DC Cir.).

FTC v. Staples, Inc. (1997). 970 F. Supp. 1066 (DDC).

FTC v. Swedish Match (2000). 131 F. Supp. 2d 151 (DDC).

GE/Instrumentarium (2003). Case No. COMP/M.3083 (EC).

New York v. Kraft General Foods, Inc. (1995). 926 F. Supp. 321 (SDNY).

Heary Bros. Lightning Protection Co., Inc. v. Lightning Protection Institute (2003). 287 F. Supp. 2d 1038 (D. Ariz.).

United States v. Columbia Steel Co. (1948). 334 US 495.

United States v. Echostar Communications Corp. (2002). No. 02-02138 (DDC).

United States v. Georgia-Pacific Corp. (2001). No. 00-02824 (DDC), 66 Federal Register 9096.

United States v. Gillette Co. (1993). 828 F. Supp. 78 (DDC).

United States v. Interstate Bakeries Corp. (1995). No. 95-4194 (ED Ill.), 60 Federal Register 40195.

United States v. Kimberly-Clark Corp. (1995). No. 95-3055-P (ND Tex.), 60 Federal Register 66557.

United States v. Long Island Jewish Medical Center (1997). 983 F. Supp. 121 (EDNY).

United States v. Oracle Corp. (2004). 331 F. Supp. 2d 1098 (ND Cal.).

United States v. Philadelphia National Bank (1963). 374 US 321.

United States v. Vail Resorts, Inc. (1997). No. 97-B-10 (D Colo.), 62 Federal Register 5037.

United States v. WorldCom, Inc. (2000). No. 00-01526 (DDC).

Volvo/Scania (2000). Case No. COMP/M.1672 (EC).

3 The Coordinated Effects of Mergers

Kai-Uwe Kühn

Coordinated effects of mergers have become of much greater concern for antitrust authorities in recent years. In Europe, coordinated effects have become an important consideration only in the 1990s. In the United States, they have always been part of merger policy but have been pushed in the background by recent improved techniques for unilateral effects analysis. However, recent discussions in Europe and the United States have led to a consensus that coordinated effects of mergers have to be interpreted as the impact of a merger on the incentives to collude (explicitly or implicitly). This has put collusion theory at the center of arguments on coordinated effects.

For this reason this chapter starts by reviewing the relevant economic literature on collusion for the assessment of the coordinated effects of mergers. The emphasis is on an analysis of how much the scope for collusion is changed as a result of a merger. I first discuss what I will call "standard collusion theory." The framework is based on the theory of infinitely repeated games. Most economic policy prescriptions on collusion are derived from standard collusion theory. Recent applications of this framework to coordinated effects have given us valuable insights. For example, the literature has provided the surprising result that mergers often lead to *reductions* in collusion incentives. A second recent development that helps in the assessment of coordinated effects of mergers is a shift in focus toward the robustness of theoretical results about collusion. For policy applications, the literature is problematic because many results appear nonrobust. I show that some of the problems with robustness are due to an improper use of theory, and I discuss what results should be considered robust. In contrast, a close look at the theory also reveals that features treated by policy makers as robust in fact are not.

However, there are limitations to the framework of standard collusion theory that have to be taken into account when designing policies for the evaluation of coordinated effects of mergers. These limitations primarily concern the way in which firms can achieve agreements among a plethora of equilibria. In section 3.2, I discuss these issues and arguments that have been advanced in antitrust practice about the precise difficulties of achieving agreement. I demonstrate that there is a lack of theory in this area and that many of the arguments that have been advanced cannot possibly be robust. In particular, arguments on complexity are often not very convincing theoretically although they are regularly embraced in practice.

In section 3.3, I survey the relevant empirical work to assess the most important factors that might be of relevance for assessing the coordinated effects of mergers, and I survey the very small literature that has directly tried to estimate these effects. Both the numerical work in the theoretical literature and the empirical work suggest that coordinated effects of mergers may be small but significantly more research is needed to make a clear assessment. At a minimum these warn us against an excessively aggressive approach toward coordinated effects.

Section 3.4 contains an assessment of reasonable policy rules, reviewing developments in Europe and the United States and suggesting a path forward to a coherent system of tests for coordinated effects in merger analysis. Section 3.5 concludes.

3.1 Standard Collusion Theory and the Coordinated Effects of Mergers

3.1.1 Unilateral versus Coordinated Effects

Any merger involves the recombination of assets of the merging firms. A merger is therefore never equivalent to the simple disappearance of a firm. The combined firm faces changed production costs, larger capacity, a broader product line, or changes in its access to financial markets. However, in the absence of cost synergies (e.g., reduced marginal cost through the merger or relaxation of financial constraints), the consolidation of firms in a merger always leads to incentives to raise prices in the short run. More precisely, the best-response function for prices on all products in which the merging firms produced substitutes, shifts upward as indicated in figure 3.1 by the move from the solid thick line to the

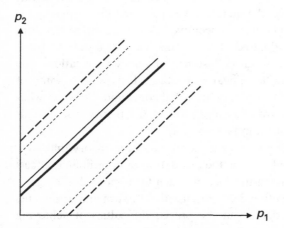

Figure 3.1
Best response prices of merging and nonmerging firms

solid thin line. Note that the short-run best-response functions of nonmerging firms are unaffected. In equilibrium, rivals will set higher prices only because they anticipate the merging firms to increase their prices. The short-run *equilibrium* price change induced by an asset transfer, holding production costs constant, is the *unilateral effect of the merger.* (e.g., see Farrell and Shapiro 1990a, b; McAfee and Williams 1992).

Collusion generally refers to the ability of firms to raise prices above the best response prices through a system of rewards and punishments in the future triggered by current behavior. The more collusion is achievable, the further these limits (drawn as thick dashed lines in figure 3.1) can be pushed away from the short-run best-response function. In a collusive mechanism firms can achieve higher prices than by short-run best responding. But they can also achieve lower prices by threatening to start a punishment phase if the low price is not charged and rewarding compliance with a low price otherwise. This possibility of sustaining lower prices than the best-response price makes the punishment significantly more severe than the return to a short-run Nash equilibrium.

The study of coordinated effects focuses on how changes in the asset distribution between firms, be it through asset trades or outright merger, change the ability of firms to credibly sustain prices above the short-run best response. The most important insight from the theoretical literature has been that asset transactions between firms that make the best-response function move up do not necessarily move the upper dashed lines upward as well. Indeed the literature has shown that asset transactions that increase unilateral market power may tighten the constraints for collusion and thus lead to favorable coordinated effects from mergers. (This is indicated by the thin dashed lines.) The reason is that maximally collusive prices are driven by the incentive constraints on collusion, which may tighten when short-run best response prices rise.

3.1.2 Comparative Statics of Collusion and the Interpretation of Collusion Theory

While the difference between unilateral and coordinated effects of mergers might seem intuitively simple in the discussion of the previous subsection, there are important conceptual problems in defining what the coordinated effect is. These problems arise because collusion theory necessarily produces a vast number of equilibria with a potentially large range of equilibrium outcomes. Generally, for policy purposes we want to answer questions like: How do prices and quantities change as a result of a merger? or Does collusion get easier or more difficult after the merger? But what exactly do these questions mean, when there is a vast multiplicity of equilibria? To give an answer, we have to be slightly more formal about the structure of collusive models.

Collusive equilibria in an infinitely repeated game are simply characterized by a set of two incentive conditions for each of the colluding firms. A firm has to comply with the collusive action a_i^c instead of playing a short-run best response $a_i^*(a_{-i}^c)$ to the vector of collusive actions of other firms a_{-i}^c. This is achieved by promising a good equilibrium outcome

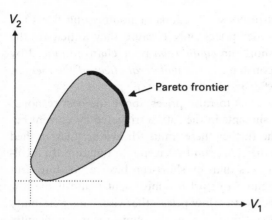

Figure 3.2
Typical value set of a repeated game

with value V_i in the future after complying with a^c and threatening to switch to a bad equilibrium outcome for firm i, $\underline{V}_i$, if deviation by firm i occurs. Formally,

$$\pi(a_i^c, a_{-i}^c) + \delta V_i \geq \pi(a_i^*, a_{-i}^c) + \delta \underline{V}_i, \qquad i = 1, \ldots, n,$$

where δ is the discount factor. For optimal punishment equilibria, the continuation value $\underline{V}_i$ is the lowest value among all equilibria for player i. Note that the inequality implies that deviations from a path that gives the lowest continuation value $\underline{V}_i$ will be sustained by restarting this path in case of a deviation. Since the work of Abreu (1988) and Abreu, Pearce, and Stacchetti (1990) we know that we can precisely characterize the equilibrium value set in a repeated game and that we can calculate this set numerically. Figure 3.2 depicts a typical value set. There is a continuum of equilibria. Note that on the boundary of the value set some incentive constraints always must be binding. However, for equilibria that have values in the interior of the set, incentive constraints are generically not binding.

In what sense can we now answer the question: How does behavior change as the environment changes? Let us approach this question with a specific example about one particular change in the environment. Suppose that the interest rate increases. In the standard model this would be reflected by a lower discount factor δ. Abreu, Pearce, and Stacchetti (1990) show that the whole equilibrium value set shrinks. The new set is nested within the equilibrium value set that is generated by the larger discount factor. There is then a clear sense in which this implies that collusion is more difficult when the interest rate is greater: the set of potential outcomes is strictly smaller. However, this observation by itself makes no prediction about behavior (i.e., prices set or quantities produced). We can therefore not make any prediction about future collusive behavior as a result of a change in the interest rate.[1]

The predictive power of changes in the equilibrium value set is even smaller when we study the comparative statics of other variables, specifically of transfers of assets as occur in mergers. Transfers of assets will change the relative size of firms and impact incentives asymmetrically. Almost any such asset redistribution will lead to a nonnested change in the equilibrium value set (see Kühn 2004; Kühn and Rimler 2006). There is therefore none of the predictive power we had in the example of comparative statics in the interest rate.

Fundamentally, this problem reflects the fact that the standard collusion model is not truly a closed model. It allows one to determine all the outcomes that are incentive compatible but not make predictions about which equilibrium will be played. What the standard theory is missing is a mechanism by which firms select the equilibrium to be played. If we add such a mechanism and (reasonably) assume that it remains the same when the environment changes, we can generate meaningful comparative statics of collusive behavior under the selection mechanism. The natural assumption for models of explicit collusion is that firms bargain over the equilibrium value set. Under symmetric information this will lead to the selection of an equilibrium on the Pareto frontier of the equilibrium value set. For example, Harrington (1991) and Kühn (2004) have assumed the Nash bargaining solution as the selection device. Recent work on renegotiation by Abreu, Pearce, and Stacchetti (1993) uses a similar selection device based on bargaining. Bargaining to the Pareto frontier of the equilibrium value set appears to be an appropriate assumption for explicit collusion.[2]

This approach to closing the model has an important caveat. In the case of tacit collusion, a selection based on explicit negotiation is clearly not appropriate for selecting a collusive equilibrium from the set. There is currently no suggestion in the literature on how to solve the problem of generating predictions for tacitly collusive behavior from standard collusion theory. I discuss the issues that arise when attempting to close the model for the case of tacit collusion in section 3.2. At this point I pursue the argument focusing exclusively on the case of *explicit collusion*.

Although the basic theory of infinitely repeated games generates an elegant characterization of the equilibrium value set as demonstrated by Abreu, Pearce, and Stacchetti (1990), it is technically very difficult, if not impossible, to obtain analytical comparative statics. This remains true even when one assumes the selection of an equilibrium by bargaining. Especially in asymmetric settings, as arise naturally in the study of the coordinated effects of mergers, one will almost always have to resort to numerical calculation of the equilibrium value set. Traditionally the literature has tried to avoid such difficulties by studying the comparative statics of subsets of the equilibrium value set. However, it has been known since Abreu (1988) that these approaches cannot detect equilibria on the frontier of the equilibrium value set. However, such analyses proceeded on the hope that the comparative statics obtained looking at equilibria for a specific constrained set of equilibria would yield qualitatively the same comparative statics as those one would obtain for the full equilibrium value set. The most popular approach in this vein has been to study the set of (symmetric) equilibria that results by reverting to the static Nash equilibrium forever after any deviation from collusion. This choice was made primarily because the calculation of punishment payoffs becomes particularly easy. More sophisticated studies have looked at symmetric optimal punishment equilibria in symmetric models. These equilibria have a similar structure to those supporting the full equilibrium set: Any deviation from the most collusive outcome is responded to by switching to the equilibrium with the lowest continuation value among symmetric equilibria. Most of this literature implicitly considers a selection rule from the equilibrium value set that, like Nash bargaining, selects a Pareto optimal point from the set of equilibria: the equilibrium in which the most profitable collusive price is set.

It turns out that the comparative statics from studying the set of symmetric equilibria and restricting punishments to reversion from the one-shot Nash equilibrium can be highly nonrobust even in symmetric models. The resulting qualitative comparative statics may contradict the comparative statics when analyzing the full equilibrium set (see Kühn and Rimler 2005). Results can depend on the functional form and on specific parameter values. In contrast, the comparative statics of the full equilibrium set are typically very robust in symmetric models. In addition in symmetric models the comparative statics obtained from symmetric optimal punishments tend to have the same qualitative properties as those for the full equilibrium set.

For asymmetric models there are no known restriction to subsets of equilibrium value sets that can give reliable predictions for behavior. For example, in Kühn (2004), I obtain strong comparative statics results for mergers in differentiated goods markets by restricting firms to use symmetric pricing strategies.[3] However, this comparative statics analysis in prices is misleading. Numerical calculation of the bargaining solution on the full equilibrium value set reveals that prices for firms that gets larger through an asset transaction may increase while prices for the firms that get smaller will decrease. In collusive models with product differentiation there is therefore no way around the numerical analysis of the equilibrium value set to determine meaningful comparative statics of mergers. In models for homogeneous goods markets with capacity constraints authors have accounted for asymmetries by studying quasi-symmetric optimal punishment equilibria that allocate market share in proportion to capacity (see Compte, Jenny, and Rey 2002; Vasconcelos 2004). This restriction is imposed in these papers for collusive and punishment phases. Technically this procedure allows one to analyze optimal collusion as if one were analyzing equilibria with a restriction to symmetric strategies. However, the restriction to quasi-symmetric strategies may not be as innocuous as the restriction to symmetric optimal punishments in symmetric models. To date there is no work that has tested whether the results obtained for quasi-symmetric optimal punishment equilibria in homogeneous goods models are robust relative to results obtained by looking at the whole equilibrium value set.

Despite these caveats about the existing literature on explicit collusion, there are some general conclusions we can draw. Overall, the literature suggests that policy implications from collusion theory should be drawn only based on models employing some form of optimal punishment strategies. Furthermore, where asymmetries and changes in the degree of asymmetry are important, numerical analysis of the equilibrium value set is necessary to obtain meaningful behavioral predictions of the impact of a change in the environment.

We should note at this point that this conclusion is not shared by everyone. For example, it is often argued that Nash reversion is a more realistic assumption because it is less "complex" than employing optimal punishment strategies (see Feuerstein 2005). One could justify using Nash reversion if there were good reasons to believe that firms play such strategies. However, this does not seem to be the case. The empirical evidence (see Levenstein and Suslow 2002) seems to suggest that cartel break down tends to be followed by attempts to reestablish cartels. There is therefore no sense in which an expectation to play Nash forever would be a particularly good assumption to make. The selection of Nash punishments would therefore have to be considered an arbitrary one.[4]

A more empirically based argument for restrictions on the equilibrium value set has been made by Vasconcelos (2004) to justify the use of quasi-symmetric optimal punishment strategies of the kind used by Compte et al. (2002) and Vasconcelos (2004). He documents that many cartels in homogeneous goods markets operate according to rules in which the market shares under collusion are proportional to capacities. While this is a nice empirical observation, it does not justify a restriction to quasi-symmetric strategies. The method of allocating market share may simply document the use of a simple method to resolving bargaining over the equilibrium value set. Firms may save on bargaining costs by establishing a fixed rule of how collusive profits are shared. The observation is not enough to justify restricting strategies generally: a cartel that uses a proportionality rule for selecting the collusive equilibrium may not use this rule in a punishment phase because there are harsher punishments available. To obtain robust results, we have to be careful in distinguishing between outcomes that are feasible due to incentive constraints and the selection rules by which firms reach an agreement within the feasible set. This distinction is currently not made carefully enough in the theoretical literature, and thus leads to considerable confusion when the implications of collusion for practical policy are considered. In the rest of this section I will discuss the literature with an emphasis on robust results, to avoid as much as possible any reference to results that may depend on arbitrary restrictions on the equilibrium value set.

A final remark about the interpretation of collusion theory is necessary before we look at the implications of the theory in the context of mergers. We have seen that behavioral predictions can only be made by making some assumptions on the method by which firms select the equilibrium they play. If the selection rule remains unchanged, there can be no simple dichotomy between collusive equilibria and noncollusive equilibria. In other words, when the environment changes firms may become more collusive or less collusive depending on the changes to the incentive constraints. But generally, the best equilibrium selected by something like a Nash bargaining solution over the equilibrium value set will support some collusion. This statement is only false in the simplest models of collusion with homogeneous goods and no capacity constraints. In that case either all prices below the monopoly price are sustainable in some collusive equilibrium or none is. For any positive degree of product differentiation, there is always a range of collusive outcomes above the one-shot Nash equilibrium as long as firms do not ignore future profits. This is important for interpreting the theory for policy purposes. Policy discussions often resort to arguments that imply that there is some tipping point (e.g., in industry concentration) at which collusion in an industry becomes feasible. Before the tipping point is reached, no collusion exists; beyond the tipping point, firms fully collude. The theory does not support such a view. Instead, it distinguishes market circumstances in which all collusive equilibria are close to the one-shot Nash equilibrium. In that case behavior is indistinguishable from one shot behavior in the market. By this view of collusion theory, little is gained for coordinated effects analysis to determine "how collusive" a market was before the merger. What is important is how behavior changes as a result of the merger. Given that the collusive model always applies, we should, in principle, be able to analyze all mergers on the basis of coordinated effects analysis only. According to the theory, such an analysis would simply coincide with unilateral effects analysis in markets in which collusion is relatively difficult.[5]

3.1.3   How to Assess the Impact of a Merger on Collusion

It should be clear that not every result on the comparative statics of collusion models is relevant for the assessment of the coordinated effects from a merger. Only those results that can inform us about the change in behavior induced by a merger are relevant for the analysis of coordinated effects of mergers. There are two types of results that could potentially enlighten such an assessment. First is a direct analysis of the comparative statics of consolidating the assets of two firms and its impact on collusion—assuming some consistent equilibrium selection argument. This approach can lead to a distinction between collusion-enhancing and collusion-reducing mergers. It could also be the basis for a merger simulation exercise. Second is an identification of market circumstances under which collusion would be very hard even after a merger. This approach would allow us to characterize circumstances under which the coordinated effects of mergers have to be small without a need to resort to a more detailed analysis. Such results would give us criteria to decide when the analysis of unilateral effects of a merger are sufficient to assess the potential impact of a merger. In this subsection we first discuss theoretical results that directly deal with the coordinated effects of mergers. Then I consider the implications for coordinated effects analysis of the rest of the collusion literature.

Theoretical Results on the Coordinated Effects of Mergers   There is a small theoretical literature, pioneered by Compte, Rey, and Jenny (2002), that has attemted directly to assess the impact of asset redistributions, including mergers, on the incentives for collusion. This literature (see also Vasconcelos 2004; Kühn and Motta 2001; Kühn 2004) has firmly established that the coordinated effects of mergers need not facilitate collusion.[6] On the contrary, collusion can be made more difficult by mergers in which the largest firm gets larger relative to the smallest firm in the market. While the exact workings of the mechanism differ depending on whether one considers capacity as the relevant asset of the firm (as in Compte et al. 2002 or Vasconcelos 2004) or if it is products in a product line (as in Kühn 2004), there is a clear result that mergers in a market that is not too asymmetric and increases asymmetries in asset holdings will make collusion harder: the joint profits of the merging firms decrease from asymmetry increasing mergers.

Unfortunately, the impression in the policy literature on the impact of asset redistribution through merger is that this outcome is the combination of two effects: (1) reducing the number of firms facilitates collusion and (2) increasing asymmetry makes collusion more difficult (see Dick 2002). This view is based on a misunderstanding of the results in this literature. This can best be seen in the model with product lines I discuss in Kühn (2004). When two firms merge in a model in which firms each produce a range of differentiated products in a product line, the product line of the merging firm becomes longer. If no product leaves the market, the short-run incentives of the nonmerging firms to undercut any given collusive price vector or deviate from any given punishment price vector are unchanged by the merger. Note that this is very different when a firm disappears from the market. In this case all firms would have an incentive to raise their prices because, at the margin, they now lose demand to less products. The incentives to undercut collusive prices would unambiguously decline. The effect of changing the number of firms is therefore fundamentally different in a merger because the assets do not leave the market.

To understand what happens to collusion after the merger it is useful to focus on the incentives of the merging firms. Merging firms have a greater incentive to raise prices from any punishment price and a smaller incentive to reduce prices from any collusive price vector than either of the merging firms pre-merger. If the merging firm is the largest in the market it has the smallest incentive to deviate from the collusive outcome—even before the merger. This typically implies that its incentive constraint is not the binding constraint on the point of the Pareto frontier of the value set that is chosen by a range of bargaining outcomes. If neither of the merging firms was previously the smallest firm, the change in the reduced incentives to deviate from collusion for the merging firms then has no direct impact on the postmerger behavior. The main effect comes from the merger's impact on the punishment incentives of the merging firms. Since there is a greater incentive to deviate from any punishments and the largest firm's incentive constraint must be binding at the start of a punishment equilibrium, collusion gets harder to sustain. The joint profits of the merging firms fall. The prices of the nonmerging firms also fall, but the prices of the merging firms may go up. This price rise is not a result of an increase in market power, but a way to shift market share to the smaller remaining firms in order to limit the price reduction necessary to keep them colluding.[7]

   As this discussion shows, the price effects of mergers under coordinated effects are difficult to characterize analytically. As a result, welfare effects are also hard to assess. However, numerical analysis can potentially help. In Kühn (2004), I make some progress in this direction by studying the effect of asset transfers between two firms. While this analysis does not directly address mergers, a number of conclusions emerge that appear fairly robust: First, small moves away from symmetry will tend to generate welfare improvements. The reason is that the argument above implies that the fall in the price of the smaller firms as a response to merger outweighs any potential price increases by the merging firms. Second, for very asymmetric duopoly market structures merger to monopoly may be Pareto improving. The intuition is that for very asymmetric distributions of assets, the larger firm will keep prices above the monopoly price to keep the smaller firm with sufficient market share to be willing to raise the price above its best response price. Merger to monopoly brings all prices to the monopoly price, which implies a reduction in most prices. Third, the price responses to asset transactions between firms that significantly change the asymmetry of market structure are surprisingly small. Fourth, it is a robust result that the joint profits from asymmetry-increasing asset transfers between firms go down unless the initial asymmetry in asset holding is already large. Most asymmetry increasing mergers cannot be justified by a motivation to enjoy increased profits from the coordinated effects of a merger.

   The current state of the theoretical literature thus tells a strongly cautionary tale about extending the use of coordinated effects arguments. Contrary to the prevailing policy view, mergers can make collusion more difficult. Furthermore it is not clear whether the coordinated effects of mergers are large enough to consider them a substantial effect of a merger. Of course, in policy the main concern appears to be about a switch from noncollusive behavior to collusive behavior. This sharp distinction is not really supported by theory. There is nothing in the theory I have surveyed that suggests that there is some threshold beyond which the market will exhibit one-shot behavior. In the models that make such a prediction it is an artifact of either assuming homogeneous goods with constant marginal cost or restricting the set of equilibrium strategies allowed. The first is empirically unrealistic; the second is arbitrary. This means that arguments that seek such categorization have to be based on reasoning outside of standard collusion theory.

When Are the Coordinated Effects of Mergers Small?   Besides the small literature that directly seeks to analyze the effects of mergers on the incentives to collude, there is a large body of collusion literature that is potentially helpful in assessing the coordinated effects of mergers. Any analysis that can demonstrate that collusion is extremely difficult to sustain or that the impact of collusion would be minimal in the post merger scenario, can be used to argue that the merger cannot have significant coordinated effects. The second benefit of this body of theory is that it can help in the design of remedies in merger cases with coordinated effects. I will discuss in this subsection which type of results can possibly be used for such arguments and whether the results in the literature can be considered robust. One of the problems with coordinated effects analysis in mergers is that some of the common wisdom about the sign of effects and the robustness of effects does not square with the theoretical results. I will highlight such discrepancies below.

The Number of Competitors The result of collusive models that is most robust to any change in model assumptions is that collusion gets harder when there are more firms. Hence, it has been concluded that in markets with a large number of firms collusion is very difficult. Unfortunately, there is a slight flaw even in this argument. Strictly speaking, the argument holds when we replicating the assets of firms as we increase the number of firms in an industry. This increases the amount of assets relative to demand. Then as the number of firms gets large, collusion becomes more and more difficult. However, in many policy contexts, as in mergers, we are interested in distributing a given number of assets among a greater number of firms. For example, when restructuring formerly regulated utilities, as in the electricity industry, it is a common policy prescription to split up the production capacity. This does, of course, reduce the short run incentives to raise prices. However, as I show in Kühn (2006), the scope for collusion is increased by splitting up capacity symmetrically among more firms whether the cost function of Compte, Jenny, and Rey (2002) is used or that of Vasconcelos (2004). Intuitively, smaller firms have less of an incentive to fill up capacity. But also unilateral deviations from punishments are less effective if other firms have enough of a proportion of the capacity to serve the market. This shows that the results in Compte, Jenny, and Rey (2002) are not purely driven by asymmetries between firms, but that fragmentation in itself can facilitate collusion. Counting the number of firms can therefore not be considered a good predictor for the likelihood of collusion in a homogeneous goods industry with capacity constraints.[8]

Homogeneous Goods Markets versus Markets with Horizontal Product Differentiation Many of the arguments used in competition policy about factors helping or hindering collusion go back to Scherer's classic textbook (see Scherer and Ross 1990). One of the claims made in this book is that collusion is more difficult in markets with heterogeneous products. It has since become the conventional wisdom in competition policy that homogeneous goods markets are more susceptible to collusion than markets with differentiated goods. From the point of view of standard collusion theory this is less than obvious. With differentiated products the incentives to deviate from a collusive price are reduced. However, it may also be the case that the intensity of punishments is reduced due to product differentiation. Therefore there appears to be a trade-off, in general. The work by Deneckere (1982) seemed to support the conclusion that product homogeneity facilitates collusion. He showed that in a product differentiation model with two firms and linear demand, an increase in product differentiation reduces the scope for collusion. To obtain such a result, he was assuming that punishments consist of infinite reversion to the one shot Nash equilibrium. Later work on the model that changed the functional form of demand by Ross (1992) and work that did not restrict punishments to Nash reversion by Lambertini and Sasaki (1999) obtained the opposite result. Kühn and Rimler (2005) have recently shown that Nash punishment results are generally highly nonrobust to the functional form of demand and the number of firms in the industry. In contrast, they show that for a wide class of product differentiation models (including all of those used in the applied literature) product differentiation facilitates collusion robustly when one does not restrict punishments to Nash reversion. The reason is that optimal punishments are so harsh that the effect of product differentiation on punishments is of second order relative to the effect on the incentives to deviate from collusion. The theory therefore gives no strong implication for the impact of product differentiation for the likelihood of coordinated effects. Neither for homogeneous goods nor for (sufficiently) differentiated goods can it be claimed that collusion is very unlikely.

It should be noted, however, that the literature has only invalidated one version of a range of arguments that could be used to support the claim that product heterogeneity undermines collusion. Scherer's argument referred primarily to issues of complexities in defining and negotiating a collusive agreement. These arguments are outside the analysis of standard collusion theory. We discuss them in the next section.

Market Transparency   In collusion theory market transparency has a very precise meaning. Markets are considered imperfectly transparent if actions of competitors cannot be monitored and *at the same time* demand conditions are sufficiently uncertain to make it impossible to infer the actions from market data. (see Green and Porter 1984; Kandori 1992) When markets are imperfectly transparent in this sense, price wars triggered by unexpectedly low demand are unavoidable. Indeed, the greater the uncertainty, the less collusion is sustainable. This robust result is a good basis for a policy rule. The main problem with evaluating transparency, however, is how to measure it. When can we be sure that observability is imperfect? How large is demand uncertainty in the market and what is a sufficient degree of uncertainty to come to the conclusion that collusion is highly unlikely? Theory has so far given little guidance as to the indicators for sufficiently low market transparency to make coordinated effects arguments irrelevant. But it may be feasible, in practice, to find a market that is so obviously intransparent that coordinated effects of mergers can be excluded.[9]

Note that these arguments differ from the claim that market transparency changes as a result of a merger. Dick (2002) has argued that mergers will typically increase market transparency and that coordinated effects analysis should evaluate such a change. He argues that the mere consolidation of the information of the merging firms would have the effect of facilitating collusion.

The argument that mergers increase market transparency is weak at best. What is relevant for collusion after the merger is information about the remaining rivals, not about the merged firms. It is not clear that a deviation by any of the remaining firms would be more easily detected after a merger. For example, if firms are subject to idiosyncratic shocks to their demands, the residual demands faced by the merged firms may be more volatile after the merger than before, making it harder to detect deviations from collusive conduct. On the other hand, it may be the case for common demand shocks that the residual demand faced by a firm becomes less volatile so that the merger facilitates collusion. The problem with using criteria like the "change in transparency due to a merger" in a policy context is that the theory underlying it has not been worked out and is certainly not trivial. The large number of surprising results in collusion theory should prevent us from being overeager to apply simple intuitions.

Asymmetries   As I have shown with the theoretical literature that looks directly at the coordinated effects of mergers, the analysis of asymmetries is essential to understanding the coordinated effects of mergers. However, having large asymmetries between firms in a pre-merger situation does not guarantee that mergers would have small coordinated effects. For example, a merger may have the effect of substantially raising the prices of larger firms that get more similar after the merger relative to smaller firms that are very different from the larger ones. It is not the case that the presence of a small firm with very different incentives alone guarantees that collusion may be undermined. Collusion between similar firms can be very effective even in the presence of small fringe firms. This is in fact one of the insights in Kühn (2004) and a fundamental problem with simplistic applications of the so-called maverick approach, as discussed further below.[10]

The most widely studied case of asymmetries in the literature has been that of cost-asymmetries (e.g., see Rothschild 1999). Consider an increase in the (constant) marginal cost of one firm in a duopoly from a previously fully symmetric situation. The incentives to deviate from the collusive price of the firm for which the costs have not changed are unchanged. There is typically a direct effect on the incentives to deviate downward from any given collusive price vector. A firm with lower marginal costs has a higher incentive to deviate from any collusive price. This is the first-order effect in any such model.

The question is whether cost asymmetries are a good factor to consider for the assessment of coordinated effects. Cost changes induced by the merger should be studied when looking at the comparative statics of collusion and are covered, for example, in Vasconcelos (2004). Beyond that it is questionable whether it is possible to define a "sufficient" degree of cost asymmetry at which collusion should be considered unlikely before and after the merger. The scope for using cost asymmetries in coordinated effects analysis is therefore limited.

It is also important to note that the analysis of asymmetries in asset holdings or costs does not necessarily extend to all asymmetries in the market. Take the case of cross-ownership holdings. An increase in cross-ownership holding by one firm and not by others will make the incentive structure more asymmetric. However, collusion is facilitated with any such consolidating move—even if asymmetries are increased. Some of the intuition obviously comes from the fact that an increase in shareholdings in other firms makes it less attractive for a firm to deviate from a collusive price. But the increase in shareholdings also makes it less feasible to escape punishments. When a firm unilaterally deviates from punishment behavior, a larger cross-ownership share will increase the weight on profit streams of rival firms, which remains low. A firm that acquires cross-ownership unambiguously increases its ability to collude. Conversely, giving shares in one's own firm to competitors also facilitates collusion. It (weakly) reduces the weight of own profits relative to competitors profits in a firm's objective function.[11] Note that this robust result on cross-shareholdings is in striking contrast to the results on mergers reported earlier. In the merger case concentration increasing mergers can lead to lower prices and make collusion less likely. This is never the case for the transfer of shareholdings. The fundamental difference is that the granting of cross-shareholdings does not entail the transfer of control rights over assets, which implies very different incentives. This reasoning suggests that the coordinated effects of joint ventures and other types of minority engagements should lead much more robustly to well-founded concerns about coordinated effects.

This cross-ownership example shows that it is not the asymmetry as such that makes collusion difficult. The scope for collusion is simply driven by the firms facing the greatest difficulties with collusion. As a simple example consider two firms producing substitutes. For one of the firms demand is decreasing over time and for the other it is increasing.[12] The firm that limits the scope for collusion is the firm with decreasing demand. What undermines collusion is that one of the firms is facing declining demand and therefore has a large incentive to deviate from collusion. Increasing heterogeneity by increasing the rate of demand growth for the other firm does little to undermine collusion further. It will only have an effect if imposition of harsh punishments become less credible for the firm with growing demand.

Another example for pitfalls in the assessment of asymmetries is the treatment of vertical integration in merger analysis. Citing the literature on the effect of cost heterogeneity on collusion, it is often claimed that a more similar vertical structure between different firms will lead to more symmetric cost structures. However, heterogeneity in vertical structure is not necessarily inconsistent with homogeneous cost structures. A change in vertical integration may simply reflect a change in the relative costs and benefits of vertical integration at the margin, leading more firms to become vertically integrated. Even if that is the case, the observed heterogeneity in the institutional structure is of little use in assessing asymmetries in the incentives to collude. This is not to argue that vertical integration may not in some cases facilitate collusive behavior (e.g., see Jullien and Rey 2000; Nocke and White 2003). Vertical integration can even generate a more homogeneous cost structure in some industries. But the automatic assumption that a more similar vertical structure eliminates the relevant asymmetries and thus facilitates collusion does not meet the standard of rigorous merger analysis.

The lesson from the theoretical literature is therefore not that any asymmetries indicate difficulties for collusion and that decreases in asymmetries through mergers can be considered to generate significant coordinated effects. It is that the incentive structure for collusion for any one of the heterogeneities considered that has to be assessed for any specific merger in order to do justice to the present state of the theoretical literature.

Irreversibilities Irreversibilities in decisions can have an effect of dramatically undermining collusion. A simple example in this class of arguments does not come from the formal literature but from competition policy folklore. Suppose that potentially colluding firms have few large customers and that there is the possibility of writing short- or long-run contracts when competing for customers. A collusive agreement would stipulate frequent contracting at a high collusive price (essentially as in a bidding ring). However, any firm can deviate from such an arrangement by offering a long term contract that guarantees better contract terms than those expected from rivals over a longer horizon. The commitment to a long-term contract effectively makes any price cut irreversible. If there are no limits to the contract length, then collusion is dramatically undermined in any such market.

In Kühn (2001), I show in a simple model a different argument on irreversible investment whereby collusion in capacity investments is qualitatively very difficult to achieve. In fact there exists no discount factor at which collusion in capacities can be sustained. Similar to the long-run contracting argument, a deviation changes the state of competition in the industry permanently. A firm deviating from a collusive capacity agreement can deviate to a large preemptive capacity level. A return to full collusion is not possible since the capacity is already in place. So firms facing the deviator have to decide whether to punish the firm by responding with large capacity expansion or accommodate in their capacity choices. This means any collusive agreement creates incentives for one of the parties to dramatically redistribute profits permanently through a preemptive irreversible capacity decision.

These are the strongest type of theoretical results possible. While much of the literature on collusion derives results on whether collusion is a little more likely under some circumstances than others, these examples are quite different. They describe circumstances, namely irreversibilites in a standard collusion model, that will make collusion impossible to sustain. Even if we would make the theory slightly more realistic, these results indicate that irreversibilities make collusion qualitatively much less likely. Unfortunately, there are few results in collusion theory that are as clear cut. However, there may be a general lesson to learn: namely that irreversible decisions should lead to coordinated effects being condidered highly unlikely.

Impact of R&D One of the points that is considered common wisdom in competition policy practice is that collusion is harder in industries with greater R&D intensity. Unfortunately, there is very little literature on collusion in multiple decision variables and decisions that change the industry state. But some insights from standard collusion theory can generate intuition about the impact of R&D on the ability to collude.

One argument may be that regular R&D activities will make industries persistently asymmetric and hence reduce the likelihood of collusion in prices. The current state of the theory makes this implausible. The work of Compte, Jenny, and Rey (2002) and Kühn (2004) has shown that there is a tendency for industry profits to increase when the industry becomes more symmetric. But this creates a force toward the persistence of "collective" dominance, as we know from the patent races literature, because innovations that increase industry profits are more likely. Generally, insights from the patent race literature should be applicable. It will matter whether R&D competition is likely to be of the action-reaction type (see Vickers 1987; Budd, Harris, and Vickers 1993) or whether dramatic innovations push the industry toward increasing dominance of a single firm. In the first case, it is not clear that collusion is undermined. In the second case, collusion is much harder to sustain in the anticipation of highly asymmetric structures after successful innovation.

Note that the foregoing arguments do not suggest any link between the R&D intensity of the industry and collusion. Instead they describe the relationship between R&D activities and collusion in prices.

3.2   What Does Standard Collusion Theory Miss?

Industrial organization economists depend on standard collusion theory for tackling policy questions regarding collusion. However, it cannot be ignored that many arguments made about the likelihood of collusion in specific markets in competition policy practice are not based on this body of theory at all. Policy papers tend to discuss the potential difficulties in *reaching* a collusive agreement, the complexity of such agreements necessary to be effective, the frequency of negotiation sessions necessary to sustain agreements, and other related issues. Standard collusion theory is silent, however, on such "coordination activities." As I showed above, some modeling of coordination has to be done to obtain meaningful comparative statics of collusion. But in standard collusion theory such coordination is achieved through a form of full information bargaining. This modeling approach assumes away all problems in coming to an agreement that feature so prominently in many policy discussions.

If coordination activities are central to the success of coordinated conduct, then the impact of a merger on coordination activities will be as or more important than the comparative statics derived in such papers as Compte et al. (2002). But unlike the analysis of the incentive constraints for collusion, there is no accepted theoretical framework to systematically analyze the question of how coordination activities can be affected by a merger. On the other hand, in policy papers both issues are often discussed together without any clarity whether the claims made rely on standard collusion theory or on the problems arising from coordination activities. In this section I attempt to sort through these issues and explain why simple intuitions might not be enough to deal with the "coordination activities" in the assessment of coordinated effects of mergers.

3.2.1 Renegotiation

The first issue to consider is an inconsistency in the theory itself as presented. As discussed above, in many circumstances, and especially in asymmetric models, equilibrium value sets are not nested. To derive comparative statics results, we have to rely on some selection device like a bargaining solution over the equilibrium value set. Of course, this immediately raises the question why negotiation can only take place at the beginning of time, as was implicitly assumed in the last section. For example, after a deviation firms may realize that a punishment phase can be very costly and try to renegotiate to a better outcome for all parties involved. It should be clear that any such renegotiation would limit the degree to which punishments could be imposed.

There is a great deal of theoretical literature on renegotiation in infinitely repeated games (e.g., see Farrell and Maskin 1989). The literature in this vein starts from a candidate equilibrium value set and excludes punishments for which the players have incentives to renegotiate to a Pareto superior point in this set. "Renegotiation proof" equilibria require that "punishments" be selected from the Pareto frontier of the equilibrium value set. To achieve severe punishment, the deviating firm has to be moved to its least favorable point on the Pareto frontier of the equilibrium value set. So, if we restrict ourselves to symmetric strategies in symmetric models, no renegotiation proof equilibrium exists except for the infinite repetition of the one-shot equilibrium.

This approach to renegotiation in infinitely repeated games is not only fairly intractable for applied work, it also is a conceptually questionable approach to renegotiation. Essentially it allows firms to renegotiate to equilibria that can only be sustained by punishments that firms know they will renegotiate away from in the future. This means that renegotiation outcomes depend on noncredible threats, which is not a desirable feature for a theory of collusion with renegotiation. Pearce (1987) worked out a more satisfactory theory of renegotiation for symmetric punishment equilibria in symmetric games in which the colluding firms anticipate future renegotiation. Essentially it is imposed that any credible punishment cannot rely on future punishments that are more severe than itself. Hence Nash reversion is such a credible punishment. However, Pearce shows that renegotiation always leads to a punishment less severe than Nash reversion. Indeed, he proves that the whole equilibrium value set for symmetric equilibria converges to the monopoly outcome as the discount factor goes to 1. Abreu, Pearce, and Stacchetti (1993) extend this theory to allow for asymmetric strategies in symmetric games. The framework the authors provide can be used to assess how much an analysis of renegotiation would add to our understanding of collusion.

Should we expect the theoretical conclusions drawn from the standard literature to be robust under the more realistic assumption of renegotiation? Note first that the incentive constraint for the highest sustainable collusive prices is not affected directly by renegotiation. Only the incentive constraint for punishment prices is replaced by a renegotiation condition. This condition means that the value of the continuation game in the most severe punishment equilibrium is very different from that in the standard theory.

Qualitatively the renegotiation condition should matter very little when we analyze asymmetries among firms. Again, firms with the most extreme incentives will be the ones that most constrain outcomes. But there is also some hope that in general the comparative statics of collusion will remain qualitatively robust more generally. Recall that many results in collusion theory can be derived robustly because the change of punishment at an optimal punishment equilibrium is of smaller order than the changes in the incentives to deviate from collusion on the Pareto frontier of the equilibrium value set. The results from equilibria when punishments are generated from Nash reversion are not robust precisely because this is not true for Nash reversion. What makes optimal punishment equilibria more robust is that punishments are front loaded. This feature of optimal punishments is preserved, even with renegotiation constraints, so many of the robust results should carry over to the renegotiation concept of Pearce.

3.2.2 Bargaining Inefficiencies

Most arguments made in the policy literature on why collusion might not work arise from claims that firms have difficulties in coming to an agreement and that the extent of the difficulties can be predicted. Indeed often there is an implicit claim that certain industry characteristics will prevent firms from reaching the Pareto frontier of the equilibrium value set. For example, Dick (2002) writes:

..., there is a tendency for it to be harder to reach and sustain a consensus on price, outputs, or market allocations, the larger is the number of suppliers who must be brought together....

This quote presents a version of the traditional argument that conflicts of interest would make bargaining harder and that increasing the number of bargainers increases conflicts of interest. Basic bargaining theory under symmetric information does not support that theory. It predicts that players will achieve a point on the Pareto frontier of the equilibrium value set. Afterall, if there is a Pareto superior outcome, firms should continue bargaining. In bargaining models with sequential offers we will therefore always see agreement on the Pareto frontier (see Rubinstein 1982). Games with simultaneous offers have a plethora of efficient equilibria but also inefficient mixed strategy equilibria. In a very simple coordination game with conflict of interest, Farrell (1987) showed that for the symmetric mixed strategy equilibrium, conflict of interest will delay agreement because bargainers become more unyielding. More important, he demonstrated that there is a positive probability of disagreement even at the limit, since bargaining can continue forever. While nicely intuitive, the result is achieved through specific equilibrium selection. It relies on the inefficiency of simultaneous move bargaining.

More satisfactory models of bargaining that can lead to inefficient outcomes arise when there are asymmetries in information. These asymmetries exist when firms are uncertain about their rivals' costs, demand information, and discount factors. Cost asymmetries can affect both the set of sustainable collusive strategies and the bargaining. Indeed the two cannot be nicely separated. Kihlstrom and Vives (1992) have addressed a related problem in which they look for agreements in which firms truthfully report their unobserved costs before engaging in an agreement. However, a centralized agency in their model makes bargaining unnecessary. To my knowledge, the problem of integrating in the same model bargaining over collusive agreements and incentive compatibility of collusive agreements under the condition of asymmetric information has not yet been resolved. In standard bargaining models with asymmetric information, inefficiencies arise only if there is uncertainty about gains from trade between parties. This means that one of the parties must find it sufficiently likely that its profits are higher when there is no agreement. Applying this idea to the more complicated issue of bargaining over a collusive agreement is difficult. But the simple bargaining model suggests that extreme cost realizations should trigger bargaining breakdown. We should also see bargaining breakdown when a firm makes significant cost or product improvements that it cannot demonstrate to its competitor. This prediction is very different from that of the standard collusion model. In the standard model extreme unobserved cost realizations lead to deviations from the collusive agreement, potentially followed by a price war. If there are bargaining inefficiencies, asymmetries should lead to *bargaining* breakdown.[13]

Note that the reference to bargaining theory does limit the ways in which arguments about bargaining inefficiencies can be reasonably made. For example, it is sometimes argued that it is more difficult to come to an agreement about collusion in differentiated goods industries because firms are uncertain about how closely goods are substitutable. That alone should not prevent an efficient bargain. Only *private* information about substitutability, meaning problems of asymmetric information, can generate inefficient bargaining outcomes.

We come next to the most important question of whether a merger changes the efficiency of bargaining among colluding firms in a way that can be systematically predicted. Only in this case can we use arguments about bargaining difficulties as theoretical support for policy recommendations. Dick (2002), for example, argues that as more firms attempt to collude, bargaining inefficiencies are more likely to arise. However, at least to my knowledge, there is little theoretical research that can back up such a claim. It is quite conceivable that in bargaining with asymmetric information, the merger of two independent bargaining entities into a single entity would increase the problem of asymmetric information and thus the scope for inefficiencies in the bargaining process. Furthermore, even if Dick's claim were true, it is not clear that the impact of a merger on the bargaining inefficiencies would necessarily be large. Suppose adding one firm to the bargain would significantly increase the probability of no agreement being reached. Then a subset of firms can still exclude this firm from the collusive bargain and obtain a higher probability of achieving agreement. Excluding a firm with $1/n$ share in the productive assets in the market will typically have a small effect on the collusive outcome. Hence a single merger will not necessarily have a very large impact on the bargaining out come.

3.2.3 Complexity

Without doubt, complexity is an important issue in collusion, but the theoretical literature has not successfully incorporated complexity into the analysis. Collusive strategies immediately raise a complexity problem because they have to specify activities conditional on past behavior for an infinite horizon. However, the literature on infinitely repeated games has taught us that optimal collusive rules are surprisingly simple (see Abreu, Pearce, and Stacchetti 1990). Furthermore these rules do not call for conditioning on precise actions of competitors but on aggregate variables. Since aggregate information does extremely well in sustaining simple collusive rules, it is not very plausible that mergers would reduce the complexity of formulating collusive rules in an industry. This does not mean that complexity does not matter for collusion. For example, in markets with significant uncertainty, state contingent collusive rules are most efficient but complexity may make it impossible to achieve such state contingencies in the collusive agreement. Nevertheless, often inefficient collusive rules are more harmful than efficient ones, so that it cannot be claimed that such complexities make policy intervention less important.

Most arguments supporting the claim that complexity limits collusion therefore quite naturally focus on the ability to achieve an agreement and monitor it, not the incentive to comply with an agreement. One typical argument, found in Scherer and Ross (1990), is that product heterogeneity can generate complexity that makes it difficult to come to an agreement. But is it plausible that a merger changes the degree of complexity in such an industry? Consider my 2004 model (Kühn 2004). In it a merger combines the product lines of two formerly independent firms, but the merger does not change the number of products. Agreement still has to be achieved over the same number of differentiated products, making it implausible that complexity has changed. The example shows how important it is to have a clear measure of complexity to assess the link between a merger and the degree of complexity of collusive contracting.

A related claim is that collusion on multiple dimensions creates more complexity, making collusion harder to sustain. Take *New York v. Kraft General Foods*. The court observed that manufacturers in the ready-to-eat breakfast cereal industry compete on price, quality, product innovation, promotions, and advertising. They argued that "for collusion to be successful it would have to control most or all of these forms of competition." The court thought this observation implied that anticompetitive coordinated effects were unlikely. The court may be right that complexity in this case makes it difficult to collude on all dimensions of interaction. However, the problem with the argument is that welfare reducing collusion does *not* require firms to collude on all dimensions on which they interact. For example, take a market in which firms compete in prices and demand enhancing (but completely dissipative) advertising. Suppose that the market is too complex for firms to reach agreement in both variables but that agreement in prices can be reached. Since advertising incentives are greater with higher margins, advertising intensity will increase with the collusive agreement on prices. This is socially worse than complete collusion. With full collusion the same prices would be obtained in our example, but the firms would agree on making no advertising expenditures. While complexity could well have an impact on the collusive agreement achieved in a market with multidimensional interactions, the policy conclusion that complexity makes collusion unsustainable is entirely wrong. Complexity of the kind discussed cannot exclude the existence of coordinated effects of mergers.

Arguments on complexity are hard to make operational because the degree of complexity is difficult to define in the first place. Beyond this fundamental problem my discussion shows that complexity may not be affected by mergers. There are furthermore potentially other ways to structure collusive agreements that greatly mitigate the issue of complexity.

3.2.4 Incomplete Contracts

Complexity can cause collusive contracts to be incomplete. Often collusive agreements are incomplete in the sense that responses to shocks in the environment are not agreed upon. This may in fact be of less consequence to firms' ability to collude than one may think. When firms cannot fully specify to react to future demand shocks, the contracts can nevertheless be completed by a rule that requires firms to come to an explicit understanding before they adjust to such shocks. Simple rules for such negotiations and how firms are compensated for past adverse events are sufficient to sustain an agreement that looks like a complete collusive contract.

Contractual incompleteness may therefore primarily create the need for firms to meet regularly and negotiate over contingencies that had not previously been considered. In contrast to renegotiation in a standard model of repeated games, renegotiation in an incomplete contracts setting can increase the profits obtained by colluding firms. What are the implications of this for a coordinated effects analysis? The main point is that contractual incompleteness does not prevent coordinated effects from mergers because firms can develop simple ways of dealing with incompleteness problems.

3.2.5 Tacit Collusion

A particularly difficult problem for coordinated effects analysis in merger cases is tacit collusion. Traditionally economists have not made any distinction between explicit collusion and implicit collusion, since the incentive constraints describing the sustainable outcomes under collusion do not depend on whether coordination is achieved through explicit or implicit means. However, from experimental evidence we know that in the absence of communication (i.e., in the absence of explicit bargaining over outcomes) coordination games are often inefficiently resolved (see Van Huyck, Battalio, and Beil 1990 and the discussion of its implication for communication in collusion in Kühn 2001). As this evidence shows, considerations of risk dominance often result in the selection of very inefficient outcomes from the point of view of the firms. This is because gambling on others to play a collusive strategy depends on the reasoning of others, so a firm risks loosing a lot of money if the reasoning of other firms is different. Setting lower prices will guarantee positive sales revenues in a much larger set of circumstances.

In the absence of explicit negotiation there is therefore no reason to expect that firms play an equilibrium on the Pareto frontier of the value set. Unfortunately, we have currently no theoretical framework that can help us predict what firms will play in the absence of communication opportunities when they are concerned about strategic risk. This means that the predictions we obtain from the framework of standard collusion theory may not have any relevance in the context of tacit collusion.

It is also questionable whether optimal punishment strategies can be expected under tacit collusion. For firms optimal punishment strategies may be very difficult to learn. Firms may therefore reasonably revert to one-shot Nash equilibrium behavior after a deviation. Note that this does not mean that the comparative statics of collusion with Nash reversion punishments is a good model for tacit collusion. An assumption of Nash punishments does not eliminate the strategic uncertainty I discussed above.

This state of the theory is particularly problematic when considering the coordinated effects of mergers. Negotiations among firms about future conduct are already prosecuted under antitrust law as explicit collusion. To prevent spontaneous understandings where there is no explicit communication (i.e., tacit collusion), is therefore the primary purpose of coordinated effects analysis in mergers. It is precisely for this set of problems that we do not have a theoretically satisfactory framework of analysis.

3.3 Empirical Regularities on Collusion and Coordinated Effects

In this section we examine to what extent the insights into the incentives for collusion produced by the theoretical literature are supported empirically. There are two issues to consider. First the empirical literature helps us assess which factors undermining or facilitating collusion are of particular importance. This can help us identify the market characteristics that make collusion unlikely and, as a consequence, coordinated effects of mergers small. The second, and more important issue, is to ask whether coordinated effects from horizontal mergers have been detected empirically, and if so, whether they are large or small.

3.3.1 Cross-sectional Investigations of Factors Facilitating Collusion

Methodological Issues   The literature on cross-sectional studies of collusion has recently been surveyed by Levenstein and Suslow (2002). There are a number of fundamental methodological problems in this literature. First, measuring cartel success cross-sectionally is difficult. A few studies have attempted to measure profits or to estimate Lerner indexes (see Eckbo 1976; Griffin 1989). Other studies rely generally on cartel duration (see Posner 1970; Suslow 1991; Dick 1996). The reasoning is that the period until cartel breakdown gives an indication about the factors that facilitate or hinder collusion. One problem with such studies is that cartel breakdown is hard to define exactly. For example, in theory a period of lower prices does not necessarily mean that a cartel has broken down. On the other hand, a lack of formal cartel structure may be consistent with an effective continuation of a cartel. There is considerable informal evidence that formal cartel structures can predetermine an industry's behavior when such structures are abandoned. But more fundamentally there is an issue of how to interpret the estimated impact of industry characteristics on cartel duration. Is it reasonable to think that the factors that theoretically make cartels more difficult to sustain will lead to shorter cartel duration? The answer is no! One important reason derives from a simple endogeneity problem. Collusion is easier to sustain (in most models) the smaller markup. If the ease of collusion directly maps into cartel duration, then firms have a trade-off between aiming for high markup and short-duration cartels and aiming for low markup and long-duration cartels. What exactly does cartel duration tell as to the presence of such a trade-off?

An alternative to duration analysis is to look at the types of changes in the market environment that precipitate the end of a cartel. This can tell us something about the type of characteristics that make *continued* collusion difficult. This means that one estimates the probability of cartel breakdown in the next period conditional on current market characteristics. The question asked would not be: What characteristics imply shorter duration? Instead we should ask: Which changes in characteristics precipitate the breakdown of collusion? This approach would use the impact of changes in the environment to identify the variables that affect the ability of firms to collude. Duration analysis instead focuses on the persistent features of the industry to predict whether the duration of collusion will be long or short. While I am not aware of papers that follow the approach of making inferences about factors facilitating collusion, case studies of collusion as reported by Levenstein and Suslow (2002) have precisely this flavor.[14] Such studies could potentially provide clearer insights into the main factors affecting collusion than duration analysis.

A second problem of a large subset of studies is that they rely heavily on data about DOJ enforcement actions against cartels (see Posner 1970; Hay and Kelley 1974; Asch and Seneca 1975; Fraas and Greer 1977). Cartels are included in the data set if there has been a DOJ enforcement action. This approach can lead to important sample selection biases in two different directions. On the one hand, if some market characteristics make it easier to detect collusion, these characteristics will be overrepresented in the sample. On the other hand, if investigation decisions condition on economic criteria about the likelihood of collusion, the enforcement effort will be concentrated on industries in which collusion is considered more likely. Cartels with characteristics that are thought to make collusion unlikely are therefore likely to be less scrutinized and underrepresented in enforcement actions. Some of the literature has avoided this problem by studying legal international cartels. The cleanest data set for these purposes is that of Dick (1996) who has analyzed legal cartels under the Webb-Pommerene Export Trade Act. These cartels are legal in the sense that they were allowed to be freely formed but their cartel agreements were not enforced in court. Work by Suslow (1991) on international commodity cartels and by Jacquemin, Nambu, and Dewez (1981) similarly has avoided the selection bias. However, both papers suffer from the problem that the cartels in question are often assisted by governments so that agreements are coordinated. These studies are probably best interpreted as looking for characteristics that reduce the firms' ability to reach a cartel agreement. They give no information about the ability to sustain a cartel.

The Main Regularities Despite the potential methodological problems the studies document a number of important results for the analysis of coordinated effects of mergers.

Heterogeneity between Colluding Firms In the studies that look at cartel profitability as the measure of success, heterogeneity between firms is a main explanatory variable. Eckbo (1976) finds that successful cartels tend to consist of firms with similar costs, whereas Griffin (1989) finds that cartels made up of a small number of similar sized firms tend to raise price. Surprisingly, duration studies do not look at heterogeneity between firms. However, these papers give examples of cartel breakdown that support the idea of heterogeneity playing a crucial role. For example, Dick (1996) reports that the Potash Export Association broke up because of conflicts of interest between producers with Canadian and without Canadian deposits. The explanation for this conflict reveals that such problems arise precisely because the incentives of firms started to differ: "In view of their plentiful new supply, certain firms began to chafe at the quotas assigned to them." This is the typical kind of heterogeneity in assets for which the theoretical work predicts difficulties for collusion. A closer look at the work by Eckbo (1976), Griffin (1989), and Suslow (1991) on the causes for cartel breakdown reveals that some of their categories, like "cheating and disagreement" and "external shock," also capture heterogeneity driving cartel breakdown. Indeed a more systematic look at heterogeneity may reveal that many categories that are routinely studied simply proxy for forms of heterogeneity in the incentives. Other case study work that explicitly looks at heterogeneity supports this view. For example, Alexander (1997) has shown in a case study of the pasta industry in the 1930s that under the National Recovery Administration heterogeneity in cost structure led to the breakdown of cooperation. This relationship between heterogeneity and collusion is probably the most established regularity in the empirical literature.

Monitoring and Demand Uncertainty Case studies indicate that cartels also fail because of monitoring problems. This observation fits well with formal econometric results by Suslow (1991) and Dick (1996). They find that demand uncertainty strongly undermines cartel duration. Suslow, in particular, finds that "demand uncertainty is the most important single variable in explaining cartel contract duration." Again, this finding is supportive of the theory by showing that monitoring the environment is critical for successful collusion.

On the other hand, Levenstein and Suslow (2002) document contradicting evidence between studies in the measured impact of unanticipated demand shocks. If imperfect monitoring models predict collusive behavior well, unanticipated demand shocks should trigger the break down of collusion. Suslow (1991) obtains this result in her data set. However, Dick (1996) obtains a result that unanticipated demand shocks have insignificant effects. A close look reveals that this result is fully consistent with collusion theories under imperfect monitoring. The theory relates to unanticipated shocks in industry-specific demands. With such shocks firms cannot distinguish perfectly between deviations from collusion and periods of low demand. However, Dick uses data on unanticipated shocks to the aggregate economy. If firms have low demand in an industry, this reflects widespread low demand, which makes it unlikely that the decrease of demand comes from an industry-specific shock. Dick's result is therefore perfectly consistent with imperfect monitoring models of collusion.

Imperfect observability and high demand uncertainty can therefore safely be considered criteria that would make coordinated effects of mergers unlikely. Note, however, that these results give no indication whether a merger can significantly facilitate monitoring.

Market Share of the Cartel   That a large market share facilitates the stability of a cartel appears to be a robust result. Eckbo (1976) finds his measure of cartel success increased in the market share of the cartel. Similarly Dick (1996), Marquez (1994), and Suslow (1991) find that market share significantly increases cartel duration. Nevertheless, these results seem to be of less relevance for the coordinated effects of mergers. The question that remains open is what exactly causes an industry configuration in which a small subset of firms colludes leaving the rest of the industry outside the cartel. In Kühn (2004), I suggest that effective collusion will only occur between relatively homogeneous firms. A small market share of the cartel is then simply a reflection of the underlying heterogeneity among the cartelized and noncartelized firms. The analysis of coordinated effects of mergers should therefore focus on any change in heterogeneity resulting from the merger instead of the pre-merger market share of the cartel.

Anticipated Demand Changes   Dick (1996) demonstrates how well collusion theory predicts the impact of anticipated demand changes. In his sample he shows that cartels are more likely to break up at anticipated downturns in demand. This contradicts the standard practitioner's view that there is more danger of collusion in downturns, but accords with the theory that declining demand makes collusion difficult (see Haltiwanger and Harrington 1990).

Barriers to Entry   An important feature of any market is ease of market entry. Collusion appears to break down quickly where barriers to entry do not exist (see Eckbo 1974; Griffin 1989). This result is not necessarily supported by collusion theory. In theory, firms can agree to respond extremely aggressively to entry, which would deter any entry. Optimal collusion can therefore create barriers to entry endogenously (see Stenbacka 1990). Entry is then an important criterion to assess the scope for coordinated effects. However, the literature only shows that breakdown of collusion follows entry. It does not show when entry is likely to occur.

Number of Firms   There is significant disagreement among empincal studies as to the impact of the number of firms on the duration of collusion. The number of firms is one of the variables where it matters for the interpretation of many studies, that the data sets come from cartel interventions. Posner (1970) suggested that his sample was biased toward relatively large cartels because the detection of large cartels is easier. He used this selection bias to explain why he found longer cartel durations for markets with a larger number of firms. On the other hand, Dick (1996), whose data set on Webb-Pommerene cartels does not generate such a selection bias nevertheless obtains the same result. Although surprising, especially in light of cartel destabilizing role of entry, both results are consistent with the theory when goods are homogeneous and capacity constraints matter.

3.3.2   Direct Tests of Coordinated Effects of Mergers

There is almost no empirical research on coordinated effects of mergers. The only exception to my knowledge is Ganslandt and Norbäck (2004). These authors study mergers in the Swedish retail market for gasoline over the period 1986 to 2002. In this period there were several mergers and restructurings in the industry that significantly changed concentration. The authors estimate aggregate demand for gasoline in Sweden. Marginal costs are approximated by wholesale gasoline prices plus taxes. This allows the authors to compute the average Lerner index. By standard arguments multiplying the Lerner index by the estimated market demand elasticity generates a measure for the average behavior in the market. This can generally be expressed as a parameter that depends on market behavior and the Herfindahl index. The authors then estimate the dependence of the behavioral parameter on an index of market concentration, namely the Herfindahl index. If most of the variation in the Herfindahl index comes from mergers and restructurings, the coordinated effects of mergers can be identified.

Ganslandt and Norbäck find no effect of the Herfindahl index on the behavioral parameter. Theoretically that may not be surprising for two reasons. First, my numerical results in Kühn (2004) show that under coordinated effects price changes from relatively large asset reallocations can be extremely small. So it is very difficult to detect any such effect in the data. Second, the Herfindahl index will not only increase with greater concentration but also when market share dispersion is greater. According to the theoretical work by Compte et al. (2002) and Kühn (2004), market share dispersion is the main factor that will lead to market collusion difficulties. The absence of a systematic impact of the Herfindahl index in empirical work therefore does not prove that there are no coordinated effects of mergers (see Kühn 2002 for a discussion). However, the general empirical approach of Ganslandt and Norbäck could be adapted to estimate the impact of mergers using theory. For example, one could investigate the dependence of behavioral parameters on other variables.

Other work on "coordinated effects" has not directly analyzed mergers. Nevo (2001) and Slade (2004) propose a decomposition of the Lerner index in studies of the coordinated effects arising in differentiated goods markets. As in Ganslandt and Norbäck (2004), they take an observable measure of marginal cost to compute the Lerner index from data. From demand elasticity estimates and marginal costs it is possible to numerically compute the noncollusive Nash equilibrium for the market and to compare the hypothetical Lerner index from that exercise to the actual Lerner index obtained. The difference can be interpreted as the coordinated effect of the merger. Both Nevo (2001) for the American breakfast cereal industry and Slade (2004) for UK brewing find very small estimates for coordinated effects in this sense. Slade goes a little further by suggesting to estimate the impact of mergers on the difference between the realized Lerner index and the Lerner index of the one-shot Nash equilibrium. This estimate can then be interpreted as the coordinated effects of mergers in differentiated goods industries.

All these approaches nevertheless rely on cost data, which is not always a valid representation of marginal cost. For example, some of Slade's estimations show that the realized Lerner index is smaller than the Bertrand-Nash benchmark. This may come from misspecification of demand, as is argued in the paper, but it can also be generated from excessively high marginal cost measures. For example, Slade's marginal cost measure includes a per unit advertising cost, which may well reflect fixed costs. The empirical evidence for coordinated effects from mergers appears therefore still to be weak.

3.4   Policy Approaches to Coordinated Effects

Both in Europe and in the United States the policy approach to coordinated effects has dramatically changed over time. Europe has only recently looked at coordinated effects of mergers starting with the *Kali and Salz* decision. The framework for coordinated effects was clarified only recently in the judgment of the Court of First Instance in the *Airtours* case. This decision showed that a systematic approach consistent with the theory of collusion had not been applied. US policy has always been concerned about coordinated effects. The use of the Herfindahl index in the merger guidelines was thought to capture this concern. Today it is clear that the Herfindahl is a poor measure of coordinated effects, since it implicitly considers asymmetric market structures to be less desirable than symmetric ones. The United States has recently had a thorough review of their practices of evaluating coordinated effects (see Kolasky 2002; Dick 2002). In this section, I discuss some policy approaches that have been suggested and the robustness of these approaches.

3.4.1   Should Coordinated Effects be Analyzed in Merger Proceedings?
To design a reasonable policy on coordinated effects, we first have to ask the question whether this should be a policy instrument at all. Antitrust policy already has a prohibition of collusive behavior. If large fines for collusion are possible then collusion can be deterred

perfectly. In such a world prevention of mergers because of coordinated effects can only be efficiency decreasing. Suppose that antitrust policy could deter all collusion because fines are high enough. If the competition authority does not take into account this fact, mergers would be blocked on the basis of coordinated effects, although there is no chance of collusion. Hence such policy can only have negative effects because efficiency enhancing mergers might be prohibited.

Any policy that requires intervention based on coordinated effects of mergers therefore has to answer the question: Why is ex ante intervention better than ex post fines? This challenge to the use of coordinated effects in merger policy has, to my knowledge, never been addressed. But the use of coordinated effects in merger policy implies that we must believe that there are systematic imperfections in enforcement policy against cartels that make it impossible for ex post intervention to create sufficient incentives to control collusion. One argument may be that punishments cannot be made harsh enough, for example, because of limited liability. But criminal penalties for managers involved in collusion are very severe. Although it is clear that not all collusion is deterred by the antitrust penalties in place, this argument is not compelling enough to use coordinated effects in merger policy. A more reasonable policy response may be to increase the penalties.

The strongest argument that supports a merger policy that considers coordinated effects is that, in the real world, collusion is impossible to prove in the absence of explicit coordination of conduct. (on the detection of cartels, see Harrington's chapter 6 in this volume). The main motivation for having a coordinated effects instrument in merger policy is to prevent tacit collusion. If we believe that this is true, our current policy approach to coordinated effects may be on weaker grounds than we think. As I have discussed, there is not yet a coherent theory that can give behavioral predictions for the impact of mergers on the conduct of tacitly colluding firms. While it is true that incentive compatibility constraints have to be satisfied for tacit collusion to be sustainable, behavior in the selected equilibrium will depend on the selection rule from the set of potential equilibrium outcomes. We currently know next to nothing about whether the predictions we can draw from standard collusion theory can be expected to hold under such circumstances.

In my further discussion below I will ignore this conceptual challenge to coordinated effects analysis in merger policy. Although most economists probably believe that such a policy is beneficial, it is important to keep in mind that this belief is not based on solid economic arguments and does not always take into consideration the whole range of policy options against collusion.

3.4.2 The Checklist Approach
In practice, the simplest approach to coordinated effects has been to ask the question whether collusion is easy or difficult to achieve in a market. The collusion-enhancing features or collusion-inhibiting features present in a market can, in principle, be determined from the literature on collusion. Coordinated effects analysis is then simply con-

ducted as going through a checklist of known industry characteristics. This approach has several disadvantages. First, it does not focus on the *change* induced by a merger. Coordinated effects are assumed to be present when a market has characteristics that make collusion likely. Such an approach would be reasonable if the elimination of a firm always increased the scope for collusion. However, theory has shown that this is not the case.

A second problem with checklist approaches is that the checklist criteria are hard to quantify. For example, how do we assess how "transparent" a market is? Is there some cutoff at which collusion gets very likely? How are different checklist criteria weighted? These problems require a lot of discretion in the use of such criteria so that the particular intuition of the person assessing the merger becomes decisive and not some objective criterion.

Some improvements on a simplistic checklist approach can be made by recognizing that not all checklist criteria should have equal weight. Checklist criteria should have more weight when a criterion is known to be relatively robust theoretically and to have credible empirical support. As I noted earlier, this is not the case for arguments about market homogeneity. Likewise the oft-stated criterion that collusion is more likely in declining markets contradicts the theory and is not confirmed by careful empirical study (see Dick 1996). On the other hand, arguments about monitoring, demand uncertainty, and market asymmetries have been carefully studied, are robust, and strongly confirmed by empirical evidence. Only such criteria should ever make a checklist.

Checklists essentially can only produce negative tests for coordinated effects. We know that under some circumstances collusion can be difficult to sustain, and in those circumstances we should exclude coordinated effects. Checklist criteria could be used to determine circumstances under which collusion is so unlikely that there should be a presumption that coordinated effects are unimportant. But we have no valid criterion to determine whether, for example, there is a sufficient degree of market transparency to make collusion unlikely. The only information that might help is hard evidence of past collusion, and this is rare in most coordinated effects cases. As a result a pure checklist approach sets an arbitrary standard for finding coordinated effects.

3.4.3 Mavericks and Other Ad hoc Empirical Tests

In the United States past practice has attempted to find simple empirical criteria that would indicate that coordinated effects are present. The criterion that has made it into the merger guidelines is that of "maverick." It is usually used as a label for a particularly aggressive competitor. Scheffman and Coleman (2003) write: "In simple terms, the significance of a maverick is significantly greater than would be indicated by its market share."[15] What exactly does that mean? Are we interested in firms irrationally setting low prices? What exactly are the criteria we can use to argue that a firm is a maverick?

Baker (2002) has made an attempt to add some discipline to the maverick analysis by focusing on the degree to which a candidate maverick firm constrains some set of firms in their ability to increase prices collusively. Baker's approach is, in principle, consistent with the theoretical analyses of asymmetries in asset holdings. For example, if a small firm is constraining collusive behavior, then a merger with that small firm will tend to facilitate collusion. This is called "elimination of a maverick" by Baker (2002). But other suggestions in Baker's paper are not quite as convincing in the view of the theory. For example, he argues that if the incentives of the maverick are not changed through a merger the merger should be deemed competitively neutral. Theoretically, however, the merger could increase the scope for collusion among other firms in the market and thus induce all firms, including the "maverick," to raise their prices. The degree of collusion could still be constrained by the presence of a firm with greater incentives to set lower prices, but the constraint does not ensure that prices will not move up. The analysis of Baker is appropriate if firms perfectly collude subject to the constraint by the maverick. But we should generally expect collusion to induce less than the profit-maximizing profits among the collusive group and therefore some scope for mergers to change the collusive incentives whether or not we identify a maverick. We will return to this issue when we come to the two-part test below.

While the maverick analysis of Baker has a rationale based on the theoretical analysis, other ad hoc empirical approaches, most important, Scheffman and Coleman (2003), rely on a leap of faith. Scheffman and Coleman take variation in prices across customers as evidence that collusion is difficult. However, such variation can be expected also from a monopolist discriminating among different customers. An optimal collusive agreement should provide for price variation as well. Indeed, when contracts are negotiated customer by customer, typical collusive agreements essentially determine a winner of each bidding game for a customer such that the bidding schemes allow prices to vary among contracts. Similar concerns arise when variability of pricing over time is taken as evidence against collusion. Variability of prices is likely to be seen in any market in which prices are individually negotiated with customers. This will even be the case in monopoly markets. Unless one has some evidence about losing bids, there is little information about the likelihood of collusion in the market.

Any analysis of list versus transaction prices is similarly ad hoc. Scheffman and Coleman point out that in their example transaction prices remain below list prices and tend to increase less than one to one with list prices. It is unclear what the implication of this observation for potential collusion is, given that there is no theory of how list and transaction prices would be related under competition or collusion. In effect it is unclear whether these authors consider the patterns they find as a lack of market transparency or as evidence for the absence of collusion. But the fundamental problem these analyses have is that they cannot help answer the fundamental question: What changes through the merger?

3.4.4 Discretionary Assessment of Changes to the Incentives to Collude

In contrast to the ad hoc empirical analysis à la Scheffman and Coleman (2003), the recent review (by the Department of Justice) of coordinated effects analysis has focused on the *changes* in collusive incentives due to a merger (see Dick 2002; Kolasky 2002). The approach suggested by the DOJ is, however, highly discretionary and relies exclusively on the accumulated empirical and anecdotal evidence. The problem of this approach is a lack of grounding in theory that would allow a better assessment of the robustness of claims.

One example is the discussion of asymmetries among firms, which the US review has placed firmly at the center of the analysis. This is in line with theoretical thinking. However, a lack of careful application of the theory is revealed in the details. For example, it is suggested to separately analyze the reduction in the number of firms as an anticompetitive effect and the potential increase in asymmetries as a countervailing effect. As has been shown in the discussion of the theoretical work on the subject there is no sense in which this separation can be made.

Second, the US review's bias toward empirical methods also limits the types of asymmetries considered. As I noted earlier, cost asymmetries are a well-documented factor hindering collusion in empirical studies. Based on these findings, Dick (2002) advocates considering the changes in cost asymmetries due to a merger. Such an assessment would require making predictions about the efficiency effects of the merger. In unilateral effects analysis there is a healthy tradition to separate the impact of asset transfers from the assessment of potential efficiencies generated by a merger. Separate analyses could be done in coordinated effects analysis as well. For example, the impact of capacity consolidation or product line consolidation could be analyzed independently of potential cost advantages from a merger. This is a way to avoid conflating predictions about cost effects with predictions made on the basis of pre-merger market data.

Currently US practice does use predictions about the changes in costs to analyze coordinated effects. For example, in *US v. Premdor and Masonite* it was argued that firms had differing cost structures before the merger because some firms were vertically integrated and others firms were not. The competitive impact statement in the case claimed that vertical integration implied that cost structures would become more aligned as a result of the merger. As discussed previously, this claim does not necessarily follow from the theory of vertical integration. The argument in the *Premdor/Masonite* case therefore made assumptions about the efficiency effects of the merger in the coordinated effects analysis. A coordinated effects analysis could be much more disciplined if it were to separate effects that arise from the reassignment of assets for a given cost structure. As in unilateral effects analysis it can then be decided how much of a cost reduction is necessary to overcome anticompetitive effects.

While the analysis of changes in asymmetries among firms has solid grounding in theory, other changes in the incentives to collude suggested by Dick (2002) have less solid grounding. Nevertheless, they have been used in US cases. For example, it has been suggested that mergers increase transparency in markets and thus facilitate collusion. Again, *Premdor/Masonite* is given as a leading example. However, as I noted earlier, it is unclear whether this argument can be made robustly. The relevant market transparency can go up or down as a result of the merger. Again the tendency in US practice is to base such arguments on pure intuition without solid theoretical or empirical support. This does not mean that there cannot be arguments that solidly support the point that market transparency is increased through a merger. But such arguments must depend on the particular features of a case.

Besides the focus on changes to collusion incentives the United States has retained arguments about market conditions that make collusion highly unlikely. Such arguments, however, can be problematic because arguments based on the incentives to comply with collusive agreements and arguments based on the problem of reaching agreement are not carefully separated. So there is little distinction between the former, for which we have solid theoretical frameworks, and the latter, about which we know very little. A reasonable policy has to acknowledge that arguments based on collusion incentives have a much stronger basis in economics than those about difficulties to reach agreement. But it appears that most frequently arguments are based on the problem of achieving agreement. An example is the *New York v. Kraft General Foods* case. It is a particularly worrying example of how arguments on complexity are abused. Multidimensional competition was treated in the *New York/Kraft* case as an impediment to collusion even though theory would suggest partial collusion as an alternative for firms. Indeed, as I noted earlier, partial collusion can have greater adverse effects than those of complete collusion.

What has emerged from the DOJ review reflected in Dick (2002) is a very discretionary set of arguments focusing on changes induced by a merger. But the approach lacks a clear set of screening criteria and empirical benchmarks. As a result it is hard for firms to predict whether coordinated effects will be a problem in a merger. Because it also dispenses with determining an order of magnitude of the effects of a merger on potential collusion, it is much weaker then Baker's (2002) empirical approach to "mavericks."

3.4.5 A System of Negative Tests and Selective Positive Criteria

In this section I propose a system of tests that are consistent with our current knowledge of the economics of coordinated effects and have advantages over pure discretion by reducing the regulatory risk for firms and limiting the scope for ad hoc reasoning. It is useful for policy toward coordinated effects in mergers to develop both negative tests (i.e., safe haven tests) and positive tests. A first step in a negative test is to identify features of the market that make collusion so unlikely, even after a merger, that there should be a presumption that coordinated effects cannot arise after a merger. A second step is to look for changes due to the merger in the market structure and to identify mergers that are unlikely to have substantial impact on the possibility of collusion.

Positive tests are much harder to establish. For this reason any positive test would have to rely to some degree on benchmarks establishing a presumption that tacit coordination is possible after a merger. Furthermore a positive test would require that the change in the ability to collude due to the merger should theoretically have significant impact. Because such a test is somewhat speculative in nature, only very conservative benchmarks for coordinated effects are warranted.

Potential Negative Tests I suggest a negative test along the lines of the definition of collective dominance advanced in the European Court of First Instance (CFI) in the judgment on the *Airtours* case. The judgment highlights the ability to punish and the feasibility of monitoring of rivals' actions. I structure this test to start with criteria that are least demanding of the data needed to verify.

First, certain features of the market can make the operation of a collusive mechanism highly unlikely. One such feature is tight capacity constraints. Then punishment mechanisms that would raise prices above the competitive level (given the capacities) will simply not be feasible. For example, I showed in Kühn (2001) that with irreversible capacity decisions, collusion in reducing capacity investments is not feasible in an important class of models. This type of economic result makes collusion qualitatively so unlikely that coordinated effects cannot be present in the industry.

Second, there is the issue of how easy it is to monitor the actions of rivals in the market. Again, this is something difficult to quantify. Nevertheless, it is possible to carefully document when decisions are essentially unobservable to rivals and when inferences about behavior are limited because of significant uncertainty in the market. Theory states that intransparent markets very significantly reduce the scope for collusion, and this is supported by evidence. On the other hand, there is no indication that high market transparency automatically implies high likelihood of coordinated effects. An analysis has to go way beyond the pure assertions of intransparency or transparency that have been made in most collective dominance cases in Europe. The CFI in the *Airtours* case, for example, very carefully checked how often rivals observed each other's interactions with hotels, showing that a careful analysis of market data can lead to a fairly convincing rejection of market transparency.

Third, there is the question whether the potentially collusive group can at all significantly increase prices. Here one should analyze by how much this potentially collusive group would raise prices if they could perfectly collude. This is just analogous to the price test for the merging firms, when we ask whether the merging firms would have an incentive to raise prices by at least 5 percent. Below 5 percent can be considered as a safe haven in that context, at which a potential price increase would not be considered significant. In a coordinated effects test, however, a somewhat higher safe haven benchmark should be set. The reason is that there exists no precise test to show how high a degree of collusion can be attained in a particular market setting. However, the incentive constraints on collusion will always make collusion to the joint optimum less likely than if the firms were a single entity. Furthermore the incentive constraints will tend to restrict optimal collusion to levels below full collusion. We should therefore never expect a collusive group to fully raise prices to the joint profit maximum. The safe haven benchmark should therefore be set above the 5 percent mark of a unilateral effects test. As in other safe haven tests it is a judgment call where to set this benchmark. At a minimum this would establish a negative test that has some qualitative justification, is in the spirit of Baker's (2002) maverick test, and could be anticipated by the parties in a merger.

The last point begs the question what should be considered the potential collusive group. For this purpose the recent theoretical literature is helpful (Compte et al. 2002; Kühn 2004). It has established that firms that are fairly similar have similar incentives to collude, whereas firms that are different in their assets will have a harder time to coordinate behavior. A potential collusive group should therefore have members that have sufficiently similar asset structures within the group but fairly different asset structures from firms outside the group. As I explain in Kühn (2001), it is appropriate to proxy the asset distributions among firms by their market share distributions. Think of firms that are within 10 or 20 percent of each other's sizes as "similar," but as "dissimilar" if one firm is, say, at least 50 percent larger than the other. Then define groups of firms as potentially collectively dominant if their market shares are similar enough within the group and sufficiently larger in size than firms outside that group. In Kühn (2001), I discuss why this procedure can best capture the qualitative results derived from the theory. Intuitively the justification comes from a striking difference in the effects of asset transactions among similar and different firms under collusion theory (see Kühn 2004). When firms are sufficiently similar, the effects of asset transactions are best described by the predictions based on collusion theory. For sufficient heterogeneity, the analysis predicts that all feasible behavior will be close to short-run best-response behavior. An alternative, but complementary approach, would be a type of maverick analysis that looks at which firms behave similarly in the markets and which firms differ. Then the collusive group should include those firms whose pricing behavior appears sufficiently similar.

Following this line of argument, the creation or strengthening of a jointly dominant position or the presence of coordinated effects of a merger can be rejected directly on the basis of an analysis of the change in asset distributions induced by the merger. If a merger makes the asymmetry between the largest and smallest firm in the candidate collectively dominant group of firms larger, profits for the colluding firms will go down (see Kühn 2004). If profits fall, the presumption is that the merger has not created significant coordinated effects, so it is very likely that the merger was motivated by other factors than anticompetitive effects. The increased asymmetry argument should therefore always be accepted as a defense against the claim of creating or strengthening a collective dominant position.

The list of negative tests should not be an inexhaustible checklist. Unless some comparative static result for collusion gives a strong indication of a low likelihood of a collusion-enhancing merger, the argument should not be considered. In particular, arguments about complexity, and the like, appear far too speculative to warrant inclusion in a negative tests list.

Potential Positive Tests   Developing a battery of safe haven tests that reject the assumption of collective dominance is relatively easy. However, it is much harder to develop reliable positive tests that provide economically reasonable evidence to conclude that collective dominance is strengthened or created. There are no market characteristics that guarantee that collusion in the market will be facilitated by a merger. While we can sometimes exclude collusion for theoretical reasons, there is no way to assert that collusion is the only possible outcome under some circumstances. This makes valid negative and positive tests very asymmetric in structure.

What could be attempted is a combination of tests that assess the price-increasing potential of a merger due to collusion and the likelihood that the price increase can credibly be realized given the asset transactions involved in the merger. First, we can use the same analysis as that suggested for one of the negative tests: measure how much the firms in the jointly collusive group would increase their prices if they could fully collude and how other firms would best respond. This gives the maximal potential for anticompetitive effects. Mergers should be more readily blocked the larger that potential is. Currently there is no such evaluation at all.

Second, we need some test for the likelihood of collusion in the group postmerger. This is difficult to achieve because this is a counterfactual that cannot be directly inferred from pre-merger market behavior. Currently there is no other choice but to resort to some market share distribution benchmark for which we regard the achievement of collusion highly plausible. Because of the speculative nature of such a benchmark, this would have to be conservative to avoid allowing private beliefs about market power to have undue effects on merger decisions. It has been suggested (see Kühn 2001) that for two-firm dominance such a benchmark should not be below 60 percent market share and a fairly symmetric distribution of market shares between the two firms. For larger potentially collectively dominant groups such market share tests should be much tighter. Certainly cross-sectional empirical work assessing the impact of asset distribution on collusive behavior in the market could help determine such benchmarks.

Finally, a systematic procedure could also apply the basic theoretical findings to assess the change in incentives to collude. Evidence of a significant accretion of market share to the collectively collusive group, and/or an increase in the symmetry of the market positions of the largest and smallest firm in the collusive group after the merger, can be used to raise the concerns about coordinated effects. Arguments on increased market transparency due to a merger could be included at this stage if a theoretically robust argument can be made for such claims. Purely intuitive arguments should generally be rejected.

The positive test I suggest here is clearly not an entirely satisfactory test. My hope is that economic research will refine such a testing procedure over time. However, the proposed positive test would impose some discipline on the analysis of coordinated effects.

3.4.6 Simulating Coordinated Effects of Mergers

A more sophisticated approach to the positive tests, as suggested in the previous section, is to simulate the coordinated effects of mergers. Analogously to a unilateral effects simulation this would model the dynamic equilibrium of the market (given some selection from the value set) and evaluate the change induced by a change in the most relevant assets.

A first stab at simulation was taken by Compte et al. (2002). They calibrated their simple model of collusion on the data from the *Nestle Perrier* case and calculated how much the minimal discount factor necessary to support collusion changed. This way they were able to show which remedies were likely to be effective and which would have been required to reduce the anticompetitive effects of the merger. This is precisely the type of analysis for which a simulation exercise can help: the assessment of relative merits of different remedies.

The model of Compte et al. (2002) cannot predict price effects in the market. But a more general a numerical exercise analogous to the unilateral merger analysis as, for example in Nevo (2001) for differentiated products may be feasible. This procedure involves first estimating demand in the industry. Then the Nash equilibrium assumption is replaced by the assumption that firms play a collusive equilibrium determined by Nash bargaining over the equilibrium value set. Because the dependence of profits on specific asset is explicitly modeled, this alternative behavioral assumption allows us to estimate costs. The impact of a change in the asset distribution can then be numerically simulated. This approach involves a complicated merging of techniques for calculating equilibrium value sets and estimation methods. Its value most likely will not come from its implementation in specific cases. However, such simulations may allow us a better understanding of the orders of magnitude of coordinated effects of mergers. There is as yet no evidence that these effects are significant and better evidence on this score is important to assess how aggressive policies towards coordinated effects should be.

3.5 Conclusion

In this chapter, I reviewed the emerging literature on coordinated effects of mergers and contrasted it with policy practice. I have highlighted the fact that standard collusion theory does provide a fairly robust framework for the assessment of *explicit* collusion. However, I also showed that the foundations for policy arguments based on the "difficulty of reaching" agreements are poorly founded in economic research. In particular, current theory does not allow any convincing conclusions on the issue of tacit collusion, which may be thought of as central for the application of coordinated effects analysis to mergers. In this sense much of what has been written on coordinated effects is tentative and a very conservative approach to the use of coordinated effects analysis in mergers is appropriate.

Notes

1. A popular question on the change in equilibrium behavior is: How does the behavior in an equilibrium in the interior of the equilibrium value set change when the environment changes? This is not a meaningful question. First, for any equilibrium in the interior, the incentive constraints are (generically) strictly slack. A small change in the environment will leave them slack. There is nothing that will induce firms that have chosen this equilibrium to change their behavior. On the other hand, firms can change to a different equilibrium, but there is no systematic prediction that theory can make about such a switch without a theory of equilibrium selection.

2. The specific bargaining solution assumed does not appear to have much influence on the qualitative comparative statics obtained (see Kühn and Rimler 2006).

3. See also the precursor paper by Kühn and Motta (2001) and the discussion of coordinated effects in Motta (2004).

4. Paolo Buccirossi has suggested to me that considering Nash reversion may be natural in the context of *tacit* collusion. I discuss this issue in section 3.4.

5. One interpretation is that standard collusion theory does not give us a good model of collusion. There seems to be some evidence that there are starting points for distinctly collusive periods and possibly even endpoints. These points cannot be explained by standard collusion theory.

6. A discussion of this literature can also be found in Motta (2004).

7. While the details of the changed incentives in Compte et al. (2002) and Vasconcelos (2004) are different, the reasoning is similar in those models.

8. Increasing fragmentation in the product lines model of Kühn (2004) does not have this effect. It is therefore specific to homogeneous goods markets in which the main assets are productive capital.

9. Note, however, that a finding that a market is transparent says little about the likelihood of collusion and nothing about how the likelihood of collusion will change after a merger.

10. Baker (2002) is more careful in restricting his definition of a maverick to the ability of the maverick firm to limit the ability of groups of others to raise prices. I discuss further below how the analyses he suggests can be fit into a broader framework consistent with the theory.

11. This is another example for how misleading the analysis of Nash reversion can be. Under Nash reversion an increase in cross-shareholdings increases the profits from a one-shot Nash equilibrium. Hence the intensity of punishment is reduced with cross-shareholdings. For this reason earlier authors (e.g., Malueg 1992) had pointed out countervailing effects of cross-shareholdings on collusion. No such countervailing effects exist when we look at the whole set of equilibria.

12. Think of two substitute products where one is becoming more popular than the other. Or consider a vertically differentiated market in which the marginal valuation of quality increases with income. The relative movement in demand could then be generated from a positive trend in income.

13. There are other ways in which departures from simple bargainig models permit the breakdown of agreement or the selection of inefficient outcomes in equilibrium. For example, Anderlini and Felli (2001) show in a simple alternating offer bargaining game that transaction costs will often preclude the existence of efficient outcomes. They point out that there is a holdup problem in alternating offer bargaining games with transaction costs. Once the transaction costs are paid, the proposer does not have to make a proposal that covers the transaction costs of the responder. This theory has little bite when the transaction costs are small relative to the potential gain and its relevance to collusion is then unclear.

14. There are studies that look at the causes of breakdown. However, they do not look at changes in variables that are generally considered to have an impact on collusion. Instead they look at categories like "cheating and disagreement," "external shock," and "entry and substitution" (see Levenstein and Suslow 2002).

15. To confuse matters even more, Scheffman and Coleman (2003) categorize the "maverick theory" as a nonunilateral effects theory that is not a part of coordinated effects. Since the logic of equilibrium theory does not allow

for such a category (either we look at the equilibrium price change from a merger in a static equilibrium or we look at it in an infinite horizon equilibrium), I will treat the maverick concept as an aspect of coordinated effects.

References

Abreu, D. 1988. On the theory of infinitely repeated games with discounting. *Econometrica* 56: 383–96.

Abreu, D., D. Pearce, and E. Stacchetti. 1990. Toward a theory of discounted repeated games with imperfect monitoring. *Econometrica* 58: 1041–63.

Abreu, D., D. Pearce, and E. Stacchetti. 1993. Renegotiation and symmetry in repeated games. *Journal of Economic Theory* 60: 217–40.

Alexander, B. 1997. Failed cooperation in heterogeneous industries under the national recovery administration. *Journal of Economic History* 57: 322–44.

Asch, P., and J. J. Seneca. 1975. Characteristics of collusive firms. *Journal of Industrial Economics* 23: 223–37.

Baker, J. B. 2002. Mavericks, mergers, and exclusion: Proving coordinated competitive effects under the antitrust laws. *New York University Law Review* 77: 135–203.

Budd, C., C. Harris, and J. Vickers. 1993. A model of evolution of duopoly: Does the asymmetry between firms tend to increase or decrease? *Review of Economic Studies* 60: 543–73.

Coleman, M., and D. T. Scheffman. 2003. Quantitative analyses of potential competitivce effects from a merger. *George Mason Law Review* 12(2): 319–70.

Compte, O., F. Jenny, and P. Rey. 2002. Capacity constraints, mergers, and collusion. *European Economic Review* 46: 1–29.

Deneckere, R. 1983. Duopoly supergames with product differentiation. *Economic Letters* 11: 37–42.

Dick, A. 2002. Coordinated interaction: Pre-merger constraints and post-merger effects. Mimeo. US Department of Justice. Available at ⟨http://www.crai.com/Agenda/Dick.pdf⟩.

Dick, A. 1996. When are cartels stable contracts. *Journal of Law and Economics* 39: 241–83.

Dick, A. 1996a. Identifying contracts, combinations and conspiracies in restraint of trade. *Managerial and Decision Economics* 17: 203–16.

Eckbo, P. L. 1976. *The Future of World Oil*. Cambridge: Ballinger.

Farrell, J. 1987. Cheap talk, coordination, and entry. *RAND Journal of Economics* 18: 34–39.

Farrell, J., and E. Maskin. 1989. Renegotiation in repeated games. *Games and Economic Behavior* 1: 327–60.

Farrell, J., and C. Shapiro. 1990a. Horizontal mergers: An equilibrium analysis. *American Economic Review* 80: 107–26.

Farrell, J., and C. Shapiro. 1990b. Asset ownership and market structure in oligopoly. *RAND Journal of Economics* 21: 275–92.

Feuerstein, S. 2005. Collusion in industrial economics: A survey. *Journal of Industry, Competition, and Trade* 5: 163–98.

Fraas, A. G., and D. Greer. 1977. Market structure and price collusion: An empirical analysis. *Journal of Industrial Economics* 26: 21–44.

Ganslandt, M., and P.-J. Norback. 2004. Do mergers result in collusion. Working paper 621. IUI, Stockholm.

Green, J., and R. Porter. 1984. Noncooperative collusion under imperfect price information. *Econometrica* 52: 87–100.

Griffin, J. M. 1989. Previous cartel experience: Any lesson for OPEC? In L. R. Klein and J. Marquez, eds., *Economics in Theory and Practice: An Eclectic Approach*. Dordrecht: Kluwer Academic, pp. 179–206.

Gilbert, C., and D. Newbery. 1982. Preemptive patenting and the persistence of monopoly. *American Economic Review* 72: 514–26.

Haltiwanger, J., and J. Harrington. 1991. The impact of cyclical demand movements on collusive behavior. *RAND Journal of Economics* 22: 89–106.

Harrington, J. 1989. Collusion among asymmetric firms: The case of different discount factors. *International Journal of Industrial Organization* 7: 289–307.

Harrington, J. 1991. The determination of price and output quotas in a heterogeneous cartel. *International Economic Review* 32: 767–92.

Hay, G. A., and D. Kelley. 1974. An empirical study of price fixing conspiracies. *Journal of Law and Economics* 17: 13–38.

Jacquemin, A., T. Nambu, and I. Dewez. 1981. A dynamic analysis of export cartels. *Economic Journal* 91: 685–96.

Jullien, B., and P. Rey. 2000. Retail price maintenance and collusion. Mimeo. University of Toulouse.

Kandori, M. 1992. The use of information in repeated games with imperfect monitoring. *Review of Economic Studies* 59: 581–93.

Kihlstrohm, R., and X. Vives. 1992. Collusion by asymmetrically informed firms. *Journal of Economics and Management Strategy* 1: 371–96.

Kolasky, J. W. 2002. Coordinated effects in merger review: From dead frenchmen to beautiful minds and mavericks. Mimeo. US Department of Justice.

Kühn, K.-U. 2001. Fighting collusion by regulating competition between firms. *Economic Policy* 32: 169–97.

Kühn, K.-U. 2002a. Reforming European merger review: Targeting problem areas in policy outcomes. *Journal of Industry, Competition, and Trade* 2: 311–64.

Kühn, K.-U. 2002b. Closing Pandora's box? Joint dominance after the Airtours judgement. In *The Pros and Cons of Merger Control*. The Swedish Competition Authority, Stockholm.

Kühn, K.-U. 2004. Coordinated effects of mergers in differentiated products markets. CEPR discussion paper 4769.

Kühn, K.-U. 2006. How market fragmentation can facilitate collusion. CEPR discussion paper 5948.

Kühn, K.-U., and M. Rimler. 2006. The comparative statics of collusion models. CEPR discussion paper 5742.

Kühn, K.-U., and M. Motta. 1999. The economics of joint dominance. Mimeo. University of Michigan.

Lambertini, L., and D. Sasaki. 1999. Optimal punishments in linear duopoly supergames with product differentiation. *Journal of Economics* 69: 173–88.

Levenstein, M., and V. Suslow. 2004. Studies of cartel stability: A comparison of methodological approaches. In P. Z. Grossman, ed., *How Cartels Endure and How they Fail: Studies of Industrial Collusion*, Cheltenham, UK: Edward Elgar, pp. 9–52.

Marquez, J. 1994. Life expectancy of international cartels: An empirical analysis. *Review of Industrial Organization* 9: 331–41.

McAfee, R. P., and M. Williams. 1992. Horizontal mergers and antitrust policy. *Journal of Industrial Economics* 40: 181–87.

Motta, M. 2004. *Competition Policy: Theory and Practice*. Cambridge: Cambridge University Press.

Nevo, A. 2001. Measuring market power in the ready-to-eat breakfast cereal industry. *Econometrica* 69: 307–42.

Nocke, V., and L. White. 2003. Do vertical mergers facilitate upstream collusion? Mimeo. University of Pennsylvania.

Pearce, D. 1987. Renegotiation proof equilibria: Collective rationality and intertemporal cooperation. Cowles Foundation discussion paper 855.

Posner, R. A. 1970. A statistical study of antitrust enforcement. *Journal of Law and Economics* 13: 365–419.

Ross, T. 1992. Cartel stability and product differentiation. *International Journal of Industrial Organization* 10: 1–13.

Rothschild, R. 1999. Cartel stability when costs are heterogeneous. *International Journal of Industrial Organization* 17: 717–34.

Scherer, F. M., and D. Ross. 1990. *Industrial Market Structure and Economic Performance*, 3rd ed. Boston: Houghton Mifflin.

Slade, M. E. 2004. Market power and joint dominance in U.K. brewing. *Journal of Industrial Economics* 52: 133–63.

Stenbacka, R. 1990. Collusion in dynamic oligopolies in the presence of entry threats. *Journal of Industrial Economics* 39: 147–54.

Suslow, V. 1991. Cartel contract duration: Empirical evidence from international cartels. Mimeo. University of Michigan.

Van Damme, E. 1989. Renegotiation-proof equilibria in repeated prisoners' dilemma. *Journal of Economic Theory* 47: 206–17.

Van Huyck, J. B., R. C. Battalio, and R. O. Beil. 1990. Tacit coordination games, strategic uncertainty, and coordination failure. *American Economic Review* 80: 234–48.

Vasconcelos, H. 2004. Tacit collusion, cost asymmetries, and mergers. *Rand Journal of Economics*, forthcoming.

Vives, X. 1999. Oligopoly Pricing: Old Ideas and New Tools. Cambridge: MIT Press.

Vickers, J. S. 1986. The evolution of market structure when there is a sequence of innovations. *Journal of Industrial Economics* 35: 1–12.

4   Competitive Effects of Vertical Integration

Michael H. Riordan

Vertical integration is an enduring topic for economics. The structure–conduct–performance perspective of the 1950s and 1960s viewed vertical integration suspiciously, worrying about exclusionary practices that foreclose competitors and leverage monopoly from one market to another. The Chicago school of the 1960s and 1970s rebutted these concerns by pointing out the weak microeconomic foundations of leverage theory, and explaining why vertical integration increases economic efficiency. Transaction cost economics of the 1970s and 1980s staked a middle ground, identifying new efficiency rationales for vertical integration, while cautioning that firms with market power might have strategic goals poorly aligned with consumer welfare (Williamson 1975, 1985). Most recently a new literature on vertical foreclosure (aka post-Chicago economics) applied game-theoretic tools to develop new theories of strategic vertical integration and identify circumstances in which vertical integration alters industry conduct to the detriment of competitors and consumers. The rich intellectual history of industrial organization economics thus reveals assorted approaches to the topic.

Vertical integration raises contentious issues for antitrust policy and industry regulation. Antitrust policy in the United States recognizes that a vertical merger can create incentives for anticompetitive foreclosure or facilitate collusion, while remaining mindful that vertical integration can achieve efficiencies (ABA 2003).[1] Vertical integration raises a similar conflict for the economic regulation of industries. Whereas foreclosure concerns offer a rationale to restrict the conduct of vertically integrated firms, faith in market efficiency and doubt about regulatory benevolence support a trend toward deregulation (Stigler 1971). Whereas Chicago school critiques of foreclosure theory and cautions about the difficulties of collusion (Stigler 1964) urge a permissive approach to vertical mergers and the regulation of vertically integrated industries, post-Chicago theories of harmful vertical integration nevertheless feature prominently in some recent merger reviews and regulatory proceedings.

My purpose in this chapter is to review the economics literature on the competitive effects of vertical integration, and assess its relevance for competition policy and industry regulation. Section 4.1 organizes my literature review around five major theories, after discussing some preliminary issues. The theories depend on assumptions both about the market power of firms to raise prices above costs and to exclude competitors, and about the power of contracts to control and align the incentives of parties. Two theories, dubbed "single monopoly profit" and "eliminating markups," derive from the Chicago school. Two other theories, "restoring monopoly power" and "raising rivals' costs," are from post-Chicago economics. The remaining theory, "facilitating collusion" has long roots in competition policy, but only recently began to receive a firmer grounding in the modern economic theory of collusion. Section 4.2 examines the relevance of these and related theories in the context of three recent cases. The first case is the acquisition of DirectTV, a distributor of video programming, by News Corp., a diversified media company (FCC 2004). The Federal Communications Commission (FCC) reviewed this vertical merger under its authority to approve the transfer of certain licenses. The FCC's conditional approval of the acquisition placed certain restraints on the conduct of the new vertically integrated firm. The second case is the airline computer reservation system (CRS) proceeding of the Department of Transportation (DOT 2004). CRSs provide information, booking, and ticketing services for scheduled airline flights. Airlines once owned these systems, but divested their ownership interests by the end of the proceeding. In the wake of vertical disintegration, the DOT allowed all regulations of the CRS industry to lapse. The third case is the acquisition of Masonite, a manufacturer of an intermediate good in the production of molded doors, by Premdor, a partially vertically integrated manufacturer of molded doors (*US v. Premdor* 2001). The Department of Justice (DOJ) agreed to the merger with a consent order requiring Masonite to divest one of its plants to a new entrant in the intermediate good market. Section 4.3 outlines a simple framework for the economic analysis of the competitive effects of vertical integration, based on a more elaborate framework in Riordan and Salop (1995). The simple framework is explained with reference to the three cases introduced in the previous section. Section 4.4 concludes with some general comments about the state of economic knowledge regarding the competitive effects of vertical integration.

4.1 Economic Analysis of Vertical Integration

4.1.1 Preliminary Issues

Vertical integration is the organization of successive production processes within a single firm, a firm being an entity that produces goods and services (Riordan 1990).[2] A firm can be interpreted as a unified ownership of assets used in production (Grossman and Hart 1986) and as a nexus of contracts linking its owners to factors of production, managers, and creditors (Jensen and Meckling 1976). The owners of a firm directly or indirectly control the use of assets, and they keep the profits from production after compensating other claimants. Thus vertical integration brings upstream and downstream assets and production under unified ownership and control.

There are varieties of vertical integration. Consider for illustration a supply chain in which raw materials and other inputs are used to produce an intermediate good, which in turn is a component input into the production of a final good; the final good is distributed to consumers through a retail channel. Forward vertical integration occurs when a firm expands the scope of its activities to both produce and distribute the final good. For example, shoe manufacturer Brown Shoe Company integrated forward when it acquired shoe retailer Kinney (*US v. Brown Shoe Co.*, 370 US 294, 1962). A firm integrates backward when it produces an intermediate good that is a component in the assembly of a final product. For example, Ford sought to acquire Autolite to produce the sparkplugs for its automobiles (*US v. Ford Motor Co.*, 405 US 562, 1972). A firm also integrates backward by producing materials or capital goods used in the production of a final output. For example, Alcoa acquired bauxite mines to supply its alumina refineries (*US v. Alcoa*, 377 US 271, 1945). Moreover vertical integration in either or both directions can be partial or full, depending on whether the firm produces all its requirements for an input, or distributes its final product exclusively through its own distribution channels. Vertical integration can also be partial if a firm acquires an ownership share of an upstream supplier or downstream customer, possibly with limited control rights (O'Brien and Salop 2000).

Vertical integration can occur by internal growth or by merger. A firm integrates backward internally by building its own facilities for manufacturing an intermediate good, or forward internally by creating its own distribution facilities. Vertical integration by investment in new productive assets usually expands markets, and therefore presumably does not raise competitive concerns. This is not to say that a vertically integrated market structure necessarily outperforms a non-integrated one; for industries subject to regulation, restrictions on the conduct of vertically integrated firms might even improve market performance. A firm also vertically integrates by acquiring productive assets from a firm already participating in a relevant upstream or downstream market, or by acquiring stock in a firm owning those assets. A vertical merger by asset acquisition or stock acquisition potentially raises competitive concerns, in which case conduct restrictions or a divestiture of assets might make acceptable an otherwise anticompetitive vertical merger.

Economic analysis demonstrates that the competitive effects of vertical integration depend on the structure of upstream and downstream markets. Among the most important elements of market structure is the market power of firms in the relevant industries. Market power is the profitable ability to raise price above cost or to exclude competitors, and is traced usually to conditions of industry concentration, product differentiation, or cost advantages. Durable market power that yields supra-competitive profits is protected by "barriers to entry," a label that applies generally to market conditions that prevent the erosion of supra-competitive profits by new entry (Bain 1956; DOJ 1997).[3] Vertical integration that fails to increase market power by eliminating competitors or raising entry barriers is unlikely to have adverse consequences for consumers.

An equally important element of market structure for analyzing vertical integration is the power of contracts to align incentives and control the conduct of firms. Generally, "contract power" refers to the ability of firms to commit credibly not to behave opportunistically (Williamson 1975, 1985, 1989), either via explicit legally enforceable contracts or via implicit contracts supported by self-enforcing behavioral norms (Baker, Gibbons, and Murphy 2002). If contracts have sufficient power to control conduct, then there is little scope for improvement by vertical integration. For example, under some circumstances non-linear pricing and appropriate vertical restraints can achieve similar profit-maximizing outcomes as vertical integration (Mathewson and Winter 1984). However, by closing gaps in incomplete contracts, common ownership enables production decisions to adapt better to market conditions (Williamson 1975) or to improve investment incentives (Grossman and Hart 1986; Hart and Moore 1990). To the extent that contracts are incomplete, vertical integration can alter incentives for opportunistic behavior in ways that increase market power.

Important issues surrounding the power of contracts concern the ability and incentive of upstream firms for price discrimination.[4] Price discrimination is infeasible if a supplier cannot control effectively the use of purchased quantities by limiting resale and preventing arbitrage (Tirole 1988). In the absence of price discrimination, upstream suppliers charge a uniform price for each unit sold to downstream customers. The ability to price discriminate can be a mixed blessing. On the one hand, the full exploitation of market power can require a more complicated pricing strategy than setting a uniform price, such as two-part tariffs or other forms of quantity discounting (Mathewson and Winter 1984). On the other hand, credible "most favored customer" clauses that limit price discrimination can control opportunistic behavior by an upstream supplier that otherwise might undermine its ability to extract monopoly profits from the downstream industry (Hart and Tirole 1990; O'Brien and Shaffer 1992; McAfee and Schwartz 1994; Rey and Tirole 2007). Such issues regarding the ability and incentive for price discrimination appear in various guises in the economic theories of the competitive effects of vertical integration reviewed below.

My review adopts a couple of simplifying assumptions for expositional convenience and clarity. First, there are well-defined relevant upstream and downstream product and geographic markets. Relevant markets include all products that are reasonably good demand substitutes. Market definition is the customary first step for market power analysis (DOJ 1997). Second, the objective of a firm is profit maximization. In particular, a vertically integrated firm aims to maximize the joint profit of its upstream and downstream operations. A corollary assumption is that vertical integration eliminates information asymmetries between the upstream and downstream divisions, thus enabling better coordination (Riordan 1990).[5]

4.1.2 Single Monopoly Profit

The Chicago school contends that an upstream monopolist protected by durable barriers to entry can claim a monopoly profit but once. If an upstream monopolist can use contracts to extract fully a monopoly profit from a downstream market, then there is no role for vertical integration to play in leveraging monopoly power to obtain any additional profit. The single monopoly profit theory presumes that vertical integration has some purpose other than leveraging monopoly power.

The single monopoly profit theory is clearest in the simple case of an upstream monopoly supplying an intermediate good to a downstream perfectly competitive industry. If downstream firms are equally efficient, then it is sufficient to consider uniform pricing in this case. A critical assumption is that requirements of the intermediate good are in fixed proportion to the final good. In this case the upstream monopolist maximizes profits by setting a wholesale price for the intermediate good that results in a price to consumers that is the same as would charge a fully integrated monopolist. Since the perfectly competitive downstream industry earns only normal returns, the full monopoly profit is returned to the upstream firm in wholesale revenues. If the upstream monopolist were to integrate forward and acquire a downstream firm, then the integrated firm would continue to earn exactly the same level of economic profits, assuming the remaining firms in the downstream industry continue to behave competitively.[6]

This simple version of the single monopoly profit theory is formalized as follows: Suppose that a vertically integrated monopolist producing a homogeneous final good can sell quantity Q at price $P(Q)$ by incurring manufacturing and distribution costs $C(Q)$. Therefore the profit of the monopolist is $\Pi(Q) = P(Q)Q - C(Q)$. Assuming this profit function has a unique maximum, the quantity that maximizes monopoly profit is Q^* satisfying the first-order condition for a maximum $P(Q^*) + Q^*P'(Q^*) = C'(Q^*)$, where a prime indicates the slope of a function. This condition is the familiar rule of equating marginal revenue and marginal cost. In contrast, consider an upstream monopolist who manufactures the good and distributes it through a perfectly competitive retail industry by setting a uniform wholesale price W. If the constant average cost of retail distribution is c_d, and there are no cost economies of vertical integration, then upstream manufacturing cost is necessarily $C_u(Q) = C(Q) - c_d Q$. A perfectly competitive downstream industry earns zero profits, requiring $P(Q) = W + c_d$. Therefore the competitive equilibrium quantity equals the monopoly quantity if $W = C'(Q^*) - Q^*P'(Q^*) - c_d$.

The single monopoly profit theory is robust to a variety of downstream market structures, once the upstream monopolist is unshackled from uniform pricing or can enforce appropriate vertical restraints (Mathewson and Winter 1984). Consider, for example, a symmetric downstream industry selling either homogeneous or differentiated products, and competing by choosing either quantities à la Cournot or prices à la Bertrand.[7] The upstream monopolist can set a wholesale two-part tariff $W(Q) = F + WQ$ such that the (marginal) wholesale price W elicits monopoly pricing downstream, and the fixed fee F extracts profits. For example, suppose that the downstream industry is a symmetric Cournot oligopoly with N firms and constant average cost c_d. Then equilibrium conduct results in a total industry output satisfying $P(Q) + (Q/N)P'(Q) = c_d + W$.[8] Therefore the monopoly output is elicited by setting a wholesale price $W^* = P(Q^*) - c_d + (Q^*/N)P'(Q^*)$, and monopoly profit is extracted by setting a franchise fee $F^* = -(Q^*/N)^2 P'(Q^*)$.[9] Thus, with two-part tariffs, the upstream monopolist collects its single monopoly profit contractually, and gains no further monopoly profit by vertical integration. Clearly, the two-part tariff solution requires that the upstream supplier is able to prevent resale. Otherwise, savvy downstream firms would decline to pay the franchise fee and purchase the good on the secondary market on terms reflecting the wholesale price.

The single monopoly profit theory assumes that bargaining power is concentrated in the hands of the upstream monopolist. The upstream firm presents its downstream customers with a harsh take-it-or-leave-it offer: either purchase the intermediate good under the terms of the two-part tariff, or withdraw from the downstream market. This extreme bargaining posture is most plausible in unregulated markets when the downstream industry is unconcentrated and price discrimination is impossible. If the downstream industry is concentrated and contracts negotiated individually, then the assumption of one-sided bargaining power seems less plausible. Is it credible for the upstream monopolist to refuse to deal if an important customer rejects the firm's initial offer? It obviously is difficult for the firm to commit not to even consider a profitable counteroffer, and the give and take of bilateral bargaining can limit the ability of an upstream firm to fully extract rents from the downstream industry (Rogerson 2003; Salop and Woodbury 2003).

Vertical integration can alter bargaining power (de Fontenay and Gans 2002). According to the theory of bilateral bargaining, a greater cost of delay in reaching agreement weakens a party's bargaining power, resulting in an agreement that is less favorable to the more impatient party (Rubinstein 1982). Suppose that an upstream monopolist (U) is bargaining separately with two downstream firms (D_1 and D_2) that compete with each other. Suppose that U makes a separate initial offer to each downstream firm. If both accept, then the downstream firms each earn some level of profit. If instead D_1 accepts and D_2 rejects U's offer, then D_1 experiences a gain in profit by virtue of a temporary competitive advantage over D_2. If contracts are bilateral, so that terms are not contingent on acceptance by the other downstream firm, then this windfall accrues purely to D_1 and does not influence continued bargaining between U and D_2. Now suppose that U and D_1 are integrated. If D_2 rejects U's initial offer, then the downstream windfall accrues directly the integrated firm. Thus the costs of delay in reaching agreement with D_2 are less when U is vertically integrated, which strengthens U's bargaining power in dealing with D_2. The increased bargaining power is an effect of and possible motive for vertical integration.[10]

Grimm, Winston, and Evans (1992) test the single monopoly profit theory by examining railroad markets with "interlining." The typical situation they consider is one in which a railroad is a monopolist on a route between two locations, A and C, but faces interline competition from one or more other railroads on shorter segments of this route, such as between B and C, where location B is "on the way" to C from A. Thus, in order to ship between A and C, the interliner must have access to the A–B segment. According to the single monopoly profit theory, the amount of interlining is irrelevant for the ability of the monopolist to extract rents from shippers on the $A-C$ route, yet the data show that shippers between A and C fare significantly better with more interline competition on the $B-C$ segment. How can this be? The result could be due to maximum rate regulation of noncompetitive routes, despite the general deregulatory stance of the Interstate Commerce Commission (ICC) at the time.[11] Obviously the integrated railroad cannot extract a monopoly profit from the $A-B$ segment if regulators prevent it from raising the price of this input to the monopoly level. Alternatively, the take-it-or-leave-it bargaining assumption of the single monopoly profit theory may be too strong, particularly if the interliners bring some brand differentiation advantages to the table.

4.1.3 Restoring Monopoly Power

A new literature on vertical foreclosure counters the single monopoly profit theory by arguing that an inability to make enforceable multilateral commitments prevents an upstream monopolist from using contracts to extract monopoly profits from a downstream industry, and that vertical integration helps overcome the commitment problem and "restore" monopoly power (Rey and Tirole 2007). The commitment problem is illustrated by reconsidering the two-part tariff solution proposed above for the case of symmetric downstream Cournot oligopoly. According to this version of the single monopoly profit theory, the upstream monopolist sets a wholesale price W^* above its marginal cost in order to induce the downstream monopoly outcome, and then fully extracts the monopoly profit from the downstream industry with a fixed fee F^*. Suppose, however, that the upstream firm has successfully negotiated this contract with $(N-1)$ of the downstream competitors who thereby are committed to pay the fixed fee. The upstream firm has an incentive to deviate and secretly offer the remaining downstream firm a contract with a lower wholesale price. In doing so, the upstream firm essentially offers firm N a variable cost advantage over its rivals, for which firm N is willing to pay a higher fixed fee. Once the $(N-1)$ rivals learn about this "sweetheart deal," they regret their contracts because more intense competition from the advantaged firm N makes it impossible for the others to earn enough operating profits to recover F^*.[12] Anticipating the predicament the $(N-1)$ firms refuse to accept the monopolizing contracts in the first place. Such skepticism by the downstream industry leads to a lower wholesale price and more competitive downstream price that limits the ability of the upstream supplier to extract the monopoly profit with a two-part tariff (Hart and Tirole 1990; McAfee and Schwartz 1994; O'Brien and Shaffer 1992; Rey and Tirole 2007).[13]

A key assumption of the restoring monopoly profit theory is that the upstream monopolist cannot make multilateral commitments. In the Hart and Tirole (1990) model, an upstream firm makes simultaneous take-it-or-leave-it contract offers to supply a fixed proportions intermediate good to N downstream firms who sell a homogeneous product to final consumers. In this model it is important that contracts be both bilateral and private.

If contract offers were public, then there could be no surprise sweetheart deals, since downstream firms would observe the contract offers to rivals and make a rational acceptance decision. More generally, the privacy of contracts is less crucial if the take-it-or-leave-it bargaining assumption is relaxed. Even if contract offers are public, downstream firms that lock themselves into a long-term contract risk the misfortune of being "surprised" by a rival who rejects the initial offer and subsequently negotiates a sweetheart deal (McAfee and Schwartz 1994).

Partial vertical integration by merging with one of the downstream firms restores the upstream firm's ability to extract monopoly profit, since sweetheart deals with downstream competitors are costly to the downstream division of the integrated enterprise. The cannibalized profits of the downstream division become an opportunity cost of selling more through an independent retail channel. These opportunity costs provide the needed discipline to discourage sweetheart deals that erode downstream prices and prevent the full extraction of monopoly profits (Hart and Tirole 1990; Rey and Tirole 2007).

Sufficiently powerful contracts solve the commitment problem without vertical integration. For example, if the final good is homogeneous, then exclusive dealing can mimic the exclusionary effects of vertical integration and similarly restore monopoly power (Hart and Tirole 1990; Rey and Tirole 2007). Market-wide retail price maintenance with a return option has similar efficacy (Rey and Tirole 2007). Obviously such contractual solutions must be enforceable to be effective. Surprisingly, most favored customer (MFC) clauses are less successful at restoring monopoly power. The reason is that a sweetheart deal may not be attractive to a competitor whose rival has already accepted the deal (McAfee and Schwartz 1994). For instance, suppose that a downstream duopolist gains a competitive advantage by accepting a two-part tariff with a lower (marginal) wholesale price and a higher fixed fee that extracts additional profits. The rival duopolist would decline the same deal, since more vigorous competition at the lower wholesale price would make it impossible to recover the higher fixed fee. In this case an MFC clause fails to deter opportunism.[14]

The theory of restoring monopoly power via vertical integration extends to an upstream market structure in which the market power of a low-cost supplier is constrained by a higher cost potential supplier (Hart and Tirole 1990; Rey and Tirole 2007). In this case the available single monopoly profit is no higher than the efficiency rents of the low cost supplier. Similarly to the case of upstream monopoly, a commitment problem prevents the low-cost upstream firm from fully capturing these efficiency rents, and vertical integration overcomes the commitment problem and restores monopoly power to the detriment of final consumers. Matters are different if the upstream industry is a homogeneous price-setting oligopoly whose members are equally efficient. In this case there are no efficiency rents, and therefore no monopoly power to restore by vertical merger. Thus the theory of restoring monopoly power only provides an explanation for forward integration by the cost leader of an upstream oligopoly.[15]

The extent to which vertical integration solves the commitment problem and restores monopoly power depends on downstream market structure. If the downstream market is homogeneous, and there are nondecreasing returns to scale at the firm level, then a vertically integrated firm can collect monopoly profits by refusing to deal with independent downstream competitors.[16] Matters are more complicated if downstream final products are differentiated or exhibit decreasing returns to scale, in which case partial vertical integration leads to less competitive outcomes but does not enable the full extraction of monopoly profits from the downstream industry.[17]

There is little empirical evidence bearing directly on the restoring monopoly power theory.[18] A recent case study of the cement and ready-mix concrete industries shows that downstream concrete prices tend to fall and quantities rise as local markets become more vertically integrated, contrary to the predictions of the restoring monopoly power theory and other foreclosure theories,[19] but consistent with an alternative efficiency explanation (Hortacsu and Syverson 2005). These findings support a presumption that most cement/concrete mergers in the sample were pro-competitive, while not necessarily ruling out that some mergers were anticompetitive. Thus a task for advocates of the restoring monopoly theory is to propose observable conditions under which harmful foreclosure effects are likely to dominate pro-competitive efficiencies.[20]

Experimental research similarly finds mixed support for the restoring monopoly power theory. Martin, Norman, and Snyder (2001) devised an experimental game patterned closely on the Hart and Tirole (1990) model of vertical foreclosure. The experimental results support the basic contention of the theory that private bilateral contracting makes it difficult for an upstream monopolist to restrict quantity, and that a partially integrated firm is more able to overcome this commitment problem and earn higher profits. At the same time the results cast doubt on the ability of upstream firms to extract profits fully from the downstream industry with take-it-or-leave-it offers. Consistent with the broader experimental literature on "ultimatum games," downstream players often reject "unfair" offers that leave too little on the table.[21]

4.1.4 Eliminating Markups

The case for a permissive approach to vertical mergers is stronger if firms have market power in both upstream and downstream markets, and if effective price discrimination in the intermediate goods market is difficult. The argument is clearest in the artificial case of successive monopoly and no price discrimination.[22] The upstream monopolist sets a uniform wholesale price W for the intermediate good. Taking W as given, the downstream monopolist chooses a quantity Q to maximize $[P(Q) - W]Q - C_d(Q)$. If the downstream cost function $C_d(Q)$ is smooth, and has a well defined slope $C_d'(Q)$ then the quantity choice determines a final price $P = P(Q)$ that adds a monopoly markup to the downstream marginal cost $[W + C_d'(Q)]$. This yields the same outcome as an integrated monopoly if and only if the wholesale price is equal to upstream marginal cost, which is $W = C'_u(Q^*)$. The problem is that the upstream monopolist has an incentive to raise W above its marginal cost. The upstream markup raises the marginal cost of the downstream firm, leading to a final price P above what an integrated monopolist would charge. The vertical integration of successive monopolies eliminates this "double marginalization" and results in a lower price of the final good. By this argument, vertical integration both raises profits and benefits consumers (Spengler 1950).

The double marginalization argument for vertical integration breaks down if sufficiently powerful contracts enable efficient price discrimination. Two-part pricing is sufficient to the carry the argument. Let Q^* denote the fully integrated monopoly quantity, and let $W^* = C'_u(Q^*)$ the upstream marginal cost corresponding to this quantity. If the upstream monopolist sets a two-part tariff schedule $W(Q) = F + W^*Q$, then the downstream firm maximizes its profit by choosing Q^*. The upstream firm sets F appropriately to fully extract the monopoly profit.[23] Thus, consistent with the single monopoly profit theory, two-part pricing enables the upstream monopolist to achieve the same profit as a vertically integrated monopoly, and results in the same downstream equilibrium price to consumers.[24]

The double-marginalization hypothesis is relevant, however, if inefficient bargaining results in a wholesale price above upstream marginal cost. Bargaining is likely to be inefficient if there is an information asymmetry between the upstream and downstream firms. In this case it is hard for the upstream firm to know the value of Q^*, and therefore the firm is unsure of the correct value of W^*. Bargaining with incomplete information generally results in marginal wholesale prices above marginal cost (Maskin and Riley 1984), creating a double marginalization problem when the downstream firm sets the final price.[25] In eliminating the information asymmetry between the upstream and downstream division, vertical integration eliminates a double markup and lowers the final price to the monopoly level.[26]

The single monopoly profit theory assumes that the monopolized intermediate good is in a fixed proportion to the final good. The theory also fails if the downstream technology uses the monopolized upstream input in variable proportions with other inputs and it is not possible to control input usage contractually. Then any attempt of the upstream monopolist to raise W prompts the downstream industry to substitute toward other inputs. Thus upstream monopoly pricing creates an input distortion compared to the cost-minimizing input combination of a vertically integrated firm. The unified control of production in a vertically integrated firm achieves a cost economy by correcting the input distortion.[27] The variable proportions case further illustrates the importance of the power of contracts. Here an inability of an upstream monopolist to dictate the input usage of downstream customers undermines the logic of the single monopoly profit theory.

Empirical evidence on eliminating markups with vertical integration is mixed. Chipty (2001) and Waterman and Weiss (1996) study the backward integration into programming by cable systems operators (CSOs) and find various pieces of evidence consistent with double marginalization. First, vertically integrated CSOs are more likely to carry their own premium programming (e.g., subscription movie channels), rather than share rents with a rival programmer. Second, and more important, integrated CSOs sell more basic cable and premium subscriptions. Double marginalization is particularly plausible in cable programming because it is the usual industry practice to price exhibition rights for programming on a per subscription basis. Villas-Boas (2007), on the other hand, finds no evidence of double marginalization in the pricing of yoghurt, consistent either with the hypothesis that contracts between manufacturers and retailers solve the double-marginalization problem, or with the hypothesis that yoghurt manufacturers lack market power.

4.1.5 Raising Rivals' Costs (RRC)

A vertically integrated firm might engineer an increase in rivals' costs by driving up the price of a scarce input (Salop and Scheffman 1987; Riordan 1998). Scarcity is indicated by an upward-sloping curve for a competitively supplied input, meaning that a positive shift in demand for the input elicits an expansion of supply only at a higher price. By artificially increasing its own demand for the scarce input, the vertically integrated firm elevates the market price of the input, thus raising the costs of its unintegrated rivals. Vertical integration matters for this incentive, since self-supplied input requirements are insulated from the price increase.[28] Consequently the higher input price impacts the costs of the integrated firm and its downstream competitors asymmetrically. This cost-raising strategy benefits the downstream operation of the integrated firm in causing rivals to exit the market or otherwise reduce their supply of the final good. While final consumers are harmed by higher downstream prices, the exclusion of less efficient rivals contributes to overall economic efficiency to the extent that market share shifts toward the more efficient vertically integrated firm. Riordan (1998) demonstrates that net effect on economic efficiency is negative when an integrated dominant firm's output market share is high relative to its input market share.[29]

Vertical integration might similarly benefit the downstream division of an integrated firm by reducing competition in the upstream market (Ordover, Saloner, and Salop 1990). Consider an upstream oligopoly selling a homogeneous input to a downstream oligopoly at a uniform wholesale price. Withdrawal of the integrated firm from the input market, except for self-supply, might increase the market power of the remaining upstream oligopolists, causing these firms to raise prices to the downstream market.[30] The resulting higher procurement costs disadvantage rival downstream firms in competition with the downstream division of the integrated firm. If the independent downstream firms pass through these cost increases to final consumers even partially, then market share is likely to shift in favor of the integrated firm. Consumers will suffer higher prices, unless there is a countervailing effect on prices from eliminating double marginalization (Reiffen and Vita 1995), and less choice if independent downstream firms exit the market.

An issue for this RRC theory is the credibility of the upstream division's refusal to deal with downstream competitors (Reiffen 1992; Hart and Tirole 1990). The problem is that it may be irresistible for the vertically integrated firm to undercut the input prices of upstream rivals. After all, if there are profits to be earned by selling to downstream competitors, then the vertically integrated firm would like to capture those profits as long as the expense to its downstream profits is sufficiently small. If the upstream products are differentiated so that upstream firms have a limited ability to steal business from a rival with a small price cut, then credibility is less of an issue and a vertical integrated firm has a greater incentive actually to execute a refusal-to-deal strategy.[31] In contrast, if the upstream product market is homogeneous, then the vigor of competition in the upstream market might be unaffected by vertical integration, leaving both competitors and consumers unharmed.[32]

There are a number of ways that a vertically integrated firm might commit to refuse to deal with downstream competitors. First, the vertically integrated firm might establish a reputation for exclusive self-supply. Suppose that a credible withdrawal by the upstream division from the input market benefited the downstream division by causing higher input prices to downstream rivals, as described above. Suppose further that any deviation from the refusal-to-deal policy, presumably in the quest of short-term profits, creates expectations by upstream competitors that the vertically integrated firm would deviate similarly in the future. In anticipation of this behavior, upstream competitors cut prices, and the raising rivals' cost strategy unravels. If the long-term benefits of a credible refusal to deal exceed the short-term profit opportunities, then a reputation for refusing to deal with competitors is a credible one. Second, the upstream division of the vertically integrated firm might design its product to be incompatible with products or manufacturing processes of downstream competitors (Church and Gandal 2000; Choi and Yi 2000). This mechanism requires that design changes be sufficiently costly, and that the technological incompatibility be effectively irreversible in the short-run.[33] Third, downstream competitors might be concerned that a vertically integrated supplier would have an incentive to reduce the quality of the input, or reduce the quality of complementary services. In this case the distorted incentives of a vertically integrated firm automatically disadvantage its upstream division, thereby increasing the market power of upstream rivals.

Downstream competitors might consider countermeasures to limit the damage from a rival's vertical merger with an upstream supplier, including integrating backwards also, or cultivating an alternative source of supply. In some cases the threat of defensive backward integration by rivals limits the raising rivals cost effect of vertical integration (Ordover, Salop, and Saloner 1990). An interesting, and at first surprising, countermeasure for independent downstream firms is to "make a deal with the devil" and contract with the vertically integrated supplier at a supra-competitive price (Chen 2002). A rival downstream firm, by promising to pay the integrated supplier a profit on upstream sales, weakens the integrated firm's incentive to compete aggressively in the downstream market. This collusive effect of vertical contracting arises because the integrated firm treats the forgone upstream profit as an opportunity cost of winning a downstream sale (Chen and Riordan 2004). Thus the independent downstream firm, by contracting with the upstream firm, effectively raises the opportunity cost of its integrated rival, thereby driving up downstream prices and profits, to the detriment of final consumers. In this case the countermeasure reinforces the anticompetitive effect of vertical integration.

If two-part tariffs are available,[34] then the raising rivals' cost effect of vertical integration might reduce participation in the downstream market with no offsetting double marginalization effect. Suppose that an equally efficient rival upstream firm offers a two-part tariff that sets the wholesale price equal to its marginal cost, while exercising market power by setting a positive fixed fee. Then vertical integration has no effect on the variable costs of the downstream industry, and does not result in higher downstream prices unless independent downstream firms exit the market in response to the changed vertical structure. If the vertically integrated firm refuses to deal with independent downstream firms, then the resulting increased market power of upstream rivals could translate into higher fixed fees charged to downstream customers, and the resulting higher fixed costs of market participation could cause some downstream firms to exit the industry. A more concentrated downstream market profits the integrated firm, while presenting consumers with less choice and higher prices.

Similarly a raising rivals' costs strategy can preserve the market power of a vertically integrated firm by deterring entry into upstream and downstream markets. Suppose that a potential entrant has the *present* ability to enter the downstream market with a superior product by sinking a fixed cost, and a *future* ability to enter the upstream market by investing in R&D. If the firm enters the downstream market only, then bargaining with the upstream incumbent results in some distribution of rents between the two firms.[35] The new entrant might be able to capture additional rents from its superior downstream product by integrating backward when its R&D investment comes to fruition. Thus the most profitable entry strategy might be to enter the downstream market presently and to enter the upstream market in the future. The vertically integrated incumbent might deter this two-level entry strategy by depriving the entrant of present revenue or raising the entrant's present cost by refusing to deal. By effectively "tying" the sale of its intermediate good to the sale of its final good, perhaps technologically, the vertically integrated firm forecloses competition in the downstream market, deters entry into the upstream market, and preserves its market power (Carlton and Waldman 2002).

Alternatively, a technological tie that forecloses downstream rivals protects a vertically integrated upstream monopolist from downstream innovation competition (Gilbert and Riordan 2007). In reducing compatibility with a monopolized intermediate good, the vertically integrated firm discourages innovation by possibly more efficient downstream competitors, and thereby protects the return from its own innovations. Such technological tying by a vertically integrated firm harms consumers and reduces economic efficiency if it forecloses more innovative downstream competitors.[36] In some cases, however, technological foreclosure can increase economic efficiency by improving innovation incentives of the vertically integrated firm.

In an early contribution to the new vertical foreclosure literature, Salinger (1988) made the important observation that RRC effects can coexist with eliminating double-marginalization effects. Salinger (1988) considers a model of successive Cournot oligopoly in which an intermediate good is transformed into a final good in fixed proportions. In the model, upstream oligopolists (simultaneously and independently) choose quantities, determining a uniform price of the intermediate good. Downstream firms, taking the intermediate goods price as given, then choose their quantities and determine the price of the final good.[37] The exercise of market power at each stage of production determines a markup of price above marginal cost. A vertical merger eliminates an upstream supplier because the vertically integrated firm refuses to deal with independent downstream firms. Thus the vertical merger increases the market power of remaining upstream oligopolists, while creating a more aggressive downstream competitor who is able to produce at marginal cost. The net competitive effect is ambiguous in general. Klass and Salinger (1995) contends that calculation of the net competitive effect usually is impractical, since it requires too much detailed information about market structure.

The Ordover, Saloner, and Salop (1990) RRC model assumes that upstream competitors lack market power in the absence of vertical integration, thus eliminating any possible efficiency gain from eliminating double marginalization. In this basic model, vertical integration creates market power in the upstream market, whose exercise results in higher wholesale prices to independent downstream firms. It is straightforward to modify the theory to assume upstream market power in the non-integrated environment, such as by assuming product differentiation. Such modifications introduce an eliminating double-marginalization effect that stands side by side with the raising rivals' costs effect of vertical integration (Reiffen and Vita 1995).[38] If both effects are present, with the raising rivals' cost effect driving prices lower and the double-marginalization effect driving prices higher, then the net welfare effect is ambiguous.

Empirical evidence provides some limited support for RRC theory. Chipty (2001) and Waterman and Weiss (1996), discussed above in the context of double marginalization, show that backward integration of CSOs into programming does result in some market foreclosure. Vertically integrated CSOs tend to carry fewer premium movie services, in addition to being more likely to carry their own, and are less likely to carry a rival basic movie service. Similarly integrated CSOs are less likely to carry a rival shopping network in addition to their own. This evidence is consistent with the hypothesis that vertically integrated CSOs refuse to deal with rival programmers, or to hold out for more favorable terms. Gilbert and Hastings (2005) study gasoline distribution and present evidence that a vertically integrated refiner charges higher wholesale prices in cities where it competes more with independent gas stations. This is direct evidence in favor of the hypothesis that a vertically integrated firm seeks to raise the cost of downstream rivals by raising wholesale prices. More complete supporting evidence would demonstrate that rival refiners are capacity constrained and/or raise their wholesale prices as well. Hortacsu and Syverson (2005), discussed earlier, present preliminary evidence that vertical integration of cement and concrete manufacturers leads to lower final prices, contrary to RRC theories.

4.1.6 Facilitating Collusion

Antitrust and regulatory authorities have remained concerned that vertical integration might facilitate collusion at upstream or downstream levels. Generally, successful express or tacit collusion requires reaching an agreement, monitoring compliance, and punishing defections. Vertical integration might facilitate collusion by aiding any of these activities.

The 1984 Non-horizontal Merger Guidelines of the US Department of Justice informally articulates several theories of harmful vertical integration. A primary concern expressed in the Guidelines is that forward integration might increase market power by raising barriers to entry (DOJ 1984, Section 4.21):

In certain circumstances, the vertical integration resulting from vertical mergers could create competitively objectionable barriers to entry. Stated generally, three conditions are necessary (but not sufficient) for this problem to exist. First, the degree of vertical integration between the two markets must be so extensive that entrants to one market (the "primary market") also would have to enter the other market (the "secondary market") simultaneously. Second, the requirement of entry at the secondary level must make entry at the primary level significantly more difficult and less likely to occur. Finally, the structure and other characteristics of the primary market must be otherwise so conducive to noncompetitive performance that the increased difficulty of entry is likely to affect its performance.

A second concern of the Guidelines is that forward integration might facilitate collusion because it is easier for an upstream firm to monitor retail prices (DOJ 1984, Section 4.221):

A high level of vertical integration by upstream firms into the associated retail market may facilitate collusion in the upstream market by making it easier to monitor price. Retail prices are generally more visible than prices in upstream markets, and vertical mergers may increase the level of vertical integration to the point at which the monitoring effect becomes significant. Adverse competitive consequences are unlikely unless the upstream market is generally conducive to collusion and a large percentage of the products produced there are sold through vertically integrated retail outlets.

A third concern of the Guidelines is that a vertical merger might eliminate a "disruptive buyer" who has a strong incentive to encourage a defection from a collusive agreement (DOJ 1984, Section 4.222):

The elimination by vertical merger of a particularly disruptive buyer in a downstream market may facilitate collusion in the upstream market. If upstream firms view sales to a particular buyer as sufficiently important, they may deviate from the terms of a collusive agreement in an effort to secure that business, therefore disrupting the operation of the agreement. The merger of such a buyer with an upstream firm may eliminate that rivalry, making it easier for the upstream firms to collude effectively.

These theories, particularly the last two, have not received much formal attention in the economics literature.[39]

Nocke and White (2007) formalizes collusion by an upstream industry as a subgame perfect equilibrium of a repeated game, at each stage of which downstream product market competition follows the negotiation of supply contracts with upstream firms. The theory demonstrates how vertical integration possibly facilitates collusion by an "outlets effect," a "reaction effect," and a "lack of commitment effect." The outlet effect means that by foreclosing part of the downstream market, a vertically integrated firm reduces the incentive of upstream rivals to defect from an agreement. The reaction effect means that a vertically integrated firm is better able to punish defections of upstream competitors by quickly increasing competition in the downstream market. In contrast, a non-integrated market structure must wait to renegotiate supply contracts before punishing a defection effectively. Finally, the lack-of-commitment effect means that a vertically integrated firm finds a departure from upstream collusion less profitable because of rivalry in the downstream market. Independent downstream firms are less willing to deal with a vertically integrated firm because of a rational expectation that the vertically integrated firm will expand in the downstream market if the collusion breaks down. Weighing against these adverse effects of vertical integration is a "punishment effect" of vertical integration. The punishment effect refers to the possibility that acquisition of a downstream firm might increase the integrated firm's incentive to defect from an upstream collusion by securing profits in the downstream market should the collusion collapse. An important result of the Nocke and White paper is to show that the outlet effect of a single vertical integration outweighs the punishment effect for a homogeneous-good upstream industry. The paper also loosely relates the reaction effect to the Non-horizontal Merger Guidelines' theory that vertical integration facilitates collusion by making it easier to monitor downstream prices, and the outlets effect to the Guidelines's disruptive buyer theory. Nevertheless, these legal theories from the Guidelines still have a long way to go before finding a solid foundation in modern economic analysis.

Riordan and Salop (1995) sketches an informal theory of how information exchange through a vertically integrated firm facilitates upstream collusion. Suppose that the vertically integrated firm does not satisfy all of its input requirements internally, and solicits bids from rival upstream firms to supply its remaining requirements. The vertically integrated firm potentially can use this information to monitor its upstream rivals' compliance with a collusive agreement. Moreover the downstream division, in the course of its ongoing communications with upstream rivals, might be able to engineer an agreement to keep input prices high. For example, upstream firms might be able to signal a proposed agreement via their bids to the downstream division. This way the downstream division acts as a conduit for communication for the upstream industry. Several conditions are necessary for such an exchange to have an anticompetitive effect. First, the upstream industry must be otherwise conducive to horizontal collusion. Second, the bid information received by the downstream division must be "projectable," meaning that it is informative about prices upstream rivals charge to other downstream firms. This is most likely to be the case if price discrimination is infeasible. Third, the information must be unique, meaning it must not be available from an alternative source. These requirements greatly narrow the circumstances in which a facilitating-collusion theory based on information exchange potentially is applicable. In any case, the Riordan-Salop theory awaits formalization.

Chen and Riordan (2004) argues that vertical integration might facilitate an effective cartelization of a downstream industry via exclusive contracts. Generally, an upstream supplier might organize a cartel by contracting with a downstream industry to restrict output and prices to final consumers. A multilateral agreement toward this end would run afoul of Section 1 of the Sherman Act, which bars contracts and conspiracies "in restraint of trade." The question remains whether an upstream supplier could achieve much the same outcome by entering into purely bilateral contracts with individual members of the downstream industry. Exclusive contracts could prevent downstream participants from defecting by contracting with alternative upstream suppliers. However, the endeavor still has to overcome a "commitment problem" similar to the one in the restoring monopoly power theory. That is, having engineered a cartel with exclusive bilateral contracts, the upstream "cartel ringmaster"[40] might have an incentive to cheat by offering individual sweetheart deals that destabilize the cartel, and the ability to do so because there is no multilateral agreement to prevent it. Just as in the restoring monopoly profit theory, vertical integration helps overcome the commitment problem by changing the incentives of the upstream supplier, whose downstream division suffers the consequences of any sweetheart deal extended to a downstream competitor. If the integrated firm cannot commit credibly to restrict its own sales to consumers, then the effective cartelization is only partial and fails to replicate the monopoly outcome. Nevertheless, the theory does explain higher prices in the downstream market as a consequence of vertical integration cum exclusive dealing, together with the exclusion of equally or even more efficient competitors in the upstream market.

4.2 Selected Cases

4.2.1 News Corp.–DirectTV Acquisition

News Corp. (NC) acquired from General Motors a controlling interest of Hughes Electronics in 2003.[41] The FCC approved the acquisition subject to certain conditions.[42] The FCC conditions among other things required NC to make its programming available to multichannel video program distributors (MVPDs) on a nonexclusive and nondiscriminatory basis, and required the commercial arbitration of disputes regarding certain kinds of programming. The Justice Department determined not to challenge the merger, stating that the FCC conditions addressed its main concerns about the transaction.

The FCC correctly identified the NC acquisition as a vertical merger of video programming and distribution assets. Hughes Electronics owned DirectTV, one of the two major direct broadcast satellite (DBS) companies in the United States, the other being EchoStar. The DBS providers compete in the MVPD market with cable system operators (CSOs) across the United States, although cable service is not available in some rural areas. Typically there is a single CSO in local markets. NC, through its subsidiary Fox, owns an assortment of video programming assets, including regional sports networks (RSNs) and local broadcast television stations.

The FCC identified the relevant upstream product market as video programming services, distinguishing separate markets for RSNs among others.[43] The Fox RSNs have exclusive rights to exhibit major sports events, including games played by popular regional sports teams. The FCC identified the relevant downstream product market to be MVPD services. The FCC rejected the idea that television broadcast stations are sufficiently close substitutes to be included in the same downstream market, and it therefore found that the merger raised no horizontal concerns. The FCC also determined the relevant geographic market for regional sports programming to be the distribution footprint of the RSN and the geographic market for MVPD services to be the franchise area of the rival CSO.[44]

The FCC recognized that MVPD markets are highly concentrated. Most relevant MVPD markets have three major participants, the two DBS companies and the local CSO. The CSOs typically have the lion's share of these markets. At the time of the acquisition, DirectTV had 13 percent and EchoStar an even smaller share of MVPD markets nationally. There are evidently substantial barriers to entry into MVPD markets. The FCC concluded that NC had significant power in the market for RSN programming. The argument relied on the idea that for many consumers, there is not a close substitute for the ability to watch their favorite teams on a regular basis. Thus the market power of an RSN derives from the underlying market power of the sports teams for which it holds exclusive exhibition rights.

The FCC described contracting practices in the relevant intermediate product market only briefly. License fees for video programming depend on the number of subscribers and may involve quantity discounts. Other conditions might include control of advertising slots and concessions to carry additional programming.

The FCC considered a raising rivals' cost theory based on the idea that the merged entity might have an incentive to foreclose permanently rival MVPDs access to Fox RSNs. The FCC staff analysis employed straightforward vertical arithmetic. In the event that NC refuses permanently to supply RSN programming to a CSO with whom it competes in a local MVPD market, NC loses the affiliate fees paid by CSO for the right to carry the RSN, as well as advertising revenues attached to subscribers of the CSO. Some subscribers who care about the rival RSN will defect to DirectTV. Therefore NC will earn increased affiliate fees from DirectTV and, by virtue of its partial ownership of DirectTV, a share of the profits from these new subscribers including associated advertising revenues. The FCC concluded that the losses outweighed the gains from permanent foreclosure under plausible assumptions about consumer behavior (FCC 2004, app. D).

The FCC nevertheless concluded that the vertical merger would enable NC to increase the price of RSN programming to MVPDs. This conclusion was based on a novel theory that the merger would increase NC's bargaining power by increasing its incentive and ability to withdraw programming temporarily in the course of negotiations over terms and conditions of carriage. The FCC summarized its theory as follows (FCC 2004, para. 4):

[O]ur analysis of the principal allegations of competitive harm in the record demonstrates that this vertical integration has the potential to increase the incentive and ability of News Corp. to engage in temporary foreclosure bargaining strategies during carriage negotiations with competing MVPDs for two types of "must have" video programming products—broadcast television station signals and regional cable programming sports networks—in order to secure higher prices for its programming. Although New Corp., like other broadcast networks, engages or attempts to engage in this sort of behavior today, ownership of a competing MVPD platform with a national footprint means that News Corp. would stand to gain from any subscriber losses the affected MVPD suffers during the period of foreclosure when those subscribers move over to its competing MVPD platform to access the desired programming. The ability to gain revenues via its ownership interest in DirectTV thereby helps offset any temporary losses that News Corp. would suffer from withdrawal of its programming from the competing MPVD in terms of lost advertising and/or affiliate fee revenues. This offsetting revenue gain makes use of the strategy more tolerable to News Corp. post-transaction than it was pre-transaction and thereby increases the likelihood and frequency of its use. This lowering of the cost of foreclosure to News Corp. from present levels fundamentally and substantially alters the bargaining dynamic between the program supplier and the competing programming distributor to the benefit of the former at the expense of the latter and its subscribers. To the extent that News Corp. succeeds in using temporary foreclosure strategies to extract supra-competitive prices for its programming, these transaction-specific higher programming costs are likely to be passed through as higher MVPD prices, which in turn would harm consumers.

Thus the FCC concluded that vertical integration increased NC's bargaining leverage in negotiation of carriage agreements with CSOs to the detriment of consumers.

To further justify its temporary foreclosure theory, the FCC resorted to what seems to be an odd theory of consumer inertia (FCC 2004, para. 79):

In markets exhibiting consumer inertia, among other things, temporary foreclosure may be profitable even where permanent foreclosure is not, because, during the period of foreclosure, downstream customers may switch to the integrated firm's downstream product and, due to inertia, then not immediately switch back to the competitor's product once the foreclosure has ended. Consumers choosing an MVPD are subject to inertia and partial lock-in, because, among other things, there are switching costs associated with changing providers and some MVPDs, including DirectTV generally require one-year contracts. Thus, temporary foreclosure may generate profits that continue for a longer period than the period of upstream losses caused by the reduction in demand for the input.

The theory seems odd because it appears to assume that inertia only works in one direction, suggesting consumer irrationality. Inertia that discourages consumers from switching back to a preferred MVPD might be expected also to give the same consumers pause before switching MVPD providers to avoid an only temporary loss in their favorite programming. If switching costs are large, then a rational consumer would not switch if they expected only a short-lived withdrawal of programming from their otherwise preferred MVPD. Moreover it is not clear why rival MVPDs do not solve the problem of consumers leaving for temporary reasons by requiring a one-year contract.

The FCC nevertheless concluded that NC had a heightened postmerger incentive for temporary foreclosure based on an analysis that assumed foreclosure lasted only one month, while defecting consumers returned to their previous MVPD only slowly. The short-lived withdrawal of the RSN from a rival CSO obviously limited the lost profits of the upstream division, while consumer inertia stretched out the downstream gains from foreclosure over a sustained period. The FCC based its projections of consumer behavior in response to temporary foreclosure on an empirical analysis of a previous isolated incident in which a regional sports network temporarily withheld programming from a CSO.

The FCC argued that NC's enhanced bargaining power from the vertical merger would harm consumers in two ways. First, higher priced RSN programming resulting from NC's enhanced bargaining power would at least partly be passed on to consumers in the form of higher subscription prices. Second, consumers would be deprived temporarily of valuable sports entertainment if NC actually executed a temporary foreclosure strategy. Standard bargaining theory suggests that the first effect is the more important one. A greater threat of temporary foreclosure should enable NC to obtain more favorable terms without ever having to carry out the threat.

It is interesting to consider the relevance of the single monopoly profit theory for this case. Suppose that, prior to the merger, NC made a profit-maximizing take-it-or-leave-it offer of terms and conditions to a CSO for the right to carry its RSN programming. Then, according to the single monopoly profit theory, vertical integration with DirectTV does not enable NC to extract any additional profit from the CSO, since NC is already fully extracting a maximized profit. A defect of the single monopoly profit theory is its assumption that, prior to the merger, NC commits to withhold programming permanently if its take-it-or-leave-it offer is rejected by the CSO. A problem with the assumption is that, if the CSO rejects the offer, then NC has an incentive to make a concession in order to retain the MVPD's business. In other words, the take-it-or-leave-it offer is not credible, in which case the give-and-take of bilateral bargaining might frustrate NC from fully extracting monopoly profits. Indeed, the FCC concluded that a permanent withdrawal of programming was not a credible threat. The FCC concluded that the vertical integration would strengthen NC bargaining power in bilateral negotiations, by reducing the opportunity cost of a temporary withholding of programming. Thus, while there is only a single monopoly profit on the table, vertical integration allows an upstream firm to claim more of it because of increased bargaining power.[45]

The restoring monopoly profit theory was given little weight in the case, partly because the FCC's program access rules limited NC's opportunities for exclusion and price discrimination, and the vertical merger did not lessen these limitations. Moreover NC offered to commit not to discriminate or enter into exclusive arrangements even beyond the scope of the program access rules. The FCC incorporated these commitments into its conditions for approval of the merger. It is ironic that according to the restoring monopoly power theory, such commitments enforced by a government agency can increase the ability of an upstream firm to extract monopoly profits from the downstream industry (Whinston 2003). Thus it is conceivable that the nondiscrimination conditions of the merger had an anticompetitive effect, apart from any effect of vertical integration. Such a concern apparently was not explored in the case.

Other possible theories of competitive effects or vertical integration were not given much attention. The FCC recognized possible efficiencies from the elimination of double marginalization but doubted that these efficiencies were sufficient to overcome the raising rivals' cost effect of the merger on consumer prices. The FCC did not consider explicitly the effect of NC's changed incentives on the market power of other providers of sports programming.

4.2.2 CRS Proceeding

In 2004 the US Department of Transportation (DOT) determined to deregulate airline computer reservation systems (CRSs). The final rulemaking phased out a host of nondiscrimination requirements and contracting prohibitions installed by the Civil Aeronautics Board (CAB) from 1984, and by the DOT from 1982 when it took over regulatory authority. Prominent among the regulations was a rule against "display bias"—a CRS could not present information in a format that gave preferential treatment to a particular airline. The DOT concluded that market conditions had changed to make continued regulation of the CRS industry unnecessary. The changed market conditions included divestures of CRS ownership by the airlines and especially the growing importance of the Internet for booking flights.

The market for CRS services is a "two-sided market." The CRS industry provides airline flight information, booking, and ticketing services to travel agents. To produce these services, CRS firms grant access to airlines to provide flight information and receive booking through the system. The airlines typically pay the CRS firm a fee for each booking, with the size of the fee depending on the "level of service," meaning the quality of information and booking capabilities the airline is able to provide on the system. Most travel agents obtain CRS access for free, and many receive signing bonuses and rebates for bookings. In addition CRS providers give volume-related incentives to induce a subscriber to increase its bookings through that system. The two sets of transactions—with airlines, on the one hand, and travel agents, on the other—obviously are complementary.

The two-sided nature of the CRS market makes product market definition tricky. The US CRS industry is comprised of four firms: Amadeus, Galileo, Sabre, and WorldSpan. From the perspective of travel agents, the different CRSs are close substitutes in the long run. The market for travel agent services apparently is highly competitive, and travel agents who fail to serve consumers well by providing clear and accurate information on alternatives lose consumers to competitors offering better service. Consequently travel agents have an incentive to favor a CRS that eschews display bias to serve consumers better. Moreover larger travel agents subscribe to multiple CRSs, and can switch between systems easily. In the short run, however, many smaller travel agents use a single CRS, apparently because of the time and training it takes to learn how to use a particular system. Consequently airlines need access to a particular system to reach the consumers served by the travel agents who use only that system. Thus, from the perspective of airlines, the different CRSs are not perfect substitutes for reaching customers. Accordingly the DOT viewed the CRS firms each to be a monopoly access provider to airlines and determined that each of the four systems comprised a relevant market. With this market definition in hand, the DOT concluded that CRS firms possess significant market power toward the airlines, while observing the continuing erosion of this market power by Internet distribution.

US airlines were integrated forward into the CRS market when the DOT (and previously the CAB) adopted its rules governing the market. For example, United owned Galileo, and American, Delta, and Northwest jointly owned Worldspan. This vertical integration raised concerns that the CRS firms would discriminate in favor of their owners, and that airlines would discriminate in favor of CRS firms in which they had an ownership interest. The first concern led to rules prohibiting display bias, effectively requiring the CRS industry to provide nondiscriminatory access to airlines. The second concern led to a misguided rule requiring airlines with a significant ownership interest in a CRS to purchase access to other systems at "reasonable" fees. This purchase mandate seemed destined to create or increase the market power of a CRS, given inevitable ambiguity about the meaning of reasonable.

Over the course of the DOT proceeding, all US airlines divested their ownership interest in CRSs.[46] This change in market structure, together with the growing importance of Internet distribution, helped motivate the DOT's deregulation of the industry.[47] The DOT assumed that independent CRSs had an incentive to sell display bias to the highest bidders, and recognized that the practice could mislead consumers and distort competition. Nevertheless, the DOT determined to eliminate its rule against display bias after six months (effective July 2004). Its explanation was that "ongoing developments" (aka the Internet) would continue to erode CRS market power over time and provide travel agents and consumers with alternative sources of information.

The DOT expressed its concerns about display bias with the following raising rivals' cost theory. First, busy travel agents are more likely to book flights displayed first, even if those flights are less convenient or more costly to consumers. Second, by shifting demand to favored airlines, display bias might cause disadvantaged rivals to offer fewer flights, or even to exit a market. Third, a consequent reduction in the capacity or the number of competitors might result in higher fares and fewer flights to the detriment of consumers. The last step of this argument is a slippery one, since, by the same logic of the first two steps, display preference can cause the favored airline to add more flights and enter new markets.

Indeed it seems a fair presumption that a display preference purchased by an airline lacking significant market power increases competition. But a pro-competitive defense does not apply to a dominant firm using display bias to deter entry or eliminate competition and maintain or extend its market power.

It is interesting that the DOT did not argue that vertical integration necessarily increased the incentive for display bias, even though it alluded to the changed vertical structure of the CRS industry as a motivation for its deregulation. The DOT noted that "(o)bviously a system that is not owned or controlled by a US airline will not have the same incentives to prejudice the competitive position or rival airlines." Nevertheless, the DOT went on to conclude that an independent CRS likely would have the ability and incentive to sell preferential display treatment. Moreover it is at least conceivable that a dominant firm has an incentive to purchase preferential treatment with an exclusionary intent. Thus the DOT's analysis begs the question of whether vertical divestiture reduced the ability or incentive for anticompetitive display bias.

The single monopoly profit theory seems to apply to the CRS market. The DOT found that each CRS firm had monopoly power toward the airlines. If selling preferential display treatment to an airline maximizes profits, then a CRS will do so, and there is no further monopoly profit gained by vertical integration with an airline. An airline can bid for preferential treatment from the independent CRS firm, and should not expect that acquiring an ownership share is a less expensive means of purchase. Therefore the demand for preferential display bias is not obviously a motive for vertical integration, and this may explain why airlines divested their ownership in CRSs by the end of the proceeding.

The restoring monopoly power theory also plausibly applies to the CRS industry, although the DOT did not explicitly consider this. Suppose that a CRS firm can maximize profit by committing not to engage in preferential display bias, but that such a commitment is unenforceable because of contractual incompleteness. If airlines were to agree to high booking fees on the promise of neutral display bias, then the CRS firm might have an incentive to break its promise and offer preferential treatment to one of them. Anticipating this incentive, the airlines would refuse to pay such high fees in the first place. If this commitment problem were a serious one, then the CRS industry presumably would have lobbied the DOT to keep its display bias rules in place. Apparently, this was not the case. And if commitment were not a problem, then a most-favored-customer clause would seem to be an effective contractual device for dealing with the problem.

4.2.3 Premdor–Masonite Merger

In 2001 the DOJ challenged Premdor's acquisition of Masonite from International Paper Company. The DOJ identified the relevant downstream market to be molded doors, and the relevant upstream market to be molded doorskins. Molded doors are manufactured by pressing molded doorskins onto a flat door. Premdor manufactured molded doors, and Masonite manufactured molded doorskins among other things. Prior to the merger,

Premdor had only limited capacity to produce molded doorskins, and purchased most of its doorskins requirements from Masonite. There was one other major competitor in each of the two markets, a vertically integrated molded door manufacturer, referred to as the "non-party firm," who produced molded doorskins mostly but not exclusively for its own requirements, as well as fringe door-makers. The DOJ settled its complaint with a consent agreement requiring Masonite to divest one of its doorskin plants to a new entrant into the upstream market.

The DOJ was concerned primarily that the vertical merger would facilitate collusive pricing in the upstream market for molded doorskins. The DOJ argued that the ability of Premdor to integrate backward by internal growth disciplined coordinated pricing by Masonite and the non-party firm in the molded doorskin markets, and that the merger would eliminate this discipline. Thus the DOJ identified facilitating collusion in the upstream market to be an anticompetitive horizontal effect of the merger.

The DOJ was concerned also that the merger facilitated collusion in the downstream market for molded doors (*US v. Premdor*, 2001, p. 6):

In addition, Masonite acts as a significant competitive constraint in the interior molded door market. Premdor and the non-party firm have an incentive to coordinate pricing to reduce output. Coordination would reduce the output of interior molded doors, and lead to higher door prices. However, such an output reduction would also reduce the output of interior molded doorskins sold in the United States, harming Masonite. Thus, Masonite would have an incentive to disrupt such coordination through increased sales to the other non-vertically integrated door manufacturers. After the proposed transaction, a vertically integrated Premdor/Masonite combination will not have the same incentive to defeat coordination in the interior molded door market by increasing sales to the non-integrated door manufacturers since the combined company would be competing against those door manufacturers, and would benefit from an increase in the prices of interior molded doors.

The DOJ's sketchy theory that vertical integration facilitates tacit collusion downstream to my knowledge does not have any counterpart in the game-theoretic economics literature on collusion. The DOJ's theory of coordinated conduct, however, does seem related to a raising rivals' cost theory of unilateral upstream conduct. By the merger Masonite gains an incentive to raise the price of doorskins to unintegrated downstream rivals, because of the benefit to Premdor of softer downstream competition. This incentive to raise the costs of downstream rivals' after the merger undermines a prior incentive of Masonite to counteract downstream collusion by cutting prices to fringe door-makers. Thus, the merger facilitates downstream collusion according to a raising rivals' costs theory.

The DOJ also implicitly identified a possible double-marginalization effect, but in such a way as to argue that the cost economies from the vertical merger would facilitate collusion in the downstream market. The DOJ argued that because of cost advantages, "the non-party firm acts as significant competitive constraint in both the upstream and downstream markets." The DOJ argued that this cost advantage would largely evaporate after the merger, possibly because of eliminating markups or coordination economies. The DOJ argued that cost economies from the vertical merger would facilitate collusion by narrowing the non-party firm's cost advantage and thereby blunt its incentive to deviate from coordinated pricing to gain additional market share.

Finally, the DOJ suggested that the vertical merger would facilitate collusion by changing the information structure of the market. Collusion in the upstream market was impeded because Masonite could not monitor easily the vertically integrated non-party firm's supply of molded doorskins to itself. Masonite gained better information on the downstream market for molded doors once it integrated with Premdor. Thus it seemed easier for the two vertically integrated firms to coordinate downstream prices of molded doors. This is an interesting idea that, to my knowledge, has not been analyzed formally in the economics literature.

4.3 Framework

A general presumption that vertical integration is pro-competitive is warranted by a substantial economics literature identifying efficiency benefits of vertical integration, including empirical studies demonstrating positive effects of vertical integration in various industries. However, there is also a growing body of academic literature identifying possible anticompetitive effects of vertical integration in particular circumstances, including empirical evidence that particular vertical integrations may have had harmful or mixed competitive effects. Moreover even a convincing demonstration that vertical integration in a particular industry is pro-competitive "on average" does not eliminate the possibility of harmful effects in a significant fraction of cases. Thus a task for legal and economic analysis to identify those particular (and perhaps relatively few) circumstances in which vertical mergers reduce, or regulatory restraints on vertically integrated firms increase, consumer welfare.

This section sets forth a three-step framework for evaluating the competitive effects of vertical integration based on the more elaborate framework proposed in Riordan and Salop (1995).[48] The first step evaluates if vertical integration is likely to raise the costs or otherwise damage the viability of competitors, or make collusion easier. The second step evaluates likely adverse consequences for consumers, such as higher prices, lower quality, or less product variety. The final step puts possible efficiencies of vertical integration into the balance to evaluate net competitive effects. The three-step framework is useful either for weighing the merits of a vertical merger, such as the NC/DirectTV and Premdor/Masonite mergers, or for pondering the usefulness of restrictions on the conduct of a regulated industry, such as the CRS industry.

A usual preliminary step is to evaluate market power at the upstream and downstream levels by analyzing the structure of these markets. If upstream and downstream markets both are unconcentrated, then vertical integration is unlikely to enable or extend the exercise of market power unless it is by superior efficiency. Similarly low-entry barriers into the upstream and downstream industries might preclude anything but a fleeting increase in market power from vertical integration. If entry is easy, then any attempt by a vertically integrated firm to raise prices likely would be met by timely new entry or expansion of competitors sufficient to restore consumer welfare.

A preliminary analysis of market power, however, often is premature. A problem with a market concentration screen is that it focuses controversy on market definition, and distracts from the fundamental question of whether vertical integration is likely to raise prices or otherwise injure consumers. In the CRS proceeding, the DOT determined that each CRS was a monopoly but did not analyze satisfactorily how vertical integration changed incentives for display bias. DOT therefore did not explain clearly whether and how the vertical divestiture of CRSs by airlines helped justify its decision to deregulate the CRS industry. Similarly a potential problem with a preliminary entry barrier screen is that it is difficult to determine the likelihood, timeliness, and sufficiency of entry without first evaluating the competitive effects of vertical integration (Salop 2000). Moreover reliable quantitative measures of entry barriers are difficult to come by, and a convincing evaluation of entry barriers often ultimately requires a coherent analysis of competitive effects.

Step 1: Impact on Rivals' Costs and Viability and on Facility to Collusion

The first step evaluates the likely effects of vertical integration on the unilateral and coordinated conduct of participants in relevant markets. Vertical integration might increase the costs or otherwise damage the viability of competitors, or it might better enable tacit or express collusion. Such effects can occur either in upstream or downstream relevant markets. A vertical merger potentially injures downstream competitors by raising their costs or by making their product less attractive to consumers. Such injuries might be accomplished by denying, degrading, or raising the price of access to an important input for which there are no close substitutes ("input foreclosure"). Vertical integration also potentially harms upstream competitors. A refusal to deal by the downstream division of a vertically integrated firm might shrink the customer base of upstream rivals ("customer foreclosure"). A reduced customer base can threaten the viability of downstream rivals by compromising economies of scale and discouraging investments in product and process improvements necessary to remain competitive.

A convincing input foreclosure theory of harmful vertical integration has two crucial elements. First, equally cost-effective substitute inputs are unavailable. Second, a vertically integrated firm has an incentive to withdraw from the input market or raise the price of the input. If a vertically integrated firm remains ready and willing to compete aggressively to supply downstream rivals, then vertical integration does not increase the market power of rival input suppliers.

A convincing theory of customer foreclosure similarly has two major elements. First, vertical integration must reduce the customer base of rival upstream firms at given prices. For this to happen, the downstream division of the integrated firm must have the incentive to refuse to deal with or to reduce its purchases from outside suppliers. Moreover rival upstream firms must lack the incentive or be unable easily to expand sales to other downstream customers. If the upstream division of the integrated firm is capacity constrained, or if the integrated firm withdraws from supplying the downstream market, perhaps pursuant to an input foreclosure strategy, then rival upstream suppliers arguably would suffer little or no net decrease in demand from the resulting realignment of customer-supplier relationships. Second, the reduced customer base must place rival upstream firms at a competitive disadvantage to the integrated firm. There are various ways for this to happen. On the one hand, a reduced customer base could sacrifice economies of scale or scope, thus raising the marginal costs of rival upstream firms. If the resulting cost disadvantage becomes sufficiently great, then rivals will leave the market. Otherwise, higher marginal costs will cause rivals to stem profit losses by raising prices, resulting in a further loss of customers. On the other hand, a reduced customer base could cause upstream rivals to reduce investments in process innovation or product improvement. Innovation is itself a source of scale economies because any reduction in the unit cost or a price premium for higher quality is captured on the entire customer case. Thus a reduced customer base reduces the returns to innovation.

Input foreclosure was a central concern of the FCC in NC/DirectTV. The FCC identified RSNs as "must have" programming for many MVPD consumers because there is no good substitute for watching their favorite teams on television. Resale of the programming is illegal, and piracy is not very attractive because of the time-sensitive nature of sports entertainment. The key issue was whether, after acquiring DirectTV, Fox had a heightened incentive to withhold access to RSN programming or raise the price of RSN programming to MVPD competitors. The FCC concluded that after the merger Fox would not have an incentive permanently to deny competitors access to RSN programming, but did have a greater incentive temporarily to withhold programming in the course of bargaining over terms of program carriage. The enhanced threat of temporary foreclosure would increase Fox's bargaining power, and enable Fox to raise the price of RSN programming to MVPD competitors.

Input foreclosure was also at issue in the CRS proceeding. Display bias in favor of a vertically integrated airline potentially disadvantages rival airlines. While access to each CRS was crucial for an airline to reach all customers, the Internet was fast becoming an alternative important source of access. Extrapolating the rising importance of Internet distribution, the DOT determined that display bias by a CRS was less likely seriously to disadvantage rival airlines in the future. In other words, the DOT believed that Internet bookings were quickly becoming an equally cost-effective substitute for bookings with traditional travel agents.

In the Premdor case, the DOJ argued that after the merger, Masonite had an incentive to raise the price of molded doorskins to independent molded door manufacturers. The DOJ did not address explicitly the possibility that the non-party firm might expand to serve independent downstream competitors, but if the case had gone to trial, the DOJ could well have argued that the vertically integrated non-party firm would exercise increased market power by likewise raising prices to independent downstream rivals. The DOJ did express the doubt that entry in the molded doorskin market would be "timely, likely or sufficient to prevent the exercise of market power that the two dominant, vertically integrated firms would be able to collectively exercise following the merger."

Vertical integration could increase the ability and incentive for tacit or express collusion by changing the information structure of markets. If a vertically integrated firm contracts out for some of its input requirements, then the downstream division must obtain price quotes and possibly other competitively sensitive information from upstream competitors. The downstream division can transmit this information to the upstream division, and similarly can transmit information in the opposite direction in the course of commercial communications with outside suppliers. Thus the downstream division of a vertically integrated firm potentially is a conduit for information exchange that potentially increases the likelihood of coordinated conduct.

For information exchange stemming from vertical integration to raise competitive concerns, several conditions are necessary. First, the input market must otherwise be conducive to collusive conduct. For example, if the input market is unconcentrated, then information exchange is unlikely to increase the likelihood of coordinated conduct. Second, the exchanged information must be "projectable" to other competitive bidding situations. For example, if the vertically integrated firm is uniquely situated, then the input prices quoted to the downstream division may not be indicative of the prices quoted to other customers. Finally, the exchange information must be "unique," in the sense that the same or closely similar information cannot be communicated readily via other legal channels. Absent these conditions, it is unlikely that the changed information structure resulting from vertical integration facilitates collusion.

In the Premdor case, the DOJ argued that the upstream market was conducive to coordinated conduct because of high concentration and a homogeneous product, and DOJ argued further that the merger eliminated Premdor's incentive to integrate backward in response to higher doorskin prices. In the DOJ's view, the reduced cost asymmetries between Premdor-Masonite and the vertically integrated nonparty firm made it easier for the two firms to monitor and punish defections from an express or tacit agreement. For example, prior to the merger, Masonite did not operate in the downstream market and consequently lacked information on the conduct of its vertically integrated rival. Thus the DOJ suggested, at least obliquely, that the merger improved communication between upstream firms by giving Masonite a presence in the downstream market.

Step 2: Anticompetitive Impact on the Output Market
It is widely agreed that competition policy should concern itself with injury to consumers rather than mere injury to competitors. Competitive markets generally improve economic welfare by weeding out less efficient competitors. Consequently policies that protect inefficient competitors can undermine competitive processes to the ultimate detriment of con-

sumers. Consumer injury results from input or customer foreclosure only if output prices rise, product quality decreases, or consumer have fewer choices.

Final consumers are injured by vertical integration if upstream suppliers raise prices, because of either increased market power or higher costs, and downstream firms pass on these price increases. Input foreclosure provides a basis for increased market power, while customer foreclosure provides a basis for higher upstream costs. Consumers are also harmed if left with fewer choices as downstream firms exit, or lesser quality choices as downstream or upstream firms reduce investments in product improvement. In the NC/DirectTV case the FCC concluded that Fox would exercise increased bargaining power resulting from vertical integration by raising the price per subscriber of RSN programming,[49] and concluded with little discussion that rival MVPD firms would pass on these higher costs of RSN programming to consumers in the form of higher prices.

In the Premdor case the DOJ argued the merger facilitated upstream market collusion via a raising rivals' cost effect on independent rivals in the downstream market for molded doors. A possible problem with this theory is that after the merger, Premdor might have a greater incentive to expand in the downstream market, which could disrupt upstream collusion with the vertically integrated non-party firm. The DOJ, however, simultaneously advanced a theory of downstream market collusion. It is conceivable that successful downstream market collusion would control Premdor's incentive for expansion. The interplay between these theories of collusion at two different market levels is complex, and the DOJ did not fully articulate or defend an integrated theory in its brief competitive impact statement.

Step 3: Efficiencies and Net Competitive Impact
Eliminating markups potentially is an important theory of pro-competitive vertical integration. Perceiving a lower marginal cost of production, a vertically integrated firm has an incentive to reduce price and expand output. Other possible efficiencies of vertical integration are better coordination of design and production decisions, improved incentives for relationship-specific investments, and better provision of point of sale services.

A conceivable efficiency argument in the NC/DirectTV case is that vertical integration could eliminate bargaining failures between NC and DirectTV and avoid a temporary withdrawal of Fox RSN programming from DirectTV. This might be understood as a kind of variable proportions distortion, particularly if DirectTV should substitute other programming to fill the channel space during any lapse. FCC did not address such an argument, perhaps because it regarded temporary foreclosure strategies unlikely prior to the acquisition.

A possible efficiency defense for display bias in the CRS proceeding is that a preferential display potentially is a form of product promotion that helps an airline expand capacity and enter new markets, or even simply to "advertise" its existing flights. By this theory, a ban on display bias might be a barrier to entry and expansion. For this efficiency theory to be persuasive against a convincing theory of competitive harm, it would be important to argue that entrants and competitors did not have access to an equally efficient alternative advertising channel to promote their service. Moreover a valid concern is that the efficiency theory does not apply to incumbents who are well established and already well known to travel agents and consumers. The DOT did not consider these issues explicitly.

In the Premdor case the DOJ argued that cost economies from the merger facilitated collusion between two vertically integrated firms by reducing the incentive of the previous cost leader to defect from an agreement. This is at best a roughly plausible theory based on the modern theory of collusive oligopoly. A cost-leader indeed could have the greater incentive to defect from a collusive agreement, but this depends on market shares. One possibility is that a cost-leader receives a larger market share under the collusive agreement in order to control its incentive to defect (Nocke and White 2007). Thus a narrowing cost advantage due to merger-related efficiencies could cause only a realignment of collusive market shares in favor of Premdor-Masonite without any substantial disruption of coordinated pricing. At the same time the cost economies of the merger might push down prices to final consumers if firms behave noncollusively, and possibly even under collusive pricing. After all, a collusive vertically integrated duopoly ideally mimics a horizontally integrated monopoly. Typically a profit-maximizing firm does lower prices in response to a cost reduction of some of its products. The DOJ recognized cost efficiencies from the vertical merger, while arguing that the required divestiture of one of Masonite's molded doorskin plants would limit collusion.

Summary

My proposed three-step framework treats the evaluation of the net competitive impact of vertical integration in merger cases or regulatory proceedings ultimately as a "battle of theories" with the following rules of engagement. The complaining party must prove injury to competitors and to consumers in steps 1 and 2 of my proposed framework. The merging parties or an integrated firm must have an opportunity to defend with evidence in support of a pro-competitive theory in step 3. Finally, a court or regulatory authority must weigh the merits of the alternative theories, recognizing the possibilities that one or the other or both might be correct, and make a reasoned assessment of whether on balance vertical integration is likely to harm final consumers. This assessment should encompass whether the facts of the case validate the critical assumptions of the alternative theories, and whether the competitive effects predicted by a valid theory are likely to be significant quantitatively. The controlling questions are whether vertical integration is likely to cause significantly higher prices, less product variety, or lower product quality.

4.4   Conclusions

Competitive effects of vertical integration remains an active topic of industrial organization research, and a challenge for antitrust and regulatory policies. The Chicago school's single monopoly profit theory is still a touchstone for academic research and policy analysis. The assumptions of the theory are a point of departure for any alternative theory, and for any analysis of real market structures. Although the single monopoly profit theory's extreme assumption of concentrated bargaining power has not received much attention in the academic literature, a more realistic theory of give-and-take bargaining lay behind the FCC's decision in the NC/DirectTV case. The restoring monopoly power theory is a clear and well-articulated alternative to the single monopoly profit theory, but it has not been influential in recent cases. In contrast, variants of raising rivals' costs theory played a prominent role in recent cases concerning the conduct of vertically integrated firms, including the NC/DirectTV merger, the CRS deregulation proceeding, and the Premdor-Masonite merger. Eliminating markups lurks as an available efficiency defense but has not been given much weight in recent cases. Finally, collusion continues to be a concern in vertical merger cases, including Premdor-Masonite, although economic theory has been slow to formalize models of how vertical integration facilitate collusion. The further development of economic theory in this area could contribute to more rigorous applications of facilitating collusion theories of vertical integration.

Hovenkamp (2001) among others argues that post-Chicago theories of anticompetitive vertical integration "may not be quite ready for prime time" because of administrative impracticality. The objection usually is raised with general concerns that such theories might be employed too aggressively in antitrust or regulatory proceedings. The essence of the objection is that raising rivals' costs and eliminating markups theories both apply to concentrated upstream and downstream industries with market power, so it is difficult to find factual evidence that distinguishes one from the other. I disagree that this is necessarily the case, and propose that courts often do have the ability to balance the significance of alternative theories for economic welfare even when both have some validity.

Market power is only one important structural element for discerning the competitive effects of vertical integration. Another is the power of contracts. An eliminating markups defense for vertical integration requires that firms be unable to achieve this efficiency with arm's-length contracts. This is most clearly the case when price discrimination is difficult. Contracts in many intermediate markets, however, feature restraints and nonlinear pricing. Thus there should be some burden on defendants to show that factual conditions regarding contracts support an eliminating markups defense. At the same time a different set of contractual failures might support a raising rivals' costs theory or restoring monopoly power theory, requiring a similar burden on plaintiffs. Such a framework suggests a "battle of theories" with courts and regulatory authorities adjudicating the relative merits of the alternatives.

Generally, it is a mistake to suppose that only one theory of competitive effects can be valid in any given case. Both a raising rivals' costs theory and an eliminating markups theory might be plausible. In such circumstances parties to the debate should provide evidence on factual conditions supporting the theories and on the actual importance of the theories for economic welfare. The court or regulatory authority should weigh the evidence to determine which theory is the more important one for understanding the competitive effects of vertical integration on a case-by-case basis. Hovencamp (2001) observes that such balancing requires the courts and regulatory authorities to exercise significant sophistication. This is true, but it seems too cynical merely to assume that these institutions are not up to the task. The balancing of the magnitude of competitive effects calls for a structured rule of reason to weigh the evidence and evaluate the likely consequences of vertical integration for economic welfare. Meanwhile further progress on the academic front should assist the courts and regulatory authorities in developing a rigorous approach to evaluating the competitive effects of vertical integration.

Notes

I thank participants at the June 2005 LEAR conference and participants at a seminar at Columbia University for their comments. I also thank Steven Salop for extensive comments on earlier drafts, and Sergei Koulayev for excellent research assistance.

1. The US Department of Justice's *1984 Merger Guidelines* also recognize "evading regulation" as an additional anticompetitive motive for vertical integration (DOJ 1984). This issue is beyond the scope of this chapter.

2. There are, of course, different legal forms of a firm, ranging from sole proprietorships, to partnerships, to corporations.

3. There is a continuing debate on the most appropriate economic definition of "entry barriers"; see *American Economic Review, Papers and Proceeding* (2004).

4. Price discrimination traditionally is categorized into three types. First-degree price discrimination refers to bargaining over terms on a customer-by-customer basis. Second-degree price discrimination involves different customers paying different prices because they make different choices from the same menu of possibilities. Quantity discounts are an important example of second-degree price discrimination, as customers electing different quantities end up paying different average prices. Finally, third-degree price discrimination means setting prices for different groups of customers, for example, setting different prices in geographically distinct markets.

5. This assumption sidesteps thorny problems about decentralized incentives inside the firm, in particular, the difficulty of aligning the incentives of owners and managers. See Mookherjee (2003) and Baldenius (2006).

6. Essentially the same argument applies to backward integration if the downstream industry is a monopoly and the upstream industry is perfectly competitive. In this case the downstream monopolist also is a monopsonist on the input market. Moreover the argument generalizes if monopolist or monopsonist were to integrate partially by acquiring a fraction of the assets of the downstream or upstream industry.

7. Generally, the Cournot quantity-setting model of oligopoly is appropriate for modeling the capacity decisions of firms in a homogeneous product industry, while the Bertrand price-setting model is more appropriate for a produce-to-order differentiated product industry.

8. See Amir and Lambson (2000) for sufficient conditions for unique symmetric Cournot equilibrium.

9. If the downstream firms are asymmetric, then the terms of the two-part tariffs can be customized for each customer in order to achieve the goal of fully monopolizing the downstream industry.

10. There are bargaining reasons for vertical integration even if D_1 and D_2 do not compete with each other and operate in independent markets. Suppose that U bargains to allocate a scarce supply of the upstream good. Thus the opportunity cost of supplying an incremental amount of the upstream good to D_2 is that the good could be supplied alternatively to D_1. Suppose further that the demands of consumers depend positively on relationship-specific investments that D_1 and D_2 must undertake prior to negotiating with U. A vertically integrated firm U-D_1 has a profitable incentive to "overinvest" in order to increase its bargaining strength in dealing with D_2 (Bolton and Whinston 1993; Kranton and Minehart 2004).

11. See Snyder (1995) for a critique of the conclusion that this evidence indicates vertical foreclosure.

12. If the $(N-1)$ rivals face a two part tariff (W^*, F^*) and each produce Q^*/N and D_1 produces q, then the joint profit of U and D_1 is $(N-1)F^* + W^*(Q-q) + [P(Q) - c_d]q - C_u(Q)$, where $Q = q + (N-1)Q^*/N$. This joint profit function is maximized where $P(Q) + P'(Q)q = C'(Q)$. Under the usual regularity conditions for the existence and uniqueness of Cournot equilibrium, the solution has $q > Q^*/N$, resulting in a downstream price below the monopoly level. Consequently the rival firms earn negative profits net of F^*. The deviant contract that induces this q from D_1 sets $W = P(Q) + P'(Q)q - c_d$. Thus $W < W^*$. The fixed fee that extracts supra-competitive profits from D_1 is $F = -P'(Q)q^2 > F^*$.

13. More formally, in the perfect Bayesian equilibrium of this game, the upstream firm (U) offers each of the N downstream firms $(D_1, \ldots, D_N)$ a contract that is immune to deviation. The equilibrium concept requires a specification of beliefs when D_1 is offered an out-of-equilibrium contract. Rey and Tirole (2007) argue that "passive beliefs" are most reasonable when firms set quantities in advance of sales and contracts are secret, that is, when offered a deviation contract, D_1 continues to believe that downstream rivals have been offered their equilibrium contracts and continue to choose their equilibrium quantities. Thus, in the symmetric Cournot case, a two-part tariff that is immune to deviation incentives satisfies $W = P(Q) + P'(Q)q - c_d < W^*$, where $Q = Nq$ satisfies $P(Q) + P'(Q)q = C'(Q)$; see the previous note. If $C_u(Q) = c_u Q$, then this solution corresponds to Cournot competition between n symmetric vertically integrated firms with constant average costs $c = c_d + c_u$. Rey and Tirole (2007) acknowledge that passive-beliefs equilibria are less compelling when downstream firms set prices for differentiated products. In the price-setting case, however, even under an alternative belief system ("wary beliefs") incentives for opportunistic behavior by U result in a more competitive outcome compared to a vertically and horizontally integrated monopoly (Rey and Verge 2003).

14. DeGraba (1996) clarifies that a most-favored customer clause deters opportunism if a downstream firm can "pick and choose" among individual terms of two-part tariffs. Consequently, if the monopolist offers a lower marginal wholesale price to any competitor, then all competitors are able to access this reduced marginal price without suffering a higher fixed fee.

15. Chen and Riordan (2004) demonstrate that if exclusive dealing is enforceable, then a vertically integrated supplier may be able to exclude equally efficient upstream competitors and effectively cartelize the downstream industry with two-part tariffs. In this scenario the integrated supplier effectively organizes a downstream cartel by compensating downstream competitors for committing not to deal with alternative suppliers.

16. In the symmetric Cournot case, if U integrates forward, then U simply refuses to deal with independent downstream competitors, foreclosing them from the market. This foreclosure does not sacrifice any monopoly profits under the assumption of constant average costs (Hart and Tirole 1990).

17. See, for example, Chen and Riordan (2004) who study a price-setting spatially differentiated downstream oligopoly.

18. Event studies yield ambiguous evidence on the competitive effects of vertical integration (Rosengren and Meehan 1994; Snyder 1995; Mullin and Mullin 1997).

19. These effects also contradict the raising rivals' cost and facilitating-collusion theories discussed below.

20. This undoubtedly is a difficult task, since the predictions of the theory depend on out-of-equilibrium beliefs, about which observable evidence must be difficult to come by. What are lacking from the general theory are robust predictions across a set of plausible beliefs (Segal and Whinston 2003).

21. Martin, Norman, and Snyder (2001) also casts doubt on the validity of passive beliefs that Rey and Tirole (2007) argue is appropriate when downstream firms choose quantities in advance of sales.

22. The artificiality is plain. If there is only a single customer for the intermediate good, then there can be no resale market for the input, and therefore no reason for the contracting parties to restrict their attention to uniform pricing. The argument makes more sense if the downstream industry is an oligopoly, and the upstream monopolist cannot control resale. Even then, the monopolist might be able to depart from simple uniform pricing by restricting the quantities it sells to individual firms. For example, in the symmetric case the upstream monopolist could simply offer a quantity $q^* = Q^*/N$ to each downstream firm for a take-it-or-leave it price that extracted the monopoly profits. The downstream firms each would take the deal, have no incentive for resale, and the upstream firm would earn the full monopoly profit. Such simple quantity forcing is less attractive if the monopolist is incompletely informed about downstream profits and therefore unable to calculate Q^*. Quantity forcing also fails if the upstream monopolist is unable to make multilateral commitments (Hart and Tirole 1990; Rey and Tirole 2007).

23. Alternatively, the upstream and downstream monopolists bargain over F to divide the surplus. Efficient bargaining maximizes the joint surplus by setting the slope of the wholesale price schedule equal to $C_u(Q)$.

24. A drawback of the two-part tariff solution is that it provides poor incentives for quality, both at the upstream and downstream level (Mathewson and Winter 1984).

25. The metering argument for tying (Telser 1979) is an early version of this theory.

26. See Riordan (1990) for a discussion of how vertical integration alters information structure.

27. While the cost reduction from vertical integration puts downward pressure on prices, an accompanying horizontal consolidation of the downstream industry has the opposite effect. Consequently in the variable proportions case the net competitive effect of forward integration by an upstream monopolist is difficult to determine without detailed information about industry structure (Perry 1989). Abiru (1988) analyzes a successive Cournot oligopoly in which the downstream industry has a constant elasticity of substitution in production and with a constant elasticity of final demand, and presents conditions under which, holding downstream horizontal industry structure constant, vertical integration results in lower final prices. These conditions require that the raising rivals' cost effect of partial vertical integration is not too great (Salinger 1988), as discussed in the next section.

28. Put another way, by driving up the market price of input, the vertically integrated firm increases the value of its own upstream assets. The greater returns of downstream foreclosure outweigh the higher opportunity cost of these assets.

29. This conclusion depends on the specifics of the dominant firm model: large dominant firm competing downstream against a competitive fringe, perfectly competitive upstream market, no price discrimination in upstream or downstream markets (Riordan 1998).

30. The vertically integrated firm might raise rivals' costs by raising its input price rather than withdraw entirely from the input market. Indeed a refusal to deal by the vertically integrated supplier could be ill advised if it causes rival downstream firms to integrate backward (Ordover, Salop, and Saloner 1990, 1992).

31. Ma (1997) studies a model with differentiated upstream goods in which a vertical integrated firm has a short-run incentive to completely foreclose its downstream rival. An interesting feature of this model, motivated by telecommunications and health care markets, is that the downstream firms sells to consumers "options" to purchase products in the future.

32. This felicitous outcome does not occur if upstream competition has the structure of a descending price auction in which competing suppliers, observing each other's offers, sequentially bid down prices. In this case the vertically integrated firm looks ahead and realizes that its bid for the business of independent downstream firms will be met by further price-cutting by the upstream rivals. Such foresight convinces the vertically integrated firm to offer higher prices or to stay out of the bidding altogether (Ordover, Salop, and Saloner 1992). This defense of the theory does not work, however, if intermediate goods contracts are bilateral and private, in which case upstream rivals do not observe, and therefore are unable directly to respond to, competing offers (Hart and Tirole 1990).

33. The significance of technological compatibility is also emphasized in the economics literature on tying (Whinston 1990).

34. Two-part tariffs should not necessarily be interpreted as an exact description of contracting practices. An equivalent pricing strategy is a step tariff such that infra-marginal units sell at a higher price than marginal units do. The premia paid on the infra-marginal units is equivalent to the fixed fee. Other forms of volume discounting can be interpreted similarly.

35. This division of rents from bilateral bargaining deflects the single monopoly profit theory.

36. The single monopoly profit theory fails in the Gilbert-Riordan model because the upstream monopolist is unable to price discriminate between alternative uses of the intermediate good, and therefore is unable fully to extract monopoly profits from the downstream competitor.

37. On the surface this appears to be an odd behavioral assumption. Even though the intermediate good is in a fixed proportion of the final good, a downstream firm acts as price-taker when purchasing the intermediate good but a quantity-setter when producing the final good. This conduct might be rationalized, however, by assuming that firms first at each stage simultaneously choose quantities à la Cournot and then simultaneously choose prices à la Bertrand (Kreps and Scheinkman 1983). Nevertheless, it is unclear to what extent this interpretation depends on assumptions about rationing in the intermediate goods market (Davidson and Deneckere 1986).

38. If upstream market power is due to quantity competition, then a vertical merger that increases upstream market power is not necessarily profitable (Salant, Switzer, and Reynolds 1983).

39. In addition to these three theories, the Guidelines also worry that vertical integration might enable public utilities to evade rate regulation (DOJ 1984, sec. 4.23).

40. Krattenmaker and Salop (1986) originally introduced the "cartel ringmaster" theory to describe a situation in which a downstream firm organized a supplier cartel to exclude downstream competitors.

41. News Corp. acquired 34 percent of Direct TV shares, and a corresponding entitlement to several seats on the board of directors.

42. FCC authority for approval of the merger stemmed from its obligation to determine that the transfer of certain licenses and authorizations from General Motors to News Corp. were in the public interest.

43. The FCC also identified a separate market for local broadcast television programming, and a separate market for nonsports and national sports programming. Our discussion ignores these markets for the sake of brevity.

44. Thus the FCC implicitly ignored rural markets lacking a CSO.

45. Rogerson (2003b, app.) argued this point with a simple reduced form model of Nash bargaining. Nash's theory of bargaining assumes that parties to a transaction proportionally divide the surplus value of a transaction, which is the value over and above the value of the "outside" opportunities of the parties should bargaining break down. Vertical integration arguably increased NC's outside opportunity because NC partially internalized the benefit to DirectTV of temporary or permanent foreclosure of DirectTV's cable competitors. See also Salop and Woodbury (2003, app.) for a similar argument in the context of the CRS proceeding discussed next.

46. Amadeus was owned partially by three European airlines.

47. Salop and Woodbury (2003) argued on Sabre's behalf that a vertically integrated CRS had an RRC incentive to raise the price of CRS access to rival airlines, and presented a bargaining model to that effect.

48. Riordan and Salop (1995) separately consider input and customer foreclosure, and address competitive effects in ancillary markets. Riordan and Salop (1995) also discuss evasion-of-regulation theories beyond the scope of the present essay.

49. My understanding is that cable programming contracts typically establish a wholesale price per subscriber. The reason for this standard contracting practice may be to create an incentive to produce high-quality programming. RSN programming contracts are "blind," meaning the sports games have not been played yet. Bargaining over fixed fees while controlling final prices is a better way to divide profits, but could also provide unfortunate incentives to degrade quality by cutting production costs.

References

Abiru, M. 1988. Vertical integration, variable proportions and successive oligopolies. *Journal of Industrial Economics* 36: 315–25.

American Bar Association Antitrust Law Section (ABA). 2003. *Antitrust Law Developments*, 5th ed. Madison, WI: ABA Publishing.

Amir, R., and V. E. Lambson. 2000. On the effects of entry in Cournot markets. *Review of Economic Studies* 67: 235–54.

Bain, J. S. 1965. *Barriers to New Competition*. Cambridge: Harvard University Press.

Baker, G., R. Gibbons, and K. Murphy. 2002. Relational contracts and the theory of the firm. *Quarterly Journal of Economics* 117: 39–84.

Baldenius, T. 2006. Ownership, incentives, and the hold-up problem. *RAND Journal of Economics* 37: 276–99.

Bolton, P., and M. Whinston. 1993. Incomplete contracts, vertical integration, and supply assurance. *Review of Economic Studies* 60: 121–48.

Carlton, D. W., and M. Waldman. 2002. The strategic use of tying to preserve and create market power in evolving industries. *RAND Journal of Economics* 33: 194–220.

Chen, Y. 2002. On vertical mergers and their competitive effects. *RAND Journal of Economics* 33: 667–85.

Chen, Y., and M. H. Riordan. 2004. Vertical integration, exclusive dealing, and ex post cartelization. *RAND Journal of Economics*, forthcoming.

Chipty, T. 2001. Vertical integration, market foreclosure, and consumer welfare in the cable television industry. *American Economic Review* 91: 428–53.

Choi, J. P., and S.-S. Yi. 2000. Vertical foreclosure with the choice of input specifications. *RAND Journal of Economics* 31: 717–43.

Church, J., and N. Gandal. 2000. Systems competition, vertical merger, and foreclosure. *Journal of Economics and Strategy Management* 9: 25–52.

Coase, R. 1972. Durable goods monopolists. *Journal of Law and Economics* 15: 143–50.

Davidson, C., and R. Deneckere. 1986. Long-run competition in capacity, short-run competition in price, and the Cournot outcome. *RAND Journal of Economics* 17: 404–15.

de Fontenay, C., and J. S. Gans. 2002. Vertical integration in the presence of upstream competition. Working paper, forthcoming in *RAND Journal of Economics*.

DeGraba, P. 1996. Most-favored-customer clauses and multilateral contracting: When nondiscrimination implies uniformity. *Journal of Economics and Management Strategy* 5: 565–79.

Department of Transportation (DOT). 2004. *Computer Reservation System Regulations: Final Rule*. Available at ⟨http://www.dot.gov/affairs/ComputerReservationsSystem.htm⟩.

Federal Communications Commission (FCC). 2004. Memorandum and order in the matter of General Motors Corporation and Hughes Electronics Corporation, transferors, and The News Corporation, transferee, for authority to transfer control. MB docket 03-124, adopted December 19, 2003, and released January 14, 2004.

Gilbert, R., and J. Hastings. 2005. Market power, vertical integration, and the wholesale price of gasoline. Yale University working paper. *Journal of Industrial Economics* 53: 469–92.

Gilbert, R., and M. Riordan. 2007. Product improvement and technological tying in a winner-take-all market. *Journal of Industrial Economics* 55: 113–39.

Grimm, C. M., C. Winston, and C. A. Evans. 1992. Foreclosure of railroad markets: A test of Chicago leverage theory. *Journal of Law and Economics* 35: 295–310.

Grossman, S., and O. Hart. 1986. The costs and benefits of ownership: A theory of vertical integration. *Journal of Political Economy* 94: 691–719.

Hart, O., and J. Moore. 1990. Property rights and the nature of the firm. *Journal of Political Economy* 98: 1119–58.

Hart, O., and J. Tirole. 1990. Vertical integration and market foreclosure. *Brookings Papers on Economic Activity: Microeconomics* (special issue): 205–76.

Hortacsu, A., and C. Syverson. 2005. Cementing relationships: Vertical integration, foreclosure, productivity, and prices. Working paper. University of Chicago.

Hovenkamp, H. 2001. Post-Chicago antitrust: A review and critique. *Columbia Business Law Review*: 257–337.

Jensen, M. C., and W. H. Meckling. 1976. Theory of the firm: Managerial behavior, agency costs, and ownership structure. *Journal of Financial Economics* 3: 305–60.

Klass, M. W., and M. A. Salinger. 1995. Do new theories of vertical foreclosure provide sound guidance for consent agreements in vertical merger cases? *Antitrust Bulletin* 45: 667–98.

Kranton, R. E., and D. F. Minehart. 2004. Vertical integration and specific investments: A tale of the second best. Working paper. University of Maryland.

Krattenmaker, T. G., and S. C. Salop. 1986. Anticompetitive exclusion: Raising rivals' costs to achieve power over price. *Yale Law Journal* 96: 209–93.

Kreps, D., and J. Scheinkman. 1983. Quantity precommitment and Bertand competition yield Cournot outcomes. *Bell Journal of Economics* 14: 326–37.

McAfee, R. P., and M. Schwartz. 1994. Opportunism in multilateral vertical contracting: Nondiscrimination, exclusivity, and uniformity. *American Economic Review* 84: 210–30.

Ma, C.-T. A. 1997. Option contracts and vertical foreclosure. *Journal of Economics and Management Strategy* 6: 725–53.

Martin, S., H.-T. Norman, and C. Snyder. 2002. Vertical foreclosure in experimental markets. *RAND Journal of Economics* 19: 219–34.

Maskin, E., and J. Riley. 1984. Monopoly with incomplete information. *RAND Journal of Economics* 15: 171–96.

Matthewson, G. F., and R. A. Winter. 1984. An economic theory of vertical restraints. *RAND Journal of Economics* 15: 27–38.

Mookherjee, D. 2003. Delegation and contractual hierarchies: An overview. Working paper. Boston University.

Mullin, J. C., and W. P. Mullin. 1997. United States Steel's acquisition of the Great Northern Ore properties: Vertical foreclosure or efficient contractual governance? *Journal of Law, Economics, and Organization* 13: 74–100.

Nocke, V., and L. White. 2007. Do vertical mergers facilitate upstream collusion? *American Economic Review* 97: 1321–39.

O'Brien, D. P., and S. C. Salop. 2000. Competitive effects of partial ownership: Financial interest and corporate control. *Antitrust Law Journal* 67: 559–614.

O'Brien, D., and G. Shaffer. 1992. Vertical control with bilateral contracts. *RAND Journal of Economics* 23: 299–308.

Ordover, J. A., S. C. Salop, and G. Saloner. 1990. Equilibrium vertical foreclosure. *American Economic Review* 80: 127–42.

Ordover, J. A., S. C. Salop, and G. Saloner. 1992. Equilibrium vertical foreclosure: Reply. *American Economic Review* 82: 698–703.

Perry, M. 1989. Vertical integration: Determinants and effects. In R. Schmalensee and R. Willig, eds., *Handbook of Industrial Organization I*. Amsterdam: Elsevier.

Reiffen, D. 1992. Equilibrium vertical foreclosure: Comment. *American Economic Review* 82: 694–97.

Reiffen, D., and M. Vita. 1995. Is there new thinking on vertical mergers? A comment. *Antitrust Law Journal* 63: 917–42.

Rey, P., and J. Tirole. 2007. A primer on foreclosure. In M. Armstrong and R. Porter, eds., *Handbook of Industrial Organization III*. Amsterdam: Elsevier.

Rey, P., and T. Verge. 2003. Bilateral control with vertical contracts. Working paper. University of Toulouse.

Riordan, M. H. 1990. What is vertical integration? In M. Aoki, B. Gustafsson, and O. Williamson, eds., *The Firm as a Nexus of Treaties*. Thousand Oaks, CA: Sage Publications.

Riordan, M. H. 1998. Anticompetitive vertical integration by a dominant firm. *American Economic Review* 88: 1232–48.

Riordan, M. H., and S. C. Salop. 1995. Evaluating vertical mergers: A post-Chicago approach. *Antitrust Law Journal* 63: 513–68.

Rogerson, W. 2003a. An economic analysis of the competitive effects of the takeover of DirectTV by News Corp. FCC filing, June 13, MB docket no. 03-124.

Rogerson, W. 2003b. A further economic analysis of the News Corp. takeover of DirectTV. FCC filing, August 4, MB docket no. 03-124.

Rosengren, E. S., and J. W. Meehan Jr. 1994. Empirical evidence on vertical foreclosure. *Economic Inquiry* 32: 303–17.

Rubinfeld, D. L., and H. J. Singer. 2001. Open access to broadband networks: A case study of the AOL-Time Warner merger. *Berkeley Technology Law Journal*: 631–75.

Rubinstein, A. 1992. Perfect equilibrium in a bargaining model. *Econometrica* 50: 97–100.

Salant, S., S. Switzer, and R. J. Reynolds. 1983. Losses due to merger: The effects of an exogenous change in industry structure on Cournot-Nash equilibrium. *Quarterly Journal of Economics* 98: 185–99.

Salinger, M. 1988. Vertical mergers and market foreclosure. *Quarterly Journal of Economics* 103: 345–56.

Salop, S. C. 2000. First principles approach to antitrust, *Kodak*, and antitrust at the millennium. *Antitrust Law Journal* 68: 187–202.

Salop, S. C., and D. T. Scheffman. 1987. Cost-raising strategies. *Journal of Industrial Economics* 36: 19–34.

Salop, S. C., and J. R. Woodbury. 2003. Economic analysis of the DOT's NPRM proposals. DOT filing, March 17, Docket nos. OST-97-2881, OST-97-3014, OST-98-4775.

Segal, I., and M. D. Whinston. 2003. Robust predictions for bilateral contracting with externalities. *Econometrica* 71: 757–91.

Snyder, C. M. 1995. Empirical studies of vertical foreclosure. *Industry Economics Conference Papers and Proceedings* (University of Melbourne and Bureau of Industry Economics), 95/23: 98–127.

Spengler, J. J. 1950. Vertical integration and antitrust policy. *Journal of Political Economy* 58: 347–52.

Stigler, G. 1964. A theory of oligopoly. *Journal of Political Economy* 72: 44–61.

Stigler, G. 1971. The theory of economic regulation. *Bell Journal of Economics* 71: 3–21.

Telser, L. 1979. A theory of monopoly of complementary goods. *Journal of Business* 52: 211–30.

Tirole, J. 1988. *The Theory of Industrial Organization*. Cambridge: MIT Press.

US Department of Justice (DOJ). 1984. *Non-horizontal Merger Guidelines*. Available at ⟨http://www.usdoj.gov/atr/public/guidelines/2614.pdf⟩.

US Department of Justice and Federal Trade Commission (DOJ). 1997. *Horizontal Merger Guidelines*. Available at ⟨http://www.usdoj.gov/atr/public/guidelines/horiz_book/hmg1.html⟩.

US v. Premdor. 2001. Competitive impact statement. Civil no. 1:01CV01696. Available at ⟨http://www.usdoj.gov/atr/cases/f9000/9017.htm⟩.

Villas-Boas, S. 2007. Vertical contracts between manufacturers and retailers: Inference with limited data. *Review of Economic Studies* 74: 625–52.

Waterman, D., and A. A. Weiss. 1996. The effects of vertical integration between cable television systems and pay cable networks. *Journal of Econometrics* 72: 357–95.

Whinston, M. 1990. Tying, foreclosure, and exclusion. *American Economic Review* 80: 837–59.

Whinston, M. 2001. Exclusivity and tying in *U.S. v. Microsoft*: What we know, and don't know. *Journal of Economic Perspectives* 15: 63–80.

Williamson, O. E. 1975. *Markets and Hierarchies: Analysis and Antitrust Implications*. New York: Free Press.

Williamson, O. E. 1985. *The Economic Institutions of Capitalism*. New York: Free Press.

Williamson, O. E. 1989. Transaction Cost Economics. In R. Schmalensee and R. Willig, eds., *Handbook of Industrial Organization*, vol. 1. Amsterdam: Elsevier.

5 Analysis of Conglomerate Effects in EU Merger Control

Damien J. Neven

Concern about "conglomerate" effects has weighed on the European Commission for some time.[1] Conglomerate effects appear, for instance, in early decisions like *Tetra Pak/ Alfa-Laval* and are the motive behind the first (ever) prohibition of a merger in *ATR/de Havilland*. A number of prohibitions in the European Union have moreover recently been based almost exclusively on conglomerate effects, in particular, *Tetra Laval/Sidel*[2] and *General Electric/Honeywell*. In other cases significant remedies, involving divestitures, have been imposed by the Commission in order to alleviate their concerns about conglomerate effects (e.g., *Guinness/Grand Metropolitan* or *SEB/Moulinex*). Decisions on both *Tetra Laval/Sidel* and *General Electric/Honeywell* have been appealed. In the case of *Tetra Laval/Sidel*, the Commission's decision was annulled by the Court of First Instance (CFI). The decision by the CFI was further appealed to the European Court of Justice (ECJ) by the Commission. The Court not only reaffirmed the decision of the CFI but also made an important pronouncement on the standards of proof and review that should apply in merger control decisions, and specifically in cases where conglomerate effects have been alleged. *General Electric/Honeywell* led to bitter exchange between the EU and US authorities who had cleared the deal.[3] The decision was confirmed by the CFI, but importantly, the analysis of the conglomerate effects undertaken by the Commission was annulled (and the prohibition thus eventually rested on minor horizontal overlaps). In all these instances the economic analysis undertaken by the European Commission has been a central element of the controversy whether in Court or in public debate.

The time is therefore ripe to take stock of these developments.[4] In this chapter, I consider the various anticompetitive effects that have been alleged by the European Commission in conglomerate mergers and review the economic literature on those practices. My objective is to contribute to the development of policy on conglomerate effects; to that effect I will seek to identify the circumstances where the anticompetitive concerns raised by the Commission are likely to be severe and discuss whether those circumstances can be identified empirically. I will also aim at identifying the elements of proof that can be gathered in order to meet the standards of proof that have been established by the ECJ. This entails a discussion of whether priors toward particular practices are such that they can be considered to be neutral, as well as a discussion of the circumstances where these practices could be anti-anticompetitive and elements of proof that can be deemed sufficient to establish that these circumstances prevail.

In section 5.1, I provide an overview of the anticompetitive concerns that have been raised by the Commission under the label of conglomerate effects. I briefly analyze four minor concerns: the prospect that merging parties will enjoy economies of scale and scope as a result of being active in several market, the prospect that buyers will enjoy economies of scale and scope because their supplier is active in several markets, the prospect that strong brands belonging to the merging parties will provide spillover benefits to their weaker brands, and finally the concern that the substitution between products belonging to separate antitrust markets will be exploited by the merging parties or that the merger will affect potential competition. I also identify a recurrent concern that firms can make contingent sales through practices like bundling, tying, or full line forcing. This will be discussed in section 5.2. In section 5.3, I attempt to develop some standards of proof in identifying these practices. In section 5.4, I conclude.

5.1 Overview of Case Law

Because there is no standard definition of conglomerate effects, a simple taxonomy may prove useful at the outset. Both unilateral and coordinated effects can take place within an antitrust market (i.e., by a set of products that substitute for one another to a sufficient degree that a firm controlling them could significantly raise price above the competitive level). By contrast, conglomerate effects take place across different antitrust markets.

In principle, products that do not belong to the same antitrust market can be complements, independent in demand, or "weak" substitutes. Weak is understood here as meaning that the substitution between the products is not strong enough to place them in the same antitrust market. Weak substitutes are often referred to as products that belong to "neighboring" markets. Hence, if a broad definition of conglomerate effects is adopted, such that potential anticompetitive effects span the whole range of possible demand relationships and conglomerate effects are taken as a residual category, these effects could include all three types of circumstances: complements, weak substitutes, and independent in demand. Conglomerate effects can thus be thought of as "indirect" effects, by contrast with the direct effects that take place within antitrust markets. Importantly, however, such indirect effects will only take place if there are common buyers. In the absence of any common buyers, there is no relationship between the products from the prospective of the seller and thus no anticompetitive effect.[5]

There is a specific type of competitive relationship that deserves attention, namely that by which complements are packaged together for resale to final users. Mergers involving such products are referred to as vertical mergers. Indeed the product of a manufacturer and the service of a distributor are such complements when they are offered jointly to final users. Anticompetitive effects arising from vertical integration have a long tradition in antitrust and are typically analyzed separately from conglomerate effects. The main concern here relates to a potential foreclosure downstream, leaving distributors without access to the product of the manufacturer, or upstream, leaving manufacturers without access to distributors.

Overall, this taxonomy indicates that conglomerate effects can involve products in neighboring markets, products independent in demand, and complements that are sold independently to final users (or at least can be sold separately). In what follows I will adopt the convention that weak substitutes include products independent in demand (as a limit case) and thus focus on products that are either weak substitutes or complements.

It is worth noting how this taxonomy relates to the European Commission's approach toward conglomerate effects. The Commission has proposed a definition of conglomerate mergers in a submission to the OECD (OECD 2002). This definition was also adopted by the CFI in its judgment on *Tetra Laval/Sidel*. It reads as follows:

Conglomerate mergers are mergers between firms that have no existing or potential competitive relationship either as competitors or as suppliers or customers. Under some circumstances, conglomerate mergers may raise competitive concerns where the merging firms are suppliers of complementary, noncompeting but closely related products requested by the same set of customers.

Because this EC definition appears to exclude vertical mergers (complements repackaged for final users that involve supplier or customer relationships) as well as mergers involving firms selling products within the same relevant markets ("competitors"), by this perspective it is consistent with the taxonomy developed above. However, it also appears ready to disallow "complements," and to exclude weak substitutes, at least if "complementary" is taken as a synonym for complement.

In the same submission the Commission developed further what is meant by complementary products: the European Union distinguishes between technical complements ("when one product cannot function without the other"), economic complements ("products that are consumed together like milk and coffee"), and commercial complements ("when they form part of range that downstream agents, such as multiple retailers, need to carry"). This statement clarifies a potential misunderstanding and also that the Commission's approach is consistent with the taxonomy developed above—such that conglomerate mergers involve weak substitutes or complements sold to final users.

A comment on what is referred to by "portfolio effects" may be appropriate. Although sometimes taken as a synonym for conglomerate effects, most often in case law portfolio effects refer to products that are weak substitutes.[6]

Let us now turn to case law. It is not my ambition to provide a comprehensive account of cases where conglomerate effects have been considered but rather to provide a reasonably complete overview of the type of anticompetitive effects that have been raised by the Commission. Besides the cases mentioned earlier—*Tetra Laval/Sidel, GE/Honeywell, Tetra Pak/Alfa Laval, ATR/de Havilland, SEB/Moulinex, Guinness/Grand Med*—prominent cases involving conglomerate effects include *Coca Cola/Carlsberg, Coca Cola/ Amalgamated Beverages, Pernod Ricard/Diageo/Seagram, Akzo Nobel/Hoechst Roussel Vet, Procter&Gamble/Gillette,* and *Johnson&Johnson/Guidant.* Hopefully the range of issues raised by these cases will faithfully reflect those raised by the Commission.[7]

The Commission raised five concerns. Four can be characterized as relatively minor, both in terms of frequency and in the importance that the Commission attached to them. As discussed below, economic analysis confirms that there is little need to pay much attention to these concerns. A fifth concern, the prospect that the merged entity will make contingent sales, has been the main reason behind the prohibition of conglomerate mergers, and this practice has received a lot of attention in the economics literature. I consider these five issues in turn.

5.1.1   Four Minor Issues

Among the minor concerns raised have been the prospect that merging parties will enjoy economies of scale and scope as result of being active in several markets, the prospect that buyers will enjoy economies of scale and scope because their supplier is active in several markets, the prospect that strong brands belonging to the merging parties will provide spillover benefit to their weaker brands, and the prospect that merging parties will exploit the residual substitution between weak substitutes or prevent the development of potential competition.

Economies of Scale and Scope in Supplying Products in Neighboring Markets   An instance of concern with this type of effect can be found in *Coca Cola/Amalgamated beverages* (at Section 149):

A further strength of CCSB is the large volume throughput generated by a combination of Coca-Cola and the other brands in its portfolio which enables CCSB to take advantage of economies of scale in purchasing, production and distribution. For example CCSB's Wakefield plant, the largest in Europe, produced nearly [...] litres in 1995 (about [...%] of CCSB's total production), whereas Britvic's total output from all its plants in 1995 was [... of approximately the same magnitude]. In addition, the large volumes enable CCSB to deliver products to customers at a lower transport cost per unit.

Similar concern was expressed in *Guinness/Grand Med* and *Coca Cola/Carlsberg.*

Economies of Scale for the Buyers of Products from Neighboring Markets   The Commission considered this advantage in the instance of *Coca Cola/Carlsberg* (at Section 69):

In Denmark, beer and packaged water are often co-distributed with CSDs. This is an advantage for both the brewer and the customers.... For customers, it is an advantage to buy a complete portfolio from one supplier, since it involves fewer deliveries.

The same concern is echoed in *Coca Cola/Amalgamated beverages, Guinness/Grand Med,* and *Lagardère/Natexis/VUP*. However, in the more recent *Procter&Gamble/Gillette* decision the Commission explicitly considered efficiencies as a defense (at Section 131).

Economies of scale or scope either for the merging parties or the buyers will, of course, make the merging parties more competitive and put additional pressure on competitors. But we cannot always presume that buyers suffer. There is in fact a very limited literature that examines whether efficiencies that accrue to merging parties can hurt consumers. Motta and Vasconcelos (2005) consider an industry in which firms that control a larger share of industry capital enjoy lower marginal cost. Firms sell homogeneous products and compete à la Cournot. They find that there is a range of efficiency benefits for the merging parties such that consumers can be hurt if competitors exit the market as a result of a merger. Exit can nevertheless be a necessary but not sufficient condition when efficiency benefits are so high that consumers gain as competitors exit even though their capital becomes idle.[8]

These insights from Motta and Vasconcelos (2005) apply particularly in circumstances where products belong to neighboring markets. The prospect that competitors may be induced to exit is often remote in such circumstances. Hence it can be presumed that improving the efficiencies for merging parties is not an antitrust offence. This presumption might be discarded if it can be shown that competitors exit. There was no claim to that effect in the cases mentioned above.

Spillovers Benefits from Strong to Weak Brands in Neighboring Markets   An example of a spillover benefit can be found in *Guinness/Grand Metropolitan* (at Section 99). It is suggested that:

[The presence of strong brands will] allow GGM to reposition their weaker brands upwards by expanding their share at the expense of competing brands. The parties have argued that such pull through effect has not occurred in the past and is accordingly unlikely in the future. However, this argument ignores the substantial increase in the parties' market share and resources that the merger will create.

A similar "pull-through" effect from strong to weak brand has been analyzed by Rabassa (1999). In Rabassa's model, firms initially invest resources in order to enhance the quality of their products and subsequently compete in prices. A merger in such circumstances raises the incentive to invest in upgrading the quality of the brands if the merging parties had strong preexisting positions (i.e., if the merging parties sold higher qualities before the merger). In comparison with a situation where qualities are exogenous, the equilibrium qualities and market share for the merging parties are higher and the profit of competitors is lower. The results are, however, sensitive to the specification of the link between upfront investment and quality that is assumed. The effect on consumers surplus can also be expected to be ambiguous (relative to the counterfactual in which qualities are exogenous) as consumers gain from the increase in quality.

Overall, there cannot be a presumption that a pull through from strong to weak brands can have significant anticompetitive effects, let alone that firms have an incentive to implement it. More generally, this is also a concern about the effect that a merger can have on marketing strategies. Those normally stay out of the radar screen of antitrust authorities because of their ambiguous effect on consumer welfare.

Residual Substitution and Potential Competition with Products in Neighboring Markets   In *Tetra Laval/Sidel* the Commission first found that the carton packaging machines (sold by Tetra Laval) and the machines used to form polyethylene terephthalate (PET) bottles (sold by Sidel) were substitutes, since buyers would see them as alternative packaging methods for certain types of liquids. After an extensive investigation, the Commission found that the substitution effect was sufficiently weak to place these products in different (but neighboring) antitrust markets. The Commission was still worried about the effect of the merger on carton machines (at Section 330):

By acquiring Sidel, Tetra would ensure that its dominant position in aseptic carton was retained and strengthened by eliminating Sidel as a source of competitive constraint.

These statements on unilateral effects across different antitrust markets, however, appear to be in contradiction with the delineation of the relevant market in the first place. If products are deemed to belong to different markets, a hypothetical monopolist in either market would not be in a position to increase price further if it controlled both. This will a fortiori be the case for a firm that does not enjoy a monopoly position.

The cross-price elasticities that are relevant to determine the antitrust market will still differ from those that determine the optimal price increase after the merger. If the delineation of the market started with carton packaging, the own-price elasticity of demand for carton packaging is equal to the sum of the elasticities of demand for substitutes with respect to the price of a carton. After the merger, the optimal price increase for the carton equipment will be affected by both cross-price effects (the elasticity of demand for cartons with respect to the prices of substitutes will also matter). This nevertheless is a second-order effect because cross-price effects are often assumed to be symmetric. The importance of cross-pricing is unlikely to compensate quantitatively for the fact that a firm that does not enjoy a monopoly position will increase price by a smaller amount than a hypothetical monopolist.

The Commission also expressed concern about the development of competition between carton and PET packaging (at Section 331):

Absent the merger, Tetra would have to compete vigorously in order for carton not to lose market share to PET by innovating... and lowering carton prices. The merger would eliminate this competition and enable Tetra to monitor and anticipate any switch from carton to PET.

Whether or not the Commission produced convincing evidence in support of its claim, the concern about potential competition highlights the fact that the horizon relevant for market definition may be different from the horizon relevant for the analysis of competition.

5.1.2 Contingent Sales

This concern has been expressed in different forms. There is a generic concern about "must stock" brands as well as more specific concerns outlined in *Tetra Laval/Sidel* and *GE/Honeywell*.

Must Stock Brands According to the Commission a "must stock" brand is a brand over which the supplier enjoys some market power, so retailers can hardly avoid listing the brand.[9] When merging parties control such powerful brands, they might, according to the Commission, make "implicit or explicit threats of refusing to supply them" in order to impose weaker brands or avoid delisting them. In addition they might show "greater flexibility to structure prices, promotions, and discounts" across brands. Market power might allow the merging firms to use "overrider" discounts, meaning "discounts granted retrospectively on the basis of volume targets to be achieved over a certain period," to encourage retailers to purchase the largest possible volumes. By these strategies competitors could be, according to the Commission, "foreclosed" or "marginalized." These concerns have been expressed in many cases, including *Coca Cola/Amalgamated beverages*, *Coca Cola/Carlsberg*, *Guinness/Grand Med*, *Nestlé/Coca Cola*, *Scottish/Newcastle*, *SEB/Moulinex*, *Newell/Rubermaid*, *Pernod/Diageo/Seagram*, and *Procter&Gamble/Gillette*.

A review of these cases confirm that anticompetitive effects are more likely when must stock brand are relatively important; as indicated in *SEB/Moulinex*, the combined turnover in markets where the merging parties sell must stock brands must exceed 35 percent of their turnover across all neighboring markets. One can presume that in the Commission's perspective, the refusal to supply will otherwise not be sufficiently costly for the distributors to accept weaker brands.

Conversely, the Commission has expressed the view that merging parties should not be able to exercise market power (even with very high market shares) in "small" markets where the combined turnover of the merging parties is less than 10 percent of their overall turnover in the concerned countries (*SEB/Moulinex*). Presumably retailers can credibly threaten the merging parties with delisting of their products if the merging parties increase price.[10] In the recent decision on *Procter&Gamble/Gillette*, the Commission has also analyzed in detail the power of retailers that may arise from the control of shelf space, the introduction of private labels, or the sponsoring of entry. Finally, the Commission has considered that anticompetitive effects are unlikely in the presence of strong competitors, and in particular, competitors with a matching portfolio of brands.

The anticompetitive strategies identified by the Commission with respect to must stock brands can be understood as tying or full line forcing by firms facing retailers with some buyer power.[11] The literature on those practices will be reviewed in the next section.

Tetra Laval/Sidel As mentioned above, the Commission found that carton packaging machines and PET packaging machines belonged to different antitrust markets. Tetra

Laval held a dominant position in the carton packaging segment, whereas Sidel held a "leading" position (around 60 percent) in one segment of the PET packaging market, namely the market for Strech-Blow-Moulding (SBM) machines. The Commission focused on the so-called sensitive markets for which both carton and PET packaging are used (i.e., juice, fruit-flavored drink, tea and coffee based drinks, and milk). The use of PET in those markets was small (in particular, for milk and juice, which are the two important segments in quantitative terms) but was expected to grow and it accounted for about 5 percent of total PET sales (see figure 5.1 for an overview of the packaging market).

The Commission's argument that Tetra Laval would leverage its position from carton to SBM machines was expressed in the following terms (Section 364–65):

Leveraging its dominant position in aseptic carton in a number of ways, Tetra/Sidel would be able to marginalize competitors and dominate the PET equipment market, in particular SBM machines. Tetra/Sidel would have the ability to tie carton packaging and equipment and consumables with PET packaging equipment and, possibly, preforms (in particular, barrier-enhanced preforms).

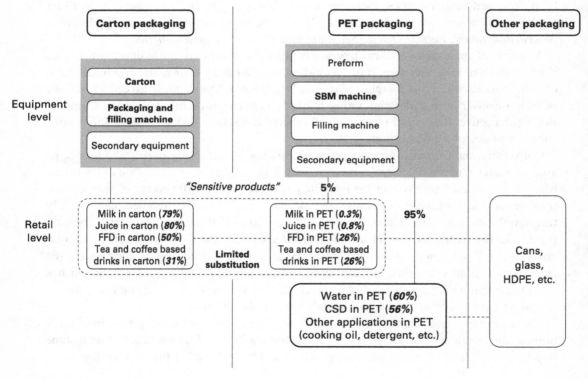

Figure 5.1
Overview of the packaging market

Tetra/Sidel would also have the ability to use pressure and incentives (such as predatory pricing or price wars and loyalty rebates) so that its carton customers buy PET equipment and, possibly, preforms from the Tetra/Sidel and not from its competitors or converters.

Many customers who will continue to need carton packaging for part of their production needs could be forced or provided with incentives to source both their carton and PET equipment from a single supplier of carton and PET packaging equipment. Customers having long-term agreements with Tetra for the carton packaging needs will be particularly vulnerable. Tetra may offer them renewed contract terms allowing them to switch part of their production to PET provided they take PET equipment and services from Sidel or customers may be dependent on Tetra through long term contracts (most customers will not make a complete switch from carton so will continue to need Tetra in the carton field). In this way, Sidel's position in PET equipment and in particular SBM machines would be enhanced in all the new PET product segments (LDPs, juice, still drinks and tea/coffee drinks).

The strategy described by the Commission here would seem to involve the sale of carton machines at a discount if customers would also buy SBM machines from Sidel. Given the large number of customers who are not interested in SBM machines, one would also expect Tetra Laval to sell carton machines on a stand-alone basis (this was not explicitly confirmed by the Commission). The Commission acknowledged (Section 367) that Tetra Laval/Sidel would continue to sell SBM machines on a stand-alone basis but claimed that it would be able to discriminate between end users. Leaving aside the question whether Sidel is indeed able of discriminate across segments (this was highly disputed), the Commission seemed to envisage that Tetra Laval/Sidel would focus their sale of SBM machines to nonsensitive segments, and hence that the tied good would not be sold on a stand-alone basis for the sensitive segments. Importantly, the tying and tied good can be described as "weak substitutes." It is also striking that the Commission provided little evidence that such a strategy would take place (i.e., would be profitable) and would be harmful. The Commission only focused on the existence of a common pool of buyers, and for the rest it summarily dismissed the arguments of Tetra Laval that tying the sales of carton and SBM machines would not be profitable nor anticompetitive. In other words, the Commission focused on the ability to tie the sales and hardly considered the incentives to do so.

GE/Honeywell   General Electric was found to have a dominant position in the market for large jet aircraft engines, with a market share between 43 and 65 percent, depending on how market share is calculated. Honeywell was found to have a leading position in the avionics and non-avionics airspace component markets.

Airspace components are sometimes chosen by the aircraft manufacturers, who will then typically certify a single component for a given aircraft. These components are referred to as supplier furnished. Some components like engines are, however, chosen by the buyer of the aircraft, either an airline or a leasing company undertaking speculative purchases. These components are referred to as buyer furnished. The manufacturers will then certify alternative components (see figure 5.2 for an overview of the aerospace market).

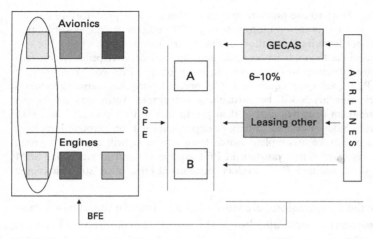

Figure 5.2
Overview of the aerospace market

The Commission first expressed concern that with respect to buyer-furnished equipment the merged entity could make "bundled" offers for engines as well avionics and non-avionics components. Engines and components can be considered complements (a reduction in the price of engines will increase the demand for aircrafts and hence the demand for avionics and non-avionics components). The Commission nevertheless acknowledged that the merged entity could also offer components on a stand-alone basis. Hence the strategy envisaged by the Commission would entail "mixed bundling" over complements sold in fixed proportions.

As indicated by the CFI judgment, the Commission seems to have emphasized in Court proceedings that bundling should be treated as a predatory strategy in that the merging parties may sacrifice profits in the short term in order to induce the exit of competitors (who will subsequently not be in a position to re-enter). In the short to medium term this strategy may, according to the Commission, marginalize competitors by depriving them of revenues in excess of their fixed costs. In turn the spending destined for research and development may decline for the next generation of products to the extent that they may not compete effectively with respect to future platforms. This "dynamic" view of bundling differs from the "static" prospective that was emphasized in the administrative proceedings, such that bundling is undertaken simply because it is profitable in the short term for the merging parties. The Commission did not, however, provide much evidence in support of either theory, relying mostly on a few examples in which multiproduct bids had been offered by Honeywell (see Grant and Neven 2005 for details).

The Commission also considered the leasing operation of GE Capital Aviation Services (GECAS). This GE division undertakes speculative purchases of aircrafts and accounts for some 6 to 10 percent of the purchases of new aircrafts. The Commission was concerned that GECAS might apply a "GE only" policy not only with respect to engines but also with respect to components. Particular concern arose about supplier-furnished equipment: the Commission feared that GECAS could "tip" the market and lead the aircraft manufacturer to choose Honeywell equipment (as the only certified equipment) on new platforms. This strategy, referred to as Archimedean leveraging, could be particularly effective where aircraft manufacturers are relatively indifferent between different components. It could again marginalize competitors and eventually lead to exits.[12] As an anticompetitive effect this is somewhat unconventional, and the Commission relied on a specific model supplied by United Technologies (UTC), a multiproduct competitor of GE. It is essentially a vertical issue to the extent that GE is supplying strict complements, namely engines, components, and financing, and repackages and resells them to final users, with a concern about foreclosure upstream. But there are at least two differences. First, part of the repackaging is undertaken by the aircraft manufacturers so that upstream foreclosure is indirect. It works changing the incentives of those manufacturers. Second, the final consumers can bypass the final stage in which financing is bundled with the aircrafts, to the extent that airlines can directly purchase the aircraft and finance their acquisition through other means than leasing (e.g., unlike what would happen with distribution services).

Hence there is no well-established economic theory that can be reviewed with respect to this leveraging strategy. The knife-edged character of the anticompetitive effect should still be emphasized. The anticompetitive effects can hardly be presumed, and accordingly one would expect the Commission to provide ample evidence that these effects are likely in the particular circumstances of the case. It is far from clear that the Commission provided enough evidence (see Nalebuff 2003 and Grant and Neven 2005 for details).

5.1.3 Summary

Overall, the Commission's concern about the prospect that the residual substitution across different antitrust markets could be exploited seems a little far-fetched and is probably the least convincing claim that it has made. It was also troubled about anticompetitive effects arising from efficiency benefits and changes in incentive with respect to product positioning. The economics literature offers little support for these approaches and admittedly the Commission has not emphasized these effects in recent cases (with some notable exceptions, e.g., *Lagardère/Natexis/VUP*) and has sometimes reversed its position (e.g., toward efficiencies). Nevertheless, the Commission has rightly raised the issue of potential competition.

The Commission has also rightly focused on various forms of contingent sales, such that the conditions of sales of one product are linked to the purchase of others. Importantly, anticompetitive effects have been alleged both with respect to complements and with respect to "weak" substitutes belonging to neighboring markets. The Commission has considered contingent sales to final consumers[13] as well as to retailers. The next section provides a review of the economic literature on such contingent contracts.

Finally, the Commission has sometimes considered purely vertical effects under the label of conglomerate effects. *Lagardère/Natexis/VUP* is a case in point. The Commission worried that unlike competitors, the merged entity would be present in the press market and hence could give privileged access to its own books in terms of promotion. To enhance readability of its own policy, it may be appropriate for the Commission to implement a systematic approach and handle vertical effects independently of conglomerate effects (it has done so in many cases). The Commission could rely on the large and relatively specific literature that informs the analysis of anticompetitive effects in this area.

5.2 Contingent Sales—An Overview of the Literature

As outlined above, the market structure that the Commission has focused on involves one market in which the merged entity is dominant and one or several markets in which it has a leading position. In this section, I present the main insights from the literature. I start with a simple taxonomy, provide a benchmark case, and then discuss variations from the benchmark.

5.2.1 Framework

To fix ideas, let us assume that the merged entity (henceforth firm 1) has a monopoly in the provision of product A. It can also supply product B_1 in a second market, in which it faces a competitor (firm 2) selling product B_2. In order to examine the possible strategies that the merged entity could deploy, it is useful to distinguish between those instances in which it has one single offer involving product A and those instances in which it proposes multiple offers, and to distinguish further between fixed and variable proportions of products A and B_1.

To see the competitive effects inherent in these strategies, it may be useful to think about them as a change to the demand system faced by firms. When products A, B_1, and B_2 are sold independently, there is a demand system for three products. If one product is no longer offered (B_1) and/or a new product is offered (with features of A and B_1 combined), a new demand system will be generated. Consumers will adjust their choices to a new product configuration, and the resulting demand system will induce different competitive interactions between the firms. For instance, even when products A and B are independent in demand, a bundle involving A and B_1 will be a substitute for B_2.

Single Offer Firm 1 could sell product A and B_1 only and in fixed proportions. This is often referred to as pure bundling. Bundling in this case can be achieved by integrating the two goods physically (e.g., Windows and Explorer) or by contractual means (e.g., hotels and travel are sold together in a package holiday). The question may arise whether pure bundling is credible (i.e., whether firm 1 can commit not to sell the products on a stand-alone basis). In some instances, as in contractual bundling, this is not a reasonable assumption. Firm 1 may wish to sell product A only if product B_1 is also purchased. Hence the proportion between the purchases of product A and those of product B_1 will vary among buyers. This is often referred to as full line forcing.

A particular instance of such contracting that has received a lot of attention in the literature is when products A and B_1 are complements (e.g., a photocopier and paper) and B_1 is purchased over time (a consumable product used in conjunction with hardware). This situation is often referred to as dynamic tying (see Nalebuff 2003).

Multiple Offers   Firm 1 could sell products A and B_1 in fixed proportions and also products A and B_1 on a stand-alone basis. This is referred to as mixed bundling, and it is the strategy that was alleged in *GE/Honeywell*. Of course, the bundle A/B_1 has to be sold at a discount relative to the sum of stand-alone prices for A and B_1 in order to attract demand. In some instances firm 1 may decide to offer an incomplete range: that is, A/B_1 could be sold alongside A only, or B_1 only. This is sometimes called incomplete mixed bundling.

As an illustration of A/B_1 and B_1 sold, take A to be the access to premier league matches and B_1 to be the access to a satellite channel. If the subscription to a satellite channel is sold independently, access to the premier league matches is only possible with a subscription to the channel.

As an instance of A/B_1 and A being sold, A could be a carton packaging machine and B_1 a PET packaging machine for some particular use. Firm 1 may want to sell A and B_1 together while selling A on a stand-alone basis, presumably for customers with a high willingness to pay for carton packaging machines. This may be main strategy that was alleged in *Tetra Laval/Sidel*.

Firm 1 could sell product A only if product B_1 is also purchased, together with product A and product B_1 on a stand-alone basis. Such strategy, which involves the sale of all three, has been dubbed "mixed tying" by Nalebuff (2004).

5.2.2   The Chicago School Benchmark

Suppose that consumers buy at most one unit of product A and one unit of product B. Suppose further that all consumers have the same reservation price for product A and that perfect competition prevails in market B. That is, products B_1 and B_2 are not differentiated and product is available at marginal cost. There is a distribution of consumers' willingness to pay for product B. In these circumstances the demand for products A and B is independent (a change in the price of A does not change the demand for B, and vice versa).

Firm 1 facing these circumstances does not find it profitable to sell the bundle AB_1 only. The reasoning is as follows: If products A and B are sold independently, firm 1 charges a price equal to the reservation price for product A, and all consumers buy, then firm 1 makes no profit in market B. If the price of the bundle is equal to the reservation price of consumers for product A and the marginal cost of product B, then firm 1 will make the same profit. This profit is, however, the maximum profit that the firm can make. If the price of the bundle is increased further,[14] then all consumers will be better off just buying product B_2. Consumers have no surplus from buying the monopoly good, and hence they are not willing to pay a little more for product B in order to secure product A. This is the Chicago school argument that there is only one monopoly profit. Making the sale of product A contingent on buying B (pure bundling) is not profitable. Mixed bundling is not profitable either.

We next consider a number of variations from this benchmark. Two features help structure the discussion, namely whether or not products A and B are strict complements (used in fixed proportions) and whether or not contingent contracts have dynamic effects. The importance of strict complementarity accords with intuition: when products A and B are strict complements, they are, so to speak, already tied by the consumers, and it is not clear what firm 1 can achieve by selling them together. Below we focus first on static framework in which firm 1 simply choose the range of products that it wants to offer and their prices. Then we consider models with a dynamic component in which the range of products offered in a given period affects market structures in the future.

5.2.3 Competition in the Absence of Complementarity

Imperfect Competition and Different Consumer Valuation   As a first variation on the benchmark, we will relax the assumption of perfect competition in the B market and the assumption that consumers have the same valuation for product A. We start with the former and assume that products B_1 and B_2 are differentiated and produced under increasing returns, for instance, with a fixed cost and constant marginal cost. As a result we can no longer take it for granted that product B_2 is available at a given price that reflects marginal cost. If firm 1 is selling A and B_1 independently, it will make monopoly profit in market A and some profit in market B. In these circumstances firm 1 may find it profitable to offer a pure bundle, meaning to sell A/B_1 only (Whinston 1990), and this strategy will lead to the exit of firm 2. By selling A/B_1, firm 1 can effectively commit to an aggressive response to the price charged by firm 2. Indeed firm 1 will obtain its monopoly rent only if it sells the bundle. Hence relative to the competition that would arise if firm 1 would sell only B_1, firm 2 faces a tougher competitor.[15] Firm 1 may be willing to price at such a low level that there is no price at which firm 2 can cover its fixed cost. It will thus prefer to exit. This strategy may be profitable for firm 1: it will suffer from reduced flexibility in the prices of its products and some consumers will drop out, but it will also reduce competition in market B. As we might expect (Whinston 1990), the strategy will be profitable as long as consumers' willingness to pay for product B_1 (relative to B_2) is strong enough. Importantly, bundling is only profitable if it leads to exit, and firm 1 needs to be able to commit to this strategy.

Now we will relax the assumption that consumers have the same preferences for product A. Suppose that there is a distribution of consumers' willingness to pay. The relationship in demand among products A/B_1, B_1, and B_2 is then a function of the correlation in consumers' valuations of those products and the dispersion of these valuations. There is no comprehensive treatment of this case in the literature but a number of specific models exist. Carbajo et al. (1990) assume that there is no differentiation in market B and a perfect positive correlation in consumer valuation for products A and B. The demand structure that arises when A/B_1 and B_2 are sold is then similar to that found with vertical differentiation.[16] Pure bundling will soften competition. Relative to the independent pricing game, the profits of both firms will increase. Consumer surplus falls, but the effect on welfare is ambiguous.

As observed by Carbajo et al. (1990), if firms compete à la Cournot, the independent output game will be less competitive. Pure bundling will be less attractive, and it will involve higher output for firm 1. Market B will become more competitive. The output and profit of firm 2 will fall. As before, although consumer surplus falls, welfare may increase.

The insights from Carbajo et al. (1990) can be easily extended to different distributions of consumer valuations between product A and B.[17] Table 5.1 shows the extreme cases of

Table 5.1
Pure bundling and softening

		Mixed bundling	Pure bundling	Independent pricing
Correlation 0	Benefits and prices	$\Pi_1 = 0 + 0.25 = 0.25$ $P_1^A = P_1^x = 0.5$ and $P_1^B = 0$ $\Pi_2 = 0$ $P_2^B = 0$	$\Pi_1 = 0.366$ $P_1^x = 0.59$ $\Pi_2 = 0.064$ $P_2^B = 0.24$	$\Pi_1 = 0 + 0.25 = 0.25$ $P_1^A = 0.5$ and $P_1^B = 0$ $\Pi_2 = 0$ $P_2^B = 0$
	Consumer surplus	0.625	0.485	0.625
	Total surplus	0.875	0.915	0.875
Correlation 1	Benefits and prices	$\Pi_1 = 0 + 0.25 = 0.25$ $P_1^A = P_1^x = 0.5$ and $P_1^B = 0$ $\Pi_2 = 0$ $P_2^B = 0$	$\Pi_1 = 0.33$ $P_1^x = 0.57$ $\Pi_2 = 0.04$ $P_2^B = 0.14$	$\Pi_1 = 0 + 0.25 = 0.25$ $P_1^A = 0.5$ and $P_1^B = 0$ $\Pi_2 = 0$ $P_2^B = 0$
	Consumer surplus	0.625	0.564	0.625
	Total surplus	0.875	0.898	0.875
Correlation −1	Benefits and prices	$\Pi_1 = 0 + 0.25 = 0.25$ $P_1^A = P_1^x = 0.5$ and $P_1^B = 0$ $\Pi_2 = 0$ $P_2^B = 0$	$\Pi_1 = 0.44$ $P_1^x = 2/3$ $\Pi_2 = 0.11$ $P_2^B = 1/3$	$\Pi_1 = 0 + 0.25 = 0.25$ $P_1^A = 0.5$ and $P_1^B = 0$ $\Pi_2 = 0$ $P_2^B = 0$
	Consumer surplus	0.625	0.39445	0.625
	Total surplus	0.875	0.94445	0.875

perfect negative and zero correlations. The equilibrium prices are computed using the model of Carbajo et al. (1990) with Bertrand competition based on zero marginal cost. It appears that firm 2 always benefits from pure bundling. Consumer surplus always falls. Welfare always increases, and it increases most when consumer valuations are negatively correlated. This presumably arises because of the scope for price discrimination that negative correlations allow for (see Adams and Yellen 1976).

Whinston (1990) considers another model where products B_1 and B_2 are differentiated, namely when consumer valuations for those products are not identical. He finds that the demand for products A/B_1 and B_2 may or may not exhibit the feature of vertical differentiation found above depending on the degree of product differentiation between B_1 and B_2 and the dispersion in consumers' valuation for product A. In this model pure bundling can lead either to foreclosure or the softening of competition. The profits of firm 2 can either increase or fall as result of pure bundling. In addition pure bundling that leads to exclusion may not be attractive. Whinston assumes zero correlation in consumer valuation and shows that mixed bundling may be attractive. It allows for some discrimination but also affects the profits of firm 2. In Whinston's example the profit of firm 2 decreases. There is a foreclosure effect, but it is weaker than that arising with pure bundling.

To sum up, it appears that with unit demand pure bundling can lead either to the softening of competition or to foreclosure, depending on the distribution and correlation in consumer valuation for the products. It is not clear a priori that one effect should dominate. A perfect correlation in consumer valuation in the B market appears to be sufficient to generate the softening of competition. In addition, when exclusion takes place, bundling may be profitable even if does not lead to the exit of competitors (as long as there is a dispersion in consumers' willingness to pay for the product A). Finally effects on welfare are ambiguous, but consumer surplus does fall.

Imperfect Competition and Downward-sloping Demand   As a second variation, let us relax the assumption that consumers have a unit demand but keep the assumption that consumers are identical and the assumption of perfect competition. We start with the former (Bernstein 1960; Mathewson and Winter 1997).[18] With downward-sloping demand each consumer makes a positive surplus when products A and B_1 are sold independently. Firm 1 will then find it attractive to sell A/B_1 only because it will be a way of extracting more surplus in the monopoly market. Unlike what happened in the Chicago school benchmark, consumers will be ready to pay a little more for product B_1 in order to retain the surplus that they have in market A.[19] Product B_2 will have no demand (but the fact that B_2 is available at marginal cost will constraint the price that is charged for the bundle).

Let us relax the assumption of perfect competition. Martin (1999) considers independent and linear demands for products A and B,[20] no product differentiation in market B, and Cournot competition. He finds that firm 1 has an incentive to sell a pure bundle, which reduces the profit of firm 2. This result is actually formally equivalent to the result of Car-

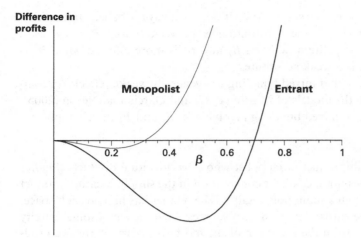

Figure 5.3
Foreclosure versus competition softening: Differences in profits between pure bundling and independent pricing (or mixed bundling) for the incumbent and the entrant

bajo et al. (1990) discussed above. Indeed customer valuations for products A and B that are perfectly correlated and uniformly distributed generate the same demand for products A/B_1 and B_2 as a system of linear demands for the underlying products.[21]

The results of Martin (1999) have been extended by Garcia and Neven (2005). These authors consider Bertrand competition and allow for product differentiation between B_1 and B_2. Garcia and Neven also consider the case where products A and B are substitutes. The results are illustrated in figure 5.3. In the figure β denotes the degree of product differentiation in the B market, with $0 < \beta < 1$. When $\beta = 0$, the two products are independent (product differentiation is maximum), and when $\beta = 1$, B_1 and B_2 are perfect substitutes. This figure presents the incremental profits of firms 1 and 2 if firm 1 undertakes pure bundling, relative to the outcome of independent pricing. Three regions can be distinguished. First, for $\beta > 0.7$, both firms gain from pure bundling. Competition is softened. Second, for $0.3 < \beta < 0.7$, firm 1 gains and the competitor looses. There is foreclosure. Bundling may be profitable even if does not induce the exit of competitors. At the appropriate fixed cost, the exit of firm 2 could be induced. Finally, for $\beta < 0.3$, firm 1 has no incentive to sell a pure bundle. These results confirm that pure bundling is not necessarily profitable. Accordingly it can hardly be presumed ex ante that a merging firm will implement this strategy. The results also confirm that bundling can lead to both softening and foreclosure depending on the degree of product differentiation in market B. Since both effects occur within significant and comparable ranges of parameter values, it does not seem that one effect can be considered a priori more likely than the other. With respect to the substitution between products A and B, Garcia and Neven (2005) find that under the assumption of no differentiation in market B, competition is always softened. In addition the effect is also stronger, the lower the substitution is between A and B. This result accords with intuition, since competition between B_1 and B_2 is more affected when B_1 is associated with a product that is a weak substitute.

Finally, it is worth mentioning that mixed bundling has generally weaker effects on competitors than pure bundling. In the models of Martin (1997) and Garcia and Neven (2005), in which consumers are identical, mixed bundling involving A/B_1 and B_1 merely replicates the independent pricing game.

Retailer Power   Consider a multiproduct monopolist who sells substitute products (Shaffer 1991). Suppose first that he does not face direct competition in the supply of either product but has to sell his product through a monopoly retailer. The retailer has limited shelf space. As shown by Shaffer (1991), he earns rents from two sources. First, he earns some scarcity rent, namely the profit forgone from the exclusion of the most attractive alternative product. Second, he also earns some strategic rents by stocking a brand that is a substitute for a brand that he already carries. The profits that he earns on the former brand will fall, but he will seek compensation for this fall in profit. As shown by Shaffer (1991), brand-specific two-part tariffs do not suffice to eliminate the strategic rents. Full line forcing (i.e., the monopolist requires carrying both products or none at all) will enable the monopolist to restore full monopoly profit.

As pointed out by Vergé (2001), consumers can benefit from full line forcing because it eliminates price distortions. Vergé also extends the analysis of Shaffer and shows that even if more general (nonlinear) contracts become more attractive than two-part tariffs, full line forcing will still be superior to those alternatives for the monopolist and will increase welfare.

Vergé (2004) considers a monopoly over product A and perfect competition in the provision of product B, and proposes a dynamic theory of leveraging. A new variety can be introduced by a competitor who faces a lower cost than that incurred by the monopolist in market A, but it is unclear ex ante whether the new product is a substitute for product A or product B. The product needs to be available on the shelf to be considered by consumers. After a trial it will become clear how consumers perceive the product. The retailer contemplates offers from both firms. In this context an incumbent firm may find it profitable to offer a contract in which he sells both products in the first period and prevents entry. This offer is accepted by the retailer if the profit that he would forgo by not selling product A in the first period is large relative to the relative efficiency of the entrant, and hence if the gain that he can make from an entrant's product is a substitute for A.

5.2.4   Competition with Complements

As mentioned above, when products A and B are strict complements (used in fixed proportions), they are effectively "tied" by consumers, to the extent that there is no demand for the B products unless product A is also available. As a result the merged entity should obtain the full rent from the sales of A and B through the pricing of A, and it is not clear what the merged entity might achieve by selling A/B_1 as a bundle. This arrangement will trivially exclude firm 2 and yield no benefit to firm 1. As shown by Whinston (1990), firm 1 will actually act to ensure that firm 2 remains active: to the extent that B_2 is differentiated from B_1, as will increase the demand for product A, firm 1 will be able to obtain additional rent.

Whinston (1990) describes two sets of circumstances where firm 1 may still want to sell the A/B_1 bundle. If there is an alternative to product A, products A and B will no longer be strict complements (consumers may consider buying B_2 and the alternative), and firm 1 will no longer necessarily benefit from the presence of B_2. Alternatively, if product B has another use besides the combination with A, firm 1 no longer benefits from the presence of firm 2 in that market. Firm 1 may find it profitable to exclude firm 2 in order to monopolize this second market, and it has the means to do so if the market for the A/B components is large enough. By selling the A/B_1 bundle, firm 1 can exclude firm 2 from that market. Its revenues from the second market may not be sufficient to cover fixed cost.

As shown by Whinston (1990), these two examples illustrate the extreme case where strict complementarity and monopoly are one component. It is important to remember that whenever product A is no longer essential, the incentives of firm 1 are similar to those discussed above. Both softening and foreclosure can result from the sale of a pure bundle.

In general, there is a potential efficiency gain associated with conglomerate mergers that involve complements. The pricing of complementary products is typically inefficient when it is undertaken by different firms. This is because these firms do not internalize positive external effects across markets (e.g., a fall in price for one component also increases the demand for the other component). A merger that brings such products under the control of a single entity can actually lead to lower prices (to the benefit of consumers).[22] For instance, the independent pricing solution that arises when product A and B_1 are controlled by the same firm is more efficient than the outcome that obtains when all three products are sold independently.

This behavior is important for the analysis of bundling when there is some competition for the provision of both products (which is arguably the appropriate framework to think about competitive effects in *GE/Honeywell*). The merging firm that controls two components and faces competitors selling individual components in both markets will internalize the cross-market effect, even if the products are not sold together. But it will do so only to a limited extent when a significant share of the increased demand for complements that is triggered by a reduction in price can be captured by competitors. Hence the merging firm may find it attractive to bundle the products as long as lower prices for the bundle do not trigger a tough response from competitors. As shown by Nalebuff (2000), pure bundling will often not be attractive. Mixed bundling may or may not be attractive depending on particular features of demand and, in particular, on the extent to which the decrease in the price of the bundle enlarges aggregate demand, as opposed to shifting market share (see Nalebuff 2002). However, bundling is typically more profitable when it involves a large number of components. This arises because of a Counot effect in "reverse": in lowering its price to lure away consumers of the bundle, the manufacturer of any given component will produce a large external benefit to manufacturers of other components. Indeed, as he switches away from the bundle, each consumer will have to choose a variety of components. This external effect will not be internalized and lead to higher prices (a weaker response) by competitors. Overall, if the profitability of bundling is somewhat uncertain, bundling will generally tend to lower the demand faced by competitors in each market. They can expect to suffer both because of lower prices and because bundling allows for some price discrimination (which effectively enhances the bundling firms' ability to extract profits from buyers). The extent to which they will suffer is nevertheless dependent on many parameters and modeling assumptions. Bundling is generally likely to benefit consumers.

Carton and Waldman (2000) consider a dynamic theory of leveraging that rests on the idea that the sale of B_2 helps firm 2 develop a product that is a substitute for A. If B_2 is sold in the previous period, there will be sufficient demand for the development of a substitute for A, whereas in the absence of B_2, demand may be insufficient. Then, even though B_2 increases the profitability of A in the first period, firm 1 could choose to exclude B_2 (by selling only the pure bundle A/B_1) in order to prevent the development of system competition.

An alternative intertemporal linkage between current bundling and future competition is discussed in Kühn (2001).[23] Kühn focuses on application network effects, such as when product A is an operating system and product B is software (e.g., a browser) that could be developed into middleware. Bundling A/B_1 will reduce the sales of B_2 so that application softwares are more likely to be written for A. This reduces consumers' willingness to pay for B_2, which may further reduced by self-fulfilling expectations. In this framework network effects will magnify the small shift in demand (foreclosure) that bundling leads to in the short term.

5.3 Standards of Proof

As indicated in section 5.1, the European Commission had not considered the effects of tying and bundling in much detail in its main decision. There is little effort for supporting its claims. It may be that the Commission presumed such strategies to be profitable and anticompetitive and had little need for evidence to be brought forward. The discussion in the previous section certainly suggests that such a position would not be well founded.

Alternatively, it may be that the Commission perceived that its decision was not subject to a high burden of proof.

In what follows, I first discuss the standards of proof that the Commission is subject to, in light of recent cases. Recent pronouncements of the Court suggest that the Commission is subject to a high standard of proof, and possibly one that is higher than the standard it had anticipated at the time of these decisions. I subsequently discuss some insights in my review of the literature on a possible way to handle tying and bundling in light of these standards.

5.3.1 Standards of Proofs and Review in Recent Cases

Various standards of proof can be used in legal proceedings. As discussed by Vesterdorf (2004), a standard of "balance of probabilities" is often found in civil proceedings, whereas the stricter standard such that proof should be established "beyond reasonable doubt" is often found in criminal cases. What standard should be applied in merger cases has not been considered at great length by the Court until recent cases.

In *Tetra Laval/Sidel*, the CFI held that the Commission should prove that the merger will have anticompetitive effects "in all likelihood." The CFI further insisted that the evidence brought forward by the Commission should be "convincing." These pronouncements suggest that the standard of proof may be stricter than a mere balance of probabilities. Importantly, the CFI also indicated that the standard of proof was particularly high in this case because conglomerate mergers are often expected to be neutral or even beneficial in terms of competition (at Section 155):

As the Court has already held, where the Commission takes the view that a merger should be prohibited because it will create or strengthen a dominant position within a foreseeable period, it is incumbent upon it to produce convincing evidence thereof (*Airtours v. Commission*, paragraph 63). Since the effects of a conglomerate-type merger are generally considered to be neutral, or even beneficial, for competition on the markets concerned, as is recognised in the present case by the economic writings cited in the analyses annexed to the parties' written pleadings, the proof of anti-competitive conglomerate effects of such a merger calls for a precise examination, supported by convincing evidence, of the circumstances which allegedly produce those effects (see, by analogy, *Airtours v. Commission*, paragraph 63).

The Commission appealed this judgment partly on the ground that the CFI had raised the standards. The Court, however, confirmed the finding of the CFI (at Section 45):

The Court of First Instance did not err in law when it set out the tests to be applied in the exercise of its power of judicial review or when it specified the quality of the evidence which the Commission is required to produce in order to demonstrate that the requirements of Article 2(3) of the Regulation are satisfied.

The CFI and the Court additionally strengthened the standard of proof by insisting on a standard of review that the Courts should apply. The Courts indicated that the scope of their review should not be restricted to mere factual issues but should also include an examination of the Commission's reasoning (including economic reasoning) and its inferences. This naturally raises the accountability that the Commission is subject to and enhances the credibility of the standard of proof that it is meant to respect (in particular, at Section 39):

> Whilst the Court recognises that the Commission has a margin of discretion with regard to economic matters, that does not mean that the Community Courts must refrain from reviewing the Commission's interpretation of information of an economic nature. Not only must the Community Courts, inter alia, establish whether the evidence relied on is factually accurate, reliable and consistent but also whether that evidence contains all the information which must be taken into account in order to assess a complex situation and whether it is capable of substantiating the conclusions drawn from it. Such a review is all the more necessary in the case of a prospective analysis required when examining a planned merger with conglomerate effect.

These standards have been amply referred by the CFI in the *GE/Honeywell* judgment. Throughout the judgment the CFI emphasizes the fact that a merger review involves a prospective analysis and accordingly that the Commission should show that behavior that is deemed anticompetitive is likely to take place. In this respect the CFI has affirmed the distinction between the ability to engage into a particular behavior and the incentive to do so, as well as the need to show that the particular behavior is anticompetitive (e.g., see Section 327).

Hence recent Court decisions have confirmed that the Commission is subject to high standard of proof. The Court has also established that the standard of proof should be particularly high when it is generally considered that particular practices do not raise anticompetitive concerns.[24] The observation that the Commission challenged these standards in Court (and lost) is certainly consistent with the view that it had not anticipated them at the time of the decisions.

If the Courts have clearly established what evidence is not sufficient to meet the standard of proof, they have naturally been less clear (given the nature of the decisions under appeal) about the type of evidence that would be considered as sufficient.[25] Given that some conglomerate mergers involving contingent sales may in some circumstances raise anticompetitive concerns (as discussed above and recognized by the Court, in particular in *GE/Honeywell*), the issue of what evidence will (or should) be deemed convincing is largely open. The next section attempts to contribute to this question.

5.3.2 Some Features of a Possible Approach toward Contingent Sales

As indicated above, there is certainly no presumption that tying and bundling have anticompetitive effects. As confirmed by the Court, the Commission should thus provide detailed evidence that the strategies are attractive and have anticompetitive effects in the case at hand. In what follows, I draw from the literature the types of circumstances that the Commission may want to focus on in building evidence. Among the insights from the literature, I consider both the likelihood of anticompetitive effects in particular circumstances and the scope for identifying these circumstances empirically. This discussion inevitably involves a great deal of judgment in interpreting a literature that remains incomplete and should be taken as merely indicative. It is also highly contingent on the current state of the literature and might have to be revised as the literature develops.

First, it appears that the existence of a monopoly in at least one market matters. That is, when the merging party has a monopoly in one market, it is hard to find circumstances where bundling/tying will benefit consumers. By contrast, in the absence of a monopoly, these strategies can benefit consumers, and in particular, when products are complements. If is, of course, tempting to translate this observation into the antitrust practice by drawing distinctions in terms of whether the merging parties have a dominant position in at least one market. This has been, by and large, the practice of the Commission, which has never found anticompetitive effects in the absence of a dominant position. This approach may be misguided, however, as the effect of tying and bundling, as described in the literature, may actually hinge of the existence of monopoly (or near monopoly) in one market (the case of complements in Whinston 1990 is a case in point). What is considered a dominant position (e.g., a 40 to 50 percent market share) in one market may fit more naturally with models in which there is competition. Hence it may be appropriate to draw a distinction between the case where there is no effective competition and others (e.g., the market for aseptic carton packaging machines in which Tetra Laval has held a market share in excess of 80 percent for a long period of time could be characterized by an absence of effective competition, whereas the market for engines for large aircrafts in which GE has held a market share of 40 to 60 percent with ample variations over time can probably not). Priors (and possibly the standard of proof that should be imposed on the Commission) should thus differ depending on whether the merging parties are active in a market where there is no effective competition.

Second, it appears that tying/bundling strategies are not necessarily profitable. This is an important departure from the area of unilateral or coordinated effects. In these areas we can presume that firms find it profitable to take advantage of the substitution between their product lines and find it profitable to coordinate where they can. There is no equivalent presumption with respect to bundling/tying strategies. Hence the Commission should provide evidence that firms will find it profitable to implement these strategies.

This may suggest that in the absence of a market with no effective competition, bundling/tying strategies may appropriately be considered as per se lawful; given that these strategies will not necessarily be implemented and may benefit consumers if they are and given that it is difficult to identify circumstances where consumers may be hurt, so that the implementation of a rule of reason may involve significant errors (i.e., so that the Commission is unlikely to be able to meet a high standard of proof), per se legality may be superior to a rule of reason.

In the absence of effective competition in one market, matters are different. The Commission may want to investigate the consequences of bundling/tying strategies. The Commission may still wonder whether the merger affects firm's ability to make contingent sales. This test may be relatively easy to pass, but it is worth wondering what prevented the firm without effective competition in one market to enter into to tied good market in the first place (absent the merger) or whether contractual arrangements with existing firms with the same effects as tying/bundling would have been feasible. If this test is passed, the Commission may want to establish whether some conditions that are necessary for bundling/tying strategies to be profitable are met. Because mixed bundling is unlikely to be harmful if it is profitable, the Commission may also want to focus on pure bundling and incomplete mixed bundling strategies. Necessary conditions include the existence of a pool of common buyers that is large relative to the pool of buyers for either tying or tied good (so that there is large overlap). A second condition involves the relative size of the two markets. If sales of the tying good are small relative to those of the tied good, competition between tied goods is unlikely to be much affected (the benefit will be small).

Having established these conditions, the Commission could presumably focus on trying to identify whether the circumstances of the cases fit with those in which tying/bundling is most anticompetitive. This approach seems warranted given that the effects of bundling/ tying strategies depend, in general, on parameters that may be difficult to estimate with confidence (so that a full rule of reason would involve significant errors or in other words, so that the Commission is unlikely to be able to meet a high standard of proof). Accordingly a modified per se rule such that a full rule of reason is triggered by particular circumstances, which can be identified with some confidence, may be appropriate. As indicated above, tying/bundling strategies can lead either to exclusion or a softening of competition. The severest type of softening should, in principle, arise when there is little product differentiation in the tied good market and when there is a wide dispersion in consumers' willingness to pay for the tying good (and the scope for entry in the tied good market is limited). These circumstances may not be all that difficult to document, for instance, through evidence of cutthroat competition in the tied good market and evidence of different segments in the tying good. If this evidence is supplemented by internal documents suggesting that the merging parties understand the logic of this strategy, it may be sufficient to raise concern. These circumstances can, however, be expected to be very rare (in particular, the combination of high-entry barriers and little product differentiation in the tied good market). The argument that tying/bundling can be used to soften competition has not been used in the case law, as far as I can tell.

As outlined above, exclusion can take place (in the absence of strict complementarity) when there is little dispersion in consumers' willingness to pay for the tying good, so the tied goods are differentiated (but not "too much"). In those circumstances tying/bundling may only be attractive if it leads to the exit of competitors, and thus it may require an ability to commit. It is not clear that much attention should be paid to this case as it may be difficult to identify the circumstances in which exclusion would take place (so a rule of reason would involve important errors).

Exclusion can also take place when there is a strict complementarity between tying and tied good. In those circumstances exclusion is easy to achieve, but as indicated above, it is not necessarily attractive. The severest type of exclusion can still be expected to take place when the merging firm has an incentive to exclude, for instance, as due to the existence of an inferior substitute for the tying good or the prospect that a complement to the tying good will turn into a substitute, and when exclusion has long-term dynamic consequences (e.g., through a network effect). In those circumstances there is a clear gain from exclusion as well as an ability to do so (which arises from the strict complementarity and the dynamic effect). The conditions are also relatively easy to document (strict complementarity is a factual matter that is not subject to much dispute and the prospect for a dynamic effect can presumably be established from analogous cases in which they have been observed). It may thus be appropriate for the Commission to identify such circumstances.

Overall, the following decision rule emerges: If the merging firm is not active in a market characterized by the absence of effective competition, bunding/tying ought not raise concern (per se lawful). If there is no effective competition in one market (and the merger changes the scope for making contingent sales), but that tying/bundling is unlikely to be profitable because the overlap between customers is small or the size of the tying good market is small, it ought not raise concern either. If there is no effective competition in one market and the necessary conditions for pure bundling (or incomplete mixed bundling) to be attractive are met, two circumstances should trigger a rule of reason. First, the observations that the tied good market is highly competitive and that the demand for the tying good is segmented should suggest a possible softening of competition. Second, the observation that the tying and tied good are strict complements, that the merged entity has an incentive to exclude, and that there is the prospect of dynamic consequences from exclusion, should suggest an investigation into the possible exclusion. In the absence of these two sets of circumstances, the merger ought not raise concern.

A full rule of reason analysis should, of course, include an assessment of possible efficiency gains associated with bundling/tying strategies. An assessment of such efficiency gains will be naturally undertaken when the Commission investigates their anticompetitive effects (in the two cases mentioned above) and accordingly seeks to uncover what the motivations are behind these strategies. Efficiency gains accruing from tying/bundling essentially rest on the idea that assembly (in the case of complements) or joint delivery are more efficiently undertaken by the seller than by the buyer.[26] Indeed economies of scope in the production of the tying and tied goods are not relevant (they can be achieved without tying/bundling—which is only a sales strategy) and only economies arising from joint sales matter.

5.4   Conclusion

The analysis of conglomerate effects in the European Union has changed markedly in the last couple of years. The Courts have instigated important changes by clarifying the standards of proof and review that apply in merger control in general and with respect to conglomerate effects in particular. They have made it clear that what matters is the incentive rather than the ability to implement a strategy and that anticompetitive effects cannot be presumed. In the *GE/Honeywell* judgment, the CFI has made also made a detailed analysis of the anticompetitive effects that can arise with complements. The Commission in its recent case law has also developed and clarified the analysis of anticompetitive effects regarding weak substitutes (in *Procter&Gamble/Gillette*) while focusing on important economic dimensions (in particular, the presence of effective competition). With some unfortunate exceptions, the relatively minor but unconvincing issues that the Commission had raised in earlier case law are no longer referred to in recent decisions.

As discussed in the chapter, there are some circumstances that can potentially be identified empirically in which contingent sales will be anticompetitive. It is not clear at the moment what type of evidence will (should) be considered to establish that these circumstances prevail. My discussion has presented some ways for the Commission to develop policy in this area. The question remains whether remedies can potentially be implemented in the presence of such concerns and, in particular, whether behavioral remedies will suffice. In *Tetra Laval/Sidel*, the Court has clarified that behavioral remedies could be appropriate, contrary to what the Commission claimed.[27] This is a welcome development to the extent that a commitment not to bundle products or even to make joint offer can potentially be monitored. Bundling/tying are strategies that, unlike others like prices, involve discrete changes that buyers can easily observe and report to the Commission. This could supply firms with adequate incentives to abide by law.

Notes

I thank L.-H. Röller, B. Lyons, and P. Mavroidis for comments on an earlier version of this chapter.

1. What is meant by "conglomerate" effects will be discussed in detail below.

2. The author acted as an advisor to *Tetra Laval* in this case. The discussion of the case throughout the chapter relies solely on public information.

3. See Grant and Neven (2005) for a detailed account.

4. In the recent past the Commission has also taken high profile decisions under Article 82 ECT on practices that are similar to those alleged as conglomerate effects in merger control cases. The issue of bundling and tying, in particular, has been prominent both in the *Microsoft* case as well as in *Tetra Laval/Sidel* and *General Electric/Honeywell*. This provides a benchmark for comparison and raises the issue of how the standard of proof regarding a given practice should differ according to the perspective at hand, namely ex post (under Article 82 ECT) and ex ante (under the merger regulation). A discussion of this issue, however, goes beyond the scope of this chapter.

5. When products are substitutes or complements, we can expect that common buyers will exist. This is not necessarily the case when products are independent in demand; for instance, there may not be common (direct) buyers of steel and toothpaste but there may be common buyers of batteries and toothpaste (assuming that these prod-

ucts are independent in demand). Rather confusingly, the term "conglomerates" often refers to companies that sell products that are completely unrelated and sold to different customers. Anticompetitive conglomerate effects do thus not arise from "conglomerates."

6. The Commission and commentaries also use the term "range" effects, as a synonym for portfolio effects.

7. I have searched all published decision for various keywords (conglomerate, range, portfolio) and considered all decisions uncovered by this method. The set of decision that I focus on is meant to reflect the competitive effects mentioned in those decisions.

8. They assume that capital is fixed but that a fixed capital cost is incurred per period (so exit can be induced and capital can become idle). Under the alternative assumption that capital is sunk, exit would not take place and prospect for an efficiency offense would be even less.

9. See, for instance, the EU submission to the OECD, page 241 (OECD, 2002).

10. This argument was challenged in court by competitors, who prevailed (*BaByliss v. Commission*, case T–114/02, 3 April 2003). The CFI held that the Commission has not established its position to the requisite legal standard (see Sections 362–63). The CFI did not question the economics of the argument but considered that the retailers would effectively prevent the merging parties from abusing their dominant position (rather than preventing the combined entity from achieving this dominant position). Since, the CFI reasoned, the merger regulation prohibits the creation of a dominant position, and not its abuse, the argument could not be accepted. This reasoning, firms cannot achieve high market shares even if it does not increase price. This sort of reasoning is odd, and hopefully it will no longer be feasible with the new merger standard (which focuses on whether effective competition is impeded).

11. The practice of "overrider" discounts can also be understood as a form of tying. The contestable sales are being tied to the sales of the must stock brands. See Ridyard (2003) for a discussion of this concept.

12. See Reynolds and Ordover, (2002)

13. Besides *Tetra Laval/Sidel* and *GE/Honeywell*, the Commission has dealt with tying toward final consumers in *Akzo Nobel/Hoechst Roussel Vet*. This case involved tying of complements products (different endocrine treatments used one after the other), substitutes (Fertagyl and Receptal), or products independent in demand (vaccines). See also *VNU/AC Nielsen* and *ATR/De Havilland*.

14. A lower price will also obviously yield a lower profit.

15. As noted by Whinston (1990), everything happens as if the cost of B_1 was reduced by the extent of the margin earned over A.

16. Indeed all consumers will attach more value to A/B_1 than B_2.

17. In the model of Carbajo et al. (1990) mixed bundling is not attractive; with a perfect correlation in consumer valuation, there is no scope for discrimination. In addition, as long as there is perfect competition in market B, mixed bundling replicates the outcome of independent pricing.

18. See also Slade (1997) who considers a model where the tying and tied goods are complements (not strict complements, however), and the provision of the tied good is competitive but its price is given exogenously. She finds that tying is profitable.

19. As noted by Mathewson and Winter (1997), a two-part tariff will do as well. If consumers have heterogeneous preferences, bundling may nevertheless be attractive.

20. This system of linear demand is derived from a quadratic utility function.

21. This is easy to check. The formal equivalence between Carbajo et al. (1990) and Martin (1999) is also apparent by comparing table IV (p. 290) in Carbajo et al. (1990) and equations 4.6 and 4.7 (p. 374) in Martin (1999), in assuming that $c_a = c_b = c$.

22. This is sometimes referred to as the Cournot effect.

23. See also Kühn, Stillman, and Caffarra (2004).

24. The Court did not, however, go as far as establishing a presumption that conglomerate merger do not involve anticompetitive effects.

25. The Court's approach toward empirical evidence in *GE/Honeywell* is, in some respect, a little puzzling. The CFI seems to give excessive credence to isolated observations (e.g., in its discussion of whether GECAS contributed to the dominance of GE). The problem is that these isolated observations appear to be generated by highly biased processes.

26. See Ahlborn, Evans, and Padilla (2003) and Kühn et al. (2004) for a discussion.

27. At Section 86 of the judgment: "Contrary to what the Commission claims, it is not apparent from that judgment that the Court of First Instance ruled out consideration of behavioural commitments. On the contrary, in paragraph 318, the Court of First Instance laid down the principle that the commitments offered by the undertakings concerned must enable the Commission to conclude that the concentration at issue will not create or strengthen a dominant position within the meaning of Article 2(2) and (3) of the Regulation. Then, in paragraph 319, it inferred from that principle that the categorisation of a proposed commitment as behavioural or structural is immaterial and that the possibility cannot automatically be ruled out that commitments which are prima facie behavioural, for instance a commitment not to use a trade mark for a certain period or to make part of the production capacity of the entity arising from the concentration available to third-party competitors or, more generally, to grant access to essential facilities on non-discriminatory terms, may also be capable of preventing the emergence or strengthening of a dominant position."

References

Adams, W., and J. Yellen. 1976. Commodity bundling and the burden of monopoly. *Quarterly Journal of Economics* 90: 475–98.

Ahlborn, C., D. Evans, and J. Padilla. 2003. The antitrust economics: A farewell to per se illegality. *Antitrust Bulletin* (Winter).

Bustein, M. 1960. The Economics of tie-in sales. *Review of Economics and Statistics* 42(1): 68–73.

Carbajo, J., D. De Meza, and D. Seidman. 1990. A strategic motivation for commodity bundling. *Journal of Industrial Economics* 38(3): 283–98.

Carlton, D., and M. Waldman. 2002. The strategic use of tying to preserve and create market power in evolving industries. *RAND Journal of Economics* 33.

Garcia, J., and D. Neven. 2005. The attempted merger between General Electrics and Honeywell: A case study of transatlantic conflict. *Journal of Competition Law and Economics* 1(3): 595–633.

Kühn, K.-U. 2001. The incentive to degrade intereoperability in the market for work group server operating systems: A simple modeling approach. Mimeo. University of Michigan.

Kühn, K.-U., R. Stillman, and C. Caffarra. 2004. Economic theories of bundling and their policy implications in abuse cases: an assessment in light of the Microsoft case. Discussion paper 04-19. John M. Olin Center for Law and Economics, University of Michigan.

Mathewson, F., and R. Winter. 1997. Tying as a response to demand uncertainty, *RAND Journal of Economics* 28(3): 566–83.

Motta, M., and H. Vasconcelos. 2005. Efficiency gains and myopic antitrust authority in a dynamic merger game. *International Journal of Industrial Organization* 23: 777–801.

Nalebuff, B. 2000. Competing against bundles. In P. Hammond and G. Myles, eds., *Incentives, Organization, Public Economics*. Oxford: Oxford University Press, pp. 323–36.

Nalebuff, B. 2002. Bundling and the GE/Honeywell merger. Working paper 22. Yale School of Management.

Nalebuff, B. 2003. Bundling, tying and portfolio effects. Part 2. Case studies. DTI Economic Paper 1. London.

Rabassa, V. 1999. Portfolio power as a new European doctrine in merger control: A theoretical justification. Mimeo. Toulouse.

Reynolds, R., and J. Ordover. 2002. Archimedean leveraging and the GE/Honeywell transaction. *Antitrust Law Journal* 70: 171.

Sheffer, G. 1991. Capturing strategic rents: full-line forcing, brand discounts, aggregate rebates and maximum resale price maintenance. *Journal of Industrial Economics* 39(5): 557–75.

Slade, M. 1997. The leverage theory of tying revisited: Evidence from newspaper advertising. *Southern Economic Journal* 65(2): 204–22.

Ridyard, D. 2003. Article 82 price abuses—Towards a more economic approach. *Proceeding of the 2003 EU Competition Law and Policy Workshop*. Oxford: Hart Publishing, pp. 441–60.

Vergé, T. 2001. Multi-product monopolist and full-line forcing: The efficiency argument revisited. *Economics Bulletin* 12(4): 1–9.

Vergé, T. 2004. Portfolio effects and merger control: Full-line forcing as an entry-deterrence strategy. Mimeo. University of Southampton.

Vesterdorf, B. 2004. Standards of proof in merger cases: Reflections in the light of recent case law of the Community Courts, *Proceeding of the Third Annual Merger Control Conference*. London: BICL.

Whinston, M. 1990. Tying, foreclosure and exclusion. *American Economic Review* 80(4): 837–59.

6   Detecting Cartels

Joseph E. Harrington Jr.

Cartels are among us. Their attempts to coordinate the prices they set and the quantities they produce are often effective. A recent comprehensive survey found the median increase in price attributable to collusion to be around 25 percent (Connor 2004). So cartels exist and are bad. When we find them, we ought to prosecute and penalize them. But how do we find them?

Broadly speaking, market collusion can be detected through structural or behavioral means. Structural methods of discovering cartels entail identifying markets with traits thought to be conducive to collusion. For example, it has been shown that structurally, cartel formation is more likely to exist where there are fewer firms, more homogeneous products, and more stable demand.[1] Grout and Sonderegger (2005, p. 15) is representative of this approach:

...the fundamental background reduces to three core issues—product, volatility, and company criteria. The first core question is whether the industry has a homogeneous product or not. Cartels are far more likely if the product is fairly homogeneous between companies in the market....Second, does the industry display volatile turnover over a sustained period of time?

Cartels are more likely if output and market conditions are normally stable....Finally, are the leading players in the market large and relatively constant? If there are significant changes in the market shares or regular exits and entrants, then cartels are less likely.

One could imagine investigating industries who score high on these relevant traits with the hope of finding evidence of a cartel.

In contrast, uncovering cartel behavior through behavioral methods involves observing the means by which firms coordinate or the end result of that coordination. The means of coordination can be some form of direct communication, and many cartels have been detected by evidence of such communication. The evidence could come from a person party to the cartel or from an employee who stumbles across documents suggestive of collusion. For example, the monochloroacetic acid cartel was discovered because the management of Clariant, after acquiring the Hoechst chemicals business, found evidence of Hoechst being part of a cartel. They chose to come forward to the American and European antitrust authorities.[2] In the case of lysine, it was an employee of Archer Daniels Midland, engaged in the conspiracy, who came forward in exchange for immunity. With the employee acting as an FBI informant, cartel meetings were recorded on videotape for the FBI.[3] In both cases it was the means by which firms colluded that ultimately led to the cartel's discovery.

Alternatively, cartel behavior can be revealed by the market impact of the coordination of firms' prices or quantities, or other aspects of their market behavior. Buyers could become suspicious of parallel movements in prices or an inexplicable increase in prices. A sales representative for a colluding firm may become suspicious because she is instructed not to bid for the business of certain potential customers (as part of a customer allocation scheme) or not to offer reasonable price concessions when business might be lost to competitors. For example, the European Commission investigated the stainless steel industry (and found collusion) after buyers complained to the Commission about a sharp increase in prices.[4] Although we do not know the specifics of the complaints, the cartels in graphite electrodes[5] and thermal facsimile paper[6] were reportedly discovered also after buyer complaints.[7]

This chapter explores the role of *economists as detectives* and, more specifically, detection through the analysis of prices, market shares, and other economic data. The focus on the behavioral method is mainly due to its more apparent efficacy in uncovering collusion. To see the weakness to a structural approach, imagine the "ideal" market for collusion: two firms, homogeneous products, stable demand, no large buyers, excess capacity, and so forth. Even though such a market would surely be flagged by a structural investigative tool, my own prior belief is that a very high fraction of those markets are not cartelized. Based on what we know (admittedly from only discovered cartels), the frequency of collusion in most economies is rather low. Hence, given a low prior probability of collusion, the posterior probability—conditional on all those structural variables taking values conducive to collusion—is still probably quite low. In other words, I think the likelihood of false positives with a structural approach is quite high. By contrast, a behavioral approach will be shown to focus on potentially more informative measures so that one might imagine a lower rate of false positives. Of course, all this is speculative but it does serve to reveal my own prior beliefs.

Having cavalierly dismissed structural methods, let me immediately qualify that view as I have been told that the Dutch competition authority has deployed structural methods with some success including, for example, uncovering collusion in the shrimp industry. But then it has also been mentioned to me that the Dutch economy may be rife with cartels in which case the prior probability of collusion is far from being low.[8] If that is indeed the case then the posterior probability of a cartel being present, conditional on many of the right structural traits, may be high enough to make such an approach useful. However, most economies probably have a low rate of collusion in which case structural methods are much less likely to be efficacious.

This chapter will then explore how the analysis of economic data—prices, quantities, market shares, demand shifters, cost shifters, and the like—can allow us to discriminate between collusion and competition to identify the presence of a cartel. The process of detection involves a sequence of screening, verification, and prosecution. During the *screening* of markets, a kind of triage is used to identify industries worthy of close scrutiny. *Verification* then is necessary to systematically exclude competition as an explanation for observed behavior and gather evidence in support of collusion. Whereas screening may entail studying price patterns, verification requires controlling for demand and cost factors and any other variables necessary to distinguish between collusion and competition. The final task of *prosecution* comes when sufficient economic evidence is developed to persuade a court or some other administrative body that there has been violation of law. One may interpret this exercise as the same as verification though with a different set of standards. With respect to US case law, economic evidence is not typically sufficient to prove guilt; there must be some evidence of coordination.[9] The discussion of this chapter will be centered on the role of economic analysis in screening and verification.

The systematic search for illegal activity is a common practice. In identifying fraudulent tax returns, tax authorities—such as the US Internal Revenue Service—are proactive in developing models that flag certain returns as worthy of investigation. In their lookout for insider trading, securities authorities—such as the US Securities and Exchange Commission—ex post monitor volume leading up to a significant announcement. In tracking down fraud, credit card companies use statistical models to identify aberrations in spending patterns. As these cases attest, government agencies and private corporations actively search for illegal activity. However, there are really no analogous policies when it comes to illegal cartels. Although attempts are made over time, it is fair to say that economic analysis—as occurs in government, academe, or private consulting—has not been applied to the discovery of cartels. Economic analysis can be instrumental to the prosecutorial argument and essential in assessing damages, but as yet it has not been applied to detecting cartels. My objective is therefore to review the theoretical and empirical methods available for cartel detection and to show how economic analysis can assist in the task of identifying industries worthy of close inspection.

Section 6.1 reviews the four methods generally used in detecting collusion and the research that implements these methods. Section 6.2 focuses on collusive markers for price and market share based on discussions from the theoretical literature on collusive pricing. Section 6.3 explores how a cartel may be able to beat a test for collusion. Section 6.4 concludes by discussing the feasibility of a more aggressive screening policy by the antitrust authorities.

6.1 Empirical Methods for Detecting Cartels

It is important to be clear as to what it is we are searching for. The objective is not to identify industries with high price-cost margins but rather to uncover prosecutoriable cases of collusion. In terms of current antitrust practice this generally means explicit collusion—

where firms have engaged in direct communication and obvious coordination—rather than tacit collusion—where firms are able to coordinate through some mutual understanding and without the aid of direct communication. From both a legal and economic perspective, explicit collusion is conceived as a discrete event; firms are or are not explicitly colluding. Of course, the impact of collusion, whether explicit or tacit, on price and welfare can be of varying degrees, and the extent of collusion is certainly pertinent to the calculation of damages and the appropriate enforcement policy. What is different about the presence of a cartel is that firms are explicitly coordinating their behavior through illegal means of communication. Having drawn this distinction between explicit and tacit collusion, I am sorry to say, because of inadequacies in the underlying theory, my ensuing analysis will largely ignore this distinction. Nevertheless, it is important to know that this distinction exists, and that future research may move it to the front of our collective mind.

Verification of episodes of collusion is a data-intensive and time-intensive task that requires controlling for the many determinants of behavior. It can involve identifying a competitive benchmark and comparing the behavior of suspected colluders to it. It can involve estimating collusive and competitive models to see which better fits the data. It is not practical to engage in such an exercise except where there are already some suspicions, that is, some evidence that collusion is afoot in an industry.

It is the role of screening to identify candidates for verification. In most antitrust cases, screening doesn't occur through economic analysis but rather through such avenues as buyer complaints, upset competitors, and the corporate leniency program. Although economic analysis can serve a screening function, the "suspicious" behavior it identifies does not provide "conclusive" evidence of collusion. Economic analysis may establish that behavior is inconsistent with a class of competitive models but not that it is consistent with some collusive model. It may show that there has been a structural break in behavior but leave unaddressed whether it is due to the formation of a cartel or some other change. Like verification, screening can be intensive in terms of data, modeling, and estimation. When it is, it is then not a practical undertaking without other evidence that collusion may be present.

In this section, I review four empirical methods that have been used for detecting collusion. Match a clever economist with a suspected cartel and a unique method of detecting collusion may emerge. Indeed there are apt to be useful methods hidden in consultants' drawers or buried in court documents. In limiting this review to the published literature, four methods are reviewed for detecting collusion, and these methods are based on asking the following questions: (A) Is behavior inconsistent with competition? (B) Is there a structural break in behavior? (C) Does the behavior of suspected colluding firms differ from that of competitive firms? and (D) Does a collusive model fit the data better than a competitive model? Methods A and B are generally screening methods in that they do not call for evidence of collusion but rather evidence that doesn't sit well with competition. Methods C and D address contrasting competition and collusion as alternative explanations of firm behavior and thus serve verification purposes. A key difference between those two methods is that in method D the competitive benchmark is estimated using data from suspected colluding firms, whereas in method C it is done using data from unsuspected firms (or markets). These various methods are reviewed in sections 6.1.1 through 6.1.4. In section 6.1.5, I show why high price–cost margins are not an adequate screening device, and in section 6.1.6, I provide a critique of these four methods.[10]

6.1.1   Is Firm Behavior Inconsistent with Competition?

This approach is based on identifying properties of behavior that would always hold under competition—or at least for a wide class of competitive models—and to test whether they are present for a particular industry. The null hypothesis is competition and the empirical task is to accept or reject that hypothesis. Of course, rejection does not imply collusion, only that behavior is inconsistent with the specified class of competitive models. As I will show, this approach is complimentary to later ones that test for collusion in that together they can be used to identify which firms may be members of a cartel by determining whose behavior is inconsistent with competition. The properties analyzed could be how firms' prices are related—for example, are they correlated when they should be independent?—or how a firm's price responds to cost and demand shocks—for example, do prices fail to rise with cost?

Testing for consistency of behavior with a competitive model is conducted in Porter and Zona (1993, 1999) and Bajari and Ye (2003). I will focus on the latter paper and cover Porter and Zona (1993, 1999) in section 6.1.3.

Bajari and Ye (2003)   The setting is a first-price sealed bid procurement auction in which the product or service is homogeneous and bidders costs are independent.[11] Bidder i's cost valuation has the cdf $F(c_i \mid z_i, \theta) : t[\underline{c}, \overline{c}] \to [0, 1]$, where θ is a vector of parameters common across bidders and z_i is a vector of publicly observed independent variables that, are unique to firm i but may be correlated across firms.

The competitive model is based on the unique equilibrium to the following game: Bidder i's expected profit from bidding b_i is

$$(b_i - c_i) \prod_{j \neq i} [1 - F_j(B_j^{-1}(b_i))],$$

which is the gain from winning, $b_i - c_i$, times the probability that bidder i wins, where $B_j(\cdot)$ is the bidding function of j. Competitive bids can then be correlated if one fails to control for z_i. However, controlling for them, costs and thereby bids are independent. Thus this is a (conditional) independent private values (IPV) setting.

The competitive model predicts that after controlling for publicly available information ($z_1, \ldots, z_N$), firms' bids are independent (more specifically, the unexplained part of one firm's bid is independent of the unexplained part of another firm's bid). Second, firms' bids are exchangeable: a permutation of the publicly available information analogously permutes the bids. In other words, firms' bidding functions are identical. Note that these properties do not pertain to a single firm but rather collections of firms; the competitive theory is being used in terms of what it predicts about the relationship among firms' bids. For example, it is not being proposed to determine whether a firm's bid is increasing in the distance between its office and the project site (which would be natural as then transportation costs are higher) but rather whether firms' bids respond the same way to distance.

The implementation of this model involves estimating a pricing equation for each firm and then testing whether independence and exchangeability hold for various (perhaps all) subsets of firms. A test for independence determines whether the unexplained part of each firm's bid is independent. A test for exchangeability determines whether firms' estimated coefficients are the same.

Bajari and Ye (2003) use this approach in analyzing procurement auctions for seal coating (a highway maintenance process) in Minnesota, North Dakota, and South Dakota in 1994 to 1998. Their data set has 138 projects for which there are eleven main companies. These contracts are awarded through a sealed bid auction with the contract going to the lowest bidder. From the engineering estimates of the cost of each project, the dependent variable is the ratio of the bid of firm i on project t, $BID_{i,t}$, to the engineering cost estimate for project t, EST_t. The bid equation is

$$\frac{BID_{i,t}}{EST_t} = \beta_0 + \beta_{i1} LDIST_{I,t} + \beta_{i2} CAP_{i,t} + \beta_{i3} MAXP_{i,t} + \beta_{i4} LMDIST_{i,t} + \beta_{i5} CON_{i,t} + \epsilon_{i,t}.$$

$LDIST_{i,t}$ is a measure of the distance between firm i and project t, so cost (and thus a competitive firm's bid) can be expected to be increasing with distance. In procurement auctions, capacity is an important factor in that it can influence production cost—if cost is increasing as capacity tightens—but also opportunity cost as a project won today may prevent the firm from bidding on a potentially more lucrative project tomorrow. $CAP_{i,t}$ is utilized capacity of firm i at the time of project t, which is measured as the ratio of the firm's total winning contracts up to the time of auction t to the firm's total of winning contracts in the entire season. $CON_{i,t}$ is the proportion of work done (by dollar volume) by firm i in the state where project t is located and is intended to capture familiarity with local regulators and local material suppliers. Finally, $LMDIST_{i,t}$ measures the minimum distance among rivals and $MAXP_{i,t}$ is maximal free capacity among rivals. Both variables pertain to the competitiveness of firm i's environment in terms of its rivals' cost.

The estimated coefficients are found to be sensible; a firm's bid is increasing (and statistically significant) in the log of distance, used capacity, and minimum distance among rivals and is decreasing in concentration. The estimated coefficient on the maximal free capacity of rivals is not significantly different from zero.

To test for independence, the residuals are calculated for each firm's bid function, $\epsilon_{i,t}$. A test of independence between firms i and j involves testing the hypothesis that the coefficient of correlation for $\epsilon_{i,t}$ and $\epsilon_{j,t}$ is zero. Among the 23 pairs of 11 largest firms that have at least four bids in the same auction, the null hypothesis of independence cannot be rejected at the 5 percent level in all but four cases. However, of these four pairs, three of them only bid against each other at most two or three times a year which, it is argued, doesn't suggest they interact enough to make collusion worthwhile. This leaves firms 2 and 4 as the lone candidates for being a cartel.

Exchangeability means that the independent variables enter the firm's bid function in a symmetric way, so the hypothesis is $\beta_{ik} = \beta_{jk}$, $\forall i \neq j$, $\forall k$. They conduct a test for exchangeability among all 11 main firms—thus running a regression that pools all 11 firms—and also test it for each pair of main firms—pooling only those two firms. The null hypothesis is rejected at the 5 percent level only when all 11 main firms are pooled and when firms 2 and 5 are pooled.

In sum, the analysis reveals that all pairs of firms satisfy both the test of independence and exchangeability except for firms 2 and 4 and firms 2 and 5. This approach not only suggests that collusion may be present—as some firms act contrary to a competitive model—but also which firms may be colluding. Out of the eleven firms in their data, two candidate cartels are identified: firms 2 and 4 and firms 2 and 5. Given that there are many feasible cartels, this is a highly useful exercise and is complementary to later approaches to be reviewed.[12]

The next natural question is whether the observed departures from competition are consistent with some model of collusion. Consider a collusive model in which the identities of the cartel's members are common knowledge to the other bidders and the cartel bids optimally, using the lowest cost among the cartel members. Further suppose that colluding firms are submitting complementary bids that exceed the bid of the designated member. This could lead to a lack of independence if, for example, complementary bids are some multiple of the designated firm's bid. It could also lead to a failure of exchangeability. If two cartel members don't compete against each other, then this could mean that factors affecting the cost of one doesn't affect the bid of the other. This case will be discussed in greater depth later. A second question is whether firms could be colluding and still satisfy independence and exchangeability. The answer is clearly yes, and all they have to do is to proportionately scale their "competitive" bids. This is an important point to which I will return later.

6.1.2   Has There Been a Structural Break in Firm Behavior?
A second general approach to identifying collusion is to look for a structural break in firm behavior. This break could be associated with the formation of a cartel but also with its

demise. In either case there ought to be a discrete change in the firm's pricing function. As opposed to the other methods described earlier, this method requires data before the time of suspected collusion. While it can be implemented without prior information as to what patterns are consistent with collusion, theory and past evidence on cartels would enhance its power by suggesting what properties to focus upon and what we ought to observe if indeed a cartel has formed. Has average price changed? Has the relationship between the firm's price and cost changed? Has the relationship among firms' prices changed? Has the variance of price and market share changed?[13] Of course, econometric evidence of structural change is far from conclusive evidence of collusion if this has not been distinguished from other sources of a break. It is then appropriate to think about this method as a screening device that is to be followed with verification methods (described later) if a structural break is found in the data.

The classical Chow test is a useful test for structural change *if* there is prior information as to when a cartel could have formed (or could have collapsed). However, if observation of, say, a price series is used to identify a possible break in market conduct, then the Chow test is inappropriate and can lead to spurious rejection of parameter stability. Thus, the prior information must not be the series for which one will be econometrically testing for a structural break.

Appropriate events for identifying a candidate breakpoint are those that either are conducive to cartel formation (i.e., make collusion easier or more profitable) or are observed along with cartel formation (e.g., allow the cartel to operate more effectively). It has been documented that trade associations are used as a cover for cartel meetings, and more to the point, trade associations have been created for that express purpose. For example, the Amino Acid Manufacturers International Association was formed by members of the lysine cartel (Connor 2001) and the Oklahoma Highway Department only started receiving identical bids at procurement auctions some time after the Asphalt Refiners Association was formed (Funderburk 1974). A test for a break in the relationship among firms' bids around the time of the creation of the association would be useful. Nevertheless, structural change can occur even if firms are not colluding. For example, the formation of an association can lead to enhanced correlation of firms' prices because it promotes the exchange of information that homogenizes firms' beliefs. It is not clear, however, that such homogenization will lead to higher average prices. It is then important to consider the various implications of a trade association and identify those effects unique to collusion.[14]

There are other events that can contribute to cartel formation and thus serve as candidate breakpoints. One should be concerned that there will be structural change even if the event does not trigger collusion. Exit or merger (particularly of a maverick firm) might allow a cartel to form, but an exit will change the noncollusive solution as well. Though average price is predicted to rise in response to an exit or a merger (whether or not a cartel forms), there may still be distinguishing effects of collusion. For example, cartel formation might predict more parallel behavior among firms, while noncollusion will have no such prediction. To properly address the question of collusion, one must deal with the endogeneity of the event toward understanding the factors behind it. For example, if a firm with an inferior technology exits and technology is more uniform among the remaining firms, then there might be more correlation among these firms' prices because of the greater homogeneity in their cost-generating processes. All this serves as a note of caution but need not rule out using these events as a date for which to test for structural change in firm behavior.

There are further events—such as entry—that provide candidate breakpoints for the collapse of a cartel. A case in point is the growing expansion of Chinese manufacturers in the market for vitamin C that eventually led to the collapse of the cartel in that market (Levenstein and Suslow 2001). While, even under noncollusion, a change in firms' prices can be expected in response to the expansion of new competitors, a discrete change in that pricing relationship does not occur *unless* it causes a cartel to dismantle itself.

Although it presumes there is already some suspicions about the presence of a cartel, one can test for structural change at the time at which suspected colluding firms become aware of a government price-fixing investigation or private litigation because such is likely to lead to a collapse of the cartel. Abrantes-Metz et al. (2006) use that type of event and find a significant decrease in the price variance. These cartel-destabilizing events could even occur in other (related) markets when firms take it as a signal that the authorities are going to investigate them as well. On this point Block, Nold, and Sidak (1981) find that a price-fixing case in the bread market for one city reduced the markups for bread in neighboring cities. While a comparison of prices before and after the launching of an investigation is often used to measure the impact of collusion on price,[15] it can be used to provide evidence of collusion as well.

Another method, but one that should be used cautiously, is to relate one feature to some other feature of the data serving to identify a possible breakpoint for structural change. For example, a plot of the average price series could establish a date at which price begins to follow a rising trend. That date could then be used as a breakpoint to test whether there is a break in, say, the correlation among firms' prices. However, care needs to be given to avoid a bias in looking for evidence of structural change. The result will very much depend on the class of noncollusive price-generating processes that is specified.

Even if there is not a candidate breakpoint, econometric methods exist for determining whether there is an unknown time at which structural change occurred. One approach goes back to Quandt (1960), who conducted a test for each possible breakpoint and then used the largest test statistic. The distribution theory for that test statistic has since been developed, beginning with Andrews (1993).[16] Once again, any evidence of structural change must be followed by an examination of the properties of the change and whether the change conforms with our understanding of collusive behavior.

A search for explicit collusion by identifying structural change can be confounded by a breakdown of tacit collusion. To see this, suppose that firms are currently tacitly colluding and a persistent demand shock hits that destabilizes the equilibrium. The sharp fall in demand could induce an abrupt shift to another equilibrium or a period of disequilibrium before a new equilibrium is reached. On this point, it is noteworthy that some cartels were preceded by abnormally low prices, such as the cartels in graphite electrodes (Levenstein and Suslow 2001) and citric acid (Connor 2001). One conjectured explanation is that firms were tacitly colluding but collusion fell apart on account of some shock. Failure to get the industry back to some tolerable level of prices through tacit means could have induced explicit collusion.[17]

6.1.3 Does the Behavior of Suspected Colluding Firms Differ from That of Competitive Firms?

Firms were suspected of colluding at procurement auctions of asphalt contracts by the Oklahoma Highway Department (OHD) over the span of 1954 to 1965 (Funderburk 1974). During the time of suspected collusion, bids were identical and, beginning in 1957, were constant at 10.25 cents a gallon. With identical bids, the OHD awarded the contract to the nearest firm to the job site in order to minimize the delivery costs incurred by the state, which, it was later argued, acted as a market allocation scheme. During the same time period, these suppliers made bids and won contracts in other states at an average price of only 6 cents a gallon, and furthermore the uniformity in bids in Oklahoma was not observed there. It was estimated that the maximum freight cost for these Oklahoma contracts was 2.48 cents a gallon, which meant that any of these firms could have won additional contracts with a price of 10.24 cents a gallon and, even if they absorbed freight costs, would receive a net price of 7.76 cents a gallon, exceeding the price of 6 cents that these same firms bid in other states.

The approach just described involves comparing the behavior of suspected colluders with some competitive benchmark. In the case of asphalt contracts, the benchmark is comparable markets in which firms are not thought to be colluding; specifically, among the distinct geographic markets for the same product or service, the firms are suspected of colluding in some but not all of these markets. Porter and Zona (1999) use the benchmark approach in examining collusion in school milk contracts. Alternatively, if there is prior information about the identities of the cartel members and the cartel is not all inclusive, a benchmark can be provided by the behavior of noncolluding firms. A third benchmark is when data show periods of suspected collusion but also of competition, such as before or after the suspected time of collusion. Data are more problematic from the time when collusion is thought to have temporarily broken down because a price war could be part of the collusion, and so need not be an appropriate competitive benchmark.[18]

The usual implementation of this concept is to estimate reduced-form price equations by regressing price on cost and demand shifters. After a price equation for (suspected) cartel members and a price equation for noncolluding firms are estimated, a test is conducted to determine whether the prices are statistically different. If they are statistically different, then prices of the noncolluding firms must be checked to see if they are consistent with those of a competitive model and if the colluding firms act in a manner consistent with some model of collusion.

Porter and Zona (1993)   The setting is a first-price sealed bid procurement auction as in Bajari and Ye (2003). Bidding behavior is specified to satisfy a log-linear bidding rule, $\log(b_{it}) = \alpha_t + \beta X_{it} + \epsilon_{it}$, where i is the firm and t is the project, α_t is an auction-specific effect, and X_{it} is a vector of observable variables affecting cost and the probability of winning.

The data are from 116 auctions conducted by the New York State Department of Transportation (DOT) for highway construction contracts over the span of 1979 to 1985. There was prior information about who might be members of the bidding ring. One of the firms was previously convicted for rigging bids on a Long Island highway construction project and four other firms were listed as unindicted conspirators, all at auctions that took place prior to the data set. This prior information was used to identify a candidate cartel comprised of these five firms. As a reality check, the authors provide some evidence that, in the absence of collusion, the suspected firms would have competed, so that the set of auctions at which they would have participated significantly intersect. If that were not the case, then there was little reason for them to collude. The maintained hypothesis was that unsuspected firms were acting competitively.

Porter and Zona first consider whether the determination of firms' bid levels differ between cartel firms and competitive firms. For the bid equation the exogenous variables are (1) the backlog of a firm at the time of an auction as measured by the dollar value of contracts won but not yet completed, (2) the capacity of a firm as measured by the maximum backlog (capacity squared is included as well), (3) a firm's capacity utilization rate, which is backlog divided by capacity (and capacity utilization squared), and (4) a dummy variable for whether a firm's headquarters is on Long Island (which serves to measure geographic proximity to a job). The bid equation is estimated separately for competitive firms and cartel firms.

The estimated bid function for competitive firms is reasonable with all estimated coefficients being highly significant. A firm's bid is initially decreasing and then increasing in utilization and initially decreasing and then increasing in capacity. In contrast, the estimated bid function for cartel firms shows that their bids are not statistically significantly related to utilization and are initially increasing and then decreasing in capacity, contrary to that for competitive firms. To test for differences in these estimated coefficients, the bid equation is estimated using all bids. Under the null hypothesis that there is no collusion, the two subsamples—competitive firms and cartel firms—should have the same estimates as those using the entire sample. A Chow test allows that hypothesis to be rejected. The authors conclude that the estimated model fits the bids of competitive firms reasonably well and the bids of cartel firms are statistically different from those of competitive firms.

A more interesting test is conducted on the ranking of bids. In terms of a multinomial logit (MNL), the likelihood of the observed ranking of bids for auction t is

$$\Pr(b_{r_1 t} < \cdots < b_{r_{n_i} t}) = \prod_{i=1}^{n_t} \frac{e^{\beta Z_{r_i t}}}{\sum_{j=i}^{n_t} e^{\beta Z_{r_j t}}},$$

where r_m denotes the firm with the mth lowest bid, $Z_{r_m t}$ are exogenous variables, and n_t is the number of bidders at auction t. The crucial property of the MNL is that the model (if correctly specified) can be estimated from any subset of bids. For example, compare using the lowest bid,

$$\prod_{t=1}^{T} \frac{e^{\beta Z_{r_1 t}}}{\sum_{j=1}^{n_t} e^{\beta Z_{r_j t}}}, \tag{6.1}$$

and the remaining higher bids,

$$\prod_{t=1}^{T} \prod_{i=2}^{n_t} \frac{e^{\beta Z_{r_i t}}}{\sum_{j=i}^{n_t} e^{\beta Z_{r_j t}}}. \tag{6.2}$$

Porter and Zona estimate the model with all ranks, the lowest rank, and the higher ranks. The null hypothesis is that the estimated coefficients are the same and is tested using a likelihood ratio test. Based on the bids of competitive bidders, the null hypothesis cannot be rejected; the estimates of the lowest competitive bid and the higher competitive bids are not statistically different. However, when estimated with the bids of the suspected cartel members, the null hypothesis is soundly rejected.

With this distinguishing empirical property of suspected cartel members, the next task is to show that it is consistent with some model of collusion. Why would collusion result in the process determining the lowest bid differing from that of higher bids? Porter and Zona suggest the following collusive scheme: The cartel identifies a firm to submit the lowest bid with the other firms instructed to offer higher bids. The designated firm's bid will be driven by its cost and the desire to trade off the probability of winning and the surplus it receives if it wins, just as with competitive firms. In contrast, the phantom bids of the other cartel members are only required to be higher and thus need not be generated by an analogous process. Their bids are not set so as to maximize their expected payoff but rather only to give the appearance of competition. Such a collusive model could explain why there would be this disparity between the process generating the lowest cartel member's bid and that of the bids of the other cartel members.

As with the independence and exchangeability tests of Bajari and Ye (2003), testing whether the estimated coefficients for (6.1) and (6.2) are the same for suspected colluding firms is a test of competition and can be conducted without a competitive benchmark. Nevertheless, a rejection of this test can be more confidently concluded as due to collusion, rather than some other form of misspecification, if the test is not rejected for firms not suspected of colluding.

Porter and Zona (1999)   A similar approach is taken in Porter and Zona (1999) in examining collusion at procurement auctions for school milk.[19] The market is a city school district that awards an annual contract for the supply of school milk. School districts conduct their auctions independently. The analysis focuses on the school districts in the Cincinnati area for which there were three defendants: Coors, Meyer, and Louis Trauth (two of them having confessed to rigging bids). Furthermore the defendants testified that the cartel used an incumbency scheme whereby if a cartel member had served a particular district in the previous year, then the other firms were to either not participate or submit high complementary bids.

The approach is similiar to that of the earlier study. A reduced form model of a firm's bid level is estimated, though, in this case, it is done simultaneously with a probit specification for whether a bid was submitted. The strategy is to determine whether there are systematic differences between the estimated bid equations for cartel members and competitive firms and, if so, whether these differences can be explained with a particular model of collusion.

The authors have detailed data on the characteristics of a contract which relate to cost—for example, the distance between the processing plant and the school district (*Distance*) and the size of the school district—and the competitive environment—for example, if a firm is the closest one to the district (and thus has a cost advantage over other bidders). Using data for all competitive firms plus a particular defendant, Porter and Zona regressed the bids on various factors (along with estimating the probability that a bid is submitted). This is done assuming the slope coefficients are the same for all firms and when the slope coefficients for the defendant are allowed to differ from those of the other firms. Both intercepts are allowed to differ. Under the null hypothesis the estimated coefficients should be the same for the two estimations, and this hypothesis is tested by a likelihood ratio test for each of the three suspected cartel members. It is worth noting that the test is not whether colluders bid more but rather whether their bids are determined differently from that of competitive firms. Higher bids could simply be due to drawing valuations from a different distribution.

For each of these three firms the null hypothesis is rejected at any conventional significance level, which means that suspected colluding firms' bids are determined by a different process than that of unsuspected firms. The unsuspected firms' bids respond in a manner consistent with the competitive model—for example, their bids are increasing in *Distance*, while the bids of two colluding firms are *decreasing* in *Distance* (all three colluding firms' bids are decreasing in distance relative to that of the other firms). The estimates for the bid submission equation show that bids are significantly lower in the distance ranges for which these firms are more likely to bid than competitive firms. This result is inconsistent with the competitive model as well. As cost is increasing in distance, a firm's bid should be increasing in distance. Furthermore, if there is a fixed cost to submitting a bid (or there is an opportunity cost to winning a contract), a firm should be more inclined to do so where it thinks it can win with a higher price–cost margin, which, controlling for cost factors, suggests that a firm's bid should be relatively *higher* where it is relatively more likely to bid.

Because unsuspected colluders are the competitive benchmark, it is clear that suspected colluders' bids have systematically departed from the behavior of competitive firms. Nevertheless, collusion is only one possible explanation for this departure. What is needed is a collusive model that predicts the direction of these departures. Before turning to that task, I discuss below what was learned from the estimates of the probability of a firm submitting a bid on a contract.

A reduced-form probit model was estimated in which the dependent variable takes the value 1 if a firm submitted a bid on a contract. Estimates for competitive firms are generally consistent with competition—for example, firms are less likely to submit a bid when *Distance* is longer. Relative to nondefendants' behavior, the three suspected colluders were much more likely to submit bids when *Distance* is 30 miles or less. Furthermore the decision to submit bids was found not to be independent across colluding firms, as ought to hold for the competitive model after controlling for all public information. By way of the estimated probit equation for competitive firms, the residual was calculated for each auction for each of the colluding firms. For each of the three pairs of these firms, the unexplained portion of each firm's submission decision was positively and significantly correlated. That the submission of bids was positively correlated across cartel members suggests parallel behavior. As additional evidence, the authors examined the residuals to the bid level equations and found that they were also positively correlated; a high bid by one of them makes it more likely that the others bid high.

Porter and Zona provide a collusive story to explain why bid levels and bid submissions depart from the competitive benchmark. That colluding firms' bids may not be increasing in distance makes sense if more distant school districts are not collusive. There are many firms and districts and, if indeed these firms are coordinating their behavior, it'll be effective only in those markets for which non-colluding firms are neither numerous nor have a significant cost advantage (e.g., situated as the closest processors). Firms then would be submitting higher bids in districts for which they have a distance advantage—so collusion works—whereas in more distant markets they would be forced by competition to submit lower bids (despite the higher transportation costs). As to the correlation in the submission of bids, this is consistent with complementary bidding that is intended to give the impression of competition. A cartel member who is not selected to win a contract (e.g., by the incumbency scheme) submits a higher bid than the incumbent to provide the appearance of competition. Ironically this correlation of the decision to submit a bid is interpreted as evidence of collusion!

6.1.4 Is Firm Behavior More Consistent with Collusion Than with Competition?

Now consider an approach that puts collusive and competitive models into a horse race to determine which better fits the data. The general strategy is to specify structural competitive and collusive models of firms' prices or bids and to estimate them using cost and demand shifters. There is evidence of collusion if a collusive model better fits the data. All the approaches reviewed here use functional forms and thus are subject to specification error. More recently attention has moved to less parametric methods for estimating oligopolistic behavior (at auctions), though they have not yet been applied to the issue of distinguishing collusion from competition.[20]

Porter (1983a) and Ellison (1994) There is another rationale for looking for structural breaks, which is that sharp changes in price—inexplicable in light of cost and demand shifts—are consistent with theories of collusive pricing under imperfect monitoring while not being easily reconcilable within a competitive theory. As originally established by Green and Porter (1984) for a context in which cartel members can only imperfectly monitor the behavior of each other, sustaining collusion may require periodic reversions to low prices as a form of punishment to induce compliance. In particular, a price war will ensue when the realized price is relatively low as such an event is suggestive of a firm having cheated and produced too much. The details of the theoretical argument are provided in section 6.2; here I describe the empirical test for distinguishing collusion from competition.

The focus is on the Joint Executive Committee, which was a cartel among railroads created to coordinate the rate charged for transporting grain from Chicago to the US East Coast. Existing in the late nineteenth century, the cartel is well documented as it preceded the establishment of the Sherman Act (and subsequent court cases) that made price-fixing illegal.

The empirical model being estimated in Porter (1983a) is a two-equation structural model that seeks to explain the determination of price and quantity using cost and demand shifters:

$$\log Q_t = \alpha_0 + \alpha_1 \log P_t + \alpha_2 LAKES_t + \epsilon_{1t}, \tag{6.3}$$

$$\log P_t = \beta_0 + \beta_1 \log Q_t + \beta_2 S_t + \beta_3 I_t + \epsilon_{2t}. \tag{6.4}$$

The demand equation (6.3) for rail services for grain relates the volume of grain shipped, Q_t, to the rate for rail services, P_t, and a demand shifter, $LAKES_t$, which takes the value 1 (0) when the Great Lakes is (not) open for shipping; the Great Lakes provide an alternative means of transportation so one expects $\alpha_2 < 0$. Equation (6.4) is referred to as a "supply relation" and is a re-arrangement of the profix-maximizing (first-order) condition defining the optimal supply of firms. S_t is an exogenous variable capturing changes in the composition of the cartel due to entry and acquisitions. The key variable here is I_t, which, according to the theory (and presuming $\beta_3 > 0$), takes the value 1 when firms are in the collusive phase (producing a relatively low quantity) and 0 when they are in the punishment phase (producing a relatively high quantity and engaging in a price war). I_t is unknown to the economist and is presumed to be determined by a stochastic process. The empirical model is then a switching regression in which the stochastic process governing I_t is estimated along with the other parameters, in particular, β_3, which measures the effect on price from a regime switch.

The test for collusion is based on the following comparison: The competitive model predicts there will be no regime switches, which means no systematic changes in price unrelated to movements in cost and demand functions. The collusive model, according to the theory of Green and Porter (1984), predicts that there will be regime switches, with firms moving between high prices and low prices (after controlling for cost and demand shifters). Furthermore the theory predicts that these switches will occur when there is a low (unobserved) demand shock. The shock will produce the low price that induces a temporary price war.

Central to testing this theory of collusion is the structure placed on the stochastic process determining I_t. Using only the feature of the theory that there are regime switches, Porter (1983a) assumes I_t is independently and identically distributed (iid) over time. The stochastic process is then defined by a single parameter, which is the probability of being in the collusive phase in a given period ($I_t = 1$). Porter finds evidence in support of the collusive model as six to eleven regime switches are identified. Furthermore price falls significantly—about 40 percent—when firms move to a price war.

Of course, the theory does not just say there are regime switches; they occur when there is evidence consistent with a firm having cheated. This more refined implication of the collusive theory is tested by Ellison (1994).[21] He actually enriches the structure placed on I_t in two ways. First, he assumes the regime—whether collusive or punishment—follows a Markov process so that the probability of being in a collusive phase tomorrow depends on the current phase, that is, whether firms are currently colluding or engaging in a price war. Second, this Markov process is allowed to depend on "triggers" that might, according to the logic of the theory, induce a shift to a price war. The intent of these triggers is to proxy for a firm receiving a "suspiciously high market share." For example, one variable measures the largest difference, among all firms, between a firm's realized quantity and a benchmark value (think of this as a firm's cartel quota). The prediction is that a higher value for these variables will make a switch from a collusive regime to a price war more likely.

Ellison (1994) finds persistence in regimes as the estimated probability of colluding tomorrow, given firms are colluding today, is very high at 0.975, while the probability of colluding tomorrow, given firms are currently engaged in a price war, is only 0.067. As to the estimated effects of the price war triggers, the evidence is more ambiguous, though some of the variables do make it more likely to transit from colluding to a price war. In sum, the evidence tends to support the Green-Porter model of collusion over standard noncollusive oligopolistic competition. From a cartel detection perspective, this approach provides a structure for looking for the regime switching that might occur when firms are colluding.[22]

Baldwin, Marshall, and Richard (1997)   The task is to determine whether a cartel was operating at some or all of 108 oral ascending timber auctions in the Pacific Northwest over a span of 1975 to 1981. A class of competitive models is specified and includes the maintained hypothesis that once controlling for publicly observed variables, it is IPV. When a single unit is auctioned, competition results in the winning bid being the second highest valuation. However, the specified class of competitive models also allows multiple units to be auctioned. If there are m units to be auctioned (and $m < n$, where n is the number of bidders), then with each bidder bidding for at most one unit, the winning bid is the $m + 1$-order statistic over n valuations.

Collusion is modeled using the collusive auction model of Graham and Marshall (1987), which allows for side payments. There is at most one cartel (a maintained assumption) and it contains l members. The cartel elicits members' valuations prior to the auction and a cartel representative submits the highest valuation of the cartel members. For the case of a single unit, if the cartel fails to contain the two highest valuations, then the price paid by the winning bidder is, as usual, distributed as a second-order statistic. More generally, if the cartel includes those firms with the highest k values, then the price is distributed as a $k + 1$-order statistic. Thus under collusion the price is distributed as a mixture among these order statistics. Finally, Baldwin, Marshall, and Richard nest the two models by allowing for both the possibility of a bidding ring and multiple units to be auctioned off.

This class of models provides two possible reasons why bidding can be less aggressive—collusion (or a bigger cartel) and a larger supply is being auctioned off. The setup makes these two alternatives analogous in that both m and l are assumed to be unobserved and independent across auctions. The independence of the size of the cartel is a bit problematic, though the authors argue that it is plausible given the auctions are geographically dispersed and occur over several years. The functional forms for the probability distribution over m and l are identical and allowed to depend on various factors. Though the determination of m and l is reduced form, the bidding models are structural given m and l.

The independent variables influencing bidding behavior and the size of the cartel include the volume of timber offered for sale on a tract, the time over which the timber is required to be cut (i.e., the contract length), a measure of logging cost, and a measure of the quality of the timber. The probability of joining the coalition depends on the volume of timber and, so as to control for geographic proximity among bidders, a "bidder proximity dummy" takes the value 1 when the highest and second highest bidders are in the same county.

The models are estimated using maximum likelihood. By the log-likelihood criterion, the single-unit collusive model noticeably outperforms the single-unit competitive model.[23] This suggests that the competitive model is misspecified, but it could be for reasons other than that firms are actually colluding. Baldwin, Marshall, and Richard dismiss one likely alternative, which is that the assumption that the distribution on valuations is lognormal is incorrect. Performance of the nested models is not enhanced when multiple supply is added to collusion. The authors conclude that the best model—based on performance and parsimony—is the single-unit collusive model.

Banerji and Meenakshi (2004)   Banerji and Meenakshi (2004) compare the performance of collusive and competitive models in examining oral ascending bid wheat auctions in India. Their prior information is that the three largest buyers (with a total market share of about 45 percent) may be colluding. The competitive model is IPV with asymmetric distributions; the three largest buyers are allowed to draw valuations from different distributions than that of the remaining buyers (all who are assumed to have the same distribution). Hence the winning bid for the competitive model is the second-order statistic over the valuations of three large buyers and the small buyers. Banerji and Meenakshi specify the collusive model to be one of bid rotation, whereby the three largest buyers randomly decide on the buyer to participate in a particular auction. The winning bid is then the second-order statistic over the valuations of one large buyer and the small buyers. It is assumed that the identity of the participating cartel member is determined prior to observing the specifics of the lot up for auction.

The data they have is for 421 auctions from two months in 1999. The data include some quality variables, the number of bidders who cast bids during the auction, the winning price, and the identity of winning bidder. They apply a structural model that incorporates a result from Athey and Haile (2004) to identify the latent distributions: identification only requires the second-order statistic and the identity of the winning bidder. The various criteria used in comparing the performance of the two models include the log-likelihood value and the mean sum of squared residuals. The collusive model fits the data better than the competitive model.

Bajari and Ye (2003)   This study also compares structural models of collusion and competition to see which performs better. Recall that their initial tests identified two candidate cartels: firms 2 and 4 and firms 2 and 5. The three candidate models are then a competitive model (where there is no collusion), cartel 24 (where firms 2 and 4 collude and all other firms do not), and cartel 25 (where firms 2 and 5 collude and all other firms do not). Their approach is Bayesian as they calculate a posterior probability distribution over these three models based on the observed markups.

The first step is to specify a prior distribution over the three models; this is arbitrarily assumed to be the uniform distribution. The next step is estimating the likelihood of observing the actual markups given a particular model. Finally, Bayes's rule is used to derive a posterior set of beliefs on the set of models.

To execute this approach, one first needs a measure of actual markups. Specifying a structural model of bidding provides a first-order condition defining a firm's bid, which is a function of its cost and the distribution on other firms' bids. By estimating that distribution and using the observed bid, one can backout the firm's cost and get an estimate of the markup. The competitive model is specified to be the IPV model with asymmetric bidder valuation distributions. The cartel model is the competitive model but where the two colluding firms act as a single profit-maximizing bidder with cost equal to their minimum cost (thus presuming they can make side payments). This procedure is done for each of the three models to yield the observed markups.

The more challenging task is to estimate the likelihood of these markups for a particular model. Toward this end, structural cost parameter estimates are needed, and these are derived by eliciting a distribution on markups from industry experts. From this markup distribution, a random draw is made for each bidder for each auction. From the observed bid one can infer the latent cost. This latent cost is then regressed on the exogenous factors, which yields a set of estimates for the structural model. With these estimates and a model, the likelihood of a particular set of costs is calculated. Simulation methods are used to then calculate an expected likelihood based on an estimated prior distribution over costs and structural parameter values.

The predicted markup at the 50th percentile for the estimated distribution is 3.33 percent for the competitive model, 4.13 percent for cartel 24, and 4.47 percent for cartel 25. As the industry experts put it at 5 percent, the cartel models fit the median markup better. However, at the 99th percentile, the cartel models predict a markup vastly higher than the 15 percent predicted by the industry experts. Cartel 24 has it at 33.54 percent and cartel 25 at 58.26 percent, while the competitive model is much closer at 23.81 percent. Because of its poor performance in the tails, the posterior probability that the model is competitive is very close to one.

There are two methodological innovations worth noting. First, the use of industry experts to provide ancillary information is novel and potentially fruitful but there are concerns. Industry experts might be good at predicting median markups but—due to fewer observations—much less effective at extreme markups: recall that it was the poor fit between the experts and the cartel models on extreme markups that allowed the competitive model to be assigned such a high posterior probability. In addition there is a concern that if experts' beliefs are based on what they infer about cost from bids, their judgment depends on the model they are using. Did they presume competition? Or did they suspect collusion? If they presumed firms competed, then was the approach biased in favor of the competitive model?

Second, the Bayesian approach provides an alternative to having two discrete categories: "Yes, there is collusion" and "No, there isn't collusion." It does indeed seem more useful to potential plaintiffs and antitrust authorities to be able to assign some (well-defined) strength to the hypothesis of collusion in deciding whether to bring a case. One could also imagine having a more informed prior distribution on there being a cartel by using the empirical frequency of discovered cartels. Although there are sure to be many undiscovered cartels, this would at least provide a lower bound to the prior probability of there being a cartel.

6.1.5 The Pitfalls of Using a High Price–Cost Margin as a Screen for Collusion

Because the ultimate objective in forming a cartel is a high price–cost margin—defined as (Price − Marginal cost)/Price—it is natural to think about using a high price–cost margin as a screen for collusion. It can be directly measured if one has both good price and cost data. Although not many economists find themselves in that situation (especially with regards to cost data), there are indirect estimation methods; indeed many of the methods thus far reviewed do exactly that.[24] With information on price, quantity, and cost and demand shifters, an industry price–cost margin can then be estimated. So, why not then use a high price–cost margin as a screen for collusion?

The problem with this approach is that we know from past studies that there is considerable variation in price–cost margins across industries—it is not as if most industries have values consistent with the dominant models of competition—and that there are many industries with high price–cost margins for which there is no evidence or even suspicion about collusion. A high price–cost margin (properly measured) is evidence of *market power* and does not imply collusion. Other reasons for a high price–cost margin are greatly differentiated products, production technologies protected by patents and trade secrets, and high search costs for consumers. All these cases are much more ubiquitous than collusion. Many industries might have high price–cost margins, but my own prior belief is that only a precious few are cartelized.

It is also worth noting when a high price–cost margin is not a necessary implication of collusion. For example, consider an industry subject to Bertrand price competition so that the noncollusive price–cost margin hovers around zero. Collusion may then have the impact of raising the price–cost margin to a level, say, commensurate with Cournot quantity competition. A naïve economist unaware of the appropriate competitive benchmark may infer from the observed price–cost margin that a cartel is not present because the price–cost margin is consistent with *some* model of competition.

In light of this critique of the efficacy of using a high price–cost margin as a screen for collusion, let us review the relative advantages of some of the approaches I have recommended. Although a high price–cost margin should not necessarily raise suspicions about collusion, a sharp *increase* in the price–cost margin ought to. While one can easily rationalize a high price–cost margin without resorting to the presence of a cartel, notable changes in the price–cost margin are not so easily rationalized without it. Of course, big changes in demand and cost will suffice, but they ought to be observable (by virtue of their size) and thereby one can take account of them. Hence the method described in section

6.1.2—screening for abrupt changes in price (or price–cost margins)—is likely to be a more effective screen than looking for high price–cost margins.

In stating that some level of the price–cost margin is suggestive of collusion, one is inferring that it is high *relative* to some competitive benchmark. Without any further analysis, this competitive benchmark would have to be chosen arbitrarily by assuming the form of competition (e.g., price or quantity competition), the degree of product differentiation, the ease of consumer search, and so forth. When this was done in the past, it was typical to assume homogeneous products, zero search costs (and there are no other source of frictions that may create market power), and firms compete in quantities, all of which are quite arbitrary. An attractive feature of the method described in section 6.1.3 is that a competitive benchmark is identified for the market in question by examining comparable markets not suspected of collusion, comparable firms not suspected of colluding, or a time period for which the suspected firms are believed not to have been colluding. These benchmarks are superior to making an arbitrary selection of the noncollusive solution.

The arbitrariness of the competitive model does plague the method described in section 6.1.4 in that the economist must choose a lot of structure without much guidance from the data; this includes the competitive model that will be estimated and serve as the benchmark for the estimated collusive model. It is this structure, however, that allows testing for more informative and telling implications of collusion. One is not just requiring that a collusive model explain the level of prices better than a competitive model but also that it explain better how prices respond to cost and demand shifters. For example, the approach of Porter (1983a) doesn't try to find evidence of collusion by determining whether prices are, in some sense, high but rather whether the price-generating process is subject to regime switches that cannot be explained by cost and demand shifters. That is a more refined and informative implication of the collusive theory. It also has the virtue that it can detect the presence of a cartel even if price–cost margins are not, in some economywide sense, high.

6.1.6 Discussion

In summary, we reviewed four methods that can be used in connection with detecting collusion: (A) determining whether firm behavior is inconsistent with competition, (B) determining whether there is a structural break in firm behavior, (C) determining whether the behavior of suspected colluding firms differs from that of (presumed) competitive firms, and (D) determining whether a collusive model better fits the data than a competitive model.

In their least sophisticated forms, methods A and B provide no direct evidence in support of collusion. Rather, they seek to establish whether observed behavior has a difficult time being explained by competitive models. If a set of firms fails that test—their behavior is inconsistent with competition or there is an inexplicable change in behavior—it is necessary to turn to one of the other methods to assess whether collusion is the most natural explanation.

With regard to method A, the issue is whether the competitive model is misspecified, and if so, it could be due to there being collusion or to assumptions on cost and demand being wrong. Misspecification due to omitted variables is particularly a concern here. To confidently reject the competitive model in Bajari and Ye (2003) on the ground that firms' bids are not independent requires that one has not left out relevant variables that would result in firms' costs being correlated. Bajari and Ye stress this caveat and, for example, note that if two firms use the same subcontractor in calculating cost and the other firms do not, then the bids of those two firms will be positively correlated and thus violate independence without there being collusion. Although it is a tall order to confidently reject the null hypothesis of competition, one is less concerned if such a test is used only as a preliminary diagnostic tool.

Methods C and D allow a researcher to compare collusion and competition but in very different ways. Method C requires finding a competitive benchmark, either firms in the market who are not thought to be part of the suspected cartel, a comparable market (e.g., a different geographic market for the same product or service) that is thought to be competitive, or a time period during which the suspected firms were thought to have been competing. There must then be prior information as to which firms may be colluding, in which markets there may be collusion, and over what time there might have been collusion. This method is then inapplicable to an all-inclusive global cartel for which data are only available during the time of suspected collusion.

A general concern with method C has to do with the endogeneity of the competitive benchmark. For example, if the benchmark comes from firms who were not members of the cartel, why weren't they members? It is natural to suppose they are different in some way from the cartel members, so then the issue is whether the data one has are adequate to control for those differences. A model of endogenous cartel formation could shed light on how to handle such concerns. Furthermore there is a presumption that noncolluding firms will act the same in an industry with a cartel as they would without a cartel. Their conduct obviously depends on particular behavioral properties, since noncolluding firms will generally produce less when other firms are colluding but their quantities and prices will still be increasing in cost. Nevertheless, it would be interesting to more broadly explore which properties of firm behavior are robust to whether its competitors are (knowingly) colluding and whether it depends on the collusive scheme deployed.

When the competitive benchmark is based on data from comparable markets for which there is no prior information about collusion, one has to be concerned that collusion might simply be more effective there. For example, suppose firms are able to tacitly collude in market X but not in market Y. As a result firms may resort to explicit collusion in market Y, and as a result collusion is suspected there but not in market X. The "competitive" benchmark is then, unbeknown to the researcher, not so competitive after all. Failure to find higher prices in market Y would then be misleading. Indeed one could find lower prices in market Y. If the inability to tacitly collude in market Y is a reflection of the competitiveness of the industry, it is possible that the highest sustainable price is greater in market X where less competitiveness allows tacit collusion to work. That is, there are certain factors that determine whether firms tacitly or explicitly collude (ceteris paribus, firms prefer the former as they are not as much at risk of paying penalties), and these factors might also determine the collusive outcome. Explicit collusion may only occur where collusion is difficult, and thus collusive outcomes might be more competitive.[25] But even if the price level is not noticeably different in the two markets, behavior—say, in how price responds to cost and demand shifters—might still vary significantly because explicit collusion operates differently from tacit collusion. Unfortunately, theory provides little help here.

After finding there are differences between suspected colluding firms' behavior and some competitive benchmark, there are two follow-up issues. First, the difference could be due to, say, omitted variables and not due to market conduct. Second, any difference must be rationalized with some collusive model. The ultimate objective is not to show that behavior is inconsistent with competition but rather that it is most naturally explained by collusion. Certain collusive models provide predicted directions as to how collusion is apt to depart from competition. For example, Porter and Zona (1999) argue that collusion in markets geographically close to cartel members' plants, and competition in more distant markets would make a firm's bid less of an increasing function of distance and perhaps even a decreasing function of distance. Thus Porter and Zona took the observed empirical departure from the competitive benchmark and offered a collusive equilibrium to rationalize it. An issue is how much discretion a researcher has in terms of various collusive schemes. Providing ancillary evidence in support of a particular collusive scheme is highly useful.

By contrast, method D builds into it both competitive and collusive models. Thus one can offer criteria for comparing the performance of the two behavioral models. This method is also the most widely applicable in that it can be used even if there is no prior information as to collusion, the cartel is all-inclusive (all firms and all markets), and data are only available during the cartel regime. The major disadvantage is misspecification. In that structural models are being estimated, there is the usual enhanced concern of misspecification compared to the reduced form price equations of method C. For example, firm symmetry is a maintained hypothesis in Baldwin, Marshall, and Richard (1997), but it is quite possible for the collusive model to outperform because buyers have different distributions over valuations. Misspecification of cost and demand conditions may then cause the competitive model to underperform.

Misspecification is apt to be an even more serious concern for the collusive model. Although there is typically a limited number of competitive models and equilibria to them, there are many more collusive equilibria even for a single model; that is, there are many more equilibria for the repeated game than for the static game. Collusive solutions can differ in terms of bid rotation, territorial allocation, side payments, market share allocations, and so forth. On these grounds, one is more likely to erroneously reject the collusive model than the competitive model. Ancillary evidence as to how firms might be colluding can be useful here. For example, there is evidence that a Florida school milk cartel used side payments, and this suggests that market shares can fluctuate over time as contracts go to the most efficient, with the others receiving transfers as compensation. In contrast, there is no evidence of side payments for a Texas school milk cartel, which suggests that collusion requires stable market shares. In both cases Pesendorfer (2000) finds the data in his study to be consistent with these hypotheses. This reminds us how the collusive solutions can vary greatly but also how other evidence can help with the multiplicity problem.

Another source of bias can arise due to mislabeling firms, markets, and periods as being noncollusive when they actually are collusive, and vice versa. Incentives of cartel members to hide evidence is recognized by Porter and Zona (1993) in noting that some of their "competitive" firms could actually have been part of the cartel. They use past convictions to identify likely suspects—if they found it profitable to collude once, they may find it profitable again—but then this misses out on firms who previously avoided convictions or have since found it optimal to join the cartel. Similarly, lack of observed interaction among firms—such as not bidding on the same contracts—can lead one to conclude that these firms are not candidates for collusion when in fact their lack of interaction is due to collusion. The usual example is a collusive scheme in which a designated cartel member submits a bid and the others do not. There could then be a bias against certain firms being considered as candidate cartels.

6.2 Collusive Markers

For developing economic evidence of collusion, one needs to know what to look for—what behavioral patterns are indicative of collusion? An important line of work is then to provide collusive markers—behavior that distinguishes collusion from competition. These markers can be developed through theoretical models or by documenting the behavior of price-fixing cartels. In this section, I review what theory has to offer and, in some cases, provide examples of cartel exhibiting these markers. A more systematic and detailed summary of documented cartel behavioral patterns—along with experimental evidence—will have to await another paper.

Theory has a crucial role to play in providing collusive markers, and theory is essential if one pursues the empirical method of contrasting the behavior of suspected colluders with that of competitive firms. When one finds a difference, it is important to know whether the difference is consistent with some collusive story. If instead the empirical method of detection is to look for structural breaks—perhaps to identify the formation of a cartel—having collusive markers can indicate what kind of change in behavior to look for. Markers are particularly valuable from the perspective of screening, where one wants easily measured traits to suggest which industries might have a cartel.[26]

Before embarking on this review, I should add an important disclaimer that evidence supporting collusion need not imply evidence against competition. The ensuing work will derive distinguishing features of collusion and competition *for a particular class of models.* Even with evidence of collusion, there is always the possibility that there actually is no collusion and the problem is we've misspecified the noncollusive model. Similarly failure to find evidence of collusion may be due to misspecifying the collusive model; for example, we've focused on the wrong collusive equilibrium. At best, collusive markers can serve to screen industries to determine whether they are worthy of more intense investigation.

My discussion will focus on what theory has to say about patterns in prices and market shares and how it depends on whether firms are colluding. Theory offers insight into how collusion affects: (1) the relationship between firms' prices and demand movements, (2) the stability of price and market share, and (3) the relationship between firms' prices. A wide array of collusive models will be covered, and it is useful to identify five crucial dimensions along which they may differ. First, a collusive model can be static or dynamic. A static approach compares what Nash equilibrium yields and what is gotten from either exogenously imposing some collective preferences (e.g., joint profit maximization) or requiring adherence of individual firm behavior to the prescription of a cartel manager. A dynamic approach assumes an infinite horizon setting in which outcomes less competitive than static Nash equilibria are sustained using strategies that punish deviations from the collusive agreement. By the dynamic approach, collusion is often distinguished from competition when equilibrium conditions bind, which is the case when collusion is not so easy. Second, models differ in terms of the market institution, which is generally either posted price—which characterizes most retail markets—or an auction. Third, models differ in terms of whether the cartel is allowed to make side payments to each other. Indeed, implicit in assuming joint profit maximization is that transfers are allowed, for otherwise it is not clear why some firms would go along with such an objective. Fourth, a model may allow firms to send messages to each other prior to choosing price or quantity. Where this is pertinent is when firms have private information about their preferences, such as cost or, in the context of an auction, their valuation. One necessarily thinks of models with direct communication as being associated with explicit rather than tacit collusion. Fifth, most models assume firms are colluding without concern for being detected by the antitrust authorities. There are a few studies, however, for which detection may occur and firms are cognizant of how their behavior can influence detection, which then has implications for the price path.

The decision to focus on the unique implications of collusion for price and market share is largely due to the relative ease with which such data are available. There are clearly other identifying markers associated with collusion. For example, unit profit is uncorrelated with firm size under competition but is negatively correlated with firm size under collusion (Osborne and Pitchik 1987), noncollusive prices depend on whether nearby products are owned by rival firms though that is not true when firms collude and maximize joint profits (Bresnahan 1987), and there is greater excess capacity under collusion (Benoît and Krishna 1987; Davidson and Deneckere 1990). Finally, the theoretical literature on collusive pricing is rich in identifying industry traits that are conducive to collusion.[27] Thus the search for collusive markers can be supplemented with attention to certain industry traits. Research has found that collusion is easier to sustain or is more profitable when concentration is higher, orders are more frequent, firms are more symmetric (Compte, Jenny, and Ray 2002; Vasconcelos 2005), multi-market contact is greater (Bernheim and Whinston 1990), and cost is more volatile (Harrington and Chen 2006).

6.2.1 Predictions on Price

The basic logic whereby collusion is sustainable as an equilibrium in a repeated game model is predicated upon rewards and punishments.[28] A Nash equilibrium for the static game is one where each firm's behavior (which is typically a price, bid, or quantity) is optimal given the (correctly anticipated) behavior of other firms. Firms collude for the purpose of raising price above the static Nash equilibrium level so as to yield higher profits. This necessarily means that a firm's behavior doesn't maximize current profit; a firm's collusive quantity is below that which maximizes current profit or its collusive price exceeds that which maximizes current profit. As cheating on the collusive outcome raises current profit, firms can only be deterred from doing so if they experience a future loss. This future loss from cheating comes from an intensification of competition in response to cheating. Thus, if firms act collusively, then they continue colluding, but if a firm cheats, then firms revert to some low-profit punishment path. This may mean going to the static Nash equilibrium for some length of time or an outcome with even lower profits (perhaps pricing below cost) or an asymmetric equilibrium that is particularly detrimental to the firm that deviated (perhaps requiring that the firm produce very little). It follows that a firm that considers deviating from a collusive outcome realizes that it can raise current profit but lower its future profit stream. The equilibrium condition or incentive compatibility constraint (ICC) requires that the forgone future profit stream is at least as great as the gain in current from deviating. When the punishment is reversion to the noncollusive outcome for T periods, the ICC is

$$\sum_{\tau=1}^{T} \delta^\tau (\pi^c - \pi^{nc}) \geq \pi^d - \pi^c,$$

where π^c, π^{nc}, and π^d are the collusive profit, noncollusive profit, and the (optimal) profit from deviating, respectively. $\delta \in (0, 1)$ is the common discount factor across firms. In this simple case the model is stationary and the solution is symmetric. Deviation yields higher current profit of $\pi^d - \pi^c$ but lower future profit of $\pi^c - \pi^{nc}$ over the next T periods (with firms returning to the collusive outcome thereafter). Equilibrium requires that this condition hold so that abiding by the collusive agreement is optimal for all firms. Since

$\pi^c > \pi^{nc}$, this will hold when T is sufficiently high and δ is sufficiently close to one, so firms sufficiently value future profits.

To derive our first collusive marker, let us modify that setting to where the demand curve changes over time. Firms jointly observe the demand shock and then choose prices. At this point, demand could be independently and identically distributed (iid) over time or show some persistence or follow some cyclical pattern. Suppose that the demand shifts are well-behaved in that "higher demand" corresponds to the demand curve shifting out and both the monopoly price and the static Nash equilibrium price rising.[29] Hence the static Nash equilibrium price (which we are taking as the noncollusive benchmark) would follow movements in demand—price rises when demand increases—and thus price and quantity are positively correlated over time. These properties also hold under perfect collusion where (symmetric) firms charge the joint profit-maximizing price.

Thus far the relationship between the price path and demand movements is not distinguishable between competition and collusion. Now suppose that firms are not so patient and thus cannot perfectly collude; that is, firms achieve the collusive outcome that yields the highest profit subject to satisfying the ICCs. This necessarily implies that the ICCs bind, which will serve to produce some useful collusive markers.

The initial work on this class of models is Rotemberg and Saloner (1986) who considered (observable) iid demand shocks. Their result is that when ICCs bind, price is *lower* when demand is stronger and thus price and quantity are *negatively* correlated. As demand shocks are iid, the future loss from cheating is always the same, since the expected future forgone collusive profit is independent of the current demand realization. However, the current gain from cheating is higher when demand is stronger because, with the price fixed, the gain in sales from undercutting rival firms' price is greater. Since the incentive to cheat is then more powerful when demand is greater, cartel stability requires setting a lower collusive price as this weakens the incentive to cheat. As a result price can move opposite to demand in a collusive equilibrium, but for the same demand and cost structures, price moves with demand in a noncollusive equilibrium.[30]

Haltiwanger and Harrington (1991) pursued this idea further but considered instead a deterministic demand cycle in which demand gradually shifts out then shifts in, with the pattern repeating itself. Such a demand pattern fits seasonal movements in demand that are relatively well anticipated. In contrast to the preceding analysis, both the current gain and future loss from cheating change over time. Take two points on the cycle where the current demand function is the same but differ in that one point is during the boom phase—demand is rising (and thus will be higher in the immediately ensuing periods)—and the other is during the bust phase—demand is falling. For the same price the current gain from cheating is the same at both points because demand is the same. However, the future loss from cheating is higher during the boom because a firm forgoes more profits from competition (compared to collusion), since demand is anticipated to be relatively strong. Thus, contrary to Rotemberg and Saloner (1986), collusion is easier during the boom phase so the firms set higher prices.[31] When the peak of the cycle and the period prior to it are compared, it is clear that the stronger demand at the peak implies a higher current gain from cheating and forgone future profits are lower (i.e., cheating before the peak means forgoing collusion when demand is strongest). Thus collusion is more difficult at the peak, which requires price to be set lower. The implication is that the price path will peak prior to demand, so the price path will lead the demand cycle. Once again, this is a pricing pattern that runs counter to noncollusive pricing where the price path follows the demand cycle.[32]

As described in section 6.1.4, another key collusive marker is that price and quantity can be subject to large and persistent changes *in the absence of large demand and cost changes*. This work begins with the seminal paper of Green and Porter (1984; also see Porter 1983b). The context is the repeated quantity game but with imperfect information. In each period firms choose quantities and then observe price. Price depends on firms' quantities and an unobserved iid demand shock (recall that such shocks were observed in Rotemberg and Saloner 1986). As a firm's quantity is never observed by other firms, a deviation cannot be directly observed. However, price is observed, and in expectation, a higher quantity will result in a lower price. Of course, since price depends on an unobserved demand shock, a low price could be due to a low demand shock rather than some firm cheating by producing above their collusive quota. There is then imperfect monitoring of collusion by the cartel's members.

An equilibrium is characterized in which, during the collusive phase, firms choose some designated collusive quantity. If the realized price is ever too low (a threshold price is specified as part of the collusive strategy), then firms switch to a punishment phase that is static Nash equilibrium quantities for T periods, after which they return to the collusive phase. A collusive equilibrium quantity is one in which a firm maximizes its payoff, taking into account that a higher quantity increases current expected profit but lowers future expected profits by making a punishment more likely (where the probability of a punishment is the probability that the realized price falls below the threshold price). Equilibrium then entails stochastic regime switches where a one-time low demand shock triggers a movement from the collusive phase to the punishment phase—associated with it is a fall in the average price—and after T periods there is a regime switch back to the collusive phase—with a rise in the average price.[33] One then observes abrupt changes in average price that cannot be explained by contemporaneous demand and cost movements.[34]

A summary of the discussion above is as follows:

Collusive Marker   Under certain conditions, price and quantity are negatively correlated, price leads a demand cycle, and the stochastic process on price is subject to regime switches under collusion; whereas price and quantity are positively correlated, price follows a demand cycle, and price is not subject to regime switches under competition.

A second collusive marker concerns price stability. Two papers taking very different approaches show that under certain conditions, prices are more stable under collusion. Consider a setting in which firms choose price, and each firm's cost is iid over time and across firms and is private information. In each period colluding firms exchange messages about their costs and then choose price. These messages are not required to be truthful, and side payments are not permitted. In characterizing an optimal collusive mechanism, there is a tension between efficiency and the amount of collusion. Because the firms have homogeneous products, the unconstrained joint profit-maximizing scheme is to have the firm with the lowest cost produce all output in that period at its monopoly price. The problem is inducing firms to truthfully reveal their cost, since a firm with high cost may want to signal it has low cost in order to be able to produce. To induce a high-cost firm to provide an accurate cost report, the collusive price may need to be set relatively low when a firm's cost report is low, for then a high-cost firm would not find it profitable to mimic a low-cost firm. Although a mechanism may exist to induce truthful revelation of firms' costs, it may not be optimal for firms to use it because it requires such low prices.

Athey, Bagwell, and Sanchirico (2004) characterize the best strongly symmetric perfect public equilibria in this setting.[35] When firms are sufficiently patient, the collusive equilibrium is to have price and (equal) market shares fixed over time, and not to respond to firms' costs. Inefficiency prevails as it is too costly to induce revelation. Thus prices are perfectly stable in response to cost fluctuations, and this also means that price is more stable than in the absence of collusion.[36] When firms are moderately patient, there is partially rigid pricing, so the price function is a step function of cost in which case price is often unchanged but then experiences a large change. This also serves to distinguish collusion from competition.[37]

In all the models reviewed thus far, firms were not concerned about detection. Suppose instead that buyers detect collusion from suspicious price changes.[38] In exploring how detection avoidance impacts cartel pricing, Harrington and Chen (2006) do not presume that buyers know how a cartel prices, nor are consciously looking for collusion. Rather, it is assumed that buyers become suspicious when the observed price series is sufficiently anomalous or inexplicable where their beliefs as to what is anomalous depend on the history of prices.

Suppose that cost is a random walk with normally distributed shocks. Hence the noncollusive price is similarly structured. Buyers believe price changes are normally distributed but do not know the moments of the distribution. With bounded memory, they observe price changes and use the sampling moments in their beliefs. This gives buyers a set of beliefs on the current price change. With these beliefs, they can then determine the likelihood of observing the actual price change and in fact do so for a series of price changes. It is assumed that detection is more likely when buyers perceive the most recent price series as being less likely. The cartel is aware of how its price path affects beliefs and thereby the probability of detection. Upon cartel formation, firms inherit the noncollusive price and buyers' beliefs that are predicated on price changes when firms were not colluding. In a sense, detection occurs when buyers pick up the "break" in the pricing function associated with cartel formation. Ideally a cartel would like to raise price fast and have it adjust quickly to cost shocks, but it must temper any such price movements by the prospect of detection.

The optimal cartel price path is found to have a transition phase—in which price rises largely irrespective of cost—and a stationary phase—in which price is responsive to cost. While price is sensitive to cost in the stationary phase, it is much less variable than cost, the noncollusive price, or the simple monopoly price. Intuitively, though the cartel might want to raise price considerably in response to a series of large positive cost shocks, such a price series may be perceived as unlikely by buyers and thus induce an investigation. To avoid triggering detection, the cartel doesn't respond commensurately to large cost shocks. Relative to noncollusive pricing, the impact of cost shocks on price is muted and takes a longer time to pass through. Thus the variance of price is lower with collusion. Examining collusion at auctions of frozen perch, Abrantes-Metz et al. (2006) find that the price variance during collusion is indeed distinctly lower then what is observed after the cartel was discovered (excluding the transition from collusion to noncollusion). Mixed evidence is provided by Bolotova, Connor, and Miller (2005) who find a lower price variance under collusion for lysine but a higher price variance for citric acid.

Collusive Marker   Under certain conditions the variance of price is lower under collusion.

A notable caveat to the preceding claim is that the price variance can be higher under the collusive theory of Green and Porter (1984). Although collusion does not result in a higher price variance within either a collusive regime or a punishment regime, the price variance is higher when data span the two regimes.[39] Of course, none of the collusive markers identified are universal, and each must be used with caution.

The last set of collusive price markers concerns the relationship between firms' prices. It is common wisdom that parallel price movements are a collusive marker. Although there is a fair amount of documentation of identical bids at auctions (e.g., see Mund 1960, Joint Executive Committee 1961, and Comanor and Schankerman 1976), in very few cases has collusion been found. More broadly, evidence that parallel pricing is a feature of collusion is ambiguous.

Let us first consider this issue in the context of an auction. McAfee and McMillan (1992) explore a symmetric IPV first-price sealed bid auction with the objective of characterizing the best collusive mechanism. A mechanism takes bidders' reports of their valuations and then assigns bids (and possibly side payments) to the ring members. The mechanism is required to be incentive compatible in the sense that reports are truthful. To ensure the incentive compatibility of the prescribed bidding behavior at the auction, one can suppose the situation is infinitely repeated and the identity of the winning bidder and the amount bid are revealed after each auction. Thus any cartel member that cheated by bidding too high (or participating when they were not suppose to) would be discovered in the event of success (i.e., winning the auction) and be subsequently punished in future auctions. As long as bidders are sufficiently patient, no cheating at the auction will occur.

If side payments are not allowed, the optimal mechanism is one in which all bidders report their valuation to the "cartel manager" prior to the auction, and bidders whose valuation exceeds the auction's reserve price are supposed to submit a bid equal to the reserve price. Because the cartel includes all bidders, the auctioneer randomly selects a winner from among those submitting the reserve price. To show that it is incentive compatible for buyers to truthfully report their valuations in the pre-auction cartel meeting, first note that all that matters is that a firm truthfully report that its valuation is either above or below the reserve price. If its valuation is above the reserve price, truthfully saying so gives it a chance to win the item at a price below its valuation and saying otherwise forgoes that profitable opportunity. A bidder whose valuation is below the reserve price will not want to say it is above it, since this means winning the item and paying a price above its valuation. Furthermore, if the mechanism was such that a bidder's report (above the reserve price) influenced its chances of being the winning bidder, bidders would have an incentive to report that their valuation is higher than it actually is. Thus the cartel can do no better than this scheme, even though it is inefficient, since the bidder with the highest valuation does not win for sure. The notable property is that all bidders bid the same price (which is the reserve price). Thus one gets a strong prediction of parallel pricing behavior.[40]

Two points are worth adding. An equivalent mechanism is bid rotation where one selected bidder (whose report exceeds the reserve price) bids the reserve price and all others do not participate (or submit bids below the reserve price). (I will return to bid rotation below where I discuss collusive markers based on market share.) Second, if the cartel can engage in side payments, then the optimal mechanism is efficient because the bidder with the highest valuation wins as long as its value exceeds the reserve price. One such mechanism is for the cartel members to hold their own first-price sealed bid auction prior to the actual auction. If the highest bid exceeds the reserve price, then that bidder bids the reserve price (all others don't bid or bid less) and pays each of the other bidders an equal share of the difference between his bid in the first auction and the reserve price.[41]

An important assumption in ensuring that cartel members will bid or participate as prescribed is that the winning bidder and the winning price be revealed after each auction. To see what would happen if that information is not available, consider the case of no side payments. According to the collusive scheme, all bidders (who declared their valuation exceeds the reserve price) are to bid the reserve price with the auctioneer randomly choosing a winner. Alternatively, a bidder could bid a little bit higher than the reserve price and win the auction for sure. As long as the winning bid is not revealed, there will be no evidence that any bidder cheated. Since no punishment will ensue, there is an incentive to deviate from the collusive bids. Therefore this mechanism does not work if the auctioneer does not reveal the winning bid.[42]

Recent work by Marshall and Marx (2007) explores such an information setting in which no ex post information is provided regarding the identity of the winning bidder and the winning bid. Furthermore Marshall and Marx enrich the first-price sealed bid auction setting with heterogeneous IPV and allow for the cartel to be less than all-inclusive—some bidders are not members of the cartel. With this informational setting, the situation is one of imperfect monitoring. The cartel member who was designated to submit the highest bid cannot distinguish failing to win the item because a noncartel member outbid it or another cartel member cheated and outbid it.

To ensure that cartel members want to bid as prescribed, Marshall and Marx (2007) show that for some valuations, two cartel members' bids will need to be clustered. Using the (truthful) reports of their valuations at the pre-auction meeting, the cartel selects the bidder with the highest report—let us refer to him as the cartel representative (at the auction)—to bid at a certain level with all other cartel members told to bid less. Absent concerns about cheating, the cartel representative would bid optimally in line with the cartel's valuation and the distribution on noncartel members' bids. The problem, however, is that if the bid is too low, another cartel member may cheat by outbidding the cartel representative's bid. To destroy that incentive to cheat, the cartel representative must set a higher bid so that the other cartel members do not want to outbid it and are content to set a lesser bid. But now suppose these other cartel members all set very low bids. The problem that emerges is that the cartel representative will have an incentive to bid lower because the only reason to bid so high was to discourage cheating. To keep that from happening, one of the other cartel members must set a bid a little below the cartel representative's bid. This will keep the cartel representative from cheating without affecting whether the cartel representative wins. Bids clustered in this way are unique to when bidders collude.[43]

Collusive Marker   Under certain conditions firms' prices are more strongly positively correlated under collusion.

In a standard static oligopoly model, some recent work has considered whether parallel pricing is more common under collusion. Buccirossi (2006) considers a static setting with stochastic cost and demand shocks and compares Nash equilibrium prices with joint profit-maximizing prices. It is shown that more parallel behavior generally does not occur under collusion. Although noncollusive prices are more correlated when there are independent demand shocks, they are *less* correlated under independent cost shocks. At Nash equilibrium a firm's price is increasing in both firms' costs, which induces some correlation even if shocks are independent. Interestingly the joint profit-maximizing price of a firm depends only on its own cost, so firms' prices are independent.[44]

One final result is worth mentioning. Blair and Romano (1989) offer a simple test for identifying who is and who is not a member of a cartel. Upon cartel formation the members will generally lower their quantities. The aggregate supply of cartel members must decline,[45] though individual firm's supply need not when firms have different costs. But what is true for standard oligopoly models is that nonmembers will always *raise* their quantity as they take advantage of the cartel members' reducing their supply. A firm reducing its quantity then identifies as a cartel member while a firm raising its quantity as not a member of the cartel. This does not provide a marker for collusion, but it does offer a way in which to identify a cartel's members.

6.2.2 Predictions on Market Share

The markers relating to market share show how collusion imposes more intertermporal structure on market share. To establish this point, let us return to the Bertrand price-setting when firms' costs are stochastic and private information. Cartel members can convey messages about their costs prior to setting price and quantity. As mentioned earlier, an optimal equilibrium can have firms keeping prices and market shares fixed, so there are indeed stable market shares. This was mentioned for when costs are iid across firms and over time, but it also holds when firms' costs are persistent over time (Athey and Bagwell 2004). In general, firms settle on a collusive outcome with stable market shares when cost persistence is sufficiently high relative to firms' patience.

This result is due to the following logic: When cost persistence increases, it becomes more valuable to a firm to signal that it has low cost, since it influences not only current beliefs (and potentially the current collusive output quotas) but also future beliefs on cost and thus can enhance a firm's future market share. Given this augmented incentive for a firm to report its cost is low (even when its cost is actually high), inducing truthful revelation either requires firms to be more patient—so they are content to wait for higher market share in the more distant future when they may truly have low cost—or to set lower prices (thus reducing the gain in current profit to a high cost firm from reporting it is low cost). When firms are not very patient, the preference is to forgo efficiency in order to support higher collusive prices. Market shares are then more stable over time under collusion.

Collusive Marker Under certain conditions market share is more stable under collusion.

When instead patience is high relative to persistence, the best collusive equilibrium may have market shares moving over time as firms achieve a more efficient mechanism in which a firm with lower cost has a higher market share (Athey and Bagwell 2001, 2004). This is shown in a simple situation where cost is high or low. The way the mechanism works is to engage in intertemporal market share favors. A firm that announces low cost and receives a high market share in the current period can expect a lower market share in the next period. This induces the firm to truthfully reveal. That is, if it is high cost and announces low cost, the firm sacrifices future market share when indeed it might truly be low cost. (Note that market share is especially valuable to a firm when it has low cost.) Thus market shares are predicted to change over time (with firms' costs), and furthermore a firm's market share is negatively correlated over time. This is a history-dependent modification of a bid rotation scheme. Note that with this cost structure, market share will be iid over time in the absence of collusion.[46]

Similar results of intertemporal market sharing arise in models of repeated auctions, which, contrary to the preceding model, do not allow messages to be sent and assume prices to be private information. The solution is a history-dependent bid rotation scheme; the probability of winning is decreasing in the frequency with which a bidder has won in the past. Thus firms are favored that have tended to lose recent auctions (Blume and Heidhues 2003; Skrzypacz and Hopenhayn 2004).[47]

Collusive Marker   Under certain conditions a firm's market share is more negatively correlated over time under collusion relative to competition.

Several recent price-fixing cartels engaged in various forms of intertemporal market sharing, including the citric acid cartel of 1991–95 (Connor 2001), the graphite electrodes cartel of 1992–97 (Levenstein, Suslow, and Oswald 2004), and the vitamins cartel, in particular, vitamins A and E, over 1989–99 (European Commission 2003).

6.2.3   Discussion

Although the collusive pricing literature is rich and offers some behavioral patterns that can help us distinguish collusion from competition, it is deficient in some serious ways. Ideally we would want markers that are fairly universal and require minimal data. None of the markers just mentioned satisfy these criteria. While some markers require only price data—such as the collusive marker of lower price variance—others require ancillary information—such as controlling for demand movements—which makes an intensive investigation necessary. Regardless of the data requirements, these markers are far from universal. Distinguishing features of collusion may only emerge when collusion is sufficiently imperfect so that ICCs bind. Thus strong cartels may not be identified by some of these markers. But the problem is well known to be much more severe than that; there are many collusive equilibria, and a marker may be peculiar to a particular equilibrium selection. Of special concern is that collusion may be present but a marker is not satisfied.

Collusive theory is in addition beset by two methodological weaknesses. With a few rare exceptions, existing models do not distinguish between tacit and explicit collusion. Yet the objective is to have markers of explicit collusion; it is not just to distinguish collusion from competition but also explicit collusion from tacit collusion. Features unique to explicit collusion include communication among firms and side payments. Since communication is a defining feature of explicit collusion, research that encompasses it is particularly valuable and includes McAfee and McMillan (1992), Athey and Bagwell (2001, 2004), Athey, Bagwell, and Sanchirico (2004), and Marshall and Marx (2007). Despite this work a major lacuna exists in both our understanding of when firms explicitly collude and what are its distinguishing features. In that tacit collusion is generally not subject to antitrust penalties, firms choosing to explicitly collude either means (1) they were unable to tacitly collude or (2) the incremental profit from colluding explicitly rather than tacitly exceeds the expected penalties. Yet there is really no research that addresses these two issues. For example, research that characterizes industry traits conducive to collusion does not distinguish between explicit and tacit collusion. But what are the traits that result in explicit collusion rather than tacit collusion? There is then the second issue about how the operating practices of an explicit cartel differs from that of firms who are tacitly colluding. This speaks directly to identifying markers of explicit collusion.

A second methodological problem is that most theories presume cartel members are ignorant of detection.[48] The characterization of firm behavior does not take account of the incentive to avoid creating suspicions among buyers, competitors outside of the cartel, and the antitrust authorities. This results in a failure of theory to address two critical issues. First, it fails to describe the properties of the cartel price path during the transition from the inherited noncollusive price to a stationary collusive outcome. In the absence of detection concerns, existing logic argues that once cartelized, the price path would immediately jump to the new collusive price. Just to the contrary, actual cartel price series show a clear transition with the price path gradually moving up from the noncollusive price level. Some documented examples include citric acid (see figure 6.1), lysine (Connor 2001), graphite electrodes (Harrington 2004a), and vitamin C (Levenstein and Suslow 2001). In essence, most theories characterize the stationary phase, even though the transition phase may offer the greatest hope for detecting cartels since it is during that phase that cartel members must surely raise the price–cost margin. To my knowledge, Harrington (2004b, 2005) and Harrington and Chen (2006) are the only papers to characterize the transition from a noncollusive stationary outcome to a collusive stationary outcome; figure 6.1 provides a typical simulated price path from Harrington and Chen (2006). If we are to detect cartels, a necessary condition is having theories that are able to produce cartel price paths that match the data, and this requires taking account of the transitional phase as well as the stationary phase.

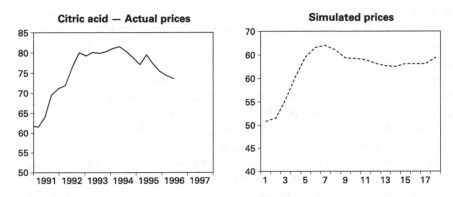

Figure 6.1
Actual (Connor 2001) and simulated (Harrington and Chen 2004) cartel price paths

A second issue is that by ignoring the possibility of detection, models do not address the issue of how a cartel can avoid "failing" a test for collusion by acting strategically. This is both a matter of whether it is feasible for the cartel to beat such a test and, if it is feasible, whether it is costly to do so. It is obviously a crucial issue when designing a test. I discuss it more fully in the next section.

6.3   Beating a Test for Collusion

An important issue about any detection method is: Can a cartel easily beat the test? In Bajari and Ye (2003) firms' bids are independent under the competitive model and lack of independence is taken as evidence consistent with collusion. However, as the authors note, this test can be circumvented by the cartel members appropriately scaling their "competitive bids" (which means scaling up in the case of a procurement auction). Since the competitive bids are independent, an affine transformation of them will be independent and thus be consistent with competition. The same is true for the bid-ranking test of Porter and Zona (1993). Similarly exchangeability can be beat with such a transformation of competitive bids. Although colluding firms' bid functions may then be different, they cannot be distinguished from a noncollusive solution where firms' valuations are drawn from different distributions. The ability of colluding firms in an auction to beat such tests is nicely shown in LaCasse (1995). The model is one in which bidders at an auction decide whether to collude and the antitrust authority decides whether to pursue an investigation based on the observed bids. At a Bayes-Nash equilibrium the posterior probability that a cartel has formed depends only on the winning bid and is independent of all other bids; the reason is that they are strategically chosen to be uninformative.

Although a cartel *could* beat these tests, there is the empirical issue as to whether they *do* beat them. In fact Porter and Zona (1993) and Bajari and Ye (2003) reject independence of firms' bids, so, if firms are not colluding, they are not being very smart about it. Bajari and Summers (2002, p. 145) note that: "...in all case studies of collusion of which we are aware, failures of conditional independence and exhangeability accompanied collusion." However, one can infer that cartels are not being smart—which may indeed be the case—or instead that this is evidence *against* collusion because a smart cartel will not behave in this manner. It is certainly evidence against the collusive theory of LaCasse (1995), since one can instead infer that there is misspecification in cost and demand conditions. A troubling element here is the dependence of inferences on the specification of the collusive model and the selection of an equilibrium. The modeler has a lot of discretion, and whether one assumes a smart or naïve cartel makes a big difference.

Fortunately there are other tests of collusion for which it is not costless for firms to beat. In Porter and Zona (1999), an unconstrained cartel finds it optimal to bid high in nearby collusive markets but to bid low in more distant competitive markets. The resulting bids decrease in distance, which was taken as evidence of collusion. Cartel members could avoid failing this test by making their bids increasing in distance, but that would require lowering their bids in collusive markets—which means earning less profit on contracts won—and/or raising their bids in competitive markets—which means reducing the chance of winning those contracts. In choosing their bids, a smart cartel will trade off cartel profit with the probability of detection. It can then reduce the power of a test but not eliminate it entirely.

It may also be difficult for cartel members to beat some tests based on identifying a structural break (the method described in section 6.1.2). Because collusion must mean a change in the process generating price—for that is the express purpose of forming a cartel—in principle, one should be able to pick up a break by monitoring the average price change. Once again, a cartel can reduce the power of this test by manipulating price changes—for example, making them modest and including price decreases amongst price increases—but it forgoes profit in doing so. In general, the transition from the non-collusive outcome to the collusive stationary path—as opposed to properties of the collusive stationary path—can be particularly fruitful for detection because mimicking competition is especially costly in terms of profit given that the cartel inherits a price well below where it likes it to be.

As the discussion above reveals, some tests of collusion have power even with smart cartels because it means lower profit from circumventing them.[49] A second reason that tests have power comes from the need to maintain cartel stability. Ensuring that a price path respects ICCs can restrict the feasibility of looking "competitive." In Marshall and Marx (2007), the cartel needs to cluster bids to avoid cheating. In Rotemberg and Saloner (1986), the cartel needs to lower prices during times of strong demand. Alternatively, they could have price move with demand, but that would require yet lower prices. The cartel may prefer to have countercyclical pricing and to trade off higher prices with a higher chance of detection. The feasibility in beating a test for collusion is further exacerbated when firms are heterogeneous, since then the cartel must balance diverse preferences. For example, in Harrington (1989), less patient firms must be given higher market shares to stabilize the cartel. Generally, it is the firm that has the greatest incentive to deviate, which limits the set of feasible policies and thus makes it harder to both maintain cartel stability and avoid detection. All this becomes even more acute when there is imperfect monitoring. Periodic reversion to lower prices may be required to maintain collusion, but the resulting structural break could trigger detection. Can a cartel design a policy that deters cheating without inducing rejection of the null hypothesis of no structural change? Or is there a fundamental tension between practices that promote compliance and those that avoid detection?

6.4 An Activist Policy of Screening for Collusion

Screening refers to a cost-effective method for identifying industries whose behavior is sufficiently suggestive of collusion so as to warrant verification, which refers to an intense investigation that directly contrasts collusion and competition as competing explanations of market behavior. Although the antitrust authorities do not currently screen for price-fixing, history is scattered with attempts. Going back to at least the 1950s, the US Department of Justice collected reports of identical bids at government procurement auctions (Joint Executive Committee 1961). Over twenty-five years ago, Joseph Gallo proposed a computer program to identify collusion at sealed-bid auctions (Gallo 1977). More recently, attempts have been made at various antitrust authorities. At the Bureau of Economics of the US Federal Trade Commission, Director Jonathan Baker used price increases after an industry-specific trough in demand to identify the exercise of market power (*FTC History* 2003, pp. 108–110), while Director Luke Froeb made progress in developing a screen in terms of the price variance (Abrantes-Metz et al. 2006). The question is: Can we effectively screen for collusion and, if so, what will it take to make it work?

There are at least three criteria for systematic and ubiquitous screening. First, evidence of collusion (preferably explicit collusion) must be discernible by just looking at prices, market shares, or other easily available data. Second, the test to be conducted should be routinizable so that it can be conducted with minimal human input. These first two criteria indicate that one is imagining an empirical exercise far removed from the typical industry analysis involving data on price, quantity, and cost and demand shifters, and then performing many modifications to a sophisticated econometric model. The third criterion is that the screen should be costly for the cartel to beat.

The objective is to screen industries as a matter of course, even where there is no hint of collusion. To be practical, screening must then rely on easily available data, which in many cases will mean exclusively price data. However, in some instances quantity and some cost or demand shifters may also be accessible at low cost. Consider a product with a primary input that trades on commodity markets. An example is raw sugar used in the production of refined sugar (Genesove and Mullin 1998). If cartel members manufacture in one country and sell in another—such as with the vitamins cartel—then exchange rate fluctuations provide an easily available cost shifter.

Although high-frequency price data are not often easily available, there is a growing number of possibilities. The government has access to bid data from auctions for which it is involved, ranging from defense procurement to Treasury bills. Online price data is another source. There is a growing amount of online retailing, and many scholars have already "scraped" data off of Web pages. Shopbots are present to perform some of this work. Furthermore some Web sites are beginning to collect price data from conventional retailers. This is currently being done with gasoline prices,[50] though the voluntary nature of reports makes the data sketchy. Then some markets—like financial markets, electric power, and some commodity markets—offer high-frequency data that, at a price, are available.

With these data the empirical exercise must be simple enough to be largely automated. One possibility is looking for certain collusive markers such as low price variance, low market share variance, high correlation in bids at an auction, negative correlation in market shares, and negative correlation in price and quantity. For example, Abrantes-Metz et al. (2006) make progress in developing a screen for low-price variance.

A second approach is to identify structural breaks in the stochastic process producing prices or some other measure of firm behavior. As new data arrive, a test for a structural break is conducted. The problem with using, say, a Chow test is that one can expect to eventually reject the hypothesis of parameter stability even if the model is stable. Fortunately, Chu, Stinchcombe, and White (1996) provide appropriate tests for conducting continual monitoring for structural breaks. Examination of spreads for certain Nasdaq securities shows a very quick switch from quoting all eighths to avoiding odd eighths, and this is reflected in a sharp increase in the spread (see Christie and Schultz 1999, fig. 2). A monitoring of structural change would have probably picked it up. Likely structural breaks to look for include an increase in the average price change, a fall in the price variance, an enhanced correlation among firms' prices, and greater market share stability.

Another possibility is to develop software that picks up anomalies. By an anomaly is meant, for example, the avoidance of odd-eighth quotes in Nasdaq markets or the inclusion of low-digit numbers on a million dollar bid, which, in the case of the FCC spectrum auctions, acted as a signal between bidders (Cramton and Schwartz 2000). To see how a bit of thought here might produce some interesting screens, consider the recent use of an empirical regularity to detect tax fraud. Benford's law (Hill 1995) is the property of many data series whereby the first digit, the second digit, and so forth, have a particular distribution that is, surprisingly, not uniform but rather logarithmic. The probability distribution on the first k digits is

$$\log_{10}\left[1+\left(\sum_{i=1}^{k} d_i \times 10^{k-i}\right)^{-1}\right],$$

where $d_i \in \{0, 1, \ldots, 9\}$ is the ith digit. For example, the frequency with which the first digit is 1 is about 30 percent and is 2 is about 18 percent. This also has the implication that digits are not independent. For example, the unconditional distribution on the second digit differs from the distribution on the second digit conditional on the first digit. This bizarre regularity helped uncover tax fraud because the fraudulent accounting numbers did not satisfy Benford's law (Geyer and Williamson 2004).

Ideally any data screen should also satisfy the property that it is costly for the cartel to beat the test. A screen that became sufficiently successful and can be costlessly beat may ultimately be beat. This is not entirely obvious, however, because new cartels are continually born and some could be naïve if information about detection methods doesn't easily spread across industries. Furthermore a firm's management that learns about how detection is being conducted may learn too late if it is by being caught colluding. The point is that the learning environment—in terms of the extent of learning from others and the opportunities for experiential learning—may be such that the learning process does not converge to where all or even most prospective cartels know how authorities detect. Nevertheless, it is certainly a desirable property for a test to be costly to beat, as then it will have power even against smart cartels.

Screening appears to be effectively used in a wide variety of contexts, including insider trading, credit card fraud, and tax evasion. What allows detection is an ample supply of data—whether it is hourly trading volume and bid and ask prices for a security, daily credit card purchases, or annual tax returns. These data serve two key purposes. First, data are available to be screened. Second, many ex post verifiable cases allow fraud to be empirically identified. Two general methods are deployed in utilizing the data. Supervised methods involve the development of canonical models of fraudulent and nonfraudulent behavior using samples of such behavior. A particular case is then classified into one of those two categories. In contrast, unsupervised methods look for deviations from some benchmark, searching for anomalies or outliers.

How could we implement screening for collusion as part of an activist policy? First, build a library of cartels and use it to empirically identify collusive markers. Although there is a wealth of cases,[51] there has not been much research distilling behavioral patterns among them. We do have some tentative findings that the variance of prices is lower with collusion (Abrantes-Metz et al. 2006; Bolotova et al. 2005) and that cartel formation is preceded with a steep price decline (Grout and Sonderegger 2005), but much more needs to be done. The antitrust authorities could be of great assistance here if they were to establish a policy that, as part of a plea agreement with colluding firms, all relevant data be made public. There is certainly a social justification for such a policy, since making data available to scholars will promote advances in our understanding of cartels, which is the basis for more effective antitrust enforcement. Second, construct high-frequency price data series for more markets. Perhaps the government could induce buyers to provide these data under the condition of privacy, especially as there is a potential benefit to them from doing so. Third, develop new empirical methods for picking up structural change and statistical anomalies. These are likely to be the most robust methods for identifying markets worthy of closer scrutiny.

Notes

I am grateful to Susan Athey, Iwan Bos, Leslie Marx, Maarten Pieter Schinkel, and Margaret Slade for their comments. My research was supported by the National Science Foundation under grant SES-0209486.

1. For some industry traits associated with collusion, see Symeonedis (2003), Motta (2004), and Grout and Sonderegger (2005).

2. See *Chemical Week*, vol. 164, issue 24, June 12, 2002.

3. Useful references are Lieber (2000), Connor (2001), and Eichenwald (2001).

4. "The industry was investigated for cartel activity after buyers complained to the European Commission about the rapid increase in prices." Graham Hind, "English cutlers 'hit by cartel'," *The Times* (London), August 21, 1994; cited in Levenstein, Suslow, and Oswald (2004).

5. *Ferromin International Trade Corporation et al. v. UCAR et al.*, In the United States District Court for the Eastern District of Pennsylvania, Second amended complaint, filed May 1, 1999, at para. 50.

6. John Clifford and Bill Rowley, "Tackling cross-border conspiracy," *International Corporate Law*, May 1995.

7. A survey of the manner in which some cartels were detected is provided in Hay and Kelley (1974).

8. This information is based on private communication with Peter A. G. van Bergeijk of the Nederlandse Mededingingsautoriteit (December 16, 2004).

9. For a detailed discussion of the role of economic analysis in judicial decisions, see Werden (2004).

10. The term "competition" will mean that firms are not colluding but not necessarily that competition is perfect. Whether competition includes tacit collusion is left unanswered as the distinction between tacit and explicit collusion is a murky one in the economics literature. I will use "competitive" and "noncollusive" interchangeably.

11. For some related work on this method, see Bajari (2001), and for a more general discussion, Bajari and Summers (2002). Hendricks and Porter (1989) is an early general discussion of detecting collusion at auctions.

12. As supporting ancillary evidence, in the late 1980s (prior to this data set), firm 2 received a prison sentence for bid rigging while firms 4 and 5 paid damages for colluding with firm 2.

13. Section 6.2 provides details on what theory suggests to look for.

14. Kühn (2001) provides a nice discussion about communication practices in connection with collusion.

15. For an analysis of how this approach—using post-cartel prices to estimate the impact of collusion on price—leads to underestimates of the effect of collusion, see Harrington (2004a).

16. For a general discussion of these econometric methods, see Hansen (2001).

17. There is another rationale for looking for structural breaks which is that sharp changes in price—inexplicable in light of cost and demand shifts—are consistent with theories of collusive pricing under imperfect monitoring, while not being easily reconcilable within a competitive theory. However, this is better thought of as an example of the method described in section 6.1.4—where I do discuss it—in that the model nests competition (the case of no regime switches) and collusion (the case of regime switches) and the issue is which model better fits the data.

18. However, as shown in section 6.1.4, such data could still be used to substantiate collusion.

19. For other analyses of collusion in the school milk market, see Lanzilotti (1996) and Scott (2000).

20. For a review of nonparametric approaches to analyzing behavior at auctions, see Athey and Haile (2004).

21. Also see Porter (1985).

22. For a related approach, see Bresnahan (1987).

23. It is also true that the noncollusive model with multiple supply performs significantly better than the single-unit noncollusive model and only marginally worse than the single-unit collusive model.

24. For a discussion of these methods, see Bresnahan (1989).

25. Interestingly Asch and Seneca (1976) find that collusive industries are less profitable than noncollusive industries.

26. A second role for theory is to provide models of competition and collusion that can be estimated and contrasted. This fits into the empirical method based on finding the model that best fits the data.

27. A useful reference is Motta (2004).

28. Standard treatments can be found in Tirole (1988) and Vives (1999).

29. This would hold, for example, if demand is linear and "higher demand" means a rise in the intercept.

30. Under certain conditions these results are robust to when demand shocks are serially correlated (Kandori 1991). Recall that a noncollusive equilibrium for a different model can generate a similar prediction. For example, suppose that when demand increases, firm demand becomes more elastic. Then price competition will intensify as demand becomes stronger, so price can fall as demand rises even when firms do not collude. Increased firm demand elasticity due to greater consumer search has been used to explain why retail prices are lower for many items during the Christmas season despite demand having shifted out.

31. However, if there are sufficiently tight capacity constraints, then price can return to being pro-cyclical (Fabra 2004).

32. For further work on demand fluctuations, see Bagwell and Staiger (1997) who find that if the demand growth rate is positively correlated over time, then the price path is sometimes procyclical but never countercyclical.

However, if the growth rate is negatively correlated, then the price path is sometimes countercyclical but never procyclical.

33. This equilibrium can be modified to allow T to be randomly selected at the start of each punishment phase, so the length of time in the punishment regime is random.

34. Abreu, Pearce, and Stachetti (1986) consider maximal punishments in this setting and also get regime switches, though characterized by a different stochastic process. Like the previous model, movement from the collusive to the punishment regime occurs when price is sufficiently low and thus when the contemporaneous demand shock is low. In contrast, the punishment phase does not entail static Nash equilibrium but yet higher quantities (and thus lower profits). Firms get out of this punishment phase only when the realized price is sufficiently *low*. There are then regime switches but the process is always Markovian; the probability distribution on price in a period depends only on the previous period's price and regime (cooperative or punishment).

35. These equilibria have the property that continuation payoffs are the same for all firms, but can vary across histories. Punishment then entails low profits for all firms. This model assumes a continuum of costs and downward-sloping demand, while further work—which I will review shortly—generally assumes two cost types and perfectly inelastic demand (Athey and Bagwell 2001, 2004).

36. When colluding firms instead have private information about the market demand function (but do not exchange messages), Hanazono and Yang (2005) similarly show that collusion can result in rigid prices. When firms are sufficiently patient and signals are sufficiently uninformative, the best strongly symmetric perfect public equilibria has firms' prices being unresponsive to demand signals.

37. As described later, in other circumstances collusive prices and market shares can be sensitive to firms' costs for this class of models.

38. In many price-fixing cases these are industrial buyers, involving vitamins, lysine, and graphite electrodes, for example. Generally, the antitrust authorities do not actively engage in detection but rather respond to complaints (McAnney 1991).

39. I thank Margaret Slade for this point.

40. LaCasse (1995) also considers this setting but where the antitrust authority actively engages in detection and the bidders, who might form a cartel, are cognizant of this fact. The challenge from the authority's standpoint is that a low winning bid might be due to the existence of a cartel or instead that all bidders have low valuations. Equilibrium entails bidders using a mixed strategy to determine whether to form a cartel and the authority randomizing in their decision to perform an investigation with that probability decreasing in the winning bid.

41. Also see Graham and Marshall (1987) and Mailath and Zemsky (1991) for analyses of collusion at second-price auctions.

42. One way around this is with bid rotation for, even if nothing is revealed about the auction outcome, at least the bidder that was chosen to win and the bidder that cheated know that a deviation occurred and thus could respond aggressively.

43. The authors note that at a (noncollusive) equilibrium for a complete information auction setting, the bidder with the highest valuation bids at the second highest valuation and the second highest bid mixes just below his valuation. Although there is clustered bidding as well, it is necessarily among the two highest bids, while this needn't be the case in Marshall and Marx (2007).

44. Smith (2003) derives a similar result in a setting with cost shocks and firms choosing quantities.

45. This is proved in Farrell and Shapiro (1990) for a joint profit-maximizing cartel.

46. This analysis assumes firms' costs are independent. Aoyagi (2002) considers when firms' costs are correlated and also finds collusion entails an intertemporal market-sharing scheme.

47. One problem with a collusive marker of negatively correlated market shares is that such a prediction would seem consistent with a noncollusive model in which firms have capacity constraints which apply over multiple periods. For example, a firm that wins a large contract in the current procurement auction may not have the capacity left to bid for contracts in the next period, or even if it does, there is an opportunity cost to using up capacity. A firm with little spare capacity ought to bid less aggressively knowing that if it wins then it'll have no capacity for the next auction, which might involve a particularly profitable contract being auctioned off.

48. Exceptions include Besanko and Spulber (1989, 1990), LaCasse (1995), McCutcheon (1997), Cyrenne (1999), Harrington (2004b, 2005), and Harrington and Chen (2006).

49. An insightful discussion on this issue is provided in Porter (2005) who poses five problems that a cartel must solve to be effective and how, in solving those problems, they might reveal that a cartel exists.

50. For example, www.gaspricewatch.com.

51. Some are reviewed in Connor (2001) and Levenstein and Suslow (2001).

References

Abrantes-Metz, R. M., L. M. Froeb, J. Geweke, and C. T. Taylor. 2006. A variance screen for collusion. *International Journal of Industrial Organization* 24: 467–86.

Abreu, D., D. Pearce, and E. Stacchetti. 1986. Optimal cartel equilibria with imperfect monitoring. *Journal of Economic Theory* 39: 251–69.

Andrews, D. W. K. 1993. Tests for parameter instability and structural change with unknown change point. *Econometrica* 61: 821–56.

Aoyagi, M. 2002. Collusion in dynamic Bertrand oligopoly with correlated private signals and communication. *Journal of Economic Theory* 102: 229–48.

Asch, P., and J. J. Seneca. 1976. Is collusion profitable? *Review of Economics and Statistics* 58: 1–12.

Athey, S., and K. Bagwell. 2001. Optimal collusion with private information. *RAND Journal of Economics* 32: 428–65.

Athey, S., and K. Bagwell. 2004. Collusion with persistent cost shocks. Unpublished paper. Columbia University.

Athey, S., K. Bagwell, and C. Sanchirico. 2004. Collusion and price rigidity. *Review of Economic Studies* 71: 317–49.

Athey, S., and P. A. Haile. 2004. Nonparametric approaches to auctions. Unpublished paper. Stanford University.

Bagwell, K., and R. Staiger. 1997. Collusion over the business cycle. *RAND Journal of Economics* 28: 82–106.

Bajari, P. 2001. Comparing competition and collusion: A numerical approach. *Economic Theory* 18: 187–205.

Bajari, P., and L. Ye. 2003. Deciding between competition and collusion. *Review of Economics and Statistics* 85: 971–89.

Bajari, P., and G. Summers. 2002. Detecting collusion in procurement auctions. *Antitrust Law Journal* 70: 143–70.

Baldwin, L. H., R. C. Marshall, and J.-F. Richard. 1997. Bidder collusion at forest service timber auctions. *Journal of Political Economy* 105: 657–99.

Banerji, A., and J. V. Meenakshi. 2004. Buyer collusion and efficiency of government intervention in wheat markets in northern India: An asymmetric structural auctions analysis. *American Journal of Agricultural Economics* 86: 236–53.

Benoît, J.-P., and V. Krishna. 1987. Dynamic duopoly: Prices and quantities. *Review of Economic Studies* 54: 23–35.

Besanko, D., and D. F. Spulber. 1989. Antitrust enforcement under asymmetric information. *Economic Journal* 99: 408–25.

Besanko, D., and D. F. Spulber. 1990. Are treble damages neutral? Sequential equilibrium and private antitrust enforcement. *American Economic Review* 80: 870–87.

Blair, R. D., and R. E. Romano. 1989. Proof of nonparticipation in a price fixing conspiracy. *Review of Industrial Organization* 4: 101–17.

Block, M. K., F. C. Nold, and J. G. Sidak. 1981. The deterrent effect of antitrust enforcement. *Journal of Political Economy* 89: 429–45.

Blume, A., and P. Heidhues. 2003. Modeling tacit collusion in auctions. Unpublished manuscript. University of Pittsburgh.

Bolotova, Y., J. M. Connor, and D. J. Miller. 2005. The impact of collusion on price behavior: Empirical results from two recent cases. Unpublished manuscript. Department of Agricultural Economics, Purdue University.

Bernheim, B. D., and M. D. Whinston. 1990. Multimarket contact and collusive behavior. *RAND Journal of Economics* 21: 1–26.

Bresnahan, T. F. 1987. Competition and collusion in the American automobile industry: The 1955 price war. *Journal of Industrial Economics* 35: 457–82.

Bresnahan, T. F. 1989. Empirical studies of industries with market power. In R. Schmalensee and R. Willig, eds., *Handbook of Industrial Organization*, Vol. 2. Amsterdam: Elsevier.

Buccirossi, P. 2006. Does parallel behavior provide some evidence of collusion? *Review of Law and Economics* 2: 85–102.

Christie, W. G., and P. H. Schultz. 1994. Why do Nasdaq market makers avoid odd-eighth quotes? *Journal of Finance* 49: 1813–40.

Christie, W. G., and P. H. Schultz. The initiation and withdrawl of odd-eighth quotes among Nasdaq stocks: An empirical analysis. *Journal of Financial Economics* 52: 409–42.

Chu, C.-S. J., M. Stinchcombe, and H. White. 1996. Monitoring structural change. *Econometrica* 64: 1045–65.

Comanor, W. S., and M. Schankerman. 1976. Identical bids and cartel behavior. *Bell Journal of Economics* 9: 281–86.

Compte, O., F. Jenny, and P. Rey. 2002. Capacity constraints, mergers and collusion. *European Economic Review* 46: 1–29.

Connor, J. M. 2001. *Global Price Fixing: Our Customers are the Enemy*, Boston: Kluwer Academic.

Connor, J. M. 2004. How high do cartels raise prices? Implications for reform of the antitrust sentencing guidelines. Working paper 04-01. American Antitrust Institute.

Cramton, P., and J. A. Schwartz. 2000. Collusive bidding: Lessons from the FCC spectrum auctions. *Journal of Regulatory Economics* 17: 229–52.

Cyrenne, P. 1999. On antitrust enforcement and the deterrence of collusive behavior. *Review of Industrial Organization* 14: 257–72.

Davidson, C., and R. Deneckere. 1990. Excess capacity and collusion. *International Economic Review* 31: 521–41.

Eichenwald, K. 2001. *Informant: A True Story*. New York: Broadway Books.

Ellison, G. 1994. Theories of cartel stability and the joint executive committee. *RAND Journal of Economics* 25: 37–57.

European Commission. 2003. Case COMP/E-1/37.512—Vitamins. *Official Journal of the European Communities*, October 1, 2003.

Fabra, N. 2006. Collusion with capacity constraints over the business cycle. Universidad Carlos III de Madrid. *International Journal of Industrial Organization* 24: 69–81.

Farrell, J., and C. Shapiro. 1990. Horizontal mergers: An equilibrium analysis. *American Economic Review* 80: 107–26.

FTC History: Bureau of Economics Contributions to Law Enforcement, Reseach, and Economic Knowledge and Policy. Transcript of Roundtable with Former Directors of the Bureau of Economics, September 4, 2003. Available at ⟨http://www.ftc.gov/be/workshops/directorsconference/index.htm⟩.

Funderburk, D. R. 1974. Price fixing in the liquid-asphalt industry: Economic analysis versus the "hot document." *Antitrust Law and Economics Review* 7: 61–74.

Gallo, J. C. 1977. A computerized approach to detect collusion in the sealed-bid market. *Antitrust Bulletin* 22: 593–620.

Genesove, D., and W. P. Mullin. 1998. Testing static oligopoly models: Conduct and cost in the sugar industry, 1890–1914. *RAND Journal of Economics* 29: 355–77.

Geyer, C. L., and P. P. Williamson. 2004. Detecting fraud in data sets using Benford's law. *Communications in Statistics* 33: 229–46.

Graham, D. A., and R. C. Marshall. 1987. Collusive bidder behavior at single-object second-price and English auctions. *Journal of Political Economy* 95: 1217–39.

Green, E., and R. H. Porter. 1984. Noncooperative collusion under imperfect price information. *Econometrica* 52: 87–100.

Grout, P. A., and S. Sonderegger. 2005. Predicting cartels. Economic discussion paper. Office of Fair Trading.

Haltiwanger, J., and J. E. Harrington, Jr. 1991. The impact of cyclical demand movements on collusive behavior. *RAND Journal of Economics* 22: 89–106.

Hanazono, M., and H. Yang. 2005. Collusion, fluctuating demand, and price rigidity. Unpublished manuscript. Kyoto University.

Hansen, B. E. 2001. The new econometrics of structural change: Dating breaks in U.S. labor productivity. *Journal of Economic Perspectives* 15: 117–28.

Harrington, J. E., Jr. 1989. Collusion among asymmetric firms: The case of different discount factors. *International Journal of Industrial Organization* 7: 289–307.

Harrington, J. E., Jr. 2004a. Post-cartel pricing during litigation. *Journal of Industrial Economics* 52: 517–33.

Harrington, J. E., Jr. 2004b. Cartel pricing dynamics in the presence of an antitrust authority. *RAND Journal of Economics* 35: 651–73.

Harrington, J. E., Jr. 2005. Optimal cartel pricing in the presence of an antitrust authority. *International Economic Review* 46: 145–69.

Harrington, J. E., Jr., and J. Chen. 2006. Cartel pricing dynamics with cost variability and endogenous buyer detection. *International Journal of Industrial Organization* 24: 1185–1212.

Hay, G., and D. Kelly. 1974. An empirical survey of price fixing conspiracies. *Journal of Law and Economics* 17: 13–38.

Hendricks, K., and R. H. Porter. 1989. Collusion in auctions. *Annales d'Économie et de Statistique* 15–16: 217–30.

Hill, T. P. 1995. A statistical derivation of the significant-digit law. *Statistical Science* 10: 354–63.

Joint Economic Committee, US Congress. 1961. 93 lots of bids involving identical bids. Reported to the Department of Justice by the Federal Procurement Agencies in the years 1955–1960. Washington, DC: GPO.

Kandori, M. 1991. Correlated demand shocks and price wars during booms. *Review of Economic Studies* 58: 171–80.

Kühn, K.-U. 2001. Fighting collusion: Regulation of communication between firms. *Economic Policy* 32: 167–97.

LaCasse, C. 1995. Bid rigging and the threat of government prosecution. *RAND Journal of Economics* 26: 398–417.

Lanzilotti, R. F. 1996. The great milk conspiracies of the 1980s. *Review of Industrial Organization* 11: 413–58.

Lieber, J. B. 2000. *Rats in the Grain: The Dirty Tricks and Trials of Archer Daniels Midland*. New York: Four Walls Eight Windows.

Levenstein, M., and V. Suslow. 2001. Private international cartels and their effect on developing countries. Unpublished manuscript. University of Massachusetts.

Levenstein, M. C., V. Y. Suslow, and L. J. Oswald. 2004. Contemporary international cartels and developing countries: Economic effects and implications for competition policy. *Antitrust Law Journal* 71: 801–52.

Mailath, G., and P. Zemsky. 1991. Collusion in second price auctions with heterogeneous bidders. *Games and Economic Behavior* 3: 467–86.

Marshall, R., and L. Marx. 2007. Bidder collusion. *Journal of Economic Theory* 133: 374–402.

McAfee, R. P., and J. McMillan. 1992. Bidding rings. *American Economic Review* 82: 579–99.

McAnney, J. W. 1991. The justice department's crusade against price-fixing: Initiative or reaction? *Antitrust Bulletin* (Fall): 521–42.

McCutcheon, B. 1997. Do meetings in smoke-filled rooms facilitate collusion? *Journal of Political Economy* 105: 330–50.

Motta, M. 2004. *Competition Policy: Theory and Practice*. Cambridge: Cambridge University Press.

Mund, V. A. 1960. Identical bid prices. *Journal of Political Economy* 68: 150–69.

Osborne, M. J., and C. Pitchik. 1987. Cartels, profits, and excess capacity. *International Economic Review* 28: 413–28.

Pesendorfer, M. 2000. A study of collusion in first-price auctions. *Review of Economic Studies* 67: 381–411.

Porter, R. H. 1983a. A study of cartel stability: The joint executive committee, 1880–1886. *Bell Journal of Economics* 14: 301–14.

Porter, R. H. 1983b. Optimal cartel trigger price strategies. *Journal of Economic Theory* 29: 313–38.

Porter, R. H. 1985. On the incidence and duration of price wars. *Journal of Industrial Economics* 33: 415–26.

Porter, R. H. 2005. Detecting collusion. *Review of Industrial Organization* 26: 147–67.

Porter, R. H., and J. D. Zona. 1993. Detection of bid rigging in procurement auctions. *Journal of Political Economy* 101: 79–99.

Porter, R. H., and J. D. Zona. 1999. Ohio school milk markets: An analysis of bidding. *RAND Journal of Economics* 30: 263–88.

Quandt, R. 1960. Tests of the hypothesis that a linear regression obeys two separate regimes. *Journal of the American Statistical Association* 55: 324–30.

Rotemberg, J. J., and G. Saloner. 1986. A supergame-theoretic model of price wars during booms. *American Economic Review* 76: 390–407.

Scott, F. A., Jr. 2000. Great school milk conspiracies revisited. *Review of Industrial Organization* 17: 325–41.

Skrzypacz, A., and H. Hopenhayn. 2004. Tacit collusion in repeated auctions. *Journal of Economic Theory* 114: 153–69.

Smith, J. L. 2003. Distinguishable patterns of competition, collusion, and parallel action. Unpublished paper. Southern Methodist University.

Staiger, R. W., and F. A. Wolak. 1992. Collusive pricing with capacity constraints in the presence of demand uncertainty. *RAND Journal of Economics* 23: 203–20.

Symeonedis, G. 2003. In which industries is collusion more likely? Evidence from the UK. *Journal of Industrial Economics* 51: 45–74.

Tirole, J. 1988. *The Theory of Industrial Organization*. Cambridge: MIT Press.

Vasconcelos, H. 2005. Tacit collusion, cost asymmetries and mergers. *RAND Journal of Economics* 36: 39–62.

Vives, X. 1999. *Oligopoly Pricing: Old Ideas and New Tools*. Cambridge: MIT Press.

Werden, G. J. 2004. Economic evidence on the existence of collusion: Reconciling antitrust law with oligopoly theory. *Antitrust Law Journal* 71: 719–99.

7   Leniency and Whistleblowers in Antitrust

Giancarlo Spagnolo

The last ten years have witnessed what one could call, with little or no exaggeration, a revolution in competition policy and antitrust enforcement, "the leniency revolution." Since the US Department of Justice's new leniency policies were introduced in 1993 (the *Corporate Leniency Policies*) and 1994 (the *Individual Leniency Policy*), and began displaying their effects, antitrust authorities' "normal way" to detect, prosecute, and hopefully also deter cartels appears to have radically changed. Buyers' complaints, audits, and dawn raids have been replaced by well-designed leniency policies and self-reporting cartel participants, only followed by the traditional methods.

Leniency policies, or programs, reduce sanctions against colluding firms that report information on their cartel to the Antitrust Authority and cooperate with it along the prosecution phase to help convict their former partners. The achievements of the new US leniency policies are described in a number of public speeches by the DOJ staff (available at http://www.usdoj.gov/atr/public/criminal.htm) and in several international reports (e.g., OECD 2002, 2003). Since their introduction, an unprecedented number of cartels has been detected and successfully prosecuted, much higher fines have been levied against participants, and several top executives from different countries have served jail sentences in the United States. This led the European Union and many other countries around the world to introduce analogous programs.[1]

This leniency revolution also led an increasing number of economists to look beyond the surface of the number of cartels detected or prosecuted and fines levied at how these programs work, what are their likely (positive and even negative) economic effects, and how they can be improved upon.

In this chapter, I review the recent evolution of leniency programs in the United States and the European Union, theoretical economic analyses of leniency programs, and the scarce empirical and experimental evidence available on the subject.[2] I then discuss recent proposals to reward the first cartel member or manager that reports "hard information" on an yet undetected cartel, and look briefly at the related experience of rewarding individuals that blow the whistle against corporations committing fraud against the US government (following the False Claim Act). I conclude with a list of desiderata for leniency programs in antitrust, some suggestions how to improve current ones and eventually introduce whistleblower compensation schemes, and an agenda of open issues for future research. I make no pretense of being objective: having worked extensively on the subject, I have developed strong views on the crucial issues at stake, and my survey will reflect these views.

My discussion is also relevant to the fight of many other forms of multi-agent organized crime—corruption, auditor-manager collusion, and corporate crime in general—because these share with cartels the crucial features that well-designed leniency and whistleblower-reward programs exploit.[3] For simplicity, I write under the assumption that all cartels are bad for society and should ideally be deterred. However, it is important to keep in mind that there are situations where competition can harm consumers, for example, where non-contractible qualitative aspects are very important in terms of gains from trade. Then agreements to restraint competition may increase welfare.[4]

7.1 Important Preliminaries

7.1.1 What Is Special about Cartels and Analogous Forms of Organized Crime?

Cartels are a form of illegal activity involving the joint, coordinated effort of several agents aimed at restricting competition by fixing prices, allocating market shares, preventing entry, and so on. In this sense, cartels can be considered a mild form of *organized crime*.[5] As emphasized in Spagnolo (2000a, b), organized crimes like cartels share three fundamental features that make them very different from the standard isolated criminal act committed by an individual wrongdoer at the core of the modern economic literature on public law enforcement.[6]

• The first feature is that cooperation among several agents is required to perform the illegal activity, so problems of free-riding, holdup, moral hazard in teams, and opportunism in general become relevant: each individual wrongdoer could "run away with the money" and must be prevented from doing it. This "governance problem" cannot be solved in standard ways in illegal organizations because—to curb opportunism of its individual members and ensure internal cooperation—these cannot rely on explicit contracts enforced by the legal system, as do legal organizations. Stigler (1964) made forcefully this point for cartels, arguing that they are intrinsically unstable because of the individual cartel member's incentive to profit from "cheating" on the cartel, namely to undercut other cartel members by offering profitable and secret price cuts to their customers.
• The second important feature is that organized criminal activity typically takes the form of ongoing relationships: instead of isolated criminal acts with given benefit and harm, it delivers *flows* of present and expected future benefits and costs. This is, of course, a direct consequence of the first feature. Since free-riding and individual opportunism cannot be limited by explicit contracts enforced by the legal system, internal cohesion of the criminal organization must be ensured by the agents themselves, illegal arrangements must be "self-

enforcing." And the typical way to ensure this is long-term interaction, namely developing in time a reputation for being tough against who violates the agreement and/or establishing relational contracts sustained by the expectation of future gains from continued cooperation. In both cases a dynamic continued activity—"the shadow of the future"—is essential. Again, Stigler (1964) made this point implicitly for cartels, arguing that besides being profitable, to be feasible a cartel must, among other things, be able to police cartel members' compliance with the collusive agreement and credibly threaten to react to defections with analogous price cuts, so that these will not "cheat," for fear of provoking a price war or other forms of retaliation.[7]

• The third, crucial feature, only noticed by economists in recent years, is that cooperating wrongdoers, by acting together, inevitably end up having—as a by-product—information on each others' misbehavior that could then in principle be reported to third parties, including law enforcers. This third feature is in turn a consequence of the first two, and is at the very hart of the effects of leniency programs. When crime is committed by a single agent, this will be very careful about being alone and unobserved, so that nobody can betray him but his own mistakes. With cartels and organized crime, instead, each wrongdoer must coordinate with and monitor the others, and automatically acquires information on the others' wrongdoing that can potentially be induced to reveal. How to extract this freely available information is the main issue in the optimal design of leniency programs and whistleblower schemes.

These three peculiar features imply complex dynamic incentive structures for the agents involved that are crucial to the optimal design of law enforcement policies. In particular, the fact that cartels are only feasible if participants are able to deter unilateral defections— like secret price cuts—by monitoring and threatening credible retaliation, introduces *a novel kind of deterrence*, not considered in the literature on law enforcement preceding recent dynamic analyses of antitrust enforcement and leniency programs, beginning with Cyrenne (1999) and Motta and Polo (2003). This condition, necessary for any cartel or illegal agreement because of the impossibility to use explicit contracts, is called "incentive compatibility" or "self-enforcing" constraint, in contrast to the "participation" constraint simply requiring that expected additional profits from entering a cartel net of expected antitrust consequences be positive.

Both participation and incentive constraints must necessarily be satisfied for a cartel to be viable so that if at least one of the two is violated, the cartel is deterred.[8] It turns out that it is much easier for law enforcers to ensure that the incentive constraint is violated than the participation one, in particular by using leniency and whistleblower programs. Many agree that these programs can increase deterrence by increasing the likelihood that cartels are convicted, but a crucial and often disregarded point is, in my view, that they can deter cartels with much lower expected sanctions than standard law enforcement. These programs may ensure that the self-enforcing constraint is not satisfied even when sanctions are still way below the level needed to make participation to the cartel unprofitable in expectation, which is what static theories of public law enforcement would require for crime deterrence.[9]

Another crucial thing to note already at this stage is that this novel kind of deterrence is maximized when the incentive for an individual firm to unilaterally deviate and undercut the cartel are maximal, that is, when individual and collective interests of cartel members are most divergent. This means that the problem of maximizing cartel deterrence through leniency can be seen as the inverse of a public good contribution problem. Such an interpretation naturally suggests a "winner take all" approach that concentrates all benefits on one individual—the first one to self-report—maximizing the conflict of interest with the rest of the group/cartel.

7.1.2 Leniency Programs: "Nothing New under the Sky"?

Promises of lenient treatment or rewards to elements of an opponent front that "betray" their partners have always been used in warlike situations, and do not have a crystal clear reputation.[10] In law enforcement, offering captured wrongdoers a lenient treatment in exchange for information valuable to prosecution has been a standard tool for centuries practically everywhere.[11] In the United States, *plea bargains,* kind of postdetection exchanges of a lenient treatment against self-reporting have been taking place long before the introduction of leniency programs. Analogous postdetection exchanges during prosecution are still routinely used (and sometimes misused) in the United States and other countries to fight drug-dealing and other organized crime, even though no publicly announced leniency policy is present.[12] Public promises of prizes or leniency *before* detection and/or prosecution have also often been used in the past.[13] These promises, however, where typically decided case by case, crime by crime.

So what's new about leniency programs in antitrust?

In my view, the feature that makes the leniency programs in antitrust somewhat special, apart from the new field of law enforcement they are directed to, is their being ex ante, general, and public.

Leniency programs are ex ante because—in their first and most innovative parts—they are directed at wrongdoers that have not yet been identified/detected, encouraging these to self-report. Therefore leniency policies may act before detection and the prosecution stage, not only after detection occurred and prosecution began, as plea bargains.

Leniency programs are general in the sense that they apply anonymously to anyone who is in a certain codified situation and behaves or may think of potentially behaving in a certain way.

Leniency programs are public in the sense that even in the United States, where prosecutorial discretion has always allowed for exchanges of leniency against evidence, they take the form of codified, automatic (hence predictable), and publicly advertised policies.

Codification is actually instrumental to both generality and publicity. It helps reducing uncertainty and discretionality, two aspects that greatly discourage self-reports. Publicity is crucial for leniency programs because the crucial objectives of law enforcement are as follows:

1. Deterring (preventing) cartel formation by undermining trust among potential co-conspirators with the increased likelihood that one of them could then loose confidence and turn the others in;
2. Detecting (discovering) cartels that were not deterred, by eliciting information on and from them.

Both objectives require that the program be general, public, transparent, predictable, and well advertised in the legal and—above all—business community. This is perhaps one reason why DOJ officials are (and should) be spending so much time going around at business managers' and lawyers' meetings to present the results of these programs in terms of convicted cartels.

General, formalized, and anonymous policies promising leniency, protection, and sometimes rewards against collaboration to not-yet-detected individuals have recently and successfully been used in Italy to fight Sicilian Mafia and Red Brigades' terrorists. These public policies are probably the closest ever to the current leniency policies in antitrust, although their (successful) implementation, at least in Italy, has been much less careful than one would have hoped for.[14]

A third, important function of leniency programs in antitrust is ex post:

3. Facilitating prosecution through exchanges of a lenient treatment against information and/or testimony on the infringement *after* a cartel has been detected in other ways.

This function is particularly important in adversarial systems like the United States, where a jury must be persuaded rather than an administrative, trained body, because it is typically hard to find sufficient hard evidence on cartels to persuade a jury without direct witnesses. However, this function does not require the generality and publicity of a public Leniency Policy. Postdetection leniency/information exchanges can be done, and have always been done—with plea bargaining in Anglo-Saxon countries and Prisoner's Dilemma style promises in other systems—with direct, "private," tailor-made agreements between prosecutors and the specific individual wrongdoers. In this regard leniency programs appear therefore to bring less novelty to law enforcement. This view appears consistent with that of some practitioners involved with these programs. For example, according to the staff of the most experienced agency on the subject, the DOJ, the main issue about leniency programs is: "How do you build a leniency program that will cause a company to come forward and voluntarily report its participation in a cartel that has gone previously undetected?" (Hammond 2004, p. 2).

7.1.3 The Objectives of (Antitrust) Laws: What Is a "Success" in Law Enforcement?

Most antitrust practitioners, prosecutors and lawyers, and most casual observers have celebrated leniency programs as a terrific success. Can we be really sure that leniency programs are such a success? I believe they are effective, but we don't *know* it. To answer this simple question, which few have asked in the policy debate, we have to clarify what exactly is a success in antitrust law enforcement against cartels. To do this, we must go back to the objectives of antitrust laws. The discussion may appear redundant to many readers, but again my personal experience is that there is a lot of confusion around, in particular, between instruments and objectives, that makes an introductory discussion worthwhile.

As for most other laws, the main objective of antitrust law enforcement against cartels is avoiding that the outlawed courses of action—in our case collusive product market agreements—take place. There are, of course, other objectives, including victim compensation and justice/fairness per se. But these are clearly of second-order relevance: the main reason why societies invest large amounts of resources to enforce the law is to reduce the frequency of inefficient, outlawed courses of action, namely crime *deterrence* (Beccaria 1763, sec. XII).

With respect to cartels this general objective can take at least two forms:

• The first, and by far the most important objective, is *ex ante* or *general deterrence* (or just *deterrence* in the remainder of the chapter), that is, preventing cartel formation with the threat of sufficiently heavy and prompt expected sanctions against violators, and with other mechanisms that make cartels either unprofitable or unstable (on the dominance of prevention on any other target of law enforcement, see again Beccaria 1763 sec. XLI).

• A second, and secondary objective, is *ex post deterrence* or *desistance*, that is, ensuring that those among the cartels that could not be deterred ex ante, but are then detected and prosecuted by law enforcers, are induced to interrupt the illegal practice. This can be either by threat of even higher expected sanctions for repeat offenders, or by other, tougher mechanisms, like incapacitation through imprisonment or disqualification.

Ex ante deterrence is by far the most important because it can be achieved for a very large number of potential infringements and at a much lower social and individual cost than desistance.

Potential cartels that are not deterred will form, and then either go undetected, in which case they will directly reduce social welfare for the time of their existence, or be detected at some point by law enforcers. As they are prosecuted, the direct cost to society is reduced by the shorter life of the cartel (provided prosecution leads to desistance), though additional substantial social costs of prosecution are incurred.[15]

Potential cartels that law enforcement deter ex ante (prevents from forming) do not imply these social costs, nor does ex ante deterrence require that law enforcement agencies detect each particular potential violator, as is the case for desistance. Deterrence therefore acts *generally* on a much larger number of potential infringements. The more deterrence is produced by a law enforcement system, the less desistance is needed and occurs. So society enjoys larger savings in prosecution costs.

For these reasons ex ante deterrence is, and must be the primary objective of law enforcement, and the foremost criterion for the evaluation of its optimality/efficiency.

Note that if we abstract from its effects on deterrence, prosecution is a pure deadweight loss to society. If prosecution had no deterrence effects, for example, because sanctions are too low (e.g., lower than gains from the infringement), from an economic efficiency point of view it should simply be avoided.[16]

The preceding discussion should have clarified that since law enforcement is a costly activity for society, the success of a (antitrust or other) law enforcement policy should be principally measured by the welfare increase from its *deterrence effects*, particularly ex ante ones, relative to its costs. A general problem therefore in evaluating the appropriateness and effectiveness of law enforcement policies is that it is hard (though not impossible) to estimate their deterrence effects. It requires identifying and measuring the costs of illegal acts that did not take place but that would have taken place in the absence of the law enforcement policy under scrutiny, and to compare them with the costs of the policy.

Going back to our leniency revolution, in the last decades we observed a steep increase in the number of successfully prosecuted cartels and in the size of imposed sanctions. This tells us something about the change in prosecution costs (they may have fallen, thanks to the improved information from leniency applicants, and their total may have increased together with the number of prosecuted infringements) but little about changes in deterrence. This is why we may well believe that in the United States the increase in convictions and prosecution costs should have fed up into increased deterrence, but clearly we don't *know* this.[17] One should keep in mind that in case of a "complete" success—complete prevention/deterrence—we would observe a *decrease* (to zero) in the number of detected and prosecuted infringements, not an increase.

To conclude, the optimistic view that the increase in convicted cartels reflects an increase in cartel deterrence is plausible, but the actual change in active cartels caused by the Corporate Leniency Policy is not directly observable. Therefore, in principle, the observed increase in convicted cartels could be due to an increase in cartel activity.[18] And even if we knew that current leniency programs increased cartel deterrence, we would not know whether differently designed ones would have done better. This calls loud for theoretical, experimental, and econometric research.

7.2 Evolution of Leniency Programs

In this section, I briefly discuss the evolution of leniency programs in the two world largest jurisdictions that introduced them, as they exemplify the two main legal frameworks within which antitrust law is being enforced around the world: an adversarial system, where juries and judges decide on the case since the first instance, and an administrative/

inquisitorial system, where a public agency has both prosecutorial and judicial power that is subject to appeal to higher courts.

7.2.1   The Evolution of US LPs

The DOJ introduced a first leniency policy for cartels already in 1978. This older policy was much less generous than the one introduced in 1993, both in terms of reductions in sanctions awarded to spontaneously reporting firms and the possibility to award leniency when firms under investigation start cooperating. The first program was not very transparent, not at all "automatic," leaving the DOJ with much discretion in its implementation, and prospective applicants with a lot of uncertainty on the likely outcome of a leniency application. As a result very few firms applied for leniency under the 1978 US leniency program.

The program revised in 1993 was also changed significantly, making the scope of amnesty much clearer and broader. In particular, Section A of the new Corporate Leniency Policy makes the awarding of complete amnesty to the first cartel member that self-reports *automatic* under the condition that no investigation is underway before the applicant comes forward. Its Section B awards leniency to the first reporting firm even when it reports after an investigation has begun, as long as at the time of the report the DOJ does not have already evidence "likely to result in a sustainable conviction." As long as reporting is a "truly corporate act," under the new policy amnesty is granted to all individual officers, directors, and employees of the applicant firm who cooperate with the investigation.

In addition the Individual Leniency Policy was introduced in 1994 to complement the corporate policy by offering individuals involved in a conspiracy the possibility to directly apply and receive amnesty independently of their company. However, the company and all fellow managers involved are not covered by leniency.

These revisions had a profound impact on the program. Since their introduction the number of applications increased more than tenfold and was accompanied by a dramatic increase in the magnitude of penalties imposed. Leniency applications appear directly responsible for successful prosecutions in several if not most recent high profile US cases. According to the OECD (2002, 2003), the dramatic increase in leniency applications is also due to the substantial increase in sanctions, both corporate and individual fines and jail sentences, that took place in recent years. But the two forces are likely to have operated together, reinforcing each other. The improved quality and quantity of evidence provided by leniency applicants are probably an important determinant of the DOJ's improved ability to obtain higher sanctions from US courts, and these higher and well-advertised sanctions in turn increased the attractiveness of leniency programs.

The combination of high sanctions and guaranteed amnesty for the first comer appears to have created strong incentives for corporations to come forward. According to Scott Hammond, former director of Criminal Enforcement of the DOJ Antitrust Division, more than 50 percent of the leniency applications are taking place before an investigation is opened, falling therefore within Section A of the Corporate Leniency Policy (personal communication). In his words, "over the last five years, the Amnesty Program has been responsible for detecting and prosecuting more antitrust violation than all of our [other investigating tools]" (2001). Similar statements can be found in Spratling (1998, 1999).[19]

Even after the enormous increase in convictions and fines of the last decade, concerns remained in the Antitrust Division and among commentators (e.g., Rey 2003; Spagnolo 2000a, 2004) that the prospect of treble-damage lawsuits was dissuading some antitrust wrongdoers from participating in the program. In particular, cartel participants had to weight the benefits of immunity from criminal prosecution against the likelihood of federal and state treble-damage claims based on their admitted wrongdoing. Leniency applicants might have found themselves liable not only for triple the damages suffered by customers that they dealt with but also for three times the damages of their co-conspirators' customers under joint and several liability rules.

Many of these concerns were removed by the 2004 Criminal Penalty Enhancement and Reform Act. This new legislation limits the total private civil liability of corporations that have entered into leniency agreements with the Antitrust Division (combined with that of their officers, directors, and employees who are covered by the agreement) to actual damages "attributable to the commerce done by the applicant in the goods or services affected by the violation" plus attorneys' fees, costs, and interest. That is, corporations that meet the requirements and obtain amnesty are no longer liable for treble but only single damages, and are no longer jointly and severally liable for damages suffered by their co-conspirators' customers. Conversely, the legislation increases the potential liability for cartel participants that do *not* obtain leniency, since in addition to their previous liability they may now also be jointly and severally liable for twice the actual damages suffered by customers of the leniency applicant. It also dramatically increases potential criminal penalties (much higher fines and up to ten years of jail) for price-fixing and analogous infringements.

7.2.2 Evolution of the EU LPs
The European Commission was among the first jurisdictions to follow the example of the DOJ, introducing a leniency program in 1996. As happened with the first US Leniency Policy, the first EU Leniency Notice was not very effective in eliciting reports from cartel members, as the amount of fine reduction was uncertain and discretional. Moreover fines had been low before 1996, and in the absence of criminal sanctions the incentive to come forward was rather low for corporations.

In February 2002 the Commission revised its six-year-old leniency program by reducing its discretion in its implementation and increasing the size of fine reductions leniency applicants could expect. The Commission also started to offer almost *automatic* immunity from fines to the first member of a cartel that reports valuable information before an investigation is opened (Secs. 8a, 9) or when the EU has very little information (Secs. 8b, 10) on the cartel. Moreover the 2002 Leniency Notice substantially reduced the amount of information an applicant needs to report to obtain leniency when applying before an investigation is opened.

If a leniency application takes place before an investigation is open and falls under paragraphs 8a and 9 of the new Notice, then the amount of reported information required for leniency to be awarded must only be sufficient *to enable the Commission to carry out an investigation*. If, instead, the report takes place after the investigation started, falling under paragraphs 8b and 10 of the 2002 Notice, the requirement remains more stringent: the amount of reported information must be sufficient for the commission to *find an infringement*. Also the new EU Leniency Notice offers extended coverage. Ringleaders can now obtain leniency, provided they did not force other firms to join the cartel.

In the years following the February 2002 revision a clear "structural break" occurred in the path of reports, much like what happened in the United States after 1993, as something like a tenfold increase in the rate of application took place (Van Barlingen 2003). This trend intensified in the following years, with about half of the applications falling under paragraphs 8a and 9. This dramatic increase forced DG Competition to undertake an internal reorganization without which it would not have been able to handle all the cartel cases that are being reported. Meanwhile average EU fines also increased substantially, and likely further contributed to the strong increase in number of firms reporting to obtain leniency.

7.2.3 Main Differences

The US and EU leniency policies are often regarded as different in several respects. In my view, the two instruments are more similar than how often described, though they do differ in some respects and, most important, in how they are interpreted and implemented.

A first difference regards the treatment of ringleaders. Allowing also ringleaders to obtain leniency, as in the European Union but contrary to what is done in the United States, can (1) elicit self-reporting, as it may not be clear to a firm considering whether to apply for leniency if it risks being regarded as a ringleader, and (2) increase ex ante deterrence, since even the ringleader cannot be completely "trusted" not to lose confidence and rush to report under the leniency program. In contrast, in an adversarial system, where testimony is crucial to persuade juries, testimony by a ringleader may not be convincing. Such reasoning may be sufficient ground for the DOJ decision to exclude ringleaders from their winner-take-all leniency policy.[20]

A perhaps more critical difference is that the EU program offers milder forms of leniency also to all other firms that are not the first to come forward, provided that the additional information they report is sufficiently valuable to prove the case. The US program does not allow leniency to a second reporting firm; it only awards amnesty to the very first firm providing valuable information. Plea bargaining was practically eliminated from US antitrust enforcement in 1989, so the DOJ does not have formal instruments left to reward a second or third firm that reports helpful information where sentences of wrongdoers do not qualify for leniency to judges and sentencing Guidelines.[21] However, even this difference is less sharp than appears on paper. The US courts have been given increasing discretion in setting sanctions, and can reduce them for firms that cooperate with investigators but do not qualify for amnesty.

It is sometimes argued that in the United States the first firm reporting information on a cartel automatically receives amnesty, whereas in the European Union whether a firm reporting after an investigation started receives leniency depends on the amount and novelty of the information reported (Section 10 of the EU Notice; as noted, the requirement of Section 9 for reports before an investigation started are milder). In my view, the two stated policies are not that different, though they may certainly be implemented in very different ways, since the US program places conditions on the information reported by an applicant.[22] If implemented strictly, these conditions limit the awarding of leniency to situations where the information provided is highly valuable, either because it reveals an unknown cartel or because the Division has very little such evidence against the firms it is investigating. This implicitly creates the link between the value of reported information and the awarding of leniency that is made explicit in the EU leniency program. Therefore, in principle, both programs can be implemented strictly, denying leniency—for example—when the reported information is not that valuable, to limit pro forma or strategic applications from firms withholding important information.

In my view, the most important statutory difference is that in the United States there is individual liability for cartel infringements and therefore a correspondent Individual Leniency Policy that complements the Corporate Policy. The ability of individual employees to obtain leniency on their own can generate agency problems in colluding firms and cause such firms to come forward more often, before a manager or employee decides to come forward on its own under the Individual Leniency Policy, or not to collude in the first place (see Sections 7.3.4 and 7.4.3 below).

7.3 Economic Theories of Leniency

From a theoretical viewpoint, the Prisoner's Dilemma game is perhaps the first and best-known model of a leniency/information exchange: the sanctions for a detected wrongdoer are reduced to induce him to confess and prove guilty his former partner(s). The Prisoner's Dilemma refers to a situation in which the joint law violators have already been detected, and leniency seeks to elicit additional information to facilitate prosecution, much like what happens in multilateral plea bargaining (e.g., Kobayashi 1992).

As argued before, the most novel and distinctive feature of leniency policies, not present in multilateral plea bargaining, is instead their potential ability to deter organized crime directly, rather than indirectly trough improved prosecution:

1. By preventing cartel formation with the increased likelihood that a leniency application will be their conclusion. That is, cartels are discouraged by "undermining trust" between wrongdoers with the increased risk that someone will unilaterally report to enjoy the benefit of leniency, which is typically restricted to the first reporting party.
2. By improving cartel detection by inducing undetected wrongdoers that lose confidence or interest in the cartel to spontaneously self-report and "turn in" their partners even when the law enforcement agency has no clue about the cartel.

Despite the prominence of the Prisoner's Dilemma game in economics and the importance of organized crime in society, until very recently there was no systematic economic investigation of the effects of leniency programs on long-term, dynamic forms of organized crime like cartels (or large-scale fraud, corruption, etc.).

The literature on law enforcement did analyze leniency and self-reporting, but relating to individual wrongdoers committing occasional crimes. For example, Kaplow and Shavell (1994) elegantly show how reducing sanctions against wrongdoers that spontaneously self-report lowers law enforcement costs by reducing the number of wrongdoers to be detected, and that when agents are risk averse, offering leniency to wrongdoers that self-report increases welfare by reducing the overall risk agents bear. Both these insights apply to leniency policies, in general. Malik (1993) discusses the role of self-reporting in reducing auditing costs in environmental regulation, while Innes (1999) discusses the value of the early remediation of damages that fine reductions for self-reporting wrongdoers allow for. Koffman and Lawarrée (1996) offer a first model how collusion in a hierarchy can be prevented by leniency: in a static principal–supervisor–agent model à la Tirole (1986), they propose to bring in a second supervisor and structure the two supervisors' incentives as a Prisoner's Dilemma. Then the second supervisor has incentive to report against the first supervisor just in case he entered a collusive agreement with the agent.

These papers highlight important benefits that lenient treatment of self-reporting wrongdoers can bring about, but they are static models, mostly of a single-agent crime, that cannot capture the new type of deterrence leniency brings in, the dynamic effects of leniency on cartels and other organized self-enforcing criminal relationships with the features discussed in section 7.1.1. Collusive agreements between price-fixing firms, like those between auditors and managers or CEOs and captured directors, are typically long-term, dynamic, and self-enforcing. Indeed a full understanding of dynamic phenomenon typically requires dynamic analysis.

The literature on plea bargaining is of course also strictly related to leniency programs, as it discusses the efficiency of exchanges of a lenient treatment against information/ cooperation from wrongdoers, although taking place only after detection (e.g., Grossman and Katz 1983; Reinganum 1988). The closest paper in this literature is probably Kobayashi (1992), who presents a model with multiple heterogeneous and jointly liable defendants with different amounts of information on each others' wrongdoing. Kobayashi finds that it may be optimal to award maximal leniency to the "worst" wrongdoer when this person has better information. As mentioned earlier, plea bargains are nevertheless exchanges of leniency against collaboration that only take place at the prosecution stage, meaning after wrongdoers have been already detected by other means. Therefore the plea bargains do not capture the most novel effects linked to leniency programs, which are the ex ante effects relative to wrongdoers that have not yet been detected.

In the remainder of this section, I will survey recent economic analyses of leniency programs in antitrust, focusing on contributions that I regard as illuminating. I will follow the timing with which the contribution were produced and circulated among researchers. At this point two things are worth noting:

1. As for most other forms of corporate crime, rational choice analysis is particularly well suited to analyze cartels and policies against them. The wrongdoers are well-educated, calculating firm managers, trained in evaluating costs and benefits of choices and to react to incentives, rather than to rage, passions, or instinct.[23]
2. The optimal design of leniency programs aims at destroying possibilities for illegal cooperation among competitors. It tends to destroy collusive equilibria in oligopolies and—ideally—leave only the competitive one. Because of this tendency to reduce/eliminate multiple equilibria, dynamic analyses of leniency are much less subject to the caveats imposed by the presence of many equilibria to other research fields based on dynamic game analyses.

7.3.1 Leniency Programs and Cartel Prosecution

The first, seminal paper explicitly dedicated to addressing the effects of leniency policies on cartels in an appropriately dynamic analytical framework is Motta and Polo (2003).[24] In this rich model, firms interact repeatedly in an oligopoly and choose whether or not to collude given the risk of being detected and prosecuted by an Antitrust Authority. If firms collude, they are subject to the risk of conviction; if they either do not collude or unilaterally defect from a collusive agreement, they are not. There is an exogenous budget of the Antitrust Authority that can be allocated to its two different tasks, detection and prosecution of detected cartels. A leniency program can be introduced that reduces fines against cartel members that provide information on the cartel, and that option may or may not be open to colluding firms that only begin collaborating after having been detected, during prosecution. Detection of a cartel by the Antitrust Authority leads to conviction only with some probability, and this probability is increased by leniency. Convicted cartels do not collude for some period of time, but they then slide back to collusion (previous versions used the alternative assumption that convicted firms would not again attempt collusion, with little change in results).

With its focus on prosecution this model takes on the spirit of plea bargaining literature. It is designed to answer a precise question: Should firms that report information when being already under investigation be also eligible to some leniency? The main object of this study therefore is Section B of the Corporate Leniency Policy, relative to firms that cooperate with the Antitrust Authority only when they are already under investigation, which is similar to plea bargaining. Both the welfare effects in terms of ex ante deterrence and of ex post desistance are considered (this study is the first, to my knowledge to introduce this clarifying distinction).

The central result the model delivers is that although lenient treatment of cartel members already under prosecution in exchange for information and collaboration has a negative effect on deterrence by reducing overall sanctions against the cartel, it also tends to have a positive effect on deterrence by making prosecution faster/cheaper and more effective. This positive effect tends to dominate the first, negative effect on deterrence. Increasing the probability of being convicted if detected by making for the prosecution a stronger case frees resources from prosecution and reallocates them to improving cartel detection (the assumption is that the Antitrust Authority is benevolent and does not sit on the laurels of the increased number of successfully prosecuted cartels).

To obtain this central result, the model had to be simplified by the following assumptions:

1. Firms sustain collusive agreements with grim trigger strategies.
2. A defecting firm cannot be convicted for having been part of a cartel nor can it report on former partners.

Under these simplifying assumptions, however, cartel members report information only when they all agree to do so as part of the collusive strategy. So leniency programs appear unable to induce agents to spontaneously and noncooperatively self-report. This leads to three secondary, less intuitive conclusions of the Motta and Polo model:

1. To have any effect, a leniency program must be open to firms under investigation (a kind of "irrelevance result" for Section A of the US and Sections 8a–9 of the EU leniency programs).
2. The same lenient treatment should be offered to all firms that apply for leniency, independent of the order with which they report (under the two assumptions above removing the "first comer rule"—the benefit of being the first firm to report—has no cost).
3. Leniency programs are second-best. If the Antitrust Authority has sufficient resources to deter cartels through fines and inspections, it should not introduce leniency programs.[25]

7.3.2 Leniency Programs and Direct Deterrence

The three secondary conclusions of Motta and Polo (2003) are somewhat counterintuitive and contrast with the DOJ's statements on what are, in their view, the crucial features of an effective leniency program (e.g., see Hammond 2004). Also, because of the emphasis on postdetection prosecution that model was not open to important novel possibilities for leniency programs different from their indirect effects of easier prosecution: the potential to *generally* and *directly* deter organized crime by (1) inducing undetected wrongdoers to spontaneously self-report and "turn in" their partners, and (2) preventing cartel formation by undermining trust among wrongdoers with the increased probability that one among them reports in order to benefit from the leniency program.

To highlight these direct effects in the simplest possible way Spagnolo (2000a) develops a stylized dynamic model of self-enforcing collusive/criminal agreements within a law enforcement system that brings Motta and Polo's (2003) approach closer to Becker (1968) and Kaplow and Shavell (1994), who focus on ex ante deterrence and spontaneous self-reporting rather than on postdetection leniency/information exchanges at the prosecution stage, albeit in static single-agent contexts. In regard to the three conclusions given above, Spagnolo (2000a) withdraws the possibility of leniency through reporting after having been detected and put under investigation, the object of Motta and Polo (2003). He focuses exclusively on the first sections of LPs, reserved only to firms that spontaneously report when their cartel has not been detected.

The first version of Spagnolo (2000a), directly building on Motta and Polo's work, inherits its assumption 2 that if a cartel member unilaterally defects undercutting the cartel price, he risks no more to be convicted for his past collusive activities. Because of this, the first version of the model delivered three main results:

1. Optimal leniency programs (their part on spontaneous reports before an investigation is opened) restrict maximum benefits to the first reporting party only.[26]

2. A program that rewards with a fines-financed bounty the first reporting firm could completely deter cartels at a finite level of fines without any prosecution or inspection costs. From the beginning the proposed reward is fine-financed, so that it does not weight on the public budget, and more important, in being (weakly) smaller than the sum of fines levied on other cartel members, *it cannot be exploited* by groups of individuals that take turn to report and cash the bonus.[27]

3. Leniency programs that only reduce/cancel fines have deterrence effect when repeat offenders are subject to higher expected sanctions. In that case a *protection from punishment* effect emerges because a firm that deviates from the cartel can soften the toughest two-phase punishment à la Abreu (1986). Firms can protect themselves by reporting the cartel under the leniency program when defecting: this reduces future expected cartel profits—the carrot that makes the stick credible—and therefore the maximal "toughness" of the punishment phase other firms can credibly threaten to impose.

Assumption 2 that a cartel member that unilaterally defects can no more be convicted is rather unrealistic and hides one of the most immediate effects of leniency leading to an "irrelevance results" analogous to Motta and Polo's result 1. Rey's (2003) rich survey also discussed this assumption and noted that it is often not realistic, hindering other possible effects. In extended versions of Spagnolo's model, circulating after (2001), assumption 2 was dropped. Allowing for a positive expected fine for a firm that defects by undercutting its cartel, Rey (2003) and Spagnolo (2004) clarified that the "irrelevance result" was fruit of that simplifying assumption and highlighted other possible deterrence effects of leniency policies, even without rewards. In particular, to results 1 through 3 above, Spagnolo (2004) added:

4. Absent leniency programs, law enforcing agencies should commit not to target agents that unilaterally defect from collusive strategies, and should make this policy public.[28]
5. Leniency programs that do not pay rewards but are restricted (or much more generous) with the first reporting party also deter cartel through a *protection from fines* effect. This effect is present as long as the reduced fines of the leniency program are below the expected fine of a defecting agent that does not report, an effect also discussed in Rey (2003). By increasing the expected payoff of an agent that defects and reports above that of an agent that just defects, the leniency program tightens individual firms' incentive constraint for colluding and destabilizes cartels.
6. Leniency programs that do not pay rewards may have a third direct deterrence effect by making illegal agreement more "risky." As often stressed by DOJ officials, leniency can generate "breakdowns in trust" among wrongdoers. To capture this effect, *strategic risk* considerations (in the spirit of John Harsanyi and Reinhardt Selten's 1988 risk dominance concept) are introduced in the model. It is shown that moderate leniency programs always strictly increase the riskiness of entering/sticking to a given collusive agreement relative to abandoning it; the riskiness increases strictly more when eligibility to the program is restricted only to the first reporting party, as in the United States. This last finding offers direct support to DOJ officials' claim that the first-comer rule is crucial in generating breakdowns of trust in cartels and the consequent rushes to report.

Other studies shortly followed on the general direct deterrence effects of leniency programs for cartels members spontaneously self-reporting before an investigation is opened. Ellis and Wilson (2001) suggested an additional reason for cartel members to spontaneously apply to a leniency program before an investigation is opened. Within a dynamic oligopoly model, it shows that a leniency program can induce colluding firms to report information under the leniency program in order to damage competitors, meaning *to raise (future) rivals' costs* through fines and imprisonment of their management, thereby gaining a profitable strategic advantage in the following competitive phase. This incentive to use leniency to raise rivals' costs is anticipated by firms, and therefore adds to previously discussed direct effects in deterring cartel formation. Ellis and Wilson's model also indicates that leniency can have a stabilizing effect on cartels whose formation was not deterred; this negative effect will be further discussed later. Hinloopen (2003) considers a dynamic oligopoly model where probabilities of detection change over time. In this model, cartel deterrence increases with the generosity of the leniency program and with a higher probabilities of detection in any future period. Both Ellis and Wilson (2001) and Hinloopen

(2003) focus on two possible deviations from collusive strategies, the usual one of unilaterally undercutting the cartel and the novel one of self-reporting the agreement. In both models, however, the optimal unilateral defection appears to be unilaterally undercutting the cartel price (to increase profits) *and* reporting under the leniency program (to reduce the expected fine). It would be interesting to know which results would go through anyway and which would not by taking the optimal defection into account.[29]

7.3.3 Negative Side Effects of Leniency: Self-reporting as a *Threat*

Motta and Polo (2003) noted that by reducing sanctions for firms that cooperate at the prosecution stage, leniency programs have a negative effect on imposed fines. So deterrence is reduced, though this effect tends to be overcompensated by the positive effect of a higher probability of conviction. Economic analysis has identified other possible negative side effects of imperfectly designed leniency.

I mentioned that leniency makes self-reporting more attractive, and this may induce cartel members to defect and report. When self-reporting becomes attractive, the *threat* of self-reporting to punish an agent that did not behave as agreed upon by the cartel may also become credible. The threat to self-report in turn could be used by smart wrongdoers to enforce cartels that would not be sustainable in the absence of this law-induced threat. Such an issue did not arise in most models discussed until now because, simply put, the information cartel members generate and can report in each period is assumed to evaporate after one period.

Buccirossi and Spagnolo (2001, 2006) model this side effect of leniency on bilateral, sequential, and asymmetric illegal transactions, such as corruption or manager/auditor collusion. In this model an illegal action (a favor) is exchanged sequentially against a bribe, and the illegal partners can optimally choose both the level of the bribe and the timing of the transaction (who delivers first), after having observed the parameters of the law enforcement systems. The model shows that the "moderate" forms of leniency typically implemented in the real world can have the counterproductive side effect of facilitating occasional, and even some repeated, illegal transactions. The possibility to obtain a reduced sanction by self-reporting can be used as a credible threat to enforce otherwise unenforceable occasional (one-shot) illegal deals. The first party that performs can force the second party to comply and reciprocate by credibly threatening to report the crime in case of noncompliance. Even in corrupt relationships where transactions are frequently repeated, moderate leniency programs can increase the parties' ability to punish deviations, thereby stabilizing the illegal arrangements by reducing gains from defecting. In practice, the information that wrongdoers have on each other plays the role of a "hostage" that is used as a credible threat to govern the illegal exchange and punish failures to comply with the agreement. The model also shows that offering "rewards" to parties that blow the whistle destroys this counterproductive side effect of leniency by making the "promise" not to report no longer credible.

Spagnolo (2000b) studies this negative side effect with respect to cartels in oligopolistic industries and to bidding rings in multi-unit auction markets. He finds that when information on a collusive agreement is durable, a leniency program that reduces sanctions for agents that self-report can enforce collusive behavior in occasional (one-shot or infrequently repeated) multi-unit auctions, in particular, in procurement cases. Again, the leniency program has the side effect of conferring credibility to the threat to report the collusive agreement if a member of the ring undercuts it.

The model shows that this negative side effect applies to multi-unit auctions and it is strongly reinforced by current (EU and US) procurement regulation, which requires that if it turns out that bids were rigged, such as because the bid rigging agreement is reported under a leniency program, the outcome of the procurement auction is nullified and the auction is repeated. This rule is aimed at increasing the ability to monitor the awarding decisions and reduce the likelihood of corruption or favoritism, but it also guarantees that it is not profitable for a firm in a ring to undercut the bid-rigging agreement and simultaneously report under the leniency program. Then the auction must be re-run so that all gains from defection disappear. Spagnolo (2000b) also shows that the mechanism tends not to apply to "smooth deviation games," like standard oligopolies with many small buyers, since it requires a discontinuous payoff function—typical of multi-unit auctions but not of oligopolies with well-divisible demand. As a result a defecting party cannot smoothly fine-tune its defection and thus leave other cartel members lower but sufficient collusive rent that they prefer not to report after such partial defection.

Ellis and Wilson (2001) obtain a related effect in their model. Besides the potential incentive to report to raise rival costs mentioned in the previous section, their model shows that for cartels not deterred by this risk—and it turns out that these cartels are the most important to deter, those with worse social welfare consequences—the leniency program has the effect of stabilizing them. The reason is that if the cartel is formed, then leniency induces cartel members to self-report after any defection from agreed collusive strategies. The punishment for defection is thereby strengthened by an amount equal to antitrust fines, much like in the models just discussed.[30]

Brisset and Thomas (2004) analyze the effect of leniency programs on a ring's ability to exchange private cost information to organize a bidding ring in a first price sealed bid auction. Focusing on coordination while assuming enforcement, they find that also from a coordination point of view, a poorly designed "low-powered" leniency program does not have the desired deterrence effects while it can act as a threat that facilitates information exchanges among ring members. They show numerically that a program that rewards ring members reporting before an investigation is open does not have counterproductive effects; it increases deterrence by hindering a ring's ability to credibly exchange the private cost information necessary to form the ring.

Analogous counterproductive side effects of leniency emerge in several more recent models (Aubert et al. 2006; Motchenkova 2005; Harrington 2005; Chen and Harrigton

2007; Festerling 2005a), confirming and reinforcing this section's message that leniency policies must be designed and implemented with *extreme care*, as they may otherwise produce rather negative effects.

7.3.4 Leniency Programs and Rewards to Whistleblowers

The best-known result in Spagnolo (2000a, 2004) is probably that in a dynamic multi-agent version of a model à la Becker (1968) for organized crimes like cartels, the *first best* (complete deterrence without inspection/prosecution costs) can be achieved with high enough *finite* fines by promising the first wrongdoer that applies for leniency and self-reports a sufficiently high "fines-financed" reward (i.e., a reward smaller than the sum of fines levied on other co-conspirators). To my knowledge, this is the first law enforcement instrument that delivers the first best since Becker (1968), who showed that with standard instruments the first best cannot be achieved even with *infinite* fines, as with zero inspection costs/probability of detection even infinite fines have zero deterrence effect.[31]

Spagnolo's (2000a, 2004) models do not distinguish between colluding individuals and colluding organizations, as it is conceived to address optimal deterrence for many forms of organized crime besides cartels, most of which involve multiple collaborating individuals, but not multiple organizations. When colluding agents are organizations, as is the case for cartels, and rewards can be paid to individual employees of these organizations, a number of novel issues emerge.

Rewards to Individuals   The model of Aubert, Kovacic, and Rey (2006) also focuses on the direct, general deterrence effects of leniency and rewards, and allows defecting firms to face the risk of conviction for past collusion. It greatly extends the approach to address novel issues linked to the effects of leniency and rewards offered to individual managers/employees on the internal organization of colluding and noncolluding firms. The model analyzes the costs and benefits of creating an agency problem between firms and their employees by allowing the latter to directly cash rewards when blowing the whistle and reporting their own firm's collusive behavior to the Antitrust Authority.

On the benefits side, the model shows that allowing employees of colluding firms that report information to obtain leniency and a cash reward increases the number of potential informants that a colluding firm must "bribe" to keep silent, directly increasing the cost of colluding and therefore the general deterrence effect of any given reward scheme. It also shows that rewards for individuals tend to be complementary to corporate leniency programs, as they make a colluding firm's strategy to defect, report, and stop "bribing" its own informed employees even more attractive, further destabilizing collusion.

On the cost side, they examine the main arguments put forward in the policy debate against offering (leniency and) rewards to individual employees that report a cartel, mainly based on the possible negative effects of this practice on firms' internal organization and performance.

These schemes may deter productive cooperation (e.g., welfare enhancing information-sharing on demand uncertainty) that could mistakenly be regarded as collusion by increasing the incentive to report it in the attempt to cash the reward. Aubert, Kovacic, and Rey show, however, that if mistakes are not too frequent, a reward scheme could, in principle, be built that only induces truthful reports.

Rewards for individuals can induce firms to inefficiently reduce turnover in order to minimize the number of parties informed about the collusive agreement. These authors' conclusion is that this inefficiency increases the cost of colluding but not of noncolluding firms. So rewards for self-reporting appear to have mostly positive cartel deterrence effects.

Colluding firms may be induced by schemes to adopt "innocent" attitudes, in particular, increasing investment in productivity enhancing technology, a type of investment that typically falls in cartelized industries. But these practices can have positive welfare effects because they induce colluding firms to be more efficient. Nevertheless, such schemes are costly, which makes collusion less attractive.

Aubert, Kovacic, and Rey offer several explanations for why firms continue keeping much "hard" information on their cartel at the risk of being detected by competition authorities. Among the explanations advanced and analyzed are that firms need information to persuade cartel partners that they did not "cheat" and undercut the agreement in situations of uncertainty and imperfect information. Such information is useful when a cartel breaks up because of an exogenous (e.g., productivity) shock.

Other Literature on Individual Whistleblowers   The literature just discussed was the first to analyze rewards schemes in antitrust. Problems related to individual whistleblowers have been subject to economic analysis with respect to crimes other than those of cartels, mostly in relation to the US False Claim Act that rewards employees who reveal fraud to the federal government. Obviously all the literature cannot be surveyed here for lack of space. I will nevertheless offer a short overview of the issues involved.

First, there is an extensive sociological literature, typically about innocent employees discovering and reporting wrongdoing by their firms, internally or externally, without expecting any monetary reward for it. Glazer and Glazer (1991) and Alford (2002) provide some good case studies and include many references. The literature on such "pure" whistleblowers is rich, but the points of interest for us that it stresses are fundamentally two:

1. Whistleblowers experience (as documented) trouble finding work and a troubled social and private life after reporting. Potential employers throughout the industry, colleagues, friends, neighbors, and often even family members turn against them. So whistleblowers *must* be both rewarded and protected extremely well; otherwise, they will come forward only by mistake.[32]

2. Rewards for whistleblowers can lower morale in organizations, reducing trust, cooperation, and efficiency (e.g., Dwarkin and Near 1997).

There is a legal literature on whistleblower reward schemes. Two excellent examples are Howse and Daniels (1995) and Kovacic (2001). The former provides an informal law and economic analysis of the costs and benefits of rewarding whistleblowers under the False Claim Act, brilliantly examining the experience from multiple points of view, with a rather positive take on whistleblowing schemes.[33] The latter proposes to extends the experience to antitrust and discusses the legal issues that this may raise. Both cite many references on legal analyses for related subjects.

More or less formal economic analyses of whistleblowing in contexts different from antitrust take two forms. The first type deals with teams of colluding wrongdoers, typically employees of an organization. Among the contributors to this literature are Felli (1996), the already mentioned Koffman-Lawarree (1996), Leppamaki (1997), and Cooter and Garoupa (2000). Common to these analyses is the message of the Prisoner's Dilemma whereby rewards for whistleblowing can deter illegal cooperation. But they also adopt a static approach that does not endogenize how wrongdoers govern or enforce the illegal cooperation in the first place, and cannot capture the effects of rewarding whistleblowers' on self-enforcing relationships like cartels. Acemoglu (1997) is the first model I am aware of that considers whistleblowing while endogenizing self-enforcing collusion between a manager and an auditor. However, in this model whistleblowing (against improper managerial choices) is the statutory task of the auditor, hindered by manager–agent collusion, and is not seen as something to reward in order to hinder collusion on other dimensions.

The second type of economic analysis includes Tokar (2000) and Buccirossi et al. (2005). They focus on the conflicting objectives created between a firm and its employees when rewards schemes are available for individual whistleblowers, particularly when courts make mistakes and employees may find it convenient to "fabricate" information in the attempt to cash a reward. A more or less explicit conclusion of these papers is that high rewards for whistleblowers may require tougher sanctions against information fabrication to avoid negative effects on deterrence also in terms of courts choosing a higher standard of proof.

Two recent economic analyses of whistleblowing not fitting this classification are Heyes (2004) and Berentsen et al. (2005). Heyes models several kinds of intrinsic/behavioral motivations that can push employees to blow the whistle in the absence of rewards and incur high economic and social costs this implies without expecting any monetary benefit. Berentson et al. shows in an incomplete information framework how whistleblowers can deter forbidden "doping" equilibria in sport contests when competing agents do not collude but share private information on each other's behavior (on whether or not illegal means were used to obtain a competitive advantage in the contest).

Although interesting and closely related in spirit to the debate in antitrust, none of these analyses develop a dynamic model of self-enforcing collusion able to capture the trade-offs typical of a cartel and the novel kind of deterrence they lead to when coupled with leniency and whistleblower reward schemes.

7.3.5   Recent Developments

Equilibrium Reports   The models focusing on direct deterrence effects discussed in sections 7.3.2 and in the subsection above keep the analysis simple by remaining in the tradition of complete information models of dynamic oligopoly (e.g., Friedman 1976; Abreu 1986, 1988). One cost of simplicity is that if one were to take these models literally, reports would be predicted only from cartels formed before an unanticipated leniency program was introduced, as a disequilibrium phenomenon. After that, since agents are forward-looking and there is no parameter uncertainty, either cartels form and are sustained, or they are deterred and do not form. In both cases no one spontaneously reports, just as in complete information oligopoly models in equilibrium punishments/price wars never occur. Nevertheless, the results of these models are clearly robust to the introduction of small stochastic shocks in various parameters (e.g., in the discount factor, or in the "disutility from sanctions") or simple forms of imperfect information (e.g., on the implementation of the leniency program). Either occurrence will generate equilibrium reports without changing much else. Richer models that obtain equilibrium reports in less obvious ways are helpful in verifying the robustness of early findings and possibly their novel effects.

A first analysis aimed at obtaining spontaneous equilibrium reports under a leniency program is Alexander and Cohen (2004). This is a static model of crime participation. It is different from the dynamic models discussed previously but close to Spagnolo (2000a, 2004) and Aubert et al. (2004) in its focus on general deterrence rather than desistance and prosecution. In this model gains from offending are ex ante uncertain, while the legal sanctions wrongdoers face if convicted—in addition to confiscation of illegal gains—are fixed, meaning the sanctions are not related to the realized profitability of the crime. The model shows, among other things, that ex post, wrongdoers whose realized criminal gains are low can be induced to spontaneously self-report to have their sanctions waived while giving up the (low) criminal gain. The contrary happens for wrongdoers whose realized criminal gains are high: they prefer not to report and face the risk of being caught and fully sanctioned to have the chance of keeping the high realized illegal gains. While the analysis is rich and elegant, and addresses several issues, the model is static and does not consider enforcement problems within a criminal team. So the results cannot be applied to cartels and similar forms of organized crime where firms/agents interact dynamically, face repeatedly both the choice of self-reporting and the risk of being discovered, and are subject to retaliation from competitors.

A more recent model that does take the dynamic features of cartels fully into account and obtains equilibrium reports, although only from colluding firms already under investigation, is Harrington (2005). It is a rich repeated oligopoly model that merges elements of several previous models and enriches them with a stochastically fluctuating continuous probability of successful prosecution after detection. The model is closest to Motta and Polo (2003), in that leniency is awarded to firms that report after their cartel has been detected and an investigation has been opened (Sections B of the current US leniency program and paragraphs 8b and 10 of the EU one) namely at the prosecution stage. Also the focus is mainly on the ex post desistance effects of such reports and of the corporate leniency program in general, under the assumption that convicted cartels do not start colluding again. The model follows Rey (2003) and Spagnolo (2004) in allowing a defecting cartel member to face conviction for past collusion if caught. It therefore obtains the same "protection from fines" effect discussed in section 7.3.2 (re-named as Defector Amnesty Effect), together with the trade-off discussed in section 7.3.1 between the lower expected fines due to leniency obtained by reporting after having been detected (named Cartel Amnesty Effect) and the higher probability of conviction caused by the additional information obtained from firms' cooperating under the leniency program. A novel feature of this model is that when along the equilibrium path a cartel is put under investigation, firms may rush *noncooperatively* to report information under a sufficiently generous leniency program (an effect named Race to the Courthouse Effect).[34]

Equilibrium reports during prosecution, after colluding firms have been detected and an investigation has been opened, take place in this model when the realization of the probability of a successful conviction (and therefore of expected sanctions after the investigation started) is high.[35] When the realization of the probability of successful prosecution is low, it is equilibrium for detected firms not to collaborate and report even at the prosecution stage.

The model confirms that it is optimal to restrict amnesty to the first reporting agent. So in most cases maximal leniency is optimal (in terms of desistance). In other cases there may be a slight increase in leniency that is harmful. In general, it is optimal to award leniency only when the additional information it produces is sufficiently valuable in terms of its impact on the probability that the investigation ends with a successful conviction, as explicitly prescribed by the 2002 EU leniency program.

How Much Information?

Asymmetrically Informed Co-Conspirators   For plea bargaining the first economic analysis of the role of asymmetries in self-reporting "team crimes" is the already mentioned one by Kobayashi (1992). In this model multiple defendants indicted for a jointly carried out organized crime face prosecution. The "most guilty" defendant, usually the ringleader, also has the most information about the criminal activity of the group, and therefore on that of other wrongdoers. The model shows that to maximize the probability of convicting the others and breaking apart the cartel, it is then optimal for the prosecutor to award the best deal exactly to the most culpable among the partner wrongdoers. Although the model is static and the focus is on postdetection prosecution, the intuition is rather strong and independent of dynamic incentive compatibility constraints. So the logic of the result is likely to extend to leniency and deterrence in dynamic frameworks, as suggested by Motta and Polo (2003, fn. 12). This policy implication is confirmed by Feess and Walz (2004b) who explore the differences between the US and EC leniency program, among other things relative to the different minimum amount of revealed information necessary to obtain leniency. Feess and Walz derive a result with a flavor similar to Kobayashi's one but with respect to leniency and deterrence: it finds that a more informed party that self reports providing more information should indeed be allowed to receive more generous benefits under the leniency programs than a less informed reporting party. This model is static as well, so it evaluates deterrence in terms of violation of the participation constraint rather than violation of the more stringent incentive/self-enforcing constraints that any cartel must satisfy. However, the intuition behind the result is again linked to the impact of different informational endowments on the information revelation game induced by leniency, and therefore it might apply as well for dynamic multi-agent crimes like cartels.

A good reason why the force highlighted by these two papers might lead to different policy prescriptions in a dynamic environment that take properly into account cartel enforcement issues is that agents could anticipate and react to this, distorting the allocation of cartel shares so that the leader is also the one who gains more from a stable cartel and therefore loses more by self-reporting. The solidity of these conjectures in an appropriately dynamic framework, however, awaits future research.

Minimum Information Requirements   DG Competition officials have have long suspected that some companies reporting a cartel under the new Leniency Notice had been strategically withholding information or made conflicting corporate statements. Because prosecuted applicants may face litigation and damages in this or other jurisdictions, they may perhaps be trying to obtain leniency and at the same time avoiding prosecution of the cartel.

Both the EU and US leniency programs explicitly condition immunity on open, complete, candid, and continued cooperation. The EU program even explicitly requires the reported information to be a substantial improvement in knowledge about the cartel for the DG Comp if the investigation started. These qualifications to the leniency policies can (and, in my view, should) be implemented strictly, since they are designed precisely to avoid strategic games of partial or distorted information revelation of the kind that took place in Italy when leniency programs were implemented against the Mafia and terrorism. Although these qualifications are there and, if properly implemented, should deter strategically limited or manipulated information reporting, DG Comp officials still appear to feel unable to fully prevent attempts to "game the system" by applying for leniency but reporting only a small part of available information or distorting it.

Harrington's (forthcoming) is the first model to analyze the critical issue of how valuable the reported information must be to make awarding amnesty worthwhile. The model allows for reports with different impacts on the likelihood of conviction. In most models discussed before, information reported is assumed to be "hard," that is, verifiable by third parties like judges, and enough in quantity and precision to lead to a conviction (i.e. it was implicitly assumed that "soft" information, like testimony not supported by documents, pictures, or other tangible incriminating elements, would not be sufficient to give immunity). In Harrington's model also information is "hard" and, if reported, leads to sure conviction, but the probability that an open investigation ends up with a conviction is a continuous stochastic variable. When the realization of this probability is high, further information from reporting firms has little value. With low realizations instead, the additional information from reporting firms is highly valuable. Exploiting this source of variation, Harrington shows that to maximize desistance, leniency should only be awarded if it increases sufficiently the likelihood that prosecution ends up with a successful conviction. Otherwise, the negative effect on desistance of the Cartel Amnesty Effect could dominate other effects, and then leniency during prosecution would decrease desistance. This result supports a strict implementation of the explicit qualifications in the leniency programs about the minimum value of information and the candid, *complete* cooperation from the beginning required to award leniency. It also suggests that—to avoid strategically limited or distorted reports, Antitrust Agencies must always deny leniency when it is learned that an applicant withheld some information, and even consider it an important aggravating factor when setting sanctions. It would be useful, of course, if future research could look at the ex ante general deterrence effects of these requirements.

Prices, Timing, Asymmetries, and Other Issues

Leniency and Prices   The deterrence effects of leniency programs of different generosities are modeled and numerically simulated in Chen and Harrington (2007). Chen and Harrington consider a dynamic homogeneous good Bertrand oligopoly model where the probability of being detected and convicted is endogenous and is a function of transaction price changes (with Bertrand competition the transaction price is the minimum among the quoted prices in each period). The sanctions include damages and are increasing in present and past realized profits. The model therefore brings together both the literature on leniency programs and on cartel pricing in the presence of an Antitrust Authority (e.g., Harrington 2004). Numerical simulations show that sufficiently generous leniency policies are beneficial in terms of direct deterrence, as they either deter cartel formation all together or reduce the optimal collusive price path of cartels that could not be deterred. This happens because they exacerbate the "protection from punishment" (or deviator amnesty) effect discussed in sections 7.3.2, 7.3.4, and 7.3.5. However, the simulations also show that intermediate levels of leniency (i.e., leniency that is not very generous) can end up stabilizing collusion, since it is then only used as a reaction after a defection takes place, as in the models discussed in section 7.3.3 with the consequence of contributing to punishing deviations and stabilizing the cartel.

Timing   More specific timing issues are considered in Motchenkova (2004), whose dynamic model consists of a continuous-time two-firm preemption game to try capture better the time dimension of the "rush to report" idea so often stressed by DOJ officials. This innovative approach shows, among other things, that limiting amnesty (the strongest fine reduction) only to the first firm applying for leniency is essential to induce such a "rush," and that less strict leniency programs that are also generous toward the firms reporting after the first can display negative side effects of the kind discussed in section 7.3.3. Although dynamic, to keep mathematical complexity under control, most of the analysis of this model does not take into account the incentive constraints that make cartels strategies self-enforcing and the novel kind of deterrence that leniency brings in through them. However, a final extension of the model does it, and the main results appear robust in this important respect.

Firm Size, Reputation, and Leniency   Within a repeated duopoly model most close to Motta and Polo (2003), Motchenkova and van der Laan (2005) show that colluding firms that are heterogeneous in size and degree of diversification will react differently to the introduction of leniency programs if antitrust convictions have substantial negative reputational effects in terms of customer losses. Larger, more diversified firms are likely to be active in more markets than those in which they are colluding. If the reputational loss from an antitrust conviction in a market is substantial and spills over to other markets in which they are active, larger firms active in many markets will suffer larger reputational losses from conviction that cannot be reduced by leniency. Thus larger firms may then be, ceteris paribus, less prone to report their cartel under a leniency program but also to enter a cartel in the first place. Motchenkova and van der Laan also derive implications about the optimal "strictness" of the leniency program. They confirm that a larger difference in benefits awarded to the first and second firm reporting increases cartel deterrence.[36]

Individual versus Corporate Leniency   The interaction between the individual leniency program and the corporate leniency program in the United States is the focus of a rich model by Festerling (2005a). Since the introduction of the corporate and then the individual leniency programs in the United States, there have been only applications to the former program. Aubert et al. (2005) already discussed complementarities between leniency offered to a firm and leniency plus rewards offered to its employees that report. Festerling, however, focuses on the case where managers fix prices contrary to their employers' wishes, and directly validates theoretically the DOJ's claim (see Hammond 2004) that the individual leniency program is effective despite no individual reports ever being observed. The main implied effect is that more corporate leniency applications result from threats of individual managers to self-report otherwise.[37] In this dynamic duopoly model, each firm is a hierarchy composed of a principal, firm owners, and an agent/manager with conflicting objectives regarding the legal consequences of antitrust convictions (e.g., exposure to private damage lawsuits, or limited ability to pay). The assumption is that the agent/manager chooses prices and whether to fix these prices with competitors without firm owners' consent. Nevertheless, when owners find out about a manager's misbehavior, they can report it to the Antitrust Authority. Corporate and individual sanctions and leniency policies give rise to a multistage revelation game where either the firm owner or the agent/manager can report information about a cartel. The individual leniency program turns out never to be used, but its presence does generate in certain parameter configurations additional corporate leniency applications. In other parameters configurations, however, the possibility that the manager will report will "force" the owner to accept the cartel, which is a negative effect related to those discussed in section 7.3.3.

Optimal Fines, Imprisonment, Leniency, and Whistleblowers Leniency and whistleblowers schemes suggest the need for different kinds of sanctions. Buccirossi and Spagnolo (2007a) consider how the theory and practice of antitrust sanctions is, or at least should be, influenced by the presence of these schemes. They show that earlier simulations of the deterrence effects of fines ignore the different type of deterrence that leniency programs bring about, and therefore grossly overstate the minimum fine likely to have deterrence effects. With schemes that reward whistleblowers, the minimum fine with deterrence effects is shown to fall to extremely low levels (below 10 percent of the optimal "Beckerian" fine estimated before). With *well-designed and correctly implemented* schemes of this type, the implication is that problems of limited ability to pay and "judgment proofness" may lose their bite, and therefore that imprisonment may not be necessary to obtain sufficient deterrence. This contrasts with arguments many present without considering the potential of well-designed and implemented leniency and whistleblowers' reward schemes.

7.4   Empirical and Experimental Evidence

There is limited empirical and experimental evidence available on the effects of leniency programs in antitrust. In the following I discuss the three experimental studies and the two econometric analyses of leniency programs I am aware of. I then contribute a little to the empirical debate by informally examining what can be learned at this very early stage from the "natural experiments" of the changes in the design of leniency programs that took place respectively in 1993 in the United States and in 2002 in the European Union. The section ends with a short review of the recent experience of the US False Claim Act in terms of rewarding whistleblowers that help discover frauds against the US federal government with large bounties financed by recovered fines and damages.

7.4.1   Laboratory Experiments
The experimental method is highly indicated for analyses of leniency programs, particularly in terms of their otherwise unobservable general deterrence effects. Apesteguja, Dufwemberg and Selten (2006) take the first elegant step in this direction. They develop a stylized theoretical framework that attempts to capture the main points made in the recent literature on the direct effects of leniency policies on cartel deterrence, and they undertake an interesting experimental analysis of these effects. The market game analyzed is a one-shot homogeneous good Bertrand oligopoly with a discrete demand function embedded in

four legal frameworks: in the Ideal treatment there is no antitrust law at all, and communication across competitors (forming cartels) is not possible; in the Standard treatment
convicted firms face fines equal to 10 percent of their revenue (and no fines at all if they
have no revenue that period) and no reduction if they report; in the Leniency treatment
firms that report a cartel they took part in receive a reduction in their fine; in the Bonus
treatment reporting firms receive a percentage of the fines paid by other firms as a reward.
Strategically equivalent collusive subgame perfect equilibria exist (in fact full folk theorems
hold) in both the Standard and Leniency treatments, sustained by the threat of reporting if
a defection takes place as in the models described in section 7.3.3. The experimental results
confirm that agents understand and use the threat of reporting to sustain collusion, more
in the Standard than in the Leniency type, and do not find that deterrence increases with
the introduction of rewards.

The extremely stylized framework used in this first study, while adding to its elegance,
opens a number of issues regarding the interpretation of its results. One issue is that the
oligopoly game is not repeated, and that the experiment allows for only one round of decisions, leaving agents no way to learn the game, while the differences among Standard, Leniency, and Bonus treatments are not that easy to understand. It is therefore possible that
some of the counterintuitive results, like that agents do not react to rewards, are driven by
subjects not fully grasping the situation, as it happened to most early experiments on public good contribution, also not sufficiently often repeated.

A second issue is the somewhat unrealistic assumption that fines equal 10 percent of
convicted firms' revenue in the relevant market and *zero* if these have in that period no
revenue in such market. Together with the assumption of homogeneous good Bertrand
competition, the low fines ensure that if a partner-cartelist "cheats" on the collusive agreement, reporting it is a "credible threat" (in the sense of section 7.3.3) already in the Standard treatment, even without leniency.[38] In the underlying model it is already implied that
because of the absence of leniency in the Standard treatment, antitrust law enforcement
has only the counterproductive function of enforcing collusion, which in this static framework would otherwise not be sustainable (as long as "cartel contracts" remain void). With
this starting point the best scenario would be no antitrust law enforcement at all: declaring
collusive agreements/contracts legally void may suffice to prevent any cartel formation,
but the question would then be why not get rid of antitrust laws (and related costly enforcement agencies, lawyers and experts) all together, rather than playing around with
counterproductive fines, leniency, and bonuses. In my reading, this first experiment
strongly suggests that subjects understand how to use self-reporting as a "threat" to enforce collusion in occasional interactions, as discussed in models reviewed in Section
7.3.3. But this experiment is based on such particular and crucial assumptions that it is
not easy to relate its results to the effectiveness of real world leniency or bonus schemes
against long-term, hard-core cartels.

A second experimental study by Hamaguchi and Kawagoe (2005) considers the effects
of cartel size and the restriction of amnesty to the first applicant on the likelihood that a

cartel is reported. The study finds the expected result that the larger is the cartel, the more effective is a given leniency program; and the less expected result that the effectiveness of a leniency program in inducing cartel members to self-report is not affected by whether only the first party or all parties that self-report are eligible to leniency. This experiment, however, does not capture the effect of leniency on cartel formation, meaning on general deterrence, since it first *forces* all the subjects to collude and then checks which cartels are reported.

A third recent experimental study that overcomes most drawbacks of the first two is that of Hinloopen and Soetevent (2005). In this study the underlying oligopoly game is repeated, communication is controlled for and allowed at different degrees; subjects are free to choose whether or not to agree on a collusive price. When leniency is introduced, cartel members can only report and obtain a fine discount before (knowing whether) an investigation is (will be) opened, and the first reporting party receives full amnesty, the second a 50 percent fine reduction, and the rest no fine reduction at all. This way the study addresses both direct general deterrence and desistance effects, but not the indirect effects linked to faster and cheaper prosecution nor rewards. The study uses Apesteguja et al.'s (2006) oligopoly model as a stage game of a repeated game with uncertain horizon, and adds to the legal framework a small fixed cost of reporting (1 point). This cost is present even when revenue is "zero" because competition is à la Bertrand and a cartel partner defected undercutting and stealing all customers from the others. Although small (an additional fixed cost/fine, limited to no-leniency treatments, would have further increased realism), this positive reporting cost partly captures the real world feature that—absent a leniency policy—if a cheated-upon cartel member reports, he is still subject to a fine. In this more realistic framework, incorporating the "protection from fines" (and in my view also part of the "increased riskiness") deterrence effect(s) discussed in section 7.3.2, this study confirms the potential of the positive ex ante deterrence effects linked to Sections A of the US Leniency Policy, restricted to the first "spontaneously" reporting party (the study does not consider rewards). It finds that with the introduction of a leniency program, on one hand, fewer cartels are established (i.e., a significant direct general ex ante deterrence effect of leniency programs restricted to firms reporting before an investigation is opened) and the life spans of cartels that were not deterred are reduced, but on the other hand, it also finds a constant high rate of "recidivism," in the sense that the same percentage of detected and convicted cartels starts colluding again after some time with and without leniency programs.

The lack of desistance effects implied by the recidivism is probably a consequence of the absence of higher fines or higher probability of detection for repeated offenders. That is to say, after a conviction, collusion is practically as attractive as before for the convicted cartel.

7.4.2 Econometric Studies

I am aware of only two econometric studies of the effects of leniency programs on cartels, both focusing on the 1996 version of the EU Leniency Program.

Brenner (2005) first analyzed econometrically the relationship between leniency applications, the size of actually imposed fines, and the duration of the investigation. Assuming that higher imposed fines signal, ceteris paribus, better information available to prosecution, Brenner finds that the program did help elicit information from cartel participants but not to the point of increasing deterrence (fines are higher in cases where some firms cooperated under the leniency program, but not much higher). No significant effects of leniency were found on the speed with which investigations were concluded nor on the hazard rate at which cartels break apart.

Arlman (2005) also analyzes econometrically the effects of the 1996 EC leniency program. In the 14 cases where leniency was awarded under the old program's section reserved to cases where the investigation was not yet open, Arlman finds 12 to have received a 100 percent fine reduction, one 90 percent, and one 80 percent. The remaining 140 firms received very partial leniency for collaborating during prosecution. The econometric analysis confirms that fines tend to be somewhat higher when leniency is used. But contrary to Brenner (2005), Arlman finds a significant effect of leniency on the speed with which a decision is taken by using the *maximal* amount of leniency awarded as explanatory variable rather than whether or not leniency was awarded. This result, contrasted with that of Brenner (2005), suggests that the speeding up of prosecution is linked to timely and substantial forms of reports under leniency, to which higher fine discounts are awarded, rather than to later and minor forms of cooperation more similar to plea bargains. Again contrary to Brenner (2005), Arlman finds that leniency does not provide prosecutors with better information. However, Arlman proxies available information with the number of words in the decision, and the interpretation of this variable in terms of better information is somewhat awkward.[39]

Both studies note that only five of the fourteen cases that obtained substantial leniency were really novel cases, the remaining being international cartels already detected and under prosecution (or already convicted) by the DOJ in the United States. This makes the judgment on the likely deterrence effects of the 1996 EU program rather conservative.[40] This is consistent with theoretical studies suggesting that to have a serious impact, a leniency program must be sufficiently transparent and generous; the 1996 EU program was criticized for leaving too much discretionality to the Commission. Since the incentive power of a leniency program directly depends on the severity of the sanctions a wrongdoer faces if caught because someone else reported, these studies confirm Buccirossi and Spagnolo's (2007a) evaluation that EU fines are likely to have been too low to have strong deterrence effects, even with current leniency programs.

7.4.3 Two Natural Experiments

As mentioned in section 7.2, the US and EU leniency programs changed over time. The main changes, in 1993 for the United States and 2002 for the European Union took place in discrete steps, and were not likely to have been fully anticipated by firms and lawyers.

So they can be regarded as kinds of "natural experiments." I also mentioned that according to informal communications of antitrust officials, the number of reports under the leniency program increased substantially after these changes. Here I explore these changes to obtain some preliminary and tentative indications on what features of a leniency program are likely to have a strong impact on the number of detected/reported cartels. However, these indications should be taken with due care, as they are based on nonverified aggregate information coming from informal communications and are drawn without controlling for other external changes that could have influenced firms' incentives to self-report. Further, as I explained in section 7.1.3, these indications have a rather far and uncertain connection with the likely deterrence effects of these programs, which is what ultimately matters.

The United States, 1993   Recall that in 1993 the US leniency program was changed dramatically, along the following dimensions:

1. *Increased generosity/transparency*   The DOJ committed to award *automatic* full amnesty for the first applicant, providing information at early stages and making clear in advance the benefits of cooperation to the amnesty-seeker.
2. *Extended coverage I*   Amnesty was made available to the first reporting party even after an investigation has been opened, provided that the DOJ did not already have evidence likely to result in a sustainable conviction.
3. *Extended coverage II*   Amnesty obtained by the first reporting firm—if it reports as a true corporate act—was extended to cover all its directors, officers, and employees that collaborate.
4. *Positive rewards*   Under the "Amnesty Plus" program, introduced a bit later, firms/managers convicted or under prosecution for one cartel for which they did not obtain immunity are invited to unveil other cartels they are or were involved with. If they reveal a new cartel, not only do they receive full amnesty with respect to this new cartel, they also get a substantial reduction in the sanctions/fines they would otherwise face for the first cartel, a net—though hidden—reward.

   Before the 1993 changes, the DOJ received about one application for leniency per year. After 1993, it started receiving up to three applications per month on average, an obviously significant (more than tenfold) increase. Of all these post-1993 applications, more than half fell under Section A of the Corporate Leniency Policy, meaning they came in before an investigation was open, when the DOJ had either no or very little information on the cartel (personal communications, Scott Hammond and Gregory Werden, DOJ).

Tentative Conclusion   It is not easy to distinguish among the relative contributions of the four changes listed above. All probably were relevant in determining the almost twentyfold increase in leniency applications after 1993. Yet clearly the more than half applications made before an investigation is opened should be linked to changes 1, 3, and/or 4.

The European Union, 2002   The main changes in the EU Leniency Program that took place in 2002 were as follows:

1. *Increase in generosity and transparency*   Prospective applicants to the EU leniency program can now expect *automatic* full amnesty if they are the first to report information sufficiently useful to prosecutors before an investigation is opened.
2. *Extended coverage*   Leniency is now also open to ringleaders, provided that they did not coerce other firms to join the cartel.

Both the 1996 and the 2002 EU leniency notices allowed firms to obtain partial fine-reductions when applying for leniency and reporting only after an investigation of their industry was already opened.

As mentioned earlier, in the first six years of the EU leniency program, between 1996 and 2002, only 16 applications for immunity were filed, of which just three led to the granting of immunity. In the three years following the 2002 changes, leniency applications and cases of immunity granted increased about tenfold: between February 2002 and June 2005 about 140 leniency applications were received, and about half of them fell under Sections 8a–9 of the Notice. That is, they took place before an investigation was opened, when DG Comp had little or no information on the cartel (personal communication, Bertus Van Barlingen, DG Comp).

Tentative Conclusion   The numbers above appear to indicate that the most crucial part of a leniency program may be the one reserved to the first party reporting when the cartels is not yet under an investigation, which should be sufficiently generous and automatic.

7.4.4   Examples of Rewards to Whistleblowers

Spagnolo (2000a, 2004), Kovacic (2001), Rey (2003), Buccirossi and Spagnolo (2001, 2006), and Aubert et al. (2006) suggest that a carefully designed and implemented policy that rewards the first firm or agent that blows the whistle and turns in former partners can greatly increase cartel deterrence and simultaneously reduce the cost of antitrust law enforcement. Some observers have been highly skeptical about this possibly, suggesting that it is likely to bring in more costs than benefits, particularly in terms of false information fabricated and reported in order to cash rewards. In this section I briefly review three recent real world experiences with practices that reward whistleblowers.

Amnesty Plus in the United States   In antitrust schemes that reward colluding firms/ individuals that report information are already used with some success. As mentioned before, the DOJ is actively using rewards in exchange for information on new cartels on which it did not have information through its Amnesty Plus program directed at cartel members detected and successfully prosecuted (or under prosecution) that did not qualify for fine reductions under the leniency program. Amnesty Plus offers them, in case they reveal a second cartel they are or were involved with but about which the DOJ was not aware, a substantial reduction in the fine due for the first cartel for which they were convicted, besides full amnesty for the new one reported. The additional reduction in the fine for the first cartel can then be regarded as a net reward. According to DOJ officials, this is the most successful part of the US leniency program, and it is directly responsible for the detection of most unknown cartels (Hammond 2005).

Korea's Rewards Scheme Korea has been a front-runner in the introduction of rewards to individual whistleblowers, even more than for leniency programs, introduced in 1996 together with the European Union. In 2002, Korea openly introduced cash rewards— not hidden as reduced fines—for whistleblowers reporting information on cartels. The rewards, aimed at reinforcing the leniency program, much as discussed in Aubert et al. (2006), were initially very low (the ceiling was about US$20,000) and, not surprisingly, did not generate reports. In November 2003, the ceiling was increased (to about US$100,000), and until May 2005, it generated five reports. In May 2005, the ceiling to rewards was raised tenfold (to approximately US$1 million), and we will soon know how will economic agents react. I believe these maximal rewards are still too small to encourage whistleblowing, given the economic and social costs whistleblowers tend to face, which are probably higher in a small country with tightly knit economic and social networks like Korea. The sociological literature on whistleblowers (e.g., see section 7.3.4) makes it clear that individuals that blow the whistle face very harsh sanctions from their former business partners, peers, and the business community in general. The exclusion from future business and social relations, which may include physical harassment, may last for the several years during which prosecution takes place. Because of this, when directed at individuals, it is evident that only programs with very high expected rewards, like the US False Claim Act, are likely to be effective in inducing informed parties to spontaneously blow the whistle.

The US False Claim Act The most famous and successful program that rewards whistle-blowers is probably the US False Claim Act against frauds to the federal government (the Sarbanes-Oxley Act appears to be catching up in fame but probably not in performance). It allows individual whistleblowers to file "qui tam" lawsuits against companies or individuals that committed fraud against the federal government, and to claim a fraction of fines and recovered funds.[41] In 1986 the False Claims Act was revised by Congress following reports of large-scale fraud against the government, especially by defense contractors. In order to give more incentives for whistleblowers to come forward and for private attorneys to use their own resources to investigate fraud, the False Claims Act was amended to include the provision of treble damages, mandating the defendant to pay a successful qui tam relator's his or her legal expenses, increasing the relator's share to 15 to 30 percent of total recovery, and protecting relators from retaliation.

Cases that can be filed as qui tam actions regard false claims that are either directly or indirectly presented to the government for "paying or approval." Along with a complaint the qui tam relator must file a "written disclosure of substantially all material evidence and information the person possesses." The DOJ can then choose whether or not it will join the whistleblower in the lawsuit. If the DOJ declines to join in a qui tam action, the relator has the right to investigate and prosecute the case. If the government does not join and the relator is successful in pursuing the case, the relator, generally, will receive a larger percentage of the award. The relator cannot receive the award if he or she is convicted for criminal infringements related to the fraud. So, to elicit information from parties involved in the fraud, immunity must be offered together with the possibility to file a qui tam lawsuit. Leniency and rewards are then complementary, much as discussed in Aubert et al. (2006).

The 1986 amendments to the False Claims Act have proved very effective in terms of generated government recovery. The scheme is now working in many other areas than defense, including prescription drug purchases, natural resource contracts, and low-income housing. Since 1987, the number of successful whistleblower lawsuits has increased continuously (see the instructive statistics at http://www.taf.org/statistics.htm). The highest level of recoveries yet was achieved in 2003, at about $1.5 billion, and was achieved at a comparatively low level of qui tam cases filed, 334, with total relators' awards of about $350 millions and *average* relator award above $1 million in over 20 percent of recoveries. This suggests that rewards for whistleblowers can reach very high levels without apparently causing strong negative side effects.[42]

Some observers have shown extreme skepticism about the proposal of offering rewards to whistleblowers in antitrust because of the possible increase in various types of legal enforcement costs these can bring about. As far as can be observed, the experience of the US False Claim Act does not support such extreme skepticism for well-designed and competently administered schemes.

7.5 Conclusions

In taking stock of the work discussed above, it can be safely concluded that a *well-designed* and *properly administered* leniency program appears to be an important and useful tool of antitrust law enforcement. It should be a tool that can *readily* be retrieved from the toolkit of an Antitrust Authority, independently of its budget. On the other hand, as in any incentive scheme, a poorly designed or administered leniency program can have serious counterproductive effects, some of which I have discussed here. In this concluding section, I will summarize the main features of what appears to be a well-designed leniency program in the light of current knowledge and discuss some issues that call for further research.

7.5.1 Characteristics of Well-designed Programs

Since the objective of a leniency program is deterring cartels by making them hard to sustain, a well-designed and implemented leniency program is one that makes the incentives of an individual (potential or real) cartel member as conflicting as possible with the interest of the cartel taken together. This means that a well-designed program must maximize incentives to betray the cartel by reporting important information to the Antitrust Authority, while at the same time limiting as much as possible the reduction in fines imposed on the whole cartel.

This objective can be achieved by maximizing the benefits an individual cartel member can receive from reporting under the leniency program, but restricting such maximal benefit to one and only one reporting party, the first comer. This extreme "winner take all" approach maximizes the conflict between individual and collective incentives in the cartel, and is likely to be the most crucial success factor in terms of deterrence.

Limited benefits in terms of partial reduced fines to parties reporting second may be useful to further increase the chances of winning the case, but they should be used only in extreme cases, when the information reported by the first reporting party, though useful, turns out insufficient to achieve a high probability of conviction by complementing it with all other ways to collect additional information that do not require further reductions in fines or other sanctions (dawn raids, records of further cartel activities obtained asking the first reporting party to go on "playing" the cartel member part, with a microphone and/or camera, etc.). The obvious reason is that although it may further facilitate prosecution, being lenient with more than one party tends to reduce both the total fines imposed on the cartel and the conflict between individual and collective incentives within the cartel, the two main sources of cartel deterrence. The aim of leniency programs is (at least should) not be making the job of prosecutors easier, but rather increasing cartel deterrence. So fine reductions for second or third reporting parties should be avoided unless it is clearly impossible to achieve conviction with the first report and more effort in traditional fact-finding strategies.

Well-designed and implemented leniency programs must be sufficiently generous with the first party that reports sufficiently important and possibly "hard" information. Otherwise, reporting can be used as a credible "threat" to enforce rather than to destabilize collusion. In this sense, protecting as much as possible the first and only the first reporting party from damage lawsuits is advisable, and I believe the US Congress should go all the way toward completely removing the possibility to obtain damages from a party that received amnesty under the leniency program. Conversely, requiring "restitution" of past collusive profits, as currently done by the US leniency program, is suboptimal from the deterrence perspective, and should be avoided.

Along the same lines, powering the leniency program with a well-designed and carefully implemented bounty scheme that rewards corporate and individual whistleblowing appears feasible and worthwhile, as it is likely to improve cartel deterrence strongly at rather low cost. No major problem emerges from the empirical observation of the (well-designed and managed) US experiences with fraud, nor from economic and legal analyses of whistleblowers. Poorly designed or implemented schemes, on the other hand, are likely to produce negative effects of various types, as is the case for any other law enforcement instrument or incentive scheme.

Leniency should also be offered to the first party reporting after an investigation has already been opened, but if sanctions are sufficiently robust and the leniency and reward program sufficiently generous, the maximal reward should be restricted only to applicants that spontaneously report before an investigation is opened, when the Antitrust Authority has not yet knowledge about the cartel. The reason is that leniency awarded to parties reporting after an investigation has been opened, meaning after the existence of the cartel has been detected, has a real cost in terms of reduced deterrence linked to the lower expected fines for a cartel it may generate (it increases the attractiveness of the "wait and see" strategy of reporting only if the cartel is detected), and should therefore be less generous than for spontaneous reports of nondetected cartels.

As for any incentive scheme, the design and implementation of leniency and whistleblower reward programs must be transparent and predictable. Every observer should be able to easily assess how attractive it is for a firm or individual participating to a cartel to betray his partners, and thereby lose confidence from the beginning that a cartel can be stable and lead to sustained high profits rather than to a costly antitrust conviction.

7.5.2 Open Issues for Further Research
Many issues in need of further research have been discussed in the previous sections. Here I would like to underline those I regard as most urgent.

As I already stressed, more empirical and experimental evidence would be extremely welcome on all the aspects of leniency and whistleblower programs discussed in this chapter. In particular, researchers and the relevant competition authorities could collaborate in producing reliable *databases* and making them generally available for analysis. There are some issues, however, where more theoretical work is needed besides empirical analysis.

First, of course, is the *international dimension* of these programs and of antitrust law enforcement in general. It is obvious that if only a subset of countries where an antitrust policy is seriously implemented (i.e., with serious sanctions against infringements) introduces a well-designed leniency program, the effect on international cartels will be hindered by the threat to be sanctioned in the latter countries when applying for leniency in the former. This is why in the discussions around the *Empagram* case the European Union argued that allowing foreign victims to file civil damage claims in US courts against infringements in the EU member states will reduce the effectiveness of the EU leniency program, as this cannot protect applicants from the threat of such claims abroad. Clearly, when only a subset of countries uses serious sanctions to deter cartels, it may fail to deter international cartels when their gains from collusion are very large and proportional to their world market. This is why many observers argued in the *Empagram* discussion that foreign customers should be allowed to file damage claims in US courts against international cartels in order to compensate for the lack of sanctions in these and other countries (e.g., Bush et al. 2004).

An international "one-stop shop" where the first applicant reporting sufficient information becomes eligible for amnesty in all countries where a leniency program is present and the cartel was active, accompanied by a full protection from any damage lawsuits in any country for this applicant, is likely to be the best solution to solve the coordination problems. However, more formal analyses are needed on this issue.[43]

A second important subject in need of further research in my view is *the type and quantity of reported information and the risks of strategic manipulation of these programs.* So far most, if not all, theoretical work has focused on exchanges of leniency against "hard information," that is, against information difficult to falsify and easy to use as proof of the infringement. The most recent tendency in practice appears instead to accept more and more purely "oral statements," in order to encourage reports from cartel members that are afraid of facilitating lawsuits for damages following the cartel conviction if they were to report more "concrete" information. The obvious problem is that oral statements are harder to verify, and can open the door to falsifications or distortions, as has happened sometimes in Italy with the leniency programs against Mafia. And as I mentioned in section 7.3.5, some antitrust officials have the feeling that some companies coming forward and reporting a cartel could have been strategically withholding or distorting information, even though leniency programs explicitly condition immunity on open, complete, candid, and continued cooperation.

Of course, there may have been problems in the implementation of these rules. Nevertheless, the issue of how much and what type of information provided at the first and later stages by a leniency applicant should be sufficient to award immunity or rewards remains a delicate and unsettled one. On one hand, with high-powered incentives like rewards for whistleblowers one would think that a substantial amount of "hard evidence" should be required to minimize the risk of facing plenty of "reward-hunters" reporting insignificant or false/fabricated information. On the other hand, given the paucity of resources devoted to antitrust policy and the large number of industries and procurements to monitor, even very little, very "soft," but truthful information can be extremely helpful in terms of cartel deterrence. The simple but correct indication that there is a cartel in a given industry can lead to a successful dawn raid and to detection and conviction of an unknown cartel. How to be sure then that the first reporting party said it all? It could have judged it profitable to leak as few morsels as necessary to obtain the first place in the leniency line, and concealed or destroyed remaining evidence to reduce the probability of a real conviction.

Finally, a third issue I believe somewhat under-researched is the interplay between these programs, the inevitable *mistakes* in courts' decisions and the *standards of proof* chosen by courts at various levels. Elsewhere I have argued that courts are likely to increase the standard of proof when facing information reported in exchange for a reward, but also that increasing sanctions against agents convicted for false reports is likely to have a deterrence effect on false reporting that may neutralize the first force. These effects depend in turn on the strength of the sanctions against each type of wrongdoing, and the outcome of this complex interaction may affect in subtle ways the optimal design of antitrust law enforcement policy against cartels.

Notes

Many thanks to Paolo Buccirossi, Philipp Festerling, Joe Harrington, Massimo Motta, Evgenia Motchenkova, and Gregory Werden, for comments on previous drafts; to Scott Hammond at the DOJ and Kirtikuram Metha and Bertus van Barlingen at DG Comp for patiently answering my insistent email requests; to Patrick Rey for our many stimulating discussion and his constant encouragement; and particularly, to my father Giuseppe Spagnolo, Professor of Criminal Law at the University of Bari and winner of the Falcone-Borsellino Prize for his work on the fight of organized crime. My many discussions with him greatly sharpened my understanding of the costs and benefits of leniency, as well as of many other important things. Financial support from the Swedish Competition Authority is gratefully aknowledged. The views expressed here are my own and do not necessarily coincide with the views of the institutions I work for.

1. Those policies differ substantially across countries—for example, in their generosity and in their treatment of firms reporting second. They are formalized and can be downloaded in many languages from the homepages of the antitrust authorities that introduced them.

2. Rey (2003) offers a thorough discussion of the importance of implementation and enforcement issues in antitrust, with particular focus on cartel deterrence and leniency program (see also Motta 2004). This survey complements Rey (2003) by offering an update on the specific and fast growing literature on leniency and whistleblower reward programs, and on the evidence that has started to become available.

3. The debate on antitrust has been followed at short distance by a smaller, parallel debate on the treatment of whistleblowers in financial crimes, sparkled by the recent episodes of corporate mismanagement, from Enron to Parmalat, and by the consequent introduction of the Sarbane-Oxley Act in the United States. See, for example, Zingales (2004) and Friebel and Guriev (2005).

4. Lande (1983) discusses first examples of cartels whose social benefits counterbalance their social costs. Stiglitz (1989) notes that investments in high product quality supply backed by reputation are worth only if there are supracompetitive profits to win in the future. Fershtman and Pakes (2000), Kranton (2003), and Calzolari and Spagnolo (2005) present dynamic models where reducing competition by fixing prices can be beneficial for both producers and consumers.

5. This section may sound obvious and can perhaps be skipped by readers with a robust industrial organization and/or dynamic games background, or that have read Stigler (1964) with due care. The section is, however, crucial for other readers. My experience is that many economists (some top journal referees) brilliant in law and economics but without industrial organization background have a hard time understanding the crucial peculiarities of organized crime like cartels. So I take here the chance to discuss cartels as simply and clearly as possible.

6. This literature stems from Becker's (1968) seminal contribution. Polisnky and Shavell (2000) offer an elegant encompassing survey of this literature. See also Garoupa (1997), who, however, focuses mostly on why fines should not always be maximal.

7. This is why, as cartels, most organized crime *must* take the form of—or be conducted within—long-term dynamic criminal *relationships*. As we know since Schelling (1960) and Friedman (1971), only in a dynamic environment can there be reactions and threats, credible punishment against partners that defect, accounted for. See Polo (1995) for an economic analysis of internal cohesiveness and competition problems for criminal organizations.

8. In addition to these two constraints, there are a number of other conditions that must also be simultaneously satisfied for a cartel to be viable, including that the cartel is able to prevent entry, achieve coordination, and establish internal trust (in section 7.3.2, I discuss how leniency can deter cartels by reducing internal trust, increasing the perceived riskiness of such illegal collaboration).

9. Simulations in Buccirossi and Spagnolo (2007a) show that the minimal expected fines with deterrence effects in this case can be less that 10 percent the minimal "Beckerian" expected fines that violate the participation constraint.

10. The mot *Divide et impera*, of uncertain but ancient origin, describes Julius Cesar and other commanders' strategy of breaking coalitions of enemies by striking advantageous deals with one or few of them. Nazi occupants used rewards for "snitches" or a lenient treatment for them and their relatives to fight resistance in France and Italy. More recently Saddam Hussein and his sons and some Al Quaeda terrorists have been located by the same system.

11. The fact that leniency/information exchanges at the prosecution stage—namely after wrongdoers have been discovered—have been "standard practice" for centuries is also witnessed by how natural it appeared to Albert Tucker in 1950 to cast in terms of a Prisoner's Dilemma story the strategic situation studied by Merrill Flood and Melvin Dresher at the Rand Corporation in order to facilitate its understanding by a Stanford psychology class.

12. The misuse occurs when prosecutors and courts rely exclusively on a testimony obtained in exchange for leniency. A useful introduction to the drawbacks of this practice is at http://www.pbs.org/wgbh/pages/frontline/shows/snitch/. Throughout the chapter I will assume that the party applying for leniency must report "hard information" against his partners to obtain it, and that his testimony is only admitted when corroborated by "hard" pieces of evidence.

13. Schemes that reward whistleblowers with part of recovered funds have been used to reduce the cost of law enforcement since thirteen-century England. Bounties for "wanted" criminals have been common in many different countries and historical periods, and often did not distinguish between whether it was a gang member or an innocent witness (or a bounty killer) to turn in the wanted.

14. Obvious mistakes in the implementation of these programs—particularly in terms of letting applicants reveal information selectively, piece after piece, and in relying too much on them as witness rather than as sources of "hard information"—have led in Italy to their practical downfall despite their demonstrated effectiveness in the fight against Mafia and terrorism.

15. Prosecution costs include, among other things, the budgets of involved courts and agencies plus the cost of distortionary taxation required to finance them; the costs of prosecution/litigation not included in those budgets, like the cost of defence lawyers, expert witnesses, and the time loss of their clients; the social costs of type I errors in convictions of innocents; and the costs of imposing sanctions on (rightly or wrongly) convicted parties.

16. Again I am exaggerating a bit to clarify. Of course, there are other reasons to prosecute criminals, including pursuing "justice," which may directly produce utility in a society of justice-lovers, and offering compensation to victims. But the main motive is deterrence, and in case of cartels this objective appears even more critical.

17. Perhaps the strongest indication that US antitrust policy is having deterrence effects (and that the EU policy is not) is the observation that some recently uncovered international cartels chose to collude and meet in all markets around the world but the US market (see Hammond 2004).

18. This is a conclusion of the only two econometric analyses of leniency programs I am aware of, for the European Union between 1996 and 2002.

19. One must be careful to separate really spontaneous reports by members of yet undetected cartels from (a) reports when the DOJ is suspicious and may be about to start an investigation of the industry, e.g. because a cartel in that industry has been detected elsewhere, and (b) reports about a new cartel obtained by members of a detected cartel under prosecution asked whether they have anything else to report (the "omnibus question"). It would be useful if the DOJ and other Antitrust Authorities could help out by providing more precise data on this important issue.

20. I thank Gregory Werden for drawing my attention on this point. It would be nice to see these trade-offs analyzed formally.

21. Of course, the DOJ does have informal instruments to be lenient with a second cartel participant if it wishes to. As will become clear in the remainder of this chapter, I am in favor of the US stricter winner-take-all approach, with generous leniency and rewards but awarded only to the first applicant and only if enough information is reported (or collected ex post with a secret microphone/camera). Not least, reducing sanctions to several (possibly all) cartel members—as is possible in the European Union—besides reducing incentives to report first (wait and report only if somebody else does it first may become the optimal strategy for cartel members that would otherwise rush to report hoping not to arrive second or third with a winner-take-all program) tends to reduce total fines paid by the cartel. Both effects can substantially reduce deterrence, the very first objective of

antitrust law, and if the positive effect in terms of facilitating prosecution is not really dramatic (it may just consist in a easier life for the Antitrust Authorities' officials), such generosity can end up increasing prosecution costs (through the increased number of prosecuted cartels and staff required) while reducing general deterrence (by reducing expected sanctions), the worst that can happen.

22. The US program states that leniency can be awarded if either A) no investigation has been opened and "*1. At the time the corporation comes forward to report the illegal activity, the Division has not received information about the illegal activity being reported from any other source;*" or, independent of whether an investigation was opened, B) "*1. The corporation is the first one to come forward and qualify for leniency with respect to the illegal activity being reported;*" and "*2. The Division, at the time the corporation comes in, does not yet have evidence against the company that is likely to result in a sustainable conviction.*" Moreover the US program requires that "*the corporation reports the wrongdoing with candor and completeness and provides full, continuing and complete cooperation to the Division throughout the investigation.*" If it is discovered that some information was withheld by the reporting firm, leniency will not be awarded and the behavior of the reporting firm will be considered an aggravating factor (as in "Penalty Plus"; see Hammond 2004).

23. Recent experimental work has shown how agents often behave far from how a rational homo economicus might be expected to behave (e.g., see Camerer 2003). But if there is one field in law enforcement where rational choice models are likely to be useful to capture important features of the problem, this is the analysis of corporate crime, and in particular, of cartel deterrence. The pricing decision is typically a thought-over decision taken by skilled, strategic, forward-looking managers. While these agents can also make mistakes, they are obviously much less likely to make them regularly than less trained and calculating individuals.

24. The (1999) working paper version of this path-breaking paper is sufficiently different from the published version to be also worth reading.

25. This last conclusion is also due to the model's assumption that antitrust enforcement costs are exogenously given, do not enter social welfare, and cannot be traded off against higher fines or more effective leniency policies.

26. Allowing more agents to obtain leniency reduces deterrence by reducing the number of wrongdoers that must pay the full fine, without having any countervailing positive effects on detection and deterrence.

27. See Spagnolo (2000a, 2004) and Buccirossi and Spagnolo (2007a). The optimal policy, of course, also maximizes fines. High fines are now valuable not only because they reduce the expected value of collusive criminal relations, as in Becker (1968) but also because they allow offers of higher rewards to agents that self-report by both financing the reward and preventing agents to exploit it (again, only if the reward is larger than the fines it generates, agents could exploit the scheme by taking turns to report).

28. The reason is close to the logic of leniency: if agents know that they will not be fined for their past wrongdoing when they defect from the collusive agreement, they are more prone to do so, and this makes such agreements harder to sustain. The result is related to that of Cyrenne (1999). He finds that if Antitrust Authorities use price wars as signals of the presence of a cartel, they can end up stabilizing cartels *by increasing the strength of the punishment phases* (see also Harrington 2004). Relatedly, but differently, Spagnolo (2004) shows that by prosecuting firms that unilaterally defected from a cartel, Antitrust Authorities can end up stabilizing cartels *by reducing firms' expected gains from unilaterally defecting.*

29. A model by Fees and Walzl (2004a) also highlights the potential direct deterrence effects of a leniency program on multi-agent forms of crime like cartels. However, this model is static, and in the analysis the ability of the criminal team to cooperate/collude under different law enforcement regimes is assumed rather than derived. It is not clear therefore how its results can be interpreted relative to intrinsically dynamic and self-enforcing illegal relationships like cartels and most other forms of organized crime.

30. However, as mentioned before, with full immunity or with sufficiently generous fine reductions for the first comer the defection strategy of undercutting the cartel *and* reporting weakly dominates those of simply undercutting or reporting. It is unclear whether this result would survive taking the optimal defection into account.

31. The requirement that the reward paid to the first leniency applicant should not be larger than the sum of the fines paid by convicted cartel members is not an ad hoc budget-balancing constraint, as some have claimed. It is rather an endogenous constraint without which any reward system is doomed to fail in any real world situation akin to the model: absent other sanctions than fines, if the reward is larger than the sum of the fines it generates, there is the obvious risk that plenty of people will start building up fake or real cartels just in order to immediately denounce them, cash the reward, pay the fines, and keep and share the positive difference between the two.

32. According to Alford (2002), about half of all whistleblowers get fired, and many of them lose their homes, and then their families too.

33. See also Arlen's (1995) comment in the same volume. A more recent law and economics analysis of this issue is Depoorter and De Mot (2004); it formalizes a subset of the issues discussed by Howse and Daniels (1995).

34. Such rushes do not take place in Motta and Polo (2003) because in that model firms choose *cooperatively* whether or not to report when an investigation is opened. The possibility of such *noncooperative* rushes to report is the source of cartel deterrence in the models discussed in section 7.3.2 and 7.3.4, but such possibility never realizes along the equilibrium path because agents forecast it perfectly and in that case they do not start colluding in the first place.

35. This model therefore produces equilibrium reports from cartels already under an investigation, as in Motta and Polo (2003), but has no implications regarding equilibrium reports before detection, the focus of Spagnolo (2000a, 2004), Ellis and Wilson (2001), and Aubert et al. (2004).

36. The model is dynamic and evaluates the deterrence effects of leniency programs taking into account self-enforcement constraints. It seems to focus, however, on a specific set of strategies (Enter cartel and self-report; Enter cartel and not self-report; Not enter the cartel in the first place), and not to considering optimal defections for cartel members, which at the interim stage appears again to be Undercut the cartel *and* Self-report. It would be useful if the authors could extend their work to encompass optimal defections at all stages, or if future work would verify whether and how their results change with optimal defections.

37. In Hammond's words: "The real value and measure of the Individual Leniency Program is not in the number of individual applications we receive, but in the number of corporate applications it generates. It works because it acts as a watchdog to ensure that companies report the conduct themselves." (Hammond 2004, p. 12). On this issue, see also Mullin and Snyder (2005) and Buccirossi and Spagnolo (2007b).

38. The 10 percent of revenue rule was inspired by the EU cap of 10 percent of yearly revenue on antitrust fines. However, EU fines would never be zero in the absence of a leniency program. The 10 percent revenue cap for EU fines is relative to firms' overall yearly turnover in all lines of business and geographical markets, while the EU basic, minimum fine for horizontal cartels, independent of revenue, was for a long time 20 million euros. Moreover respect for the collusive price is considered *an aggravating factor* that increases the minimum fine. It is not easy to envisage a market where, if a firm undercuts the cartel, other firms in the cartel have zero revenue for one full year. Absent leniency policies, a firm with positive revenue that reports a cartel would be subject to a positive fine. The multiplicity of equilibria in Standard would then disappear as after a defection reporting is dominated by not doing it (and avoiding the fine), the outcome of Standard and Ideal would then most likely be similar and Leniency would fare much worse than how depicted, like predicted by models discussed in section 7.3.3.

39. It is at least debatable whether one needs more or fewer words to support a decision when better information is available. An inverse relation, more concise decisions when the evidence is very strong, appears at least as plausible as the one postulated in the study.

40. However, this does not automatically imply that the European Union was wrong in awarding full amnesty to overseas cartel members seeking amnesty in the European Union. In the absence of an international one-stop-shop for leniency, when one international cartel member first applies for leniency in the United States, and then later on in the European Union, the optimal thing to do for the European Union is to also award full leniency, even if it already had information on that cartel from the DOJ's investigation. Such a policy tends to encourage self-reporting in the United States, and therefore facilitates the detection of international cartels in general.

41. The words "qui tam" come from *Qui tam pro domino rege quam pro se ipso*, which means "he who brings an action on behalf of the king, as well as for himself." The organized use of whistleblowers in law enforcement in terms of qui tam seems to originate in thirteenth-century England, when, because of a lack of an organized police force, English common law adopted various qui tam provisions in order to enforce the king's laws. To make such actions attractive, a bounty was paid to the private party who enforced the law. The founders of the United States followed the English example and included qui tam provisions into most of the penal statutes enacted by the Continental Congress, America's first ruling body. On March 2, 1863, the False Claims Act, also known as the "Lincoln law," was passed by Congress at the urging of President Abraham Lincoln, following the report of widespread contractor fraud at the expenses of the Union Army. The law applied not only to military but to all government contractors.

42. In general, recoveries in cases declined by the DOJ fluctuate much more than those accepted and are also much lower, which implies that sustaining and winning a case without the government's support is very hard, and/or the screening activity of the DOJ is precise in selecting most important cases.

43. See Festerling (2005b) for a first step in this direction.

References

Abreu, D. 1986. Extremal equilibria of oligopolistic supergames. *Journal of Economic Theory* 39(1): 191–225.

Abreu, D. 1988. On the theory of infinitely repeated games with discounting. *Econometrica* 56: 383–96.

Acemoglu, D. 1995. Career concerns and cover-ups: A Dynamic Model of Collusion. Unpublished manuscript. Department of Economics. MIT.

Alexander, C., and D. Reiffen. 2004. Regret without detection: How leniency can deter corporate and organizational offences. Unpublished manuscript. US Securities and Exchange Commission.

Alford, F. C. 2002. *Whistleblowers: Broken Lives and Organizational Power.* Ithaca: Cornell University Press.

Apesteguia, J., M. Duwfemberg, and R. Selten. 2004. Blowing the whistle. Mimeo. Universities of Arizona, Bonn, and Navarra.

Aubert, C., W. Kovacic, and P. Rey. 2006. The impact of leniency programs on cartels. *International Journal of Industrial Organization* 24: 1241–66.

Aumann, R. J., and L. Shapley. 1976. Long term competition: A game theoretic analysis. Unpublished manuscript. Stanford University.

Beccaria, C. 1763. *Dei Delitti e Delle Pene.* Available at ⟨http://www.filosofico.net/index024.htm⟩; available in English as *On Crimes and Punishments and Other Writings*, edited by Richard Bellamy, New York: Cambridge University Press, 1995.

Becker, G. 1968. Crime and punishment: An economic approach. *Journal of Political Economy* 76(2): 169–217.

Berentsen, A., E. Bruegger, and S. Loertscher. 2005. On cheating and whistleblowing. Economics Department, University of Basel.

Bush, D., J. Connor, J. Hlynn, S. Ghosh, W. Grimes, J. Harrington, N. Hawker, R. Lande, W. Shepherd, and S. Semeraro. 2004. How to block cartel formation and price-fixing. AEI Brookings Joint Center Brief *amicus curiae* 04-01, April.

Brenner, S. 2005. An empirical study of the European corporate leniency program. Unpublished manuscrtipt. University of Berlin.

Brisset, K., and T. Lionel. 2004. Leniency program: A new tool in competition policy to deter cartel activity in procurement auctions. *European Journal of Law and Economics* 17(1): 5–19.

Buccirossi, P., and G. Spagnolo. 2001. Leniency programs and illegal exchange: How (not) to fight corruption. Working Paper in Economics and Finance 451. Stockholm School of Economics. Available at ⟨www.hhs.se and www.ssrn.com⟩.

Buccirossi, P., and G. Spagnolo. 2006. Leniency programs and illegal transactions. *Journal of Public Economics* 90(6–7): 1281–97.

Buccirossi, P., G. Palumbo, and G. Spagnolo. 2005. Whistleblowers and financial fraud. Manuscript in progress. Lear, Bank of Italy, and Stockholm School of Economics.

Buccirossi, P., and G. Spagnolo. 2007a. Optimal fines in the era of whistleblowers: Should price fixers still go to prison? In V. Goshal, and J. Stennek, eds., *The Political Economy of Antitrust.* Amsterdam: Elsevier, ch. 4.

Buccirossi, P., and G. Spagnolo. 2007b. Corporate governance and collusive behhavior. In W. D. Collins, ed., *Issues in Competition Law and Policy.* Chicago: American Bar Association, Antitrust Section.

Calzolari, G., and G. Spagnolo. 2005. Reputation and collusion in procurement. Unpublished manuscript. University of Bologna and Stockholm School of Economics.

Cyrenne, P. 1999. On antitrust enforcement and the deterrence of collusive behavior. *Review of Industrial Organization* 14: 257–72.

Chen, J., and J. E. Harrington Jr. 2007. The impact of the cartel price path. In V. Ghosal and J. Stennek, eds., *The Political Economy of Antitrust.* Amsterdam: Elsevier.

Clarke, J. L., and S. J. Evenett. 2003. The deterrent effects of national anticartellaws: Evidence from the international vitamins cartel. *Antitrust Bulletin* 48(3): 689.

Cooter, D. R., and N. Garoupa. 2000. The virtuous circle of distrust: A mechanism to deter bribes and other cooperative crimes. *Berkeley Law and Economics Working Papers*, article 13, vol. 2000 (Fall 2001).

Connor, J. 2003. Private international cartels: Effectiveness, welfare, and anticartel enforcement. Purdue Agricultural Economics working paper 03-12. Available at ⟨www.ssrn.com⟩.

Depoorter, B., and J. De Mot. 2004. Whistle blowing. Berkeley Law and Economics working paper 13, vol. 2004.

Dworkin, T. M., and J. P. Near. 1997. A better statutory approach to whistleblowing. *Business Ethics Quarterly* 7: 1–16.

Ellis, C., and W. Wilson. 2001. Cartels, price-fixing, and corporate leniency policy: What doesn't kill us makes us stronger. Unpublished manuscript. University of Oregon.

Feess, E., and M. Walzl. 2004a. Self-reporting in optimal law enforcement when there are criminal teams. *Economica* 71: 333–48.

Feess, E., and M. Walzl. 2004b. An analysis of corporate leniency programs and lessons to learn for US and EU policies. Unpublished manuscript. Department of Economics, University of Aachen.

Festerling, P. 2005a. Cartel prosecution and leniency programs: Corporate versus individual leniency. Working paper 2005-20. Aarhus University. Available at ⟨ftp://ftp.econ.au.dk/afn/wp/05/⟩.

Festerling, P. 2005b. International cartel prosecution. Unpublished manuscript. Aarhus University.

Felli, L. 1996. Preventing collusion through discretion. Working paper. London School of Economics.

Fershtman, C., and A. Pakes. 2000. A dynamic game with collusion and price wars. *RAND Journal of Economics* 31(2): 207–36.

Fiorentini, G., and S. Pelzman, eds. 1995. *The Economics of Organized Crime*. Cambridge: Cambridge University Press.

Friebel, G., and S. Guriev. 2005. Earnings manipulation and internal incentives. CEPR discussion paper 4861.

Friedman, J. 1971. A noncooperative equilibrium for supergames. *Review of Economic Studies* 38(113): 1–12.

Gambetta, D., and P. Reuter. 1995. Conspiracy among the many: The mafia in legitimate industries. In G. Fiorentini and S. Peltzman, eds., *The Economics of Organised Crime*. Cambridge: Cambridge University Press.

Glazer, M. P., and P. M. Glazer. 1991. *The Whistleblowers: Exposing Corruption in Government and Industry*, New York: Basic Books.

Grossman, G. M., and M. L. Katz. 1983. Plea bargaining and social welfare. *American Economic Review* 73: 749–57.

Hamaguchi, Y., and T. Kawagoe. 2005. An experimental study of leniency programs. RIETI discussion paper series 05-E-003.

Hammond, S. D. 2005. An overview of recent developments. In *The Antitrust Division's Criminal Enforcement Program*. Available at ⟨http://www.usdoj.gov⟩.

Hammond, S. D. 2004. Cornerstones of an effective leniency program. US Department of Justice. Available at ⟨http://www.usdoj.gov/⟩.

Hammond, S. D. 2000. Detecting and deterring cartel activity through an effective leniency program. Available at ⟨http://www.usdoj.gov⟩.

Hammond, S. D. 2001. When calculating the costs and benefits of applying for corporate amnesty, how do you put a price tag on an individual freedom? Available at ⟨http://www.usdoj.gov⟩.

Hammond, S. D. 2000. Fighting cartels—Why and how? Lessons common to detecting and deterring cartel activity. Available at ⟨http://www.usdoj.gov⟩.

Harrington, J., Jr. 2004. Cartel pricing dynamics in the presence of an antitrust authority. *RAND Journal of Economics* 35(4): 651–73.

Harrington, J., Jr. 2005. Optimal corporate leniency programs. *Journal of Industrial Economics*, forthcoming.

Harsanyi, J., and R. Selten. 1998. *A General Theory of Equilibrium Selection in Games*. Cambridge: MIT Press.

Healy, P. H., and G. P. Krishna. 2003. The fall of Enron. *Journal of Economic Perspective* 17(2): 3–26.

Heyes, A. G. 2004. Whistleblowers and the regulation of environmental risk. Unpublished manuscript. Royal Holloway, University of London.

Hinloopen, J. 2003. An economic analysis of leniency programs in antitrust law. *De Economist* 151(4): 415–32.

Hinloopen, J., and A. Soetevent. 2005. An experimental investigation of the effects of leniency programs for antitrust enforcement. Unpublished manuscript. University of Amsterdam and ENCORE.

Howse, R. L., and R. Daniels. 1995. Rewarding whistleblowers: Costs and benefits of an incentive-based compliance strategy. In R. Daniels and R. Morck, eds., *Corporate Decisionmaking in Canada.* Calgary: University of Calgary Press, 1995.

Innes, R. 1999. Remediation and self-reporting in optimal law enforcement. *Journal of Public Economics* 72(3): 379–93.

Innes, R. 1999. Self-policing and optimal law enforcement when violator remediation is valuable. *Journal of Political Economy* 107(6): 1305–25.

Kaplow, L., and S. Shavell. 1994. Optimal law enforcement with self-reporting of behavior. *Journal of Political Economy* 102(3): 583–606.

Kobayashi, B. 1992. Deterrence with multiple defendants: An explanation for "unfair" plea bargains. *RAND Journal of Economics* 23(4): 507–17.

Kobayashi, B. 2004. Antitrust, agency and amnesty: An economic analysis of the criminal enforcement of the antitrust laws against corporations. Unpublished manuscript. George Mason University School of Law.

Koffman, F., and J. Lawaree. 1996. A prisoner's dilemma model of collusion deterrence. *Journal of Public Economics* 59: 117–36.

Kornhauser, L. A., and R. L. Revesz. 1994. Multidefendant settlements under joint and several liability: The problem of insolvency. *Journal of Legal Studies* 23.

Kovacic, W. 2001. Private monitoring and antitrust enforcement: Paying informants to reveal cartels. *George Washington Law Review* 69: 766–97.

Kranton, R. E. 2003. Competition and the incentive to produce high quality. *Economica* 70: 385–404.

Landes, W. M. 1983. Optimal sanctions for antitrust violations. *University of Chicago Law Review* 50(2): 652–78.

Leppamaki, M. 1997. An economic theory of collusion, blackmail and whistle-blowing in organisations. PhD thesis. London School of Economics.

Malik, A. 1993. Self-reporting and the design of policies for regulating stochastic pollution. *Journal of Environmental Economics and Management* 24(3): 241–57.

Motchenkova, E. 2004. Effects of leniency programs on cartel stability. Center discussion paper 2004-98. Tilburg University. Available at ⟨www.ssrn.com⟩.

Motchenkova, E., and R. van der Laan. 2005. Stricness of leniency programs and cartels of asymmetric firms. Center discussion paper 2005-74. Tilburg University. Available at ⟨www.ssrn.com⟩.

Motta, M., and M. Polo. 1999. Leniency programs and cartel prosecution. Working paper. European University Institute.

Motta, M., and M. Polo. 2003. Leniency programs and cartel prosecution. *International Journal of Industrial Organization* 21(3): 347–79.

Motta, M. 2004. *Competition Policy: Theory and Practice.* Cambridge: Cambridge University Press.

Mullin, W. P., and C. M. Snyder. 2005. Targeting employees for corporate crime and forbidding their indemnification. Working paper. George Washington University. Available at ⟨www.ssrn.com⟩.

OECD. 2002. *Fighting Hard Core Cartels: Harm, Effective Sanctions and Leniency Programmes.* Paris.

OECD. 2003. *Hard Core Cartels: Recent Progress and Challenges Ahead.* Paris.

OECD. 2005. *Cartels: Sanctions against Individuals.* DAF/COMP39.

Polinsky, M., and S. Shavell. 2000. The economic theory of public enforcement of law. *Journal of Economic Literature* 38: 45–76.

Polo, M. 1995. Internal cohesion and competition among criminal organisations. In G. Fiorentini and S. Peltzman, eds., *The Economics of Organised Crime.* Cambridge: Cambridge University Press.

Reinganum, J. F. 1988. Plea bargaining and prosecutorial discretion. *American Economic Review* 78(4): 713–28.

Rey, P. 2003. Towards a theory of competition policy. Ch. 3. In M. Dewatripont, L. P. Hansen, and S. J. Turnovsky, eds., *Advances in Economics and Econometrics: Theory and Applications, Eight World Congress.* Cambridge: Cambridge University Press.

Schelling, T. 1960. *The Strategy of Conflict.* Cambridge: Harvard University Press.

Selten, R. 1965. Spieltheoretische Behandlung eines Oligopolmodells mit Nachfragentragheit. *Zeitschrift fur die gesamte Staatswissenschaft* 12: 201–324.

Spagnolo, G. 2000. Optimal leniency programs. FEEM Nota di Lavoro 42.00, Fondazione ENI "Enrico Mattei," Milan. Available at ⟨http://www.ssrn.com and http://www.feem.it/⟩.

Spagnolo, G. 2000. Self-defeating antitrust laws: How leniency programs solve Bertrand's paradox and enforce collusion in auctions. FEEM Nota di Lavoro 52.00, Fondazione ENI "Enrico Mattei," Milan. Available at ⟨http://www.ssrn.com and http://www.feem.it/⟩.

Spagnolo, G. 2004. Divide et impera: Optimal leniency programs. CEPR discussion paper 4840. Available at ⟨www.cepr.org and www.ssrn.com⟩.

Spagnolo, G. 2005. Cartels criminalization and their internal organization. In M. Schinkel, K. J. Cseres and F. O. W. Vogelaar, eds., *Remedies and Sanctions in Competition Policy: Economic and Legal Implications of the Tendency to Criminalize Antitrust Enforcement in the EU Member States.* London: Edwar Elgar.

Spratling, G. R. 1998. The corporate leniency policy: Answers to recurring questions. Presented at ABA Meeting, Antitrust Section. Available at ⟨http://www.usdoj.gov/atr/public/speeches/1626.htm⟩.

Spratling, G. R. 1999. Making companies an offer they shoudn't refuse. Available at ⟨http://www.usdoj.gov/atr/public/speeches/2247.htm⟩.

Stigler, G. J. 1964. A theory of oligopoly. *Journal of Political Economy* 72(1): 44–61.

Stiglitz, J. 1989. Imperfect information in the product market. In R. Schmalensee and R. Willig, eds., *Handbook of Industrial Organization,* vol. 1. Amsterdam: Elsevier, pp. 771–847.

Schroeder, D., and H. Silke. 2005. Requests for leniency in the EU: Experience and legal puzzles. In M. Schinkel, K. J. Cseres, and F. O. W. Vogelaar, eds., *Remedies and Sanctions in Competition Policy: Economic and Legal Implications of the Tendency to Criminalize antitrust Enforcement in the EU Member States.* London: Edwar Elgar.

Tokar, S. 2000. Whistleblowing and corporate crime. Unpublished manuscript. European University Institute.

Van Barlingen, B. 2003. The European Comission's leniency notice after one year of operation. *Competition Policy Newsletter* 2: 16–21.

Werden, G. J., and M. J. Simon. 1987. Why price fixers should go to prison. *Antitrust Bulletin* 32: 917–37.

Zingales, L. 2004. Want to stop corporate fraud? Pay off those whistle-blowers. *Washington Post* (Outlook Section), January 19, p. B2.

8 Facilitating Practices

Paolo Buccirossi

The economic and legal antitrust literature qualifies facilitating practices as actions that foster collusion (Hovenkamp 1994, ch. 4; Church and Ware 2000 ch. 10). However, the exact scope of this definition depends on what we mean by "collusion." Unfortunately, this expression is often employed with different meanings by lawyers and economists, and even within the economic profession it is not always adopted consistently.

In the legal literature, collusion mainly refers to a situation where firms coordinate their strategies through some form of concerted activity with the aim to restrict competition. Although a formal agreement is not strictly necessary, collusion requires some "meeting of the minds," "mutual assent," or "concerted practice." In short, collusion identifies one of the conducts generally prohibited by antitrust law (Article 81 of the EC Treaty, Section 1 of the Sherman Act).

The economic notion of collusion contrasts with the legal notion, as it refers directly to the market outcome. Collusion occurs if prices are above those that would result with competitive conditions.[1] This definition poses the problem of identifying the competitive benchmark. To this end, the outcome of a perfectly competitive market, marginal cost pricing, is inadequate, as it would probably lead to an overinclusive definition of collusion. Hence it is now prevalent in the economic literature to equate the competitive benchmark to the outcome of a static game (Phlipps 1995; Motta 2004). As a consequence collusion is considered a strategic phenomenon that rests fundamentally on a dynamic interaction. It arises only if firms are able to sustain higher prices by threatening to punish in the future rivals that deviate from their collusive strategy profile (Ivaldi et al. 2007).

By definition then, a practice facilitates collusion if it helps firms to coordinate on a price above the static equilibrium in their repeated interaction. However, this definition may be inadequate for the opposite reason of the perfect competitive benchmarking. It leads to an under-inclusive definition of collusion and of facilitating practices. Indeed a large number of papers on facilitating practices study static games with the stated intention to assess their impact on "collusion." Clearly, if the purpose of antitrust law is to avoid the exercise of market power when it reduces social welfare, a practice that makes a static market game less competitive might be as harmful as one that makes a dynamic game less competitive.

To take into account the vast literature that only considers static games and to avoid further confusion, I will use "collusion" only to refer to the dynamic phenomenon (as prevailing in the economic antitrust literature) and will borrow from the economic and policy analysis of mergers the distinction between *unilateral* and *coordinated* effects. Unilateral effects stem from the modification of one-shot oligopoly games such that, even if firms maximize their short-term profits without taking into account the impact of their choices on future rivals' behavior, they end up charging higher prices. Coordinated effects arise if firms are able to collude within a dynamic game as explained above.

In effect, a practice constitutes a facilitating practice if it makes the prevailing market equilibrium less competitive either because firms move to a less competitive *static* equilibrium (unilateral effects) or because firms move from a static equilibrium to a dynamic collusive equilibrium (coordinated effects).[2] As I show in the next section, this wide definition of "facilitating practice" can have some problems as, in some circumstances, unilateral and coordinated effects can be conflicting phenomena.

Facilitating practices differ from other conducts targeted by antitrust prescriptions (i.e., mergers, abuse of dominance, and cartels) in three respects. First, there is no modification of the firms' control structure, as in a merger. Hence facilitating conduct does not entail a reduction of the number of independent competitors. Second, all firms are made better off, whereas anticompetitive strategies caught by some antitrust prohibitions, such as those established in Section 2 of the Sherman Act or in Article 82 of the EC Treaty, are those adopted by some firms (usually just one firm) aimed at excluding or disadvantaging rivals so as to reduce their competitive threat. Third, the collusive result can be due either to a collective decision or to individual decisions taken autonomously by each firm, whereas cartels are inherently a collective phenomenon. These distinctive features of facilitating practices, and especially the third one, raise important legal and policy issues related to their antitrust treatment. Antitrust agencies and courts tend to examine the existence of facilitating practices under three different perspectives, which give rise to three different questions. The first is whether an *agreement* to adopt such practices constitutes an infringement of Article 81 of the EC Treaty or of Section 1 of the Sherman Act. The second is whether the adoption of a facilitating practice independently of an agreement is or should be prohibited by antitrust law and, in case of an affirmative answer, what is the legal basis for such prohibition. The third is whether the adoption of facilitating practices provides evidence of a collusive agreement. I will discuss answers to these three questions in the concluding section 8.6. Before that I will survey the economic literature on facilitating practices and relate it to some leading antitrust cases and policy documents both in the European Union and in the United States. Section 8.1 presents a recapitulation of the theory of collusion. Sections 8.2 and 8.3 deal with those practices that affect the information firms possess when competing, namely pre-play communication (section 8.2) and the exchange of information (section 8.3). Sections 8.4 and 8.5 deal with those practices that can change firms' payoff functions either through a modification of their ownership structure (section 8.4) or through the adoption of best-price clauses (section 8.5).

8.1   The Essential Theory of Collusion

8.1.1   The Coordination Problem

Collusion, either express or tacit, entails two fundamental problems. The first one is how to choose a profile of coordinated strategies. From a theoretical point of view, any vector of prices that improves firms' payoff with respect to the static equilibrium could be the equilibrium outcome of an infinitely repeated game. If firms want to raise price, they must solve the strategic uncertainty that stems from the existence of such multiplicity of equilibria. In order to identify those practices that can facilitate the solution of the coordination problem, we must have an equilibrium selection theory that explains how players select an equilibrium in a game with multiple equilibria. For our purposes this theory should ascertain what factors reduce the risk of a coordination failure and/or allow players to coordinate on a Pareto superior equilibrium. Unfortunately, there not exits such a general theory but rather several theories, each focusing on some aspect of how players make their strategic decisions. However, most of the proposed criteria for equilibrium selections hinge on a fundamental intuition. The idea is that each player wonders whether there is something that justifies a prior belief on which strategies his opponents will select among the many possible strategies that belong to an equilibrium profile. These priors are provided by some prominent characteristic of the game (the strategy space or the payoff functions), history, communication, or external institutions. Following this approach, we can say that a practice facilitates coordination if it helps firms to form prior beliefs on how rivals will play that improve the likelihood of coordinated and more privately efficient strategies.

8.1.2   The Enforcement Problem

Even if firms are able to overcome the "coordination problem," collusion entails a second fundamental problem: how to enforce the coordinated profile of strategies. Although all firms, collectively and individually, gain from coordinating, each firm (or at least some of them) has the possibility to gain even more if it deviates unilaterally from the coordinated action.[3] Firms cannot rely on the legal system to enforce the collusive strategies. They must find a market mechanism that makes collusion self-enforcing. In the repeated dynamic game this mechanism is provided by the anticipated reactions of rivals. These reactions comprise the promise to keep colluding as long as rivals reciprocate and the threat to punish any deviation from the collusive path, by adopting more aggressive market conducts. If for all the colluding firms the short-run extra profits gained by deviating are lower than the present value of the long-run loss imposed by the substitution of the promise with the threat, any colluding firm will find it rational to adopt the collusive strategy and stick to it.

The incentive constraint conditions can be described as

$$\pi_i^d - \pi_i^c \leq \delta(C_i - P_i),\tag{8.1}$$

where δ denotes the discount factor, π_i^d and π_i^c represent the profit a firm gains by respectively deviating from and adhering to the coordinated behavior, and C_i and P_i denote the present value of the flow of profits gained by firm i in the continuation game if all firms always adopt the collusive profile or if a "punishment phase" is triggered by a deviation. The same constraint can be written as

$$\delta \geq \frac{\pi_i^d - \pi_i^c}{C_i - P_i}.\tag{8.2}$$

Equation (8.1) states that collusion is sustainable if the extra profit stemming from an optimal deviation, $\pi_i^d - \pi_i^c$, does not exceed the present value of the difference between the profit of the continuation game associated with the collusive action (promise) and those of the continuation game associated with this deviation (threat). Equation (8.2) restates the same condition in terms of the discount factor. It states that if firms are patient, in the sense that they give sufficient importance to future profits, the higher profits associated to a collusive path offset the short-run benefit they can obtain by deviating. We can identify factors that improve the sustainability of collusion as they loosen the incentive constraints defined by equations (8.1) and (8.2). Generally speaking, the stability of collusion depends on the accuracy of monitoring, the level of collusive and deviation profits, and the degree of punishment.

Monitoring   History-dependent strategies, necessary to enforce collusion, imply that firms are able to learn what happened in the past. To do so, they need to monitor the market and other firms' behavior. The degree and the accuracy of monitoring may be described according to two dimensions. One is the rapidity with which a deviation is detected and punished. The second is the degree of certainty of such discovery and reaction.[4] Monitoring is the more accurate the swifter a deviation is detected and punished and/or the lower the incidence of errors, where an error occurs both if a punishment follows a collusive action and if a deviation goes unpunished. The faster the detection and punishment of a defection, the lower the short-run gain from deviating and the higher the present value of the loss that stems from the punishment. Both effects relax the incentive constraint. Accurate monitoring may also reduce the probability of errors. Denote with α_p (false positive or type I error) probability that a firm gets punished even if it does not deviate and with α_n (false negative or type II error) the probability that a deviation is not detected. The incentive constraint described by equation (8.1) can be written as

$$A_i(\alpha_p) = \pi_i^c + (1 - \alpha_p)\delta C_i(\alpha_p) + \alpha_p \delta P_i \geq \pi_i^d + (1 - \alpha_n)\delta P_i + \alpha_n \delta D_i(\alpha_n) = B_i(\alpha_n), \qquad (8.3)$$

where C_i and D_i represent the present value of the flow of profits gained by firm i in the continuation game if it colludes and if it deviates, as long as the punishment is not implemented so that $\partial C_i / \partial \alpha_p \leq 0$ and $\partial D_i / \partial \alpha_n \geq 0$.

We have that

$$\frac{\partial A_i(\alpha_p)}{\partial \alpha_p} = \delta(P_i - C_i) + \frac{\partial C_i}{\partial \alpha_p} < 0, \qquad (8.4)$$

$$\frac{\partial B_i(\alpha_n)}{\partial \alpha_n} = \delta(D_i - P_i) + \frac{\partial D_i}{\partial \alpha_n} > 0. \qquad (8.5)$$

Therefore, if a more accurate monitoring reduces the probability of false negatives and/or of false positives, collusion becomes more easily enforceable. Errors reduce the incentive to collude for two reasons: first, a firm may get punished also if it behaves "well," and this reduces the expected profit of a collusive action; second, a firm may get away with a deviation, and this increases the expected profit of a deviation.

Collusive and Deviation Profits Collusion is more easily sustainable if collusive profits are higher and/or if deviation profits are lower. Simple inspection of condition (8.1) confirms this statement. If firms can reap larger profits by colluding the left-hand side of equation (8.1) decreases, while the right-hand side increases, making the inequality more easily satisfied; the same occurs if any firm obtains a lower level of profit by deviating. It must be noted, however, that collusive and deviation profits often move together, in the sense that some market features or some practices have an impact of the same sign on both levels of profits. In these cases the consequence on the sustainability of collusion depends on the magnitude of the two impacts. As a general result we can say that if a factor increases (decreases) collusive profits and deviation profits in the same proportion, it does not hinder (facilitate) collusion and possibly facilitates (hinders) it. To see this, suppose that both collusive and deviation profits change by a factor of x. The incentive constraint becomes

$$(1 + x)(\pi_i^d - \pi_i^c) \leq \frac{\delta(1 + x)}{1 - \delta} \pi_i^c - \delta P_i,$$

which is the same as

$$(\pi_i^d - \pi_i^c) \leq \delta C_i - \frac{\delta}{1 + x} P_i.$$

It is immediate that

$$\delta C_i - \frac{\delta}{1 + x} P_i \geq \delta(C_i - P_i)$$

if and only if $x \geq 0$. So the variation of profits facilitates collusion if $x > 0$ and hinders collusion if $x < 0$. However, if the punishment is zero the critical discount factor is $1 - (x\pi_i^c / x\pi_i^d)$ and is not affected by x.

Punishment   Punishment must satisfy two conditions to sustain collusion. It must be credible and it must be sufficiently severe to offset the short-term gains from deviation. The first condition is captured by the "subgame perfection" refinement of a Nash equilibrium. In a subgame perfect Nash equilibrium the strategies are the best response to the rivals' strategies at any possible subgame. This means that any player adopts his best response to the conduct of other players, not only along the equilibrium path but also in subgames that will never be played if all the players follow their equilibrium strategy. The simplest punishment strategy that satisfies this perfection requirement consists in the reversion to the static Nash equilibrium. By definition, the Nash reversal punishment is rational in any possible repetition of the stage game. However, this punishment might not be sufficiently harsh to sustain some level of collusive profits, given the actual level of the discount factor and the other features of the game.

Abreu (1986, 1988) has shown that firms can improve their ability to sustain a collusive equilibrium if they adopt a stick-and-carrot strategy in the punishment phase. The "optimal" punishment requires firms to adopt a market behavior such that the deviator is very strongly punished in the repetition that immediately follows a deviation (the stick). Firms will then revert to the collusive path (the carrot), if and only if all firms have previously adopted the stick portion of their strategy. The carrot part of this strategy is essential to make it credible. Since the actions that lead to the stick do not form a Nash equilibrium in the static game, their adoption can be rational only if motivated by the prosecution of the game. A player may be willing to punish other firms *and himself*, only if he knows that by doing so he will gain higher profits in the future. Abreu proves that there exist subgame perfect stick-and-carrot strategies that allows firms to reduce the present value of profits gained by firms in the punishment phase, which is P of equations (8.1) and (8.2). These strategies make collusion more stable as they relax the incentive constraints defined by these inequalities. If such a strategy makes P vanish, we obtain the minimal critical discount factor that supports a collusive equilibrium.

It would be important to know what type of punishment strategies firms actually adopt when they collude either tacitly or expressly. Abreu claims that stick-and-carrot strategies identify "optimal penal codes" in the sense that they allow firms to sustain a collusive outcome for the largest set of values of the discount factor. However, this does not necessarily implies that rational firms will adopt this type of strategies to enforce collusion. Although stick-and-carrot strategies are optimal in the narrow sense defined by Abreu, they might not be optimal if we take into account other factors. First stick-and-carrot strategies are more complex than Nash reversal, in that they require some form of coordination and therefore of monitoring, also in the punishment phase. If monitoring is costly, firms may prefer to adopt punishments that do not require it. Second, imperfect monitoring may provoke unwarranted punishment that impose unnecessary costs. If there is a positive probability of such errors, firms may be better off if they adopt collusive strategies that call for less harsh punishment as the expected gain stemming from an improved likelihood of a successful collusion could be outweighed by the expected loss of an erroneous price war. According to some commentators, Nash reversal seems to be the most obvious way to punish deviators. For instance, Hovenkamp (1994, p. 147) argues that "there is good reason to think that competitive pricing is one of the most common mechanisms by which cartels discipline cheaters. One reason is that it is natural and may happen without any communication among the cartel members." Levenstein (1997) and Genesove and Mullin (2001) find that in actual cases firms usually punish cheaters by matching their conduct. This is a less severe punishment than Nash reversal and Abreu's stick and carrot.

8.1.3 The "Topsy-Turvy Principle" of Tacit Collusion

If the static equilibrium is used as a credible threat to sustain collusion in supergames, by increasing the profits gained in the static equilibrium, firms render punishment *less severe* and therefore tighten the incentive constraint that must be satisfied to sustain collusion. Shapiro (1989) calls this fact the *topsy-turvy* principle of tacit collusion: "anything (e.g., unlimited capacities) that makes more *competitive* behavior feasible or credible actually promotes collusion" (p. 357).[5] Hence there seems to be an inherent conflict between unilateral and coordinated effects.

However, even if the conflict arises in several market models, it is not a condition of general validity. First, a practice that engenders unilateral effects does not prevent firms to sustain coordinated effects through the threat of aggressive market behavior that does not correspond to the static equilibrium. Second, even if collusion is supported by a Nash reversal, a practice that determines unilateral effects may still give rise to coordinated effects if it modifies the other conditions conducive to tacit collusion, meaning if it helps to solve the coordination problem, improves monitoring, decreases deviation profits, or increases collusive profits. In conclusion, I believe that unilateral and coordinated effects are distinct phenomena that call for specific analyses. No conclusions can be simply drawn on the latter by limiting the analysis to one-shot games.

8.2 Pre-play Communication

The simplest way firms may try to solve their coordination problem is by talking to each other and agreeing on future conduct. Most people would consider such behavior socially harmful. Indeed such conduct is the archetype of an anticompetitive conduct and probably is the only conduct that is still subject to an undisputed per se rule. Yet, the apparent simplicity of this prescription hides two very complex issues.

First, it is not immediately clear why and how some forms of pre-play communication should alter the way players actually behave in the markets. Suppose that two firms meet, discuss, and agree their pricing strategies. Once they leave the conference room and have to decide their price, nothing in the game they are going to play is really changed. The only novelty is that each player knows that the rival has agreed (or simply declared) that she will charge a given price and that each player knows that the rival knows that he has agreed to charge a given price, and so on. However, the two firms' strategy space and pay-off functions have not changed.

Second, if pre-play communication is the essential factor that gives an agreement its pro-collusive properties, then there exist many ways in which firms can communicate. Some forms of communication do not require the direct exchange of messages and may even re-sult from normal market behavior. For instance, a firm that publishes its future prices makes this information available also to its competitors. An understanding between two firms may also result from a unilateral message. If a firm "proposes" a new price to its competitor, the message receiver's market behavior may suffice to communicate its agree-ment or disagreement. This poses the problem of where we should draw the line between lawful forms of communication and unlawful ones.

The two issues are strongly related. An attempt to answer the latter question calls for an understanding of the impact of pre-play communication on competition.

8.2.1 Insights from the Economic Literature

The issue of the impact of pre-play communication on the outcome of noncooperative games has been addressed on a theoretical ground by many authors and has spurred a large number of experiments.[6] It is interesting that most of these contributions have been motivated by the intention to explain why and how communication helps players coordi-nate their strategies and reach more efficient equilibria. In fact the proposition that com-munication favors coordination seems intuitively so persuasive that it is a wonder why we need a theory to explain it. However, if we look at the more subtle questions, such as what type of communication facilitates coordination and in what circumstances and to what ex-tent, then the need for a theory becomes clear.

The models developed so far have followed two different approaches: one discusses the possibility of expanding the set of equilibria beyond that of the Nash equilibria of the game without communication,[7] while the other focuses on the role of communication in selecting one Nash equilibrium out of a set of many equilibria.[8] We are interested in the second approach as collusion entails the problem of choosing one of the multiple equilibria of a repeated market game. The literature on "cheap talk"[9] has emphasized the impor-tance of the payoff structure of the game. In their seminal paper Crawford and Sobel (1982) show that the more the preferences of the players diverge, the less they are able to communicate in a useful way. Therefore we can examine the impact of pre-play communi-cation in different contexts characterized by different degree of conflict.

Table 8.1
Example 1

	A	*B*
A	3, 3	0, 1
B	1, 0	2, 2

In a pure coordination game, communication easily helps the players to address the strategic uncertainty that stems from the existence of a multiplicity of equilibria, by providing them with some prior beliefs on what strategies their opponents will select among the many possible strategies that belong to an equilibrium profile.

The simplest case is one of pure coordination, in which there exist multiple equilibria that are completely ranked according to the Pareto dominance criterion.[10] Consider the game in table 8.1 where player 1 chooses rows and player 2 columns. Both (A, A) and (B, B) are Nash equilibria, but (A, A) Pareto dominates (B, B). Still there exists a third equilibrium, in which both players choose each action with probability 1/2, that gives an individual payoff of 3/2. We can assume that in a situation of strategic uncertainty the mixed-strategy equilibrium prevails.[11] Hence each player has a prior belief that the opponent will play one of the two pure strategies with equal probability. Let us add a preliminary stage of one-way pre-play communication, in which only player 1 can send a message. A simple form of communication in which player 1 informs his rival about his future conduct can allow them to coordinate on (A, A) in the second stage. If player 1 declares that he will play A, he will provide his opponent with a message that is *self-committing* and *self-signaling*. The message is self-committing in the sense that if player 2 believes it and plays accordingly, it is in the interest of player 1 to fulfill it. It is self-signaling because if player 1 intends to play A, it is in his interest that player 2 believes that he is going to play A; if he intends to play B, it is not in his interest that player 2 believes that he will play A.

Now assume that player 2 updates her beliefs so that the probability of player 1 choosing *x* is 1 if he declares that he will play *x* and the message is credible (i.e., both self-committing and self-signaling). Then the only equilibrium of the Two-Stage Game is that in which player 1 declares A in the first stage and both choose A in the second stage.[12] In this example the credibility of the message stems from being both "self-committing" and "self-signaling." Let us consider, however, a slightly different game (table 8.2) that is a variation of the Stag Hunt Game.[13]

In example 2 there are three equilibria as well, two in pure strategies, ordered according to the Pareto dominance criterion, and one in mixed strategies in which both players randomize between their strategies with equal probability. Again, the expected payoff corresponding to the mixed-strategy equilibrium is 3/2, and we can assume that this would be the outcome in a situation of strategic uncertainty. However, in this game both players

Table 8.2
Example 2

	A	*B*
A	3, 3	0, 2
B	2, 0	1, 1

Table 8.3
Example 3

	A	*B*
A	3, 3	−10, 2
B	2, −10	1, 1

strongly prefer that their opponent picks up A instead of B. The consequence of this different payoff structure may prove decisive. Indeed, the communication stage in which player 1 is allowed to send a message *might* not solve the coordination problem. This is so because if player 1 says that he will play A, his message is self-committing but is not self-signaling. Indeed, whatever he plans to do, it is in his interest that player 2 believes that he is going to choose A. Aumann (1990) argues that such a message does not convey any information and should be disregarded by the receiver. Farrel and Rabin (1996) acknowledge Aumann's argument but conjecture that communication helps player coordinate on the more efficient equilibrium. If Aumann's point of view is correct, then pre-play communication does not help players to solve their strategic uncertainty if their messages are not self-signaling. If, on the contrary, we believe that a self-committing signal that is not self-signaling remains to some extent credible, then communication and the way messages are exchanged have the same effects as in a pure coordination game. Which of the two conjectures is correct may depend on the degree of risk embedded in each of the available strategies.

Let us modify example 2 as in table 8.3. In example 3, (A, A) and (B, B) are still the two pure Nash strategy equilibria of the game with the first dominating the second. However, now strategy A is very risky for both players as in the case of a coordination failure it imposes on them a significant loss. If we follow the risk dominance criterion proposed by Harsanyi and Selten (1988) we can see that (B, B) is the selected equilibrium. We can thus conjecture that in games like those shown in examples 2 and 3 the ability of a non–self-signaling message to facilitate coordination changes dramatically.

The Aumann–Farrell and Rabin controversy, possibly augmented by risk dominance considerations, has been investigated through experiments. The results are mixed. Charness (1998, 2000) rejects the argument put forward by Aumann. In his experiments one-way communication allows players to significantly increase the probability of achieving the efficient, but risky, equilibrium. Clark et al. (2001) tested the impact of two-way communication in two types of coordination games. In the first game players do not have a strict preference on the rival's strategy choice, whereas in the second they do, so their messages are not self-signaling. Their results support the Aumann's conjecture, in that communication in the second type of game is significantly less effective in reaching the Pareto dominant outcome. However, they find that in both types of games, communication *improves* players' ability to coordinate on the efficient equilibrium. They investigate the relation between announcements and actions and argue that the main difference in the two settings is the credibility of messages, also when they call for the same efficient coordinated choice. In the first game, players predominantly announce the efficient strategy and tend to behave according to their message if the opponent message is the same. In the second game, there is still a tendency to announce the efficient strategy, but then players tend to favor the less risky strategy even when the opponent has sent the same message. This suggests that they are less willing to change their beliefs when messages are not self-signaling, as argued by Aumann. Yet communication is not without consequences, and also the point of view of Farrel and Rabin may be supported by these results.

Finally, communication is not only a means to coordinate players' behaviors but also an instrument useful to solve their conflict. In a seminal paper, Farrell (1987) shows that cheap talk can improve the equilibrium payoffs in a game with the structure of the Battle of the Sexes.[14] He proves that allowing firms to communicate *repeatedly* by exchanging *simultaneous* messages reduces the probability of coordination failure. However, this probability remains positive even if the degree of conflict is small and if players are allowed to repeat infinitely their pre-play communication stage.

To summarize, in coordination games, where symmetric firms have perfectly aligned interests, very simple forms of communication, such as public price announcements, are likely to suffice to solve the coordination problem. When the market environment becomes more complex and the attempt to coordinate a more risky endeavor, simple communication may prove insufficient to achieve a coordinated equilibrium. Firms must find a way to overcome the credibility problem. This can be done through a sequence of messages which aim to provide assurance about the true intentions of the sender. Finally, where firms have asymmetric interests, they must communicate repeatedly to find an acceptable solution to what is both a coordination and a bargaining problem.

These results suggest that "rich" communication protocols are most effective in coordinating players' choices. Indeed what might prove fundamental, and at the same time is difficult to grasp in highly stylized models, is that different forms of communication are likely to affect the set of meaningful messages that players can exchange.[15] For instance, a firm publicly announcing its future (uncommitted) price simply states "in the future I intend to charge x." If it sends the same piece of information as a private message to its rival, it adds a new meaning, that is, "I want *you* to know that....." The two types of messages are clearly different in that the choice of the intended receiver signals that the message *must* mean something to the receiver. Therefore the messages are likely to bear differently on how players try to solve their strategic uncertainty. A *sequential* private communication is even more powerful, as it allows the receiver to express his agreement or disagreement, which corresponds to new meaning attached to the messages. The possibility to exchange meaningful messages depends also on the complexity of the environment in which firms make their decisions. In a duopoly for homogeneous products, public speeches may convey enough information to reduce uncertainty and facilitate coordination. In a market with many firms, public messages are clearly less effective.

8.2.2 Some Selected Cases on Pre-play Communication

In some antitrust cases *discussions*, *negotiations*, and finally the *agreement* occur by means of indirect forms of communication. In *Airline Tariff Publishing Company (ATP)*[16] the DOJ filed a civil antitrust suit against eight airlines and ATP, alleging that they had conspired to fix fares through the ATP fare dissemination system. ATP was a joint venture of the air carriers that collected and disseminated airfares data.[17] The ATP database was accessible to all carriers and to the major computer reservation systems that serve travel agents. It was updated everytime a carrier transmitted an information about an airfare change. The information contained also "first ticket dates," "last ticket dates," and "footnote designators." First and last ticket dates indicated the future date when the new fare would be applicable (first) and when it would no longer be applicable (last). Footnotes designators were used to link the markets and the fare types involved by using the same footnote designator on all fare that were supposed to change. According to the DOJ, by filing fares with a first ticket date in the future, the airlines were able to go through an iterative process of proposals and counterproposals before actually changing the existing fares, thus eliminating the risk of loosing sales. Airlines could also use a first ticket date to signal when a new fare should take effect, and could impose "punishment fares" effective immediately, with a last ticket date signaling an offer to remove it if the offending airline had changed its behavior. Through these repeated cheap talks, airlines were able to raise fares, change fare restrictions, and eliminate discounts in hundreds of city-pair markets. The DOJ obtained a consent decrees that prohibited the use of first ticket dates and (except for advertised promotions) last ticket dates on any of the airlines' fares.[18]

In the European Union, price announcements have been considered as a means of indirect communication among firms in some leading cases. In *Dyestuffs*[19] the European Commission maintained that parallel price movements occurred as a result of a concerted practice between ten producers of aniline dyes. The European Court of Justice (ECJ) upheld the Commission's decision[20] relying on the evidence that price increases were announced in advance. According to the ECJ, the announcements had the effect of increasing market transparency and of eliminating the uncertainty about the future conduct of the firms and the risk of independent pricing. It must be said that the Commission had found evidence of direct and indirect contacts between the parties, including records of meetings in which prices were discussed and the dates of intended price increases announced. Therefore price pre-announcements were not the only element considered in its finding of an Article 81 infringement. In a subsequent case, *Wood Pulp*,[21] the Commission relied mostly on the existence of an advance price announcement to support its claim of an illegal concerted practice and fined forty-three wood pulp producers.

The ECJ annulled the decision.[22] It held that the system of quarterly price announcements served legitimate business purposes, as it constituted a rational response to the fact that the pulp market was a long-term market and to the need of both buyers and sellers to limit commercial risk. Therefore the ECJ held that the system of announcements did not amount to a means of artificial indirect communication and it did not infringe Article 81. Interestingly the Commission argued that the fragmented market structure was supportive of its position, as the absence of a narrow ologipolistic market made parallel business behavior not a naturally rational outcome. The ECJ considered instead that the price parallelism was satisfactorily explained by the oligopolistic tendencies of the market. Beyond the contradictory assessment of a factual point, what at a first glance may strike as surprising is that the oligopolistic structure of the market, or its absence, seems to have opposite implications to the ones that the economic theory would suggest. For the Commission the market fragmentation founds the illegality claim, whereas for the ECJ the oligopolistic tendencies of the market justifies the observed parties' behavior. To reconcile this with our understanding of the collusive risk of facilitating practices, we must recognize that the Commission and the ECJ were not assessing the advanced price announcements on their own merit, but rather their qualification as circumstantial evidence of a more cogent form of express collusion. This perspective may reflect the lack in the European Union of a legal basis to address directly the anticompetitive effects of unilateral facilitating practices that do not stem from an agreement or a concerted practice.

8.3 Exchange of Information

Exchange of information among competitors is a form of communication. What distinguishes this practice from those discussed in the previous section is the type of information exchanged. While pre-play communication normally refers to an exchange of views about future plans regarding prices, sales, and other strategic variables, the practice I discuss in this section consists in sharing information on past firms' conduct or on past and current market conditions. In other words, communication refers to schemes used to convey information on subjective intentions, whereas the exchange of information refers to a scheme whereby firms acquire data on objective features of the market or on the firms' past behavior.

The main reason why antitrust authorities are concerned with the exchange of information among competitors is that this practice can help firms in monitoring each other's behavior. We have already seen that monitoring is an essential element of collusion and that anything that allows firms to better and more promptly detect deviations facilitates the emergence of a collusive outcome.

This statement seems to warrant a simple rule that bans information sharing outright. However, there are several reasons to follow a more prudent approach. First, the practical application of such a simple rule would be far from simple. Information is too wide a concept to establish such a strict prohibition, and as for communication, there are several and extremely different ways by which firms can exchange information or engage in practices that result in the dissemination of business information. Second, by exchanging information, firms may pursue goals other than collusion. Therefore we need to assess the impact of this practice on welfare in the case firms do not collude. If information sharing is welfare enhancing in the one-shot game, the application of a per se illegality rule might prevent firms from improving market efficiency. On the contrary, if information sharing leads to a less efficient static equilibrium, then its prohibition does not have any of the adverse effects that we want to avoid.

Another issue addressed in the literature is whether firms individually are willing to reveal their private information to rivals. This question is important in order to understand if the exchange of information is always a form of coordinated action, or if it might be the outcome of individually rational decision-making.

In a nutshell, the antitrust treatment of information sharing depends on the answers to three questions:

- What type of information sharing facilitates collusion?
- What are the welfare effects of information sharing, absent collusion?
- Is revealing private information an individually rational decision?

I will discuss the answer to each question in turn.

8.3.1 Information Exchanges That Facilitate Collusion

The first question has received little direct attention in the theoretical economic literature. To be sure, several models of collusion investigate repeated oligopolistic interaction with imperfect monitoring and show that public and private information can allow firms to enforce a collusive outcome. These models, however, do not discuss directly what types of information-sharing mechanisms are more likely to have collusive effects. Hence, to arrive to an answer, we can rely on the criteria adopted by antitrust authorities to distinguish lawful from unlawful information-sharing mechanisms and check whether these criteria are consistent with the economic literature, in the sense that they outlaw the mechanisms that are most likely to solve the absence of perfect monitoring, and only them.

In the United States useful insights can be found in the *Antitrust Guidelines for Collaborations Among Competitors* (AGCAC), issued jointly by the Federal Trade Commission and the US Department of Justice in April 2002. The US Agencies recognize that pro-collusive effects may stem from the dissemination of competitively sensitive information on past and future conducts or from the modification of the incentives firms have to compete with each other. At paragraph 3.31(b) AGCAC reads: "Agreement that facilitate collusion sometimes involve the exchange or disclosure of information. . . . The competitive concern depends on the nature of the information shared. Other things being equal, the sharing of information relating to price, output, costs, or strategic planning is more likely to raise competitive concern than the sharing of information relating to less competitively sensitive variables. Similarly, other things being equal, the sharing of information on current operating and future business plans is more likely to raise concerns than the sharing of historical information. Finally, other things being equal, the sharing of individual company data is more likely to raise concern than the sharing of aggregated data that does not permit recipients to identify individual firm data." These principles have been applied in several cases.[23] Recently they have been clarified in the *Todd v. Exxon* case[24] in which the Court of Appeal argued that alongside the structure of the industry involved, the major factors to consider in a data exchange case are the nature of the information exchanged, the time frame covered by the data, the specificity of the information, and whether the data were made publicly available or disseminated only among the firms.

In the European Union, the position of the European Commission on facilitating practices can be mainly traced from its case law, rather than from its policy documents.[25] The leading case about information sharing is *UK Agricultural Tractor Registration Exchange.*[26] The decision, adopted by the Commission in 1992, found that the complex system for the exchange of information adopted in the UK tractor market violated Article 81. The UK tractor market was a tiny, but highly concentrated, market with significant barriers to entry that protected firms from overseas competition. Through their trade association, the Agricultural Engineers Association (AEA), the parties exchanged the information that had to be transmitted to the British Ministry of Transport to obtain a license plate for a new tractor, which included the name of the manufacturer, the brand, the serial number, the identity of the sales agent, and the postal code of the buyer. This information allowed firms to identify any sale made by their competitors.

The Commission affirmed that the information exchange system put in place by the AEA restrained competition because of the oligopolistic structure of the market, the confidential nature of the information exchanged, and the high level of data disaggregation, in terms of both its geographical and its time coverage. The Commission concluded that this system created an artificial market transparency that increased the likelihood of a collusive outcome. Both the Court of First Instance (CFI) and the ECJ upheld the Commission's decision. The ECJ stated that "the information exchange system reduces or removes the degree of uncertainty as to the operation of the market and that the system is therefore liable to have adverse influence on competition between manufacturers."[27]

The principles of this case were subsequently applied by the Commission in several cases.[28] In *CEPI-Cartonboard*[29] the Commission required the parties to aggregate the statistical data over more than one country, or with other products, when only two or very few producers were present in certain geographical or product markets, so as to impede the identification of the business decisions of individual firms through the market statistics. In *Wirtschaftsvereinigung*[30] the Commission reaffirmed the importance of the market structure and of other market conditions for the assessment of the information-sharing mechanism. According to the logic of antitrust authorities, the exchange of information among competitors is likely to have dangerous pro-collusive effects when it takes place in an oligopolistic market that is already prone to collusion and when it allows to communicate disaggregated and recent data concerning firms business variables such as prices, output, volume sales, customers, costs, and investments. According to this general rule, the legal treatment of the exchange of information depends on the following:

• The structural characteristics of the market
• The degree of aggregation of the data
• The age of the data
• The nature of the information exchanged

The analysis of the market structure is relevant as it limits the scope of the antitrust prohibition to those circumstances in which there is a serious risk of collusion or where collusion is likely to significantly reduce welfare. Consideration has to be given to the degree of concentration, barriers to entry, product homogeneity, symmetry among the firms, and other structural factors. Such analysis is similar to that required to investigate the risk of coordinated effects stemming from mergers.

The degree of aggregation plays a central role in the assessment of information sharing. An antitrust authority must ascertain whether the exchanged data provide sufficient statistics to identify the conduct of individual firms. In general, the more firms, customers, products, territories and time periods are included in any data point made available through the information-sharing mechanism, the less apparent will be a deviation that may consist in a secret price cut granted to *some* customers, for the sale of *some* products in *some* territories, for *some* period of time. Aggregated data make the inference of deviation less certain and are likely to lead to errors of both types that, as I have already argued, make collusion less likely. This indication can be checked against some findings in the formal economic literature. Green and Porter (1983) describe a market where quantity-setting firms cannot observe their rivals' actions and are uncertain about demand. However, they can observe the market-clearing price. Collusion can be sustained by trigger strategies in which the firms produce the collusive output as long as the market price is above a certain level and enter in a finite phase of "price wars" whenever a price below the triggering level is observed. In the Green and Porter model collusion is not perfect as noncooperative conducts are needed to sustain the collusive outcome. As the source of this inefficiency is the lack of knowledge of the true state of demand; firms can improve the equilibrium if this type of uncertainty is reduced. Porter (1983) has indeed proved that firms approach the perfectly collusive outcome as information about demand is improved. In the Green and

Porter trigger strategy equilibrium, firms actually never defect. Hence only type I errors occur, as firms get "punished" also when there is no deviation. The exchange of information among competitors can clearly reduce the occurrence of this type of error and improve the stability of collusion. The exchange of individual data on output clearly eliminates all type I errors and allows the firms to reach the fully collusive outcome. However, also information on aggregate sales suffices to solve the demand uncertainty and leads to perfect collusion. Hence the only insight we can draw from their model is that the exchange of information among competitors is a facilitating factor, but we are not able to make a clear distinction between the type of data that has pro-collusive effects. Models of cooperation with private information have been developed by Kandori and Matsushima (1988) and Compte (1998). They study markets in which there are no public signals that can trigger a punishment phase, but where firms receive only private signals. They show that communication among firms can overcome their enforcement problem and allow firms to obtain a collusive outcome. In their models firms do not reveal their action but their private signal, which represents disaggregated information. They prove that this type of information sharing can improve collusion, as it allows the implementation of individualized punishment strategies that reduce the inefficiency associated with a general punishment phase. In summary, models of collusion with imperfect monitoring seem to support the position taken by antitrust authorities, in that they show that imperfect monitoring is a source of inefficiency from the colluding firms point of view that can be overcome with the exchange of individual data on firms' past strategies. Aggregate data instead do not always suffice to reach the fully collusive equilibrium, though there are cases where this type of data can be sufficient.

Unfortunately, we do not have sophisticated instruments to go beyond this very general statement and identify precise policy rules. Indeed the level of detail needed to detect deviations depends on several market features, such as the number of players, the mode of competition, the product and geographic extension of the relevant markets, and the stability of demand. Hence how much aggregation is sufficient to make a prohibition unwarranted would depend on many market conditions, most of which are not observable or verifiable in court. We have to add that the method employed to exchange information may also be important. Trade associations often collect information on individual firm, elaborate the individual data and report market data to their members. Even if the final reports contain only aggregated data, the entire process can provide occasions in which firms come to know each others' strategies or discuss their future behavior. It is not infrequent that the design of the information system and its implementation is delegated to some group within the association that includes representatives of all the firms. In these cases the filter of the trade association is only apparent, as the information exchange takes place between individual firms for any practical purposes. The age of data and the frequency with which firms exchange data are also crucial to determine whether this practice is likely to facilitate collusion.

According to the stance taken by competition authorities, recent and frequent data allow firms to react timely to deviations, reducing the scope for profitable cheating. Although this logic is impeccable in cases of perfect monitoring (i.e., when firms through their exchange of information perfectly and truthfully reveal their strategy), formal analysis has proved that less frequent information release, which delays the dissemination of public or private information, increases the possibility of collusion. This result has been established by Abreu et al. (1991) for the case of public information and confirmed by Compte (1998) for the private information case. The intuition behind this formal result is that with imperfect monitoring, a delayed revelation of private signals increases the precision of the information, as the revealed signal combines with new private signals. This allows firms to envisage more efficient punishment strategies that improve the likelihood of a collusive outcome. It must be clarified that this result does not contradict the previous statement that aggregation of data relative to a longer time period reduces the scope for collusion, as it only alludes to the time when the information is released but not a change in its content.

The third relevant attribute of an information exchange mechanism regards the nature of the information exchanged. Since this practice facilitates collusion as long as it makes firms' conduct more transparent, any type of information that directly, or indirectly, is capable of showing a deviation from a collusive equilibrium cannot be exchanged without causing antitrust concerns. Hence information on prices, output, customers, and volume sales is clearly sensitive, and data on these variables at a firm level make the identification of cheaters a simple matter. However, also information on costs can help colluding firms in spotting deviation episodes,[31] when the collusive understanding is about the price–cost margin and firms are able to observe their rivals' prices but not their costs.

8.3.2 Welfare Effects of Information Sharing without Collusion

Since some information-sharing mechanisms have facilitating properties, it is important to know what their effects are on consumer surplus and on profits when firms do not collude. To do so, we must compare the equilibrium of a market game with and without information sharing. Many scholars have tackled this issue.[32] Unfortunately, the only general conclusion that can be drawn from this vast research effort is that the consequences of information sharing mechanisms on welfare are ambiguous, as they depend (in a complex way) on whether firms compete in price or quantity, whether strategies are complement or substitute, whether the uncertainty concerns demand or cost, and whether the random parameters entering into individual payoffs are perfectly correlated, independent, or imperfectly correlated, and firms receive perfect signals. Some factors influence the impact on welfare of a system that makes firms better informed also in the absence of any strategic interaction. Thus a simple monopoly model suffices to illustrate some relevant forces at work. Suppose that a monopolist with zero marginal cost faces a linear inverse demand, as in equation (8.6), whose intercept depends on a random variable θ that can take two values, θ_H and θ_L, with $\theta_H > \theta_L$, and probabilities respectively β and $(1 - \beta)$:

$$p = a + \theta - q. \tag{8.6}$$

Suppose further that the expected value of θ is zero, which implies that

$$\theta_H = \frac{(\beta - 1)}{\beta} \theta_L.$$

This relation also implies that the variance of the uncertain parameter is

$$\sigma_\theta^2 = \frac{(1 - \beta)\theta_L^2}{\beta} = \frac{\beta\theta_H^2}{(1 - \beta)}.$$

Let us consider first the case where the monopolist chooses the quantity. If the monopolist does not have any information on θ, it maximizes its expected profits and sets $q = a/2$ whatever is the true realization of θ. The market clears through price adjustments. The monopolist's expected profits are $E\pi = a^2/4$, and the expected consumer surplus is $ECS = a^2/8$. Now suppose that the monopolist can acquire information that perfectly reveals the true state of the demand. It will produce more in the high-demand state and less in the low-demand state, meaning the output will be $q = (a + \theta_i)/2$ with $i = H, L$. Therefore the monopolist will gain higher profits when it is informed, whatever the true state of the demand.

The expected increase in profits is

$$E\Delta\pi = \frac{(1 - \beta)\theta_L^2}{4\beta} = \frac{\beta\theta_H^2}{4(1 - \beta)} = \frac{\sigma_\theta^2}{4}. \tag{8.7}$$

Consumers benefit from having a more informed monopolist when demand is high ($\theta = \theta_H$) as they consume a larger quantity at a lower price, but they lose out when demand is low ($\theta = \theta_L$) as they consume less at a higher price. However, the first effect dominates the second because the expected consumer surplus is a convex function of the equilibrium quantity. Indeed the modification of the expected consumer surplus is

$$E\Delta CS = \frac{(1 - \beta)\theta_L^2}{8\beta} = \frac{\beta\theta_H^2}{8(1 - \beta)} = \frac{\sigma_\theta^2}{8}. \tag{8.8}$$

Result (8.8) is reversed in the case of a price-setting monopolist. The reason is that without information, the monopolist sets the price based on the expected demand and the market clears through quantity adjustments. If the monopolist is perfectly informed (or better informed), it will rise its price in the high-demand state and lower it in the low-demand state. As a consequence consumers will consume less when demand is high and more when demand is low. For the same reasons as those discussed above the net result is a lower expected surplus. Note that the increase in the expected profits is given by equation (8.7) also for the price-setting monopolist, although in this case the variation of the expected consumer surplus is

$$E\Delta CS = -\frac{\sigma_\theta^2}{2}.$$

Clearly, total welfare (profit plus consumer surplus) always increases with information. However, the antitrust implications depend on the objective function of the antitrust authority. If the antitrust authority is concerned only (or predominantly) about consumers' welfare, then improving the information of a monopolist is undesirable in a price-setting monopoly.

With linear demand and constant marginal cost, uncertainty about the level of the cost is always undesirable, whichever the variable set by the monopolist. In both cases better information leads to more output in low-cost states and less output in high-cost states. This improves both the expected level profits and the expected consumer surplus. In the simple model where marginal cost depends on a random shifter that can take values θ_H and θ_L, with $\theta_H > \theta_L$, and probabilities respectively β and $(1 - \beta)$, with a zero expected value, expected profits increase as described by equation (8.7) and the expected consumer surplus increases according to equation (8.8).

This simple example allows also to see that according to equation (8.7) the value of the information for the monopolist depends on the variability of demand or costs. More precisely, the higher is the reduction in uncertainty due to the acquisition of information, which in turn depends on the initial degree of uncertainty and on the precision of signals, the higher the increase in the expected profits. The same holds true for the consumer surplus, with the only difference that if the uncertainty is about demand, the sign of the effect on consumer surplus depends on the market variable set by the monopolist. The monopoly example identifies one important effect of information acquisition that can be called the "precision effect," as it depends on the degree of precision gained with the information or lost without it. If we consider the demand described by (8.6) as the residual demand of a firm, once all strategic effects have been taken into account, the monopoly model shows that a firm benefits from having a better knowledge of its market conditions. Such a better knowledge increases also the consumer surplus in many circumstances, when it leads to output adjustments such that output is larger in high-demand/low-cost states, and vice versa.

In an oligopoly, however, sharing information has also strategic effects that must be explicitly taken into consideration. To understand these strategic effects, it is important to distinguish between a situation where the uncertainty concerns variables that are perfectly correlated (common value case) and a situation where the uncertain variables are perfectly firm-specific, and therefore independent (private value case), or are partially correlated and each firm receives a perfect signal about the true value of the variable entering into its own profit function (perfect signal case). This distinction is important because the precision effect, outlined in the monopoly model, occurs only in the common value case. In the private value case and in the perfect signal case, by exchanging information firms do not improve their knowledge of their own specific market conditions, but only obtain a better knowledge of the type of firms they are competing with. If the uncertainty is about variables that are totally uncorrelated (private value), a firm does not receive any information about its own variable by knowing the signal received by another player. If individual variables are partially correlated and firms receive perfect signals for their own variables, receiving information from a rival gives some knowledge about the true value of the variable of the receiver's payoff function, but this is totally unnecessary as the receiver has already, and perfectly, solved this uncertainty.

In both cases exchanging information does not *improve* the knowledge that firms have about their specific variables. Hence precision effects are possible only in the common value setting. In all settings, however, there are strategic effects as firms change their strategies due to the information sharing. These effects can be called "direct adjustment" and "strategic adjustment" effects. The former stems from the modification of a firm strategy due to an improved knowledge of its own market conditions. The latter stems from the modification of a firm strategy due to an improved knowledge of its rivals' type. For the reasons explained above, while in common value games both strategic effects are present, in private value/perfect signal games there are only strategic adjustments.

To understand how these effects modify the market equilibrium, we must study how information sharing alters the correlation of firms' strategies as a consequence of the two strategic effects described above. To this end a further distinction becomes relevant: the one between games with strategic substitutes and games with strategic complements. Since we are considering the exchange of information among competitors, we restrict the exposition to the case of substitute goods. Hence strategies are substitutes if firms compete in quantity (Cournot) and are complements if the compete in price (Bertrand). The direct adjustment effect (better knowledge of a firm's market conditions due to the information sharing) always increases the correlation of strategies. On the contrary, the strategic adjustment effect (better knowledge of the rivals' type due to the information sharing) decreases the correlation of strategies if firms compete in quantity (strategic substitutes) and increases it if firms compete in price (strategic complements). The intuitive explanation is that in a quantity game (strategic substitutes) if firm i knows that its type is such that it will increase its output, by revealing this information to rivals it will induce them to produce less; if, on the contrary, its type is such that it will produce less, the information makes rivals produce more. In a price game (strategic complements), the opposite is true: by revealing its type, firm i makes rivals change their price in its same direction.

We can sum up all these intermediate results and define the impact of information sharing on firms' profits and consumer surplus. Some generalization is possible if we leave out of the picture the case of Bertrand competition with cost uncertainty. We can say that "normally" an increased correlation of the strategies is efficient from the viewpoint of the firms if the strategies are complements, and is inefficient if strategies are substitutes. This implies that in a common value model (where the prevailing impact of the direct adjustment effect over the strategic adjustment effect leads to a higher correlation) firms always gain by exchanging information if they compete in price. If they compete in quantity, the higher correlation brings about a reduction in profits, whereas the precision effect (outlined in the discussion of the monopoly case) has an opposite impact. Which of the two effects prevails depends on the relevance of the strategic interaction, which in turn depends on the degree of substitutability among the oligopolists' products. For close substitutes, firms loose by sharing information. The opposite occurs when products are poor substitutes. Consumers benefit from information sharing only because of the precision effect and if firms compete in quantity. If firms compete in price with an uncertain demand, both the precision effect and the strategic effects reduce consumer surplus. Therefore, with common value, firms and consumers interests are aligned only if there is quantity competition and there is a weak strategic interaction because of a low degree of substitutability among products. Hence, when these conditions are fulfilled, information sharing is clearly efficient from the point of view of an antitrust authority whatever its objective function.

In the private value/perfect signal model information sharing does not produce any precision effects and the only strategic effect is the strategic adjustment. The latter always alters the correlation of strategies in a direction profitable for the firms. Hence firms always gain from sharing information. However, consumers suffer for the improved strategic interaction among firms and therefore, absent any precision effect, are always worse off because of the exchange of information. Since, in this case, firms and consumers have conflicting interests, the welfare assessment depends on the relative importance attributed to them by the antitrust authority.

With Bertrand competition and cost uncertainty the results are ambiguous. Although information sharing always increases the correlation of the strategies, a higher correlation is not always profitable. Gal-Or (1986) proves that, in a duopoly model, information sharing makes firms worse off. However, Raith (1996) argues that this result does not extend to larger markets, as it is dependent on the parameters of the specific model. These results are summarized in table 8.4 where the + and − signs indicate whether information sharing has a positive or a negative impact on the relevant variable.

8.3.3 Individual Incentives to Unilaterally Reveal Information

So far we have discussed how information sharing affects firms collectively. A different question is whether firms would have an incentive to reveal information to their rivals in the absence of an industrywide agreement. This issue can be addressed by studying a two-stage game where in the first stage each firm decides its revelation behavior and in the second stage each firm receives its private signal, reveals it or not, depending on its first stage

Table 8.4
Effects of information sharing on consumer surplus and profits

Strategic variable	Common value		Private value/perfect signal	
	Demand	Cost	Demand	Cost
Quantity (strategic substitute)	CS: +	CS: +	CS: −	CS: −
	$\pi: \begin{cases} -a \\ +b \end{cases}$	$\pi: \begin{cases} -a \\ +b \end{cases}$	π: +	π: +
Price (strategic complements)	CS: −	Ambiguous effects	CS: −	Ambiguous effects
	π: +		π: +	

Note: a if products are good substitutes; b if products are poor substitutes. CS is consumer surplus.

Table 8.5
Dominant revelation behavior

Strategic variable	Common value		Private value/perfect signal	
	Demand	Cost	Demand	Cost
Quantity (strategic substitute)	Concealing	Concealing	Revealing	Revealing
Price (strategic complements)	Revealing	Ambiguous	Revealing	Ambiguous

decision, gets the information revealed by those firms who decided to transmit it and then sets its strategic variable.[33]

In this setting it is interesting to know whether firms have a dominant strategy in the first stage. Yet, to give an answer, it is necessary to know the type of uncertainty and the mode of competition. As proved by Raith (1996), in all cases, with the exception of the Bertrand market with cost uncertainty, firms have dominant strategies in the first stage. This dominant strategy is to always reveal their private information in private value/perfect signal settings and to do so in common value settings only if they compete in price (strategic complements). On the contrary, in the common value model, if firms compete in quantity, the dominant revelation strategy is to conceal private information, both with demand and cost uncertainty. The intuition behind these results is that in the first stage the individual decision to reveal information depends only on the correlation effect, as a firm does not modify its own knowledge by revealing or concealing its information. Since in private value/ perfect signal games revealing always alters the correlation between conducts in a profitable way the dominant strategy is always to reveal. In the common value case revealing always increases the correlation which is profitable if firms compete in price but it is not if they compete in quantity. These results are reported in table 8.5.

Comparing tables 8.4 and 8.5 we can note that the equilibrium of the two-stage game is always efficient from the firms' point of view when the dominant strategy is to reveal, whereas it can be either efficient or inefficient if firms compete in quantity, when the dominant strategy is to conceal, depending on the degree of competition. For example, in a Cournot market with largely differentiated products, complete information sharing is profitable, but the dominant strategy is not to reveal.

8.3.4 Conclusions on Information Sharing

It is extremely difficult to derive clear policy indications from the formal analysis of information sharing. However, some implications seem quite robust. First, information sharing does not provide evidence supporting the claim that firms entered into an explicit agreement. In many circumstances firms have the incentive to unilaterally reveal their information to rivals. Hence the existence of many circumstances in which information sharing is an equilibrium formed by dominant strategies makes an inference of an explicit agreement unfounded. Moreover the only setting in which the exchange of information might be taken as a clear indication of an agreement is that with common value uncertainty and quantity competition, that is also the setting in which information sharing, absent collusion, benefits consumers and possibly increases profits.

The second implication concerns the possibility that the prohibition of some information sharing mechanisms may prevent efficiency enhancing practices. As argued in section 8.3.1, the exchange of aggregated data is likely to be deemed innocuous and, therefore, permitted, whereas the exchange of individual data may rise antitrust concerns. Now the discussion of the formal literature on information sharing in oligopoly shows that the information sharing mechanisms that are more likely to improve welfare are those that provide firms with a better knowledge of industrywide conditions. This knowledge can be improved through the exchange of aggregated data. Therefore there seems to be a good reason to allow firms to exchange this type of information, as it has little impact on the risk of collusion and, absent collusion, it is likely to have a positive impact on welfare. On the other hand, the exchange of private data has more ambiguous effects on welfare (and certainly a negative impact on consumer surplus). Therefore there does not seem to be a convincing argument that preventing such type of information sharing, which significantly increases the risk of collusion, is likely to result in a welfare inferior equilibrium. The case is even stronger for those markets where there exist structural conditions that make collusion a serious threat.

Finally, in this section and in the previous one I discussed some practices that have as their direct objective a modification of firms knowledge or beliefs. The same goal may be pursued indirectly by means of practices that make the environment in which firms operate more transparent or predictable. Examples are the adoption of rules of conducts, or ethic codes, the standardization of products or of ancillary services, the imposition of vertical restraints, joint marketing or buying agreements, price computation manuals, cost books, interlocking directorates, basic point pricing, and R&D joint ventures. Many of these practices have clear efficiency justifications and are unlikely to be challenged on their own. However, they could create market conditions that favor the emergence of a collusive equilibrium when they are connected to a merger or to other forms of collaboration among competitors.

8.4 Partial Ownership Arrangements

8.4.1 Theory

Firms or firm's owners may acquire stocks in rival firms that grant them the right to part of the rivals' profits. If, by doing so, they acquire (possibly joint) control over the other company, the operation becomes a merger, and it will be subject to an antitrust scrutiny. However, a partial ownership arrangement (POA) may be a mere "passive investment," in that the acquirer does not gain any direct influence on the strategic decisions of the target firm.[34]

Nonetheless, such silent financial interest may affect the firms' conducts so as to lead to a less competitive outcome. The reason why a POA may lessen competition by provoking either unilateral effects or coordinated effects, or possibly both, is intuitively easy. A competitive conduct causes a negative effect on rivals' profits. In a static game, if a firm lowers its price or increases its output, it makes its rivals worse off. In a dynamic game, a deviation from the collusive path improves the payoff of the deviator and reduces the profits of rivals. A firm that does not hold financial interests in its rivals does not take into consideration these negative effects. The acquisition of a financial interest in some competitors has the consequence of, at least partially, internalizing the "negative externalities" of competitive strategies. This reduces the incentive of the acquiring firm to adopt aggressive market conducts in one-shot games, or to abandon a coordinated behavior in repeated games. In short, an investment in rival firms, even if it is completely passive, reduces the return of competitive actions to the extent that competition lowers the value of the investment.

This intuition has been formally proved in several models, most of which deals with static games.[35] The first formal analysis has been provided by Reynolds and Snapp (1986), who show that in a static Cournot game, where firms sell substitute products, any modification of the ownership structure such that a firm's controller raises its ownership interest in a rival reduces the equilibrium market output. In the limit, n firms can secure monopoly profits without any collusive agreement if each of their controllers owns $1/n$ of all the firms.

In the model of Reynolds and Snapp, the firms' controllers own shares in rival firms so that the controller of firm i receives the following payoff:

$$u_i^c = \sum_{j=1}^{n} \gamma_{ij} \hat{\pi}_j(\sigma), \tag{8.9}$$

where γ_{ij} is the share of controller i in firm j, and $\hat{\pi}_j(\sigma)$ indicates the operating earning of firm j associated to the strategy profile σ. A different POA occurs if *firms* (rather than controllers) own stakes in rivals. In this case the profit of each firm with direct or indirect stakes in rivals is given by

$$\pi_i = \hat{\pi}_i(\sigma) + \sum_{j \neq i} a_{ij}\pi_j,$$

where the first term, $\hat{\pi}_i(\sigma)$, indicates the operating earning of firm i associated to the strategy profile σ and the second term, $\sum_{j \neq i} a_{ij}\pi_j$, is the return of the equity hold by firm i in any other firm $j \neq i$, and is given by the fraction of the shares of firm j owned by firm i, a_{ij}, times the profit of firm j. In matrix notation the vector of the firms' profits is given by the solution of the following equation system:

$$\pi = \hat{\pi}(\sigma) + A\pi,$$

where $\hat{\pi}(\sigma)$ is the column vector of the operating earnings associated to the profile σ and A is a Leontief matrix whose elements are denoted by a_{ij}. This equation system has a solution that is defined by

$$\pi(\sigma) = B\hat{\pi}(\sigma),$$

where $B = I + A + A^2 + A^3 + \cdots$.

Hence a firm's profit consist of three parts: (1) its own operating earning, (2) the direct share in the operating earning of other firms, and (3) the indirect effect of its shareholding in its rivals. It follows that total firms' profits exceed the total industry operating earning. However, the total profits for the external "real" shareholders (i.e., controllers and other equity-holders) equal the total operating earning in the industry. In particular, the controller of firm i, who owns γ_{ii} shares of firm i, obtains a payoff of

$$u_i^f = \gamma_{ii}\pi_i(\sigma) = \gamma_{ii} \sum_{j=1}^{n} b_{ij}\hat{\pi}_j(\sigma), \tag{8.10}$$

where b_{ij} is the entry in the ith row and jth column of matrix B.

The two types of arrangements can be combined so that each controller receives

$$u_i^{fc} = \sum_{j=1}^{n} \gamma_{ij}\pi_j(\sigma) = \sum_{j=1}^{n} \gamma_{ij} \sum_{k=1}^{n} b_{jk}\hat{\pi}_k(\sigma). \tag{8.11}$$

Note that equation (8.11) is the same as equation (8.9) when there are no POAs between firms, as in this case $b_{ii} = 1$ for any i, and $b_{ij} = 0$ for any $j \neq i$.

The distinction between "controller's POAs" and "firm's POAs" is not trivial and has some relevant policy implications.[36] Consider first the case where either only the controllers or only the firms own shares in rival firms so that the controllers' payoff are described by equation (8.9) and (8.10). Let x_i be any competitive variable such that π_i is a concave function of x_i, $\partial\pi_j/\partial x_i < 0$, for any $j \neq i$ and such that the market equilibrium is more competitive the higher the value of x_i.[37] From a simple inspection of equations (8.9) and (8.10) it is immediate to see that the level of x_i that would be chosen by a controller that maximizes his payoff is lower if there exist a POA, as he weights the negative impact of rising x_i on the rivals' profits. There are, however, two relevant differences between the two ownership structures. Equation (8.9) shows that a controller that owns stakes in its rivals can lower his incentive to compete also by diluting his ownership in his own firm. By doing so, he increases the relative weight he will give to the well-being of its rivals, further reducing his incentive to choose a high value of x_i. This shows that an antitrust concern may arise not only when a controller invests in rivals but also when he partially divests his own firm, provided that he owns a financial interest in some competitors.

This result does not hold true when only firms partially own some competitors. However, if this latter arrangement is in place, the incentive controllers have to compete is affected not only by their firms' direct interest in rivals but also by their indirect interests. Further it can be inferred that a firm's passive investment in a rival will diminish not only the incentive to compete of the controller of the acquiring firm but also the incentive to compete of the controllers of the firms that have a direct or indirect interest in the acquirer, so that the anticompetitive effect may be stronger with a firm POA. Paradoxically, when the two ownership structures are combined, an increase in a firm's stake in a rival can increase some firm's incentive to compete. For simplicity, consider the case of two firms. From equation (8.11) we have that firm 1's controller payoff is

$$u_1^{cf} = (\gamma_{11}b_{11} + \gamma_{12}b_{21})\pi_1 + (\gamma_{11}b_{12} + \gamma_{12}b_{22})\pi_2,$$

so the weight he gives to the profit of the controlled firm (firm 1) depends positively also on the shares of firm 1 owned by firm 2 (remember that b_{21} increases if a_{21} increases). Hence, if firm 2 raises its stake in firm 1, this passive investment makes firm 1's controller relatively more sensible to the profit of his own firm so that his incentive to compete increases.

These results carry over, to a large extent, to the analysis of repeated games, though with some caveats. The first caveat is that to study the coordinated effects of POAs, we cannot consider only how a passive investment modifies the firms' incentive to compete aggressively. A modification of the ownership structure affects the firms' optimal deviation strategies and their deviation payoffs, and also the level of their profit along the collusive path and, possibly, in the punishment phase. Gilo et al. (2006) prove that in a pure Bertrand game (price competition and homogeneous products) the acquisition by a *firm* of some shares of a competitor never hinders collusion and in fact relaxes the incentive constraint for the acquiring firm and for all the firms with a direct or indirect interest in the acquiring firm.[38] In their model the POA does not modify the payoff associated to the punishment phase, but as we have seen, the POA softens market competition in a one-shot game. Hence, if firms punish a deviation by reversing to the static equilibrium forever, the "topsy-turvy principle" of tacit collusion (see section 8.1.3) applies. As shown by Maleug

(1992), this makes the effect of the POA ambiguous, since the less harsh punishment can tighten the incentive constraint and hinder collusion.

The second caveat is that a POA affects the ability of firms to collude only if it lowers the critical discount factor of the firm with the highest incentive to deviate. This firm may be referred to as the industry maverick. Consideration about the involvement of a maverick in a share transaction are not novel to antitrust. In the analysis of mergers the acquisition of a maverick by one of the leading firms raises the concern that the ability of the new controller to influence the market conduct of the maverick will remove an important competitive constraint. However, when an investment is passive so that the acquirer cannot directly influence the decisions of the target firm, and only the incentives of the parties in the transaction are modified, the risk of coordinated effect arises if the role of the maverick in the transaction is reversed, that is, if the maverick invests in some competitors. If the maverick does not hold equity interests in rivals, its incentive to deviate is not changed by other share transactions in the industry. More important, if the maverick is the target of the partial ownership acquisition, its incentive to deviate is either unaffected or, possibly, increased.[39]

Notwithstanding these important qualifications, the results of the formal literature on POAs seem to found serious antitrust concerns about these ownership structures. These concerns may be extended to other complex ownership and market relationships such as pyramids, debt relationships, interlocking directorates, and networks.[40] Such arrangements seem also to lack any redeeming virtue.[41] However, the anticompetitive motive may be insufficient to explain such a widespread phenomenon. Moreover, while POAs (like mergers), in the absence of efficiencies, always lessen competition, it remains to be proved that (like mergers) they are individually rational. In a linear and symmetric Cournot model, Reitman (1994) investigates whether firms have an incentive to form POAs in the absence of bilateral gains from complementary technology or expertise. This reminds of the question tackled by Salant, Switzer, and Reynolds (1983) who proved in a similar game that a merger that does not create a monopoly is not individually rational. Reitman shows that a similar result obtains for POAs. As in a horizontal merger a POA bestows positive external effects on other firms, since the firms not involved in the POA benefit from the less competitive outcome and from the decision of the participating firms to lower their output. However, for the participating firms the POA is not profitable, unless other POAs form simultaneously.

Farrell and Shapiro (1990) prove that horizontal mergers in Cournot markets are rational, from the point of view of the merging parties, if the transaction improves their efficiency. We can carry their result over the issue of POAs and conjecture that some efficiency reasons can explain why some POAs are formed. Allen and Phillips (2000) examine why corporations purchase large equity positions in other companies and argue that long-term partial ownership arrangements are useful in aligning the incentives of the firms involved in alliances or joint ventures when these projects require ex ante relationship-specific investments.[42] They find that corporate equity ownership stakes, together with product market relationships, lead, in R&D-intensive industries, to an improvement in operating performances and a substantial increase in investment expenditures by target firms. This indicates that partial ownership arrangements are useful to consolidate other market relationships and that, when they exist, the competition authorities should assess the overall competitive effects of these relationships rather than the effects of the cross-ownership arrangement in isolation.[43]

8.4.2   The Antitrust Treatment of POA

In the United States, stock acquisition is treated under Section 7 of the Clayton Act, which condemns the acquisition of "the whole or any part of the stock" of another firm if "the effect of such acquisition may be substantially to lessen competition." However, the third paragraph of the same Section makes the prohibition not applicable "to persons purchasing such stock solely for investment and not using the same by voting or otherwise to bring about, or in attempting to bring about, the substantial lessening of competition." The scope of this "solely for investment" exemption is not clear. According to some commentators it is not much of an exception at all. Hovenkamp (1994) argues that any stock purchase may be challenged on the ground that it has the effect of substantially lessening competition. If this effect is proved, the exception does not apply.

If the acquisition does not substantially lessen competition, it is not illegal in the first place, so there are no reasons to look for an exception.[44] An opposite view is expressed by Gilo (2000) who notices that according to the leading case law, the solely for investment condition has been equated to its being "passive," that is it holds if the acquirer does not gain influence over the actions of the firm whose stock has been acquired. According to Gilo, in case of passive investments the exemption does not apply only if the plaintiff is able to prove that the acquirer *uses* its ownership right so as to bring about a lessening of competition. That is, the prohibition is warranted only if the anticompetitive effects are actual rather than probable. This would grant a de facto exemption to all passive stock acquisitions. The case law does not clarify which of these two interpretations is appropriate.

In most cases antitrust agencies and courts have mainly addressed the question of whether the stock acquisition granted the acquirer some influence on the strategic decisions of the target firm. In case it did not, this was considered sufficient to clear the transaction.[45] In a recent case concerning the diary market,[46] the DOJ alleged that the partial acquisition by Dairy Farmers of America, Inc. (DFA) of Southern Belle, combined with its 50 percent ownership interest in competing National Dairy Holdings, L.P., would substantially lessen future competition in the sale of milk by dairies to Kentucky and Tennessee schools because it would give the parties the incentive and the opportunity to collude. The Court rejected this claim. Even if it agreed that a company need not acquire control of another company in order to violate Section 7 of the Clayton Act, the Court argued that causation between the acquisition and the competitive harm is made less likely when the acquiring company does not have the ability to be involved in the decision-making that forms the basis of the alleged anticompetitive effects. The Court concluded that since DFA could not participate in Southern Belle's pricing, bidding or day-to-day business operations, the DOJ had failed to prove that DFA's nonvoting interest in Southern Belle was likely to cause anticompetitive effects. This reasoning clearly misses the argument put forward by the economic theory of the collusive effects of POAs.

Indeed the only purpose of the economic theory summarized above is to show that a passive investment can lessen competition between the acquirer and the target firm (and in the market) even if the acquirer *does not* participate in the strategic decision of a competitor. However, there are cases where the "solely for investment" exception has not been applied, even where the stock acquisition did not allow the acquirer to participate to the business decision making of the target firm[47] or where an adequate weight was given to the consequences of the passive investment on the incentives of the parties involved. In 1998 the merger between AT&T and Tele-Communications Inc. (TCI) was given regulatory approval by the DOJ conditioned on the undertaking of TCI to divest its 23,5 percent stake in Sprint PCS Group. In its complaint the DOJ argued:

AT&T's ownership of a substantial equity interest in Sprint PCS may substantially lessen competition in the relevant markets. By acquiring a partial ownership of Sprint PCS, AT&T will reduce its incentives to prevent customers from choosing Sprint PCS, rather than AT&T, as a provider of mobile wireless telephone services. As a result of the acquisition, AT&T will indirectly benefit, as an owner of Sprint PCS stock, when a customer chooses Sprint PCS rather than AT&T. Because of this ownership, AT&T will have less incentive to lower prices (or to increase the quality of its service) in order to prevent customers from switching to other providers of mobile wireless telephone services in areas in which Sprint PCS is a significant rival. This anticompetitive effect is exacerbated by the fact that AT&T and Sprint PCS are particularly close substitutes for one another for many customers, especially for those customers who are attracted by their strong brands and the nearly nationwide footprint offered by both AT&T and Sprint PCS.

In the European Union the Merger Regulation applies only if the acquisition entail a modification of the control structure of the acquired firm. Therefore a passive investment does not give rise to a merger and is not subject to preventive scrutiny. However, it can be assessed under Article 81. The antitrust treatment of partial ownership arrangements is still largely based on the judgment of the ECJ in the *Philip Morris* case. In 1984 Philip Morris and Rembrandt Group Ltd, two of the six largest companies active in the European market for cigarettes, entered an agreement whereby Philip Morris would acquire 30.8 percent of the shares of Rothmans International, representing 24.9 percent of the votes, whereas Rembrand would held also 30.8 percent of Rothman's shares, with 43.6 percent of the voting rights. Philip Morris had undertook not to have its own representatives in the management of Rothmans. The ECJ maintained that "although the acquisition by one company of an equity interest in a competitor does not in itself constitute conduct restricting compe-

Facilitating Practices   335

tition, such an acquisition may nevertheless serve as an instrument for influencing the commercial conduct of the companies in question so as to restrict or distort competition."[48]

It should be noted that at that time the EC Merger Regulation was not in force yet. Therefore we can read the *Philip Morris* judgment as an attempt to use Article 81 to close the gap. Since then the Commission has never enjoined or tried to modify agreements that established partial ownership arrangements.[49] It has, however, taken into account the existence of such agreements in the analysis of mergers that could create or strengthen a collective dominant position (coordinated effects).

8.5 Best-Price Policies

A best-price policy is a commitment made by a firm either to match or beat the lower price charged by other firms (price matching guarantee and price beating guarantee) or by itself to other current or future customers (most-favored customer clause).

8.5.1 Price-Matching and Price-Beating Guarantees

Price-matching (PMG) and price-beating guarantees (PBG) (collectively referred to as low price guarantees) are facilitating practices as they can lead to supracompetitive prices by preventing firms to be undercut by rivals, or by reducing the rivals' incentives to undercut.[50] The argument was first informally developed by Hay (1982) and Salop (1986), and subsequently explored formally by several authors. The simplest setting that can illustrate the anticompetitive potential of low price guarantees is that of a symmetric market with Bertrand competition in which firms can promise to match competitors' prices. A firm that adopts a PMG has two prices (which may coincide). One is the posted price and the other is the actual or selling price, which is a function of all prices charged in the market. A PMG implies that the actual price is the minimum of all available prices. Since consumers choose among firms according to their selling price, a firm with a PMG cannot be effectively undercut.

If all firms adopt PMGs, then charging the monopoly price becomes a weakly dominant strategy for all players and forms an equilibrium of the one-shot game. Indeed, if a PMG firm raises its posted price, the selling price does not change. If a firm (with or without a PMG) lowers the posted price, rivals automatically match it provoking a reduction of total profits that remain equally shared. A deviation consisting in modifying the price, and abandoning the PMG strategy does not change the situation in the case of a price reduction and provoke the loss of all consumers in the case of a price increase. Any price between the competitive and the monopoly price forms an equilibrium. However, all PMG firms gain at least the same profits if they set the listed price equal to the monopoly level.

How robust is this result to its underlying assumptions? A PMG can generate supracompetitive prices also if firms sell differentiated products or if they bear different costs and/or face different demands that cause the competitive profiles to exhibit some price dispersion, provided that there exists a vector of identical prices at which firms are not unilaterally willing to deviate by moving their prices in opposite directions (Hviid and Shaffer 1999). Somehow counterintuitively, the threat of a more aggressive response to an attempt by rivals to lower the price embedded in the PBG strategy may restore the competitive equilibrium. Dixit and Nalebuff (1991) noted that a firm facing rivals with a PBG cannot undercut competitors' prices by *lowering* the posted price. If they do so they end up reducing even further the effective price of PBG competitors. This seems to reinforce the anticompetitive effects of PMGs. However, as pointed out by Corts (1995) and by Hviid and Shaffer (1994), the same firm can steal consumers away from PBG firms by adopting a PBG strategy and "overcutting" rivals, namely by *increasing* its posted price.

A higher posted price then triggers the PBG and lowers the selling price below the prices of competing firms. Since PBGs reintroduce the possibility of undercutting, they bring firms back to the competitive equilibrium. Yet Edlin (1997) and Kaplan (2000) show that the argument put forward by Corts and Hviid and Shaffer is correct if PBGs apply only to listed prices. Indeed it is immediate to see that if a firm promises to beat not only any rivals' posted price but also their effective prices (included those that might result from the application of a PBG), the possibility to undercut the price of a PBG firm by raising the posted price disappears,[51] making a PBG at least as valid as a PMG in order to support supracompetitive prices.[52]

The Hay-Salop insight is robust to different model specifications of the supply side of the market.[53] Yet their conjecture turns out to be less robust if we consider different models of consumers' behavior. So far we have imagined that low price guarantees imply automatic price adjustments, which is effectively correct if all consumers redeem their guarantee as soon as they find a lower (posted or selling) price. Hviid and Shaffer (1999) point out that for most consumers the activation of a price guarantee entails "hassle" costs, as they must go back to the firm where they made their purchase, provide evidence of the lower price, argue with a salesperson, and so on. The size of these hassle costs depends on many variables attaining both to consumer's preferences and to the low price guarantee policy. However, it is probably correct that for many (all) consumers the prospect of a *small* price reduction is not sufficient to compensate the waste of time required to claim it. Whatever is the value that we consider *small*, this implies that hassle costs are positive.

Hviid and Shaffer show that the presence of positive hassle costs, no matter how much small, in a symmetric market is sufficient to deprive PMGs of their anticompetitive consequences. Their reasoning is easily grasped in the simple context of homogeneous products. If, for all consumers, the hassle cost is $z > 0$ and two firms posted prices p_A and p_B are such that $p_A > p_B$, but $p_A - p_B < z$, then even if firm A has a PMG, there are no consumers who are willing to activate firm A's PMG, whose actual price remains p_A. In an homogeneous market with price competition, all consumers will buy from firm B. Since for any value of z and any price charged by competitors a firm can always charge a price that is below all competing prices and such that the difference between the minimum available price and its price is less than z, all firms have the possibility and the incentive to undercut their competitors.

The only equilibrium that survives is therefore the competitive equilibrium. Hviid and Shaffer prove that "hassle costs" do not always eliminate the possibility of anticompetitive PMGs. However, they show that hassle costs significantly limit the negative impact of these strategies as their capability of increasing final prices and reducing welfare depends negatively on the size of hassle costs borne by consumers. This finding paves the way of a possible counterargument. Firms have the possibility to substitute consumers in their activity or compensate consumers for their hassle costs. For instance, they can announce and implement the policy of monitoring rivals prices and adjust their pricing policy accordingly so to keep valid their low price claim. The second strategy may be implemented by a PBG in which competitors price are beaten by a lump sum that compensates the guarantee holder for the resources she must spend to redeem her guarantee.

Low-price guarantees can also serve the purpose of price discriminating among consumers. Belton (1987) Png and Hirshleifer (1987) and Corts (1996) investigate models where there are two classes of customers who incur a different cost to obtain information. They show that the employment of low price guarantees in these cases can allow firms to raise the price charged to uninformed consumers without risk of loosing informed consumers.

In all models where firms achieve supracompetitive prices through low price guarantees, welfare decreases both if we consider only the consumer surplus and if we take into account also the firms' profits. Edlin and Emch (1999) argue that the total welfare loss of low-price guarantees might be much greater than the "Harberger triangle" because of the allocative inefficiency of high prices. They consider a market with free entry and fixed costs and show that price-matching policies that sustain a high price attract entry until firms' average costs rise to the equilibrium price. Over-entry entails higher industrywide average costs that dissipate any collusive profit and add the "Posner rectangle" to the total welfare loss.

As for other facilitating practices discussed in previous sections, formal economic research on low-price guarantees has restricted attention to static games, showing their potential anticompetitive *unilateral* effects. Whether low price guarantees have coordinated effects is not clear. They do not seem to provide means to solve the coordination problem as they do not convey any information on the desired price level. However, they can contribute in different ways to solve the enforcement problem. Since a low-price guarantee normally imposes on consumers the burden of providing evidence of a cheaper offer, this policy can constitute an indirect means to which firms turn to collect information and monitor rivals' behavior. It may be thought that low-price guarantees can produce coordinated effects because they reduce the profits a firm can reap by deviating from the concerted actions, as they render punishment more rapid.

If we exclude the consideration above on monitoring, it is not clear whether the conjecture on the ability of low-price guarantees to alleviate the enforcement problem is correct. In the simple model of Bertrand competition with homogeneous products and PMGs either the monopoly outcome is obtained in the static equilibrium (which makes any preoccupation of coordinated effects redundant) or, in the presence of hassle costs, the competitive equilibrium prevails in the one-shot game. Hence the existence of PMGs does not alter the incentive constraints for a collusive equilibrium of the repeated games. When low-price guarantees alter the static equilibrium without bringing firms to the joint maximization level, as in the Hviid and Shaffer model with asymmetric firms, the impact of low-price guarantees on the incentive constraints cannot be predicted without a formal analysis.

The economic analysis of low-price guarantees has significantly contributed to the their bad name, to the point where several legal scholars have taken stance against them. This attitude depends also on the seeming lack of business justifications for price protection clauses other than anticompetitive goals. For instance, Hovenkamp (1994, p. 178) maintains that "the social cost of enjoining the practices would not be high, for there was no convincing evidence that the practices were efficiency creating." Recently, however, Moorthey and Winter (2002) have presented a duopoly model with differentiated products in which in equilibrium one firm uses a PMG to signal to uninformed consumers its low-price strategy.

The essential element that drives the Moorthey and Winter result is that the two firms differ in their unit costs and that the cost difference is sufficiently large. In this situation the high-cost firm is not willing to adopt a PMG that "delegates" its selling price for informed consumers to the low-cost firm because, although the PMG leads to a collusive price, the collusive level is set by the low-cost firm at *its* monopoly price, and this price might be too low for the high-cost firm. If the number of informed consumers is sufficiently large, uninformed consumers, who do not have information on the price levels but observe the pricing *policy* of the two firms, know that the disciplining behavior of informed consumers would penalize the high-cost firm that offers a PMG and therefore could correctly infer that the firm that offers the PMG is the one that charges the lowest price. However, the effects of PMGs on consumer welfare are ambiguous. Moorthy and Winter prove that the adoption of a PMG by the low-cost firm leads to a price increase for the low-cost firm and a price decrease for the high-cost firm. Uninformed consumers normally benefit from the information conveyed by the pricing policy, while informed consumers who buy from the low-cost firm are always worse off.

In conclusion, although, the Moorthey and Winter model does not provide a convincing efficiency reason against the bad reputation of low-price guarantees, at least it offers a rationale for the adoption of price protection clauses different from their anticompetitive motives (unilateral effects, price discrimination, and collusion). This rationale is strengthened by some experimental results obtained in the marketing literature that investigates the consumers perception of low-price guarantees. Jain and Srivastava (2000), Srivastava and Lurie (2001) and Chatterjee et al. (2003) find that buyers prefer markets where sellers offer LPGs, perceive the store with the price-matching policy to have lower prices, and are more likely to choose the store with a refund policy. These findings seem to point out the need to incorporate a bounded rationality hypothesis to explain the wide adoption of low-price guarantees by retailers. Empirical research appears to indicate that such aspect might explain the strategic decision to adopt a low-price guarantee and their actual features.

Arbatskaya et al. (2004), studying a sample of newspaper ads of low-price guarantees, find that a very large portion of them are inconsistent with their use as facilitating devices. They conjecture that one reason for such pricing policy is to induce consumers to buy immediately rather than wait for a product to go on sale or continue searching for a lower price. According to these suggestions, low-price guarantees can be thought as a form of "nonprice" competition aimed to satisfy some consumer preferences for feeling "protected" from rip-offs. Whether this conjecture is correct and, more important, whether these preferences (if they exist) should be taken into account in welfare analyses, are questions that need further research to be answered.

8.5.2 Most-Favored Customer

A most-favored-customer clause (MFCC) obliges a firm to charge a buyer the same price charged by the same firm to other customers. It can be either retroactive or contemporaneous. A retroactive MFCC entitles the buyer to receive a discount (or a refund) if the seller charges anyone a lower price within a given period of time in the future. A contemporaneous MFCC corresponds to a commitment not to price discriminate as it forces the firm to charge the same price to all buyers.

MFCCs have similar effects as LPGs. The main difference is that while the latter reduce the rivals' incentive to lower the price, the former reduce the incentive of the firm that adopts the clause to lower its own price in the future or to some selected customers.[54] As shown by Cooper (1986), by adopting a retroactive MFCC in a two-period game, a firm credibly commits to act less competitively in the second period, as a price reduction entails the payment of a penalty to past consumers that may exceed the gains from increased sales. Therefore the second-period reaction function with the MFCC has a flat portion, showing that the best response to any rival's price in the relevant interval is to charge the first-period price. This induces the rival to charge a higher price in the second period, since prices are strategic complements. Hence the firm with the MFCC can increase its flow of profits (and the rival's flow of profit) by setting a first-period price above the static Bertrand equilibrium.[55] Since the MFCC increases the profit of both firms, there is a perfect equilibrium in which one firm offers such a clause before the market game opens.[56]

While the unilateral effects of MFCCs are clearly proved by the formal literature,[57] their coordinated effects are less obvious. Here I repeat what I said about LPGs: there are nor formal studies on the impact of MFCCs on the ability of firms to sustain collusion in an infinitely repeated game. Baker (1996) has pointed out that MFFCs can reduce firms' incentive to deviate because they effectively impede them to offer discounts to a single customer. Hence a selective price deviation may become unprofitable if the price reduction must apply to all customers. However, for the same reason selective punishment strategies become unfeasible, and the impossibility to punish deviators selectively may increase the cost of imposing a penalty on the deviating firm. Moreover, as already argued for other facilitating practices, if a MFCC improves the equilibrium payoffs in the one-shot game, and collusion is sustained by the threat of a Nash reversal, such a clause may hinder collusion as it makes the punishment less severe.

As for other facilitating practices, MFCCs have some efficiency justifications. They can support long-term relationships with relation-specific investments, by protecting one party from opportunistic behavior by the other party. In such long-term contracts a fixed price can be unattractive, as it would impede efficient adjustments to new demand and cost conditions. However, a frequent price negotiation can put the party who has made the relation-specific investment at the mercy of the other party. A MFCC constrains the bargaining position of the strongest party and allows the price to change as market conditions vary.[58] When this business justification applies, the efficiency properties of MFCCs must be balanced against their anticompetitive effects under the rule of reason.

8.5.3 Some Antitrust Cases

Most of the economic literature has been spurred by two US cases. The first, *GE-Westinghouse*,[59] resulted in a modification of a preexisting consent decree concerning an open and explicit agreement and therefore was not litigated. The DOJ observed in the early 1960s that the market for large turbine generators had experienced a dramatic reduction in the degree of competition. The DOJ argued that this was the consequence of a new pricing policy introduced by GE in 1963 and adopted by Westinghouse a year later. The new policy contained several facilitating practices, including a "price protection" clause, according to which in the event GE had lowered its price to any customer it would have paid a retroactive discount to any buyer who paid the list price within the past six months. Once informed of the intention of the DOJ to file a civil suit, GE and Westinghouse accepted all the relief sought by the DOJ.

The second case, *Ethyl*,[60] was brought by the Federal Trade Commission under the Section 5 of the FTC Act.[61] The case involved four producers of lead antiknock additives for gasoline. The two largest producers adopted three practices that allegedly led to supracompetitive prices: (1) a uniform delivered pricing, (2) price announcements, and (3) most-favored customer clauses. The administrative law judge and the full Commission found that these practices facilitated a collusive coordination by reducing the firms' incentive to discount. However, the court of appeals dismissed the complaint. According to the opinion of the court, the FTC had not proved that the firms had adopted these practices with the intent to accomplish tacit collusion. Even if these practices, at some point in time, resulted in a substantial lessening of competition, the court feared that such a test would have been too vague and would have allowed an undue interference with the freedom of action that characterizes the market system.[62]

The European Commission has never carried out an investigation on best-price policies as practices that facilitate collusion.[63]

8.6 Conclusions

At the start of the chapter, I asked three questions relevant for proper antitrust treatment of facilitating practices: (1) Does an *agreement* to adopt facilitating practices violate some antitrust prohibitions as those stated in Article 81 of the EC Treaty or Section 1 of the Sherman Act? (2) Should the adoption of a facilitating practice independently of an agreement be prohibited by antitrust law? And, in case of an affirmative answer, what is the legal basis for such prohibition? (3) Does the adoption of facilitating practices provide evidence of a collusive agreement?

To answer these questions, I summarized the main findings of the economic literature: (1) Practices that affect the information structure of the game or the players' payoff functions can have anticompetitive effects by softening competition in static games or by making collusion more stable in infinitely repeated games. (2) The anticompetitive effects of facilitating practices occur only if some market conditions are satisfied; in particular, they are more likely to emerge in highly concentrated markets that are already prone to collusion. (3) Anticompetitive effects do not necessarily stem from a collective action as they can result from the unilateral adoption of a facilitating practice by just one firm. (4) In some cases the adoption of a facilitating practice is a dominant strategy. (5) All the facilitating practices examined can serve also some efficiency purposes.

In my opinion, these results suffice to answer the first two questions but not the third one. As for the first question, it is apparent that an *agreement* to implement one or more facilitating practices, insofar as these practices lessen competition, should be considered a violation of the antitrust prohibition of anticompetitive agreements. Article 81 of the EC Treaty or Section 1 of the Sherman Act is clearly applicable, with the only caveat that either application should be subject to the rule of reason, given the existence of possible efficiency justifications. A related issue is who should bear the burden of proof in such cases. My position is that the plaintiff or the antitrust authority should prove that the market conditions that make the emergence of likely anticompetitive effects are fulfilled. When this condition is met, a rebuttable presumption of illegality is established. The defendant then should bear the burden of proving that the implementation of the practice is justified by efficiency reasons and that its efficiency outweighs its anticompetitive effects.

As for the second question, I believe that antitrust laws should contain a prohibition (subject to the rule of reason) of facilitating practices, even when they are adopted in the absence of an agreement to do so. However, I believe that the prohibition of anticompetitive agreements contained in Article 81 or Section 1 is not applicable in most cases. My position hinges on the conviction that an *agreement* is a requisite for the application of these norms, which leads to the question of what is an agreement in antitrust law. Two opposite views can be taken on this issue (Hay 2000). On one hand, its meaning can be restricted so as to include only those cases in which firms explicitly, and through some form of direct communication, try to coordinate their behavior. On the other hand, the meaning of "agreement" can cover any form of coordination that may arise with or without an explicit communication or any communication at all.

It is well established by jurisprudence, and accepted by most legal scholars, that while the first meaning is too limited, as it leaves out of the scope of antitrust law some forms of cooperation or concerted action that are likely to harm competition, the antitrust prohibition does not extend to cover parallel conduct that is only the consequence of oligopolistic interdependence, even if it results in a less competitive equilibrium. The main reason why "conscious parallelism" does not constitute an antitrust violation is that it only requires that firms make rational decisions, so it is impossible to identify conducts that can be described as "avoidable" or "culpable."[64]

Notwithstanding the limitation on the notion of *agreement*, there is room to expand the meaning beyond the clear instance of an *explicit agreement* and so to capture *some* avoidable and potentially harmful conducts. These more subtle forms of coordination are sometimes referred to as *tacit agreements*. However, I believe that the meaning of "agreement" is too stretched if by tacit agreement we mean any form of coordination that arises from some avoidable conduct, including a conduct unilaterally adopted by one firm.[65] Market coordination, even if it is the result of a culpable conduct, is not an agreement.

Since an agreement—no matter whether express or tacit—requires at least *two* parties, it can be established only if a culpable conduct can be attributed to at least two firms. If just a firm adopts a facilitating practice, for instance, a best-price policy, its conduct is culpable and may be subject to an antitrust prohibition. However, the conduct of its rivals, that set their market strategies taking into account the likely reaction of their competitors, as affected by the facilitating practice adopted by one of them, is not culpable, as it is not culpable any rational conduct that stems only from oligopolistic interdependence. The existence of a culpable conduct by one firm does not suffice to give rise to an agreement that is and should remain a collective infringement.

My position here should not be read as supporting a formalistic approach. Indeed some instances of two-way pre-play communication are capable of coordinating firms' market behavior and may constitute an agreement, even if communication takes place indirectly and through means other than the natural language. Nothing prevents an application of Article 81 or Section 1 to these practices. In all the other cases in which a facilitating practice is adopted unilaterally, I believe that a different norm should be applied. In the United States, this role can be played by Section 5 of the Federal Trade Commission Act, which outlaws "unfair method of competition," without requiring proof of an agreement. In the European Union, a similar norm is missing and should be introduced to fill an important gap.

Finally, as for the third question, on whether the implementation of a facilitating practice provides circumstantial evidence of an express collusive agreement, I believe that we are not in the position to give a clear answer. First, if the alleged agreement concerns the adoption of the facilitating practice, it must be recognized that theoretical analysis shows that in most cases the adoption of a facilitating practice is a dominant strategy. This excludes that firms *must* agree to adopt them. Second, if the alleged agreement concerns a different strategic choice, for instance, as in the case of a price-fixing agreement, then the answer depends mostly on an empirical question that has not been adequately investigated. Indeed the matter is whether the probability of observing a facilitating practice is higher when a collusive agreement is in place rather when it is not. Only if this is the case, we can argue that the ex post probability we have to assign to the existence of a collusive agreement is higher when we observe the implementation of a facilitating practice so that this fact supports an allegation of an unlawful agreement.

On a pure theoretical ground there are no reason to believe that the probability of a facilitating practice conditioned to the existence of a conspiracy is higher or lower. On one hand, a facilitating practice may be useful to sustain a collusive agreement that otherwise would fail. Hence we may argue that when firms decide to collude explicitly, they are likely to adopt some facilitating practice. On the other hand, firms may adopt a facilitating practice to reach a collusive equilibrium for the very reason that they do not want to enter an illegal explicit agreement. Moreover firms that collude explicitly may not need to resort to some facilitating practice to reach the same outcome. This would imply a lower occurrence of facilitating practices when firms collude explicitly. So the issue is whether firms see facilitating practices and overt collusion as complements or substitutes. The issue is only solvable empirically, and this will require new research.

Notes

I thank Marco Pistagnesi and Cristiana Vitale for their helpful comments, and Paolo Siciliani for his research assistance.

1. For the sake of simplicity in the chapter, I use "price" to refer to any strategic variable that may be affected through facilitating practices so as to increase profits and reduce consumer welfare.

2. Baker (1996) uses "facilitating practices" to refer to conduct that would permit firms to achieve higher prices in a noncooperative repeated game framework and the term "dampening competition" to refer to conduct that would lead to higher prices in a static setting.

3. This is true by definition: if no firm can increase profits by deviating unilaterally, then the profile of strategies is a Nash equilibrium of the static game. But I define collusion here as a departure from the equilibrium of the static game.

4. The formal literature on collusion in supergames with imperfect monitoring started with the contributions of Porter (1983) and Green and Porter (1984) and was further developed by Abreu et al. (1986). These papers study the feasibility of collusion in markets where firms have imperfect information and condition their behavior upon

some public signal. More recent contributions are those of Compte (1998) and Kandori and Matsushima (1998), who discuss the role of communication among firms to sustain a collusive equilibrium when they can only observe private signals.

5. Shapiro (1989, p. 365, n. 65) attributes to Avinash Dixit the saying "Competition is collusion."

6. Numerous experiments have been conducted to study the impact of communication on coordination. Most results support the theoretical prediction that communication is a powerful coordinator device. Dawes et al. (1977) show that pre-play communications generally improve cooperation in Prisoner's Dilemma games; Daughety and Forsythe (1987a, b) and Binger et al. (1990) report that group discussions are effective in raising price in repeated Cournot games. Similar results in auction markets are reported by Isaac and Walker (1985). Burton et al. (2005) and Blume and Ortmann (2007) present other experimental results on the same subject. Holt (1995), Ledyrad (1995), Wellford (2002), and Haan et al. (2005) offer very rich surveys of experiments on the role of communication in coordination games.

7. See Aumann and Hart (2003) for a discussion of this literature.

8. Farrel and Rabin (1996) provide a nontechnical discussion of the main issues of this approach.

9. "Cheap talk" refers to a form of communication that does not affect the players' payoffs as it carries no cost. This characteristic distinguishes cheap talk from signaling that involves the transmission of costly information.

10. In a pure matching game the same payoff is associated to all coordinated strategy profile, so players do not care which coordinated equilibrium they reach. However, the relevant common feature of a pure matching game and the game discussed in the text is that in both games the interests of all players are aligned and that no player has an incentive to disguise his intentions.

11. This assumption is consistent with the interpretation of a mixed-strategy equilibrium as an equilibrium in beliefs when players are uncertain about the actual choice of rivals (e.g., see Aumann and Brandenburger 1995) that fits with the following discussion on how communication can change these beliefs.

12. In a communication game with cheap talk all the strategy profiles that form an equilibrium in the action stage are still an equilibrium in the Two-Stage Game, if messages are simply ignored by the players. These equilibria are called "babbling equilibria," as they posit that the players babble and not really communicate. If we maintain that the players can exchange *meaningful* messages, the elimination of all babbling equilibria seems a sensible refinement that is implicitly assumed in the text.

13. In the classical Stag Hunt Game the payoff of both players when they choose B would be independent of the strategy chosen by the opponent.

14. Arvan et al. (1999) prove that this improvement is not only a possibility, but that cheap talk *must* imply an improvement in equilibrium payoffs.

15. Miller and Moser (2004) show that, in an evolutionary setting, giving agents the ability to communicate even a priori meaningless messages may promote the emergence of coordinated behaviors that lead to superior outcomes.

16. *United States v. Airline Tariff Publ'g Co.* 836 F. Supp. 9 (DDC 1993).

17. Borenstein (1994) provides a discussion of the *ATP* case.

18. Another interesting case of coordination through some form of indirect communication is described by Cramton and Schwartz (2000). For a summary of this case, see chapter 16 by Klemperer in this volume.

19. Commission Decision, case IV/26.267 *Dyestuffs*, O.J. 1969 L 195/11.

20. Cases 48, 49, 51–7/69 *ICI v. Commission* (1972) ECR 619.

21. Commission Decision, case IV/29.725 *Wood Pulp*, O.J. 1985 L 85/1.

22. Cases 89, 104, 114, 116–17, 125–29/85, *Ahlström Osakeyhtiö and others v. Commission* (1988) ECR 5193.

23. Key cases include: *Maple Flooring Manufacturers Ass'n v. United States*, 268 US 563 (1925); *United States v Container Corp.*, 393 US 333 (1969); *United States v. Citizens and Nat'l Bank*, 422 US 86, 113 (1975) and *United States v. US Gypsum Co.*, 438 US 422,441 (1978).

24. *Todd v. Exxon Corp.*, 275 F.3d 191 (2d Cir. 2001). In this case the plaintiff alleged that fourteen major companies in the integrated oil and petrochemical industry, collectively accounting for 80 to 90 percent of the industry's revenues and employing approximately the same percentage of the industry's workforce, had violated Section 1 of the Sherman Act by regularly sharing detailed information regarding compensation paid to nonunion managerial, professional, and technical employees and using this information in setting the salaries of these employees at artificially low levels. Therefore, even if the case concerns the exchange of data about an input mar-

ket rather than the product market, the Court followed and clarified the same approach discussed in the more typical case in which the information concerns the market in which firms act as sellers.

25. Indeed the *Guidelines on Horizontal Cooperation Agreement* (OJ 2001/C 3/02) and the *Guidelines on the Application of Article 81(3) of the Treaty* (OJ 2004/C 101/08), which provided an opportunity to give guidance on the position of the European enforcement body, deliberately leave out of their scope a discussion of the competitive assessment of exchange of information. Some statements can be found in much older documents such as the 1968 *Notice concerning Decisions and Concerted Practices in the field of Co-operation between Enterprises* (OJ 1968/C 75/3) and in the 1977 *7th Report on Competition Policy*. In both cases the Commission affirmed that the assessment of facilitating practices such as the exchange of information is conducted under a rule of reason approach. The 1977 Report qualifies the Commission position by establishing three criteria to be followed to assess such arrangements. They regard (1) the structure of the market, (2) the nature and the scope of the information exchanged, and (3) the private or public nature of the information dissemination mechanism. According to the Commission, information sharing is likely to be an infringement of Article 81 if it takes place in a market whose conditions make collusion a serious risk, if it concerns sensitive information or trade secrets, and if it improves only the seller's knowledge of the market, without creating an opportunity for customers to compare the various offers and increase rivalry.

26. Commission Decision, cases IV/31.370 and 31.446 *UK Agricultural Tractor Registration Exchange*, O.J. 1992, L68/19.

27. Case T-35/92, *J. Deree v. Commission* (1994) ECR I-3111, par. 90.

28. For a discussion of the Commission's practice after *UK Agricultural Tractor*, see Capobianco (2004).

29. Commission Notice, case IV/34.936 *CEPI-Cartonboard*, O.J. 1996, C 310/3.

30. Commission Decision, case IV/36.069 *Wirtschaftsvereinigung Stahl*, O.J. 1998, L 1/10.

31. Information on costs can also facilitate the solution of the "coordination problem." The knowledge of players' costs might prove essential to finding a common price or output policy that satisfies all firms. Moreover, if firms follow a cost-plus approach in setting their prices, cost information provides reliable hints of their future pricing decisions.

32. The first formal models were developed by Novshek and Sonnenschein (1982), Clarke (1983), and Vives (1984). Important contributions are those of Gal-Or (1985, 1986), Li (1985), Shapiro (1986), Sakai (1986), and Kirby (1988). This literature investigates information sharing in an oligopoly where firms face either a stochastic intercept of a linear demand function or a stochastic marginal cost. Michael Raith (1996) has developed a model that retains some simplifying assumptions (mainly: linear-quadratic profit functions and normally distributed random variables) but generalizes the previous literature. The policy implications of this literature are discussed by Kuhn and Vives (1995) and by Kuhn (2001). This and the following sections are largely based on Raith's general model.

33. This formulation of the problem assumes that firms are somehow able to commit to some revelation behavior so that this does not depend on the type of signal received. However, as argued by Raith (1993), the distinction between deciding the revelation behavior before or after private information is received is imposed by the static structure of the model. Indeed, if the Two-Stage Game is taken as a reduced form of a repeated interaction, then the commitment can be considered as a metaphor of a behavior meant to possibly sacrifice short-run gains in order maximize long-run profits.

34. Examples of such passive investments are Microsoft's acquisition of nonvoting stock of Apple and Northwest Airlines' acquisition of 14 percent of the common stock of Continental Airlines. For a discussion of these and several other cases, see Gilo (2000).

35. Reynolds and Snapp (1986), Flath (1991, 1992), Merlone (2001), and Dietzenbacher et al. (2000) study the effects of POAs in static games. The only papers that investigate the consequences of POAs on tacit collusion in repeated games are Maleug (1992) and Gilo et al. (2006).

36. The results of Reynolds and Snapp (1986) extend to the case of "firms POAs" as proved by Flath (1992) in a symmetric Cournot game with symmetric financial control. The existence of unilateral effects of firms POAs has been proved also in case of asymmetric Cournot markets (Merlone 2001) and Betrand differentiated markets (Dietzenbacher et al. 2000).

37. For instance, x_i is the level of output of firm i or the discount firm i offers with respect to the choke-off price.

38. The firms whose incentive constraint is not affected by the share acquisition are those that do not hold an interest in the acquiring firm and the target firm.

39. The role of the maverick in the transaction (if any) is still important although less crucial for the analysis of unilateral effects of POAs.

40. See Buccirossi and Spagnolo (2006) for a survey of the literature on the complex theme of collusion relating to ownership and corporate governance.

41. For instance, Hovenkamp (1994, p. 498) argues that "Mergers . . . receive rather complex rule of reason treatment because they . . . have the potential to create substantial economies. . . . If A acquires 15% of the shares of its competitor B, A may not have enough equity to 'control' B. Neither, however, will the firms have common management or other bases for obtaining the kinds of economies that make mergers socially valuable. In this case, . . . the potential for social good has been reduced to nearly zero."

42. Klein et al. (1978) and Williamson (1979, 1985) argue that specific investments give rise to opportunistic behavior and holdup problems that create inefficiencies when transactions are governed only by arm's-length contracts. Williamson claims that equity can lower contracting costs or the costs of monitoring agreements. Aghion and Tirole (1994) model vertical relationships in which the specific investment problem is alleviated by partial ownership arrangements. Although these contributions focus on vertical relationships, whereas competitive concerns can arise when firms acquire stakes in horizontal competitors, their insights apply in all cases where firms contribute in a common project with complementary products.

43. The empirical analysis carried out by Alley (1997) casts some doubts on the impact of cross-ownership on collusion. He applies a conjectural variation model to the Japanese and US automobile industries and finds that although the Japanese market is collusive, it remains more competitive than the US market. Berglöf and Perotti (1994) argue that the predominance of shareholding within a Japanese *keiretsu* may be rationalized as an efficient way of enforcing collaboration and long-term commitment of group members.

44. The same position is expressed by Areeda and Turner (1980, p. 1024) who maintain that the "solely for investment" exemption is superfluous. They explain that "the true exception' issue would squarely arise only in an acquisition that is deemed both (a) to be solely for investment and (b) to have a probable anticompetitive effect. But there could be no such a case if the acquirer were presumed to intend the probable consequences of his act." Hence the exception is not applicable also if it is interpreted as a reference to the "intention" of the acquirer and not to the effects of the acquisition as presumably these effects are a necessary part of the acquirer's motives.

45. A leading case is the acquisition by Gillette of 22.9 percent of the nonvoting stock of Wilkinson Sword, *United States v. Gillette Co.*, 55 Fed. Reg. 28 (1990). Gilo (2000) discusses this and some related cases.

46. *United States v. Dairy Farmers of Am., Inc.*, 2004-2 Trade Cas. (CCH) P74, 537, (2004) US Dist. LEXIS 17814.

47. See Gilo (2000) for a survey and a discussion of such cases.

48. Cases 142, 156/84, *British–American Tabacco Company Ltd an R. J. Reynolds Industries Inc. v. Commission* (1987) ECR I-4487, par. 37.

49. The European Commission has addressed agreements for the acquisition of minority shareholding in the cases IV/34.857 *BT/MCI*, O.J. 1994 L223/36, and IV/34.410 *Olivetti/Digital*, O.J. 1994 L309/24. For a discussion of the *Philip Morris* case and the subsequent decisions of the European Commission, see Caronna (2004).

50. LPGs can also serve an entry deterrence purpose (e.g., see Arbatskaya 2001). I do not discuss this issues as it is outside the scope of this chapter.

51. The computation of selling prices when PBGs apply to actual prices might be quite complex, since any price reduction stemming from the application of the PBG of one firm triggers the competitors PBGs, and so on. However, the iterative process converges quite quickly to a vector of practically identical prices (especially if we admit that any difference in the value of two prices stemming from the third decimal is inessential for almost all products).

52. Experiments conducted by Deck and Wilson (2003) and by Fatas et al. (2005), however, seem to confirm that PMGs are better policies to support collusive equilibria. They both find that PBGs lead prices near or below the static Nash equilibrium prediction, while PMGs lead to supracompetitive prices.

53. The robustness of the Hay-Salop result with respect to some model specifications has been proved also by Doyle (1988) (number of firms) and Chen (1995) (simultaneous or sequential choice of prices and LPGs, and firms asymmetry). Schnitzer (1994) analyzes the effects of LPGs in a dynamic but finite duopoly game. In her model the LPG takes the form of a "meet or release" clause such that if firm A charges p_A^{t-1} in period $t-1$ and firm B charges p_B^t in the following period, the buyer is entitled to receive the rebate $p_B^t - p_A^{t-1}$. She shows that there exists a perfect equilibrium in which one seller offers the "meet or release" clause and both sellers charge the monopoly price in all but the last period.

54. A MFCC may also solve the problem faced by the durable good monopolist, pointed out by Coase (1972). If a durable good monopolist is not able to make a price commitment, it will find attractive to lower the price to its residual demand and ends up limiting its own market power. The nondiscrimination commitment embodied in the MFCC facilitates the exploitation of market power (see Butz 1990; Png 1991).

55. Holt and Scheffman (1987) and Schnitzer (1994) prove that in a price competition game with homogeneous goods, in which buyers select randomly the firm to buy from when they offer the same price, a MFCC leads to the same outcome as the Cournot equilibrium outcome.

56. Neilson and Winter (1993) show that unless some unreasonable conditions hold, only one firm adopts the MFCC in equilibrium. This indicates that the adoption of a MFCC as a facilitating practice may pose a coordination problem. Moreover Besanko and Lyon (1993) demonstrate that in contrast to the work on retroactive MFCC, not adopting a contemporaneous MFCC can be a dominant strategy. Their result highlights an important differences between retroactive and contemporaneous MFCC and suggests that MFCC are a less powerful facilitating practice than retroactive MFCC.

57. The effectiveness of these clauses has been investigated also experimentally by Grether and Plott (1984). Their research was motivated by the *Ethyl* case (see section 8.5.3) in which the FTC alleged that the practices adopted by the main producers of lead-based antiknock compunds, namely advance price announcements, most-favored customer, and delivered pricing were in breach of Section 5 of the FTC Act as they had favored the emergence of a noncompetitive outcome. In the experiment carried out by Grether and Plott the combination of these practices leads to a significant departure from the competitive price level. However, their results do not clarify which practice is most responsible for this outcome.

58. See Crocker and Lyon (1994) for a detailed description of this efficiency justification and for an empirical analysis of its applicability in the natural gas market.

59. *United States v. General Electric Co.*, 42 Fed. Reg. 17005 (1977).

60. *E.I. du Pont de Nemours & Co. v. Federal Trade Commission*, 729 F.2d 128 (2d Cir. 1984).

61. Hay (1989, 2000) and Vita (2001) provide a detailed discussion of this case.

62. More recently the DoJ and the FTC have brought several cases involving the adoption of MFCCs in the health care market. These and other private litigations have had mixed results. For a discussion of these cases, see DOJ and FTC (2004).

63. Some cases might have been litigated at the national level. For instance, in the United Kingdom the Monopolies and Mergers Commission, in 1999, issued a report that led to the enactment of an order prohibiting tour operators from including MFCCs in their contracts with travel agents. The order was then partially annulled by the court of appeals. The case is discussed by Akman and Hviid (2005).

64. An avoidable or culpable conduct may be that of charging a price that is "too" high. However, this then changes the nature of the antitrust intervention into a form of direct price regulation.

65. For a different point of view, see Hay (2005).

References

Abreu, D. 1986. Extremal Equilibria of Oligopoly Supergames. *Journal of Economic Theory* 39: 191–228.

Abreu, D. 1988. On the theory of infinitely repeated games with discounting. *Econometrica* 56(2): 383–96.

Abreu, D., P. R. Milgrom, and D. G. Pearce. 1991. Information and timing in repeated partnership. *Econometrica* 59(6): 1713–33.

Abreu, D., D. G. Pearce, and E. Stacchetti. 1990. Toward a theory of discounted repeated games with imperfect monitoring. *Econometrica* 58(5): 1041–64.

Aghion, P., and J. Tirole. 1994. The management of innovation. *Quarterly Journal of Economics* 109(4): 1185–1209.

Akman, P., and M. Hviid. 2005. A most-favoured-customer guarantee with a twist. CCP working paper 05-8. Centre for Competition Policy. University of East Anglia.

Allen, J., and G. M. Phillips. 2000. Corporate equity ownership, strategic alliances and product market relationships. *Journal of Finance* 55(6): 2791–2815.

Alley, W. A. 1997. Partial ownership arrangements and collusion in the automobile industry. *Journal of Industrial Economics* 45(2): 191–205.

Arbatskaya, M. 2001. Can low-price guarantees deter entry? *International Journal of Industrial Organization* 19(9): 1387–1406.

Arbatskaya, M., M. Hviid, and G. Shaffer. 2004. On the incidence and variety of low-price guarantees. *Journal of Law and Economics* 47: 307–32.

Areeda, P., and D. F. Turner. 1980. *Antitrust Law*. Boston: Little Brown.

Arvan, L., L. Cabral, and V. Santos. 1999. Meaningful cheap talk must improve equilibrium payoffs. *Mathematical Social Sciences* 37: 97–106.

Aumann, R. J. 1990. Nash equilibria are not self-enforcing. In J. J. Gabsewicz, J. F. Richard, and L. A. Wolsey, eds., *Economic Decision-Making: Games, Economics and Optimisation*. Amsterdam: Eslevier.

Aumann, R. J., and A. Brandenburger. 1995. Epistemic conditions for Nash equilibrium. *Econometrica* 63(5): 1161–80.

Aumann, R. J., and S. Hart. 2003. Long cheap talk. *Econometrica* 71(6): 1619–60.

Baker, J. B. 1996. Vertical restraints with horizontal consequences: Competitive effects of "most-favored-customer" clauses. *Antitrust Law Journal* 64(3): 517–34.

Belton, T. M. 1987. A model of duopoly and meeting or beating competition. *International Journal of Industrial Organization* 5(4): 399–417.

Berglof, E., and E. Perotti. 1994. The governance structure of the Japanese financial *keiretsu*. *Journal of Financial Economics* 36(2): 259–84.

Besanko, D., and T. P. Lyon. 1993. Equilibrium incentives for most-favored customer clauses in oligopolistic industry. *International Journal of Industrial Organization* 11(3): 347–67.

Binger, B. R., E. Hoffmanm, and G. D. Libecap. 1990. An experimetric study of the Cournot theory of firm behavior. Working paper. University of Arizona.

Blume, A., and A. Ortmann. 2007. The effects of costless pre-play communication: Experimental evidence from games with Pareto-ranked equilibria. *Journal of Economic Theory* 132(1): 274–90.

Borenstein, S. 1994. Rapid price communication and coordination: The airline tariff publishing case. In J. E. Kwoka Jr. and L. J. White, eds., *The Antitrust Revolution: Economics, Competition, and Policy*, 3rd ed. Oxford: Oxford University Press.

Buccirossi, P., and G. Spagnolo. 2006. Corportate goverance and collusive behavior. Lear research paper 06-01. Forthcoming in W. D. Collins, ed., *ABA Competition Law and Policy*, ABA.

Burton, A., G. Loomes, and M. Sefton. 2005. Communication and Efficiency in Coordination Game Experiments. In J. Morgan, ed., *Experimental and Behavioral Economics*. Amsterdam: Elsevier.

Butz, D. A. 1990. Durable-good monopoly and best-price provisions. *American Economic Review* 80(5): 1062–76.

Capobianco, A. 2004. Information exchange under EC competition law. *Common Market Law Review* 41: 1247–76.

Caronna, F. 2004. Article 81 as a tool for controlling minority cross-shareholding between competitors. *European Law Review* 29: 485–500.

Cason, T. N., and C. F. Mason. 1999. Information sharing and tacit collusion in laboratory duopoly markets. *Economic Inquiry* 37(2): 258–81.

Charness, G. 1998. Pre-play communication and credibility: A test of Aumann's conjecture. Economics Working Paper 293. Department of Economics and Business, Universitat Pompeu Fabra.

Charness, G. 2000. Self-serving cheap talk: A test of Aumann's conjecture. *Games and Economic Behavior* 33(2): 177–94.

Chatterjee, S., T. B. Heath, and S. Basuroy. 2003. Failing to suspect collusion in price-matching guarantees: Consumer limitations in game-theoretic reasoning. *Journal of Consumer Psychology* 13(3): 255–67.

Chen, Z. 1995. How low is a guaranteed-lowest price. *Canadian Journal of Economics* 28(3): 683–701.

Church, J., and R. Ware. 2000. *Industrial Organization: A Strategic Approach*. New York: Irwin, McGraw-Hill.

Clark, K., S. Kay, and M. Sefton. 2001. When are Nash equilibria self-enforcing? An experimental analysis. *International Journal of Game Theory* 29(4): 495–515.

Clarke, R. 1983. Collusion and the incentives for information sharing. *Bell Journal of Economics* 14(2): 383–94.

Coase, R. H. 1972. Durability and monopoly. *Journal of Law and Economics* 15(1): 143–49.

Compte, O. 1998. Communication in repeated games with imperfect private monitoring. *Econometrica* 66(3): 597–626.

Cooper, T. E. 1986. Most-favored-customer pricing and tacit collusion. *RAND Journal of Economics* 17(3): 377–88.

Corts, K. S. 1995. On the robustness of the argument that price-matching is anti-competitive. *Economics Letters* 47(3–4): 417–21.

Corts, K. S. 1996. On the competitive effects of price-matching policies. *International Journal of Industrial Organization* 15(3): 283–99.

Cramton, P., and J. A. Schwartz. 2000. Collusive bidding: Lessons from the FCC spectrum auctions. *Journal of Regulatory Economics* 17(3): 229–52.

Crawford, V. P., and J. Sobel. 1982. Strategic information transmission. *Econometrica* 50(6): 1431–1531.

Crocker, K., and T. Lyon. 1994. What do "facilitating practices" facilitate? Am empirical investigation of most-favored-nations clauses in natural gas contracts. *Journal of Law and Economics* 37(2): 297–322.

Daughety, A. F., and R. Forsythe. 1987a. Industrywide regulation and the formation of reputation: A laboratory analysis. In E. Bailey, ed., *Public Regulation: New Perspectives on Institutions and Policies*. Cambridge: MIT Press, pp. 346–79.

Daughety, A. F., and R. Forsythe. 1987b. Regulatory-induced industrial organization. *Journal of Law, Economics and Organization* 3: 397–434.

Dawes, R. M., J. McTavish, and H. Shaklee. 1977. Behavior, communication and assumptions about other people's behavior in a commons dilemma situation. *Journal of Personality and Social Psichology* 35: 1–11.

Deck, C. A., and B. J. Wilson. 2003. Automated pricing rules in electronic posted offer markets. *Economic Enquiry* 41(2): 208–23.

Dietzenbacher, E., B. Smid, and B. Volkerink. 2000. Horizontal Integration in the Dutch financial sector. *International Journal of Industrial Organization* 18(8): 1223–42.

Dixit, A., and B. Nalebuff. 1991. *Thinking Strategically*. New York: Norton.

DoJ and FTC. 2004. *Improving Health Care: A Dose of Competition*, A Report by the Federal Trade Commission and the Department of Justice. Available at ⟨http://www.usdoj.gov/atr/public/health_care/204694.htm#toc⟩.

Doyle, C. 1988. Different selling strategies in Bertrand oligopoly. *Economic Letters* 28(4): 387–90.

Edlin, A. S. 1997. Do guaranteed-low-price policies guarantee high prices, and can antitrust rise to the challenge? *Harvard Law Review* 111: 528–75.

Edlin, A. S., and E. Emch. 1999. The welfare losses from price matching policies. *Journal of Industrial Economics* 47(2): 145–68.

Farrell, J. 1987. Cheap talk, coordination and entry. *RAND Journal of Economics* 18(1): 34–39.

Farrel, J., and M. Rabin. 1996. Cheap talk. *Journal of Economic Perspectives* 10(3): 103–18.

Farrell, J., and C. Shapiro. 1990. Horizontal mergers: An equilibrium analysis. *American Economic Review* 80(1): 107–26.

Fatas, E., N. Georgantzís, G. Sabater, and J. Mañez. 2005. Pro-competitive price beating guarantees: Experimental evidence. *Review of Industrial Organization* 26(1): 115–36.

Flath, D. 1991. When is it rational for firms to acquire silent interests in rivals? *International Journal of Industrial Organization* 9(4): 573–83.

Flath, D. 1992. Horizontal shareholding interlocks. *Managerial and Decision Economics* 13: 75–77.

Gal-Or, E. 1985. Information sharing in oligopoly. *Econometrica* 53(2): 329–43.

Gal-Or, E. 1986. Information transmission—Cournot and Bertrand equilibria. *Review of Economic Studies* 53(1): 85–92.

Genesove, D., and W. P. Mullin. 2001. Rules, communication, and collusion: Narrative evidence from the Sugar Institute case. *American Economic Review* 91(3): 379–98.

Gilo, D. 2000. The anticompetitive effect of passive investment. *Michigan Law Review* 99: 1–47.

Gilo, D., Y. Moshe, and Y. Spiegel. 2006. Partial cross ownership and tacit collusion. *RAND Journal of Economics* 37(1): 81–99.

Green, E., and R. Porter. 1984. Non-cooperative collusion under imperfect price information. *Econometrica* 52(1): 87–100.

Grether, D. M., and C. R. Plott. 1984. The effects of market practices in oligopolistic markets: An experimental examination of the *Ethyl* case. *Economic Inquiry* 22(4): 479–507.

Haan, M. A., L. Schoonbeek, and B. M. Winkel. 2005. Experimental results on collusion: The role of information and communication. Unpublished manuscript. University of Groningen.

Harsanyi, J. C., and R. Selten. 1988. *A General Theory of Equilibrium Selection in Games*. Cambridge: MIT Press.

Hay, G. 1982. Oligopoly, shared monopoly, and antitrust law. *Cornell Law Review* 28: 439–81.

Hay, G. 1989. Practices that facilitate cooperation: The *Ethyl* case. In J. E. Kwoka Jr. and L. J. White, eds., *The Antitrust Revolution: Economics, Competition, and Policy*, 3rd ed. Oxford: Oxford University Press.

Hay, G. 2000. The meaning of "agreement" under the Sherman Act: Thoughts from the "facilitating practices" experience. *Review of Industrial Organization* 16: 113–29.

Hay, G. 2005. Facilitating practices. Cornell Law School research paper 05-027. Forthcoming in W. D. Collins, ed., *ABA Competition Law and Policy*, ABA.

Holt, C. A. 1995. Industrial organization: A survey of laboratory research. In J. H. Kagel and A. E. Roth, eds., *Handbook of Experimental Economics*. Princeton: Princeton University Press.

Holt, C. A., and D. T. Scheffman. 1987. Facilitating practices: The effects of advance notice and best-price policies. *RAND Journal of Economics* 18(2): 187–97.

Hovenkamp, H. 1994. *Federal Antitrust Policy: The Law of Competition and its Practice*. St. Paul: West Publishing Co.

Hviid, M., and G. Shaffer. 1994. Do low-price guarantees facilitate tacit collusion? Working Paper 94-02. University of Michigan.

Hviid, M., and G. Shaffer. 1999. Hassle costs: The Achilles heel of price matching guarantees. *Journal of Economics and Management Strategy* 8(4): 489–521.

Isaac, R. M., and J. Walker. 1985. Information and conspiracy in sealed bid auction. *Journal of Economic Behavior and Organization* 6(2): 139–59.

Ivaldi, M., B. Jullien, P. Rey, P. Seabright, and J. Tirole. 2007. The economics of tacit collusion: Implications for merger control. In V. Ghosal and J. Stennek, eds., *The Political Economy of Antitrust*. Amsterdam: Elsevier, pp. 217–39.

Jain, S., and J. Srivastava. 2000. An experimental and theoretical analysis of price-matching refund policies. *Journal of Marketing Research* 37(3): 351–62.

Kandori, M., and H. Matsushima. 1988. Private observation, communication and collusion. *Econometrica* 66(3): 627–52.

Kaplan, T. R. 2000. Effective price-matching: A comment. *International Journal of Industrial Organization* 18(8): 1291–94.

Kirby, A. J. 1988. Trade associations as information exchange mechanisms. *RAND Journal of Economics* 19(1): 138–46.

Klein, B., R. G. Crawford, and A. A. Alchian. 1978. Vertical integration, appropriable rents, and the competitive contracting process. *Journal of Law and Economics* 21(2): 297–326.

Kühn, K.-U. 2001. Fighting collusion by regulating communication between firms. *Economic Policy* 16(32): 167–97.

Kühn, K.-U., and X. Vives. 1995. *Information Exchanges among Firms and Their Impact on Competition*. Luxemburg: Office for Official Publications of the European Community.

Ledyard, J. O. 1995. Public goods: A survey of experimental research. In J. H. Kagel and A. E. Roth, eds., *Handbook of Experimental Economics*. Princeton: Princeton University Press.

Levenstein, M. C. 1997. Price wars and the stability of collusion: A study of the pre–World War I bromine industry. *Journal of Industrial Economics* 45(2): 117–37.

Li, L. 1985. Cournot oligopoly with information sharing. *RAND Journal of Economics* 16(4): 521–36.

Malueg, D. A. 1992. Collusive behavior and partial ownership of rivals. *International Journal of Industrial Organization* 10(1): 27–34.

Merlone, U. 2001. Cartelizing effects of horizontal shareholding interlocks. *Managerial and Decision Economics* 22(6): 333–37.

Miller, J. H., and S. Moser. 2004. Communication and coordination. SFI working paper 03-03-019. Santa Fe Institute.

Moorthy, S., and R. A. Winter. 2002. Price-matching guarantees. *Review of Marketing Science Working Papers* 2(1), article 2. Available at ⟨http://www.bepress.com/roms/vol2/iss1/paper2⟩.

Motta, M. 2004. *Competition Policy. Theory and Practice*. Cambridge: Cambridge University Press.

Neilson, W. S., and H. Winter. 1993. Bilateral most-favored-customer pricing and collusion. *RAND Journal of Economics* 24(1): 147–55.

Novshek, W., and H. Sonnenschein. 1982. Fulfilled expectations Cournot duopoly with information acquisition and release. *Bell Journal of Economics* 13(1): 214–18.

Phlipps, L. 1995. *Competition Policy: A Game-Theoretic Perspective*. Cambridge: Cambridge University Press.

Png, I. P. L. 1991. Most-favored-customer protection versus price discrimination. *Journal of Political Economy* 99(5): 1010–28.

Png, I. P. L., and D. Hirschleifer. 1987. Price discrimination through offers to match price. *Journal of Business* 60(3): 365–83.

Porter, R. 1983. Optimal cartel trigger-price strategies. *Journal of Economic Theory* 29(2): 313–38.

Raith, M. 1993. A general model of information sharing in oligopoly. STICERD discussion paper TE-93-260.

Raith, M. 1996. A general model of information sharing in oligopoly. *Journal of Economic Theory* 71(1): 260–88.

Reitman, D. 1994. Partial ownership arrangements and the potential for collusion. *Journal of Industrial Economics* 42(3): 313–22.

Reynolds, R., and B. Snapp. 1986. The competitive effects of partial equity interests and joint ventures. *International Journal of Industrial Organization* 4(2): 141–53.

Sakai, Y. 1986. Cournot and Bertrand equilibria under imperfect information. *Journal of Economics* 46(3): 213–32.

Salant, S., S. Switzer, and R. Reynolds. 1983. Losses due to merger: The effects of an exogenous change in industry structure on Cournot-Nash equilibrium. *Quarterly Journal of Economics* 98(2): 185–99.

Salop, S. 1986. Practices that (credibly) facilitate oligopoly coordination. In J. Stiglitz and G. F. Mathewson, eds., *New Developments in the Analysis of Market Structure*. Cambridge: MIT Press, pp. 265–94.

Schnitzer, M. 1994. Dynamic duopoly with best-price clauses. *RAND Journal of Economics* 25(1): 186–96.

Shapiro, C. 1986. Exchange of cost information in oligopoly. *Review of Economic Studies* 53(3): 433–46.

Shapiro, C. 1989. Theories of oligopoly behavior. In R. Schmalensee and R. D. Willig, eds., *The Handbook of Industrial Organization*. Amsterdam: North Holland.

Srivastava, J., and N. Lurie. 2001. A consumer perspective on price-matching refund policies: Effect on price perceptions and search behavior. *Journal of Consumer Research* 28(2): 296–307.

Vita, M. 2001. Fifteen years after ethyl: The past and future of facilitating practices. *Antitrust Law Journal* 68(2): 991–1005.

Vives, X. 1984. Duopoly information equilibrium: Cournot and Bertrand. *Journal of Economic Theory* 34(1): 71–94.

Wellford, C. 2002. Antitrust: Results from the laboratory. In C. A. Holt and R. M. Isaac, eds., *Experiments Investigating Market Power*. Oxford: Elsevier Science.

Williamson, O. 1979. Transaction-cost economics: The governance of contractual relations. *Journal of Law and Economics* 22(2): 233–61.

Williamson, O. 1985. *The Economic Institution of Capitalism: Firms, Markets, Relational Contracting*. New York: Free Press.

9 Economics of Vertical Restraints

Patrick Rey and Thibaud Vergé

Most relationships between producers and distributors consist of sophisticated contracts. These contracts use more than the simple linear pricing rules that are the heart of microeconomic textbooks. Often contracts are governed by contractual provisions, referred to as *vertical restraints*, that not only set more general terms for payments (nonlinear prices–two-part tariffs, quantity discounts, royalties, slotting allowances) but also include terms limiting one party's decisions (resale price maintenance, quantity fixing, tie-ins) or softening competition (exclusive dealing, franchising, exclusive territories).

The motivations for vertical restraints and their impact on economic welfare have been actively debated by academics. Some believe that vertical agreements are very different from agreements between competing firms and appear only when they can improve the efficiency of the vertical structure. Competition agencies should therefore let firms design these arrangements as they wish. Others believe that any contractual term that restricts one party's freedom of trade—and this would be the case for most if not all vertical restraints—can only be harmful and should thus be banned. This chapter aims at providing an economic perspective on this debate.

The chapter is organized as follows: In section 9.1, we briefly describe the most common vertical restraints building on the classification proposed by Rey and Tirole (1986). We then present the past and current legal treatment of vertical restraints in the United States and the European Union (section 9.2). In section 9.3, we elaborate on vertical coordination issues: we show that vertical restraints can be used to restore the efficiency of the vertical interaction (e.g., by solving double-marginalization or free-riding problems), although the impact on consumer surplus and economic efficiency are unclear. In section 9.4, we review how vertical restraints can eliminate or reduce the competition between rival vertical structures. Finally, in section 9.5, we summarize the findings and discuss their implications for competition policy.

9.1 Common Vertical Restraints

9.1.1 Payment Schemes

A uniform price constitutes a linear pricing rule according to which the payment is proportional to the quantity bought by the distributor. Several provisions allow the firms to depart from this constant unit price.

• *Nonlinear tariffs* The simplest form of nonlinear pricing consists in including, besides the uniform wholesale price (w), a franchise fee (F). This combination ($T(q) = F + wq$) is also referred to as a *two-part tariff*. Other forms of nonlinear tariffs include progressive rebates on the quantity bought by the distributor (*quantity discounts*). Note that it suffices to observe who carries the manufacturer's products to enforce a franchise fee provision, whereas more general nonlinear prices may be more difficult to enforce if arbitrage is possible. For instance, if the manufacturer is unable to observe the quantity sold by each retailer, the distributors might then be able to get a higher rebate by pooling their orders.
• *Royalties* Royalties are another kind of payment, based on the distributor's sales measured either in units or in revenues. Contrarily to linear or nonlinear wholesale tariffs, royalties do not depend solely on the quantity bought to the manufacturer but also on the quantity actually sold by the distributor. Royalties may depend as well on the sales of other goods by the retailer, thereby allowing the manufacturer to impose a tax on the rivals' products. Note that royalties are effective only if the manufacturer is able to closely monitor the distributor's sales.

All these different payment structures directly affect the way that joint profit is shared between the producer and the distributor, and also indirectly the "targets" (retail prices, promotional effort, etc.) that determine the joint profit.

9.1.2 Provisions Limiting the Parties' Rights

• *Resale price maintenance (RPM)* Resale price maintenance is a provision according to which the final price charged to consumers is not set by the distributor but imposed by the producer. This restriction has several variants, including maximum retail price (price ceiling), minimum price (price floor), nonbinding "recommended retail price" or advertised price. Resale price maintenance or price floors supposes that price cuts can be detected at a sufficiently low cost. Note that these price cuts can take the form of nonmonetary concessions such as free delivery.
• *Quantity fixing* Quantity fixing is a provision that specifies the quantity to be bought and resold by the retailer. Variants include quantity forcing, which imposes a purchase of a minimum quantity, and quantity rationing, which specifies a maximum quota. If demand is known and depends only on the final price, then quantity forcing is equivalent to a price ceiling and quantity rationing to a price floor. Therefore quantity fixing is equivalent to resale price maintenance.[1]

• *Tie-in* Tie-in provisions impose on the distributor to buy one or more goods from the manufacturer over and above that which the distributor initially wants to carry. *Full-line forcing* is a particular type of tie-in that requires the distributor to carry the manufacturer's whole range of products. The use of tie-in supposes that the manufacturer can verify the range of goods carried by the distributor.

• *Exclusivity clauses* Producer and distributor may also sign exclusivity agreements. These exclusivity clauses might limit only the distributor's or both parties rights.

Under an *exclusive dealing* agreement, the distributor agrees not to engage in any other business that competes directly with the manufacturer's activities (or even in any other business). A variant consists of *exclusive purchasing* which requires the distributor to buy all goods exclusively from the manufacturer.

Territorial or customer provisions may limit the "territory," either geographical or defined as a specific segment of the market (e.g., distribution through mail rather than through retail stores), or limit the group of customers (small vs. large businesses, individual customers vs. business clients) that a particular distributor is allowed to serve. On the other hand, by granting an *exclusive territory*, the manufacturer commits itself not to allow any other distributor to serve the customer in this territory thereby eliminating any intra-brand competition. Enforcing territorial provisions can be rather difficult: while it is relatively straightforward to set the number of outlets at a given location, it is more difficult to check whether a distributor is competing outside its territory.

This list is, of course, not exhaustive. The manufacturer may, for example, commit itself to a minimum quality, to specific (nationwide) advertising, or to technical support; the distributor may commit itself to specific level of promotional effort or customer services (e.g., after-sales services). Some other clauses may limit one party's right to compete with the other after termination of the relationship.

9.2 Legal Treatment

In this section we briefly present the legal situation of vertical restraints in the United States and the European Union. In both jurisdictions, cases involving vertical contracts can be deemed illegal either because they restrict competition (Section 1 of the US Sherman Act or Article 81 of the European Communities Treaty) or because they constitute an abuse of dominant position (Section 2 or Article 82).

9.2.1 US Competition Policy toward Vertical Restraints

Vertical restraints have been part of antitrust enforcement in the United States for a long time. It was as early as 1911 that the Supreme Court ruled in *Dr. Miles* that resale price maintenance was illegal per se, and this ruling still governs such agreements.[2] Although there is a long history of antitrust toward vertical restraints, policies have not been consistent over time and have often changed sharply over relatively short periods of time.[3] If the attitude of competition authorities and enforcement agencies toward minimum RPM has been constant over time (per se illegality), this has not been the case for nonprice restraints especially over the past thirty or forty years. In the early 1920s, following cases such as *Standard Oil* or *Colgate*, vertical restraints were usually assessed on a case-by-case basis.[4] This was then confirmed in 1963 in *White Motors* when the Supreme Court stated that it knew *"too little of the actual impact of (exclusive territories)"* and that *"the legality of the territorial and customer limitations should be determined only after a trial."*[5] A sharp turn occurred in 1967 following the *Schwinn* ruling when all vertical restraints became illegal per se.[6] This very tough attitude toward all vertical restraints was heavily criticized—especially by the so-called Chicago School—and the authorities eventually adopted a more permissive attitude toward nonprice restraints ten years later: in 1977 the Supreme Court concluded in *GTE Sylvania* that pro- and anticompetitive effects should be evaluated and that these restraints should therefore be treated under the rule of reason.[7] Price restraints (e.g., RPM) however remained illegal per se. A further move toward a very lenient policy started when the Reagan administration took office in 1981. It was then widely accepted that vertical restraints were likely to be pro-competitive, and when the *Vertical Restraints Guidelines* where published by the US Department of Justice in 1985, they were regarded as rendering all nonprice restraints legal. As noted by Comanor and Rey (1997), it is then *"hardly surprising that neither federal antitrust agency brought a single case against a vertical restraint during the twelve Reagan–Bush years."*

Following another change of administration, competition policy switched back toward an active enforcement under the rule of reason as it was stated in 1996 by Robert Pitofsky, the then Federal Trade Commission (FTC) chairman:

The Commission of the 1990s has tried to strike a middle ground between what many people believe was an excessively active enforcement in the 1960s and the minimalist enforcement of the 1980s. In the process we have restored much of the antitrust agenda that was abandoned during the period 1980 through 1988. For example, the Commission investigates and is prepared to enforce the law against resale price maintenance agreements, some carefully selected nonprice vertical restrictions, attempts to monopolize, boycotts and vertical and conglomerate mergers—all areas of antitrust that were left completely or largely unenforced during much of the 1980s.

This move toward active enforcement was confirmed as early as in May 1996 when the FTC brought charges against *Toys 'R' Us* for abuse of dominant position and exclusionary practices. In 1998 *Toys 'R' Us* was requested to stop the "warehouse policy" that it had first introduced in 1992.[8] The FTC (as expressed by its then chairman Robert Pitofsky) explained that *"Toys 'R' Us wanted to prevent consumers from comparing the price and quality of products in the clubs to the price and quality of the same toys displayed and sold at Toys 'R' Us, and thereby to reduce the effectiveness of the clubs as competitors."* *Toys 'R' Us* was in essence forcing the manufacturers not to sell to the warehouse clubs that were threatening its market shares.

The agreement between *Toys 'R' Us* and its main suppliers (including major toy manu-facturers, e.g., *Mattel, Fisher Price*, and *Tyco*) imposed, for instance, that all special, exclu-sive, or clearance products had to be offered first to *Toys 'R' Us* to see if it wanted to buy the product. New or promoted products could be sold to warehouse clubs only if they were carrying the manufacturer's entire line. It appeared that the *Toys 'R' Us* was carefully enforcing the agreement by threatening to stop buying from any producer that was reported to have "cheated the agreement" and sold to warehouse clubs. This policy proved to be very effective as noted by the FTC: "*After the boycott took hold in 1993, Costco's toy sales decreased by 1.6 percent despite total sales growth of 19.5 percent. . . . [R]eversal of the clubs' success as toy retailers can also be seen by examining individual toy manufacturer's sales to the clubs. For example, Mattel's sales to warehouse clubs declined from over $23 mil-lion in 1991 to $7.5 million in 1993.*" In 1997, forty-four states, the District of Columbia, and Puerto Rico sued *Toy 'R' Us* (and the manufacturers involved in the boycott), and in a settlement in 1999, the firms agreed to pay an aggregate sum of more $56 million (in cash for costs of suits and fees, and in charitable distribution of toys).[9] As noted by Comanor and Rey (1997), this was "*a sharp break from past enforcement practices, under which such restraints were rarely if ever challenged.*" Another important implication of the case is that large distributors could be sued for abuse of dominant position although their market shares might not be very large. In his case, *Toys 'R' Us* share of toys sales nationally was only 20 percent. However, the FTC noted that although "*Toys 'R' Us market share as a toy retailer was measured, it was clear that its boycott was having an effect on the market.*"

The *Toys 'R' Us* case marked a major change toward a more vigourous enforcement, and since then, US authorities have continued their efforts and opened a number of cases involving major firms, the most famous one being the everlasting case against *Microsoft*. Recent cases with important vertical components such as *United States v. Microsoft, Le-Page v. 3M*, or the DOJ investigation of *Orbitz* seem to signal a more active enforcement policy toward vertical restraints.[10] Although these are all important cases, we will not de-tail them here as they involve issues on tying and foreclosure that are considered in another chapter.

9.2.2 European Competition Policy toward Vertical Restraints

In contrast to US antitrust laws, which date back to 1890 and are primarily concerned with the promotion of competition, European competition law is much more recent and promoting competition is not a goal in itself but only a mean to achieve single market integration. Under Article 81(1) of the European Communities Treaty, any agreement "*which may affect trade between member states and which has as (its) object or effect the prevention, restriction or distortion of competition within the common market*" is prohibited. As mentioned by Verouden (2003), "*the Commission has fairly consistently chosen a strict interpretation of the concept of restriction of competition.*"[11] This has been and is still par-ticularly true for territorial restraints especially if the boundaries of these territories are national borders and such agreements are used to restrict parallel imports. In 1964 the Commission concluded in *Grundig-Consten* that an exclusive dealing agreement that made *Consten* the exclusive supplier of various *Grundig* products in France was restrictive because it was preventing re-exports by *Consten*.[12] This case was also the first to establish that vertical and not only horizontal agreements fell under Article 81(1). More recently *Nintendo* (and some of its distributors), *Volkswagen A.G., Opel Netherlands B.V.* and *DaimlerChrysler A.G.* were respectively fined €168 million, 90 million, 43 million, and 72 million for attempting to restrict parallel imports.[13]

A particular feature of European competition law is that, under Article 81(3), agreements that fall under the scope of Article 81(1), and should therefore be banned, may be exempted if they *"contribute to improving the production or distribution of goods or to promoting technical or economic progress while allowing consumers a fair share of the resulting benefit."* When the implementation of Article 81 came into force in 1962, under regulation 17/1962 an agreement had to be notified to the Commission in order to benefit from an exemption. As a result within a few years the Commission was overwhelmed by the number of notifications. To speed up the process, the European Commission then identified categories of distribution arrangements (e.g., exclusive dealing or franchising agreements) that were exempted in block. This rather formalistic and bureaucratic approach was often criticized for creating "straitjackets," and calls were made for a more flexible, economic-based approach. In 1996, the Commission published a *Green Paper on Vertical Restraints*, which included an economic analysis of the impact of vertical restraints on competition. The conclusions of this *Green Paper* and the debate that followed led to the adoption of a new block exemption regime in 1999, the publication of new guidelines in 2000, and the removal of the obligation of notification in May 2004.[14] These new guidelines take on board most insights from the economic literature and constitute a major shift of policy; in particular, decisions are no longer based primarily on the type of restraint considered but also account for the market environment: *"For most vertical restraints, competition concerns can only arise if there is insufficient inter-brand competition, i.e., if there is some degree of market power at the level of the supplier or the buyer or at both levels. If there is insufficient inter-brand, the protection of inter- and intra-brand competition becomes important."*

Although the enforcement of Article 81 has changed over the years, price restraints such as resale price maintenance (RPM) have always been banned per se (although recommended retail prices and maximum prices are acceptable). The Commission's view can be summarized by the *Pronuptia* decision in which the Commission found that RPM was restricting intra-brand competition: *"certain provisions restrict competition between the members of the network. That is true of provisions... which prevent franchisees from engaging in price competition with each other."*[15] RPM is thus on a "blacklist" of practices that would prevent any exclusive dealing or franchising agreement to be granted exemption under the block exemption regime.

The authorities attitude toward nonprice restraints is much more lenient. Territorial or customer restrictions may be granted exemption under Article 81(3) except if they prevent parallel imports: exclusive territories provisions have, for instance, been granted exemption in the *Pronuptia* case, and in a number of other franchising agreements considered by the Commission, territorial or customer restrictions qualified for exemption. At the same time similar arrangements have been deemed illegal in the *Grundig-Consten* case, since their effect was to restrict parallel imports. Following a very similar line of argument, exclusive purchasing clauses that are seen as restriction of competition, and thus fall under Article 81(1), have often been exempted under Article 81(3). This is usually the case for franchising agreements in which *"an obligation not to buy from alternative suppliers must be justified by the need to protect the identity or reputation of the network or the franchisor's intellectual property."* It should nevertheless be noted that the decision to grant exemption for territorial restrictions or exclusive purchasing requirements depends on the type of distribution arrangements. Although they are usually acceptable when included in franchising agreements, they tend not to be exempted under exclusive or selective distribution agreements.

Some major recent antitrust cases outside cartel enforcement have been in relation to restriction of parallel imports, thereby confirming the importance of single market integration as a goal. Some recent decisions are direct evaluations of the anticompetitive effects of vertical restraints. In 2001, *Michelin* was fined €20 million for abuse of dominant position (Article 82) for using a system of rebates (a particular kind of nonlinear tariff) that induces retailers to buy exclusively from *Michelin* and thus prevented them from choosing freely.[16] In March 2004, *Microsoft* was fined a record €497 million for abuse of dominant position on the market for operation systems for PCs for practices amounting to bundling.[17]

In October 2004, the European Commission moved closer to reach a settlement with *The Coca-Cola Company (TCCC)* to end its five-year long investigation of the company's practices.[18] Using a new competition policy tool that offers firms the possibility to make voluntary binding commitments to settle a case, *TCCC* offered to remove some majors conditions from its contracts with its customers. It will thus stop offering target and growth rebates or exclusivity arrangements. It will also stop requiring customers to buy less popular products such as *Vanilla Coke* or *Sprite* in order to obtain the best-selling products that are *Coca-Cola* and *Fanta Orange*. Finally, customer will be allowed to use 20 percent of the space in the coolers provided for free by *TCCC* to store any product of their choice.[19] According the Commission, these commitments *"will bring more competition to the European market for carbonated soft drinks and increase consumer choice in shops and at cafés."* This case seems to confirm the idea that vertical restraints are seen as having strong anticompetitive effects when there is a lack of inter-brand competition.

9.3 Vertical Coordination

The theme of vertical coordination has been the first and most often analyzed in the economic literature. The emphasis is placed on coordination problems within a given vertical structure, namely between a producer and its retailer(s), rather than on the interaction with other vertical structures. Hence most of the contributions consider the case of a unique producer dealing with one or more retailers.

The vertical structure considered as a whole faces a number of decision variables: some affect the joint profit (retail prices, quantity sold to consumers, selling efforts, etc.) while others affect the way this joint profit is shared between the different parties (wholesale price, franchise fee, etc.). The decentralization of the decision variables that affect the joint profit (the "targets") to the retailers can cause inefficiencies because they create externalities that have to be correctly accounted for. Vertical restraints can then be used as means to coordinate and restore the efficiency of the vertical structure. As we will now show, this does not necessarily mean that it is in the consumers' (or society as a whole) best interest to eliminate or correct these externalities.

9.3.1 Double Marginalization

Double marginalization has been the first coordination problem formally analyzed (Spengler 1950). It refers to situations where both the producer and the retailer enjoy some market power. In such situations they both add a markup to their costs, thereby leading to excessive prices. The externality arises from the fact that each firm, when setting its markup does not take into account the impact of this decision on the other firm's profit. For instance, when setting the final price, the retailer trades off an increase in its margin against a decrease in the quantity sold, but does not take into account the reduction in the producer's profit due to the decrease in the quantity.

For example, consider the case of successive monopolies (as shown in figure 9.1) with constant marginal costs, c for the producer and γ for the distributor. Denote respectively by w and p the producer's (uniform) wholesale price and the distributor's retail price, and by $q = D(p)$ the consumer demand.

The aggregate profit of the two firms depends only on the retail price p and the monopoly (or joint-profit-maximizing) price is characterized by

$$p^M(c) = \arg\max_p [(p - c - \gamma)D(p)].$$

In such a situation each of the two firms has an incentive to set its price above its perceived marginal cost. To achieve a positive profit, the producer will thus set a wholesale price above its marginal cost ($w > c$) and the retailer will then choose the retail price p that maximizes its profit, that is,

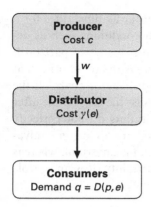

Figure 9.1
Successive monopolies and the double-marginalization problem

$$p^M(w) = \arg\max_{p}[(p - w - \gamma)D(p)],$$

which leads to a final price larger than the monopoly price and to a joint profit below its maximum level (monopoly profit).[20]

This double-marginalization problem can be solved using a variety of vertical restraints:

• An obvious solution consists in controlling the retail price using resale price maintenance (imposing $p = p^M(c)$) and setting the wholesale price so as to achieve the desired sharing of the monopoly profit. A price ceiling $(p \leq p^M(c))$ would actually suffice here and a minimum quota $(q \geq D(p^M(c)))$ would be equivalent.
• Alternative solutions include nonlinear tariffs, the simplest form being a two-part tariff, $T(q) = cq + F$. By setting a wholesale price equal to its marginal cost c, the producer gives the right incentives to the distributor who now faces a perceived marginal cost equal to $c + \gamma$ and set the retail price at the monopoly level $p^M(c)$. The franchise fee F can then be used to share the profit as desired.

This simple analysis yields several insights. First, vertical restraints allow the manufacturer and the retailer to maximize joint profits. Second, these restraints used to solve the double-marginalization problem not only maximize the joint profit, but they also lead to lower prices thereby benefiting consumers and hence increasing the total welfare.

Notice that vertical restraints are not necessarily needed to solve the double-marginalization problem. Introducing strong intra-brand competition (using several perfectly substitutable retailers) would remove the retail markup. The manufacturer could then set the wholesale price equal to $p^M(c) - \gamma$, thus to a retail price equal to the monopoly price $p^M(c)$.

Different types of restraints (RPM, quotas, nonlinear tariffs) appear as substitutes for a better efficiency. However, this equivalence vanishes when market conditions such as demand or distribution costs are uncertain and the retailer is risk-averse. A two-part tariff (of the form $T(q) = cq + F$) ensures that the distributor selects always the retail price that maximizes the aggregate profit of the vertical structure, but the distributor bears all the risk. RPM, on the other hand, does not allow the distributor to adjust the retail price after a demand or (retail) cost shock. This means that the vertical restraints do not perfectly solve the double-marginalization problem if there is uncertainty and are no longer equivalent. For instance, RPM is preferred to two-part tariffs when demand is uncertain, whereas two-part tariffs yield a higher joint profit than RPM under cost uncertainty (Rey and Tirole 1986).

9.3.2 Retail Services

Distributors usually provide a range of services that affect the demand for the products that are on offer: services such as free delivery, pre-sale advice to potential buyers, use of salespersons or cashiers to reduce waiting times. Showrooms, after-sales services, or parking facilities tend to attract more customers to a store and can play an essential role in the success of some products.

These efforts will not only generate vertical externalities between the producer and its retailers but also horizontal externalities among the different distributors of the same product. The degree of appropriability of such services will play a crucial role in our analysis. Providing pre-sale advice to customers can create horizontal externalities (giving rise to the well-known *free-riding* problem), but competing retailers are unlikely to benefit from an increase in the number of cashiers.

Successive Monopolies   To illustrate, let us start with the simplest model and extend the successive monopolies setting presented earlier by introducing an additional choice variable, e, representing retail effort. As shown in figure 9.2, the distributor now chooses both the retail price p and an effort level e, which increases consumer demand $q = D(p, e)$ (with $\partial_e D > 0$) and the retail cost $\gamma(e)$ (with $\gamma'(e) > 0$).[21]

Only p and e matter for the vertical structure and these two variables are now the two "targets" that affect the joint profit. It would also be equivalent to reason with quantity sold rather than retail price considering the inverse demand function $p = P(q, e)$ (which then satisfies $\partial_q P < 0$ and $\partial_e P > 0$). The two "targets" are now the quantity q and the effort level e, and their optimal values are given by

$$(q^M(c), e^M(c)) = \arg\max_{(q,e)}[(P(q, e) - c - \gamma(e))q].$$

When facing a simple linear tariff (i.e., a uniform wholesale price w), the distributor perceives a marginal cost equal to $w + \gamma(e)$ and thus chooses the same quantity ($q^M(w)$) and

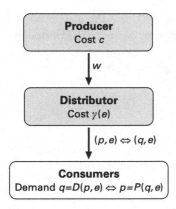

Figure 9.2
Successive monopolies with retail services

effort level ($e^M(w)$) than would a vertical structure with aggregate marginal cost $w + \gamma(e)$. The producer will hence choose the wholesale price w so as to maximize the its own profit given the distributor's reaction to this wholesale tariff:

$$w^* = \arg\max_w[(w - c)q^M(w)].$$

The manufacturer thus chooses a wholesale price higher than its marginal cost ($w^* > c$). The distributor will in turn choose a quantity below the optimal level, that is, an excessive retail price (double marginalization) and too little effort. The basic reason is that when choosing level of effort and its price, the distributor does not take into account the impact of these decisions on the producer's profit $(w - c)D(p, e)$.

Once again the joint profit is not maximized. The main reason is that the producer has only one instrument (the wholesale price w) to control the two targets that affect the joint profit (p- or q- and e) as well as the allocation of this profit. There are again several equivalent ways (at least under perfect information) to solve this coordination problem:

• RPM (or a price ceiling) alone would not be sufficient because it would not control efficiently the effort level. However, a price ceiling combined with the requirement to provide a minimum level of retail services would restore the efficiency of the vertical structure: the manufacturer directly monitors the two "targets" and can then use the wholesale price to achieve the desired allocation of the joint profit.
• A two-part tariff could as well be efficient and does not require the producer to be able to closely monitor the level of effort. Charging $T(q) = cq + F$ leads the distributor to choose both the level of effort (e^M) and the retail price (p^M, with $p^M = P(q^M, e^M)$) that maximize the joint profit, since retail profit coincides—up to a constant—with joint profit. The franchise fee can then be adjusted to achieve the desired sharing of profit.

Once again, several types of vertical restraints allow the producer and the distributor to achieve joint-profit maximization. However, as originally shown by Spence (1975), in contrast with the case of pure double marginalization, solving the coordination problem is not necessarily socially desirable. The socially optimal quantity (q^S) and effort level (e^S) are solution of the total welfare maximization:

$$(q^S, e^S) = \arg\max_{(q,e)}[S(q,e) - (c + \gamma(e))q],$$

where $S(q, e) = \int_0^q P(x, e)\, dx$ represents the consumer surplus. Under the standard regularity assumptions, the socially optimal values are the unique solutions of the first-order conditions and are characterized by

$$P(q^S, e^S) - c - \gamma(e^S) = 0$$

and

$$\gamma'(e^S)q^S = \partial_e S(q^S, e^S) = \int_0^{q^S} \partial_e P(x, e^S)\, dx,$$

whereas the joint-profit maximizing quantity and effort levels are given by

$$P(q^M, e^M) - c - \gamma(e^M) = -\partial_q P(q^M, e^M)q^M$$

and

$$\gamma'(e^M)q^M = \partial_e P(q^M, e^M).$$

Firms and consumers and likely to disagree over the optimal level of services, or more precisely, over the right balance between retail prices and services. An increase in the level of services (together with an increase in the retail price) that increases the level of aggregate profit may well reduce consumer surplus and even total welfare. The reason is that the vertical structure is interested in attracting the marginal consumers and thus tends to neglect the impact of such decision on the infra-marginal consumers. It may well be the case that marginal consumers would be willing to pay more for an increase in the level of services but that this might hurt the majority of consumers, thereby decreasing consumer surplus.[22]

Intra-brand Competition In contrast to the pure double-marginalization case, intra-brand competition is not necessarily enough to facilitate coordination (on the right price/retail service mix) within the vertical structure and to ensure that joint profits are maximized. While the manufacturer chooses a wholesale price above its marginal cost in order to maximize its own profit, intra-brand competition pushes the distributors to choose the effort level (and therefore retail prices) that maximize the consumers' surplus: in other words, competition among identical retailers eliminates the retail markup and induces retailers to choose the consumers' preferred balance between retail price and level of services. As a result the joint profit is not maximized.[23]

Once again the use of vertical restraints can restore the efficiency of the vertical structure and some combinations are equivalent:

• RPM, this time in the form of a price floor, is sufficient. Intra-brand competition induces the distributor to choose the highest level of effort compatible with nonnegative profit, that is, where $\gamma(e) = p - w$. The producer can therefore use RPM to control the price level ($p = p^M$), and the wholesale price to monitor the level of effort ($w = p^M - \gamma(e^M)$).
• Two-part tariffs alone are not sufficient. However, the joint-profit maximizing outcome can be achieved by combining a two-part tariffs with the assignment of exclusive territories to the retailers. Exclusive territories will then remove any intra-brand competition and the two-part tariff (of the form $T(q) = cq + F$) makes the distributor the residual claimant of the joint profit as in the single distributor case.

However, from the economic welfare point of view, the comparison between the joint-profit-maximizing outcome and the outcome achieved with linear tariffs only is usually ambiguous (e.g., see Caillaud and Rey 1987; Comanor 1985; Sherer 1983). This comes again from the divergence between the preferences of the marginal consumers and those of the infra-marginal ones. This divergence is likely to be important when the vertical structure enjoys substantial market power: if consumers have alternative solutions, an increase in the price and level of services is unlikely to harm the consumers as they would then be able to switch to an alternative product.[24]

Finally, if the retail services are subject to free-riding (e.g., as relevant for pre-sales advice), vertical restraints can be used to mitigate this problem. With exclusive territories a retailer can no longer free-ride on the retail effort exerted by a competitor (see Mathewson and Winter 1994).[25] In such a situation the competition between retailers is likely to generate an insufficient level of services from both the firms' and the consumers' point of view. Vertical restraints are thus likely to be socially desirable.

9.3.3 Multi-product Manufacturer and the Retailer's Rent

As we have seen, vertical restraints can be used to achieve joint-profit maximization either by solving a double marginalization or by giving the right incentives to the retailer(s) to provide the appropriate level of services to the customers. Strategic motives (e.g., rent shifting) within a given vertical structure may also play a role and give rise to the use of some restraints. This is, for instance, the case when a monopolist producer sells several imperfectly substitutable products through a monopolist distributor (as shown in figure 9.3). Vertical restraints now play two roles: to solve the double-marginalization problem (which can arise if the manufacturer uses linear wholesale tariffs) but also to affect the way the joint profits are shared. However, the two-part tariffs that would be sufficient to maximize the joint profit in the single product case are no longer sufficient.

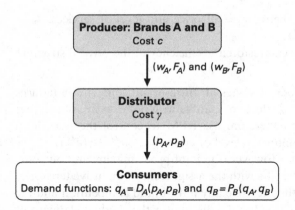

Figure 9.3
Multi-product monopolist producer

As shown by Shaffer (1991a), the joint-profit-sharing problem comes from the fact that the retailer earns a strictly positive rent attributable to its discretion over brand choice. The producer thus faces a trade-off between maximizing the joint profit and reducing the rent it leaves to the distributor. Suppose that the producer offers two brand-specific two-part tariffs (for $i = A, B : T_i(q_i) = w_i q_i + F_i$). If it carries both brands, the distributor chooses the retail prices $p_A^M(w_A, w_B)$ and $p_B^M(w_A, w_B)$ that maximize its own profit:

$$\pi^M(p_A, p_B) = (p_A - w_A - \gamma)D_A(p_A, p_B) + (p_B - w_B - \gamma)D_B(p_A, p_B).$$

Let $\pi_{A+B}^M(w_A, w_B)$ denote the corresponding maximum. If the distributor accepts to carry both brands, the retailer earns profit equal to

$$\pi^R(A, B) = \pi_{A+B}^M(w_A, w_B) - F_A - F_B.$$

Note that if the manufacturer were to set both wholesale prices equal to its marginal cost c, the distributor would be the residual claimant of the joint profits and would thus set retail prices at their monopoly levels.

Because the two brands are imperfect substitutes, introducing brand B reduces the sales of product A. This means that the retailer could also decide to carry one brand only (e.g., brand B), and its profit would then be

$$\pi^R(B) = \pi_B^M(w_B) - F_B,$$

with $\quad \pi_B^M(w_B) = \max_{p_B}[(p_B - w_B - \gamma)D_B(\emptyset, p_B)].$

If the retailer has accepted to carry brand B, the maximal franchise fee that the manufacturer can set for brand A is therefore equal to the marginal contribution of brand A to the joint profit, that is,

$$F_A = \pi_{A+B}^M(w_A, w_B) - \pi_B^M(w_B).$$

Because this contribution is usually increasing in w_B, the manufacturer will increase the wholesale prices above the joint-profit maximizing level ($w_A, w_B > c$), thereby bringing prices above their monopoly levels. Thus brand-specific two-part tariffs are not enough to ensure joint-profit maximization.

Vergé (2001) notes, however, that more general nonlinear tariffs would do better than two-part tariffs. With two-part tariffs, the manufacturer of brand A must, for example, leave to the retailer a relatively large rent because, if deciding to carry only product B, the retailer can increase the quantity q_B so as to maximize its profit on that product. If instead the manufacturer offers more restrictive contracts (e.g., quantity forcing contracts of the form (q_i, t_i)), the retailer can no longer increase the quantity q_B when dealing exclusively with B, and the rent to be left by the manufacturer could therefore be lower.[26]

Additional restraints can thus be used to restore the efficiency of the vertical structure. Full-line forcing (imposing to buy both brands) is one obvious consideration. Because the retailer can only choose to carry both brands or neither brand, the strategic rent effect vanishes. Setting wholesale prices equal to the marginal production cost thus leads to joint-profit maximization. RPM (price ceilings are again sufficient), aggregate rebates (discounts based on the total quantity sold), or brand discounts (based on the number of brands carried by the distributor) will have the same effect.

As in the standard double-marginalization case, vertical restraints are not only privately optimal but are also socially desirable as they reduce the retail prices to their monopoly levels.

9.3.4 Vertical Restraints and the Commitment Problem

When a monopolist manufacturer supplies several competing retailers, it has an interest to restrict its supply so as to maintain high prices and profits, which it can then share with the retailers. However, when dealing with one of the retailers, the producer has an incentive to cheat on the other competitors. As first shown by Hart and Tirole (1990), such opportunism may prevent the manufacturer from fully exerting its market power.

Suppose, for example, that a monopolist manufacturer sells its product through two retailers (assume that distribution costs are equal to 0) who compete à la Cournot (setting quantities rather than prices) on the final market. Denote by q^M the joint-profit-maximizing quantity and by π^M the corresponding profit. The manufacturer would like to sell $q^M/2$ to each retailer against a fixed payment equal to $\pi^M/2$. This is feasible if offers are observable. However, if the manufacturer can secretly renegotiate with one of the retailers, it can increase the quantity sold to that retailer against a larger payment. This renegotiation would, however, be anticipated by the second retailer who could then choose not to accept the initial offer. The same argument applies to any quantity: whatever quantitiy q it is offered, a retailer anticipates the manufacturer to offer to its rival, the quantity that would be the best-reply to q in the standard Cournot framework:

$$BR(q) = \arg\max_{q'}[P(q', q)q' - C(q')].$$

In this context, the only sustainable outcome is therefore the standard Cournot outcome.

Opportunistic behavior also arises if the manufacturer contracts sequentially with competing retailers: it then has an incentive to free-ride on early signing retailers when negotiating later deals. If negotiations are simultaneous but secret, each retailer may still worry that its competitors receive secret deals (e.g., lower prices per unit).[27]

In order to restore the efficiency of the vertical structure, the monopolist producer has an incentive to reduce retail competition using different kinds of vertical restraints: exclusive rights (or vertical integration) or an industrywide price floor will eliminate such competition. Whereas Hart and Tirole (1990) consider Cournot competition, O'Brien and Shaffer (1992) analyze a similar issue when differentiated retailers compete in prices. Using the concept of contract equilibrium à la Crémer and Riordan (1987), they show that the opportunism problem leads to the "competitive outcome" (the marginal wholesale price is equal to the marginal cost) and point out that RPM (combined with two-part tariffs) eliminates this risk. The problem is very similar to Hart and Tirole: when negotiating the wholesale contract, a retailer and the manufacturer take the contracts offered to the competing distributors as given and therefore do not internalize the retail margins on those products: by setting the retail and wholesale prices equal to the monopoly price, the producer becomes the residual claimant on all retail sales and is no longer willing to free ride on the other retailers' sales when making an offer to one of the downstream firms.[28]

In this context, vertical restraints are used to restore the ability of the vertical structure to maintain high prices. This will not only harm the consumers but also reduce total economic welfare.

9.3.5 Other Coordination Motives

A distributor usually distributes goods for several producers at the same time. Consider now a vertical structure consisting of the retailer and one of the manufacturers. If the wholesale price for one of the products from the competing manufacturers is lower than the (marginal) cost of that product, the distributor may be induced to favor the sales of that other product. From the point of view of the vertical structure, however, this introduces a distortion in the mix of products and reduces total profits. This distortion vanishes if the manufacturer imposes exclusive dealing arrangements. Absent the distortion, the products of the other manufacturers will not be present in the retailer's shelves. The use of two-part tariffs is often sufficient to restore the maximization of the industrywide profit. Free-riding between producers on customer services can create the same problems: marketing activities can have spillovers on other products that are not properly accounted for by the vertical structure in the absence of vertical restraints. We will come back to these issues when we consider inter-brand competition.

Some of the manufacturers' choices also affect their distributors' profits indirectly: this is certainly the case for decisions regarding either nationwide advertising campaigns or product quality. There again, in the absence of specific arrangements a simple linear price is likely to generate vertical externalities and to fail to achieve joint-profit maximization, whereas adequately chosen vertical restraints can correct for these externalities and to achieve (or to get closer to) joint-profit maximization.

Last, one of the parties must sometimes make specific investments that have little residual value if the relationship is terminated. In that case the return on such investments must be guaranteed through some long-term commitment; otherwise, the fear of opportunistic behavior (*holdup* problem) can lead to underinvestment (see Williamson 1985, 1989). Various provisions can again be used to prevent such opportunistic behavior from one or the other party: exclusive territories can, for example, be granted to protect distributors' investments, while noncompetition or exclusive dealing provisions can be used to protect a manufacturer's image and reputation (e.g., see Besanko and Perry 1993).

9.4 Inter-brand Competition

We have so far limited our attention to coordination problems within a given vertical structure. We now analyze the impact of vertical restraints on inter-brand competition, that is, on the strategic interactions between competing vertical structures. We start with short-term or static effects and try to see whether vertical restraints can be used to maintain or even increase existing market power. We see how these restraints can be used to exacerbate market imperfections—for example, by reducing competition on the upstream market or even leading to manufacturers' cartels—or to help maintain joint-profit-maximizing prices at both the upstream and downstream levels (global cartel). We end with a discussion of long-term or dynamic effects of vertical restraints on the structure of the market.

9.4.1 Competition Dampening
Vertical restraints used within a given vertical structure are likely to affect the strategic interactions between this distribution channel and rival vertical structures. The terms of the contracts accepted by the distributors affect the nature of the competition between these retailers on the downstream market. Vertical restraints used in a vertical structure will therefore indirectly influence the behavior of rival manufacturers when they set the terms of the contracts with their own distributors. Particular restraints can thus be used by a manufacturer to credibly commit not to behave aggressively vis-à-vis its rivals. Several authors have applied this idea of pre-commitment as way to limit inter-brand competition.

Bonanno and Vickers (1988), for instance, explore the idea, earlier formulated by Vickers (1985), that producers may prefer, for strategic purposes, to delegate the marketing of their products to independent retailers: when two independent vertical structures compete, each manufacturer finds it optimal to increase its wholesale prices. If its retailer is not so agressive when setting the retail price, the rival structure may be less agressive in response. In a similar setting Rey and Stiglitz (1988, 1995) show that vertical restraints such as exclusive territories, which eliminate intra-brand competition within a vertical structure, can help reduce inter-brand competition.[29] If the manufacturers maintain a high degree of intra-brand competition, then the final retail price will closely reflect the wholesale price of that particular product. In this sense, direct marketing by the producers is equivalent to having perfect competition among retailers within each vertical structure. If instead the manufacturers assign exclusive territories to their distributors and thus eliminate intra-brand competition within their distribution network, distributors will freely set their final prices. These final retail prices will then respond to any change in the retail price set by the rival manufacturer's retailers, and will therefore indirectly react to any change in the wholesale price set by rival manufacturer. Assigning exclusive territories can thus act as a pre-commitment to be less "aggressive" and give incentives to the rival manufacturer to set higher prices.[30]

To illustrate this point consider the following situation summarized in figure 9.4: two manufacturers (1 and 2) produce imperfect substitutes and face the same constant marginal cost of production c. The producers delegate the marketing to a network of independent retailers (a retailer can only sell one product) and the marginal cost of distribution is constant and equal to γ. When retail prices are p_1 and p_2, the demand for product i $(i = 1, 2)$ is $D_i(p_1, p_2)$.

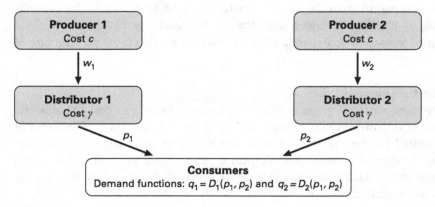

Figure 9.4
Competing vertical structures

Suppose first that each retail network consists of several identical retailers who compete in prices. In this case retail prices simply reflect perceived costs, and we have $p_i = w_i + \gamma$. Everything happens as if the manufacturers were either marketing the products themselves (with the same distribution cost γ) or dictating the retail prices (e.g., using RPM). The resulting price equilibrium is therefore characterized by

$$\frac{p_i - c - \gamma}{p_i} = \frac{1}{\varepsilon_{ii}(p_1, p_2)},$$

where $\varepsilon_{ii}(p_1, p_2) = -(p_i/D_i)(\partial D_i/\partial p_i)$ denotes the direct price elasticity of the demand for product i.

Suppose now that that one of the two manufacturers—manufacturer 1, say—assigns exclusive territories to its distributors and assumes that each exclusive territory is representative of the overall population. As a result each distributor of manufacturer 1's product faces competition only from the retailers distributing manufacturer 2's products. These retailers continue to sell at price $p_2 = w_2 + \gamma$, but the retailers selling manufacturer 1's product choose their best response to that price, given a perceived marginal cost equal to $w_1 + \gamma$. That is, they sell at price $p_1^r(p_2; w_1)$ given by

$$\frac{p_1^r(p_2; w_1) - w_1 - \gamma}{p_1^r(p_2; w_1)} = \frac{1}{\varepsilon_{11}(p_1^r(p_2; w_1), p_2)}.$$

Given w_2, manufacturer 1 can still control the retail price of its product by adjusting its wholesale price, and it can recover any retail margin, for example, through franchise fees. But the retail competition stage now alters the elasticity of the demand perceived by the rival manufacturer, which becomes

$$D_2^r(w_1, w_2) = D_2(p_1^r(w_2 + \gamma; w_1), w_2 + \gamma).$$

The elasticity of this demand is thus given by

$$\varepsilon_{22}^r(w_1, w_2) = -\frac{w_2}{D_2^r(w_1, w_2)} \frac{\partial D_2^r(w_1, w_2)}{\partial w_2}$$

$$= \varepsilon_{22}(p_1^r(p_2; w_1), p_2) + \lambda_{12}(w_1, w_2)\varepsilon_{21}(p_1^r(p_2; w_1), p_2),$$

where $\lambda_{12} = (p_2/p_1^r)(\partial p_1^r/\partial p_2)$ denotes the elasticity of the best response p_1^r with respect to the rival retail price p_2 and $\varepsilon_{21} = -(p_1/D_2)(\partial D_2/\partial p_1)$ denotes the cross-elasticity of the demand for product 2 with respect to the price of product 1. If the two products are substitutes, $\varepsilon_{21} < 0$. Moreover an increase in manufacturer 2's wholesale price w_2 increases the retail price for its product and thus relaxes the competitive pressure on the retailers of product 1, who are then likely to increase their own prices. So $\lambda_{12} > 0$, meaning retail prices are likely to be strategic complements. This attenuates the elasticity of demand perceived by manufacturer 2 who will therefore be less agressive and set a higher wholesale price (for a given p_1). Retailers facing this price increase will be induced to set higher retail prices.[31]

By granting exclusive territories to its retailers, a manufacturer commits to follow up any price increase. Because this encourages its rival to be less agressive (even when that rival does not impose territorial restrictions), competition is dampened and higher wholesale and retail prices result.[32]

Note that all vertical restraints do not generate such competition-dampening effects. The key idea is that manufacturers use vertical restraints as a mean to commit themselves not to compete aggressively against their rivals. This is achieved through the delegation of some decision power to the distributors: for instance, granting exclusive territories gives some freedom to the retailers in their choice of retail prices, freedom that is nonexistent if intra-brand competition is fierce (in this case a retail price is simply the sum of the corresponding wholesale price and the retailing cost). Therefore vertical restraints that increase the direct control of manufacturers over their retailers, such as RPM, cannot be used here.

As we said earlier, the key issue is the ability for the manufacturers to pre-commit not to compete fiercely against each other. Assigning exclusive territories is therefore a powerful restraint in this setting as it is easily observable by the rivals and not easily renegotiated. They are also likely to have a better commitment power than nonlinear contracts (e.g., delegation of pricing decision to a retailer using two-part tariffs as in Bonanno and Vickers 1988): for example, manufacturers are more likely to observe whether rivals have assigned exclusive territories to their retailers (it does take time to set up a new retail outlet) than to have information on whether wholesale tariffs include franchise fees (which could anyway be easily renegotiated). The impact of territorial restraints on the equilibrium retail prices is thus likely to be higher. Although they do not necessarily need to have full information on the terms of the contracts offered by the rival manufacturer to its retailers, it is nevertheless important that the distributors have some knowledge of these wholesale tariffs.[33] Another issue is to identify the set of admissible contracts: in the absence of any restriction, firms could easily achieve the fully collusive outcome as shown by Katz (1991).[34]

Note finally that the key ideas presented here do not rely on the fact that producers have the all bargaining power: think, for instance, of the Bonanno and Vickers (1988) setting in which the retailers would propose wholesale tariffs to the manufacturers. It would still be the case that vertical restraints can be used within a vertical structure to reduce inter-brand competition. Shaffer (1991b) shows that in this case retailers would offer wholesale prices above the marginal cost of production in order to soften competition on the retail market (and thus maintain high prices) and recover the wholesale profit through negative franchise fees ("slotting allowances").

9.4.2 Collusion

Courts have often argued that vertical price restraints can help manufacturers to sustain a cartel. The US Supreme Court in its decision in *Business Electronics* repeated its previous judgment that *"there was support for the proposition that vertical price restraints reduce intra-brand competition because they facilitate cartelization."*[35] This argument has been informally used by Telser (1960), and more recently Mathewson and Winter (1998, p. 65) argued that the use of RPM could have an even bigger impact when retailing costs can change over time: "If wholesale prices are not easily observed by each cartel member, cartel stability would suffer because members would have difficulty distinguishing changes in retail prices that were cause by cost changes from cheating the cartel. RPM can enhance cartel stability by eliminating retail price variation."

However, it is only recently that this argument has been formalized. Jullien and Rey (2007) show that by leading to more uniform retail prices, RPM makes price cuts easier to detect, and therefore RPM facilitates collusion when retailers compete in prices. In the absence of RPM, retail prices are driven by wholesale prices but also by local shocks on retailing costs or demand conditions. Because observing the retail prices does not allow the manufacturers to perfectly infer the wholesale prices, deviations from the collusive agreement cannot be easily identified. When RPM leads to uniform retail prices, it allows manufacturers to detect deviations at once and therefore makes collusion easier to sustain. Retailers cannot respond to changes in demand conditions or retailing cost, so price uniformity is not efficient and manufacturers have to trade off this inefficiency against the benefits of collusion.

Nevertheless, Jullien and Rey (2007) find situations where the additional profit generated by the collusive agreement offsets the loss of profit due to price rigidity. For instance, in the case where shocks affect only retail costs, equilibrium prices are both higher (on average) and more rigid when firms adopt RPM. When instead local shocks affect only the demand, the impact of RPM is potentially more ambiguous, since this will lead to prices that are higher (on average) but that do not react to demand fluctuations. Jullien and Rey find, however, that RPM can only reduce welfare when goods are sufficiently differentiated.

9.4.3 Interlocking Relationships

We have so far focused on situations where manufacturers distribute their products through distinct retail channels. Clearly, for most consumer goods, retailers carry competing products.

One Common Agent   Bernheim and Whinston (1985) show that if two manufacturers decide to sell their goods via the same retailer (this situation is usually referred to as "common agency"), it will give rise to joint-profit maximizing prices being charged in equilibrium.[36] Their results remain valid for a fairly large set of common agency situations as long as two-part tariffs can be used.

The intuition for this result is fairly simple. Suppose that two manufacturers, A and B, producing differentiated goods sell these goods through a monopolist retailer R. Production and distribution technologies exhibit constant returns to scale and the marginal cost of production and distribution are denoted c and γ respectively. We denote by $D_i(p_A, p_B)$ the demand for good $i = A, B$ when retail prices are p_A and p_B. The manufacturers simultaneously offer two-part tariffs (w_i, F_i) to the retailer, who then sets the retail prices.

Given the wholesale prices that have been offered by the two manufacturers, the retailer will set the prices that maximize its retail profit, that is,

$$(p_A^M(w_A, w_B), p_B^M(w_A, w_B)) = \arg\max_{(p_A, p_B)} \sum_{i=A, B} (p_i - w_i - \gamma) D_i(p_A, p_B).$$

Let denote $\pi_{A+B}^M(w_A, w_B)$ the corresponding maximum and by $q_A^M(w_A, w_B)$ and $q_B^M(w_A, w_B)$ the corresponding quantities. Note that if the two manufacturers were to set the wholesale prices equal to their marginal production cost c, the distributor would be the residual claimant of the joint profits and would thus set retail prices at their monopoly levels.

This situation presents some similarities with the problem of the multi-product monopolist presented earlier. Consider an equilibrium in which the retailer accepts both offers. Because the two goods are imperfectly substitutable, introducing product B reduces the sales of product A. Therefore, to induce the retailer to sell its product, a manufacturer has to leave a rent to the common agent. If it accepts to carry both brands, the retailer earns a profit equal to

$$\pi^R(A, B) = \pi_{A+B}^M(w_A, w_B) - F_A - F_B.$$

If it accepts the offer made by manufacturer i only, the retailer earns a profit equal to

$$\pi^R(i) = \pi_i^M(w_i) - F_i,$$

with $\pi_i^M(w_i) = \max_{p_i}[(p_i - w_i - \gamma) D_i(\emptyset, p_i)].$

The highest fixed fee that manufacturer A can set in order to have its offer accepted is therefore

$$\bar{F}_A = \pi_{A+B}^M(w_A, w_B) - \pi_B^M(w_B).$$

Manufacturer A will thus choose the wholesale price w_A that maximizes its profit, knowing it cannot charge a fixed fee higher than $\bar{F}_A$. The equilibrium wholesale price w_A^* is therefore

$$w_A^* = \arg\max_w [(p_A^M(w, w_B^*) - c - \gamma) q_A^M(w, w_B^*)$$

$$+ (p_B^M(w, w_B^*) - w_B^* - \gamma) q_B^M(w, w_B^*) - \pi_B^M(w_B^*) - F_B^*]$$

If the two manufacturers set wholesale prices equal to the marginal cost of production c, the retailer sets the retail prices at their joint-profit maximizing level. Therefore, if manufacturer B chooses $w_B^* = c$, it is optimal for manufacturer A to set $w_A^* = c$, since its profit is then equal to the industry profit up to constant. Under standard regularity assumptions, this is the unique equilibrium outcome. The main difference from the multi-product monopolist case is that although it has to leave a rent to the retailer, a manufacturer cannot influence that rent because it only controls one wholesale price. When it sets its wholesale price, each manufacturer internalizes only partially the impact that this choice has on the sales of the rival's product—more specifically it cares only about the retail markup and not the total markup on that product. However, if the rival manufacturer has set its wholesale price equal to marginal cost, retail and total markup are identical, and a manufacturer's profit now coincides (up to a constant) with the industry profit.

Two Common Agents More interesting are situations in which there is competition both upstream and downstream, and each manufacturer deals with several retailers but each retailer also deals with several retailers. Dobson and Waterson (2007) study a bilateral duopoly with interlocking relationships and show that the welfare effects of RPM depend on the relative degree of upstream and downstream differentiation as well as on retailers' and manufacturers' relative bargaining power. Double-marginalization problems are more severe when producers have more bargaining power, so RPM can be socially preferable in such circumstances. This result nevertheless depends critically on the restriction to linear wholesale prices.[37]

In a similar context of "interlocking relationships" but allowing for two-part tariffs, Rey and Vergé (2002) show that RPM can be used to eliminate both upstream and downstream competition. To see the argument, consider the situation summarized in figure 9.5. Two

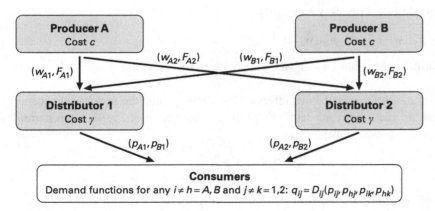

Figure 9.5
Interlocking relationships

manufacturers, A and B, each produce their own brand of a good and market them through two differentiated retailers, 1 and 2 (e.g., retailers can differ in the services they provide to consumers, the location of their stores, etc.). There are thus four relevant "products" for the consumers who can choose between brands and between stores. Demand for product ij (i.e., brand $i \in \{A, B\}$ sold in store $j \in \{1, 2\}$) is

$$D_{ij}(\mathbf{p}) \equiv D(p_{ij}, p_{hj}, p_{ik}, p_{hk})$$

(for any $i \neq h \in \{A, B\}$ and any $j \neq k \in \{1, 2\}$),

and the marginal costs of production and distribution are constant and equal to c and γ respectively.

Manufacturers simultaneously offer two-part tariffs to both retailers and, when possible, impose the retail price of their products. To keep the presentation as simple as possible, we assume that if one of the four offers is rejected, the market fails and manufacturers and retailers earn zero profit. This ensures that retailers are willing to accept an offer as long as they make nonnegative profit. Rey and Vergé (2002) propose several more realistic frameworks for which the results presented here remain valid: this will generally be the case there is no retail bottleneck, in the sense that manufacturers can find equally efficient alternative channels for each relevant retail location, that is, if the following two features hold:

• Retailers have no market power, so manufacturers extract all profits.
• Manufacturers cannot exclude their rivals from any retail location.

If all offers have been accepted, each retailer $j = 1, 2$ sets its prices p_{Aj} and p_{Bj} so as to maximize its profit, given by

$$\pi_j = (p_{Aj} - w_{Aj} - \gamma)D_{Aj}(\mathbf{p}) + (p_{Bj} - w_{Bj} - \gamma)D_{Bj}(\mathbf{p}) - F_{Aj} - F_{Bj}.$$

For any vector of wholesale prices, we denote by

$$\mathbf{p}^r(\mathbf{w}) = (p_{A1}^r(\mathbf{w}), p_{B1}^r(\mathbf{w}), p_{A2}^r(\mathbf{w}), p_{B2}^r(\mathbf{w}))$$

the retail equilibrium prices and by $D_{ij}^r(\mathbf{w}) = D_{ij}(\mathbf{p}^r(\mathbf{w}))$ the resulting demand for each product.

Because retailers can only accept both offers or earn zero profit, the maximum acceptable franchise fees are such that each retailer's profit is nonnegative ($\pi_j \geq 0$). Each manufacturer $i = A, B$ thus seeks to solve

$$\max_{w_{i1}, w_{i2}, F_{i1}, F_{i2}} (w_{i1} - c)D_{i1}^r(\mathbf{w}) + F_{i1} + (w_{i2} - c)D_{i2}^r(\mathbf{w}) + F_{i2},$$

subject to $(p_{i1}^r(\mathbf{w}) - w_{i1} - \gamma)D_{i1}^r(\mathbf{w}) - F_{i1} + (p_{j1}^r(\mathbf{w}) - w_{j1} - \gamma)D_{j1}^r(\mathbf{w}) - F_{j1} \geq 0,$

$(p_{i2}^r(\mathbf{w}) - w_{i2} - \gamma)D_{i2}^r(\mathbf{w}) - F_{i2} + (p_{j2}^r(\mathbf{w}) - w_{j2} - \gamma)D_{j2}^r(\mathbf{w}) - F_{j2} \geq 0.$

Since the participation constraints are clearly binding, this program is equivalent to

$$\max_{w_{i1}, w_{i2}} \Pi_i^r(\mathbf{w}) \equiv \sum_{j=1,2} (p_{ij}^r(\mathbf{w}) - c - \gamma) D_{ij}^r(\mathbf{w}) + (p_{hj}^r(\mathbf{w}) - w_{hj} - \gamma) D_{hj}^r(\mathbf{w}). \tag{9.1}$$

When contracts consist of two-part tariffs only, competition leads to a somewhat competitive outcome. This result is not entirely obvious. Retailers act as "common agents" for both manufacturers, as Bernheim and Whinston (1985, 1986) emphasize, and their common agency helps maintain monopoly prices and quantities. The essential difference here is that there exists competition on both the upstream and the downstream market. Using the same retailers (the "common agents") eliminates the impact of the upstream competition. However, to prevent the competition between retailers from driving prices down, manufacturers must charge wholesale prices above marginal costs. But then, as seen from the manufacturers' maximization program (9.1), each manufacturer does not internalize the total markup on the rival's products (but only the retail margin) and therefore has an incentive to free-ride on the rival's upstream margin. This state of affairs eventually leads to prices below the industrywide profit-maximizing level (hereafter "monopoly level").

If manufacturers can use RPM, they no longer need to rely on wholesale prices to maintain high retail prices. They can proceed thus as follows:

1. Set retail prices to the monopoly level.
2. Charge wholesale prices that simply reflect production costs ($w_{ij} = c$).
3. Use franchise fees to recover the resulting profits.

If one manufacturer does this, it is its rival's best interest to do it too. For example, when manufacturer B adopts the above-mentioned strategy, manufacturer A's profit boils down to (with $\mathbf{p} = (p_{A1}, p_{B1}^M, p_{A2}, p_{B2}^M)$):

$$\Pi_A = \sum_{j=1,2} ((p_{Aj} - c - \gamma) D_{Aj}(\mathbf{p}) + (p_{Bj}^M - c - \gamma) D_{B1}(\mathbf{p}) - F_{Bj}).$$

Thus manufacturer A's profit coincides (up to a constant) with the industry profits, so manufacturer A has an incentive to maintain monopoly prices for its products. In addition, because profits can be shared through franchise fees as well as through wholesale prices, manufacturer A can always "sell at cost" ($w_{Aj} = c$) and recover profits solely through the franchise fees. Therefore RPM allows firms to sustain monopoly prices, despite the competition in both the upstream and downstream segments.

9.4.4 Exclusive Dealing and Foreclosure

In some circumstances vertical restraints can be used to foreclose market access and prevent the entry of potentially more efficient competitors. One possible strategy might be to sign up available distributors into exclusive dealing arrangements, thereby forcing potentially new suppliers to set up their own distribution systems. If there are large economies of scope or scale in the distribution sector, these exclusive arrangements will raise the entry cost of potential rivals: for example, if the manufacturer is distributing its products through retailers who can also distribute the products of a potential competing manufacturer, and if there are synergies from distributing both lines of products, a potential competitor entering the market will have low retailing costs; exclusive dealing provisions will rule this arrangement out and thus force a potential competitor to distribute its products in a less efficient way. Then the increased distribution costs can deter entry.

A similar entry barrier might be created if entry at the downstream level is difficult and costly, such as if there is a limited supply of retailers, at least of comparable quality, or a scarcity of comparably good retail locations. Then again, tying-up the best retailers or locations through long-term exclusive dealing provisions will increase distribution costs for newcomers and thus rule out entry from a potential competitor.

These strategies are part of more general "raising rivals' costs strategies" that have been informally explored in the US institutional context by Krattenmaker and Salop (1986). Such strategies can be used against actual competitors to force them out of the market or at least substantially reduce their market shares, as well as to prevent potential competitors from entering the market or at least to delay their entry. Exclusive agreements can, of course, hurt retailers (who may prefer to carry both lines of products, and may also eventually face increased competition if entry does occur). But retailers can be compensated for this risk by a share of the extra profits generated so long as entry is successfully deterred.

A formal analysis of these strategies has been proposed by Comanor and Frech (1985) and then developed by Mathewson and Winter (1987) and Schwartz (1987), who have recognized the role of incumbent manufacturers' competition for distributors. More recently Bernheim and Whinston (1998) have further extended the analysis by considering larger class of contracts (previous works had focused on linear wholesale tariffs). They show that exclusive contracts can again be used to foreclosure markets, except if vertical arrangements allow upstream and downstream firms to achieve perfect coordination.

The role of exclusive provisions as entry deterrent has long been contested especially by the so-called Chicago school who have argued using such provisions to deter entry cannot be profitable. Even assuming that exclusive dealing provisions can effectively deter the entry of potential manufacturers, why would distributors agree with such arrangements, thereby forgoing opportunities to deal with more efficient suppliers and to generate more competition among their suppliers? Posner (1976) and Bork (1978) claim that for a retailer to accept an exclusive dealing agreement, it should be compensated for the loss of profits that could have been generated using more efficient suppliers. This strategy would then necessarily be unprofitable for the incumbent manufacturer.

Aghion and Bolton (1987) provide a first answer to the Chicago school critique stressing that an incumbent manufacturer could use part of the extra profit generated to "bribe" the distributors into the agreements. More precisely consider the situation presented in figure 9.6.

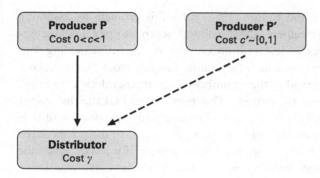

Figure 9.6
Potential entry on the upstream market (Aghion and Bolton 1987)

An incumbent producer P has a constant marginal cost of production c $(0 < c < 1)$ and faces a potential entrant P' whose marginal cost is uniformly distributed over the interval $[0, 1]$. To market its product, the manufacturer has to deal with a monopolist distributor D. The marginal cost of distribution is constant and equal to γ, and the final demand is assumed to be inelastic and equal to $Q = 1$ as long as the retail price is not higher than $r > c + \gamma$.

Suppose first that exclusive dealing is banned. The game is then as follows: The potential entrant decides whether to enter or not. The incumbent manufacturer and the entrant (if entry occurs) simultaneously set their wholesale prices w and w'. The retailer buys from the cheapest manufacturer and resells at price r on the final market. The entrant chooses to enter only when it is more efficient than the incumbent ($c' < c$, which occurs with probability c), and it sets a price equal to c that attracts the whole demand. The producers' (P and P') and the distributor's profits are then respectively

$$\pi_P(E) = 0, \quad \pi_{P'}(E) = c' - c, \quad \text{and} \quad \pi_D(E) = r - c - \gamma.$$

When the entrant is less efficient, entry does not occur, and the incumbent producer acting as a monopolist sets a price equal to r. The firms' profits are

$$\pi_P(N) = r - c - \gamma, \quad \pi_{P'}(N) = 0 \quad \text{and} \quad \pi_D(N) = 0.$$

The (ex ante) expected profits for the incumbent producers and the retailer are therefore

$$\pi_P^* = (1 - c)(r - c - \gamma) \quad \text{and} \quad \pi_D^* = c(r - c - \gamma).$$

Consider now what happens if the distributor has signed an exclusive dealing agreement with the incumbent manufacturer. Confirming the Chicago school argument, such an agreement cannot simply consist of a commitment to deal exclusively with the incumbent even when a more efficient producer is active; the retailer would never be willing to accept such an agreement. However, Aghion and Bolton (1987) solve this problem by assuming that by signing an exclusive dealing agreement, the distributor accepts to pay a compensation to the incumbent in case it decides to deal with the entrant. An exclusive dealing contract thus consists of a wholesale price w at which the retailer can buy from the incumbent manufacturer and of a penalty p to be paid to the incumbent if the retailer decides to break the exclusivity agreement and deal with the entrant. This now means that the distributor will accept to deal with the entrant only if $w' + p \leq w$. The alternative producer will thus enter when $c' \leq w - p$. Given that the entrant will charge a price equal to the price offered by the incumbent minus the penalty ($w' = w - p$), the retailer's profit if it has accepted the exclusive dealing offer (w, p) is simply $\pi_D = r - w - \gamma$. The incumbent manufacturer's maximization program is therefore:

$$\max_{(w,p)} [(w - p)p + (1 - w + p)(w - c)]$$

subject to $r - w - \gamma \geq c(r - c - \gamma)$,

The solution of this program is then

$$w^* = r - \gamma - c(r - c - \gamma) \quad \text{and} \quad p^* = w^* - \frac{c}{2} = (1 - c)(r - c - \gamma) + \frac{c}{2}.$$

The incumbent's expected profit under this exclusive dealing agreement is

$$\pi_P^{ED} = (1 - c)(r - c - \gamma) + \frac{c^2}{4} = \pi_P^* + \frac{c^2}{4}.$$

This solution shows that entry can be at least partially prevented (entry occurs when the entrant is much more efficient than the incumbent, $c' \leq c/2$), although the entrant is more efficient than the incumbent manufacturer. The entry barrier is achieved through the provision for liquidation damages that allow the retailer to break the exclusive dealing agreement by paying a penalty to the incumbent manufacturer. To enter the market, the entrant will have to compensate the retailer for exactly the amount of this penalty, and everything happens as if the damages were paid directly by the entrant. When entry occurs, the damages increase the joint profit of the pair $P - D$, who can then share this increase in joint profit through the wholesale price. Exclusive dealing is thus an attractive option for both the incumbent manufacturer and the retailer because it allows them to extract some of the profit that the entrant could generate in case of entry.

In an extension to this model, Spiegel (1994) shows that liquidation damages may rather enhance welfare (although ex post entry deterrence may be excessive). For example, the manufacturer could make an investment to decrease its marginal cost prior to the negotiation with the retailer.

Rasmusen, Ramseyer, and Wiley (1991) showed that exclusive dealing provisions can be used to deter entry of more efficient competitors, even in the absence of "rent extraction," that is, by way of simple contracts without the liquidation damage inherent in the Aghion and Bolton (1987) framework. Their argument relies on poor coordination among distributors and on the assumption that entry is viable only if the entrant is able to sell its products to a minimum number of consumers (e.g., because of large fixed costs of entry). The idea is that if the incumbent can convince a sufficient number of retailers to enter in an exclusive dealing agreement, entry will become unprofitable for the rival. This can be done by sharing with the retailers that enter the exclusive agreement the extra rent that the manufacturer can gain from dealing with the remaining retailers who have no alternative supplier. If offers are made simultaneously to all retailers, there must then exist an equilibrium in which all retailers accept the exclusive dealing agreement: because one retailer alone would never buy a large enough quantity to make entry viable for the rival supplier, it has no incentive to deviate and reject the exclusive deal.

More recently Segal and Whinston (2000) show that if offers cannot be discriminatory, the equilibrium suggested by Rasmusen, Ramseyer, and Wiley (1991) is not coalition-proof. When discrimination is possible (i.e., when the manufacturer can make different offers to different retailers), the existence of a perfect coalition-proof equilibrium can still be restored. In this case the "exclusion equilibrium" is not based on a lack of coordination between retailers but simply on the externality that distributors accepting the exclusivity deal create on the remaining retailers. These two models suppose that the downstream firms are the final buyers of the good. Implicit is the assumption that the retailers then resell on independent markets, that is, act as local monopolists.

Fumagalli and Motta (2006) extend the analysis of Segal and Whinston and allow for competition among retailers. They show that exclusive dealing cannot occur in equilibrium if competition among the retailers is fierce enough. Consider, for instance, the extreme in which retailers are identical and compete in prices on the final market. If all its rivals accept the exclusive deal offered by the incumbent, a retailer has a strong incentive to deal with the alternative supplier. If that supplier is a more efficient entrant, it will attract all the consumers, and this will make entry viable. So exclusive dealing can be profitable only if intra-brand competition is limited.

Comanor and Rey (2000) also show that exclusive dealing can occur and prevent efficient entry even without "rent-extraction." Their argument relies instead in the idea that entry of a new competitor at one stage (either at the upstream or downstream stage) not only introduces or reinforces competition at that stage but also triggers or reinforces competition at the other stage. This is then likely to result in a decrease in the joint profit of the incumbent firms, who then have an incentive to prevent entry in order to protect their rents. Consider, for instance, the extension of the Aghion and Bolton (1987) framework to allow potential entry at both stages, as illustrated by figure 9.7.

An incumbent producer P has a constant marginal cost of production c and markets its product through an incumbent distributor D with constant marginal cost of distribution γ. The final demand is assumed to be inelastic and equal to $Q = 1$ as long as the retail price is

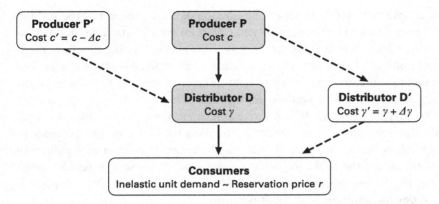

Figure 9.7
Potential entry in both markets (Comanor and Rey 2000)

not higher than $r > c + \gamma$. If the two firms act as monopolists at their respective stages, the distributor sells at price r, and the two firms can share the corresponding profit

$$\pi_P^* + \pi_D^* = r - c - \gamma.$$

Suppose now that the retailer has access to a more efficient manufacturer who produces at cost $c' = c - \Delta c$ and that the incumbent producer has access to an alternative distributor (or can set up its own distribution network). This alternative retailer is, however, less efficient than the incumbent retailer and faces a marginal cost of distribution equal to $\gamma' = \gamma + \Delta\gamma$. Assume finally that the alternative supplier does not have access to the alternative distributor.[38] This means that three vertical structures can be created (also only at most two are likely to coexist). Assume that all three are viable, that is, $c + \gamma' \leq r$.

In the absence of any pre-commitment between the two incumbents, the incumbent distributor will switch and deal with the more efficient producer. This leaves the incumbent manufacturer with no other choice than to deal with the alternative retailer. Entry at the upstream level thus not only generates competition between the two producers but also triggers competition between two vertical structures: the efficient pair $P' - D$ with cost $c + \gamma - \Delta c$ faces competition from the less efficient pair $P - D'$ with cost $c + \gamma + \Delta\gamma$. Bertrand competition between producers leads to a wholesale price equal to c, while competition between the two vertical structures leads to a retail price equal to $c + \gamma + \Delta\gamma$. In equilibrium, only the most efficient structure ($P' - D$) is active and the equilibrium profits are

$$\pi_P^{**} = \pi_{D'}^{**} = 0, \quad \pi_{P'}^{**} = \Delta c, \quad \text{and} \quad \pi_D^{**} = \Delta\gamma.$$

The important result in this case is that the joint profits of the incumbent firms are now lower than in the absence of the alternative firms:

$$\pi_P^{**} + \pi_D^{**} = \Delta\gamma < r - c - \gamma = \pi_P^* + \pi_D^*.$$

Hence the two incumbents could find it advantageous to enter in an exclusive dealing arrangement and thereby rule out any entry. Note that this is true even when the incumbent producer P has all the bargaining power vis-à-vis the incumbent distributor D (and thus $\pi_D^* = 0$), in which case D would a priori be eager to promote upstream competition. However, because the joint profits will be higher under the exclusive dealing agreement, P can always convince D by offering a compensating reduction in wholesale price.

Lately Marx and Shaffer (2006) have shown that the increase in retailers' bargaining power can lead to retailers' securing upfront payments from the manufacturer ("slotting allowances") and that this type of vertical contracts can be exclusionary, leading to fewer choices for consumers. In particular, they look at a standard intra-brand competition model similar to O'Brien and Shaffer (1992) but now assuming that the retailers make take-it-or-leave-it offers to the producer. If the offers are made by the manufacturer, the joint-profit maximization can be achieved using two-part tariffs, through (1) a wholesale price above cost to compensate for the impact of intra-brand competition and maintain monopoly retail prices, and (2) fixed fees used to recover any retail margin. But when instead the offers are made by the retailers and include both an upfront fee U paid when the contract is signed and a fixed fee F paid when the retailer actually buys the product from the manufacturer, as well as a wholesale price w, the manufacturer is always excluded from the shelves of at least one retailer. This goes against the intuition of standard common agency models (e.g., Bernheim and Whinston 1985) which predicts joint-profit maximization.

Suppose, for instance, that there exist two retailers—say, A and B—to distribute the manufacturer's product. The marginal costs of production and distribution are constant and equal to c and γ respectively, and there are no fixed costs. Denote by Π_i^M ($i = A, B$) the industry's maximizing profit when only retailer B is active and assume that retailer A is the dominant retailer, that is, $\Pi_A^M \geq \Pi_B^M$.

Let us first understand why common agency cannot occur in equilibrium. If common agency is to arise in equilibrium, the manufacturer must be indifferent between accepting both offers and accepting one offer only; otherwise, the other retailer can increase its upfront payment. But if the manufacturer accepts to deal exclusively with retailer B, that retailer will earn more than in the common agency situation. Therefore in equilibrium the manufacturer and retailer B get together less than if the manufacturer were to deal exclusively with retailer B, and thus exclusion is profitable.

Conversely, there always exists an equilibrium in which the weaker retailer B is excluded. Suppose that retailer A requests a wholesale price equal to cost c and an upfront payment of $\Pi_A^M - \Pi_B^M$ from the manufacturer, and accepts in exchange to pay, if it actually buys the product, a fixed fee equal to Π_A^M. If the manufacturer accepts that offer only, it earns Π_B^M while A earns $\Pi_A^M - \Pi_B^M$ and B is excluded. Obviously the manufacturer cannot do better by dealing exclusively with retailer B, and if the manufacturer accepted both offers, A can decide to remain inactive because retail competition will drive its revenue below Π_A^M. Again, the manufacturer will de facto deal only with retailer B and thus cannot get more than $\Pi_B^M - (\Pi_A^M - \Pi_B^M) < \Pi_B^M$. In other words, accepting to pay a large fixed fee if it eventually buys from the manufacturer allows the dominant retailer to enforce exclusive dealing. If the manufacturer accepts both contracts, the dominant retailer can then decide not to purchase because its flow profit will no longer cover the fixed fee.

If the retailers could offer make offers contingent on exlusive dealing or common agency (as in Bernheim and Whinston 1998), exclusion would, however, be unlikely to occur in equilibrium. Rey, Thal, and Vergé (2006) show, for example, that with contingent three-part tariffs (which include upfront payments and fixed fees conditional on buying, as above) nonexclusionary equilibria always exist and can even sustain the industry monopoly outcome. In this case upfront payments ("slotting allowances") always occur whenever retailers have some bargaining power, but the welfare effect of such three-part tariffs is unclear. On the one hand, they lead to the higher prices than those that standard two-part tariffs would generate, but on the other hand, they ensure that consumers can find the product on both retailers' shelves. The global effect will more likely to be positive when intra-brand competition is strong because exclusionary equilibria are more likely.

Other types of vertical restraints can be used to deter entry. Generally, vertical restraints that modify the partners' attitudes toward their competitors are likely to have this impact. Hence incumbent firms can use these restraints to commit themselves to a tough attitude in the event of entry. For example, it has been argued that long-term exclusive dealing provisions that tie distributors to a given brand induce fiercer competition if competing products appear. Similarly exclusive territories can induce a tougher response in the event of geographically limited entry. In the absence of such arrangements, if a new competitor enters in a given area, an already well-established manufacturer might be reluctant to engage in a price war, which will also affect neighboring areas. By contrast, an independent retailer with an exclusive right on an area will not take into account the impact of the local price cut on neighboring areas, and thus will be likely to engage in a tougher competition with the local entrant.[39]

9.5 Implications for Competition Policy toward Vertical Restraints

The first lesson that can be drawn from the preceding analysis is that no simple conclusion can be derived on whether any particular type of vertical restraint is pro- or anticompetitive. Both price (e.g., resale price maintenance) and nonprice restraints (e.g., exclusive dealing or territories) can either increase or decrease economic welfare. What really matters is not the restraint used but the context in which it is used and the goal that it is supposed to achieve.

Decisions taken by all firms—a manufacturer and its retailer—within a vertical structure affect the profits of all firms in that structure as well as the economic welfare. Because each firm is likely to ignore the impact of its decisions on other firms profits, each individual firm will usually fail to maximize the aggregate profits of the vertical structure. Provisions that increase coordination within the vertical structure will therefore restore the efficiency of that structure, and this will happen in different ways. First, coordination can be achieved by granting to the manufacturer the right to set the retail prices or specify the level of services offered by the distributors. Second, vertical restraints such as two-part tariffs can make the distributor feel the full effect of its decisions by making its profits equal to the aggregate profits of the vertical structure (up to a constant). Finally, when spillover effects occur among retailers, vertical restraints such as territorial or customer restrictions can eliminate intra-brand competition and thereby remove the externality. Typically different combinations of vertical restraints can be used to deal with a particular combination of problems.

If the impact on the aggregate profits of the vertical structure is positive, the impact on economic welfare or consumer surplus is not always so clear-cut. For example, provisions that eliminate double marginalization will reduce the retail price. Hence economic welfare increases because both profits and consumer surplus increase. On the other hand, the choice of retail service that maximizes profit does not necessarily maximize consumer or total surplus.

Our review of the literature has highlighted several ways in which vertical restraints can be used strategically to impede or even entirely eliminate the benefit of inter-brand competition on consumers and social welfare. From a theoretical point of view, the optimal policy toward vertical restraints then cannot be one such that some particular provisions are deemed illegal per se while some others are always acceptable. Per se rules may nevertheless be desirable if, for example, they significantly reduce transaction costs and legal uncertainty, as compared with a case-by-case treatment by courts or competition authorities.

The economic analysis does not only stress the complexity of the evaluation of the effects of vertical restraints; it also identifies some ideas on the likely impact of vertical restraints that can provide guidelines for competition authorities. In particular, the market structure and more specifically the extent of inter-brand competition from other manufacturers and retailers is a crucial factor in the analysis of the effects of vertical restraints. For example, when inter-brand competition is limited, firms and consumers are less likely to agree on the services that should be provided to consumers. This is because firms will tailor their services to attract marginal consumers, who are then likely to be different from the average infra-marginal consumer. Improving vertical coordination may well decrease total surplus. However, when the vertical structure faces strong competition from other suppliers, consumers buying a given brand are likely to be more homogeneous, and the vertically made choices are more likely to benefit all consumers. Hence, if the market structure—level of concentration, conditions of entry, dynamics, and so forth—ensures vigorous competition among rival vertical structures, vertical restraints are unlikely to harm economic efficiency or reduce competition. Conversely, in less competitive markets the risk is much greater that vertical restraints can be used to reduce competition or otherwise reduce economic efficiency. Likewise the strategic impact of vertical restraints on inter-brand competition critically depends on the structure of the market and on the nature of upstream and downstream competition.

Competition policy should focus on the extent of inter-brand competition and on the role of alternative distribution systems (e.g., hard discount vs. more conventional channels) rather than on intra-brand competition only. Even when vertical restraints eliminate intra-brand competition, sufficient competition from other structures will not decrease economic welfare because the structure will be unable to exercise market power. Similarly the strategic impact of vertical restraints on inter-brand competition will critically depend on the structure of the market and on the nature of upstream and downstream competition.

Finally, vertical restraints (especially price restraints) can have anticompetitive effects even when there is strong inter-brand competition. Price restraints can facilitate full cartellization of the market if the two vertical structures are not independent and the manufacturers deal will the same retailers. Complete analysis of such markets with intricate relationships between producers and distributors is, however, complicated, and more research needs to be carried out to understand the impact of vertical restraints in such situations.

Notes

We thank Yossi Spiegel for useful comments.

1. This equivalence between price and quantity controls vanishes if the distributor can sell to or buy from other distributors.

2. See *Dr. Miles v. John D. Park & Sons Co., 220* US 373 (1911).

3. For a more exhaustive presentation of the evolution of competition policy in the United States, see Kovacic and Shapiro (2000).

4. See *Standard Oil Co. v. United States, 221* US 1 (1911) and *United States v. Colgate & Co.*, 250 US 300 (1919).

5. See *White Motors Co. v. United States*, 372 US 253 (1967).

6. See, for instance, *United States v. Arnold, Schwinn & Co.*, 388 US 365 (1988).

7. See *Continental T.V, Inc. v. GTE Sylvania*, 433 US 36 (1977).

8. This decision was later confirmed by the Court of Appeals (7th Circuit) in 2000. See *Toy 'R' Us, Inc. v. FTC*, Docket 9278.

9. See *State of New York, et al. v. Toys 'R' Us, et al.* (1997 MDL 1211–USDCt, Eastern District of New York).

10. See *United States v. Microsoft*, Civil Action No 98-1232 and *LePage v. 3M*, 324 F. 3d 141 (3d Circ. 2003).

11. Verouden (2003) also offers an extensive survey of the interpretation and application of Article 81(1) over the past forty years.

12. It is worth noting that the rules implementing Article 81(1), which was then known as Article 85(1) of the Treaty of Rome (signed in 1957), only came into force in 1962. This decision was confirmed in 1966 by the European Court of Justice. See Commission Decision, *Official Journal of the European Communities 161*, 20 October 1964, and European Court of Justice, *Consten and Grundin v. Commission*, joined cases 56/64 and 58/64, 13 July 1966.

13. See case *Nintendo* COMP/35.587 [Commission Decision, *OJ L255*, 8 October 2003], *Volkswagen A.G.* COMP/36.693 [Commission Decision, *OJ L262*, 2 October 2001], *Opel Nethelands B.V.* COMP36.653 [Commission Decision, *OJ L59*, 28 February 2001] and *DaimlerChrysler A.G.* COMP 38/0.64.

14. See Commission Regulation (EC) 2790/99, OJCE 1999 (L336), Commission Notice—Guidelines on Vertical Restraints, OJCE 2000 (C291) and Council Regulation (EC) 1/2003, OJCE 2003 (L1).

15. See *Official Journal of the European Communities 13*, 15 January 1987.

16. See case *Michelin* COMP/36.041 [Commission Decision, *OJ L143*, 31 May 2002].

17. See case *Microsoft* COMP/37.792.

18. See case *TCCC* COMP/39.116.

19. A similar issue had been raised in 1991 in a case involving leading ice-cream makers *Langnese-Igol* and *Schöller*. See Motta (2004, pp. 391–98) for an analysis of the case.

20. A simple revealed preference argument (see Tirole 1988) implies that the monopoly price $p^M(c)$ increases with the cost.

21. In what follows, $\partial_x F$ stands for $\partial_x F / \partial_x$.

22. See, for instance, Motta (2004, ch. 6) for a formal analysis of the impact of vertical restraints in this context.

23. This remains valid even if retailers are differentiated. See, for instance, Spiegel and Yehezkel (2003) who show that intrabrand competition between vertically differentiated retailers may be suboptimal for a manufacturer.

24. Winter (1993) offers a detailed analysis of firms' and consumers' objectives when retailers' effort aims at reducing consumers' shopping time. Schulz (2007) shows that, if some consumers do not search for the best price but buy spontaneously, RPM can reduce social welfare even if it increases services to consumers.

25. Marvel and McCafferty (1984) show that RPM can be used to solve free-riding problem when some kind of quality certification activity undertaken by a retailer is costly and can be "appropriated" by competitors.

26. Specifying a maximum quantity would suffice. Note that manufacturer still needs to leave a positive rent to the retailer, and this rent increases with the quantities supplied. As a result the manufacturer distorts the quantities it supplies and thus fails to maximize joint profits.

27. How this affects the final outcome depends on the type of beliefs formed by the retailers (see McAfee and Schwartz 1994; Rey and Vergé 2004). Martin, Normann, and Snyder (2001) have experimented alternative contracting situations between a monopolist supplier and competing retailers. They observe that the monopolist was able to maintain output close to the monopoly level significantly less often when making secret offers.

28. Nondiscrimination rules (or "most-favored customer" clauses) can in some cases limit opportunism: see DeGraba and Postlewaite (1992), McAfee and Schwartz (1994), and Marx and Shaffer (2004).

29. This argument has recently been empirically tested by Slade (1998) in the context of a change of regulation in the UK beer industry.

30. Related ideas have been developed in the marketing literature (e.g., see McGuire and Staelin 1983). Other papers such as Gal-Or (1991) have enriched the delegation model (for reviews of this literature, see Caillaud and Rey 1995; Irmen 1998).

31. See Rey and Stiglitz (1995) for a formal analysis of these conditions.

32. The level of prices in equilibrium will depend on the exact nature of wholesale contracts, and in particular, on whether or not franchise fees are allowed. For example, in the absence of franchise fees double-marginalization problems are likely to occur and lead to even higher prices. In all cases exclusive territories reduced both interbrand and intra-brand competition.

33. Caillaud, Jullien, and Picard (1995) analyze the commitment power of unobservable contracts in the presence of asymmetric information.

34. Katz (1991) also shows that under some circumstances, unobservable contracts might still have some commitment power.

35. See *Business Electronics Corp. v. Sharp Electronics*, 485 US 717 (1988) and *Continental T.V. Inc.v. GTE Sylvania Inc.*, 433 US 36 (1977).

36. There are multiple equilibria, but they only differ in the way the profit is shared among the different parties.

37. For example, in the setup used by Dobson and Waterson (2007), which is based on simultaneous Nash-bargaining, the two parties' relative bargaining power will no longer affect retail prices if the firms adopt two-part tariffs.

38. It is equivalent to assume that the producer P' can set its own retail network. But because P' has just entered the market and is not necessarily well informed, it will face retail costs that will make that vertical structure non-viable (e.g., retailing cost γ'' will be such that $c' + \gamma'' > r$).

39. See Rey and Stiglitz (1995) for a formalization of this idea.

References

Aghion, P., and P. Bolton. 1987. Contracts as a barrier to entry. *American Economic Review* 77: 388–401.

Bernheim, D., and M. Whinston. 1985. Common marketing agency as a device for facilitating collusion. *Rand Journal of Economics* 16: 269–81.

Bernheim, D., and M. Whinston. 1986. Common agency. *Econometrica* 54: 923–42.

Bernheim, D., and M. Whinston. 1998. Exclusive dealing. *Journal of Political Economy* 106: 64–103.

Besanko, D., and M. Perry. 1993. Equilibrium incentives for exclusive dealing in a differentiated products oligopoly. *Rand Journal of Economics* 24: 646–67.

Bonanno, G., and J. Vickers. 1988. Vertical separation. *Journal of Industrial Economics* 36: 257–65.

Bork, R. 1978. *The Antitrust Paradox*. New York: Basic Books.

Caillaud, B., B. Jullien, and P. Picard. 1995. Competing vertical structures: Precommitment and renegotiation. *Econometrica* 63: 621–46.

Caillaud, B., and P. Rey. 1987. A note on vertical restraints with the provision of distribution services. Working paper. INSEE and MIT.

Caillaud, B., and P. Rey. 1995. Strategic aspects of vertical delegation. *European Economic Review* 39: 421–31.

Comanor, W. 1985. Vertical price fixing and market restrictions and the new antitrust policy. *Harvard Law Review* 98: 983–1002.

Comanor, W., and H. E. Frech III. 1985. The competitive effects of vertical agreements. *American Economic Review* 75: 539–46.

Comanor, W., and P. Rey. 1997. Competition policy towards vertical restraints in Europe and the United States. *Empirica* 24: 37–52.

Comanor, W., and P. Rey. 2000. Vertical restraints and the market power of large distributors. *Review of Industrial Organization* 17: 135–53.

Crémer, J., and M. Riordan. 1987. On governing multilateral transactions with bilateral contracts. *Rand Journal of Economics* 18: 436–51.

De Graba, P., and A. Postlewaite. 1992. Exclusivity clauses and best price policies in input markets. *Journal of Economics and Management Strategy* 1: 423–54.

Dobson, P., and M. Waterson. 2007. The competition effects of industry-wide vertical price fixing in bilateral oligopoly. *International Journal of Industrial Organization*. ⟨doi:10.1016/j.ijindorg.2007.04.004⟩.

Fumagalli, C., and M. Motta. 2006. Exclusive dealing and entry when dealers compete. *American Economic Review* 96: 785–95.

Gal-Or, E. 1991. Duopolistic vertical restraints. *European Economic Review* 35: 1237–53.

Hart, O., and J. Tirole. 1990. Vertical integration and market foreclosure. *Brookings Papers on Economic Activity, Microeconomics*: 205–86.

Irmen, A. 1998. Precommitment in competing vertical chains. *Journal of Economic Surveys* 12: 333–59.

Jullien, B., and P. Rey. 2007. Resale price maintenance and collusion. *RAND Journal of Economics*, forthcoming.

Katz, M. 1991. Game-playing agents: Unobservable contracts as precommitment. *Rand Journal of Economics* 22: 307–28.

Kovacic, W., and C. Shapiro. 2000. Antitrust policy: A centrury of economic and legal thinking. *Journal of Economic Perspectives* 14: 43–60.

Krattenmaker, T., and S. Salop. 1986. Anticompetitive exclusion: Raising rivals' costs to achieve power over price. *Yale Law Journal* 96: 209–93.

Martin, S., H.-T. Normann, and C. Snyder. 2001. Vertical foreclosure in experimental markets. *RAND Journal of Economics* 32: 466–96.

Marx, L., and G. Shaffer. 2004. Opportunism in multilateral vertical contracting: Nondiscrimination, exclusivity, and uniformity; comment. *American Economic Review* 94: 796–801.

Marx, L., and G. Shaffer. 2006. Upfront payments and exclusion in downstream markets. *RAND Journal of Economics*, forthcoming.

Mathewson, F., and R. Winter. 1984. An economic theory of vertical restraints. *RAND Journal of Economics* 15: 27–38.

Mathewson, F., and R. Winter. 1987. The competitive effects of vertical agreements: Comment. *American Economic Review* 77: 1057–62.

Mathewson, F., and R. Winter. 1998. The law and economics of resale price maintenance. *Review of Industrial Organization* 13: 57–84.

McAfee, P., and M. Schwartz. 1994. Opportunism in multilateral vertical contracting: Nondiscrimination, exclusivity and uniformity. *American Economic Review* 84: 210–30.

McGuire, T., and R. Staelin. 1983. An industry equilibrium analysis of downstream vertical integration. *Marketing Science* 2: 161–91.

Motta, M. 2004. *Competition Policy: Theory and Practice*. Cambridge: Cambridge University Press.

O'Brien, D., and G. Shaffer. 1992. Vertical control with bilateral contracts. *RAND Journal of Economics* 23: 299–308.

Posner, R. 1976. *Antitrust Law: An Economic Perspective*. Chicago: University of Chicago Press.

Rasmusen, E., J. Mark Ramseyer, and J. S. Wiley Jr. 1991. Naked exclusion. *American Economic Review* 81: 1137–45.

Rey, P., and J. Stiglitz. 1988. Vertical restraints and producers competition. *European Economic Review* 32: 561–68.

Rey, P., and J. Stiglitz. 1995. The role of exclusive territories in producer's competition. *RAND Journal of Economics* 26: 431–51.

Rey, P., and J. Tirole. 1986. The logic of vertical restraints. *American Economic Review* 76: 921–39.

Rey, P., J. Thal, and T. Vergé. 2006. Slotting allowances and conditional payments. CREST working paper 2006-23.

Rey, P., and T. Vergé. 2002. Resale price maintenance and horizontal cartel. CMPO working paper 02/047. University of Bristol.

Rey, P., and T. Vergé. 2004. Bilateral control with vertical contracts. *RAND Journal of Economics* 35: 728–46.

Schwartz, M. 1987. The competitive effects of vertical agreements: Comment. *American Economic Review* 77: 1063–68.

Segal, I., and M. Whinston. 2000. Naked exclusion: A comment. *American Economic Review* 90: 296–309.

Schulz, N. 2007. Does the service argument justify resale price maintenance. *Journal of Institutional and Theoretical Economics* 163: 236–55.

Shaffer, G. 1991a. Capturing strategic rent: Full-line forcing, brand discounts, aggregate rebates, and maximum resale price maintenance. *Journal of Industrial Economics* 39: 557–75.

Shaffer, G. 1991b. Slotting allowances and resale price maintenance: A comparison of facilitating practices. *RAND Journal of Economics* 22: 120–36.

Sherer, F. M. 1983. The economics of vertical restraints. *Antitrust Law Journal* 52: 687–707.

Slade, M. 1998. Beer and the tie: Did divestiture of brewer-owned public houses lead to higher beer prices. *Economic Journal* 108: 565–602.

Spence, M. 1975. Monopoly, quality and regulation. *Bell Journal of Economics* 6: 417–29.

Spengler, J. 1950. Vertical integration and antitrust policy. *Journal of Political Economy* 58: 347–52.

Spiegel, Y. 1994. On the economic efficiency of liquidated damages. *Economics Letters* 45: 379–83.

Spiegel, Y., and Y. Yehezkel. 2003. Price and non-price restraints when retailers are vertically differentiated. *International Journal of Industrial Organization* 21: 923–47.

Telser, L. 1960. Why should manufacturer want fair trade. *Journal of Law and Economics* 3: 86–105.

Tirole, J. 1988. *The Theory of Industrial Organization*. Cambridge: MIT Press.

Vergé, T. 2001. Multi-product monopolist and full-line forcing: The efficiency argument revisited. *Economics Bulletin* 12(4): 1–9.

Verouden, V. 2003. Vertical agreements and Article 81(1) EC: The evolving role of economic analysis. *Antitrust Law Journal* 71: 525–75.

Vickers, J. 1985. Delegation and the theory of the firm. *Economic Journal* 95: 138–47.

Williamson, O. 1985. *The Economics Institutions of Capitalism: Firms, Markets Relational Contracting*. New York: Free Press.

Williamson, O. 1989. Transaction cost economics. In Richard Schmalensee and Robert Willig, eds., *Handbook of Industrial Organization*, Vol. 1. Amsterdam: North-Holland.

Winter, R. 1993. Vertical control and price versus non-price competition. *Quarterly Journal of Economics* 108: 61–76.

10 Exclusive Contracts and Vertical Restraints: Empirical Evidence and Public Policy

Francine Lafontaine and Margaret Slade

There is perhaps no aspect of competition policy that is as controversial or has been as inconsistent over time and across jurisdictions as policy toward restraints between upstream firms and their downstream retailers. Moreover conflicting and changing legal attitudes are mirrored in economic theory. Indeed theorists have constructed models that lead one to either extol the virtues or rue the consequences of vertical agreements and to advocate either per se legality or illegality.[1] In such an ambiguous legal and theoretical environment, the need for an overall empirical assessment seems particularly pressing, and we hope to shed some light on this important and controversial subject.

In this chapter we look at empirical methods that have been used to assess the consequences of vertical restraints, and we survey the findings of empirical studies that have used those methods. As much of the empirical literature has addressed the effect of restraints in the context of exclusive retail relationships, including franchise distribution, we focus almost entirely on such contracts.[2]

The chapter is organized as follows: In section 10.1, we discuss briefly a number of economic models used to explain the rationale behind the various types of vertical restraints. These models are reviewed elsewhere in this book, so we discuss only the principal paradigms. In section 10.2, we follow with an overview of US and EU government responses to such contracts. The heart of the paper is found in section 10.3. In that section, we review the methods that can be used to assess the consequences of vertical restraints and provide a survey of empirical findings. The empirical approaches can be grouped into broad classes. The first involves analyses of cross-sectional, time-series, or panel data on firms or regions, some of which employ a vertical restraint and some of which do not. These studies range from mainly descriptive to more rigorous econometric analyses. Furthermore many of the studies view changes in the legal environment as natural experiments that allow applied researchers to assess the consequences of laws and regulations by examining differential responses of two groups of firms, a treatment group that is affected by the change and a control group that is not.

Whereas the first approach evaluates the actual consequences of changes in the legal environment, a second approach uses event studies to assess market forecasts of those consequences. In particular, share-price information can be used to determine how investors perceive the implications of changes in the law.

Finally, a literature is currently emerging in which structural models that involve vertical contracts and restraints on manufacturer/retailer interactions are estimated and used to assess the consequences of current practice and proposed changes. All the approaches can generate insights into the effects of both privately agreed-upon and legally mandated restraints. Only the third, however, can be used to forecast the effects of changes that have not yet occurred.

Our review of the empirical evidence follows our discussion of methods. Since the empirical regularities that we uncover appear to be strong and consistent across industries and analytical techniques, we also attempt to draw policy implications based on those regularities.

10.1   Private Motives for Vertical Restraints

Firms are involved in a vertical relationship if they operate at different but complementary levels of the production/distribution chain. All upstream/downstream or input/output relationships are vertical, and any restriction that is imposed by one member of a vertical relationship on the other member of that relationship is a vertical restraint. Authors disagree, however, in that for some, any form of nonlinear-pricing rule constitutes a restraint, whereas in most cases nonlinear prices are excluded. Nonlinear prices do not really constitute a restriction on behavior, although some of the incentive effects that nonlinear prices are meant to generate are similar to the incentive effects that are often associated with exclusive dealing. In the remainder of this chapter, we focus on the more traditional set of price and nonprice vertical restraints. The former refers to resale price maintenance, for example, where a manufacturer sets the price or sets a maximum or minimum price that retailers can charge, and the latter includes exclusive dealing, exclusive territories, quantity forcing, and tying.

Vertical restraints most often arise in retail settings, with the upstream firm or manufacturer typically restricting its downstream retailers' choices.[3] For example, a manufacturer might limit its retailer's product line or geographic market, or it might set the retail price. Because vertical restraints are observed most often in situations where the downstream firm is a retailer, most of the empirical evidence, and hence our review of that evidence, focuses on that situation as well.

In most western economies a large fraction of retail sales through independent retailers is subject to some form of exclusive dealing clauses. For example, in the United States that fraction is over one-third.[4] Most exclusive retailing arrangements occur within franchise relationships, which take two basic forms. Traditional franchising involves an upstream manufacturer and a downstream retailer, as in gasoline retailing or car dealerships, whereas, with business format franchising, production takes place mainly at the retail outlet, such as a fast-food restaurant. Many of the studies that we survey focus on one of the types of franchising.[5]

In this section we briefly discuss the economic rationale behind vertical restraints that are voluntarily undertaken. These include efficiency as well as anticompetitive motives. We emphasize how each argument applies to the specific context of a downstream retailer, and thus, in many cases, a franchise relationship. In the next section we examine government responses to the use of restraints, given their potential anticompetitive effects. We also review the reasons why in some cases governments mandate that such restraints be used. Often such constraints restrict the activities of upstream firms. For example, a political jurisdiction might enact a law that requires that wholesalers be given exclusive territories (e.g., for auto or beer distribution).

10.1.1 Efficiency Reasons for Vertical Restraints

Double Marginalization or the Succession-of-Monopoly Problem   The typical succession-of-monopoly problem arises when an upstream monopolist sells an input to a downstream firm at a price above marginal cost. If the downstream firm also has market power, it is well known that it will choose a price that is higher, and a quantity that is lower, than the price and quantity that would maximize joint profits.[6]

A number of researchers (e.g., Barron and Umbeck 1984; Shepard 1993; Slade 1998) discuss the potential effect of double marginalization on prices in traditional franchising where the franchisor sells an input that is resold by franchisees under a fixed-proportion technology. This problem can be overcome by the use of a fixed fee (i.e., a two-part tariff), which is the standard textbook solution. Specifically, the manufacturer sells her product to the retailer at marginal cost, the retailer then chooses to sell the product at the optimal retail price from the manufacturer's perspective, and the manufacturer finally uses the franchise fee to extract the downstream surplus. In many traditional franchising setups, however, retailers do not pay franchise fees. Fixed fees, however, can take the form of rental payments. For example, manufacturers (e.g., oil companies) often own retail premises, which they rent to retailers (e.g., service-station operators) at rates that are independent of realized sales and need not equal market rates.

With business format franchising, in contrast, the amount of inputs sold by franchisors to franchisees is usually small.[7] Nevertheless, despite the lack of input sales by franchisors, a form of double marginalization still occurs because of the reliance on revenue-based royalty payments in franchise contracts. Specifically, royalties represent a tax on output that results in a downward rotation of the demand curve faced by the franchisee who is subjected to this tax. As a result a franchisee with market power will maximize his profits by choosing a quantity that is below the quantity that the franchisor would prefer and selling it at a price that, once adjusted to include the royalty on sales, is above that which would have been optimal for the franchisor.[8]

To overcome the double-marginalization problem and reduce retail prices, franchisors might want to use some form of vertical restraint. Maximum resale prices is an obvious candidate. Alternatively, franchisors could use a minimum quantity requirement or eliminate royalties on sales altogether and replace them with higher franchise fees. The latter solution corresponds to the standard two-part tariff used in traditional franchising. Finally, a manufacturer who controls the number of stores that sell her product could eliminate the double-marginalization problem by increasing outlet density and thus the intensity of intrabrand competition.[9]

When double marginalization is an issue, the imposition of vertical restraints will not only increase the overall efficiency of the vertical structure but also lead to lower prices for customers. Thus restraints are usually welfare enhancing when used to solve the successive-monopoly problem.

Dealer Services and Free-Riding Issues   Manufacturers who invest in improving retail outlets, promoting retail products, or training outlet managers might worry that dealers will free ride on those investments. For example, dealers might encourage customers who visit their store to switch to a competing brand that has a lower price—thereby making the sale easier—or that has a higher retail margin—thereby making the sale privately more profitable. Exclusive dealing resolves this problem by making it impossible for the dealer to propose an alternative brand to his customers. In such a context, exclusive dealing is a mechanism that enables manufacturers to protect their investments against potential dealer opportunism. Furthermore, in its absence, potentially profitable manufacturer investments might not be undertaken.

Alternatively, dealer services at the point of sale can enhance the demand for a manufacturer's or a franchisor's product. For example, Dunkin Donuts has a policy that requires franchisees to discard donuts that are no longer fresh.[10] Franchisees, who are residual claimants on their own unit's profits after the payment of royalties to their franchisor, obtain a benefit from the value of the brand thus generated. However, they do not fully internalize the benefit that is associated with their own decisions, as some of their customers with positive experiences will patronize other units of the same chain rather than returning to their unit in the future. In contrast, franchisees bear the full cost of the policy. As a result they will tend to provide a quality that is too low from the perspective of the franchisor. Furthermore the problem worsens as the fraction of repeat business that franchisees face falls.[11] Marvel and McCafferty (1984) suggest that resale price maintenance can be used to ensure that retailers will provide product quality certification services.

In some cases the quality problem can take the form of a dealer or franchisee wanting to use lower quality inputs in the production process.[12] This type of free-riding can be resolved with input purchase requirements (tying) or approved supplier programs as long as defection from such programs is not too difficult to detect.

In general, not only do dealers have incentives to free ride on the value of the brand and put in too little effort, a vertical externality, they also have incentives to free ride on services offered by other dealers, a horizontal externality. If service is important to the sale of a manufacturer's product, she will need to ensure that dealers provide it. Telser (1960) argued that minimum price restraints could solve this incentive problem by preventing retailers from competing on price and leading them to compete instead on quality or customer service.[13] Klein and Murphy (1988) instead proposed that manufacturers use vertical restraints such as minimum resale prices or exclusive territories to ensure that their dealers earn above normal returns, which means that those dealers have something to lose if their contracts are terminated. Such rent, in combination with ongoing quality or service monitoring and the threat of termination, will entice the dealers to provide the desired level of quality or service. In either case, since the quality and service levels in question are valued by customers—if it were otherwise manufacturers would not value them—quantities sold and hence consumer satisfaction should be enhanced.[14]

Dealer Ex ante Investment Incentives   A related but different dealer-incentive issue arises in situations where the manufacturer wants the dealer to invest ex ante in specific facilities or human capital in order to provide better service to consumers. Unless the dealer can be assured that his investments are fully protected, he will choose to underinvest or not invest at all. A vertical restraint such as an exclusive territory can provide the guarantee that the dealer needs.[15] While the exclusivity of the territory might give the dealer some market power, consumers benefit from the resulting investment and thus the restraint can have positive welfare effects.

Price Discrimination   A number of authors have shown that vertical restraints such as tying, exclusive dealing, and refusals to deal can be used by manufacturers to enforce price-discrimination schemes (e.g., see Burstein 1960; Perry 1980; Chen and Ross 1993 on each of these respectively). Of course, the welfare implications of vertical restraints in this context, as for price discrimination generally, are ambiguous and so are the expected effects on observed quantities.

10.1.2   Anticompetitive Reasons for Vertical Restraints

Vertical restraints are often viewed with suspicion because comparable horizontal practices are frowned upon. For example, resale price maintenance is viewed as vertical price fixing, exclusive territories can create monopoly power, and exclusive dealing can inhibit entry. Nevertheless, as we have just indicated, real efficiencies can be associated with these restraints. However, competitive harm can also result for reasons that we now discuss.

Dealer Cartels and Monopolization   The arguments that explain how certain types of vertical restraints can facilitate dealer cartels or monopoly power are straightforward. In particular, a manufacturer that imposes a minimum price for her product can help a dealer cartel enforce the monopoly price (e.g., see Ornstein 1985). Similarly exclusive territories, if they are large enough, can insulate retailers from competition by eliminating nearby competitors as well as preventing entry. The main issue that these arguments raise, however, is why manufacturers would find it in their own best interest to impose such restraints. If upstream firms have no market power, they will be indifferent to the imposition of restraints and might agree to adopt them to satisfy dealers. However, brand differentiation and the use of trademarks usually confer some market power on upstream firms. Another answer that appears in the literature involves a beneficial reduction in interbrand competition, a type of argument to which we now turn.

Strategic Delegation   The idea that upstream firms can soften the intensity with which they compete with one another by delegating the pricing decision to independent retailers is by now well understood. The models in this case focus on interbrand competition across vertical structures. Rey and Stiglitz (1995), for example, show that when manufacturers compete directly with each other (when they set retail prices themselves), the resulting Nash-equilibrium prices are lower than the joint-profit-maximizing prices. If, however, retailers have some market power, and if manufacturers delegate the pricing decision to their retailers, the equilibrium prices that result will be higher than in the former situation. A softening of competition occurs because prices are normally strategic complements (i.e., price reaction functions normally slope up). An increase in a manufacturer's wholesale price is therefore associated not only with higher own-dealer prices but also with higher competitor retail prices. Furthermore, with two-part tariffs, equilibrium prices will not exceed monopoly prices.[16]

The argument above is premised on the assumption that retailers or distributors have market power. The assignment of exclusive territories is one (but not the only) way of ensuring that this is so. It also relies on the assumption that retailers compete on prices, an assumption that is apt to be valid in the current context. However, if downstream firms engage in quantity competition, delegation will not benefit the vertical chain.[17]

Foreclosure and Raising Rival's Costs   The main worry of antitrust authorities in the United States and the European Union when it comes to vertical restraints is the possibility that their use will foreclose entry by competitors at some level of the vertical chain. In the context of relationships involving a retailer, such as the ones that we are concerned with here, a manufacturer that establishes an exclusive retail network (i.e., exclusive dealing) that involves most retailers, for example, might prevent her competitors from gaining access to customers at a reasonable cost, or at all. This in turn could prevent entry of potential competitors or perhaps even lead to rivals exiting the upstream industry (e.g., see Krattenmaker and Salop 1986; Aghion and Bolton 1987; Comanor and Rey 2000). This argument requires that entry into retailing be costly due to, for example, economies of scale or a scarcity of good locations.

Exclusive dealing, which has sometimes been referred to as vertical integration by contract, is the form of restraint for which foreclosure arguments are most frequently made. In addition, when there are few uses for an input, tying can foreclose entry of firms in the tied goods industry.

In the end, if vertical restraints are used to lessen competition at some level of the vertical structure through foreclosing or disadvantaging rivals, prices to consumers should be higher and quantities sold smaller than they would be in the absence of such restraints.

Aftermarkets   A final anticompetitive motive for imposing vertical restraints involves the creation of monopoly power, not in the market for the manufacturer's product but in a related market.[18] This rationale is often invoked as a motive for tying of, say, parts and service to the purchase of a machine or the purchase of paper to that of a copier. According to this argument, although consumers have many brands to choose from in the primary market, due to the tie, they have no choice in the aftermarket (e.g., in the service market). Indeed consumers are locked in ex post, and monopoly power can be exploited in the aftermarket.

A problem with this argument is that if consumers are forward-looking, they will anticipate supercompetitive prices in the tied market and will demand compensation in the form of lower prices in the primary market. Nevertheless, in a world of imperfect consumer information, this anticompetitive motive for tying persists.[19]

10.2   Public Policy toward Vertical Restraints

As noted earlier, legal policies toward vertical restraints have been inconsistent, not only over time within a jurisdiction but also across jurisdictions. To illustrate the legal ambiguity, consider the history of the US Department of Justice's (DOJ's) position toward vertical restraints (VR). Until the 1940s, most restraints on distribution were upheld as lawful.[20] By the mid-1960s, however, this lax attitude had given way to a much more aggressive stance whereby virtually every restraint had become suspect and many had become per se illegal. This new harsh view, however, was itself short-lived. Indeed a second reversal in attitude, which surfaced in the 1977 *Sylvania* Supreme Court decision, culminated in the publication of the 1985 *Vertical Restraints Guidelines*.[21] Those *Guidelines*, which were extremely lenient toward most forms of restraints, were controversial from the outset. In particular, both the US Congress and the National Association of Attorneys General (NAAG) denounced them, and one of the first acts of the new Clinton administration was to rescind them.[22] Since that time, they have not been replaced, and there is no formal vertical policy guidance in the United States.[23]

Changing legal attitudes toward vertical restraints have not been the exclusive domain of the United States. In particular, prior to enacting its *Vertical Restraints Guidelines* in 1999, the EU attitude was governed by what seemed like a blanket prohibition on vertical agreements that restrict competition,[24] combined with numerous bloc exemptions for particular types of agreements, including franchise agreements. In practice, those bloc exemptions created a very inflexible system that led firms to adopt standardized contractual terms. The new *Guidelines* provide more flexibility as they follow an approach that is closer to a rule of reason.

In our discussion of motives in section 10.1, we made it clear that vertical restraints, both price and nonprice, can enhance efficiency in some circumstances and distort competition in others. This is sometimes given as the reason why government policy toward vertical issues has been so variable.[25] However, horizontal agreements and mergers can also give rise to both efficiency gains and competitive distortions. To illustrate, when two firms in the same product market merge, there can be a trade-off between lower costs due to economies of scale and increased market power due to higher concentration. Hence, one cannot say a priori if product prices will rise or fall. Nevertheless, economists and lawyers are less apt to disagree about horizontal issues.

In addition to inconsistencies in overall policy toward vertical restraints, there are differences in the legal treatment of different types of restraints. In most countries vertical price restraints are treated much more harshly than nonprice restraints. In particular, resale price maintenance is often per se illegal, whereas most nonprice restraints are governed by a rule-of-reason standard.[26] This is despite the fact that from an economic perspective, nonprice and price restraints are often substitute methods of achieving a given objective, and that the achievement of that objective might or might not harm consumers.[27] The fairly harsh treatment of vertical price restraints is sometimes said to occur because it is wrongly associated with horizontal price fixing, which is per se illegal in most jurisdictions.

Since the late 1970s, the United States has employed a rule-of-reason approach to most nonprice vertical restraints.[28] Specifically, in *Continental T.V., Inc. v. GTE Sylvania, Inc.*, the Supreme Court found that though specific vertical restrictions can have anticompetitive effects, there had been no showing that in general vertical restrictions have a "pernicious effect on competition" or that they lack "any redeeming value." The Court therefore concluded that such restrictions should be judged under a rule of reason.

In applying this approach to vertical restraints, the courts have usually stressed horizontal anticompetitive effects. Indeed the two factors that are emphasized in assessing the potential anticompetitive effects are collusion and exclusion at one level or another of the vertical chain. On the former, it is often claimed, for example, that upstream collusion is facilitated when exclusive dealing arrangements are widespread downstream, since their presence eliminates buyer competition. This in turn reduces the incentives of sellers to undercut one another to try to entice buyers to switch. As for exclusion, it can also result from exclusive dealing arrangements, since new upstream competitors can face difficulties in reaching customers when most retailers are involved in exclusive deals with upstream firms. Similarly new downstream competitors can have difficulty obtaining supplies under such circumstances. This in turn makes entry at either level less likely.

The emphasis on horizontal consequences of nonprice restraints might be surprising given that with or without horizontal considerations, the effects of vertical restraints are usually ambiguous. However, it is reasonable to assume that vertical restraints are more apt to be harmful when markets, particularly upstream markets, are highly concentrated. When this is not the case, vigorous interbrand competition tends to offset restraints on intrabrand competition.

In the European Union the rule-of-reason approach came somewhat later, after the publication of the Commission's *Guidelines on Vertical Restraints* in 1999. Prior to that time, as we noted earlier, EU policy was somewhat contradictory. In the twenty-first century, however, policies toward VR in the two jurisdictions have converged to a substantial degree as the European Union has adopted a position closer to that of the United States.[29]

In our discussion so far, we have assumed that vertical restraints have been voluntarily undertaken by the parties to the contract and that the role of the competition authority is to monitor those contracts. However, not all vertical restraints come from within vertical relationships. Indeed it is not uncommon for jurisdictions, particularly the US states, to enact laws that restrict either downstream or upstream behavior. An example of the former is the passage of a law that requires exclusive sales territories in distribution,[30] whereas an example of the latter is a law that limits the franchisor's ability to terminate a franchise without "good cause." It is difficult to explain such laws in economic terms, and in practice, the pressure for adoption often comes from lobbying groups such as associations of dealers.[31] Furthermore, as with positions on voluntarily chosen vertical restraints, policies toward mandatory adoption of restraints have been variable and inconsistent.

Finally, whereas vertical restraints have at times been treated harshly by the law, vertically integrated firms have been able to engage in similar practices with impunity (see Katz 1989).

10.3 Empirical Evaluation of the Effects of Vertical Restraints

It is important to develop a sound basis for a consistent public policy regarding exclusive contracts. Unfortunately, as should be clear from our discussion so far, economic theorists and policy makers disagree on the most important consequences of vertical contracts. Fortunately, one need not rely solely on theory to determine the consequences of vertical restraints, since the world is a laboratory that is constantly offering experiments that can be analyzed by applied researchers. In this section we indicate how data can be used to assess the consequences of vertical restraints, and we discuss some of the many pitfalls that the applied researcher can encounter. In addition we attempt to summarize what this body of research has found. Unfortunately, like the theory, the empirical evidence is somewhat fragmented. However, it is our belief that with further work, empirical analyses will be able to provide much needed guidance to theorists, policy makers, and the courts. Our first goal is to encourage further empirical work in this area.

Most econometric analyses of exclusive contracts examine *incidence*; that is, researchers seek to determine the circumstances under which various sorts of restrictive agreements are reached by parties to a contract.[32] Our objective, by contrast, is to determine both the private profitability and the social desirability of vertical restraints, whether privately agreed upon or legally mandated. Thus our focus will be on the *consequences* of restrictive agreements. In particular, we discuss methods of assessing the effects of VR on price, consumption, and other measures of consumer well-being, and on profits and other measures of firm value.

10.3.1 Methods of Assessment

In this subsection we discuss various empirical approaches to the assessment of the effects of vertical restraints. For simplicity, we focus our discussion on the effects of vertical restrictions on price. As should be clear, the principles presented here would remain the same if other variables of interest, such as output or profit, were used instead of price.

The most straightforward way to evaluate the effects of restrictive agreements is to present some persuasive descriptive statistics. For example, one can compile information on retail prices in regions where a restrictive agreement is banned and compare them to prices in regions where the agreement is allowed. Descriptive statistics are useful in so far as they convince the reader that there is an empirical regularity that should be explained. The obvious problem, however, is that there can be many explanations for that regularity. For this reason most researchers combine descriptive statistics with econometric analysis. In what follows we describe several different econometric approaches to the problem.

Cross-sectional, Time-Series, and Panel Estimations The simplest econometric analysis of vertical restraints involves performing a multivariate regression on a cross section of firms or retail establishments. For example, one might look at retail prices across establishments that are and are not subject to a particular restraint. Although attention is focused on the coefficient of a dummy variable that indicates whether the restraint is employed, the regression typically includes a number of supply, demand, and policy variables that also affect price.

The problem with this sort of analysis is that the use of a restraint is endogenous to the relationship. In the absence of legal restrictions, the upstream firm will choose a set of restraints that maximizes its profit, and there are many unobservable characteristics of the manufacturer and retailer that can affect both retail price and the choice of restraints. For example, exclusive dealing might occur in situations where upstream firms must make substantial investments, and since those investments can influence retail cost and/or demand, they can also influence price. Under those circumstances the relationships that are uncovered are correlations, not causalities. Moreover the endogeneity problem is exacerbated by the fact that it is usually difficult to find instruments that are correlated with the use of a restriction but do not affect the dependent variable. To make matters worse, in the absence of nonsuspect instruments, it is impossible to perform a formal assessment of the validity of any instruments.

To circumvent this problem, researchers have looked at, for example, cross sections of regions where legislators ban and do not ban particular restraints. Since the ban comes from outside the vertical relationship, it is often thought to be exogenous. Nevertheless, although the endogeneity problem is lessened in this situation, it is not eliminated. To illustrate, suppose that it is discovered that prices are higher in regions where resale price maintenance is allowed. One is tempted to conclude that RPM causes higher prices. However, it is also possible that RPM is not banned exactly in those areas where both up and downstream firms have substantial market power and the potential for double marginalization is therefore greater. Under those circumstances the causality runs from high prices to tolerance toward RPM.

If the underlying factors that affect both the use of a restraint and the dependent variable are time invariant, the problem above can be overcome through the use of panel data. In particular, with panel data, one can use a fixed-effects estimator that removes the influence of the time-invariant unobserved regional, brand, or outlet characteristics that cause the endogeneity problem. With this procedure, however, the effect of a restraint is identified solely through time-series variation. In other words, one is essentially assessing how changes in the use of a restraint lead to changes in prices, and there may be little time-series variation in the data. Furthermore, if the unobservable characteristics vary over time, the endogeneity problem is not solved. With panel data, it is tempting to use lagged endogenous variables as instruments in the hope that they are predetermined. This hope will be thwarted, however, if unobserved variables are serially correlated.

Another approach is to look at a single time series of prices that includes periods before and after a legally mandated change such as the banning of a restraint. The problem with this approach is that many things change over time, and although it is tempting to attribute any significant price movement to the legal change, this attribution might not be valid.

Natural Experiments It is rare that laws are modified simply to enable economists to collect data in order to evaluate the effects of vertical restraints. In other words, in vertical markets, we rarely have access to designed experiments. Nevertheless, many legal changes can be thought of as natural experiments.[33] Although much of our discussion of empirical approaches so far has been concerned with how natural experiments can be used to assess restrictive agreements, we nevertheless reserve the term natural experiment to denote analyses that involve (1) an exogenous policy change, (2) a group of observations that is affected by the change (the treatment group), and (3) a group that is not affected (the control group). Furthermore the differential response of those two groups to the change is used to identify the effect of a restraint.

Formally, suppose that n brands of a product, $i = 1, \ldots, n$, are sold in two regions, $j = 1, 2$, in two time periods, $t = 1, 2$, and that period 1 occurs before and period 2 occurs after a change in the law. A linear regression equation for price can be written as

$$p_{it}^j = \alpha_i + \delta^j + \gamma^j D_2 + \beta^T X_{it} + u_{it}^j, \tag{10.1}$$

where D_2 is a dummy variable that equals one in period two, X_{it} is a vector of observed brand, chain, and cost characteristics, and u_{it}^j is a zero-mean random variable. The change in the price of brand i in region j is then

$$\Delta_i^j = p_{i2}^j - p_{i1}^j = \gamma^j + \beta^T (X_{i2} - X_{i1}) + u_{i2}^j - u_{i1}^j, \tag{10.2}$$

and the expected difference in the price difference across regions, DD, is

$$DD = E(\Delta_i^1 - \Delta_i^2) = \gamma^1 - \gamma^2. \tag{10.3}$$

Furthermore, as long as the error u_{it}^j is uncorrelated with the observed characteristics X_{it}, the difference-in-difference estimator of the effect of the change in the law is unbiased.[34]

Generally, with obvious modifications one can include regional variables X_{it}^j in equation (10.1). In that case the difference-in-difference estimator in equation (10.3) will no longer be constant but will depend on changes in those variables.

A difference-in-difference estimator does not require a paired sample. For example, in equation (10.1), i might index establishments rather than brands, and the number of establishments might differ in the two regions. Furthermore with either paired or nonpaired samples it is not necessary to estimate a regression equation. Assuming no region-specific changes, one can simply difference the prices in each region, average the differences across brands or establishments, and calculate the difference in those averages. That number gives the magnitude of the effect. Its statistical significance can be obtained by dividing the estimate by its standard error.[35]

Event Studies We have been concerned thus far with evaluating the realized consequences of changes in public policy toward vertical restraints. One can also estimate forecasts of the effects of those changes on firm value. The tool that is commonly used to perform that evaluation is the event study, which requires that the firms that are used in the analysis be publicly traded.

An event study is based on the assumption that stock markets are efficient and that share prices reflect all currently available information. In other words, it is assumed that the current price equals the expected value that accrues to the holder of the share— the expected discounted stream of capital gains and dividends—where expectations are formed efficiently and rationally. With efficient markets, when a "surprise" occurs, the associated change in the share price is the expected value of the change in that flow.[36]

It is common to base an event study on the Sharpe (1963) market model that relates the return on asset i in period t, R_{it}, to the market return, R_{mt}, where the market return is the return on a broadly based portfolio of traded assets,[37]

$$R_{it} = \alpha_i + \beta_i R_{mt} + u_{it}, \qquad i = 1, \ldots, n; \; t = 1, \ldots, T. \tag{10.4}$$

When assessing an event such as the enactment of a law, it is important that the event be a "surprise." Unfortunately, when, for example, a final bill is passed, there might be little news in the event. For this reason it is common to partition an event into a number of subevents in the hope that the evolution of the news can be captured. To illustrate, the sequence of subevents might be the following:

1. Legislation proposed.
2. Subcommittee formed.
3. Bill made public.
4. Bill passed by one body.
5. Bill passed by second body.
6. Compromise bill negotiated.
7. Final bill passed.

In order to evaluate the subevents, the market model can be augmented to include a series of dummy variables, D_{st}, $s = 1, \ldots, S$, with $D_{st} = 1$ if subevent s occurred in period t and zero otherwise,

$$R_{it} = \alpha_i + \beta_i R_{mt} + \sum_s \gamma_{si} D_{st} + u_{it}. \tag{10.5}$$

When there is a large number of firms in the sample, instead of estimating the $S \times n$ matrix of coefficients γ_{si}, it is common to collapse the matrix by assuming that the coefficients are functions of firm characteristics. This practice yields a parsimonious but still flexible specification.

Equation (10.5) can be estimated as a system of seemingly unrelated regressions (SUR). The estimated effects $\hat{\gamma}_{si}$ can then be summed across subevents to find the overall effect of the event for each firm or group of firms and averaged across firms or groups to find the average effect. Finally, the standard errors of each estimate can be calculated using well-known formulas.[38]

Structural Models The econometric methods that we have discussed thus far involve estimating reduced-form equations. In particular, there is no way to recover the structural parameters that characterize tastes and technology from such models. This is not a criticism in itself, but it does mean that certain types of analysis cannot be performed. In particular, it is not possible to use reduced-form equations to forecast the consequences of changes in policy ex ante.[39]

Although it is now common to estimate structural econometric models to evaluate changes in horizontal market structure such as mergers and divestitures,[40] it has not been common to use such models to assess vertical issues. Nevertheless, structural models are beginning to emerge, and there are both costs and benefits to employing such models.

The principal benefits are twofold. First, one can evaluate changes in the law before they occur by performing simulations that are based on models that have been estimated using pre-change data (e.g., see Brenkers and Verboven 2006, who evaluate the removal of exclusivity and selectivity practices in European automobile distribution). This benefit is particularly important as it is much more costly to rescind a mistaken policy after firms have adjusted to the change than it is to change the policy ex ante.

Second, in some cases estimation of a structural model facilitates the solution of the identification problem in the sense that it forces the researcher to specify all of the equations in the system and to justify exclusion restrictions. This can be analogous to the use of full-information maximum-likelihood techniques to estimate structural supply/demand models, which does not require instruments from outside of the model. However, it is more common to estimate complex structural models by GMM, which usually requires the use of additional instruments (e.g., see Mortimer 2008).

The principal costs are also twofold. First, the construction of a structural model requires one to make strong assumptions concerning market equilibrium. This requirement is particularly demanding in the vertical case because, not only must one specify the games played among firms at the same level of the vertical structure (e.g., the manufacturers), but also one must specify how firms within a vertical structure interact (e.g., a manufacturer and her affiliated retailers). Unfortunately, given the lack of agreement among theorists as to these issues, it is often difficult for empiricists to specify this information a priori. However, misspecifying the equilibrium leads to biased estimates of the structural parameters and, thus, to inaccurate forecasts of the effects of policy changes.

Second, it is always difficult to forecast changes in costs that result from a change in the structure of the market or the legal environment.[41] This issue is particularly troubling in the vertical case because many cost changes relate to the type of motivational and informational issues (i.e., agency costs) that are central to the decisions firms make about vertical structure. Nevertheless, despite the difficulties that are inherent in such exercises, we feel that this area of research is particularly promising and that the use of structural models will grow in the years ahead.

10.3.2 Empirical Findings

The results of studies that have examined the effects of vertical restraints on market outcomes are summarized in tables 10.1 through 10.3. As in earlier sections of this chapter, we stress situations where downstream firms are exclusive wholesalers or retailers. However, because of the paucity of empirical work on consequences, we also discuss some research that involves common agency (e.g., distilled spirits and glassware).

Most of the studies that are listed in the tables are concerned with the standard set of restraints that we enumerated in section 10.1. However, we also include studies that evaluate restrictions on the ability of the upstream firm to terminate the franchise agreement. Those requirements, which we label termination restrictions in the table, are usually imposed by regional governments in response to perceptions of unfair treatment of retailers by manufacturers. In other words, they are restrictions that are often indirectly imposed on upstream firms by downstream firms through the intervention of regional authorities, which are often states.

Finally, since our primary focus is on public policy, we also consider studies that evaluate divorcement. Divorcement is a legally imposed restriction on the type of contract that can be written between up and downstream firms. In particular, retail outlets can be owned by either the manufacturer or the dealer and they can also be operated by either party. To illustrate, gasoline service stations can be owned and operated by the oil company (CC), owned by the oil company but operated by an independent dealer (CD), or owned and operated by independent dealers (DD).[42] We call the prohibition of CC contracts divorcement type I and prohibition of CD contracts divorcement type II.

Table 10.1
Empirical assessment of effects of vertical contracts by method of assessment

Analysis type	Author	Year	Industry	Restraint
Descriptive	Jordan and Jaffee	1987	Beer distribution	Exclusive territories
	Hanssen	2000	Movie distribution	Block booking
Cross sectional	Smith II	1982	Auto distribution	Various
	Hass–Wilson	1987	Contact lenses	Tying
	Brickley, Dark, and Weisbach	1991	Several	Termination restrictions
	Azoulay and Shane	2001	Several	Exclusive territories
	Blass and Carlton	2001	Gasoline retailing	Divorcement (I)
	Sass	2004	Beer distribution	Exclusive dealing
Time series	Sass and Saurman	1996	Beer distribution	Exclusive territories
Panel	Ornstein and Hanssens	1987	Distilled spirits	Resale price maintenance
	Culbertson and Bradford	1991	Beer distribution	Exclusive territories
	Sass and Saurman	1993	Beer distribution	Exclusive territories
	Slade	2000	Beer distribution	Exclusive dealing
	Vita	2000	Gasoline retailing	Divorcement (I)
	Barron, Taylor, and Umbeck	2004	Gasoline retailing	Sourcing restrictions
Natural experiment	Barron and Umbeck	1984	Gasoline retailing	Divorcement (I)
	Ippolito and Overstreet	1996	Glassware	Resale price maintenance
	Slade	1998	Beer retailing	Divorcement (II)
Event study	Gilligan	1986	Many	Resale price maintenance
	Brickley, Dark, and Weisbach	1991	Many	Termination restrictions
	Ippolito and Overstreet	1996	Glassware	Resale price maintenance
Structural	Asker	2004	Beer distribution	Exclusive dealing
	Brenkers and Verboven	2006	Auto distribution	Exclusive territories

Notes: Block booking is a form of tying. Divorcement (I) means company operation of retail outlets prohibited. Divorcement (II) means company ownership of retail outlets prohibited.

Table 10.2
Empirical assessment of effects of voluntary vertical restraints

Author	Year	Industry	Variable (Y)	Effect (Y)	Effect (W)
Exclusive dealing					
Slade	2000	Beer retailing	Price	+	−
Asker	2004	Beer distribution	Cost	−	+
Sass	2004	Beer distribution	Price	+	+
			Consumption	+	
Exclusive territories					
Jordan and Jaffee	1987	Beer distribution	Price	+	−
Sass and Saurman	1993	Beer distribution	Price	+	+
			Consumption	+	
Sass and Saurman	1996	Beer distribution	Consumption	+	+
Azoulay and Shane	2001	Several	Survival	+	+
Brenkers and Verboven	2006	Auto distribution	Price	+	−
Tying					
Hanssen	2000	Movie distribution	Consumption	+	+
RPM					
Gilligan	1986	Many	Stock returns	Mixed	Ambiguous
Ippolito and Overstreet	1996	Glassware	Consumption	+	+
			Stock returns	+	
Sourcing restrictions					
Barron, Taylor, and Umbeck	2004	Gasoline	Price	−	+

Notes: Effect (Y) denotes the effect on the dependent variable. Effect (W) denotes the effect on consumer well-being. RPM denotes resale price maintenance. Sourcing restrictions are limitations on downstream input purchases.

Table 10.1 contains a list of articles where the entries are organized by method of analysis. This table shows that cross-sectional and panel analyses have been the most popular forms of assessment. Nevertheless, the other econometric methods have also been used.

Most important, once one considers that the table was constructed to include studies that assess the consequences of all types of vertical restraints and legal restrictions on vertical contracts, it highlights how very few studies there really are in each category and in total.[43] One can contrast this paucity with the very large number of theoretical articles that have been written on the subject as well as the multiplicity of retail and service industries that have used the restraints. We did indeed search broadly, so the data in table 10.1 should provide an accurate depiction of the state of empirical research on this topic. Clearly, much more work is needed in this area.

Tables 10.2 and 10.3 present the same set of studies as table 10.1. However, in this case, they are organized by type of restraint and by whether that restraint was adopted voluntarily or was forced upon the vertical structure. Specifically, table 10.2 shows those studies that focus on privately imposed vertical restraints, whereas table 10.3 contains assessments of mandated vertical restraints, for example, where the government intervenes and requires that retailers be granted exclusive territories or imposes rules governing termination.[44]

Table 10.3
Empirical assessment of effects of mandated vertical restraints

Author	Year	Industry	Variable (Y)	Effect (Y)	Effect (W)
Exclusive territories					
Smith II	1982	Auto distribution	Number of dealerships	−	Ambiguous
Culbertson and Bradford	1991	Beer distribution	Price	+	−
Tying					
Hass-Wilson	1987	Contact lenses	Price	+	−
RPM					
Ornstein and Hanssens	1987	Spirits	Price	+	−
			License values	+	
			Consumption	−	
Termination restrictions					
Smith II	1982	Auto distribution	Number of dealerships	+	Ambiguous
Brickley et al.	1991	Several	Stock returns	−	−
Dealer licensing					
Smith II	1982	Auto distribution	Price	+	−
			Consumption	+	
			Number of dealerships	−	
Divorcement					
Barron and Umbeck	1984	Gasoline	Price	+	−
			Hours	−	
Slade	1998	Beer retailing	Price	+	−
Vita	2000	Gasoline	Price	+	−
Blass and Carlton	2001	Gasoline	Cost	+	−

Notes: Effect (Y) denotes the effect on the dependent variable. Effect (W) denotes the effect on consumer well-being. RPM denotes resale price maintenance. Dealer licensing is a form of entry and resale restriction.

In both tables, the last three columns show the outcome variable under scrutiny (variable Y in the table), the direction of the estimated effect of the restraint on that variable (effect Y), and the conclusion that is reached concerning the consequence of the restraint for consumer well-being (effect W). For example, if the variable under scrutiny is consumption, a + sign in the next-to-last column means that the use of the restraint was associated with larger consumption, whereas a + sign in the last column indicates that consumers are better off as a consequence.

In performing this exercise, we looked at the overall effect of the restraint. For example, if the restraint is estimated to result in higher prices and increased consumption, we indicate that it was good for consumers,[45] whereas if only higher prices resulted, we indicate that it was bad. Unfortunately, when only the effect on prices was examined by a study, there is some ambiguity in the findings. In particular, although we classify higher prices by themselves as bad, they can be good if they result from higher quality services.

Given the small number of available studies, it is difficult to make definitive claims about robust empirical regularities. This is particularly true in light of the limitations of the various econometric approaches (particularly the identification problem) and the ambiguity in interpreting price effects by themselves. There is also an ambiguity in interpreting a restraint's effect on the number of franchises or dealerships by themselves, since there may have been too many or too few outlets to begin with.[46]

Nevertheless, the results are quite striking. Indeed table 10.2 shows that in all but three cases, privately imposed vertical restraints benefit consumers or at least do not harm them. The three exceptions are studies that show that particular restraints are associated with higher prices, and we have already discussed the difficulties associated with interpreting price effects.[47] If we ignore price effects, the results in the table imply that voluntarily adopted restraints are associated with lower costs, greater consumption, higher stock returns, and better chances of firm survival.

Table 10.3, in contrast, shows that when restraints are mandated by the government, they systematically reduce consumer welfare or at least do not improve it. It appears that when dealers or consumer groups convince the government to "redress" the unfair treatment that they allege to be suffering, the consequences are higher prices, higher costs, shorter hours of operation, and lower consumption as well as lower upstream profits.[48]

In general, the empirical evidence leads one to conclude that consumer well-being tends to be congruent with manufacturer profits, at least with respect to the voluntary adoption of vertical restraints. When the government intervenes and forces firms to adopt (or discontinue the use of) vertical restraints, it tends to make consumers worse off. This is true even when the pressure for the intervention comes from consumers themselves. When the pressure comes from downstream firms, intervention tends to lead to dealer entrenchment and the inability of manufacturers to use restraints as incentive devices.

We conclude that while there are clearly limitations to the set of available studies in terms of techniques used, industry coverage, and ability to interpret the findings, the empirical evidence is consistent and convincing. Taken at face value, tables 10.2 and 10.3 indicate that vertical restraints in manufacturer/retailer settings are publicly desirable when privately desirable, and thus government intervention is not warranted in those situations. This is not to say that their use should never be questioned, but the presumption should not be that they are detrimental to consumers. The current rule-of-reason approach, combined with "safe harbors" for manufacturers with low market shares, seem more than justified based on this evidence. Furthermore, mandated restraints tend to be welfare decreasing, and hence government policies that are aimed at helping dealers and consumers tend to be misguided, counterproductive, and inconsistent with the goals of competition policy.

10.4 Conclusions

While different theoretical models often yield diametrically opposed predictions as to the welfare effects of vertical restraints, we find that with manufacturer/retailer or franchisor/franchisee relationships the empirical evidence concerning the effects of vertical restraints on consumer well-being is surprisingly consistent. Specifically, it appears that when manufacturers choose to impose such restraints, not only do they make themselves better off but they also typically allow consumers to benefit from higher quality products and better service provision. In contrast, when restraints and contract limitations are imposed on manufacturers via government intervention, often in response to dealer pressure due to perceptions of uneven bargaining power between manufacturers and dealers, the effect is typically to reduce consumer well-being as prices increase and service levels fall. Moreover, although the law usually discriminates between price and nonprice restraints, treating the former more harshly, our conclusions regarding efficiency hold for both classes.

The evidence thus supports the conclusion that in these markets, manufacturer and consumer interests are apt to be aligned, while interference in the market is accomplished at the expense of consumers (and of course, manufacturers). This is probably true because manufacturers have every incentive to develop lean and efficient distribution systems to reach ultimate consumers, which entails imposing vertical restraints on retailers when such restraints enhance dealer services and efficiency more generally, and encouraging retailer competition by eschewing restraints when such competition yields lower distribution and sales costs.

The consistency of the findings from these empirical studies is not surprising ex post. Indeed the retail markets that we examine are relatively competitive, and upstream firms face many problems in providing their wholesalers and retailers with appropriate incentives. Given the informational and motivational constraints that they face, they have had to devise ways to circumvent those problems in order to achieve lower costs and increased sales. Moreover it seems unlikely that public agencies can come up with more efficient ways of achieving the same objectives.

While much more empirical evidence is needed before we can draw more definitive conclusions, and in particular, before we can rule out the possibility that vertical restraints lead to foreclosure or anticompetitive behavior more generally, the present empirical evidence suggests that a fairly relaxed antitrust attitude toward restraints is warranted. Moreover the notion that governments should impose restraints on manufacturers in order to protect their dealers and consumers should be viewed with skepticism. In particular, the role of the government should be limited to intervention in situations where market failures are of such magnitudes that the inevitable costs are warranted.

Finally, while we find the evidence compelling, some of the studies yield negative or ambiguous effects from restraints. Further empirical work might reveal more systematically the sets of circumstances under which particular restraints tend to be undesirable (e.g., see Gilligan 1986 for an attempt along these lines). Moreover the studies discussed here focus on relationships involving retailers. However, there is also a need to understand the effects of vertical restraints in other contexts. We believe that empirical work is especially promising in this regard, and hope that it will provide guidance for future theoretical and competition policy developments.

Notes

1. A practice is per se illegal if it suffices to provide evidence that it exists and it is unnecessary to demonstrate that it damages competition. Under a rule-of-reason approach, in contrast, there is no *a priori* presumption, and the costs and benefits of a practice must be weighed on a case-by-case basis.

2. For a survey of empirical evidence with a different emphasis and focus, see Cooper et al. (2005).

3. Slotting allowances, however, can be interpreted as a form of vertical restraint, a two-part tariff imposed by retailers (supermarkets) on manufacturers. See also Scherer (2004) on the *Toys 'R' Us* litigation, which involved a retailer imposing restraints on its suppliers, and Comanor and Rey (2000) for a related theoretical analysis.

4. See US Department of Commerce (1988).

5. Although some might be tempted to consider individual franchised outlets in a chain to be vertically integrated, franchises are independent businesses under the law. Their operations are nevertheless subject to numerous restrictions, including typically exclusive dealing and other vertical restraints, which makes this setting perfect for the study of vertical restraints and explains why most of the studies that we have found relate to one form of franchising or another.

6. A full understanding of successive monopoly dates at least to Spengler (1950), although one can find its origins in Cournot's (1838) analysis of complementary products. Greenhut and Ohta (1979) discuss the oligopoly case.

7. For example, Lafontaine (1992) shows that the value of inputs sold by franchisors in the restaurant and fast-food industry averages only about 4.5 percent of franchisees' sales. Moreover this percentage represents actual, not required, sales. In many cases franchisees choose to buy from their franchisors because it is more convenient or economical to do so. Thus required sales are even smaller than this percentage suggests. The tendency of business format franchisors to sell little to their franchisees can be traced in part to the 1971 decision in *Siegel et al. v. Chicken Delight, Inc.* where the court found that requirements that franchisees purchase inputs from their business format franchisors were a form of tying, given that such franchisors already "sell" a business format and/or trade name to their franchisees. With the business format or trade name as the tying good, any other input that a franchisor requires that franchisees purchase from him represents a tied sale (see *Siegel et al. v. Chicken Delight, Inc.*, 1971). Since that decision, business format franchisors have tended to rely more on approved supplier programs for all but the most critical inputs (see Hunt and Nevin 1975; Klein and Saft 1985; and Lafontaine 1993 for more on the issue of input tying in business format franchising).

8. See Blair and Lafontaine (2005) for more on this.

9. This solution, however, is generally inefficient. An optimal choice of outlet density does not focus exclusively on the elimination of double marginalization.

10. Similarly from its early days McDonald's implemented policies related to QSC (or quality, service, and cleanliness) so as to ensure a positive customer experience to those frequenting a McDonald's anywhere in the world and thus encourage them to visit other McDonald's restaurants in the future.

11. See, for example, Brickley (1999) and Blair and Lafontaine (2005) for more on this. Note that if the retailer were not an independent business but instead part of a vertically integrated structure, he would not necessarily bear the cost of higher service level in the unit. If paid a salary that does not depend on retail profits, there would be no reason for the retailer to free ride. A different type of incentive problem would occur, however, if service provision entailed costly effort on the part of the retailer. When monitoring the provision of this effort is costly, the retailer who is not paid based on retail profit will have every incentive to shirk, as in the traditional principal-agent problem. The solution to this problem is to make the retailer a residual claimant, in which case the free-riding problem resurfaces.

12. Input-substitution problems in vertical structures can take a different form. Specifically, downstream firms that do not operate under fixed-proportion technologies have incentives to adjust the quantity of inputs that they use away from a high-priced input that is sold by an upstream monopolist toward inputs that are obtained from competitive suppliers. This possibility has been used to explain, for example, why monopolists might vertically integrate (e.g., see Warren-Boulton 1974). Instead, the monopolist could tie the purchase of the products provided by the competitive industries to its own, requiring efficient ratios of inputs (see Blair and Kaserman 1978). We do not pursue this possibility further because most of the retail situations that we are concerned with entail relatively fixed proportions. Moreover none of the empirical studies that we have uncovered examine cases where tying is used in industries with variable proportions.

13. Thus Telser (1960) assumed that dealers would not just pocket the increased profits resulting from the lack of price competition. They would instead spend them on increased quality or service, and the increased quality and service they chose would be the same as desired by the manufacturer.

14. See also Goldberg (1984) and Meese (2004) for more on these and related arguments. Note that the welfare effects of vertical restraints that are meant to ensure the provision of dealer services are less clear, however, if consumers do not all value the services equivalently (see notably Spence 1975 on this issue).

15. For this solution to work, the upstream firm must be able to verify downstream investment and to terminate the contract if it is unsatisfactory.

16. In the absence of fixed fees, delegation can still lead to higher upstream profits but is not guaranteed to do so.

17. This is true because quantities are strategic substitutes.

18. This is a form of leveraging.

19. See, for example, MacKie-Mason (2004) for more on imperfect information and tying.

20. Resale price maintenance was an exception, as it was declared a per se violation of Section 1 of the Sherman Act by the Supreme Court in its 1911 *Dr. Miles Medical Co.* decision.

21. *Continental TV, Inc. v. GTE Sylvania, Inc.*

22. Assistant Attorney General Anne Bingaman (1993) stated in her speech that rescinded the Guidelines, that "These Guidelines seem so thoroughly to discount the anticompetitive potential of vertical intrabrand restraints and so easily assume their efficiency-enhancing potential as to predetermine the conclusion against enforcement action in almost every case. I am simply not willing to sign on to that balance."

23. The NAAG, however, published its own VR Guidelines in 1995.

24. Under Article 81 of the Treaty of Rome.

25. See, for example, Pitofsky (1997).

26. In its 1997 Khan decision, the US Supreme Court overruled the per se prohibition on maximum resale price maintenance. Ten years later the Court overruled its 1911 Dr. Myles decision and thus asserted that vertical price restraints were to be judged under a rule of reason. This decision put price and nonprice restraints on an equal footing in the United States.

27. See Blair and Kaserman (1983) and Mathewson and Winter (1984) on the substitutability of different forms of vertical restraints.

28. One exception is tying arrangements, which are treated under a modified per se rule.

29. One exception is the harsher treatment of exclusive territories in the European Union, particularly if those territories are drawn along national borders.

30. For example, some states have laws that require the use of exclusive territories in the distribution of beer, whereas others forbid the use of ET, and still others have adopted no restrictions (see Sass and Saurman 1993).

31. See, for example, Smith II (1982) for a discussion of this issue.

32. See Lafontaine and Slade (1997) for a survey of those studies.

33. The term "natural experiment" is not particularly illuminating in that there is nothing natural about changes in the law. Nevertheless, we follow the labor and public-finance literature in using the term.

34. In the short run one can assume that the characteristics are predetermined.

35. Formulas for tests of differences in means under various assumptions about the two populations can be found in Walpole and Myers (1972, p. 242).

36. See MacKinlay (1997) for a general discussion of the use of event studies in economics and finance.

37. The market model can be augmented to include other financial and nonfinancial assets, as in the APT model of Ross (1967).

38. See, for example, Campbell, Lo, and MacKinley (1997, ch. 4).

39. This is just another example of the Lucas (1976) critique.

40. See, for example, Hausman, Leonard, and Zona (1994), Nevo (2000), and Pinkse and Slade (2004).

41. This issue is often ignored by researchers who perform horizontal merger simulations. However, it is relatively straightforward to estimate a cost function that allows one to assess economies of scale and scope, and changes therein, in that context.

42. There is clearly a fourth case, DC, but it is never observed in practice.

43. As noted previously, a related literature that assesses incidence also exists, but those studies are outside the scope of this chapter.

44. Note that the restraints studied in table 10.3 were imposed, not prohibited, by a government.

45. The combination of higher prices and increased consumption is usually interpreted as being due to increased provision of services, which are costly to provide but are valued by consumers.

46. A larger number of outlets is associated not only with lower transport costs, a plus, but also with higher prices due to duplication of fixed costs and lower demand per outlet, a minus.

47. For example, Slade (2000) finds that beer prices are higher in tied houses than in independent establishments, where tied houses operate under an exclusive purchasing agreement with a brewer. One could argue that the two groups of pubs have very different characteristics, and that pubs do not really sell beer. Instead they sell "an evening in the pub." On the other hand, economic models can explain the finding without resorting to this interpretation. For example, pubs are geographically separated. So, once in the pub, customers only compare the prices of the brands that are offered. If independent houses carry more brands, price elasticities are apt to be larger in absolute value and markups are apt to be lower in those houses.

48. The increase in license values that is found by one study indicates that any benefit to downstream firms accrues to the original (not the current) holder of the license.

References

Aghion, P., and P. Bolton. 1987. Contracts as barriers to entry. *American Economic Review* 77: 388–401.

Asker, J. 2004. Measuring cost advantages from exclusive dealing: An empirical study of beer distribution. Mimeo. Stern School of Business, New York University.

Azoulay, P., and S. Shane. 2001. Entrepreneurs, contracts, and the failure of young firms. *Management Science* 47: 337–58.

Barron, J. M., and J. R. Umbeck. 1984. The effects of different contractual arrangements: The case of retail gasoline. *Journal of Law and Economics* 27: 313–28.

Barron, J. M., B. A. Taylor, and J. R. Umbeck. 2004. Will open supply lower retail gasoline prices? *Contemporary Economic Policy* 22: 63–77.

Bingaman, A. K. 1993. Antitrust enforcement, some initial thoughts and actions. Address before the Antitrust Section of the American Bar Association, New York.

Blair, R. D., and D. L. Kaserman. 1978. Vertical integration, tying, and antitrust policy. *American Economic Review* 68: 397–402.

Blair, R. D., and D. L. Kaserman. 1983. *Law and Economics of Vertical Integration and Control*. New York: Academic Press.

Blair, R. D., and F. Lafontaine. 2005. *The Economics of Franchising*. Cambridge: Cambridge University Press.

Blass, A. A., and D. W. Carlton. 2001. The choice of organizational form in gasoline retailing and the cost of laws that limit that choice. *Journal of Law and Economics* 44: 511–24.

Brenkers, R., and F. Verboven. 2006. Liberalizing a distribution system: The European car market. *Journal of the European Economic Association* 4: 216–51.

Brickley, J. A. 1999. Incentive conflicts and contractual restraints: Evidence from franchising. *Journal of Law and Economics* 42: 745–74.

Brickley, J. A., F. H. Dark, and M. S. Weisbach. 1991. The economic effects of franchise termination laws. *Journal of Law and Economics* 34: 101–32.

Burstein, M. L. 1960. The economics of tie-in sales. *Review of Economics and Statistics* 42: 68–73.

Campbell, J. Y., A. Lo, and C. MacKinley. 1997. *The Econometrics of Financial Markets*. Princeton: Princeton University Press.

Chen, Z., and T. Ross. 1993. Refusals to deal, price discrimination, and independent service organization. *Journal of Economics and Management Strategy* 2: 593–614.

Comanor, W. S., and P. Rey. 2000. Vertical restraints and the market power of large distributors. *Review of Industrial Organization* 17: 135–53.

Cooper, J. L., M. Froeb, D. O'Brien, and M. G. Vita. 2005. Vertical antitrust policy as a problem of inference. *International Journal of Industrial Organization* 23: 639–64.

Cournot, A. 1838. *Recherches sur les principes mathematiques de la theorie des richesses.* Paris.

Culbertson, W. P., and D. Bradford. 1991. The price of beer: Some evidence from interstate comparisons. *International Journal of Industrial Organization* 9: 275–89.

Dr. Miles Medical Co. v. John D. Park and Sons Co. 1911. 220 US 373.

Gilligan, T. W. 1986. The competitive effects of resale price maintenance. *RAND Journal of Economics* 17: 544–56.

Goldberg, V. P. 1984. The free-rider problem, imperfect pricing, and the economics of retailing services. *Northwestern University Law Review* 79: 736–57.

Greenhut, M. L., and H. Ohta. 1979. Vertical integrations of successive oligopolists. *American Economic Review* 69: 137–41.

Haas-Wilson, D. 1987. Tying requirements in markets with many sellers: The contact lens industry. *Review of Economics and Statistics* 69: 170–75.

Hanssen, A. 2000. The block-booking of films re-examined. *Journal of Law and Economics* 43: 395–426.

Hausman, J., G. Leonard, and D. Zona. 1994. Competitive analysis with differentiated products. *Annales d'Econometrie et de Statistique* 34: 159–80.

Ippolito, P. M., and T. R. Overstreet Jr. 1996. Resale price maintenance: An economic assessment of the Federal Trade Commission's case against the Corning Glass Works. *Journal of Law and Economics* 39: 285–328.

Jordan, J., and B. L. Jaffee. 1987. The use of exclusive territories in the distribution of beer: Theoretical and empirical observations. *Antitrust Bulletin* 32: 137–64.

Katz, M. L. 1989. Vertical contractual relations. In R. Schmalensee and R. D. Willig, eds., *Handbook of Industrial Organization.* Amsterdam: Elsevier Science.

Klein, B., and K. M. Murphy. 1988. Vertical restraints as contract enforcement mechanisms. *Journal of Law and Economics* 31: 265–97.

Klein, B., and L. F. Saft. 1985. The law and economics of franchise tying contracts. *Journal of Law and Economics* 28: 345–61.

Krattenmaker, T., and S. C. Salop. 1986. Anti-competitive exclusion: Raising rival's costs to achieve power over price. *Yale Law Journal* 96: 209–93.

Lafontaine, F. 1992. Agency theory and franchising: Some empirical results. *RAND Journal of Economics* 23: 263–83.

Lafontaine, F. 1993. Contractual arrangements as signaling devices: Evidence from franchising. *Journal of Law, Economics and Organization* 9: 256–89.

Lafontaine, F., and M. E. Slade. 1997. Retail contracting: Theory and practice. *Journal of Industrial Economics* 45: 1–25.

Lucas, R. E. 1976. Econometric policy evaluation: A critique. In K. Brunner and A. H. Meltzer, eds., *The Phillips Curve and the Labor Markets, Supplementary Series to the Journal of Monetary Economics.* Amsterdam: North-Holland, pp. 19–46.

MacKie-Mason, J. K. 2004. Links between markets and aftermarkets: Kodak (1997). In J. E. Kwoka and L. J. White, eds., *The Antitrust Revolution: Economics, Competition and Policy,* 4th ed. New York: Oxford University Press.

MacKinlay, A. G. 1997. Event studies in economics and finance. *Journal of Economic Literature* 35: 13–39.

Marvel, H., and S. McCafferty. 1984. Resale price maintenance and quality certification. *RAND Journal of Economics* 15: 340–59.

Mathewson, F., and R. Winter. 1984. An economic theory of vertical restraints. *RAND Journal of Economics* 15: 27–38.

Meese, A. J. 2004. Property rights and intrabrand restraints. *Cornell Law Review* 89: 553–620.

Mortimer, J. 2008. Vertical contracts in the video rental industry. *Review of Economic Studies*, forthcoming.

Nevo, A. 2000. Mergers with differentiated products: The case of the ready-to-eat cereal industry. *RAND Journal of Economics* 31: 395–421.

OECD. 1994. Competition policy and vertical restraints: Franchising agreements. Report. Paris.

Ornstein, S. I., and D. Hanssens. 1987. Resale price maintenance: Output increasing or restricting? The case of distilled spirits in the US. *Journal of Industrial Economics* 36: 1–18.

Ornstein, S. 1985. Resale price maintenance and cartels. *Antitrust Bulletin* 30: 401–32.

Perry, M. 1980. Forward integration by Alcoa: 1888–1930. *Journal of Industrial Economics* 29: 37–53.

Pinkse, J., and M. E. Slade. 2004. Mergers, brand competition, and the price of a pint. *European Economic Review* 48: 617–43.

Pitofsky, R. 1997. Vertical restraints and vertical aspects of mergers—A US perspective. Speech delivered to the Fordham Corporate Law Institute.

Rey, P., and J. Stiglitz. 1995. The role of exclusive territories in producers' competition. *RAND Journal of Economics* 26: 431–51.

Ross, S. A. 1976. The arbitrage theory of capital asset pricing. *Journal of Economic Theory* 13: 41–360.

Sass, T. R. 2005. The competitive effects of exclusive dealing: Evidence from the U.S. beer industry. *International Journal of Industrial Organization* 23: 203–25.

Sass, T. R., and D. S. Saurman. 1993. Mandated exclusive territories and economic efficiency: An empirical analysis of the malt-beverage industry. *Journal of Law and Economics* 36: 153–77.

Sass, T. R., and D. S. Saurman. 1996. Efficiency effects of exclusive territories: Evidence from the Indiana beer market. *Economic Inquiry* 34: 597–615.

Scherer, F. M. 2004. Retailer instigated restraints on suppliers' sales: Toys "R" Us (2000). In J. E. Kwoka and L. J. White, eds., *The Antitrust Revolution: Economics, Competition and Policy*, 4th ed. New York: Oxford University Press.

Sharpe, W. F. 1963. A simplified model for portfolio analysis. *Management Science* 9: 277–93.

Shepard, A. 1993. Contractual form, retail price, and asset characteristics. *RAND Journal of Economics* 24: 58–77.

Siegel et al. v. Chicken Delight, Inc. 448 F. 2d43 (9th Cir. 1971).

Slade, M. E. 1998. Beer and the tie: Did divestiture of brewer-owned public houses lead to higher beer prices? *Economic Journal* 108: 1–38.

Slade, M. E. 2000. Regulating manufacturers and their exclusive retailers. In Morten Berg and Einar Hope, eds., *Foundations of Competition Policy*. London: Routledge, pp. 133–49.

Smith II, R. L. 1982. Franchise regulation: An economic analysis of state restrictions on automobile distribution. *Journal of Law and Economics* 25: 125–57.

Spence, M. A. 1975. Monopoly, quality, and regulation. *Bell Journal of Economics* 6: 417–29.

Spengler, J. 1950. Vertical integration and anti-trust policy. *Journal of Political Economy* 58: 347–52.

Telser, L. 1960. Why should manufacturers want fair trade. *Journal of Law and Economics* 3: 86–105.

US Department of Commerce. 1988. *Franchising in the Economy: 1986–88*. Washington, DC: GPO.

Vita, M. G. 2000. Regulatory restrictions on vertical integration and control: The competitive impact of gasoline divorcement policies. *Journal of Regulatory Economics* 18: 217–33.

Walpole, R. E., and R. H. Myers. 1972. *Probability and Statistics for Engineers and Scientists*. New York: Macmillan.

Warren-Boulton, F. R. 1974. Vertical control with variable proportions. *Journal of Political Economy* 82: 773–802.

Abuse of Market Power

John Vickers

Competition law is a fundamental part of the ground-rules of the market economy. Its three basic elements combat anticompetitive agreements, anticompetitive mergers and abuse of market power. Competition policy in Europe in respect of the first two elements has recently been reformed toward a more economics-based approach. Many practitioners and observers of competition law believe that the same should happen with the rules on the abuse of market power. In the United States too there is much current debate about what the law against monopolization is, and should be. In this chapter I describe some of the main issues in these debates and stress the importance of economics-based development of competition law.

In recent years the balance of emphasis of EC competition policy toward agreements among firms has shifted, at least to some degree, from vertical to horizontal agreements and from legal form to economic effect. The 1999 block exemption regulation for vertical agreements created a larger safe harbor for nonprice vertical agreements in unconcentrated markets. Around the same time EC anti-cartel policy, following successes in the United States, became much more vigorous. Large fines (the stick) and more encouraging leniency arrangements (the carrot to information providers) have been used in a number of major cases in markets ranging from vitamins, lysine, and citric acid to graphite electrodes and plasterboard. The balance of incentives for potential cartelists has shifted significantly and cartel activity is accordingly less likely. Very recently, as part of the modernization of the implementation of EC competition law that came into effect on May 1, 2004, the bureaucratic notification system for agreements was ended. The result of these developments is a European policy approach toward agreements among firms that is more economics based in terms of its priorities, processes, and substantive case analysis.

May 2004 also saw the coming into force of the revised EC Merger Regulation. Among other things, this regulation changed the test for merger appraisal from whether the merger would create or strengthen a dominant market position to whether the merger would significantly impede effective competition.[1] This approach is more in tune with the economic purpose of merger policy and is close to, if not the same as, the substantial lessening of competition test in the law of the United States and a number of other countries, including, since June 2003, the United Kingdom. The new EC merger regulation was accompanied by economics-based horizontal merger guidelines. Economics now plays a stronger role in merger appraisal within the European Commission's directorate for competition, for example, through the new chief economist position. And recent judgments suggest that the European Community Courts in Luxembourg now require more economic rigor in merger analysis.

In contrast to these developments affecting agreements and mergers, EC competition law and policy toward abuse of market power have seen less development and are in a state of some uncertainty. There appear, moreover, to be significant differences between EC and US law and policy—unlike the general situation now with mergers—but even this is hard to judge in view of significant intrajurisdictional uncertainties on both sides of the Atlantic. Ultimately it will be the courts that resolve the uncertainties through cases, but in the meantime the competition authorities must apply, and competition lawyers must advise on, the law as they see it to be. Public debate on these issues should help clarity, understanding and perhaps reform. It is now under way and economics has a major part to play.

11.1 The Law

The cornerstone of European law on abuse of market power is Article 82 of the EC Treaty; the text is reprinted in the sideline. As is immediately apparent, the prohibition on abuse of dominance covers a wide and diverse range of corporate behavior. The practical meaning of the prohibition has evolved over time through the case law, especially since judgments by the European Court of Justice (ECJ) from the late 1970s, before which there were very few cases.

Article 82 of the EC Treaty

Any abuse by one or more undertakings of a dominant position within the common market or in a substantial part of it shall be prohibited as incompatible with the common market in so far as it may affect trade between Member States. Such abuse may, in particular, consist in:

(a) directly or indirectly imposing unfair purchase or selling prices or other unfair trading conditions;
(b) limiting production, markets or technical development to the prejudice of consumers;
(c) applying dissimilar conditions to equivalent transactions with other trading parties, thereby placing them at a competitive disadvantage;
(d) making the conclusion of contracts subject to acceptance by the other parties of supplementary obligations which, by their nature or according to commercial usage, have no connection with the subject of such contracts.

Article 82 applies only to firms that have dominant positions. Of course, a large body of case law deals with the assessment of dominance—market definition, market shares, entry conditions and so on. Such issues are beyond the scope of this chapter, which is concerned with abuse of market power, and so will take dominance as given.

It is worth pausing, however, to note the issue of whether inferences about dominance can ever be made from the conduct questioned as abusive. On the one hand, analysis of dominance must be based on the evidence looked at in the round, and it would seem wrong to exclude from the evidence base for dominance assessment relevant conduct by the firm in question. On the other hand, there is a danger expressed by Coase (1972, p. 67):

If an economist finds something—a business practice of one sort or another—that he does not understand, he looks for a monopoly explanation. And as in this field we are very ignorant, the number of un-understandable practices tends to be very large, and the reliance on monopoly explanation, frequent.

Although the economics of the past thirty years has reduced our ignorance, the warning is one still to heed. False inferences can be made not only about monopoly but also about anticompetitive conduct.

All but a few EC cases on abuse of dominance have concerned exclusionary conduct by dominant firms—namely conduct preventing or restricting competitors rather than behavior directly exploitative of consumers. (Exclusionary practices can, of course, be *indirectly* exploitative of consumers, and, as discussed below, there is a view that no conduct is properly characterized as exclusionary unless it is ultimately exploitative.) Many EC cases have dealt with pricing issues, such as predatory pricing, selective price cuts, margin squeezes, and discounts and rebates. Nonprice issues have included tying, bundling, exclusive dealing, and refusal to supply. The cases discussed in this chapter involve questions of pricing abuse.

Case law has established some general principles:[2]

• That a dominant firm has a special responsibility not to allow its conduct to impair genuine undistorted competition.
• That a dominant firm may not eliminate a competitor or strengthen its position by recourse to means other than those based on competition on the merits.
• That abuse involves recourse to methods different from those that condition normal competition.
• That the concept of abuse is objective, so does not require anticompetitive intent (though evidence on intent can be relevant to finding abuse).

Some of the intellectual roots for these principles can be traced to the ordo-liberal school of law and economics based in Freiburg in the 1920s and 1930s.[3] For the ordo-liberals, competition law was central to the economic constitution of society as a constraint on the exercise of both private and state power in the economic sphere. Where market power could not be eliminated, the favored competition law standard was that dominant firms should act *as if* constrained by competition. That should allow "performance competition" (*Leistungswettbewerb*)—to offer better deals to customers. But it should disallow "impediment competition" (*Behinderungswettbewerb*)—hindering rivals' ability to offer better deals to customers. In a competitive market there is naturally performance competition but no scope for impediment competition. By this standard, a dominant firm, while welcome to engage in performance competition, may not engage in impediment competition.

The United States has a much longer tradition of competition law than Europe. Section 2 of the Sherman Act of 1890 makes it illegal to "monopolize, or attempt to monopolize, or combine or conspire with any other person or persons, to monopolize any part of the trade or commerce among the several States, or with foreign nations."

Monopolization has two elements, which very roughly correspond to dominance and abuse:

• Possession of monopoly power.
• "the willful acquisition or maintenance of that power as distinguished from growth or development as a consequence of a superior product, business acumen or historic accident."[4]

In discerning the latter the challenge lies in "distinguishing between exclusionary acts, which reduce social welfare, and competitive acts, which increase it".[5]

Note that in the United States, the law is engaged only if there is a causal link from the conduct to the market power. By contrast, although Article 82 applies only if there is market power—to the extent of dominance—conduct can be abusive even if it does not maintain or strengthen that power. So in Europe, but not in the United States, pure exploitation of market power—such as excessive pricing—can breach competition law. But nearly all European cases have concerned exclusionary, rather than directly exploitative, conduct.

Here the fundamental issue, which recurs in various guises and phrases, is the same in Europe, the United States, and elsewhere: how to distinguish between (unlawful) exclusionary or competition-distorting behavior and (lawful) "competition on the merits" by firms with market power? The answer is less than clear. Indeed Elhauge (2003b), speaking of US law, goes so far as to say that "monopolization doctrine currently uses vacuous standards and conclusory labels that provide no meaningful guidance about which conduct will be condemned as exclusionary" (p. 253).

Case law does suggest standards to help distinguish between exclusionary and pro-competitive behavior for some types of dominant firm conduct, but the underlying substantive principles are not always easy to discern. Development of such principles is important, for otherwise there would be a danger that competition law toward abuse of dominance could become a set of ad hoc and unpredictable rules that are consistent neither with each other nor with the policy goals of the law.

In the next section, I outline some of the standards that have evolved, and questions that have arisen, in relation to types of pricing abuse—predatory pricing, selective price cuts, margin squeezes, and discounts and rebates—by reference to some recent EC, UK, and US cases. In the subsequent sections, I pursue the quest for general principles by discussing tests based on profit "sacrifice," productive efficiency, and consumer harm.

11.2   Some Recent Cases

11.2.1   Predatory Pricing

Competition spurs firms to offer customers good deals, and competition law should not readily condemn the offering of deals to customers that are alleged to be too good. Industrial organisation theory has, however, demonstrated that predatory pricing—low pricing that is profit maximizing only because of its exclusionary effect—is certainly not an empty box, especially where reputation and financial effects are important.[6] In this spirit a US Court of Appeals recently said that while it approached the question of predation "with caution, we do not do so with the incredulity that once prevailed."[7]

Competition law is unconcerned with low pricing by nondominant firms. For dominant firms the standard approach is to examine pricing in relation to measures of cost. Thus in the case known as *Tetra Pak II*, the ECJ, confirming the approach in the earlier *AKZO* case, held that:

First, prices below average variable costs must always be considered abusive. In such a case, there is no conceivable economic purpose other than the elimination of a competitor, since each item produced and sold entails a loss for the undertaking. Secondly, prices below average total costs but above average variable costs are only to be considered abusive if an intention to eliminate a competitor can be shown.[8]

The ECJ went on to say that, in the circumstances of the case, it was not necessary to prove in addition that Tetra Pak had a realistic chance of recouping its losses. That contrasts with US law. In 1993 the Supreme Court in *Brooke Group* held that predatory pricing violates the Sherman Act only if there is a dangerous probability that the predator will recoup its losses.[9] Arguably, however, dominance—without which there can be no abuse in European law—implies ability to recoup.

As to the first part of the ECJ standard, while pricing below AVC by a dominant firm is normally abusive, the presumption of abuse can, exceptionally, be rebutted. An interesting, but unsuccessful, attempt to rebut a finding of abuse was made in a recent UK case. (UK law mirrors EC law.) The Office of Fair Trading (OFT) found in 2001 that Napp Pharmaceutical Holdings had abused its dominant position in the supply of sustained relief morphine tablets and capsules by a combination of below-cost pricing in the hospital segment of the market and excessive pricing in the community segment. Napp sought to justify its below-cost pricing on the grounds that hospital sales led on to profitable community sales and so were not loss-making. But this was a circular argument inasmuch as the high margins on community sales depended on the exclusionary low pricing to hospitals. For this and other reasons, Napp's appeal against the OFT's decision failed. Pricing above the dominant firm's AVC but below its ATC was discussed by the Competition Appeal Tribunal in another recent UK case—*Aberdeen Journals* (though the OFT found abuse in that case on the basis of pricing below AVC). For example, the CAT said that such pricing "is likely to be abusive when undertaken in anticipation of competitive entry or in order to undercut a new entrant," and that, with prices below ATC including a proportionate share of general overheads, "sooner or later an equally efficient competitor will be forced out of the market."[10] The appropriate definition (and of course measurement) of cost can be controversial.

In 1999 the US Department of Justice (DOJ) brought a case against American Airlines saying that it had reacted—by price cuts and capacity expansion—in an unlawfully predatory way to entry by rivals on routes connecting to its Dallas hub. The DOJ argued that the conduct was predatory because it was unprofitable but for its exclusionary effect. The district court gave summary judgment (i.e., judgment without full trial) against the DOJ, which was upheld on appeal, on the ground that AA had not engaged in pricing below an appropriate measure of cost. A key point in this case, which is discussed below in relation to the "sacrifice test," was whether profit lost on existing capacity is an opportunity cost that should be counted in the reckoning when applying the cost tests for predatory pricing.

11.2.2 Selective Price Cuts

Above-cost price cuts were at issue in the case of *Compagnie Maritime Belge*, on which the ECJ gave judgment in 2000.[11] The enterprise, which had a near-monopoly position on certain shipping routes between Europe and West Africa, had selectively cut prices to match those of its competitor, though not demonstrably to below total average cost. The Court saw the risk that condemning such pricing could give inefficient rivals a safe haven from the full rigors of competition but, in the circumstances at hand, judged that there was abuse (albeit not abuse under the heading of predation) because the selective price cuts were aimed at eliminating competition while allowing continuing higher prices for uncontested services.

A very basic model, taken from Armstrong and Vickers (1993, example 3), illustrates some of the pros and cons of disallowing selective price cuts by dominant firms. Suppose that

- Overall demand is divided uniformly (but not necessarily equally) between two markets.
- Firm M is dominant over market 1 but firm E might enter market 2.
- Firm M has constant marginal cost.
- Firm E has constant returns to scale, except perhaps for a fixed cost of entry.
- The move order is that E decides whether to enter and, if so, its scale of entry k. Then M decides the prices p_1 and p_2 in the two markets.

If selective price cuts are allowed, M will set $p_1 = p^m$, the monopoly price, and $p_2 = p(k)$, where $p(k)$ is a decreasing function of the scale of entry. Let $p^e = p(k^e)$ be the price associated with the optimal scale of entry k^e for E, taking account of M's response, if it enters.

If selective price cuts are banned, M must set $p_1 = p_2$. Then M will respond less aggressively to entry than if selective price cuts are allowed, and so, if E enters, it will do so on a larger scale. In this simple model the optimal scale of entry for E is such as to induce $p_1 = p_2 = p^e$. (The mathematical intuition for this result is that the situation in the aggregate of both markets when price discrimination is banned is the same, apart from multiplication by a constant, as that in the contested market when discrimination is allowed.)

So in this simple setting, subject to the proviso below, a ban on selective price cuts would not affect price in the contested market but would cause price in the uncontested market to fall to that in the contested market. That would obviously be good for consumers in the uncontested market. However, it could be bad for productive efficiency because firm E might be considerably less efficient than firm M at serving the business that it wins from M. Firm M's incentive to compete in market 2 is blunted by the profit forgone in market 1.

The proviso is whether firm E will enter. (Recall that entry might entail a fixed cost.) It may well be that E's entry decision will be the same whether or not selective price cuts are allowed. But depending on the size of the fixed cost of entry, it is possible that E will enter if and only if selective price cuts are banned. Then, in this simple model, the monopoly price p^m will prevail in both markets if selective price cuts are allowed, but price will be p^e in both markets if they are banned.

This very simple example illustrates the wider point that a rule against *selective* price cuts in response to competition by dominant firms would have mixed effects on social welfare even if no price is reduced below variable cost, and even if the dominant firm merely meets competition and does not engage in profit sacrifice (on which see below). Such a rule could be good for competitors and consumers but costly in terms of productive efficiency. Although consumers benefited from the ban on selective price cuts in the simple example above, this is not a general result. Indeed a rule against selective price cuts could often be bad for consumers in contested markets and sometimes detrimental to consumers overall. Some of these themes will recur in the discussion below of discounts and rebates.

11.2.3 Margin Squeezes

A margin squeeze occurs when a vertically integrated dominant firm sets the wholesale price for an upstream product, on which downstream rivals rely, and the retail price for its final product such that the margin between them is unduly low, thereby anticompetitively squeezing rivals downstream. The question to consider here is what counts as unduly low.[12] Equivalently a margin squeeze occurs when the wholesale price is unduly high relative to the retail price—a kind of "raising rivals' costs"—or when the retail price is unduly low relative to the wholesale price—akin to predatory pricing. It can also be seen as akin to undue discrimination between self-supply and supply to others. These are just different descriptions of the same thing.

Two recent UK cases, with contrasting outcomes, are *Genzyme* and *BSkyB*. Genzyme is dominant in the supply of drugs for the treatment of Gaucher's disease. In 2001 it ended its distribution agreement with the homecare delivery and services provider Healthcare at Home (HH). Genzyme would thereafter only supply HH the drug at the price that Genzyme charged for the drug plus delivery and homecare services—in short, at a wholesale price equal to its retail price. Thus there was no margin for HH to make *any* contribution to its costs. The OFT found that Genzyme's margin squeeze was an abuse of dominance, and this finding was upheld on appeal.[13] Somewhat similarly, in 2003 the European Commission found that Deutsche Telekom had abused a dominant position by setting the wholesale price of local loop capacity to competitors at times higher than the retail price to final customers.

When, as in these examples, wholesale price is as high as the retail price—so that the retail–wholesale margin is zero (or less)—rivals cannot profitably operate in direct competition with the dominant firm no matter how efficient they are. But when questions of abusive margin squeeze arise, how large a positive margin should be required? While too small a margin can squeeze out "efficient" rivals, too large a required margin would shelter "inefficient" rivals to the detriment of productive efficiency. And what is the right benchmark by which to judge rivals' efficiency?

The natural answer is the efficiency of the dominant firm in the downstream activity. In other words, the benchmark is the "as-efficient" competitor. There is no need to assess any firm against some hypothetical yardstick of efficiency. The issue is whether the dominant firm is by margin squeeze preventing rivals from winning business that they would serve more efficiently than the dominant firm. So, in principle, if the dominant firm's downstream unit would be loss-making if it paid the wholesale prices charged to rivals, there is a margin squeeze; otherwise, there is not. This makes economic sense and has been recognized in European case law. For example, in a case some years ago, British Sugar was found to have abused its dominant position by setting its retail and wholesale (industrial) sugar prices such that the margin between the two was insufficient to reflect its own costs of transformation (in that case, its own repackaging costs).[14]

The margin squeeze question in the *BSkyB* case was whether BSkyB was abusing its dominance in the supply of premium pay TV channels by charging rival distribution companies too much for wholesale channel supply in relation to its own retail prices for those channels.[15] Upon examination BSkyB's downstream operation was found to be around breakeven in the period in question, so margin squeeze abuse was not shown.

11.2.4 Discounts and Rebates

One of the most topical issues regarding abuse of dominance is that of discounts and rebates. In September 2003 the European Court of First Instance upheld a Commission decision finding abusive the system of quantity rebates operated by the tire manufacturer Michelin to its dealers in France. Michelin's quantity rebates, it was held, were "loyalty-inducing," so tended to prevent dealers from being able to select their suppliers freely, and sought to prevent dealers from getting supplies from competing manufacturers. The rebates were therefore found to have a foreclosure effect. The Court said that this need not be an actual effect—to find abuse it is sufficient to show that the dominant firm's conduct "tends to restrict competition or, in other words, is capable of having that effect."[16]

In December the Court likewise upheld a European Commission decision against British Airways for its performance reward systems for UK travel agents.[17] It was held that these encouraged the agents to sell BA tickets in preference to those of other airlines, and restricted the agents' freedom of choice to the detriment of other airlines. Neither Michelin nor BA was found to have given an adequate economic justification for its rebate/discount scheme, for example, in terms of cost savings.

The issue of discounts and rebates also arose in the recent US case of *LePage's*. LePage's sued 3M for monopolizing the market for transparent tape by its policy of giving discounts and rebates to retailer customers on the basis of sales targets and the range of 3M products that they stocked—so-called bundled rebates. In a judgment of 2003 the Court of Appeals by a majority upheld a lower court verdict against 3M.[18]

These cases about discounts and rebates, on both sides of the Atlantic, illustrate sharply a fundamental dilemma for the competition law treatment of abuse of market power. A firm with market power that offers discount or rebate schemes to dealers is likely to sell more, and its rivals less, than in the absence of the incentives. But that is equally true of low pricing generally.

Superficially, then, discounts and rebates can appear at once anticompetitive and pro-competitive. So can various other forms of commercial behavior by firms with market power. Only by going beneath the surface to underlying economic principles can the clash of superficial appearances be resolved sensibly. But what are, or should be, the underlying principles by reference to which conduct that distorts and harms competition can be distinguished from normal competition on the merits?

The remaining sections discuss three related approaches to this question—the sacrifice test, the as-efficient competitor test, and the consumer harm test. The main aim is to assess some economic pros and cons of the tests, and not their consistency with existing case law, though that will be mentioned in places.

11.3   The Sacrifice Test

One general principle that has been advanced for helping to determine when dominant firm behavior is unlawfully exclusionary—as distinct from competition on the merits—is the sacrifice test, sometimes also known as the "but for" test. This test asks whether the dominant firm conduct in question would be profitable, or make business sense, but for its tendency to eliminate or lessen competition.[19]

At a general level this test has some appeal. Predatory pricing fails the test, since it entails short-run losses and is profitable only because of its tendency to eliminate (and/or deter) rivals. Meeting competition by price cuts passes the test inasmuch as the price cuts are a profitable response to the entry and expansion of rivals. Unlike with predatory pricing, such price cuts do not depend for their profitability on the subsequent exploitation of enhanced market power.

Quite apart from questions about the application of the test to the facts of cases—for example, about the requisite standard of proof—there are several prior conceptual issues. Is the test a substantive standard or just a standard to assess intent or willfulness? What is the benchmark for assessing sacrifice? In what circumstances is the test sufficient and/or necessary for conduct to be unlawful?

11.3.1 A Test of Intent or a Substantive Standard?

As to the first of these questions, an intent form of the test might say that conduct is intentionally (or willfully) exclusionary if it does not make business sense but for being exclusionary. Such a test for implied intent (or willfulness) itself says nothing about what is exclusionary, which has to be determined separately. Baumol et al. (2003), consistent with the pure intent form of the test, speak of the sacrifice test as a "tool for assessing willfulness," and as part of the "willfulness inquiry."[20]

But elsewhere they say, for example, that "the finding that the practice would not make business sense absent the additional monopoly power it provides generally reveals that the business practice is anticompetitive" (p. 5). This suggests that the sacrifice test can perhaps be interpreted as a substantive standard. Thus a "substantive" form of the test might say that conduct is exclusionary if it does not make business sense unless competition is distorted or harmed (or some such). To be saved from circularity or vacuity, however, this needs specification of what is meant by competition being distorted or harmed. A casual approach might seek to avoid this need by saying that a strategy was exclusionary if it was inexplicable unless it somehow led to monopoly power. But this would run straight into the danger expressed in the quotation from Coase above. This suggests that while the sacrifice test might be useful in assessing willfulness or intent, it does not naturally yield a substantive standard of what behavior is exclusionary. There is no escape from the fundamental question of what is harm to, or distortion of, competition.

11.3.2 Sacrifice Relative to What?

Any form of the sacrifice test must specify the benchmark for assessing whether or not there has been sacrifice.[21] In short, sacrifice relative to what? If the benchmark was the most profitable strategy (that was not anticompetitive), then, in principle, only the profit-maximizing such strategy would pass the test. If, moreover, not being anticompetitive was equated with being focused entirely on the short run, then only short-run profit maximization by the dominant firm would pass the test.

This could have very unfortunate consequences for prices, efficiency, investment, and innovation—and hence for consumers and economic welfare overall—especially if the test is taken to provide a substantive standard rather than a measure of willfulness.[22] Many of those adverse consequences might be averted by distinguishing not being anti-competitive from short-run focus. But then an alternative specification of anticompetitiveness is needed. And the test would still, in theory, be passed only if the dominant firm chose the profit-maximizing strategy from the set of not-anticompetitive strategies, which could still be bad for prices and efficiency.

It might be said that this concern is merely theoretical because in practice, the test would be failed only if the firm adopted a strategy that was manifestly and substantially less profitable (but for its anticompetitive effects) than some salient alternative strategy. But a test that is less bad in practice than in theory is not obviously a good test.

A variant that might escape some of these criticisms is a test that assesses whether *changes* in strategy entail sacrifice. Then, for a firm that alters strategy—for example, in response to entry—the benchmark would be whether the new strategy is less profitable (but for its anticompetitive effects) than the old strategy in the new situation. *American Airlines* was a case in point.[23] The DOJ argued that capacity expansion by AA in response to entry was unlawful in that it increased AA's revenues—taking into account revenue lost on preexisting AA capacity—by less than it increased costs. Put another way, the claim was that price was below cost, where cost includes the opportunity cost of profit loss on existing capacity caused by the capacity expansion. The courts did not accept this approach to cost.

The below-cost standards for assessing predatory pricing, mentioned above, can themselves be construed as variants of the sacrifice test—the benchmark being, for example, sacrifice relative to not producing (on an avoidable cost standard) or relative to producing less (on a marginal or variable cost standard). However, while such a standard might show particularly clear instances of sacrifice, it seems a curious—or at least very cautious—benchmark for a sacrifice test, especially for firms with market power. Moreover, to say that below-cost pricing generally entails sacrifice is not to derive a cost standard for predation from a sacrifice test. Rather, it is to characterize, in terms of sacrifice, a standard derived independently.

11.3.3 Necessary and/or Sufficient?

It follows from the discussion above that the sacrifice test seems incapable of providing, by itself, a *sufficient* condition for a finding of unlawfully exclusionary behavior by firms with market power. As a test of willfulness or intent—saying, for example, that conduct is intentionally (or willfully) exclusionary if it does not make business sense but for being exclusionary—it obviously has to be combined with an independent specification of what is substantively exclusionary (or anticompetitive, or competition-distorting, or whatever). Attempts to cast the test as a substantive standard appear to face a fundamental problem of being circular or ungrounded -as with, for example, saying that conduct is exclusionary if it does not make business sense but for distorting or harming competition. Such formulations restate the fundamental question, more or less helpfully, rather than answering it.

Should sacrifice nevertheless be a *necessary* condition for finding unlawfully exclusionary behavior? One aspect of this question arose in relation to the *Trinko* case recently before the US Supreme Court.[24] The central issue in the case was whether the incumbent telecommunications company Verizon had violated Section 2 of the Sherman Act by refusing to supply access to local telephone facilities to rivals, in contravention of pro-competitive regulatory requirements. The US government, in its *amicus* brief to the Supreme Court, argued that at least in the context of refusal to supply, conduct should not be found unlawful *unless* there was sacrifice.

Baumol et al. (2003), though strong supporters of the usefulness of the sacrifice test, objected on the ground that in some circumstances conduct could be willfully exclusionary without entailing sacrifice. Just such a circumstance, they contended, was if a monopolist flouted pro-competitive regulatory requirements and, indeed, that could itself show exclusionary wilfulness.

The broader issue here is whether and when conduct can harm competition, including willfully, yet not involve sacrifice. Some strategies by dominant firms to raise rivals' costs fit this description. A related question is whether and when conduct can harm competition unlawfully but without any anticompetitive intent (let alone sacrifice). Recall that in European law abuse of dominance is an objective concept and can exist without anticompetitive intent—hence Whish (2003, p. 194) says that "intention is not a key component of the concept of abuse." The dominant firm has a special responsibility not to impair undistorted competition. This suggests that the dominant firm must not only refrain from deliberately impairing such competition but on occasion, because of its special responsibility, might have to depart from what would otherwise be profitable in order not to cause impairment. Then sacrifice would in a sense be *required* of the dominant firm. As a matter of European law, therefore, sacrifice is by no means necessary for abuse.

In conclusion, the sacrifice test, appropriately specified, appears useful in a number of contexts—especially predation—but not to provide a general foundation for distinguishing competition on the merits from conduct that is exclusionary or distorting of competition. The appropriate specification of the test is anyway far from clear. As Edlin and Farrell (2003, p. 523) put it:

"Sacrifice"—behavior that would be irrational without its exclusionary effect—is logically neither necessary nor sufficient for harm to competition. It could yet be a useful test, but only because of some (still unexplored) empirical correlation, not as a matter of economic logic. So it's hardly surprising that there's so much unfocused disagreement about the right version of the test.

In any event the fundamental question remains—What is harm to competition?

11.4 The As-efficient Competitor Test

One way to approach this question is to ask whose exclusion should be prevented by the law against exclusionary practices by dominant firms? The answer cannot sensibly be rivals in general. A natural answer is in terms of rivals that are no less efficient than the dominant firm. When competition is effective, more efficient firms gain at the expense of less efficient firms, so the as-efficient competitor test appears to accord with protecting competition as distinct from competitors.

The test has some pedigree in case law. For example, as is evident from the discussion above, the standard applied to predatory pricing and margin squeeze abuse in some EC cases is related to exclusion of competitors who are efficient—at the activity in question—relative to the dominant firm. Posner (2001, pp. 194–95) proposes a general standard for deciding exclusionary claims under US antitrust law:

[T]he plaintiff must first prove that the defendant has monopoly power and second that the challenged practice is likely in the circumstances to exclude from the defendant's market an equally or more efficient competitor. The defendant can rebut by proving that although it is a monopolist and the challenged practice exclusionary, the practice is, on balance, efficient.

In the same vein Elhauge (2003a) argues that above-cost price cuts to drive out entrants are not predatory, and that costs should be defined such that prices above costs cannot inflict losses on as-efficient rivals.

Clearly, there are circumstances where the entry of less efficient rivals can improve social welfare because the gain in allocative efficiency through lower prices can outweigh the loss in productive efficiency through higher costs. (This can happen in the simple example above.) There are also circumstances where rules against above-cost price cuts might result in the entry of less efficient rivals that would not otherwise have occurred. Where these two sets of circumstances overlap, such rules would improve social welfare, despite being more restrictive of dominant firm conduct than the as-efficient competitor test would imply.

However, such rules could well have adverse welfare effects in other circumstances.[25] As well as promoting the entry of less efficient firms, they could keep prices up—especially if they had the effect of "telling a monopolist to hold the umbrella of monopoly prices over its competitors."[26] If prices fall, the entry of less efficient firms might worsen productive efficiency more than it benefits allocative efficiency. (This too can happen in the simple example above.) The less efficient firms might have entered anyway. Effects on possible rivals no less efficient than the dominant firm, and on incentives for efficiency, might also be relevant. And there may be implementation difficulties with rules stricter than the as-efficient competitor test. All in all, argues Elhauge in line with the as-efficient competitor test, it is best for competition law not to restrict above-cost price cuts.[27]

This disciplining principle has a clear logic but the breadth of its application is open to debate. For example, should it apply to all *selective* above-cost price cuts? And should it extend to all *conditional* price reductions, such as discounts conditional on exclusive dealing?

In EC law selective above-cost price cuts can sometimes be abuses of dominance. The finding of exclusionary abuse in the case of *Compagnie Maritime Belge* was mentioned earlier. Besides exclusion, selective low pricing can in some circumstances be an abuse under clause (c) of Article 82, which concerns discriminatory pricing that distorts downstream competition.[28]

In economic terms there is a dilemma. Given the apparently ambiguous welfare effects, there is little basis in economic theory for a rule that *always* permitted above-cost price discrimination by dominant firms in response to competition. Yet the natural and mostly desirable response to competition by dominant firms will often involve (above-cost) price discrimination. This suggests that hostility to this *form* of response to competition would be wrong, but that in limited economic circumstances the evidence as a whole might justify a finding of abuse (even when the price cuts are unconditional). Which circumstances is a matter in need of more economic analysis.

One factor is the undue denial of scale economies to rivals—a form of raising rivals' costs. This issue arises most sharply as regards (above-cost) price reductions *conditional* on the buyer not dealing with rivals. For example, by exclusive dealing in the presence of scale economies, it is theoretically possible for a dominant incumbent profitably to exclude from the market a rival whose cost curve is nowhere higher than its own.[29] Each customer would individually do better to accept than reject an exclusive contract with the dominant firm at a price just below the unit cost (at small scale) of the rival even if that price is substantially above the unit cost of the (large-scale) dominant firm. It would be in the collective interest of the customers to deal with the rival at a large scale, but none will do so individually because of the diseconomies of its small scale.

The dominant firm can thereby exploit to its advantage, but to the detriment of customers and efficiency, the coordination problem of the customers—a strategy of divide and rule. It is not obvious which way the as-efficient competitor principle points in this case, for the rival is by assumption as-efficient overall but is less efficient at supplying each individual customer because of its lack of scale economies. Be that as it may, this is an example of how inefficient exclusion can be profitable for a dominant firm. But this theory is not applicable unless, on the facts, the proportion of the market foreclosed would significantly affect scale economies. And it should be remembered that exclusive dealing can in some circumstances have beneficial effects (e.g., overcoming free-rider problems in the provision of retailer services).

Less restrictive than exclusive dealing conditions, but still possibly foreclosing in effect, are price terms conditional on such factors as the proportion of purchases made from the dominant firm, purchases relative to previous-period purchases and retrospective rebates based on amount purchased. In the language of EC case law, these are loyalty rebates or at least can be "loyalty-inducing." Again, there are some conditions in which such pricing practices—even if above the costs of the dominant firm—can exclude as-efficient rivals. But the *form* of the pricing practices does not by itself reveal whether or not those conditions hold; analysis of the surrounding economic circumstances (e.g., scale economies and extent of foreclosure) is needed for that. In an economics-based approach, possible benefits of the practices, depending on the facts, should also be weighed in the scales. As well as cost-saving justifications for discount schemes, it can be both natural and desirable for dominant firms to offer their customers incremental prices that are lower than average prices, which discount schemes can help achieve.

Article 81 of the EC Treaty, which deals with anticompetitive agreements, contains a framework for the assessment of possible efficiency benefits, but Article 82 does not do so explicitly. The principle of "objective justification" is, however, well established in the case law, and its scope may develop over time. It will be interesting to see whether the as-efficient competitor principle gains more extensive recognition as the case law evolves.

11.5   The Consumer Harm Test

An alternative answer to the basic question posed at the start of the previous section is that the law against exclusionary practices by dominant firms should prevent the exclusion of rivals whose presence enhances consumer welfare.[30] (Whether "consumer welfare" here means consumer surplus or social welfare more generally—that is, including profit—is a large question that occurs in a range of competition policy settings but is beyond the scope of this chapter.)

The consumer welfare (or harm) test returns us to the traditional distinction, mentioned earlier, between exclusionary and directly exploitative abuses of market power. The qualifier "directly" is important insofar as the main (only?) reason why we care about exclusionary behavior is that if unchecked, it will ultimately leave consumers worse off. Thus Fox (2002) asks "Is there only *one* type of practice that is anticompetitive: that which is exploitative?"

Stated in terms of a necessary condition, the question in short is whether there is no exclusion without exploitation.[31] The affirmative response, which Fox identifies with prominent US antitrust thinking,[32] might be put as follows: Market power is the ability to raise price and restrict output. To count as exclusionary, conduct must be reasonably capable of maintaining or strengthening market power. In this view, conduct would not be deemed to be exclusionary unless it is shown to have the effect of raising price and restricting output.[31]

This standard of anticonsumer effect, stated as a necessary condition for a finding of unlawful exclusion, would place a more or less strict limiting principle on antitrust intervention against firms with market power and a strong discipline against the pitfalls of *competitor* protection. The strictness of the limiting principle depends in part on the standard of proof needed to establish the anticompetitive effects of higher prices or lower output. Must those effects be actual or probable? Or is it enough for the conduct in question to have the tendency, a reasonable capability, or merely a possibility of causing them?

Fox argues, however, that the issue is not just about the standard of proof of output-limiting effects and that the *concept* of harm to competition is potentially much broader than negative output and price effects. In particular, should harm to competition include harm to the dynamic *process* of competition? If so, what does that mean in practical terms?

It is hard to separate the issue of the standard of proof of anticonsumer effect from the conceptual issue of whether the notion of harm to competition should extend beyond effect to process. The more that only demonstrable (and so presumably short-term) outcomes are allowed to weigh in the scales of "effect," the stronger is the case for including "process" harms. If, however, a reasonable exploitation story—not necessarily reliant on clear and present exploitation—could meet the standard, then the case for additionally including "process" harms would be less strong. In the limit, the idea that there could be harms to the competitive process, justifying competition policy intervention, that are not even capable of harming consumers is unattractive. Competition to serve the needs of the general public of consumers—not some abstract notion of competition for its own sake—is the point of competition policy.

11.6 Conclusion

The law on abuse of market power is far from settled. The law in Europe could now develop in either of two broad directions, with emphasis increasingly either on form or on economic effect. Form-based evolution of the law would further develop descriptions of conduct for dominant firms to avoid. Economics-based evolution would clarify underlying principles in terms of actual and potential economic effects, develop practically administrable rules and methods explicitly on the basis of those principles, and apply them to cases.

In the competition between economics-based and form-based approaches the former has strong advantages. It can align the law with its economic purpose and in an internally consistent manner. It can prevent form from triumphing over substance at the cost of both allowing detrimental conduct and blocking benign conduct. And it can provide clarity at fundamental, rather than superficial, level. These advantages will be realized if European competition law on abuse of dominance becomes more firmly anchored to economic principles, and where those principles are practically applicable by competition authorities, lawyers, and the courts.

To say that the law on abuse of dominance should develop a stronger economic foundation is not to say that rules of law should be replaced by discretionary decision-making based on whatever is thought to be desirable in economic terms case by case. There must be rules of law in this area of competition policy, not least for reasons of predictability and accountability. So the issue is not rules versus discretion but how well the rules are grounded in economics. To that end there is great scope for economic analysis and research to contribute to the development of the law on abuse of dominance. To be effective, however, economics must contribute in a way that competition agencies, and ultimately the courts, find practicable in deciding cases.

Notes

An earlier version of this chapter, written while John Vickers served as Chairman of the UK Office of Fair Trading, was published in the *Economic Journal*, vol. 115 (June), pp. F224–F261. The editor thanks the OFT for granting Crown copyright permission to reprint it (note of the editor). The chapter was originally presented before the thirty-first conference of the European Association for Research in Industrial Economics, in Berlin, on September 3, 2004. The author is very grateful to Mark Armstrong, Frances Barr, John Fingleton, Amelia Fletcher, Eleanor Fox, Bill Kovacic, Nic Newling, Ali Nikpay, and Richard Whish for many discussions and comments. The views expressed here are personal and not necessarily those of the Office of Fair Trading.

1. An account of recent EC and UK merger policy reform is in Vickers (2004).

2. See, for example, Whish (2003, ch. 5).

3. See Gerber (1998, especially ch. 8).

4. *United States v. Grinnell Corporation*, 384 US 563, 570–571 (1966).

5. *United States v. Microsoft Corporation*, 253 F.3d 34, 58 (D.C Cir.) (2001).

6. See Brodley et al. (2000) for a comprehensive analysis of the (US) law and economics of predatory pricing.

7. *United States v. AMR Corporation*, 335 F.3d 1109 (10th Cir.) (2003).

8. Case C-333/94P *Tetra Pak International SA v. Commission* [1996] ECR I-5951, para. 41.

9. *Brooke Group Ltd. v. Brown & Williamson Tobacco Corp.*, 509 US 209 (1993).

10. *Aberdeen Journals Limited v. OFT* [2003] CAT 11, paras. 352 and 370.

11. Case C-395/96P *Compagnie Maritime Belge SA v. Commission* [2000] ECR I-1365.

12. Of course, there is no general duty on dominant firms to supply downstream rivals. The law and economics of refusal to supply is beyond the scope of this chapter; see Whish (2003, pp. 663–78) on the position in European law. The recent *Trinko* case before the US Supreme Court, mentioned below, concerned refusal to supply telecommunications network access.

13. *Genzyme Limited v. OFT* [2004] CAT 4.

14. *Napier Brown/British Sugar* OJ [1988] L284/41, para. 66.

15. Decision of the Director General of Fair Trading, *BSkyB investigation: Alleged infringement of the Chapter II Prohibition*, 17 December 2002. Another issue in the case concerned BSkyB's "mixed bundling" pricing of premium channels such that a bundle of premium channels was priced at less than the sum of the individual prices of the channels—that is, the incremental price was below average price.

16. Case T-203/01 *Manufacture Française des Pneumatiques Michelin v. Commission*, judgment of 30 September 2003, para. 239.

17. Case T-219/99 *British Airways plc v. Commission*, judgment of 17 December 2003. BA has appealed the CFI's judgment to the ECJ (pending case C-95/04).

18. *LePage's Inc. v. 3M Co.*, 234 F.3d 141 (3rd Cir.) (2003). The Supreme Court declined to take the case. The US government advised that it was not an attractive vehicle to clarify the law on bundled rebates and that it would be preferable to allow the case law and economic analysis to develop further. A recent contribution to that economic analysis is Nalebuff (2004).

19. Note that this is not necessarily the same as asking whether the conduct is short-run profitable (see below). The degree of probability that should attach to the "tendency" is an important question not discussed in detail here.

20. At pages 13 and 11 of their *amici* brief on the *Trinko* case mentioned below.

21. Edlin and Farrell (2003) give a fuller discussion of this issue in their analysis of the *American Airlines* predation case. The Court of Appeals judgment in the case is cited in note 7 above.

22. Elhauge (2003b) makes particularly trenchant criticisms on these lines.

23. Again, see Edlin and Farrell (2003).

24. *Verizon Communications Inc. v. Law Offices of Curtis V. Trinko LLP*, 124 S. Ct. 872 (2004).

25. See Elhauge (2003a) for an extensive analysis.

26. Posner (2001, p. 238).

27. Elhauge (2003a, fn. 53) is, however, clear that *conditional* above-cost discounts (see below) should be treated differently from straight above-cost price cuts.

28. In the BA case mentioned earlier the CFI found abuse under this heading—affecting travel agents—as well as foreclosure of airline rivals.

29. See Rasmusen et al. (1991). A thorough survey of the modern economic theory of foreclosure is given by Rey and Tirole (2003).

30. In this sentence it is crucial that there is no comma after "rivals."

31. The consumer harm test could, in principle, be cast as a sufficient rather than necessary condition so that conduct was held to be exclusionary if it was likely (say) to lead to consumer harm. But this by itself seems dangerously open-ended.

32. In particular, Muris (2000).

33. On a broad interpretation, output restriction could embrace issues of quality and even innovation, not just quantity.

References

Armstrong, M., and J. Vickers. 1993. Price discrimination, competition and regulation. *Journal of Industrial Economics* 41(4): 335–59.

Baumol, W., J. Ordover, F. Warren-Boulton, and R. Willig. 2003. Brief of *amici curiae* economics professors to U.S. Supreme Court in *Verizon v. Trinko*.

Brodley, J., P. Bolton, and M. Riordan. 2000. Predatory pricing: Strategic theory and legal policy. *Georgetown Law Journal* 88(8): 2239–330.

Coase, R. 1972. Industrial organization: A proposal for research. In V. Fuchs, ed., *Policy Issues and Research Opportunities in Industrial Organization*. New York: National Bureau of Economic Research, pp. 59–73.

Edlin, A., and J. Farrell. 2003. The American Airlines case: a chance to clarify predation policy. In J. Kwoka and L. White, eds., *The Antitrust Revolution*. Oxford: Oxford University Press, pp. 502–27.

Elhauge, E. 2003a. Why above-cost price cuts to drive out entrants are not predatory. *Yale Law Journal* 112(4): 681–828.

Elhauge, E. 2003b. Defining better monopolization standards. *Stanford Law Review* 56(2): 253–344.

Fox, E. 2002. What is harm to competition? Exclusionary practices and anti-competitive effect. *Antitrust Law Journal* 70(2): 371–412.

Gerber, D. 1998. *Law and Competition in Twentieth Century Europe: Protecting Prometheus*. Oxford: Oxford University Press.

Muris, T. 2000. The FTC and the law of monopolization. *Antitrust Law Journal* 67(3): 693–723.

Nalebuff, B. 2004. Bundling as an entry barrier. *Quarterly Journal of Economics* 119(1): 159–87.

Posner, R. 2001. *Antitrust Law*, 2nd ed. Chicago: University of Chicago Press.

Rasmusen, E., M. Ramseyer, and J. Wiley. 1991. Naked exclusion. *American Economic Review* 81(5): 1137–45.

Rey, P., and J. Tirole. 2003. A primer on foreclosure. forthcoming in M. Armstrong, and R. Porter, eds., *Handbook of Industrial Organization*, vol. 3. Amsterdam: North Holland.

Vickers, J. 2004. Merger policy in Europe: Retrospect and prospect. *European Competition Law Review* 25(7): 455–63.

Whish, R. 2003. *Competition Law*, 5th ed. London: LexisNexis UK.

12 Price Discrimination

Mark Armstrong

In broad terms, one can say that price discrimination exists when two "similar" products that have the same marginal cost to produce are sold by a firm at different prices.[1] This practice is often highly controversial in terms of its impact on both consumers and rivals. This chapter aims to explain some of the main economic motives for price discrimination, and to outline when this practice will have an adverse or beneficial effect on consumers, rivals, and on total welfare.

Broadly speaking, there are three main reasons why competition policy may be concerned with price discrimination. First, a dominant firm may "exploit" final consumers by means of price discrimination, with the result that total and/or consumer welfare are reduced. Here the question that needs to be addressed is: In what circumstances does price discrimination by a dominant firm have an adverse effect on welfare? The answer, as will be clear in this survey, often depends on the welfare standard that guides the application of competition law. However, in practice, competition authorities hardly ever concern themselves with price discrimination as an exploitative device.

Second, and especially in Europe, it is sometimes a policy objective to attain a "single market" across the region. Arguably, one manifestation of a single market is that a firm does not set different prices in different regions, or at least it does not prevent arbitrageurs reselling goods sourced in the low-price region to the high-price region. That is to say, firms are often prevented from segmenting markets with a view to engaging in price discrimination. In Europe, this concern has lead to a very hostile attitude by the authorities to attempts by firms to prevent "parallel imports," for instance.

Third, and perhaps most important from a competition authority's point of view, we may be concerned that price discrimination can be used by a dominant firm to "exclude" (or weaken) actual or potential rivals. The question is: In which cases is price discrimination an effective way to put the seller's rivals (primary line injury) or the buyer's rivals (secondary line injury) at a disadvantage so as to force them to exit the market, or induce them to compete less aggressively?

The appropriate antitrust treatment of price discrimination may require consideration of more than one of these concerns. For instance, a form of price discrimination may potentially be an efficient way to supply services to final consumers, and yet it may also possess exclusionary effects. In such cases competition law and policy need to balance the risk of preventing firms from pricing their products efficiently with the risk of permitting conduct that leads to a less competitive market structure.

The plan of the chapter is as follows: Section 12.1 outlines some of the principal methods of price discrimination. Section 12.2 shows how the ability to engage in price discrimination can sometimes lead to efficient (e.g., marginal cost) prices, which clearly leads to welfare gains. Section 12.3 discusses how price discrimination can open up new markets or shut down existing markets. Section 12.4 examines when price discrimination causes total output to rise or fall. Section 12.5 discusses when the introduction of price discrimination will cause some prices to rise and other to fall, while sections 12.6 and 12.7 focus on less familiar situations in which price discrimination causes all prices to fall or all prices to rise. Section 12.8 examines the impact of price discrimination on entry incentives. Section 12.9 introduces dynamic price discrimination, while section 12.10 outlines the impact of price discrimination in vertically related markets.

The discussion throughout focuses on the underlying economics of price discrimination and its impact on profits, entry, consumer surplus, and welfare. Where relevant particularly prominent antitrust cases are mentioned.[2]

12.1 Forms of Price Discrimination

There are numerous business practices that fall under the heading of price discrimination. First, consider static situations where consumers buy all relevant products in a single period. In most markets, firms set the charge for purchase of their products by means of a simple price per unit for each product, where these prices do not depend on who makes the purchase. Such tariffs (1) are anonymous (they do not depend on the identity of the consumer), (2) do not involve quantity discounts for a specific product (i.e., there are no "intra-product" discounts), and (3) do not involve discounts for buying a range of products (i.e., there are no "inter-product" discounts). Various forms of price discrimination are found by relaxing these three restrictions.

Nonanonymous Price Discrimination Nonanonymous price discrimination occurs when a firm offers a different tariff to identifiably different consumers or consumer groups. When the tariff also involves simple per-unit pricing (rather than nonlinear pricing or bundling), this is the familiar case of *third-degree* price discrimination. Examples of this practice include selling the same train ticket at a discount to senior citizens, selling the same car at different prices in two countries, or selling the same drug at difference prices for human and animal use. Unless arbitrage between consumer groups is very easy or competition between firms is almost perfect, we expect that any firm, if permitted to do so, would wish to set different tariffs to different groups. In antitrust cases this type of price discrimination can occur when the alleged abuse consists in "selective price cuts" or "geographic price discrimination."[3]

Another example of this form of price discrimination is *first-degree* price discrimination, where each consumer is charged exactly her willingness to pay for the product(s). In its purest form, the information needed for first-degree price discrimination makes it more of a theoretical benchmark than a realistic business strategy. However, it provides a transparent limit framework in which to discuss the possible efficiency gains from price discrimination, as well as its distributional impact on consumers.

Quantity Discounts The practice of offering quantity discounts occurs when the per-unit price for a specific product decreases as the number of purchased units increases. A simple—and easily implemented—instance of this is a two-part tariff whereby a buyer must pay a fixed charge in return for the right to purchase any quantity at a constant marginal price. There are two distinct motives to use nonlinear tariffs. First, nonlinear tariffs provide a more efficient means by which to generate consumer surplus. With linear pricing, the only way to make profit is to set prices above costs, which entails deadweight losses. With a two-part tariff, however, a firm can extract profit using the fixed charge, while leaving marginal prices close to marginal costs (which then maximizes the size of the "pie" to be shared between consumer and firm). This role for nonlinear pricing exists even if all consumers are similar. A second role emerges if consumers have heterogeneous tastes for a firm's products. In this case a nonlinear tariff can be used to sort different types of consumers endogenously (called *second-degree* price discrimination).[4] If some consumers gain higher utility from the product than others, then the firm that offers a tariff where the marginal price declines with volume will typically make higher profit than the firm that offers the same marginal price to all consumers.[5]

Pure quantity discounts are generally not challenged by competition authorities if they merely reflect cost efficiencies stemming from the larger volume of product sold (and are therefore not discriminatory). However, at least in Europe, there is hostility toward a dominant firm that offers discounts that do not reflect costs.[6] This attitude seems to be overly rigid because it does not recognize the efficiencies that may stem from the pricing method, independent of the cost efficiencies related to the scale of the transaction.

Bundling Discounts A bundling discount occurs when the price for one product is reduced if the consumer also buys another product. Two variants of bundling exist: (1) *pure bundling* is where a consumer can only purchase the products as bundle and there is no scope for buying an individual item, and (2) *mixed bundling* is where the firm sets prices for a bundle and also for individual items. In general, unless products have negligible marginal costs or are perfect complements, pure bundling is a rather inefficient business practice. The reason is that it forces some consumers to purchase products for which their willingness to pay is smaller than the cost of supply. Thus we expect that "all inclusive holidays" will often be an inefficient way to market holidays, since efficiency requires that consumers only consume what they value.

In addition we will see that pure bundling can provide a means by which to deter entry by single-product firms. Mixed bundling (with two products) sorts consumers endogenously into three groups: those with a strong taste for both products (who buy the bundle from the firm), those with a strong preference for product 1 but weak preferences for product 2 (who buy just product 1), and those with the reverse tastes (who buy just product 2). Mixed bundling is closely related to two-part pricing: the "first" item from the firm is expensive, while the "second" is relatively cheap. Indeed, because it is often hard to pin down what it means for products to be "distinct," in practice, it may be hard to distinguish (intra-product) quantity discounts from (inter-product) bundling discounts. For example, should a season ticket for a concert series count as a quantity discount for purchasing several units of the same product, or as a discount for purchasing several distinct items?

Next turn to dynamic situations. There are several ways in which a firm can set different prices for essentially the same product over time. If consumers wish to buy a single item at some point in time (e.g., a new novel), then a firm might be able to make those consumers with a higher reservation price pay more than other consumers by setting a price for the item which decreases over time. This *intertemporal* price discrimination is essentially another form of second-degree discrimination. A crucial difference between static and dynamic forms of price discrimination is that in the latter case, a firm may not have the ability to commit to its future prices. That is to say, once a firm has sold its product to the initial (enthusiastic) pool of consumers, it typically has an incentive to reduce its price to extract profit from the remaining, lower value consumers. Indeed, in simple models, it turns out that the firm would prefer not to have the ability to price discriminate in this way, but it cannot help but offer declining prices over time. This is the essence of the famous Coase (1972) problem faced by firms selling to forward-looking buyers. In these situations policy that forbids price discrimination might have the effect of endowing the firm with commitment power, with the result that all prices rise. Thus it is perhaps not surprising that competition authorities have rarely investigated this type of dynamic price discrimination.

Other issues arise if consumers wish to purchase a product repeatedly (e.g., from a supermarket or an online retailer). In this case a firm may be able to base its price today on whether (or how much, or what) a consumer has purchased from it in the past. This *behavior-based* price discrimination is becoming increasingly prevalent due to the improved technological ability to track consumer behavior by means of the Internet, loyalty cards, and so on. This kind of price discrimination is a dynamic variant of nonlinear pricing, and one that raises interesting and subtle issues. However, one difference with static nonlinear pricing is that in many cases a firm does not announce its discounting strategy. Partly this is because it would often be too complicated to describe its strategy—for instance, a supermarket's personalized vouchers to a particular consumer will depend on the customer's history of purchases, and this will be impractical to communicate in detail. But partly there is the commitment problem again. For instance, a supermarket may notice that a past customer appears to have starting shopping elsewhere (e.g., his loyalty card has not been used), and it may then decide to mail the consumer a financial inducement to return to the shop. It is unlikely that the supermarket will wish to publicize such a strategy. In sum, information about shopping habits presents firms with an ability to set "personalized" (i.e., discriminatory) prices. It is intrinsically hard to commit to such personalized prices.[7]

The final class of discriminatory pricing discussed involve the pricing of inputs to downstream firms. An issue of frequent antitrust concern is the wholesale price a vertically integrated firm should be permitted to charge a downstream rival. When the firm sets too high a wholesale price (relative to its own retail price), the firm might be said to "discriminate" against its rival. The interpretation of "too high" is not obvious, however, and this issue is discussed later in the chapter. A second issue is whether a vertically separate upstream supplier should be able to discriminate in its wholesale contracts among downstream buyers. A major difference between supplying an input to downstream firms and supplying a product to final consumers is that, in the former case, the contracts are often much more complex and "personalized" than those typically offered to final consumers. As such, the contract with one downstream firm might not be known to a rival downstream firm. This "secret deals" problem again raises the issue of credibility. We will see that if the upstream supplier can offer discriminatory deals to downstream firms, it may be forced to offer generous deals which ultimately benefit final consumers. But if public policy forbids such discriminatory behavior, this may restore the monopolist's ability to set high prices to its downstream buyers.

Regardless of the method of price discrimination, it is necessary that consumer arbitrage not unravel the discriminatory prices. For instance, if a firm wishes to set a lower price in one country it is important that consumers in higher-price countries not be able easily to import the same product from the low-price country. (Prominent examples of price discrimination by country include cars and pharmaceuticals.) Similarly a season ticket holder should not be able to let others use the season ticket, or consumers should not easily be able to pretend to be new customers at a firm in order to take advantage of its introductory offers. Therefore, when policy makers wish to discourage price discrimination, they will often take the indirect route of ensuring that consumer arbitrage is as easy as possible. For instance, as mentioned earlier, European competition law is very hostile to firms preventing parallel imports of their products when those firms are dominant or enter into anticompetitive agreements with other firms.[8]

12.2 Price Discrimination Leading to Efficient Prices

In many cases the welfare problems caused by firms exploiting their market power are due to firms having insufficient information about their consumers' preferences, or being constrained (e.g., by public policy) in their ability to condition prices on their information about consumers. In some circumstances, allowing firms to engage in price discrimination can implement efficient prices. In these cases total welfare is unambiguously improved, although the impact on consumers may be negative.

One familiar example of this is first-degree discrimination, where a monopolist has perfect information about each consumer's willingness to pay for its product(s).[9] To be concrete, suppose that there is a population of consumers, each of whom wishes to consume a single unit of the firm's product. Willingness to pay for this item is denoted v, and this varies among consumers according to the distribution function $F(v)$. Thus, if a consumer has valuation v and faces the price p, he will buy if $v \geq p$. Suppose that the firm has unit cost c. If price discrimination is not permitted (or is otherwise not possible), the firm will choose its single price p to maximize profit $(p - c)(1 - F(p))$. Clearly, the chosen price will be above cost, and total surplus is not maximized. (It is efficient to serve all those consumers with $v \geq c$, but only those with $v \geq p > c$ are served.) If the firm can somehow observe each consumer's v and is permitted to discriminate on that basis, it will charge each consumer the maximum possible (i.e., $p = v$) provided this price covers its cost of supply. In other words, an efficient outcome is achieved. However, the firm appropriates the entire gains from trade and consumers are left with nothing. Thus the benefits of allowing first-degree price discrimination depend on the chosen welfare standard: with a total welfare standard such discrimination is beneficial, whereas with a consumer standard it is not. Since it is rather common that the impact of price discrimination on consumers is the opposite to its impact on overall welfare, this issue—that optimal policy toward price discrimination depends on the chosen welfare standard—appears repeatedly in the price discrimination literature.

Another example of first-degree price discrimination involves two-part tariffs. Suppose that the monopolist knows the utility each consumer gains from its product. Specifically, suppose that a particular consumer has surplus $u(q) - T$ if she consumes q units of the product in return for a payment T. Consumers must receive a nonnegative surplus if they are to buy from the firm at all. If the firm has a unit cost c, its profit-maximizing strategy is to maximize $T - cq$ subject to the consumer's participation constraint $u(q) - T \geq 0$. This entails choosing q to maximize $u(q) - cq$ so that total surplus from the interaction is maximized. This outcome can be implemented by means of a two-part tariff: the firm sets the marginal price equal to marginal cost c and sets the fixed charge to extract all the consumer's surplus. (The fixed charge will differ from consumer to consumer, depending on their preferences $u(\cdot)$.) Again, this strategy results in the efficient level of consumption, while consumers are left with no surplus.[10]

Monopoly first-degree price discrimination is merely an extreme form of a fairly common situation. Lack of information about consumer tastes, in combination with market power, leads to welfare losses as a firm faces a trade-off between volume of demand and the profit it makes from each consumer. In many cases, if the firm can price discriminate more finely, it will be able to extract consumer surplus more efficiently, and this will often lead to greater overall welfare. However, it is consumers' private information that protects them against giving up their surplus to a monopoly. Therefore, when a price-discriminating monopolist has improved information about its consumers, often a reduction in consumer surplus will result.

Competition among suppliers is another means by which consumers are protected against surplus extraction. Even if firms know everything about a consumer's tastes, competition ensures that the consumer will still be left with surplus. In competitive environments, whether consumers are better or worse off when firms can practice price discrimination is a subtle question, as we will see throughout this chapter.

Consider, for example, the effects of firms offering two-part tariffs instead of linear prices. (This discussion assumes that consumers buy all supplies from one firm or the other, i.e., there is "one-stop shopping.") With linear pricing, firms' prices will be close to their marginal costs if the market is competitive, and prices will be higher when the firms have more market power. When firms offer two-part tariffs, their marginal prices will usually be lower than when linear prices are employed. For instance, in the special case where all consumers have the same demand function, firms will sets marginal prices exactly equal to marginal cost, since that is the most profitable method for a firm to deliver a particular level of consumer surplus. Total welfare often increases if two-part tariffs are used instead of linear prices, since the marginal price falls to cost. With more intricate analysis one can also show that profit increases with this form of price discrimination, while consumers are typically worse off.[11] Thus this competitive setting resembles the monopoly setting with two-part tariffs just discussed: welfare and profits increase, but consumers are harmed by the use of two-part tariffs. The main effect of competition here is that consumer surplus is no longer driven down to zero when two-part tariffs are used. To confuse the issue, though, we will see alternative situations in section 12.6 where the reverse happens: when competing firms know everything about consumer tastes and price accordingly, firms are harmed and all consumers are better off.

Finally, in the context of *regulated* monopoly, socially optimal prices almost always exhibit price discrimination. Ramsey prices—the prices that maximize welfare subject to the regulated firm covering its costs, including fixed costs—depend on demand conditions in much the same way as an unregulated monopolist's prices do. For instance, when the firm serves a number of independent markets, each with the same marginal cost of supply, Ramsey principles suggest that the most efficient way to cover the firm's production cost is to set a higher price in those markets where consumer demand is less elastic, exactly as would be the case with an unregulated profit-maximizing firm. In sum, socially optimal prices are discriminatory whenever the regulated firm has fixed costs of operation which need to be funded by price-cost markups.

12.3 Price Discrimination Can Open (or Shut) Markets

It is possible that permitting price discrimination will open markets that would otherwise not be served at all. To see this, suppose that a monopolist faces two independent markets, one of which is "high value" and the other is "low value." When discrimination is allowed, suppose that the discriminatory price in the high-value market is significantly higher than the "choke price" that causes demand in the low-value market to fall to zero. Then, if the size of the high-value market is sufficiently large compared to the low-value market, and discrimination is not allowed, the monopoly will choose to serve only the high-value market. In such cases, granting permission to discriminate results in a Pareto improvement: the strong market's price is unchanged while the weak market is served, which increases the surplus of consumers in the weak market as well as the firm's profit.[12]

Let us consider a simple example of this phenomenon. There are two kinds of consumer: consumers in market 1 each wish to consume a single unit of the product and are willing to pay up to 4 for this unit, while consumers in market 2 each wish to consume a unit and are willing to pay 2 for this unit. Suppose that the monopoly has no cost of production. In this case, if the firm must charge the same price to both markets, it will choose to set the price 4 and serve only market 1 whenever there are more consumers in that market than in market 2. (If there are more consumers in market 2, then the firm will prefer to set the price 2 and serve all consumers.) If price discrimination is possible, then the firm will set a price 4 in market 1 and a price 2 in market 2, and this results in a Pareto improvement.[13]

Another aspect of this issue is that the higher profit that price discrimination generates can provide a more effective way for a firm to cover its fixed costs. In some cases a monopoly might be profitable overall if it can price discriminate but unprofitable if it cannot. A broadcaster, for instance, might only be profitable if it can bundle its channels together, or a rail operator might only be able to break even if it can discriminate between low-income and other travelers. In such cases *all* markets would be shut down if price discrimination were not allowed.

Further examples of how the introduction of price discrimination might open or shut a market involve nonlinear pricing. Suppose that there are two groups of consumers, high-value users and low-value users, and the firm cannot distinguish between the two groups directly. Both types of consumer potentially wish to consume up to two units of the product. Low-value users have utility of 2 from their first unit and further utility of 1 from the second unit. High-value users have utility twice as high: their utility is 4 from the first unit and 2 from the second unit. The fraction of high-value users among the consumers is λ, say. If production is costless when the firm sets a linear price, the profit-maximizing price is $p = 2$ (regardless of the fraction λ). With such a price, the low-value users consume a single unit while the high-value users consume two units. Suppose next that the firm sets a nonlinear tariff, and that its price for a consumer's first unit is p_1 while its price for a subsequent unit is p_2. Then one can show that the profit-maximizing nonlinear tariff is $p_1 = 2$, $p_2 = 1$ if $\lambda < \frac{1}{2}$, and $p_1 = 4$, $p_2 = 2$ if $\lambda > \frac{1}{2}$. Thus, when low-value users are more numerous, the introduction of nonlinear pricing causes the low-value users to consume two units, which is efficient. This results in a Pareto improvement compared to linear pricing. However, when high-value users are more numerous, the optimal strategy for the firm is to exclude the low-value users completely so as to fully extract the high-value surplus. Total welfare decreases in this case compared with linear pricing, and all consumers are weakly worse off. In particular, this simple example shows that nonlinear pricing has an ambiguous effect on welfare relative to linear pricing.

While a consideration of when markets open or shut due to price discrimination does offer some insights—in particular, the possibility of Pareto improvements is an uncontroversial benefit of price discrimination—this analysis does not take us very far. For instance, the welfare difference between a market being shut down and being open a tiny bit is not significant. Moreover, in practice, markets are rarely completely shut down when price discrimination is banned. (In virtually all countries, there is someone who is willing to pay almost any price for a luxury car or a pharmaceutical product.) For this reason in the next section we discuss the effect of price discrimination on total output.

12.4 Effect of Price Discrimination on Output

A focus of earlier work on price discrimination has been on its effect on output. If different products have different (marginal) prices when those products have the same marginal cost, then total output is suboptimally distributed from a social welfare perspective. However, it might be that output increases when firms are permitted to engage in price discrimination, and this effect might be sufficient to outweigh the undesirable "unequal marginal utilities" effect. By this insight one may deduce that if price discrimination does *not* lead the firm(s) to expand output, it will cause welfare to fall.[14] However, this does not tell us much in the event that discrimination causes total output to rise, since welfare might then be higher or lower. Thus using changes in output as a test for the welfare effects of price discrimination is capable only of delivering bad news. Moreover, outside some classroom examples, it is rarely easy to find conditions that characterize when output rises or falls with discrimination, and very detailed knowledge of consumer demand is needed to formulate accurate public policy.[15] However, if the firm is *regulated* the comparison is sometimes easier. For instance, Armstrong and Vickers (1991) and Armstrong, Cowan, and Vickers (1995) show that with common forms of average price regulation, total output necessarily increases if the firm is permitted to engage in price discrimination. As already emphasized, however, this does not imply that price discrimination will be welfare improving.[16]

Another insight is that if the strong market is also the large market, then allowing price discrimination is often good for output and welfare. To see this, consider the next example.[17] Consumers each wish to purchase a single unit of a monopolist's product. Consumers either have a high valuation v_H for the unit or a low valuation $v_L < v_H$. There are two markets, 1 and 2, and the fraction of the consumers in market i who have a high valuation is λ_i. Suppose $\lambda_1 \geq \lambda_2$ so that market 1 has the greater proportion of high-value consumers. Suppose that production is costless. If the firm is able to practice third-degree price discrimination across the two markets, it will set a high price v_H in market i if $\lambda_i v_H \geq v_L$, and otherwise, it will set the low price v_L. If the firm cannot discriminate, it will base its price on the overall fraction of high-value consumers across the two markets. If a fraction β of all consumers are in market 1, the overall fraction of high-value consumers is $\bar{\lambda} = \beta\lambda_1 + (1 - \beta)\lambda_2$. If the proportion of high-value consumers is similar in the two markets so that the discriminating firm would like to set the same price in the two markets (either both high or both low), then clearly policy toward discrimination has no impact on prices. However, if the distribution of consumers is quite asymmetric, in the sense that

$$\lambda_1 > \frac{v_L}{v_H} > \lambda_2,$$

the discriminating monopolist would set a high price in market 1 (the strong market) and a low price in market 2 (the weak market). In this case policy that prohibits price discrimination will certainly have an effect on prices. If the weak market is the larger market, in the sense that $\bar{\lambda} < v_L/v_H$, the nondiscriminating firm will choose to set a low uniform price. This will increase consumer surplus and total welfare relative to the situation with price discrimination. On the other hand, if the strong market is the larger market, in the sense that $\bar{\lambda} > v_L/v_H$, the firm will respond to a ban on discrimination by setting a high price to everyone. This high price will harm consumers in the weak market, and lower total welfare. In sum, when a weak market—a market with relatively few high-valuation consumers—is also a relatively small market, then price discrimination is likely to help consumers in this market and improve overall welfare. So policy that effects a per se ban on price discrimination by country, say, may be too blunt a policy.

Extending this monopoly analysis to situations of oligopoly does not usually make the effect of price discrimination on output easier to predict, since one must consider firm-level elasticities as well as market elasticities.[18] One exception to this occurs in Armstrong and Vickers (2001, sec. 4). Here the focus is on the competitive limit where prices are close to marginal cost, and it is shown that if the weak market is also the market with lower market elasticity then total output falls with discrimination, and hence so does welfare. In competitive environments, firms might be forced to set a lower price in the "wrong" market (i.e., in the less elastic market), since firm-level elasticities might differ drastically from market-level elasticities. By contrast, with monopoly the firm generally sets high prices in the correct (inelastic) markets.

12.5 Rise and Fall of Prices Caused by Price Discrimination

It is intuitive in many situations that when a firm is permitted to engage in price discrimination some of its prices will fall while others will rise. That is to say, the nondiscriminatory price is some kind of "average" of the discriminatory prices.

Consider first the case of monopoly supply. Suppose that a monopolist serves two markets, 1 and 2, that have independent consumer demands. The firm's profit in market i when it sets the price p_i in that market is denoted $\pi_i(p_i)$. Then the profit-maximizing discriminatory prices are characterized by $\pi_i'(p_i) = 0$, while the profit-maximizing uniform price p satisfies $\pi_1'(p) + \pi_2'(p) = 0$. Except in the knife-edge case where there is no gain from discrimination, it follows that in one market i we have $\pi_i'(p) < 0$ and in the other market $\pi_j'(p) > 0$. Assuming that profit functions are single-peaked, it follows that if the monopoly can price discriminate it will lower its price in market i and raise its price in market j.

Matters are more complicated when there are competing suppliers. As emphasized in Corts (1998), the chief difference with monopoly is that a market might be strong for one firm but weak for its rival. In such cases price discrimination can cause *all* prices to fall, as discussed in section 12.6 below. However, when firms do not differ in their judgment of which markets are strong, Corts shows that when price discrimination is permitted, prices will rise in the market that both firms view as strong and prices will fall in the market that both firms view as being weak. (Corts uses the term "best-response symmetry" when firms agree about which market is strong and which is weak.) Armstrong and Vickers (2001, sec. 4) and Armstrong (2006, sec. 3.2) provide simple examples of best-response symmetry where price discrimination causes some prices to rise and others to fall. In both examples industry profit rises when discrimination is permitted, while consumer surplus falls.

The discussion in this section has considered only the case of third-degree price discrimination so far. Consider next a monopoly bundling example.[19] There are two products, 1 and 2, provided by a monopolist. Consumers are characterized by their valuations v_1 and v_2, where v_i is a consumer's valuation for product i. Suppose that her valuation for consuming both products is just the sum $v_1 + v_2$. In general, the firm sets three prices: p_1 is the firm's price for product 1 alone, p_2 is the price for product 2 alone, and p_{12} is the price for the bundle of products 1 and 2. Figure 12.1 shows the resulting pattern of demand (when $p_{12} < p_1 + p_2$).

Suppose the marginal cost of supplying either product is zero and consumer valuations (v_1, v_2) are uniformly distributed on the unit square $[0, 1]^2$. If bundling is not possible (i.e., $p_{12} = p_1 + p_2$), the profit-maximizing price for each product is $\frac{1}{2}$ and the firm makes profit of $\frac{1}{2}$. If the firm is able to price discriminate by means of offering a discount for joint purchase ($p_{12} < p_1 + p_2$), one can show the profit-maximizing prices are $p_{12} = \frac{4}{3} - \frac{1}{3}\sqrt{2} \approx 0.862$ for the bundle of two products and $p_1 = p_2 = \frac{2}{3}$ for each stand-alone product. Thus the price for joint consumption is lower than with unbundled pricing, while the price for a single item is higher. In this example at least, the market for joint consumption is the weak market while the market for individual consumption is the strong market. This pricing policy results in profits approximately equal to 0.55, which is 10 percent higher than the profit without bundling. One can calculate that aggregate consumer surplus with this mixed bundling policy is given by 0.255, which compares to 0.25 with independent pricing. Thus aggregate consumer surplus also increases (slightly) when mixed bundling is used, although those consumers with strong taste for one product but not the other are worse off with the bundling policy since they constitute the strong market. Again,

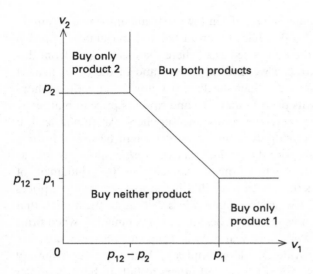

Figure 12.1
Pattern of consumer demand with monopoly bundling

we see that price discrimination is not necessarily harmful to consumers or welfare, even in a monopoly context.

12.6   Intense Competition Arising from Price Discrimination

Perhaps surprisingly, there are several situations where permitting firms to engage in price discrimination causes *all* prices to fall and competition to become intensified. The models discussed here fall into two categories: those that discriminate on the basis of consumer brand preferences and those that discriminate on the basis of competitive bundling. We discuss these in turn. (Further situations in which price discrimination leads to tougher competition are found in the dynamic context presented later in section 12.9.)

Following the analysis of the previous section, consider cases where firms differ in their view of which markets are strong and which are weak. Corts uses the term "best-response asymmetry" for these cases.[20] Take, for example, the model of Thisse and Vives (1988). There are two firms in a Hotelling market. Suppose first that firms can observe each consumer's location (or brand preference) and can price accordingly. A firm will then set a relatively high price to nearby consumers in order to exploit those consumers' unwillingness to travel so far to the other firm, so its nearby consumers constitute a firm's strong market. In particular, one firm's strong market is the other's weak market. In equilibrium, consumers purchase the product from the preferred firm, which is efficient, and those consumers who are almost indifferent between the two brands will obtain the best deal. If firms must set a uniform price to all consumers, however, Thisse and Vives show that this uniform price can be above all the discriminatory prices. Thus, when there is best-response asymmetry, it is possible that all prices decrease with price discrimination. In this model price discrimination has no impact on total welfare, since all consumers just wish to buy a single unit, and they buy this unit from the closer firm with either pricing regime.[21] All consumers clearly benefit from price discrimination. Firms, however, make lower profits when they engage in this form of price discrimination compared to when they must offer a uniform price.[22] As Thisse and Vives (1988, page 134) put it:

[D]enying a firm the right to meet the price of a competitor on a discriminatory basis provides the latter with some protection against price attacks. The effect is then to weaken competition, contrary to the belief of the proponents of naive application of legislation prohibiting price discrimination like the Robinson-Patman Act.

The fact that firms might be worse off when they practice price discrimination is one of the key differences between monopoly and competition. Ignoring issues of commitment for now (see section 12.9.1 below), a monopolist is always better off when it can price discriminate: the firm is free to choose a uniform price when discrimination is permitted, but in general, it is better off setting different prices. In the same way, an oligopolistic firm is always better off if it can price discriminate, compared to when it cannot, for *given* prices offered by its rivals. However, as in many instances of strategic interaction, once account is taken of what rivals too will do, firms in equilibrium can be worse off when price discrimination is permitted. Firms then find themselves in a classic Prisoner's Dilemma.

We turn next to examples concerning bundling. The first such example is taken from Matutes and Regibeau (1992), where two symmetric firms each offer a version of two products. Consumers wish to purchase one unit of both products. (These two products can be purchased from the same firm or from two different firms.) In their example Matutes and Regibeau show that when firms are able to offer a discount for joint consumption, the firms' prices are uniformly below the equilibrium prices without bundling. Of course, each firm's profit then falls when bundling is employed. Clearly, consumers are all better off as a result of the price reductions caused by price discrimination. However, there is *excessive loyalty*: because of the bundle discount too many consumers buy both products from the same firm than is efficient, so welfare falls with this form of discrimination.[23] The economic reason why mixed bundling acts to intensify competition is rather subtle, and awaits further clarification. (It cannot be anything to do with best-response asymmetry, since firms do not view the various kinds of consumer as strong or weak in different ways.)

The final examples in this section involve a multi-product firm facing a *single*-product rival. I discuss two such examples. The first one involves pure bundling and the second involves third-degree price discrimination. Consider this bundling example.[24] Suppose that there are two products, 1 and 2, and each consumer potentially would like a unit of each product. Firm A supplies both products and holds a monopoly over product 1, while firm B supplies a variant of product 2. Suppose that consumers have additive utility for the two products. Consumers have homogeneous preferences for product 1, and all have the same reservation value, v_1, for this item. The two firms supply imperfectly substitutable versions of product 2, and if firm A sets the (unbundled) price p_2^A while B sets the price p_2^B, firm A's product 2 demand is $q_2^A(p_2^A, p_2^B)$ and B has demand $q_2^B(p_2^A, p_2^B)$. Firm A has marginal cost $c_1^A < v_1$ for product 1 and marginal cost c_2^A for its product 2, while B has marginal cost c_2^B for its product 2. Then A's profit from product 2 is $(p_2^A - c_2^A)q_2^A(p_2^A, p_2^B)$, and B's profit is $(p_2^B - c_2^B)q_2^B(p_2^A, p_2^B)$. Given that A sets unbundled prices, its most profitable response to B's price p_2^B is denoted $p_2^A = R_{SEP}^A(p_2^B)$, and similarly B's best response to A's price p_2^A is denoted $p_2^B = R_2^B(p_2^A)$. When firm A sets unbundled prices for its two products, the prices for product 2 are determined by the intersection of these two reaction functions, as depicted by γ on figure 12.2. (Firm A sets the monopoly price $p_1^A = v_1$ for product 1.)

Next suppose that firm A commits to sell its two products as a pure bundle, while prices are determined in a second stage. Say that firm A's price for the bundle is p_{12}^A. A consumer deciding whether to buy from firm A or firm B knows that when she buys from A, she obtains an extra utility v_1 due to the additional consumption of product 1. Therefore firm A's "effective price" for product 2 is $p_2^A = p_{12}^A - v_1$, and the demand for A's bundle is just $q_2^A(p_{12}^A - v_1, p_2^B)$. Firm A's total profit is

$$(p_{12}^A - c_1^A - c_2^A)q_2^A(p_{12}^A - v_1, p_2^B) = (p_2^A - [c_2^A - \{v_1 - c_1^A\}])q_2^A(p_2^A, p_2^B).$$

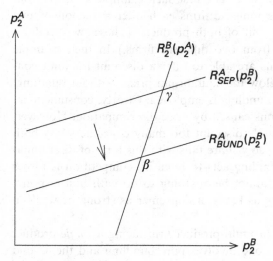

Figure 12.2
Strategic effect of pure bundling

This is similar to its profit from product 2 when there is unbundled pricing, except that its cost c_2^A is shifted down by $\{v_1 - c_1^A\}$. Therefore firm A's most profitable effective price p_2^A, given B's price p_2^B, which is denoted $p_2^A = p_{12}^A - v_1 = R_{BUND}^A(p_2^B)$, is shifted *downward* compared to the case of unbundled pricing. The (effective) prices for product 2 are now located at β on figure 12.2, which are lower for both firms. Typically both firms' profits fall when firm A offers its products as a bundle. Therefore, when there is an existing firm in market 2—so that entry deterrence is not an issue—in this particular model we would not expect the multi-product firm to choose to sell its products as a bundle.

Why does bundling by the multi-product firm lead to more intense competition? As explained by Whinston (1990), when firm A bundles its products, in order to make profitable sales of its monopolized product 1, it must also make sales of its product 2. This leads it to cut price in an effort to take sales away from firm B, an effect Whinston terms "strategic foreclosure." However, whether this strategic foreclosure effect operates or not depends on the details of the model, as we will see in section 12.7.

A closely related model involves third-degree discrimination instead of bundling.[25] Suppose that firm A serves two independent markets, 1 and 2. Market 1 is monopolized by firm A, whereas in market 2 there is a rival firm B. If firm A can price discriminate in the sense that it may offer selective price cuts and set distinct prices in the two markets, it will set the monopoly price in market 1, while prices in market 2 will be determined by the competitive interaction between the two firms. On the other hand, if firm A cannot set different prices in the two markets, it will have to trade off the benefits of setting a low price in the competitive market versus a high price in the captive market. In particular, if firm A prefers to set a higher price in the captive market than in the competitive market, so that the former is firm A's strong market, the effect of a ban on price discrimination is to reduce the price in the captive market and to raise prices in the competitive market. The profit of the single-product rival clearly increases when such a ban is imposed, while the effect on firm A's overall profit is not clear-cut.[26]

12.7 Discrimination That Can Relax Competition

There are a variety of ways in which price discrimination can act to relax competitive pressures in the markets, to the detriment of consumers.[27]

When a multi-product firm faces a single-product rival, it is possible that bundling can act to reduce the intensity of competition.[28] To see this, suppose again that there are two products, 1 and 2. Firm A supplies both products, while firm B can supply only product 2. The two firms here offer identical versions of product 2. A consumer has valuation v_1 for product 1 and v_2 for product 2 (and valuation $v_1 + v_2$ for both products). Suppose that the firms' costs of supply are normalized to zero. For simplicity, suppose that (v_1, v_2) is uniformly distributed on the unit square $[0, 1]^2$. Then, if firm A sets unbundled prices for its two products, it will set the monopoly price $p_1^A = \frac{1}{2}$ in its captive market. All profits are competed away for product 2, and that product's price is equal to zero. Therefore, with unbundled pricing, firm A's profit is $\frac{1}{4}$, while firm B makes nothing.

Suppose instead that firm A commits to bundle its two products together, prior to the two firms choosing prices. Firm A sets a price p_{12}^A for its bundle, while firm B sets the price p_2^B for its product. Figure 12.1 depicts the pattern of consumer demand (where $p_1^A = \infty$). By calculating the areas in the figure, one can calculate the equilibrium prices, which are approximately $p_{12}^A \approx 0.61$ and $p_2^B \approx 0.24$. Therefore all prices rise compared to the situation where firm A sets unbundled prices. So bundling helps differentiate the two firms' offerings: firm A offers a superior "product" (by virtue of its additional product 1 in the bundle). The respective profits of the two firms are approximately $\pi^A \approx 0.367$ and $\pi^B \approx 0.067$, which are also both higher compared to when firm A prices its products separately. This example, in combination with the discussion of the Whinston model in the previous section, indicates that the effect of bundling on a multi-product firm's incentive to be aggressive to single-product rivals is ambiguous and depends on the fine details of the model of consumer demand. Without very detailed data on consumer preferences, it is hard for an anti-trust authority to predict a priori whether bundling will relax or intensify competition.

Another way in which price discrimination might relax competition is when *price-matching* contracts are used, namely when a firm promises consumers it will match a lower price of a rival firm if consumers can find evidence of such a price. Such contracts are a form of price discrimination, since the price a consumer pays differs according to their knowledge of other firms' prices and their willingness to go to the trouble to provide evidence of a lower price. If consumers are well informed about all rivals' prices and there are no effort costs involved in documenting the lower prices, there is a clear danger of collusion: there is no incentive for one firm to undercut another because the low-priced firm will not obtain greater market share and will simply lower its and its rivals' prices. In this stark framework, public policy that prohibits the use of such "competitor-based" discrimination schemes will help restore normal competitive pressure in the market, to the benefit of consumers. However, if consumers face costs of searching for price offers or providing evidence of low prices, a more conventional price discrimination motive emerges: sorting consumers on the basis of their value of time (akin to the use of discount coupons). In such cases the collusive impact of competitor-based discrimination is blunted, and consumers might sometimes be better off when this form of price discrimination is employed.[29]

A further way in which price discrimination might act to limit competition occurs when it leads to negative network effects. Consider an telecommunications market in which subscribers join one network or another. Public policy might or might not permit firms to price discriminate on the basis of the destination network. This form of discrimination is present if a subscriber on network A faces a different call charge if his call is made to another subscriber on network A or to a subscriber on a rival network B. If firms each make it *cheaper* to make calls to people on rival networks than to people on their own network, then negative network effects are present. All else equal, subscribers will prefer to join a smaller network because then a greater fraction of their calls can be made at the cheap rate. It is well known that markets with negative network effects of this form are not very competitive, since a firm that offers a low price will not attract many new subscribers. Therefore this form of price discrimination can act to relax competition, to the detriment of consumers.[30]

12.8 Effects of Discrimination on Entry

The effects of price discrimination on entry is a central concern of competition policy. Three broad issues are discussed: (1) the effect on the equilibrium number of firms in a monopolistic competition framework, (2) the effect on a monopolist's incentive to enter an adjacent market, and (3) the effect on a potential entrant's incentive to enter a monopolized market.

12.8.1 Free Entry
Price discrimination can raise or lower equilibrium profits in a market with a given number of firms, as seen in the previous sections. When there is free entry of firms, it follows that the equilibrium number of firms will rise with price discrimination in the former case but will fall in the latter case when more intense competition will drive out some firms. In some common models of oligopolistic interaction—though by no means all—it is well known that free entry will result in too many firms entering from a total welfare perspective.[31] In those cases where price discrimination raises profits, the resulting greater entry will only exacerbate the welfare costs of excessive entry. By contrast, when price discrimination destroys profits, the excess entry problem will be mitigated (although typically not overturned).[32]

12.8.2 A Monopolist's Incentive to Enter an Adjacent Market
The second topic in this section involves a monopolist in one market entering an "adjacent" market. The motives considered here are not necessarily anticompetitive—there need not be a motive to drive firms out of the adjacent market—but rather the firm wishes to engage in price discrimination, and in some situations the only way it can do this is by participating in the adjacent market.

Ability to Offer Quantity Discounts   In this example, product 1 is monopolized by firm A, while product 2 is potentially supplied in a competitive market with price equal to cost. For simplicity, suppose that all production is costless. Product 2 is a complementary product to product 1 but consumed in variable quantities by consumers. Consumers wish to buy just one unit of product 1, however. (The classical examples of this situation are computers and punch cards, or photocopiers and toner.) Consumers differ in how much of the joint product they wish to consume. Let the demand for the joint product by a consumer with demand parameter θ be $\theta - p_2$ if the marginal price for product 2 is p_2. Let θ be uniformly distributed between 0 and 1. If p_1 is the price for product 1, a consumer's net surplus is $\frac{1}{2}(\theta - p_2)^2 - p_1$. Therefore a consumer will participate in the market if $\theta \geq \sqrt{2p_1} + p_2$, and total demand for product 1 and product 2 is respectively

$$q_1 = 1 - (\sqrt{2p_1} + p_2), \quad q_2 = \frac{1}{2}(1 - p_2)^2 - p_1.$$

If the monopolist for product 1 ties the purchase of its monopoly product to purchase of the potentially competitive product 2, it can set a price above cost for product 2. It will then choose the pair of prices (p_1, p_2) to maximize total profit $p_1q_1 + p_2q_2$, and this entails $p_1 = 0.08$ and $p_2 = 0.2$. This brings in profit of 0.08, while consumer surplus is approximately 0.043. In particular, the monopolist indeed wants to set a price above cost for product 2.[33] If the monopolist did not tie product 2 with product 1, all active consumers will buy product 2 on the competitive market with price $p_2 = 0$. This strategy will surely bring the monopolist less profit than the tying strategy (since it could choose $p_2 = 0$ under the tying regime but chose to set $p_2 = 0.2$). Therefore the monopolist has an incentive to "leverage" its monopoly position for product 1 into the market for product 2. If such tying is not permitted (so $p_2 = 0$), the monopolist would significantly increase its product 1 price to $p_1 = 0.22$. Its profit is then 0.074, while consumer surplus is essentially unchanged at 0.044. In this example total welfare is then higher if the monopolist is permitted to tie its product, although in general the comparison is ambiguous.[34] Notice also that the monopolist chooses to pursue this tying strategy even if it incurs a slightly higher cost in supplying product 2 than do the competitive rivals. (This result assumes that the monopolist cannot monitor a consumer's consumption of product 2 from rival suppliers.) In this sense the monopolist has an incentive to exclude more efficient rivals.

Ability to Offer Bundling Discounts   Since a multi-product monopolist typically gains when it can bundle its products (see the discussion in section 12.5), the multi-product monopolist makes greater total profit than if the same products were supplied by a series of single-product monopolies. (If the products were supplied by single-product firms, then prices would be product by product.) This is true even when the various products are neither complements or substitutes in the usual sense. In technical terms, there may be "informational economies of scope" involved in multi-product supply, even if more familiar economies of scope are not present.[35]

To illustrate, return to the example in section 12.5 where there are two products, 1 and 2, and consumers have valuations (v_1, v_2) for these two products individually and valuation $v_1 + v_2$ for joint consumption. If production is costless and the valuations are uniformly distributed on $[0, 1]^2$, the multi-product monopolist obtains profit of 0.55 by practicing mixed bundling, while a pair of single-product monopolies each supplying one product make a combined profit of 0.5. To see how this affects a monopolist's incentive to enter an adjacent market, consider the following broadcasting scenario: There is an incumbent broadcaster who currently holds broadcasting rights to a particular sports event. The rights to a second, perhaps unrelated, sports event then become available for auction. Because the incumbent broadcaster will be able to engage in bundling if it obtains the second rights, but a new broadcaster will not, the incumbent will be willing to pay more for the new rights than a new broadcaster. (It will be prepared to pay up to 0.3 for the new rights, whereas a new broadcaster can only pay 0.25.)

Thus, even if for no other reason, this argument suggests that an existing rights holder is likely to win a bidding war for any new rights. Indeed, in a richer model where the entrant might offer a superior service (e.g., it has lower supply costs or a higher quality service), the incumbent might be prepared to pay more for the additional rights than the superior entrant. However, set against this is the fact that consumers often benefit from bundling. For instance, in this example, consumers are better off if the incumbent wins the new rights and practices bundling. Thus, if policy makers are deciding whether to permit bundling, they might have to trade off the possible consumer benefits of bundling against the possible foreclosure of more efficient entrants. The information required to implement accurate policy in this environment is formidable.

This provides a simple example of "conglomeration" effects (or "portfolio" or "range" effects), which have risen in prominence in antitrust cases in recent years. See Neven chapter 5 in this volume for a more detailed account of such cases, which include the controversial *General Electric/Honeywell* merger. One reason why these cases are challenging for the competition authorities is that the standard approaches to market definition no longer always apply well.[36]

12.8.3 An Entrant's Incentive to Enter a Monopolized Market

One of the most controversial aspects of price discrimination is the possible impact of an incumbent's ability to price discriminate on the incentives for entry. There are a number of ways in which price discrimination by an incumbent firm affects the incentives to enter its markets. Constraining the incumbent's freedom to choose its prices affects its response to entry, and hence the expected postentry profits of the entrant.

This is illustrated in the context of the model of third-degree price discrimination based on Armstrong and Vickers (1993) discussed in section 12.6. There is a multi-market incumbent facing potential entry into one of its markets. If the incumbent is permitted to set different prices in its two markets, then it is plausible that it will react more aggressively to entry compared to when it must set the same price in the competitive and the captive market. We conclude that the postentry profit of the entrant is likely to be lower when the incumbent can price discriminate than when it cannot. If the entrant has a fixed cost of entry, it will enter only if it expects postentry profit to cover its entry cost. There are then three cases to consider. If the entry cost is large, there will be no entry regardless of whether the incumbent can price discriminate. In this case the social desirability of price discrimination is exactly as in the standard monopoly case, and this is ambiguous in general. Similarly, if the entry cost is very small, entry will take place regardless of policy toward price discrimination. The interesting case is where the cost of entry lies in the intermediate range so that entry is profitable only if the incumbent cannot price discriminate, and a ban on price discrimination then acts to induce entry. In such cases it is plausible that a ban on price discrimination will cause the prices in *both* markets to fall: if discrimination is possible, there will be no entry and the incumbent will charge monopoly prices in each market; if the incumbent must charge a common price in the two markets, this will bring in the entrant and force both of the incumbent's prices down from monopoly levels.

The general principle, as in the Thisse-Vives quote in section 12.6 above, is that denying an incumbent the right to meet the price of a competitor on a discriminatory basis provides the latter with some protection against price attacks. While the effect of a ban on price discrimination is indeed to weaken competition if the entrant is already in the market, once the ex ante incentives to enter are considered, the effect of a ban on price discrimination might actually be pro-competitive. However, the welfare effects of a ban on price discrimination in this context are not clear-cut. For instance, since the incumbent is reluctant to cut its profits in the captive market by meeting its rival's price in the competitive market, even a highly inefficient entrant might prosper. While preventing an incumbent from engaging in selective price cuts is likely to be a powerful means with which to assist entry, as with many forms of indirect entry assistance the danger of inefficient entry is never far away.

This question of whether to permit (above-cost) selective price cuts is of substantial importance in practice. For instance, many network industry incumbents (e.g., privatized telecom companies) are required to offer geographically uniform retail tariffs, even though they face competition only in particular areas (e.g., cities). While such a policy acts to encourage entry and to "bring the benefits of competition to the whole country" (as it is often put), it also induces inefficient, or excessive, entry into the attractive market segments. The question is particularly important in markets without a history of regulation. For instance, Vickers (2005, p. F249) summarizes a recent antitrust case involving shipping:

Above-cost price cuts were at issue in the case of *Compagnie Maritime Belge*, on which the ECJ gave judgment in 2000. The enterprise, which had a near-monopoly position on certain shipping routes between Europe and West Africa, had selectively cut prices to match those of its competitor, though not demonstrably to below total average cost. The Court saw the risk that condemning such pricing could give inefficient rivals a safe haven from the full rigors of competition, but in the circumstances at hand judged that there was abuse (albeit not abuse under the heading of predation) because the selective price cuts were aimed at eliminating competition while allowing continuing higher prices for uncontested services.

The situation where a firm selectively lowers its prices in more competitive markets is closely connected to the situation where a firm selectively offers low prices to customers of a rival. (I will discuss this issue in more detail in section 12.9, albeit mostly in the context of competition between symmetric firms.) When firms are symmetric, we will see that selective price cuts to a rival's past customers can reduce prices to all consumers.

A second way in which price discrimination might impede entry concerns (pure) bundling.[37] Recall from section 12.6 Whinston's (1990) model where, if a multi-product firm bundles its two products, the equilibrium profits of the single-product rival are reduced. If then the multi-product incumbent can commit to bundle its products together before the entry decision has been made, the lower bundled prices can act to deter entry. (Again, this will depend on the size of the fixed cost of entry.) Once entry is deterred, the incumbent can raise its bundle price to the monopoly level. There are a broad range of situations in which the incumbent may find it privately profitable to deter entry in this way, but at a detriment to total welfare, which will be higher if entry takes place. Such instances provide a coherent case for a ban on bundling by an incumbent.

From the incumbent's point of view, one problem with the strategy is that if entry *does* take place, the incumbent also makes lower profits with bundling than with unbundled prices. That is to say, its plan to bundle products might not be credible. The entrant might predict that the incumbent will renege on its promise to bundle if entry does take place, in which case the threat to bundle carries little weight. However, there are plenty of cases where the bundling decision is a long-term decision (e.g., if it is built into the product design), in which case it has credibility and the ability to deter entry.[38]

Another problem is that apparently minor changes to the model imply that bundling, even if credible, will not deter entry. For instance, in section 12.7 we saw that if consumers have heterogeneous valuations for the monopolized product, both firms' profits will be higher if the multi-product firm bundles its products. Bundling then acts to *encourage* entry. The incumbent may still want to deter entry so that it can set monopoly prices in both of its markets, but if there is a fixed cost of entry, the incumbent may need to commit to unbundled pricing to deter entry (even though after entry does occur, the incumbent may need to revert to the bundling strategy and so boost both firms' profits). In this example the monopolist choosing to unbundle its products obtains higher profit (0.5) than with monopoly bundling after the entry in one market (which yields the incumbent profit of only 0.367).

This discussion of bundling so far has assumed the two products enter additively into the consumer's utility: the fact that a consumer has purchased product 1 has no impact on her willingness to pay for product 2. Many examples of bundling involve complements. In the extreme case of perfect complements, a consumer places no value on product 2 unless she also has product 1. The analysis changes somewhat when the two products are perfect complements. For one thing, a firm with a monopoly on one component clearly has the *ability* to foreclose entry into the complementary product market, simply by bundling its two components together. Whether it has the incentive to do this is another question. Whinston (1990, sec. III) shows in a benchmark model that the incumbent has no such incentive. Indeed the incumbent generally benefits from the presence of a differentiated entrant in one component market. For instance, if the entrant provides an identical product 2 component but at lower cost, the incumbent will be able to extract all the entrant's profit by setting a product 2 price below its own cost, and raising its product 1 price accordingly. This is an instance of the Chicago School's insight that an incumbent has no incentive to prevent entry by a more efficient firm in a complementary product market.[39] Similarly, if the entrant offers a differentiated product 2 component that appeals more to some consumers than the incumbent's own product, the incumbent will make more profit by allowing the entrant to deliver its monopoly component to the entrant's own pool of consumers.[40]

Remaining in the context of perfect complements, Choi and Stafanadis (2001) examine the case where an entrant must innovate if it is to produce a successful substitute for one of the incumbent's components. If the incumbent bundles its two product, this implies that there is no scope for single component entry. Entry then requires successful innovation on *both* fronts. Bundling can therefore reduce the incentive to innovate, and so can increase the probability that the incumbent retains its markets. However, it is not always optimal for the incumbent to bundle, since it benefits when an entrant successfully innovates on just one component (as in the previous paragraph). Carlton and Waldman (2002) present a model where entry into the monopolized market is more likely to occur if the entrant is first active in the competitive market. If the entrant offers a superior product in the competitive market, or if its costs are lower there, then entry there is socially desirable. If entry were to be limited to that market, the incumbent would also welcome entry (as in the previous paragraph). However, the incumbent might choose to bundle its products and prevent desirable entry into the competitive market in order to discourage subsequent entry into its captive market.

12.9 Dynamic Price Discrimination

A topic that has received much recent attention is dynamic price discrimination. A publisher sets a high price for a new (hardback) book, and subsequently the price is reduced. Or a retailer uses information it has obtained from its previous dealings with a customer to offer that customer a special deal (or, as we will see, sometimes a bad deal). As discussed in the introduction, these forms of price discrimination seem to have proliferated in recent years with developments in information technology. The cases of monopoly and duopoly supply are discussed in turn.

12.9.1 Monopoly
Classical results demonstrate that (1) if a monopolist can commit to its future prices, it often does not wish to engage in intertemporal price discrimination,[41] and (2) if the firm

cannot commit to its future prices, it will decrease its price over time, its total profit is lower than in case (1) while consumers are better off compared to case (1).[42] A ban on price discrimination in this context, even if feasible, will act to boost the monopolist's profits and harm consumers, since it gives the firm commitment power.

In more detail, suppose the firm can sell its product over two periods. There are two classes of model that are relevant. First, there is the "single-sale" (or durable good) model where a consumer wishes to buy just a single unit of the good over the time horizon (e.g., a new novel). Second, there is the "repeated-sale" model, where a consumer potentially wishes to consume in both periods (e.g., at a supermarket or online retailer).

Consider first the single-sale model. Suppose that there is a diverse population of consumers, each of whom wishes to buy just a single unit of a monopolist's good. As in section 12.2 the consumer's valuation for this item v varies among consumers according to the distribution function $F(v)$.

First suppose that consumers are myopic: they will buy the good as soon as the price offered is lower than their valuation v. Then the firm can fully extract consumer surplus by offering a price that decreases over time. By moving down the demand curve in this way, first-degree price discrimination is achieved. Notice that there is no issue about the firm committing to a price path over time in this special case where consumers are myopic.

If consumers are forward-looking, however, the firm will not be able to extract consumer surplus fully, even if it can commit to future prices. Moreover the firm will lose profit if it cannot commit to a time path for prices. Initially, say that the firm can commit to a price pair $\{p_1, p_2\}$, where p_t is its price in period $t = 1, 2$. For simplicity, assume that v is uniformly distributed on $[0, 1]$ and that production is costless. It is then straightforward to show that the profit-maximizing price pair is $p_1 = p_2 = \frac{1}{2}$. Therefore, there is no inter-temporal discrimination, and consumers buy either in the first period or not at all. This analysis changes if consumers are forward-looking and the firm is able to "change its mind" in the second period. Once consumers with $v \geq \frac{1}{2}$ have purchased in the first period, the firm is left with a pool of less enthusiastic consumers. So in the second period the profit-maximizing policy is to set $p_2 = \frac{1}{4}$. Of course, if consumers foresee that the firm will behave in this opportunistic manner, their first period choice will be affected, and some consumers will strategically delay their purchase in order to receive the discounted price next period. To counteract this effect, the firm will optimally set an initial price $p_1 < \frac{1}{2}$. In sum, when the firm has the freedom to set its second-period price only after the initial period, *both* prices decrease compared to the case where the firm can commit (when $p_1 = p_2 = \frac{1}{2}$). If, somehow, public policy prohibits inter-termporal price discrimination so that the firm is forced to set $p_2 = p_1$, this will restore the firm's ability to commit to future prices, and will boost profit and harm consumers.

Next, consider the repeated-sale model. Suppose that an individual consumer has the same valuation v for a unit in each of the two periods. Now the firm has potentially three prices to choose: p_1, the price for a unit in the first period; p_2, the price in the second period if the consumer did not purchase in the first period; and $\hat{p}_2$, the price for a unit in the second period if the consumer also purchased in the first period. When the firm can commit to its second-period prices, one can show that the profit-maximizing pricing policy is just to set $p_1 = p_2 = \hat{p}_2 = \frac{1}{2}$. Therefore it is optimal not to price discriminate. When the firm cannot commit, one can show that the most profitable prices satisfy[43]

$$p_2 \leq p_1 \leq \frac{1}{2} \leq \hat{p}_2.$$

Therefore, when the firm cannot commit to its future prices, it will set a relatively low first-period price ($p_1 \leq \frac{1}{2}$), and then a high second-period price for those (high-value) consumers who purchased in the first period ($\hat{p}_2 \geq \frac{1}{2}$) and an even lower second-period price aimed at those who did not purchase in the first period ($p_2 \leq p_1$).[44] In particular, the firm views its past customers as its strong market in the second period, and new customers as its weak market. (This ranking also holds in oligopoly settings below.) All consumers are better off when the firm cannot commit, while the firm is obviously worse off. Total welfare is also higher without commitment. Again, the effect of a ban on price discrimination is to give the firm commitment power, to the detriment of consumers.[45]

12.9.2 Oligopoly

In this section I discuss two repeated-sale models involving symmetric firms. In each model the firm learns about a consumer's brand preferences from that consumer's initial choice of firm. In one model, due to Fudenberg and Tirole (2000), consumers have a stable brand preference for one of the two firms. If a consumer buys from firm A in the first period, she will most likely prefer to buy from firm A in the second period as well, all else equal, and both firms will price accordingly. In the second model, due to Chen (1997b), consumers initially view the two firms as perfect substitutes, but in the second period they incur a switching cost if they change supplier, and firms price accordingly in the second period.[46]

In each model, firms set their second-period prices, taking as given their first-period market shares. That is, the framework is one where firms offer short-term contracts, and there is no commitment to future prices. In both models the second period resembles the static model of Thisse and Vives (1988) discussed in section 12.6: whenever such price discrimination is permitted, firms will price low to try to "poach" their rival's previous customers and price high to their own previous customers. Each firm regards its own previous customers as its strong market, and there is "best-response asymmetry" in the terminology of Corts (1998). The models therefore share the feature that second-period prices are all lower than they would be if behavior-based discrimination were not feasible.[47] Moreover both models predict there to be excessive switching in the second period, in the sense that some consumers will buy from their less preferred firm because they are tempted by the low poaching price. In general, in these simple models with unit demand, behavior-based price discrimination causes welfare to fall.[48]

While the two models are similar in terms of their predicted prices in the second period, they differ greatly in their prediction for how initial prices are determined. In broad terms, when behavior-based price discrimination is employed, the Fudenberg-Tirole model predicts that prices are initially high and then decline, while Chen's model suggests that prices are initially low and then rise. (This latter result is common to most switching cost models.) Fudenberg and Tirole show in an example that profit (over the two periods) falls and consumers in aggregate are better off when firms practice price discrimination. In Chen's model firms are always better off when price discrimination is not possible, and it is ambiguous whether consumers are better or worse off. (As already mentioned, in both models total welfare falls when price discrimination is employed.)

The discussion so far has not considered the possibility within the Fudenberg-Tirole framework that consumer brand preferences might change over time. For simplicity, consider the opposite polar case where second-period brand preferences are independent of those in the first period. In this case the consumer's choice of firm in the first period gives no useful information to firms in the second period, and there is no motive for a firm to set discriminatory prices to its own past customers and its rival's past customers. Suppose now that at the start of period 1, firms can commit to a dynamic pricing strategy; that is, they can credibly announce the three prices—the initial price, the second-period price if the consumer did not buy in the first period, and the second-period price if the consumer did buy from the firm in the first period. (This setting, where firms commit to explicit loyalty schemes, is broadly applicable to frequent flier programs, and the like.) In this case the static model of competitive mixed bundling by Matutes and Regibeau (1992), discussed in section 12.6, can be applied. The dynamic loyalty scheme causes all prices to fall compared to the case where firms did not make their second-period prices depend on whether the consumer purchased from them in the first period. The lowered prices are clearly good for consumers, although social welfare is reduced because there is excessive loyalty. This result provides an interesting contrast to the Fudenberg-Tirole model without commitment, where the inefficiency was due to *insufficient* loyalty to firms. It is important to recognize, though, that both forms of dynamic price discrimination—ex post discrimination to poach rival consumers and ex ante explicit loyalty schemes—are often pro-consumer in their impact.

So far, because we have assumed that the two firms are symmetric, we have not allowed for the exit of either firm. Antitrust scrutiny of price discrimination typically focuses on the case where one firm is dominant, but little work has been done on dynamic price discrimination when firms are asymmetric. Chen (2006) takes a first step, and shows that the use of behavior-based price discrimination can induce a weak firm to leave the market. For instance, he shows that the stronger firm will often price below cost when selling to the rival's past consumers, with the aim and effect of eliminating socially desirable competition. The use of this form of price discrimination to deter entry and induce exit deserves further scrutiny.

12.10 Price Discrimination in Vertically Related Markets

In practice, many of the most pressing antitrust concerns about price discrimination relate to the pricing of inputs. For instance, Article 82(c) of the EC Treaty states explicitly that a dominant firm is abusive if it applies "dissimilar conditions to equivalent transactions with other trading parties, thereby placing them at a competitive disadvantage." My discussion here is in two parts to cover cases where the upstream monopolist is vertically integrated or vertically separated.

Consider first a vertically integrated firm that supplies an essential input to a potential entrant. Suppose that the incumbent firm has marginal cost c_1 for supplying its service to final consumers and marginal cost c_2 for supplying the input to a potential entrant. The entrant needs one unit of the input for each unit of output it supplies, and it incurs marginal cost c for converting a unit of the input into a unit of the final product. (No firm incurs any fixed costs in this simple framework.) Suppose that consumers view the final products of the two firms as perfect substitutes, and they choose to buy from the lower priced firm. Suppose that the incumbent does not know the marginal cost c of the entrant at the time it sets its two prices p and a, where p is the incumbent's price to final consumers and a is its price for the input. Suppose that the cost c is perceived to be a random variable with distribution function $F(c)$. If the incumbent sets the two prices p and a, the entrant can profitably enter if its own costs are lower than the maximum price it can charge (i.e., when $a + c < p$). In this case the incumbent will make its profit solely from selling the input to the entrant; otherwise, the incumbent makes its profit solely from selling directly to final consumers. Therefore the incumbent's expected profit is

$$\pi = F(p - a)q(p)(a - c_2) + [1 - F(p - a)]q(p)(p - c_1).$$

If we write $m = p - a$ for the *margin* offered to the entrant, the profit can be written as

$$\pi = q(p)(p - c_1) + q(p)F(m)(c_1 - c_2 - m).$$

Then, regardless of the incumbent's decision about its retail price p, if free to do so it will choose m to maximize $F(m)(c_1 - c_2 - m)$. In general, this entails $m < c_1 - c_2$, or

$$a > c_2 + [p - c_1]. \tag{12.1}$$

What does price discrimination (as broadly interpreted) mean in this context? Intuitively, as with Article 82(c), the integrated firm discriminates against the entrant when the entrant faces a different (higher) cost for its input than does the "downstream" part of the integrated firm. But what is the true economic cost to the integrated firm in supplying a unit of the input to the entrant? One naive answer is that it is its physical cost c_2. But this ignores the opportunity cost element that when the integrated firm supplies a unit of input to the entrant, it supplies one less unit to final consumers and forgoes a profit there of $p - c_1$. That is to say, the economic cost to the monopolist of supplying a unit of the input to the rival is $c_2 + [p - c_1]$, and so the nondiscriminatory input price is

$$a = c_2 + [p - c_1].   \tag{12.2}$$

With this input price the potential entrant finds it profitable to enter only if this is the more efficient way to supply the product to final consumers. (With expression 12.2, the entrant will enter only if $c + c_2 < c_1$, i.e., when this is the lower cost method of delivering the product to consumers.) That is to say, if the input price is set as in expression (12.2) then an equally efficient entrant can just survive in the market. If the input charge satisfies (12.1), however, an equally efficient entrant cannot survive in the market.[49] The reason why an integrated firm wishes sometimes to exclude a more efficient rival in this case (in contrast to the standard Chicago result) is that the entrant has private information about its cost, and the incumbent wishes to appropriate part of the entrant's efficiency advantage.[50] Therefore an unconstrained integrated firm might be expected to show undue discrimination against a rival. In such circumstances a ban on this kind of price discrimination will raise total welfare compared to a laissez-faire regime.[51]

Consider an alternative scenario in which a vertically separated upstream monopolist sells an essential input, again with cost c_2, to two competing downstream firms, A and B say. For simplicity, suppose that A and B compete in a Cournot fashion, given the input prices set by the upstream firm.[52] Suppose that the contract between the monopolist and downstream firm i takes the form of a two-part tariff, with fixed charge f^i and per unit of input price a^i. First, note that by an appropriate choice of two-part tariff, the monopolist can ensure that (1) the industry profit is maximized and (2) it appropriates the entire industry profit. (This is done by setting a high per-unit input price a—above the cost c_2—that generates high retail prices downstream, and then extracting the downstream profit via the fixed charge f.) In many relevant cases, however, the fact that buyers are firms rather than consumers implies that these contracts for input prices will be negotiated bilaterally rather than simply announced by the monopolist. Indeed, it is plausible that each downstream firm's contract with the monopolist will not be observed by the rival downstream firm. In this situation of secret deals the monopolist finds it hard to avoid offering each downstream firm a cost-based two-part tariff, with $a^i = c_2$. Of course, if both A and B pay for the input at cost, then the industry outcome will correspond to the (moderately) competitive Cournot outcome rather than the industry profit-maximizing outcome. In effect, the monopolist cannot avoid "competing with itself."

Why is the monopolist forced to set $a^i = c_2$ in this framework? Since the deal is secret, the choice of contract between the monopolist and firm A, say, cannot affect the expected output from firm B (or its input choice). The contract with A will maximize the combined profits of A and the monopolist, taking the contract with B as given. But the joint profit-maximizing contract will involve $a^A = c_2$, since in this way the downstream firm's incentives are in line with the monopolist's. A similar contract will be secretly agreed with firm B. The monopolist's market power is eroded by its inability not to negotiate efficient bilateral deals secretly with the downstream firms.

This effect is closely related to the Coasian problem for the inter-temporal monopolist, which was discussed in section 12.9.1 above. In the dynamic context the unconstrained monopolist cannot commit not to offer a good deal to the remaining (low-value) consumers in the second period, and this acts to undermine its market power. And just as with the Coase problem, a policy to ban price discrimination in input prices will act to restore the monopolist's market power. If the upstream monopolist was not allowed to offer different terms to different downstream firms, then it cannot secretly negotiate efficient bilateral contracts, and it can implement the monopoly outcome. As in the Coase problem, a policy that bans price discrimination may end up being detrimental to (final) consumers.

12.11 Conclusion

The welfare effects of allowing price discrimination are ambiguous, both with monopoly and with oligopoly supply. There is no justification for public policies that prohibit price discrimination in general. Price discrimination can lead to efficient pricing, for instance (see section 12.2). Price discrimination can lead to more intense competition which benefits consumers (see sections 12.6 and 12.9). When firms have difficulty committing to prices, they often are forced to charge low prices. In such situations a policy that forbids discrimination endows a firm with commitment power and prevents the firm competing with itself, to the detriment of consumers and welfare (sections 12.9.1 and 12.10). Firms that offer different prices to their loyal customers and to their new customers can make competition more intense, but they can also induce excessive switching between firms (section 12.9.2). By contrast, multiproduct firms might induce excessive loyalty by means of bundling discounts (section 12.6). Price discrimination can also lead firms to leave consumers with less surplus than they would enjoy in its absence (sections 12.2 and 12.7). In addition the freedom of an incumbent firm to engage in price discrimination will typically have a discouraging effect on entry (sections 12.8.3 and 12.10).

Ideally, then, policy toward price discrimination should be founded on good economic understanding of the market in question. This survey has highlighted the formidable amount of information required to determine when price discrimination is likely to be welfare enhancing or decreasing. Since it is impractical, and undesirable, to require competition bodies to have a good economic understanding of all markets, some broad rules of thumb are needed. One possible such rule is to follow a presumption that price discrimination by dominant firms aimed at final consumers should be permitted. Obviously there are many examples where such price discrimination harms consumers and welfare, but given the detailed information required to decide on this, and given that rules against excessive pricing remain available in some jurisdictions for use with particularly egregious cases, it seems sensible to give firms the benefit of the doubt. On the other hand, continued detailed scrutiny of cases involving selective price cuts and cases involving margin squeeze—which can be broadly interpreted as price discrimination—is important.

Notes

I am very grateful to Paolo Buccirossi and John Vickers for comments. More technical and detailed discussions of some of the material presented here is presented in Armstrong (2006). In preparing this survey, I have benefited from consulting the two earlier surveys by Hal Varian (1989) and Lars Stole (2007).

1. There seems to be no consensus on a precise definition. Stigler (1987) suggests a definition that applies to a wider class of cases: discrimination exists when two similar products are sold at prices that are in different ratios to their marginal costs. Which of these definitions we use makes no difference for the purpose of this chapter.

2. Varian (1989, sec. 3.7) summarizes the origins of the legal approaches to price discrimination in the United States, which initially focused on protecting small retailers against large chain stores. For a survey on the application to price discrimination of Article 82 of the EC Treaty, see Geradin and Petit (2005).

3. Prominent antitrust cases in the European Union concerning selective price cuts and geographic price discrimination are *Irish Sugar* and *Compagnie Maritime Belge*, for the first category, and *United Brands* and *Tetra Pak II* for the second.

4. There are plenty of examples of second-degree discrimination that are not to do with nonlinear pricing. For instance, many retailers use coupons placed in newspapers to segment the market. It is plausible that those consumers who take the trouble to cut out and use a coupon will also have more elastic demand, and should therefore face a lower price. See Narasimhan (1984), for example.

5. See Tirole (1988, sec. 3.5.1), for example.

6. In its judgment in *Michelin II* the European Court of First Instance suggested that if discounts are not based on cost efficiencies they should be regarded as in beach of Article 82. For further discussion of competition law and policy toward quantity discounts and related practices, see Vickers (chapter 11 in this volume, sec. 11.2.4) and the Symposium on Loyalty Rebates, in *Competition Policy International* (vol. 1, Autumn 2005).

7. The information and commitment problems are sometimes less severe when the buyers are downstream firms with which the seller has long-term relationships. The dominant seller may then offer what in the antitrust jargon are sometimes referred to as "target rebates." This practice conditions the rebate to the meeting of a threshold based on the past purchases of the buyer. Target rebates were investigated in the *Michelin I* and *II*, *British Airways* and *Irish Sugar* cases.

8. An important recent case is C-53/03 *Syfait v. GlaxoSmithKline* before the European Court of Justice. At issue was a pharmaceutical company's wishing to prevent its products, which are sold at a low price in Greece, from being re-imported into high-price countries. Advocate General Jacobs wrote an opinion in October 2004 that such constraints on parallel imports should not necessarily be considered abusive since the price differentials stemmed from state intervention in the prices for drugs in each country.

9. Armstrong (1999) and Bakos and Brynjolfsson (1999) show how a monopolist supplying *many* products can sometimes be in a position to practise (approximate) first-degree price discrimination, even if it does not know the precise willingness to pay for any individual item.

10. Price discrimination can also lead to efficient supply to *some* consumers, if not all. For instance, in standard models of nonlinear pricing, a profit-maximizing monopolist will ensure that those consumers with the strongest tastes for its product will face a marginal price equal to the firm's marginal cost. See Willig (1978), for example.

11. See Corollary 1 in Armstrong and Vickers (2001) and Yin (2004). Armstrong and Vickers (2006) show that these results extend to many situations where consumers have heterogeneous demand functions.

12. See Layson (1994) for formal analysis along these lines. I follow the literature here, that a market where the price rises with discrimination is a "strong" market whereas a market where the price falls is a "weak" market.

13. Note that a variant on this example shows that price discrimination can sometimes cause markets to shut down. Suppose that there is a third intermediate market where consumers have a valuation of 3 for a unit. Let 50 percent of consumers be in market 1, 10 percent in market 3, and 40 percent in market 2. Without price discrimination, the best strategy for the firm is to set a price of 2 and to serve all consumers. If, however, the firm can distinguish only two groups of consumers, those in market 1 and those who are in either market 2 or 3, the optimal strategy for the firm is to set a price of 2 to those in market 1 and to set a price of 4 to those in markets 2 or 3. Permitting price discrimination then actually causes the firm to abandon market 3, and as a result welfare falls.

14. The effect of discrimination on total output appears to have been first studied by Robinson (1933). Schmalensee (1981) shows that as total output increases, welfare increases with discrimination provided that demands for the products are independent and marginal costs are constant. Varian (1985) extends this argument to allow for cross-price effects, and Schwartz (1990) extends the argument to nonlinear cost functions.

15. When consumer demands are linear, and no markets are opened as a result of price discrimination, it is well-known that output is not affected by price discrimination; hence that discrimination causes welfare to fall. Schmalensee (1981, p. 245) concludes "If all demand functions are strictly concave or convex and the p_i's [the discriminatory prices] are not nearly equal, there is apparently no simple, general way to tell if monopolistic discrimination will raise or lower total output." However, see Cowan (2006) for more progress in this direction.

16. An interesting case involving price discrimination and total output is Competition Commission (1999). In 1999, the supply of milk in the United Kingdom was fixed by European quotas. One distributor, *Milk Marque*, held nearly a 50 percent market share and was heavily engaged in price discrimination to its buyers. Since its total output was fixed via the quota arrangements, this discriminatory pricing was likely to harm welfare. This factor was an important part of the Competition Commission's case against *Milk Marque*.

17. This is taken from Hal Varian, "A Big Factor in Prescription Drug Pricing: Location, Location, Location," *The New York Times*, September 21, 2000.

18. See Holmes (1989), for example.

19. Two key papers on monopoly bundling are Adams and Yellen (1976) and McAfee, McMillan, and Whinston (1989).

20. Nevo and Wolfram (2002) present evidence consistent with the hypothesis that price discrimination via coupons in the breakfast cereal market exhibits best-response asymmetry, and that the introduction of coupons leads to a fall in all prices. They also document how firms allegedly colluded to stop the use of coupons.

21. As ever, one should be wary of reaching policy conclusions on the basis of these unit demand models since price levels have little role to play in welfare terms. If consumers had elastic multi-unit demands, price reductions have a beneficial welfare impact. If in addition firms have imperfect information about brand preferences, price discrimination may induce some consumers to buy from their less preferred supplier. For instance, Bester and Petrakis (1996) consider a model where firms only know whether a consumer prefers it to its rival but not by how much. In this model, firms set lower prices to those consumers who are known to prefer the rival brand, with the result that those consumers who are almost indifferent between the two brands will prefer to buy from the (slightly) less preferred supplier in return for the reduced price. A similar feature appears in the dynamic models of price discrimination discussed in section 12.9.

22. Cooper et al. (2005) use a variant of this model to argue that mergers are less likely to be detrimental when firms practice spatial price discrimination than when they do not.

23. A variant of this model involves the two firms having to choose between separable pricing and *pure* bundling. In this case, firms' profit also falls in many cases when firms choose to sell their products only as a bundle, and typically if falls by more than when mixed bundling is employed. See Matutes and Regibeau (1988) and Economides (1989) for this analysis. The example analyzed in Matutes and Regibeau (1992) is extended in Armstrong and Vickers (2006) to allow for asymmetric products, nonuniform distributions, correlation in brand preferences, and shopping costs for purchasing from more than one supplier. They show in this more general framework that mixed bundling continues to harm profit and welfare, and to boost consumer surplus, relative to linear pricing. However, they also extend the bundling model to allow for elastic, multi-unit demand for each product, in which case the impact of price discrimination on profit, welfare and consumer surplus is shown to be ambiguous.

24. This is essentially example 2 in Whinston (1990). For more detailed discussion of the Whinston model and the literature that follows, see Neven (chapter 5 in this volume).

25. See Armstrong and Vickers (1993) for formal analysis, where we argue that the effect of allowing price discrimination on the intensity of competition is exacerbated when the multi-product firm is regulated and operates under an average-price constraint. (If the firm reduces its price in the competitive market, it can then *raise* its price in the captive market.)

26. Dobson and Waterson (2005) present a related model where a national retailer operates in a number of markets. In some of the markets, the national retailer is the sole supplier and in the remaining markets it faces a single local competitor. They show that it is possible for the chain store to benefit if it commits to a national pricing policy (i.e., if it does not price differently depending on competitive conditions in each local market).

27. See Buccirossi (chapter 8 of this volume) for a fuller account of "collusive" practices.

28. This bundling example is taken from Nalebuff (2004, sec. III.E). See Whinston (1990, sec. II), Carbajo, De Meza, and Seidman (1990), and Chen (1997a) for earlier analyses.

29. See Corts (1996), for example.

30. I have skimmed over the means by which firms agree to set lower prices to make calls to subscribers on rival networks. In the telecommunications context, this could be done via low "call termination" rates. If firms agree to set their charge for delivering calls from rival networks below the associated cost, then firms will have an incentive to set low charges for calls made to rival networks. See Laffont, Rey, and Tirole (1998), Gans and King (2001), and Berger (2005) for further details.

31. See Mankiw and Whinston (1986), for instance.

32. See Borenstein (1985), Norman and Thisse (1996), and Bhaskar and To (2004) for further analyses of the effect of price discrimination on the free-entry number of firms. Ordover and Panzar (1982) investigate the effects of an upstream monopolist's use of two-part pricing on the number of downstream firms. They find that in general, the monopolist will not set a socially optimal two-part tariff, despite the fact that it knows everything about its downstream customers. In this respect there is a contrast between selling to final consumers (when the use of two-part tariffs leads to an efficient outcome, as discussed in section 12.1 above) and selling to intermediate customers.

33. The monopolist will do even better if its sets a fully nonlinear tariff, rather than just a two-part tariff, for consumption of the joint product.

34. See Tirole (1988, sec. 3.3.1.5) for a clear account. The firm can also do well if it offers consumers an *optional* bundled tariff. Suppose that the firm offers consumers the profit-maximizing unbundled tariff ($p_1 = 0.22$, $p_2 = 0$). Say that in addition to this tariff the firm offers consumers the option of another tariff that has a lower price for the monopoly component but a higher price for the competitive good. Such a tariff will be attractive to consumers with relatively low demands. Specifically, if the firm offers the optional tariff with $\hat{p}_1 = 0.037$ and $\hat{p}_2 = 0.272$, then those consumers with $0.54 \leq \theta \leq 0.82$ will use this new tariff. (Some of these are new consumers and some are "cannibalized" from the existing tariff.) Since consumers have the option of using the unbundled tariff, consumer surplus definitely rises with the addition of this tariff. The firm's profit with the new optional tariff is 0.081, which is higher than that generated by the unbundled tariff on its own, and also higher than that generated by the optimal single two-part tariff ($p_1 = 0.08$, $p_2 = 0.2$). Therefore the introduction of the optional tariff represents a Pareto improvement compared to when the unbundled tariff is used on its own. See Nalebuff (2005) for related analysis (where the same model for consumer demand is employed).

35. See Bakos and Brynjolfsson (2000) for further analysis of this issue. The argument does not apply to third-degree price discrimination, where there are several separate markets and each consumer wishes to purchase just a single product from the multi-market firm.

36. Another way in which price discrimination interacts with market definition is that (1) when a hypothetical monopolist is able to price discriminate between two or more consumer groups, these consumer groups will make up separate antitrust markets, while (2) when the monopolist cannot price discriminate, the whole market becomes the relevant market for antitrust purposes. For instance, see the *Horizontal Merger Guidelines* issued by the United States Department of Justice and the Federal Trade Commission, 1992.

37. The most prominent case is the *Microsoft* case, and in particular the part of the case relating to the bundling of the *Internet Explorer* browser with its *Windows* operating system; see Motta (2004, sec. 7.5) for some further details. An earlier relevant case from 1979 is *Berkey Photo v. Eastman Kodak*.

38. Nalebuff (2004) mainly considers a model in which the incumbent firm not only makes its bundling decision prior to entry but decides on its prices before entry. Among other results he shows that bundling is an effective

way to deter single-product entry if the incumbent does not know in advance into *which* market the entrant will enter.

39. The Chicago argument relies on the integrated firm possessing accurate information about its rivals' capabilities. In section 12.10, I discuss a model where the integrated firm is unsure about a rival's cost of supply, and in this case the firm does have an incentive to exclude a more efficient rival.

40. Whinston shows that if the complementary products are not perfect complements, then the incumbent may again wish to exclude a rival by means of bundling.

41. See Stokey (1979). If the model is modified either so that consumers have different discount factors or so that consumers as a whole have a different discount factor to the firm, then it may be optimal to commit to a decreasing time path.

42. This point was first made by Coase (1972). See also Hart and Tirole (1988).

43. See Armstrong (2006, sec. 2.2) for further details.

44. This form of discrimination is not feasible if past consumers pretend to be new customers, for instance, by deleting their computer "cookies" or using another credit card when they deal with an online retailer.

45. Taylor (2004) analyzes a related situation where one firm sells a product in period 1 and a separate firm sells a related product in period 2. The first firm is able to sell its information about which consumers purchased from it in the first period to the second firm. The second firm is willing to pay for this information, since it provides the basis for behavior-based price discrimination toward these consumers. Since the first firm can fully extract the second firm's benefit from the information, the scenario is essentially the same as when an integrated firm supplies in both periods and cannot commit to its second-period price. Taylor distinguishes between sophisticated and naive consumers. If consumers are naive, in the sense that they do not foresee that their decisions with one firm might affect their offers from the subsequent firm, the first firm has an incentive to raise its price above the monopoly level in order to boost the value of information to the second firm. Public policy toward privacy might prohibit the passing of consumer information between firms, and this would make naive consumers better off and reduce the level of industry profit. On the other hand, when consumers are sophisticated, a ban on information transfer will surely increase industry profit.

46. See Taylor (2003) for an extension to Chen's analysis in a number of important directions, for instance, to more than two periods and more than two firms. When there are more than two periods, the fact that a consumer switched supplier in the second period indicates that the consumer has low switching costs, and this might generate more intense competition for the consumer in future periods.

47. Even if it appears to be "unfair" to the firm's existing customers that the firm's new customers often obtain a better deal, it is possible for the existing customers to be worse off if this form of price discrimination is forbidden.

48. In a richer model where consumers have elastic, multi-unit demands each period, the low second-period prices will bring welfare benefits that might outweigh the welfare losses from excessive switching.

49. In antitrust terminology, a vertically integrated incumbent is sometimes said to practice a "price squeeze" (or "margin squeeze") if an equally efficient entrant makes a loss with the offered margin; see Vickers (chapter 11 in this volume, sec. 11.2.3) for further discussion and a summary of recent price squeeze cases. Grout (2001) and Bouckaert and Verboven (2004) discuss the implementation of price squeeze rules in richer settings than discussed here (e.g., when the entrant incurs a fixed cost of entry or when the incumbent incurs extra costs if it supplies the input to the rival than it does if it supplies itself). Although price squeezes share with predatory pricing the feature that a "price" (here, the margin) is below avoided cost (here, the opportunity cost), there is nothing necessarily predatory about them. For instance, in the example presented in the text, the integrated monopolist sets a low margin not to drive out rivals with a view to subsequently raising a price but to extract some of the potential efficiency gains generated by entrant supply. (Indeed the monopolist is here better off when entry occurs.)

50. If the monopolist did know the entrant's cost c, and was permitted to base its input charge on this cost (another form of price discrimination), it would set the input price that just ensures profitable entry by an equally or more efficient entrant. The result is productive efficiency, but the entrant is left with zero profit. This outcome corresponds closely with the case of first-degree price discrimination discussed in section 12.2.

51. Armstrong and Vickers (1998) argue that from a social welfare perspective it is often better to require the incumbent to set its input price equal to its cost c_2 than to require it to satisfy condition (12.2), for the reason that (12.2) provides no constraint on the incumbent's retail price p.

52. The key papers relevant to this "secret deals" problem are Hart and Tirole (1990), O'Brien and Shaffer (1992), and McAfee and Schwartz (1994). See Rey and Tirole (2007) for a full account of this literature. In partic-

ular, the results reported in the text are also valid when the downstream firms compete in prices. I have largely taken this informal discussion from Vickers (1996).

References

Adams, W., and J. Yellen. 1976. Commodity bundling and the burden of monopoly. *Quarterly Journal of Economics* 90(3): 475–98.

Armstrong, M. 1999. Price discrimination by a many-product firm. *Review of Economic Studies* 66(1): 151–68.

Armstrong, M. 2006. Recent developments in the economics of price discrimination. In R. Blundell, W. Newey, and T. Persson, eds., *Advances in Economics and Econometrics: Theory and Applications: Ninth World Congress of the Econometric Society*, vol. 2. Cambridge: Cambridge University Press, pp. 97–141.

Armstrong, M., S. Cowan, and J. Vickers. 1995. Nonlinear pricing and price cap regulation. *Journal of Public Economics* 58(1): 33–55.

Armstrong, M., and J. Vickers. 1991. Welfare effects of price discrimination by a regulated monopolist. *RAND Journal of Economics* 22(4): 571–80.

Armstrong, M., and J. Vickers. 1993. Price discrimination, competition and regulation. *Journal of Industrial Economics* 41(4): 335–60.

Armstrong, M., and J. Vickers. 1998. The access pricing problem with deregulation: A note. *Journal of Industrial Economics* 46(1): 115–21.

Armstrong, M., and J. Vickers. 2001. Competitive price discrimination. *RAND Journal of Economics* 32(4): 579–605.

Armstrong, M., and J. Vickers. 2006. Competitive nonlinear pricing and bundling. Mimeo. University College London.

Bakos, Y., and E. Brynjolfsson. 1999. Bundling information goods: Pricing, profits, and efficiency. *Management Science* 45(12): 1613–30.

Bakos, Y., and E. Brynjolfsson. 2000. Bundling and competition on the Internet. *Marketing Science* 19(1): 63–82.

Berger, U. 2005. Bill-and-keep vs. cost-based access pricing revisited. *Economics Letters* 86(1): 107–12.

Bester, H., and E. Petrakis. 1996. Coupons and oligopolistic price discrimination. *International Journal of Industrial Organization* 14(2): 227–42.

Bhaskar, V., and T. To. 2004. Is perfect price discrimination really efficient? An analysis of free entry. *RAND Journal of Economics* 35(4): 762–76.

Borenstein, S. 1985. Price discrimination in free-entry markets. *RAND Journal of Economics* 16(3): 380–97.

Bouckaert, J., and F. Verboven. 2004. Price squeezes in a regulatory environment. *Journal of Regulatory Economics* 26(3): 321–51.

Carbajo, J., D. De Meza, and D. Seidman. 1990. A strategic motivation for commodity bundling. *Journal of Industrial Economics* 38(3): 283–98.

Carlton, D., and M. Waldman. 2002. The strategic use of tying to preserve and create market power in evolving industries. *RAND Journal of Economics* 33(2): 194–220.

Chen, Y. 1997a. Equilibrium product bundling. *Journal of Business* 70(1): 85–103.

Chen, Y. 1997b. Paying customers to switch. *Journal of Economics and Management Strategy* 6(4): 877–97.

Chen, Y. 2006. Dynamic price discrimination with asymmetric firms. Mimeo. University of Colorado.

Choi, J., and C. Stefanadis. 2001. Tying, investment, and the dynamic leverage theory. *RAND Journal of Economics* 32(1): 52–71.

Coase, R. 1972. Durability and monopoly. *Journal of Law and Economics* 15(1): 143–49.

Competition Commission. 1999. *Milk: A Report on the Supply in Great Britain of Raw Cows Milk*. London: HMSO.

Cooper, J., L. Froeb, D. O'Brien, and S. Tschantz. 2005. Does price discrimination intensify competition? Implications for antitrust. *Antitrust Law Journal* 72: 327–73.

Corts, K. 1996. On the competitive effects of price-matching policies. *International Journal of Industrial Organization* 15(3): 283–99.

Corts, K. 1998. Third-degree price discrimination in oligopoly: All-out competition and strategic commitment. *RAND Journal of Economics* 29(2): 306–23.

Cowan, S. 2006. The welfare effects of third-degree price discrimination with non-linear demand functions. *RAND Journal of Economics*, forthcoming.

Dobson, P., and M. Waterson. 2005. Chain-store pricing across local markets. *Journal of Economics and Management Strategy* 14(1): 93–119.

Economides, N. 1989. The desirability of compatibility in the absence of network externalities. *American Economic Review* 71(5): 1165–81.

Fudenberg, D., and J. Tirole. 2000. Customer poaching and brand switching. *RAND Journal of Economics* 31(4): 634–57.

Gans, J., and S. King. 2001. Using "bill and keep" interconnect agreements to soften network competition. *Economics Letters* 71(3): 413–20.

Geradin, D., and N. Petit. 2005. Price discrimination under EC competition law: The need for a case-by-case approach. GCLC Working paper 07/05.

Grout, P. 2001. Competition law in telecommunications and its implications for common carriage of water. *Utilities Policy* 10(3–4): 137–49.

Hart, O., and J. Tirole. 1988. Contract renegotiation and Coasian dynamics. *Review of Economic Studies* 55(4): 509–40.

Hart, O., and J. Tirole. 1990. Vertical integration and market foreclosure. *Brookings Papers on Economic Activity: Microeconomics*: 205–76.

Holmes, T. 1989. The effects of third-degree price discrimination in oligopoly. *American Economic Review* 79(1): 244–50.

Laffont, J.-J., P. Rey, and J. Tirole. 1998. Network competition. II. Price discrimination. *RAND Journal of Economics* 29(1): 38–56.

Layson, S. 1994. Market opening under third-degree price discrimination. *Journal of Industrial Economics* 42(3): 335–40.

Mankiw, G., and M. Whinston. 1986. Free entry and social inefficiency. *RAND Journal of Economics* 17(1): 48–58.

Matutes, C., and P. Regibeau. 1988. Mix and match: Product compatibility without network externalities. *RAND Journal of Economics* 19(2): 221–34.

Matutes, C., and P. Regibeau. 1992. Compatibility and bundling of complementary goods in a duopoly. *Journal of Industrial Economics* 40(1): 37–54.

McAfee, R. P., J. McMillan, and M. Whinston. 1989. Multiproduct monopoly, commodity bundling and correlation of values. *Quarterly Journal of Economics* 104(2): 371–84.

McAfee, R. P., and M. Schwartz. 1994. Opportunism in multilateral vertical contracting: Nondiscrimination, exclusivity and uniformity. *American Economic Review* 84(1): 210–30.

Motta, M. 2004. *Competition Policy: Theory and Practice*. Cambridge: Cambridge University Press.

Nalebuff, B. 2004. Bundling as an entry barrier. *Quarterly Journal of Economics* 119(1): 159–88.

Nalebuff, B. 2005. Bundling as a way to leverage monopoly. Mimeo. Yale University.

Narasimhan, C. 1984. A price discrimination theory of coupons. *Marketing Science* 3: 128–47.

Nevo, A., and C. Wolfram. 2002. Why do manufacturers issue coupons? An empirical analysis of breakfast cereals. *RAND Journal of Economics* 33(2): 319–39.

Norman, G., and J.-F. Thisse. 1996. Product variety and welfare under tough and soft pricing regimes. *Economic Journal* 106(1): 76–91.

O'Brien, D., and G. Shaffer. 1992. Vertical control with bilateral contracts. *RAND Journal of Economics* 23(3): 299–308.

Ordover, J., and J. Panzar. 1982. On the nonlinear pricing of inputs. *International Economic Review* 23(3): 659–75.

Rey, P., and J. Tirole. 2007. A primer on foreclosure. In M. Armstrong, and R. Porter, eds., *Handbook of Industrial Organization*, vol. 3. Amsterdam: North-Holland, pp. 2145–220.

Robinson, J. 1933. *The Economics of Imperfect Competition*. London: Macmillan.

Schmalensee, R. 1981. Output and welfare Implications of monopolistic third-degree price discrimination. *American Economic Review* 71(1): 242–47.

Schwartz, M. 1990. Third-degree price discrimination and output: Generalizing a welfare result. *American Economic Review* 80(5): 1259–62.

Stigler, G. 1987. *Theory of Price*. New York: Macmillan.

Stokey, N. 1979. Intertemporal price discrimination. *Quarterly Journal of Economics* 93(3): 355–71.

Stole, L. 2007. Price discrimination and competition. In M. Armstrong, and R. Porter, eds., *Handbook of Industrial Organization*, vol. 3. Amsterdam: North-Holland, pp. 2221–99.

Taylor, C. 2003. Supplier surfing: Competition and consumer behavior in subscription markets. *RAND Journal of Economics* 34(2): 223–46.

Taylor, C. 2004. Consumer privacy and the market for customer information. *RAND Journal of Economics* 35(4): 631–50.

Thisse, J.-F., and X. Vives. 1988. On the strategic choice of spatial price policy. *American Economic Review* 78(1): 122–37.

Tirole, J. 1988. *The Theory of Industrial Organization*. Cambridge: MIT Press.

Varian, H. 1985. Price discrimination and social welfare. *American Economic Review* 75(4): 870–75.

Varian, H. 1989. Price discrimination. In R. Schmalensee, and R. Willig, eds., *Handbook of Industrial Organization*, vol. 1. Amsterdam: North Holland, pp. 597–654.

Vickers, J. 1996. Market power and inefficiency: A contracts perspective. *Oxford Review of Economic Policy* 12(4): 11–26.

Whinston, M. 1990. Tying, foreclosure and exclusion. *American Economic Review* 80(4): 837–59.

Willig, R. 1978. Pareto-superior nonlinear outlay schedules. *Bell Journal of Economics* 9(1): 56–69.

Yin, X. 2004. Two-part tariff competition in duopoly. *International Journal of Industrial Organization* 22(6): 799–820.

13 Public Policy in Network Industries

Nicholas Economides

Network industries are a large, significant, and often fast-growing part of the world economy. A key network industry is telecommunications, providing voice and data services, including the Internet and the World Wide Web. Another key network industry is computer software and hardware. These two sectors, telecommunications and computers, have been the engines of fast growth of the world economy. In the news and entertainment sector, network industries include broadcasting and cable television, which in recent years are reaching into traditional telecommunications services. In transportation, networks include airlines, railroads, roads, and shipping, and the delivery services that "live" on these, such as the postal service and its competitors. In the financial sector, networks include traditional financial exchanges for bonds, equities, and derivatives, clearing houses, B2B and B2C exchanges, credit and debit card networks, as well as automated transactions banking networks, such as ATM networks.

Besides traditional network industries, many of the features of networks apply to *virtual networks*. A virtual network is a collection of compatible goods that share a common technical platform. For example, all VHS video players make up a virtual network. Similarly all computers running Windows can be thought of as a virtual network. Compatible computer software and hardware make up a network, and so do computer operating systems and compatible applications. More generally, networks are composed of complementary components, so they also encompass wholesale and retail networks, as well as information networks and servers such as telephone yellow pages, Yahoo, MSN, and Google.

In recent years high-technology industries have been playing an even more central role in the US and world economy, exhibiting very fast growth and high valuations of their equity. Many of the high-technology industries are based on networks (e.g., the telecommunications network and the Internet). Other high-technology industries, such as the computer software and hardware industries, exhibit properties that are typically observed in networks, as will be explained in detail. So, to understand the "new economy," we need to understand the economics of networks. Another key infrastructure industry, electricity production and distribution, is also a network industry.

Adding to the importance of networks from a public policy point of view is the fact that network industries often provide necessities. Monopolization in such a setting can have significant social and political implications.

There may be a number of anticompetitive concerns in a network industry. The focus of this chapter are the following questions: Since network industries have special common features, are there special competition policy issues arising out of key features of network industries? If yes, what is the framework of the public policies that can be pursued to address these issues?

13.1 The Logic of Competition Law

The logic of competition and antitrust law in the United States and the European Union is to guard against restrictions and impediments to competition that are not likely to be naturally corrected by competitive forces. For this chapter, I will posit that the maximization of efficiency (allocative, productive, and dynamic) is the desired outcome of competition and antitrust law, and that typically competition is the means of achieving efficiency.

As an alternative to antitrust and competition law, economic regulation has been established in three exceptional case: (1) for those markets where it is clear that competition cannot be achieved by market forces, (2) for markets where deviation from efficiency is deemed socially desirable, and (3) for markets where the social and private benefits are clearly different. In each of these cases it is clear that a market without intervention will not result in the desired outcome. In the first case, this is true by the definition of the category. In the second case, markets may lead to efficiency, but society prefers a different outcome, so intervention is necessary to achieve this. In the third case, maximization of social surplus does not coincide with maximization of the sum of profits and consumers' surplus because of "externalities."

Some key network industries are regulated at least in part or in some aspects. Telecommunications has significant regulation at both the federal and state level. Railroads, electricity, and air and ground transportation are also heavily regulated. Financial exchanges are under "light" regulation and to a significant extent under self-regulation. In contrast, B2B exchanges, credit card, and banking networks, as well as computers and their virtual networks, are almost completely unregulated.

A full discussion of the merits and problems with regulation of each of these network industries is impossible in the context of this brief chapter. Instead, I will outline the parameters that would necessitate regulation or deregulation based on the broad features of network markets. In future work, I will examine the full application of these principles in all network industries. I expect to observe that the principles of economic regulation are not applied equally to all industries, and in a number of cases, the present regulatory regime is based on historical reasons (political, social, and technological) and cannot be justified based on the application of the economic principles to the present technology.

13.2   Special Features of Markets with Network Effects

13.2.1   Sources of Network Effects and the Reversal of the Law of Demand

Many network industries exhibit increasing returns to scale in production: unit cost (average cost) decreases with as production increases. Often incremental cost is negligible, for example, in software. But these are also features of nonnetwork industries and are *not* the defining feature of network industries. Thus increasing returns to scale in production or negligible incremental production cost are not the defining feature of the competition policy issues that are rooted in the existence of networks.

Networks are composed of *complementary* nodes and links. The crucial defining feature of networks is the complementarity among the various nodes and links. A service delivered over a network requires the use of two or more network components. Thus, network components are complementary to each other.

Figure 13.1 represents the emerging *information superhighway* network. Clearly, services demanded by consumers are composed of many complementary components. For example, interactive ordering while browsing in a "department store" as it appears in successive video frames requires a number of components: a database engine at the service provider, transmission of signals, decoding through an interface, display on a TV or computer monitor, and so forth. There are substitutes for each of these components. For example, transmission can be done through a cable TV line, a fixed telephone line, a wireless satellite, or PCS; the in-home interface may be a TV-top box or an add-on to a PC. It is likely that the combinations of various components will result in substitute but not identical services.

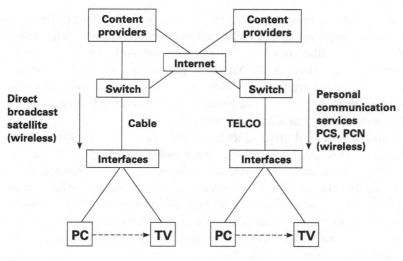

Figure 13.1
The Information superhighway

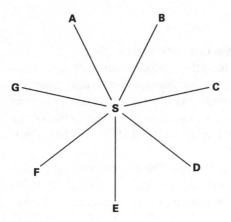

Figure 13.2
A star network

Thus the information superhighway will provide substitutes made of complements, and this is a typical feature of networks.

A common and defining feature of network industries is that they exhibit increasing returns to scale in consumption, commonly called network effects. The existence of network externalities is the key reason for the importance, growth, and profitability of network industries and the "new economy." A market exhibits network effects (or network externalities) when the value to a buyer of an extra unit is higher as more units are sold, everything else being equal.[1]

Network effects arise because of complementarities. In a traditional network, network externalities arise because a typical subscriber can reach more subscribers in a larger network. Figure 13.2 depicts a traditional telecommunications network where customers $A, B, \ldots, G$ are connected to a switch at S. Although goods "access to the switch," $AS, BS, \ldots, GS$ have the same industrial classification, and traditional economics would classify them as substitutes, they are used as *complements*. In particular, when customer A makes a phone call to customer B, he uses *both* AS and BS.

Networks where services AB and BA are distinct are called "two-way" networks. Two-way networks include railroad, road, and many telecommunications networks. When one of AB or BA is unfeasible, or does not make economic sense, or when there is no sense of direction in the network so that AB and BA are identical, then the network is called a one-way network. In a typical one-way network there are two types of components. Composite goods are formed only by combining a component of each type, and customers are often not identified with components but instead demand composite goods. For example, radio and TV broadcasting and early paging networks are one-way networks.

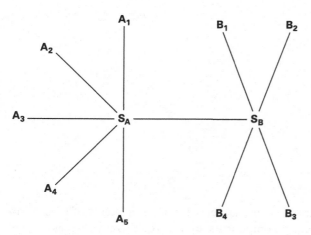

Figure 13.3
A long-distance network (alternatively, an ATM network)

The classification in network type (one-way or two-way) is not a function of the topological structure of the network. Rather, it depends on the interpretation of the structure to represent a specific service. For example, the network of figure 13.3 can be interpreted as a two-way telephone network where SA represents a local switch in city A, A_1, represents a customer in city A, and similarly for SB and B_j. We may identify end nodes, such as A_i and B_i, end links, such as A_iS_A and S_BB_j, the interface or gateway S_AS_B, and switches S_A and S_B. In this network there are two types of local phone calls $A_iS_AA_k$ and $B_jS_BB_R$, as well as long-distance phone calls $A_iS_AS_BB_j$. We can also interpret the network of figure 13.3 as an Automatic Teller Machine network Then a transaction (say a withdrawal) from bank B_j from ATM A_i is $A_iS_AS_BB_j$. Connections $A_iS_AA_k$ and $B_jS_BB_R$ may be feasible but there is no demand for them.

A *virtual network* can be thought of as a collection of compatible goods that share a common technical platform. For example, all VHS video players make up a virtual network. Similarly all computers running Windows XP can be thought of as a virtual network. More generally, a virtual network can be thought of a combination of two collections of two types of goods $\{A_1, \ldots, A_m\}$ and $\{B_1, \ldots, B_n\}$ such that (1) each of the A-type good is a substitute to any other A-type good, (2) each of the B-type good is a substitute to any other B-type good, and (3) each of the A-type good is a complement to any other A-type good. Virtual networks are one-way networks. Examples of virtual networks are computer hardware and software, computer operating systems and software applications, cameras and compatible film, and razors and compatible blades. There are many more virtual networks than traditional networks.

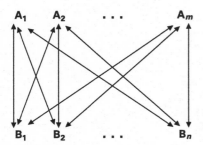

Figure 13.4
A virtual network of complementary goods

In a virtual network, externalities arise because larger sales of components of type A induce larger availability of complementary components $B_1, \ldots, B_n$, thereby increasing the value of components of type A. As figure 13.4 shows, the increased value of component A results in further positive feedback. Despite the cycle of positive feedbacks, it is typically expected that the value of component A does not explode to infinity because the additional positive feedback is expected to decrease with increases in the size of the network.[2]

The crucial relationship in both one-way and two-way networks is the complementarity between the pieces of the network. This crucial economic relationship is also often observed between different classes of goods in nonnetwork industries. Figure 13.4 can represent two industries of complementary goods A and B, where consumers demand combinations $A_i B_j$. Notice that this formulation is formally identical to the long-distance network of figure 13.3 in the ATM interpretation.

In traditional nonnetwork industries the willingness to pay for the last unit of a good decreases with the number of units sold. This is called *the law of demand*, and it is traditionally considered to hold for almost all goods.[3] However, the existence of network effects implies that as more units are sold, the willingness to pay for the last unit is higher. This means that for network goods, the fundamental law of demand is violated, so some portions of the demand curve can slope upward. In other words, for some portions of the demand curve, as sales expand, people are willing to pay more for the last unit.

The law of demand is still correct if one disregards the effects of the expansion of sales on complementary goods. But, as increased sales of a network good imply an expansion in the sales of complementary goods, the value of the last unit increases. Combining the traditional downward-slopping effect with the positive effect due to network expansion can result in a demand curve that has an upward-slopping part.

The key reason for the appearance of network externalities is the complementarity among network components. Depending on the network, the network effect may be direct or indirect. When customers are identified with components, the network effect is direct. Consider a typical two-way network, such as the local telephone network of figure 13.2.

In this n nodes two-way network, there are $n(n-1)$ potential goods. An additional $(n+1)$th customer provides direct externalities to all other customers in the network by adding $2n$ potential new goods through the provision of a complementary link (e.g., ES) to the existing links.[4]

In typical one-way networks, the network effect is only indirect. When there are m varieties of component A and n varieties of component B as in figure 13.4 (and all A-type goods are compatible with all of B-type), there are $m \times n$ potential composite goods. An extra customer yields indirect externalities to other customers, by increasing the demand for components of types A and B. In the presence of economies of scale in production, the increase in demand may potentially increase the number of varieties of each component that are available in the market.

Exchange networks or financial networks (e.g., the NYSE and NASDAQ, commodities, futures, and options exchanges as well as business-to-business "B2B" exchanges), also exhibit indirect network externalities. There are two ways in which these externalities arise. First, externalities arise in the act of exchanging assets or goods. Second, externalities may arise in the array of vertically related services that compose a financial transaction. These include the services of a broker, bringing the offer to the floor, and matching the offer. The second type of externalities are similar to other vertically related markets. The first way in which externalities arise in financial markets is more important.

The act of exchanging goods or assets brings together a trader who is willing to sell with a trader who is willing to buy. The exchange brings together the two complementary goods, "willingness to sell at price p" (the "offer") and "willingness to buy at price p" (the "counteroffer"), and this creates a composite good, the "exchange transaction." The two original goods are complementary, and each has no value without the other one. Clearly, the availability of the counteroffer is critical for the exchange to occur. Put in terms commonly used in finance, minimal liquidity is necessary for the transaction to occur.

Financial and business-to-business exchanges also exhibit positive size externalities in the sense that the increasing size (or thickness) of an exchange market increases the expected utility of all participants. Higher participation of traders on both sides of the market (drawn from the same distribution) decreases the variance of the expected market price and increases the expected utility of risk-averse traders. Ceteris paribus, higher liquidity increases traders' utility.[5] Thus financial exchange markets also exhibit network externalities.[6]

As I noted earlier, network externalities arise out of the complementarity of different network pieces. They arise naturally in both one- and two-way networks, as well as in vertically related markets. The value of good X increases as more of the complementary good Y is sold, and vice versa. Thus more of Y is sold as more X is sold. It follows that the value of X increases as more of it is sold. This positive feedback loop seems explosive, and indeed it would be, except for the inherent downward slope of the demand curve.

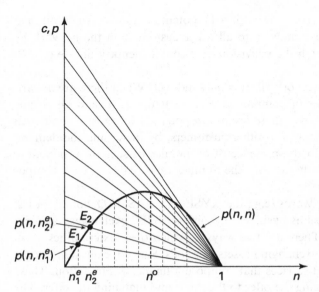

Figure 13.5
Fulfilled expectations demand and critical mass

To understand this better, consider a fulfilled expectations formulation of network externalities. Let the willingness to pay for the nth unit of the good when n^e units are expected to be sold be $p(n, n^e)$. In this formulation, n and n^e are normalized so that they represent market coverage, ranging from 0 to 1, rather than absolute quantities. Willingness to pay $p(n, n^e)$ is a decreasing function of its first argument because the demand slopes downward. As $p(n, n^e)$ increases in n^e, this captures the network externalities effect, meaning the good is more valuable when the expected sales n^e are higher. At a market equilibrium of the simple single-period world, expectations are fulfilled, $n = n^e$, and this defines the fulfilled expectations demand $p(n, n)$.

Figure 13.5 shows the construction of a typical fulfilled expectations demand in a network industry. Each willingness-to-pay curve, $p(n, n_i^e)$, $i = 1, 2, \ldots$, shows the willingness to pay for a varying quantity n, given an expectation of sales $n^e = n_i^e$. At $n = n_i^e$, expectations are fulfilled and the point belongs to $p(n, n)$ as $p(n_i^e, n_i^e)$. Thus $p(n, n)$ is constructed as a collection of points $p(n_i^e, n_i^e)$. It is reasonable to impose the condition $\lim_{n \to 1} p(n, n) = 0$. This means that as the market is more and more covered, eventually the network reaches consumers who are willing to pay very little for the good even if they are able to reap very large network externalities. It follows that $p(n, n)$ is decreasing for large n. In figure 13.5 the fulfilled expectations demand at quantity zero is $p(0, 0) = 0$. This means that consumers think that the good has negligible value when its sales (and network effect) are zero. Although this is true for many network goods, some network goods have positive inherent value even at zero sales and no network effects. If the good has an inherent value k, $p(0,0) = k$, the fulfilled expectations demand curve in figure 13.5 starts at $(0,k)$.

Economides and Himmelberg (1995), taking off from Rohlfs (1974), have shown that the fulfilled expectations demand is increasing for small n if *either one* of three conditions holds:[7]

1. The utility of every consumer in a network of zero size is zero.
2. There are immediate and large external benefits to network expansion for very small networks.
3. There are a significant number of high willingness-to-pay consumers who are just indifferent on joining a network of approximately zero size.

The first condition is straightforward and applies directly to all two-way networks, such as the telecommunications and fax networks where the good has no value unless there is another user to connect to. The other two conditions are more subtle but are commonly observed in networks and vertically related industries. The second condition holds for networks where the addition of even few users increases the value of the network significantly. A good example of this is a newsgroup on an obscure subject, where the addition of very few users starts a discussion and increases its value significantly. The third condition is most common in software markets. A software application has value to a user even if no one else uses it. The addition of an extra user has a network benefit to other users (because they can share files or find trained workers in the specifics of the application), but this benefit is small. However, when large numbers of users are added, the network benefit can be significant.

13.2.2 Critical Mass

When the fulfilled expectations demand increases for small n, we say that the network exhibits a positive critical mass under perfect competition. This means that if we imagine a constant marginal cost c decreasing as technology improves, the network will start at a positive and significant size n^0 (corresponding to marginal cost c^0). For each smaller marginal cost, $c < c^0$, there are three network sizes consistent with marginal cost pricing: a zero size network, an unstable network size at the first intersection of the horizontal line through c with $p(n,n)$, and the Pareto optimal stable network size at the largest intersection of the horizontal line with $p(n,n)$. The multiplicity of equilibria is a direct result of the coordination problem that arises naturally in the typical network externalities model. In such a setting it is natural to assume that the Pareto optimal network size will result.

The existence of an upward-slopping part of the demand curve and the multiplicity of equilibria even under perfect competition also allows for a network to start with a small size and then expand significantly. For example, take the case where marginal cost is at $c < c^0$ and a new invention creates a new product with significant network effects. Then it is possible that the industry starts at the left intersection of the horizontal at c with $p(n, n)$ as expectations are originally low, and later on advances suddenly and quickly to the right intersection of the horizontal at c with $p(n, n)$. Thus the multiplicity of equilibria in network industries can lead to sudden significant expansions of network size.

13.2.3 Features of Markets with Network Effects

Ability to Charge Prices on Both Sides of a Network   There are a number of fundamental properties of network industries that arise out of the existence of network effects.

A firm can make money from either side of the network or from both. For example, a telecommunications services provider can charge subscribers when they originate calls or when they receive calls or for both.[8] When a network consists of software clients and servers, both provided by the same firm, the firm can use the prices of the client and server software to maximize the network effect and its profits. For example, it can distribute the client software at marginal cost (free) and make all its profits from the server software. In a similar vein, Adobe distributes the "Acrobat Reader" free while it makes its profits from the "Acrobat Distiller" product, which allows the creation of files that can be read by the Acrobat Reader. The availability of prices on both sides of the network allows for complex pricing strategies and, depending on the dynamics and market shares on the two sides of the market, can be used strategically to enhance and leverage a firm's strong strategic position on one side of the network. Of course, this is not confined to high-technology or software industries; it applies wherever complementary components are present.[9]

Externalities May or May Not Be Internalized   In network industries often the additional subscriber/user is not rewarded for the benefit that he/she brings to others by subscribing. Hence typically there are "externalities," meaning benefits not fully intermediated by the market. However, firms can use price discrimination to provide favorable terms to large users to maximize their network effect contribution to the market. For example, a large customer in a financial market can be given a very low price to be compensated for the positive network effect it brings to the market.[10]

Fast Network Expansion   Generally, the pace of market penetration (network expansion) is much faster in network industries than in nonnetwork industries. In the earlier discussion on critical mass, we saw that in a one-period model, as unit cost decreases, the network starts with significant market coverage. In the presence of frictions and not perfectly elastic supply, the network expansion is not instantaneous from 0 to n^0 but rather is a rapid expansion following an S-shaped curve, as seen in figure 13.6. Notice how the market share expansion compares for a new good (diffusion) in the presence (delta = 1) and absence (delta = 0) of network effects as a function of time. The self-reinforcing nature of network effects leads to a much faster expansion when network effects are present.[11]

Market penetration

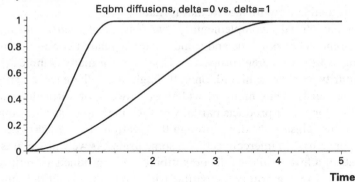

Figure 13.6
Diffusion of an innovation with and without network effects

Efficiency: Perfect Competition Is Inefficient   In the presence of network externalities, it is evident that *perfect competition is inefficient.* The marginal social benefit of network expansion is larger than the benefit that accrues to a particular firm under perfect competition. Thus perfect competition provides a smaller network than is socially optimal, and for some relatively high marginal costs, perfect competition does not provide the good while it is socially optimal to provide it.[12]

Since perfect competition is inefficient, state subsidization of network industries is beneficial to society. The Internet is a very successful network that was subsidized by the US government for many years. However, the subsidized Internet was aimed at promoting interaction among military research projects. During the period of its subsidization, almost no one imagined that the Internet would become a ubiquitous commercial network. Yet the foundation of the Internet on publicly and freely available standards has facilitated its expansion and provided a guarantee that no firm can dominate it.

Standards Wars   So far we have assumed *compatibility*, namely that various links and nodes on the network are costlessly combinable to produce demanded goods. Two complementary components A and B are compatible when they can be combined to produce a composite good or service. For example, we say that a VHS-format video player is compatible with a VHS-format tape. Two substitute components A_1 and A_2 are compatible when each of them can be combined with a complementary good B to produce a composite good or service. For example, two VHS tapes are compatible. Similarly we say that two VHS video players are compatible. Also we say that two software products are compatible (more precisely *two-way* compatible) when they each can read and write files in a common format. So compatibility may be *one-way* when the files of format B_1 of software A_1 can be read by software A_2, but the files format B_2 of software A_2 cannot be read by software

A_1. Moreover compatibility may be only partial in the sense that software A_1 is able to read files of format B_2 but unable to write files in that format.

Links on a network are potentially complementary, *but it is compatibility that makes complementarity actual.* Some network goods and some vertically related goods are immediately combinable because of their inherent properties. However, for many complex products, actual complementarity can be achieved only through the adherence to specific technical compatibility standards. Thus many providers of network or vertically related goods have the option of making their products partially or fully incompatible with components produced by other firms. This can be done through the creation of proprietary designs or the outright exclusion or refusal to interconnect with some firms. As we will see, it is not always in the best interests of a firm to allow full compatibility of its products with those of its competitors. The extent to which a firm is compatible with the products of other firms is an important strategic decision for a firm (as will be discussed in detail further on).

A key strategic decision for a firm is the extent to which it will be compatible with other firms. As I noted earlier, a network good has higher value because of the existence of network effects. Different firms conforming to the same technical standard can create a larger network effect while still competing with each other in other dimensions (e.g., quality and price). But even the decision to conform to the same technical standard is a strategic one. A firm can choose to be compatible with a rival and thereby create a larger network effect and share it with the rival. A firm could alternatively choose to be incompatible with the rival but keep all the network effects it creates to itself. Which way the decision will go depends on a number of factors. First, in some network industries, such as telecommunications, interconnection and compatibility at the level of voice and low-capacity data transmission are mandated by law. Second, the decision will depend on the expertise that a firm has on a particular standard (and therefore on the costs that it would incur to conform to it). Third, the choice on compatibility will depend on the relative benefit of keeping all the network effects to itself by choosing incompatibility versus receiving half of the larger network benefits by choosing compatibility. Fourth, the choice on compatibility depends on the ability of a firm to sustain a dominant position in an ensuing standards war if incompatibility is chosen. Finally, the compatibility choice depends on the ability of firms to leverage any monopoly power that they manage to attain in a regime of incompatibility to new markets.

Standards may be defined by the government (e.g., at the beginning of the Internet), a world engineering body (e.g., in the FAX), an industrywide committee, or just sponsored by one or more firms. Even when industrywide committees are available, firms have been known to introduce and sponsor their own standards.[13] The discussion here is on the *incentives* of firms to choose to be compatible with others. We first examine the simple case where standardization costs are different and firms play a coordination game. A 2×2 possible version of this game is presented below. Entries represent profits as shown in figure 13.7, where there is full compatibility at both noncooperative equilibria. The arrows

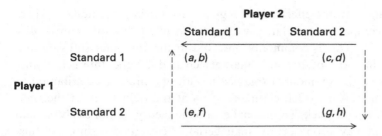

Figure 13.7
Standards war leading to incompatibility

Player 2

	Standard 1	Standard 2
Standard 1	(a, b)	(c, d)
Standard 2	(e, f)	(g, h)

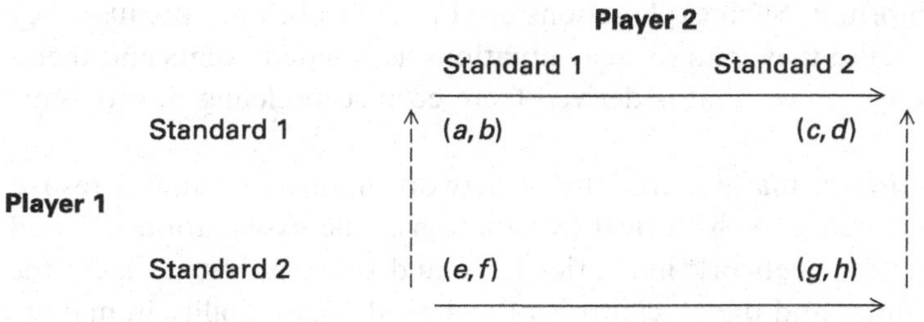

Figure 13.8
Standards war leading to incompatibility

signify the direction of individually incentives, assuming that the opponent will not change his/her strategy.

In the game of figure 13.7, standard 1 is a noncooperative equilibrium if $a > e$, $b > d$. Similarly standard 2 is an equilibrium if $g > c$, $h > f$. In this game assume that a firm has higher profits when "its" standard i get adopted, $a > g$, $b < h$. Profits, in case of disagreement, will depend on the particulars of the industry. One standard assumption that captures many industries is that in cases of disagreement profits are lower than those of argument on either standard, e, $c < g$; d, $f < b$. Under disagreement, the setting of either standard will constitute a noncooperative equilibrium. There is no guarantee that the highest joint profit standard will be adopted. Since the consumers' surplus does not appear in the payoff matrix, there is no guarantee of maximization of social welfare at the noncooperative equilibrium.

In the same setup we could have each side preferring its own sponsored standard no matter what the opponent does; that is, each side has a dominant strategy and chooses its own technical standard. This game results in an in incompatibility equilibrium.

To understand the relative benefits of the compatibility decision, we need to examine the industry structures that would arise under either choice. When all firms are compatible, one expects equality to the extent that it is the rule in nonnetwork industries. However, in industries exhibiting strong network effects, in a regime of total incompatibility (where each firm has its own incompatible standard), we expect to observe extreme inequality in market shares and profits. This is commonly observed in the computer software and hardware industries and in most of the new markets created by the Internet. Sometimes such extreme inequality is commonly explained in industry circles by attribution to history. Stories abound on who or which company "was at the right place at the right time" and therefore now leads the pack. Traditional economic theory cannot easily explain such extreme inequality and may also resort to "managerial," "entrepreneurship," or "historical" explanations that are brought over in economics only when all else fails. As a last resort, if all else fails to explain a market phenomenon, economists tend to dismiss what they cannot explain as an "aberration" or a temporary phenomenon that will certainly disappear in the long-run equilibrium! Such explanations are deficient not only because they may be incorrect but also because they tend to treat situations as isolated events and therefore lose all potential predictive power that is derived from correct modeling of economic phenomena.

There is a simple explanation of market structure in network industries without resorting to managerial, entrepreneurship, or historical explanations. The explanation is based on two fundamental features that network industries have and other industries lack: the existence of network externalities and the crucial role of technical compatibility in making the network externalities function.

Firms can make a strategic choice on if they are going to be compatible with others, and sometimes on if they will allow others to be compatible with them. The ability of a firm to exclude other firms from sharing a technical standard depends on the property rights that a firm has. For example, a firm may have a copyright or a patent on the technical platform or design, and can therefore exclude others from using it.

Compatibility with competitors brings higher network externality benefits ("network effect") and therefore is desirable. At the same time compatibility makes product X a closer substitute to competing products ("competition effect"), and it is therefore undesirable. In making a choice on compatibility, a firm has to balance these opposing incentives. In a network industry the traditional decisions of output and price take special importance, since higher output can increase the network externalities benefits that a firm can reap.

Inequality in market shares and profitability is a natural consequence of incompatibility. Under incompatibility, network externalities act as a *quality feature* that differentiates the products. Firms want to differentiate their products because they want to avoid intense competition.

In making the choice between compatibility and incompatibility, firms take into account the intensity of the network externality. The more intense the network externality, the stronger is the incentive for a firm to break away and be incompatible from substitutes. It follows that in industries with very intense network externalities, firms are more likely to choose incompatibility. As we will see in detail below, incompatibility implies inequality.

Inequality is accentuated by output expansion and an increase of the network. Moreover a firm of higher output has a higher perceived quality and is therefore able to quote a higher price. Thus the inequality in profits is even more acute than the inequality of outputs.

Inequality of Market Shares and Profits   Markets with strong network effects where firms can choose their own technical standards are "winner-take-most" markets. In these markets there is extreme market share and profits inequality. The market share of the largest firm can easily be a multiple of the market share of the second largest, the second largest firm's market share can be a multiple of the market share of the third, and so on. This geometric sequence of market shares implies that even for a small number of firms n, the nth firm's market share is tiny. In equilibrium there is extreme market share and profits inequality.[14]

The reason for the inequality is straightforward. A firm with a large market share has higher sales of complementary goods and therefore its good is more valuable to consumers. This feeds back resulting in even higher sales. Conversely, a firm with small market share has lower sales of complementary goods, and the feedback results in even lower sales. However, the low-sales firm is not necessarily driven out of business because that would require too low a price by the high-sales firm. In the absence of fixed costs, an infinite number of firms can survive, but there is tremendous inequality in market shares, prices, and profits among them. Good examples of this market structure are the PC operating systems market and many software applications markets.

To understand the extent of market share, price, and profits inequality in network industries, we provide results from Economides and Flyer (1998). As a benchmark they assume that all firms produce identical products, except for whatever quality is added to them by network externalities. Also they assume that no firm has any technical advantage in production over any other with respect to any particular platform and that there are no production costs. We consider here only the extreme case of "pure network goods" where there is no value to the good in the absence of network externalities. The summary of the equilibria under total incompatibility (which can be enforced when firms have proprietary standards) is in tables 13.1 and 13.2. The ith firm sells quantity q_i at price p_i, and firms are ordered in decreasing quantity so that $q_1 > q_2 > q_3$, meaning firm 1 has the largest sales, firm 2 is the second largest, and so on. The maximum potential sales is normalized to equal 1. At equilibrium not all consumers buy the good, that is, total sales are $\sum_{j=i}^{I} q_j < 1$.

The market equilibria exhibit extreme inequality. The ratio of outputs of consecutive firms is over 2.6. Ratios of prices of consecutive firms are higher than 7. The ratio of profits of consecutive firms is about 20. This means that a firm that has about 38 percent of the sales of the immediately larger firm, can charge only 15 percent of the price of the next larger firm, and receives only 5 percent of the profits of the immediately larger firm. Entry after the third firm has practically no influence on the output, prices, and profits of the top three firms as well as the consumers' and producers' surplus. From the fourth one on, firms are so small that their entry hardly influences the market.

Table 13.1
Quantities, market coverage, and prices under incompatibility

Num-ber of firms I	Sales of largest firm q_1	Sales of second firm q_2	Sales of third firm q_3	Market coverage $\sum_{j=1}^{I} q_j$	Price of largest firm p_1	Price of second firm p_2	Price of third firm p_3	Price of smallest firm p_I
1	0.6666			0.6666	0.222222			2.222e-1
2	0.6357	0.2428		0.8785	0.172604	0.0294		2.948e-2
3	0.6340	0.2326	0.0888	0.9555	0.170007	0.0231	0.0035	3.508e-3
4	0.6339	0.2320	0.0851	0.9837	0.169881	0.0227	0.0030	4.533e-4
5	0.6339	0.2320	0.0849	0.9940	0.169873	0.0227	0.0030	7.086e-5
6	0.6339	0.2320	0.0849	0.9999	0.169873	0.0227	0.0030	9.88e-11
7	0.6339	0.2320	0.0849	0.9999	0.169873	0.0227	0.0030	≈ 0

Note: Even with no fixed costs and an *infinite* number of firms, the Herfindahl-Hirschman index is HHI = 0.464, which corresponds to between two and three firms of equal size.

Table 13.2
Profits, consumers' and total surplus under incompatibility

Number of firms I	Π_1	Π_2	Π_3	Profits of last firm Π_I	Total industry profits $\sum_{j=i}^{I} \Pi_j$	Consumers' surplus (CS)	Total surplus (TS)
1	0.1481			0.1481	0.1481	0.148197	0.29629651
2	0.1097	7.159e-3		7.159e-3	0.1168	0.173219	0.29001881
3	0.1077	5.377e-3	3.508e-4	3.508e-4	0.1135	0.175288	0.28878819
4	0.1077	5.285e-3	3.096e-4	1.474e-5	0.1132	0.175483	0.28868321
5	0.1077	5.281e-3	2.592e-4	8.44e-7	0.1132	0.175478	0.28867817
6	0.1077	5.281e-3	2.589e-4	1.18e-14	0.1132	0.175478	0.28867799
7	0.1077	5.281e-3	2.589e-4	0	0.1132	0.175478	0.28867799

Monopoly May Maximize Total Surplus In industries with significant network externalities, under conditions of incompatibility between competing platforms, monopoly may maximize social surplus. This is because, when strong network effects are present, a very large market share of one platform creates significant network benefits for this platform, which contribute to large consumers' and producers' surpluses. It is possible to have situations where a breakup of a monopoly into two competing firms of incompatible standards *reduces* rather than increases social surplus because network externalities benefits are reduced. This is because de facto standardization is valuable, even if done by a monopolist.

In the Economides-Flyer model, although consumers' surplus is increasing in the number of active firms, total surplus is decreasing in the number of firms. That is, the more firms in the market, the lower is total welfare. This remarkable result comes from the fact that when there are fewer firms in the market there is more coordination and the network effects are larger. As the number of firms decreases, the positive network effects increase more than the deadweight loss so that total surplus is maximized in a monopoly! Total surplus is highest while consumers' surplus is lowest in a monopoly. This poses an interesting dilemma for antitrust authorities. Should they intervene or not? In nonnetwork industries typically both consumers' and total surplus are lowest in a monopoly. In this network model, maximizing consumer's surplus would imply minimizing total surplus.

Compared to the market equilibrium under compatibility, the incompatibility equilibrium is deficient along many dimensions. Consumers' and total surplus are higher under compatibility, the profits of all except the highest production firm are higher under incompatibility, and prices are lower under compatibility except possibly in a duopoly.

No Anticompetitive Acts Are *Necessary* to Create Market Inequality   Because inequality is natural in the market structure of network industries, there should be no presumption that anticompetitive actions are responsible for the creation of market share inequality or very high profitability of a top firm. Thus no anticompetitive acts are *necessary* to create this inequality. The "but for" benchmark against which anticompetitive actions in network industries are to be judged should not be "perfect competition" but an environment of significant inequality and profits.

In Network Industries, Free Entry Does Not Lead to Perfect Competition   The existence of network effects imply that in network industries, free entry does not lead to perfect competition. In a market with strong network effects, once few firms are in operation, the addition of new competitors, even under conditions of free entry, does not change the market structure in any significant way. Although eliminating barriers to entry can encourage competition, the resulting competition may not significantly affect market structure. This implies that in markets with strong network effects, antitrust authorities may not be able to significantly affect market *structure* by eliminating barriers to entry. See the earlier example where the addition of the fifth firm hardly changes the output of the first four firms.

The remarkable property of the incompatibility equilibrium is the extreme inequality in market shares and profits that is sustained under conditions of free entry. Antitrust and competition law have placed a tremendous amount of hope on the ability of free entry to spur competition, reduce prices, and ultimately eliminate profits. In network industries, free entry brings into the industry an infinity of firms, but it fails miserably to reduce inequality in market shares, prices, and profits. Entry does not eliminate the profits of the high-production firms. And it is worth noting that at the equilibrium of this market there is no anticompetitive behavior. Firms do not reach their high output and market domination by exclusion, coercion, tying, erecting barriers to entry, or any other anticompetitive behavior. The extreme inequality is a natural feature of the market equilibrium.

At the long-run equilibrium of this model with free entry, an infinity of firms have entered, yet the equilibrium is far from competitive. No anticompetitive activity has led firms to this equilibrium. Traditional antitrust intervention cannot accomplish much because the conditions that such intervention seeks to establish already exist in this market.

Can there be an improvement over the market incompatibility equilibrium? Yes, a switch to the compatibility equilibrium has higher consumers' and total surpluses for any number of firms. Is it within the scope of competition law to impose such a change? It depends. Firms might have a legally protected intellectual property right that arises from their creation of the design of the platform. Only if anticompetitive behavior was involved, can the antitrust authorities clearly intervene.

Imposing a "Competitive" Market Structure Is Likely to Be Counterproductive An implication of network effects is that antitrust interventions may be futile. Because "winner takes most" is the natural equilibrium in these markets, attempting to superimpose a different market structure (e.g., one in which all firms have approximately equal market shares) may be both futile and counterproductive.

Nature of Competition Is Different in Network Industries Strong network effects imply that competition *for the market* takes precedence over competition *in the market*. The fact that the natural equilibrium market structure in network industries is winner take most with very significant market inequality does not imply that competition is weak. Competition on which firm will create the predominant (top) platform and reap most of the benefits is often intense. In network industries there is typically an intense race to be the dominant firm. In network industries we often observe Schumpeterian races for market dominance.

A good recent example of Schumpeterian competition is the competition among dot-coms in 1999 and 2000. As explained earlier, economic models imply a high valuation of the dominant firm compared to other firms in the same network industry. The same perception prevailed on Wall Street. During that period, dot-com firms advertised very intensely and subsidized consumers so as to be able to achieve the coveted dominant position in the market. The easy availability of capital for dot-coms at the time facilitated this behavior as firms "burned" almost all the cash they had in their attempts to get the top market share. Many of the dot-coms failed because demand for their services was much lower than predicted or because of flaws in their business models. However, all the successful dot-coms, such as eBay, Amazon, Yahoo, and later Google, also followed this strategy. Generally, in network industries, the costs of entry may be higher, but the rewards of success may be higher compared to nonnetwork industries.

Path Dependence The presence of network effects gives special importance to *path dependence*. Path dependence is the dependence of a system or network on past decisions of producers and consumers. For example, the price at which a VHS player can be sold today is path dependent because it depends on the number of VHS players sold earlier (the installed base of VHS players). The existence of an installed base of consumers favors an incumbent. However, competitors with significant product advantages or a better pricing strategy can overcome the advantage of an installed base.

For example, in the market for video players, VHS overcame Beta after six years of higher installed base by Beta. This was an implication of

1. Sony's mistake in disregarding network externalities and not licensing the Beta format.
2. JVC's widespread licensing of VHS.
3. The fact that one low-end, low-priced VHS player can contribute as much to the network effect as a high-end, high-priced Beta player.

In the Beta/VHS case, it is clear that Sony mistakenly ignored the network effects that arose from the availability of rental tapes of pre-recorded movies. The main function of video recorders was originally thought to be "time delay" in watching material recorded from the TV. The pre-recorded market emerged later, first as a market where movies were sold and later as a movies rental market. The emergence of markets for "movies for sale" and "movies for rent," which had to be recorded in a particular format, created a significant complementary good for Beta and VHS players. The significant cost of physical distribution of tapes throughout the country and the costs of carrying a significant inventory of titles made the choice of what movies to bring and in what format crucially dependent on present and forecasted demand. This forecast was highly correlated with the present and forecast installed base of video players in each format. Thus, although network effects and path dependence played a crucial role in determining the fate of Beta, the outcome was far from predetermined. Early, more aggressive licensing of the Beta format by Sony or the early promotion of low-end Beta players could have reversed the demise of the Beta format.

An often cited example on path dependence is the prevalence of the QWERTY keyboard despite claims of more efficient function by the alternative Dvorak keyboard. For many business applications, and for antitrust purposes, the QWERTY example is not crucial because there was no significant strategic business interest in the success of either design. There is also a factual dispute on whether the Dvorak keyboard was significantly more efficient than the QWERTY one.[15]

13.3   Competition Policy Issues in Network Industries

13.3.1   One-sided Bottlenecks
Interconnection issues in telecommunications, railroads, airline, and other transportation networks are very common. Often one company controls exclusively a part of the network, which is required by others to provide services. We call this network part "a bottleneck." Generally, bottlenecks can be divided into two categories: one-sided and two-sided. A one-sided bottleneck is monopolized by a firm, and this firm does not require the use of a different bottleneck. Such a bottleneck is shown as link AB in figure 13.9. An example of

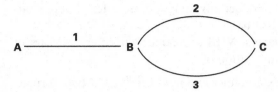

Figure 13.9
One-sided bottleneck

such a bottleneck is the connection of local service telecommunications subscribers to a switch. This is typically called "the last mile," and often called "the local loop." After the 1984 breakup of AT&T, the local loop has been monopolized by the local exchange carrier, typically a Regional Bell Operating Company (RBOC) or GTE. Excluding cellular phones, the local loop is a required input in the production of long-distance services, and typically long-distance companies do not have a comparable local loop. Similarly such a one-way bottleneck can arise when a firm monopolizes a railroad track such as *AB*. In telecommunications, the local exchange bottleneck has traditionally resulted in high prices for use of the bottleneck to originate ("access origination") or terminate calls ("access termination").

The potential anticompetitive consequences of a one-sided bottleneck are obvious, and have been understood since the early days of the telecommunications network when AT&T enjoyed a monopoly in long distance (here *AB*) but faced competition in local markets. In the context of figure 13.9, the early AT&T was in possession of links 1 (long distance) and 2 (local) but did not allow an independent firm that possessed link 3 to interconnect at *B* and provide part of the long-distance service *CBA*. For over two decades in the beginning of the twentieth century, AT&T refused to interconnect independent local telecommunications companies to its long-distance network unless they became part of the Bell System, which essentially meant unless they were acquired.[16]

The early AT&T foreclosure of independents through a refusal to interconnect shows the importance of complementarities in networks and the way that companies can leverage dominance in one market to create dominance in a market for complementary goods, especially when the complementary good requires the monopolized input to provide a final service. In this case AT&T monopolized long distance and was able to leverage its position in long distance (through the refusal to interconnect with independent locals) and gain a dominant position in local telecommunications markets throughout the country.

The continued foreclosure of the independents by AT&T and its "refusal to deal" with them caused regulation to be established at the state and federal levels in the 1930s. The 1934 Federal Communications Act ("1934 Act") imposed mandatory interconnection in an attempt to stop the foreclosure of independents and stabilized the market share of local lines held by AT&T. However, at that point AT&T's market share of local lines had increased from about 50 percent in 1914 to close to the 89 percent that AT&T had in 1981, prior to the 1982 agreement with the Department of Justice to be broken up.

A major revision of the 1934 Act, the Telecommunications Act of 1996 ("1996 Act"), mandates interconnection of all public switched telecommunications networks at any technically feasible point. The 1996 Act and similar EU regulations attempt to solve the problem of the monopolization of the key parts of local telecommunications network. They impose unbundling of the network and forced leasing to entrants of some of the monopolized parts of the network, including the local loop. The goal is to make "mix-and-match" entry strategies feasible for local voice telephone service as well as broadband Internet access through digital subscriber lines (DSL) that utilizes high-frequency transmission though copper local loops. Thus the 1996 Act and EU regulations mandate access prices for unbundled parts of the network (unbundled network elements, or UNEs) at cost-based prices. The FCC and state PUCs accepted the view that lease prices should be based on *forward-looking* costs of a network that could be built today rather than on historical, accounting, or embedded costs (as favored by RBOCs). In setting prices for unbundled network elements, the FCC and state public utility commissions (PUCs) also rejected the relevance of prices based on *private* opportunity cost, such as the efficient components pricing rule (ECPR). Such rules derive prices for components from the monopoly prices of end-to-end services. Thus the ECPR and its varieties would guarantee the monopolist's profits despite market structure changes in the markets for components that are used to create final services.[17] To prevent anticompetitive actions in telecommunications, the 1996 Act also imposes a number of rules, such as number portability, mandatory resale of services, transparency, and nondiscrimination. A full discussion of these rules can be found at Economides (1999). Still the 1996 Act missed opportunities to define technical standards and require technical compatibility of telecommunications equipment.

Unfortunately, legal maneuvers by the incumbent local exchange carriers and high prices for the unbundled network elements considerably delayed very significant entry in local telecommunications markets. Despite the delayed entry, Economides, Seim, and Viard (2007), analyzing local telecommunications entry in New York State, show that entry resulted in substantial benefits to consumers. Local telecommunications entry in residential markets through leasing of the incumbent's network by major carriers such as AT&T and MCI has practically stopped after the Court of Appeals in Washington, DC, struck down the FCC rules implementing leasing, and the new FCC rules did not enforce leasing "at cost plus reasonable profit" prices.[18]

13.3.2 Two-sided Bottlenecks

In a two-sided bottleneck, each of two firms is a monopolist, each with a different bottleneck, and each firm requires the other's bottleneck to produce its output. Take the example

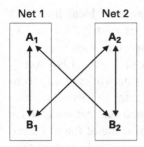

Figure 13.10
Two-sided bottleneck

of two local telephone companies. Customers subscribe only to one local telephone company but may require the other company's network to complete calls. This case is represented in figure 13.10. Calls originate at A_1 or A_2 and terminate at B_1 or B_2. In the context of this example, each of firms 1 and 2 buys *access termination* from the other. If each firm $i = 1, 2$, sells both services A_1B_2 and B_1A_2, then each firms buys both *access origination* and access termination from the other. Termination charges at B_1 or B_2 for calls from the opponent network can be used to disadvantage and foreclose the opponent network.

Many issues of traditional bottlenecks have been dealt by regulation in the United States and the European Union. In monopolized one-way bottlenecks, such as access origination and termination used in the creation of long-distance calls, access prices are regulated and there has been a tendency to decrease the regulated prices. However, prices are still high. In the two-way bottleneck of access used in the creation of local calls by competing local exchange carriers, the Telecommunications Act of 1996 imposes cost-based reciprocal fees and allows the possibility of "bill and keep," meaning zero prices. If cost-based reciprocal compensation were not the rule, and firms were able to set termination at profit-maximizing levels, Economides, Lopomo, and Woroch (1996, 2007) show that a large network will try to impose very high termination charges on an opponent's small network so that no calls terminate from the small network to the large one. Without the possibility of such across-networks calls, a small network will only be able to provide within-network calls and, being small, will be of little value to potential subscribers. As a consequence large networks would be able to provide more value to subscribers, and the small network would be foreclosed. Starting from a regime of a large local incumbent and a small potential entrant, the large incumbent could set up termination access fees to keep the entrant out of the market.[19]

In summary, in the absence of specific regulatory rules, two-sided bottlenecks can lead to foreclosure of competitors, even when each firm requires use of the bottleneck of the other to complete calls or provide a service.[20]

13.3.3 Market Power Creation Specific to Networks: The Importance of Technical Standards

The example of early AT&T's refusal to deal (interconnect) with independents (and with interconnected networks of independents) can also arise in milder terms when a firm X that has a significant position in its industry insists that firms that provide complementary products Y do not also provide them to X's competitors. For example, in the mid-1980s Nintendo refused to allow third-party games (software) to play on its game console (hardware) unless the software manufacturers agreed not to write a similar game for competing game systems for two years. Faced with this condition imposed by Nintendo, software developers had to make a choice to either write a game for Nintendo or for the competing platforms of Atari and Sega. Clearly, this restriction reduced the potential revenue of a game developer who would like, for a small additional cost, to port its game to the alternative systems. But also, more important, the restriction forced developers to predict which game system would have higher sales, and create software just for this system. Thus Nintendo used its dominance of the game market at that point in time to coerce developers to write software just for its platform, and thereby increased the value of the Nintendo virtual network (of hardware and software). Nintendo abandoned this requirement under antitrust challenge.

Because of the extreme inequality of market shares, prices, and profits in a network industry, restriction of the installed base of a firm in a network industry can be very detrimental. It can push a firm to a lower rank with significantly lower profits or, in extreme cases, push a firm to such a low market share that it has to close down because it cannot recover its fixed costs.

Another example from the computing industry illustrates a situation of market power creation specific to networks. Suppose that firm A chooses to make its product A incompatible with the products of other firms that perform similar functions, and it also subsidizes firms that produce complementary goods B to its product A.[21] Alternatively, we may assume that firm A subsidizes its own division that sells complementary goods B. The results are as follows:

1. The value of firm A's product increases.
2. The entry hurdle of firm A's rivals increases.
3. There is possible creation of market power.

Firm A's defense will be that its actions are pro-competitive, since their primary cause is the enhancement of the value of product A. From the point of view of A's competitors, the actions of A look very much like anticompetitive behavior since the abundance of complementary goods B for product A puts them at a competitive disadvantage.

Note that the existence of incompatibility is a *necessary* condition for possible creation of market power. Moreover the key to increasing social welfare is to move to compatibility. That is, assuming that innovation and product availability will not be reduced, the best of all worlds is to have public standards and full compatibility. However, it is very difficult for US antitrust authorities to intervene and/or define standards.

Besides the use of technical standards, firms can use bundling and other pricing strategies as well as non–price discrimination strategies to leverage market power across markets.

13.3.4 Vertical Integration and Vertical Control Issues in Network Industries

In networks, as in other settings, there are potentially anticompetitive issues arising from the possibility of vertical integration and the behavior of vertically integrated firms. These may include the bundling of components through vertical integration, contract, or manipulation of technical standards so that an entrant must enter both components markets even if it desires to enter only one of the markets. Often firms have expertise or a technical advantage in only one component and desire to enter only in the market for that component. An incumbent can strategically alter the market environment through acquisition or contract so that the entrant can only be successful if it enters more than one market. This increases the financial hurdle for an entrant, and it also forces it to sell components where it does not have expertise. Thus it makes it more likely that entry will not occur.

A vertically integrated firm can also use discrimination in price charged to a subsidiary compared to the price charged to a downstream competitor, or discrimination in quality provided to subsidiary compared to quality provided to a downstream competitor, that is, raising rivals' costs. These issues are discussed in more detail in Economides (1996b).

Firms in network industries can also use a variety of way to manipulate technical standards in joint ventures to achieve market power. The issue of market power then arises in "aftermarkets," where consumers are "locked in" to a service that arises out of commitments of a durable nature. For example, in an important case that reached the Supreme Court, Kodak refused to supply parts to independent firms that serviced Kodak photocopiers. Although one could argue that there was significant competition in the market for new photocopiers and Kodak did not have a dominant position in that market, once customers had bought a Kodak photocopier, they were "locked in," and faced significant costs to buy a new photocopier of a different brand. So Kodak's actions could be anticompetitive in the "aftermarket" for repair services of consumers who have already bought Kodak photocopiers. A similar case of anticompetitive actions can be made in aftermarkets where consumers are locked in by having made an investment in a durable good that is incompatible with other comparable durable goods or are locked in other ways. For example, consumers without number portability in wireless cellular and PCS markets may be "locked in" to the service of a particular provider or network. Similarly consumers can be "locked in" to the e-mail service of an Internet service provider (ISP), since there is no portability of e-mail addresses and many ISPs do not offer forwarding of incoming e-mail messages to another ISP. The problem becomes even more complex when the conditions that establish dominance in the aftermarket are set in the shrink-wrap contract that the consumer agrees to when he bys the original product. For example, what if car manufacturers imposed the condition that by buying the car, the consumer agrees to only buy replacement parts from this manufacturer? Or more generally in a network industry, what if a hardware or software platform seller imposed conditions on what software (or complementary goods) will it allow consumers to use with its platform. These are important issues that need to be examined.

13.3.5 B2B, B2C, and Other Exchanges Issues

The world of business to business (B2B) and business to consumers (B2C) exchanges lacks the regulation of traditional financial and commodity exchanges. Many proposed B2B exchanges are run by the firms that also are trading. For example, Enron was proud of the fact that it was participating as a trading party in B2B exchanges that it organized and ran. Such a situation would be strictly prohibited in traditional financial and commodity exchanges because of the possibility that the organizer of the exchange would take advantage of the information created in the trading process to fashion privately beneficial trades. In another example, Covisint, an exchange for automobile parts organized by automobile manufacturers, was accused of acting to consolidate the monopsony power of car manufacturers. In general, B2B exchanges can provide substantial benefits by consolidating trades, increasing market liquidity, improving standardization, and reducing search costs.[22] But B2B exchanges also have the potential of creating significant antitrust issues.

13.3.6 Dynamic Efficiency Issues

The world of networks and dynamic effects brings to the forefront the fact that behavior that exhibits static efficiency may lack dynamic inter-temporal efficiency. The possibility exists of a lock-in to a technology and a path that, when decisions are taken in every period, looks optimal given past decisions but is suboptimal if earlier investment decisions had been delayed and all the decisions were taken at once. In a world with network effects a "lock-in" to an inferior technology can easily occur as firms (and countries) find it more desirable to invest in the technology in which they have already invested. This can occur under perfect competition, but the problem can easily become much more important under oligopoly, as firms race to become dominant, given the importance of dominance in a network industry. With rapid technological change, firms in an oligopoly race for dominance can easily get stuck investing heavily in the currently best technology and unable to invest sufficiently in the next technology, thereby placing themselves off the optimal investment path.

13.3.7 Innovation Issues

An important antitrust issue is the speed of innovation in a network industry as affected by strategic decisions of firms and potentially anticompetitive actions. The effects of actions on innovation are important because innovation affects the welfare of future consumers, and this should be taken into consideration in an antitrust decisions. The difficulty in dealing with innovation issues in antitrust arises from the fact that the efficiency and intensity of innovation in monopoly compared to perfect competition and oligopoly are open questions in economics. Thus it is very hard to make general statements on innovation in an antitrust context.

13.3.8   Criteria to Be Used for Antitrust Intervention in Network Industries

When an antitrust intervention is considered in a network industry, a number of considerations that arise out of the nature of network industries have to be taken account. These are explained in detail in earlier sections, primarily in section 13.2. First, the benchmark of the "but for" world that should be considered is a network industries equilibrium with significant inequality, rather than a perfectly competitive equilibrium. Second, competitors' harm is not a sufficient reason for intervention. The right question is, Were consumers (past, present, future) harmed by specific actions? Third, uncertainty must be taken into account, and caution must be used in guessing how a high-technology industry would have evolved but for the anticompetitive action(s). Fourth, it is possible for monopoly to maximize total surplus. Fifth, it is not possible to sustain a long-term equilibrium with equal market shares, and a short-term equilibrium with equal market shares generally has low total surplus. Sixth, path dependence and the value of installed base are limited by Schumpeterian competition, and upheavals are not uncommon in network industries. Seventh, especially in software industries, the extent and functionality of products is flexible.[23] The definition of the market of a potential antitrust violation may be much harder.

13.3.9   Criteria to Be Used for Remedies

When a remedies phase is reached, a liability finding has already been made. The objective of remedies is to stop practices that are found to be illegal, prevent the recurrence of such practices, and restore any recurring threat posed by such practices.

Any intervention by antitrust authorities creates a disruption in the workings of markets. The objective of the remedial relief is to accomplish the objectives mentioned in the previous paragraph without damaging efficient production and competition in the market. The potential damage that antitrust intervention can produce is larger when it is applied to an industry with fast technological change, where leaps to new and more efficient technologies are expected while the specific nature of the future winning technology is unknown. Often it is difficult to predict future winning technologies, and therefore it is hard to fashion an antitrust remedy with an accurate prediction of its effect on industry structure and competition a few years down the road. Of course, this uncertainty is multiplied when the remedy creates a significant intervention in the industry. Therefore, lacking the knowledge of the effects of their actions, it is in the public interest that antitrust authorities and courts avoid extensive intervention in industries with fast technological change. It is best to intervene only to the extent that (1) intervention reverses the effects of actions for which liability was established and (2) the effects of the intervention are predictable.

In markets with network effects, as I have explained in detail above, the existence of network effects has crucial implications on market structure and the ability of antitrust authorities to affect it. In markets with strong network effects, even in the absence of anticompetitive acts, the existence of network effects in markets results in significant inequalities in market shares and profits. The resulting equilibrium market structure can be called a *natural oligopoly* where very few firms dominate the market. The structural features of natural oligopoly for a software market cannot be altered by antitrust intervention without significant losses for society. The very nature of markets with network effects implies that the ability of antitrust authorities to alter market structure in such industries is limited, as discussed above.

As an alternative to antitrust and competition law, sectoral economic regulation can and has been established in three exceptional case: (1) for markets where it is clear that competition cannot be achieved by market forces, (2) for markets where deviation from efficiency is deemed socially desirable, and (3) for markets where the social and private benefits are clearly different. In each of these cases it should be clear that a market without intervention will not result in the desired outcome. I will leave case 2 aside, since a discussion of it will lead us to a detailed discussion of specific industries. The requirements for case 3 are typically met in many network industries, since expansion of the network creates network effects that are typically not fully internalized by markets. However, it would be foolish to advocate regulation as the standard solution in network industries because of the existence of network effects. Often a much smaller intervention, such as subsidization of the network to help network effects, will be enough.

In case 1, where it is clear that competition and its benefits cannot be achieved by market forces, regulation may be a solution. The significant advantage of industry-specific regulation is that it can be tailored to the specifics of the industry, and specific rules on pricing and availability of particular products and services. Regulators, such as the FCC, also have staffs that can provide impartial technical advice that is unavailable to a court.

However, regulation has a number of drawbacks. First, it is best suited for industries with well-defined and slow-changing products and services. With stable product definitions, rules can be devised and specific pricing can be implemented if necessary. Second, as a corollary to the first observation, regulation is not well suited in industries with rapid technological change and frequently changing product definitions. Moreover, in an industry with fast technical progress, regulation can be used by the regulated companies to keep prices relatively high, as exemplified by telecommunications regulation. Third, often regulators are very close to the interests of the regulated parties rather than to the interests of the public. Fourth, experience has shown that often regulators are not well informed about key variables as well as changes in the industry. Fifth, regulators at both the state and federal levels are under pressure and influence by both the executive and the legislative part of government, so they cannot be as impartial as a court. Sixth, there is a tendency for regulators to expand their reach into related and new markets. For example, the California Public Service Commission has recently asserted its authority over the Internet.[24] These drawbacks can create significant surplus loss due to regulation.

In summary, regulation should be used sparingly in industries with stable products if it is clear that antitrust has failed. It should be kept in mind that regulation can cause a significant surplus loss as well.

13.3.10   Recent Antitrust Cases in Network Industries

The Microsoft Antitrust Cases   Over the last few years the Federal Trade Commission and the Department of Justice of the United States have investigated Microsoft on various antitrust allegations. The 1991 to 1993 and 1993 to 1994 investigations by the Federal Trade Commission (FTC) ended with no lawsuits. The 1994 investigation[25] by the United States Department of Justice (DOJ) was terminated with a consent decree in 1995.[26] The key provisions of the 1995 consent decree were as follows:

1. Microsoft agreed to end "per-processor" contracts with computer manufacturers (original equipment manufacturers, or OEMs), but it was allowed to use unrestricted quantity discounts.

2. "Microsoft shall not enter into any License Agreement in which the terms of that agreement are expressly or impliedly conditioned upon the licensing of any other Covered Product, Operating System Software product or other product (provided, however, that this provision in and of itself shall not be construed to prohibit Microsoft from developing integrated products); or the OEM not licensing, purchasing, using or distributing any non-Microsoft product."[27]

Thus the 1995 consent decree imposed two restrictions, one horizontal, and one vertical. The horizontal restriction stops Microsoft from charging an effectively zero price for the last 5 or 10 percent of the consumers sold to an OEM. By setting a lump-sum fee (based on the total number of computers manufactured by an OEM), Microsoft effectively set the price of the last 10 percent or more to zero. For example, suppose that an OEM produces 1 million units and Microsoft sets the per unit price of Windows at $40. In a per-processor contract Microsoft can offer to the OEM the option to install Windows in all 1 million units at a price of $30 million. This is equivalent to 750,000 units sold at $40 and 250,000 units sold at zero price. Thus this particular per-processor contract essentially sets the price of the last 25 percent of the production of the OEM at zero. If the OEM was installing Windows to approximately 75 percent of its production, the per-processor contract gives strong incentives to expand this percentage, since competing operating systems are sold at a positive price. The per-processor offer was an aggressive pricing contract by Microsoft that helped it gain and retain market share in competition with DR DOS and IBM's

OS-2. The 1995 consent decree stopped the zero marginal price offer but allowed quantity discounts to OEMs. Since this was not quantified and since software has practically zero marginal cost, there is no clear guidance from this case on the extent of quantity discount that would be considered illegal.

The vertical restriction of the 1995 consent decree prohibits product bundling created by contract but allows Microsoft to keep expanding the number and type of functions of its products, including Windows. In short, in the 1995 consent decree contractual bundling was disallowed, but technological bundling was explicitly allowed. As we will see, this issue is of crucial importance in the next Microsoft case. The 1995 consent decree was a crucial win for Microsoft because it allowed it to expand the functionality of Windows.

Over time a number of new functions were incorporated in Windows, including memory management, disk compression, disk defragmentation, Web browsing, and many others. On October 20, 1997, DOJ alleged that Microsoft violated the 1995 consent decree by bundling Internet Explorer (IE) with the Windows operating systems, and requiring computer manufacturers to distribute IE with Windows 95. DOJ petitioned the district court to find Microsoft in civil contempt. On December 11, 1997, Judge Thomas Penfield Jackson issued a preliminary injunction barring the bundling of IE with Windows.[28] On May 12, 1998, the court of appeals for the DC Circuit voided the 1997 preliminary injunction. On June 23, 1998, the court of appeals ruled that the 1995 consent decree did not apply to Windows 98, which was shipped with an integrated IE as part of the operating system and an IE icon on the PC desktop, arguing that "courts are ill equipped to evaluate the benefits of high-tech product design."[29]

During the week following the court of appeals stay of Judge Jackson's preliminary injunction that barred the bundling of IE with Windows because of the alleged violation of the 1995 consent decree, DOJ filed a major antitrust suit against Microsoft. In this action (DOJ Complaint 98-12320), filed on May 18, 1998, DOJ was joined by the attorneys general of 20 states and the District of Columbia. The court of appeals in its June 23, 1998, decision affirmed that Microsoft's practice of bundling IE with Windows was legal under the terms of the 1995 consent decree. To overcome this interpretation of the law as far as the integration of the browser is concerned, DOJ argued that Microsoft's bundling of IE with Windows and its attempt to eliminate Netscape as a competitor in the browser market was much more than adding functionality to Windows and marginalizing a series of add-on software manufacturers. DOJ alleged (and the district court concurred) that Microsoft added browser functionality to Windows and marginalized Netscape because Netscape posed a potential competitive threat to the Windows operating system. This distinctive threat posed by Netscape was a crucial part of the DOJ allegations. DOJ alleged that applications could be written to be executed "on top" of Netscape; since Netscape could be run on a number of operating systems, DOJ alleged that Netscape could erode the market power of Windows. In DOJ's logic, Microsoft gave away IE and integrated it in Windows so that Netscape would not become a platform that would compete with Windows. Thus DOJ alleged that Microsoft's free distribution of IE, its bundling with Windows, and all its attempts to win the browser wars were *defensive* moves by Microsoft to protect its Windows monopoly, which DOJ and Microsoft agreed was originally created legally.[30]

Formally, the allegations were as follows:

1. Microsoft illegally monopolized the market for operating systems (OSs) for personal computers (PCs) under Section 2 of the Sherman Antitrust Act.

2. Microsoft had anticompetitive contractual arrangements with various vendors of related goods, such as with computer manufacturers (OEMs) and Internet service providers (ISPs), and had taken other actions to preserve and enhance its monopoly; these contractual arrangements and other actions were illegal under Section 2 of the Sherman Antitrust Act.

3. Microsoft illegally attempted to monopolize the market for Internet browsers (but failed to succeed), an act that is illegal under Section 2 of the Sherman Antitrust Act.

4. Microsoft bundled anticompetitively its Internet browser, IE, the Microsoft Internet browser, with its Windows operating systems; this is illegal under Section 1 of the Sherman Antitrust Act.

The Microsoft trial took place at an accelerated schedule at the US District Court for the District of Columbia from October 19, 1998, to June 24, 1999.[31] Microsoft's CEO Bill Gates was not called as a witness, but his video-taped deposition was extensively used during the trial. Judge Jackson pre-announced that he would announce his "findings of fact" *before* his "conclusions of law." This was widely interpreted as implying that the judge was trying to give an opportunity to the sides to reach a compromise and resolve the case through a consent decree.

On November 5, 1999, Judge Jackson issued his "findings of fact," siding very strongly with the plaintiffs. In December 1999, Richard Posner, a prominent antitrust scholar and the Chief Judge of the Court of Appeals for the Seventh Circuit, agreed to serve as mediator for settlement discussions.[32] On April 1, 2000, settlement talks broke down after some states reportedly disagreed with the proposed agreement.[33] On April 3, 2000, Judge Jackson issued his "conclusions of law" finding for the plaintiffs on almost all points. In particular, Judge Jackson found Microsoft liable for monopolization and anticompetitive tying of IE with Windows but found that Microsoft's exclusive contracts did not make it liable for preventing Netscape from being distributed. On June 7, 2000, after an extremely short hearing,[34] Judge Jackson issued his remedies decision, splitting Microsoft into two companies, one for operating systems and one for applications and everything else, and imposing severe business conduct restrictions.

There a number of fundamental mistakes with Judge Jackson's decision on Microsoft. First, the judge did not consider the natural equilibrium in network industries. Instead, implicitly it was assumed that in the absence of anticompetitive actions, the natural equilibrium would be perfect competition. However, there is ample theoretical and empirical evidence discussed earlier in this chapter that markets with strong network effects, such as the OS market, are "winner-take-most" markets with significant market share and profits inequality as well as high concentration. Thus from the high profits and high concentration in these markets there does not necessarily follow the presumption of anticompetitive behavior. That is, the market share inequality and high profits for top firms are not necessarily the effects of anticompetitive actions but rather part of the natural equilibrium in these industries. Second, imposing a breakup will create an egalitarian market structure, since the natural equilibrium is "winner take most."

Third, there was the issue of exercising monopoly power in the OS market. In antitrust it is generally understood that a firm has monopoly power when it has the sustained ability to control price or exclude competitors. The existence of significant barriers to entry and the very high market share of Microsoft in the operating systems market gave indications that Microsoft had monopoly power. But there was also a very strong indication to the contrary. Microsoft priced its operating system to original equipment manufacturers (OEMs) at an average price of $40 to $60, a ridiculously low price compared to the static monopoly price.[35] Microsoft's economic witness showed that the static monopoly price was about $1,800, a large multiple of Microsoft's actual price.[36] At first glance, it seems that Microsoft could not possibly have monopoly power in OSs when its OS price is about 3 percent of the monopoly price.

Why was the price of Windows low compared to the monopoly price? I have argued elsewhere that all other explanations fail except that the price was low because of potential competition.[37] Briefly, Microsoft might have set the price of Windows low to hook consumers. But the low prices prevailed even when Microsoft had 90 percent market share. When would Microsoft increase the price? An alternative explanation might be that price was low because of competition from the installed base of Windows. However, (1) it is very difficult to uninstall Windows, (2) consumers buy much better new PCs faster than traditional obsolescence rates imply, and (3) Windows' price is small compared to the PC plus Windows bundle. Thus this explanation is also unlikely. Yet another explanation might be to reduce pirating. However, the price of other Microsoft products, notably MS-Office, was high. This is not consistent with the piracy explanation. Finally, another proposed explanation of the low Windows price is because it allows for higher prices of complementary goods. But since MS does not monopolize *all* the complementary goods markets, it would be optimal to charge the monopoly price on Windows. The only remaining explanation is the low price was due to the existence of actual and potential competition. Since actual competition was very limited, the remaining explanation is that potential competition constrained the price of Windows.

The Appeals Court in Washington, DC, ruled on Microsoft's appeal on June 28, 2001. The Court vacated Microsoft's breakup and other remedies imposed by the District Court. Microsoft was found liable of monopolization of the operating systems market for PCs. Microsoft was found not liable of bundling. Microsoft was found not liable of attempting to monopolize the Internet browser market. Judge Thomas Penfield Jackson of the District Court was taken off the case for improper behavior.[38] The case was remanded to the District Court for remedies determination for the monopolization charge. The Appeals Court instructed the District Court to examine the bundling of IE and Windows (if plaintiffs bring it up) under "a rule of reason" where the consumer benefits of bundling are balanced against the damage of anticompetitive actions. In face of the Appeals Court decision, DOJ decided not to pursue the bundling issue and announced that it would not seek the breakup of Microsoft.

On November 6, 2001, the United States—New York, Illinois, North Carolina, Kentucky, Michigan, Louisiana, Wisconsin, Maryland, and Ohio—and Microsoft proposed a settlement in the major antitrust case. California, Connecticut, Iowa, Massachusetts, Minnesota, West Virginia, Florida, Kansas, Utah, and the District of Columbia pursued the suit further to a full remedies trial (started March 11, 2002) in front of US District Judge Colleen Kollar-Kotelly. These states proposed making the source code of Windows and IE public, "freezing Windows" so that additional functionality would be sold as an additional good, making all APIs public, and other severe remedies.

On November 12, 2002, Judge Colleen Kollar-Kotelly imposed the final judgment that had only small differences from the original proposed settlement. The settlement terms are as follows:

• Provisions seen as favorable to Microsoft
1. No breakup
2. Microsoft can expand functions of Windows
3. No general restrictions on bundling
4. No wide disclosure of source code
• Provisions seen as favorable to the plaintiffs
1. Broad scope of definition of middleware products (browser, e-mail clients, media players, instant messaging software, etc.)
2. Requirement to partially disclose middleware interfaces. Microsoft is required to provide software developers with the interfaces used by Microsoft's middleware to interoperate with the operating system.
3. Requirement to partially disclose server protocols. The settlement imposes interoperability between Windows and non-Microsoft servers of the same level as between Windows and Microsoft servers.
4. Freedom to install middleware software. Computer manufacturers and consumers will be free to substitute competing middleware software on Microsoft's operating system.
5. Ban on retaliation. Microsoft will be prohibited from retaliating against computer manufacturers or software developers for supporting or developing certain competing software.
6. Uniform pricing of Windows for same volume sale. Microsoft will be required to license its operating system to key computer manufacturers on uniform terms for five years. Microsoft will be allowed to provide quantity discounts.

7. Ban on exclusive agreements; contract restrictions. Microsoft is prohibited from entering into agreements requiring the exclusive support or development of certain Microsoft software.

8. Compliance and enforcement. A panel of three independent, on-site, full-time computer experts will help enforce the settlement.[39]

In my opinion, this was a fair settlement. It seems that DOJ got a bit more than what it would have gotten in a full remedies trial. It is unlikely that the dissenting states will, in the end, be able to get anything substantially different from this settlement.[40]

The EU Competition Commission under Mario Monti started an important proceeding against Microsoft in August 2000. It alleged that Microsoft abused its dominant position in operating systems for PCs by leveraging this power (1) in server software and (2) in media players. In the server market, the European Union alleged that Microsoft was using its market power in PC clients to disadvantage the non-Microsoft server (in particular, Sun servers) by not disclosing sufficient information that would allow full interoperability between Microsoft clients and servers and non-Microsoft servers. In the media player market, the European Union alleged that Microsoft was using its dominant position in PC operating systems and bundling the Windows Media Player (WMP) with Windows to disadvantage RealAudio and other media players. The statement of objections was finalized in August 2003. The European Commission found Microsoft liable on both counts in March 2004 and imposed a $497.2 million fine. Microsoft was also required (1) to fully disclose the interface that would allow non-Microsoft servers to achieve full interoperability with Windows PCs and servers and (2) to offer to PC manufacturers a version of its Windows without WMP.[41] Microsoft appealed but did not win a stay. The EU decision was affirmed by the Court of First Instance in September 2007.

I have very serious concerns about the usefulness of the requirement imposed by the European Union to create a version of Windows without WMP. Competing media players such as RealAudio and Quicken are easily downloadable and available for free. Thus the cost to consumers of any of these players is just the five minutes or so it takes to download them. Even if the European Union is perfectly correct on liability, the remedy it imposed is way out of proportion and, in the end, may reduce rather than increase consumers' welfare. Since the version of Windows without WMP was sold at the same price as the one with the media player—the European Union had not imposed any restrictions on pricing—practically no computer manufacturer bought Windows without WMP. On the issue of interoperability, it is hard to offer an opinion without full knowledge of facts that are not publicly available. However, it is clear that even with full disclosure of the interface there may be advantages to components (e.g., clients and servers) produced by the same company.

Local Telecommunications, Trinko, and the Sacrifice Principle The *Trinko* case is the most important recent Section 2 case in the intersection of antitrust and regulation. The Law

Offices of Curtis V. Trinko bought local telecommunications services from AT&T. AT&T was providing these services by combining leased parts of the Verizon local telecommunications network (unbundled network elements, or UNEs) and adding retail services of its own, such as billing and marketing. Under the rules of the Telecommunications Act of 1996, incumbent local exchange carriers, including Verizon, were obligated to lease parts of their local telecommunications network to any firm at "cost plus a reasonable profit" prices that could combine them at will, add retailing services, and sell local telecommunication service as a rival to the incumbent.

The 1996 Act was a brave but failed attempt to introduce competition in all telecommunications markets.[42] Congress understood that it was uneconomic for firms to enter in local telecommunications by replicating the infrastructure of the incumbents.[43] Thus it set up two additional possibilities for entrants (besides entering with their own facilities): (1) to enter by leasing parts of the incumbents' local telecommunications network (leasing unbundled network elements (UNEs)[44] and (2) to enter by buying in wholesale the incumbents services and reselling them. The most important avenue to entry was leasing UNEs, combining them with the entrant's retailing services (e.g., marketing and billing) and selling to final consumers. To facilitate entry, the 1996 Act set the price for UNEs at "cost plus reasonable profit."[45] The 1996 Act additionally mandated that unbundled network elements be sold at "rates, terms, and conditions that are just, reasonable, and nondiscriminatory."[46] To facilitate entry, the 1996 Act also imposed the requirement on an incumbent to allow for physical collocation of equipment at its premises,[47] and on all companies the duty to provide number portability, so that consumers can keep their phone numbers if they change local service provider.[48]

In *Verizon Communications Inc. v. Law Offices of Curtis V. Trinko*,[49] Trinko sued Verizon for raising the costs of its retail rival AT&T (which had entered the market as a competitive local exchange carrier, or CLEC) and otherwise disadvantaging AT&T through anticompetitive conduct (including discrimination in fulfilling customer transfer orders to entrants) under Section 2 of the Sherman Act.[50] The Supreme Court held that Trinko's complaint failed to state a claim under Section 2 of the Sherman Act, and dismissed the complaint.

In arguing for dismissal, the Supreme Court noted that the markets for leasing parts of the local telecommunications network were created by the 1996 Act and did not exist voluntarily earlier. The Court somehow believed that Verizon's refusal to deal and its related raising rivals' costs practices were justified because infrastructure leasing prices were based on cost plus a reasonable profit: "Verizon's reluctance to interconnect at the cost-based rate of compensation available under Section 251(c)(3) tells us nothing about dreams of monopoly."[51] But Verizon was a monopolist in the network infrastructure and in the network services markets.[52] In my opinion, reluctance to sell leases at above average cost prices is a clear indication that the monopolist in the networks infrastructure market is attempting through this action to prevent entry in the network services market, which requires access to the networks infrastructure market. In my opinion, the fact that Verizon was obligated to lease local telecommunications infrastructure at cost plus a reasonable profit and did not write such leases at any price earlier does not imply that Verizon's refusal to deal and raising rivals' costs strategies does not create antitrust liability.

Additionally the Court missed the vertical leveraging issue in *Trinko*. Verizon provides two local telecommunications services: (1) network infrastructure services (NET services), which it provides to itself and to competitors in local telecommunications, and (2) retail services. End-users consume a composite service comprised of NET services and retail services. Competitors to Verizon in retail local telecommunications buy only NET services, adding their own retailing services for sale to end-users. At the point of the initial implementation of the 1996 Act, Verizon had a monopoly in both NET services and retail services. The conduct of Verizon in *Trinko* can be seen as the result of Verizon leveraging its monopoly in NET services to preserve its monopoly in retail services. This was recognized by the Second Circuit, which noted that Trinko could have "a monopoly leveraging claim" based on the fact that "the defendant '(1) possessed monopoly power in one market; (2) used that power to gain a competitive advantage . . . in another distinct market; and (3) caused injury by such anticompetitive conduct.'"[53] In contrast, the Supreme Court dismissed the vertical issue, using a fallacious circular argument in footnote four of its decision, stating, "*In any event, leveraging presupposes anticompetitive conduct, which in this case could only be the refusal-to-deal claim we have rejected.*"[54] In my opinion, the key anticompetitive conduct was the leveraging from NET services to retailing services and the Court missed that.[55]

It is hard to offer a definitive opinion on the implications of *Trinko*. Some believe that its importance is confined to regulated industries. Others believe that it has significantly weakened enforcement of Sherman Section 2. This opinion is based their view on *Trinko* Courts statement: "*Aspen Skiing* is at or near the outer boundary of Section 2 liability."[56] The facts in *Aspen Skiing* were as follows: Aspen Skiing Co. controlled three out of four ski slopes in Aspen, Colorado, with the fourth slope controlled by Aspen Highlands. Aspen Skiing and Aspen Highlands offered a joint ticket that allowed the buyer to ski on all four slopes with revenue shared according to use. Aspen Skiing discontinued the joint ticket in 1978–79 and refused to sell its tickets to Aspen Highlands even at full retail price, to prevent Aspen Highlands from bundling them with its own tickets and recreating the joint ticket that had formerly been available. The Supreme Court ruled that Aspen Skiing's refusal to deal was anticompetitive.[57]

Despite the Court's statement in *Trinko*, one would expect *Trinko* to fall within the outer boundary set by *Aspen Skiing*. Because Verizon's price was set by regulation at cost plus a reasonable profit, it is reasonable to infer that Verizon's price to cost margin was lower than in the duopoly of *Aspen Skiing*. Thus, all else being equal, one would expect Verizon more likely to refuse to sell than Aspen Skiing Co. From the point of view of the firm committing the anticompetitive act, the incentive seems stronger for Verizon than for

Aspen Skiing. Therefore, if the Supreme Court deems the refusal to deal by a duopolist in *Aspen* anticompetitive, it should find the refusal to deal by the monopolist in *Trinko* even more so.

Being forced by regulation to sell below the monopoly price, and unable to discriminate in price by regulatory restraints, the monopolist in Trinko has an incentive to raise the costs of its rivals. If regulation were not present, price discrimination and monopoly pricing would have likely made raising rivals' costs strategies suboptimal form the monopolist's point of view and would not have been used. In the regulatory environment of the 1996 Act, raising rivals' costs is a natural response of a monopolist to the restraints of regulation.[58] Raising rivals' costs strategies reduce competition and social welfare associated from the existence of a free market.[59] In applying the Aspen Skiing standard, the Court erred in not considering the significant difference in incentives of the potentially liable party between the unregulated environment in *Aspen Skiing* and the regulated environment of *Trinko*.

In *Trinko* the Supreme Court did not state a rule under which specific conduct will be found to be "willful monopolization." In its brief in *Trinko* the government proposed such a standard based on the "sacrifice principle."[60] I define the sacrifice principle as follows: *a defendant is liable of anticompetitive behavior if its conduct "involves a sacrifice of short-term profits or goodwill that makes sense only insofar as it helps the defendant maintain or obtain monopoly power."*[61] This definition only partially coincides with the definition of the same principle in the government's brief in *Trinko*. Specifically, the government's brief allows *all* behavior that does *not* involve sacrifice of short-term profits to be characterized as not "exclusionary" and not "predatory."[62] I disagree. *Conduct can be exclusionary even without a sacrifice of short-term profits.* But when such a sacrifice is observed, it shows directly that this conduct is anticompetitive.

In my opinion, the vertical leveraging in *Trinko* passes the "sacrifice test." The behavior of Verizon to raise the costs of rivals in local telecommunications services entailed a sacrifice of profits from potential leasing of UNEs. This sacrifice would not have occurred if Verizon were not trying to protect its monopoly in the retail market for local telecommunications services. Thus, in applying the sacrifice principle, Verizon's actions are found to be anticompetitive. If Verizon did not have a retailing division, it would have no incentive to foreclose or disadvantage independent retailing firms. Instead, if its strategy were not to preserve its monopoly position in retailing, Verizon would have had every incentive to sell its NET services to all at prices above cost, as mandated by the 1996 Act. Since Verizon sells its NET services to its retailing division at cost while any NET services price sold to third parties includes a reasonable profit (according to the 1996 Act's rules), raising rivals' costs actions that disadvantage third party retailing service firms and result in smaller sales of NET services to these firms clearly imposes a sacrifice of profits for Verizon. Therefore the "sacrifice" principle can be applied in the *Trinko* case in the same way that the Supreme Court articulated it in *Aspen Skiing* to conclude that Verizon's raising rivals costs actions resulted in a short-term sacrifice of profits and therefore would not have been taken except to preserve its monopoly.

Market Power in Broadband Internet Access and Net Neutrality   The Internet is a global network of interconnected networks that connect computers. The Internet allows data transfers as well as the provision of a variety of interactive real-time and time-delayed telecommunications services. Internet communication is based on common and public protocols. Hundreds of millions of computers are presently connected to the Internet. The vast majority of computers owned by individuals or businesses connect to the Internet through commercial Internet service providers (ISPs).[63] Users connect to the Internet either by dialing their ISP, connecting through cable modems, residential DSL, or through corporate networks. Typically routers and switches owned by the ISP send the caller's packets to a local point of presence (POP) of the Internet. Dial-up, cable modem, and DSL access POPs as well as corporate networks dedicated access circuits connect to high-speed hubs. High-speed circuits, leased from or owned by telephone companies, connect the high-speed hubs forming an Internet backbone network (IBN).

The Internet is based on three basic separate levels of functions of the network:

1. The hardware/electronics level of the physical network
2. The (logical) network level where basic communication and interoperability are established
3. The applications/services level

Thus the Internet separates the network interoperability level from the applications/services level. Unlike earlier centralized digital electronic communications networks, such as CompuServe, AT&T Mail, Prodigy, and early AOL, the Internet allows a large variety of applications and services to be run "at the edge" of the network and not centrally.

An example of complex pricing discussed in section 13.2.3 is the present attempt of AT&T, Verizon, Deutsche Telecom, and other broadband Internet access providers to implement a complex price discrimination scheme on the Internet. A number of different services are provided on the Internet, including e-mail, browsing (using Internet Explorer, Firefox, Opera, etc.), peer-to-peer services, Internet telephony (voice over Internet protocol, or VOIP), among many others. A number of different functions/applications run on top of the Internet browser, including information services (Google, Yahoo, MSN), display of images, and transmission of video. Since the advent of Mosaic in 1993 and Netscape in 1994, the text-based Internet was enhanced to allow for images and video to be transmitted on it in digital form.

On the Internet, users pay ISPs for access to the whole Internet. Similarly ISPs pay backbones for access to the whole Internet.[64] ISPs pay per month for a pipe of a certain bandwidth, presumably according to their expected use.[65] When digital content, for example, is downloaded by consumer A from provider B, both sides; that is, both A and B pay.

A pays to his ISP through his monthly subscription, and *B* pays similarly. In turn ISPs pay to their respective backbones through their monthly subscription. The present regime on the Internet does not distinguish in terms of price (or in any other way) among bits or information packets depending on the services that these bits and packets are used for. This regime, called "net neutrality," has prevailed on the Internet since its inception. Presently a bit or information packet used for VOIP, for e-mail, for an image, or for a video is priced equally as a part of the large number of packets that correspond to the subscription services of the originating and terminating ISP.

After the acquisition of AT&T by SBC[66] and of MCI by Verizon, taking advantage of a change in regulatory rules by the Federal Communications Commission, AT&T and Verizon now advocate price discrimination based on which application and on which provider the bits they transport came from. AT&T and Verizon would like to abolish the regime of net neutrality and substitute for it a complex pricing schedule where, besides the basic service for transmission of bits, there will be additional charges by the Internet access operator applied to the originating party (e.g., Google, Yahoo, or MSN) even when the application provider is not directly connected to AT&T or Verizon, that is, even when Google's Internet service provider (ISP) is not AT&T or Verizon.[67]

The proposal is to impose price discrimination on the provider side of the market and not on the subscriber; that is, it is a version of two-sided pricing. This is uniquely possible to firms operating within a network structure. Besides traditional networks, such two-sided pricing is also possible by intermediaries in exchange networks (e.g., the exchanges themselves). There is presently considerable debate on the legality as well as the efficiency properties of the implementation of such complex rules by broadband Internet access firms mainly because of the very considerable market power of such firms.

Residential retail customers may well have difficulty changing ISPs. In the United States at least 95 percent of households have only one or two broadband Internet access choices, a digital subscriber line (DSL), or through cable TV, and their resellers, and many households are facing a monopoly of either cable or DSL. There are also switching costs to residential customers when changing equipment. Finally, residential customers are much more affected by contracts that bundle broadband Internet access with other services such as telecommunications and cable television.

As discussed earlier, the Internet under net neutrality separated the network layer from the applications/services layer. Net neutrality has allowed firms to innovate "at the edge of the network" without seeking approval from network operator(s). The decentralization of the Internet based on net neutrality facilitated innovation resulting in big successes such as Google, MSN, Yahoo, and Skype. Net neutrality also increased competition among the applications and services "at the edge of the network," which did not need to own a network to compete. Additionally the existence of network effects on the Internet implies that efficient prices to users on both sides (consumers and applications) should be lower than in a market without network effects. We see instead an attempt to increase prices, which will reduce network effects and innovation.

Abolition of net neutrality raises both horizontal and vertical antitrust issues. Starting with horizontal issues, last mile carriers (who are in duopoly or monopoly) may reduce capacity of "plain" broadband Internet access service and/or degrade it so that they can establish a "premium" service for which they will charge additionally content/applications provider. Coordinated reduction of capacity in "plain" service is reminiscent of cartel behavior. In general, the coordinated introduction of price discrimination schemes may reduce output. There is a general theorem in economics that price discrimination that reduces output reduces total surplus.[68] Therefore introduction of coordinated price discrimination may have anticompetitive consequences.

There is a also a variety of potentially anticompetitive vertical effects. For example, a carrier may favor its own content or application over that of an independent. VOIP provided over broadband Internet competes with traditional circuit-switched service provided by AT&T and Verizon and can be subject to discrimination. Additionally both AT&T and Verizon are gearing to distribute video, so they may favor their video service over that of others. But the anticompetitive concerns are hardly limited to products and services currently provided by the firms with market power in the access market. The carriers can also leverage market power in broadband access to the content or applications markets through contractual relationships. For example, a carrier can contract with a Internet search engine to put it in "premium" service while searches using other search engines have considerable delays using "plain" service.

The question posed before the US Congress is whether it should intervene immediately by imposing nondiscrimination restrictions or wait instead for antitrust suits. In my opinion, it is better to impose the nondiscrimination restrictions by law for a number of good reasons:

1. Suits take time, and much damage can be done before they are resolved. The legal system is slow, and lawsuits do not get resolved in "Internet time."

2. There are a variety of antitrust concerns, whereas typically each suit will deal with one issue. Thus delays can be compounded.

3. The Internet is a key essential network for growth of the US economy. The United States is already lagging behind fourteen less developed and lower income countries in Internet market penetration, as seen in figure 13.11.

4. Increasing prices through two-sided pricing will not increase network traffic nor grow the network!

5. Even if in the end there are no antitrust violations connected with the abolition of net neutrality (which I think is very unlikely), the abolition of net neutrality is likely to have significant negative consequences for innovation on the Internet, and therefore it is in the public interest to prevent it by law.

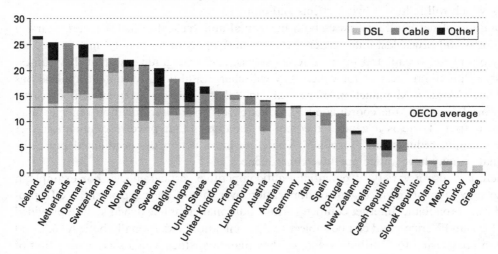

Figure 13.11
Internet broadband penetration among OECD countries (source: OECD)

Competitiveness of the Internet Backbone and the MCI Mergers   When WorldCom proposed to buy MCI, the European Union objected,[69] with concern that the combined Internet backbones of MCI and WorldCom would dominate the European market with anticompetitive consequences. As a result of EU objections, MCI agreed to spin off its backbone, MCIi, which was bought by Cable and Wireless. The subsequent proposed merger of WorldCom and Sprint faced similar objections by the European Union and in the United States by the DOJ, as well as objections by DOJ in the long-distance and unswitched private lines markets, so that was shelved as well. The market shares at the time and contemporary projections are summarized in table 13.3.[70]

In papers filed in support of the merger of SBC and AT&T as well as of the merger of Verizon with MCI, there was mention of two recent traffic studies by RHK. These studies showing traffic for 2004, summarized in table 13.4, show a dramatic change in the ranking of the networks, with AT&T now being first and MCI being fourth. They also show that now a much bigger share of traffic (over 40 percent) is carried by smaller networks. These latest traffic studies show that the concern of the European Union and of the DOJ in the United States that the Internet backbone market would tilt to monopoly has proved to be overstated.

GTE, which had made a smaller bid for MCI than WorldCom, supported by Cremer et al. (1998, 2000), raised a number of anticompetitive concerns for networks that obey the following assumptions:

Table 13.3
Market shares of national Internet backbones

Company	1997	1999	2001 (projected in 1999)	2003 (projected in 1999)
MCI WorldCom	43%	38%	35%	32%
GTE-BBN	13%	15%	16%	17%
AT&T	12%	11%	14%	19%
Sprint	12%	9%	8%	7%
Cable and wireless	9%	6%	6%	6%
All other	11%	21%	22%	19%
Total	100%	100%	100%	100%

Source: *Hearing on the MCI WorldCom-Sprint Merger before the Senate Committee on the Judiciary*, Exhibit 3 (November 4, 1999). Testimony of Tod A. Jacobs, Senior Telecommunications Analyst, Sanford C. Bernstein & Co., Inc. Bernstein Research, *MCI WorldCom* (March 1999) at p. 51.

Table 13.4
Carrier traffic in petabytes per month in 2004

Company	Traffic				Market share among all networks
	1Q2004	2Q2004	3Q2004	4Q2004	4Q2004
A (AT&T)	37.19	38.66	44.54	52.33	12.58%
B	36.48	36.50	41.41	51.31	12.33%
C	34.11	35.60	36.75	45.89	11.03%
D (MCI)	24.71	25.81	26.86	30.87	7.42%
E	18.04	18.89	21.08	25.46	6.12%
F	16.33	17.78	17.47	19.33	4.65%
G	16.67	15.04	14.93	15.19	3.65%
Total traffic top 7 networks	183.53	188.28	203.04	240.38	57.78%
Total traffic all networks	313	313	353	416	100%

Source: Data from *RHK Traffic Analysis—Methodology and Results*, May 2005.
Note: The identities of all networks are not provided, but it is likely that B, C, E, and F are level 3; Quest, Sprint, and SBC are in unknown order.

1. Consumers do *not* demand universal connectivity.

2. There is an installed base of clients (ISPs) of Internet backbone networks who cannot migrate to other providers.

Using these assumptions, Cremer et al. (1998, 2000) argue that (1) a large IBN has an incentive to introduce incompatibilities and to degrade interconnection with one rival but not with all rivals, (2) even small differences in network size will lead to a spiral of ever-increasing dominance by a larger IBN, since dominance is defined by size, (3) large IBN will refuse to cooperate with small networks, and (4) in the case where switching costs are low, large IBNs will still be able to dominate small networks.

These results are based on assumptions that do not presently hold on the Internet backbone. First, customers on the Internet demand *universal connectivity*. Users of the Internet do not know in advance what Internet site they may want to contact or to whom they might want to send e-mail. Thus Internet users demand from their ISPs and expect to receive universal connectivity. This is the same expectation that users of telephones, mail, and fax machines have: that they can connect to any other user of the network without concern about compatibility, location, or, in the case of telephone or fax, any concern about the manufacturer of the appliance, the type of connection (wireline or wireless) or the owners of the networks over which the connection is made. Because of the users' demand for universal connectivity, ISPs providing services to end-users or to Web sites must make arrangements with other networks so that they can exchange traffic with *any* Internet customer.

Second, there are no "captive customers" on the Internet backbone. The reasons for this are as follows:

1. ISPs can easily and with low cost migrate all or part of their transport traffic to other network providers.

2. Many ISPs already purchase transport from more than one backbone to guard against network failures and for competitive reasons (ISP "multihoming").

3. Many large Web sites/providers use more than one ISP for their sites ("customer multihoming").

4. Competitive pressure from their customers makes ISPs agile and likely to respond quickly to changes in conditions in the backbone market.

Competitive conditions imply that significant price increases, or raising rivals' costs or degrading interconnection, are unlikely to be profitable on the Internet backbone. If the large Internet backbone connectivity provider's strategy were to impose equal increases in transport costs on all customers, the response of other backbone providers and ISPs will be to reduce the traffic for which they buy transit from the large IBN, and to instead reroute traffic and purchase more transit from each other. Thus, in response to a price increase by the large Internet backbone, other IBNs and ISPs reduce the traffic for which they buy transit from the large IBN down to the minimum level necessary to reach IBNs that are *exclusively* connected to the large IBN. All other IBNs and ISPs exchange all other traffic with each other, bypassing the large IBN. For these and other reasons it is unlikely that large IBNs at the time of the MCI mergers will find it profitable to limit connectivity to other backbones.[71]

13.4 Concluding Remarks

The discussion of this chapter is a start of an in-depth study of public policy in network industries. The legal system does not yet have a framework for analysis of competition policy issues in network industries. This was to a large extent exemplified in *United States v. Microsoft.*

The Microsoft case has certainly been the most important antitrust case of the "new economy" this far. Unfortunately, its legal battle was fought to a large extent without the use of the economics tools discussed above, which are at the foundation of the new economy and were key to the business success of Microsoft. There are several explanations for this omission. First, often legal cases are created and filed before an economist is found who will create the appropriate economic model to support the case. Second, the economic theory of networks is so incomplete and unsettled that there is no commonly accepted body of knowledge on market structure with network effects. Based on such theory one could have evaluated deviations toward anticompetitive behavior. Third, the legal system has tremendous inertia to new ideas and models. Fourth, the legal system is ill-equipped to deal with complex technical matters. Fifth, because of all these facts lawyers on both sides find it easier to fight the issues on well-trotted ground even if the problems are really of a different nature. It is as if there is a dispute among two parties in the middle of a heavily forested area, but the lawyers of both parties fight it as if the dispute happened on the open plains. They know the way that disputes on the plains are resolved, whereas the law of dispute resolution in forests has yet to be established.

The bottom line is that as things stand today, there are many areas of antitrust law where there is significant uncertainty on how to apply the law in network industries and when to judge various practices as legal or illegal. Guidance to firms on avoidance of anticompetitive actions is further complicated by the divergence of competition policy standards between the European Union and the United States.

With further academic analysis of antitrust issues, I hope that when the next major new economy antitrust case appears, there will be a deeper understanding and application of the economics of networks and of the way that antitrust law should be applied to network industries.

Notes

1. I will typically use the term "network effects" and reserve the term "network externalities" for those cases where a market fails to fully intermediate network effects.

2. Some authors consider two-sided networks a separate category than markets with network effects. *See* Armstrong (2005), Evans (2003), Jullien (2004), and Rochet and Tirole (2003, 2004). However, the two-sided setup is a standard setup that has been discussed in the economics of networks literature since the middle 1980s, and there is no crucial distinguishing factor to separate the analysis of two-sided networks from the traditional analysis of virtual networks.

3. More precisely, the law of demand is true for *normal* goods, that is, for goods for which an increase in income leads to a higher quantity of sales. If increases in income drove sales sharply down, the possibility of a *Giffen good* arises where sales increase as prices increase. Giffen goods are truly exceptional and rarely observed.

4. Besides the positive network effects described in detail in this chapter, there is the possibility of negative effects, such as congestion in transportation networks, or interference in radio, broadcast TV, and wireless telecommunications networks.

5. See Economides and Siow (1988).

6. The existence of network externalities in exchange markets is one of the reasons behind the proposal of Economides-Schwartz to bunch orders and execute them at once in pre-defined times, thereby creating a *call market* concurrent with the continuous NYSE market; see Economides and Schwartz (1995a). A call market has higher liquidity than continuous markets and can provide anonymity to large orders. A survey of equity traders has established that most of traders are willing to wait for execution of their orders in a call market; see Economides and Schwartz (1995b).

7. Suppose that consumers expect a network of size n^e, $0 \leq n^e \leq 1$. Let network externalities be summarized by function $h(n^e) = k + f(ne)$, with $f(0) = 0$, $f'(\cdot) > 0$, $f''(\cdot) \leq 0$. Consumer of type y has utility $u(y, n^e) = yh(n^e)$ from one unit of the good, and let the distribution of consumer types be $G(y)$. Then the marginal consumer y^* is defined by $u(y^*, n^e) = p$. Therefore $y^* = p/h(n^e)$ for $0 < p/h(n^e) < 1$. It follows that demand is $n = 1 - G(y^*) \Rightarrow p(n, n^e) = h(n^e)G^{-1}(1 - n)$. Imposing fulfilled expectation, $n = n^e$, we derive the fulfilled expectations demand $p(n, n) = h(n)G^{-1}(1 - n)$. Now we check for upward-slopping demand at $n = 0$. In general, the slope of the fulfilled expectations demand is $dp(n, n)/dn = -h(n)/G' + h'(n)G^{-1}(1 - n)$. The slope at $n = 0$ is positive if and only if $\lim_{n \to 0} dp(n, n)/dn = \lim_{n \to 0} h'(n) - \lim_{n \to 0} h/G'(1) = \lim_{n \to 0} f'(n) - k/G'(1) > 0$. Therefore the fulfilled expectations demand slopes upward at $n = 0$ in the three cases:

• When $k = 0$ (pure network good)
• When $\lim_{n \to 0} f'(n)$ large (very strong marginal network externalities)
• When $G'(1)$ large (density of high-valuation types is sufficiently large)

8. The pricing schemes used vary considerably depending on the telecommunications service. Traditionally, in fixed networks, as in most places in the United States, local calls are free with a local connection that requires a fixed monthly fee. Long-distance subscribers were charged only for outgoing calls. In the last three decades 800, 866, 877, 888–prefix "toll-free" services allow for no charge to the calling party but impose a fee to the receiving party, while 900–prefix services allow the receiving party to charge a positive price to the initiator. In wireless cellular and PCS telecommunications, subscribers in the United States pay for both incoming and outgoing calls, whereas in most of the rest of the world, wireless subscribers pay only for outgoing calls. On the Internet, typically retail subscribers pay a flat fee regardless of the amount of time they use the service, the number of bits exchanged, or whether the calls are incoming or outgoing, and regardless of the destination. Similarly Internet service providers buy backbone connectivity at rates that depend just on the size of the pipe they utilize and regardless of utilization or whether the information packets are incoming or outgoing, and regardless of the destination.

9. Low-technology examples are razors and blades and cameras and film.

10. It is anecdotally known that Cantor Fitzgerald, which has a 70 percent market share in the secondary market for US government thirty-year bonds, offered to Salomon (the largest "primary dealer" and trader of US bonds) prices equal to 1/10 to 1/5 of those charged to small traders. This is consistent with profit maximization by Cantor Fitzgerald because of the liquidity (network effect) brought to the market by Salomon, which is by far the largest buyer ("primary dealer") in the auctions of US government bonds.

11. For a detailed discussion, see Economides and Himmelberg (1995).

12. This is easy to prove mathematically in the model of Economides and Himmelberg (1995) discussed earlier. Let $B(n, n) = \int_0^n p(q, n) \, dq$ be the gross benefit function at sales level n. Then the incremental benefit of network expansion is $B(n, n)/dn = p(n, n) + \int_0^n \partial p(q, n)/\partial n \, dq > p(n, n)$, since $\partial p(q, n)/\partial n > 0$ represents the positive network effect of expansion of the network on the willingness to pay of other network participants. Under perfect

competition, consumers face a price equal to marginal cost. Since the incremental benefit of network expansion exceeds price, perfect competition is inefficient.

13. See Stango (2004) for a recent survey of the economics of standards setting. There are a number of recent empirical studies on standard competition and competition with competing with incompatible standards. Dranove and Gandal (2001) discuss the effects of the "preannouncement" of the DIVX standard on adoption of DVDs. Also see the earlier analyses of Farrell and Saloner (1985, 1986), the survey of Besen and Saloner (1994), and Lerner and Tirole (2004). Additionally often firms pre-announce new products to make consumers delay their purchasing decisions and therefore make it less likely that consumers will buy products from competitors. Often, products are pre-announced and never appear in the market, although the pre-announcement had the effect discussed above. Such products that never appear have been called "vaporware." For a more detailed discussion, see Choi et al. (2005).

14. If the distribution of the willingness to pay is distributed away from 0, an industry with network effects exhibits the finiteness property (Shaked and Sutton 1983), with a finite maximum number of active firms despite all realizing strictly positive profits.

15. See David (1985) and Liebowitz and Margolis (1990).

16. AT&T claimed that the main reason for its refusal to interconnect was the low technical standards of the independents, as well as incompatibilities, that would jeopardize AT&T's network after interconnection. While there is some truth to those claims, it is unlikely that they applied to all independents. Moreover, once acquired by AT&T, independents were interconnected with AT&T's network, after some modifications. This shows that the refusal to interconnect was mainly a strategic and commercial decision rather than a technical one.

17. See Economides and White (1995) and Economides (2003).

18. AT&T, the largest long-distance company, announced in the summer of 2004 that it stopped marketing both local and long-distance service to residential customers, and MCI followed the same strategy without a formal announcement. In 2005 SBC announced that it would buy AT&T, and Verizon announced that it would buy MCI. Both mergers cleared antitrust and regulatory review in March 2007. In filings to the US Department of Justice and the FCC, both AT&T and MCI claimed that they had abandoned the residential local and long-distance markets. For a detailed discussion, see Economides (2005a, b).

19. This is not just a theoretical possibility. Telecom New Zealand (TNZ), operating in an environment of weak antitrust and regulatory intervention (so called light-handed regulation), offered such high termination fees that the first entrant into local telecommunications, Clear, survives only by refusing to pay interconnection fees to TNZ, whereas the second entrant, BellSouth New Zealand, exited the local telecommunications market.

20. Also see Armstrong (1998), Cambini and Valletti and (2005), Carter and Wright (2003), Dessein (2004), Gans and King (2001), and Laffont et al. (1998).

21. For example, one can think of A as a computer operating system (OS), and B as an application. OS manufacturers can and do embed software routines that are useful to application software developers, since they reduce the cost of writing applications.

22. See Economides and Siow (1988) for a discussion of the benefits of B2B and other exchanges.

23. This can help an incumbent because it can expand the functionality of its product, but can also help its rivals as they may incorporate functionalities of the incumbent's product into theirs.

24. The California Public Utilities Commission investigated the WorldCom-Sprint proposed merger in the context of the "transfer of licenses" to the merged entity. However, after the merger proposal was withdrawn by the parties, the CPUC continued to investigate the participation of these two firms on the Internet, and asserted its regulatory authority over the part of the Internet that is physically located in California.

25. DOJ sued Microsoft on July 15, 1994, under 15 USC §2 of the Sherman Act, alleging that Microsoft had entered into licensing agreements with OEMs that prevented other operating system vendors from gaining widespread distribution of their products.

26. The Microsoft court entered the consent decree as its Final Judgment on April 21, 1995.

27. Final Judgment, Civil Action No. 94-1564.

28. The Microsoft court also referred the issue to a special master, Professor Lawrence Lessig of Stanford.

29. The court of appeals further noted that "the limited competence of courts to evaluate high-tech product designs and the high cost of error should make them wary of second-guessing the claimed benefits of a particular design decision"; see 147 F.3d at 950 n. 13.

30. For a detailed discussion of *United States v. Microsoft*, see Economides (2001a, 2001b, 2002) and http://www.stern.nyu.edu/networks/.

31. Only twelve witnesses testified for each side.

32. As mediator, Judge Posner was *not* acting in his judicial capacity.

33. See generally, *New York Times*, April 2, 2000.

34. The hearing was on May 24, 2000. It started at 10:15 am, ended around 3:30 pm, and included a two-hour lunch break.

35. It is likely that the marginal price for the last unit sold to the same OEM was extremely low, since the 1995 consent decree allowed Microsoft to have quantity discounts but barred it from zero marginal cost pricing.

36. The derivation of the monopoly price for Windows follows. Let p_H be the price of the PC hardware (everything except Windows), and let p_W be the price of Windows. Assume that Windows is installed on all PCs, meaning Microsoft has 100 percent market share. Since hardware and software are combined in a ratio of $1:1$, the demand of a PC with Windows is $D(p_H + p_W)$. Profits of Microsoft from Windows sales are

$$\Pi_W = p_W D(p_H + p_W) - F_W,$$

where F_W is the fixed cost of developing Windows, and the marginal cost is negligible. Maximizing Π_W implies marginal revenue equals marginal cost:

$$\frac{D(p_H + p_W) + p_W\,dD}{dp_W} = 0 \Leftrightarrow 1 + \left(\frac{p_W}{p_H + p_W}\right)\left(\frac{p_H + p_W}{D}\right)\left(\frac{dD}{dp_W}\right) = 0 \Leftrightarrow \frac{p_W}{p_H + p_W} = \frac{1}{|\varepsilon|},$$

or equivalently, the monopoly price of Windows is

$$p_W = \frac{p_H}{|\varepsilon| - 1},$$

where $|\varepsilon| = -[(p_H + p_W)/D]/[dD/dp_W]$ is the market elasticity of demand for PCs with Windows. Say that the average price of PC hardware is \$1,800 and the elasticity is $|\varepsilon| = 2$. Then the monopoly price of Windows is $p_W = \$1,800$. Even if the elasticity were much higher $|\varepsilon| = 3$, and the average price of PC hardware much lower at \$1,200, the monopoly price would be \$600, which is ten to twelve times the price charged by Microsoft to OEMs. An elasticity of $|\varepsilon| = 31$ is required to get a Windows monopoly price of \$60. It is extremely unlikely that the market for PCs exhibits such large market elasticities.

37. See Economides (2001a, b).

38. During the trial Judge Jackson gave extensive interviews on his views of the case. In one of them, he compared the leadership of Microsoft (Bill Gates, Steve Ballmer) to a drug-dealing gang that he had convicted in a recent case.

39. One panel member is selected by Microsoft, one by the Justice Department, and one by both. The panel has full access to all of Microsoft's books, records, systems, and personnel, including source code, and helps resolve disputes about Microsoft's compliance with the disclosure provisions of the settlement.

40. See my detailed position at my amicus brief, Economides, Nicholas (2002), *http://www.usdoj.gov/atr/cases/ms_tuncom/major/mtc-00022465.htm*.

41. See "EU Commission Concludes Microsoft Investigation, Imposes Conduct Remedies and a Fine," *at http://www.eurunion.org/news/press/2004/20040045.htm*.

42. For an extensive discussion of the 1996 Act, see Economides (2005a, 2003).

43. As the Federal Communications Commission stated:

Because an incumbent LEC currently serves virtually all subscribers in its local serving area, an incumbent LEC has little economic incentive to assist new entrants in their efforts to secure a greater share of that market. An incumbent LEC also has the ability to act on its incentive to discourage entry and robust competition by not interconnecting its network with the new entrant's network or by insisting on supracompetitive prices or other unreasonable conditions for terminating calls from the entrant's customers to the incumbent LEC's subscribers.

   Congress addressed these problems in the 1996 Act by mandating that the most significant economic impediments to efficient entry into the monopolized local market must be removed. The incumbent LECs have economies of density, connectivity, and scale; traditionally, these have been viewed as creating a natural monopoly. As we pointed out in our NPRM, the local competition provisions of the Act require that these economies be shared with entrants. (Federal Communications Commission, First Report and Order, FCC No. 96-325, at ¶ 10–11 [August 1, 1996])

44. 47 USC §§251(c)(3), (c)(6). The Federal Communications Commission defined the key UNEs as the "local loop," local switching, and local transport. See Federal Communications Commission, First Report and Order, FCC No. 96-325, at §51.319 (August 1, 1996).

45. The 1996 Act at 47 USC §252(d)(1) orders that pricing of interconnection or unbundled network elements:

(A) shall be
(i) based on the cost (determined without reference to a rate-of-return or other rate-based proceeding) of providing the interconnection or network element (whichever is applicable), and
(ii) nondiscriminatory, and
(B) may include a reasonable profit.

46. 47 USC §251(c)(3).

47. 47 USC §251(c)(6).

48. 47 USC §251(b)(2).

49. 540 US 398 (2004).

50. Ibid. at 402–405. Trinko originally sued NYNEX, which was later bought by Bell Atlantic. Bell Atlantic merged with GTE to created Verizon.

51. *Trinko*, 540 US at 409.

52. *See* Economides, Seim, and Viard (2007).

53. *Trinko*, 305 F.3d at 108.

54. *Trinko*, 540 US at 415 n. 4.

55. For a full discussion of the *Trinko* case, see Economides (2005b, 2007).

56. *Trinko*, 540 US at 409.

57. *Aspen Skiing*, 472 US at 593–608.

58. *See* Economides (1998).

59. See generally, Salop and Scheffman (1983) and Krattenmaker and Salop (1986).

60. Brief of Amici Curiae United States and the Federal Trade Commission in support of *Trinko*, 540 US 398 (2004) (No. 02-682) at 16.

61. As the government's brief notes, the sacrifice principle has been used in various versions in *Aspen Skiing*, 472 US at 608, 610–611 (conduct that "sacrifice[s] short-run benefits," such as immediate income and consumer goodwill, undertaken because it "reduc[es] competition over the long run"); *General Industries Corp. v. Hartz Mountain Corp.*, 810 F.2d 795, 803 (8th Cir. 1987) (conduct anticompetitive if "its 'anticipated benefits were dependent upon its tendency to discipline or eliminate competition and thereby enhance the firm's long term ability to reap the benefits of monopoly power.'"); *Stearns Airport Equipment Co. v. FMC Corp.*, 170 F.3d 518, 523–524 n. 3 (5th Cir. 1999) (conduct exclusionary if it harms the monopolist but is justified because it causes rivals more harm); *Advanced Health-Care Services v. Radford Community Hospital*, 910 F.2d 139, 148 (4th Cir. 1990) ("making a short-term sacrifice" that "harm[s] consumers and competition" to further "exclusive, anti-competitive objectives"). Ibid.

62. "Conduct is not exclusionary or predatory unless it would make no economic sense for the defendant but for its tendency to eliminate or lessen competition." Brief of Amici Curiae United States and the Federal Trade Commission at 15, *Verizon Communications Inc. v. Law Offices of Curtis V. Trinko*, 540 US 398 (2004) (No. 02-682). For a more detailed discussion of the *Trinko* case, see Economides (2005b, 2007).

63. Educational institutions and government departments are also connected to the Internet but do not offer commercial ISP services.

64. This service is called "transit." See Economides (2005c).

65. See Economides (2005c, fig. 2).

66. SBC changed its name to AT&T after it acquired AT&T.

67. The proposed Internet model without net neutrality would be closer to the traditional pre–Internet telecommunications model where customers pay per service. See Economides (2005b).

68. This is contingent on all markets are served under uniform pricing, which holds here because we are starting with all markets served under net neutrality.

69. See European Union Commission (1998).

70. See Economides (2005c).

71. For a more detailed discussion, see Economides (2005c).

References

Armstrong, M. 1998. Network interconnection in telecommunications. *Economic Journal* 108: 545–64.

Armstrong, M. 2005. Competition in two-sided markets. *RAND Journal of Economics* 37: 668–91.

Advanced Health-Care Services v. Radford Community Hospital. 910 F.2d 139, 148 (4th Cir. 1990).

Aspen Skiing Co. v. Aspen Highlands Skiing Corp. 472 US 585, 593–608 (1985).

Besen, S., and J. Farrell. 1994. Choosing how to compete: Strategies and tactics in standardization. *Journal of Economic Perspectives* 8: 117–31.

Brief of Amici Curiae United States and the Federal Trade Commission. Verizon Communications Inc. v. Law Offices of Curtis V. Trinko, 540 US 398 (2004).

Carter, M., and J. Wright. 2003. Asymmetric network interconnection. *Review of Industrial Organization* 22: 27–46.

Choi, J. P., E. G. Kristiansen, and J. Nahm. 2005. An economic analysis of product pre-announcements. *CESifo Economic Studies* 51(2–3): 299–319.

Chou, C.-F., and O. Shy. 1990. Network effects without network externalities. *International Journal of Industrial Organization* 8: 259–70.

Church, J., and N. Gandal. 1993. Complementary network externalities and technology adoption. *International Journal of Industrial Organization* 11: 239–60.

Cremer, J., P. Rey, and J. Tirole. 1998. The degradation of quality and the domination of the Internet. *Submission of GTE to the European Union for the merger of MCI with WorldCom*, app. 5.

Cremer, J., P. Rey, and J. Tirole. 2000. Connectivity in the commercial Internet. *Journal of Industrial Economics* 48: 433–72.

David, P. A. 1986. Understanding the economics of QWERTY. In W. N. Parker, ed., *Economic History and the Modern Economist*. Oxford: Basil Blackwell.

Dessein, W. 2003. Network competition in nonlinear pricing. *RAND Journal of Economics* 34(4): 593–611.

Dranove, D., and N. Gandal. 2003. The DVD vs. DIVX standard war: Empirical evidence of preannouncement effects. *Journal of Economics and Management Strategy* 12: 363–86.

Economides, N. 1996. The economics of networks. *International Journal of Industrial Organization* 16(4): 675–99. Prepublication copy available at ⟨http://www.stern.nyu.edu/networks/Economics_of_Networks.pdf⟩.

Economides, N. 1998. The incentive for non-price discrimination by an input monopolist. *International Journal of Industrial Organization* 16: 271–84. Prepublication copy available at ⟨http://www.stern.nyu.edu/networks/1136.pdf⟩.

Economides, N. 1999. The Telecommunications Act of 1996 and its impact. *Japan and the World Economy* 11: 455–83. Prepublication copy available at ⟨http://www.stern.nyu.edu/networks/98-08.pdf⟩.

Economides, N. 2001a. The Microsoft antitrust case. *Journal of Industry, Competition and Trade: From Theory to Policy*. Prepublication copy available at ⟨http://www.stern.nyu.edu/networks/Microsoft_Antitrust.final.pdf⟩.

Economides, N. 2001b. The Microsoft antitrust case: Rejoinder. *Journal of Industry, Competition and Trade: From Theory to Policy* 1(1): 71–79. Prepublication copy available at ⟨http://www.stern.nyu.edu/networks/Microsoft_Antitrust.Rejoinder.pdf⟩.

Economides, N. 2002. Amicus brief of Nicholas S. Economides on the revised proposed final judgment in the Microsoft case. Submitted to the United States Department of Justice. Available at ⟨http://www.usdoj.gov/atr/cases/ms_tuncom/major/mtc-00022465.htm⟩.

Economides, N. 2003a. US telecommunications today. In C. V. Brown and H. Topi, eds., *IS Management Handbook*. Boca Raton, FL: Auerbach Publications, pp. 191–212. Prepublication electronic copy available at ⟨http://www.stern.nyu.edu/networks/Economides_US_Telecommunications_Today_October_2002.pdf⟩.

Economides, N. 2003b. The tragic inefficiency of M-ECPR. In A. Shampine, ed., *Down to the Wire: Studies in the Diffusion and Regulation of Telecommunications Technologies*. New York: Nova Science Publishers, pp. 142–54. Prepublication copy available at ⟨http://www.stern.nyu.edu/networks/tragic.pdf⟩.

Economides, N. 2005a. Telecommunications regulation: An introduction. In R. R. Nelson, ed., *The Limits and Complexity of Organizations*. New York: Russell Sage Foundation Press, pp. 48–76. Prepublication copy available at ⟨http://www.stern.nyu.edu/networks/Telecommunications_Regulation.pdf⟩.

Economides, N. 2005b. Vertical leverage and the sacrifice principle: Why the Supreme Court got Trinko wrong. *New York University Annual Survey of American Law* 63(3): 379–413. Prepublication copy available at ⟨http://www.stern.nyu.edu/networks/Trinko.pdf⟩.

Economides, N. 2005c. The economics of the Internet backbone. In I. Vogelsang, ed., *Handbook of Telecommunications*. Amsterdam: Elsevier. Prepublication copy available at ⟨http://www.stern.nyu.edu/networks/Economides_ECONOMICS_OF_THE_INTERNET_BACKBONE.pdf⟩.

Economides, N. 2007. Hit and miss: Leverage, sacrifice, and refusal to deal and the supreme court decision in *Trinko*. Forthcoming in *Vanderbilt Journal of Entertainment and Technology Law*. Prepublication available copy at ⟨http://www.stern.nyu.edu/networks/Hit_and_Miss.pdf⟩.

Economides, N. 2008. Net neutrality, non-discrimination, and digital distribution of content through the Internet. Forthcoming in *I/S: A Journal of Law and Policy for the Information Soceity*. Prepublication copy available at ⟨http://www.stern.nyu.edu/networks/Economides_Net_Neutrality.pdf⟩.

Economides, N., and F. Flyer. 1998. Compatibility and market structure for network goods. Discussion paper EC-98-02. Stern School of Business, NYU. Available at ⟨http://www.stern.nyu.edu/networks/98-02.pdf⟩.

Economides, N., and C. Himmelberg. 1995. Critical mass and network evolution in telecommunications. In G. Brock, ed., *Toward a Competitive Telecommunications Industry: Selected Papers from the 1994 Telecommunications Policy Research Conference*. Prepublication copy available at ⟨http://www.stern.nyu.edu/networks/tprc.pdf⟩.

Economides, N., G. Lopomo, and G. Woroch. 1996. Regulatory pricing policies to neutralize network dominance. *Industrial and Corporate Change* 5(4): 1013–28. Prepublication copy available at ⟨http://www.stern.nyu.edu/networks/96-14.pdf⟩.

Economides, N., G. Lopomo, and G. Woroch. 2007. Strategic commitments and the principle of reciprocity in interconnection pricing. In G. Madden, ed., *The Economics of Digital Markets*. Cheltenham, UK: Edward Elgaz. Available at ⟨http://www.stern.nyu.edu/networks/reciprocity.pdf⟩.

Economides, N., and R. Schwartz. 1995a. Electronic call market trading. *Journal of Portfolio Management* 21(3): 10–18. Prepublication copy available at ⟨http://www.stern.nyu.edu/networks/Electronic_Call_Market_Trading.pdf⟩.

Economides, N., and R. Schwartz. 1995b. Equity trading practices and market structure: Assessing asset managers' demand for immediacy. *Financial Markets, Institutions and Instruments* 4(4): 1–46. Prepublication copy available at ⟨http://www.stern.nyu.edu/networks/Equity_Trading_Practices.pdf⟩.

Economides, N., K. Seim, and B. Viard. 2007. Quantifying the benefits of entry into local phone service. Available at ⟨http://www.stern.nyu.edu/networks/Local_Telecommunications.pdf⟩.

Economides, N., and A. Siow. 1988. The division of markets is limited by the extent of liquidity. *American Economic Review* 78(1): 108–21. Available at ⟨http://www.stern.nyu.edu/networks/aer88.pdf⟩.

Economides, N., and J. Tåg 2007. Net neutrality on the Internet: A two-sided market analysis. Available at ⟨http://www.stern.nyu.edu/networks/Economides_Tag_Net_Neutrality.pdf⟩.

Economides, N., and L. J. White. 1994. Networks and compatibility: Implications for antitrust. *European Economic Review* 38: 651–62.

Economides, N., and L. J. White. 1995. Access and interconnection pricing: How efficient is the efficient component pricing rule? *Antitrust Bulletin* 40(3): 557–79. Prepublication copy available at ⟨http://www.stern.nyu.edu/networks/Access_and_interconnection_pricing.pdf⟩.

Economides, N., and L. J. White. 1998. The inefficiency of the ECPR yet again: A reply to Larson. *Antitrust Bulletin* 43(2): 429–44. Prepublication copy available at ⟨http://www.stern.nyu.edu/networks/The_Inefficiency_of_the_ECPR.pdf⟩.

European Union Commission. 1998. *Statement of Objections to the MCI WorldCom Merger.*

Evans, D. 2003. The antitrust economics of multi-sided platform markets. *Yale Journal on Regulation* 20(2): 324–81.

Farrell, J., and P. Klemperer. 2003. Coordination and lock-in: Competition with switching costs and network effects. In R. Schmalensee and R. Willig, eds., *Handbook of Industrial Organization*, vol. 3. Amsterdam: North Holland.

Farrell, J., and G. Saloner. 1985. Standardization, compatibility and innovation. *RAND Journal of Economics* 16: 70–83.

Farrell, J., and G. Saloner. 1986. Installed base and compatibility: Innovation, product preannoucements, and predation. *American Economic Review* 76: 940–55.

Federal Communications Commission. 1996. *First Report and Order*, FCC No. 96-325 (August 1, 1996).

Gabel, D., and D. F. Weiman. 1994. Historical perspectives on interconnection between competing local operating companies: The United States, 1894–1914. In D. Gabel and D. F. Weiman, eds., *Opening Networks to Competition: The Regulation and Pricing of Access.* Norwell, MA: Kluwer Academic, pp. 75–105.

Gans, J., and S. King. 2001. Using "bill and keep" interconnect arrangements to soften network competition. *Economic Letters* 71(3): 413–20.

General Industries Corp. v. Hartz Mountain Corp. 810 F.2d 795, 803 (8th Cir. 1987).

Katz, M. L., and C. Shapiro. 1992. Product introduction with network externalities. *Journal of Industrial Economics* 40: 55–83.

Katz, M. L., and C. Shapiro. 1994. Systems competition and network effects. *Journal of Economic Perspectives* 8: 93–115.

Katz, M. L., and C. Shapiro. 1986. Technology adoption in the presence of network externalities. *Journal of Political Economy* 94: 822–41.

Krattenmaker, T. G., and S. C. Salop. 1986. Anticompetitive exclusion: Raising rivals' costs to achieve power over price. *Yale Law Journal* 96: 209.

Laffont, J.-J., P. Rey, and J. Tirole. 1998. Network competition. II: Price discrimination. *RAND Journal of Economics* 29(1): 38–56.

Lerner, J., and J. Tirole. 2006. A model of forum shopping, with special reference to standard setting organizations. *American Economic Review* 96: 1091–103.

Liebowitz, S. J., and S. E. Margolis. 1990. The fable of the keys. *Journal of Law and Economics* 33: 1–25.

Matutes, C., and P. Regibeau. 1988. Mix and match: Product compatibility without network externalities. *RAND Journal of Economics* 19: 221–34.

Posner, R. A. 2000. Antitrust in the new economy. *Tech Law Journal.* Available at ⟨http://www.techlawjournal .com/atr/20000914posner.asp⟩.

Rochet, J.-C., and J. Tirole. 2003. Platform competition in two-sided markets. *Journal of the European Economic Association* 1(4): 990–1029.

Rochet, J.-C., and J. Tirole. 2004. Two-sided markets: An overview. Mimeo. University of Toulonse.

Rohlfs, J. 1974. A theory of interdependent demand for a communications service. *Bell Journal of Economics* 5(1): 16–37.

Rohlfs, J. 2003. *Bandwagon Effects in High Technology Industries.* Cambridge: MIT Press.

Salop, S. C., and D. T. Scheffman. 1983. Raising rivals' cost. American Economic Review 73: 267.

Shaked, A., and J. Sutton. 1983. Natural oligopolies. *Econometrica* 51: 1469–84.

Stango, V. 2004. The economics of standards wars. *Review of Network Economics* 3(1): 1–19.

Stearns Airport Equipment Co. v. FMC Corp. 170 F.3d 518, 523–524 n. 3 (5th Cir. 1999).

Valletti, T. M., and C. Cambini. 2005. Investments and network competition. *RAND Journal of Economics* 36: 446–67.

Verizon Communications Inc. v. Law Offices of Curtis V. Trinko. 540 US 398 (2004).

14 Competition Policy for Intellectual Property

Richard J. Gilbert

Intellectual property rights afford inventors, and authors in the case of copyright, protection from imitation. The intellectual property laws give rights-holders substantial discretion over how to use or license their intellectual property. The antitrust laws prohibit arrangements that restrain competition. One body of law promotes higher prices by excluding some potential competitors, while the other body of law promotes lower prices by prohibiting some conduct that limits competition. Courts and academics have attempted to reconcile the conflict by noting that both the intellectual property laws and the antitrust laws enhance competition, the former by creating incentives to develop new products and processes.[1] Yet the two legal doctrines continue to clash in antitrust cases involving intellectual property in both the United States and the European Union.

I begin the chapter with a brief history of antitrust law for intellectual property in the United States (section 14.1) and describe the general approaches used in the United States and the European Union to analyze competition involving intellectual property rights (section 14.2). In section 14.3, I discuss the characteristics of intellectual property that may justify antitrust treatment that differs from antitrust policy for ordinary property.

In section 14.4, I briefly examine the antitrust treatment of patent pools. Department of Justice advisory letters and EU guidelines clarify how the enforcement agencies analyze the competitive risks posed by patent pools and help resolve a muddled history of legal opinions in this area. Both US and EU policy documents look favorably upon a condition that a patent pool offer licenses for individual patents in the pool, and recent theoretical work further suggests that this condition can be used as a screen to identify patent pools that may be anticompetitive. In section 14.4, I also show that a requirement to unbundle licenses can have unintended effects when licensees invent around the patents in the pool. Individual licenses encourage inefficient investment to escape royalties on licensed patents, which can be avoided if the pool licenses all of its patents as a package.

14.1 Cycles of Antitrust Enforcement for Intellectual Property

In the early years following the passage of the Sherman Act in 1890, courts in antitrust cases involving intellectual property deferred to the rights of intellectual property owners, even in matters that involved arrangements between actual or potential competitors.[2] For example, in *E. Bement & Sons v. National Harrow Co.* the US Supreme Court decided in 1902 that a patent pool that set royalties for patents used by most manufacturers and sellers of float spring tooth harrows[3] and prohibited licensees from selling other products did not violate the antitrust laws. The Court reasoned that the pool was legal because:

[T]he general rule is absolute freedom in the use or sale of rights under the patent laws of the United States. The very object of these laws is monopoly, and the rule is, with few exceptions, that any conditions which are not in their very nature illegal with regard to this kind of property, imposed by the patentee and agreed to by the licensee for the right to manufacture or use or sell the article, will be upheld by the courts. The fact that the conditions in the contracts keep up the monopoly or fix prices does not render them illegal.[4]

The themes expressed by the Court in *National Harrow* are that patent laws trump antitrust laws, pooling arrangements confer benefits by avoiding costly litigation over patent scope and validity, and licensing terms that fix prices are not unlawful because patentees have the right to specify the prices at which their products are sold.

The Supreme Court soon abandoned the first theme, holding in *Standard Sanitary Manufacturing v. US* that a joint licensing arrangement for patents relating to an enameling process for sanitary ironware violated the antitrust laws. Antitrust policy generally, and with respect to intellectual property in particular, became more stringent in the 1960s. Over a span of ten years the Supreme Court decided cases that restricted the ability of a patentee or a patent pool to issue geographically limited licenses (*US v. Singer Manufacturing Co.*), declared as patent misuse the requirement that a licensee pay royalties on products that do not use the teaching of the patent (*Zenith Radio Corp. v. Hazeltine Research, Inc.*), limited provisions in licensing agreements that prohibit the licensee from challenging the validity of the patent (*Lear, Inc. v. Adkins*), and made enforcement of a patent procured by fraud on the Patent Office a monopolization offense (*Walker Process Equipment, Inc. v. Food Machinery & Chemical Corp.*). The Federal Trade Commission (FTC) brought an antitrust claim for charging discriminatory royalties for the use of a patented machine (*Emile M. LaPeyre et al. v. Federal Trade Commission*) and the US Department of Justice (DOJ) brought a complaint challenging the grant of exclusive licenses (*US v. Studiengesellschaft Kohle, MBH*).

In 1972, a speech by Bruce Wilson, then Deputy Assistant Attorney in the US Department of Justice, set out the enforcement posture of the Antitrust Division with a list of what came to be known as the "nine no-no's" of patent licensing:[5]

1. Requiring a licensee to purchase unpatented materials.
2. Requiring a licensee to assign future patents.
3. Restricting a purchaser of a patented product in the resale of the product.
4. Restricting a licensee's ability to deal in products or services not within the scope of the patent.

5. Agreeing with a licensee not to grant future licenses to others without the licensee's consent.
6. Mandatory package licensing.
7. Royalties on the total sales price of products containing unpatented items.
8. Restricting a licensee's sale of products made by use of the patented process.
9. Requiring a licensee to adhere to a minimum price with respect to the licensee's sale of the licensed product.

It is doubtful whether US antitrust policy toward licensing arrangements was ever as inflexible as the nine no-no's would suggest. In any case the DOJ's enforcement posture with respect to intellectual property softened during the next decade. By 1979 the Antitrust Division's position was that "patent licensing agreements should be analyzed under the same standards as other agreements."[6] Agency officials described a policy toward licensing arrangements that gave patentees wide discretion to fashion different licensing arrangements under the principle that the owner of the patent has the right to refuse to license anyone. The 1982 *DOJ Guidelines for International Operations* included a section on intellectual property licensing that formalized this view and also stated that the owner of a patent is entitled to the "full value of the patent."[7] The full value referred to the area under the derived demand curve for patent licenses. However, the International Guidelines did not offer policy guidance for licensing practices that might shift the location or change the elasticity of the derived demand curve. For example, is it within the scope of the patent grant to license a patent on the condition that the licensee refrains from using a competing product? Subsequent guidance from the Agencies addressed this question.

14.2 Current State of US and EU Antitrust Policy for Intellectual Property

The DOJ/FTC *Antitrust Guidelines for the Licensing of Intellectual Property* (IP Guidelines), published in 1995, describe the approach currently used by the US federal antitrust agencies to analyze licensing arrangements involving intellectual property.[8] The IP Guidelines state three fundamental principles that apply to intellectual property licensing:[9]

1. For the purpose of antitrust analysis, the Agencies regard intellectual property as being essentially comparable to any other form of property.
2. The Agencies do not presume that intellectual property creates market power in the antitrust context.
3. The Agencies recognize that intellectual property licensing allows firms to combine complementary factors of production and is generally procompetitive.

In 2004 the European Commission enacted a new block exemption regulation that applies to technology transfer agreements involving patents, know-how, and software copyright (EC Regulation[10]) and also released guidelines for applying the new block exemption and for evaluating the antitrust risks of licensing agreements that fall outside the scope of the new EC Regulation.[11] The new EC Regulation and the accompanying EC Guidelines develop an analytical framework that is similar to the framework described in the IP Guidelines. Both the IP Guidelines and EC Regulation/Guidelines:

• Describe the approach that the Agencies use to evaluate licensing arrangements.
• Affirm that technology licensing is generally procompetitive.
• State that for the purpose of antitrust policy, intellectual property is similar to other forms of property.
• Do not presume that intellectual property creates market power.
• Distinguish licensing transactions that occur between competitors and noncompetitors.
• Recognize that applicable law balances efficiencies against any negative effects on competition from licensing arrangements that do not clearly fix minimum prices or reduce output.
• Recognize that exclusive licenses promote the adoption of new technologies in many circumstances.
• Include "safety zones" within which certain licensing arrangements are automatically exempted.

There are, however, important differences that reflect the different governing principles in US and EU competition law. A central concept in the US IP Guidelines is the counterfactual proposition that "antitrust concerns may arise when a licensing arrangement harms competition among entities that would have been actual or likely potential competitors in a relevant market in the absence of the license."[12] The EC Regulation and Guidelines do not endorse this analytical principle and specifically address concerns that may arise in licensing arrangements between parties that could not compete in the absence of a license. The EC Guidelines state:

The assessment of whether a licence agreement restricts competition must be made within the actual context in which competition would occur in the absence of the agreement with its alleged restrictions. In making this assessment it is necessary to take account of the likely impact of the agreement on inter-technology competition (i.e., competition between undertakings using competing technologies) and on intra-technology competition (i.e., competition between undertakings using the same technology). Article 81(1) prohibits restrictions of both inter-technology competition and intra-technology competition. It is therefore necessary to assess to what extent the agreement affects or is likely to affect these two aspects of competition on the market.[13]

The emphasis in the US Guidelines is solely on intertechnology competition. The US Guidelines say "The Agencies will not require the owner of intellectual property to create competition in its own technology."[14] The EC Guidelines are more qualified: "A technology owner cannot normally be expected to create direct competition with himself on the basis of his own technology."[15] Although similar, these two statements reflect important differences in antitrust philosophies.

Which approach is more likely to screen anticompetitive licensing arrangements from the vast number of arrangements that enhance economic welfare? The principle of "harm to competition in the absence of the license" is useful to assess when a licensing arrangement has a horizontal dimension that may threaten competition. For example, suppose two firms cross-license patents on technologies to produce a new chemical compound. If the patents are blocking, the cross-license does not harm competition that could occur in its absence. However, if each patent covers a technology that could be used to produce the chemical, the cross-license could harm competition that would occur in its absence. This finding does not automatically lead to a conclusion of antitrust liability, but is instead a screen to identify conduct that requires further analysis.

For licensing arrangements that do not harm competition that would have occurred in the absence of the license, the US Guidelines suggest that a patentee has considerable discretion over how to license its intellectual property. The patentee may limit the number of licensees, allow only an exclusive licensee, or restrict licensees by geography or field of use.

A criticism of the principle of "harm to competition in the absence of the license" is that it does not provide a framework that adequately addresses the potential harms to competition from vertical restraints in licensing agreements. Vertical restraints are of particular concern in the European Union, with its objective to promote trade among the member states.

For example, in the antitrust case brought by the US Department of Justice and several states against Microsoft, the plaintiffs alleged that Microsoft harmed competition by, among other things, entering into agreements with Internet access providers and Internet content providers that caused them not to distribute or promote competitive browsers.[16] These are allegations of anticompetitive exclusive dealing. However, the competition allegedly harmed by this exclusive dealing may not have occurred if Microsoft did not issue software licenses for its intellectual property.

The EU approach to the licensing of intellectual property essentially replicates the policies it applies to vertical agreements for other types of property.[17] Consistency in policy guidance is desirable, but the traditional EU concerns about vertical restraints can be counterproductive when applied to intellectual property. For example, both the EC technology transfer regulation and the EC block exemption for vertical agreements deny a block exemption for licenses that restrict active or passive sales to end-users by a licensee that is a member of a selective distribution system and operates at the retail level, even though the licensor and the licensee are not competitors. Yet one should not presume that territorial exclusivity in technology licenses restricts trade. The license provides the licensee with a product or technology that the licensee would not have without the license. In that respect the license promotes trade, even if it limits access to the product or technology to only a portion of the European Union.

Neither the US nor the EU policy documents relating to antitrust and intellectual property provide an entirely satisfactory template to analyze arrangements involving intellectual property that can harm competition and economic welfare. The next section considers antitrust policy for intellectual property more broadly and identifies ways in which intellectual property may justify a different antitrust approach than for ordinary property.

14.3 Should Antitrust Differ for Intellectual Property?

A central tenet of US and EU policy for intellectual property is that for the purpose of antitrust policy, intellectual property is essentially comparable to any other form of property. There are, however, a number of ways in which intellectual property differs from ordinary property, although these differences do not necessarily justify a unique antitrust policy. I begin with a list of important distinctions, which I then discuss in more detail:

- Intellectual property enjoys special legal prerogatives.
- Intellectual property's role in stimulating innovation.
- The boundaries that define intellectual property are uncertain.
- Intellectual property motivates strategic conduct.
- Intellectual property owners may require conditions on licensees to discourage imitation and to appropriate the value of their inventions.
- The owners of intellectual property may have means to impose licensing conditions that extend beyond what is feasible for ordinary property.
- Intellectual property is often complementary to other assets.

14.3.1 Intellectual Property Enjoys Special Legal Prerogatives

Patents confer rights to exclude others from making, using, or selling the invention claimed by the patent. Because a patentee can exclude others from using the patent, a license that conveys partial rights to a patent does not alone harm competition. However, license restrictions that are harmless in isolation can adversely affect competition when part of a broader context. A license for a patented chemical that gives the licensee the exclusive right to sell the chemical west of the Mississippi does not alone restrict competition that would have occurred if the patentee chose not to license the patent at all. But if the owners of patents on two similar chemicals agree to license one of the patents for sale exclusively west of the Mississippi and the other for sale exclusively east of the Mississippi, the agreement not to pursue sales in each other's exclusive territory can adversely affect competition that would have occurred in the absence of the license.

US patent law expressly states that "no patent holder . . . shall be denied relief or deemed guilty of misuse or illegal extension of the patent right by reason of his having . . . (4) refused to license or use any rights to the patent . . . ."[18] In *CSU v. Xerox*,[19] the US Court of Appeals for the Federal Circuit affirmed this principle, holding that Xerox was not obliged to sell patented parts and license diagnostic software required to service its copiers to independent service organizations (ISOs). However, other courts have reached different conclusions. In *Eastman Kodak Co. v. Image Technical Services, Inc.*, a group of ISOs accused Kodak of unlawfully monopolizing and attempting to monopolize the sale of service for Kodak equipment by refusing to sell replacement parts except to customers who purchased service from Kodak or who repaired their own machines. Kodak asserted that many of its parts and diagnostic software were protected by patent and copyright, and therefore it could not be found to have violated the antitrust laws by refusing to make its parts and software available to ISOs. An appellate court dismissed Kodak's argument, finding that its intellectual property defense was a pretext and not a valid business justification for its conduct.

The extent to which intellectual property rights can immunize conduct that is otherwise unlawful under the antitrust laws remains unsettled. In *CSU v. Xerox* the Federal Circuit Court noted that "intellectual property rights do not confer a privilege to violate the antitrust laws," but opined that:

In the absence of any indication of illegal tying, fraud in the Patent and Trademark Office, or sham litigation, the patent holder may enforce the statutory right to exclude others from making, using, or selling the claimed invention free from liability under the antitrust laws.[20]

Other courts and enforcement agencies have not agreed with the Federal Circuit's limited view of potential antitrust liability for patent holders.[21] The US Department of Justice filed an antitrust complaint against General Electric's licensing practices for its medical imaging equipment. GE's licenses required that each licensee not compete with GE in servicing any other facilities' medical equipment, including non-GE equipment. The DOJ alleged that this restriction violated the Sherman Act. The DOJ also challenged territorial and field of use restrictions imposed by Pilkington in licenses for trade secrets related to its float glass technologies. The US Federal Trade Commission alleged that Intel's refusal to provide advanced technical information to Intergraph violated the antitrust laws.[22] Both agencies have imposed licensing requirements as conditions to conclude mergers. In *US v. Microsoft*, the District Court denied Microsoft's defense that its software copyrights offered protection from antitrust liability.

In *C.R. Bard v. M3 Systems, Inc.*, a divided panel of the Court of Appeals for the Federal Circuit issued an opinion that appears at odds with *CSU v. Xerox*. Bard held patents on a biopsy gun and on needles used with the gun to take tissue samples. Faced with competition from M3 Systems for replacement needles, Bard redesigned the gun and needle assembly to be incompatible with the needles sold by M3 Systems. Bard's redesign of its biopsy gun was a technological tie. Although not a simple refusal to deal, the tie had the effect of denying access to Bard's patented biopsy gun, which M3 Systems required to sell its needles. A district court jury held that Bard had engaged in predatory conduct to exclude competition from M3 Systems, a finding that the Federal Circuit upheld.[23]

14.3.2 Intellectual Property's Role in Stimulating Innovation

Intellectual property rights enhance market power by excluding imitators and impose a potential drag on the economy if rights-holders can raise prices above marginal production costs. At the same time intellectual property rights promote research and development by making it easier for innovators to profit from the fruits of their efforts. Some market power in the supply of goods or services can be an acceptable price to pay for the creation of new or improved goods or services.

Does this trade-off justify a different, and perhaps less restrictive, antitrust policy for intellectual property? The argument against a weaker antitrust policy for intellectual property is that intellectual property rights-holders are entitled to profit from the exclusionary power of their rights, which they can do without imposing other restraints on competition. It is not an antitrust violation to charge a high royalty for an invention.[24] The owner of an intellectual property right is entitled to benefit from the market power created by that right, which in turn should be related to the social value of the intellectual property.

The principle that an inventor is entitled to the value the invention creates does not permit an inventor of a new product in market X to raise prices in market Y simply because the profits in market Y would encourage invention in market X. Yet in some basic sense, intellectual property policies do just this. They link profits in one sphere of economic activity—the market for the invention—to incentives in another sphere—the activity of research and development to create the invention. A coherent theory of socially desirable policies to promote innovation should not rely on arbitrary market distinctions but rather should begin with first principles. One way to pose the problem is to maximize social welfare subject to the constraint that the profits from innovation are sufficient to cover its costs. Viewed this way, the optimal promotion of research and development (R&D) takes on the flavor of a Ramsey (1927) pricing problem. The social costs of collecting the funds necessary to compensate an R&D program are minimized by raising prices in *every* market by an amount that is inversely proportional to the market elasticity of demand.

Ramsey pricing has obvious limitations as the foundation for a competition policy to reward innovation. There is no obvious way to know how much distortion should be permitted in each market. Compensation typically cannot be limited to R&D costs because the costs of R&D are not public information and may not even be known by the innovator. Even if costs could be calculated after an invention is made, it would be difficult to know how to direct compensation to those who were responsible for the innovation in a way to provide correct incentives for R&D. Kaplow (1984) develops an insightful variation on the Ramsey pricing theme to assess the value of restraints that affect intellectual property and to choose policies that promote innovation at the lowest social cost. Kaplow ranks each policy according to a figure of merit equal to the policy's profit contribution for R&D divided by the social cost imposed by the policy. One measure of social cost is the deadweight loss imposed by the policy, measured by the difference between total economic surplus without the policy and total economic surplus with the policy. Other measures of social cost can be used such as consumer surplus or a weighted average of consumer surplus and producer profits.

An ideal policy would reward innovation with no social cost. An ineffective policy would provide no profit contribution for R&D, or would make a very small profit contribution with a very large social cost. Consider policies indexed by k. Each policy describes allowable conduct by the IP rights-holder, with the consequences of each policy for market prices presumed to be known. Let p^k represent the set of all prices corresponding to policy k. The policy $k = 0$ corresponds to a market with no restraints, including no intellectual property rights. Each additional policy generates a profit contribution of $\Delta \pi(p^k)$ and reduces total surplus by $\Delta V(p^k)$, where $\Delta \pi(p^k) = \pi(p^k) - \pi(p^{k-1})$ and $\Delta V(p^k) = -(V(p^k) - V(p^{k-1}))$.[25] If a policy-maker allows the set of policies $k = 1, 2, \ldots, K$, then together the policies generate a profit of $\pi(p^0) + \sum_{k=1}^{K} \Delta \pi(p^k)$ and a total surplus of $V(p^0) - \sum_{k=1}^{K} \Delta V(p^k)$. The question is: What policies should be allowed? Absent integer constraints, the optimal rule is to choose policies in descending order of $\Delta \pi(p^k)/\Delta V(p^k)$ until the set of all chosen policies generates enough profit to pay for the cost of R&D.[26]

This approach is the ratio test described by Kaplow (1984). For example, consider whether patentees should be permitted to offer licenses with discriminatory royalties.[27] Such a policy would make a large contribution to profit, while the aggregate welfare loss is likely to be low; some consumers would pay more relative to a policy of no price discrimination, while others would pay less. According to the Kaplow ratio test, discriminatory royalties should be permitted, unless other policies are available that would generate sufficient profits to fund R&D with even lower reduction in surplus. Interestingly it does not immediately follow from the Kaplow ratio test that the efficient set of policies to promote R&D should even include patent rights. Other policies could be available that raise funds for R&D with lower social costs.[28]

14.3.3 The Boundaries That Define Intellectual Property Are Uncertain

Compared to intellectual property, it is typically easier to describe the boundaries of ordinary property and to prevent theft and trespassing. Accidental infringement of intellectual property can occur because the infringer was unaware of the scope of the property right or even its existence. Patents are registered with the Patent and Trademark Office in the United States, and with analogous agencies in other countries, but registration has little notification value in technological areas where there are thousands of patents. The US Patent and Trademark Office database includes almost 4 million utility patents. A search of the database reveals 54,635 patents related to semiconductor device manufacturing issued between January 1, 1990, and May 1, 2005. Even in relatively narrow technological areas it can be impractical for a user of a technology to be aware of all the patents that could be infringed.

Even if a firm is aware of the existence of patents in a relevant area, it can be difficult to discern the scope of these rights. Patent grants often include multiple claims, any one of which can be infringed. The "doctrine of equivalents" allows a patent holder to prove infringement for the use or sale of products or methods that are similar to, but do not literally infringe, the patent's claims. The doctrine prevents a potential infringer from escaping liability by making trivial changes to a patented product or method, but "equivalence" is not clearly defined and may extend to nontrivial differences.

Patents don't come with "no-trespassing" signs. Even if they did, for many patents the signs would have to list numerous tracts that could be trespassed scattered over many locations, and even the patent holder could not clearly describe the "lot lines" that define the property protected by the patent. A consequence of this uncertainty is that accidental infringement is common in many industries and adds a risk premium to investments that require access to intellectual property rights.

Patent validity is also uncertain. About 45 percent of litigated patents are held to be invalid (Allison and Lemley 1998). Many others are not enforced or are enforced with nominal royalties. Uncertain patent validity adds risk to investments in R&D, although the net effect depends on both types of errors: "good" patents that are held to be invalid and "bad" patents that are held to be valid or not challenged. Research in Motion, supplier of the Blackberry wireless messaging device, paid $450 million to settle an infringement action brought by NTP for patents that Research in Motion characterized as too general and broad to be valid.[29] Ayres and Klemperer (1999) make the argument that allowing some latitude for users to infringe "good" patents without penalty can be socially beneficial. A probability of infringement is similar to a cap on the royalty that the patentee can charge. A small reduction in the royalty has no first-order effect on the patentee's profit, but it has a positive first-order effect on social surplus by reducing deadweight loss. Applying Kaplow's ratio test, a small probability of infringement is a good deal for society because it lowers deadweight loss with little effect on the innovator's profit.

Courts have been reluctant to assess patent validity and scope in the context of antitrust cases. Patent validity and scope are central to the competitive effects of settlement agreements between a patentee and a potential entrant into the market for the patented product. If the patent is valid and would be infringed, the patent gives its owner the right to exclude a firm that employs the teaching of the patent. On the other hand, if the patent is not valid or would not be infringed, a settlement between a patentee and a potential entrant could harm competition that would have occurred in the absence of the settlement.

The US Federal Trade Commission challenged several settlement agreements between manufacturers of a patented drug and its generic equivalent, arguing that they are payments by the patentee to avoid or delay competition from the generic supplier. An appellate court ruled against the Commission in a recent decision, *Schering-Plough Corp. v. FTC*. The case involved the drug K-Dur 20, a patented extended release form of potassium chloride used to treat hypertension or congestive heart disease. Schering-Plough, the patentee, reached settlement agreements with Upsher-Smith Laboratories and ESI Lederle requiring that Upsher and ESI not introduce a generic equivalent of K-Dur 20 before a certain date, which preceded the expiration of the patent. The Commission held that the settlement was an anticompetitive attempt to protect Schering's monopoly profit by eliminating a challenge to its K-Dur patent. The court reversed the Commission's finding "for a rather simple reason: one of the parties owned a patent."[30] The opinion emphasized the benefits of settlements of patent disputes and noted that "without any evidence to the contrary, there is a presumption that the ... patent is a valid one, which gives Schering the ability to exclude those who infringe its product."[31] The court did not explicitly explore the likelihood that Upsher or ESI might successfully challenge the validity or scope of Schering's patent.

Courts encourage parties to settle their differences privately because negotiated outcomes are efficient in many cases and economize on scarce legal resources. However, private bargaining does not necessarily lead to efficient outcomes for disputes that involve patent rights. If a patent is not valid or has only limited ability to exclude competitors, a settlement that protects the patent from a challenge to its validity or scope can have economic consequences that extend beyond the parties to the settlement. Consumers bear the burden of settlements that sustain otherwise invalid or narrow intellectual property rights. Nonetheless, even settlements of patent disputes have efficiency benefits that can outweigh the competitive risks.[32]

14.3.4   Intellectual Property Motivates Strategic Conduct

Patents and the procedures for awarding patents create opportunities for strategic conduct. Although strategic behavior is the norm in business, the potential to act strategically to the detriment of consumers can be particularly severe for intellectual property. The US Patent and Trademark Office allows patent applicants to file continuation applications in an effort to obtain additional or broader claims. If these claims are granted, they receive the priority date of the original application. Several patents issued to Jerome Lemelson, who earned a fortune from patent royalties, spent decades in the PTO under continuation proceedings. One of his patent applications, covering machines and methods for printing and reading bar codes, remained at the patent office for more than 44 years before it issued as patent number 5,966,457.[33]

Lemley and Moore (2003) argue that continuations have allowed patent applicants to gain a strategic advantage over competitors by allowing the applicant to observe products that succeed in the market and then to draft claims that cover those products. Critics of the continuation process use the term "submarine patents" to describe patents that remain in the PTO for many years and then surface to destroy infringers. Recent legislation limits the harm from patent continuations by changing the US patent term to 20 years from the date a patent application is *filed* instead of 17 years from the date the patent is *issued*.[34] The new patent term prevents a patentee from effectively lengthening the patent term by filing continuations, but it applies only to patents filed before 1995. Furthermore a patent applicant who files after 1995 may delay the issue date to capitalize on sunk investments made by users of the patent technology, even if the delay reduces the effective patent term.[35]

The combination of uncertainty, strategic behavior, and sunk investments can lead to "holdups" that add greatly to investment risk. In economic terms, a holdup occurs when a supplier of an input exploits investments made by a buyer that are specific to the use of the input. The specific investments provide the supplier with the opportunity to collect rents from the buyer. These rents exist because the buyer has incurred costs that cannot be recovered if it switches to another supplier. In some circumstances buyers can take actions to protect themselves from strategic behavior; for example, by making contractual commitments that reduce the risk of exposure to patent claims after sunk investments have been made.

There is a risk of holdup when a patent covers a product or method that is necessary to implement a standard that has wide consumer acceptance and the patent was not disclosed before the standard was adopted.[36] Participants in a standard-setting organization may have the choice of several standard specifications that offer comparable benefits, but switching to a different standard after one has been adopted can be costly. High switching costs may give the owner of a patent that is essential to the standard the power to impose high royalties. Some standard-setting organizations have adopted rules that require participants to notify the organization if they own intellectual property rights that are necessary to implement a proposed standard, and in some cases require that these rights be licensed at "fair, reasonable and nondiscriminatory" terms.

The US Federal Trade Commission has played a watchdog role in cases where participants in a standard-setting process have failed to disclose patents. In 1992 the Video Electronics Standards Association established a standard for the VL-bus, a mechanism to transfer instructions between a computer's microprocessor and its peripheral devices. The FTC accused Dell Computer of creating a holdup by failing to disclose that it owned intellectual property that was necessary to implement the VL-bus standard until after the standard had been adopted.[37] According to the FTC, Dell's actions hindered industry acceptance of the VL-bus standard pending resolution of the patent issue, deterred companies from using the VL-bus, created uncertainties that increased the costs of using the VL-bus, and chilled the willingness of companies to participate in standard-setting efforts.

The Federal Trade Commission pursued similar allegations against Rambus, Inc. and the Union Oil Company (Unocal). In a complaint announced on June 18, 2002, the FTC accused Rambus of concealing from the JEDEC Solid State Technology Association the existence of patents it either owned or had applied for relating to technological standards for synchronous dynamic random access (DRAM) computer memory, in violation of JEDEC's rules.[38] According to the Commission, this conduct allowed Rambus to monopolize and attempt to monopolize markets relating to technological features necessary for the design and manufacture of DRAM memory devices, resulting in adverse effects on competition and consumers.

An FTC Administrative Law judge dismissed the complaint against Rambus on February 17, 2004. The judge held that Rambus did not deceive JEDEC or its members and that

Rambus had a legitimate business justification for its actions. Furthermore the judge found that the challenged conduct did not cause JEDEC to be locked-in to using Rambus's technologies in its standardization efforts and did not result in any anticompetitive effects. The FTC staff appealed the decision. On August 2, 2006, the Commission reversed the findings of the Administrative Law Judge and ruled that Rambus had engaged in anticompetitive conduct.

In a complaint announced on March 4, 2003, the FTC charged Unocal with committing fraud in connection with regulatory proceedings that established environmental standards for gasoline sold in California. The California Air Resources Board (CARB) initiated rule-making proceedings in the late 1980s to determine standards governing the composition of low-emissions reformulated gasoline (RFG). The FTC alleged that during the RFG rule-making process Unocal made materially false and misleading statements to CARB and other regulatory participants regarding its emissions research results. According to the complaint, Unocal offered emissions research results that it claimed were nonproprietary but failed to disclose that it had pending patent claims on these results and that it intended to assert its proprietary interests in the future.

On November 25, 2003, the Administrative Law Judge in the Unocal matter dismissed the FTC's complaint on the grounds that Unocal's conduct constituted petitioning of a governmental authority (in this case the CARB) and as such was entitled to antitrust immunity. The judge also said that other aspects of Unocal's conduct would require analysis of substantial issues of patent law that he believed were not within the Commission's jurisdiction. The FTC staff's complaint contended that in the absence of Unocal's alleged fraud, either CARB would not have adopted RFG regulations that substantially overlapped with Unocal's patent claims or would have negotiated terms to deal with Unocal's market power.

The FTC commissioners disagreed with the findings of the Administrative Law Judge and on July 7, 2004, voted to reverse and vacate the decision by the Administrative Law Judge and remand the case for a new trial. Soon after, the proposed merger of Unocal and Chevron allowed the FTC to resolve its concerns by conditioning approval of the merger on a requirement that Unocal license the relevant patents on a royalty-free basis.

Market power that arises from a failure to disclose patent rights to a standard-setting committee can cause firms to underinvest to avoid placing themselves at risk of a patent holdup or to overinvest in defensive measures. At the same time an overly broad disclosure requirement can dull incentives for innovation. Antitrust enforcement that deals with the exploitation of patent rights necessary to implement a standard raises a number of difficult questions. What are the obligations of an intellectual property rights-holder to disclose its property rights? What are the obligations of the standard-setting organization to require disclosure? Is the organization liable for anticompetitive conduct if it neglects to require disclosure or does not take reasonable actions to mitigate the potential harm from an undisclosed patent? When does the conduct of a participant constitute fraud? Do disclosure requirements and limits on the exercise of patent rights discourage innovation? Is antitrust enforcement necessary to protect consumers from failure to disclose intellectual property rights in the standards process? In other situations, parties can make commitments that potentially expose themselves to holdup, such as investing in an expensive aluminum factory that is close to a low-cost supply of bauxite. Yet antitrust agencies rarely intervene if the parties fail to protect themselves from opportunistic behavior. Why should standard-setting be different? One possible answer is that standards affect the welfare of consumers who are not directly represented by the standard-setting organization, and it is the job of the antitrust agencies to protect these consumers (Farrell 2004). But how much protection is sufficient?

As of this writing, none of the FTC cases alleging concealment of intellectual property rights have resulted in a final determination of antitrust liability. Dell settled the FTC's charges by agreeing not to enforce its patent against computer manufacturers incorporating the VL-bus design. Unocal settled as a condition of its merger with Chevron, and the Rambus case is still under appeal.

14.3.5 Intellectual Property Owners May Require Conditions on Licensees to Discourage Imitation and to Appropriate the Value of Their Inventions

Just as uncertainty about the location of patent mines can be a reason to limit the scope of a patentee's lawful conduct, uncertainty about the value of a technology and whether a patent has been infringed can justify licensing conditions that depart from simple royalty obligations on the use of the licensed technology.[39] Suppose a patent covers a new machine used to manufacture magnetic disks. The patentee could have no way to know that a supplier of magnetic disks used the patented machine, but the patentee could charge a royalty on sales of magnetic disks without regard to how they were manufactured, or even on sales of disk drives. Limited information could justify other licensing restrictions to appropriate the value of an invention. These could include restrictions on sales of competing technologies by a licensee as a means to better monitor a licensee's use of the licensed technology. These types of licensing restraints could also adversely affect competition that would have occurred in the absence of the license. The efficiency justifications for restrictive licensing terms would depend on particular circumstances and would have to be weighed against possible anticompetitive effects.

Microsoft's MS-DOS "per-processor" licensing arrangement charged licensees a royalty for each computer sold with a particular type of microprocessor, rather than for each operating system sold with a computer. Microsoft claimed that the per-processor licensing scheme discouraged piracy because computer manufacturers could not escape Microsoft's royalty obligation by selling a machine without an operating system (which would allow the manufacturer or the user to load a pirated copy). In other respects Microsoft's licensing scheme was similar to a royalty based on total sales, which the Supreme Court frowned upon in *Zenith Radio Corp. v. Hazeltine Research, Inc.*

14.3.6   The Owners of Intellectual Property May Have Means to Impose Licensing Conditions That Extend Beyond What Is Feasible for Ordinary Property

The prerogatives of intellectual property complement vertical restraints that are lawful for ordinary property and may amplify their effects. Software licenses, sometimes in the form of click-wrap or shrink-wrap licenses, often include detailed limitations on how and where the software may be used. The market for agricultural seeds illustrates the power of intellectual property. The 1998 version of a technology licensing agreement between Monsanto and farmers regulating the use of genetically modified hybrid soybean seeds required that farmers: use the seed containing the Monsanto gene technologies for planting a commercial crop only in a single season, not supply any of this seed to any other person or entity for planting; not save any crop produced from this seed for replanting or supply saved seed to anyone for replanting, and not use the seed or provide it to anyone for crop breeding, research, generation of herbicide registration data or seed production. Failure to abide by these conditions would expose the farmer to significant penalties.[40]

A seller of unpatented hybrid seeds can demand that the farmer pay a fee and may impose other conditions, but the scope of the seller's control is limited. A farmer can replant seed or purchase seed from other suppliers, and unless the seed includes a tag or marker analogous to a patented gene, it would be difficult for the seller to prove that the farmer's conduct violated a contractual agreement.

The wide scope afforded by intellectual property to impose and enforce conditions on a licensee's behavior reinforces the role for antitrust law to limit contractual restraints that harm competition in commerce for products protected by intellectual property rights.[41]

14.3.7   Intellectual Property Is Often Complementary to Other Assets

Intellectual property typically has to be combined with other assets and capabilities to supply a useful product or service. In most cases a discovery is an input to future inventions as well as an output of research and development efforts. Coordinating the supply, including pricing, of factors that are complements to each other can enhance economic welfare. A single supplier of complements may choose a lower price than the sum of prices chosen by individual suppliers and may take actions to promote the adoption and use of the entire package of complementary products or services. This basic principle motivates favorable treatment for patent pools and package licensing of complementary patents, which is the subject of the next section.

14.4   Patent Pools and Cross-licensing Arrangements

In 1997 the US Department of Justice issued the first in a series of business review letters relating to patent pools. This short document is notable because it provides an economic framework to evaluate patent pooling arrangements that was largely absent in prior judicial decisions. The 1997 DOJ business review letter addressed the pool formed to resolve patent disputes and to license patents necessary to implement the MPEG-2 audio and video digital compression standard.[42] The DOJ determined that the pool achieved potential efficiencies by aggregating complementary and blocking intellectual property rights. The DOJ subsequently issued additional business review letters relating to patent pools to develop digital versatile discs compliant with the DVD-ROM and DVD-video formats[43] and third-generation mobile communication systems.[44]

In expressing its view that these pools are unlikely to violate the antitrust laws, the DOJ highlighted the following factors:

1. The pool is limited to patents that are essential to implement the standard.
2. The pool grants nonexclusive licenses that do not prevent licensees from developing alternative technologies.
3. Patents can be licensed individually as well as in a package.
4. Licensees are required to grant back licenses to use patents they hold that are essential to comply with the technology.

If a pool only includes essential patents, which by definition would individually block the use of the technology licensed by the pool, then economic theory implies that pooling the patents and licensing them by a single entity is pro-competitive relative to individual licensing. Individual licensing of blocking patents incurs a risk of inefficiently high royalties because each patentee would ignore the effect of its royalty on the demand for other patents necessary to implement the technology. A single entity that licenses all the patents would internalize this effect and have an incentive to charge a lower total royalty for the pooled patents than the sum of all the royalties charged by individual licensees.[45] Furthermore, if individual patentees fail to coordinate their licensing, this could delay the implementation of the technology. Pooling the patents also potentially reduces the transaction costs of negotiating individual licenses.

Whether a patent pool is limited to essential patents is a central issue in the determination of whether the pool is pro-competitive or potentially anticompetitive. It is, however, difficult to ensure that a pool includes only essential patents. The use of an independent patent expert to assess essentiality provides some comfort, but essentiality is often difficult to determine. Furthermore, even an independent expert could find that his or her interests are aligned with the welfare of the pool and its members.

Allowing pool members to license their patents individually provides a safety valve to protect against anticompetitive effects from including nonessential patents in the pool. If patents are substitutes, individual patentees can license their technologies to develop competing technologies or to promote the development of the pooled technology along alternative paths. Indeed the Guidelines issued by the European Commission specifically mention provisions for independent licensing as a pro-competitive characteristic of patent pools.

Lerner and Tirole (2004) provide analytical support for the emphasis on independent licensing in the DOJ business review letters and the European Commission Guidelines. They consider a pool comprised of n symmetric patents. The profit that the pool can earn by licensing a package consisting of all the patents is $V(n)$. If the pooled patents are perfect complements, then $V(n - m) = 0$ for $m \geq 1$. If they are perfect complements, then each patent can block the use of all of the other patents and render them valueless. If the pooled patents are perfect substitutes, then $V(n - m) = V(n)$ for $m \geq 1$. In this case each patent is as good as any other patent or any collection of other patents. Lerner and Tirole show that the pool is pro-competitive if and only if it is robust to independent licensing, meaning that the profits of the pool would not be threatened if the pool members were permitted to offer separate licenses for individual patents, under the assumption that the pool members set royalties for individual patents in a noncooperative fashion.

Take the example of the pool that consists of symmetric essential patents (i.e., perfect complements). A profit-maximizing pool would set a price P^m for a license to use all of the patents. Separate owners of essential patents who license independently would choose prices that in the aggregate are no less than P^m and would exceed P^m if demand is not perfectly inelastic. This is an example of the double-marginalization outcome for separate suppliers of complementary products. Thus the profits earned by a pool comprised of essential patents would not be threatened if the pool members were permitted to license their patents individually, and the pool should not object to including a provision for independent licensing in its by-laws.

The Lerner and Tirole result provides a potentially useful way to screen pools that should not be allowed because they include patents that are substitutes for each other. Such pools would be undermined by a provision for independent licensing by the pool members and therefore one would expect the pool as an entity to object to such a provision. In contrast, the profits that could be earned by a pool that consists only of essential patents would not be threatened by a requirement to offer individual licenses.

Unfortunately, the Lerner and Tirole rule encounters difficulties when firms can invent around the patents in the pool. Suppose that potential users of the pooled patents can invest in R&D to find substitutes. This R&D activity is socially wasteful if the alternatives are close substitutes for the patents offered by the pool, since the R&D is costly and the alternatives would contribute little additional social value. Relative to independent licensing, with some conditions on the costs of inventing around the patents, a package license issued by the pool for all of its patents reduces the incentives for users of the pool's technology to invest in duplicative R&D.[46]

For example, suppose that the pool consists of two patents, both of which are essential to implement a technology. The value of the technology to a user is B, which I assume is also its social value. The user can invent around either patent with probability q by spending $R(q)$. The invent-around, if successful, is a perfect substitute for the patent. Suppose that the pool offers only a package license for both patents at a price P^m. A user who accepts the package license has a net value of $B - P^m$. If instead the user attempts to invent around the package license, it can do so only if it succeeds in inventing around both patents, since it would have to pay P^m even if it licensed only one. This occurs with probability q^2 at a cost of $2R(q)$. It is more profitable for the user to accept a package license and not attempt to invent around the pool's patents if

$$q^2 B + (1 - q^2)(B - P^m) - 2R(q) < B - P^m. \tag{14.1}$$

The left-hand side of inequality (14.1) is the expected value of attempting to invent around the pool's patents. The first term is the expected value of a successful invent-around, which occurs with probability q^2. The second term is the expected value of the package license, which the user accepts with probability $1 - q^2$. The right-hand side of inequality (14.1) is the value of taking a package license without attempting to invent around the patents. The user profits by accepting a package license and not inventing around the patents if

$$q^2 P^m - 2R(q) < 0 \tag{14.2}$$

for all $0 < q \le 1$.

Now suppose that the user can accept a package license or separately license either or both of the patents in the pool at a price p. I assume $p < P^m$ (otherwise, a user would never accept an individual license) and $2p > P^m$ (otherwise, a user would never license the patents as a package). Rather than accept a package license, it is profitable for the user to license one of the patents and attempt to invent around the other patent if

$$q(B - p) + (1 - q)(B - P^m) - R(q) > B - P^m. \tag{14.3}$$

The first term on the left-hand side of inequality (14.3) is the probability that an invent-around is successful, in which case the user pays p for one of the patents. The second term is the probability that the invent-around fails, in which case the user must license both patents at a cost P^m. Inequality (14.3) is satisfied for any $0 < q \le 1$ if

$$q(P^m - p) > R(q). \tag{14.4}$$

Suppose that the cost of R&D is a convex increasing function of q, with $R(0) = R'(0) = 0$ and $R''(q) > 0$. Then there always exists a q for which inequality (14.4) is satisfied.[47] If the user could negotiate a license for one of the patents with $p < P^m$, it would be profitable to do so and to attempt to invent around the other patent. Furthermore inequality (14.2) is satisfied for a range of R&D functions. For example, if $R(q) = Aq^\beta$ with $1 < \beta < 2$ and $A > B/2$, it would not be profitable to attempt to invent around a package license.

From a social perspective, if the invent-around technology is a perfect substitute for the licensed technology and offers no other benefits, it would be undesirable to compel the pool to offer individual licenses because that would promote inefficient investment in R&D. Consumers may benefit from the option to license individual patents. The ability to license individual patents increases a technology user's attainable surplus relative to pure package licensing and may force the pool to lower the price of its package license to discourage R&D. (Inequality 14.4 is less likely to be satisfied if $P^m - p$ is small.) If antitrust enforcement is biased toward consumer welfare, a policy that requires individual licensing of the pool's patent might be desirable even if it promotes socially inefficient R&D. However, requiring pools to offer individual licenses need not make consumers better off. If antitrust policy compels pools to offer individual licenses, the gains to consumers are at the expense of profit for the pool. Under some conditions the pool's profit may be insufficient to justify the formation or the continued operation of the pool. Then a policy that compels individual licensing by pool members is undesirable from both a social and consumer perspective. Although the pool might have the potential to offer consumer benefits, it might not be economically viable if it has to offer licenses for individual patents and cannot offer only a package license for all of its patents.

14.5 Concluding Remarks

In this chapter I have briefly reviewed the development of antitrust policy for intellectual property in the United States and compared the current antitrust guidelines published by the United States and the European Union for the licensing of intellectual property. Over the period of more than a century, antitrust policy for intellectual property has come to recognize a balance between providing incentives for innovation and limiting practices that might harm competition. The balance is present in policy statements by both the United States and European Union, although differences remain that reflect different policy objectives, such as promoting trade among the member-states of the European Union.

Antitrust policy for intellectual property in both the United States and the European Union currently strikes the balance between providing a reward for innovation and limiting harm to competition by treating intellectual property as essentially the same as other forms of property for the purpose of antitrust analysis. The logic of this approach is not entirely clear. Intellectual property does differ from other forms of property in many respects. These differences largely stem from the unique legal prerogatives enjoyed by intellectual property, the role of intellectual property in stimulating innovation, the uncertain scope of intellectual property rights, the potential for strategic conduct in the exercise of intellectual property rights, the need to discourage imitation and increase appropriation, the availability of contractual means to protect and extend intellectual property, and the fact that intellectual property is often complementary to other tangible and intangible property rights.

The ratio test developed by Kaplow (1984) provides an economically sound basis to choose policies that reward innovation at the lowest possible social cost. In principle, the ideal mix of policies could differ substantially from current policies, which constrain the exercise of patents and other forms of intellectual property in much the same way that competition policy constrains the use of other property. Unfortunately, there are great practical difficulties in applying the Kaplow ratio test to obtain a quantitative ranking of alternative policies to reward innovation, and even if one could rank alternative policies, the obstacles to implementing the preferred policies would be formidable indeed. We are left with a conclusion that mirrors the views expressed by Pitofsky (2001) and Hovenkamp (2004), that considering the difficulties of moving to a better system, the present application of antitrust principles to intellectual property appears to be an acceptable case of the second-best.

This chapter also considers antitrust policies for patent pools and, in particular, a requirement that patent pools offer licenses for individual patents. Although such a requirement may have the desirable effect of identifying pools that are potentially anticompetitive, it also can encourage socially excessive investment to invent around individual patents. This in turn can reduce the profits of the pool and impede the formation of some patent pools that would be socially desirable.

Notes

I am grateful for helpful discussions with Joseph Farrell, Michael Katz, Michael Riordan, Carl Shapiro, and Alan Weinschel.

1. In *Atari Games v. Nintendo*, the court opined that "When [a] patented product is so successful that it creates its own economic market or consumes a large section of an existing market, the aims and objectives of patent and antitrust laws may seem, at first glance, wholly at odds. However, the two bodies of law are actually complementary, as both are aimed at encouraging innovation, industry and competition." 897 F.2d 1572 (Fed. Cir. 1990).

2. See Tom and Newberg (1997) for an excellent discussion of the evolution of antitrust policy for intellectual property. Carlton (1999) and Gilbert (2004) survey the historical antitrust treatment of patent pools and cross-licensing arrangements.

3. A harrow is an agricultural device for spreading crop residue on fields, usually before planting.

4. *E. Bement & Sons v. Nat'l Harrow, Co.*, 186 US 70, 91 (1902).

5. Bruce B. Wilson, Deputy Assistant Attorney General, Antitrust Division, Address before the Michigan State Bar Antitrust Section and the Patent Trademark and Copyright Section (September 21, 1972), *partial text reprinted in* 4 Trade Reg. Rep. (CCH) ¶ 13,125. See Gilbert and Shapiro (1997) for a discussion of the competitive risks associated with these licensing restrictions.

6. Kyle P. Ewing, Deputy Assistant Attorney General, Antitrust Division, Address Before the San Francisco Patent Law Association (May 5, 1979), reprinted in 4 Trade Reg. Rep. (CCH) ¶ 13,128, at 20,717.

7. The 1982 *Guidelines for International Operations* no longer apply but are relevant to describe the evolution of antitrust policy in the United States for intellectual property.

8. In 2000 the DOJ and FTC published *Antitrust Guidelines for Collaborations among Competitors*, which further refine the agencies' methodology for analyzing certain types of collaborations involving intellectual property. For mergers or acquisitions of intellectual property, the DOJ/FTC Merger Guidelines apply.

9. IP Guidelines at §2.0.

10. Commission Regulation 772/2004. A block exemption exempts a practice, such as a restraint in a license, from antitrust liability under Article 81 of the Treaty of Rome.

11. *Guidelines on the Application of Article 81 of the EC Treaty to Technology Transfer Agreements* (2004/C 101/02) (EC Guidelines).

12. IP Guidelines at §3.1.

13. EC Guidelines at para. 11. (footnotes omitted)

14. IP Guidelines at §3.1.

15. EC Guidelines at para. 172.

16. *US et al. v. Microsoft, Memorandum and Order*, US District Court for the District of Columbia, Civil Action No. 98-1232-3, September 1998.

17. See Commission Regulation No 2790/1999 of December 22, 1999, on the application of Article 81(3) of the Treaty to categories of vertical agreements and concerted practices.

18. Pub. L. 100-703, codified at 35 USC §271(d).

19. *In re* Independent Service Organizations Antitrust Litig. (*CSU, L.L.C. v. Xerox Corp.*), 203 F.3d 1322 (Fed. Cir. 2000).

20. *Id.* at 1328.

21. See, for example, Pitofsky (2001).

22. See *In the Matter of Intel Corporation*. The FTC complaint ended with a consent decree that prohibits Intel from withholding advanced technical information from a customer for reasons related to an intellectual property dispute, provided that the customer does not seek an injunction against the manufacture, use or sale of Intel's microprocessors. See Decision and Order, *In re* Intel Corp.

23. The precedent value of this decision is limited because Bard advanced only limited arguments in its appeal of the jury verdict.

24. "A patent empowers the owner to exact royalties as high as he can negotiate with the leverage of that monopoly." *Brulotte v. Thys Co.*, 379 US 29 (1964).

25. For example, $k = 1$ could correspond to exclusive territories and $k = 2$ to resale price maintenance. I make a strong assumption that policies are additive in their contributions to both profits and surplus.

26. This assumes that the K policies exactly satisfy the profit constraint. If not, the optimal set of policies could substitute a policy with a larger welfare loss per R&D dollar for another policy that has a smaller total welfare loss.

27. The US Federal Trade Commission challenged discriminatory royalties in a series of cases involving licenses for shrimp-peeling machines. See, for example, *Emile M. LaPeyre et al. v. Federal Trade Commission*.

28. Of course there are other ways to think about rules for selecting policies that promote R&D. For discussions of other ways to design intellectual property rights, see, for example, Tandon (1982), Gilbert and Shapiro (1990), Klemperer (1990), Kremer (1998), Ayres and Klemperer (1999), and Scotchmer (2005). Maurer and Scotchmer (2004) argue that policies should not penalize licensing compared to other organizational forms and should generate profits related to the social value of the invention with as few restrictions as necessary.

29. *New York Times*, March 17, 2005, p. C5.

30. The court cited a previous decision by the same circuit, *Valley Drug Co. v. Geneva Pharmaceuticals, Inc.*, 344 F.3d 1294 (11th Cir. 2003).

31. *Id.* at 1231.

32. See, for example, Shapiro (2003) and Judge Posner's analysis of the benefits from settlements in *Asahi Glass v. Pentech*. Furthermore a settlement does not prevent a patent challenge by others.

33. The patent issued on October 12, 1999. The patent history is illuminating. It refers to more than 25 continued or abandoned patent applications by Lemelson dating back to June 14, 1955.

34. 35 USC §154(a)(2).

35. US patent law now requires publication of many applications 18 months after they are filed. This has the potential to limit holdup, but the law applies only to patent applications that have to be published for other reasons. See Lemley and Moore (2003).

36. See Anton and Yao (1995) and the ABA section of Antitrust Law (2004) for review and analysis of antitrust enforcement actions regarding standard setting.

37. *Dell Computer Co.*, 121 F.T.C. 616, 617–18 (1996).

38. JEDEC, formerly known as the Joint Electron Device Engineering Council, is the semiconductor engineering standardization body of the Electronic Industries Alliance.

39. Efficient technology transfer can require restraints on conduct and royalty terms when one party to a license has better information about the value of the technology. See, for example, Gallini and Wright (1990) and Lewis and Yao (1995). If the licensee is privately informed about demand conditions before contracting with the licensor, Blair and Lewis (1994) show that an efficient license exhibits some form of resale price maintenance and quantity fixing.

40. *Monsanto Co. v. Homan McFarling*, US Court of Appeals for the Federal Circuit, 363 F.3d 1336 (decided April 9, 2004).

41. Proposed amendments to US commercial law would allow licensors to impose additional conditions on licensees. See Lemley (1999).

42. Letter from Joel I. Klein, Assistant Attorney General, US Department of Justice, to Garrard R. Beeney, Sullivan & Cromwell (June 26, 1997). MPEG stands for Moving Picture Experts Group. Originally founded to license patents required to use the MPEG-2 standard, the pool included 27 essential patents in 1997. It has since grown to include more than 640 patents and licenses patents necessary to implement several other standards.

43. Letter from Joel I. Klein, Assistant Attorney General, US Department of Justice, to Garrard R. Beeney, Sullivan & Cromwell (December 16, 1998); Letter from Joel I. Klein, Assistant Attorney General, US Department of Justice, to Carey R. Ramos, Paul, Weiss, Rifkind, Wharton & Garrison (June 10, 1999).

44. Letter from Charles A. James, Assistant Attorney General, US Department of Justice, to Ky P. Ewing, Vinson & Elkins (November 12, 2002). As of June 2000, a total of 45 firms had claimed ownership of at least one patent essential to compliance with one or more of the third-generation radio interface standards.

45. See Shapiro (2001) and Gilbert (2004).

46. Gilbert and Katz (2004) derive a sufficient condition for package licensing to discourage R&D to invent around the licensed patents. The following example relies on Gilbert and Katz (2004).

47. By L'Hospital's rule, $\lim_{q \to 0} R(q)/q = R'(0) = 0$. Therefore inequality (14.4) must be satisfied if q is sufficiently small and $p < P^m$.

References

ABA Section of Antitrust Law. 2004. *Handbook on the Antitrust Aspects of Standard Setting*. American Bar Association.

Allison, J. R., and M. A. Lemley. 1998. Empirical evidence on the validity of litigated patents. *AIPLA Quarterly Journal* 26: 185–277.

Anton, J. J., and D. A. Yao. 1995. Standard-setting consortia, antitrust, and high-technology industries. *Antitrust Law Journal* 64: 247–65.

Ayres, I., and P. Klemperer. 1999. Limiting patentees' market power without reducing innovation incentives: The perverse benefits of uncertainty and non-injunctive remedies. *Michigan Law Review* 97: 985–1033.

Blair, B. F., and T. R. Lewis. 1994. Optimal retail contracts with asymmetric information and moral hazard. *RAND Journal of Economics* 25: 284–96.

Carlton, S. C. 1999. Note: Patent pools and the antitrust dilemma. *Yale Journal of Regulation* 16: 358–99.

Farrell, J. 2004. Listening to interested parties in antitrust investigations: Competitors, customers, complementors, and relativity. *Antitrust* 18 (Spring): 64–68.

Gallini, N. T., and B. D. Wright. 1990. Technology transfer under asymmetric information. *RAND Journal of Economics* 21: 147–60.

Gilbert, R. J., and C. Shapiro. 1990. Optimal patent length and breadth. *RAND Journal of Economics* 21(1): 106–12.

Gilbert, R. J., and C. Shapiro. 1997. Antitrust issues in the licensing of intellectual property: The nine no–no's meet the nineties. *Brookings Papers: Microeconomics*: 283–336.

Gilbert, R. J. 2004. Antitrust for patent pools: A century of policy evolution. *Stanford Technology Law Review* (April).

Gilbert, R. J., and M. L. Katz. 2005. Should good patents come in small packages? A welfare analysis of intellectual property bundling. *International Journal of Industrial Organization* 24(5): 931–52.

Hovenkamp, H. J. 2004. United States antitrust policy in an age of IP expansion. Research paper 04-03. University of Iowa Legal Studies.

Kaplow, L. 1984. The patent-antitrust intersection: A reappraisal. *Harvard Law Review* 97: 1813–92.

Klemperer, P. 1990. How broad should the scope of patent protection be? *RAND Journal of Economics* 21 (Spring): 113–30.

Kremer, M. 1998. Patent buyouts: A mechanism for encouraging innovation. *Quarterly Journal of Economics* 113: 1137–67.

Landes, W. A., and R. A. Posner. 2003. *The Economic Structure of Intellectual Property Law.* Cambridge: Harvard University Press.

Lemley, M. A., and K. A. Moore. 2004. Ending abuse of patent continuations. *Boston University Law Review* 84: 63.

Lemley, M. A. 1999. Beyond preemption: The law and policy of intellectual property licensing. *California Law Review* 87: 111–72.

Lerner, J., and J. Tirole. 2004. Efficient patent pools. *American Economic Review* 94: 691–711.

Lewis, T. R., and D. A. Yao. 1995. Some reflections on the antitrust treatment of intellectual property. *Antitrust Law Journal* 63: 603–19.

Maurer, S. M., and S. Scotchmer. 2004. Profit neutrality in licensing: The boundary between antitrust law and patent law. NBER working paper 10546.

Pitofsky, R. 2001. Challenges of the new economy: Issues at the intersection of antitrust and intellectual property. *Antitrust Law Journal* 68: 913–24.

Ramsey, F. P. 1927. A contribution to the theory of taxation. *Economic Journal* 37: 47–61.

Scotchmer, S. 2005. *Innovation Incentives.* Cambridge: MIT Press.

Shapiro, C. 2001. Navigating the patent thicket: Cross licenses, patent pools, and standard setting. In A. Jaffee, J. Lerner, and S. Stern, eds., *Innovation Policy and the Economy*, vol. 1. Cambridge: MIT Press.

Shapiro, C. 2003. Antitrust limits to patent settlements. *RAND Journal of Economics* 34: 391–411.

Shapiro, C. 2002. Competition policy and innovation. STI working paper 2002/11. OECD. Paris.

Tandon, P. 1982. Optimal patents with compulsory licensing. *Journal of Political Economy* 90: 470–86.

Tom, W. K., and J. A. Newberg. 1997. Antitrust and intellectual property: From separate spheres to unified field. *Antitrust Law Journal* 66: 167–229.

European Commission Regulation 772/2004 of 27 April 2004 on the Application of Article 81(3) of the Treaty to Categories of Technology Transfer Agreements.

European Commission Guidelines on the Application of Article 81 of the EC Treaty to Technology Transfer Agreements (2004/C 101/02).

US Department of Justice and Federal Trade Commission. 1985. *Antitrust Guidelines for the Licensing of Intellectual Property.* Reprinted in 4 Trade Reg. Rep. (CCH) ¶13,132. Available at ⟨http://www.usdoj.gov/atr/public/guidelines/ipguide.htm⟩.

Case References

Asahi Glass Co., Ltd. v. Pentech Pharmaceuticals, Inc. 289 F.Supp. 2d 986 (2003).

Atari Games v. Nintendo. Court of Appeals for the Federal Circuit, 975 F.2d 832 (1992).

Bement v. National Harrow Co. 186 US 70 (1902).

Brulotte v. Thys Co. 379 US 29 (1964).

C.R. Bard v. M3 Systems, Inc. 157 F.3d 1340 (Fed. Cir. 1998).

Image Technical Services, Inc. et al. v. Eastman Kodak Co. 504 US 451 (1992), 125 F.3d 1195 (1997).

Emile M. LaPeyre, et al. v. Federal Trade Commission. Court of Appeals for the 5th Cir., 366 F.2d 117 (1966).

In re Independent Service Organizations Antitrust Litig. (*CSU, L.L.C. v. Xerox Corp.*), 203 F.3d 1322, Court of Appeals for the Federal Circuit (2000).

Lear, Inc. v. Adkins. 395 US 653 (1969).

Miles Medical Co. v. John D. Park & Sons Co. 220 US 373 (1911).

Monsanto Co. v. Homan McFarling. Court of Appeals for the Federal Circuit, 363 F.3d 1336 (2004).

Schering-Plough Corp. v. FTC. Docket No. 04-10688, Court of Appeals for the 11th Circuit (2005).

Standard Sanitary Manufacturing v. US. 226 US 20 (1912).

United States Federal Trade Commission. In re CIBA-Geigy Limited, CIBA-Geigy Corporation, Chiron Corporation, Sandoz Ltd., Sandoz Corporation, and Novartis AG, File No. 961 0055, Docket No. C-3725, Complaint (1997).

United States Federal Trade Commission. In re Intel Corporation, Docket No. 9288, Complaint (1998).

United States Federal Trade Commission. In re Rambus Inc., Docket No. 9302, Complaint (2002).

United States Federal Trade Commission. In re Rambus, Inc., Docket No. 9302, Opinion of the Commission (2006).

United States Federal Trade Commission. In re Union Oil Co., Docket No. 9305, Complaint (2003).

United States v. General Electric Co. 272 US 476 (1926).

United States v. General Electric Co. Complaint (1996).

United States et al. v. Microsoft. Memorandum and Order, District Court for the District of Columbia, Civil Action No. 98-1232-3 (1998).

United States v. Pilkington. Complaint (1994).

United States v. Singer Manufacturing Co. 374 US 174 (1963).

United States v. Studiengesellschaft Kohle, M.B.H. Court of Appeals for the District of Columbia, 670 F.2d 1122 (1981).

Walker Process Equipment, Inc. v. Food Machinery & Chemical Corp. 382 US 172 (1965).

Zenith Radio Corp. v. Hazeltine Research, Inc., et al. 395 US 100 (1969).

15 Competition Policy in Two-Sided Markets, with a Special Emphasis on Payment Cards

Jean-Charles Rochet and Jean Tirole

Two-sided (or more generally, multi-sided) markets are markets in which platforms offer interaction services to two (or several) categories of end-users. The fundamental question for these platforms is how to allocate surplus to the different end-users in order to get the two (or multiple) sides on board while making money overall.

Such markets include videogame platforms (aimed toward gamers and developers), software producers (aimed toward users and application developers), newspapers (aimed toward reading public and advertisers), and payment card systems (aimed toward merchants and consumers).

Conceptually the theory of two-sided markets is related to the theories of network externalities and of (market or regulated) multi-product pricing. From the former, it borrows the notion that there are non-internalized externalities among end-users.[1] From the latter, it borrows the focus on the price structure and the idea that price structures are less likely to be distorted by market power than price levels. The multi-product pricing literature, however, does not allow for externalities in the consumption of different products: to use a celebrated example, the buyer of a razor internalizes in his purchase decision the net surplus that he will derive from buying razor blades. The starting point of the theory of two-sided markets, by contrast, is that an end-user does not internalize the welfare impact of his use of the platform on other end-users.

To refine the analysis, it is important to distinguish usage and membership fees. The platforms' usage or variable charges impact the two sides' willingness to trade, and thereby their net surpluses from potential interactions; the platforms' membership, or fixed charges, in turn condition the end-users' presence on the platform. The platforms' fine design of the structure of variable and fixed charges is relevant only if the two sides do not negotiate away the corresponding usage and membership externalities.

After characterizing the two types of externalities (usage and membership) present in two-sided markets (section 15.1), we review the price (section 15.2) and nonprice (section 15.3) strategies employed by unregulated platforms to generate activity: membership and usage pricing, nonprice screening of membership, and regulation of interaction among end-users. We show how these strategies respond to platform competition and to users' multi-homing.

We then proceed to analyze the implications of two-sidedness for competition policy, with a particular focus on payment card networks, which have been drawing a growing amount of attention from antitrust authorities lately. In section 15.4, we discuss the fundamental externalities inherent to the payment card industry. In section 15.5, we offer a simple model of this industry that allows us to discuss in section 15.6 the determinants of the price structure. In section 15.7, we demonstrate the robustness of the predictions of our model. Finally, in section 15.8, we conclude by assessing regulatory and antitrust policies for payment card networks.

15.1   Membership and Usage Externalities

15.1.1   Definitions and Notation

Consider a platform enabling or facilitating the interaction between two end-users. For convenience we will call these users buyer B and seller S. In videogames, for example, such an interaction occurs when a buyer (gamer) buys a game created by a seller (developer) and plays it using the console built by the platform. Similarly, in an operating system (OS), an interaction occurs when the buyer (user) buys an application built by the seller (developer) on the platform. In the case of payment cards, an interaction occurs when a buyer (cardholder) uses his card to settle a transaction with a seller (merchant).[2] The interaction between a buyer (viewer) and an advertiser mediated by a newspaper or a TV channel occurs when the viewer notices and reads the ad. The interaction between a caller and a receiver in a telecommunications network is a phone conversation, and that between a Web site and a Web user on the Internet is a data transfer.

We distinguish between membership charges and usage charges, and between membership externalities and usage externalities. Gains from trade between end-users almost always arise from usage:[3] the cardholder and the merchant derive convenience benefits when the former uses a card rather than cash, a caller and a callee benefit from their communication but not per se from having a phone, and so forth. Usage decisions depend on how much the platform charges for the usage. As depicted in figure 15.1, the platform usually charges a price or access charge p^S to the seller and p^B to the buyer for enabling the interaction. In the case of American Express, the merchant gets charged a fee, some percentage of the item's price, so $p^S > 0$; however, the buyer pays nothing for using the American Express card, $p^B = 0$.[4] Similarly a caller chatting on a mobile phone is charged a per-minute calling charge and the receiver a per-minute reception charge. This way usage externalities arise from usage decisions. If I strictly benefit from using my card rather than cash, then the merchant exerts a (positive) externality by taking the card. Similarly, if I benefit from being able to call a friend on his mobile phone, then this friend's willingness to give me his number and receive the call exerts a positive externality on me.

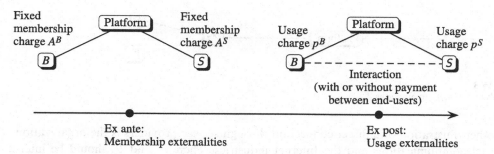

Figure 15.1
Ex ante and ex post externalities

Figure 15.2
Connection through service providers

Ex ante, the platform may charge interaction-independent *fixed fees* A^S and A^B. For example, American Express charges yearly fees to cardholders ($A^B > 0$). In the case of videogames, platforms may charge game developers fees for development kits ($A^S \geq 0$), but they do charge gamers for the videogame console ($A^B > 0$) and also charge per-game royalties (e.g., about \$8 per game) that they levy on the seller ($p^S > 0$). (As we will later discover, it does not matter whether game developers or gamers are taxed in this particular example.) For Windows, Microsoft charges a usage-independent fee to consumers ($A^B > 0$) but no variable fees ($p^S = p^B = 0$). Microsoft by and large does not charge the application developers (in particular, access to the applications programming interfaces come for free). To the extent that an end-user on side i derives a strictly positive net surplus from interacting with additional end-users on side $j \neq i$, membership decisions generate membership externalities.

Figure 15.2 depicts a more complex situation where end-users connect to the platform through intermediaries or "service providers," depicted by $\mathcal{B}$ and $\mathcal{S}$. For example, Visa card or MasterCard holders and the merchants affiliated with these two payment platforms are served by service providers called "issuers" and "acquirers," respectively. The merchant's bank, the acquirer, pays an interchange fee p^S to the cardholder's bank, the issuer, who receives p^B. This means that for a not-for-profit platform, and with our assuming away per-transaction costs, $p^S = -p^B > 0$.[5] Any interaction costs perceived by the end-users, $\hat{p}^B$ and $\hat{p}^S$ in the figure, depend on the commercial conditions offered by the intermediaries, and coincide with p^B and p^S only under conditions of perfect competition among service providers.[6]

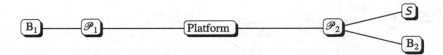

Figure 15.3
"On us" or "on-net" interactions

Another illustration of indirect connection through service providers is the organization of the telecommunications and the Internet industries. There $\mathscr{B}$ and $\mathscr{S}$ should be interpreted as telecommunications operators in the case of telecommunications and, say, exchange points in the case of Internet.[7] The similarity with payment card associations requires some elaboration. In the telecommunications and Internet applications, there are no "buyers" and "sellers" in the traditional sense of a sales transaction. There is a flow of communication between a caller and a callee, or from a Web site to a Web user. The object to study is the particular communication between the two end-users. One end-user (the caller or the Web site) is technically at the origin of the connection. Purely by convention, we will label this end-user S; the other (the receiver, the Web user) we will label B. To the extent that S and B are on two different but interconnected networks $\mathscr{S}$ and $\mathscr{B}$, the latter have an agreement for terminating the connection initiated on the former. This agreement specifies a (per-minute or per-megabyte) termination charge $p^S = -p^B > 0$ to be paid by network $\mathscr{S}$ to network $\mathscr{B}$. The networks $\mathscr{B}$ and $\mathscr{S}$ then pass through this termination charge or revenue to the end-users in the form of per-minute calling and receiving charges or outgoing and incoming traffic fees. Note that the "platform" in this case is a communication protocol, and thus it is largely virtual. It is no different than a mechanism recording "off-net" traffic and operating settlements.

To the extent that end-users use service providers, these service providers (e.g., $\mathscr{P}_2$ in figure 15.3) may, in some instances, connect two end-users (S and B_2), without their having to interact with other service providers (e.g., $\mathscr{P}_1$). Such interactions are called "on us" interactions in the case of payment cards, and correspond to the case where the same bank is both the customer's issuer and the merchant's acquirer. Similarly a telephone operator may service both the caller and the callee, and the exchange points may service the Web site and the Web user; the traffic is then said to be "on net."

A more illustrative example may be a homeowner who lists her house with a real estate agency (the platform) but retains the right to sell the house independently. There is always the chance that an interaction between the buyer and the seller will not come through the platform.

Finally that there may be multiple non-interconnected platforms. For example, in the absence of a common listing, a seller of a house may want to enter nonexclusive arrangements with multiple real estate agencies in order to reach a wider range of potential buyers; alternatively, a buyer may choose to deal with multiple real estate agencies. Videogame

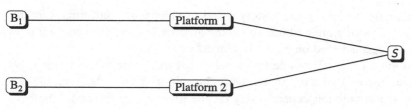

Figure 15.4
Multi-homing

developers may port their game to several game platforms, and more generally, software developers may multi-home to competing but incompatible software platforms. Then, again, because different payment card systems are not interconnected, a Visa cardholder cannot use her card at a merchant that accepts American Express or MasterCard, but not Visa, and for convenience merchants often accept and consumers often hold multiple cards. In fact multi-homing by at least one side of the market is necessary for gains from trade to be reaped when platforms are incompatible or not interconnected.

15.1.2 Pure Usage Externalities

Suppose that there are no membership externalities. Our interest is here in whether end-users intensively use the platform and not whether they join it.[8]

In isolating usage, an important distinction to make is that between the *price level*, which is the total price charged by the platform to the two sides, and the *price structure*, which refers to the distribution or apportioning of the total price between the buyer and the seller. Underlying the recent surge of academic work on two-sided markets is the widespread belief among economists and public and private decision-makers that the price structure affects profits and economic efficiency as well.

Managers, of course, devote considerable time and resources to determine which side should bear the pricing burden. Commonly their firms end up making little money on one side (and sometimes using this side as a loss-leader) and recouping their costs on the other side. Policy-makers also seem to strongly believe in the importance of price structure. The locus of policy intervention in price structure proceeds on the premise that economic efficiency can be improved by charging more to one side and less to the other relative to what the market delivers. The monitoring of termination charges in telecommunications (and soon the Internet) and antitrust involvement in the computation of interchange fees in payment systems reflect this belief of policy-makers.

Private and public decision-makers, on the other hand, would be wasting their time if the price structure were neutral, that is, if a price reallocation between the two sides had no impact on economic outcomes. Nonneutrality is not a foregone conclusion, however. Every Econ 101 student learns that for a given level of VAT, it does not matter who, whether merchant or consumer, is charged for it. The transaction price between the two parties adjusts accordingly. The per-game royalty levied by videogame platforms is similar to a VAT in that the prices of games adjust, so (in the absence of collection costs) it does not matter whether the cost is levied on game developers or on users.

A necessary condition for a market to be two-sided is that the Coase theorem not apply to the relation between the two sides of the markets. The gain from trade between the two parties generated by the interaction depends only on the total charge levied by the platform, and so in a Coase (1960) world the price structure is neutral.[9]

15.1.3 Membership Externalities

Besides the regulatory attention to termination charges and interchange fees, the recent literature on the telecommunications, Internet, and credit card industries has focused on pure usage externalities. This literature complements the earlier literature on indirect network externalities[10] as well as the more recent studies (e.g., Armstrong 2004) on the polar case of pure membership externalities.

Membership is associated with transaction-insensitive end-user costs. Membership costs include fixed fees levied by the platform as well as technological fixed costs on the user side. For example, a software developer incurs both a fixed payment for the development kit and attendance at trade shows and a fixed cost of developing the software.

The dividing line between the two transaction-insensitive costs is sometimes a bit unclear. A software platform may try to attract software developers by charging a low price for the development kit (a fixed fee) and/or by giving away software development support or designing developer-friendly APIs. On the other hand, only the total transaction-insensitive cost matters for the end-user. So we will not be concerned here in making such artificial distinction between fixed fees and fixed technological costs.

Under transaction-insensitive costs, the allocation of fixed fees between buyers and sellers matters unless small changes in fixed fees leave memberships (the set of end-users who decide to incur the transaction-insentive costs) invariant on both sides, a rather unlikely situation. An increase in the buyers' fixed fee A^B, say, is usually not passed through to the sellers. To be certain, one can find examples where membership decisions are coordinated. For example, divisions of a firm buying client and server software, or a family joining a tennis club to play each other, will make a concerted membership decision. The package offered to the firm, or the family, is the only relevant aspect of pricing, and not the way in which the total price is decomposed among divisions or members of the family. But such instances of "ex ante Coasian bargaining" are rare.

When the two sides transact ex post, fixed costs are sunk and therefore are irrelevant. For example, an increase in A^B compensated by a decrease in A^S computed so as to keep the platform's profit constant changes the volume of trade and social welfare, in general. Fewer buyers will find the platform attractive, although this effect is somewhat alleviated by the prospect of being able to transact with more sellers, and conversely for the sellers. The nonneutrality of fixed fees is most dramatically illustrated by an extreme but telling example, due to Wright (2003). Suppose that consumers all derive the same per-transaction surplus b^B from the convenience of paying merchants by credit card rather than by cash. The merchants are not prevented by the transaction costs nor by a card system's nondiscrimination rule to charge different prices for card and cash payments. Consider a merchant (a monopolist, to simplify the exposition) selling a merchandise with value v (when purchased by cash) to consumers. It is optimal for this merchant to charge v for cash payments and $v + b^B$ for card payments. Thus a cardholder obtains no transaction-specific surplus from holding a card. If she must pay an annual fee or a transaction cost in applying for a card, she does not want to hold a card in the first place. The corresponding "investment" is then "held up" ex post by the merchants' surcharge (to use Williamson's 1975 terminology).[11]

15.2 Pricing Strategies by Platforms

15.2.1 Pricing Principles for Two-sided Platforms

A few factors affect prices charged to end-users, and departures from standard business strategies may result in a platform's internalization of the other side's welfare. The linkage between the two sides, from the platform's viewpoint, is particularly apparent when the platform makes no or loses money on one side. For example, media platforms will periodically give away newspapers or offer free TV programs not to prey on rival platforms but to be able to charge higher markups to advertisers.[12] Such linkage also shows up in the form of the simple "see-saw principle." Whatever factor is conducive to a high price on one side, to the extent that it raises the platform's margin on that side, also is conducive to a low price on the other side, attracting members and helps that side become more profitable.

Elasticities and Externalities   As the analyses in Anderson-Coate (2005), Armstrong (2004), and Rochet-Tirole (2003) make clear, demand elasticities on both sides are essential determinants of the pricing of platforms. For example, in Rochet-Tirole (2003), a factor affecting elasticities on a given side is the size of the installed base of end-users on that side. When, say, the number of captive buyers increases, the buyer's price naturally increases, and the seller's price decreases, since attracting sellers yields a higher collateral profit on the buyer's side.

Similarly, the attraction of a lowered price on one side may be profitable for the platform if this side creates substantial externalities on the other side. For example, "marquee buyers" are courted as they allow platforms to charge high prices to sellers.[13]

Relative Market Power of Service Providers   If end-users are served through intermediaries (as in figure 15.2), the platform may try to undermine the intermediaries' market power by charging lower access fees. If, for example, a service provider decides to charge a high markup to buyers, the platform must in turn reduce a^B so as to limit the double margin-alization on that side, and increase a^S (since offering a surplus to buyers by enlisting sellers becomes relatively less attractive).

Platform Competition and Multi-Homing   Platform competition may have ambiguous conse-quences on the price structure. For example, a fraction of buyers are known to multi-home (connect to multiple platforms). On the one hand, the elasticity of buyers' demand for a given platform increases because these buyers are able to switch to a competing platform. On the other hand, the elasticity of sellers' demand is corrected by what Rochet-Tirole (2003) call the "single-homing index." Roughly speaking, buyers' multi-homing allows platforms to "steer" sellers, that is, to induce them to opt out of the competing plat-forms.[14] The smaller is the single-homing index of buyers, the higher is the incentive for platforms to steer sellers. Platform competition thus creates downward pressure on prices on both sides of the market, and the impact on relative prices is ambiguous.[15] Therefore platform competition does not necessarily lead to an efficient price structure.[16]

Bundling   Platforms offering several types of interaction services can benefit from bundling them. For example, the payment card platforms of American Express, Visa, and Master-Card offer both debit and credit cards and, until recently, engaged in a tie-in on the merchant side through the so-called honor-all-cards rule. The motivations for tying in two-sided markets may be different from the usual ones in classical markets (e.g., price discrimination or entry deterrence).[17] In a two-sided market, tying allows platforms to per-form better the balancing act between buyers and sellers, and the concomitant rebalancing of the price structure is not necessarily detrimental to social welfare.

15.2.2   Platforms' Motivations for Charging Membership Fees
Platforms have several motivations to recoup their costs (and perhaps make a profit) by levying membership fees.

The Platform Unable to Tax Interactions Properly   The interaction among the end-users may not be perfectly observed, as illustrated by the case of dating clubs. More generally, even if a transaction is observed, it may not be the entire transaction. Buyers and suppliers may find each other and trade once on a B2B exchange, and then bypass the exchange alto-gether for future trade. Or they may underreport the trading price and operate side trans-fers. The platform's ability to tax transactions depends on how much anonymity it can impose on trades. Another factor is advertising. Whether the reader who carefully reads the ad acts on it and thereby generates the desired "transaction" is not ensured.[18] The media's purchase price and the advertising fees can be viewed as fixed costs relative to such individual transactions.

Fixed Fees as an Efficient Way of Capturing End-user Surplus   As is well known from price discrimination and Ramsey pricing theories, it is often efficient (both privately and socially) to recoup the platform's fixed cost (e.g., the cost of writing the platform's software) through charges on both the variable use of the platform and on general access to the platform. The need for fixed fees is particularly strong when the platform subsidizes usage.

Suppose that a software platform is concerned with independent developers' exercising market power over platform users (Hagiu 2004). The platform can reduce the price of applications through a proportional subsidy on applications. This policy, while encouraging efficient trade, is costly to the platform and may leave large surpluses to both application developers and consumers. Fixed fees levied on both sides are ways of capturing the end-user surpluses and of enabling subsidization.

15.3   Other Platform Strategies

We have seen that payment card platforms often try to discourage merchants from charging cardholders for card usage, and that a platform may want to subsidize sales of applications developed for the platform (see Hagiu 2004). In this section we document how platforms more generally woe end-users not only through the tariffs $\{a_i, A_i\}_{i=1,2}$ they charge them[19] but also by regulating the interactions between these end-users. That is, platforms must perform a balancing act with respect to their price structure as well as other policy dimensions. Generally, platforms encourage positive externalities and discourage negative ones, and to do so, they constrain one side to the benefit of the other.

In reviewing platform regulation of interactions among end-users, we will show that it is useful to compare platform choices with those that prevail under the more standard *vertical view*, whereby the platform interacts with only one side (e.g., the seller side) and has no direct interaction with the other side (e.g., the buyer side); see figure 15.5.

15.3.1   Regulation of End-user Interactions
Asymmetric information among end-users, and the concomitant rent extraction concerns, keep the platform's price structure neutral (see Rochet-Tirole 2004), but it is nonetheless

Figure 15.5
Vertical view

a source of suboptimal trade among end-users. Thus, if the seller side has market power over the buyer side (as in Hagiu 2004), buyers derive too small a surplus from joining the platform. The platform then has an incentive to alter, through a subsidy, the price charged to buyers so as to boost the buyers' surplus and their willingness to join the platform. This way the platform behaves much like a public utility commission that addresses a market power problem by setting a price cap or by subsidizing some services through a fund levied from other services.

Two remarks are in order. First, the rationale for constraining the price charged by the seller to the buyer would vanish if the industry were organized according to the vertical view. That is, were the platform not to deal directly with buyers, the platform could provide sellers with the maximal profit in their relationship with buyers and therefore would grant them maximal commercial freedom.[20] It is only because the platform can extract surplus on the buyer side that it is willing to "displease" the seller side by constraining it.

Second, even though interactions among end-users often exhibit monopoly or monopsony power, platforms do not always attempt to regulate transaction prices among end-users. There are often good (and standard) reasons for laissez-faire as well. The platform may not be able to price discriminate as well as the price-setting end-user, or, in situations where an end-user (e.g., an application developer) sinks a substantial investment cost so that the efficient transaction price varies substantially among applications. Then the prices paid by end-users should not be fixed by the platform, and the resultant laissez-faire policy by the platform is viewed as a commitment not to up hold the application developer's investment through an expropriatory price cap on the sale of the application to platform users.

15.3.2 Screening Members

End-users often care not only about the price (which they pay to the platform and to the other side) but also about the quality of the interaction. In some industries the platform is concerned about the identity of participants, as the latter creates externalities on the other side. Supermarkets, for example, do not auction off shelf space to the highest bidder; otherwise, the outcome might be less of the desired diversity of brands to the average shopper.[21] Nightclubs, dating agencies, conferences, and exchange markets try to avoid rowdy patrons or screen potential patrons for undesirable character traits and unacceptable behavior. Exchanges have rules against front-running, and other rules on collateral requirements that address the risk of default by their members. Media networks put some minimum constraints on advertisers and advertisements so as not to offend their audiences. In this regard platforms resemble regulatory commissions (e.g., in banking, finance, electricity, or telecommunications) that impose minimum standards on operators in order to spare consumers negative externalities (as when the operator goes bankrupt).

Again, such nonprice discrimination would be meaningless under the vertical view. A platform that does not internalize buyer welfare has no incentive to be selective in choosing sellers.[22]

15.3.3 The Platform as a Competition Authority

In some circumstances the platform may make itself attractive to one side of the market by encouraging competition on the other side. The competition on the other side may be expected to bring prices closer to the marginal cost, and the volume of interactions closer to the efficient volume. Competition may also protect against the holdup of one's specific investments.

Accordingly, a two-sided platform can benefit from allowing competition on one side if it can at least partly recoup the associated benefits on the other side. The same as a competition authority it cares about the benefits associated with competition (Belleflamme-Toulemonde 2004; Ellison et al. 2003). Note, again, that the platform does not internalize these benefits if it has contracted with only one side. As an illustration of the vertical view, consider a patent owner (the platform) that generally grants licenses to one or a small number of licensees (sellers), who then market a final good to consumers (buyers).[23] If the patent owner could control access to the final goods and thereby charge consumers for their indirect use of the patent, she would grant licenses much more generously because she could recoup the consumer benefits of competition among licensees. One should therefore expect less foreclosure in a two-sided market than in a vertical environment. This example provides yet another demonstration that the application of standard economic institutions developed in vertical contexts to two-sided markets is misleading.

15.4 An Illustration of Usage Externalities in Two-sided Markets: The Payment Cards Industry

As the discussion above shows, the analysis of two-sided markets is complex, in particular, when dealing with the interactions between usage and membership externalities. Two-sided markets also differ from each another: Economic theory has yet to establish a corpus of knowledge able to provide clear and robust recommendations for competition policy in two-sided markets in general. The payment cards industry, however, has received a fair amount of attention in recent years from academics, competition authorities, and regulators. It is also simpler than other two-sided markets because membership externalities can be neglected, at least in a first analysis. The rest of the chapter is devoted to the payment card industry. In this section we discuss the fundamental externalities inherent to this industry. In section 15.5, we will present a simple model of this industry, to be used in the last part of the chapter for illustrating the specificities of two-sided markets in the design of a competition policy.

15.4.1 Externalities in the Payment Card Industry

The choice of a payment instrument to settle a transaction affects the costs and benefits of both parties to the transaction and therefore involves a fundamental externality. As we noted earlier, it is standard for other industries to distinguish between membership externalities (do I have a phone?) and usage externalities (do I call or turn it on?). In the case of payment systems, the distinction is on the merchant side muddled by (one feature of) the honor-all-cards (HAC) rule that forces a merchant to accept all payments by card within a given system or none. Thus, conditional on accepting the card, the merchant's usage decision is largely outside his control. To illustrate usage externalities, it is therefore useful to envision an hypothetical world in which a merchant is allowed to keep discretion on acceptance of a *given* card (i.e., the merchant accepts the platform's card as he wishes, depending on the circumstances).

If the buyer[24] insists on paying by cash (which is legal tender), the seller incurs the costs of handling and holding the cash (i.e., indirect costs of theft, counterfeit bills, and counting the cash). On the other hand, a cash payment allows the seller to save the merchant discount charged by his bank for managing card payments. Equivalently a seller who refuses a payment by card typically forces the buyer to incur the cost of finding an ATM and withdrawing cash. Paying cash may prevent the buyer from receiving the benefits that are often associated with a card payment (e.g., deferred debit or free interest period, frequent flyers miles, or cash back bonuses). The transaction may be even made infeasible if the card is a credit card and the buyer needs the credit facility to buy the good or service sold by the seller. This externality can be characterized as a "usage" externality.

Payment card networks are also characterized by a more classical network externality. A seller who joins a payment card network implicitly commits to accepting the cards issued by the members of this network and increases the potential utility of buyers who hold the cards by offering them an opportunity for using their cards. This is similar to the positive externality generated when a new user joins a telecom network. This externality is called a "membership" externality. The social cost of an incomplete membership decreases as the network matures, namely after most potential users have joined. By contrast, even in a mature network (where most buyers hold cards and most sellers accept them), the usage externality identified above remains important: the choice of the payment instrument is ultimately a decision of the buyer, and it impacts the net cost of the seller. Our objective in this section is to study the consequences of this usage externality.

To simplify the analysis, we assume that transactions can only be settled by using either a card or cash, and we start with the case where the number of transactions is fixed. The efficiency of card usage is this way determined by buyers choosing which transactions to settle by a card and which by cash.

The choice depends on the difference between the net utilities accruing to buyers and sellers for a card payment and for a cash payment. For a typical transaction let b^B denote this difference in gross utility for the buyer and b^S that for the seller. Let c denote the total cost of a card payment for the two banks who provide the payment service:[25] the buyer's bank, called the *issuer*, and the seller's bank, called the *acquirer*. Because the issuer and the acquirer (or anyone else for that matter) incur no direct cost when the transaction is settled in cash,[26] c can also be interpreted as the incremental cost of card versus cash. Social welfare is maximized (i.e., the use of cards is socially efficient) whenever card payments occur if and only if

$$b^B + b^S \geq c. \qquad (15.1)$$

15.4.2 Baxter's Analysis

Baxter (1983) was the first to emphasize that perfect competition among banks does not, on its own, lead to an efficient choice of payment instruments in the absence of an interchange fee. That is, perfect competition without transfers implies that p^B (the unit price of card services for buyers) equals c^B (the issuers' marginal cost), and similarly that p^S (the unit price of card services for sellers) equals c^S (the acquirers' marginal cost), where $c^S + c^B = c$. In the absence of side payments and strategic considerations by sellers (both aspects are studied later), a card payment takes place if and only if both parties agree:

$$b^B \geq p^B = c^B \qquad (15.2)$$

and

$$b^S \geq p^S = c^S. \qquad (15.3)$$

As illustrated by figure 15.6, condition (15.2) is more restrictive than condition (15.1). So the usage of card services is suboptimal even if banks are perfectly competitive.[27] This is due to the externality described above. Consider for example the case where $b^B = 1$, $b^S = 8$, $c^B = 4$ (this corresponds to point A in figure 15.1), and $c^S = 4$. By not using the

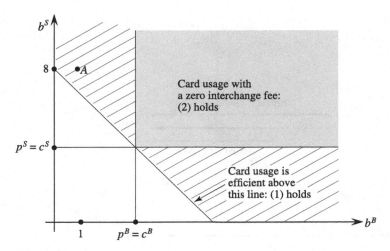

Figure 15.6
Underefficient usage of card services when the interchange fee is zero. The hatched area represents forgone card transactions that would have been efficient.

card (which is rational for the buyer, since $b^B < p^B = c^B$), the buyer inflicts a negative externality ($c^S - b^S = -4$) on the seller and prevents a socially efficient card payment (since $b^B + b^S = 9 > c^B + c^S = 8$).

When sellers are homogeneous (i.e., b^S is the same for all sellers) and banks are perfectly competitive, Baxter (1983) shows that this inefficiency can be eliminated by having the acquirer pay an interchange fee of $a_0 = b^S - c^S$ to the issuer. This interchange fee leaves the merchants indifferent between a cash and a card transaction because the merchant's discount, $a_0 + c^S$, is equal to their gross surplus, b^S, from the transaction. The net cost of the issuer becomes $c^B + c^S - b^S = c - b^S$. Therefore the issuers internalize the total cost of the card transaction net of the seller's benefit. Under perfect competition among issuing banks, this change in the issuer's cost is fully passed to the buyers (p^B becomes $c - b^S$), and the card transaction takes place if and only if

$$b^B \geq c - b^S, \tag{15.4}$$

which is equivalent to (15.1), the social efficiency condition. In a perfectly competitive world an interchange fee set at the optimal level a_0 allows the internalization of the fundamental externality described above and restores efficiency of card usage.[28]

These conclusions are illustrated in figures 15.7 and 15.8.

15.4.3 Criticisms of Baxter's Analysis
In their criticism of Baxter's analysis, Carlton and Frankel (1995) argue that this externality can alternatively be internalized, in the absence of interchange fee, by allowing sellers

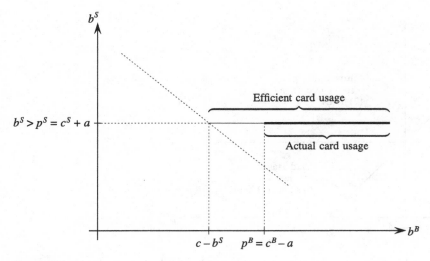

Figure 15.7
Card usage with homogeneous sellers and an inefficiently low interchange fee $a < a_0 = b^S - c^S$

to charge differentiated prices for cash and card payments. Indeed, if sellers themselves are perfectly competitive and if they and their customers incur no transaction costs from a dual (cash/card) price system, they fully pass through their net cost $c^S - b^S$ of card payments to buyers by surcharging (or discounting) card payments relative to cash payments. Buyers then use their card if and only if

$$b^B - p^B \geq c^S - b^S. \tag{15.5}$$

In the case of competitive issuers ($p^B = c^B$), this condition is equivalent to the efficiency condition:

$$b^B + b^S \geq c^B + c^S = c.$$

As Carlton and Frankel point out, however, in countries where it is allowed, differentiated pricing for cash and card payments is seldom used by sellers (this phenomenon is called "price coherence" by Frankel 1998) due to transaction costs. Casual evidence from the United Kingdom or some US states, where there is no "no-discrimination rule," shows that in practice such transaction costs prevent a large proportion of merchants from charging differentiated prices for cash and cards. More systematic survey evidence from the Netherlands and Sweden also points at a small occurrence of surcharging.[29]

But if the majority of sellers do not surcharge buyers, the volume of payments (which depends both on the proportion of sellers who accept cards and on the proportion of buyers who are willing to pay by cards) is a function of both prices p^B and p^S and not only on their sum. In this case the level of the interchange fee matters.

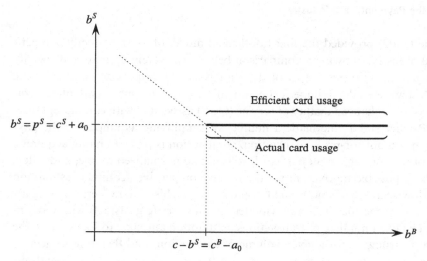

Figure 15.8
Card usage is efficient when $a = a_0 = b^S - c^S$ (Baxter's interchange fee)

A second criticism can be leveled at the Carlton-Frankel analysis. Suppose that transaction costs were low enough so that the merchants would differentiate prices and pass through to cardholders any increase in the interchange fee and therefore in the merchant discount. On the cardholder side the cost charged by the issuer for using the card decreases by the increase in the interchange fee, but the price paid to the merchant also increases by the same amount. The interchange fee is therefore "irrelevant" or "neutral," in that its level has no impact on card usage.[30] Consequently in the world depicted by Carlton and Frankel the interchange fee should not be a topic of interest to competition authorities, retailers, or any other player in the industry.

Returning to the absence of price differentiation, we next ask whether credit card networks choose an appropriate level of the interchange fee or there is a systematic bias toward under- or overprovision of card services? Unfortunately, Baxter's framework cannot provide an answer to this question, because in a perfectly competitive world, banks make no profit regardless of the level of the interchange fee. Because Baxter further focused on not-for-profit networks, it is therefore impossible to predict how the payment card network will select its interchange fees. In order to predict the interchange fee, one must allow the network owners' profit be affected by the interchange fee, either because they are imperfectly competitive users of the network or because the network is for-profit, or both. Indeed, banking industries are not perfectly competitive in many countries. Carlton and Frankel (1995) have expressed the concern that interchange fees could be used as collusive devices when banks have market power. The model presented in the next section allows us to examine this question.

15.5 A Model of the Payment Card Industry

Rochet and Tirole (2002) provided the first full-fledged model of an imperfectly competitive payment card industry, allowing a comparison between privately optimal and socially optimal interchange fees. With respect to Baxter's analysis, two important features of the payment card industry were added: imperfect competition between issuers, and internalization by the sellers of the enhanced quality of service (QOS) associated with card acceptance. For tractability, Rochet and Tirole made a number of simplifying assumptions: the payment card partform is a not-for-profit association, competition is perfect among acquirers, the total number of transactions (cash plus card) is fixed and normalized to one, and sellers are homogeneous. A possible motivation for the highly competitive acquirers assumption is the merchants' low search cost and limited brand loyalty. This is, however, a strong assumption, and certainly one that is grossly violated in countries (e.g., Israel) with monopolized acquiring. The fixed-number-of-transactions assumption amounts to focusing on the choice of payment instruments for a given volume of transactions and therefore neglecting the impact of price variations in payment services on the demand for final goods and services: it also seems reasonable in a first step.[31]

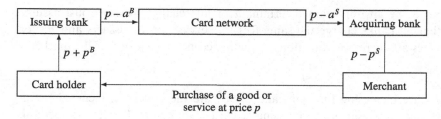

Figure 15.9
Flows of funds associated with a card payment

We extend the model of Rochet and Tirole (2002) in order to make it applicable to other contexts. In particular, we allow for a possibility of a for-profit network (Rochet and Tirole 2002 considers only not-for-profit associations).

For expository purposes, in section 15.5.1 we abstract from competition with other networks. In section 15.5.2 we then introduce a second platform, and study the consequences of platform competition.

15.5.1 The Case of a Single Platform

Our model is illustrated in figure 15.9. When a cardholder (who, for convenience, will be called the buyer) uses his card to purchase a good or service in a store at price p, the amount $p + p^B$ is debited from his account at the issuing bank, where p^B represents the cardholder fee.[32]

The issuing bank then transfers $p - a^B$ to the network, where a^B represents the interchange fee on the buyer's side. The network in turn transfers $p - a^S$ to the acquiring bank, where a^S represents the interchange fee on the seller's (i.e., merchant's) side. Finally, the account of the merchant in the acquiring bank is credited of the amount $p - p^S$, where p^S represents the merchant fee or discount.

When the platform is operated on a not-for-profit basis, the two interchange fees coincide ($a^S = a^B = a$): This is the case studied by Rochet and Tirole (2002). We extend their analysis by allowing the network operator to keep a margin ($a^S - a^B$) on each transaction. Often for-profit systems choose not to distribute substantial dividends, and therefore these systems behave as if they had a single interchange fee ($a^S \simeq a^B$). On the other hand, for-profit systems may choose to make a profit on the platform ($a^S > a^B$).[33] We consider both for-profit and not-for-profit systems.

The timing of our model is as follows:

• The network owner (or owners) sets the two interchange fees a^B and a^S (with $a^S = a^B$ if it is not-for-profit).
• Banks compete for providing services to consumers and merchants. We do not make restrictive assumptions on the intensities of competition on these downstream markets, since

they will turn out to be an important determinant of interchange fees. We just assume for tractability that all banks charge the same fees for service, p^B for issuers and p^S for acquirers. These fees are increasing functions of the net costs on each side of the market:

$$p^B = f^B(c^B - a^B), \quad p^S = f^S(c^S + a^S),$$

where f^B and f^S are increasing functions and c^B, c^S are the unit costs incurred by respectively issuers and acquirers for processing a card transaction. Perfect competition corresponds to the limit case where $f^B(c^B - a^B) = c^B - a^B$ and $f^S(c^S - a^S) = c^S - a^S$. In general, prices are strictly above costs: $f^B(c^B - a^B) > c^B - a^B$ and $f^S(c^S + a^S) > c^S + a^S$. For our illustrations, we will often consider the case of *constant margins*: $f^B(c^B - a^B) = c^B - a^B + \pi^B$ and $f^S(c^S + a^S) = c^S + a^S + \pi^S$, where π^B and π^S are strictly positive.[34]

• Merchants compete for attracting consumers, not only by setting retail prices p but also by deciding whether they accept debit card payments.

• Consumers observe retail prices and which shops accept cards. They decide where to buy and which means of payment to use for their purchase.

For simplicity, we assume (as in Wright 2004a and Guthrie-Wright 2003) that consumers are identical, but that the convenience benefit[35] b^B of paying by card differs from one transaction to the other.[36] For expositional simplicity also, we assume that the cardholder chooses the retailer before knowing the specific convenience benefit b^B that he will experience in the store. The expected net convenience benefit conditional on wanting to use the card in the store is

$$v^B(p^B) \equiv E[b^B - p^B | b^B > p^B].$$

The proportion of transactions with a gross convenience benefit greater than p^B is denoted $D^B(p^B)$ and interpreted as a "demand" function for card transactions on the buyers' side. For simplicity, we assume that merchants are identical:[37] the gross convenience benefit of a card payment for a merchant is denoted b^S.

Taking into account the increase in store attractiveness generated by card acceptance, a merchant will rationally accept the card if and only if the merchant fee p^S is less than or equal to the sum of his own convenience benefit b^S and the expected convenience benefit derived from the card by the buyer:

$$v^B(p^B) \equiv E[b^B - p^B | b^B > p^B].$$

Accepting the card provides the merchant with an increase in store attractiveness for which the merchant is willing to pay—besides the convenience benefit b^S and the increase $v^B(p^B)$ in the willingness of consumers to pay for his good or service—as is shown in Rochet and Tirole (2002), and also in Wright (2003c) and Guthrie and Wright (2007). The merchant's net benefit of accepting the card is therefore equal to $b^S + v^B(p^B) - p^S$.

Merchants accept the card if and only if this net benefit is nonnegative:

$$p^S \leq b^S + v^B(p^B).$$

15.5.2   Competing Platforms

We extend here our basic model of the payment card industry by introducing two platforms (indexed by $i = 1, 2$). End-users on both sides of the market then have the choice between using only one of the two platforms (single-homing) or both (multi-homing). In Rochet and Tirole (2003) we analyze how network competition is affected by the intensity of consumer multi-homing, measured by a multi-homing index σ. In this report we focus for simplicity on the two polar cases $\sigma = 0$ (single-homing) and $\sigma = 1$ (complete multi-homing).

Consider first the case of *single-homing* consumers: each consumer has at most one card. In this case each system is effectively a monopolist on the merchant side. The only way a merchant can benefit from a card payment by any given consumer is to accept the (unique) card owned by the consumer in question. In the single-homing case, merchants' acceptance decisions are thus the same as if each platform were a monopoly. Card i is accepted by merchants if and only if their net benefit is nonnegative:

$$p_i^S \leq b^S + v^B(p_i^B).$$

By contrast, in the polar case of complete *multi-homing* ($\sigma = 1$), the merchant knows that each consumer holds both cards in his wallet. Thus, by refusing one card, the merchant can still benefit from the convenience of a card payment by "steering" the consumer, that is, by forcing him to pay with the other card. In the case (which we consider here for simplicity) where the two cards are perfect substitutes for both categories of users, merchants accept only the card(s) that provides(s) maximum total user surplus

$$[v^B(p_i^B) + b^S - p_i^S]D^B(p_i^B),$$

among the two cards $i = 1, 2$, and $D^B(\cdot)$ denotes the usage of the card. That is, if $H^B(\cdot)$ denotes the cumulative distribution function of b^B, $H^B(b^B) = 1 - D^B(b^B)$.

15.6   Determinants of the Price Structure in the Payment Card Industry

In this section we first determine the interchange fee that would be chosen by a social planner aiming at maximizing social welfare; we then use the benchmark model presented in section 15.5 to characterize the interchange fee chosen by the system's owners as function of the structure of the industry and the intensity of competition both within and between networks. We conclude by suggesting criteria so as to determine whether interchange fees can be considered excessive.

15.6.1 Socially Optimal Interchange Fees

In our benchmark model, social welfare W is equal to the integral, for actual card transactions, of the difference between total user benefit $b^B + b^S$ and total provider cost $c^B + c^S$. In equilibrium, merchants always accept cards and buyers use them only if their convenience benefit for the transaction exceeds the (marginal) price p^B. Thus card transactions occur whenever $b^B > p^B$, and we can write social welfare as a function of p^B:

$$W(p^B) = \int_{p^B}^{\infty} (b^B + b^S - c^B - c^S) \, dH^B(b^B).$$

Note that social welfare depends only on p^B, as long as p^S is such that merchants accept cards:

$$p^S \leq b^S + v^B(p^B).$$

Thus, if the social planner has no redistributive objectives, that is, if it weighs equally the profits made by the banks and the platform(s) and the surplus obtained by final users, the socially optimal price structure is obtained when p^B maximizes W: for

$$p_W^B = c^B + c^S - b^S.$$

The merchant fee p^S only has to satisfy the inequality above. Thus there is only one socially optimal interchange fee on the buyer side, defined implicitly by

$$f^B(c^B - a_W^B) = p_W^B.$$

In the case of a constant margin π^B on the issuing side, namely when $f^B(c^B - a_W^B) = c^B - a_W^B + \pi^B$, the socially optimal interchange fee on the issuers' side is given explicitly by

$$a_W^B = b^S - c^S + \pi^B$$

$$= a_0 + \pi^B.$$

Note that the fee exceeds Baxter's interchange fee a_0 because it internalizes the imperfectly competitive margin π^B on the issuers' side. Put differently, the interchange fee is raised so as to offset the demand contraction effect of market power on the issuing side.

By contrast, the merchants' inelastic demand creates an indeterminacy in the socially optimal interchange fee on the acquirers' side. This fee only has to satisfy the inequality:

$$f^S(c^S + a_W^S) \leq b^S + v^B(p_W^B).$$

In the case of a constant margin π^S on the acquirers' side, this inequality becomes

$$a_W^S \leq b^S - c^S + v^B(p_W^B) - \pi^S.$$

Note that this latter inequality is compatible with budget balance of the platform only when

$$a_W^S \geq a_W^B,$$

that is,

$$v^B(p_W^B) \geq \pi^B + \pi^S.$$

This means that when market power in the banking industry is important (when $\pi^B + \pi^S$ is large), the socially optimal price structure is only attainable in a situation where the platform loses money.

15.6.2 Privately Optimal Interchange Fees

We now derive the interchange fee chosen by the network's owners as function of the intensity of competition both within and between networks. We first need to specify the platform's objective function.

The Platform's Objective Function The platform's profit is given by

$$B^P = (a^S - a^B)D^B(p^B),$$

provided that merchants accept the card, that is, provided that

$$p^S \leq b^S + v^B(p^B).$$

For simplicity, we assume from now on that margins in downstream markets are constant:

$$p^B = c^B - a^B + \pi^B, \quad p^S = c^S + a^S + \pi^S.$$

We can express interchange fees as functions of final user prices:

$$a^B = c^B + \pi^B - p^B, \quad a^S = p^S - c^S - \pi^S,$$

so that the platform's profit can be written as

$$B^P = (p^B + p^S - c^B - c^S - \pi^B - \pi^S)D^B(p^B).$$

To the extent that the platform may be owned by the main banks, its pricing policy (a^S and a^B, or equivalently p^S and p^B) can take into account not only the profit of the platform itself but also the profits of the downstream banks (issuers and acquirers). To accommodate the variety of situations, we consider that the objective function of the platform is a weighted sum of the three profits:

$$B = B^P + y^A B^A + y^I B^I,$$

where B^A (respectively, B^I) is the profit of acquirers (respectively, issuers) and y^A (respectively, y^I) measures the influence of acquirers (respectively, issuers) on the platform's board of directors.

A few illustrations demonstrate the flexibility of this objective function:

• *Not-for-profit platform controlled by issuers.* A not-for-profit platform controlled by the issuers maximizes B^I subject to the platform's breakeven constraint $B^P = 0$ (and, of course, merchant acceptance). So $y^I = \infty$ and $y^A = 0$.

More generally, the objective function of a not-for-profit platform whose decision-making is determined through bargaining between issuers and acquirers is obtained by setting y^I/y^A equal to the relative weights of issuers and acquirers in the negotiation and either by setting both variables tend to infinity or by setting $B^P = 0$ right away.

• *For-profit platform owned by issuers, acquirers, and independent parties (the "investors").* Independent ownership or more generally a board of directors controlled by investors corresponds to $y^I = y^A = 0$. Suppose that the acquirers control the board and own a fraction α of the platform's cash-flow rights. They then maximize $\{\alpha B^P + B^A\}$, and so $y^A = 1/\alpha$ and $y^I = 0$. Symmetrically, an issuer-controlled platform maximizes $\{\beta B^P + B^I\}$ when issuers have a fraction β of the platform's cash-flow rights and so $y^I = 1/\beta$ and $y^A = 0$. One could envision a bargaining process among issuers, acquirers, and investors, or a subset of these, yielding an objective function that is a weighted average of the three objective functions just derived. For example, if acquirers and issuers have cash-flow stakes α and β in the platform with $\alpha + \beta = 1$ and respective weights w^A and w^I ($w^A + w^I = 1$) in bargaining, and dividing by $(w^A\alpha + w^I B)$ in order to be consistent with the linear form posited above, then

$$B = \frac{w^A[B^A + \alpha B^P] + w^I(B^I + \beta B^P)}{w^A\alpha + w^I\beta},$$

and correspondingly

$$y^A = \frac{w^A}{w^A\alpha + w^I\beta}$$

and

$$y^I = \frac{w^I}{w^A\alpha + w^I\beta}.$$

• *Coasian (efficient) bargaining controlled by all providers.* All issuers, platform, and acquirers reach an agreement that maximizes their total profit,[38] which corresponds to $y^A = y^I = 1$.

The objective function becomes

$$B = (p^B + p^S - c^B - c^S - (1 - y^A)\pi^S - (1 - y^I)\pi^B)D^B(p^B). \tag{15.6}$$

Because of possible differences between issuers and acquirers in ownership and cash-flow rights on the platform, the objective function of the platform may thus diverge from the total industry profit. Let us denote by $\pi \equiv (1 - y^A)\pi^S + (1 - y^I)\pi^B$ the correcting term that appears in the above formula. By definition of y^A and y^I, we have

$$\pi = \frac{(w^A - w^I)(\alpha\pi^B - \beta\pi^S)}{w^A\alpha + w^B\beta}.$$

When bargaining between the banks is efficient, we know that $y^A = y^I = 1$, and thus $\pi = 0$. This is also the case if issuers and acquirers have the same weight in bargaining ($w^A = w^I$). In the general case, π may be positive or negative, depending on whether acquirers or issuers have more weight ($w^A > w^I$ or the contrary) and whether profit margins (weighted by cash flow stakes) are bigger on the acquiring or issuing side ($\alpha\pi^B > \beta\pi^S$ or the contrary).

Monopoly Platform   In the monopoly platform situation, p^S is set at the maximum level compatible with acceptance of the card by merchants:[39]

$$p^S = b^S + v^B(p^B).$$

In this case the objective function of the platform can be rewritten as

$$B = \int_{p^B}^{\infty} (b^B + b^S - c^B - c^S - (1 - y^A)\pi^S - (1 - y^I)\pi^B)\, dH^B(b^B).$$

For a for-profit platform, this expression is maximized when

$$p^B = p_m^B \equiv c^B + c^S + (1 - y^A)\pi^S + (1 - y^I)\pi^B - b^S. \tag{15.7}$$

Notice that the price structure $\{p_m^B, p_m^S = b^S + v^B(p_m^B)\}$ may imply that the platform loses money: $a_m^S < a_m^B$. As this occurs, the platform's owners will need to inject cash on a regular basis. The formulas above give

$$a_m^S - a_m^B = v^B(p_m^B) - y^I\pi^B - y^A\pi^S.$$

This expression becomes negative when margins π^B and π^S are high. When the platform is not for profit, the objective function becomes

$$B = (y^A\pi^A + y^I\pi^I)D^B(p^B).$$

Therefore the platform's owners will choose the interchange fee that maximizes buyers' usage, i.e. the maximum interchange fee that is compatible with merchant acceptance.

For-profit Joint Venture   If we now assume away any ownership stake by independent investors (as in section 15.5.1), the optimal interchange fee is

$$a_m^B = c^B + \pi^B - p_m^B = b^S - c^S + y^I\pi^B + (y^A - 1)\pi^S.$$

We need to compare this fee with the socially optimal interchange fee

$$a_W^B = b^S - c^S + \pi^B.$$

We get

$$a_m^B = a_W^B + (y^I - 1)\pi^B + (y^A - 1)\pi^S = a_W^B - \pi. \tag{15.8}$$

Thus interchange fees for buyers are too high whenever π is negative.

Not-for-Profit Cooperative   For the case of a not-for-profit platform we add a zero-profit constraint:

$$p^B + p^S = c^B + c^S + \pi^B + \pi^S.$$

Regardless of $\{y^I, y^A\}$, the platform chooses the maximum interchange fee that is compatible with merchant acceptance, leading to

$$p^B = p_A^B \equiv c^B + c^S - b^S - v^B(p^B).$$

The corresponding interchange fee is implicitly[40] determined by

$$a_A^B = a_W^B + v^B(p_A^B) - \pi^B - \pi^S,$$

where A stands for association. The interchange fee chosen by an association is too low (as compared with the social optimum) whenever the total profit margin $\pi^B + \pi^S$ exceeds net buyer surplus v^B.

Competing Platforms   The analysis of platform competition admits several alternative hypotheses. Here we assume "member duality." That is, all issuers and acquirers are members of the two platforms and therefore offer both card services to end-users. However, we assume away board duality in order to rule out coordinated platform policies.[41] That is, an issuer owning a cash-flow and control right over a given platform owns no share in and has no control right over the other platform, and similarly on the acquirer's side. Platforms offer perfectly substitutable cards, and we look for symmetric equilibrium.[42] The pricing strategy of the two platforms crucially depends on consumers' multi-homing index σ, namely the proportion of consumers who hold the other card and therefore can substitute when their preferred card is not accepted by the merchant. We analyze the two extreme cases $\sigma = 0$ (single-homing) and $\sigma = 1$ (complete multi-homing).

The analysis of competitive platforms is more complex than that of a monopoly platform because banks have two incarnations: as users of the networks and as owners. For example, a set of issuers may own a platform and use the rival platform if the latter offers a higher interchange fee. The following results have been proved only in four polar cases:

(1) independent platforms, (2) platforms controlled by issuers, (3) platforms controlled by acquirers, (4) Coasian outcome (maximization of total profit). We suspect that the results are more general.

Consumer Single-Homing In this case each platform is effectively a monopolist on the merchant side, since consumers have only one card. The platforms charge the maximum merchant fee that merchants are ready to accept, taking into account the increase in store attractiveness generated by card acceptance. Thus

$$p_i^S = b^S + v^B(p_i^B),$$

and the total surplus of final users is driven down to zero.

Competition between the platforms to attract issuers yields[43] $a^B = a^S$. This in turn implies

$$a_{SH}^B = a_W^B + [v^B(p^B) - \pi^B - \pi^S].$$

Thus the outcome of platform competition with consumer single-homing is formally equivalent to that of a monopoly not-for-profit platform.

Consumer Complete Multi-Homing In contrast to the previous case, merchants can steer consumers who have the two cards in their wallets, so platforms compete to attract merchants. In the case of independent platforms, each platform chooses the price structure that maximizes total user surplus under the breakeven constraint:

$$\max_{p^B, p^S}(v^B(p^B) + b^S - p^S)D^B(p^B)$$

subject to $p^S \geq c^S + \pi^S + c^B + \pi^B - p^B.$

After some computations this yields

$$p^B = c^B + c^S - b^S + (\pi^B + \pi^S),$$

or

$$a_{MH}^B = a_W^B - (\pi^B + \pi^S).$$

Thus interchange fee received by issuers is too low, as compared with the social optimum. The next section summarizes the main implications of our results.

15.6.3 When Can Interchange Fees Be Considered Excessive?

Our results are summarized in table 15.1, which shows the interchange fee received by issuers, a^B the level of total users surplus, and the profit of the banking sector by industry structure. From the table it is clear that the privately optimal interchange fee typically

Table 15.1
Industry structure and interchange fees

	Interchange fee	User surplus	Industry profit
Monopoly (or collusion)	$a_m^B = a_W^B + (y^I - 1)\pi^B + (y^A - 1)\pi^S$	0	Maximum
Monopoly (not for profit)	$a_A^B = a_W^B + v^B(p^B) - \pi^B - \pi^S$	0	Moderate
Competition + single-homing	$a_{SH}^B = a_W^B + v^B(p^B) - \pi^B - \pi^S$	0	Moderate
Competition + multi-homing	$a_{MH}^B = a_W^B - \pi^B - \pi^S$	Maximum	Small

Note: The socially optimal interchange fee is $a_W^B = b^S - c^S + \pi^B$.

differs from the socially optimal level a_W^B. However, note that there is no systematic bias. Note also that the interchange fee received by issuers impacts the volume of card transactions, and thus social welfare, whereas the interchange fee paid by acquirers only impacts the split of social welfare between user surplus and industry profit.

A few comments are in order:

• When there is a single platform, (monopoly), or when several platforms collude, interchange fees received by issuers are not necessarily excessive. The difference between a^B and a_W^B may be positive or negative, depending on the market power of banks (the level of π^B and π^S), the governance structure of platforms (reflected by the values of y^I and y^A), and the average net surplus of buyers $v^B(p^B)$. When issuers and acquirers have the same weight in the decision made by the platforms, the interchange fee received by issuers is socially optimal. Otherwise, it may be biased.

• Social welfare (i.e., the sum of user surplus and industry's profit) is maximized whenever $a^B = a_W^B$. This occurs when there is a monopoly platform (or collusion between competing platforms) and Coasian bargaining ($y^A = y^I = 1$).

• When there is a monopoly platform, or when several platforms collude, the interchange fee minimizes total user surplus.

• Platform competition does not guarantee a positive user surplus. Inter-platform competition creates surplus for end-users when the two platforms do not collude or when they are not for profit, and when consumers multi-home.

15.7 Robustness of Our Conclusions

For expository purposes we have taken as a benchmark a simple model of the payment card industry. In this section we analyze the robustness of our conclusions to the relaxation of several simplifying assumptions of the model.

15.7.1 Imperfectly Informed Consumers

As before, we assume that consumers are perfectly informed about card acceptance policies by merchants. Alternatively, we could assume, as Baxter (1983) did in his early contribution, that merchants' acceptance decisions were unknown to consumers or at least that they did not have any impact on consumers' choice of stores to patronize. (A more general specification that encompasses the two cases would introduce a new parameter τ, interpreted as the proportion, $0 \leq \tau \leq 1$, of consumers who are aware of merchants' card acceptance policy, or else the fraction of purchases made by a given consumer and for which the consumer is aware of the card acceptance policies before choosing a store.) Our benchmark model corresponds to $\tau = 1$, whereas Baxter's case corresponds to $\tau = 0$.

When $\tau < 1$, the maximum fee that merchants are ready to pay (in the case of a single platform, or two platforms and consumer single-homing) is reduced to $b^S + \tau v^B(p^B)$.[44] This implies that the formulas of table 15.1 have to be modified. The socially optimal interchange fees are unaffected,[45] at least when b^S is large enough. The interchange fees chosen by the platforms are reduced in two cases: a monopoly not-for-profit platform (second row of table 15.1) and competition between two platforms when consumers single-home (third row of table 15.1). Generally, when $\tau < 1$, merchant resistance is stronger and the likelihood that privately optimal interchange fees are excessive is reduced. Consider the case of a monopoly (for profit) platform and Coasian bargaining. The objective function of the platform is

$$B = (p^B + p^S - c^B - c^S)D^B(p^B).$$

Replacing p^S by the formula above, we get

$$B = \int_{p^B}^{\infty} (p^B + b^S + \tau(b^B - p^B) - c^B - c^S)\, dH^B(b^B).$$

B is maximized when

$$p^B = p_m^B \equiv c - b^S + \frac{(1 - \tau)}{\eta},$$

where $\eta = -(D^B)'/D^B$ is the semi-elasticity of buyer demand. Finally

$$p_m^S = b^S + \tau v^B(p_m^B).$$

So the price paid by cardholders is too high (as compared with the socially optimal price $p_W^B = c - b^S$).

15.7.2 Unobservable Merchant Heterogeneity

Another simplifying assumption we used is that the merchants' convenience benefit b^S for a card payment is identical across merchants. A straightforward reinterpretation of our model accommodates observable heterogeneity, since platforms can select interchange fees that depend on observable characteristics of merchants. For example, supermarkets typically face lower interchange fees than other retail stores. However, the empirical observation of actual refusal by merchants to accept cards suggests that unobserved merchant heterogeneity is a relevant factor. If unobservable heterogeneity across merchants is introduced, the situation becomes more complex, since a situation where different merchants are confronted with nondifferentiated merchant discounts generates a (finite) elasticity of merchant demand for cards. So our conclusions have to be amended. Rochet and Tirole (2003) show that the socially optimal price structure becomes relatively complex because it depends on demand elasticities and average surpluses on both sides of the market. In the case of a monopoly not-for-profit platform, Rochet (2003) shows that the platform will select an interchange fee that is either too high or too low as compared with the socially optimal one. In other words, there is no systematic bias. More specifically, the privately optimal interchange fee (the one chosen by the platform) is too low (as compared with the social optimum) when the average net surplus of sellers $v^S(p^S) = E[b^S - p^S | b^S > p^S]$ is smaller than the average net surplus of buyers,[46] $v^B(p^B)$. A more general analysis can be found in Rochet (2003).

15.7.3 Fixed Fees

We have assumed that buyers pay per-transaction fees, whereas in practice, cardholders often pay fixed (yearly) fees. In Rochet and Tirole (2002) we study the impact of such fixed fees in a model where consumers differ ex ante in their convenience benefit b^B for a card payment (nonobservable consumer heterogeneity). The results are similar to those of the present model, the main difference being that net buyer surplus $v^B(p^B)$ has to be replaced by gross buyer surplus $\beta^B(p^B) = v^B(p^B) + p^B$. This increases the likelihood that interchange fees received by issuers are excessive.

15.7.4 How Proprietary Systems Perform the Balancing Act

In proprietary (three-party) systems (e.g., American Express in most countries or Discover), the network is the only intermediary in the payment card transaction between a cardholder and a merchant. The flow of funds is described in Figure 15.10.

The levels of the customer fee p^B and the merchant discount p^S are chosen by the managers of the proprietary system so as to maximize its profit. We can easily adapt our model of section 15.5 to study the determinants of p^B and p^S, the prices faced by final users.

Consider the case of a monopoly system, and suppose that only a fraction $\tau < 1$ of the buyers are aware of merchants' acceptance decisions. The maximum fee that merchants are ready to accept becomes

$$p^S = b^S + \tau v^B(p^B).$$

The profit of the platform is

$$B = (p^B + p^S - c^B - c^S)D^B(p^B).$$

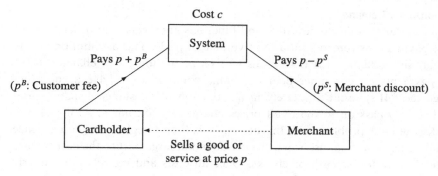

Figure 15.10
Flow of payments in a card transaction within a proprietary system

Replacing p^S by the formula above, we get

$$B = \int_{p^B}^{\infty} (p^B + b^S + \tau(b^B - p^B) - c^B - c^S)\, dH^B(b^B).$$

This is maximum for

$$p^B = p_m^B \equiv c - b^S + \frac{(1 - \tau)}{\eta},$$

where $\eta = -(D^B)'/D^B$ is the semi-elasticity of buyers' demand. Finally

$$p_m^S = b^S + \tau v^B(p_m^B).$$

Thus the price paid by cardholders is too high (as compared with the socially optimal price $p_W^B = c - b^S$). Notice that the analysis is identical to the case where an open platform maximizes the industry's profit (Coasian bargaining, $y^I = y^A = 1$).

In the polar case of competition between proprietary platforms offering perfectly substitutable cards, we obtain instead[47]

$$p_c^B = p_m^B$$

and

$$p_c^S = c - p_c^B.$$

Thus perfect competition between proprietary platforms leads to a positive user surplus (and zero profit for the platforms) but does not correct the price distortion for cardholders. In the case (studied here) where merchants' demand is inelastic, prices are unambiguously too high for cardholders. In a more general model with elasticities on both sides, the direction of the bias may be reversed.

15.7.5 Elastic Consumer Demand

We have assumed so far that consumers' demand functions are inelastic in order to focus on the choice of payment instruments for a fixed volume of trade. This assumption clearly simplifies the analysis. Relaxing it will allow us to look at the impact of changes in the prices of card payments on consumer demand. Some commentators have argued that high interchange fees (IFs) result ultimately in a reduction of consumer demand, since merchants are likely to pass on to the retail prices charged to consumers an increase in the merchants discounts. A problem with this argument is that it neglects the convenience benefits of card payments for final users, which correspond in large part to the cost savings associated to not having to use cash or checks. Once all costs and benefits are properly taken into account, empirical evidence shows that card payments are, on average, more efficient than paper instruments. Thus consumer price indexes are not the appropriate metric for assessing the impact of IFs on consumer demand. Consumer demand is more likely to react to changes in "net" retail price, that is, the retail price net of the average cost of payment instruments. In our model this net retail price varies one to one with total user surplus. Introducing elastic consumer demand would therefore not alter significantly our results.

15.8 Regulatory and Antitrust Policies for Payment Card Networks

Interchange fees differ across countries and across transaction types. In several regions of the world (European Union, Australia, Israel) the mode of determination of IFs has come under scrutiny by competition authorities, spurred by complaints formulated by large retailers' associations.[48] In this section we build on the results of our theoretical model, presented in section 15.6, and to lay out, in a nontechnical fashion, the basic economic principles for choosing an interchange fee. We also examine the case for a public regulation of interchange fees.

15.8.1 Payment Systems Are Two-Sided Markets

Recall that a fundamental characteristic of card payment systems is that every card transaction involves two users: a cardholder and a merchant. Thus it is appropriate to view payment card systems as providing interdependent services to cardholders and merchants. Cardholders benefit from their holding a card only if their cards are accepted by a wide range of merchants, and merchants benefit from the card only if consumers use it. Therefore a payment card network can function effectively only if sufficient numbers of both cardholders and merchants participate in the network. To this "membership externality" must be added a "usage externality." In particular, merchants do not benefit from their patrons' holding a card if the latter use it only sporadically.

Thus it is crucial for payment networks to find an effective method for balancing the prices on the two sides of the market. As we saw in section 15.1, card payment systems are but one of many examples of such two-sided markets. Detailed analyses of other examples, such as the software industry, videogames, internet portals, medias, and shopping malls, are provided by Armstrong (2006), Evans (2003), and Rochet-Tirole (2003, 2006). In all these industries as well, the crucial challenge for the platforms is to get both sides of the market "on board" while making a profit overall.

Where there exist positive externalities between different categories of users, it may even happen that one side of the market is left entirely free of charge. For example, cardholders are often exempt of transaction fees. This happens when cardholders are highly resistant to transaction charges. Another example is the pricing policy of Adobe (and many other programs) in the software industry. Adobe Inc. sells Acrobat Exchange, the software needed to transform electronic files into the PDF format. The economic value of this software comes in great part from the fact that any potential reader can download for free the complementary software, needed to read PDF files (Acrobat Reader) on Adobe's web site. This reader is a "damaged" version of Acrobat Exchange. This price structure results from the fact that readers have a lower willingness to pay for the software than writers. Other examples involving substantial cross-subsidies between the two sides of the market include portals, free TV networks, and low-price newspapers, and videogames.

15.8.2 How Do Payment Card Associations Perform the Balancing Act?

A payment card association such as Visa has two key characteristics: It is *open* and *not for profit*. The two properties need not come hand in glove. An infrastructure or a piece of intellectual property that is licensed on a nondiscriminatory basis is open but often for profit. Conversely, cooperatives are not always open. A proprietary platform such as Amex is both closed and for profit. The openess and budget balance properties of Visa in turn imply two important distinctions with Amex, which is both closed and for profit:

As we saw in section 15.5, in an open system the network's influence on the determination of final user prices is only indirect: it operates through the setting of interchange fees between member banks. Final users' prices p^B and p^S are not fixed by the network but result from competition among member banks within the network in the issuing and acquiring markets.[49] By contrast, a proprietary system directly sets p^B and p^S and receives the associated revenues (see figure 15.10).

Second, like for-profit systems a cooperative system has to perform a balancing act between the two sides of the market, and has to allocate the total cost between them in a proper fashion. However, as we noted above, it can do so only indirectly through the level of the interchange fee (IF).

Impact of Banning the No-Discrimination Rule   It is often argued, as we saw in section 15.4, that merchants' charging different prices for cash and card transactions is an alternative mechanism to the IF for internalizing externalities between merchants and cardholders, and that the no-discrimination rule (NDR) should be banned. The NDR is a rule that in some countries prevents the merchants affiliated with payment card networks from charging different prices for customers who pay by cash (or check) and customers who pay by card.

Despite the caveats we stated in section 15.4, let us assume that payment-based price discrimination by merchants is costless. The IF becomes totally ineffective if merchants charge different prices for cash and card payments.[50] In the model above merchants fully pass on their net cost for a card payment (merchant discount minus convenience benefit) to the customer who pays by card. If cardholders' fees to issuers are exactly proportional to transactions (in particular, there is no yearly fee) and if cardholders are perfectly informed before selecting a merchant of card and cash prices charged by competing merchants, the choice of the payment instrument is determined by the sum of the fees paid by cardholders and merchants, which implies that the IF no longer plays a role.

Furthermore, if the issuing and acquiring markets are perfectly competitive, the prices faced by merchants and cardholders are not distorted by banks' market power and so the externality between merchants and cardholders is perfectly internalized, resulting in an efficient usage of cards, as suggested by Katz (2001).

However, when the issuing and/or acquiring markets are not perfectly competitive, the second leg of the reasoning no longer applies. For example, we show in Rochet and Tirole (2002) that when issuers have market power, banning the NDR may result in an underprovision of card services. In contrast, with the NDR in place, the IF chosen by an association can result in efficient card usage.

In a different approach Wright (2003a) shows that when merchants have market power and cardholders' payments to issuers are not proportional to transactions because consumers pay a nonnegligible yearly fee, merchants may be able to extract consumer surplus from card usage. So there is no incentive to hold a payment card.

Does the No-Discrimination Rule Generate Distortions in the Choice of Payment Instruments? It is sometimes argued that cash (and check) users are penalized by the NDR, since undifferentiated retail prices incorporate average transaction costs of merchants (including merchant discounts for card transactions). Thus customers who pay by cash incur a fraction of the costs of card payments, which provides an additional incentive for them to switch to cards. However, this does not imply that IFs selected by card associations distort the choice of payment instruments by consumers in favor of cards and at the expense of other payment instruments like cash or check. This choice is also distorted by the markups charged by issuers and acquirers, if these intermediaries enjoy market power. In a situation of underutilization of payment cards, policies (e.g., the NDR) that encourage card usage increase rather than decrease welfare.[51]

A second argument in favor of the NDR builds on the fact that in most countries the prices of these other instruments may not fully reflect their costs. In particular, in many countries check users do not internalize the costs of these checks because there are no check fees for the vast majority of users. As a consequence surcharging card users, while check users do not pay for their costs, would certainly not go in the direction of economic efficiency but instead hinder the development of electronic transactions.[52]

15.8.3 Public Policy Regarding Interchange Fees

Merchants have repeatedly lobbied competition authorities to regulate IFs. This is easy to understand: retailers have a vested interest in bringing IFs down,[53] since such reductions would be partly reflected in reduced merchant discounts. Of course, cardholders have a vested interest in high IFs, since decreases in IFs can cause cardholder fees to rise. A cardholders' lobby, assuming that one exists, will then have some vested interest to push for a regulation that increases IFs and thereby raises cardholders' benefits.[54]

As a rule, public policy should be guided by social interest rather than special interests; public policy should rest on a full-fledged economic analysis of market failures. In this section we examine the market failures that have been advanced in relation to the use of IFs within payment card associations, and we argue that public regulation of the associations' IFs, if any, should be based on a deeper analysis than the one employed so far.

The Interchange Fee Is Not a Fee for Service   The proponents of a cost-based regulation of interchange fees implicitly refer to a vertical structure, considering that issuers provide an intermediation service to acquirers, who then supply the final service to merchants. This view is erroneous because it ignores the role of cardholders as consumers of the payment services, on an equal footing with merchants. It fails to recognize the two-sidedness of the payment card industry, and the resulting need for balancing the demands of the two types of users. Unlike a fee for service in a vertically organized industry, the interchange fee affects not only the marginal cost of merchants but also the size of the cardholder clientele and the usage of cards.[55]

Concerns about Anticompetitive Behavior in Relation with Interchange Fees   Do we expect the IFs chosen by platforms to be set at the "wrong level"? The results represented in section 15.6 (see table 15.1) show that although the socially optimal and privately optimal levels of IFs both depend on the same factors (issuers' and acquirers' costs, issuers' and acquirers' margins, etc.), they are not equal in general. However, given the profession's current state of knowledge, it is hard to decide whether the IFs chosen by a platform are systematically too high or too low as compared with socially optimal levels. In general, it is not in the interest of a platform to choose IFs that deviate markedly from social optima for three reasons. First, network externalities can weaken the other side of the business and reduce the demand on one's own side. Second, competition within networks can reduce the issuers' marginal cost of doing business partly or fully in favor of cardholders. Third, competition between networks allows merchants and/or cardholders to switch providers when one network decides to increase its prices. Let us briefly examine these three points.

Network Externalities   Even a monopoly issuer (respectively, a monopoly acquirer) would not benefit from a very high (respectively, very low) IF. A high IF would result in substantial merchant resistance and would induce many merchants to reject the card. Therefore, although a very high IF results in a low marginal cost to the issuer of offering payment services to cardholders, it does not benefit the issuer if the cardholders reduce the use of the card because many merchants do not accept it. Symmetrically, even a monopoly acquirer can exercise restraint in setting the IF, since a very low IF leads to a correspondingly high cardholder fee and so discourages consumers from holding and using the card. Thus network externalities by themselves induce *some* restraint. This restraint, however, is not sufficient to bring the IF to the socially optimal level.

Within-Network Competition   An increase in the IF does not just go into the issuers' pockets. It reduces the marginal cost of all issuers, and correspondingly reduces the price charged to cardholders. Indeed some standard models of competition used in economic theory[56] predict that the increase in the IF is fully passed through to cardholders. While there may not be a full pass-through to cardholders, it is reasonable to assume that a reasonable fraction of the increase in the IF is competed away (passed on to consumers). In this case issuers appropriate only a fraction of the increase in the IF and lose if this increase in the IF induces a substantial fraction of merchants not to take the card. To sum up, the fact that an increase in the IF is partly competed away reinforces the benefits to issuers from exercising restraint.

Between-Networks Competition   Competition between networks is an additional force that restrains payment associations in their choice of prices. Suppose that issuers control the association and therefore would like to levy a high interchange fee. However, when the association competes with other payment systems and when a substantial fraction of cardholders multi-home, merchants are tempted to reject the cards of payment systems that charge high merchant discounts (see section 15.5.2). System competition combined with cardholder multi-homing therefore force issuer-controlled association to exercise further restraint in their choice of interchange fee.

Rochet and Tirole (2002) and Guthrie and Wright (2007) show that competition between not-for-profit networks does not necessarily lead to a higher social welfare than a monopoly network. The intuition goes as follows: First, a standard benefit of competition is to bring the price *level* down. However, this benefit of competition does not exist when systems are associations whose not-for-profit status prevents exercise of market power. Competition therefore alters the price *structure* (the allocation of cost between the two sides of the market) rather than the price level. As shown in these papers, competition may lead systems to leave a large rent to a side of the market that has a credible threat to sever its relationship with one of the systems. As this rent comes at the expense of the other side of the market, the balancing act is perturbed.

15.8.4 Comparison with Other Industries

To be certain, the fact that an association's members, whether predominantly issuers or acquirers, have the socially worthwhile objective to bring both sides of the market on board does not mean that the association, whoever controls it, will pick just the socially optimal IF. But this feature is not specific to the payment card industry: no industry ever engenders the socially optimal decisions. There is no reason to believe that airlines select the perfect bundle of routes, frequencies and prices, that patent holders perfectly maximize social welfare in their licensing choices, or that biotechnology start-ups perform the socially optimal amount of R&D.

The standard approach to public intervention in industries involves two steps:

1. The theoretical identification of a serious market failure and the validation of its empirical relevance.
2. The identification of the least distortionary way of addressing the market failure and a check that the remedy will not be worse than the illness.

For example, the regulation of telecommunications, electricity, and railroad industries has traditionally been based on a broad intellectual consensus that certain segments represent natural monopolies and provide their owners with incentives to charge largely inflated, distortionary prices (part 1). Concerning part 2, there has been much debate as to the proper mode of regulation as well as again a broad consensus that regulation itself introduces nonnegligible distortions. Yet most economists feel strongly enough about part 1 that they are willing to accept the need for regulatory intervention in those industries, despite the concomitant regulatory distortions.

Proponents of a regulation of the IF must first build a theoretical paradigm that gathers broad intellectual consensus and demonstrates a clear market failure, shows the resulting distortions to have a clear and sizable impact on welfare, and proposes a form of regulation consistent with the underlying theory and better than nonintervention. So far no such theoretical paradigm has been achieved. On the contrary, recent academic work concurs to establishing that in the absence of empirical work showing that one of the effects analyzed in this chapter dominates, there is no systematic bias in the IFs selected by cooperative networks. Put differently, there is no a priori theoretical reason to think that privately optimal IFs are higher or lower than socially optimal ones. Substantial distortions in the industry can come from policy misunderstanding the economics of the two-sided markets and imposing cost-based regulation.

A cost-based regulation of the IF might be an unfortunate precedent for two-sided markets. The same logic may then imply that advertisers' fees paid to TV networks, newspapers, and portals[57] should be regulated on a cost basis so as to stop the subsidization of eyeballs by advertisers; that videogame developers be entitled to regulated royalties and development kits' prices, and to above-cost console pricing; that the Internet should be regulated so as to stop the subsidization of Web sites by dial-up customers through bill-and-keep; that software reader programs be charged the same price as software writer programs (they cost the same); and that social gatherings be regulated so as to prevent payments to or free entry for attractive participants (e.g., celebrities) while others pay for entry. We do not think that these implications are fully understood by the proponents of cost-based IFs.

Notes

1. The theory of network externalities has largely ignored price structure issues, as well as many of the themes of the two sided-market literature such as multi-homing (focusing on the design of converters by platforms rather) or the control of interactions among end-users.

2. The outside option for both users, which provides a benchmark for a surplus analysis, is to settle the transaction in cash or with a check.

3. An exception is the benefit that some people draw from being associated in membership with selected others within a club.

4. $p^B < 0$ if the customer receives frequent flyer miles or cash-back bonuses.

5. We here ignore "system fees," which are fees paid to the credit card associations in order to cover the associations' capital and operating costs.

6. We assume that the latter incur no per-interaction cost. If they do, add these costs onto p^B and p^S to obtain $\hat{p}_B$ and $\hat{p}^S$ under perfect competition.

7. There are often multiple layers of intermediaries, for example, an ISP between the end-user and the backbone.

8. While restrictive, this situation already encompasses a number of industries of interest, for example, a mature telecommunications market in which everyone has a phone, or a mature payment system in which no substantial fixed cost or charge stands in the way of membership.

9. As we show in Rochet-Tirole (2006), the failure of the Coase theorem to apply is not sufficient for the price structure to matter. We accordingly identify the conditions that do make a market two-sided.

10. For example, see Katz-Shapiro (1985, 1986) and Farrell-Saloner (1985, 1986).

11. By contrast, the allocation of the variable fees p^B and p^S keeping the total variable fee $p = p^B + p^S$ constant is still neutral, provided that there are no transaction costs that install grains of sand in the pass-through mechanism. First, the volume of ex post transactions is insensitive to the variable fees allocation for given membership levels. Second, the split of the total end-user surplus between the two sides can be shown to be unaffected by the allocation of the total variable fee. Membership on either side is therefore unchanged.

12. The cause of asymmetry most studied in the literature is a differential in (semi-)elasticities. Several papers (Ambrus-Argenziano 2004, Bakos-Katsamakas 2004, Caillaud-Jullien 2003) have shown that pricing and other asymmetries arise even when the two sides are symmetric.

13. See Rochet-Tirole (2003) for details.

14. What matters here is membership multi-homing rather than usage multi-homing (Rysman 2004 presents some evidence that cardholders multi-home much more in membership than in actual usage).

15. For linear demands, platform competition does not alter the price structure. So, for example, competition among not-for-profit associations (for which the break-even-constraint fixes the price level) does not alter prices under linear demands.

16. See Anderson-Coate (2003), Armstrong (2006), Guthrie-Wright (2007), Hagiu (2006), and Rochet-Tirole (2004) for further analyses of multi-homing. Multi-homing on both sides also raises fascinating questions with respect to the decision of which platform to route on (Hermalin-Katz 2004).

17. See Rochet-Tirole (2004).

18. To be sure, there have always been attempts at measuring these. For example, the seller may ask the buyer to refer to the newspaper or magazine where the buyer learned about the product. On the Web there have been attempts at measuring an eyeball's path of clicks, and referral payments are now common.

19. In matching markets the platform can also alter the distribution of the surplus among end-users through the choice of auction design. See Bulow-Levin (2006) and Damiano-Li (2003). Parker-van Alstyne (2004), in the context of software platforms, look at nonprice dimensions of licensing contracts (openness of code/disclosure, length of license). Bakos-Katsamakas (2004) consider the impact of the platform's technological design on the end-users' per transaction benefits.

20. Under the vertical view the platform could impose resale price maintenance (RPM) on the sellers so as to avoid double marginalization. But RPM is then (at least under symmetric information between platform and sellers) only a substitute for a missing nonlinearity of the tariff charged to the sellers. Therefore RPM is not an intrinsic feature of the relationship between platform and seller.

21. Another issue in this case is that a seller's willingness to pay for shelf space depends on how much shelf space and prominent display is purchased by rival brands. So, at the very least, such auctions should be combinatorial.

22. In a repeated purchase context the platform might care about the impact of seller behavior on its reputation.

23. See Rey-Tirole (2003) for an overview of foreclosure theory and practice.

24. For simplicity, we will call these parties the buyer and the seller, instead of using the technical terms: payor and payee.

25. c may also include the marginal cost of the card network, but we neglect it in this analysis.

26. Consumers and merchants handle cash through their banks. The banks' cost of handling cash may at the margin not be equal to what they charge for the service, however. Similarly, the cost of ATM services may or may not at the margin be aligned with their pricing to ATM cardholders. If cash services are priced below cost, then card payments are further encouraged in comparison to the no-distortion-of-pricing-of-the-cash-service benchmark studied in this chapter. The analysis must be amended as explained in the next note (which is set in the context of check services).

27. This is a fortiori true if the alternative payment instrument is a check, of total cost c_0. The incremental cost of cards becomes negative, whereas because of regulation, checks are free of charge for users in a number of countries. In this case the condition for efficient usage of cards becomes $b^B + b^S \geq c - c_0$, whereas in the competitive equilibrium without interchange fees, the condition for card usage remains $\{b^B \geq c^B \text{ and } b^S \geq c^S\}$ when check payments are not charged by banks. If checks were charged at their unit costs, say c_0^B and c_0^S, the reasoning of the text would apply, provided that the costs of card payments are replaced by the incremental costs of card versus checks. Notice that in this case an interchange fee on checks could suffice to restore efficiency. In practice, more than two payment instruments are available, which complicates the analysis. In particular, an efficient use of payment modes requires that interchange fees be set appropriately for all payment instruments.

28. If b^S varies across sellers but is observable, Baxter's result remains valid if the network sets differentiated interchange fees. Notice that no network effect is involved in this example. Network effects only become important when fixed fees and fixed costs are introduced, or when one of the parties (typically the seller) has to commit ex ante to accept cards. In this case a seller's acceptance decision is influenced by the number of cardholders.

29. See ITM (2000). In the United States, surcharges for card payments are forbidden (at least in some states; see Chakravorti and Shah 2001 for a detailed discussion of surcharges and discounts), but cash discounts are allowed. In the United Kingdom, any form of restriction is illegal, yet differentiated pricing is not frequently observed.

30. This intuition was verified in a restricted setting by Rochet and Tirole (2002). Gans and King (2003) prove it in an extremely general setup.

31. Two papers by Schwartz and Vincent (2000, 2002) relax this assumption in a particular context.

32. In practice, p^B is often zero or even negative (when cardholders receive frequent-flyer awards or cash-back bonuses). Sometimes p^B is paid as an annual cardholder fee independent of the number of transactions. This case is considered in Rochet-Tirole (2002) and leads to similar results.

33. In some cases it is optimal for the platform owners (who are also the platform users) to choose a negative margin, that is, to let the platform make a deficit, and therefore to accept to re-inject cash periodically in the platform. We analyze these cases in section 15.6.

34. The assumption that markups π^B and π^S are fixed simplifies the analysis, but it is a strong one. An example is the acquiring and issuing sides described in a Hotelling model of product differentiation.

35. Both convenience benefits and costs are measured with respect to an alternative payment means (cash or check) taken as benchmark.

36. Rochet and Tirole (2002) assume instead that consumers are ex ante heterogeneous, which introduces additional complexities.

37. The reader may wonder whether merchant inelastic demand is consistent with a fixed markup π^S. In the Hotelling model margins are compressed when the firms' (here, acquirers') marginal cost is close to the consumers' (here, the merchants') valuations. So consider this variation on the Hotelling/Lerner/Salop model. First, fees $\{a^S, a^B\}$ are set by the platform. Second (ex ante identical), merchants must pay a fixed cost C_0 in order to be able to use cards. They then learn their location in the product space. Third, acquirers set their prices. Then $\pi^S = t/n$ if t is the transportation cost, there are n acquirers and the circle has length 1. The average transportation cost is $t/2n$. Let b_0^S denote the gross convenience benefit. The merchants invest C_0 at the second stage if and only if $b_0^S + v^B(p^B) - [a^S + c^S + \pi^S + \frac{t}{2n}] \geq C_0$. Let $b^S \equiv b_0^S - (C_0 + \frac{t}{2n})$. Then we are back to the basic model. Furthermore, if C_0 is not too small, acquirer prices are not in the region where markups are compressed.

38. Side transfers could be used to reach a desired sharing of this profit.

39. This implies that total user surplus is driven down to zero.

40. The determination of a_A^B is only implicit because p_A^B depends on a_A^B.

41. The case of perfect collusion between platforms is formally equivalent to the case of a monopoly platform studied above.

42. In practice, the cards may not be perfect substitutes and the market share of the two networks may not be equal; but our symmetric model is used as a benchmark.

43. In the case of issuer-owner platforms (or acquirer-owned platform by symmetry, or else in the Coasian case), would the issuers want to subsidize the platform? Suppose that a given platform is owned by half of the issuers (the case for subsidies is even weaker if it is owned by fewer than half). Then it can be shown that subsidies are indeed suboptimal if

$$\left| \frac{(D^B)'^B}{D^B(p^B)} \right| < 2/\pi^B,$$

where the factor 2 refers to the fact that the subsidy will be enjoyed not only by the owners but also by non-owners.

44. This functional form requires some further assumptions (see e.g., Rochet-Tirole 2002). On the other hand, the comparative statics with respect to τ don't rely on it.

45. This is clear for a_W^B, since p_W^B is not affected by the reduction of τ. This is also true for a_S^B if merchants still accept cards, that is, when $p_W^S \leq b^S + \tau v^B(p_W^B)$.

46. This condition is very rough; it does not provide a simple empirical test of excessively high interchange fees, since these surpluses are endogenous. However, the condition is satisfied when merchants are identical, since then $v^S = 0$.

47. The result is the same whether consumers have a single card (single-homing) or both (multi-homing).

48. The Australian case is particularly interesting. In 2003, the Reserve Bank of Australia mandated a substantial reduction of the interchange fee for Visa and MasterCard credit cards. See Chang et al. (2005) for more detail and a first assessment.

49. Note that a change in a induces changes in p^B and p^S, although not necessarily one for one, except if downstream markets are perfectly competitive.

50. Rochet-Tirole (2002). Gans and King (2001), (2003) show that this neutrality of IFs when the NDR is banned holds under very weak assumptions.

51. We assume that consumers do not "overshoot," that is, that they do not create overconsumption.

52. This argument applies to the present situation in most European countries where the cost of checks is not reflected in the prices for users. A different reasoning would apply to countries like Canada, where check fees are high.

53. This is only true up to a limit since a low interchange fee reduces the number of cardholders: A decrease in merchant discounts, compensated by an increase in cardholder fees, may be detrimental to the welfare of merchants themselves. Indeed, when the elasticity of cardholders demand is high, even a small increase in cardholder

fees may result in a large decrease in cardholders' card usage, and thus in the economic value of cards for merchants.

54. Again, there is a limit to the IF increase, since cardholders want their card to be accepted by merchants.

55. Moreover it must be kept in mind that in the case of an association, the IF is not retained as profit but rather goes toward lowering the net costs on the side of the system that receives the IF. Ultimately issuers receiving interchange tend to pass on some of the reduction in net costs in the form of lower cardholder prices.

56. These include the perfectly competitive model and the Hotelling model of product differentiation.

57. These examples are developed in several small case studies in Evans (2003) and Rochet and Tirole (2003). Wright (2004b) discusses, in a very illuminating way, eight fallacies that can arise from using conventional wisdom from one-sided markets in two-sided market settings.

References

Ambrus, A., and R. Argenziano. 2004. Network markets and consumers coordination. Mimeo. Harvard University/Yale University.

Anderson, S., and S. Coate. 2005. Market provision of broadcasting: A welfare analysis. *Review of Economic Studies* 72(4): 947–72.

Armstrong, M. 2006. Competition in two-sided markets. *RAND Journal of Economics* 37(3): 668–91.

Bakos, Y., and E. Katsamakas. 2004. Design and ownership of two-sided networks. Mimeo. New York University.

Baxter, W. F. 1983. Bank interchange of transactional paper: Legal perspectives. *Journal of Law and Economics* 26: 541–88.

Belleflamme, P., and E. Toulemonde. 2004. Competing B2B marketplaces. Mimeo. ULB, Brussels.

Bulow, J., and J. Levin. 2006. Matching and price competition. *American Economic Review* 96(3): 652–68.

Caillaud, B., and B. Jullien. 2003. Chicken and egg: Competition among intermediation service providers. *RAND Journal of Economics* 34(2): 309–28.

Carlton, D. W., and A. S. Frankel. 1995. The antitrust economics of payment card networks. *Antitrust Law Journal* 63(2): 643–68.

Chakravorti, S., and A. Shah. 2001. A study of the interrelated bilateral transactions in credit card networks. Federal Reserve Bank of Chicago Emerging Payments occasional paper EPS-2001-2.

Chang, H., D. Evans, and D. Garcia Swartz. 2005. The effect of regulatory intervention in two-sided markets: An assessment of interchange-fee capping in Australia. *Review of Network Economics* 4(4): 328–58.

Damiano, E., and H. Li. 2003. Price discrimination in matching markets. Working paper. University of Toronto.

Ellison, G., D. Fudenberg, and M. Màbius. 2004. Competing auctions. *Journal of European Economic Association* 1: 30–66.

Evans, D. 2003. The antitrust economics of two-sided markets. *Yale Journal on Regulation* 20(2): 325–82.

Farrell, J., and G. Saloner. 1985. Standardization, compatibility, and innovation. *RAND Journal of Economics* 16: 70–83.

Farrell, J., and G. Saloner. 1986. Installed base and compatibility: Innovation, product preannouncements, and predation. *American Economic Review* 76: 940–55.

Frankel, A. S. 1998. Monopoly and competition in the supply and exchange of money. *Antitrust Law Journal* 66(2): 313–61.

Gans, J. S., and S. P. King. 2001. Regulating interchange fees in payment systems. Working paper. University of Melbourne.

Gans, J. S., and S. P. King. 2003. The neutrality of interchange fees in payment systems. *Topics in Economic Analysis and Policy* 3(1): 1–18.

Guthrie, G., and J. Wright. 2007. Competing payment schemes. *Journal of Industrial Economics* 55(1): 37–67.

Hagiu, A. 2006. Pricing and commitment by two-sided platforms. *RAND Journal of Economics* 37(3): 720–37.

Hermalin, B. E., and M. Katz. 2006. Your network or mine? The economics of routing rules. *RAND Journal of Economics* 37(3): 692–719.

Institaut v. Telefonisch Marktorderzoek (ITM). 2000a. *Study Regarding the Effects of the Abolition of the Non-discrimination Rule in Sweden for European Commission Competition Directorate General.* Amsterdam: ITM.

Katz, M. L. 2001. Reform of credit card schemes in Australia. Commissioned report for the Reserve Bank of Australia.

Katz, M., and C. Shapiro. 1985. Network externalities, competition, and compatibility. *American Economic Review* 75: 424–40.

Katz, M., and C. Shapiro. 1986. Technology adoption in the presence of network externalities. *Journal of Political Economy* 94: 822–41.

Parker, G., and M. Van Alstyne. 2005. Two sided network effects: A theory of information production design. *Management Science* 51: 1494–1504.

Rey, P., and J. Tirole. 2003. A primer on foreclosure. In M. Armstrong and R. Porter, eds., *Handbook of Industrial Organization.* Amsterdam: North Holland.

Rochet, J. C. 2003. The theory of interchange fees: A synthesis of recent contributions. *Review of Network Economics* 2(2): 97–124.

Rochet, J. C., and J. Tirole. 2002. Cooperation among competitors: Some economics of payment card associations. *RAND Journal of Economics* 33(4): 1–22.

Rochet, J. C., and J. Tirole. 2003. Platform competition in two-sided markets. *Journal of the European Economic Association* 1(4): 990–1029.

Rochet, J. C., and J. Tirole. 2004. Tying in two-sided markets and the honor-all-cards rule. Mimeo. Toulouse University.

Rochet, J. C., and J. Tirole. 2006. Two-sided markets: A progress report. *RAND Journal of Economics* 37(3): 645–67.

Rysman, M. 2004. An empirical analysis of payment card usage. Mimeo. Boston University.

Schwartz, M., and D. R. Vincent. 2000. The no-surcharge rule in electronic payments markets: A mitigation of pricing distortions. Mimeo. Georgetown University.

Schwartz, M., and D. R. Vincent. 2002. Same price, cash or credit: Vertical control by payment networks. Working paper 02-01. Department of Economics, Georgetown University.

Schwartz, M., and G. Werden. 1996. A quality-signaling rationale for aftermarket tying. *Antitrust Law Journal* 64: 387–404.

Williamson, O. 1975. *Markets and Hierarchies: Analysis of Antitrust Implications.* New York: Free Press.

Wright, J. 2003a. Optimal card payment systems. *European Economic Review* 47(4): 587–612.

Wright, J. 2003b. Why do firms accept credit cards? Mimeo. University of Auckland.

Wright, J. 2004a. Determinants of optimal interchange fees in payment systems. *Journal of Industrial Economics* 52: 1–26.

Wright, J. 2004b. One-sided logic in two-sided markets. *Review of Network Economics* 3(1): 44–65.

16 Competition Policy in Auctions and "Bidding Markets"

Paul Klemperer

The existence of a "bidding market" is commonly cited as a reason to tolerate the creation or maintenance of highly concentrated markets. I discuss three erroneous arguments to that effect: the "consultants' fallacy" that "market power is impossible," the "academics' fallacy" that (often) "market power does not matter," and the "regulators' fallacy" that "intervention against pernicious market power is unnecessary," in markets characterized by auctions or bidding processes.

Furthermore I argue that the term "bidding market" as it is widely used in antitrust is unhelpful or misleading. Auctions and bidding processes do have some special features—including their price formation processes, common-values behavior, and bid-taker power—but the significance of these features has been overemphasized, and they often imply a need for stricter rather than more lenient competition policy.

16.1 Context and Overview

The rise of e-commerce, government privatizations, and both public and private outsourcing has greatly increased the role of auctions in the economy.[1] At the same time auctions are often regarded as "different" from ordinary markets, and antitrust policy is often conspicuous by its absence.

Similarly many market transactions, especially business-to-business, are conducted through informal bidding processes, but it is often claimed that these "bidding markets" have such desirable features that ordinary competition policy concerns do not apply. Moreover it has become commonplace for companies to contend that they compete primarily in "bidding markets" and that there is therefore little need for further antitrust scrutiny.[2] Perhaps because of the frequency with which such arguments have been made, they seem also to have seeped into some antitrust agency thinking, and "the existence of a bidding market is a commonly cited reason by competition authorities to tolerate the creation or maintenance of highly concentrated markets" (UK Office of Fair Trading 2004a, para. 5.33).[3]

Three distinct strands of thought seem to lie behind the widespread view that antitrust can safely ignore markets conducted through bidding processes:

First are the claims, heavily pushed by legal and economic consulting firms, that in "bidding markets," market share does not imply market power, that the existence of two firms is enough to imply perfect competition, or even that just one firm is enough. Second, some academic literature argues that collusion, cartels and mergers can actually be desirable in an important class of auctions. Third, some regulators have themselves contended that even if market power can in principle be both present and pernicious in auctions and bidding processes, there is nevertheless often no need for regulatory intervention.

This chapter explores and, I hope, explodes, these myths. More generally, this chapter analyses the (limited) extent to which the special features of auctions and bidding processes mean that competition policy should indeed be different than in "ordinary" economic markets.

I begin with the "consultants' fallacy" that (roughly) "market power is impossible" in a bidding market.[4] I discuss the characteristics that are often claimed for bidding markets, and note that the extreme assumptions of an idealized bidding market can indeed yield the extreme conclusions that are often claimed for them. However, neither many auctions, nor many more informal bidding processes, satisfy all these extreme assumptions, and once we relax any of them we are quickly back into the familiar world of problems of dominance and unilateral and coordinated effects.

Furthermore the characteristics of (imperfect) bidding markets that cause these problems are the standard ones that are commonplace in the checklists that competition authorities use worldwide to identify these problems in "ordinary markets."

The "academics' fallacy" that (often) "market power does not matter" in an auction[5] starts from the fact that auctions and bidding processes are often used precisely because different market participants have different, and poor, information. In these settings each bidder has to worry about the "winner's curse" that it is more likely to win the auction when its rivals have discouraging information about the value of the prize. So bidders are more cautious than if they were more confident about their own information. In this context a cartel or merger that allows bidders access to more information reduces their winner's curses and so, it is argued, makes them bid more aggressively. Unfortunately, this analysis is incomplete: I show this so-called common-value effect does not much affect the overall costs of collusion to the bid-taker. More generally, I emphasize that in either the "common values" or the (more standard) "private values" case, the clear formal rules of auctions can facilitate predation and collusion.

Furthermore markets that operate though "ascending" auctions can be both more conducive to coordinated effects and collusion, and less attractive to potential entrants (especially in the "common values" case), than either markets with "sealed-bid" processes or "ordinary" markets. These issues have become more significant since the ease of running ascending auctions over the internet has made them far more common than previously, when it was harder to conduct them unless bidders were physically in the same location.

Finally, the "regulators' fallacy" that (put in extreme form) "intervention against pernicious market power is unnecessary" contains some truth: it is based on the view that bid-takers' power to set the rules and procedures of the auction can resolve any competitive problems.[6] However, if the bid-taker cannot commit to its future behavior, or is susceptible to lobbying, that can undermine its power. Moreover the bid-taker is often severely restricted by legal and political constraints, or its own organizational structure. (This is particularly likely if the bid-taker is a government agency.) It is true that with enough care and determination it is usually possible to design an auction that can overcome all these problems,[7] but it is often unrealistic to expect this to be achieved in practice. Competition policy must sometimes take the decision-making structure of other organizations as given—just as it must sometimes accept the current industrial structure. In short, we should not be overly sanguine about what bid-taker power can achieve.

Section 16.2 gives a typical definition of an ideal "bidding market," but shows that auctions and bidding processes are often far from this ideal, and section 16.3 argues that the resulting competition problems are therefore essentially the same as those of "ordinary" markets. The remainder of the chapter discusses the limited differences. Section 16.4 outlines the special price-formation process in auctions and bidding processes, and shows how their clearly defined rules often facilitate anticompetitive behavior, especially in ascending auctions. Section 16.5 demonstrates that cartels and mergers are probably no less damaging to bid-takers in "common-value" auctions than ordinarily, while the predatory and entry deterring possibilities are greater, so the existence of common values is probably an argument for tougher rather than more lenient competition policy. Section 16.6 shows how bid-takers' monopsonistic power to set the rules of bidding contests can in principle mitigate the competition problems, but why this power is often much less effective in practice. Section 16.7 briefly discusses a number of special topics, and section 16.8 concludes.

16.2   Auctions *versus* "Bidding Markets"

I begin by discussing the features that are often associated with "bidding markets," and the extent to which they are found in auctions and bidding processes.

16.2.1   (Ideal) "Bidding Markets"

While the term "bidding market" is frequently used informally there seems to be no agreed definition of one.[8] However, Patterson and Shapiro (2001) write "the [European] Commission described a true bidding market as one where 'tenders take place infrequently, while the value of each individual contract is usually very significant. Contracts are typically awarded to a single successful bidder (so-called "winner-takes-all" principle),'" and although it can be debated whether the European Commission actually intended this to be a general definition of a "bidding market," this is certainly a common interpretation.[9] That is, the term is associated with contests where:

1. Competition is "winner take all," so each supplier either wins all or none of the order. There is therefore no smooth trade-off between the price offered and the quantity sold.[10] (This is the last part of the European Commission's definition quoted above.)

2. Competition is "lumpy." That is, each contest is large relative to a supplier's total sales in a period, so that there is an element of "bet your company" in any contest. (Or, in the European Commission's definition quoted above, "the value of each individual contract is usually very significant.")

3. "Competition begins afresh for each contract, and for each customer." That is, if there is any repetition of a contest, there is no "lock-in" by which the outcome of one contest importantly determines another. This corresponds roughly to the part of the European Commission's definition quoted above "tenders take place infrequently," together with its statement elsewhere that "in bidding markets, market shares may not be informative of the likely competitive impact of a merger" (European Commission 2002, para. 14).[11]

Sometimes a fourth characteristic is assumed either implicitly or explicitly:

4*. Entry of new suppliers into the market is easy.[12]

Finally, users of the term "bidding market" typically implicitly or explicitly assume that:

5. A "bidding system" or "bidding process" is involved.[13]

Note that assumption 5 is a description of the price-formation process whereas assumptions 1 through 4* reflect deeper structural features of the market.[14]

The kind of example often offered as a prototypical bidding market is a large, indivisible, defense contract for a major weapons system (though this would probably not satisfy the additional assumption 4*). At the opposite extreme, competition between supermarkets for consumers exhibits none of these features. Of course, many markets lie between the extremes.

Clearly, these assumptions neatly lead to the conclusion that there are few antitrust problems in bidding markets:

With two identical firms, characteristics 1 through 3 perfectly fit a once-and-for-all, Bertrand (price-setting) competition for a single consumer who accepts the lowest offered price. Such a competition is, of course, also equivalent to the standard Bertrand competition in a homogeneous-product market with many consumers that is described in elementary textbooks.

It is straightforward that the existence of two identical firms is indeed sufficient for perfect competition (assuming constant marginal costs and no capacity constraints), and that historic market shares imply neither future success nor market power.[15]

If we add the "easy entry" assumption 4*, we then have a perfectly contestable market (as described by Baumol, Panzar, and Willig 1982), and in this case it follows that an optimal outcome is obtained even when only one firm is actually present.

Thus, using assumptions 1 through 3, or 1 through 4* to define a bidding market, it makes sense that "the existence of a bidding market is a commonly cited reason by competition authorities to tolerate the creation or maintenance of highly concentrated markets" (UK Office of Fair Trading 2004a, para. 5.33).

16.2.2 Auctions and "Bidding Markets"

The question, of course, is the extent to which the real markets that are described as "bidding markets" in practice actually correspond to the idealized markets described by assumptions 1–3 or 1–4*. In fact, as I now discuss, many markets associated with bidding systems or auctions (i.e., markets satisfying 5) violate at least one of the assumptions 1–3, while assumption 4* may very often not be satisfied and, in particular, may apply only rarely when 1 and 2 also apply.

First, many formal auction processes are multi-unit auctions with several winners, so violate the "winner take all" assumption 1. In particular, in a uniform-price auction, or in a simultaneous-ascending auction for multiple homogeneous units, all bidders receive (essentially) the same price and any bidder who lowers his quantity offer can improve his terms of trade (and the terms of trade for all winners). These auctions are common for electricity, financial securities, and radiospectrum, for example, though some of them—a one-off sale of radiospectrum by the government, for example—may well satisfy conditions 2 and 3.

Furthermore even many *single*-unit sealed-bid auctions effectively violate condition 1: if a bidder cannot predict the required level of a winning bid (perhaps because the bidder doesn't know its opponents' costs, or perhaps because bidders' products or services are differentiated so that it is not clear how the bid-taker will respond to any given price difference) then the bidder faces a trade-off between the price and the *expected* quantity sold. If bidders are risk-neutral, the effects on price-setting behavior and the incentives to exploit market power are identical to the case in which there is a smooth trade-off between price and actual quantity. And even if bidders are risk-averse there is no fundamental difference.[16]

Transactions in many industries are characterized by more or less formal bidding processes that may perhaps satisfy assumption 1 and 3 but not the "lumpy competition" assumption 2. For example, the supply of consulting, architectural, building, or other professional services, or contracts to supply retailers, or the supply of steel pilings (as in the UK Competition Commission's recent investigation of Arcelor/Corus) might all be characterized by many small essentially independent contracts and so fail (at least) criterion (2).

On the other hand, a contract to supply information technology to a large public health authority such as the UK National Health Service, or competition for a rail or bus franchise, or to run the UK National Lottery, might satisfy assumptions 1 and 2 but not 3, because whichever company wins the current contract will have a significant advantage in winning a subsequent competition when the current technology needs updating or the current franchise expires. The winning bidder may also have an advantage in similar contests in other jurisdictions.

Indeed the "every competition begins afresh" condition 3 is quite likely not to apply if there is repetition of an auction or bidding process, especially if assumptions 1 and 2 do apply. The reasons for holding an auction include that there is poor information about the right price, in which case the winner of the first contract learns valuable information about how to bid in future, which makes entering to compete with him very dangerous— see my discussion on "common values" in section 16.5 below. If assumption 1 applies, so there is only one winner, that single winner may gain a learning-by-doing advantage. And if assumptions 1 and 2 both apply, this may be because of economics of scale deriving from sunk costs, again, contradicting assumption 3.

Many auctions fail the "easy entry" assumption 4*. Of course, many auctions that fail assumption 3, such as because of lock-in, fail assumption 4* for the same reasons. More important, satisfying assumptions 1–3 is likely to be associated with new entry being hard, i.e., assumption 4* failing, for several reasons: first, the investment and organization required to credibly demonstrate to a bid-taker the ability to enter the market on the large "lumpy competition" scale implied by (2), is likely to require at least some sunk costs. If it is efficient to have a single winner, as suggested by (1), the economies of scale this implies may derive from sunk costs that again make entry hard.[17] The very fact that there will be only a single winner blocks small-scale entry that an incumbent might otherwise accommodate, and guarantees any potential entrant a fierce reception. More generally, if assumptions 1–3 apply so competition would be very fierce with two or more firms, then entry is not very attractive to a second firm even if a single incumbent is currently earning substantial rents. So relatively small barriers to entry may successfully deter entry, and assumption 4* fails more easily than if assumptions 1–3 did not hold.

Some auctions may satisfy *none* of our criteria. For example, the repeated auctions that characterize many modern electricity wholesale markets clearly violate assumptions 1, 2, and 4*, and also—because of the effects of the frequent repetition on bidders' strategic behavior—often violate assumption 3. The same may apply to some financial-securities auctions.

Indeed whether or not the detailed process of price formation is an auction—meaning assumption 5 holds—may be a completely academic point. For example, airline tickets are sold both through traditional nonauction retail routes, and through priceline.com's auction procedure in which each consumer first enters details of a proposed itinerary and airlines then bid electronically to offer the best schedule and fare.[18] But, although airlines nominally bid for each customer individually in priceline's auction, they must in practice have prespecified rules that automatically determine their responses to particular requested itineraries, just as in their traditional retailing.[19] Furthermore this market (whether run using a formal bidding process or not) seems little different from our example of supermarket pricing, which exemplified the *opposite* of a bidding market and satisfies *none* of assumptions 1–4*: setting a slightly higher fare for a particular offering slightly reduces an airline's sales in just the same way as it would slightly reduce a supermarket's sales;[20] no single transaction is significant; previous sales affect the likelihood of future sales (if only because of the existence of frequent-flyer programs, etc.); and, contrary to views expressed in the 1980s, it is now generally accepted that there are substantial sunk costs of entering the air travel market.

In short, just like "ordinary" economic markets, auction markets cover a wide spectrum from being close to the ideal "bidding market" described above, to being very far away from it.

So using the term "bidding market" as it is now widely used, to mean either Bertrand market (restricting to assumptions 1–3), or contestable market (if the "easy entry" assumption 4* is added), seems, at best, unnecessary, since the terms "Bertrand market" and "contestable market" are perfectly adequate. More often—and one fears this is why the "bidding market" term is so often used by antitrust advocates—the confusion between assumptions 1–4* about the market structure, and assumption 5 about details of the price formation process, is positively misleading. As I now discuss (in section 16.3), and as should come as no surprise, auctions and bidding processes are beset by the same range of competitive problems as "ordinary" economic markets.

Nevertheless, so-called bidding market issues often arise particularly starkly in auctions. While an auction process is neither necessary nor sufficient for a "bidding market," markets with one or more of the ideal characteristics I described are very often organized using a more or less formal bidding process or auction. (The reason is that a large transaction size [cf. assumption 2], poor information about the "right" price—more likely for a "one-off" contest [cf. assumption 3], or for an idiosyncratic transaction that is likely to be efficiently handled by just one winner [cf. assumption 1], or poor information even about who the bidders are [cf. assumption 4*], all make an auction relatively more efficient and posted prices relatively less efficient.)

Furthermore there are several ways in which the antitrust of auctions and bidding processes can be a little different from usual, and sections 16.4 through 16.7 of this chapter will consider these.

Thus the remainder of this chapter focuses on (all) those markets that satisfy assumption 5, namely those markets that involve a "bidding system" or a "bidding process."[21]

16.3   How Auctions and Bidding Processes are like "Ordinary" Markets

The competition problems of auctions are broadly the same as those of "ordinary" economic markets. Statements such as "in bidding markets . . . competition can be as vigorous with two firms as with three or more" (Lexecon 1995)—cited approvingly in the South African Competition Tribunal's recent decision permitting a "three-to-two" merger[22]—depend on the two firms being genuinely identical and genuinely competing, just as in an "ordinary" (nonauction) market. If one firm is advantaged, such as by lower costs or reputation, it has market power; if firms are differentiated, both have market power; and even if they are identical, they can jointly exercise market power if they can coordinate. With more firms there are generally fewer problems, but problems are more likely if some or all of assumptions 1–4* fail—all just as usual.[23]

16.3.1 Dominance

As discussed above, especially when contracts are large and specialized, the winner of the current contract will often have a substantial advantage at the re-contracting stage, and new entry is likely to be hard and unattractive (i.e., assumptions 3 and 4* are likely to fail). For example, after being the winner among eight bidders of the contest for the seven-year monopoly franchise to run the UK National Lottery when it was founded in 1994, Camelot had developed substantial learning-by-doing and reputation advantages by the time of the subsequent contest in 2000. Not surprisingly there was far less competition (just two bids) in the second contest.[24]

This is just the standard problem of competition in markets with "switching costs" as elaborated, for example, by Klemperer (1995), Farrell and Klemperer (2007), and Klemperer (forthcoming a). As those papers emphasize, this does not necessarily mean competition is weak or inefficient overall—the reduced second-stage competition can be compensated for by correspondingly fiercer first-stage competition that reflects the (quasi) rents that the first-stage winner expects to earn at the second-stage.[25] However, as those papers also explain, the resulting bargain-then-rip-off offers that the buyer (or bid-taker) receives often do create inefficiencies, and make competition more fragile, for example, making predatory behavior easier and more tempting. In the second National Lottery competition the first-stage winner (Camelot) brought substantial public relations, legal, and other resources to bear in defeating its sole challenger (Virgin's People's Lottery), including successfully overturning the government's initial decision to award the second franchise to the challenger,[26] and the experience of this has certainly had a chilling effect on the possibility of serious challenges emerging to contest the award of the third franchise due in 2006.[27]

A distinction from the standard analysis of "switching cost" markets is that the bid-taker may have more control over the auction process than buyers have over the rules of competition in an ordinary market. However, this distinction is less important than it might seem, as I discuss later (section 16.6). The main message is that the ordinary economics of dominance applies.[28]

16.3.2 Coordinated Effects

Where entry is hard (i.e., assumption 4* fails), and especially when bidding is not winner-takes-all (i.e., assumption 1 also fails), coordinated effects (i.e., tacit collusion) can emerge as easily in auctions and bidding processes as in "ordinary" economic markets.[29] The standard kinds of repeated-game analysis apply, and the standard checklists of factors that competition authorities use worldwide remain appropriate for predicting the likely emergence of coordinated effects. The UK Competition Commission, for example, cites all of the following as facilitating coordination: few firms, high degree of market transparency, high frequency of firms' interactions,[30] predictability of demand and costs, low likelihood of disruptive innovation, similarity of firms, lack of serious financial constraints on firms, long-term commitment of firms to the market, standardization of the product, inability of buyers to self-supply, and difficulty of entry by new firms.

It is no surprise therefore that the UK electricity (auction) market, which satisfied almost the Competition Commission's entire checklist,[31] is suspected of having fallen prey to coordinated effects in the late 1990s.[32] It may be that the specific auction rules contributed to the problems (see Klemperer 1999b, 2002a, 2003b), and it was partly in response to this concern that the UK regulator introduced New Electricity Trading Arrangements (NETA) in 2001. However, it is clear that independent of the price-formation process the electricity market would be very vulnerable to coordinated effects as long as it satisfied so much of the Competition Commission's checklist. Indeed a common view is that the post-NETA fall in prices is much more due to the substantial reduction in market concentration that occurred around the same time than to the change in the market rules (e.g., see Newbery 2004). That is, the standard factors facilitating collusion mattered; changing the auction process did not much matter.

I will discuss below some special issues about how the details of auction-market rules can facilitate coordinated effects (and explicit collusion) and, in particular, through creating the standard checklist conditions of market transparency, high frequency of firms' interactions, and difficult entry. But the main message is that the fundamental issues are no different than in "ordinary" markets.

16.3.3   Unilateral Effects

Just as for ordinary markets, several of the most important factors supporting coordinated effects including, especially, high concentration, lack of buyer power and difficulty of entry, also facilitate standard unilateral effects (i.e., monopolistic supply reduction or monopsonistic demand reduction).

Thus, for example, while the extent to which electricity markets have suffered from coordinated effects can be debated, there is a broad array of evidence that they have at least suffered from the unilateral exercise of market power (e.g., see Wolfram 1998 on the UK electricity market, and Borenstein et al. 2002, Joskow and Kahn 2002, and Wolak 2003 on the Californian market[33]).

To take another example, Cramton (2002) writes that in the 1994 US Nationwide Narrowband spectrum auction, "The largest bidder, PageNet [which he advised] reduced its demand from three of the large licences to two, at a point when prices were still well below its marginal valuation for the third unit. [It] felt that if it continued to demand a third

license, it would drive up the prices on all the others to disadvantageously high levels."
This seems to have been unilateral behavior, rather than (attempted) coordinated behavior, since there is no suggestion or evidence that the bidder expected any other bidder to
behave more cooperatively in response to its demand reduction, nor that any other bidder
did so.[34] Cramton also provides evidence of unilateral effects in the subsequent 1995–96
"CBlock" US spectrum auction.

In these multi-unit auction examples the bidder's quantity reduction is explicit. In a single-unit auction the unilateral effect involves making a less attractive bid that reduces the
bidder's probability of victory (i.e., reduces the bidder's *expected* quantity transacted), but
this too is analytically equivalent to raising price, and so lowering sales, in an "ordinary"
market. Thus in single-unit auctions unilateral effects are manifested in rises in expected
price-cost margins as the number of bidders falls.[35]

As usual, while auction-market rules may sometimes exacerbate some of the standard
conditions supporting unilateral effects (e.g., by making entry hard; see sections 16.4.3
and 16.4.4) the fundamental principles are the same as in "ordinary" markets.[36]

16.4   Bidding Rules and Procedures

Both the formalization of a bidding process into an auction with a small number of clearly
defined rules, and those rules themselves, sometimes facilitate predatory and/or collusive
strategies, especially in ascending auction processes, as I now discuss.

16.4.1   Price Formation in Auctions and Bidding Processes

Formal Auctions   When formal auction procedures are used, two basic designs of auction,
and variants of these designs, are most common. The first basic design is the ascending
auction, in which the price is raised successively until only one bidder remains, and that
bidder wins the object at the final price she bid, as is common in sales of art and antiques.[37] The other standard design is the first-price sealed-bid or "pay-your-bid" auction,
in which each bidder independently submits a single bid without seeing others' bids, the
object is sold to the bidder who makes the highest bid, and the winner pays her bid, as is
common in sales of oil or mineral rights, or in bidding for procurement contracts (although in the latter cases it is the low- rather than high-bidder who is the winner).

Informal Bidding Processes   In more informal bidding processes, it may be unclear how best
to think of the "auction." If a seller conducts parallel negotiations with two or more potential buyers simultaneously, this is probably in effect a standard ascending auction. But
even in a so-called (first-price) sealed-bid auction, if the bidders repeatedly interact with the
bid taker, asking "what kind of bid is likely to be successful?" the process can mimic what

an economist would call an ascending auction. Furthermore bidders may not believe a nominally "sealed-bid" process will end when the bids are opened: it is always in the bid taker's interest to entertain further bids, and shareholders might sue him if he turns down a subsequent improved bid; disappointed bidders who would like a further bid may also bring legal proceedings.[38] Even if the bid taker originally attempted to precommit to not accepting further bids, reasons can usually be found why the original bidding failed to satisfy some rule, or why the situation has changed so additional bids are needed.[39] And if bidders expect the process will later turn into an ascending auction, they will bid as if it was an ascending auction in the first place.

On the other hand, superficially ascending processes may really be sealed bid. When bidding for a house you may not know whether you'll get another chance to bid.[40] When buying a car, you can in principle go back and forth between dealers soliciting improved offers, but in practice a dealer may refuse to put its offer in writing and so prevent you from credibly communicating it to a competitor; if so you are in effect running a sealed-bid contest. Sometimes when companies put themselves up for sale it is understood that there will be a series of rounds (even though these may all be called "final"), with the investment bankers talking up the price between rounds, but if there is no hard information about competitors' bids until after a deal is sealed, only the final round really counts.[41]

Bidding is closer to sealed-bidding if bidders are differentiated and the criteria for evaluating bids are not fully transparent, so that bidders would not necessarily know whose bid would win even if they were fully informed about others' offers.

Note that sealed-bidding corresponds to standard Bertrand price-setting. With perfect information, the sealed-bid process corresponds to Bertrand competition in a market in which all consumers make the same choice between firms. And, as noted above, with imperfect information about rivals' costs or about the bid-taker's preferences, bidders making sealed bids face a trade-off between the price and their *expected* sales that is similar to the price-quantity trade-off firms face in standard differentiated-products Bertrand competition (and also similar to the similar trade-off in Cournot competition).

Unfortunately, though our understanding of whether particular informal industrial bidding processes are best thought of as ascending or sealed-bid is often poor,[42] the distinction is also often crucial as I now discuss.

16.4.2 Ascending Auctions *versus* Sealed-Bid and Ordinary Markets I: Efficiency

A key distinction between ascending and sealed-bid auctions for a single fixed prize is that the efficient bidder generally wins an ascending auction, because if a high-valuation bidder is initially outbid it can always raise its bid later. By contrast, a sealed-bid auction may be efficient when bidders are symmetric, but is not generally efficient.[43] The reason is that bidders cannot revise their initial bids, and a bidder with a lower valuation may therefore win at a price that a bidder with a higher valuation could have beaten but did not because it was hoping to win more cheaply. Likewise "ordinary" economic markets that are not "winner-take-all" are typically inefficient, because less efficient firms typically make some sales.

Thus, for example, a merger that makes an industry asymmetric may be less socially desirable if prices are set in sealed-bid auctions or in "ordinary" economic markets, than if prices are set in ascending auctions.[44] However, a regulator who cares about bid-taker welfare (as most antitrust regulators do, if consumers are bid-takers) rather than efficiency may have the opposite preferences, since bid-taker surplus is the same under the two auctions if bidders are symmetric but is often higher in a sealed-bid auction if bidders are asymmetric (see Maskin and Riley 2000). (Put differently, efficiency savings of asymmetry-creating mergers are more likely to be passed through to bid-takers in the sealed-bid case.) Furthermore, if the auction reveals information that improves the efficiency of the sealed-bid auction (perhaps merely by sharing information between the merging partners), both efficiency-maximizing and consumer surplus-maximizing regulators may be more enthusiastic about mergers when prices are set in sealed-bid auctions than when they are set in ascending auctions.

However, one suspects that these direct efficiency effects on the relative attractiveness of mergers in different auction regimes, and further results that can be developed along these lines,[45] are much less important than the indirect effects to which I now turn.

16.4.3 Ascending Auctions *versus* Sealed-Bid and Ordinary Markets II: Entry

Because ascending auctions are always won by the strongest party, it is also often known who that winner will be. There is then no incentive for any other bidders to turn up—a disastrous outcome for the bid-taker, especially if he does not have the ability to set a reserve price (perhaps because he lacks the information).

Klemperer (2002a) provides several examples of this, for example, Glaxo's 1995 takeover of Wellcome without serious competition, and for literally billions of dollars less than its valuation, after the largest shareholder in the target company had made commitments that forced the sales process to be essentially an ascending auction. By contrast, entry is more attractive into a sealed-bid auction in which there is usually some uncertainty about who the winner will be,[46] or into an "ordinary" economic market in which a slightly-inferior firm may win an only slightly inferior market share.[47] Klemperer (1999a,b, 2002a, 2003a) argue that this is a crucial issue in auction design; see also section 16.6.1.[48]

Furthermore, since entry into an ascending auction can be deterred by even a small disadvantage, entry deterring and predatory strategies of reducing one's own costs, or raising rivals' costs, or making threatening statements, can all be far more profitable than in a sealed-bid auction, or in an "ordinary" economic market. Indeed a common tactic for an incumbent or otherwise advantaged firm is to attempt to (re)structure the bidding process as an ascending auction.[49]

16.4.4   Formal Rules Facilitate Communication

One of the biggest problems faced by firms who wish to collude or predate is how to signal their intentions to rivals when ordinary communication is illegal. Unfortunately for regulators, the formal rules of auctions often solve firms' problem by defining a "language" that bidders can use to communicate with each other. Klemperer (2002a) gives many examples, including a multi-license US spectrum auction in 1996–97, in which US West was competing vigorously with McLeod for lot number 378—a license in Rochester, Minnesota. Although most bids in the auction had been in exact thousands of dollars, US West bid \$313,378 and \$62,378 for two licenses in Iowa in which it had earlier shown no interest, overbidding McLeod, who had seemed to be the uncontested high-bidder for these licenses. McLeod got the point that it was being punished for competing in Rochester, and dropped out of that market. Since McLeod made subsequent higher bids on the Iowa licenses, the "punishment" bids cost US West nothing (see Cramton and Schwartz 2000).[50]

Thus clear rules permit clear communication, and so facilitate both predatory and collusive behavior.

Furthermore auctions like the one described provide a rich enough vocabulary to communicate without providing too much. A simple single (sealed) bid auction would have made the behavior described impossible; an ascending auction with fixed increments (e.g., each new bid must be exactly 10 percent higher than the bid it is beating) would have made it very hard.[51] On the other hand an "ordinary" market with many different strategies available to firms may yield too rich a vocabulary for clear communication. For example, it is very hard for consumer-goods retailers who are selling hundreds of products, many of which are at least slightly differentiated from their rivals' products, and who can also follow different strategies in advertising, service quality, and so forth, to communicate suggestions about how to coordinate prices or divide markets, and to monitor whether their rivals are sticking to tacit agreements, without breaking the laws prohibiting explicit communication.[52]

Although the problems are worst for ascending auctions they are not restricted to them. For example, in repeated sealed-bid auctions the clearly defined history of past behavior may allow enough communication to permit coordinated pricing.[53]

Thus a key distinction between a bidding process with formal rules and an "ordinary" market is that the formality of the rules itself makes market behavior much more transparent, and so much more vulnerable to competition problems.

16.4.5   Ascending Auctions *versus* Sealed-Bid and Ordinary Markets III: Collusion

One-off Markets   Where ascending auctions clearly allow more strategic behavior than single-bid auctions or ordinary markets is in "one-off" markets that will never be repeated. Because an ascending auction turns a one-off market into a multi-stage game, it permits complex interactions and communications between bidders that would be impossible in a one-shot game. A good example is the behavior in Iowa described in the previous subsection; see Klemperer (2002a) for more examples.[54]

It is important to observe, however, that the reason ascending auctions encourage anti-competitive behavior is that they create the standard conditions that facilitate it. This is clearly seen in that they provide easy answers to the four problems that firms must solve in order to support collusion in an ordinary industrial market—these problems are listed in, for example, the European Commission's current (2004) merger guidelines, and in standard industrial organization textbooks—(1) how can firms reach agreement on a division of the market? (2) how can they monitor adherence to the agreement? (3) how can they credibly punish any observed deviation from the agreement? (4) how can they deter non-participants in the agreement from entering the industry?

In terms of the checklist of section 16.3.2, ascending auctions make the market very transparent helping to solve problems 1 and 2 much more effectively than in an "ordinary" industrial market whose definition may not be obvious, so in which efficient agreements are unclear, and in which defection is often ambiguous and slow to observe. Ascending auctions enormously increase the frequency of interaction,[55] so bids can be used to signal proposals about how to divide the "pie," to signal agreement with others' proposals, and to quickly and easily punish defectors, helping to solve problems 1 and 3 (especially since punishing a defector by raising price only on objects it will win, as in Iowa—see section 16.4.4—is costless to the punisher). And ascending auctions help deter entry, solving problem 4 (see section 16.4.3).[56]

To a limited extent similar strategic behavior is possible in other auctions and "ordinary" one-off markets. For example, by offering "meet the competition" clauses (MCCs) or "we will never be undersold" promises that guarantee rebates to any customer who finds a better price at a rival, firms can sustain collusive prices in a one-shot game—in effect MCCs introduce a dynamic component into the game by promising a reaction in the event an opponent deviates from a tacitly understood agreement. However, MCCs cannot help firms signal or negotiate what that agreement might be (at least in a one-off context). And a MCC is also risky if you may face an opponent who has very low costs.

Likewise in uniform-price multi-unit auctions (in which all the units are sold at the (same) price that equates supply and demand), bidders can in principle achieve collusive prices as an "implicitly collusive" equilibrium by choosing bids that would result in very competitive outcomes in the out-of-equilibrium event that the opponents fail to cooperate in the collusion.[57] Again, however, it is unclear how in a one-off market bidders can agree what the collusive shares should be,[58] and the strategy is vulnerable to opponents' mistakes in understanding these shares or to additional bidders entering unexpectedly. So the existence of these equilibria in theoretical models may be more relevant in practice to assisting collusion in repeated markets than to allowing it in actual one-off markets.[59]

However, the greater danger of collusion in one-off ascending auction markets can also be exaggerated. Coordinated effects are harder with more firms, or less similar firms (see section 16.3.2), and bidders often seem more imaginative in their attempts to signal than in their understanding of others' signals—as usual, something is much more obvious after it has been explained.[60] Even with ascending auctions, it is much harder to build up mutual understanding in a one-off market than in a regularly repeated one. Finally, as I discuss in section 16.6.1, even minor modifications to an ascending auction's rules can often reduce the risk of collusion.

Market Division Bidding processes may also facilitate collusive market division by turning a one-shot game for a whole market into a long series of individual customer-specific contests.[61] Especially when all bids are observable, this may make it much easier to segment the market, such as allocating customers geographically, though firms may, to some extent, be able to achieve similar segmentation in an "ordinary" market through price discrimination.

How Many Bidders are Enough? It is often asked, "How many bidders are enough to make a market competitive?" The answer is no clearer than in an "ordinary" market, but experience suggests that (contrary to the simple theory of "bidding markets"; see section 16.2.1) one more bidder than the number of prizes is *not* enough in an ascending auction, even in a one-off auction in which bidders can win at most one prize each (so there is no question of colluding to divide the prizes). For example, in the year 2000 Netherlands' 3G (ascending) auction in which six bidders competed for five licenses, the auction finished early raising less than one-third the revenue expected, after what many interpreted as predatory behavior that eliminated a bidder (see section 16.5.2 and Klemperer 2002b, 2003a). Similarly the Italian 3G (ascending) auction held just three months later, also with six bidders for five licenses, collapsed almost as soon as it had begun amid allegations of collusion and with a proportionately similar loss of government revenue (see Klemperer 2002b).[62]

16.5 Common Values

Auctions and bidding processes are often used precisely because different participants have different, and poor, information—auctions are famously good at efficiently aggregating and using dispersed information, while with perfect information using posted prices is more straightforward. But if competitors have information or opinions about the value of winning a contract or prize that would be useful to other competitors, this creates "common values" issues. In particular, a bidder wins the prize only when it has very optimistic information about its value (indeed in symmetric equilibrium it wins the prize only when it has the highest signal)—this is the "winner's curse." Failure to take into account the bad news about others' signals that comes with any victory would lead to the winner paying more, on average, than the prize is worth. So bidders adjust their bids downwards (in either sealed-bid or ascending auctions) to allow for the winner's curse.

It is sometimes argued that "winner's curse" issues reduce competition problems. However, while they may perhaps mitigate the problems of collusion (this is unclear; see below), they certainly do not negate them. Indeed, overall, the existence of common values is probably an argument for *stronger* rather than weaker competition policy.

Furthermore in many cases it is hard to distinguish whether or not an auction or market is common or private values—that is, from a given bidder's perspective does other bidders' private information relate to others' valuations, or also to this bidder's actual valuation?[63] Moreover, even if the situation is truly common values, do bidders bid as if others' information matters to them, or do they bid as if there were private values? If the latter, then any common value effects are even less important.

16.5.1   Common Values and Collusion

It is well understood that the more competitors a bidder faces, the greater is the winner's curse, (i.e., the worse is the news from winning) and the more the bidder must adjust his bid to account for the curse. So, if a subset of bidders colludes, it faces a lesser curse from winning, and therefore, it is argued, it may bid more aggressively and raise bid-taker surplus. So, it is contended, bid-takers *gain* from bidders' collusion! But although bids are adjusted less for the winner's curse, this effect is offset both by the reduced winner's curse, and by the standard loss-of-competition effects; ceteris paribus (absent winner's curse effects), bidders with fewer competitors bid less aggressively, and even if they bid equally aggressively, the winning bid among fewer bidders is, on average, less aggressive. While the details of functional forms are crucial, the simplest examples suggest mergers with common values are as anticompetitive as mergers with private values:[64]

First, consider the "maximum game" introduced by Bulow and Klemperer (2002) in which each bidder, i, initially receives a signal, t_i, and the actual common value, v, of the single prize is the maximum of these signals, that is, $v = \max_i\{t_i\}$.[65] In the symmetric equilibrium of an ascending auction, each bidder drops out at his own signal. After any mergers, a merged entity behaves as if it had a signal equal to the maximum of all its signals. Clearly, revenue is unaltered unless the bidders with the two highest signals happened to merge in which case revenue falls to equal the highest signal not held by the winner. Note that the results are *identical* to those of a pure private-value model in which each bidder's actual value is t_i, and a merged entity's actual value is the maximum of the values held by its constituents.[66]

A second example is provided by the "wallet game" introduced by Bulow and Klemperer (1997) and Klemperer (1998), in which the actual common value of the single prize is the sum of all the signals, that is, $v = \sum_i t_i$. Here too, it is very easy to show that mergers that result in two firms each holding half the signals reduce bid-taker surplus,[67] and Mares and Shor (2004) extend this to show that any sequence of mergers that results in a symmetric industry structure reduces bid-taker surplus.[68] These results hold for both ascending and sealed-bid auctions.[69] Analyzing mergers that yield asymmetric industry structures is much harder, but those results that are available suggest that here too mergers reduce bid-taker surplus with common values, just as with private values.[70]

Of course, all these results contrast with those of Bulow and Klemperer (2002) who show that reducing the number of bidders by simply excluding some of them always raises bid-taker surplus in the "maximum" game, and often does so in the "wallet" game. The crucial difference is that Bulow and Klemperer assume excluding bidders also excludes their private information from being used in the bidding, whereas a consortium (joint) bidder retains and uses all the information of the constituent bidders. In common-value auctions, the bidders' rents reflect the expected difference in information between the winner and the runner up, so if reducing participation excludes particularly valuable private information it can reduce the difference between bidders' information and so increase bid-taker surplus. By contrast, joint bidding hurts the bid-taker if it increases the differences in private information available to different bidders by giving different merged bidders access to more different signals. Indeed the most profitable strategy for an uninformed bid-taker is to exclude all bidders and sell to a completely uninformed bidder who will be willing to bid the full expected value of the prize; a very unprofitable strategy is to allow all the informed bidders to combine, even if you can make them a take-it-or-leave-it offer. Nonetheless it is not surprising that Bulow and Klemperer's (2002) work (and empirical support for it in; e.g., Hong and Shum 2002) has been misinterpreted as suggesting a possible merit of joint bidding in common-value auctions.[71]

Other previous papers also seem to have been misinterpreted as suggesting common values mean joint bidding is less damaging than usual:

Hoffman et al.'s (1991) and Hendricks and Porter's (1992) empirical work emphasizes that joint-bidding in common-value oil-industry auctions allows informed bidders more access to capital, so bid-takers could gain. But with private values or in "ordinary" (nonauction) markets, a joint venture can also be pro-competitive if it relaxes capital constraints, and Hendricks and Porter's evidence suggests joint bidding may also increase bidder rents, just as in ordinary markets, for the usual reduction of competition reasons (Hendricks and Porter 1992, p. 511).

In a similar vein, de Brock and Smith (1983) present a theoretical example in which joint bidding rarely reduces the bid-taker's surplus very much, and for some parameterizations actually increases it. But in their example there are (social) efficiency gains from mergers, since bidders' improved information means oil tracts are developed more efficiently. So, again, this is nothing new. This is very similar to the standard argument that an R&D joint venture that pools information efficiently can both be socially beneficial and can benefit consumers (or benefit bid-takers in a private-values auction). Indeed in de Brock and Smith's example mergers *always* increase bidders' expected profits and, just as in "ordinary" markets, the anticompetitive effect of increased market power can only be out-weighed by the efficiency effects if the industry is sufficiently unconcentrated. (In their examples the bid-taker is always left worse off unless at least ten(!) bidders remain after the merger.)

Perhaps there are greater information-pooling and/or capital-constraint-relaxing bene-fits of mergers in common-value auctions than in private-value auctions or "ordinary" markets, because common-value issues are driven by poor and different information and so also firms may face greater risks. On the other hand, in a common-value auc-tion it is a matter of social indifference who wins,[72] whereas in ordinary markets mergers that transfer more output to lower cost firms (as is usually the case) are socially bene-ficial. So, on balance, efficiency benefits of mergers may be more likely in "ordinary" markets.[73]

Some other arguments also suggest joint bidding may be more deleterious in common-value than in private-value auctions: if participants underestimate the common-value effects, or otherwise fail to compensate sufficiently for them, they will lose more from the winner's curse the more bidders there are, so in practice common-value effects may exacer-bate (and certainly not reduce) the costliness to bid-takers of collusion or mergers. Fur-thermore the strategy of incumbents merging to strengthen themselves and prevent the entry of further rivals may be particularly effective in common-value contexts (see the next subsection).[74]

Mares and Shor's (2004) experiments provide further evidence that joint bidding hurts bid-takers in common-value auctions.

Finally, and *crucially*, and far more significant than the issue of joint bidding when some competition remains, is the issue of joint bidding or collusion among *all* bidders. A very real danger is that (just as in private-value contests) the more joint bidding is permitted, the easier it is for industrywide collusion to develop.

In sum, while these issues are still not well understood, the current evidence is that joint bidding is unlikely to be much more benign in common-value auctions than in private-value auctions or in "ordinary" markets.

16.5.2 Common Values and Predation

With "almost common values," that is, in common-value cases in which one bidder is slightly stronger than the other(s), the disadvantages of weaker bidders in ascending auc-tions that I discussed in section 16.4.3 are exacerbated by the winner's curse effects.

The reason is that winning against a bidder whose value of winning is greater than yours is even worse news than usual about the opponent's valuation of the prize; so you must bid extra cautiously. And because he knows you are being extra cautious, beating you is not very bad news for him about your valuation; so he need not worry much about the win-ner's curse and can bid more aggressively than if you and he were symmetrically placed. So the effect is self reinforcing—because the weak bidder faces a very severe winner's curse and is bidding extra cautiously, the advantaged bidder faces very little winner's curse and is bidding extra aggressively. This substantially reduces bid-taker surplus even if entry to the auction is unaffected. Moreover, since the weaker bidder's potential profits from bidding are so low, it may also be discouraged from even entering, further hurting the bid-taker.

Thus antitrust policy must be more careful than usual to protect against actions that magnify weaker bidders' disadvantages in ascending auctions. Such actions may include mergers. For example, prior to the Netherlands 3G auction in 2000 of five licenses (which, for good technological and antitrust reasons, were indivisible and had each to be won by a different firm), there were four strong incumbent 2G operators and one weaker incumbent 2G operator (Ben). There were also a number of potential entrants, of whom Deutsche Telekom (DT) was particularly strong since it was both financially unconstrained and had potential synergies with its substantial operations in neighboring Germany. Since even the weak incumbent had some advantages, based on past sunk investments in technology, base stations, customer loyalty and brand-name recognition, there might have been a competitive auction if Ben and DT had bid independently. But after Ben merged with DT it seemed very clear who the five winners would be, and only one of the remaining potential entrants bothered to bid.[75] Furthermore that remaining entrant only bid weakly, and gave up altogether after being discouraged by further actions that some argued were predatory and deserved government investigation. The result was a disaster for the bid-taker (the Netherlands' government), which earned less than one-third of the revenue that a well-managed process could have yielded.

The Netherlands' ascending auction design would have made it unattractive to potential entrants even absent the special common-value considerations. But the common-value issues seem to have exacerbated this problem, and they also greatly increased the disadvantages faced by the one new entrant who did bid.[76] (See Klemperer 2002b, 2003a, for further details.)

Although the most obvious advantage one bidder might have over another is a higher valuation for the prize, other possible advantages include a commitment to maintain a reputation for aggressive bidding (Bikhchandani 1988), or a small ownership stake, or "toehold," in the prize being competed for (which provides an incentive to push the price up further than otherwise; see Bulow, Huang, and Klemperer 1999). Klemperer (1998) gives details and examples.[77]

The UK Monopolies and Mergers Commission took this last issue very seriously when it blocked BSkyB (the leading UK satellite TV company) from acquiring Manchester United (then Europe's leading football club) in 1999.[78] The concern was that Manchester United received 7 percent of the Premiership's TV revenues that were sold as a bundle in an ascending auction. Acquiring this 7 percent "toehold" in the prize would have made BSkyB most likely to win the auction, and ownership of the football TV rights would have reinforced BSkyB's market power in the pay-TV market.[79]

One argument against the Commission's decision was that if bidders behaved as if the auction was private values, the auction would have been much less affected because the logic given at the beginning of the subsection only fully applies if participants understand it and believe it. With private values, or if bidders behave as if there are private values, a small advantage of the right kind may still deter entry, but otherwise may not much affect the auction, by contrast with the common-values case, in which not only is entry even more likely to be deterred, but a small advantage creates a much less competitive auction. However, the Commission took the view that while bidder behavior might not be as extreme as in the theoretical models, the common-values aspect would make BSkyB's rivals at least somewhat more cautious.[80] Sadly, the prominence given to my papers, Klemperer (1998), and Bulow, Huang, and Klemperer (1999), in the debate, probably made it more likely that bidders would behave according to the theory. Similarly other advantaged firms have made a point of emphasizing the common-values theory—and their own belief in it. For example, Pacific Telephone paid an auction theorist[81] to give seminars explaining the "winner's curse" at industry gatherings prior to a US mobile phone license auction in which it was the advantaged incumbent.[82]

Another argument against the Commission's decision was that the TV rights did not need to be sold using an ascending auction, and "toehold" problems are unlikely to be significant in, for example, a sealed-bid auction: I will address this argument in the next section.[83]

16.6   Bid-Taker Power

An important feature of auctions and bidding processes is that the bid-taker often has far more control over the competitive process than an ordinary consumer does. Skillful use of the bid-taker's monopsonistic power to design and run the contest can mitigate the competition problems.[84]

However, there are also many constraints and limitations on bid-takers' power. Although good auction design may be able to overcome these problems in principle, regulators must be careful not to take too rosy a view of what bid-takers can realistically achieve in practice. Indeed, where bidders can lobby against or otherwise subvert the rules and/or the bid-taker cannot precommit his future behavior, the bid-taker's "power" can actually work against him and aggravate the competitive problems.

16.6.1   Tailoring the Rules

Sealed-Bid Auctions   It will be apparent from the previous discussion that many problems of entry deterrence, predation, and collusion can be avoided by choosing sealed-bid rather than ascending auction rules. Sealed-bid auctions may also be more profitable for bid-takers even absent these problems, especially when bidders' risk-aversion is important, as is likely in a large "winner-take-all" "bet-your-company" contest (i.e., when conditions 1 and 2 of an ideal "bidding market" are satisfied). See, especially, sections 16.4.3 through 16.4.5 and 16.5.2 above, and Klemperer (1999a, 2002a) for more details.

Anglo-Dutch Auctions Although a sealed-bid auction has many advantages, it is often socially less efficient than an ascending auction (see section 16.4.2). A solution to the dilemma of choosing between the ascending (often called "English") and sealed-bid (or "Dutch") forms is to combine the two in a hybrid, the "Anglo-Dutch," which often captures the best features of both, and was first described and proposed in Klemperer (1998). Assuming, for simplicity, a single object is to be auctioned, the auctioneer begins by running an ascending auction in which price is raised continuously until all but two bidders have dropped out. These two bidders are then each required to make a final sealed-bid offer that is not lower than the current asking price, and the winner pays his bid.[85]

Among its other advantages, the Anglo-Dutch auction encourages entry and discourages collusion (just like a sealed bid auction) but is more likely to sell to the highest valuer than a pure sealed-bid auction, both because it directly reduces the numbers allowed into the sealed-bid stage and also because the two finalists can learn something about each other's and the remaining bidders' perceptions of the object's value from behavior during the ascending stage. See Klemperer (1998, 2002a) for a fuller discussion of the Anglo-Dutch auction's advantages.

It was first developed for practical use in the design of the UK 3G auction where it was proposed to use it to encourage entry in the event only four licences were available for sale, since the UK industry had exactly four strong incumbent operators. There is evidence that it might have been successful in this, but in the event a fifth license became available for sale so it was no longer appropriate to use it (see Binmore and Klemperer 2002). However, formal Anglo-Dutch procedures have subsequently been used very successfully in auctions of electricity (e.g., see Woo et al. 2004), automobile components, and real estate (Moreland 2004).[86]

Fine-tuning Ascending Auctions An alternative approach is to try to make the ascending auction more robust. For example, requiring bids to be "round" numbers, prespecifying the exact increments, and making bids anonymous, make it harder to use bids to signal other buyers.[87] Aggregating lots into larger packages makes it harder for bidders to "divide the spoils," and keeping secret the number of bidders remaining also makes collusion harder (Cramton and Schwartz 2000; Salant 2000). But these measures do not eliminate the risks of collusion, and do very little to mitigate the discouraging effect of ascending auctions on entry. Moreover bidders can often adapt their behavior to overcome such minor "fixes" faster than bid-takers can develop new fixes (see also section 16.6.2).

Other New Procedures There has recently been enormous interest in designing new auction procedures, though there is a paucity of theory about how effective many of them are—especially the multi-unit ones.[88] Of particular note for resolving antitrust concerns is

Ausubel's (2004) popularization of a modification of the multi-unit ascending auction that creates a dynamic version of the Vickrey auction and so eliminates classical "unilateral effects," that is, it eliminates bidders' incentives to scale back their demands (or supplies) in order to end the auction quickly at an uncompetitive price.[89] However, this auction can reduce bid-taker surplus so may not fit most regulators' objectives.[90] Furthermore its relative complexity both makes it difficult to explain, and means that bidding may be affected less in practice than in theory (some experiments suggest this). Perhaps for these reasons, I am not aware of it having been applied in practice. In practical auction design, simplicity is crucial, and it is much easier to "sell" designs that are similar to well-known institutions. (For example, the adoption of the Anglo-Dutch auction for practical use has been helped by describing it as a formalization of the informal process that is traditionally used to sell many houses.[91])

Secrecy   An important aspect of sealed-bid auction rules is whether or not bids are secret. Just as in "ordinary" markets, keeping bids secret makes it harder for bidders to coordinate their activities and makes defection from a collusive agreement harder to observe and therefore more attractive. So secrecy fights collusion between bidders. Unfortunately, secrecy may also facilitate collusion between the bid-taker and one or more bidders,[92] and the fear of this may also sometimes discourage entry.

Allowing each bidder to submit multiple sealed bids over a period of time can help frustrate collusion by making it harder for bidders to monitor each other, and keeping the number and identities of bidders secret can also make an auction more competitive (especially if bidders are risk averse) and encourage entry.[93]

Reserve Prices, etc.   A very powerful use of the bid-taker's monopoly (or monopsony) position is in setting a reserve price. Of course, it must be credible that the bid-taker will stick to the announced reserve (see section 16.6.2).

In multi-unit auctions, the bid-taker may wish to make the quantity traded uncertain and/or depend on the price to eliminate "implicitly collusive" equilibria of the kind described in section 16.4.5 (e.g., see Klemperer and Meyer 1989; Kremer and Nyborg 2000; Li Calzi and Pavan 2005; McAdams 2001).

Discrimination   Discriminating between bidders by setting different reserve prices, or by giving bidding credits to particular bidders or particular classes of bidders, corresponds exactly to price discrimination in ordinary markets in forcing stronger bidders to bid more aggressively (see Bulow and Roberts 1989). It can also encourage the entry of weaker bidders into the auction.[94]

Sometimes it is possible to pay bidders to enter an auction; for example, firms' bid-preparation costs can be reimbursed,[95] or "white knights" can be offered options to enter a takeover battle against an advantaged bidder.

Where awarding a contract means evaluating multiple criteria, for example, price and quality, it may be possible to induce more competitive bidding by precommitting to underweight or ignore one criterion. An illustration of this is that part of the power of a buying group (e.g., a hospital) may be that the average preference of their members (e.g., doctors and nurses) is closer to the average of different brands than is the preference of an individual member. Central procurement from a single vendor may therefore achieve a better price (Farrell and Klemperer 2000).

Bundling and Packaging   Another reason why procuring from a single vendor may be desirable is that it takes advantage of bidder's risk aversion. By making a contract larger, it may be possible to turn it into a "must-win" for one or more bidders, who will then bid more competitively.[96] Bundling can also prevent both unilateral and coordinated effects (e.g., see sections 16.3.2, 16.3.3, 16.4.4, and 16.4.5), by making it impossible for bidders to "divide the pie" among themselves. On the other hand, committing to divide a prize among multiple winners can sometimes attract entry of weaker bidders, and may also induce more competitive bidding by reducing winner's curses.[97]

Bundling and packaging can often reduce inefficiency when complementary goods or contracts are auctioned—in the absence of bundling, some bidders may end up stuck with objects that are worth very little to them because they failed to win complementary objects (the "exposure" problem), while other bidders may fail to bid at all (or quit an ascending auction early) in fear of this.

On the other hand, bundling can also increase inefficiency while raising bid-taker surplus, in exactly the same way that bundling products, or offering nonlinear pricing and quantity discounts, can raise an "ordinary" monopolist's profits at the same time as lowering social surplus. The antitrust issues parallel issues of monopoly bundling and exclusion in "ordinary" markets.

Bundling and packaging is especially critical when an auction creates a new market (e.g., as the 3G spectrum auctions created the 3G mobile phone markets). Allowing the industry structure to be determined in the auction (e.g., by selling many small blocks of spectrum, but allowing each firm to win multiple blocks) has the advantage that the outcome depends on bidders' private information, but the disadvantage that bidders' objectives are not the social objectives. So it may be better to determine the industry structure in advance (e.g., by fixing the number and sizes of licenses for sale, and allowing firms to win at most one each). The choice between these approaches is a topic of active research (e.g., see Hoppe, Jehiel, and Moldovanu 2006), but it is not yet easy to make many general statements.

Controlling Resale   Resale can render both discrimination and bundling ineffective, so in the simplest models with a fixed number of bidders who know their own current and future values, a bid-taker wants to prevent resale—exactly as a price-discriminating monopolist in an "ordinary" market needs to prevent resale. However, the possibility of resale can also give arbitrageurs an incentive to participate in the auction (which increases its competitiveness),[98] and resale also allows bidders to respond to new information about their valuations of the assets.[99] So the effects on an auction of the knowledge that resale will subsequently be permitted are complex. A natural instinct is that it is likely to be broadly efficient (even though it will not always maximize bid-taker surplus) to permit the resale of assets such as licences in the same way, and subject to similar rules, as mergers of firms. However, more research is needed to confirm or refute this.

Antitrust Rules   Finally, as must by now be clear, where bid-takers have the power (e.g., when they are governments), it is important for them to ensure normal antitrust rules apply (see section 16.7).

16.6.2   Constraints on Bid-Taker Power

Although in theory bid-takers have many instruments available to them, they also face important constraints including governmental or supragovernmental legislation or procedures, internal-organizational issues, bidders' countervailing tactics, and the difficulty of committing their own future behavior. Bid-takers that are government agencies are often especially severely constrained.

For example, a prohibition on resale may be hard to enforce, so strategies involving discriminating between bidders and/or bundling may be ineffective.[100] Moreover State Aid (and other) legislation generally prevents European governments from explicitly discriminating between bidders (e.g., using targeted bidding credits), and while similar ends can often be achieved using technically neutral rules, (e.g., placing more weight on criteria that favor the preferred bidder(s)) this is usually less efficient. For example, in the UK 3G auction we were advised that bidding credits to encourage entry were not permissible. However, choosing auction rules that favored entry, specifically an Anglo-Dutch auction, was possible. So was dividing the available spectrum into a large enough number of licenses that one would have to be won by an entrant—in other words, running a "split award" auction (in fact broader competition policy reasons dictated this choice anyway, once it became clear it was technically feasible).[101]

UK government legislation imposed other constraints on the 3G auction design that could only have been removed by parliamentary legislation—an option that was not favored by Ministers for whom parliamentary time is a scarce resource; fortunately further legislation turned out to be unnecessary in this case. (See Binmore and Klemperer 2002.)[102]

Political constraints are much broader than purely legal ones. For example, when the UK Competition Commission ruled on the proposed merger of private prison operators Falck and Wackenhut,[103] an important issue was whether the UK Prison Service could realistically use its monopsony power to eliminate competitive problems—for example, the political imperatives of privatization limited the scope to threaten public provision as an alternative to private procurement.

Internal-organizational issues can importantly affect behavior in both the public and the private sector, since decision-makers' incentives are rarely perfectly aligned with their organization's. For example, managers may be much more interested in obtaining short-term cost savings than in avoiding "lock-in" problems developing on follow-on contracts after they have moved on from their current jobs—it is very hard to structure incentives to overcome this problem. Decentralized decision-making also creates severe problems. The drug-purchasing decisions made by UK hospitals, for example, effectively determine many "follow-on" drug purchases in the community—which are paid for by different parts of the National Health Service. It seems naïve to argue that because the NHS could in principle centralize its drug procurement, the competition authorities should not be concerned about the kind of predatory behavior alleged in the NAPP case:[104] effective competition policy must sometimes take the larger organizational structure of bid-takers as given—just as it must often accept the current industrial structure.

Another constraint on bid-takers is that auction designs (especially government ones) are often susceptible to lobbying. In this context the bid-taker's ability to set and amend the rules can be a liability. I have described elsewhere how the Hong Kong 3G auction designers found their auction publicly vilified as the "dark auction" and were forced to make a superficially small change to the rules that vitiated the point of the design and had disastrous consequences (Klemperer 2003a). Industry lobbying also seems to have been effective in damaging the Netherlands 3G sales process—it is clear that the Netherlands' government's choice of auction design was a very poor one for it, but a very profitable one for the incumbent operators (see section 16.5.2).[105]

The UK design team had a happier experience when proposing two alternative similar designs meant that lobbyists for the incumbent operators (who hated both designs) concentrated much of their energy on the choice between them. Perhaps as a result, and even though (it is rumored) they spent considerably more money in a few weeks lobbying against the designs than the UK government spent on economic advice, modeling, and testing, over the whole two and a half year process, our proposal that (either) one of the designs would be used survived their onslaught. (We graciously acceded to the lobbyists' choice between the two designs—as we anticipated, they preferred the same design that we did.) It was unsurprising that the incumbents spent so much money on lobbying, since a design that was different from either of the two we proposed could easily have saved them fifteen billion pounds.

Bidders are powerful in other ways too. For example, they may be able to subvert an auction if the bid-taker cannot commit to keeping information about bids secret. For example, a concern about the proposed BSkyB/Manchester United combination discussed above (section 16.5.2) was that the risk of information leaking through Manchester United to BSkyB would leave the Premier League (of which Manchester United is one member) unable to negotiate effectively with broadcasters.

Even bigger problems can arise if bidders refuse to accept the outcome of an auction, and the bid-taker cannot precommit to sticking to it (perhaps because shareholders, or more senior managers, or political masters cannot be precommitted, or because of legal constraints). As discussed above (section 16.4.1) this turns a "sealed-bid" auction into an ascending auction.[106] Thus, for example, although as I discussed in section 16.5.2 the Premier League could in principle have alleviated any "toehold" problems by using a sealed-bid auction, the Monopolies and Mergers Commission took the view that the Premier League would be unable to stop the sales process degenerating into an ascending auction if that were in BSkyB's interest. This would be especially true after a BSkyB/Manchester United combination, since Manchester United could then help undermine the bidding process,[107] but the Commission noted that even on previous occasions, when no such combination existed, "Although the sale of Premier League rights ... had the appearance of a sealed-bid auction, the reality was rather different."[108]

16.7   Other Antitrust Issues

Efficiencies in Mergers   In "ordinary" markets mergers often generate efficiencies through the transfer of more of the industry's output to a lower-cost firm, even if the merger does not reduce the component businesses' costs. In a "winner-take-all" market efficiencies, if any, are of a different kind; a merger increases efficiency only if it increases the chance of the most efficient bidder winning. So, for example, in a private-values ascending auction there are no social efficiencies from merging, and in other kinds of auctions any merger that makes a previously symmetric industry asymmetric usually reduces efficiency.[109]

Merger Simulation   Just as there is now a significant literature on simulation of the unilateral effects of mergers in "ordinary" markets, so there is a subliterature on simulating unilateral effects when prices are set in auctions (looking at how the static Nash equilibrium of a market is altered by a merger); see Werden and Froeb (chapter 2 in this volume).

Detecting Collusion   On the one hand detecting collusion in auctions is potentially problematic, because of the low quality of information that is often available—often, the reason an auction rather than a more traditional posted-price process is used is precisely because bid-takers have poor information, and bidders have significant private information, about costs and valuations, perhaps for an idiosyncratic transaction. On the other hand, there is often extremely good data about all bids and, especially when many similar contracts are auctioned, it is possible to test whether suspected colluders behave similarly to assumed-competitive firms and, more generally, whether firm behavior better fits a competitive or collusive model.[110] The literature on the econometrics of detecting collusion in auction markets is ably summarized in Harrington (chapter 6 in this volume.[111]

Enforcement   A main theme of this chapter (and of Klemperer 2002a) is that the key antitrust challenge is simply to recognize that the particular method of price-formation in auctions and bidding processes does not affect the fundamental principles of antitrust. Historically antitrust agencies have largely failed to grasp this. Bidders have openly taken actions in auctions that would never have been regarded as acceptable in "ordinary" markets.

For example, regulators did not pursue the apparent use of bids in some of the early US mobile-phone license auctions to signal to rivals in the manner illustrated in section 16.4.4. (One problem is persuading courts that observed bidding is necessarily anticompetitive signaling; usually *some* competitive story can be concocted.) Similarly statements that would be classed as predatory in "ordinary" markets passed unchallenged, and the ARCO vice president who originally encouraged his staff to coin the evocative term, the "winner's curse," and discuss it at industry gatherings and so persuade competitors to bid less aggressively, actually described his strategy as "legalized collusion".[112] Collusion in takeover battles for companies is legal in the United States. However, the US Department of Justice did successfully pursue a case of using bids to signal in a more recent spectrum auction,[113] and the US competition authorities are arguably more sophisticated in their treatment of bidding markets than sometimes seems to be the case elsewhere in the world.

European antitrust has been even more feeble than in the United States. Regulators have tolerated a range of explicit collusive and predatory statements about auctions that would surely be unacceptable if made about a "normal" economic market,[114] and accepted joint-bidding agreements that are, in effect, open collusion.[115] It may be that the antitrust climate for auctions has toughened a little: T-Mobil was willing to explicitly confirm the way its rival and it had used bids as signals to co-ordinate a rapid end to a German spectrum auction in 1999, but the same firm (and its competitors) refused to confirm officially that they were signaling to rivals when apparently similar behavior was observed in the German 3G spectrum auction a year later.[116] However, European regulators have shown little appetite for pursuing such matters,[117] and often persist in treating auction markets more laxly than "ordinary" economic markets. The European Commission's treatment of some recent bidding-market cases suggests some improvement in the level of its analysis. But Europe still has a long way to go in its handling of auctions and bidding processes.

16.8 Conclusion

Discussions of "bidding markets" often confuse details of the price formation process (whether or not there is an auction or bidding system) with deeper structural features of the market. While these structural features are often associated with auction processes, they need not be. Furthermore, while these structural features would—if they obtained— lead to very optimistic conclusions about the welfare consequences of the markets, this is nothing new. And if—as is common—they do not apply, similar competition problems arise in auction markets as in "ordinary" economic markets, and for similar reasons.

Moreover, even where behavior in auctions is a little different, or more extreme, than in an "ordinary market"—in particular, in some "ascending auction" cases—these differences can usually be understood in terms of the standard principles of antitrust.

In short, the term "bidding market" as it is widely used in antitrust seems unhelpful or misleading.

Auctions and bidding processes do have special features, including their special price-formation processes, common-values behavior, and bid-taker power. However, the significance of some of these features has been greatly overemphasized, while others imply a need for stricter rather than more lenient antitrust policy.

Notes

This chapter was circulated under the title "Bidding Markets" by the UK Competition Commission as the first in its series of *Occasional Papers* in June 2005, but the views expressed are personal and should not be attributed to the Commission or to any past or present individual Member other than myself. I had neither any advisory nor any decision-making role in any of the Commission's cases discussed below. Furthermore, although some observers thought some of the behavior described below warranted regulatory investigation, I do not intend to suggest that any of it violates any applicable rules or laws. I am very grateful to all the consultants, academics, and regulators, who helped and advised me on it. Special thanks are due to Claes Bengtsson, Paolo Buccirossi, John Davies, Giulio Federico, Paul Geroski, Christian Kobaldt, Daniel Marszalec, Marco Pagnozzi, David Reitman, Amanda Rowlatt, Max Tse, and Mark Williams.

1. See *Auctions: Theory and Practice*, Klemperer (2004). Chapter 1 is an introduction to the theory of auctions. See also Klemperer (2000).

2. This has been argued in at least five cases before the UK Competition Commission in the last year.

3. The UK Office of Fair Trading has identified bidding markets in about one-quarter of the merger cases it has handled since it started publishing decisions in 2000.

4. It is expressed almost this extremely in some consultants' submissions to the competition authorities.

5. Of course, none of my academic colleagues would dream of expressing this statement without hedging it around with many qualifications; the danger is that the qualifications get lost as the ideas enter the policy arena.

6. This is the fallacy that is least easy to pin on any one group. But I have heard it more often in debates about public policy (albeit from policy-makers pushing for less regulation) than either from advocates in specific cases, or in more academic forums. Perhaps it should be called the "*de*regulator's fallacy." Certainly, as will become clear, I exempt my colleagues at the UK Competition Commission from this error.

7. The UK 3G auction (which Ken Binmore and I designed) overcame challenges of most of these kinds, but that auction design process lasted over two years and was for an auction worth billions of pounds (see Binmore and Klemperer 2002).

8. I will use the term "market" in an informal economic sense. I am not intending to delimit formal antitrust markets. See note 23.

9. Patterson and Shapiro have quoted the Commission's statement from Pirelli/BICC merger (European Commission, 2000). Shapiro had left his position as Chief Economist at the US Department of Justice at the time of writing.

10. Or quantity bought, if the contestants are potential buyers. Whether the bidders are suppliers competing to sell, or purchasers competing to buy, makes no difference to the economic analysis.

11. It fits even more closely with parties' arguments I have seen (but not accepted) at the UK Competition Commission that, for example, "in a pure bidding market, the obstacles to switching from one supplier to another are low, and every tender is a new contest to be won solely on the merits of the bid." In publicly available testimony in another case (in which I was not involved) before the Competition Commission, Arcelor said "the supply of steel sheet piling in the UK has ... the characteristics of a 'bidding market' [that] there are no switching costs be-

tween piling from different manufacturers; and most orders are tendered for, project-by-project so that, in consequence, market shares in this case do not offer any significant indication of market power." See UK Competition Commission (2005, para 6.48). US sources often describe a "bidding market" as a "'$1/n$' market" in which "all firms are equal" with an implicit or explicit assumption that firms have no capacity constraints. In a similar spirit, Owen (2004) writes "A bidding market is one in which the competitive significance of each firm, . . . , is not correlated with its past success and not limited by its current capacity."

12. Typical parties' arguments I have seen (and rejected) at the UK Competition Commission include that "because a market is a bidding market it is easy for non-incumbents to win contracts—most or all sales could easily be lost to a competitor in the next round—so existing market shares are of little relevance." For example, in publicly available testimony in a case (in which I had no involvement) before the Competition Commission, Dräger submitted that "The existence of a bidding market makes the relevance of historic market shares questionable . . . The sales process allows competitors to showcase their products on an equal footing with established players. . . . Purchases are made by tender process and as such all potential competitors have the chance to offer a contract to supply. . . ." See UK Competition Commission (2004b).

13. For example, Lexecon (2003) writes . . . "In many industries, firms purchase services or products through a bidding system. . . . The "all or nothing" characteristic of such markets implies . . . in particular when the size of the tender is high relative to the size of the bidder and when new tenders are infrequent . . . ," thus combining (5) with statements with the flavor of (1), (2), and (3), respectively.

14. The other assumptions can also depend on the details of price formation. For example, as in the theory of contestability, (4*) may partly depend on incumbents' prices responding only slowly to new entry.

15. In one recently completed case at the UK Competition Commission, one of the merging parties submitted that "the CLSM/MPR and MPLSM sectors should be characterized as bidding markets. As a result a competition assessment based on the analysis of market shares is not useful for assessing the level of competition in these markets, as market shares are not indicative of market power . . . any increase of share resulting from the merger is irrelevant due to the existence of the bidding market." See UK Competition Commission (2004a).

Other recent submissions to competition authorities include "in bidding markets, historical market share conveys no market power whatsoever," and "economists define a bidding market as one in which all suppliers have an incentive to bid at competitive levels." And, as of Spring 2005, there seems to be no diminution of submissions of this kind to either the European Commission or other European regulatory agencies—perhaps even the opposite—according to officials of those agencies I have talked to.

The UK Office of Fair Trading (2004b) is correct to write in its current guideline on the assessment of market power "if competition at the bidding stage is effective, . . . currently higher market share would not necessarily reflect market power." The European Commission (2002) was treading more dangerous ground when it wrote that "in bidding markets, market shares may not be informative of the likely competitive impact of a merger"— the problem of course comes when the OFT's qualifying statement, or the EC's "may," is omitted.

16. That is, there is still a smooth trade-off between price and the bid-taker's *expected* utility.

17. A sufficiently large bid-taker may be able to strategically use its "buyer power" to attract a new entrant, even if that entrant is slightly disadvantaged or there are sunk-costs of entry, for example, by subsidizing the entrant's costs—but see section 16.6's discussion of the constraints on bid-taker power.

18. There are other services in which airlines simply compete to offer the lowest fare, and Priceline is also famous for a "name your price" service.

19. Considering the retail and auction segments as different, or as different markets, *might* make sense if the different sales routes accessed different customers, but *not* because of any difference in the price-formation process.

20. As noted above, even if there is only one or a small number of passengers on a particular route, a slight increase in fare slightly reduces the probability of making a sale.

21. I am reluctant to engage in further semantic issues by defining "bidding systems" or "bidding processes," but their important characteristic is "customer-by-customer pricing" by contrast with an ordinary retail market in which a seller makes the *same* offer to *many* buyers. That is, when "bidders" are sellers, each bidder generally treats each buyer separately and so makes a separate offer (or no offer) to each buyer. (Conversely, bidders who are buyers each make a separate offer to any seller they deal with.) The offer may be a price, or may include other dimensions. The offer may be improved, or refined, during the bidding process, perhaps in response to discussions or negotiations with the bid-taker (though a formal definition would probably exclude full-blown one-on-one bargaining in a bilateral monopoly). Assuming bidders are sellers, the buyer may be the final customer, or may (e.g., in an electricity pool) represent several final customers. However, as discussed above, the buyer may split

her purchases between several bidders (contradicting assumption 1), may be one of many buyers (contradicting 2) and may have substantial costs of switching sellers (contradicting 3), and there may be significant costs of developing the capability to approach her with a credible bid (contradicting 4*).

22. The merger of Murray & Roberts Ltd and The Cementation Company Ltd.—see Competition Tribunal South Africa (2004).

23. The claim that one firm is enough for an optimal outcome is as highly sensitive as usual to (generally implausible) assumptions of speedy, costless, entry.

As I noted above in my discussion of airline-ticket sales, whether or not the detailed process of price formation is an auction is sometimes completely unimportant.

On the other hand, simplistically measured past market shares may reflect market power even less accurately in auction markets than usual. Most obviously, if a "market" consists of only a single winner-take-all contract, even symmetrically placed firms have ex post shares of 0 or 100 percent (and it would be ridiculous to argue all possible mergers are therefore irrelevant). Measures of firms' capabilities and capacities, perhaps summarized by their estimated ex ante probabilities of winning a contest, or average shares over a longer history may be helpful. (Also, if each bidding contest is, technically, a separate antitrust market, then "multi-market contact" effects between these "separate" markets supporting predation or collusion are particularly likely; Bernheim and Whinston 1990.)

24. Arguably the surprise was that there was a second bidder at all.

25. So policy must consider whether observed current rents merely reflect a competitive return on past investments.

26. I am not suggesting that Camelot's behavior was in any way improper or that it contravened any laws or regulations.

27. Lock-in effects have been found to be important in what were claimed to be bidding markets in several recent cases before the UK Competition Commission.

28. In some cases a lock over the market may be jointly held by several firms. (This could perhaps be described as a case of "joint dominance," though the term is usually used in the context of concerns about collusion rather than exclusion.) For example, when in 2000 the Netherlands auctioned five 3G mobile-phone licenses it was very hard for any other bidder to compete with the five incumbent mobile-phone operators in the market, and the only new entrant that dared to bid was swiftly eliminated by what many described as predatory behaviour, so the auction raised less than one-third of what the winners valued the licenses at. (See sections 16.5.2 and 16.6.2 below, and Klemperer 2002b, 2003a for more details; in principle, the government's control of the sales process should have allowed it to mitigate the problems; in practice, it exacerbated them.)

29. Explicit collusion is also common in auction markets. For example, according to McMillan (1991), *two-thirds* of the criminal cases brought by the US Department of Justice's Antitrust Division in 1981 to 1988 involved bid-rigging by construction firms.

30. This feature is not explicitly in the Competition Commission's list, but is implicit in its (and other agencies') Guidelines.

31. There were exceptions. For example, the firms were not all similar, though the *relevant* firms—namely the firms that had flexible capacity (not Nuclear Electric)—arguably were similar.

32. Sweeting (2004) finds that generator behaviour after 1996 was inconsistent with static Nash equilibrium and consistent with tacit collusion, Macatangay (2002) finds evidence of coordinated bidding patterns in 1996–97, and Evans and Green (2003) also seems to support suspicions about coordinated effects. Similar suspicions have been voiced about the Spanish electricity market. See, for example, Fabra and Toro (2005).

33. Tapes of telephone conversations obtained in the FBI's investigation of Enron show the extreme way in which that company unilaterally exercised market power to raise prices, including arranging to shut down a power plant supplying energy to California on January 17, 2001, when blackouts affected up to a half million consumers (see Egan 2005).

More generally, "The many investigations of the causes of the California Electricity Crisis currently underway have not uncovered evidence that suggests suppliers coordinated their actions to raise prices in California" (Wolak 2003), suggesting that the significant market power effects that many studies have found for California in 2000–2001 were unilateral effects.

34. On the contrary, if there was any response, it seems to have been to try to persuade the largest bidder to reduce its demand further without any recompense. See also Cramton (1995).

35. Auctions with common values are a partial exception; see the discussion of Bulow and Klemperer (2002) in section 16.5.1.

36. See Klemperer (forthcoming c) for further discussion.

37. Of course, this design becomes a *descending* one when the bidders are sellers. In this case the price is lowered until only one bidder remains and that bidder wins the object at the final price bid. For simplicity, I will continue to refer to such an auction as an ascending auction.

38. For example, the government commission's original 2000 decision to award the UK National Lottery to a new-entrant bidder was overturned by a legal challenge from the incumbent which then won the contract after improving the terms of its offer. See section 16.3.1. See also the discussion of the proposed Manchester United/ BSkyB combination in section 16.6.2.

39. For example, in the sale of RJR-Nabisco there were several successive rounds of supposedly final sealed-bids: after the first set of "final" sealed-bids had been opened (and revealed to all), an extension was arranged to allow a bidder time to clarify some details of its offer prior to a second "final" round of sealed-bids; one of the losers in this second round then submitted and made public a further, unsolicited, higher bid to pressure the Board into reopening the sale, and yet more bids then followed as the process degenerated into something more closely resembling an ascending auction (see Burrough and Helyar 1990, pp. 415–16, 479–502).

40. Agents may have little incentive to extend the process, preferring to manage the matching of buyers and sellers than to maximize price on any one transaction (in the UK agents typically receive 1.5 percent of the transaction price and it can be hard to arrange higher powered incentives), or a competing bidder may credibly make a take-it-or-leave-it offer (which seems more common in the real world than the current theoretical literature can easily explain).

41. As a demonstration of this, I have heard of sales in which the winner's final bid exceeded its initial bid, *and* its initial bid exceeded *all* subsequent competitive bids.

42. Interestingly, when reviewing the recent merger between Oracle and PeopleSoft, the US Department of Justice and the European Commission came to quite different views on whether the bidding process was best described as an ascending auction or as a sealed-bid auction. It seems the two authorities (which both originally opposed the transaction) had differing views on whether buyers could be believed when they told competing bidders what the other bidder(s) had offered. So the US DOJ (which felt buyers could credibly report bidders' offers) did modeling based on the assumption that sales were ascending auctions, while the European Commission (which felt buyers couldn't do this) looked at studies that modeled the sales processes as sealed-bid auctions. (See European Commission, 2004; *US et al. v. Oracle Corporation.*)

43. In reality the strategic uncertainty induced by a sealed-bid auction means that it may not be efficient even with symmetric bidders. This probably does not affect our argument. Pure common value auctions are an exception, since any allocation is efficient. See section 16.5.

44. In this discussion I assume mergers do not affect the price-formation process.

45. Marshall et al. (1994), Dalkir, Logan, and Masson (2000) and Tschantz, Crooke, and Froeb (2000) make detailed comparisons of the price effects of mergers in sealed-bid and ascending auctions, assuming particular functional forms for distributions of valuations. However, the results are sensitive to the functional forms assumed. Changing the functional forms can reverse the relative magnitudes of the price effects of mergers in sealed-bid and ascending auctions. So the suggestion (Froeb and Shor 2005) that we use the magnitude of the effect in an ascending auction as an upper bound for the magnitude of the effect in a sealed-bid auction may be risky.

46. But sealed-bid auctions may discourage potential bidders who have only small amounts to trade, since such bidders need better information about their rivals to bid intelligently than they would need in ascending or uniform-price auctions, and the costs of obtaining good information might not be worth their paying (see Klemperer 2002a).

47. As in, for example, a Cournot market, or a Bertrand market with heterogeneous consumers without price discrimination.

48. More generally, Bulow and Klemperer (1996, 2007) show the importance for a bid-taker of attracting as many bidders as possible.

49. For example, governments are often lobbied heavily for ascending auction processes for this reason. The 2001 Hong Kong 3G auction is just one example in which the government disastrously gave in to this lobbying (see section 16.6.2).

Note that it also follows that the US Robinson-Patman Act, which outlaws price discrimination where this "reduces competition," and is generally thought to be intended to protect weaker competitors, is less well designed for this purpose than often assumed. The exemption in the Act that allows a firm (e.g., a large firm or an incumbent) that has previously made sales at a higher price to discount its price to meet the price of a competitor (e.g., a small firm or new entrant) but not to beat the competitor's price, essentially permits the large firm to compete in an ascending auction contest, but would rule out its participation in a sealed-bid contest (or at least put the large firm in a very weak position since it could not take the risk of beating its rival by more than a trivial margin). If the Act really wished to encourage smaller firms, it should instead make *ascending* auctions hard for larger firms to participate in, but encourage "sealed-bid" sales processes that favor weaker firms.

50. For another example of bidders using their bids to signal to each other see note 54.

51. It might still have been possible for US West to signal the same message by overbidding on the Iowa licenses whenever McLeod bid on Rochester. But it would certainly have been harder for US West to be confident its message was understood; perhaps McLeod would have pretended not to understand and, without common knowledge that its message was understood, US West might have given up trying to communicate in this way.

52. Note that communication is made harder when firms have incentive to feign at least partial misunderstanding of their rivals. This is often the case (and was certainly the case in the US West/McLeod example discussed above).

53. For example, the kind of price coordination that has been alleged about some concentrated electricity markets might perhaps arise in any repeated single-bid auction, including pay-your-bid and uniform price auctions.
  Fabra (2003) argues that collusion is easier in repeated uniform-price multi-unit auctions than in repeated discriminatory multi-unit auctions. See also note 61.

54. Another favorite example of bidders' ability to "collude" in a "one-off" ascending auction was provided by the 1999 German DCS-1800 auction: ten blocks of spectrum were sold, with the rule that any new bid on a block had to exceed the previous high bid by at least 10 percent. There were just two credible bidders, the two largest German mobile-phone companies T-Mobil and Mannesman, and Mannesman's first bids were 18.18 million Deutschmarks per megahertz on blocks 1–5 and 20 million Deutschmarks per MHz on blocks 6–10. T-Mobil— who bid even less in the first round—later said "There were no agreements with Mannesman. But [we] interpreted Mannesman's first bid as an offer" (Stuewe 1999, p. 13). The point is that 18.18 plus a 10 percent raise equals 20.00. Clearly, T-Mobil understood that if it bid 20 million Deutschmarks per MHz on blocks 1–5, but did not bid again on blocks 6–10, the two companies would then live and let live with neither company challenging the other on the other's half. Exactly that happened. So the auction closed after just two rounds with each of the bidders acquiring half the blocks for the same low price, which was a small fraction of the valuations that the bidders actually placed on the blocks.

55. And so also mean that simply being in the one-off market is as good as a "long-term commitment," in terms of the checklist of section 16.3.2.

56. At a more formal level, Grimm, Riedel and Wolfstetter (2002) argue that the rules of ascending auctions turn the outcomes of one-shot oligopolistic games that we call "collusive" into noncooperative Nash equilibria of repeated oligopoly games. Grimm et al. demonstrate this point in the context of the 1999 German DCS-1800 auction described in note 54.

57. For example, if two buyers each bid very high prices for less than half the available quantity, but low prices for half or more, then each buyer receives half the quantity at the low price, and both players would be worse off if either player deviated to bid more aggressively for more than half the quantity.

58. Although these "implicitly collusive" equilibria are Nash equilibria of the one-shot game, the problem of finding the collusive outcome is much harder than that of, for example, finding an "ordinary" Cournot-Nash equilibrium, because of the infinite multiplicity of equilibria to choose among here. (See Federico and Rahman 2003 for discussion in the context of electricity markets.)

59. Sade, Schnitzlein, and Zender (2004) have found collusion to be no more common in experimental markets that use uniform-price auctions than those that use discriminatory auctions—in fact they find the contrary.

60. It is often entertaining to hear after an auction what bidders thought they were communicating. I'm not sure I fully believe the southern European bidding team who explained how its bid in a major auction had an 'obvious' interpretation from the Bible, but the horrified reactions of the northern European consultants who had spent considerable effort trying (and failing) to decode the bid during the auction were a treat to behold. Culture matters.

Coordination is particularly problematic when more than one bidder thinks it is, or should be, the leader coordinating the others. See Klemperer (2002d, 2003a).

61. The theoretical literature on collusion in repeated auctions (Blume and Heidhues mimeo 2002; Aoyagi 2003; Skrzypacz and Hopenhayn 2004; McAfee and McMillan 1992) shows how schemes such as bid-rotation (in which firms take turns to submit the winning bid) can achieve collusive outcomes in the absence of side transfers between bidders.

62. The forgone revenue was similar per head of population. The sets of bidders were different in the two auctions, and there is no suggestion that there was any important connection between these auctions (though Klemperer 2002b argues that bidders did learn how to "play the game" better through the course of the European 3G auctions more generally).

On a personal note, it has sometimes been put to me that the investment bankers who advised on the UK 3G auction (which I, together with Ken Binmore, designed) had no useful role. But I believe they performed (at least) a very valuable marketing job in persuading 13 bidders to compete for the five UK licenses. Though some of the bidders seemed unlikely winners even at the time, 13 bidders were enough that neither predation nor collusion was a realistic strategy. (See Binmore and Klemperer 2002.)

63. It is often difficult to distinguish private values from common values even based on ex post bidding data. See, for example, Laffont and Vuong (1996) and Pinkse and Tan (2005). However, there are some econometric tests, see, for example, Armantier (2002), Athey and Haile (2002), Haile, Hong, and Shum (2004), Hendricks, Pinkse, and Porter (2003), and Paarsch (1992; see also Bulow and Klemperer 2002 for some relevant theory), and some empirical literature distinguishes the different contexts. For example, Hendricks, Pinkse, and Porter provide evidence that oil and gas leases (where rivals have private information about yields) are mostly common value assets. Construction contracts (where rivals have private information about costs) are also typically thought to be largely common values. Purchases for resale may also have large common-value components.

64. Hendricks, Porter, and Tan (2003) show that joint-bidding consortia are less likely to be formed in common-values contests, since bidders who think they have good information may prefer to bid noncooperatively than to share their possible gains with less-informed rivals. A positive interpretation of this result is that any consortium is likely to reflect strong efficiency benefits. A negative interpretation is that it may have been formed for its entry-deterring effects (see below and section 16.5.2; Hendricks et al. ignore the effects of joint-bidding on further entry). A neutral interpretation is that if we do observe a consortium, the auction is more likely to be private values than common values.

65. This model, or an approximation to it, may be appropriate when bidding for mineral rights, if a positive signal "finding gold" makes all other prospecting results irrelevant. Harstad and Bordley (1996) and Parlour and Rajan (2005) present more complex models with very similar properties to the "maximum game."

66. These results extend to sealed-bid auctions for mergers that result in a symmetric industry structure (when bidders are risk-neutral and their information signals are independent), by an elementary application of the revenue equivalence theorem.

67. In the symmetric equilibrium, the last bidder to drop out quits at what the actual value would be, if the actual winner's signal were in fact tied with his own. Thus writing $t_{(i)}$ for the actual ith highest signal, before any mergers obtains the winner's profit as $t_{(1)} - t_{(2)}$ and expected auction revenue as $E[v - (t_{(1)} - t_{(2)})]$. Postmergers, each firm's private information is represented by the sum of its signals and each firm again bids up to what the actual value would be if its opponent were tied with it, so the winning firm's profit is the difference between the sum of its signals and the sum of its opponent's signals. Then, conditional on $t_{(1)}$ and $t_{(2)}$ being held by separate merged firms, let the sums of all the other signals held by these two merged firms be S_1 and S_2, respectively, so expected seller revenue is $E\{v - |(t_{(1)} + S_1) - (t_{(2)} + S_2)|\} < E\{v - ((t_{(1)} + S_1) - (t_{(2)} + S_2))\} = E\{v - (t_{(1)} - t_{(2)})\}$. Of course, conditional on $t_{(1)}$ and $t_{(2)}$ being held by the same firm, the expected difference between the winning firm's information and the losing firm's information is even higher, so expected seller revenue is even lower.

68. Mares and Shor assume nm bidders, each of which owns a single signal, merge to create n firms, each of which owns m signals.

69. The extension to sealed-bid auctions is an elementary application of the revenue equivalence theorem; I assume bidders are risk-neutral, that their information signals are independent, and that they play the symmetric equilibrium in an ascending auction.

70. For sealed-bid auctions, see Klemperer (forthcoming b). For ascending auctions, a general analysis is hard because there is a multiplicity of equilibria, and is hard to pick it among them after a merger that leaves bidders

asymmetric. However, Pagnozzi (2004a) argues that the result that mergers are anticompetitive generalizes to asymmetric cases by analyzing the game as the limit of an "almost common-value model."

71. Further confusion has resulted from an influential paper by Krishna and Morgan (1997) that made valuable contributions to the study of common-value auctions but also contended that joint bidding could benefit bid-takers in wallet games. Unfortunately, that part of their paper was flawed, and joint bidding *cannot* benefit bid-takers in Krishna and Morgan's model, as Mares and Shor (2004) demonstrated. Furthermore Levin (2004) showed that in multi-unit auctions it is even more likely that joint bidding hurts the bid-taker.

72. Of course, this also means that if we care about social welfare rather than about bid-taker's or consumers' welfare, we should not care about mergers in pure common-value auctions.

73. In winner-take-all, sealed-bid, private-value auctions, efficiency can be increased or decreased by mergers. See section 16.4.2.

74. Of course, it also follows that a merger that combines two weak bidders, and thereby reduces the difference between the amount of private information available to the resulting (merged) bidder and the amount of private information available to a stronger bidder, could be particularly desirable in preventing the entry-deterring and predatory possibilities discussed in the next subsection. This parallels the result that in a "normal market," a merger may create a more effective competitor to an otherwise dominant firm.

75. In addition to Deutsche Telekom, Hutchison had also been considered a strong potential entrant, but it also entered a partnership with an incumbent (KPN). Other potential entrants were also co-opted into joint-ventures with incumbents, or dropped out altogether.

76. The common-value issues were sufficiently important and well-understood that they were discussed in the press in advance of the Netherlands' auction. Although this auction might have been uncompetitive even without common values, the antitrust concern I describe below (caused by the proposed BSkyB-Manchester United merger) would probably not have been an issue at all, absent common values.

77. Levin and Kagel (2005) show that the effects can be smaller, though still important, when there are more than two bidders.

78. See Monopolies and Mergers Commission (1999). Prior to 2003 the Commission (the predecessor body to the Competition Commission) could only make recommendations, so this decision was technically a recommendation, but it was accepted by the government.

79. Though the theories discussed in the Commission's decision appealed to my papers Klemperer (1998), Bulow, Huang, and Klemperer (1999), I did not discuss the case with the Commission or with any interested party before the decision (which was prior to my appointment as a member of the Competition Commission).

80. See Monopolies and Mergers Commission (1999, para. 2.116).

81. Not me!

82. Conversely, one major oil company is said to have deliberately cultivated a reputation for *not* believing in economic theory.

83. An alternative view was that antitrust policy did not go far enough: after BSkyB was prohibited from taking over Manchester United it very quickly took small minority stakes in all of Manchester United, Manchester City, Chelsea, Leeds, and Sunderland, thus to some degree recreating the "toehold" stake in football TV revenues that had caused concern, while evading the Commission's scrutiny because the stakes were too small to qualify as mergers. (In principle, the Office of Fair Trading could have taken action, but this might have been hard.) Perhaps since BSkyB already had a very strong position, it should have been prohibited from developing a toehold, but it would have helped "level the playing field," and so been good for competition, if any of BSkyB's rivals had developed a toehold. In fact NTL dropped a bid to acquire Newcastle but took minority stakes in Aston Villa, Leeds, Middlesborough, and Newcastle.

84. Of course, a bid-taker's power cannot generally prevent it being hurt by mergers of bidders who have private information (including, as discussed in section 16.5.1, in most common-value contexts).

85. Many houses are sold using a similar, but less formal, process. Similarly, in W. R. Hambrecht's OpenBook auctions for corporate bonds, the early bidding is public and ascending but higher bidders are given an advantage in a final sealed-bid stage (although in this case all bidders are permitted to enter the final stage). The process also has some similarity to auctions on eBay which are ascending price, but with a fixed ending time so that many bidders often bid only in the last few seconds in essentially sealed-bid style.

86. I am aware of the formal Anglo-Dutch auction having been recently used in Florida, Texas, Germany, and the Netherlands. I would be eager to hear about other practical applications.

87. See Salmon (2004) for discussion of some of these ideas.

88. Milgrom (2004) is an excellent introduction to the state of the art in multi-unit auctions. Note that in multi-unit contexts, uniform-price multi-unit auctions are generally more attractive to new entrants than are discriminatory-price multi-unit auctions.

89. Similar unilateral effects, in which bidders reduce demands (or supplies) to make the auction price(s) less competitive for their remaining demands (or supplies), also arise in other multi-unit auctions (or sequential single-unit auctions).

90. There are also other difficulties: for example, high valuers are often required to pay less than low-valuers (which seems odd to policy makers), it creates difficult-to-guard-against opportunities for collusion, and it may deter entry of new bidders, so it is probably only useful in carefully controlled environments.

91. See also note 85. By contrast, the attempt to implement a slightly novel design in Hong Kong was a disaster; see the next subsection and Klemperer (2003a).

92. A very simple form of collusion is for the bid-taker to tell a bidder what its competitors have bid. This may be prevented by having all bids publicly opened.

93. For example, when Denmark ran the last of the 2000–2001 European 3G auctions, the government was rightly concerned whether it could attract any new entrant given that the number of licenses equalled the number of incumbents; see our discussion of the Netherlands' auction in section 16.5.2 (and since also the telecom market had by then gone so sour). They followed all the strategies in this ("secrecy") sub-subsection, and ran a highly successful auction. See Klemperer (2002b, 2003a). McAfee and McMillan (1987, 1988) argue that the Canadian utility company Ontario Hydro benefited from keeping the number of bidders secret in auctions it ran.

94. Ayres and Cramton (1996) estimate that offering 40 percent bidding credits to "designated bidders" (the bid-taker agreed to refund 40 percent of winning bids by firms controlled by women, minorities, etc.), together with favorable terms for payment by installment, actually *raised* the federal government's revenue (by $45m, or about 12 percent) in the 1994 sale of regional narrowband PCS spectrum.

95. Similarly the UK Inland Revenue (i.e., tax-collecting authority) recently paid bidders to undertake exploratory studies about how a large IT project might be designed and managed, as a way of reducing these bidders' information disadvantages relative to the better-informed incumbent who had won the previous contract.

96. One way to make a contract larger is to aggregate several auctions that would otherwise take place at different times.

97. See sections 16.4.3 and 16.5.2, Gilbert and Klemperer (2000), and Bulow and Klemperer (2002). Using such "split-award" auctions is just a form of offering "second prizes" and, when it would be efficient and/or would ex post maximize bid-taker surplus to have a single winner, can be seen as a form of discriminating in favour of weaker bidders.

98. Pagnozzi (2004b) models how the bargaining in the aftermarket is itself affected by the outcome of the auction, and how the possibility of entering the resale market can both induce bidders to drop out of an auction early and give arbitrageurs a strong incentive to participate.

99. But resale does not resolve all inefficiencies, even when firms' private objectives are the social objectives (Cai 2000; Myerson and Satterthwaite 1983; Cramton, Gibbons, and Klemperer 1987).

100. For example, on one occasion when the US government offered bidding credits to firms controlled by women (i.e., the government agreed to refund a percentage of winning bids by such firms), a female executive resigned her position at a large established firm to form a new company to bid in the auction and re-sell the rights to her original employer with—it is said—the resale terms settled in advance of her departure and a promise that she could return to her original job if her new company failed to win the auction. Such strategies obviously vitiate the point of bidding credits.

101. State Aid rules create broader constraints. For example when I advised the UK government on the design of the world's first auction of greenhouse gas emissions, the EU Commission insisted on rules that made a minimum number of winners sufficiently likely, and negotiating State Aid clearance was an important issue. (See Klemperer et al., forthcoming.) Nevertheless, the overall effect of State Aid legislation is probably to promote competition.

A Netherlands auction worth hundreds of millions of euros famously fell foul of the EU rules and was—it is said—hurriedly redesigned on a Friday afternoon, with laughable results (see van Damme 1999).

102. The Freedom of Information Act is a very recent piece of UK government legislation that weakens bidtakers' power, by making it hard or impossible to keep auction outcomes secret (see section 16.6.1).

103. See UK Competition Commission (2002).

104. NAPP Pharmaceutical Holdings Ltd. was able to preclude entry into the hospital market for sustained release morphine products. Sales to hospitals led to "follow-on" community sales where NAPP's prices were more than ten times higher. See Farrell and Klemperer (2007). In principle, the problems could probably have been resolved if purchases for hospitals and the community were made simultaneously by a single organization.

105. The industry also lobbied effectively against a better (i.e., earlier) timing for the auction, which might have made the flawed design less vulnerable. (The first European auction was always likely to attract the most potential entrants—see Klemperer 2002b, 2003a—and the Netherlands' industry lobbying helped ensure that the United Kingdom won the race to be first by a clear margin.)

106. This has often been a problem in the sale of companies—including of Glaxo (see section 16.4.3) and RJR-Nabisco (see note 39).

107. The Commission wrote "if it looked as if [BSkyB's] bid ... was not going to be successful ... Manchester United could come to the meeting of the Premier League at which final rights bids from broadcasters were due to be considered armed with authority from BSkyB to make an improved bid on BSkyB's behalf. Even if the introduction of an improved bid at the meeting were against the Premier League's bidding rules, we see no practical way in which it could be prevented. ... We think that it would not be too difficult to [at least force] the rights auction to go to another round ... by converting a sealed bid auction into an ascending price one it would gain an additional advantage from the toehold effect" (Monopolies and Mergers Commission 1999, paras. 2.129–2.130).

108. Monopolies and Mergers Commission (1999, para. 2.115).

109. In theory symmetric auctions usually have efficient outcomes. In practice, outcomes are not always efficient, and a merger that created a sufficiently strong firm *might* improve efficiency.

Furthermore a merger can, of course, create efficiencies if it lowers the merged firm's costs below the minimum of either merging party's costs—for example, if it turns two small firms, who could not realistically compete independently for a contract, into a single operator with the scale to compete for the contract—but this point applies equally to "ordinary" markets.

110. The data are often better for sealed-bid auctions (since losing bids are often available) than for ascending auctions (where only the final loser's dropout price is generally known), but on the other hand the relationship between bids and valuations or costs is much simpler in an ascending auction.

For example, Porter and Zona (1993) and Bajari and Ye (2003) examine data sets of first-price sealed-bid procurement auctions for highway construction contracts and for highway maintenance projects, respectively, while Porter and Zona (1999), Lanzillotti (1996), Scott (2000), and Pesendorfer (2000) all look at such auctions for school milk; Baldwin, Marshall, and Richard (1997) and Banerji and Meenakshi (2004) look at ascending auctions of timber and wheat, respectively.

One issue is that a clever-enough collusive mechanism could, in principle, mimic what would be the competitive outcome with different costs or valuations. Another issue is that the tests in these papers may be sensitive to misspecification of, for example, costs, and I have already noted that although there may be good data about bids, other data about auctions are often poor. In practice, however, these studies seem to have some success in identifying collusion; some of their results are corroborated by independent information about whether collusion was present.

111. See also Porter (2004). Harrington also analyses broader implications of collusion that apply to "ordinary" as well as auction markets.

112. See American Association of Petroleum Geologists (2004), describing the process leading Atlantic Richfield Company staff to the publication of Capen, Clapp, and Campbell (1971). Of course, the line between legitimate dissemination of research results and other efficiency-enhancing information sharing on the one hand, and illegitimate behavior on the other, is a hard one to draw. But Klemperer (2002a) suggests Pacific Telephone should perhaps have been regarded as having crossed that line with their remark prior to the main US 1995 mobile phone license auction that "if somebody takes California away from us, they'll never make any money"—this seems to correspond to threatening that "if anyone tries to compete with us, we'll cut the price until they lose money." Likewise Pacific Telephone's hiring of an auction theorist to explain the winner's curse to competitors might correspond to hiring an industrial economist to explain the theory of the difficulties of entering new markets to potential entrants.

113. The case resulted in consent decrees against Mercury PCS II, L.L.C., Omnipoint Corporation, and 21st Century Bidding Corp. See *US v. Mercury PCS II, L.L.C.* (1998).

114. Klemperer (2002a) cites many examples: for example, before the Austrian third-generation spectrum auction Telekom Austria, the largest incumbent and presumably the strongest among the six bidders, said it "would be satisfied with just 2 of the 12 blocks of frequency on offer" and "if the [five other bidders] behaved similarly it should be possible to get the frequencies on sensible terms," but "it would bid for a 3rd block if one of its rivals did" (Reuters, 31/10/2000). It seems inconceivable that a dominant firm in a "normal" market would be allowed to make the equivalent offer and threat that it "would be satisfied with a market share of just (1/6)" and "if the other five firms also stick to (1/6) of the market each, it should be possible to sell at high prices," but "it would compete aggressively for a larger share, if any of its rivals aimed for more than (1/6)."

Similarly, during the German third-generation spectrum auction, MobilCom told a newspaper that "should [Debitel] fail to secure a license [it could] become a "virtual network operator" using MobilCom's network while saving on the cost of the license" (Benoît 2000, p. 28). This translates roughly to a firm in a "normal" market saying it "would supply a rival should it choose to exit the market," but MobilCom's remarks went unpunished.

Glaxo let it be known that it "would almost certainly top a rival bid" (Wighton 1995b) in the takeover battle discussed in section 16.4.3, which would roughly translate to an incumbent firm in a "normal" economic market saying it "would almost certainly undercut any new entrant's price."

115. The 2000–2001 European 3G auctions provide numerous illustrations. See Klemperer (2002b).

One issue is that bidders are buyers rather than sellers in many auctions, and the European Commission guidelines on cooperation agreements (European Commission 2001) are much more tolerant of cooperation among buyers than of cooperation among sellers. This is another respect in which US antitrust seems to differ from European antitrust.

116. The coordination in the 1999 German auction is described in note 54. On the occasion of the later 3G auction, *The Financial Times* reported: "One operator has privately admitted to altering the last digit of its bid in a semi-serious attempt to signal to other participants that it was willing to accept [fewer lots to end the auction]" (Roberts and Ward 2000, p. 21), but the firms were not willing to confirm this. See Klemperer (2003a, 2002d) for more discussion of these two auctions.

117. This kind of signaling behavior could perhaps be challenged as an abuse of "joint dominance" under EC and UK law.

References

American Association of Petroleum Geologists. 2004 Bidding science saved $$. *Explorer* (December).

Aoyagi, M. 2003. Bid rotation and collusion in repeated auctions. *Journal of Economic Theory* 112(1): 79–105.

Armantier, O. 2002. Deciding between the common and private values paradigm: An application to experimental data. *International Economic Review* 43(3): 783–801.

Athey, S., and P. A. Haile. 2002. Identification of standard auction models. *Econometrica* 70(6): 2107–40.

Ausubel, L. 2004. An efficient ascending-bid auction for multiple objects. *American Economic Review* 94(5): 1452–75.

Ayres, I., and P. Cramton. 1996. Deficit reduction through diversity: How affirmative action at the FCC increased auction competition. *Stanford Law Review* 48(4): 761–815.

Bajari, P., and L. Ye. 2003. Deciding between competition and collusion. *Review of Economics and Statistics*. 85(4): 971–89.

Baldwin, L., H. R. C. Marshall, and J. F. Richard. 1997. Bidder collusion at forest service timber sales. *Journal of Political Economy* 105(4): 657–99.

Banerji, A., and J. V. Meenakshi. 2004. Millers, commission agents and collusion in grain auction markets: Evidence from basmati auctions in North India. Working paper. Centre for Development Economics, Delhi School of Economics.

Baumol, W. J., J. C. Panzar, and R. Willig. 1982. *Contestable Markets and the Theory of Industry Structure*. New York: Harcourt Brace Jovanovich.

Benoît, B. 2000. Bidders warned in German 3G phone auction. *Financial Times*, August 2, p. 28.

Bernheim, B. D., and M. D. Whinston. 1990. Multimarket contact and collusive behavior. *Rand Journal of Economics* 21(1): 1–26.

Bikhchandani, S. 1988. Reputation in Repeated Second-Price Auctions. *Journal of Economic Theory* 46(1): 97–119.

Binmore, K., and P. Klemperer. 2002. The biggest auction ever: The sale of the British 3G telecom licences. *Economic Journal* 112(478): C74–C96.

Blume, A., and P. Heidhues. 2002. Modeling tacit collusion in auctions. Working paper. University of Pittsburgh and WZB, Berlin.

Borenstein, S., J. B. Bushnell, and F. A. Wolak. 2002. Measuring market inefficiencies in California's restructured wholesale electricity market. *American Economic Review* 92(5): 1376–405.

Bulow, J., M. Huang, and P. Klemperer. 1999. Toeholds and takeovers. *Journal of Political Economy* 107(3): 427–54.

Bulow, J., and P. Klemperer. 1996. Auctions versus negotiations. *American Economic Review* 86(1): 180–94.

Bulow, J., and P. Klemperer. 1997. Prices and the winner's curse. Working paper. Nuffield College, Oxford University.

Bulow, J., and P. Klemperer. 2002. Prices and the winner's curse. *Rand Journal of Economics* 33(1): 1–21.

Bulow, J., and P. Klemperer. 2007. When are auctions best? Working paper. Nuffield College, Oxford University.

Bulow, J., and J. Roberts. 1989. The simple economics of optimal auctions. *Journal of Political Economy* 97(5): 1060–90.

Burrough, B., and J. Helyar. 1990. *Barbarians at the Gate: The Fall of RJR Nabisco*. London: Arrow.

Cai, H.-B. 2000. Delay in multilateral bargaining under complete information. *Journal of Economic Theory* 93(2): 260–76.

Capen, E., R. Clapp, and W. Campbell. 1971. Competitive bidding in high-risk situations. *Journal of Petroleum Technology* 28: 641–53.

Competition Tribunal South Africa. 2004. *Murray & Roberts Limited and The Cementation Company (Africa) Limited*, available at ⟨http://www.comptrib.co.za⟩.

Cramton, P. 1995. Money out of thin air: The nationwide narrowband PCS auction. *Journal of Economics & Management Strategy* 4(2): 267–343.

Cramton, P. 2002. Spectrum Auctions. In M. Cave, S. Majumdar, and I. Vogelsang, eds. *The Handbook of Telecommunications Economics*. Amsterdam: Elsevier.

Cramton, P., R. Gibbons, and P. Klemperer. 1987. Dissolving a partnership efficiently. *Econometrica* 55(3): 615–32.

Cramton, P., and J. A. Schwartz. 2000. Collusive bidding: Lessons from the FCC spectrum auctions. *Journal of Regulatory Economics* 17(3): 229–52.

Dalkir, S., J. W. Logan, and R. T. Masson. 2000. Mergers in symmetric and asymmetric noncooperative auction markets: The effects on prices and efficiency. *International Journal of Industrial Organization* 18(3): 383–413.

DeBrock, L. M., and J. L. Smith. 1983. Joint bidding, information pooling, and the performance of petroleum lease auctions. *Bell Journal of Economics* 14(2) 395–404.

de Silva, D., T. Dunne, and G. Kosmopoulou. 2003. An empirical analysis of entrant and incumbent bidding in road construction auctions. *Journal of Industrial Economics* 51(3): 295–316.

Department of Justice/Federal Trade Commission. 1997. *1992 Horizontal Merger Guidelines*. Available at ⟨http://www.ftc.gov/bc/docs/horizmer.htm⟩.

Egan, T. 2005. Tapes reveal Enron took a role in crisis. *International Herald Tribune*, February 5–6, p. 12.

Evans, J., and R. Green. 2003. Why did British electricity prices fall after 1998? Working paper. MIT.

European Commission. 2000. Case No. Comp/M 1882-Pirelli/BICC. *Official Journal* L70/35.

European Commission. 2001. Guidelines on the applicability of Article 81 of the EC Treaty to horizontal cooperation agreements. *Official Journal* 2001/C 3/02.

European Commission. 2002. Draft Commission Notice on the appraisal of horizontal mergers under the Council Regulation on the control of concentrations between undertakings. *Official Journal* 2002/C 331/03.

European Commission. 2004. Case No. COMP/M 3216-Oracle/Peoplesoft. *Official Journal* L218/6.

Fabra, N. 2003. Tacit collusion in repeated auctions: Uniform versus discriminatory. *Journal of Industrial Economics* L1(3): 271–93.

Fabra, N., and J. Toro. 2005. Price wars and collusion in the Spanish electricity market. *International Journal of Industrial Organization* 23 (3–4): 155–81.

Farrell, J., and P. Klemperer. 2000. Coordination and lock-in: Competition with switching costs and network effects. Working paper. University of California, Berkeley, and Nuffield College, Oxford.

Farrell, J., and P. Klemperer. 2007. Coordination and lock-in: Competition with switching costs and network effects. In M. Armstrong and R. Porter, eds., *Handbook of Industrial Organization*, vol. 3. Amsterdam: North-Holland.

Federico, G., and D. Rahman. 2003. Bidding in an electricity pay-as-bid auction. *Journal of Regulatory Economics* 24(2): 175–311.

Froeb, L. M., and M. Shor. 2005. Auction Models. In J. Harkrider, *ed. Econometrics: Legal, Practical, and Technical Issues.* ABA Section of Antitrust Law: 225–46.

Gilbert, R. J., and P. D. Klemperer. 2000. An equilibrium theory of rationing. *RAND Journal of Economics* 31(1): 1–21.

Grimm, V., F. Riedel, and E. Wolfstetter. 2002. The third generation (UMTS) spectrum auction in Germany. *ifo Studien* 48: 123–43.

Haile, P. A., H. Hong, and M. Shum. 2004. Nonparametric tests for common values at first-price auctions. Discussion paper 1445. Cowles Foundation.

Harstad, R. M., and R. F. Bordley. 1996. Lottery qualification auctions. In M. R. Baye, ed. *Advances in Applied Micro-Economics*, vol. 6. Greenwich, CT: JAI Publications, pp. 157–83.

Hendricks, K., J. Pinkse, and R. H. Porter. 2003. Empirical implications of equilibrium bidding in first-price, symmetric, common value auctions. *Review of Economic Studies* 70(1): 115–45.

Hendricks, K., and R. H. Porter. 1992. Joint Bidding in Federal OCS Auctions. *American Economic Review* 82(2): 506–11.

Hendricks, K., R. H. Porter, and G. Tan. 2003. Bidding rings and the winner's curse: The case of federal offshore oil and gas lease auctions. Research Paper No. C03-25.USC CLEO.

Hoffman, E., J. R. Marsden, and R. Saidi. 1991. Are joint bidding and competitive common value auction markets compatible?—Some evidence from offshore oil auctions. *Journal of Environmental Economics and Management* 20: 99–112.

Hong, H., and M. Shum. 2002. Increasing competition and the winner's curse: Evidence from procurement. *Review of Economic Studies* 69(4): 871–98.

Hoppe, H., P. Jehiel, and B. Moldovanu. 2006. License auctions and market structure. *Journal of Economics and Management Strategy*. 15(2): 371–96.

Jehiel, P., and B. Moldovanu. 2001. Efficient design with interdependent valuations. *Econometrica* 69(5): 1237–59.

Joskow, P., and E. Kahn. 2002. A quantitative analysis of pricing behavior in California's wholesale electricity market during summer 2000. *Energy Journal* 23(4): 1–35.

Klemperer, P. D. 1995. Competition when consumers have switching costs: An overview with applications to industrial-organization, macroeconomics, and international-trade. *Review of Economic Studies* 62(4): 515–39.

Klemperer, P. D. 1998. Auctions with almost common values: The "wallet game" and its applications. *European Economic Review* 42(3–5): 757–69.

Klemperer, P. D. 1999a. Auction theory: A guide to the literature. *Journal of Economic Surveys* 13: 227–86.

Klemperer, P. 1999b. Applying auction theory to economics. Draft of invited lecture to Eighth World Congress of the Econometric Society. Available at ⟨www.paulklemperer.org⟩.

Klemperer, P. D., ed. 2000. *The Economic Theory of Auctions*, Cheltenham, UK: Edward Elgar.

Klemperer, P. D. 2002a. What really matters in auction design. *Journal of Economic Perspectives* 16: 169–89.

Klemperer, P. D. 2002b. How (not) to run auctions: The European 3G telecom auctions. *European Economic Review* 46(4–5): 829–45.

Klemperer, P. D. 2002c. Some observations on the British 3G telecom auction: Comments on Börgers and Dustmann. *ifo Studien* 48: 115–20.

Klemperer, P. D. 2002d. Some observations on the German 3G Telecom auction: Comments on Grimm, Riedel, and Wolfstetter. *ifo Studien* 48: 145–56.

Klemperer, P. D. 2003a. Using and abusing economic theory. *Journal of the European Economic Association* 1: 272–300.

Klemperer, P. D. 2003b. Why every economist should learn some auction theory. In M. Dewatripont, L. Hansen, and S. Turnovsky, eds. *Advances in Economics and Econometrics: Theory and Applications*, vol. 1. Cambridge: Cambridge University Press, Cambridge, pp. 25–55.

Klemperer, P. D. 2004. *Auctions: Theory and Practice*, Princeton: Princeton University Press.

Klemperer, P. D. 2005. Bidding Markets. Occasional Paper 1. UK Competition Commission.

Klemperer, P. D. forthcoming a. Switching costs. In L. Blume, and S. Durlauf, eds. *The New Palgrave Dictionary of Economics*, Basingstoke, UK: Palgrave Macmillan.

Klemperer, P. D. forthcoming b. Notes on mergers in common-value auctions. Mimeo. Nuffield College, Oxford University.

Klemperer, P. D., et al. forthcoming. Auctions for environmental improvements: The UK ETS auction. Working paper. Nuffield College, Oxford University.

Klemperer, P. D., and M. A. Meyer. 1989. Supply function equilibria in oligopoly under uncertainty. *Econometrica* 57: 1243–77.

Kremer, I., and K. G. Nyborg. 2000. Underpricing and market power in uniform price auctions. *Review of Financial Studies* 17: 849–77.

Krishna, V., and J. Morgan. 1997 (Anti-)competitive effects of joint bidding and bidder restrictions. Working paper. Penn State University and Princeton University.

Laffont, J.-J., and Q. Vuong. 1996. Structural analysis of auction data. *American Economic Review* 86(2): 414–20.

Lanzillotti, R. F. 1996. The great milk conspiracies of the 1980s. *Review of Industrial Organization* 11: 413–58.

Levin, D. 2004. The competitiveness of joint bidding in multi-unit uniform-price auctions. *RAND Journal of Economics* 35(2): 373–85.

Levin, D., and J. H. Kagel. 2005. Almost common values auctions revisited. *European Economic Review* 49(5): 1125–36.

Lexecon. 1995. When two is enough: Competition in bidding markets. Lexecon Competition Memo. June 1995. (Reprinted in S. Bishop, and W. Bishop. 1996. *European Competition Law Review* 17(1): 3–5.)

Lexecon. 2003. *An Introduction to Quantitative Techniques in Competition Analysis*. Available at ⟨http://www.lexecon.co.uk/publications/2003/index.htm⟩.

Li Calzi, M., and A. Pavan. 2005. Tilting the supply schedule enhances competition in uniform-price auctions. *European Economic Review* 49: 227–50.

Macatangay, R. E. A. 2002. Tacit collusion in the frequently repeated multi-unit uniform price auction for wholesale electricity in England and Wales. *European Journal of Law and Economics* 13(3): 257–73.

Mares, V., and M. Shor. 2004. Industry concentration in common value auctions: Theory and evidence. Working paper. Olin School of Business, Washington University and Owen Graduate School of Management, Vanderbilt University.

Marshall, R. C., M. J. Meurer, J. F. Richard, and W. Stromquist. 1994. Numerical analysis of asymmetric first price auctions. *Games and Economic Behavior* 7(2): 193–220.

Maskin, E., and J. Riley. 2000. Asymmetric auctions. *Review of Economic Studies* 67(3): 413–38.

McAdams, D. 2002. Modifying the uniform-price auction to eliminate "collusive-seeming equilibria." Working paper. MIT.

McAfee, R. P., and J. McMillan. 1992. Bidding rings. *American Economic Review* 82(3): 579–99.

McAfee, R. P., and J. McMillan. 1987. Auctions with a stochastic number of bidders. *Journal of Economic Theory* 43: 1–19.

McAfee, R. P., and J. McMillan. 1988. *Incentives in Government Contracting*, Toronto: University of Toronto Press.

McMillan, J. 1991. "*DANGO*: Japan's price-fixing conspiracies. *Economics and Politics* 3: 201–18.

Milgrom, P. R. 2004. *Putting Auction Theory to Work*. Cambridge: Cambridge University Press.

Monopolies and Mergers Commission. 1999. *British Sky Broadcasting Group plc: A Report on the Proposed Merger*. The Stationery Office Ltd., UK.

Moreland, F. 2004. Private communication.

Myerson, R. B. and M. A. Satterthwaite. 1983. Efficient mechanisms for bilateral trading. *Journal of Economic Theory* 29(2): 265–81.

Newbery, D. 2004. Electricity liberalisation in Britain: the quest for a satisfactory wholesale market design. Working paper. MIT.

Owen, B. M. 2004. Confusing success with access: "Correctly" measuring concentration of ownership and control in mass media and online services. SIEPR Discussion paper. Stanford University.

Paarsch, H. J. 1992. Deciding between the common and private value paradigms in empirical-models of auctions. *Journal of Econometrics* 51(1): 191–215.

Pagnozzi, M. 2004a. Bids as a vehicle of (mis)information: Collusion in English auctions with affiliated values. Working paper. University of Naples.

Pagnozzi, M. 2004b. Bidding to lose? Auctions with resale. Working paper. University of Naples.

Parlour, C., and U. Rajan. 2005. Rationing in IPOs. *Review of Finance* 9(1): 33–63.

Patterson, D., and C. Shapiro. 2001. Trans-Atlantic divergence in GE/Honeywell: Causes and lessons. *Antitrust Magazine*. Fall 2001: 18–26.

Pesendorfer, M. 2000. A study of collusion in first-price auctions. *Review of Economic Studies* 67(3): 381–411.

Pinkse, J., and G. Tan. 2005. The affiliation effect in first-price auctions. *Econometrica* 73(1): 263–77.

Porter, R. H. 2004. Detecting collusion. Working paper. CSIO, Northwestern University.

Porter, R. H., and J. D. Zona. 1993. Detection of bid rigging in procurement auctions. *Journal of Political Economy* 101(3): 518–38.

Porter, R. H., and J. D. Zona. 1999. Ohio school milk markets: An analysis of bidding. *RAND Journal of Economics* 30(2): 263–88.

Roberts, J., and A. Ward. 2000. Little gold at the end of the spectrum. *Financial Times*, November 3, p. 21.

Sade, O., C. Schnitzlein, and J. F. Zender. 2004. Competition and cooperation in divisible good auctions: An experimental examination. Working paper. Hebrew University of Jerusalem, University of Central Florida, and University of Colorado at Boulder.

Salant, D. 2000. Auctions and regulation: Reengineering of regulatory mechanisms. *Journal of Regulatory Economics* 17(3): 195–204.

Salmon, T. 2004. Preventing collusion between firms in auctions. In M. C. W. Janssen, ed. *Auctioning Public Assets: Analysis and Alternatives*. Cambridge: Cambridge University Press.

Scott, F. A. 2000. Great school milk conspiracies revisited. *Review of Industrial Organization* 17(3): 325–41.

Skrzypacz, A., and H. Hopenhayn. 2004. Tacit collusion in repeated auctions. *Journal of Economic Theory* 114(1): 153–69.

Stuewe, H. 1999. Auktion von Telefonfrequenzen: Pannung bis zur letzten Minute. *Frankfurter Allgemeine Zeitung*, October 29.

Sweeting, A. 2004. Market power in the England and Wales wholesale electricity market 1995–2000. Working paper. Northwestern University.

Tschantz, S., P. Crooke, and L. Froeb. 2000. Mergers in sealed vs. oral auctions. *International Journal of the Economics of Business* 7(2): 201–13.

UK Competition Commission. 2002. *Group 4 Falck A/S and The Wackenhut Corporation: A Report on the Merger Situation.* The Stationery Office Ltd., UK Cm 5624.

UK Competition Commission. 2003. *Merger References: Competition Commission Guidelines.* Available at ⟨http://www.competition-commission.org.uk⟩.

UK Competition Commission. 2004a. *Carl Zeiss GmbH / Bio-Rad Laboratories Inc: Main Party Submission from Bio-Rad Laboratories Inc.* Available at ⟨http://www.competition-commission.org.uk⟩.

UK Competition Commission. 2004b. *Dräger Medical AG & Co KgaA / Air-Shields: Main Party Submission from Dräger Medical AG.* Available at ⟨http://www.competition-commission.org.uk⟩.

UK Competition Commission. 2005. *Arcelor SA and Corus Group plc: Final Report.* Available at ⟨http://www.competition-commission.org.uk⟩.

UK Office of Fair Trading. 2004a. *Empirical Indicators for Market Investigations, Part 2: Main Report.* Prepared by NERA. Available at ⟨http://www.oft.gov.uk⟩.

UK Office of Fair Trading. 2004b. *Competition Act Guideline on the Assessment of Market Power.* Available at ⟨http://www.oft.gov.uk⟩.

US v. Mercury PCS II, L.L.C. 1998. Civil Action 98-2751 in the US District Court for the District of Columbia. Available at ⟨http://www.usdoj.gov/atr/cases/indx87.htm⟩.

US et al. v. Oracle Corporation. 2004. Case No. C 04-0807 in the US District Court for the Northern District of California.

van Damme, E. 1999. The Dutch Dcs-1800 auction. In F. Patrone, I. Garcia-Jurado, and S. Tijs, eds., *Game Practice: Contributions from Applied Game Theory*, New York: Kluwer, pp. 53–73.

Wighton, D. 1995. Wellcome still smarting over handling of trust's stake. *Financial Times*, March 8, p. 32.

Wolak, F. A. 2003. Measuring unilateral market power in wholesale electricity markets: The California market 1998 to 2000. *American Economic Review* 93: 425–30.

Wolfram, C. 1998. Strategic bidding in a multi-unit auction: An empirical analysis of bids to supply electricity in England and Wales. *RAND Journal of Economics* 29(4): 703–25.

Woo, C. K., D. Lloyd, M. Borden, R. Warrington, and C. Baskette. 2004. A robust Internet-based auction to procure electricity forwards. *Energy* 29: 1–11.

17   European State Aid Control: An Economic Framework

Hans W. Friederiszick, Lars-Hendrik Röller, and Vincent Verouden

European state aid control is currently at a turning point. The European Union and its member states are increasingly recognizing the need to rethink the balance between the various objectives of state intervention. Constraints on state budgets and concerns about the effectiveness of state aid have increased the political pressure toward a more economic effects-based approach in state aid and state aid control. Both at national and European level, the political mandate is for "less and better targeted state aid."[1]

In this chapter we explore how increased reliance on economic insights in state aid control can contribute toward enhancing the effectiveness of state aid control. The economics of state aid control is related to several areas of economics: first, to public economics, since state aid is a form of public intervention in the economy; second, to the economics of competition, as state aid confers an advantage to some firms and thus has the potential to affect the competitive process; and third, to international trade theory, as state aid can affect trading conditions. This latter aspect creates incentives for national governments to pursue national economic or political goals, which in turn provides a rationale for supranational (European) state aid control.

Although state aid control is related to these well-developed fields of economics, most of the analysis in the practice of European state aid control is not firmly rooted in economic principles. There are a number of reasons for this state of affairs. One factor for the relative lack of economics in state aid control (relative to other areas of competition policy) is that the economic and legal principles underlying state aid control are by their very nature more challenging. For example, European state aid control involves more than a single objective: it involves economic efficiency as well as equity objectives. Another example is that there are several relevant theories of competitive harm at work, including some that are more dynamic—such as keeping inefficient rivals in the market. There is also the added complication that the cost of the aid to the taxpayer needs to be taken into account.

Another reason that might explain the underdevelopment of economic-based analysis in state aid control is that the field is invariably more political. As a result existing state aid procedures reflect largely the desire to limit political influence, rather than a focus on economic effectiveness. Accordingly, a strict legal tradition has developed in which state aid is deemed illegal, unless certain (largely form-based) criteria are met. It is sometimes argued that this tradition would be incompatible with a more effects-based approach, which includes the balancing of positive and negative effects. A related view—which has also been expressed in other areas of competition policy—is that predictability is better served by a stricter form-based approach.

In this chapter we address these issues and suggest an economic framework of assessment for European state aid control. We argue that the time is right for a more effects-based approach as it is a means to better distinguish "good" aid from "bad" aid. In this context, we advocate the use of a general balancing test as a conceptual framework for analyzing state aid cases. In essence, this test asks whether (1) the state aid alleviates a market failure or addresses another objective of common interest, (2) the state aid is well targeted, and (3) the distortions of competition are sufficiently limited so that the overall balance is positive. This approach is appropriate both in the design of the state aid rules and in the analysis of individual state aid cases, in particular, in those cases involving large amounts of aid.

In our opinion, the effects-based approach outlined in this chapter can contribute toward the policy goal of "less and better targeted aid." We also conclude that such an approach, provided that it is properly implemented, does not lead to an overall softening of state aid control and that predictability can be ensured. Moreover it is likely, as well as intended, that an effects-based approach will shift the argumentation from legal and accounting battles toward a battle over the impact of the aid on markets and ultimately on consumers. Such a change would not only greatly contribute toward the effectiveness of European state aid control but enhance predictability as well. Finally, we argue that an effects-based approach allows for a better prioritization in the field of state aid control.

This chapter is organized as follows: Section 17.1 provides a brief overview of the current legal context of European state aid control and discusses possible entry points for more economic analysis. Section 17.2 summarizes the most relevant economic concepts applicable to state aid control from a national perspective, and section 17.3 focuses on the international aspects. Section 17.4 addresses the debate on the relevant policy standard in state aid control. Finally, we present elements of an economic framework of analysis for state aid control in section 17.5. The chapter ends with some concluding remarks on the broader issues discussed in this introduction.

17.1   The Legal Framework—Room for Economic Assessment?

The main provision in the EC Treaty[2] dealing with state aid control is Article 87. Article 87 EC specifies a two stage approach. First, with a view to establish *jurisdiction*, it is assessed whether a specific state measure constitutes "state aid" within the meaning of Article 87(1). Only state measures that constitute "state aid" within the meaning of Article

87(1) are subject to EU state aid control. Second, there is the assessment of *compatibility*, to assess whether the aid measure can be allowed under the provisions of the EC Treaty.

The Treaty applies a negative presumption to all forms of state aid, declaring those measures incompatible with the common market.[3] The Commission may grant an exemption, however, and declare state aid "compatible" under Article 87(2) or Article 87(3) EC. Measures falling under Article 87(2) are compatible as such.[4] Measures falling under Article 87(3), which are in practice more important, can be declared compatible under the discretion of the Commission. In order to enable the Commission to exercise its control, all measures covered by EU jurisdiction have, in principle, to be notified to the Commission ex ante, and then approved by the Commission before they are implemented.

The way in which the Commission exercises its discretionary powers is outlined in a number of Regulations and in so-called soft law provisions, such as Guidelines and Communications. Specific categories of training aid, employment aid and aid to SMEs are exempted by the so-called block exemption regulations. These measures have to be brought to the Commission's attention only ex post and information requirements are reduced. In addition specific soft law provisions exist providing criteria to assess compatibility for aid measures of a horizontal (i.e., nonsectoral) nature, for certain sectoral measures, for measures in relation to public enterprises and with respect to specific types of state aid (state aid "instruments"), such as state guarantees.[5] Smaller amounts of aid are considered to fall outside EU jurisdiction and hence do not have to be notified (*de minimis* approach). Measures which do not fulfill the criteria outlined in the soft law provisions or regulations can, in exceptional circumstances, be approved by direct application of Article 87(3).

We next briefly outline the criteria for assessing jurisdiction, followed by the approach to assess compatibility. We also address to what extent economic analysis is currently undertaken and indicate the scope for further economic analysis.

17.1.1 Jurisdiction—The Legal Definition of State Aid

Article 87(1) of the EC Treaty states: "Save as otherwise provided in this Treaty, any aid granted by a Member State or through State resources in any form whatsoever which distorts or threatens to distort competition by favouring certain undertakings or the production of certain goods shall, insofar as it affects trade between Member States, be incompatible with the common market." The case law identifies four conditions to be fulfilled jointly for a measure to constitute state aid in the meaning of Article 87(1) EC:[6]

1. *Transfer of state resources*   There must be an intervention by the state or through state resources.
2. *Economic advantage*   The measure must confer an advantage on the recipient.
3. *Distortion of competition*   The measure must distort or threaten to distort competition.
4. *Effect on trade*   The measure must be liable to affect trade between member states.

It is important to note that in most cases the last two criteria ("distortion of competition" and "effect on trade") are considered to be fulfilled if the measure is "selective" in terms of granting an advantage. A measure can be selective in terms of favoring certain companies, the production of specific products, or the development of a specific region. Under this approach the assessment of the criteria "distortion of competition" and "effect on trade" under Article 87(1) is rather rudimentary. In addition it is left unclear whether both the competition and the trade criterion have a separate relevance in assessing jurisdiction.[7]

There are three areas in which economic analysis plays, or could play, an important role in the assessment of jurisdiction. First, economic analysis is relevant for establishing the extent to which an aid measure confers an economic advantage to the recipient of the aid. In practice, this is the most important entry point for economic analysis. In many cases it is fairly straightforward to determine the size of the economic advantage, such as for direct subsidies granted to firms. In many other situations, however, it is much less straightforward—in particular, in the context where governments invest in companies or provide loans or guarantees. In such cases the market economy investor principle (MEIP), or one of its derivatives (e.g., the private creditor principle) may become relevant. The MEIP is relevant in cases where the state intervenes by means comparable to private investors. The credit approved or the investment undertaken are only considered state aid in the meaning of Article 87(1) if the (monetary) compensation the state receives in exchange for the investment or loan is lower than what a private investor would have requested under such circumstances.[8]

Second, economic analysis has, at least potentially, a role to play in determining whether or not a measure is "selective." State aid must be selective for it to be capable of affecting the balance between the recipient firms and their competitors.[9] "Selectivity" is what differentiates state aid measures from so-called general measures, which apply equally to all firms in all economic sectors in a member state (e.g., most nationwide fiscal measures). A scheme is also considered selective if the authorities administering the scheme enjoy a degree of discretionary power. The selectivity criterion is further satisfied if the scheme applies to only part of the territory or a specific industry of a member state (this is the case for all regional and sectoral aid schemes). Measures that are de jure not selective could de facto have a highly divergent economic impact on firms, sectors, or regions. Economic analysis can help identifying the de facto impact of an aid measure on specific firms or industries.

Third, economic analysis may be relevant in analyzing whether the selectivity of the aid translates into actual or likely distortive effects on competition or trade. For instance, even where the aid is selective, it is possible that the aid does not affect trade among member states, as might be the case when the aid supports the provision of nontradable goods or services. In view of the Commission's expertise in other areas of competition policy (merger control, antitrust), this area seems to be a natural candidate for economic analysis. Case law, however, requires a rather low "intervention threshold" as regards the criteria of distortion of competition and effect on trade under Article 87(1).[10] In particular, the Court of First Instance has held that *"... there is no requirement in case-law that the distortions of competition, or the threat of such distortion, and the effect on intra-Community trade, must be significant or substantial."*[11] As indicated above, it appears that in practice,[12] distortions of competition and effects on trade are assumed to be present when the measure is selective, that is, when the market position of the aid beneficiary vis-à-vis its competitors is improved by the aid. Accordingly the scope for more economic analysis appears to be fairly limited in this regard.

The rather wide interpretation of the concepts of distortion of competition and effect on trade under Article 87(1) is a reflection of the fact that state aid, unlike mergers and (most) contractual agreements concluded by companies, is presumed to be distortive. By throwing a wide net around Article 87(1), the Court seeks to provide a central role to the Commission in determining the legality of state support to companies.

In certain areas the Court has adopted an approach that is more sophisticated and geared toward the economic circumstances of a particular case. For example, in the context of public service obligations (services of general economic interest) the Court has held that subsidies given to a company providing the public service do not constitute state aid in the sense of Article 87(1) when specific conditions are met relating to, among other things, the amount of the subsidy and the way in which it has been granted.[13]

17.1.2 Compatibility Criteria

As pointed out before, despite the negative presumption of Article 87(1), measures can be declared compatible if one of the exemptions of Article 87(2) or 87(3) are fulfilled. Article 87(2) provides an automatic exemption; Article 87(3) gives a certain discretion to the Commission in assessing compatibility. We will focus on the latter provision as it is, in practice, the more important legal basis for approving state aid measures. Article 87(3) states:

The following may be considered to be compatible with the common market:

(a) aid to promote the economic development of areas where the standard of living is abnormally low or where there is serious underemployment;
(b) aid to promote the execution of an important project of common European interest or to remedy a serious disturbance in the economy of a Member State;
(c) aid to facilitate the development of certain economic activities or of certain economic areas, where such aid does not adversely affect trading conditions to an extent contrary to the common interest;
(d) aid to promote culture and heritage conservation where such aid does not affect trading conditions and competition in the Community to an extent that is contrary to the common interest;
(e) such other categories of aid as may be specified by decision of the Council acting by a qualified majority on a proposal from the Commission.

Paragraphs (a) and (c) constitute the legal base for approving regional investment aid,[14] where paragraph (a) is interpreted to refer to regions with income levels per head significantly below the EU average and paragraph (c) to regions with income and employment levels below the average of the particular member state concerned. Paragraph (c) is also the basis for most other soft law provisions: for instance, the R&D framework,[15] the Rescue and Restructuring Guidelines,[16] the rules applicable to Services of General Economic Interest,[17] and the Environmental Guidelines.[18] It also provides the basis for the existing block exemption regulations in the field of training aid, employment aid, and aid to SMEs.

The general principle behind the Commission's compatibility assessment is to balance the positive impact of the aid measure (pursuing an objective of common interest) against its potential negative effects (distortions of trade and competition).[19] In most cases such a balancing will not be carried out explicitly. The approach taken in most block exemption regulations and soft law provisions is to define a set of "eligible costs" by which companies may receive state aid. The amount of subsidy is specified in terms of maximum aid intensities of the eligible costs (e.g., 50 percent of R&D expenditure at the stage of industrial research can be covered by state aid). The implicit balancing inherent in this approach is to obtain the positive impact of the aid measure by declaring expenses eligible that target objectives of common interest (e.g., some specific R&D expenditure) while restricting the possible distortions of competition by limiting the aid intensity (e.g., to 50 percent).

The various soft law provisions have typically been applied in a rather strict, formalistic way. There is little scope for approving state aid measures that do not meet the conditions set out in the provisions but that are very likely benign. Alternatively, disallowing state aid measures that meet the conditions but are likely to be ineffective or distort competition is not envisaged.

Novel measures or measures that are for other reasons exceptional and therefore not covered by existing soft law provisions are assessed "directly under Article 87(3)."[20] These cases remain, however, very limited in number and scope.

Over the years the Commission's approach has been to fine-tune the soft law provisions in order to improve their precision. Such fine-tuning has, for instance, been applied to the regional aid guidelines, which stipulate under which conditions member states can give aid to finance investments by companies setting up in particular regions. Whereas the traditional criteria applied in regional aid cases have been the level of GDP per capita relative to the EU average and, in certain cases, relative employment figures, a complementary set of rules has been introduced in order to limit the distortions of competition and trade.[21] These rules thus define lower maximum aid intensity levels for large investment projects and specify that firms cannot receive regional aid when they hold a market share above 25 percent or when they are active in a sector which is in relative decline.

Another example is given by the R&D Guidelines, which distinguish between different types of R&D, according to whether the R&D activity relates to fundamental research or rather to R&D activity "close to the market." Furthermore R&D aid to large firms has to induce an expansion of research activity (so-called incentive effect).

A special approach is taken in the guidelines on risk capital, which support equity funds that provide risk capital to smaller firms.[22] In this context higher amounts of risk capital aid are approved if it is shown that the aid is proportional to the size of the market failure addressed.[23]

Despite the increased fine tuning of soft law provisions, EU state aid rules remain rather form-based, leaving little room for assessing the impact of the measure on competition and trade. Explicit economic analysis of state aid measures has been of minor importance for compatibility assessment.[24]

In the few cases where the Commission undertook a more explicit analysis of the competitive impact of the state aid measure, the following principles emerge. First, state aid is more distortive in markets that are more competitive.[25] The underlying idea is that in markets where profit margins are already rather slim (due to competition) or where market shares are fairly volatile, state aid granted to a specific firm (or group of firms) may have a greater impact. Second, operational aid is almost always considered highly distortive, more than aid to finance investment.[26] As operational aid is directed toward the variable costs, it can directly affect firms' ability to compete and capture market share.

In sum, in the existing legal context of European state aid control, the competition analysis and the assessment of the negative effects on trade are rather rudimentary. Economic analysis of the state aid character of a given measure is limited mainly to the assessment of the "economic advantage" of the measure. As far as compatibility is concerned, a balancing of the benefits of the aid with the distortive effects of aid is, in principle, foreseen. In practice, however, the approach taken rests largely on the definition of the eligible costs and the use of maximum aid intensities. An explicit competition analysis or assessment of the effect on trade is done only in the few cases directly assessed under Article 87(3) or is limited to a partial analysis.

The resulting approach—while perhaps being relatively simple to administer—does not seek to identify the effectiveness of aid and the actual impact on markets. In combination with a rather broad approach taken when considering whether or not a measure constitutes state aid (see above), the state aid approval system thus bears the risk of being overly broad (to look at too many measures) and at the same time to be too imprecise, in the sense of not discriminating enough between "good" aid measures and "bad" aid measures.[27]

17.2 The Economics of State Aid (Control): Basic Concepts

The economic underpinnings of European state aid control draw on three fields of economics: (1) public economics (to analyze the purpose and effectiveness of state intervention in the national economy), (2) the economics of competition (to analyze the impact of state aid on competition), and (3) international trade theory (to study state aid policy in an international context). In this section we first focus on the public economics perspective of state aid policy: Why do national authorities resort to state aid to intervene in the economy?

It is important to understand the motives for state aid policy. If and when member states adopt state aid measures, they are likely to do so for a reason. The more state aid policies are used in pursuing (national) welfare objectives, the more likely it is that these national policies are also in line with EU objectives (e.g., those described in Article 87(3) EC), provided that negative spillovers in the European Union are limited. As a result appropriate state aid policies at the national level should be a positive element in the EU appraisal of state aid.

A proper assessment of the economic costs and benefits of state aid control also has to address the effectiveness of state aid. The last part of this section reviews a number of limitations of state aid, in terms of its effectiveness in achieving public policy objectives, as well as its exposure to political influences by specific stakeholders.

17.2.1 Rationale for State Aid

At the beginning of the twentieth century economists developed the analytical tool of a *social welfare function*.[28] A social welfare function maps the utilities of single individuals into an aggregate measure of social welfare, using a system of weights representing the importance attached to the utility of the respective individuals.

The fundamental theorems of welfare economics postulate conditions under which the market mechanism results in a Pareto efficient allocation:[29] the first welfare theorem defines the conditions under which any competitive economy results in a Pareto efficient allocation of goods and services; the second theorem says that under such conditions any Pareto efficient allocation may be obtained by a suitable lump-sum transfer of resources. The welfare theorems thus allow, in principle, to separate the two welfare elements of *efficiency* and *equity*.

Following this line, this subsection addresses two—even though in practice not necessarily independent—ways of increasing social welfare through state intervention. The first is by increasing the efficiency of an economy and thereby "pushing the welfare frontier outward" (sometimes referred to as "making the cake bigger"). The second way is to redistribute the available resources in a way that maximizes the preferences of society for equity and redistribution. This is about "moving along the welfare frontier" ("dividing the cake better").[30]

Efficiency Rationales   Economic efficiency is often analyzed in terms of total welfare, i.e. the sum of consumer welfare (the difference between customers' willingness to pay and the actual price) and producer welfare (profits) in the markets concerned.[31] A public intervention should be implemented when total welfare increases by more than the cost of the intervention.[32]

When can government intervention be efficiency enhancing? State intervention may improve the functioning of markets (and thereby pass the welfare test) when competition, if left to its own devices, is unlikely to produce efficient outcomes in terms of prices, output, and use of resources. These instances are referred to as "market failures."[33] Markets fail when the market (based on private actors) does not provide a good or service even though the economic benefits outweigh the economic costs. Sound public policy should be directed at improving the efficient functioning of markets by correcting market failures, as long as the benefits of intervention outweigh the costs.

Economists (backed by the first welfare theorem) have pointed to a number of situations where market failures exist. The most important in the field of state aid are as follows:[34]

Externalities   Externalities exist when actions by one agent have consequences for other agents. This "side effect" may be negative ("negative externalities") or positive ("positive externalities"). An example of a negative externality is the situation where environmental side effects are not taken into account by producers. An example of a positive externality can be found in the sphere of R&D. When a company undertakes R&D, this activity can have positive spillover effects for other companies (diffusion of knowledge; technological breakthroughs). Such side effects drive a wedge between the private benefits of a given action (to the actor) and the overall economic benefits of the action, which can lead to an inefficient market outcome.

Public goods (form of externality)   Public goods are goods for which it is difficult or impossible to exclude anyone from using the goods (and hence making them pay for the goods).[35] Here one can think of national defense, public broadcasting services, but also of services of general economic interest. In a sense, public goods represent an extreme case of externalities, since suppliers of such goods cannot appropriate the benefits to other people. As a result public goods are not provided by the market up to an efficient level. According to the first welfare theorem, the public financing of such goods or services may then be an efficient response to correct the problem of underprovision of public goods and to achieve a more efficient outcome.

Information asymmetries/missing markets   In certain markets, there is a discrepancy between the information available to one side of the market (e.g., the supply side) and the information available to the other side of the market (the demand side). A well-known example is the financial market where the company demanding finance (loans or equity) is typically better informed about the state and prospects of the company than banks or investors. If companies have little scope for credibly transmitting this type of information (as is often thought to be the case for SME activity in innovative industries), it is difficult for banks or investors to distinguish "good" from "bad" loans or investments. As a result the market may not come off the ground, even where there is a considerable group of SMEs with projects worth the investment. According to the first welfare theorem then, providing incentives to the financial sector to increase SME investments can be an appropriate response from the viewpoint of efficiency.

Coordination problems   Markets may also not function efficiently when there is a coordination problem between market actors. This aspect plays a key role in standards setting.

While state intervention can play an important role in providing for better coordination, the specific role for state aid is less clear in this context.

Market power   Another reason why the market may not lead to an efficient outcome is the existence of market power ("failure of competition"). Notably market power leads to prices that are too high from society's point of view, thereby not achieving efficiency. State aid measures can, in principle, reduce market power (e.g., by fostering entry into a given market that would not occur without the state aid). State aid measures can, of course, also create market power. State aid can lead to a buildup of market power in the hands of some firms, for instance, when companies that do not receive state aid (e.g., nondomestic firms) have to cut down on their market presence, or where state aid is used to erect entry barriers.

Equity Rationales and Potential Trade-Offs   Functioning markets establish an efficient allocation of goods. They also provide opportunity to individuals to engage in an open and fair competitive process. However, the outcome of this process might be perceived as inequitable. Governments may wish to intervene for purposes of creating a more equitable outcome of the market process. This provides a rationale for state intervention, for example in the form of social or regional aid.[36]

Economic theory is not determinative in identifying the "optimal" redistribution of wealth and resources, as this depends on the citizens' preferences.[37] In most textbooks on the application of economic theory to antitrust and regulation, a utilitarian welfare approach is taken so as to focus on efficiency considerations.[38] The criterion of efficiency offers a neutral concept, allowing economists to identify situations off the social welfare frontier independent of political concerns about distribution. In principle, integrating equity considerations into the analysis undermines the normative strength of economic concepts such as "perfect competition," or the idea of Adam Smith's invisible hand. A representative quote can be found in the industrial organization textbook by Jean Tirole (1993, p. 12):

In this book, I will treat income distribution as irrelevant. In other words, the redistribution of income from one consumer to another is assumed to have no welfare effect. (The marginal social utilities of income are equalized.) I certainly do not feel that actual income distributions are optimal, even with an optimal income-tax structure (because there are limits and costs to income taxation, as is emphasized by the optimal-taxation literature). Market intervention does have desirable or undesirable income-redistribution effects. But I will focus on the efficiency of markets, using Musgraves's (1959) framework in which the distribution branch of government worries about distribution and the allocation branch (the one considered in this book) deals with efficiency.[39]

A similar approach that limits attention to the efficiency of markets (i.e., to total welfare) appears not to be appropriate in the context of state aid control. First, in the area of state aid control, redistribution is often among the very objectives of state aid measures. Social and regional cohesion policy is explicitly mentioned in the Treaty as a possible ground for allowing state aid measures. In fact equity-oriented state aid measures—in particular, regional growth measures and, often linked, aid for sectoral adjustment—account for roughly 40 percent of all state aid granted.[40] Therefore redistributional concerns are taken into account in the approval of state aid and cannot be disregarded in an overall assessment.

One could argue, as in other fields of antitrust policy, that state aid is only one of many instruments governments have at their disposal to address redistributional issues. General transfers to individuals, in particular lump-sum, income or consumption related, are not subject to the EU state aid control. In addition a broad set of measures partially targeting efficiency objectives have strong distributional effects and are not covered by the notion of state aid either. This is the case for most measures in public education, health care, and general infrastructure. Therefore one might question whether an individual state aid measure (or state aid as such) is the appropriate instrument to address redistributional concerns or whether other—less distortive—instruments exist for redistributional objectives.[41]

Second, it has to be recognized that many public policy measures that focus on redistribution have strong side effects on efficiency, and vice-versa.[42] These side effects may result in a trade-off between equity and efficiency objectives. An important role of economic analysis is to identify any such trade-off.

For instance, state aid to improve living standards in disadvantaged regions by subsidizing local firms may have the side effect of distorting competition in product markets. These side effects may be strongly negative from an efficiency point of view. In fact, rather than solving any market failures, they introduce new ones (in the form of distortions of competition). Also, when redistribution is expensive in view of the shadow costs of taxation, no "cost-free" redistribution is possible. One of the reasons why redistributive transfers may not be optimal is linked to the incentive problems they tend to create. For instance, regions may reduce their effort to balance their budget or to eliminate structural rigidities in their economies if the negative implications of budget deficits and slow growth performance are compensated by higher aid receivables. In other words, financial compensations from richer to poorer regions may, if not properly implemented, induce moral hazard problems and thereby decrease economic efficiency.

Alternatively, providing R&D aid for large-scale research projects in order to tackle market failures in this field may imply additional resources to already well-equipped research centers in the "core" regions to the detriment of the "periphery." Similarly both environmental problems (due to congestion and concentration of industries) and income levels may be largest in urban areas, making them the main beneficiary of environmental aid schemes. Such measures may then accentuate existing differences in economic wealth among regions.

Sometimes there is no trade-off between efficiency and equity objectives—either due to positive side effects or to redistribution itself being an instrument to solve market failures. Consider two countries with an equal endowment of a specific input factor, say, capital.[43]

Suppose that the production function is concave in this input factor. The country with a more equal distribution of the input factor will exhibit a higher output than the other country. If perfect capital markets exist, those agents with a higher input endowment would lend resources to agents with lower endowments, and output in the country with less equally distributed income would rise to the level of the other country. If capital markets are imperfect, a government redistribution policy with respect to the input factor could at least partially replicate the perfect market equilibrium.[44] In such a scenario, redistribution may increase welfare, allowing different regimes to be ranked under an efficiency criterion. In fact, one can derive the level of "efficient redistribution" as the amount of redistribution that maximizes welfare.

In this context Sleuwaegen et al. (2000) argue that relocalization of firms between assisted regions (regions obtaining funds to attract investment) is often welfare decreasing due to "subsidy-shopping motives."[45] By contrast, relocalization between nonassisted and assisted regions would increase efficiency on average, and can be considered "efficient redistribution."

Similarly Besley and Seabright (1999) have pointed toward an interdependency between efficiency and equity in the context of aid to attract regional investments. When a company chooses to locate in a particular region, this may give benefits to other players in the region concerned as well, benefits that are not taken into account by the investing company. This is also the reason why regions often "compete" to attract the investment. From an overall efficiency point of view, it would be optimal if the region where the spillover effects are highest would obtain the investment concerned. If so, a "bidding contest" between regions would allow the region with the highest benefits to obtain the investment.[46] However, this result—which is optimal from an economic point of view—may not be achieved when countries are resource constrained. In such a case poor countries will easily be outbid by rich countries independently of whether the investment is most efficient in the region or not. Redistribution may then improve the efficiency of the process of attracting regional investment.[47]

In sum, it seems appropriate and—in contrast to merger control or antitrust—necessary to include redistributional concerns in the assessment of state aid measures, such as by explicitly addressing the trade-off between equity and efficiency in a general welfare test. In most cases, however, the weighting can only be of a qualitative nature as the pecuniary value of social benefits is often not measurable and entails a social judgment. Nevertheless, those judgements are necessary on a political level. De Graaff formulated, referring to Lionel Robbins, already in 1957: "...economists do not really mean that interpersonal comparisons are 'impossible.' All that they mean is that they cannot be made without judgements of an essentially ethical nature."

17.2.2 The Limits of State Aid

More controversial is the issue of how to correct for market failures. There are several significant problems to be addressed before one can be sure that state aid is effective and leads to a welfare enhancing outcome.

The first issue is measurability. The existence and, in particular, the magnitude of a particular market failure is hard to measure. Consider, for example, granting an R&D aid to a firm in order to create the "right" incentive to innovate. The market failure associated with this kind of aid may be related to the fact that the social return to R&D investment is higher than the private return. The exact size of the market failure depends on the difference between the social and the private returns, which in turn depends on a large number of other factors such as market structure, the ability to appropriate intellectual property, the patent system, the importance of the innovation, and the R&D production function, to name just a few. In practice, it is almost impossible to determine the precise size of the market failure. Nevertheless, it is certainly possible to investigate whether a market failure is likely to exist at all and whether it is significant. In other words a qualitative assessment is possible, while a quantitative approach will not be very reliable in most cases.

A second related issue is that the intended benefit of state aid need not be larger than the costs. State aid is costly. It involves using state funds that could have been used in other domains of government (opportunity costs of state aid) as well as the cost of raising the funds required (shadow costs of taxation). Even if one assumes that state aid is employed in the right kind of situations and in the right manner, it may still not be worth it, especially if its impact is smaller than anticipated (presumably because the market failure is small), or the costs are high.

Third, there may be undesirable side effects of state aid. Much of state aid has an impact on the functioning of the market. This may create anticompetitive side effects,[48] which may ultimately hurt the consumer. Some of these side effects affect national market participants only; others affect firms or customers in neighboring countries as well. The latter—so-called international spillover effects—will be discussed in more detail in the following section on European state aid control as they provide one of the strongest justifications for a European state aid control system.

A final area of difficulty is termed "government failures." A prominent example is the claim that governments are not good at "picking winners" either because they lack the relevant information, and/or because they are passing out favors to further their own goals. The literature on political economy has produced a number of insights as to when these informational or commitment problems lead to ineffective policy decisions.[49] The argument is based on politicians or regulators pursuing their private goals, which in some circumstances do not coincide with the public goals. For instance, in the so-called representative democracy model, politicians strive to be reelected and choose their policies accordingly. In this setup, policies are not always effective in raising social welfare. A particular concern is the existence of commitment problems of governments.[50] To achieve an effective policy, design issues such as accountability and transparency of government become important parameters.[51]

The discussion above suggests that although market failures may be the economic rationale for state aid, the effectiveness of state aid is determined by many other factors. Only in a world where a "perfectly informed and benevolent dictator" decides on state aid policies would one expect state aid to be perfectly effective.

17.3   The Rationale for European State Aid Control

This section analyzes the rationale for (supranational) state aid *control*, which is different from the rationale of national state aid. National intervention relates to situations where there is a wedge between private benefits and social benefits. EU state aid control is needed when "private" (country-specific) benefits of state intervention are not aligned with "social" (EU-wide) benefits. In other words, state aid is about the behavior of (national) market participants, whereas state aid control is about the behavior of national governments.

In principle, one can distinguish between three justifications for supranational state aid control. The first and most prominent one is that cross-border externalities may drive a wedge between national and international interests. Second, insofar as national authorities face commitment problems, delegating state aid control to a supranational authority may be beneficial. Third, safeguarding the proper functioning of the internal European market provides a justification for European state aid control. The latter rationale is closely linked to the first two, though.

17.3.1   Cross-border Externalities

Cross-border externalities occur when national governments do not take into account the (negative) side effects of their intervention on other European states.[52] In economics the literature on "strategic trade policy" (Brander and Spencer 1985, 1987) provides the strongest theoretical basis for having a supranational (European) system of state aid control. This literature studies settings in which countries compete with each other in an individually rational, but collectively wasteful subsidy competition, with the prospect to appropriate a larger share of international oligopoly profits. While this concept was originally put forward in relation to export subsidies, comparable prisoners' dilemma type of situations are common to a broad set of situations involving various forms of state aid, from launch aid in the aviation industry or other types of R&D aid to the attraction of foreign direct investment (FDI) or rescue and restructuring aid.

To give an example, consider a situation where rescue and restructuring aid is given to a failing firm in one member state producing products for markets located outside the European Union and facing competitors located in other European countries. Assume that the industry is in decline, forcing a gradual exit of certain producers. In such a situation the order of exit will typically depend on firms' ability to commit to stay in the industry.[53] A unilateral commitment to subsidize one of the firms can alter the order of exit, and induce the immediate closure of other (nondomestic) firms.

The insights of the strategic trade literature point to the importance of imperfect competition, in particular, resulting from scale economies, as a factor influencing the scope for strategic trade conduct. Under imperfect competition the reaction function of aid benefi-ciaries is shifted outward, resulting in less foreign output and, under the assumptions of the model, to higher price levels. By contrast, in perfectly competitive markets, aid to indi-vidual firms will affect profits of individual firms but not change the competitive price level and output. Finally, at the other extreme, export subsidies to a monopolist tend to expand output and lower prices toward efficient levels. Overall, we thus have an inverted-U rela-tionship in terms of the most distortive effects in the various market structures.

The second insight is that negative spillovers are a necessary precondition for pri-soners' dilemma situations to emerge.[54] When a prisoners' dilemma situation is present, a ban on export subsidies is optimal from the point of view of the group of countries as a whole.

Two particular caveats/extensions should be mentioned when applying this doctrine to European state aid control. First, the strategic trade literature does not take into account the specificities of an integrated European market. Second, if there are externalities that are location specific, subsidy races may not result in prisoners' dilemma situations.

As regards the first point, Collie (2005, 2002, 2000) extends the traditional strategic trade framework to an integrated economy, that is, the subsidized product is not exported to a third nonproducing country but produced for consumption in an unsegmented com-mon market between several countries. Within such an environment it is no longer only firm profits that determine national (and European) interest but also consumers' interests: consumers tend to benefit from expanded output, and hence from lower prices induced by state subsidies. In such an environment Collie shows that the prohibition of state aid is still welfare enhancing if the costs of funding the subsidies are sufficiently high and prod-ucts are close substitutes.[55] Collie therefore extends the main result of the strategic trade literature—subsidy competition may give rise to a prisoners' dilemma type of situation—to the conditions of an integrated economy. However, if products are highly differentiated the negative impact on competing firms is reduced while the beneficial effects on consumers is increased, resulting in state aid becoming welfare enhancing.[56]

With respect to the second point, the conclusions of the "strategic trade policy" litera-ture have to be qualified by an important argument put forward by Besley and Seabright (1999) in an FDI setting: if countries are heterogeneous and therefore the benefits to at-tract investment vary over regions, competition between countries to attract FDI can re-sult in an efficient allocation of investment across regions. As described in the previous section, despite the existence of negative externalities between regions, subsidy competition may induce an overall efficient outcome as it results in regions attracting FDI which derive the highest economic benefit from attracting FDI. The broader policy conclusion drawn by the authors is the need to focus on the institutional particularities of intergovernmental subsidy competition; issues like accountability, commitment capability in a dynamic con-text, or institutional restrictions on bidding become the focus of assessment. Those issues will be addressed further below.

To conclude, negative cross-country externalities are a strong justification for a supranational control system of national state aid measures. So, for instance, Fingleton et al. (1999, p. 76) have advocated an approach emphasizing international spillovers: "We conclude that a supranational system of state aid control might be appropriate in order to prevent countries giving aids that have strongly negative externalities on other countries without sufficient positive effects in the home country."

17.3.2 National Commitment Problems

A second possible justification for European state aid control is based on a potential commitment problem faced by national governments. Kornai (1980) generally referred to this problem as the "soft budget constraint." The idea is that governments may not be able to commit to clear rules and a fixed budget ex ante. In such a situation firms have smaller incentives to become efficient, as they (correctly) anticipate that the government will have no choice but to bail them out when the need arises. As a result efficiency and welfare is reduced.[57]

Dynamic commitment problems of such a type induce important economic inefficiencies. They are common problems in rescue and restructuring cases, but equally important for regional measures where national governments "bail out" regional governments, under R&D schemes where inefficient start-ups or R&D projects receive ongoing funding due to such dynamic commitment problems. Similarly projects that start off as public-private partnerships (PPI) sometimes continue, after some years, as fully public entities.

An important question in this context is whether national commitment problems justify intervention by a supranational authority. Are they not a purely national problem and—perhaps even more importantly—can a supranational control authority solve the problem?

Assume for a moment that the economic effects are de facto national, that is, the aid beneficiary operates on a local national market. Kornai (1980) defined two conditions for commitment problems to arise in such a context: first, the possibility for the beneficiary to renegotiate the terms of the funding ex post and, second, the existence of a close administrative relationship leading to some form of regulatory capture. Whether these conditions are met in the context of European state aid control is a matter of debate. It may be argued that the European Commission is less able or possibly even less willing[58] to enter into ex post renegotiation than national governments would. The closeness of the administrative relationship relates to the issue of whether national governments are more prone to lobbying on the part of firms than the European Commission, which may be more distant from national firms' interests.

Another aspect to consider is that a supranational institution may be better placed to spread "best practice," or even ensure consistency across jurisdictions, thereby increasing the efficiency of aid funding authorities.

In sum, a supranational institution may in principle be an instrument to solve national commitment problems. The extent to which national commitment problems are a justification for supranational state aid control remains controversial, however. While the European Commission may be better placed so resolve commitment problems, it is likely to be also less well informed about national circumstances.

17.3.3 Internal Market Rationale

The internal market is one of the pillars of the European Union. It is based on the rationale that a more integrated European market will—by increasing competition and by allowing companies to achieve scale—promote economic growth.[59] Given this view, national state aid measures are counterproductive. That is, they not only directly harm other countries (the basic externality argument) but also undermine the functioning of the European internal market, by preventing firms from achieving scale and effectively competing.

Supranational state aid control can be thought of as a commitment device to a principle —the internal market principle—which is in everybody's interest ex ante but difficult to abide by ex post. In a zone where trade barriers are abolished, governments may be tempted to resort to state aid to support their national industries and firms. State aid control keeps a lid on those actions that distort the functioning of the internal market. Likewise, member states tend to be reluctant to open up their markets when national incumbents are not "fit" for competition. In such a situation inefficient national industries or firms often go hand in hand with a slower liberalization process. State aid control can play a vital role in breaking such cycles.[60]

Accordingly Biondi and Eeckhout (2004) point to the priority of internal market considerations in state aid control: "... the assumption upon which the entire reasoning is based is the recognition that both sets of rules [internal market vs. state aid rules] are pursuing an identical aim, namely that of ensuring the free movement of goods under normal conditions of competition."[61]

17.4 The Policy Standard for Assessing State Aid at the European Level

The first step toward a more refined economic approach is to define a relevant policy standard in the assessment of state aid measures. Recall that Article 87(1) EC prohibits state aid measures that distort competition, insofar as they affect trade. Article 87(3) EC identifies a number of conditions under which state aid measures are compatible, which relate to both economic development and social and regional cohesion objectives. The common element underlying these conditions is that the measure should be in line with the "common interest." The crucial question is what interpretation should be given to the concept of common interest, that is, what is the relevant standard for assessing whether an aid measure is in the common interest?

In this section we argue that maximizing total (European) welfare, subject to redistributional objectives, is the proper interpretation of the concept of "common interest." Accordingly we advocate an approach that differentiates between a total welfare approach—that focuses on the efficiency of markets and the economy at large[62]—and a "social welfare function" approach that takes redistributive concerns into account. In other words, we propose to conceptually separate efficiency and equity objectives. Much of what economists can say is about efficiency (e.g., that state aid has the potential to increase efficiency if and only if market failures are addressed). With respect to distributional objectives, economics can provide certain guidance, such as with a view to minimize the cost in terms of efficiency of achieving such objectives (or even to identify measures that can contribute to both). The judgment on the value to be placed on equity and efficiency is ultimately one of a political nature. Nevertheless, to be clear about any trade-offs between the two is an important element in properly identifying measures that are in the common interest.

The remainder of this section will address the appropriate *policy standard* (i.e., the yardstick to be applied by the control agency when deciding to allow or disallow state aid) for assessing measures aimed at economic efficiency. We do not address the relevant standard under equity considerations. This does not imply that the equity considerations are less important though.

In developing our arguments, we begin by commenting on the welfare standard approach in the context of other areas of competition policy (in particular, in Article 81 and merger control) and then focus on state aid control.

17.4.1   Policy Standards in Other Fields of Competition Policy

Recall that other fields of competition policy—notably antitrust and merger control—have converged in recent years to what is, by and large, a consumer welfare policy standard. In the context of Article 81, the Commission holds that "[t]he objective of Article 81 is to protect competition on the market as a means of enhancing consumer welfare and of ensuring an efficient allocation of resources."[63] The reference to "efficient allocation of resources" could be interpreted in terms of total welfare. However, given that Article 81(3) explicitly refers to "consumer benefit," it appears that the Commission is to focus on consumer welfare.[64]

In merger control, the emphasis is now firmly on consumer welfare. The recently adopted Merger Guidelines indicate that "[e]ffective competition brings benefits to consumers, such as low prices, high quality products, a wide selection of goods and services, and innovation. Through its control of mergers, the Commission prevents mergers that would be likely to deprive customers of these benefits by significantly increasing the market power of firms."[65] In the context of the analysis of efficiencies claimed by the merging parties, the Guidelines specify that the "relevant benchmark in assessing efficiency claims is that consumers will not be worse off as a result of the merger."[66]

It is worth reflecting on the rationale put forward in support of a consumer welfare policy standard in these areas (as opposed to a total welfare standard). In principle, economists advocate a *total* welfare standard—an approach going back to Williamson's analysis in the late 1960s—that encompasses a balancing of rents to producers and consumers. Nevertheless, there are several arguments in support of entrusting a competition agency with a consumer welfare standard. These are based on the following considerations: (1) informational advantages, (2) merger selection bias, and (3) lobbying activities. In addition a consumer standard is considered to be easier to implement.[67] It is important to emphasize that none of the rationales for a consumer standard are normative. Instead, it is the presence of regulatory imperfections or regulatory failures that can justify the consumer standard as a policy standard. In particular, such imperfections can turn a consumer standard into the policy standard that in fact maximizes total welfare.

We now review the arguments briefly in some more detail, starting with informational advantages on the part of firms. Besanko and Spulber (1993) argue that consumer welfare should have more weight in merger assessments in order to counterbalance a certain underenforcement bias due to a problem of asymmetric information (the competition authority having less information regarding efficiency gains resulting from mergers than the merging parties themselves). The basic idea is that under a total welfare standard, firms tend to propose mergers that exhibit relatively large efficiencies. As a result of the problem of asymmetric information, it becomes optimal for the competition authority to adopt a low probability to block mergers, leading to underenforcement from a total welfare perspective. The underenforcement can be avoided by the agency committing to a consumer standard ex ante.[68]

The second line of argument—a selection bias—starts from the observation that competition authorities can only assess mergers that are notified (see Lyons 2002). Under a total welfare standard firms will put forward mergers that meet the total welfare test (to obtain approval) but that, under this constraint, maximize firm profits. Inasmuch as profits and consumer rent are negatively correlated, it will not be the total welfare-maximizing mergers that are put forward by firms. Implementing a consumer welfare standard can counterbalance this bias.

Finally, Neven and Röller (2005) analyze a political economy environment using a common agency framework (see Bernheim and Whinston 1986b) where firms (both merging firms and nonmerging competitors but not consumers)[69] can provide to the enforcement agency (the common agent) inducements that are contingent on the outcome of the merger review. They show that—under certain institutional settings—a consumer standard maximizes total welfare. In particular, an institutional environment of low transparency (which allows effective lobbying) and low accountability of the agency implies that a consumer standard is superior to a total welfare standard.

In sum, there are a number of arguments that support a consumer welfare approach in merger control. Whether these arguments carry over to the field of state aid control is an open question, to which we now turn.

17.4.2 The Policy Standard in the Field of State Aid Control

As we have mentioned above, total welfare is the appropriate standard as far as economic efficiency is concerned. Nevertheless, in certain political and institutional environments, entrusting a control agency with a consumer welfare standard may be optimal from the point of view of maximizing total welfare. Before investigating this issue in state aid, let us note that in contrast to other areas of competition policy, total welfare in state aid does not only include the sum of producer and consumer surplus but also the cost to tax payers. This is an important difference to other areas of competition policy, and we will return to this difference later.

We begin by asking whether the policy standard in state aid should be based on total welfare or on consumer welfare. In light of the discussion above, the answer will depend on whether there is a potential enforcement bias (as in merger control) inherent in an explicit total welfare standard that is likely to be reduced or avoided by a consumer standard.

As we mention above, one of the distinguishing features of state aid control is that the European Commission has to deal primarily with member states and not with firms. Information as well as potential lobbying efforts run from the aid beneficiary (the firms or the industry favored by the measure) via the national government to the Commission. To the extent that state authorities are prone to be captured by individual interest groups, the Commission is confronted with governments supporting vested interests (i.e., those of the beneficiaries of the aid). Given the institutional architecture of the European Union, it is likely that governments' influence and bargaining powers vis-à-vis the Commission is not smaller than that of individual firms. Hence there is an institutional risk that distorted interests are carried forward, via national governments, to the Commission.

In terms of systematic empirical evidence there are not many studies to our knowledge that investigate the political economy of European state aid control. One example is the study by Neven and Röller (2000) who investigate the political economy of state aid allocation. They find that the allocation of state aid can be explained to a very large degree with political and institutional variables. Even though the evidence provided is not based on any structural estimation, it is nevertheless striking that most of the variation is due to noneconomic factors.

A related question is then whether national governments are more likely to support certain types of vested interests. The OECD Roundtable on subsidies and state aid in 2001 concluded that domestic opposition to subsidies is relatively low, while domestic support is relatively large as long the negatively affected firms are located in a foreign country.[70] Furthermore, as in other fields of competition policy, the aid beneficiaries tend to be concentrated, while the negative externalities tend to be spread widely over the population. All this suggests that national governments are more likely to support national producers.[71]

Overall, we consider it likely that the political pressure in state aid is substantial, and certainly not lower that in other areas of competition policy. In addition it appears that national governments are more likely to support domestic producers, rather than domestic consumers (and obviously not foreign interests). It is also unlikely that nondomestic rivals are underrepresented in state aid control procedures, either directly or through their respective governments. Accordingly we argue that decision-making at the EU level can benefit from more emphasis on consumers for similar reasons as in merger control: informational disadvantages, selection, and lobbying.

With regard to the informational disadvantages, the Commission's investigative powers to collect market information are rather limited in the field of state aid control. In the first phase of the investigation—before the opening of the "formal investigation procedure"—information exchange is channeled through the aid-granting member state by means of the notification process (it may be triggered by a third party complaint, however). After opening the formal investigation procedure the consultation of third parties is carried out by a publication in the EU Official Journal asking for comments from interested parties. A more direct exchange (as in hearings) or a proactive market inquiry is not envisaged, even though not excluded either.[72] In any case, a legal instrument to facilitate the collection of market information through third parties does not exist.

As far as selection bias is concerned, note that the European Commission mostly assesses state aid measures that are notified. Under a standard of review focusing on total welfare, member states would tend to select measures that marginally meet the total welfare standard, yet maximize domestic producer surplus.[73]

Finally, with respect to the lobbying bias, recall that the political economy literature shows that a government takes efficient decisions either when the government is benevolent itself (i.e., it is immune to lobbying) or when *all* affected parties are represented by a lobby.[74] Given that consumers are not fully represented in the state aid procedure, it follows that a total welfare standard may be subject to an enforcement bias.

In sum, the main arguments put forward in the literature on merger control in favor of a consumer standard appear also to be valid in the context of state aid control. As a result a consumer standard—rather than a total welfare approach—seems more prudent. In other words, a policy standard focusing explicitly on consumer welfare appears better suited to foster total welfare than a standard of review focusing explicitly on total welfare.

A possible criticism of the consumer standard might be that state aid measures always tend to affect consumers positively, at least in a static context. For example, assume some market power ex ante, then a production subsidy will typically result in an output expansion and a reduction in prices, to the benefit of consumers.

However, the same criticism might be expressed toward the use of a total welfare standard, if one were to define total welfare as the sum of consumer and producer welfare. In the example above, with some market power ex ante, the production subsidy tends to foster both consumer welfare and total welfare alike (output moves toward the total welfare optimum, thereby increasing allocative efficiency).[75]

Apart from this, it is important not to forget about the cost of financing state aid. The positive correspondence between state aid and consumer benefit no longer holds when consumers are also considered in their capacity as taxpayers. In this light we propose that the opportunity costs of funding, that is, the direct cost of the subsidy and the deadweight loss due to distortionary taxes, need to be part of the policy standard for state aid. Collie

(2005, 2002, 2000) has shown that within such an environment, state aid control enhances total welfare for reasonable estimates for the opportunity cost of funding. Importantly Collie's results are derived under a total welfare standard, but they apply equally under a consumer/tax standard.

In operational terms, by including the tax dimension, a consumer standard bolsters the requirement that state aid is effective in changing firms' behavior and not resulting in mere windfall profits. This issue (also called the "incentive effect") is crucial in many areas of state aid—for instance, in state aid directed toward firms' location decisions or whether R&D aid results in crowding out or crowding in of private investment. In all these cases a consumer/tax standard is a significant safeguard to ensure the effectiveness of aid measures and to ensure that aid increases total welfare.

A further aspect of the effect of state aid on consumers is that the short-run and the long-run impact on consumers may be very different. As in other areas of competition policy, short-run benefits might translate into long-run losses if aid leads to exclusionary conduct. If aid is used to predate rivals or to prevent exit, short-term lower prices have to be compared to possible future increases. Even in the short run, aid may not always benefit consumers if it leads to anticompetitive behavior, such as when aid forecloses or marginalizes foreign competitors. Incumbents that cross-subsidize competitive segments may deter entry and harm consumers in the short run.

A related question is whether a consumer standard in state aid is tougher than a total welfare standard. In general, this will depend on how the aid affects firms' profits. Firms' profits are composed of two groups: beneficiaries and rivals. Under most standard assumptions it stands to reason that the beneficiary benefits while the rivals are being harmed. Whether aggregate industry profits are increasing depends on the precise circumstances. Nevertheless, to the extent that subsidies increase industry profits, a consumer standard would be tougher, meaning all aid that is compatible under a consumer surplus standard would also be compatible under a total welfare standard, but not the reverse.

Let us briefly turn to two other possible standards often cited in the field of state aid: the effect-on-rivals standard and the internal market standard.[76] The effect-on-rivals standard is closely linked to the idea of a "level playing field." The idea of a level playing field focuses on achieving ex ante fairness: a measure is not distortive if it leaves the market position of all competitors unchanged. From a conceptual perspective this approach could essentially lead to all aid being "bad," since the inherent effect of most aid measures is to change the relative market position of the companies in the market. In this sense, the effect-on-rivals standard is consistent with the legal presumption that state aid is illegal.

The main shortcoming of the effects-on-rivals standard is that it does not directly assess the effect of an aid measure, on markets, competition, or consumers. This approach makes it difficult to use the standard as an overarching standard in the field of state aid, as it does not recognize potential benefits of aid both at the national and the European level. On the other hand, an effect-on-rivals standard is closely linked to a consumer standard in more dynamic settings. An advantage obtained through state intervention (and not through superior performance) is likely to reduce the incentives to compete. In other words, the effect-on-rivals can be a proxy for the negative impact on consumers in a dynamic sense. The greater the negative impact on rivals, the more likely it is that consumers will be negatively affected in the longer run.[77] At this point one can not help but mention the similarities with the debate of "competition on the merits" as well as "protecting competitors instead of the competitive process" surrounding the Article 82 reform. There are, however, important differences here.[78] The conduct in question in state aid is not undertaken by private firms, but by governments. In this sense an approach that minimizes the impact on competitors might be more justified in the context of state aid control than in the context of the antitrust rules.

Finally, the internal market standard is usually not associated with balancing positive versus negative effects of a particular measure. Rather, it is often interpreted as one where any obstacle to the proper functioning of the internal market is prohibited.[79] This per se approach makes it difficult, as in the case of the effect-on-rivals standard, to use the internal market standard as an overarching standard in the field of state aid, as it does not recognize potential benefits of aid at the national or European level.

In sum, we see merit in implementing a policy standard that emphasizes consumers and taxpayers in the assessment of state aid measures. Emphasizing these categories of actors is likely to bolster the requirement that state aid is effective and increases total (EU) welfare. The effect on rivals could play a role in terms of understanding the dynamic effects of state aid on competition (e.g., keeping inefficient firms alive). However, as a final objective we do not think that the effect-on-rivals standard should be endorsed.

17.5   Elements of a General Framework—Toward an Effects-Based Approach

In this section we outline some elements of a framework for the assessment of state aid measures. To recall, state aid that affects trade between member states and distorts competition is prohibited under Article 87(1), unless the European Commission exempts the aid from this prohibition under Article 87(3). The common element for exempting aid under Article 87(3) is that the aid is in the "common interest." As mentioned above, we propose to interpret the meaning of "common interest" as encompassing two fundamental aspects, efficiency and equity. To the extent that an aid measure is analyzed in terms of its impact on efficiency, we argue that there are good reasons to employ a welfare standard that takes explicitly into account consumer benefit and the effect on taxpayers.

As a conceptual framework for evaluating state aid measures, we advocate the use of a general balancing test. In essence, this test asks whether (1) the state aid addresses a market failure or other objective of common interest, (2) the state aid is well targeted (i.e., is the aid an appropriate instrument, does it provide an incentive effect and is it kept to the minimum necessary), and (3) the distortions of competition are sufficiently limited so that the overall balance is positive.

Further we argue that in order to increase the effectiveness of EU state aid control, a more *effects-based* approach is warranted. Whereas traditionally most aid measures are scrutinised under a "one size fits all" approach based on formal criteria, a more systematic assessment of the positive and negative effects of the aid is warranted, in particular, for aid measures involving large amounts of aid. Such an approach would be a means to enhance the effectiveness of state aid control, to better distinguish "good" aid from "bad" aid.

17.5.1 A Structured Assessment of State Aid Measures: The Balancing Test

We propose to implement an effects-based approach in state aid control through a "balancing test." In particular, we suggest the following three-step test for assessing the compatibility of a state aid measure under Article 87(3):[80]

1. Is there a market failure or another objective of common interest? (e.g., social or regional cohesion)?
2. Is the aid measure targeted (i.e., does the proposed aid address the market failure or other objective)? In particular,
a. Is the aid measure an appropriate instrument, or are there other, better placed instruments?
b. Is there an incentive effect, does the aid change the behavior of firms?
c. Is the aid kept to the minimum, or could the same change in behavior be obtained with less aid?
3. Are the distortions of competition and effect on trade sufficiently limited so that the overall balance is positive?

Fundamentally, the test balances the positive and negative effects of state aid. This can be done by first analyzing the "benefits" of a state aid measure under steps 1 and 2. Finally, the "cost" or negative effects of an aid measure are assessed under step 3, including the balancing.

Before commenting on the three legs in more detail, let us mention one other issue. It may be argued that when state aid is properly used to solve a market failure (conditions 1 and 2), then there may be no "real" distortion of competition (there may be a distortion of competition in the strict sense of Article 87(1), but not in the sense that there are concrete negative effects against which the positive effects of the aid measure have to be balanced). In other words, some form of "integrated" approach might seem more appropriate, leading to a two-legged test rather than a three-legged test.

We believe that the idea of balancing two sides under the compatibility criteria—that is, to distinguish positive and negative elements in the sense of a cost-benefit analysis—is a more practical approach.[81] The legal notions of "distortion of competition" and "effect on trade" are terms describing the negative side of aid, with "common interest" the positive side. Solving market failures or addressing cohesion objectives adds to the positive side, while introducing (new) distortions is a negative. In practice, the two sides are often separable, and the "integration" can be done under the balancing in step 3. Consider the following example.[82]

Example: Environmental Aid   A pipeline for the transportation of a chemical product A is built with public support. Suppose that state aid is justified because the pipeline reduces the risk of environmental damage relative to other means of transportation, such as motorways. Consider two types of distortion of competition. Suppose that product B, which is a close substitute for product A in the downstream market, cannot use the pipeline for technical reasons. The state funds provided for the construction of the pipeline therefore put producers of product B at a competitive disadvantage, resulting in a lower market presence and lower profitability. This manifests a first distortion of competition. A second potential distortion could arise vis-à-vis other modes of transportation, such as road transport: compared to a situation without aid, fewer products will be transported via those alternative modes. The first type of distortion is (at least conceptually) separable from the addressed market failure: internalizing the environmental externality does not automatically lead to discrimination between products A and B. As a result whether or not one chooses an integrated approach is irrelevant. The second distortion, however, is inherently linked to the market failure. Within an integrated approach, the latter effect might not be considered a "distortion" in the market for transportation, in that it simply corrects a market failure and improves the functioning of the market. Under a balancing approach, it would be considered a "distortion," but would be balanced against the possible positive environmental benefits. The result of the assessment—compatibility or prohibition—would be the same under both approaches though.

The example illustrates that some distortions are inevitably linked with market failures, while others are a side effect (new market failures). However, it also shows that there is no problem in identifying both effects as a distortion in the legal sense of Article 87(1) and leaving it up to the final balancing under Article 87(3) to decide on compatibility. It is worth noting in this context the concepts of "distortion of competition" and "effect on trade" are not necessarily identical under Article 87(1) and Article 87(3). Article 87(1) has an important *jurisdictional* dimension that is based on spillovers across member states. In particular, the mere *existence* or likelihood of an effect on nondomestic rivals is relevant under Article 87(1). Such an approach may be reasonable, as long as the *magnitude* and *importance* of these effects are assessed under Article 87(3).

Linked to the question of an integrated versus a balancing approach is the question of sequencing of the individual steps. The balancing test as presented here is considered a complete test requiring a full assessment of all legs in order to come to an overall assessment. Alternatively, the test could also be implemented in a sequential way. In this case a "weak" performance on one of the first steps would lead to incompatibility of the aid measure. Such a sequential approach results in lower resource requirements and in an overall tougher regime. The disadvantage of such an approach is, however, that aid measures may be declared incompatible without proper assessment of the distortionary effects of the aid on competition and trade—the limitation of that provides the main justification for a European state aid control though. Consequently such an approach seems to be appropriate only if those elements are addressed sufficiently under Art. 87(1) or through other pre-selection filters, such as within block exemption regulations or guidelines.

We now discuss the individual legs of the test in more detail.

Assessing the Benefits—Steps 1 and 2 of the Test   An appropriate starting point in any case assessment is to ask whether there is a market failure or an objective of common interest (step 1 of the balancing test). This transparency vis-à-vis the objective of the aid measure is needed to assess the effectiveness and necessity of the aid. Only if there is a market failure can a measure have the potential to increase economic efficiency. Furthermore addressing efficiency and equity upfront clarifies possible trade-offs between the two. The existence of a market failure or a cohesion objective is, however, a *necessary but not sufficient* condition for state aid to be effective and appropriate.

Step 2 ensures that the aid targets the market failure or achieves another common interest objective, meaning it asks whether the aid solves the problem. This step touches upon the problem of "government failure." Specifically, building on past practice in state aid control, the test addresses three aspects. The first part of step 2 asks whether the aid instrument is the *appropriate instrument*. In other words, it asks whether there are other, better-placed instruments that are either more effective or less costly in reaching the objective chosen. Clearly, a certain type of state aid measure may not be the most effective way at achieving the stated goal. There may be other government instruments—inside and outside state aid—that might be better placed to improve the functioning of markets or achieve a social objective. From an economic point of view, many different policies outside state aid can be thought of, such as infrastructure provision, education, labor market policy, and product market regulation. Similarly problems of regional or social cohesion can be addressed through state aid but also through other, possibly more generic, policies. How far the net should be spun in terms of a search for better-placed instruments is a matter of policy decision. At a minimum alternative measures inside state aid should be assessed.

The second part of step 2 asks whether there is an *incentive effect*, namely does the aid change the behavior of firms. Without an incentive effect, firms behavior is not affected and consumers are not affected either, since the aid is simply transferred from the taxpayer to the firms. Note the crucial role that a consumer standard plays in this context. If there is no incentive effect, there cannot be any benefit to consumers, hence the necessity of the incentive effect. In this sense the consumer standard (as operationalized by the incentive effect) is a safeguard against windfall profits to firms.

The issue of the incentive effect is related to, but not identical to, the third part of step 2. While the second part asks whether the aid measure will result in the company adopting the required behavior, the third part asks whether the same change in behavior can be obtained with a lower amount of aid. The second question thus relates to the *impact* of the state aid measure, the third to the *efficiency* of the state aid measure.

When assessing the benefits of an aid measure, different questions will arise depending on the objective that is pursued. An example from the area of state aid to risk capital funds might be instructive at this point.

Example: Risk Capital Schemes Financing the Earliest Phase of Enterprise Formation

Consider a risk capital fund (created, in part, with public money) that is financing the earliest phase of enterprise formation, the seeding phase. Why could public funding of such type of activity be justified from a market failure perspective? Assume that the expected return on investment is very low, or even negative. By contrast, suppose that the provision of risk capital at later stages is highly profitable. If firms cannot write complete contracts committing themselves to stay with venture capitalists throughout the different stages of development, cream skimming behavior may be observed: private venture capitalists provide funding for later stages only and free-ride on early fund providers. Based on this market failure, an in-depth assessment of the measure is possible. First, it has to be assessed whether there are other, better placed instruments than state aid available. Could, for instance, a relatively simple change in financial market regulations allow complete contracts? Second, does the aid measure change the behavior of private investors so that the objective is reached; that is, does the measure attract ("crowd-in") additional private funds by solving the bottleneck in the seeding phase of funding? Past examples of successfully implemented schemes can be useful evidence in support of the case. Finally, it has to be assessed whether the same change in behavior could have been obtained with less aid. This involves questions relating to the endowment of the fund, as well as the financial conditions under which funding is provided to start-ups.

Another example might be a regional development scheme. The objective here is on whether the scheme leads to higher levels of economic activity in the region, an objective that is in principle not a market failure objective. Nevertheless, even when one is concerned with regional or social cohesion, it is possible that targeting market failures is the best way forward, as certain state aid measures may well be capable of pursuing both efficiency and equity rationales at the same time. Using state funds to resolve market failures in disadvantaged regions has the effect of both increasing economic efficiency and fostering regional cohesion within the country.[83]

Example: Risk Capital Schemes in Less Prosperous Regions

Consider a risk capital fund set up in a less prosperous region of Europe.[84] Assume that due to exogenous factors—such as political instability—both the amount and the conditions at which private risk capital is provided are less favorable than in other regions. The number of start-ups and fast-growing SMEs is smaller than in regions of comparable size. In such circumstances providing public funds to develop the regional risk capital market can be a sensible policy instrument for more economic activity and growth in this region. Experience of other regions with comparable shortcomings could give some guidance.

Three further points should be emphasized when assessing the benefits of aid measures: First, the concept of market failure is still a relatively broad concept. There are several market failures that can be argued. State aid control should, however, concentrate on a small set of well-defined market failures and specify those clearly in its guidelines.

Second, market failures are difficult to measure. We therefore suggest that the empirical assessment should focus on whether the underlying conditions for a particular market failure do exist (e.g., Do incomplete contracts exist? Is the return on investment for seed capital negative?) and whether the market outcome is consistent with the existence of a market failure (e.g., whether the private market for seed capital is underdeveloped as compared to regions not affected by this market failure).

Third, as already mentioned, the focus and depth of analysis depends on the particular area of state aid. For instance, the incentive effect is a particular concern in cases of environmental aid, regional investment aid, and R&D. Appropriateness of the aid is of particular concern in the context of regional investment aid. For instance, labor market policies, infrastructure development, or improved stability of the regulatory and legal environment are in most cases more important elements of an effective policy to attract regional investments.

Assessing and Balancing the Negative Effects—Step 3 of the Test Even if a state aid measure targets a defined market failure (steps 1 and 2 of the test), it may cause significant distortions of competition in the European Union (i.e., the aid may introduce other types of market failures). For this reason the overall balance needs to be assessed, which is done at step 3. A proper balancing would seek to identify and analyze the effects on competition and on trade. Not all forms of state aid are likely to distort competition in an appreciable way. This insight is particularly important in the context of Article 87(3), where the balancing is to take place.[85] We begin by defining a typology of theories of harm and then mention possible criteria that can be used in the assessment.

A Typology of the Distortions of Competition We propose to differentiate between four different (but mutually dependent) types of distortion of competition. The first three relate to the impact of aid on *effective competition* between *firms*. The fourth relates to the impact of aid on competition between *member states*. We will address these in turn.

1. *Reducing effective competition by supporting inefficient production* A first potentially harmful effect of state aid is that it keeps inefficient firms or sectors in place. Consequently

it negatively affects productive efficiency, as well as the efficiency of the economy as a whole (total welfare). In particular, aid granted in markets featuring overcapacity and aid given in declining industries is likely to be problematic in that it risks creating or maintaining inefficient market structures. These industries normally witness exit or consolidation so as to restore the profitability of the industry to normal levels. State aid to individual companies may alter this process by cementing the market position of any given recipient. Also, when aid is not given to particularly inefficient firms, market structures may arise that feature several players operating significantly below efficient scale.

Examples include state aid to rescue firms in financial difficulty, financial arrangements in the electricity sector whereby state bodies purchase power at inflated prices shielding incumbent operators from effective competition, sector specific aid (e.g., to sectors using outdated technologies), as well as aid to particular regions that may be used to allocate production factors inefficiently across regions.

2. *Reducing effective competition by distorting dynamic incentives*   State aid may alter the investment incentives of firms, thereby decreasing dynamic efficiency (welfare in the long run). When a company receives aid to invest in production capacity or R&D, for example, this generally increases the presence of this company in the (future) product market. This increased presence may lead rivals to revise their future revenue prospects from their own investments downward and to adjust their own investment plans accordingly.

Two reactions from rivals can be envisaged. Either they reduce the scope of their original investment plans (crowding-out effect), or they maintain or increase the scope of their plans. In both cases rivals are affected. In our view, one should be concerned primarily about crowding-out effects as they may result in a lower overall increase (or even in an overall decrease) in the level of investment activity in the markets. Further it must be borne in mind that "soft budget constraint"[86] problems might erode the beneficiary firms' incentive to become efficient.

3. *Reducing effective competition by increasing market power*   State aid measures can be used by a single firm (or a group of firms) to increase or maintain market power, by foreclosing actual or potential competitors. For instance, subsidizing firms in their "home market" may create entry barriers for (nondomestic) competitors, while the resulting monopoly profits can be used by the recipient firms for expansion into new (foreign) markets. In the context of R&D, if funding of public R&D is done through a large incumbent firm only, R&D competition may be significantly impeded, especially if other players would have been better placed to undertake the R&D project.

The degree to which the recipients of state aid have a degree of control over the various markets concerned is important. Where the recipient is already dominant on a product market, the aid measure may reinforce this dominance by further weakening the competitive constraint that rivals can exert on the recipient company.

4. *Distorting production and location decisions across member states*   By supporting domestic production and attracting foreign investors, member states directly intervene in the

international allocation of resources, thereby affecting trade flows and potentially inducing a shift in the localization of economic activities across member states. In principle, two main concerns can be identified: First, trade may be affected in that the aid measure affects trade flows in goods and services in the European Union, taking location choices as a given. Second, aid measures may alter the location of productive assets in the European Union.

In both instances national governments may have an interest in supporting domestic production and in attracting foreign investors, because of the positive implications for employment, tax revenues, and the business environment in the member state. These measures may result in an inefficient production structure throughout Europe. In addition these measures may create negative spillovers for other member states when the good or service is traded. As discussed above, such type of negative international spillover may induce subsidy races between member states whereby every member state ends up worse off.

Criteria for Assessing the Negative Effects of State Aid   After having identified the possible distortions of competition—or, if one likes, the "theories of harm"—the significance of these negative effects has to be assessed. Under a proper balancing, distortions of competition become relevant only to the extent that they significantly affect trade in the European Union. State aid measures that reduce effective competition but primarily at a local or regional level should be assessed more positively at the EU level. In other words, the analysis of the impact on competition and trade under Article 87(3) should go beyond that of Article 87(1).

We now describe a number of potentially relevant elements for assessing the significance of the distortive effects of aid measures and their effect on trade. We identify three main groups of criteria: procedural aspects of the granting process, market characteristics, and criteria linked to the amount and type of aid.[87]

Procedural Aspects of the Granting Decision   The level of distortion of an aid is likely to depend on procedural aspects of the granting process such as selectivity of the process, aid schemes versus ad hoc aid, and open tender procedure. Aid measures may have strong potential to distort competition insofar as the granting process is not transparent and does not follow an open and nondiscriminatory procedure. In such cases there is a potential that aid measures may be designed to support specific firms, such as national champions. Accordingly, in general terms, aid schemes tend to be less distortive than ad hoc aid measures. Open tender procedures are to be regarded as less distortive as well: open tenders reduce the risk of "picking winners."

Even though aid schemes may be a priori less distortive than ad hoc aid, they are not without effect. Schemes may have a serious impact on the location of production within Europe, in particular, when the scheme is de facto sector specific. Further, specific selection factors may exist, which result in de facto selectivity for a small group of firms with significant market power or potential to obtain significant market power as a result of the measure. This may in particular be the case if the measure addresses only a small number of beneficiaries, or when there are no safeguards to exclude firms with significant market power. For instance, high intensity aid schemes may de facto direct a large share of the scheme budget to a small group of firms. In such cases, the aid scheme may need to be assessed under the same criteria as individual aid measures.

Market Characteristics   Market characteristics are important elements to assess the negative effects of an aid measure, both with respect to its impact on effective competition and production shifts between different jurisdictions. A list of such market characteristics includes the following:[88]

- Size or market share of recipient or asymmetry of market shares.
- Entry barriers like R&D intensity of the beneficiary's markets.
- The degree of product differentiation and complementarities with neighboring markets.
- Segmentation of markets among member states.
- Tradability of the goods; impact on location choices.

For individual aid measures, the market share of the beneficiary in the affected markets may indicate market power.[89] Distortions are more likely to arise if the aid measures increase the asymmetry among competitors, in the sense of making large firms (in terms of market share) even larger. Other relevant factors for assessing the capacity of aid to increase the beneficiary's market power include the level of product differentiation, the significance of entry barriers, as well as the presence of buyer power.[90]

When firm-specific information is not available, general information about the concentration in the affected markets may still be relevant. An existing track record of competition problems in the affected markets (e.g., past or ongoing antitrust cases or the fact that the beneficiary is a strong national incumbent in a recently liberalized sector) may provide additional indications.

Market characteristics are important to asses the potential of a measure to significantly influence trade flows, either by shifting production between jurisdictions or by influencing localization decisions by firms. The degree to which goods or services are tradable is important in this respect. The potential to affect trade may also be higher if the aid beneficiary is a large firm with economic activities in several member states. Furthermore the potential to shift rents between jurisdictions depends on the concentration in the affected markets.

Significant negative effects may also exist even when the targeted product is nontradable, as it may have an impact on upstream, downstream, or complementary markets. In particular, a state aid decreasing the price of an input may adversely affect the production possibilities of a downstream product in other member states by increasing the relative cost of production. Aid measures in important input markets (e.g., banking) or in large markets with a Europeanwide dimension (e.g., markets in the automotive sector) have a higher potential to affect trade flows in a significant way than aid to niche segments.[91] Aid measures in markets characterized by structural overcapacity or stagnation at EU level are of particular concern, especially when inefficient capacity is kept in place or even expanded as a result of the aid measure.

Amount and Type of Aid   In addition to the procedural aspects of the granting process and the market characteristics, the amount and type of aid instrument is of importance. Criteria in this category include the following:

- The absolute amount of aid and aid intensities.
- "One time last time principle," repetition and duration.
- Aid to variable cost or aid to investment cost affecting entry or quality.
- Granted as direct subsidy, tax reduction or guarantee.

In general, the larger the amount of aid, the higher is the potential to reduce effective competition and to affect location decisions. The same logic applies to aid measures repeatedly given to the same beneficiary in order to preserve a market position, such as aid granted to a (large) firm in financial difficulties.

In terms of the *type of aid*, one can differentiate between operational aid and investment aid. Operational aid tends to have a direct impact on the level of variable cost, and thus on the price level and consumers. As a result operational aid can be expected to have a stronger impact on the flow of goods and services. Investment aid can also affect effective competition and trade, but its impact is typically more long-term, such as through the location decision of firms.

Naturally the multiple effects of all the above-mentioned criteria—procedural aspects, market characteristics, as well as the amount and type of aid—are interrelated. For example, a large investment aid to an individual firm has a clear potential to distort competition and affect trade in the European market. This potential is larger when the granting process is not transparent and does not follow an open and nondiscriminatory procedure. Moreover, if the beneficiary is a significant player in the relevant market concerned, then the investment will further affect trading conditions, as well as likely induce a shift in the localization of economic activities across member states. A proper balancing should aim at analyzing these aspects in an integrated way.

Analyzing the various interdependencies will require a certain amount of sophistication and investigation effort. This should not lead toward less effective state aid control, or to less predictability. Careful attention should be given in this respect to the architecture of state aid control.

17.5.2   The Architecture of State Aid Control: Precision and Predictability

A more effects-based approach in state aid control—as envisaged by the balancing test proposed in the previous section—should lead to more precision in terms of discriminating between "good" aid and "bad" aid. At the same time there is a need for a sufficient level of predictability for the member states when designing state aid measures. In our view, an economic approach does not necessarily mean fewer rules—the focus should be on *better* rules, thereby preserving predictability. Moreover an explicit analysis of the economic effects of aid measures on markets and consumers is needed *in certain cases*. This requires that it be clear under what conditions a more effects-based analysis is triggered. It also implies that the effect-based analysis must be clearly spelled out in guidelines and other soft law provisions, including the theories of harm and the empirical evidence required to assess them.

An economic approach is relevant for a number of stages. First, it is relevant for designing explicit provisions (e.g., safe harbors identifying measures that are per se allowed and prohibition regions identifying measures that are per se prohibited). Second, and related, it can be used for identifying under what conditions a more effects-based analysis is required (linked with priority setting). Third, an economic approach can be applied to provide an analytical framework (which may include the formulation of presumptions) to assess individual aid measures where this is appropriate.

It is useful to start by looking at the approach as it has traditionally been used by the Commission up to the *State Aid Action Plan*[92] (see figure 17.1). The assessment is largely based on defining aid intensity *thresholds*, below which the aid measure is allowed (safe harbor region) and above which it is prohibited (prohibition region)—both within the context of guidelines and block exemptions. Detailed rules have been devised that specify the cost categories eligible for state support, the maximum aid intensities to be applied, and

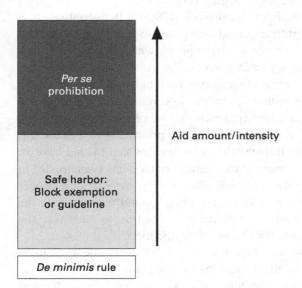

Figure 17.1
Traditional architecture

a number of criteria that, if they are met, allow for higher maximum aid intensities ("top-ups").

For the majority of cases, the case handler's standard assessment accordingly concentrates on evaluating the proper classification of the costs covered by the measure and whether the criteria for higher aid intensities are met. Hence the assessment is in most cases of a black-and-white type. For instance, if a measure is found to target investment in a disadvantaged region and the aid intensity is below $x\%$, it is declared compatible; otherwise, it is declared incompatible. Likewise, if a measure is found to target industrial research and is restricted to SMEs, it is declared compatible as long as the aid intensity is below $y\%$.

The traditional compatibility assessment concentrates largely on the correct categorization of aid measures by member states: Is the measure an R&D aid or in fact a restructuring aid? Do the costs relate to "industrial research" or rather to "pre-competitive research"? Are the target companies SMEs or are they larger companies? Clearly, this assessment must continue to be an important element of any effective state aid control system. However, it falls short of an effects-based appraisal of the economic justifications of a measure or of the consequences of the measure in terms of the effect on competition and trade.

In general, the appropriateness of such a per se approach depends on whether (1) the rules, in general, are designed correctly and (2) the degree to which the individual measures and the circumstances under which they are implemented vary.

Take, for example, a rule applied in the R&D framework (1996).[93] Industrial research activities are considered as not very distortive and relatively prone to market failures. As a result industrial research may get up to 50 percent state support, which is more than pre-competitive research when it can only get up to 25 percent. The rule "industrial research may get up to 50 percent" may be right on average, yet it may be wrong in individual, but important cases. Allowing for further economic analysis in certain cases where the average is not met is at the root of the effects-based approach that we propose in this section.

Only in very few cases is an effects-based analysis—at least in principle—part of the traditional approach. For example, the R&D framework (1996) requires that the aid have an incentive effect,[94] but in practice, the assessment of the relevant criteria has been applied in a rather rudimentary form. Furthermore the incentive effect is only one part of a proper balancing test, one that seeks to compare the positive aspects of an aid measure with the negative aspects. An aid measure that provides an incentive to the firm to undertake the intended action may still result in significant distortions of competition.

As indicated above, an economic approach does not mean a full economic assessment in all cases. The obvious solution—as in all other areas of competition policy, such as mergers and antitrust—has to be a sensible combination of safe harbour thresholds and prohibition thresholds and a more complete economic assessment for those cases (limited in number) that fall between these two thresholds.

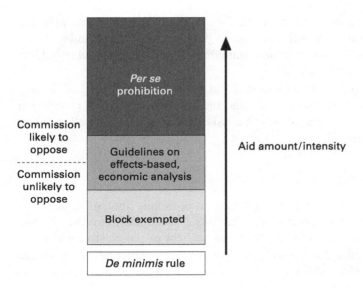

Figure 17.2
Possible architecture

Figure 17.2 outlines the proposed architecture. Under such an approach one could choose to keep the per se prohibition region unchanged. At the other end of the spectrum strict safe harbor regions may be identified for measures for which one is confident that no substantial distortions of competition and effects on trade will arise. Those measures could be block-exempted.

In principle, the thresholds could be based on aid intensity, aid amount, size of the aid beneficiary, market share of aid beneficiary, or other specific (e.g., sectoral) criteria, or a combination of these factors. In our opinion, however, a reasonable approach to trigger an effects-based approach in individual cases could be based on aid amounts as, first, it provides for a simple threshold and, second, larger aid amounts, generally speaking, tend to go with greater potential distortions of competition.

Guidelines should outline the analytical framework applied for an effects-based, economic assessment of the individual measures. Within these guidelines the Commission could make use of "soft" safe harbor regions, for instance, indicating that below certain aid intensity thresholds or when certain specific criteria are met, the Commission would be *unlikely* to take a negative decision on the aid measure. In figure 17.2 the soft safe harbor threshold is indicated by a dashed line.

It should be noted that the "burden of proof" in case the thresholds are not met, should lie, at least in part, with the member state. In other words, member states should come forward with evidence allowing the Commission to assess whether the aid meets the economic test, as they are best placed regarding the relevant information needed on, for example, the presence of market failures. This approach also creates the right incentives (similar to efficiencies in merger control), since it is the member state that should know best when achieving the objective requires the use of state aid.

In sum, the proposed approach implies two aspects of design. First, the level of the safe harbor thresholds (both "strict" and "soft" ones) and the thresholds for per se prohibition need to be assessed. Second, the effects-based analysis has to be clearly spelled-out in guidelines and block exemptions.

17.6   Concluding Remarks

In our view, the main benefit of an increased reliance on economic analysis in state aid control is to make the positive and negative implications of state aid more explicit and their balancing more systematic. A more systematic assessment of the positive and negative effects of the aid, in particular, for aid measures involving large amounts of aid, would be a means to enhance the effectiveness of state aid control, to better distinguish "targeted" aid from "untargeted" aid.

We do not believe that an effects-based approach will lead to overall softening of state aid control. Many of the economic indicators and fact-based assessments can be rigorously implemented. This includes the assessment of market failures, as well as the distortions of competition. A consistent implementation of such an approach could contribute substantially to a policy shift toward both less and better targeted aid. A cautious implementation of the more economic approach is needed, however. Procedural shortcomings still hamper a rigorous economic assessment: obtaining much of the information necessary hinges on a sufficient level of cooperation by member states. Such an implementation would imply designing an adequate state aid architecture and requiring a high standard of proof as regards the positive benefits of state aid claimed by member states.

We also like to emphasize that predictability of the state aid regime may well gain from a more effects-based approach. It is far from obvious that the current form-based approach provides optimal predictability. The current regime has not yet reached the point where the often cited trade-off between precision and predictability becomes relevant. Moreover it is likely, as well as intended, that an effect-based approach will shift the argumentation from legal and accounting battles toward a battle over the impact of the aid on markets and ultimately on consumers. Such a change would greatly contribute not only to the precision and effectiveness of European state aid control but also to its predictability.

A further advantage of an effect-based approach—if implemented cautiously—is that it holds the potential to reduce the scope for politics in the field of state aid control. To be sure, we do not believe, or even advocate, that political factors will or should not play a role in state aid control. However, de-emphasizing politics is helpful in terms of increasing the effectiveness and predictability of state aid control.

Finally, an effects-based approach has the potential to raise the awareness on the costs and benefits of state aid, both at the level of the European Union and at the level of the member states. As far as economic objectives are concerned, similar cost–benefit analysis—as implicit in our proposed economic test—would need to be done at the member state level, at least for those cases requiring individual analysis. In this sense an effects-based economic approach in state aid control would be complementary to efforts to improve the effectiveness of state expenditures at national levels.

Notes

This chapter has been written while Röller was Chief Economist at the European Commission, DG Competition and Friederiszick member of the Chief Economist Team. We would like to thank our colleagues at DG Competition, in particular, Alain Alexis, Thomas Deisenhofer, Thibaut Kleiner, Nicola Pesaresi, Oliver Stehmann, and Marc Van Hoof for helpful discussions. The chapter also benefited from discussions with Mathias Dewatripont, Paul Seabright, Marcel Canoy, and Rod Meiklejohn. Finally, we would like to thank the seminar participants at a number of public events, in particular, the Wilmer Cutler Pickering Hale and Dorr Conference on State Aid 2005, the UK Presidency Event on State Aid 2005, the European Economic Association Annual Meeting in Amsterdam 2005, as well as the Beesley Lecture 2005 in London. The views expressed are those of the authors and do not necessarily reflect those of the European Commission.

1. The political mandate for an economic approach towards "less and better targeted state aid" has been expressed in various conclusions of the European Council since the launch of the Lisbon agenda in 2000, as well as in the Commission's *State Aid Action Plan, Less and Better Targeted State Aid: A Roadmap for State Aid Reform 2005 to 2009*, available at ⟨http://ec.europa.eu/comm/competition/state_aid/reform/saap_en.pdf⟩.

2. The legal framework of the European Union is based on a number of treaties. In the economic domain, the 1957 Treaty of Rome, which established the European Community (EC), contains the central provisions.

3. In the European context the term "common market" stands for the European (EU) market.

4. These measures primarily relate to social measures aimed at individuals, as well as measures addressing damage due to natural disasters.

5. See Hancher et al. (1999), Biondi et al. (2004), and Rydelski (2006) for comprehensive overviews. A brief description of the main soft law provisions is provided in the Vademecum on Community Rules on State Aid, 2003, available at ⟨http://ec.europa.eu/comm/competition/state_aid/others/vademecum/vademecumen2003_en.pdf⟩.

6. See Judgement of the European Court of Justice of July 24, 2003, Case C-280/00, *Altmark Trans GmbH and Regierungspräsidium Magdeburg v. Nahverkehrsgesellschaft Altmark GmbH* ("*Altmark* judgment"), paragraph 75.

7. See, for instance, the Commission's *Vademecum: Community Rules on State Aid* (2003), p. 3, referring to the two criteria as one criterion.

8. Note that the exact quantification of the economic advantage received becomes relevant, in particular, when the aid is found unlawful and has to be repaid by the aid beneficiary to the aid-granting state authority (so-called recovery).

9. Commission's *Vademecum: Community rules on state aid* (2003), *supra* note 7, p. 3.

10. See Ahlborn and Berg (2004) and Bishop (1997). See also Frédéric Louis, *EC State Aid Control*, presentation at the conference on EC State Aid Control: The Case for Reform, Brussels, 14.06.2005 (referring to the judgment of the Court of March 13, 1985, in joined cases 296 and 318/82, *Kingdom of the Netherlands and Leeuwarder Papierwarenfabriek BV v. Commission of the European Communities*).

11. Judgment of the Court of First Instance, September 29, 2000, Case T-55/99, *Confederación Española de Transporte de Mercancías (CETM) v. Commission of the European Communities*. In this judgment the Court furthermore held that:

... the Commission is not required to carry out an economic analysis of the actual situation on the relevant market, of the market share of the undertakings in receipt of the aid, of the position of competing undertakings and of trade flows of the services in question between Member States, provided that it has explained how the aid in question distorted competition and affected trade between Member States. (id., para. 7)

However, in a recent judgment of the Court of First Instance, Case T-34/02, *Le Levant v. Commission* (February 22, 2006), the Court followed the reasoning of the parties, who claimed that the Commission had failed to identify the relevant product and geographic markets and, consequently, had failed to appropriately specify the distortions of competition and the effects on trade under Article 87(1). The degree of economic analysis required to meet the legal standard under Article 87(1) is not yet fully spelled out by the Court. See paragraphs 104, 123, and 124 of the judgment.

12. *See* Opinion of Advocate-General Capotorti delivered on June 18, 1980, Case 730/79, *Philip Morris Holland BV v. Commission of the European Communities*. It should be mentioned that the Commission has taken the view that very small amounts of aid (*de minimis* aid) do not have a potential effect on competition and trade between member states. It therefore considers that such aid falls outside the scope of Article 87(1).

13. *Altmark* judgment, *supra* note 6, paragraph 95. Public subsidies compensating public service obligations are not caught by Article 87(1) when:

first, the recipient undertaking is actually required to discharge public service obligations and those obligations have been clearly defined; second, the parameters on the basis of which the compensation is calculated have been established beforehand in an objective and transparent manner; third, the compensation does not exceed what is necessary to cover all or part of the costs incurred in discharging the public service obligations, taking into account the relevant receipts and a reasonable profit for discharging those obligations; fourth, where the undertaking which is to discharge public service obligations is not chosen in a public procurement procedure, the level of compensation needed has been determined on the basis of an analysis of the costs which a typical undertaking, well run and adequately provided with means of transport so as to be able to meet the necessary public service requirements, would have incurred in discharging those obligations, taking into account the relevant receipts and a reasonable profit for discharging the obligations.

14. Community Guidelines on national regional aid (1998), Official Journal C 74, 10.03.1998, pp. 9–31. The Regional Aid Guidelines stipulate under which conditions member states can give aid to finance investments by companies setting up in particular regions.

15. Community Framework for state aid for research and development (1996, prolonged in 2002), Official Journal C 045, 17.02.1996, pp. 5–16.

16. Community Guidelines on state aid for rescuing and restructuring firms in difficulty (2004), Official Journal C 244, 01.10.2004, pp. 2–17.

17. Community Framework for state aid in the form of public service compensation (2005), Official Journal C 297/4, 29.11.2005, pp. 4–7.

18. Community Guidelines on state aid for environmental protection (2001), Official Journal C 37, 03.02.2001, pp. 3–15.

19. See, for instance, the Commission's *State Aid Action Plan* (2005), *supra* note 2.

20. Examples are the cases relating to aid in support of the development of broadband provision in Wales (Commission decision of June 1, 2005; see also Competition Policy Newsletter 2005, 1, p. 8; ⟨http://ec.europa.eu/comm/competition/publications/cpn/⟩) and aid for the construction of a propylene pipeline connecting Rotterdam, Antwerp and the German Ruhr area (Commission decision of June 16, 2004, case C67/03, Official Journal L56/15 2005).

21. Multisectoral Framework on regional aid for large investment projects (2002), Official Journal C 70, 19.03.2002, pp. 8–20.

22. Commission communication on state aid and risk capital (2001), Official Journal C 235, 21.08.2001, pp. 3–11.

23. See section 17.2 for a description of the concept of market failure.

24. For similar opinions, see Ahlborn and Berg (2004) and Bishop (1997). The UK Office of Fair Trading (2005, at 2.20) has noted in this context: "The Commission has published guidelines outlining in more detail types of compatible state aid under Article 87(3) EC. However, these guidelines do not apply economic criteria to assess the extent to which such state aid distorts competition."

25. So the Court of First Instance stated that "it is settled case-law that even aid of a relatively small amount is liable to affect trade between Member States where there is strong competition in the sector in which the recipient

operates." Case /-288/97 Regione Autonoma Friuli-Venezia Giulia v. Commission [2001] ECR II-1169, para. 44. Similarly, "Moreover, because of the structure of the market, a feature of which is the presence of a large number of small-scale undertakings in the road haulage sector, even relatively modest aid is liable to strengthen the position of the recipient undertaking as compared with its competitors in intra-Community trade." (Id., para. 46). See also Case 259/85 *France v. Commission* (para. 24).

26. The Court of First Instance has held that "operating aid, that is to say aid which, like the aid in question, is intended to relieve an undertaking of the expenses which it would normally have had to bear in its day-to-day management or its usual activities, in principle distorts competition." Case T-214/95 *Het Vlaams Gewest v. Commission* (1998) ECR II-717, para. 43.

27. Economists usually measure the precision of a test by assessing type I and type II errors. A type I error is the prohibition of a welfare-increasing state intervention. A type II error is the approval of a welfare-decreasing state intervention.

28. The concept of the social welfare function goes back to Bergson (1938). It goes beyond the scope of this paper to discuss the critics on the concept of a social welfare function. See, for instance, Stiglitz (2000) for a discussion.

29. Pareto (1896) observed that social welfare is unambiguously increased by a change that makes at least one individual better off, without making anybody else worse off. From this principle economists have derived the concept of "Pareto improvement," "Pareto optimality," or "Pareto efficiency." A situation is considered Pareto efficient if it is impossible to make further changes that satisfy the Pareto principle.

30. Note that in the latter case interpersonal utility comparisons become necessary while for the former interpersonal utility comparisons can be avoided by applying the Pareto criterion: the utility of every citizen is (weakly) increased.

31. A situation in which total welfare is maximised is characterized by Pareto efficiency. It should be noted that the exact measure of the effect of a change on consumer surplus is the *equivalent* or *compensating variation*, which takes into account income effects. The concept of consumer surplus only corresponds under the restrictive assumption of quasi-linear utility functions to those concepts, but is applied in most applications for practical reasons (see Varian 1992, p. 160).

32. Note that the economic cost of the intervention includes the opportunity cost of the funds employed as well as the cost of raising the funds (i.e., the shadow cost of taxation). We will come back to these points in section 17.2 when we discuss the limits of state aid.

33. Stiglitz (2000, p. 77): "The first fundamental theorem of welfare economics asserts that the economy is Pareto efficient only under certain conditions. There are six important conditions under which the market is not Pareto efficient. These are referred to as market failures, and they provide a set of rationales for government activity."

34. For summaries of the arguments regarding market failures, see Stiglitz (2000), Meiklejohn (1999), or Gual et al. (1998).

35. In addition public goods are characterized by nonrivalry in consumption: the use or consumption of the good by one person does not reduce the possibilities of others persons to use or consume it.

36. Also a policy aimed at cultural diversity and pluriformity of the media may be viewed under the heading of equity, as it relates to society's perception that the market outcome—though efficient—is not satisfactory in preserving or promoting cultural and democratic values.

37. See, however, the concept of "efficient redistribution" discussed later on.

38. Two classical concepts put forward in this regard by economists are the utilitarian approach of putting equal weight on individual utilities and the Rawlsian approach of putting all weight on the individual with lowest utility. However, an infinite amount of possible preference functions are possible.

39. Similarly Laffont and Tirole's (1993) textbook on market regulation employs a utilitarian approach maximizing the sum of the individual utilities. A comparable position is expressed in the text book by Viscusi et al. (2000, p. 9):

Ideally, the purpose of antitrust and regulation policies is to foster improvements judged in efficiency terms. We should move closer to the perfectly competitive ideal than we would have in the absence of this type of intervention.... Put somewhat differently, our task is to maximize the net benefits of these regulations to society. Such concern requires that we assess both benefits and the cost of these regulatory policies and attempt to maximize their differences. If all groups in society are treated symmetrically, then this benefit-cost calculus represents a straightforward maximization of economic efficiency.

They proceed by saying: "Alternatively, we might choose to weight the benefits to the disadvantaged differently or make other kinds of distinctions, in which case we can incorporate a broader range of concerns than efficiency alone."

40. See the State Aid Scoreboard, available at ⟨http://ec.europa.eu/comm/competition/state_aid/scoreboard/⟩.

41. A related argument is that in an environment of vested political influence a restriction to efficiency considerations may be appropriate given the availability of redistributional instruments outside the set of state aid instruments.

42. Trade-offs are also present in the world of antitrust. Consider the example of perfect price discrimination mentioned in Tirole (1993). Introducing perfect price discrimination by a monopolist enhances efficiency. At the same time it has a strong (negative) distributional side effect on consumers: the entire consumer rent is appropriated by the monopolist.

43. Note, however, that in richer theoretical settings (incorporating, in particular, the political system to vote for redistribution, and the inclusion of individual leisure) the property of Pareto rankability might get lost in general. Benabou (2000), for instance, concludes:

This leads to two stable steady states, the archetype for which could be the United States and Western Europe: one with high inequality yet low redistribution, the other with the reverse configuration. These two societies are not Pareto rankable, and which one has faster income growth depends on the balance between tax distortions to efforts and the greater productivity of investment resources (particularly in education) reallocation to more severely credit-constrained agents.

44. See Przeworski (2003, p. 185).

45. Sleuwaegen et al. (2000, p. 75).

46. This result is established within a multi-auction approach (Bernheim and Whinston 1986a) where regions can provide "bids" contingent on firms' investment decision.

47. Another important example why equity considerations may become relevant is the situation of a country being hit by a demand shock in one of its sectors resulting in unemployment. If employment in the particular sector would go down without state aid, the wage cost becomes part of the total welfare assessment. See for instance Brander and Spencer (1987) or Lahiri and Ono (2004, p. 85).

48. See also the survey by Fingleton et al. (1999) and UK Office of Fair Trading (2004).

49. A comprehensive introduction into this literature is provided by Persson and Tabellini (2000).

50. Such commitment problems may, for instance, be due to the election cycle: governments may be willing to renegotiate contracts agreed upon by their predecessors, resulting in dynamic inefficiencies.

51. See, for instance, Neven and Röller (2000) and Duso (2002) for some empirical evidence. Neven and Röller (2005) provide a model analyzing the design of merger control policy in a political economy framework. See Vickers (2005) for similar views.

52. In principle, the same type of reasoning holds for positive externalities like international information spillover. Governments may provide insufficient funding from a European perspective or may not support those projects that maximize European welfare, even though they may be regarded as positive.

53. The classical reference on such type of exit models are Fudenberg and Tirole (1989) and Ghemawat and Nalebuff (1985, 1990). For a survey of the literature, see Neven et al. (2004, p. 16).

54. See Besley and Seabright (1999, p. 21).

55. These results hold both for Bertrand and Cournot settings (Collie 2002).

56. It has to be mentioned that the current body of literature does not consider settings involving other market failures besides imperfect competition. More research is needed to obtain a fuller picture in this regard.

57. See Kornai et al. (2003) and Dewatripont and Maskin (1995). Conceptually, consider a bank providing a credit for a private investment project (e.g., the expansion of a national firm into a neighboring EU market). The project could be of two types: a less profitable one that exhibits a negative net present value and a profitable one that exhibits a positive net present value. The bank cannot observe the profitability of the project when deciding about the credit approval. After the investment the bank observes the project's profitability. When the project is not profitable, the bank has two options. It can close down the firm or grant a second credit. Depending on the parameters it may be profit maximizing for the bank to provide a second credit in order to recover some of its

losses on the first credit. In a dynamic context this is fatal, however. Managers who know the profitability of the project ex ante and have some private benefits in starting the project and keeping it alive are willing to propose unprofitable projects, given that the bank will bail them out later, if need be. Thereby ex ante inefficient projects are implemented. Note that this commitment problem arises in a purely profit-maximizing environment, and will be exaggerated if the funding source is not a profit-maximizing entity. An example of this is provided by the Hungarian economy in the 1970s. Hungary, at that time still a socialist economy, was experimenting with the introduction of market reforms. Despite the introduction of incentives for state-owned firms to maximize their profits, firms were always bailed out when exhibiting long-term losses. This "insurance against bankruptcy" resulted in severe dynamic inefficiencies.

58. A supra-national authority may have higher reputation losses. This may be the case as the Commission has to approve measures such as rescue and restructuring aid on a regular basis while national governments provide those means less often. Furthermore a negative European precedent results in dynamic inefficiencies across Europe changing the relation of short-term benefits (which are national only) and long-term losses in dynamic incentives (which are Europe-wide).

59. See also Midelfart-Knarvik and Overman (2002, p. 325).

60. The internal market argument has recently been linked to the strategic trade/exit game literature cited before. Martin and Valbonesi (2006) argue that market integration triggers an exit process of firms and therefore creates incentives of governments to subsidize inefficient, domestic incumbents to the detriment of European-wide welfare.

61. Biondi and Eeckhout (2004, p. 108).

62. The concept of total welfare in the context of state aid does not only include the sum of consumer and producer welfare in the markets concerned but also the cost to taxpayers associated to the funding of state aid.

63. Guidelines on the application of Article 81(3) of the treaty, Official Journal C 101, 27.04.2004, pp. 97–118, at para. 13. See also Kjølbye (2004).

64. It should be mentioned that the overall EU "market integration" objective plays a role in the application of Article 81, especially in the context of territorial restraints. In addition to not reducing consumer welfare, agreements between companies should not add to segmentation of national markets. To a certain degree the two objectives are aligned (see Peeperkorn 1999, p. 65).

65. Guidelines on the assessment of horizontal mergers under the Council Regulation on the control of concentrations between undertakings ("Merger Guidelines"), at para. 8.

66. Merger Guidelines, at para. 79.

67. Werden (1996), for instance, argues that the assessment of a differentiated product merger by the enforcement agency is made much easier under a consumer standard because an estimation of firms' profits requires additional, strong assumptions about the functional form of demand. In this context Ilzkovitz and Meiklejohn (2001) also point to the practical problem of assigning the European part of firms' profit under a (European) total welfare standard.

68. A related argument is put forward by Lagerlöf and Heidhues (2005). They analyze the incentives of firms to deliver verifiable but costly information on efficiencies under different merger control regimes. As it is the firm that decides on whether or not to collect the information, efficiency assessments are carried out in favorable cases only. They conclude that an efficiency defense is optimal from a total welfare perspective in case of (high) efficiencies resulting in price reductions postmerger (so that the merger would meet a consumer standard).

69. The assumption that consumers are underrepresented in merger proceedings is supported by two arguments. First, consumers may not be well informed about the consequences of proposed mergers and accordingly may not be able to formulate their interest appropriately. Second, consumers may face prohibitive transaction costs in representing their interests. These costs can be associated with the traditional problems of free-riding and collective action with numerous agents.

70. OECD (2001, p. 8).

71. Id.

72. Paragraph 8, Council Regulation (EC) No 659/1999 of March 22, 1999, states: "... the formal investigation procedure should be opened in order to enable the Commission to gather all the information it needs to assess the compatibility of the aid and to allow the interested parties to submit their comments...."

73. Note that a selection bias can provide a rationale for the European funds, as the Commission proposes and selects measures which aim at maximizing European welfare.

74. In the latter case a balanced lobbying process results in an "efficient lobbying equilibrium," where national interests are neutralized by the other parties' lobbying effort. For instance, a recent working paper suggests that the "empirical puzzle in the literature concerning the apparently nearly "welfare-maximizing" behavior of the US government in setting trade policy" can partially be explained by efficient lobbying competition. See Gawande and Krishna (2005). An introduction to this literature is provided by Persson and Tabellini (2000, p. 172). The standard common agent model—on which most lobbying models build upon—was developed by Bernheim and Whinston (1986b); an application to trade issues is developed by Grossman and Helpman (1994).

75. In a monopoly setting these arguments converge into the classical regulation literature on "natural monopolies." A production subsidy driving prices down to marginal cost minimizes the deadweight loss associated with monopoly and is welfare enhancing as long as the benefits to the customers exceed total cost. See, for instance, Viscusi et al. (2000, ch. 11), for an introductory discussion. For an analysis within an oligopoly setting, see Garcia and Neven (2004).

76. In fact, both standards are closely linked. Biondi and Eeckhout (2004, p. 105) summarize the internal market jurisprudence by stating that "in a nutshell, the language of free movement is one of discrimination, obstacles, and market access." These are the same elements one would assess under an effect-on-rivals standard trying to establish an equal, nondiscriminatory level playing field.

77. This correspondence has led Martin and Strasse (2005) to propose a consumer welfare standard for assessing state aid. Under their approach a positive impact on consumer welfare in the long run is taken as an indication that the aid measure benefits the competitive process and is unlikely to harm rivals in a significant way.

78. Furthermore in situations where the relative positions of competitors are strongly affected, lobbying efforts of firms may be high, justifying a more careful assessment by the European Commission. The argument was put forward by Garcia and Neven (2004, p. 10). Note that in contrast to a welfare reducing horizontal merger, rivals' interests are not aligned with the aid beneficiary's interests. Profits of competitors not benefiting from the aid measure are usually always negatively affected. Hence one can expect that the criticism that has been made in the context of merger control, namely that the Commission protects competitors at the expense of consumers, is less likely to apply in the context of state aid control.

79. See Biondi and Eeckhout (2004, p. 108).

80. See also the Commission's *State Aid Action Plan* (2005), *supra* note 1.

81. See, in a different context, Stiglitz (2000, ch. 11).

82. These stylized facts are derived from a case concerning aid for the construction of a propylene pipeline between Rotterdam, Antwerp and the Ruhr area, see Commission decision of June 16, 2004, case C67/03, OJ L56/15 2005. The example is, however, not to discuss the merits of this particular case but to explain the general idea.

83. Another concern is that regional aid does not go against regional comparative advantages. See the work done by Midelfart-Knarvik and Overman (2002) who argue—based on an empirical analysis of European and national regional aid measures—that those measures did not become effective as they went against regional comparative advantages.

84. These stylized facts are derived from two state aid cases relating to risk capital provision in the United Kingdom. The example is, however, not to discuss the merits of this particular case but to explain the general idea.

85. The mere *existence* or likelihood of an effect on nondomestic rivals is the relevant criterion under Article 87(1). Under Article 87(3) it is not the existence but rather the *magnitude* and *importance* of these effects in terms of welfare that become relevant for the analysis of whether or not the aid measure is in the "common interest" of the European Union.

86. See section 17.3.

87. For a similar list of indicators, see UK OFT (2005); for a discussion of the criteria within a theoretical framework, see Garcia and Neven (2004).

88. See Garcia and Neven (2004), UK OFT (2004), and Nitsche and Heidhues (2006) for a more detailed account.

89. For instance, market shares are implemented as a criterion in the Multisectoral Framework on Regional Aid for Large Investment Projects (2002), *supra* note 21. In the existing framework it is established that individually notifiable projects will not be eligible for investment aid if the beneficiary has a market share of more than 25

percent (before or after the aid granted). These thresholds are applied only for aid measures related to relatively large amounts of eligible cost (investment projects of more than EUR 100 million).

90. Market shares may only partially reflect the market power of a particular firm in a differentiated industry. Closest competitors of the aid beneficiary may be affected significantly stronger, for instance, increasing the possibility of exit of those competitors to the detriment of consumers.

91. Careful reflections are, however, necessary on the aid amount relative to the size of the affected sector. High aid amounts in niche markets may distort the market conditions less than small amounts in emerging markets (e.g., biotechnology).

92. *Supra*, note 1.

93. *Supra*, note 15.

94. The R&D Framework (1996, prolonged in 2002) foresees an assessment of the "incentive effect" particularly in two cases: "in the case of individual, close-to-the-market research projects to be undertaken by large firms; in all cases in which a significant proportion of the R&D expenditure has already been made prior to the aid application." Under the incentive effect it is assessed whether "planned aid will induce firms to pursue research which they would not otherwise have pursued" by taking into account inter alia changes in quantifiable factors, market failures, and additional cost connected with cross-border cooperation.

References

Ahlborn, C., and C. Berg. 2004. Can state aid learn from antitrust? The need for a greater role for competition analysis under the state aid rules. In A. Biondi, P. Eeckhout, and J. Flynn, eds., *The Law of State Aid in the European Union*. Oxford: Oxford University Press, pp. 41–66.

Bator, F. M. 1958. Anatomy of market failure. *The Quarterly Journal of Economics* (August) 72(3): 351–79.

Benabou, R. 2000. Unequal societies: Income distribution and the social contract. *American Economic Review* 90(1): 96–129.

Bernheim, D., and M. Whinston. 1986a. Menu auctions, resource allocation and economic influence. *Quarterly Journal of Economics* 101: 1–31.

Bernheim, D., and M. Whinston. 1986b. Common agency. *Econometrica* 54(4): 923–42.

Besanko, D., and D. Spulber. 1993. Contested mergers and equilibrium antitrust policy. *Journal of Law, Economics and Organization* 9(1): 1–29.

Besley, T., and P. Seabright. 1999. The effects and policy implications of state aids to industry: An economic analysis. *Economic Policy* 14(28): 15–53.

Biondi, A., and P. Eeckhout. 2004. State aid and obstacles to trade. In A. Biondi, P. Eeckhout and J. Flynn, eds., *The Law of State Aid in the European Union*. Oxford: Oxford University Press, pp. 103–16.

Biondi, A., P. Eeckhout, and J. Flynn, eds. 2004. *The Law of State Aid in the European Union*. Oxford: Oxford University Press.

Bishop, S. 1997. The European Commission's policy towards state aid: A role for rigorous competitive analysis. *European Competition Law Review* 18(2): 84–86.

Brander, J. A., and B. J. Spencer. 1985. Export subsidies and international market share rivalry. *Journal of International Economics* 18: 83–100.

Brander, J. A., and B. J. Spencer. 1987. Foreign direct investment with unemployment and endogenous taxes and tariffs. *Journal of International Economics* 22: 257–79.

Collie, D. R. 2000. State aid in the European Union: The prohibition of subsidies in an integrated market. *International Journal of Industrial Organization* 18: 867–84.

Collie, D. R. 2002. Prohibiting state aid in an integrated market. *Journal of Industry, Competition and Trade* 2(3): 215–31.

Collie, D. R. 2005. State aid to investment and R&D. *European Economy. Economic Papers* 231: 1–22.

Dewatripont, M., and E. Maskin. 1995. Credit and efficiency in centralized and decentralized economies. *Review of Economic Studies* 62: 541–55.

Duso, T. 2002. The political economy of the regulatory process: An empirical approach. Dissertation. Humboldt University, Berlin.

Ehlermann, C.-D., and M. Everson, eds. 2001. *European Competition Law Annual: 1999. Selected Issues in the Field of State Aid.* Oxford: Hart Publishing.

Fingleton, J., F. Ruane, and V. Ryan. 1998. A study of market definition in practice in state aid cases in the EU. Report to DG ECFIN.

Fingleton, J., F. Ruane, and V. Ryan. 1999. Market definition and state aid control. *European Economy* 3: 65–88.

Friederiszick, H. W., D. Neven, and L.-H. Röller. 2003. Evaluation of the effectiveness of state aid as a policy instrument. Report to DG ECFIN.

Fudenberg, D., and J. Tirole. 1989. A theory of exit in duopoly. *Econometrica* 54: 943–60.

Garcia, J., and D. Neven. 2004. Identification of sensitive sectors in which state aid may have significant distorting effects. Report for the HM Treasury, London.

Gawande, K., and P. Krishna. 2005. Lobbying competition over US trade policy. NBER working paper 11371.

Glowicka, E. 2005. Bailouts in a common market: A strategic approach. WZB discussion paper, SP II 2005-20. Berlin.

Grossman, G. M., and E. Helpman. 1994. Protection for sale. *American Economic Review* 84: 833–50.

Ghemawat, J. J., and B. Nalebuff. 1985. Exit. *RAND Journal of Economics* 16(2): 184–94.

Ghemawat, J. J., and B. Nalebuff. 1990. The devolution of declining industries. *Quarterly Journal of Economics* 105(1): 167–86.

Graaff, J. de V. 1957. *Theoretical Welfare Economics.* Cambridge: Cambridge University Press.

Gual, J., and P. Videla. 1998. State aid and convergence in the European Union. Report to DG ECFIN.

Hancher, L., T. Ottervanger, and P. J. Slot. 1999. *E.C. State Aids,* 2nd ed. London: Sweet and Maxwell.

Ilzkovitz, F., and R. Meiklejohn. 2001. European merger control: Do we need an efficiency defence? *European Economy* 5: 3–29.

Kjølbye, L. 2004. The new Commission guidelines on the application of Article 81(3). *European Competition Law Review* 25(9): 566–77.

Kornai, J. 1980. The soft budget constraint. *Kyklos* 39(1): 3–30.

Kornai, J., E. Maskin, and G. Roland. 2003. Understanding the soft budget constraint. *Journal of Economic Literature* 41: 1095–236.

Laffont, J.-J., and J. Tirole. 1993. *A Theory of Incentives in Procurement and Regulation.* Cambridge: MIT Press.

Lagerlöf, J., and P. Heidhues. 2005. On the desirability of an efficiency defense in merger control. *International Journal of Industrial Organization* 23: 803–27.

Lahiri, S., and Y. Ono. 2004. *Trade and Industrial Policy under International Oligopoly.* Cambridge: Cambridge University Press.

Lyons, B. R. 2002. Could politicians be more right than economists? A theory of merger policy. Working Paper 02-01. Centre for Competition and Regulation, UEA.

Martin, S., and C. Strasse. 2005. La politique communautaire des aides d'Etat est-elle une politique de concurrence? *Concurrences* 3: 52–59.

Martin, S., and P. Valbonesi. 2006. The state aid game. Discussion paper. Università di Padova.

Meiklejohn, R. 1999. The economies of state aid. *European Economy* 3: 25–31.

Midelfart-Knarvik, K. H., and H. G. Overman. 2002. Delocation and European integration: Is structural spending justified. *Economic Policy* 35: 323–59.

Mitchell, W. C., and M. C. Munger. 1991. Economic models of interest groups: An introductonary survey. *American Journal of Political Science* 35: 512–46.

Neven, D. J., and L.-H. Röller, eds. 2000. *The Political Economy of Industrial Policy in Europe and the Member States.* Berlin: Edition Sigma.

Neven, D. J., and L.-H. Röller. 2005. Consumer surplus vs. welfare standard in a political economy model of merger control. *International Journal of Industrial Organization* 23(9–10): 829–48.

Nitsche, R., and P. Heidhues. 2006. Study on methods to analyse the impact of state aid on competition. *European Economy* (244): 190p.

OECD. 2001. Competition policy in subsidies and state aid. DAFFE/CLP(2001)24.

Pareto, V. 1896. *Cours d'économie politique*, 2 vols. Lausanne. Reprinted by G.-H. Bousquet and G. Busino. Geneva: Librairie Droz, 1964.

Peeperkorn, L. 1999. The Commission's radical overhaul of EC competition policy towards vertical restraints. In J. Faull and A. Nikpay, eds., *The EC Law of Competition*. Oxford: Oxford University Press, pp. 553–75.

Persson, T., and G. Tabellini. 2000. *Political Economics: Explaining Economic Policy*. Cambridge: MIT Press.

Plender, R. 2004. Definition of aid. In A. Biondi, P. Eeckhout, and J. Flynn, eds., *The Law of State Aid in the European Union*. Oxford: Oxford University Press, pp. 3–47.

Przeworski, A. 2003. *States and Markets: A Primer in Political Economy*. Cambridge: Cambridge University Press.

Rehbinder, M. 2004. Recent developments in Commission state aid policy and practice. In A. Biondi, P. Eeckhout, and J. Flynn, eds., *The Law of State Aid in the European Union*. Oxford: Oxford University Press, pp. 117–33.

Rydelski, M. S., ed. 2006. *The EC State Aid Regime: Distortive Effects of State Aid on Competition and Trade*. London: Cameron May.

Sleuwaegen, L., E. Pennings, and I. De Voldere. 2000. Public aid and relocation within the European Community. Report to the European Commission, Directorate General III, Brussels.

Stennek, J., L.-H. Röller, and F. Verboven. 2001. Efficiency gains from mergers. *European Economy* (5): 31–128.

Stiglitz, J. E. 2000. *Economics of the Public Sector*, 3rd ed. New York: Norton.

Tirole, J. 1988. *The Theory of Industrial Organization*. Cambridge: MIT Press.

UK Office of Fair Trading. 2004. The effects of public subsidies on competition. Report prepared by Frontier Economics.

Varian, H. R. 1992. *Microeconomic Analysis*. New York: Norton.

Vickers, J. 2005. State aid and distortion of competition. Paper for the UK presidency conference on state aid. London, July 14.

Werden, G. 1996. A robust test for consumer welfare enhancing mergers among sellers of differentiated products. *Journal of Industrial Economics* 44: 409–13.

Williamson, O. 1968. Economies as an antitrust defense: The welfare trade-offs. *American Economic Review* 58: 18–36.

Viscusi, W. K., J. M. Vernon, and J. E. Harring von. 2000. *Economics of Regulation and Antitrust*, 3rd ed. Cambridge: MIT Press.

Index